PENGUIN BOOKS

THE PENGUIN BOOK OF MODERN INDIAN SPEECHES

Rakesh Batabyal graduated from St. Xavier's College, Ranchi, and did his master's and doctorate in modern history from Jawaharlal Nehru University, New Delhi. He was a postdoctoral fellow at the Indian Institute of Advanced Study, Shimla (1996–99) and later at the National Institute of Panjab Studies, New Delhi. He is currently assistant director of the Academic Staff College of Jawaharlal Nehru University where he trains university and college teachers from across the country. His book *Communalism in Bengal: From Famine to Noakhali, 1943–47* has been widely received as an authoritative work on communal politics in Bengal in the 1940s and on Mahatma Gandhi's Noakhali visit. He is currently writing a book on the institutional history of modern India.

The Penguin Book of Modern Indian Speeches

1877 to the Present

Edited by

RAKESH BATABYAL

PENGUIN BOOKS

PENGUIN BOOKS
Published by the Penguin Group
Penguin Books India Pvt. Ltd, 11 Community Centre, Panchsheel Park,
New Delhi 110 017, India
Penguin Group (USA) Inc., 375 Hudson Street, New York, New York 10014, USA
Penguin Group (Canada), 90 Eglinton Avenue East, Suite 700, Toronto,
Ontario, M4P 2Y3, Canada (a division of Pearson Penguin Canada Inc.)
Penguin Books Ltd, 80 Strand, London WC2R 0RL, England
Penguin Ireland, 25 St Stephen's Green, Dublin 2, Ireland
(a division of Penguin Books Ltd)
Penguin Group (Australia), 250 Camberwell Road, Camberwell,
Victoria 3124, Australia (a division of Pearson Australia Group Pty Ltd)
Penguin Group (NZ), 67 Apollo Drive, Rosedale, North Shore 0632,
New Zealand (a division of Pearson New Zealand Ltd)
Penguin Group (South Africa) (Pty) Ltd, 24 Sturdee Avenue, Rosebank,
Johannesburg 2196, South Africa

Penguin Books Ltd, Registered Offices: 80 Strand, London WC2R 0RL, England

First published by Penguin Books India 2007

10 9 8 7 6 5 4 3

ISBN-13: 978-0-14310-263-2 ISBN-10: 0-14310-263-X

Typeset in *Adobe Garamond* by SÜRYA, New Delhi
Printed at Chaman Offset Printers, New Delhi

For

Professor Bipan Chandra, my teacher
Shri Ajeet Kumar Batabyal, my father
and
Late Dr Sanjay Ambatkar, my friend

CONTENTS

ACKNOWLEDGEMENTS

Growing up in the steel city of Bokaro (then in Bihar, now in Jharkhand), living close to the headquarters of the Indian National Trade Union Congress (INTUC) and opposite the Bokaro steel plant's administrative building, my first exposure to speeches were the ones made by workers and their leaders, articulating their agonies and aspirations in public meetings. It was an interesting relationship between this world and my daily schedule of hockey or football: an evening meeting usually meant no football or hockey. Notwithstanding this contest for site, the speeches, I now realize, connected me to the daily struggle of our families to provide a better existence for us. They related me to the lives of those who worked in the steel plant and were our next-door neighbours. I still remember the clear, loud voice of Bindeswari Dube of INTUC (who later became the chief minister of Bihar) and the well-modulated baritone of Samaresh Singh (who later became a minister in the Jharkhand cabinet), then an emerging but powerful voice of the Bharatiya Majdoor Sangh. I recall vividly the speeches of a rebel trade union leader, A.K. Ray, an indomitable fighter for the rights of labourers, tribal people and coalminers, with their curious mix of Bengali and Hindi.

There was about these speeches a sense of urgency, of an ongoing struggle, a quest to transcend the present. My siblings and I developed a connectedness with the working class, the facts and figures of their lives, quite often articulated in these speeches, became a part of our existence and daily education. We had none of those comfortable middle-class dreams and aspirations that would soon constitute the dominant world view. Our education and understanding of the larger world further evolved when our own house became the headquarters of the Chotanagpur Plateau Praja Parishad through which my father tried to organize migrant and displaced tribal labourers, most of whom were regularly cheated by government officers and private contractors of the Bokaro plant and its ancillary units.

I recall with fondness people like Shibu Soren. Back then, he spoke from his heart, and one could feel his total dedication to his cause. Those were the days of Karpuri Thakur, George Fernandes and Atal Bihari Vajpayee, all of whom commanded a unique respect in our world. In the post-Emergency elections, Vajpayee was due to come to Bokaro to campaign for a local leader of the Janata Party. My mother coaxed me to go to the nearby high school grounds to listen to his address. Unaware of the fight that had broken out between two warring factions there, I, all of ten years old at the time, landed in the middle of it and ended up receiving a couple of powerful lathi blows from the Bihar police. Thankfully, one of the policemen recognized me as a boy from the neighbourhood and took me to the hospital, and from there escorted me home. My mother, eagerly waiting to hear what her favourite leader had said, had to be content with nursing my bruises for the next couple of days. Years later, in 1996, when I watched Vajpayee speaking during a confidence motion in Parliament, my right hand unconsciously went up to my left shoulder and an old wound suddenly started hurting. My mother is no more but I owe to her the natural keenness to listen to public speeches, be it of a leader of an auto-rickshaw drivers' union in a street corner or of M. Karunanidhi in the Coimbatore Corporation Ground during the 2004 election or of Mamata Banerjee in Calcutta in 1997 when she founded the Trinamool Congress.

Listening to a public speech, I have come to realize, entails not merely listening to the speaker but also becoming part of the multitude which internalizes that speech in a variety of ways. Only those who are part of the multitude can experience this. The rest can simply interpret and theorize. For this ability not only to listen to the speakers out there on the ground but also become part of the multitude, I must thank my mother. I miss her, as she would have been very happy to see this collection. My sister Shampa, living in the slums of urban Rajasthan and in its dusty villages, one of the best rural development workers in the country, has also been a great source of inspiration. She, by her unflinching devotion to the country and its rural folk, always makes me proud and I hope she finds that I have been as honest in my work as she is in hers. Without these influences, this book would have simply been a mechanical collection of speeches and if it has succeeded in not being one, the credit must go to my parents; my siblings Rajesh, Seema and Shampa; my grandparents Renu and Jivan Chakravarty; my childhood friends Jamid Qais, Arun, P.S. Suresh, Papa, Manto (Syed Numan Ashraf), Bibhash, Rakesh Haldar, Palash, Regi Verghese, Kumar, JP and PN; my elders, namely, Noori Apa, Bishram Singh, P.K. Pingua and many others with whom I shared the trials and tribulations, joys and sorrows of growing up in a world which was both exciting and humanizing.

My mind also goes back to the unnamed youth who took shelter in the vacant space near our house and worked as a cobbler during the day. He told me stories while he made his food in that kerosene lamp-lit space under the staircase. The rebellion by Spartacus, the killing of Rosa Luxemburg and Liebknecht and the escapades of M.N. Roy and Lenin and Che Guevara were part of his repertoire. He would take me to the nearby administrative ground and, while listening to the speeches of trade union leaders, indicate the factual and logical fallacies. I did not understand many of them but I learnt that speeches were to be taken seriously. At times, I would find him watching us play football and he would come and tell me what was wrong with my tactics. Probably it is from him that I unconsciously learnt that politics is not merely an instrument outside of one's body and life. It is one's personality. It is similar to how one plays football or how one appreciates a song. Narrowness in all aspects of life, not only politics, begins when things are conceived in isolation. One day, on my way back from school, I was told that he was gone and that the police had come searching for him. Today, after almost thirty years, it is my turn to say thank you. To that unnamed runaway Naxalite, I owe the big lesson of empathy for those who can sacrifice their present for some large and distant dream. I salute that storyteller. I fervently wish that my sons Ramakrishna and Vishnuvardhan too get a storyteller like him someday, somewhere.

It was sometime in 1980, while passing through Purulia district of West Bengal, that my father and I chanced upon an election meeting. A young leader was addressing a large crowd of mostly rural people on a bright Sunday afternoon near a village called Jaipur. The intensely political person that he was, my father, who himself was fighting an election in the neighbouring state of Bihar, stopped his two-wheeler and we sat down with a cup of tea and became part of that gathering. It was a fascinating speech, in Bengali, laced with humour, wit and sarcasm. I have never forgotten the effect of that speech on me. I realized that there is something in the language of each region that gets articulated in its politics and this is generally not translatable, and is best understood in the moment. For many years now I have never missed a single opportunity to listen to a roadside meeting or a public speech, irrespective of my familiarity or otherwise with the language. And on every such occasion, my memory goes back to that afternoon in Jaipur, Purulia. Now, whenever I hear that same gentleman speak in English in Parliament, I feel like whispering in his ear, 'Why don't you speak the way you did that afternoon.' It was Priya Ranjan Dasmunshi, the Congress leader from Bengal and a Union cabinet minister at present, whom I have to thank for showing me how much magic local culture brings to a political speech. Thinking back to the same afternoon, I also thank my father for teaching me never to be dismissive of the opponent. He strongly criticized the politics of that afternoon's speaker but he heard him out.

I feel a deep sense of gratitude to my teachers, particularly Father Van Troy, Father C. de Brower and Father Leo Franklin at St. Xavier's College, Ranchi, who taught me the joys of an austere life with honesty of purpose. This simple lesson has stayed with me ever since. At the same time, seeing and listening to the INTUC leaders, one was witness to how different the day-to-day lifestyle and dealings of the leaders were from what their speeches articulated. This has constantly helped me to distinguish reality from rhetoric in a substantive way. I recall what the late Justin Richard, a respected but forgotten leader of the old Jharkhand Party, who had come to inaugurate the Birsa Chowk in Bokaro, told me in response to my childlike queries about his life: that the fight against injustice and immorality demands great moral fervour and powerful vision. It is this moral vision that became the first casualty of the new state of Jharkhand. Political speeches bereft of moral concerns and values, I learnt while reading hundreds of lives and memoirs for this volume, are invariably of short-term value.

Working at the Academic Staff College of Jawaharlal Nehru University (JNU) I meet thousands of university and college teachers from across the country. It gives me the rare opportunity to interact with brilliant minds working at the frontiers of sciences and humanities in many of our institutions. Talking, lecturing or listening to their woes, worries and world views has helped me mature intellectually. I am indebted to all those from all corners of the country who helped me sustain a universal and cosmopolitan notion of Indianness. I owe special thanks to the staff at the Academic Staff College, particularly

Ramprasad, Yashpal, Rakesh Dedha, Veena Arora, P.S. Chahar and Irshad Ali, for their support.

The idea of arranging the speeches in chapters developed while I was teaching at the Faculty of Social Sciences at the University of Kelaniya, Sri Lanka. I am thankful to Prof. Sunanda Madumma Bandara and Prof. Kulasena for all their help. Ossantha, Virginia and the Fernando family provided me with a home away from home and I am ever grateful to them. My Sri Lankan sojourn gave me the opportunity to experience the beauty of Sinhala eloquence in many public meetings that I attended. As I began to follow Sinhala speeches closely, I began to respect the tradition developed by G.K. Gokhale, Pherozeshah Mehta and Dadabhai Naoroji even more. Sometimes eloquence is effected at the cost of detailed, dispassionate analysis. And this is precisely what the early Indian nationalists gifted to the Indian national movement. In fact, the generation of Mahatma Gandhi and Jawaharlal Nehru did not even need detailed economic analysis to back their anti-colonial arguments. It had already been prepared for them. It is only recently that the traditions set by them have been attacked by sophisticated and sponsored colonial analysis by sections of economic historians and we are still to find our new Gokhales or Naorojis.

I am indebted to the generation which was not only fighting one of the biggest battles for independence politically but was also unmatched in its learning and scholarship. G.A. Natesan, the legendary editor of *Indian Review*, and C.Y. Chintamani of Indian Press who published the collected speeches of almost all the leaders during the freedom struggle were two such intellectuals who took on the Herculean task of spreading the message of liberation. In more recent times, the collection of early works at the JNU library was a gold mine, notwithstanding its badly managed state. I must thank B.R. Nanda for making the Nehru Memorial Library such a rich repository of biographies, memoirs and tracts of the late nineteenth and early twentieth centuries which helped me immensely in my research for this work.

My greatest debt is to Prof. Bipan Chandra who not only taught me to understand the Indian nation in the context of world history but also locate it in an appropriate intellectual perspective. It is from him that I learnt to distinguish the substantial from the fashionable. Through his life and learning I have had a glimpse of the lives of those who have a passion to change society. It was on his persuasion that I began work on the history of Punjab, which gave me new insights. While preparing a biographical dictionary of Punjab, I discovered the way Punjabi intellectuals of the nineteenth and twentieth centuries have left a very powerful imprint on the public space of India—its politics, culture and society. It is a mere coincidence that those who encouraged me and respected my sense of independence have all grown up intellectually and politically in that robust public space. I thank all of them—in many ways this work is dedicated to the spirit of their commitment—particularly Prof. Amrik Singh, Prof. Randhir Singh and Prof. C.P. Bhambri. Prof. Amrik Singh has been very keen that I work on the history of education and I hope the chapter on education will reach the standard that he expects of me.

Among my friends, colleagues and compatriots I must thank Vicky and Usha who always have words of comfort. I acknowledge with thanks Mridula Mukherjee and Aditya Mukherjee who have respected my ideas and supported them. The Thursday Discussion Group and its members—late Mohit Sen, late Girish Mathur, Prof. V.P. Dutt, Arjun Sengupta and Girish Mishra—were not only intellectually stimulating but also helped me relate ideas to policy and politics in the world around. The powerful collective of Visalakshi Menon, Antony Thomas, Sucheta Mahajan, Bhupinder Yadav, Salil Mishra, Amit Mishra, Lata Singh and Richa Malhotra have sustained my interest in history as well as in society. It is their criticism and appreciation that I have valued most for the last twelve years or so. Susmita Dasgupta, that brilliant mind who refuses to join academia, has been my first sounding board for many ideas which she, many times, articulates better. Reshmi and Ravindranathan, Suryanath and Anita, Vivek and Karthika, Sanjay Joshi, Swapna and Gourab Banerjee, Madhushree Banerjee, Beny Kurien, Bijoy Pratihari and H.S. Shivaprakash have been very supportive friends. Deepak Yadav was a good help in times of need. Mrinal Miri, Nirmalangshu Mukherjee, Bijoy Baruah, Sushil and Mahashweta Choudhury, Avijit Pathak and Sovon Sanyal have always been supportive of my intellectual endeavours and have shown concern for my personal well-being. I thank all of them. I fondly think of Sumati Oraon who respected and trusted the arguments and conclusions that an MA student like me would voice. She, with her caring and thinking ways, helped me sustain my respect for the political class. Her untimely death robbed the tribal world of a leader who genuinely cared.

I thank Malathi Ramaswamy for being a good sounding board

with her effusive questions on history and society. Rajeswari Ramakrishnan, my mother-in-law, and her sister Gauri Subramanian, coming as they do from a family connected with social reform in Tamil Nadu, found my work quite serious and I received many interesting insights from them. K.S. Ramakrishnan, Col. Ramaswamy, Nandini and Ravi Ramaswamy have been enormously supportive in many ways. I hope Rahul Lingam, Prem and Pavan Rajagopal in the US will find in this book some answers to the many questions they have about Indian history and politics.

Today, I remember with sadness Dr Sanjay Ambatkar, an unknown struggling alumnus of Bombay University, whom I met one summer afternoon near a dhaba at JNU. Dissatisfied with the educational standards of universities in Maharashtra and the vacuity of intellectual life there, he had come to work at some good research or teaching institution in Delhi. A well-read and articulate person, Sanjay taught me a whole range of things over the four years that we remained close friends. We discussed, disagreed and debated on issues as varied as Manmohan Singh's writings on trade, Tilak's ideas on Hinduism and the economic implications of the 'Look East Policy' (in which he had just published his own economic model and of which he was very proud). He died fighting unemployment and penury. To me, the death of a self-respecting economics graduate of Bombay University at a time when we are celebrating hundreds of self-styled economists touting sensex data was ironical and full of meaning. I dedicate this book to his memory.

I have been constantly working on this book for the last three and a half years, reading hundreds of texts, biographies and parliamentary debates. My sons have quite often been at the receiving end of my tiredness and irritation. I hope they will understand one day why their father kept snapping all the time. To Ravi Singh of Penguin Books—who insisted that I was the best person to do it and found Mahalakshmi Ramakrishnan, my wife, to endorse his views—I am really indebted for forcing me to do this work. I hope I have been able to achieve what they thought I was capable of. Editing the book was arduous because of the nature of the sources and the world it was talking about. At Penguin, I was glad to see Meru and Shantanu and later Avanija talking quite passionately about the book. Meru converted immediately to the world of Gandhi and Gokhale, Naoroji and Nehru. Shantanu, with his disarming smile hiding the tough hands of an editor, was a great support. I express my gratitude to all of them. In the end, I must own up to the errors that may remain in this book.

INTRODUCTION

When this volume was conceived, I thought it would be a simple job of compiling a few famous speeches, something many other editors have done in the past. But once I began reading material for it, several new dimensions which had not struck me earlier began to emerge. Like every historian, the first question I faced was that of historicity. A historian's hindsight, intuition and his location in a historical context are what normally help him read facts and decide on their historicity or otherwise. How does one relate a particular speech to the history of the time and then call it historic? How does one confer on a speech, or even a fact, a trans-historical status and value, and then bestow on it a representative character? These were the issues which immediately needed to be grappled with before one began the process of selection and collection. For me, therefore, compiling this book was a more difficult task than it might have been for those who are innocent of the historian's dilemmas.

Which speech is historic—this is not an innocuous question. It is a question with political, social and cultural perspectives attached to it. Looking back at any specific period, there is always a danger of viewing it from the limited perspective of the brief moment in time that we inhabit. It is crucial not to look at any age in isolation from what led up to it and what came after, and as a result of, it. This led me to read the histories of the nineteenth and early twentieth centuries—which have shaped a number of contemporary trends and ideas that constitute our world view—with a long-term historical perspective. Equally, since the present too colours the way a past is viewed, I felt it important to allow a careful understanding of our times to enter into a debate with our recent history. The present volume is an outcome of this endeavour. Not all questions will be settled in these pages but they inform everything from the selection to the arrangement and presentation of the speeches.

What emerged from my reading of the history of the last two hundred years of the subcontinent was the fact of a long and continuing struggle—the struggle for freedom. Freedom premised at the universal plane may be seen as the leitmotif of human quest, and most of the speeches in this volume verbalized that quest in myriad ways. I was often surprised at the language, emotion and dream articulated especially in the important speeches made in the six or seven decades prior to independence and in the decade immediately after 1947. Leaders like Sir Syed Ahmad and M.G. Ranade most often spoke in the voice of universalism and humanism, something they themselves may not have consciously known. As a historian working in an intellectual milieu where anti-humanism and anti-universalism are often the keys to success in academia, this collection increasingly became an academic challenge for me: that of presenting as valuable and path-breaking ideas and commitments which are considered mere common sense by later generations.

I

Colonialism, or rather the intelligentsia's attempt in the late nineteenth and early twentieth centuries to understand, negotiate with, and fight colonialism, has been the most significant marker of the history of modern India. A serious reading of the intellectual premises and political arguments of men and women like Surendranath Banerjea, Dadabhai Naoroji and Annie Besant shows that, though circumscribed by their age and context, these people were making a radical departure from their moorings and were presenting a very powerful critique of the colonial system. They were not the intellectual or political collaborators of colonialism that many politically prejudiced or historically myopic writings say they are. These early nationalists were trying to evolve the economic, political and moral foundations of a new society.

The speeches and writings of public persons in nineteenth- and twentieth-century India indicate that they had not merely understood the might and exploitative agendas of the colonial power, but also realized the fact that the society from which this power had emerged had undergone an industrial revolution which had far-reaching consequences completely unprecedented in human history. They recognized the role the industrial revolution had played in making England the most modern and developed country at that historical juncture. They were also aware of the social and scientific benefits that could accrue to a backward society like India from an engagement with England. This led them to look towards England to help India transcend its internal morass and help usher in a modern society. For Naoroji and others, British colonial presence in India was providential, at least to begin with, as it provided Indian society—a stagnant one which had missed out on the scientific and industrial revolution in the West—an opportunity to catch up. In fact, they intuited what Karl Marx would write later about the regenerative role of colonialism: that the colonial state in India, through its ideas, institutions and instruments of exploitation, for example, the railways, hastened social and political change. This provided them with a blueprint for a new society for India too—a modern, industrial society. Thus, their speeches were marked less by rhetoric and more by a close and detailed analysis of the facts and processes involved in the rise and maintenance of colonialism. They were also conscious of their own role in such a context. This nuanced and complex understanding of the empire of the day and a perception of the role of intellectuals and political leaders, as glimpsed in the first few speeches in this book, laid the foundations of modern-day Indian sensibilities, whether in politics, or on social questions, or in an understanding of India's economic location and policies.

It was in their critique of the colonial system that these intellectuals made the greatest contribution. They provided a detailed analysis of the way colonialism worked through its sophisticated and elaborate system of finances, manipulation of currencies and trade policies, establishment of communication linkages for economic and administrative facilitation, integration of executive and judicial powers in local governance, and racial appropriation of the instruments of administration. The early nationalists' eye for detail and meticulous work thus 'deconstructed' the empire, exposing its internal circuitry as it were, and provided the intellectual foundation of Indian nationalism (which Bipan Chandra, one of the finest historians of modern India, has called 'economic nationalism' in his book *Rise and Growth of Economic Nationalism in India*). At the level of public engagement, their attempts to criticize the economic policies of the empire and the colonial state and at the same time develop democratic methods and institutions to fight those policies laid the foundations of India's democratic polity as well. It is here that their efforts to model institutions after the nineteenth-century British parliamentary system become significant. Their political tracts, economic treatises and speeches at various platforms indicate the evolution of a vision anchored in the core values of a parliamentary democracy which later influenced India's political and social evolution.

Interestingly, much of contemporary intellectual engagement with India's modern history, particularly in our metropolitan centres or in the West, is characterized by a downplaying of the career and vision of these early nationalists; they are dismissed as lightweight liberals or condemned as the empire's collaborators, intellectual or economic or political. Or their vision and discourse is assumed to be a matter of common-sense understanding and therefore not worthy of being studied. This has resulted in making many discussions on modern-day Indian democracy, the state and the economy a-historical, grounded on extremely superficial assumptions or currently fashionable theories in the West. A serious exploration into the foundations of many of the issues facing contemporary India—the success or failure of its democracy, the evolution of its institutions and economy—will indicate that they have their roots not in the hoary past of the Vedas or the ancient republics, but in the intellectual and political engagements of public men and women in the late nineteenth and early twentieth centuries. There is no getting away from this foundational truth.

A historically inclined perspective helps one discern that the national liberation movement was not merely one single movement of political liberation, but, as many would say in their speeches, a beautiful movement unique in human history. It was the gradual unfolding of the movement into multiple streams which made the quest for political freedom against the colonial state meaningful. This also proved the early nationalist assertions—which even Nehru made when he was president of the Congress in 1929—that Indian nationalism was entirely different from its Western counterpart. It was liberating and inclusive rather than exclusivist. It welcomed every class and all streams of political and economic thought, some of which were antagonistic to its inclusivist nature itself. Though articulating such dimensions in public speeches made the speeches substantive, it also tended to make them quite long as the speakers tried to locate the interconnectedness of issues.

The intelligentsia and public men at the turn of the twentieth century had a palpable sense of a movement in India on a vast scale. It is with such sensibilities that Surendranath Banerjea, Bal Gangadhar

Tilak and Pherozeshah Mehta were speaking and writing in that era. They were in constant search of a plan of action, a vision for India. Their speeches may sound sedate by the standards of today's political rhetoric or literary fashion, but they were expressing ideas at a time when the common Indian did not have the wherewithal to even speak up, nor could he or she thoroughly comprehend their implications. The spell of colonial rule, as Bipin Chandra Pal would say, was upon us; it was our *mai-baap.* Pal called it maya or illusion under which Indians lived. Later historians and particularly those who studied the national movement thoroughly used the word *hegemony* to explain the ideological sway that colonial rule had over Indians. The speeches of Naoroji, Mehta and Gokhale were not simple acts of eloquence; they were political acts of awakening people and impelling them to shrug off the imperial cast. Given the British arguments that India was not and never had been a nation and that it was merely a geographical imagination, an attempt was made quite often in the speeches to imagine and create an India. Thus, there were conscious efforts to argue that even if India was not a nation in the modern sense of the term, it could be constituted as one owing to its historical and economic rationale. It *could* be moulded into a nation and indeed it was *becoming* one.

At the same time, the movement was not born of any anti-foreigner or anti-alien sensibility. After all, the notion of videshi or alien has always had manifold implications in a society like India where the primary identity till recently was of one's caste or village. A journey through the speeches in this book will indicate that rarely did a leader or intellectual try to defend an anti-colonial position on nativistic grounds, i.e., India is for Indians and foreigners should leave. The Indian nationalist leadership never argued that the British should leave India only because they were foreigners. It was rather the notion of justice which constituted the core of their arguments asking the British to leave. British rule, as Naoroji famously described it, was 'un-British'. Many among India's intelligentsia of the time had envisioned that British rule in India would usher the principles of liberal democracy as voiced in the British Parliament, the press and in the works of Bentham, Mill and others. However, the gradual realization of the lack of fair play in dealing with India on several fronts, mainly economic, became the reason for an increasing disillusionment, a sense of injustice which would culminate in the demand for the withdrawal of the British from India.

The argument for the British quitting because they were foreigners did also exist, of course, though it always constituted a second line of reasoning. This fundamentally racial argument came to provide the intellectual basis for some internal movements among those Indians who wanted to voice their rejection of the hierarchies within the Indian social system. Many tribal and non-Brahmin caste movements used the nativistic and racial arguments to assert that Brahmins and upper castes were outsiders and had been exploiting the indigenous peoples who had been relegated to a low-caste status.

However, it was the economic critique that constituted the core of the argument against colonial presence and it began with the grand old man of India, Dadabhai Naoroji. His drain theory and its understanding of the exploitation of India under colonial rule was the cornerstone of the entire national movement. What Naoroji initiated in the British Parliament in 1892 and repeated at various public platforms was then carried forward by Pherozeshah Mehta, who excelled in tearing apart official claims at various forums—the legislative assembly, the Bombay Corporation or the university senate. His speeches, full of sarcasm, wit and sheer confidence, set the benchmarks for debate on public issues. Surendranath Banerjea, acknowledged as the first public leader of modern India, was completely devoted to arousing nationalistic sentiments among the people of various regions, and his speeches attracted many future leaders.

II

The colonial critique of the early nationalists also contained an awareness of India's social malaise and in this they were the inheritors of the different socio-religious movements of the nineteenth century. From Raja Rammohun Roy, whom Surendranath Banerjea referred to as the greatest Indian reformer, to Jyotiba Phule, G.K. Gokhale and Badruddin Tyabji, everyone was involved in social reform, thus broadening and enlarging the canvas of their engagement. With the heightening of political consciousness, there was a tension brewing between those championing the political question and the others who also demanded social reform. At the end of the nineteenth century, particularly after the formation of the Indian National Congress in 1885, this conflict reached a high. Attempts were made to ensure that the controversy did not cause a rift in the nascent political processes and organization. It did not, for example, take much longer than its third session for the Congress to announce that it was not going to entertain any demand for social reform of any community unless the demand had an overwhelming support from that community itself. Interestingly, this decision was taken by people who themselves were the greatest social reformers in their own respective communities, people like Tyabji and Naoroji. At the same time, the apprehensions that the controversy would have divisive effects were proved right when Syed Ahmad Khan, who was involved in modernizing the Muslim upper classes through his Aligarh movement, came to oppose the Congress. The tussle between the reformers who gradually voiced themselves through the Indian Social Reform Conference and the groups which came to critique the primacy of social reform brought the dilemma to the fore. K.T. Telang, a leading intellectual of the period, created a furore when he suggested, as a via media, that political processes should be given precedence over social reforms since this involved lesser resistance from society. It was only with the arrival of Mahatma Gandhi on the scene that the political demand and the social question came together cohesively on the same platform. Gandhi not only amalgamated the social and political movements but also launched the biggest ever social change movement in the country—the removal of untouchability. His speech at Benares in 1916 announced his arrival on the scene with a canvas much larger than what the leadership of the time had envisaged. It was a direct attack on the norms, language and composition of the leadership of the era. From 1920 onwards, one can see the political movement constantly engaging with the issues of untouchability, Hindu–Muslim unity and the amelioration of the rural poor.

Very soon the question of leadership and representation became the centre of most public speeches. As the British, strategically, decided to lend representative status to different leaders or groups, there were strong clashes for such status among India's public leaders. There were more than a few who argued that they represented the Hindus or the Muslims or, as B.R. Ambedkar claimed, the depressed classes. Gandhi, in his straight and simple manner, claimed that he represented all Hindus and all Muslims *and* the depressed classes. The language of representation gave the speeches of this period a very strong authoritative character coupled with a narrowness not evident till now. These varying claims of representation, which were heard most clearly during the Second Round Table Conference in 1931, with the British seeking different representatives for different communities—Hindus, Muslims, Sikhs, depressed classes, native princes—reached a climax when Veer Savarkar claimed in 1937 that he and his party, the Hindu Mahasabha, represented the Hindus, and M.A. Jinnah in 1940 declared that he was the sole spokesperson of the Muslim nation—a nation which he said had no common bond with the Hindu and therefore had to be given separate status as Pakistan.

III

The question of freedom that informed almost all the pre-independence speeches was also intimately related to the issue of equality. The ideal of equality that the early intelligentsia envisioned initially sprang from Queen Victoria's proclamation of 1858 which pledged the British crown to equality irrespective of race, colour and creed. For the enlightened among Indians who wanted to see their own backward society moving in the direction of the most developed country of the time, the Queen's proclamation was also a testimony to the fact that the philosophy and culture of the post-Renaissance West had virtues worth imbibing. It is, therefore, understandable that they were disappointed when the British seemed unwilling to put their pronouncements on equality into practice in India as was seen in the reactions against the Ilbert Bill which sought to provide a semblance of equality before the law to Indians vis-à-vis Europeans. The Indian leaders were also aware of the deep inequality that existed in their own society. Inequality, particularly on the basis of caste and gender, was extremely stark and all efforts at social reform were aimed at eradicating this. However, at a more basic level, deprivation and exploitation of the rural peasantry was their major concern.

The peasantry had been reeling under the weight of feudal oppression on which had been imposed the colonial revenue demand. The complete change in the character of land rights and the resultant transformation in land relations during the colonial period led to some of the worst famines rural India had ever witnessed. With the gradual unravelling of the working of the economy under colonial rule, the peasantry began to occupy central place in the political consciousness of the Indian intelligentsia. Peasants themselves, however, became the focus of political mobilization only after Gandhi entered the scene. At the same time, the rapid penetration of socialist and communist thinking in the 1920s led to radicalization of the issue of equality with the idea being transformed into a quest for an egalitarian society.

Another aspect of equality pertained to government jobs. This being the only employment avenue for educated Indians, they began demanding their share of the pie monopolized by the British. However, the issue became complicated as the relatively prosperous and educated segment among the non-Brahmin castes in Maharashtra and later in the Madras Presidency began to raise the demand for what later came to be known as communal representation. The colonial state patronized these demands, more as a means of fragmenting the nationalist liberation struggle than out of any concern for equality. Communal reservation for non-Brahmin castes (today's Other Backward Castes) was first brought about in Mysore state. But it was in Madras Presidency that the most significant developments took place regarding this issue, and the debates originating from there in the 1920s culminated in the Constituent Assembly unanimously providing for reservation of seats for Scheduled Castes and Scheduled Tribes in free India's constitution.

The sense of justice and the progressive ideas which gripped society were also fostered by the writers of the era. Subrahmanya Bharathi's nationalist poems aroused deep sympathy in the Tamil region and their seizure by the British police led to a major attack on the colonial state in Madras Presidency. Another equally powerful voice was that of Kazi Nazrul Islam who changed the canvas of poetry and its content in Bengal and filled his writings with so much protest that it became de rigueur for the authorities to proscribe them. His impact on the youth in Bengal and on revolutionary youth all over the country was immeasurable. The writers articulated freedom at a more basic level, expressing the urges and aspirations of the common man, the peasantry and the workers. In this sense, Munshi Premchand's presidential address at the Progressive Writers' meet in 1936 was historic. Unfortunately, the speech is in Hindustani and a translation mars its greatness in more ways than one, which is why I have refrained from including it in this collection.

IV

Independence was an event of great significance. Notwithstanding recent efforts in many quarters to dilute its importance by positing the partition of the country as the event of consequence and independence as a mere transfer of power from the sahibs to the brown sahibs (the Indian elite), freedom provided the Indian people the wherewithal to effect social and economic change with a speed hitherto unknown. The first manifestation of genuine independence was the drafting of the constitution which finally made the people sovereign and Parliament the highest authority to legislate. With this a new India began to wake up to the reality that it needed to change and that it *could* change. This was articulated in the speeches in the Constituent Assembly whose tenor, confidence and vitality made them trendsetters and of lasting educational value to future generations. With almost all stalwarts of the liberation movement contributing their collective might to the vision for a free India, the speeches and debates in the Constituent Assembly were fascinating in their reach and imagination and in their quest for human freedom. Visionaries like Sardar Patel, Rajendra Prasad, Jawaharlal Nehru, Maulana Azad, Gopalaswamy Ayyangar, B.R. Ambedkar, Syama Prasad Mookerjee and many others gave their best to the Constituent Assembly.

A society characterized by poverty, malnutrition, illiteracy, lack of capital and infrastructure, low productivity and many more ills was sought to be transformed by one of the greatest human efforts in history, oriented towards creating a modern, self-reliant, developed nation with a democracy organized with the help of universal adult franchise. This was the path the Constituent Assembly decided for India. The Parliament which succeeded the Constituent Assembly took it upon itself to oversee this gigantic transformation, and towards this end began to act as the watchdog not only of democracy but also of the developmental processes and their ramifications for the poor, the marginal and the underprivileged. It was in Parliament that most of these sections of people found articulation through their representatives. It is, therefore, no surprise that a majority of India's most significant and historically important speeches ever—Jaipal Singh's intervention on the appointment of a commissioner for Scheduled Castes and Scheduled Tribes, the speech on the Untouchability (Offences) Bill, Ram Manohar Lohia's speech on the daily earnings of an Indian—were made in Parliament in the first couple of decades after independence.

The international order in which India emerged as a free nation was soon to be divided into two antagonistic blocs which would have important consequences for India. Articulating India's long-held understanding of itself in the world, Nehru had declared on the eve of independence: 'We propose, as far as possible, to keep away from the power politics of groups aligned against one another, which have led in the past to world wars and which may again lead to disasters on an even vaster scale.' India felt it could play a conciliatory role in a world torn asunder due to the bitter ideological and strategic divide. It had shown its steadfast commitment for a democratic and peaceful world order by siding with the republicans in the Spanish Civil War and in criticizing Hitler and Mussolini. Its sympathies for the communist society in Soviet Union notwithstanding, it did not align itself with the communist bloc either, for which Nehru was for long criticized as a closet imperialist, a view that was strengthened when under his leadership India decided to remain within the Commonwealth. Nehru's speeches on independent India's role in relation to the world and the reasons why he felt India should remain with the Commonwealth reveal the mind of a master statesman.

Notwithstanding India's commitment to democracy and peace, the West remained suspicious of its independent ways. Erstwhile colonial countries like Britain and France and the new leader of the capitalist bloc, the US, increasingly became antagonistic. This was manifested as early as 1948 itself when India went to the United Nations complaining about Pakistan's act of aggression on its territory, Kashmir, which had recently become part of India through an instrument of accession. India soon found that the whole issue had turned on its head with the Western nations looking upon the issue as a matter of disputed territory rather than one of aggression. The blatant partiality of members of the Security Council, however, brought out the best in V.K. Krishna Menon, one of the most analytical minds of independent India. His complete command of facts, commitment to the cause of the nation, his strident anti-colonialism, and mastery of language marked by bitter sarcasm, wit and raw confidence made his speeches in the United Nations in the 1950s a delight. Particular mention must be made of his brilliant interventions on apartheid in South Africa and on Kashmir, the latter being the longest speech made in the history of the United Nations and, despite its great length, one of the most memorable in Indian history. The way he repeatedly exposed the duplicity of the West and snubbed their representatives at the august forum indicated India's resolve that despite being a poor country it would face the world with confidence and not barter its self-respect.

V

The 1960s was a time of uncertainties and crises. Globally, the Cold War had reached its zenith with the US and Soviet Russia almost going to war over the issue of installation of missiles in Cuba by the Soviets. The war in Vietnam had entered its most violent phase with US bombers destroying village after village, while in the Middle East, Israel and the Arabs were engaged in a war in 1967.

Conditions were no better at home. At the beginning of the decade, India was involved in an armed conflict with China. The Chinese aggression marked a watershed in India's independent history, shattering once and for all a complacence with regard to internal security which India had developed in pursuance of its avowed policies of peace and friendly relations with neighbours. The Chinese aggression and the events leading up to it resulted in some of the best parliamentary speeches in India, most notably J.B. Kripalani's intervention on India's policy with respect to China and Tibet, and Bhupesh Gupta's brilliant response articulating communist support to India's war effort in light of the fact that communists were being victimized and branded as traitors and unpatriotic in the wave of nationalist feelings that swept the country following the Chinese aggression.

The war with China followed by the one with Pakistan in 1965 and the drought and famine of 1966-67 had created a precarious food situation which could not but have an impact on politics and society. India's independent posture in the international arena further aggravated matters, with the US, in what amounted to nothing short of political blackmail to gain support for its position in Vietnam, refusing to consider India's urgent request for food aid. With the resultant economic instability came a large measure of political chaos. The overwhelming presence of the Congress party was eroded with many states throwing up parties and affiliations which differed with and opposed the policies of the Congress at the centre. Fissiparous tendencies also began to be manifested in various parts of the country on a number of issues, the most important of which was that of national language which had been hanging fire ever since it had been taken up in the Constituent Assembly. Tamil Nadu witnessed violent anti-Hindi agitations with a demand for the separation of the state from India. The equally powerful and militant pro-Hindi stance by political sections in the north contributed to the strong sense of instability in the country and a commensurate loss of the elegance which had characterized public speaking by eminent leaders till then.

VI

The 1970s were by far the most momentous years in the history of independent India. The economic, political and social upheavals during the decade would influence the making of modern-day India in many ways. On the political front, the decade began with the formation of new states in the north-eastern region of the country which together with the linguistic reorganization of states in the late 1950s meant that the political map of India looked very different from what it had been at the time of independence. The euphoria following the victory over Pakistan in the 1971 war dissipated soon after in the political instability resulting from middle-class unease with rising prices, unemployment and corruption in high offices. Indira Gandhi, the hero of the 1971 war, became the target of a mass movement calling for a change in the political set-up. Jayaprakash Narayan led students and a conglomerate of non-Congress political formations against the policies of Indira Gandhi and the Congress. Soon, however, the movement began exhibiting undemocratic trends with communal organizations almost hijacking it. The resultant tussle saw Indira Gandhi imposing Emergency, probably the single most important event in the sixty years of India's independence. For the first time since independence, Indians had a taste of authoritarianism as their personal freedom was curbed. The speeches made in Parliament opposing the Emergency and Indira Gandhi's speech defending it, give glimpses of the complex issues involved.

On the economic front, the decade began with Indira Gandhi's historic steps of nationalization of banks and abolition of privy purses. With independence, India had opted for a model of economic development in which the state was to play a significant part. It was believed that since India was embarking on the road to industrialization after nearly two hundred years of colonial exploitation, the state had to be involved not only to ensure the establishment of institutions which would facilitate the process but also lead to a more equitable distribution of the prosperity that would result from it. No country in the world, with the exception of the United States, had industrialized itself with democracy as the delivery system. Thus, it was a gigantic task which, the state reasoned, could not be left solely to private enterprise. With the Congress adopting a socialistic pattern of society as its objective at its annual session in Avadi in 1954, the stage was set for the state to play a major role in the economic development of the nation. Indira Gandhi's decision to nationalize private commercial banks, despite the element of populism inherent in it, was in keeping with the thinking that had shaped the economy since independence. However, state control over means of production led to increasing bureaucratic interference and corruption with commensurate stagnation of the economy which right through the 1970s grew at what was derisively termed 'the Hindu rate of growth'. By the end of the decade, it was imperative to let go of state shackles and the first hesitant steps towards liberalizing the economy were taken in the beginning of the 1980s. The process would culminate with the economic reforms announced by Manmohan Singh, finance minister in the Narasimha Rao government (1991–96), which aimed at dismantling the economic and financial structures erected in the decades following independence. His budget speech of 1992–93 heralded a new way of life in modern India. The process of integrating the Indian economy with global finance and the international economic order began to unleash forces, the impact of which is still to be assessed properly.

VII

In the last two decades of the twentieth century, India was a nation struggling to come to grips with the violence that threatened the country's unity and integrity. Punjab witnessed one of the bloodiest separatist movements in Indian history. In the north-east, Assam went up in flames. Since the 1930s, the Assamese-speaking population had been showing their uneasiness about the Bengali-speaking peasantry from East Bengal coming and occupying land in the region. In the late 1970s, they began to organize and agitate against the constant influx of Bangladeshi migrants settling in Assam. The violent overtones of the agitation, symbolized by Nellie, where a large number of Muslim villagers were massacred, destabilized the whole region for a while with the Government of India relegated to being a helpless onlooker. Kashmir erupted with sporadic violence from the late 1980s. These insurgencies raised serious questions about the ability of Indian federalism and democracy to deal with separatist tendencies.

The political scenario began to change drastically with communal and caste identities fast becoming the loci of political and social questions. By the late 1980s, these would fundamentally alter the face of the Indian body politic. The most important development was the increasing communal overtones in politics. Beginning with the Gujarat riots in 1986, it gained momentum with the Bharatiya Janata Party (BJP)-led movement for restoration of what they claimed to be the birthplace of Lord Rama, the Ram Janmabhoomi. A civil property dispute was gradually moulded into a powerful and violent movement asserting the religious rights of the majority. The period also saw the polarization of society on the basis of caste with the Dalits and Other Backward Classes becoming increasingly vocal and militant in articulating their desire for greater representation in education, employment and politics.

Sadly, the true extent and impact on the nation of the changes in the last two and a half decades are rarely glimpsed in the public speeches of this period. A whole country was being transformed—for better or worse—but you wouldn't guess this from our public discourse. The nature, content and tenor of speeches which had begun to change for the worse by the end of the 1960s, became pathetic in the years leading to the new millennium, with Parliament merely articulating the political malaise of the body politic. The speeches lost their literary standard, an indication of the gradual loss of the aesthetic in public life. G.G. Swell's speech on the Gujarat riots of 1986 and Narasimha Rao's speech in the aftermath of the destruction of the Babri Masjid are exceptions which echo the concerns of the time.

Post-1966, Congress leaders, including many stalwarts, seemed increasingly apologetic and concerned about the impact of their speeches on the 'High Command' while the opposition's ideology was limited to a deep anti-Congressism. This could not but have an impact on the quality of public discourse. The reasons for falling standards in public speaking had also to do with the changing contours of politics, with new political groups laying little store by parliamentary debates, preferring to take to the streets to settle issues. Rarely well thought out, increasingly strident and bereft of linguistic elegance, these speeches also lacked the passion which had marked the oratory of the last hundred-odd years. The logical coherence of arguments began to be replaced by neat political expediency. The emergence of the BJP heightened this aspect of public speaking with its leaders resorting to high rhetoric, reference to mythical history and direct and quite often personal attacks on its opponents. This contributed to bringing an element of vacuity in public speeches which almost always tended to be pragmatic and politically calculated.

The speeches in this collection add up, in a sense, to the story of the evolution of modern India. They reflect both the success of Indian democracy as well as a shift from substantive ideological debates on issues to pure electoral calculation. If this book contributes in any degree towards restoring substance and ideology to our public discourse, it will have served its purpose.

1

CONCEIVING A NATION

Today, we have a map which gives everyone a definite idea of a geographical and political entity called India. But it was not so even a hundred years ago. Nor were there commonly agreed notions of history, economics, polity or even the much talked about cultural unity. Anybody from another village or town or far-off country was a videshi. Caste, as Al Beruni noted in the eleventh century, or as Raja Rammohun Roy lamented in the nineteenth century, was the identifying social marker while the village was the locus of one's geographical, political or even cultural identity. An alien was not somebody racially different but someone who was not from one's own village. Interestingly, even today, people in various parts of the country, from Punjab to Maharashtra, and the entire southern peninsula, carry the village name as part of their personal names.

When British occupation and colonization began around the mid-eighteenth century, the idea of a nation as we understand it in political or even socio-economic terms today was not a powerful presence. Thus, the British found it easy to legitimize their imperial ideology by calling India a disparate community with no sense of nationhood. This idea is still powerful and Western nations, including the USA (a settlers' society by all accounts), find it difficult to understand and recognize the 'nation' in the non-Western locale where people essentially remain Hindu or Muslim, Shia or Sunni.

The nation, with its political and lately economic essences, grew as a feeling and an ideology in opposition to the idea of imperial presence in colonized countries. The French Revolution, espousing the idea of common citizenry and the idea of this citizenry as a nation, became the inspiration of people all over the world. When the French armies moved around the continent, it was for the first time that a national army was moving and not a king's army. The first war of liberation on the basis of nationalism can also be traced to the wars of independence (for example the Greek war of independence) that took place in Europe in the 1820s.

The operation of a colonial system began to foster a perceptible sense of unity in India too. By the middle of the nineteenth century, India began to have a semblance of political, administrative and economic unity far more extended than it had ever achieved after Emperor Asoka. This unifying exercise proved crucial in creating a sense of a common people. These ideas inspired the intelligentsia in India who faced a piquant situation in the nineteenth century. While the might of the British Empire was unifying territories of the Indian subcontinent into one judicial and political unit, it came about at the cost of recurrent famines and a growing decadence in society. The intelligentsia and socio-religious reformers began to analyse the reasons for this decadence and the people's inability to face the superior British power. They located it in the body politic and in the social organization of the people. Caste, untouchability and the lack of unity among people were sought to be linked. They thought in terms of political unity. While social analysis led many of them to organize the people, the idea of a nation provided them with a locus for such a notion of unity. The nation had to be visualized, concretized and a common people organized.

There is much talk about the nation being imagined. In that sense, all institutions, including the family, marriage and to an extent the self itself, are imagined. What is significant is how it is visualized and in what context the imagination takes place. The colonial authority stressed that India was not a nation but only a geographical entity. Indians looked back at their hoary past to assert that they had an old national history. India, along with China, modern-day Iraq and Egypt, is one of the oldest surviving civilizations. Though nation and nationalism entered as new ideas, elements of India's civilizational ethos continued to provide a solution to many of the problems in the making of a new nation. For example, the deep pan-Indian cultural unity, which many tried to invoke for the cause of the nation and in their mobilizational efforts, is an outcome of this civilizational continuity.

But many things were of modern origin. In fact, the colonialists were not wrong in emphasizing that it was British colonialism that created a country out of India, providing it with a political, geographical and, through the English language, a kind of linguistic unity, at the top at least. With the gradual spread of the idea of the nation, the Indian intelligentsia, while accepting that Indians were united by the British, asserted that India was not a nation yet, but was aspiring to be one. It was, in fact, 'a nation in the making', as Surendranath Banerjea evocatively argued. His speech reproduced here will give the modern generation of Indians a sense of the struggle that nineteenth-century intellectuals foresaw in creating the unity that was to be called a nation.

While civilization proved helpful in the making of this nation, the architects of this nationalism, however, consciously never allowed elements like culture or religion to become the premise or bedrock of the Indian nation. In fact, those who tried to create a common Indian nation fought the idea of a nation based on cultural, linguistic or even religious unity.

The diversity of India at the beginning of the eighteenth and nineteenth centuries was more real than it is today. In that sense, the colonialists were not wrong that India was a mere geographical expression. The intellectuals from the beginning saw economic and political unity as the cornerstone of the new nation they were trying to build. For this, they constantly looked for symbols. The symbols were chosen not because they represented any community or religion but because they represented this quest for a mobilizing metaphor. Bahadur Shah Zafar, for example, instantly became a symbol of unity for those who revolted in 1857. He represented a political unity before the British. The conception of nation had changed by the 1940s and the monarchical system had no place in the hearts and minds of the people any more. A new nation had emerged but that the Mughals were still seen as a representation of national unity is movingly symbolized by Netaji Subhas Chandra Bose's visit to the tomb of Bahadur Shah Zafar in Rangoon. Even though the idea of Mughal monarchy was at variance with Netaji's modern democratic temperament, Zafar symbolized pre-British India, which had its own history, as well as the resistance to the British and the sense of outrage at the injustice meted out to the country. Tilak's choice of Shivaji, too, had this element. It represented the quest for a symbol of protest.

How to transcend the boundaries of caste and, in some sense, communities, and weld people to the idea of a nation were the strongest urges among the intelligentsia who were located in the centres where British presence was most entrenched, that is, in the presidencies of Bombay, Calcutta and Madras. For many latter-day historians, the fact of the Indian nation is too commonsensical an idea, requiring no rigorous probe or proof except to be discarded as intellectually unfashionable. To the early intelligentsia, however, nation-making was an arduous and difficult task. They were, in fact, unlike their portrayal by many as intellectual collaborationists, in search of a critique of the most powerful system operating in the world at that point of time—the British colonial system—an exploitative system coming from the most modern and progressive society. Notwithstanding the latest fashion to debunk them as compradors or as trapped in colonial and Western mindsets, their task was a Herculean one. It seems common sense, with the benefit of hindsight. To create this nation they looked at history, memorials and metaphors. Nation-making was a gigantic and unprecedented political task and its immediacy was never lost on the people and the leadership of the country.

The selections in this chapter start with what one of the pioneers of modern-day nationalism, Surendranath Banerjea, thought of the man who for generations of Indians symbolized modern India, Raja Rammohun Roy. Surendranath Banerjea spent his life advocating, propagating and politically trying to consolidate the idea of India as a nation. He was also in some sense the first pan-Indian political personality, and his speeches invoking the unity of the people under the rubric of a nation played a crucial role in nation-building. The second speech is by Sir Syed Ahmad Khan who, like Rammohun, was a true torch-bearer of modernity in the country. The nation that he speaks of is a nation of mingling communities. Bal Gangadhar Tilak, the first mass leader of modern India, gives his understanding of the nature of patriotism in relation to the nature of society and nation. Mahadev Govind Ranade talks about locating the nation in some kind of a historical framework. In all these, the nation is conceptualized differently; but it is unmistakable that the idea of the nation is modern and that it grew in the context of colonialism.

~

SURENDRANATH BANERJEA

Rammohun Roy: The Father of Modern India

Any sensitive reader of the history of India over the last two hundred years would consider Surendranath Banerjea (1848–1925) as the first person to articulate the sense of a modern Indian nation out of what was essentially a group of diverse communities inhabiting a geographical region. The father of modern Indian nationalism, Surendranath Banerjea was a powerful and popular speaker. A passionate pan-Indian vision and a large historical canvas was what made his speeches so significant to a large number of people who found in them a message through which to forge a unity called nation. This, he argued, was a unity different from what the country had seen so far. In this historic address on 27 September 1888 at Calcutta to commemorate the birth centenary of Raja Rammohun Roy, Surendranath Banerjea argued that this modern nation emerged from the work of people like Rammohun Roy who personified the spirit of this struggle. Locating Rammohun Roy in the socio-religious and political context, quite often of Bengal, Surendranath Banerjea sees him as 'the mightiest product of English influence' and says that it was Rammohun Roy who in some sense had prepared the contours of a modern nation and therefore 'our national life [can] be said to flow from him as from a fountain'.

Fifty years ago and more, Rammohun Roy sank into his grave in a distant land amid the faithful tears ('no faithless tears' in the language of the sonnets) of his English friends, but unwept and unhonoured by his countrymen at large. They regarded him as an outcast, and his death in a foreign land as perhaps the just punishment, the merited visitation of Providence, for his open defiance of the religion of his fathers. For years he lay unnoticed in the humble tomb which the piety of his English friends had raised for him, and it was not until the arrival of Dwarkanath Tagore in England that a suitable monument was raised over the remains of the greatest Hindoo reformer of modern times. What a change has since taken place! The grandsons of those who regarded Rammohun Roy as an outcast, a heretic, as one unfit to be associated with, are now gathered round his tomb to make atonements for the sins of the past, to redeem an unfulfilled duty, and above all to draw from him—aye, from his yet unextinguished ashes—the inspiration for whatever is honourable in life, noble in conduct, and true in religion, morals, politics, in the struggle for social reform. The ceremony of today would descend into a dead and meaningless form if divorced from such a purpose as this. This ceremony would only then be instinct with life, and replete with life, and replete with interest, when associated with such a high moral purpose.

Rammohun Roy is the mightiest product of English influences so far as they have yet displayed themselves, as Chaitanya was the mightiest product of Mohamedan influences in Bengal. There is a striking similarity in the circumstances which produced these wonderful men. A great man, it has been truly remarked, is the product of his age, the reflex of the energies of his time, the embodiment of the forces of his epoch. A great man is such as his age makes him, but he is something more. He reacts upon the age, carries it to a further stage of progress, be it in morals, or in politics or in religion. He gives back to the age more than what he has received from it. The age pours into the lap of its gifted son its choicest gifts. The hero improves, refines and embellishes them, and repays them back with compound interest. Thus the age is illustrated, adorned and ennobled in the personality of its most gifted representative.

Chaitanya rose as a living protest against the abominations of Tantric worship. The struggle between Vaishnavism and Sakta worship had already commenced. The Bacchanalian orgies of those times were a disgrace to the age. Human nature rose in revolt against them. There is a divinity within us which, rough-hew it as we may, will amid darkness and despair reassert its sovereignty. There are depths beyond which human nature will not go. The divine element comes to the rescue. In the hearts of others, it speaks tremulously, in half-broken accents, and in moments of temporary illumination. In the heart of the prophet, it glows with heavenly radiance. It is an all-consuming fire. It absorbs him and overpowers him and bodies itself forth in language of deep, burning and passionate conviction. Thus rose Chaitanya, the exponent of the purity, the moral forces and the religious energies of his times. But he brought to the age something which it did not possess, something which was his own, something it derived from the abundance of his own nature. He breathed into the sweet spirit of love—the spirit of *bhakti*—that spirit of charity of which St. Paul speaks, and which finds such striking illustration in the triumphant sufferings of the martyred souls of humanity.

When Rammohun Roy appeared on the scene, the struggle between Sakta worship and Vaishnavism was in full operation. It was indeed the old struggle between right and wrong, between the principle of light and that of darkness. Rammohun Roy was peculiarly situated as regards this struggle. On his father's side he was a Vaishnava; on his mother's he was a Sakta. It seemed as if these two contending systems of thought had, after ages of conflict and struggle, met together in the same family to produce the greatest religious reformer of modern India, who, singularly enough, was neither a Sakta nor a Vaishnava, but sought to restore the religion of his fathers to its pristine purity. Rammohun Roy was singularly well-equipped for this struggle. Inferior to Chaitanya in the inexhaustible resources of deep spirituality and boundless love, he was superior to him in the incisiveness of his logic, in the breadth of his intellect, which excited the admiration of the most gifted minds of Europe, and in the keener appreciation and firmer grasp of the situation which he displayed as the result of superior culture and deeper insight. Chaitanya was such as Sanskrit learning and Mohamedan influences and his own sweet spirituality had made him. Rammohun Roy was the product of these factors, but he associated with them the inestimable benefit of English culture.

I fear we are not always sufficiently alive to the deep debt which we owe to the time of the Mohamedan conquest. The country was sunk in ignorance and superstition. To Islam belongs the credit of keeping alive in the recollections of our people the principles of the monotheistic creed, which Rammohun Roy sought to read in the olden records of our race. Rammohun Roy was deeply versed in Sanskrit as well as in Arabic, and from the outset stood forth as the champion of monotheism. But the method which he followed was peculiar and singularly characteristic of the man and the reformer. He sought to build upon the old foundations, but only so far as they were compatible with truth. The truth he worshipped; the truth he loved; the truth was the adorable divinity of his heart. God knows what he suffered for the sake of truth. But deep as was his attachment to the truth, he likewise reverenced the past. His was no violent alienation, no bitter estrangement, no sudden cutting adrift from the sheet-anchors of the past. Of course everything that the past taught was not true. There was in it a good deal of 'transcendental nonsense' in the expressive language of your illustrious chairman [*Dr Mahendra Lal Sircar, founder of the Indian Institute of Cultivation of Science in Calcutta—Ed*]. But here and there amid the decayed ruins of ancient Indian greatness there were to be found gems of priceless value. These he treasured up; these he carefully studied, and these he incorporated into that system of progressive religion of which he was to be the immortal founder.

So will it always be with the march of reform, whether it be in religion, morals or politics. The history of the English constitution is the history of steady and continuous progress, due to no violent changes, to no violent remedies, but to careful up-building upon the foundations of the past. English reform has always been actuated by deep reverence for the past, combined with careful attention to the requirements of the present, and presided over by the all-pervading spirit of truth. The history of the world furnishes the instance of a conspicuous departure from these lessons, followed by conspicuous failure. The French Revolutionists in the wildness of their revolutionary zeal dethroned their king and brought him to the guillotine. They disestablished their church, expelled the clergy, confiscated church property, and to complete the measure of their development in this new direction, they installed Reason as an object of worship in place of Almighty God. The retribution soon came. The reaction was a hundredfold more bitter and intense than the fury of that revolutionary zeal which had precipitated these changes. Those who had expelled their king and had massacred him and the members of his family submitted to a military despotism, the little finger of which was thicker than the loins of Louis XVI. Those who had disestablished the church and had expelled the priesthood, were once again, amid tears and penances, received back into the bosom of the Catholic Church; and to mark the crowning triumph of the Church, the Pope came all the way from Rome to Paris to crown Napoleon as the anointed sovereign of France.

The apostle of monotheism, the founder of the Brahmo Samaj—the activity of Rammohun Roy was not confined to religious matters. Religion shaped and guided his conduct. Deep religious convictions formed the nutriment of his soul as they were the crowning glory of his life. But he knew that duty to God comprised duty to man, and the most acceptable way of serving the Almighty is by serving his creatures. The activity of his political life was not the least conspicuous feature of his career. In these days, political agitation is viewed with disfavour and political agitators are regarded as a mischievous class. However that may be, we who belong to that class and glory in it, claim Rammohun Roy as our leader, our guide, our revered preceptor in the difficult struggle for political regeneration. He advocated the freedom of the Press at a time when the Press was not yet free. He advocated the separation of judicial from executive functions at a time when nobody had apparently thought of the reform; and this is a reform which the National Congress urges from year to year, and urges in vain. With the prescience of genius as if anticipating an evil which did not prevail in his own time, and which it was reserved for Lord Salisbury to bring about in these days, he deprecated the appointment of men who were too young to offices in the Civil Service. Rammohun Roy suggested 22 years as the minimum limit of age for admission into the Covenanted Service. The Public Services Commission have recommended 23 years as the maximum limit of age.

I have heard it said that religious reformers should not take part in politics. Why not? Is not politics a part of our duty? And does not religion embrace the whole circle of our duties? Yes, politics based upon religion or deep moral earnestness is the one thing that is needful for this country. Politics divorced from a high moral purpose becomes the paltry squabble for power in which humanity can feel no interest. Take the case of the Home Rule agitation. Withdraw from it the personality of Mr. Gladstone and his intense moral earnestness, withdraw from it the deep fervour of the Irish patriots, and it becomes a miserable struggle for political power in which the deeper interests of humanity are lost sight of. Take again the case of the Pilgrim Fathers, the founders of American greatness. They were not allowed to worship God in their own country according to the light of their consciences. They preferred exile to the miseries of a life where their conscientious convictions had to be sacrificed. They crossed the ocean and settled in a foreign land. They established their own religion and their own government. They developed themselves into statesmen, and became the founders of the noblest Government and the freest race that the world has ever seen.

The first of political agitators, and the founder of the Brahmo Samaj—Rammohun Roy was also the first of Indian social reformers. What is the essence of social reform? What is its first and last word—its vitalising principle? All social reforms consist in the elevation of women, the removal of their disabilities and the restoration to them of that position of dignity and honour which is theirs by right. Rammohun Roy was singularly well-equipped for this task. The fertilising stream of deep motherly affection had been poured into his heart from his earliest years. Nay, more. When, driven from home by the persecuting hand of his relatives, he wandered among the wilds of

Thibet [*sic*], it was again the protecting arm of a woman that saved him from a violent death. He had throughout his life received in rich abundance the sweet and healing balsam of womanly affection. How could he disregard their claims upon his consideration? He knew how sweet and loving and tender Hindoo women were; and it was therefore with a sense of cruel agony that he saw perpetrated before his eyes the deadly horrors of *Suttee*.

I have read the opinion expressed somewhere—I believe in a journal or in some book—that *Suttee*, when voluntarily performed, represents the highest effort of womanly sacrifice and devotion to the memory of a dead husband. I regret I cannot accept this view of the matter. Is there no other means of illustrating womanly regard for a departed husband except by recourse to a practice from which human nature recoils with horror and indignation? Is it to be supposed that Hindoo widows are now less devoted to the memory of their dead husbands than they were in the time of Rammohun Roy, because, forsooth, they do not enjoy the liberty of immolating themselves on the funeral pyre? Against such an assumption I desire to enter my most emphatic protest. It would be nothing less than a libel on the womanhood of our race; for though I am a warm advocate of widow-marriage, I must observe that for purity of character, meekness of disposition and devoted self-sacrifice, the Hindoo widow is an ornament to her race and her sex.

Well, against this cruel rite Rammohun Roy commenced a crusade. The first pamphlet that he wrote on the subject was in 1818, and it was not till 1829 that the law was passed by which *Suttee* was declared penal. For 11 years, he continued the agitation. Hindoo society rose in arms against him. He never hesitated, never faltered, but with the calm clear eye of faith into the things of the future, he continued his work, till the victory was his.

I have read it stated in the columns of an influential English Journal—*The Saturday Review*—that the credit of the reform does not belong to Rammohun Roy in a special sense, but that he was one of a band of reformers who for some time had been pressing for it. The question is not of any great difficulty. It can be easily settled by a reference to a few facts. Rammohun Roy was the first to advocate the reform; he was its most persistent advocate. When at last, the law was passed, he went to England armed with a petition to support it, against the protestations of the Dharma Sabha. But this is not all. Without him the law could never have been passed. The Government felt bound by every consideration of honour and expediency not to interfere in a matter which affected the religion of the people. It was not until Rammohun Roy had pointed out that *Suttee* was not sanctioned by religion or the ancient tenets of the Hindoo Shastras that the Government felt itself at liberty to take action in the matter, and to move in the interests of humanity...

The social reformer, the founder of the Brahmo Samaj, the first of political agitators—the claims of the Raja to the gratitude of his countrymen have not yet been exhausted. He was also the founder of the Bengalee Prose literature and the first of Bengalee journalists. There is hardly a field of public usefulness which he left unoccupied. Ladies and gentlemen, I do not know what your own feelings on the subject may be, but I venture to think that those who are engaged in the great task of improving our language, adorning it and perfecting it for the varied purposes of speech, are among the truest benefactors of our race. Their achievements are the most durable; their fame immortal. In the progressive development of the human race it is possible to realise a time when the fame of a Marlborough or of a Wellington may be forgotten, and the memory of their victories may pass out of the mind. But the immortal creations of a Chaucer, a Shakespeare and a Milton, the noble thoughts of an Addison, a Bolingbroke or a Burke, will always linger in the recollections of the English-speaking races. They have endowed the people with the richest heritage. When the history of our people comes to be written, as I trust it will be written by no unfaithful hand, the highest place will be accorded to the Conscript Fathers of our language; and in the immortal rolls of fame there are few names that will stand higher than those of Rammohun Roy, Iswar Chandra Gupta, Modhusudan Dutt, Akshay Kumar Datta, Iswar Chandra Vidyasagar, Hem Chandra Banerji, and last but not least of the glorious band, Bankim Chandra Chatterjee.

Such was Rammohun Roy, and such was the nature of his achievements. Our national life may be said to flow from him as from a fountain. His labours have shaped the whole course of national development. Before him all was dark and gloomy. The sun of Chaitanya had long set, and the firmament was covered with deep gloom. Then rose Rammohun Roy, the apostle of modern progress. Others have followed him. Keshub Chunder Sen, Kristo Das Pal, Ram Gopal Ghose have come and gone; but they were no more fit to wear his mantle than we are to wear theirs.

I fear we have not been sufficiently respectful to the memory of Rammohun Roy. Three years ago you resolved to raise a national memorial in his honour. Where is this memorial? Your Town Hall is filled with the statues, busts and portraits of lesser luminaries. I do not grudge them these honours, which, no doubt, they richly deserve. But where is the memorial in honour of the greatest Hindoo reformer of modern times? I ask you to redeem the honour of your race, to make good your plighted faith, and to rescue the national character from the stain of dark ingratitude. But above all, gentlemen, I would ask you to raise in the temples of your hearts a monument that would be worthy of the great Raja. Purify your souls, hold communion with his blessed spirit, seek to elevate yourselves to the height of his moral greatness, and to assimilate his principles and his teachings into your everyday conduct; and then you will have raised a memorial not unworthy of the great Raja, or of this occasion, and one which would be in conformity with the spirit of his teachings.

~

SYED AHMAD KHAN

Hindu and Mussalman

Syed Ahmad Khan (1817–98), or Sir Syed as he is affectionately called by his countrymen, was one of the most enlightened men of the nineteenth century who deeply influenced the educational and political life of the subcontinent. Coming from one of the Talukdar families of the United Provinces, Syed Ahmad witnessed the post-Mutiny British reprisals, particularly on Muslims, and became convinced that it was through a friendly attitude towards the British and by adopting modern Western education that the upper classes, particularly the Muslim upper classes in northern India, could retain their leadership and reap the advantages of British rule which was ushering an entirely new socio-political order. India, for Sir Syed, was a common nation of the two qaums, *the Hindu and Muslim. In this speech, delivered at Patna on 27 January 1883, he made the now-famous comparison of the Hindu and the Muslim as two eyes of a beautiful bride.*

Friends, in India there live two prominent nations which are distinguished by the names of Hindus and Mussulmans. Just as man has some principal organs, similarly these two nations are like the principal limbs of India. To be a Hindu or a Muslim is a matter of internal faith which has nothing to do with mutual relationship and external conditions. How good is the saying, whoever may be its author, that a human being is composed of two elements—his faith which he owes to God and his moral sympathy which he owes to his fellow being. Hence leave God's share to God and concern yourself with the share that is yours.

Gentlemen, just as many reputed people professing Hindu faith came to this country, so we also came here. The Hindu forgot the country from which they had come, they could not remember their migration from one land to another and came to consider India as their homeland, believing that their country lies between the Himalayas and Vindhyachal. Hundred of years have lapsed since we, in our turn, left the lands of our origin. We remember neither the climate nor the natural beauty of those lands, neither the freshness of the harvests nor the deliciousness of the fruits, nor even do we remember the blessings of the holy deserts. We also came to consider India as our homeland and we settled down here like the earlier immigrants. Thus India is the home of both of us. We both breathe the air of India and take the water of holy Ganges and the Yamuna. We both consume the products of the Indian soil. We are living and dying together. By living so long in India, the blood of both have changed. The colours of both have become similar. The faces of both having changed, have become similar. The Muslims have acquired hundreds of customs from the Hindus and the Hindus have also learned hundreds of things from the Mussulmans. We mixed with each other so much that we produced a new language—Urdu, which was neither our language nor theirs. Thus if we ignore that aspect of ours which we owe to God, both of us, on the basis of being common inhabitants of India, actually constitute one nation; and the progress of this country and that of both of us is possible through mutual cooperation, sympathy and love. We shall only destroy ourselves by mutual disunity and animosity and ill-will to each other. It is pitiable to see those who do not understand this point and create feeling of disunity among these two nations and fail to see that they themselves will be the victims of such a situation and inflict injury to themselves. My friends, I have repeatedly said and say it again that India is like a bride which has got two beautiful and lustrous eyes—Hindus and Mussulmans. If they quarrel against each other that beautiful bride will become ugly and if one destroys the other, she will lose one eye. Therefore, people of

Hindustan you have now the right to make this bride either squint eyed or one eyed.

Undoubtedly, what to say of Hindus and Mussulmans, a quarrel among human beings is a natural phenomenon. Within the ranks of the Hindus or Mussulmans themselves, or even between brothers as also between fathers and sons, mothers and daughters there are dissensions. But to make it perennial is a symptom of decay of the family, the country and of the nation. How blessed are those who repent and step forward to untie the knot which has, by chance, marred their mutual relations, and do not allow it to get disrupted. O! God, let the people of India change this way of thinking.

~

SURENDRANATH BANERJEA

Indian Unity

Conceiving a nation out of congeries of people, societies, languages, regions and histories of warfare was a difficult job, a matter of imagination and hard work. The work of Rammohun Roy, Veereshlingam Pontulu, M.G. Ranade, Jyotiba Phule and hundreds of social workers conditioned Indian society to modern ways. Surendranath Banerjea's first address to the people was on the history of the Sikhs, about whom, as Bipin Chandra Pal wrote in his memoirs, they had heard much. He later spoke of the Marathas in a positive vein as Maratha raids in the Bengal and Orissa territories and their atrocities had made them unpopular in those parts. It was Surendranath Banerjea who suggested a Shivaji Festival in Calcutta to rouse the spirit of unity at least between the Bengalis and the Marathas. Thus, unity of people of different regions and languages was the first task that early nationalists took upon themselves. On 16 March 1878, two days after the Vernacular Press Act was passed, Surendranath Banerjea spoke on the need and the nature of Indian unity at a meeting of the Students Association at the Medical College Theatre, Calcutta. This is one of the clearest and fullest expositions of the way the early thinkers were trying to conceive the modern Indian nation in the context of world and Indian history.

... Gentlemen, I cannot help thinking that it is our proud privilege to live in one of the most interesting epochs in the history of our country, one of those epochs, which, if I am at all allowed to make a forecast of the future, will not be without its influence on the fortunes of after generations. Those fierce animosities, those bitter dissensions, those degrading passions which in the last and the preceding centuries had converted this beautiful country of ours into one vast ensanguined plain, have now happily subsided, and we live in an era of unexampled peace, prosperity and happiness. For this great result we are indebted to the British Government. If at this moment the semi-barbarous hordes of Afghanistan, bursting our barriers, are not sweeping across our country, it is because of the omnipotent might of the British Ruler. If, at this moment, happily the sentiment of brotherhood has been universally evoked in the minds of the Indian races, it is because under the auspices of British rule, the varied and diversified peoples that inhabit this great country have been welded together into a compact and homogeneous mass. But I ask, gentlemen, is this after all a season of unmixed gratulation? Have we no mournful reflections to darken the horizon of our thoughts? May we not, occupying the vantage ground that we now happen to occupy, emancipate ourselves from the present, look back into the past and question the past? May we not resuscitate the dying embers of a by-gone age and endeavour to fan them forth into a living flame, full of light for our future guidance? May we not, occupying the intellectual eminence that we have attained, invoke the genius of history and call upon her to declare what were the circumstances, what the incidents, what the causes which brought about our fall and have perpetuated our degradation? The Goddess of History thus questioned, is sure to return one answer, and it will be an answer at once decisive and unequivocal in its character. The Goddess will answer, 'Indians, your dissensions, your jealousies, your animosities, have brought about your fall and have perpetuated your degradation. Learn to respect the holy principle of union. Learn to love one another as brothers. Learn to make common cause for the redress of common grievances, and the great God of nations, the Protector of the rights of fallen peoples may yet from his high place in Heaven look upon you with compassion, may yet in his infinite mercy ordain the dawning of a bright day for your country.' So will speak the Goddess of History and she will point to facts in Indian History in support of her statement.

But, perhaps, it will be said that the question of Indian unity, of the intellectual, moral and social union of the Indian peoples, is a dream, is a chimera, the phantom of an excited imagination. It will be said that India throughout the long period of her chequered history has presented the spectacle of a country, inhabited by peoples, separated by language, separated by religion, separated by manners, and customs, separated in short by everything that constitutes the distinctive difference between races and peoples. Why then, it will be said, at this time of day commit the monstrous absurdity of talking of Indian unity?

Gentlemen, I have stated the arguments against Indian unity as strongly as the case admits of, in order to point out that these arguments are not wholly unanswerable in their character. I invite your attention once more to the terms of the proposition you are considering: India is inhabited by people separated by language, by religion, by manners, and customs. Is their intellectual, social, moral union possible? I say such a union is possible—is practicable; and I appeal to the facts of Indian history in support of the statement. Let us take the example of Switzerland, to begin with. Switzerland, you are aware, is a federal country, enjoying the blessings of a republican government. Switzerland is divided into a number of cantons. Well, there are Roman Catholic cantons and there are Protestant cantons. There are French-speaking cantons, and there are German-speaking cantons. But in spite of these differences of language and religion, Switzerland is a united country, and never was the strength of Swiss union, the compactness of that homogeneity more strikingly exemplified, than on that memorable day when that great oppressor of our race, Napoleon Bonaparte, endeavoured to wipe out this little republic from the face of Europe. Take again the case of Belgium. Belgium is a united country, and it would have been truly remarkable if it were not, considering how limited its area is. Well, in Belgium, there are the Wallons, and there is the Flemish speaking population, there are again Roman Catholic Belgians, and there are Protestant Belgians. But Belgium is a united country in spite of religious and linguistic differences. Let us now take the case of Germany. In Germany, we do not, indeed, meet with those strongly marked linguistic differences we notice in the case of Belgium and Switzerland, but I know of no country where in modern times the spirit of religious difference, I had almost said, the spirit of bitter religious hatred, has been carried on to a greater or more extravagant length than in this confederated German Empire. And if it were not that this was the 19th century, that Germany was placed in the midst of the hallowed, the consecrated, the peaceful influences of modern civilisation, Germany would today have presented the spectacle of a country deluged with blood, shed on the altar of religious differences.

Germany is united in spite of strongly marked religious differences in her people. I shall take one more instance, and this time it will be Italy. Italy, you are aware, was united in 1870. But the idea was a very old one. Dante had sung of Italian unification. The highest minds in Italy had aspired to bring about the consummation of that great event. Again and again there rose up poets, princes, philosophers and statesmen, with whom the great dream of their lives was the dream of Italian unification. But it was believed there were insuperable obstacles to the unification of Italy. The Italians had become a degraded people. They had forgotten the glorious memories of the past. They had forgotten the great deeds of their sires. They had forgotten the patriotism of Brutus, the eloquence of Cicero, the martial achievements of Caesar. Differences of language added to the confusion. The Neapolitan understood not the Roman, the Roman understood not the Venetian. They were all brothers, born of the same illustrious progenitors, the inheritors of the same great memories, yet they knew not one another, understood not one another, they were strangers in each other's sight. But was there no hope for Italy? Was she for ever to remain in the grovelling depths of continued misery? Aye no. The day of Italy's deliverance was fast approaching. The fiat had gone forth, the celestial mandate had been issued that Italy was to be saved. The hour had arrived. The men were there. Under the guidance of Garibaldi and Mazzini Italy rose to the conception of Italian unity; and through acts of noble and unheard of self-sacrifice, which have shed lasting glory on the honoured names of the martyred patriots of Italy, the Italian people brought about the unity and the independence of their country. The unification of Italy was effected notwithstanding dialectical differences.

Thus, then, gentlemen, from the instances I have just cited, we are naturally led to conclude that there may be religious differences, there may be linguistic differences, but they do not form insuperable barriers to the consummation of a national unity. A point has thus been gained in the argument. But it is my contention that the considerations I have just urged against national unity lose much of their weight when we bear in mind the wholly altered circumstances under which we now live. Modern India is very different from ancient India. The conditions of life in modern India are very different from the conditions of life in ancient India. We may deprecate the change. We may regret the circumstance. But there is no denying the fact that we are in the midst of a great revolution along whose current we are irresistibly borne. English civilisation has been introduced into our midst, and along with it have been introduced certain revolutionary agencies of mighty potency, which are operating with powerful effect upon the framework of Indian Society, thinning away its vital parts and greatly helping the cause of Indian unity. Foremost amongst these agencies, English Education claims our attention. The traveller who visits the cities of Delhi and Agra is struck with wonderment at the magnificent works of architectural beauty which still grace these once imperial capitals. They remind us of Moslem supremacy. They are the silent monumental records of bygone times. They remind us of the generosity and humanity of Akbar, of the splendour of Shah Jehan, of the religious bigotry of Aurangzeb. England indeed cannot boast of such monuments of architectural magnificence, but her claims to the lasting gratitude of posterity will rest upon a surer, more permanent and durable basis, upon the conviction which is deep and earnest in us, viz., that under the auspices of English rule were, for the first time, sown the seeds of a civilisation containing the germs of India's future greatness, of her political, moral and intellectual regeneration.

The question might be asked: how is English Education helping the cause of Indian union. I have mentioned that one of the obstacles to national unity is the diversity of dialects that prevails in India. English Education partly removes this difficulty by supplying a common medium of communication between the educated classes. I may not know Mahrati. An educated native of Bombay may not know Bengali. But we can hold intercourse with one another, correspond with one another through the common medium of the English language. Nor is this all. English Education has uplifted all who have come under its influence to a common platform of thoughts, feelings and aspirations. Educated Indians whether of Bengal, Madras, Bombay or the North-Western Provinces are brought up under the same intellectual, moral and political influences. Kindred hopes, feelings and ideas are thus generated. The educated classes throughout India are thus brought nearer together.

Railways also are greatly helping to bring about a feeling of unity and sympathy between the Indian races. Railways have abridged distances. The distance between Calcutta and Delhi is not 1,400 miles but is only a question of about 44 hours. The distance between Calcutta and Lahore is not 1,600 miles but is only a question of about 52 hours. The distance between Calcutta and Bombay is not 1,900 miles but is only a question of about 61 hours. The means of communication being so easy, we have taken more largely to travelling. We know one another now much more intimately than we ever did before. Those prejudices which had separated us for ages are fast disappearing, and the patriot sees in the distant horizon the faint streaks of that dawn which are to usher in the day of his country's regeneration and union. Railways are thus helping to promote Indian union.

The existence of a native Press is also calculated to bring about the same result. If I had addressed you day before yesterday, I should have said that the native Press was a free Press. But within the last forty-eight hours a law has been hurriedly enacted which has put a gag into the mouth of the Vernacular Press, has enveloped its fate in deep gloom, has dealt a terrible blow at the cause of Indian progress and enlightenment. The law which has been enacted, and the circumstances under which it has been enacted strongly remind us of our degradation, of the stretches to which the exercise of arbitrary power might be carried in this country, and how it has become necessary that we should interpose an effective and at the same time a thoroughly constitutional barrier against the reckless exercise of such great power.

... Gentlemen, it appears that the circumstances under which we live are wholly different from those of ancient India. Any arguments, therefore, founded upon the past of India, can have no application in the present day, the facts being so different. But if in spite of the arguments I have urged, it should be thought that the consummation of Indian unity must necessarily take such a long time that for all practical purposes it must be pronounced to be impossible of realisation, I ask what possible difficulty would there be to the unification of the interests of the educated classes spread throughout the different parts of India? We are not separated by language; English supplies us with a common medium of communication, and removes one of the great difficulties to national union. I know there are those who would give worlds to create dissensions amongst us. I know there are those who would raise mountain barriers between us, who would interpose an ever widening gulf of bitter animosities between us, who would rend asunder the bonds of sympathy which ought to subsist between us, brothers born of the same mother. And these men would fain be our leaders, our guides, our instructors. I know not how you regard their tricks, but for my part, my feelings towards them are those of pure, simple, unmitigated contempt and abhorrence.

... There may thus be a unification of the interests of educated

India; is not such union necessary and desirable? Have we no grievances to redress? I do not put this question by way of reflection upon the Government of this country. Every country, however well governed, has its grievances. The French have their grievances, the Germans have their grievances, the Swiss have their grievances, and even the English enjoying the freest institutions in the world have their grievances also. It would indeed have been truly remarkable if a country situated as India is, without the blessings of representative institutions, had no grievances to redress, no complaints to make. And is it not necessary, in order that we might obtain the redress of our grievances, that the voice of united India should be heard with respect to them? United representations must necessarily carry much greater weight with the English nation and the English Parliament than the prayers of this particular province, or of that particular province.

... The cause of Indian unity stands in need of missionaries. No cause has ever prospered which has not had its missionaries, its apostles and prophets. The cause of Italian unity had its apostles and prophets, its Garibaldis and its Mazzinis. Who will be the Garibaldi and Mazzini of Indian unity? Who amongst us will emulate their self-sacrifice, their matchless patriotism, their unflinching devotion to the interests of their country? Their revolutionary spirit is not indeed needed for the benefit of India. The march of progress which has already commenced under English auspices must not be disturbed. May England long continue to rule India for the glory of England and the benefit of India. But we want the inspiration to noble actions to be derived from the blessed names and sanctified examples of the immortal apostles of Italian unity. I repeat, who will be the apostles of Indian unity?

Young men, whom I see around me in such large numbers, you are the hopes of your families. May I not also say, you are the hopes of your country. Your country expects great things from you. Now I ask, how many of you are prepared, when you have finished your studies at the college, to devote your lives, to consecrate your energies to the good of your country? I repeat the question and I pause for a reply. (Here the speaker paused for a few seconds. Cries of 'all, all' from all sides of the gallery.) The response is in every way worthy of yourselves and of the education which you are receiving. May you prove true to your resolve, and carry out in life the high purposes which animate your bosoms.

... In holding up for your acceptance the great principle of Indian unity, I do not lay any claims to originality. Three hundred years ago, in the Punjab, the immortal founder of Sikhism, the meek, the gentle, the blessed Nanak preached the great doctrine of Indian unity and endeavoured to knit together Hindus and Musulmans under the banner of a common faith. That attempt was eminently successful. Nanak became the spiritual founder of the Sikh Empire. He preached the great doctrine of peace and goodwill between Hindus and Musulmans. And standing in the presence of his great example, we too must preach the great doctrine of peace and goodwill between Hindus and Musulmans, Christians and Parsees, aye between all sections of the great Indian community. Let us raise aloft the banner of our country's progress. Let the word 'Unity' be inscribed there in characters of glittering gold. We have had enough of past jealousies, past dissensions, past animosities. The spirits of the dead at Paniput will testify to our bloody strifes. The spirits of the dead in other battlefields will testify to the same fact. There may be religious differences between us. There may be social differences between us. But there is a common platform where we may all meet, the platform of our country's welfare. There is a common cause which may blind [*sic*] us together, the cause of Indian progress. There is a common Divinity, to whom we may uplift our voices in adoration, the Divinity who presides over the destinies of our country. In the name then of a common country, let us all, Hindus, Musulmans, Christians, Parsees, members of the great Indian community, throw the pall of oblivion over jealousies and dissensions of bygone times and embracing one another in fraternal love and affection, live and work for the benefit of a beloved Fatherland. Under English auspices there is indeed a great future for India. I am confident of the great destinies that are in store for us. You and I may not live to see that day. These eyes of ours may not witness that spectacle of ineffable beauty. It may not be permitted to us to exclaim Simeon-like, 'Now Lord, lettest thou thy servant depart in peace.' It may not be permitted to us to exclaim like the Welsh Bard on the heights of Snowdon, 'Visions of glory, spare my aching sight.' But is it nothing to know when you are dying, when you are about to take leave of this world, of its joys and sorrows, when the past of your life is unfurled before you, when eternity opens wide its portals, is it nothing to know at that last awful, supreme moment of your lives, that you have not lived in vain, that you have lived for the benefit of others, that you have lived to help in the cause of your country's regeneration? Let us all lead worthy, honourable and patriotic lives, that we may all live and die happily and that India may be great. This is my earnest and prayerful request. May it find a response in your sympathetic hearts.

~

MAHADEV GOVIND RANADE

The Evolution of a New India

M.G. Ranade (1842–1901) is one of the founders of the modern Indian nation. Ranade achieved, by dint of his hard work, the highest of official positions available to an Indian in that period. At the same time, he worked for social reform selflessly and with dedication, and provided an intellectual critique of the British colonial system by presenting a powerful economic appraisal of the way the system was operating. He founded the Indian Social Conference and as its secretary, prepared, guided and organized the different voices for social reform throughout the country. Being one of the earliest votaries of the Indian National Congress, he saw to it that the annual convention of the Social Conference was held along with the annual session of the Congress. It meant that he saw in social reform the potential of political change. Ranade loved India, its soil, its history and had an unshakable belief about its potential to come out of the dark patch that it had entered over the past couple of centuries. He looked upon the modern times ushered with the British and the democratic ethos of the West as liberating influences which would help Indians rid their own society of superstitions and other evil practices. His private life, like that of many public men of the nineteenth century, was so simple that he was called a rishi. His addresses at the various sessions of the Social Conference, it was pointed out, were characterized by a deep empathy with society, sound historical knowledge, logic and rationale, and an overall sense of direction and conviction which influenced a whole generation of people to dedicate themselves to the cause that he espoused. In this historic address at the thirteenth session of the Social Conference held at Lucknou in 1899, Ranade tries to locate a modern India in a stream of historic consciousness and lineage. Future possibilities are seen in the light of historical connections.

The question for consideration for us at the present moment is, whether in consequence of the predominance of the Mahomedans for five centuries which intervened from the invasions of Mahmud to the ascendancy of Akbar, the people of India were benefited by the contact thus forcibly brought together between the two races. There are those among us who think that this predominance has led to the decay and corruption of the Indian character, and that the whole story of the Mahomedan ascendancy should, for all practical purposes, be regarded as a period of humiliation and sorrow. Such a view, however, appears to be unsupported by any correct appreciation of the forces which work for the elevation or depression of nations.

It cannot be easily assumed that in God's Province, such vast multitudes as those who inhabit India were placed centuries together under influences and restraints of alien domination, unless such influences and restraints were calculated to do lasting service in the building up of the strength and character of the people in directions in which the Indian races were most deficient. Of one thing we are certain, that after lasting over five hundred years, the Mahomedan Empire gave way, and made room for re-establishment of the old native races in Punjab and throughout Central Hindusthan and Southern India, and foundations of a much more solid character than those which yielded so easily before the assaults of the early Mahomedan conquerors. The domination, therefore, had not the effect of so depressing the people that they were unable to raise their heads again in greater solidarity. If the Indian races had not benefited by the contact and example of men with stronger muscles and greater powers, they would have never been able to re-assert themselves in the way in which history bears testimony they did.

Quite independently of this evidence of the broad change that took place in the early part of the 18th century when the Moghul Empire went to pieces, and its place was taken up not by foreign settlers, but by revived native powers, we have more convincing grounds to show that in a hundred ways the India of the 18th century, so far as the native races were concerned, was a stronger and better constituted India than met the eyes of the foreign travellers from Asia and Europe who visited it between the period of the first five centuries from 1,000 to 1,500. In Akbar's time this process of regenerated India first assumed a decided character which could not be well mistaken. No student of Akbar's reign will fail to notice that for the first time the conception was then realised of a united India in which Hindus and Mahomedans, such of them as had become permanently established in the country, were to take part in the building of an edifice rooted in the hearts of both by common interests and common ambitions. In place of the scorn and contempt with which the Mahomedan invaders had regarded the religion of the Hindus, their forms of worship, their manners and customs, and with which the Hindus looked down upon them as barbarous Mlechas, whose touch was pollution, a better appreciation of the good points in the character of both came to be recognised as the basis of the union.

Akbar was the first to see and realise the true nobility of soul and devotion and fidelity of the Hindu character, and satisfied himself that no union was possible as long as the old bigotry and fanaticism was allowed to guide the councils of the Empire. He soon gathered about him the best men of his time, men like Faizi, Abul Fazl and their father, Mubarak, the historians Mirza Abdur Rahim, Nizamuddin Ahmed, Budauni and others. These were set to work upon the translation of the Hindu epics and shastras and books of science and philosophy. The pride of the Rajput races was conciliated by taking in marriage the princesses of Jaipur and Jodhpur, and by conferring equal or superior commands on those princes. These latter had been hitherto treated as enemies. They were now welcomed as the props of the Empire, and Maharaja Bhagwandas, his great nephew Mansingh, for some time Governor of Bengal and Kabul, Raja Todarmal and the Brahmin companion of the Emperor, Raja Birbal, these were welcomed to court, and trusted in the full consciousness that their interests were the same as those of the Mahomedan noblemen. The Emperor himself, guided by such counsel of his Hindu and Mahomedan nobles, became the real founder of the union between the two races and this policy for a hundred years guided and swayed the councils of the Empire.

A fusion of the two races was sought to be made firmer still by the establishment of a religion of the *Din-I-Ilahi* in which the best points of the Mahomedan, Hindu and other faiths were sought to be incorporated. Invidious taxation privileges were done away with, and toleration for all faiths became the universal law of the Empire. To conciliate his subjects, Akbar abjured the use of faith except on four special occasions in the year, and he joined in the religious rites observed by his Hindu Queens. In regard to the particular customs of the people relating to points where natural humanity was shocked in a way to make union impossible, Akbar strove by wise encouragement and stern control where necessary, to help the growth of better ideas. Sati was virtually abolished by being placed under restraints which nobody could find fault with. Re-marriage was encouraged, and marriage before puberty was prohibited. In these and a hundred other ways, the fusion of the races and of their many faiths was sought to be accomplished with a success which was justified by the results for a hundred years. This process of removing all causes of friction and establishing accord went on without interruption during the reigns of Akbar, Jahangir and Shahjahan. Shahjahan's eldest son, Dara Shikuh, was himself an author of no mean repute. He translated the Upanishads, and wrote a work in which he sought to reconcile the Brahmin religion with the Mahomedan faith. He died in 1659.

This period of a hundred years may be regarded as the halcyon period of Indian history when the Hindu and Mahomedan races acted in full accord. If in place of Aurangzeb, Dara Shikuh had succeeded to power as the eldest son of Shahjahan, the influence set on foot by the genius of Akbar would have gathered strength, and possibly averted the collapse of the Moghul power for another century. This was, however, not to be so, and with Aurangzeb's ascent to the throne, a change of system commenced which gathered force during the long time that this emperor reigned. Even Aurangzeb had, however, to follow the traditions of his three predecessors. He could not dispose with Jaisingh or Jaswantsingh who were his principal military commanders. In the reign of his son, whole provinces under him were governed by Rajput, Kayastha and other Governors. The revival of fanatic bigotry was kept in check by the presence of these great Rajput chiefs, one of whom on the reimposition of the 'Zezia' addressed to the Emperor a protest couched in unmistakable terms that the God of Islam was also the God of Hindus, and the subjects of both races merited equal treatment. Aurangzeb unfortunately did not listen to this advice, and the result was that the empire built by Akbar went to pieces even when Aurangzeb was alive. No one was more aware of his failure than Aurangzeb himself, who in his last moments admitted that his whole life was a mistake. The Marathas in the South, the Sikhs in the North, and the Rajput States helped in the dismemberment of the empire in the reigns of his immediate successors with the result that nearly the whole of India was restored to its native Hindu sovereign except Bengal, Oudh, and the Deccan Hyderabad. It will be seen from this that far from suffering from decay and corruption, the native races gathered strength by reason of the Mahomedan rule when it was directed by the wise counsel of those Mahomedan and Hindu statesmen who sought the weal of the country by a policy of toleration and equality. Since the time of Asoka, the element of strength born of union was wanting in the old Hindu dynasties who succumbed so easily to the Mahomedan invaders.

Besides this source of strength, there can be no doubt that in a hundred ways the Mahomedan domination helped to refine the tastes and manners of the Hindus. The art of Government was better understood by the Mahomedans than by the old Hindu sovereigns. The art of war also was singularly defective till the Mahomedans came. They brought in the use of gunpowder and artillery. In the words of Babar, they 'taught ingenuity and mechanical invention in a number of handicraft arts', the very nomenclature of which being made up of non-Hindu words, shows their foreign origin. They introduced candles, paper, glass and household furniture and saddlery. They improved the knowledge of the people in music, instrumental and vocal, medicine and astronomy, and their example was followed by the Hindus in the perversions of both these sciences, astrology and alchemy. Geography and history were first made possible departments of knowledge and literature by their example. They made roads, aqueducts, canals, caravansaries, and the post office, and introduced the best specimens of architecture, and improved our gardening, and made us acquainted with a taste of new fruits and flowers. The revenue system as inaugurated by Todarmal in Akbar's time is the basis of the revenue system up to the present day. They carried on the entire commerce by sea with distant regions, and made India feel that it was a portion of the inhabited world with relations with all, and not cut off from all social intercourse. In all these respects, the civilisation of the united Hindu and Muslim powers represented by the Moghuls at Delhi was a distant advance beyond what was possible before the tenth century of the Christian era.

More lasting benefits have, however, accrued by the contact in the higher tone it has given to the religion and thoughts of the people. In this respect, both the Mahomedans and Hindus benefited by contact with one another. As regards the Mahomedans, their own historians admit that the Sufi heresy gathered strength from contact with the Hindu teachers, and made many Mahomedans believe in transmigration and in final union of the soul with the supreme spirit. The Moharram festival and saint worship are the best evidence of the way in which the Mahomedans were influenced by Hindu ideas. We are more directly concerned with the way in which this contact has affected the Hindus. The prevailing tone of pantheism had established toleration for polytheism among our most revered ancient teachers who rested content with separating the few from the many and established no bridge between them. This separation of the old religion has prevented its higher precepts from becoming the common possession of whole races. Under the purely Hindu system, the intellect may admit, but the heart declines to allow a common platform to all people in the sight of God. The Vaishnava movement has however succeeded in establishing the bridge noted above, and there can be no doubt that in the hands of the followers of Ramananda, especially the Kabirpanthis, Malikdasis, Dadupanthis, the followers of Mirabai, of Lord Gauranga on the Bengal side, and Baba Nanak in Punjab in the fifteenth and sixteenth centuries, the followers of Tukaram, Ekanath and Namdev in the Deccan, Babalalis, Prananathis, Sadhs, the Satnamis, the Shivnarayans and the followers of Mahant Rama Charan of the last two centuries—this elevation and the purification of the Hindu mind was accomplished to an extent which very few at the present moment realise in its significance. The Brahmo and the Arya Samaj movements of this century are the continuations of this ethical and spiritual growth. Caste, idolatry, polytheism, and gross conceptions of purity and pollution were the precise points in which the Mahomedans and Hindus were most opposed to one another, and all the sects named above had this general characteristic that they were opposed to these defects in the character of our people. Nanak's watchword was that he was neither Hindu nor Mahomedan, but that he was a worshipper of the *Nirakar* or the formless. His first companion was a Mahomedan, and his teacher is said to have been also a Mahomedan. Lord Gauranga had also Mahomedan disciples. Mahomedan saints like Shaik Mahomed, Shaik Farid and Mahomed Kazi were represented both by Hindus and Mahomedans. The abuses of polytheism were checked by the devotion of one object of worship which in the case of many of these Vaishnava Sects was supreme God, the *Paramatma*, and the abuses of caste were controlled by conceding to all, Hindus and Mahomedans alike, the right to worship and love the one God who was the God of all.

In the case of Sikhs, the *puratanic* spirit even developed under persecution, into a coarse imitation of the Mahomedan fanaticism directed against the Mahomedans themselves; but in the case of the other sectaries, both old and new, the tolerant and the suffering spirit of Vaishnavism has prevailed, breathing peace and goodwill towards all.

Such are the chief features of the influences resulting from the contact of Mahomedans and Hindus in Northern India. They brought about a fusion of thoughts and ideas which benefited both communities, making the Mahomedans less bigoted, and the Hindus more *puratanic* and more single-minded in their devotion. There was nothing like this to be found in Southern India as described by Dubois where the Hindu sectarian spirit intensified caste pride and idolatrous observances. The fusion would have been more complete but for the revival of fanaticism for which Aurangzeb must be held chiefly responsible. Owing to these circumstances, the work of fusion was left incomplete; and in the course of years, both the communities have developed weaknesses of character which still need the disciplining process to be continued for a longer time under other masters. Both Hindus and Mahomedans lack many of those virtues represented, the love of order and regulated authority. Both are wanting in the love of Municipal freedom, in the exercise of virtues necessary for civic life, and in aptitudes for mechanical skill, in the love of science and research, in the love and daring of adventurous discovery, the resolution of difficulties, and in chivalrous respect for womankind. Neither the old Hindu nor the old Mahomedan civilisation was in a condition to train these virtues in a way to bring up the races of India on a level with those of Western Europe, and so the work of education had to be renewed and it has been now going on for the past century and more under the 'pax-Britannica' with results—which all of us are witnesses to in ourselves.

If the lessons of the past have any value, one thing is quite clear, viz. that in this vast country no progress is possible unless both Hindus and Mahomedans join hands together, and are determined to follow the lead of the men who flourished in Akbar's time and were his chief advisers and councillors, and sedulously avoid the mistakes which were committed by the great grandson Aurangzeb. Joint action from a sense of common interest, and a common desire to bring about the fusion of the thoughts and feelings of men so as to tolerate small differences and bring about concord—these were the chief aims kept in view by Akbar and formed the principle of the new divine faith formulated in the *Din-I-Ilahi*. Every effort on the part of either Hindu or Mahomedans to regard their interests as separate and distinct, and every attempt made by the two communities to create separate schools and interests among themselves, and not heal up the wound inflicted by mutual hatred of caste and creed, must be deprecated on all hands. It is to be feared that this lesson has not been sufficiently kept in mind by the leaders of both communities in their struggle for existence and in the acquisition of power and predominance during recent years.

There is at times a great danger of the work of Akbar being undone by losing sight of this great lesson which the history of his reign and that of his two successors is so well calculated to teach.

The Conference which brings us together is especially intended for the propagation of this 'din' or 'Dharma', and it is in connection with that message chiefly that I have ventured to speak to you today on this important subject. The ills that we are suffering from are most of them self-inflicted evils, the cure of which is to a large extent in our own hands. Looking at the series of measures which Akbar adopted in his time to cure these evils, one feels how correct was his vision when he and his advisers put their hand on those very defects in our national character which need to be remedied first before we venture on higher enterprises. Pursuit of high ideas, mutual sympathy and cooperation, perfect tolerance, a correct understanding of the diseases from which the body politic is suffering, and an earnest desire to apply suitable remedies—this is the work cut out for the present generation. The awakening has commenced, as is witnessed by the fact that we are met in this place from such distances for joint consultation and action. All that is needed is that we must put our hands to the plough, and face the strife and the struggle. The success already achieved warrants the expectation that if we persevere on right lines, the goal we have in view may be attained. That goal is not any particular advantage to be gained in power and wealth. It is represented by the efforts to attain it, the expansion and the evolution of the heart and the mind, which will make us stronger and braver, purer and truer men.

This is at least the lesson I draw from our recent history of the past thousand years, and if these centuries have rolled away to no purpose over our heads, our cause is no doubt hopeless beyond cure. That is however not the faith in me; and I feel sure it is not the faith that moves you in this great struggle against our weak selves, than which nothing is more fatal to our individual and collective growth. Both Hindus and Mahomedans have their work cut out in this struggle. In the backwardness of female education, in the disposition to over-leap the bounds of their own religions, in matters of tolerance, in their internal dissensions between castes and creeds, in the indulgence of impure speech, thought, and action on occasions when they are disposed to enjoy themselves, in the abuses of many customs in regard to unequal and polygamous marriages, in the desire to be extravagant in their expenditure on such occasions, in the neglect of regulated charity, in the decay of public spirit in insisting on the proper management of endowments—in these and other matters both communities are equal sinners, and there is thus much ground for improvement on common lines. Of course, the Hindus being by far the majority of the population, have other difficulties of their own to combat with; and they are trying in their gatherings of separate castes and communities to remedy them each in their own way. But without cooperation and conjoint of all communities success is not possible, and it is on that account that the General Conference is held in different places each year to rouse local interest, and help people in their separate efforts by a knowledge of what their friends similarly situated are doing in other parts. This is the reason of our meeting here, and I trust that this message I have attempted to deliver to you on this occasion will satisfy you that we cannot conceive a noble work than the one for which we have met here today.

~

BAL GANGADHAR TILAK

Empires: Old and New

If Surendranath Banerjea was the first national leader of the country, Bal Gangadhar Tilak (1856–1920) was the first to go beyond the educated middle class and become a symbol of the national spirit, the spirit of sacrifice and selfless love for the nation. The whole country mourned when he was charged with sedition and sentenced by a Poona court in 1896. One of the greatest scholars in Sanskrit and Marathi, and well versed in English and law, Tilak saw in nationalism his true vocation. He tried to give it direction through his papers and public work, and through organizations like the Indian National Congress. A fiery speaker, Tilak's speeches were marked by their sense of history, logic, slight sarcasm, an acute grasp of the politics and ideology of the age and an invocation for national work which made him one of the most charismatic leaders of the times. In the speech reproduced below, given at Bellary on 5 May 1905 while inaugurating the Vani Vilas Theatre, he shows how nationalists tried to define the modern Indian nation and sense of nationalism. One cannot help but be astounded by the finesse and the cosmopolitan nature of thought that they displayed in trying to think out such attempts at nation-making, well aware that this nation had to operate under the British dominion.

In India we have to consider what are the duties of a patriot. Formerly, India was what the present-day writers called a congeries of nations. Patriotism was a non-egoistic virtue and altruistic in its operations. We have to find out from ancient history whether the administrators of petty States placed before themselves an ideal higher than the family or the individual ideal. Empires meant in those days quite a different thing from what they mean today—an empire now means a country ruled from the Himalayas to Comorin with the subject races under the same laws and regulations. An empire of this kind never existed before. There was a complete autonomy in each different province in olden days, but a tribute was levied from the minor provinces only as a mark of subordination. An Empire did not mean the assumption of the internal administration of a province by the suzerain power. The idea that a country of so many provinces has a single interest and a single ideal to look to, was not conceived because it was not necessary. This was not the intellectual fault of their ancestors. There was a kind of unity and there were ties, but those were not national, because the country was then differently circumstanced. Looking at the ideal which, to a certain extent, inspired the Mahrattas about 250 years ago, it was plain that the ancient ideals were more or less provincial. When Shivaji made his conquests, it was for the Mahratta nation only. Such an ideal would be considered narrow now; but we should look to the spirit of the ideal which laid down a policy by which one Province of India at least assumed an importance which was felt throughout the land.

Such provincial and racial ideals would not serve the purposes of a modern patriot, the limits should be made broader and more liberal, and as Lord Curzon said the ideal should be composite as circumstances are now entirely altered after the establishment of the British rule in India. India which was a geographical expression once became a single administration in the hands of the English. A nation is constituted of many elements, the element of ethnology, of language, of literature, of religion and of tradition. The first duty of an Indian patriot is to ask if the people of India are of one nation. The answer that came to the lips of everyone is that India was one nation. This answer might be prompted by self-love or self-deception. Perhaps the wish is the father to the thought. Hope being the very salt of patriotism, it is not for the patriot to be disappointed.

In considering the question whether India can be a nation, various questions crop up. One man says that from the heterogeneous communities of India one nation cannot arise; another wants the Indian social customs to be done away with; another industrial friend wants the industries to be first revived, for the country can then only accumulate wealth, and wealth is power. The question of nationality should not be looked at from only one point of view but progress must be looked for all along the line, and the mutual relation of the different parts should be understood. There is not a doctrine in the world which has not its opponents; there are no doubt differences in language, climate and religious faith; even if all these differences are obliterated for the time being, yet the vastness of the country is such that difference would again arise soon.

There are certain factors which, if properly developed and cultivated, would eventually lead to one nationality. The Hindus are governed by the Shastras, held sacred all over the country; they have the same history, they live in the same land, they are under the same government which is a new factor contributed by the British rule. The task of an Indian Patriot is not easy; he should not be daunted by difficulties, for the development of character consisted in conquering difficulties which are after all of human creation. There is no conflict between Vedantic ideals and patriotic ideals. Progress means adapting to the changed circumstances at each time. Society being a living organisation, it was unnatural if it could not adapt itself to altered circumstances. The social organisation in India is not surely dead, it is probably slumbering and sleep is no death, and there is sure to be a waking sooner or later. Patriotism in India involves nationality and welding of races. The limits should be widened, the ideal of a composite patriotism should be attained and the goal of the Indians should be to become worthy members of the British Empire having the same rights and privileges as the other members, helping each other and cooperating with each other, towards the same goal and for the glorification of one empire.

2

CRITIQUE OF COLONIALISM

India produced a galaxy of public personalities during the latter half of the nineteenth century, people unmatched in their depth of knowledge, vision and intellectual prowess even today. Generally products of English education, most of them were first-rate scholars in their own languages and traditions and, while proposing a long-term association with British rule, displayed enormous zeal in reforming their societies. Through their sustained criticism of the operation of the colonial system and the evils in their own societies, they produced not only a powerful intellectual critique of both but also gave shape to a potent political movement which would herald the dawn of a new society—democratic, free and modern in its form and substance.

Their understanding of the British administrative system made them believe that the spirit of justice and the winds of democracy blowing across the world would ultimately influence the British authorities in their dealings with the colonies. An economically developed and politically evolved Britain could be called upon to do the same for India. This encouraged them to raise the matter of India's freedom in the British Parliament. They were convinced of the necessity of taking their political vision not only to their own countrymen but also to the British people.

These statesmen worked all their lives to prove to the British people and the rulers that India had been denied justice; that under British colonialism India and her people had become poorer, that she had been drained, her industries devastated and land denuded.

Dadabhai Naoroji, Pherozeshah Mehta, Gopal Krishna Gokhale, Romesh Chandra Dutt, Surendranath Banerjea, G.V. Joshi, N.G. Chandavarkar, Ambika Charan Majumdar and many others fought an intellectual battle, the likes of which had not been seen before, against the world's mightiest empire which also had equally powerful champions to defend its case in the rising tide of intellectuals among the utilitarians and liberals in England. The spirit and vigour of these Indian intellectuals remain unmatched. Each individual life was a shining example of progressive nationalist thinking trying to rouse the soul of a sleeping civilization towards a new modernity.

The writings of these people made it clear that colonial rule was responsible for the growing poverty and unemployment among the people. Through his regular writings and speeches, Naoroji and his successors made the critique of colonialism so profound that successive generations like that of Tilak or of Gandhi and Nehru never felt the need to address the same issues again. By the time Dadabhai addressed the Calcutta session of the Congress in 1906, demanding swaraj, he and his co-workers had shattered the myth of a benevolent empire—an empire that believed and made people believe that it existed for the good of Indians. These leaders also criticized the colonial authorities for not involving Indians in the administration of the country. Surendranath Banerjea, for example, travelled across the country, educating his countrymen about the discriminating nature of colonial rule. In 1883, the Ilbert Bill tried to give an Indian judge the powers to try a European subject of the Crown. The vehement and organized protests of the British and the European public against the bill, which they thought was subverting racial hierarchy, also opened the eyes of a large section of Indians to the essentially racial character of the state. It made them conscious of their position as subject people not entitled to equality as promised in the Queen's Proclamation of 1858 or which they had hoped to acquire through education.

The organized protests by the Europeans also made the intelligentsia realize the importance of organization and unity. The formation of the Madras Native Association (1855), the Poona Sarvajanik Sabha (1870), the Indian Association (1877) and the Madras Mahajan Sabha (1884) resulted from this realization. These organizations voiced demands of increased Indian representation in the legislative and viceroy's executive councils, and called for raising the age for appearing in the civil service examination and increasing the government budget on education and other developmental activities.

Newspapers like the *Amrita Bazar Patrika*, the *Bengalee*, the *Hindu*, and the *Tribune* were started to express the concerns of the people. The Indian National Congress, too, was a product of this need. During 25–28 December 1885, Allan Octavian Hume organized the first conference of the Indian National Congress at Bombay to take up issues of national importance.

Most of these early nationalists strongly believed that the interests and well-being of all Indians were common and that they were being thwarted by the exploitative acts of the colonial state which was surely and steadily draining India of its resources. They, however, also emphasized that the colonial state was amenable to reason and once it was made to see its mistakes it would ultimately give Indians their due. They were conscious of the fact that India was not made up of one single community and was far from being a cohesive society. It was British administration, the new channels of communication and English education that had made it possible for people to become aware of belonging to one nation. This consciousness, however, was not equally developed and strong in all sections of the population. Thus, while demands for reforms were to be articulated as a nation, efforts to concretize and bring together disparate sections into the fold of the nation were also necessary. The nationalists tried to mould public opinion along these lines.

DADABHAI NAOROJI

Maiden Speech in the House of Commons

Hailing from a Parsee priestly family, Dadabhai Naoroji (1824–1906), the Grand Old Man of India, was inspired by his widowed mother to grow up as a fierce public man. One of the first to launch the social reform movement among the Parsees, through his papers Rast Goftar *and* Society, *Dadabhai gradually moved on to read and analyse the workings of the British colonial system in India and evaluate its claims of benevolent development of the people. This led him to pen the immortal work* Poverty and UnBritish Rule in India *in 1869 which laid the foundation of one of the most sophisticated critiques of colonialism through a study of the actual operation of the system.*

Politically, like all his contemporaries, he believed that the most developed country in the world, Britain, a country which had witnessed the Industrial

Revolution and where the most advanced ideas of democracy and liberty were practised, had a providential role to play in helping Indians get out of their backward-looking society. Dadabhai spoke with facts, figures, moderation, fearlessness and confidence which sprang from his selfless work, his standing among the nationalists in India and among the Britons. It was he who propagated the 'drain theory' which postulated that the British were bleeding India white. Dadabhai Naoroji dedicated his whole life to enlightening both Indians and Englishmen about how British colonialism was draining India of her wealth and potential investable surplus. As a result, not only was India getting poorer, its people more impoverished, but her capacity to come out of the poverty was also getting increasingly reduced. He argued that this was 'unBritish' rule because while it was from Britain that the ideas of justice and equality were being transmitted around the world, and even though the Queen had proclaimed that Indians would be equal citizens, the reality was in sharp contrast. Dadabhai's life personified the critique of the colonial system.

This is his maiden speech in the House of Commons delivered on 9 August 1892. The speech is historic in many senses. First, it was an Indian speaking in the British Parliament as an equal member. The early nationalist, in fact, envisioned full and equal rights for all Indians under the British system. The whole struggle of the early nationalists, even of the Indian National Congress in the first couple of decades, was to acquire the right to equality in full measure. The nationalist struggle in the late nineteenth and early twentieth centuries was focused on contesting the denial of this right through different measures like the Vernacular Press Act and the whole racial attitude shown by British administrators.

It may be considered rather rash and unwise on my part to stand before this House so immediately after my admission here: and my only excuse is that I am under a certain necessity to do so. My election for an English constituency is a unique event. For the first time during more than a century of settled British rule, an Indian is admitted into the House as a member for an English constituency. That, as I have said, is a unique event in the history of India, and, I may also venture to say, in the history of the British Empire. I desire to say a few words in analysis of this great and wonderful phenomenon. The spirit of the British rule, the instinct of British justice and generosity, from the very commencement, when they seriously took the matter of Indian policy into their hands, about the beginning of this century, decided that India was to be governed on the lines of British freedom and justice. Steps were taken without any hesitation to introduce Western education, civilisation, and political institutions in that country; and the result was that, aided by a noble and grand language in which the youth of that country began to be educated, a great movement of political life—I may say new life—was infused into that country which had been decaying for centuries. The British rulers of the country endowed it with all their own most important privileges. A few days ago, Sir, you demanded from the Throne the privileges which belong to the people, including freedom of speech, for which they fought and shed their blood. That freedom of speech you have given to us, and it enables Indians to stand before you and represent in clear and open language any desire they have felt. By conferring those privileges you have prepared for this final result of an Indian standing before you in this House, becoming a member of the great Imperial Parliament of the British Empire, and being able to express his views openly and fearlessly before you. The glory and credit of this great event—by which India is thrilled from one end to the other—of the new life, the joy, the ecstasy of India at the present moment, are all your own; it is the spirit of British institutions and the love of justice and freedom in British instincts which has produced this extraordinary result, and I stand here in the name of India to thank the British people that they have made it at all possible for an Indian to occupy this position, and to speak freely in the English language of any grievance which India may be suffering under, with the conviction that though he stands alone, with only one vote, whenever he is able to bring forward any aspiration and is supported by just and proper reasons, he will find a large number of other members from both sides of the House ready to support him and give him the justice he asks. This is the conviction which permeates the whole thinking and educated classes of India. It is that conviction that enables us to work on, day after day, without dismay, for the removal of a grievance. The question now being discussed before the House will come up from time to time in practical shape and I shall then be able to express my humble views upon them as a representative of the English constituency of Central Finsbury. I do not intend to enter into them now. Central Finsbury has earned the everlasting gratitude of the millions of India, and has made itself famous in the History of the British Empire, by electing an Indian to represent it. Its name will never be forgotten by India. This event has strengthened the British power and the loyalty and attachment of India to it ten times more than the sending out of one hundred thousand European soldiers would have done. The moral force to which the Right Hon'ble Gentleman, the member for Midlothian (Mr. W.E. Gladstone), referred is the golden link by which India is held by the British power. So long as India is satisfied with the justice and honour of Britain, so long will her Indian Empire last, and I have not the least doubt that though our progress may be slow and we may at times meet with disappointments, if we persevere, whatever justice we ask in reason we shall get. I thank you, Sir, for allowing me to say these few words and the House for so indulgently listening to me, and I hope that the connection between England and India—which forms five-sixths of the British Empire—may continue long with benefit of both countries. There will be certain Indian questions, principally of administration, which I shall have to lay before the House, and I am quite sure that when they are brought forward they will be fairly considered and if reasonable, amended to our satisfaction.

~

DADABHAI NAOROJI

Poverty of India

At the ninth session of the Indian National Congress at Lahore in 1893, Dadabhai Naoroji spoke on the subject of poverty in India, emphasizing that the issue had to be central to our political and intellectual understanding of the colonial position. The problem of increasing poverty had gradually become the bedrock on which the intelligentsia tested the bona fide of British colonial power. In fact, the philosophical and intellectual foundations of Indian nationalism lay in this economic critique of the British colonial system which was shown to be not only unable to ameliorate the conditions of the poor but also instrumental in impoverishing the people further.

But the greatest question before you, the question of all questions, is the poverty of India. (Hear, hear.) This will be, I am much afraid, the great future trouble both of the Indian people and of the British Rulers. It is the rock ahead. In this matter we are labouring under one great disadvantage. This poverty we attribute to the system, and not to the officials who administer that system. (Hear, hear and applause.) But unfortunately for us, for themselves and the British people, the officials (with clear-sighted exceptions of course) make the matter personal, and do not consider impartially and with calmness of judgement this all-important subject. The present Duke of Devonshire has well put this state of the official mind, which is peculiarly applicable in connection with this subject. He said, 'The Anglo-Indian, whatever may be his merits, and no doubt they are just, is not a person who is distinguished by an exceptionally calm judgment.' (Speech, H. of C., 23 August 1883.)

... You remember my papers on the Poverty of India, and I have asked for Returns to bring up information to date, so that a fair comparison of the present with the past may enable the House to come to a correct judgement. I am sorry the Government of India refuses to make a return of a Note prepared so late as 1881 by Sir David Barbour, upon which the then Finance Minister (Lord Cromer) based his statement in his speech in 1882 about the extreme poverty of the mass of the people. I do not see why the Government of India should refuse. The Note, I am told, is an important document. Government for its own sake should be ready to give it. In 1880, the present Duke of Devonshire, then Secretary of State for India, readily gave me some statistics and information prepared by Mr. F. Danvers, though I did not know of their existence. This enabled me to point out some errors and to explain some points which had been misunderstood. Such information is extremely necessary, not merely for the sake of the exceedingly poor masses of the people, but for the very stability of the British power itself.

The question of the Poverty of India should be fully raised, grappled with and settled. The Government ought to deal boldly and broadly with it. Let there be a return in detail, correctly calculated, made every year of the *total* annual income of all British India, per head of population, and of the requirements of a labourer to live in working health, and not as a starved beast of burden. Unless such complete and accurate information is given every year in detail, it is idle and useless to make mere unfounded assertions that India is prospering.

It must also be remembered that Lord Cromer's annual average of not more than Rs. 27 per head is for the whole population, including the rich and all classes, and not what the great mass of the population can or do actually get. Out of the total annual income of British India, all that portion must be deducted which belongs to European Planters, Manufacturers, and Mine-owners, and not to the people of British India, excepting the poor wages they received...

Another portion is enjoyed in and carried out from the country on a far larger share per head by many who are not the children of the soil—official and non-official. Then the upper and middle classes of the Indians themselves receive much more than their average share. The great mass of the poor people, therefore, have a much lower average than even the wretched 'not more than Rs. 27' per head.

You know that I had calculated the average of the income as being Rs. 20 per head per annum, and when Lord Cromer's statement of Rs. 27 appeared, I requested him to give me his calculations but he refused. However, Rs 20 or 'not more than Rs 27'—how wretched is the condition of a country of such income, after a hundred years of the most costly administration, and can such a thing last? (Cries of 'no, no'.)

It is remarkable that there is no phase of the Indian problem which clear-headed and fair-minded Anglo-Indians have not already seen and indicated. More than a hundred years ago, in 1787, Sir John Shore wrote these remarkable, far-seeing, and prophetic words:

> Whatever allowance we may make for the increased industry of the subjects of the State, owing to the enhanced demand for the produce of it (supposing the demand to be enhanced), there is reason to conclude that the benefits are more than counter-balanced by evils inseparable from the system of a remote foreign dominion. (Parl. Ret. 377 of 1812.)

And these words of prophecy are true to the present day. I pass over what has been said by other European officials at different times during the hundred years. I come to 1886, and here is a curious and complete response after a hundred years by the Secretary of State for India. In a dispatch (26 January 1886) to the Treasury, he makes a significant admission about the consequences of the character of the Government of the foreign rule of Britain. He says:

> The position of India in relation to taxation and the sources of the public revenues is very peculiar, not merely from the habits of the people and their strong aversion to change which is more specially exhibited to new forms of taxation, but likewise from the character of the Government, which is in the hands of foreigners, who hold all the principal administrative offices and form so large a part of the Army. The imposition of new taxation which would have to be borne wholly as a consequence of the foreign rule imposed on the country and virtually to meet additions to charges arising outside of

> the country would constitute a political danger, the real magnitude of which, it is to be feared, is not at all appreciated by persons who have no knowledge of or concern in the Government of India, but which those responsible for that Government have long regarded as of the most serious order.

What a strange confirmation, fulfilment and explanation of the very reason of the prophecy of a hundred years ago, and admission now that because the character of the present Government is such that '*it is in the hands of the foreigners who hold all the principal administrative offices and form so large a part of the army*', the consequence of it is a '*political danger*', the real magnitude of which is '*of the most serious order*'.

Need I, after this declaration, even despair that some of our Anglo-Indian friends would not take a lesson from the Secretary of State and understand the evil of the system under which India is suffering? Have I ever said anything clearer or stronger than this dispatch has done? It gives my whole fear of the future perils to the people of India and political danger to the British power in a nutshell. This shows that some of our Anglo-Indian authorities have not been, nor are, so dull and blind as not to have seen before or see now the whole peril of the position, and the unnatural and suicidal system of administration.

Yes, figures are quoted by some of what they call 'increase of trade', 'balance of trade in favour of India', 'increase of industry', 'hoarding of treasure in British India', etc., etc.; but our misfortune is that these people, with bias and prejudices and prepossessions, and apparently having not very clear ideas of the principles, processes, and details of commercial and banking operations and transactions, and of the perturbations of what Sir John Shore called 'the evils of a distant foreign dominion', are not able to understand and read aright these facts and figures of the commercial and economic conditions of British India. These people do not realise or seem to understand that what are called 'the trade returns of British India', are misleading, and are not the trade returns of British India. A good portion of both the imports and exports of both merchandise and treasure belong to the Native States and to countries beyond the borders, and not to British India. A separate return must be made of the imports and exports of the non-British territories, so that a correct account of the true trade of British India may be given by itself—and then there should be some statement of the exports which are not trade exports at all, but only political and private European remittances; and then only will it be seen how wretched this British Indian true trade is, and how fallacious and misleading the present returns are. A return is made every year called 'The Material and Moral Progress of India'. But that part regarding 'Material Progress' to which I am confining my observations is very imperfect and misleading. As I have already said, nothing short of a return every year of the average annual income per head of population of British India, and of the absolute necessaries of life for a healthy labourer, in detailed calculation, can give any correct idea of the progress or otherwise of the material condition of the people of British India. I ask for 'detailed calculation' in the returns, because some of the officials seem to have rather vague notions of the Arithmetic of Averages, and though the foundation figures may be correct, they bring out results far from truth. I have pointed out this with instances in my papers. I have communicated with the Secretary of State for India, and he has communicated with the Government in India. But I do not know how far this correction has been attended to by those who calculate averages.

Trade between England and India

What is grievous is that the present unnatural system, as predicted by Sir John Shore, is destructive to us, with a partial benefit to the United Kingdom with our curse upon it. But were a natural system to prevail, the commercial and industrial benefits aided by perfect free trade that exists between India and the United Kingdom will be to both countries of an extent of which we can at present form no conception.

But here is an inexhaustible market of 221,000,000 of their own civilised fellow-citizens with some 66,000,000 more of the people of the Native States, and what a great trade would arise with such an enormous market, and the United Kingdom would not for a long time hear anything about her 'unemployed'. It is only some people of the United Kingdom of the higher classes that at present draw all the benefit from India. The great mass of the people do not derive that benefit from the connection with India which they ought to get with benefit to both countries. On the other hand, it is with the Native States that there is some comparatively decent trade. With British India, as compared with its population, the trade of the United Kingdom is wretched indeed after a century of a very costly administration paid for by the poverty-stricken ryots.

My last prayer and exhortation to the Congress and to all my countrymen is: go on united and earnest, in concord and harmony, with moderation, with loyalty to the British rule and patriotism towards our country, and success is sure to attend our efforts for our just demands, and the day is not distant when the world will see the noblest spectacle of a great nation like the British holding out the hands of true fellow citizenship and of justice to the vast mass of humanity of this great and ancient land of India with benefits and blessings to the human race.

~

ROMESH CHANDRA DUTT

The Economic Condition of India

Romesh Chandra Dutt (1848–1909) was one of the earliest Indian civil servants. His work as a civil servant provided him with a close understanding of the peasant economy and its myriad aspects and problems and afforded him a chance to gain first-hand knowledge of life in villages. All these were reflected in his writings on the Indian economy and particularly in his monumental Economic History of India *which appeared in two volumes. His letters to Lord Curzon about the causes of famine were a remarkable attack on the official positions on economy and development in India. His papers on famines in India (1897) produced a great stir. He constantly championed the cause of lessening the land revenue which he felt was a great burden on the ryot as well as on the zamindars. In this speech, which he delivered at the Philosophical Institution, Glasgow, on 4 September 1901, he presented a succinct summary of his stand on the Indian economy.*

Last Monday, my esteemed and distinguished friend, Sir John Jardine, gave you a general account of that great country which now forms an important portion of the British Empire. He gave you an account of India and its people, told you of the different Provinces into which British India is divided, and also of those States which are ruled by their own Native Princes. Tonight, we shall look into the state of things in India from a different standpoint. We shall enquire into the economic condition of the people—their industries, their trades, their agriculture. We shall try to ascertain how far the sources of national wealth in India have been developed by railways, and how far the annual harvests of the people have made [*sic*] safe by irrigation works. We shall examine the incidence of the Land Tax on the agricultural population of India, and the present state of the finances of that country. In a word the material condition of the vast population of India, forming a sixth of the human race, will form the subject of our enquiry this evening.

This is a subject which must always receive the attention of all thoughtful men and women in this country, but recent events in India have invested this subject with a special importance. There is not a man or woman in Great Britain who has not felt grieved by the accounts of recent famines in India. Within the memory of men who are still in their middle age, within the last 30 years, there have been no less than ten desolating famines, causing the deaths of fifteen million people in India. And tonight, when we are assembled in this hall, half a million people are assembled in the different famine camps in Western India, and that country is passing through its third year of a continuous famine. It is necessary, therefore, that we should enquire somewhat minutely into the material condition of the people of India, and find out how far it is possible to prevent or minimise the effects of famines in India in the future, as they have been prevented in other parts of the British Empire.

I. Agriculture and the Land Tax

The material well-being of the people of India, as in every other part of the world, depends on successful agriculture, on flourishing industries, and on sound system of finance. I take agriculture first, because four-fifths of the population of India depend directly or indirectly on agriculture. It is the main industry of India, the main source of subsistence for the people. This is an important fact which we should always bear in mind in speaking about India. India, today, is essentially an agricultural country. If agriculture flourishes, if the crops are safeguarded, if the land is moderately taxed, the people are prosperous. If any of these conditions is wanting, the people must necessarily be on the verge of starvation, and must perish in years of bad harvest.

The land system of India is different from the land system of this country. Here you are familiar with the landlord who owns land, the farmer who holds farms, and the agricultural labourer who is paid by wages and has no permanent rights in the land he cultivates. In India, on the contrary, the actual cultivator, by immemorial custom, had some proprietary and heritable rights in the field which he cultivated. Sometimes, as in Bengal, he lived under his landlord, paying rent to the landlord, but owning his hereditary field from which he could not be evicted so long as he paid the customary rent. In other instances, as in Northern India and in Madras and Bombay, he lived in his village community, that ancient system of village self-government which prevailed in India for thousands of years. The landlord or the village community paid the Land Tax to the State; the individual cultivator paid his rent to the landlord or his share of produce to the community, and held his ancestral field from generation to generation, without let or hindrance. Such was the ancient land system of India—the land belonged to the nation, not to any privileged class.

How has this system been affected by British rule? In Bengal and some other places, the ancient system has been preserved and strengthened. The British Government levies the Land Tax from the landlords, and the amount of this Tax was permanently settled a hundred years ago—between 1793 and 1805. But in Northern India, as well as in Madras and Bombay, where the village community system flourished down to the early years of the nineteenth century, that old institution exists no longer. That ancient form of village self-government has unfortunately perished under the too centralised system of British administration. In Northern India, landlords have taken the place of these communities; in Madras and Bombay, generally, the cultivators are directly under the State. Therefore, if you ask me what is the actual position and status of the Indian cultivator at the present day, I can roughly describe it in one sentence. In Northern India the cultivator lives under landlords, and the landlords pay the Land Tax to the State; in Southern India the cultivator lives directly under the State, and pays the Land Tax to the State. There are exceptions to this general rule, but it will be enough for our purpose this evening to remember this broad distinction. In Northern India it is the landlord who pays the Land Tax to the State; in Southern India it is the cultivator who pays the Land Tax to the State.

Now what is this Indian Land Tax? You are aware that in England a Land Tax was raised during the wars of the Spanish Succession at the rate of 4s. in the £ of annual value, i.e. 20 per cent on the rental; and that it was reduced after the Peace of Utrecht to 2s. in the £ and then 1s. in the £, or 5 per cent on the rental.

The Land Tax in England varied between these limits, until it was made perpetual and redeemable by Pitt's Government in 1798. For a hundred years, therefore, before it was made perpetual, the Land Tax averaged between 5 and 20 per cent on the rental in England. In India the Land Tax ranges between 35 per cent and 100 per cent of the rental! Let me explain this to you in a few words.

In Bengal, where the Land Tax was permanently fixed over a hundred years ago, it now bears a proportion of 28 per cent on the rental of estates. To this should be added a newer tax of 6¼ per cent, also assessed on the rent, so that the total tax on land in this province comes to about 35 per cent.

In Northern India, the Government of Lord Dalhousie declared as far back as 1855 its intention to limit the Land Tax to 50 per cent of the rental. In his own words, the Government was determined 'to limit the demand of the State to 50 per cent or one-half of the average net assets'. This was a heavy tax, but it was a clear and definite limit. I regret to state that even this high limit has now been exceeded. A number of new taxes are now surcharged on the Land Tax, and the Land Tax itself came to be assessed at 50 per cent, not on the actual rental, but on the prospective rental of estates. In other words, if a landlord's rental is £1,200, the Government demanded a Tax, not of £600, but may be of £700, on the ground that the rental may rise hereafter. Is this not paltering with the people of India in a double sense, keeping the word of Dalhousie's promise to the ear and breaking it to the hope?

In the Central Provinces of India, Lord Dalhousie's rule of limiting the Land Tax to half the rental was accepted in 1855, but was evaded in 1863. And then the rule was openly abandoned in 1888, and the Government demanded a Land Tax up to 60 per cent of the rental, in addition to other taxes also assessed on the rent.

Lastly in Madras and Bombay, the rule of limiting the Land Tax to half the rent was also declared in 1856 and 1864, but has been evaded in practice. The Directors of the East India Company wrote in their dispatch of 1856 that the 'rights of the Government is not a rent, which consists of all the surplus produce after paying the cost of cultivation and the profits of agricultural stocks, but a land revenue only'. And after the Company was abolished, Sir Charles Wood, the first Secretary of State for India, wrote in his dispatch of 1864 that he desired to take only a share, and generally a half share, of the rent as Land Tax. This is the rule; but in practice the Government often takes one-third of the field produce as Land Tax, and this is not 50 per cent, but approximates to 100 per cent of the economic rent of the field. For in a small farm yielding £12 a year, the cost of cultivation and the profits of the agricultural stock generally exceed £6 or even £7 in the year; and the Government by demanding £4 as Land Tax sweeps away nearly the whole of the economic rent. How is this practice reconciled with Sir Charles Wood's principle? In this way. The Government says in effect to the cultivator: My good friend, we assume the cost of cultivation and profits of agricultural stock to be £4; we assume the economic rent to be £8, and our Land Tax of £4 is therefore half the rent! Is this not once more, keeping the word of Sir Charles Wood's promise to the ear, and breaking it to the hope?

These details are quite enough. They will give you an idea how the Land Tax is levied in different parts of India, in Bengal, in Northern India, in the Central Provinces and in Southern India. It is the heavy incidence of the Land Tax, and especially its uncertainty, which has a depressing effect on agriculture, which prevents land improvements and any saving, and impoverishes the people. Whatever the Land Tax may be, let it be clear, definite, intelligible. Except in Provinces where it is permanently fixed, the Land Tax is recognised by the British Government, all over India, to be one-half the rent. This rate is recognised by Lord Dalhousie's rule of 1855, by the Court of Director's dispatch of 1856, and by Sir Charles Wood's dispatch of 1864. This rate is heavy enough in all conscience, but let us at least religiously and conscientiously adhere to this rule, and not seek to evade or exceed it. Thoughtful and moderate Englishmen demand this, and educated and public-spirited Indians desire it also. In December last, a Memorial was signed by a number of retired Indian officials pressing this recommendation on the Secretary of State for India. The Right Honourable Sir Richard Garth, late Chief Justice of Bengal, was one of the signatories; Sir John Jardine, who spoke here last Monday, was another; and several other retired officials, including myself, signed it. The unrepresented people of India demand from the British Government a faithful observance of those clear and definite rules which were laid down by the Government itself forty or fifty years ago.

II. Railways and Irrigation

Gentlemen, I now turn from the important subject of the Land Tax to the Railways and Irrigation Works of India. The construction of

Railways has, I need hardly remark to this audience, been highly beneficial in India, as it is beneficial in every other part of the world. It has shortened distances, made travelling and traffic cheaper, and what is of great importance, it has made transport of food grains from one province to another in times of distress quicker and easier. Nevertheless, railways in India have been constructed with doubtful wisdom out of the revenues of the country, or under guarantee of profits out of such revenues. When the State undertakes railway construction or guarantees profits out of public revenues, the concern is never as paying as when undertaken by private companies on their own risk. And so it happens that the entire railway system in India has resulted, not in profit, but in a total loss of forty million pounds sterling to the revenues of India. This loss has added to the public debt, and the tax-payers of India are paying, year after year, a heavy tax as interest on the debt thus piled up. During the last year there was no loss, because the railway earned much by conveying vast quantities of food grains to the famine-stricken provinces. What was widespread calamity for the people was a gain to the railway. We all hope the famine will not last long; and I much fear the profits of the railways will disappear with the famine. In any case it is extremely doubtful if the Indian railways will ever make sufficient profits to wipe off the past loss of forty millions; and generations of Indian tax-payers will continue to bear the burden of taxation in consequence of this loss.

The total length of railways in India open to traffic by the end of 1898 was 22,500 miles. In that year the Indian Famine Commission stated in their published report that the lines required for famine protection purposes had been completed, and that preference should be given to irrigation works in the future. The advice was unheeded. There is a continuous pressure put on the Indian Government by capitalists and speculators for the construction of fresh railway lines out of the Indian revenues. And thus in spite of the advice of the Famine Commission of 1898 and the earlier commission of 1880, the Indian Government has shown more activity in the construction of railways than in irrigation works. The total length of railways open to traffic up to the end of 1900 was 25,000 miles.

The railway system does not add one single blade of corn to the food supply of the country, while irrigation works double the food supply, save crops, and prevent famines. Nevertheless, while 225 millions sterling pounds have been spent on railways, only 25 millions have been spent on irrigation works. Irrigation works are either canals or storage tanks or wells. Canals are only possible in level tracts of the country, along the basin of large rivers. Storage tanks and wells are possible elsewhere. During a century and a half of British rule the whole country could have been covered with irrigation works. All provinces could have been protected against the effect of droughts. The food supply of India could have been increased and made constant; famines and deaths could have been absolutely prevented; loss of revenue could have been obviated. But by a fatal unwisdom and want of foresight, railways have been fostered and irrigation neglected in India. Out of 220 million acres of cultivated land in India not much over 20 millions are protected by irrigation works. Many of these works are the works of old Hindu Rajas and Mahomedan Governors which have been preserved up to date. If you read Dr. Francis Buchanan's narrative of his journey from Madras through Mysore to Malabar—performed just a hundred years ago—you will find mention of old canals and storage tanks, made and maintained by the old Hindu and Mahomedan rulers, in every part of their dominions. In spite of their frequent wars, in spite of crude systems of Government, they knew the value of irrigation works. If the more enlightened British Government had followed their example in this respect, they could have covered the whole of India with irrigation works within a hundred years, and they could have made famines impossible under British rule. Let us hope they will take the lesson to heart today; that they will henceforth devote all the available resources of the Indian Empire to irrigation works, so that famines will be impossible twenty or thirty years hence.

III. Industries and Manufactures

I have dwelt so long on agriculture because agriculture is the one national industry of India at the present day. Four-fifths of the population of India depend upon this one industry. Other industries flourished in India in past centuries, but the history of those industries under British rule is a melancholy one; many of them have declined and some have perished altogether. If you read the account of India in the 17th century written by the eminent Frenchman, Francois Bernier, who resided there many years, you will find that in spite of the arbitrary administration of those days, the people of India were a great manufacturing nation, and exported vast quantities of cotton and silk fabrics to the markets of Asia and of Europe. And if you read the statistical account of Eastern India, recorded a hundred years ago by Dr. Francis Buchanan and edited by Montgomery Martin, you will find that one-half of the women population of India found employment in spinning and weaving in those days, and earned something from day to day and from year to year, which they added to the earnings of their husbands, their fathers, or their brothers. It is a lamentable fact that practically the whole of this industry has died out in India, and the profits from this industry are lost to the people. It first declined under the illiberal and ungenerous commercial policy of England in the early part of the nineteenth century, when prohibitive duties were imposed on Indian manufactures exported to Europe, while English manufactures were imported into India almost duty-free.

'It is a melancholy instance,' writes Horace Hayman Wilson, the well-known historian of India, 'of the wrong done to India by a country on which she has become dependent. It was stated in evidence (in 1813) that the cotton and silk goods of India up to the period could be sold for a profit in the British market at a price from 50 to 60 per cent lower than those fabricated in England. It consequently became necessary to protect the latter by duties of 70 and 80 per cent on their value, or by positive prohibition... British goods were forced upon her without paying any duty, and the foreign manufacturer employed the arm of political injustice to keep down and ultimately strangle a competitor with whom he could not have contended on equal terms.'

Later in the century, the prohibitive duties were abolished, after they had done their fatal work. Handlooms were replaced all over the world by steam, and steam-mills were started in Calcutta and in Bombay. They prospered for a time, but the imposition of an excise duty on the production of Indian mills in recent years has greatly interfered with their success. It is a duty unknown in any other part of the civilised world; it hampers our infant steam industry, and makes it difficult for us to compete with our Asiatic competitors, Japan and China. It is an unwise and illiberal tax by which the British Government disables its British subjects in India from competing on equal terms with other Asiatic nations in the markets of the world.

What has been said about the spinning and weaving industry of India applies to some extent to other old Indian industries. Dyeing and the manufactures of dyes, tanning and leather work, working in iron and other metals, the weaving of shawls and carpets, muslins and brocades, the manufacture of paper and stationery articles—all have declined. Millions of the Indian population who made a livelihood from these industries are now compelled to agriculture as the one remaining source of their subsistence; and responsible statesmen in the present day, in the House of Commons and outside, are trying to think out how they can undo the mischief done in the past, and again diversify Indian Industries. I have myself, during the many years of my service under the Indian Government, visited villages and towns which were once the homes of flourishing communities of weavers—those who produced the famous Indian muslin which was once the wonder of Europe. Those villages are now deserted and desolate; the great lakes excavated in the olden times are silted up; the temples and religious edifices are in decay; the streets are covered with jungle; and the old weaver families have migrated elsewhere to seek a scanty subsistence, and their old ancestral villages know them not.

Gentlemen, you hear very little in this country of this decline of the old national industries of India. Your attention is naturally attracted to those industries only in which British capital is employed. You read of tea and coffee, of indigo and jute, of coal mines and gold mines, which are worked by British Companies. We wish well to all these industries, for they give employment to hundreds of thousands of Indian labourers. But you cannot improve the condition of the people of India without fostering their own industries, carried on by themselves, in their towns and villages. You cannot add to the wealth of the Indian people except by wise legislation, tending to promote and help their own national undertakings. And unless you improve the material condition of the people of India, they will be but poor customers of your own commodities. Our interests and yours are closely allied and not divergent. If our manufactures were revived, and industrial prosperity once more restored to India, the three hundred million people of India could become the largest customers of your manufactures. But if they remain poor, resourceless, starving agriculturists, all your efforts to increase the consumption of your goods in India will utterly fail. India ought to be the greatest market for British goods; India could be so, if her people were prosperous under British rule.

IV. Trade

Under the present circumstances of the people of India, your imports into India show no rapid improvement. The average annual import of merchandise into India, most of which was from Great Britain, was

708 millions of rupees, or 47 million pounds, during the five years ending in 1894. In the succeeding five years ending in 1899 the average annual import into India was 736 millions of rupees or 49 million pounds. An export of 49 million of pounds to a population of 300 millions means a consumption of 3s. per head of the population. If the people of India consumed your goods at the rate of 5s. or 6s. a year per head of population—and this is a moderate estimate even for a poor Asiatic nation—your exports into India would be doubled, and you would carry on a trade with India exceeding your trade with any other country in the world. Therefore, I say that your trade interests and those of the people of India are closely allied and not divergent. It is not by restrictive excise duties on the manufactures of India, nor by draining her resources, that Great Britain can gain in the long run. It is by making the population of India prosperous that your trade with India can prosper.

V. Finances and the Economic Drain

Gentlemen, I have spoken to you of the agriculture and the Land Tax of India, of her railways and irrigation works, of her industries and trade. I have only one word to add about the financial administration of India. The net revenues of India for the current year have been estimated at 42 millions sterling. Roughly speaking you can say that 20 millions out of this comes from Land Revenue, 20 millions from other taxes including Salt, and two millions from Opium. In other words, the trades and industries of the country bring little revenue, because the trades and industries are on the decline—one half the revenue of the country is tax on land and tax on salt, and is raised from the good of the poor. If you can examine the figures closely, you will find how little reason there is for congratulation on the increase of revenues in India; that increase does not mean increasing prosperity, but only an oppressively increasing taxation on the food supply of the people. Twenty-six years ago, our present Prime Minister, Lord Salisbury, was Secretary of State for India, and condemned in the strongest terms this undue taxing of the food of the people. He wrote in 1876:

> So far as it is possible to change the Indian system, it is desirable that the cultivator should pay a smaller proportion of the whole national charge. It is not in itself a thrifty policy to draw the mass of revenue from the rural districts where capital is scarce... The injury is

> exaggerated in the case of India, where so much of the revenue is exhorted [*sic*] without a direct equivalent. As India must be bled, the lancet should be directed to the part where the blood is congested, or at least sufficient, not to those which are already feeble from the want of it.

These remarks of Lord Salisbury apply with greater force now than they did twenty-six years ago. You are bleeding the agricultural population of India at a time when they are suffering from repeated, continuous and widespread famines; and you are exporting a larger portion of that revenue out of India without a direct equivalent today, than you did 26 years ago. You are draining India annually of sixteen millions sterling for what are called 'Home charges'; while the total of charges which India has to remit annually to this country without a direct equivalent is over twenty millions! Do you think that any country can prosper under such a system of finance? Do you think Great Britain or the United States, or Germany or France or any other country could prosper if an amount equal to one half of her annual revenues was sent out of the country, year after year, to be spent in a foreign country? Do you think England is doing justice to India under a financial arrangement through which the food of twenty millions of people in India is annually sent away to England without a direct equivalent?

I have said the net revenue of India for the current year is estimated at 42 millions. The expenditure, roughly speaking is this: 17 millions for the Army, 17 millions for the Civil services, and 8 millions more for other charges. Of all these three heads the cost of the Army is felt to be most unjust and oppressive, because the great army maintained in India is not merely for the defence of India but for the defence of Great Britain's possessions in Asia and in Africa. 30,000 troops were lately sent out of India to China and to South Africa; and this proves beyond a doubt that the Indian Army is maintained as much for Imperial purposes as for India. That being so, it is only just and fair that Great Britain should pay a portion of the cost of the army maintained in India, and not try to run her empire on the cheap by throwing the whole cost of the army on the unrepresented and famine-stricken population of India.

VI. Famine and Their Remedies

Ladies and Gentlemen, I thank you for listening so patiently and with so much interest to this account of the economic condition of India.

It is a subject of the greatest importance; I do not think there is a question of graver import connected with any part of the British Empire than the present condition of India. Called upon to deal with the subject within the limits of one speech, I should have but ill discharged my duty if I had merely gleaned some facts and figures from official reports, and placed them before you without explaining their bearing on the condition of the people of India. Great Britain can look back on the past history of Indian administration—if not with unalloyed satisfaction—at least with legitimate pride. If blunders have been committed in the past, much good work too has been well and honestly done. Great Britain has restored peace and security of property to the vast population of India after a century of disorder and disturbance. Great Britain has introduced into India Western methods of education which have had the happiest results among an ancient and intellectual people. And if Great Britain has too hastily and unwisely swept aside some of our old self-governing institutions, she is making us familiar with newer methods of enlightened administration. These are results which we can contemplate with just pride and sincere satisfaction; but there are matters in which the success of British rule has not been so conspicuous; and we cannot honestly feel the same satisfaction in contemplating the economic condition of the people of India in the present day. No impartial observer in India, no unprejudiced critic in this country, can think of the wretched and almost universal poverty of the vast population of India without a feeling of commiseration and sorrow, or can read of the frequent and fatal famines of that country without a feeling of pain and of humiliation. These are facts which tell their own tale; roseate pictures of Indian prosperity, so often painted and so sedulously circulated, convince no one, and deceive no one. To you, such representations of Indian prosperity appear like an endeavour to conceal defects in administration which should be remedied and not concealed; to the mass of my countrymen, who live in a chronic state of poverty of which you have no conception, such roseate pictures painted in this country appear like an unfeeling mockery of their misfortunes. The evil is undoubtedly there; Englishmen and Englishwomen desire to know the reasons of the frequent and fatal famines in the past; and they desire also to see no more of them in the future. Therefore, standing before you tonight to speak of the economic condition of my country, I have sought to lay before you, as clearly as I could within my brief limits, the causes of this undoubted evil, and the remedies which are needed. Moderate the Land Tax within reasonable and intelligible limits; extend irrigation works all over India; revive the industries and manufactures of the people; reduce the financial drain which is impoverishing India; and admit the people themselves into some reasonable share in the control of the administration of their own concerns, and you will hear as little of famines in India in the future, as you hear of famines in Great Britain or famines in the city of Glasgow. An Empire has its responsibilities as well as its glory; and the happiness and advancement of the people of India are the highest responsibilities of Great Britain and her most glorious mission in the east.

~

DINSHAW EDULJEE WACHA

Congress Resolution on Military Expenditure

Dinshaw Eduljee Wacha (1844–1936) was a leading public figure who dedicated himself to the cause of the nation and its people. His mastery over finances, currency and the nuances of administration was evidenced in his fearless and detailed criticism of municipal governance as well as the central budget. This motivated Bombay's political workers to send him, along with G.K. Gokhale, to England before the Welby Commission in 1902. He contended before the commission—instituted by the Crown to look into fiscal management and enquire into the official expenditure of the Government of India—that the increase in expenditure and consequent financial crisis were to be ascribed principally to the enormous growth of military expenditure. He argued that it was the scheme of amalgamation of 1889 which made the Indian Army uniform in all respects to the English Army that had led to the growth in military expenditure. Wacha consistently maintained that the military arrangement between Britain and India was an unequal one 'in which the stronger and the richer partner successfully managed to foist on the weaker and the poorer burdens which really did not belong to her'. The situation worsened after the Second Anglo-Afghan War, the huge cost of which was borne by the Indian exchequer despite the fact that Indians were in no way involved in the war. In the speech reproduced here, in which he moved a resolution at the eighth session of the Indian National Congress held at Allahabad between 28 and 30 December 1892, Wacha, with evidence from British officials, clarified how military operations were responsible for draining India's resources in the service of the empire.

Mr. President, Ladies and Gentlemen. The Resolution I am about to propose to you is one which, I am sure, will not only commend itself to your approval but be carried by acclamation—such is the admitted justice of its demand and such unanimity on the subject. It is as follows:

> That having regard to the fact that the abnormal increase in the annual military expenditure of the Empire since 1885-86 is principally owing to the military activity going on beyond the natural lines of the defences of this country, in pursuance of the Imperial policy of Great Britain in its relation with some of the great Powers of Europe, this Congress is of opinion, that, in bare justice to India, an equitable portion of that expenditure should be borne by the British Treasury, and that the revenues of India should be proportionately relieved of that burden.

You would no doubt remember, gentlemen, that at previous Congresses, particularly at the one held last year at Nagpur, I expatiated at length on the enormous growth of the military expenditure since 1884-85. It has risen from 16 to 22 crores in seven years. But it is altogether needless for me on this occasion to tire your patience by referring to its particulars once more. You will, however, have understood from the drift to the resolution just read to you what is it that we now demand of the Home Government. It is acknowledged in all quarters, aye, even by those who are the unmitigated apologists of the 'Forward policy' feverishly pursued by the Government of India, that the gross injustice of throwing on this country for years past, the whole burden of the military expenditure, a considerable portion of which should, in all fairness, be borne by the British Treasury, ought no longer to be tolerated, past endurance as it is, and entailing as it does oppressively heavy sacrifices on the already over-burdened tax-payers of the land.

Responsible administrators at Calcutta and at Westminster have not only protested against the shameful injustice, but recorded their deliberate opinion as to the expediency of redressing it, considering that wealthy England partly defends herself at home at the expense of the revenues of impoverished India. Apart from the long-standing scandal of the charges in connection with the Home depots to which I drew pointed attention at the sittings of the First Congress, and apart from other unjust charges, such as those of transport, arrears of pensions, and so forth—apart from these, the Imperial policy of Great Britain in its relations with Russia, and its attitude towards the whole question, known as the Eastern question, have foisted on India the annual permanent charge of 2 crores on account of the 30,000 additional troops maintained since the acquisition of Upper Burmah and the Penjdeh incident. That this additional burden is altogether unjustifiable is well-known. So, too, all the cost of the so-called 'Special defences'. You would remember my referring to these last year and reading to you a few extracts from the minutes of two of the members of the Government of India on the subject, namely, those of the Hon'ble Mr. C.P. Ilbert and Sir Auckland Colvin. They courageously protested not only against the unfairness of the burden, but against the policy which led to that addition.

I particularly read out to the Congress that part of the joint minute of those members of the Government in which it was observed that the addition of 30,000 troops to the then existing force, under the plea of safeguarding the Empire against attack from without, was hollow, and that its veiled object was purely the kindling of the faggots of external aggression. Now, I say, that the warning of Mr. Ilbert and Sir Auckland Colvin was prophetic. This must be clear to you from the number of so-called punitive expeditions undertaken by the Government of India, under the mischievous advice of its military advisers since 1885-86—expeditions which have enabled them to acquire the Zhob valley and that portion of Baluchistan which is now known as British, and such strategical places as Gilgit, Chalt, Hunza and Nagyar, and the probability, later on, of the occupation of Chitral, not to say anything of the continued bullying and baiting attitude adopted towards the Ameer of Afghanistan, with fixed determination to have a bold 'spring forward' on a fitting opportunity. All the places I have alluded to have been almost forcibly acquired under the plea of checkmating Russia in her nearer advance to India and carrying on a filibustering policy beyond the Hindu Kush. As I informed you, it is the policy of keeping Russia away from the Bosporus, which is the sole object of Russia's advance nearer the confines of India. But for this Imperial policy of Great Britain, of which Russia's onward march is the logical sequence, all the events that have occurred on the North-West Frontier would have been nowhere, and this incubus of a large standing army, gnawing away the finances of India and eating into the vitals of the tax-payers would have never been known.

Members of the Standing Committees of the Congress at various centres would remember that in 1888, Mr. Martin Wood, an honoured gentleman and a veteran, though now retired, Anglo-Indian journalist, who has been fully in sympathy with the legitimate aspirations of the Congress, and who is unostentatiously doing great service to the cause of this country at home, had addressed a most thoughtful letter to the Congress on the subject of this disastrous 'Forward policy'... It must be in your recollection that the cardinal point to which Mr. Wood referred in that correspondence was this forward policy of the Government which is the dominant factor of the chronic embarrassment of Indian finances. It is also the key to the whole material condition of the country. I passingly referred to that cardinal point in my speech last year, but as it bears the closest relation to the subject-matter of the resolution now before you, I deem it advisable to quote the passage at whole length, and afterwards place this letter on the table also, with the permission of the President, as part of this day's proceedings. Mr. Wood observed:

> It is a maxim acknowledged by our statesmen that expenditure depends on policy. In this instance the grievous addition to the unproductive outlay from Indian revenues is wholly due to the revolutionary change entered on in 1876, followed by the disastrous invasion of Afghanistan in 1878-80, and now sought to be perpetuated by the establishment of permanent military posts far beyond the physical boundaries of India on the West, for the maintenance of which the immensely costly railways already referred to, have been constructed. You are well aware that the policy has been adopted, and forced on India under cover of partisan counsels among certain English politicians; but this does not make it any more worthy of approval or lessen the need for its being checked, or, if possible, reversed.

Thus it is the policy which is at the root of the expenditure, and all of you will agree with me in thinking that, next to seeing that expenditure controlled or its burden partially relieved by the British treasury, our constant aim should be to nag on at the mischievous policy, with a view to its reversal. But meanwhile let me further point out to you the broad considerations which we are sometimes apt to overlook or postpone, as Mr. Wood justly observes, amidst the stress of other current topics. These considerations are:

(a) The financial position of India dominates all its other material conditions.

(b) The pressure caused by the absorption of your resources, consequent on the fatal error of thrusting military outposts beyond the natural boundaries of India, transcends in its cramping and distressing effects all other financial and fiscal mistakes put together.

(c) That error, with its concomitant military extravagance, is one of executive policy, and no reform in administration nor in the local Legislative Councils will avail to obtain a reversal of that erroneous policy or security against repetitions of similar sacrifices of India's true interests.

(d) By appealing in respect of the paramount financial peril of India, to Her Majesty's Secretary of State as the one directly responsible authority, and, next, to the High Court of Parliament, your Congress will effectually convince independent English politicians of the capacity of your people to understand and deal with those large questions of policy, on the right solution of which depends the present and future welfare of the masses of your people.

Gentlemen, I need not tell you how weighty are these considerations, and what is, therefore, the duty of the Congress in reference to them. I dare say you fully comprehend the drift to the extracts just read and clearly understand the position of Indian finance as dominated by the huge octopus of military expenditure. The Currency question becomes of secondary importance in comparison with it. For though you may remedy your Currency, the financial embarrassment arising from the burdensome military expenditure will continue to prevail until the policy which entails it is absolutely reversed.

I am deeply of conviction, and, so too, I believe, you are, that were this policy to be reversed tomorrow, we would see an end to the 'prolonged wail' of our Finance Ministers in succession touching the growing difficulty of bringing an equilibrium in the annual balance sheet of the Empire. We would then at once see an end to the inspired statements put forth from time to time about the enhancement of old and the imposition of new taxation.

... I observed at the outset that not only is the entire Native press but even the Anglo-Indian press in favour of the demand made in the resolution before you. The Government of India itself has, since 1879, more than once bitterly complained in its despatches of the unjust burden saddled on the Indian Treasury in reference to that portion of the military expenditure which in all conscience and equity should be borne by the British Treasury. For it is incurred in consequence of the policy pursued by England towards Russia in Europe.

... But, gentlemen, I may further request you to remember that it is not only the Government here that has protested against the injustice of the burden of military expenditure being laid by a rich country like England on so poor a country like India. Members of the Council of India too have protested against it. When the entire cost of the unrighteous Second Afghan war was at first attempted to be foisted on India, some of those members vigorously recorded their minutes against the scandalous injustice of the attempt. Some went into the broad question we are discussing today. These minutes, I believe, are so germane to the substance of the resolution before you that I would be wanting in my task if I did not acquaint you with them. They are all taken from the Blue Books on Afghanistan published by order of the House of Commons in 1879, '80, '81. The entire cost of the Second Afghan war was, as you are aware, twenty-five crores of rupees. And it was after a memorable debate in the House of Commons that India was done paltry justice to by a contribution of five crores from the British Treasury at the rate of a crore per annum, though there was not an inconsiderable body of English opinion in favour of England bearing the whole cost.

This is what Sir Erskine Perry, one of the truest and staunchest friends of India in the India Council, whose loss we must for ever deplore, observed: 'I deny absolutely that the interest of India demand a war. Lord Lytton has told us more than once that the Central Asian question is not an Indian but a European question, but it depends on the policy of the Cabinet. I bow to the reasoning, the soundness of which I am not in a position to judge; but as our Indian policies are charged by Parliament with the protection of the revenues of India, I maintain that it is unjust to throw any of the cost of an Imperial policy on the revenues of that extremely poor country.'

The late Sir Henry Durand, then Military Member of the Council and who was afterwards Lieutenant-Governor of the Punjab, minuted: 'For the above reasons I should have been disposed to vote against the present charge on the revenues of India, but looking upon it only as an advance to the Imperial Government, feeling also that it is expedient that no time should be lost in providing for a necessity growing out of an actual war, and having been given the power under Section 23 of 21 and 22 Vict., Chapter 106, of recording my opinion, I have voted with my colleagues in the affirmative.'

Sir Barrow Ellis recorded the following minute, and I ask you to listen to it most attentively as it has a great bearing on the general question. Sir Barrow Ellis, too, you may know, was a steadfast and true friend of this country and a just and most sympathetic Civilian, the type of whom is getting rare.

> It is not for me to justify the war, nor to seek to determine the causes that have led to it, except in so far they bear on the question whether the charge ought to be borne by Indian revenues or by the Imperial

> Treasury. Had the war been undertaken on account of aggression by Shere Ali, or because the Afghans menaced the peace and security of India, then doubtless, at whatever cost, the charge would fairly have been debitable to India, but surely no one will allege these to be the causes of the war. It is not anything that Shere Ali has said or done that *per se* justifies the extreme step of declaring a war that must at least cost much money, and many valuable lives. The war is clearly the outcome of events in Europe, and the necessity for it has risen from the action of Russia, which action again was devised as a support to the schemes in Europe. It is thus in the interest of the Empire, and in furtherance of European policy, that the war has been brought about, and it is in these considerations that its justification must be found. I trust, therefore, that it will be borne in mind that the mere fact of the locale being on the Indian Frontier ought not to be made an excuse for placing a new burden upon India. In any case substantial aid will be freely given by India in the supply of war material, and in meeting the ordinary cost of a large portion of the troops engaged; the additional charges involved ought to be accepted by the British nation, and this liability, I doubt will not be generally recognised. The people of India are unrepresented, and it is the more incumbent, therefore, that the British nation should impose on India no charge of this kind that is not just and beyond challenge. Taxation is already as heavy in India as it well can be, and the people will feel the more new taxes, which in any case would cause grave dissatisfaction, not to say discontent, when the imposition of such taxes is due to an expenditure which ought in fairness to be borne by the Imperial Exchequer, and not by the already over-weighted Indian tax-payer.

Gentlemen, I ask you to consider whether the weighty reasons stated in the minute of Sir Barrow Ellis do not still hold good? Is it not time, we should reiterate them at this juncture with all the strength legitimately at our command, especially, when the expenditure, which stood at 14 crores before the breaking out of the Second Afghan war, now stands at 22 crores, and the burden of the additional cost is admitted on all sides to be intolerable?

But let us pass from the testimony of the Members of the Council of India (there is other evidence which for want of time, I refrain from referring to in this place) to that of another and distinguished official, of purely English training, who occupied the post of Finance Minister during the ever-memorable Viceroyalty of the beloved Lord Ripon, one who by his conspicuous financial ability and appreciation of real material condition of India, gave the greatest satisfaction to all classes of Her Majesty's subjects here, I mean Sir Evelyn Baring, now Lord Cromer, whom we should all gladly welcome as Viceroy, if as is rumoured, he is to succeed Lord Lansdowne. Minuting on the question of military expenditure, Sir Evelyn Baring observed:

> I do not think the financial condition of India is free from anxiety whose main source of revenue is derived from payments in silver, either fixed in perpetuity or only capable of increase at long intervals, while at the same time it owes a large sum annually in gold. The Home charges have of late years been gradually increasing. In 1881-82 they will amount to no less than 18 millions sterling. The charge is abnormally high, and moreover includes many remittances which are merely in the nature of banking transactions, but when all reasonable deductions have been made, the amount which India must send home to meet her current wants is still very large. Obviously under such conditions our essential element of State finance—stability—must be wanting.

Then, after referring to the precariousness of opium receipts and the necessity of keeping down the Salt duty as low as possible, and after reviewing other sources of revenue, Sir Evelyn further observed:

> Lastly, the pressure of population upon the soil, which year by year increases in intensity, presents an economic difficulty of the first magnitude with which, indeed, I doubt the capability of Government to cope by any direct means, but which renders it imperative upon us to reduce in every possible way the pressure of taxation. On these grounds I consider not only that it would be in the highest degree unwise to take any steps which could have for the result a larger increase of a wholly unproductive nature, but I entertain a strong opinion that the reduction of present Military expenditure is of all others the financial question which most deserves the attention of the Government of India.

Finance Minister after Finance Minister who succeeded Sir E. Baring has spoken in the same strain, so that I do not at all feel myself called upon to say aught more upon this subject after the authoritative opinions of all such experts and statesmen. I trust, therefore, that this resolution on which all India and even the Council of India are agreed, will be passed by acclamation.

~

PHEROZESHAH MERWANJI MEHTA

The Budget Speech, 1895-96

Pherozeshah M. Mehta (1845–1915) was one of the pioneers who shaped Indian political consciousness in the nineteenth century. After his initial education at Elphinstone College under teachers like Alexander Grant, Mehta qualified for the Bar from Lincoln's Inn in 1868. He was the soul of the Bombay Municipal Corporation and its most articulate and decisive leader. He energized provincial politics and gradually emerged as a dynamic and powerful spokesperson. While the Grand Old Man of India, Dadabhai Naoroji, talked, wrote and spoke about 'unBritish' rule in the British Parliament, Pherozeshah Mehta made it a point to articulate it in the Bombay legislature and in the Imperial Legislative Council where Indians were being gradually allowed to speak. Pherozeshah Mehta was ruthlessly sarcastic about British bureaucracy and his facts, figures and wit were unmatched. One of the finest intellectuals and political personalities India has produced, Pherozeshah, like Dadabhai, was also an indefatigable fighter for the Congress who in his later years was targetted by the new generation over his hold on the organization.

In the budget speech reproduced here, made at the meeting of the Legislative Council held on 28 March 1895 and in the presence of Lord Elgin who presided over the debate on the financial statement, Pherozeshah Mehta was at his best, making his point brilliantly and with wit.

...These are not the views of clumsy and pretentious Native would-be politicians, who audaciously presume to think that they could govern the Empire better, but those of distinguished men whose mature and tried knowledge and experience must command respect, confirming in the most remarkable manner the contention of the Association that it is the enormous increase of expenditure since 1885-86 which is more responsible even than the depreciated rupee for the embarrassed and critical state of Indian finance. But it has been argued that, though it is perfectly true that the expenditure has increased, the increase is justified by the needs of an expanding and progressive Empire. In discussing the present Budget I propose to go a step further than the Association did last year, and endeavour to show that, even if the need for the increase were academically incontrovertible, still it is unjustifiable, as being a burden beyond the capacity and resources of the country to bear without dangerous exhaustion. In introducing the Tariff Bill, the Hon'ble Sir James

Westland tried to satisfy the Council that 'it was not by reason of any laxity in controlling expenditure that it was rendered necessary to ask for increased powers of taxation'. In the debate on the Budget last year, the Hon'ble General Sir Henry Brackenbury was still more emphatic about the impossibility of reducing military expenditure. In replying to the invitation of the Hon'ble Mr. Playfair to meet with some degree of fullness the arguments raised in certain quarters for the reduction of the military expenditure, the honourable member said:

> My Lord, I have never seen such arguments. I have seen denunciations, I have seen invectives, I have seen statements and assertions, and have seen appeals to the Government of India to reduce expenditure, but I have never seen one single argument. I have seen no argument put forward by anybody to show that military expenditure in this country could reasonably be reduced.'

It seems to me that in these utterances both the honourable members miss one point which is indispensable for sound and solvent finance. Necessity of expenditure is after all a relative term. However great the necessity for a particular item of expenditure, that necessity must be controlled by the ways and means for incurring it and must be proportioned to the capacity for defraying the expenses of it. I have no doubt that if the increase of troops in 1886 had been 40,000 instead of 30,000 the Hon'ble Military Member would have spoken quite as peremptorily against any reasonable reduction of expenditure, and would be still roving quite as much in despair in quest of arguments. But the real question is whether the items of military and civil expenditure bear any just and reasonable proportion to the revenue that can be possibly realised from the country without incurring peril and exhaustion. What is the present position in this respect as disclosed by the Budget laid before the council? Since 1885-86 the income tax has been reimposed, or rather the license tax has been developed into an income tax and extended to Burma. A duty is levied on petroleum. A patwari cess has been levied in the North-Western Provinces and Oudh. The excise duty on salt has been raised to within eight annas of the highest figure possible if salt is not to be placed beyond reach of the mass of people. The import and cotton duties, with an excise duty on yarn, have been fully reintroduced. Altogether something like seven crores of fresh taxation have been imposed since 1885.

...What these figures mean is that military expenditure more than fully absorbs one half of the whole net revenue of the country, or, to put it in another way, if you leave out of account the opium revenue, which cannot be relied on as stable owing to the competition of the home-grown drug in China, the military expenditure absorbs the whole of what has been called taxation revenue proper, derived from salt, stamps, excise, provincial rates, customs as now fully revived, income and other assessed taxes, forests, registration, and tributes from Native States.

... In that spirit of humorous banter which I am glad the heavy monotony of figures and statistics has not driven out of the Hon'ble Finance Member, Sir James Westland was last year pleasantly sarcastic over 'the united wisdom of the Native gentlemen interested in politics, who met at Christmas at Lahore to show us how we ought to govern India', and enjoyed a hearty laugh over their proposals to reduce revenue and increase expenditure at one and the same time. Though of course they could not bear comparison with members of the most distinguished service in the world, these gentlemen are still not altogether devoid of logic and sense in their suggestions. It is not very difficult to understand that, if you economise in the right directions, you can reduce revenue and increase expenditure in others. If you could reduce your military expenditure to reasonable proportions, if you could steady your 'forward' policy so as to not to lead to incessant costly expeditions, if you could get your inflated Army Home estimates moderated, if you could devise ways by which the huge burdens of salaries and pension could be lightened, then it is not chimerical to imagine that you could improve your judicial machinery, strengthen your police, develop a sounder system of education, cover the country with useful public works and railways, undertake larger sanitary measures, cheapen the post and telegraph, and still be in a position to relieve small incomes, to press less heavily on the land, to give the cultivators breathing time, and to reduce the salt tax.

It is from this point of view that the Financial Statement which the honourable member has presented to the Council can scarcely be considered wholly satisfactory. While fully recognising that he is surrounded by adverse and difficult circumstances, and that his hand is not free, still the fact remains that the new Budget is a hand to mouth budget, and not based on enduring principles of sound finance. Fortune has smiled on him during the past year, and it is difficult not to read beneath the lines that he still entertains a lurking faith in windfalls and miracles for the new year. He shows a surplus of four and a half lakhs of rupees, but it is speculative surplus. It is obtained after the imposition of taxation to the tune of over three crores, after putting the Famine Insurance Fund in abeyance, after taking the rate of exchange probably higher than it is likely to be maintained, and after shutting his eyes to the heavy cloud that is looming in the North West. And all this in a year of prosperity and peace, when the country has remained free from famine and war, barring of course the frontier expeditions, which, as predicted by Sir Auckland Colvin, must now be accepted as a trouble quite as constant and irremediable as exchange. The prospect before us is really neither hopeful nor cheering: and, in spite of his efforts to administer some grains of consolation, the real note that the honourable member strikes is unmistakable when he winds up by saying 'that many causes for anxiety still remain and we may again be in difficulties before many months are over'. What then? is a question whose gravity it will be more easy to appreciate than to solve.

~

PHEROZESHAH MERWANJI MEHTA

The Ilbert Bill Controversy

Pherozeshah Mehta fearlessly criticized the English bureaucracy with a robust confidence arising out of his in-depth understanding of the way it operated. His dignified and measured eloquence was often laced with biting sarcasm. His trademark approach towards British officialdom is reflected in this famous speech delivered at the public meeting held in the Town Hall, Bombay, on 28 April 1883 for the purpose of considering the Ilbert Bill. Presided over by Sir Jamsetjee Jeejeebhoy, the meeting saw Badruddin Tyabji moving the following resolution: 'That in the opinion of this meeting the Bill to amend the Code of Criminal Procedure is necessary for the just and impartial administration of justice and is in consonance with the righteous policy which the British Government has followed in the administration of this country.' Pherozeshah Mehta seconded the resolution in the following speech.

Mr. Chairman and Gentlemen, in rising to second the resolution which has been just moved by my honourable friend Mr. B. Tyabji, in a speech which you will agree with me in admiring as equally remarkable for its ability and eloquence as for the studied and dignified moderation of its tone (cheers), I confess that I undertake the task which has been assigned to me with some degree of trepidation. Within the last few days we have been generously inundated with advice to preserve the utmost judicial calmness and moderation without the slightest admixture of even judicial severity, not to allow an angry word or syllable to escape us, while we are also to put forth our case with force and vigour. Now, gentlemen, this advice is more easy to preach than to practise, and though I have resolved to use my best endeavours to achieve this golden mean, I cannot quite escape a feeling of some nervousness as to the success of this rather difficult experiment. But gentlemen, I have one consolation that in whatever I may say I will be guided by two sentiments which will never permit me to say anything which will be needlessly offensive or malicious. (Hear, hear.) If I entertain one political conviction more strongly than another, it is that this country in falling under British rule, has fallen into the hands of a nation than which no other is better qualified to govern her wisely and well. Look among all the leading nations of the world, and you will not find one who, both by her faults and by her virtues, is so well adapted to steer her safe on the path of true progress and prosperity. It is true that the English are a stubborn piece of humanity who might well be asked sometimes to take to heart the exhortation addressed once to the chosen people of God, 'Circumcise, therefore, the foreskin of your heart and be no more stiff-necked', but it must be acknowledged at the same time that it is perhaps this very trait which has preserved this country from rash and extreme experiments, and has put it on a path of sure, though slow, development. (Cheers.) Secondly, in setting up as a critic of Englishmen in India, I fully recognise that I do not set up any claim of superiority. I do not set up as a superior person who could have done better under similar circumstances. On the contrary, gentlemen, I believe most of the natives who have devoted any thought to this subject, are ready to recognise that if they were placed in the position of dominant race, God knows how they might have strutted before high Heaven and performed antics which might make angels weep. At the same time, gentlemen, I feel confident that Englishmen will frankly admit that this circumstance gives them no immunity from criticism, nor gives them any right to be impatient if they are judged by the principles they themselves have introduced and taught as the principles on which their work in this country must be finally judged. (Cheers.) The nervousness which I have admitted is therefore allayed by the consciousness that, even if I err, I will not set down aught in malice. My fear and trembling however are not quite at an end, and that is in consequence of the attitude which our European friends have taken up in regard to the public expression of native opinion on this Jurisdiction Bill which we are met here to consider to-day. That attitude is not unlike that of the amiable Scotchman described by Charles Lamb, who pitched into you for your presumption if you ventured to go in for praise of his great national poet and performed the same operation on you for your ignorance if you dared to find fault with him. (Laughter.) Much in the same humour our European friends are disposed to rebuke us for our obstreperousness if we make bold to express our opinion of this Bill in public meeting assembled, and are just as ready to take advantage of us on the score of our indifference if we sit quiet without blowing the feeblest counterblast to the incessant sounding of trumpets or clashing of cymbals which is kept up even until now all over the country to fright away this poor little Bill. This attitude may lay claim, I admit, to some amount of rather grim humour, but I trust our European friends will not be very hard upon us if we refuse to be tossed about in this manner on the two horns of such a dilemma as they present to us, and prudently hold fast by the one which does us least injury. But as soon as we decide, gentlemen, after anxious consideration, to hold a public meeting, another mine is sprung upon us. We are told that we have no concern with this Bill at all, that it is only a little matter between Lord Ripon and the Europeans in India, in which the parties have got rather hot with each other, that in fact we have no *locus standi* at all to take part in the argument. Now, gentlemen, of all the cool and astonishing things which have been said in the controversy on this Bill (and they are not few), it seems to me that this is about the most cool and astonishing (laughter), for nothing can be clearer than that the natives have the most immediate and vital concern in the subject-matter of this Bill. I do not refer here to the handful of native civilians who might get extended jurisdiction under it. I do not speak here of the educated English-speaking natives who might be supposed to sympathise with native civilians. But I speak of the masses of the native population, and I say that they are as directly and strongly interested in this Bill as any European British-born subject. As sure as there are two parties to an offence, the offending party and the suffering party, both the one as well as the other are interested in the trial in which they are respectively to appear as complainant and accused. Either may suffer by a miscarriage of justice. As courts of criminal law are constituted in the mofussil, the interest of the natives is still more close and vital. If a European commits an offence against a native, the latter has seriously to consider whether it would be worth his while to bring the offender to justice, remembering that he and his witness may have to bear no inconsiderable loss of time and trouble and expense in hunting after a qualified magistrate. (Applause.) Has it ever been inquired into, in the course of this controversy, how many offences committed by Europeans have never been brought to the cognisance of court of justice in consequence of the difficulties thus created by this 'dear and cherished privilege of being tried by their peers'? (Cheers.) I can tell you, gentlemen, that the popular impression in the mofussil about this valuable privilege is that it is simply an immunity practically enjoyed by the Europeans from the consequences of a large class of offences committed by them against natives. (Loud cheers.) Only the other day I happened to be at Surat and had a conversation about this Bill, not with educated natives, but with true unsophisticated children of the soil, from the other side of the Taptee. I will relate to you, gentlemen, the conversation I had with these natives utterly unspoilt by a knowledge of English, particularly as it is advanced by the opponents of the Bill that the agitation in favour of it is created only by the educated natives in which the masses take no interest whatsoever. They, the people I speak of, asked me if we in Bombay were not going to stir in the matter and support the Bill, as they said that the privilege at present enjoyed by Europeans meant simply, in a large number of cases, immunity from prosecution altogether, as the trouble and the expense of a trial before a competent magistrate were very great, and further, as they had a very poor chance in the case of ordinary offences before a European magistrate when the offender was a European. And they gave me an instance within their own knowledge of a European (a man not highly placed be it fairly admitted) who went about bragging in their part of the country that he could ill-treat natives as he liked as no native magistrate could try him and no European magistrate would believe any d-d lot of native witness. (Laughter.) The word 'd–d' is a free translation of my own of the vernacular word used in the conversation. Gentlemen, I do not offer this European as a representative European, or this story, either, as a representative story. It is unfortunately too much the fashion both with natives and Europeans to moralise on isolated instances as if they were always typical ones. But I think this story very forcibly illustrates both the interest which the natives have in the subject-matter of this Bill and the interest which they take in the controversy and agitation about it. (Applause.) A *locus standi*, gentlemen, we most assuredly have in this controversy; if European British subjects hold that of the accused we have the *locus standi* of the complainants. Now, Gentlemen, I don't propose to take up your time by entering into a discussion of the merits of this Bill after the able and exhaustive treatment of it by Mr. Tyabji. But all his arguments rest upon one assumption, his inferences follow logically and irresistibly if there is no question about this assumption. Mr. Tyabji was perfectly justified in arguing upon the basis of this assumption, for it is founded upon the declared policy of the Crown with regard to the government of this country. But in the progress of this controversy the opponents of the Bill have perceived that their arguments cannot be maintained till they attacked the wisdom of this policy. So now they deliberately urge that this Bill is in itself a matter of little moment, but their fears are aroused as it indicates the shifting of the foundations of British power in India. Denouncing the wisdom of the declared policy of the Crown, or urging that its declarations in that respect were not meant to be practically acted upon, they boldly say that India has been conquered by force and must be governed by force. In preaching this gospel of might with regard to the government of this country, they have found a devoted supporter in England in Sir Fitzjames Stephen [*1829–1894, legal member in the Supreme Council who left his mark on Indian legislation including the passing of the Evidence Act, a revised Code of Criminal Procedure, among others—Ed.*] and a somewhat doubtful one in Lord Salisbury. They ridicule the policy of righteousness as one of the weak sentiment and seem almost to adopt, with scarcely disguised approval, the vigorous summary of their position given recently by Mr. Bright (loud cheers) in his own peculiarly happy manner, that having won India by breaking all the Ten Commandments, it is too late now to think of maintaining it on the principles of the Sermon on the Mount. (Cheers.) Our European friends will pardon me if I say that a good many of them have a sneaking, when they have not pronounced, partiality for this proposition while they consider that the platitudes about England's duty to India, and the other quotations from Lord Macaulay and others about a 'policy of national wisdom, national prosperity, and national honour', have no business to intrude in practical politics but are only good enough to be spouted by native orators on public occasions. For many years the policy of governing India on principles of justice and equality for all the Queen's subjects of whatever caste and creed has never been so openly and so furiously called in question as now. It therefore seems to me, gentlemen, that this is a time, when without overstepping the limits of our loyalty or our gratitude, we may properly and justifiably examine the propositions which have been thus advanced, and try to show that the declared policy of the Crown was adopted after long and careful consideration not on grounds of weak sentiment, that it was adopted not simply because it was a policy dictated by honour and justice (which we cheerfully and gratefully acknowledge that it is), but also because it was a policy dictated by the true interest of England herself, because in no other way could England hope to preserve her great dependency with the greatest amount of safety and profit to herself. In the first place, gentlemen, it is said that India was won by the sword. Now I say that Englishmen don't do justice to themselves when they read Indian history in this way, though it cannot be denied that there are many pages in this history blotted by error and crime. England has won India not simply by the sword, but in a large measure by the exercise of high moral and intellectual qualities which have not only guided its victories, but have always been on the alert to neutralise its baneful influences. (Cheers.) But, gentlemen, however India was won, can it be maintained with safety and profit by the sword only? This is too large a question to be treated fully in a public meeting like this, but I will lay before you three considerations which I think show that it is impossible. First, India maintained by England by the power of her armies would be a heavy burden on her in case of her being involved in European complications. It is utterly improbable that England can always escape being dragged into the contests, rivalries and ambitions of the other European powers. What with France with her desire to extend her colonial empire, with Italy anxious for the African coast right against her, with Russia intent upon extending and consolidating her power in Asia, with the other powers jealously watching these—however great and powerful England may be, the strain of such entanglements cannot but tell upon her, and one day she may find herself in a predicament in which India may simply hang as a mill-stone round her neck. (Loud applause.) We must not forget the contingency of the American powers appearing on the scene and complicating matters dreadfully. Ireland is another thorn in the side of England, and what a lesson she teaches as to how hard and difficult it is to undo the mistakes of a policy of force, centuries after they were committed! How nobly had England been struggling to redeem the consequences of such a policy and yet how slowly she succeeds in undoing the mischief of the past! But secondly, there is another Nemesis attending a policy of force. That policy would require day by day larger English armies and larger English Civil Services. In progress of time large numbers of Englishmen trained in the maxims of despotism and saturated with autocratic predilections, would return to their native home, where they could not but look with intolerance on free and constitutional forms. This is no visionary speculation. Careful English observers have already noticed traces of such a tendency. In the course of few generations, such a tendency, if not checked, would develop into a mighty influence and the free and constitutional government of England which has been so long the pride of the world would be placed in the deadliest jeopardy. (Cheers.) Rome was once proud of her sturdy freedom and her republicanism; she lost both in the extension of her despotic empire. She has left, however, a valuable lesson and it has been well and truly said that for the sake of all that she values most, her own freedom and civilisation, England must raise India to her own level or India will drag her down to hers. (Cheers.) The third consideration on this point I have to lay before you relates to the benefit to be derived from the commercial intercourse between the two countries. With a policy of force, as I have said before, the resources of India would be drained in the first instance in maintaining large costly armies and huge services; the country would be thus too much impoverished to admit of her developing the great material resources which nature has showered on her. In India, impoverished and emasculated, the English merchant would only be an emaciated attendant in the rear of the English soldier and the English Civilian, and English commercial enterprise, more glorious even than her military enterprise, would find no congenial field. I have thus, gentlemen, very hastily and very imperfectly sketched the consequences to England herself of a policy of force. Now look at the other picture. With India educated, civilised, contented and loyal, what a help she would be to England in her time of need, what a field for commercial enterprise, what reciprocal benefits from inter-communion in every way. (Loud cheers.) How great England is even now, with her Indian possessions governed on the present declared policy of the Crown? She would wax greater and greater with every legitimate development of that policy. I say, therefore, gentlemen, that of the two policies on which India could be governed, England has chosen that which will secure her own best interests with those of India herself. When in the inscrutable dispensations of Providence, India was assigned to the care of England, one can almost imagine that the choice was offered to her as to Israel of old: 'Behold, I have set before you this day a blessing and a curse: a blessing if ye will obey the commandments of the Lord your God which I have commanded this day, a curse if ye will not obey the commandment of the Lord your God, but turn aside out of the way which I have commanded this day, to go after other gods which ye have not known.' England has chosen wisely and well, she has discarded the temptations held forth by the passions of selfishness, prejudice and vainglory. She has chosen to follow 'the Eternal that maketh for righteousness'. She has deliberately declared by the mouths of her greatest and most trusted statesmen, she has proclaimed it through the lips of Her Gracious Majesty herself (cheers), that India is to be governed on the principles of justice, equality and righteousness without distinctions of colour, caste or creed. (Loud cheers.) Our English friends, therefore, gentlemen, must make up their minds to discuss this Bill on the basis of this declared policy of the Crown. (Cheers.) On this basis I say, the case for passing the Bill is simply irresistible as my friend Mr. Tyabji has shown. I will only refer to one argument which may be shortly described as the 'anomaly' argument. Now gentlemen this word 'anomaly' has a good deal to complain of as to the treatment it has received at the hands of the opponents of this Bill. Never has any word in the English language before been so cruelly maltreated. But it must sit quiet under its injuries at present, as till the Bill is passed it cannot secure conviction before a European magistrate. This anomaly argument however is perfect if it is properly regarded. It derives its force from actual fact and experience. However anomalous the position of Englishmen in India, still, it can be made, and has been made, the basis of a righteous policy. In the prosecution of that policy, native magistrates have already exercised jurisdiction over Europeans, with the most satisfactory success in the Presidency towns. Race feeling and native perjury have not been able to mar the experiment. But it is said that that is because of the existence of a public opinion in the Presidency towns which does not exist in the mofussil. But this plausible argument yields to a close examination. The argument admits that public opinion is sufficient to countervail the dreaded consequences of race prejudice and false swearing. Let us see then if in the mofussil, there is not a force which can operate in the same way. I say that there is, and a stronger one than public opinion, that of the official opinion of the European district officers, which would work on the native magistrate more directly, and more expeditiously, and more closely as all his interests and predilections and associations would closely connect him and make him dependent on them. (Applause.) I say, gentlemen, this argument takes the whole question from the domain of speculation and brings it within that of observed fact and experience which establish that native magistrates can be safely trusted with jurisdiction over Europeans. Before concluding, however, I am desirous of saying a word about the storm of passion and prejudice which, commencing in the Calcutta Town Hall, has so spread over the whole land. Some of my native friends are disposed to be very hard upon these angry and excited people. I, for one, gentlemen, however, am inclined to make great allowances for, nay, almost to treat with tenderness this sudden ebullition of anger and fury, when I realise the real character of it. Gentlemen, all men have their nobler and baser instincts struggling within them, and you will find that even in the most well-disciplined organisations, in the most well-balanced minds, after the nobler instincts have well established their sway, a moment comes when the smallest rift upsets the work of years, casts everything into confusion, and generates a whirlwind at which those who knew the men before as good and worthy stand aghast. (Cheers.) So it seems it has been the case with Europeans in India. But this abnormal ebullition lasts only for a short time and I am sure, gentlemen, that soon after this Bill is passed, as passed it will be, Englishmen will themselves smile at the wonderful things they have said and done about this Bill. At present, dire prophecies are proclaimed as to the ill-feeling which has been created between natives and Europeans by the introduction of this Bill which is to leave effects for ever so long. Gentlemen, I will, with your permission, indulge in a truer vein of prophecy. The newspapers have recently informed us that Mr. Branson has left for England. Most probably he will return a short time after this Bill is passed and there has been time for angry feelings and prejudices to cool down. I can then picture to myself Mr. Branson and Mr. Lalmohun Ghose as soon as they meet in Calcutta, rushing into each other's arms—(loud laughter)—singing the song,

> As through the land at eve we went
> And plucked the ripened ears
> We fell out, my wife and I,

O, we fell out, I know not why,
And kissed again with tears.
And blessing on the falling out,
Which all the more endears,
When we fall out with those we live,
And kiss again with tears.

(Loud cheers and laughter.) In presenting this touching tableau I say, gentlemen, that this Bill, which Lord Ripon has introduced in the honest and well-considered prosecution of his far-sighted and righteous administration, holds forth hopeful promises of improved relations between the natives and European in this country. (Loud and prolonged cheers.)

SURENDRANATH BANERJEA

The Vernacular Press Act

In March 1878, the British Indian government passed the Vernacular Press Act to gag the vernacular press which had begun criticizing policies of the government, particularly at a time when the country was facing severe famine conditions. This attack on the local press was considered by educated Indians in many parts of India as an attack on freedom. There were several public meetings in presidency towns and other cities in India to protest against the act. In Calcutta, agitators staged protest meetings, the most famous of which was held in the Town Hall on 17 April 1878. Surendranath Banerjea had by this time emerged as a fiery speaker and it was he who moved the second resolution after the first resolution had been moved, seconded and adopted.

... It has been remarked by the immortal founder of modern jurisprudence that every law is an evil. It is an infringement of the natural liberty of man, an encroachment upon his innate rights and privileges. It, therefore, becomes the bounden duty of those who introduce any measure of law, to justify it by facts and arguments. Much more is this duty incumbent on those who introduce a repressive measure of legislation, like the one under discussion. Therefore, we are driven to the conclusion that it is for Government to prove that the Act is necessary, and not for us to show that the Act is unnecessary and uncalled for. It must also be said, in justice to the Government that they have made out the strongest case possible under the circumstances, and have brought forward all the facts and arguments in support of their position. But what are they? Let us examine the facts. The justification of Government is contained in the speeches of Hon'ble Members, the statement of objects and reasons, and above all, in the translation of extracts from the vernacular journals. I hold these extracts in my hand. The main object of the law, as stated in the first paragraph of the statement of objects and reasons, is to empower the Government to suppress seditious writings more effectually than is practicable under the present law. Sir Alexander Arbuthnot remarks that, within the last three or four years, there has been a steady increase in the number of seditious writings in the vernacular papers, and that the evil has become worse than ever within the last twelve months. Thus it has become necessary to pass a special law on the subject. But the question at once occurs, is there not already a section in the Penal Code to repress sedition? Why, we all remember that in the year 1870, when Sir Fitzjames Stephen was Law member of the Supreme Council, a section was added to the Penal Code, defining disaffection and punishing sedition. But that law is pronounced to be inefficient. I ask, have you tried it? Have you experimented with it? Have there been prosecutions under it? Have editors of vernacular papers been charged under its special provision? If not, what right have you to assume that the law is inefficient? And, if inefficient and unworkable, why not rather amend and improve it than introduce a new law? But, gentlemen, the Government has strong objections to prosecute editors of vernacular papers for sedition under the Penal Code. It has, therefore, thought fit to introduce this special law. Its grounds are not many. The chief of them runs somewhat as follows: The ordinary criminal law punishes an offender after the crime has been committed; the special law seeks to prevent the commission of an offence. The Government wants to prevent, not to punish. Hence the special law. Gentlemen, I invite your attention to the terms of this argument, for upon this argument rests the entire superstructure of the Act. The ordinary criminal law punishes. This special law prevents. I must at once pause to point out the fallacy of this reasoning, which seeks to draw a distinction between the criminal law that punishes and the criminal law that prevents. Why does the criminal law punish? Is it not to prevent the commission of an offence? The end and aim of the ordinary criminal law, therefore, is to prevent. The end and aim of the special law is likewise to prevent. What need is there, then, for the special law? But the analogy does not stop here. The *modus operandi* is in both cases the same. The ordinary criminal law prevents by means of punishment. The special law prevents also by means of punishment. For that law contemplates that the offending editor will be deterred from writing seditious articles through fear of forfeiting his bail bond, which amounts to a fine, and which is therefore a punishment. Hence it will appear that the end and aim of the ordinary criminal law is precisely the same as that of the special law, and the *modus operandi* is the same in both the cases. What necessity—what justification then is there, I ask, for this law?

There is another argument adduced in support of the measure. The Government is anxious to prevent the dissemination of the poison of sedition. If prosecutions for sedition were instituted under the Penal Code, the poisonous matter complained of would be quoted in the various papers, and that would help to disseminate the poison. But what, then, if the poison were allowed to disseminate? Why, the safety of the State, says Government, requires that the poison should not be allowed to spread. The supreme law of the safety of the State is invoked, and we are asked to fall down before this dread divinity and to hold tongues in sullen silence. If the safety of the State required such a law, I am sure, my countrymen would gladly vote in favour of it. But I ask, was there ever a time in which the question of the safety of the State was more narrowly and anxiously considered than in the dark days of the Indian Mutiny? In those dark days, when the country was in flames, when the British Empire was tottering to its foundations, when the contagion of rebellion was spreading like wild-fire over an American prairie; in those dark, stern and awful days, Lord Canning and his Council thought nothing of disseminating the poison, but boldly came forward when it became necessary to prosecute certain vernacular editors who had been guilty of writing seditious libels. In 1857, the editor of the *Durbin*, the editor of the *Samachar Sudhabarsan*, the editor of the *Sultan-ul-Akhbar* were prosecuted by Lord Canning for sedition. In those dark days of the mutiny, when the political system was most prone to succumb to the deadening effects of this poison, it had vitality enough to resist its baneful influences. And now we are told in times of comparative peace, contentment, and prosperity, and with a loyal and law-abiding people, that the gigantic fabric of British Empire, this colossal and imperial structure, resting upon the willing allegiance, the steadfast loyalty and the fervent devotion of two hundred and fifty millions of human beings, stands in danger of being wrecked and ruined by the miserable pratings of a few vernacular editors, who might take it into their heads to indite articles, not the most temperate or the most respectful towards the Government.

But there is another argument which, in the opinion of Government, makes it necessary that the poison should not be allowed to disseminate. It is assumed that the readers of vernacular papers are ignorant and uncultivated men, upon whose minds the seditious criticisms of the vernacular papers would have a most fatal and prejudicial effect, and sap the foundations of their loyalty. A paternal Government must protect them, and hence the law. Now, I beg most distinctly to affirm that the readers of vernacular papers are not thoughtless, ignorant and uncultivated men. They are, for the most part, educated men. Primary education was introduced into our country only the other day, and we have not yet reached that state of blessedness, devoutly to be wished for, when the Bengal ploughman may be seen ploughing with the one hand, and holding the *Sulava Samachar* in the other. The vast masses of our people still continue in the grovelling depths of profound ignorance. They read no newspaper, vernacular or otherwise. It is educated people who read them. The *Hindu Patriot* confirms this view of the matter, and so does the *Indian Mirror*; and the *Shahachar*, whose mournful loss we deplored the other day, in that farewell letter of his which we all read with such melancholy interest, distinctly stated that all its readers were educated men and did not come from the uncultivated classes. But there is a higher authority yet who supports this view of the matter. Sir Richard Temple says as follows in his Administration Report for 1874-75 (p. 481): 'Generally speaking, it may be said that the Vernacular Press has little or no influence on the majority of the people, who are agriculturists and labourers. They do not see newspapers and are not influenced by them, either directly or indirectly.'

The arguments, then, upon which this measure of legislation is based, have fallen through, and the measure stands before us, in all its naked deformity, unjustified and unaccounted for.

~

BADRUDDIN TYABJI

Presidential Address, 1887

Badruddin Tyabji (1844–1906) was an alumnus of the famed Elphinstone College, Bombay. Apart from being an eminent lawyer, he led the social reformers in Bombay and western India and was at the forefront in advocating women's education. His speeches were marked by close reasoning, sober judgement, lucid exposition and magnetic eloquence. One of the inspirations behind the founding of the Indian National Congress, he became its third president in 1887 at its Madras session. Soon after its formation, the Congress came to be criticized by various sections of the population—zamindars and talukdars, local princes, British officialdom and community leaders like Sir Syed Ahmad—as a disloyal and seditious organization. This could have harmed the prospects of the Congress which was trying to rope in larger groups of people within its political fold. It fell to Badruddin Tyabji to preside over the session of the Congress at a time when the attacks on it had the potential of scaring sections of the population, thereby preventing them from joining it. In this address, Tyabji puts the matter straight by arguing that neither the Congress nor the educated sections who had joined it had become disloyal. While he indicated that the leadership still truly believed in the progressive nature of the British presence, there was, however, space to constitute the Congress as a representative party of the Indian voice. In this speech he also countered the assertions made by British officials as well as by people like Sir Syed that the Congress was a microscopic minority of the educated native.

Gentlemen, it has been urged in derogation of our character as a representative national gathering that one great and important community—the Mussulman community—has kept aloof from the proceedings of the two last Congresses. Now, gentlemen in the first place, this is only partially true, and applies only to one particular part of India, and is moreover, due to certain special, and local, temporary causes (hear, hear, and applause) and in the second place, no such approach can, I think, with any show of justice, be urged against this present Congress, (applause) and, gentlemen, I must honestly confess to you that one great motive which has induced me, in the present state of my health, to undertake the grave responsibilities of presiding over your deliberations, has been an earnest desire, on my part, to prove, as far as in my power lies, that I, at least, not merely in my individual capacity, but as representing the Anjuman-i-Islam of Bombay (loud applause), do not consider that there is anything whatever in the position or the relations of the different communities of Indian—be they Hindus, Mussulmans, Parsees, or Christians—which should induce the leaders of any one community to stand aloof from the others in their efforts to obtain those great general reforms, those great general rights which are for the common benefit of us all (hear hear, and applause) and which, I feel assured, have only to be earnestly and unanimously pressed upon Government to be granted to us. Gentlemen, it is undoubtedly true that each one of our great Indian communities has its own peculiar social, moral, educational and even political difficulties to surmount—but so far as general political questions affecting the whole of India, such as those which alone are discussed by this Congress, are concerned, I, for one, am utterly at a loss to understand, why Mussulmans should not work shoulder to shoulder (hear, hear, and applause) with their fellow-countrymen, of other races and creeds for the common benefit of all (applause).

Gentlemen, it has been urged as a slur upon our loyalty that this Congress is composed of what are called the educated natives of India. Now, if by this it is intended to be conveyed that we are merely a crowd of people with nothing but our education to commend us, if it is intended to be conveyed that the gentry, the nobility and the aristocracy of the land have kept aloof from us, I can only meet that assertion by the most direct and the most absolute denial (hear, hear and applause). To any person who made that assertion I should feel inclined to say, come with me into this Hall (applause) and look around you (applause) and tell me where you could wish to see a better representation of the aristocracy not only of birth and wealth, but of intellect, education and position, than you see gathered within the walls of this Hall (applause). But, gentlemen, if no such insinuation is intended to be made, I should only say that I am happy to think that this Congress does consist of the educated natives of India (hear, hear).

Gentlemen, I, for one, am proud to be called not only educated but a 'native' of this country (applause, and hear, hear). And, gentlemen, I should like to know where among all the millions of Her Majesty's subjects in India are to be found more truly loyal, nay, more devoted friends of the British empire than among these educated natives (loud and continued applause). Gentlemen, to be a true and a sincere friend of the British Government, it is necessary that one should be in a position to appreciate the great blessings which that Government has conferred upon us. And I should like to know who is in a better position to appreciate these blessings—the ignorant peasants or the educated natives? Who, for instance, will better appreciate the advantages of good roads, railways, telegraphs and post offices, schools, colleges and universities, hospitals, good laws and impartial courts of justice?—the educated natives or the ignorant peasants of this country? (Applause.) Gentlemen, if there ever were to arise—which God forbid—any great struggle between Russia and

Great Britain for supremacy in this country—who is more likely to judge better of the relative merits of the two empires? (Hear, hear.) Again I say, gentlemen, that in these matters it is the educated natives that are best qualified to judge, because it is we who know and are best able to appreciate—for instance—the blessings of the right of public meeting, the liberty of action and of speech, and high education which we enjoy under Great Britain, whereas, probably, under Russia we should have nothing but a haughty and despotic Government whose chief glory would consist in vast military organisation, aggression upon our neighbour and great military exploits (applause).

No, gentlemen, let our opponents say what they please, we, the educated natives, by the mere force of our education, must be the best appreciators of the blessings of a civilised and enlightened Government, and, therefore, in our own interests, the best and staunchest supporters of the British Government in India (Applause). But gentlemen, do those who thus charge us with disloyalty stop for a moment to consider the full meaning and effect of their argument, do they realise the full import and significance of the assertion they make? Do they understand that, in charging us with disloyalty, they are, in reality condemning and denouncing the very Government which it is their intention to support? (Hear, hear, loud and continued applause.) For, gentlemen, when they say that the educated natives of India are disloyal what does it mean? It means this: that in the opinion of the educated natives—that is to say, of all the men of light and leading, all those who have received sound, liberal and enlightened education, all those who are acquainted with the history of their own country and with the nature of the present and past government, that in the opinion of all these—the English Government is so bad that it has deserved to forfeit the confidence and the loyalty of the thinking part of the population. (Hear, hear, and applause.) Now, gentlemen is it conceivable that a more frightful and unjust condemnation of the British Government can be pronounced than is implied in this charge of disloyalty against the educated natives of India?

Gentlemen, if this charge were brought by some bitter enemies of Great Britain, if it were brought by the Russians, for example, I could understand it (hear, hear). But it is almost beyond my comprehension that it should come, not from the enemies, but from the supposed friends of British Government (loud laughter and hear, hear), not from the Russians, but from Englishmen (hear, hear), who presumably want, not to destroy, but to support their Government! I say it surpasses my comprehension (loud applause). Gentlemen, just consider for a moment the effect of this reckless allegation upon the uneducated millions of the inhabitants of this country, upon the hordes of the Russians in the North, and upon the enlightened nations of Europe! I say, therefore, that the conduct of those who thus recklessly charge us with disloyalty resembles the conduct of the 'foolish woodman' who was lopping off the very branch of the tree upon which he was standing (hear, hear, loud applause and loud laughter) unconscious that the destruction of the branch meant the destruction of himself. (Applause and laughter.)

~

GOPAL KRISHNA GOKHALE

Excessive Surpluses 'A Double Wrong': The First Budget Speech in the Imperial Legislative Council

Gopal Krishna Gokhale (1866–1915), whom Gandhi called his political guru, remains one of the finest intellectuals and public men produced by India in modern times. Educated at Elphinstone College, Bombay, Gokhale became professor of history and political economy at Fergusson College, Pune. For Gokhale, political agitation and social reform were not separate issues and he followed Ranade by committing himself entirely to the cause of social reform, so much so that he came to be regarded as the voice of social reform. At the same time, his sharp intellect and grasp of public policy and financial matters made him one of the sharpest critics of the colonial state's policies vis-à-vis India. In 1902, he became a household name after his evidence before the Royal Commission on Indian Expenditure (Welby Commission). He showed—like his teachers and predecessors, Rai Bahadur G.V. Joshi, Dadabhai Naoroji and Pherozeshah Mehta—an uncanny understanding of fiscal and financial details. It was in recognition of these qualities that he was named Pherozeshah Mehta's successor to the Imperial Legislative Council as representative of Bombay. Gokhale wrote and spoke with a mastery over facts and figures, an eye for detail and an astonishingly thorough knowledge of administrative and financial problems. This was matched by a moderate tone, clear but vigorous expression and an inspiring earnestness. These qualities made his speeches veritable works of art. The present speech, his maiden one in the Imperial Legislative Council, heralded the emergence of Gokhale on a bigger platform. It contained not only a trenchant economic critique of the colonial state but also a review of its fiscal policy as it tore apart the arguments put forward for the surplus budget. The speech was delivered on Wednesday, 26 March 1902, and the opening line—'I fear I cannot conscientiously join in the congratulations which have been offered'—still reverberates in the annals of Indian history.

Your Excellency, I fear I cannot conscientiously join in the congratulations which have been offered to the Hon'ble Finance Member on the huge surplus which the revised estimates show for last year. A surplus of seven crores of rupees is perfectly unprecedented in the history of Indian finance, and coming as it does on the top of a series of similar surpluses realised when the country has been admittedly passing through very trying times, it illustrates to my mind, in a painfully clear manner, the utter absence of a due correspondence between the condition of the people and the condition of the finances of the country. Indeed, my Lord, the more I think about this matter the more I feel—and I trust your Lordship will pardon me for speaking somewhat bluntly—that the surpluses constitute a double wrong to the community. They are a wrong in the first instance in that they exist at all—that Government should take so much more from the people than is needed in times of serious depression and suffering; and they are also a wrong, because they lend themselves to easy misinterpretation and, among other things, render possible the phenomenal optimism of the Secretary of State for India, who seems to imagine that all is for the best in this best of lands. A slight examination of these surpluses suffices to show that they are mainly, almost entirely, currency surpluses, resulting from the fact that Government still maintain the same high level of taxation which they considered to be necessary to secure financial equilibrium when the rupee stood at its lowest. The year when the rupee touched this lowest exchange value was 1894-95, the average rate of exchange realised in that year being only 13-1*d*. to the rupee. Government, however, had, in the face of the falling rupee, resolutely maintained an equilibrium between their revenue and expenditure by large and continuous additions to the taxation of the country, and thus even in the year 1894-95, when the rupee touched its lowest level, the national account-sheet showed a surplus of seventy lakhs of rupees. From this point onwards, the currency legislation, passed by Government in 1893, began to bear fruit and the exchange value of the rupee began to rise steadily. In 1895-96, the average rate of exchange realised was 13-64*d*. respectively, but the year turned out to be famine year and the second year also one of a costly frontier war necessitating extraordinary expenditure for direct famine relief and military operations of 2.1 crores in the first year and 9.2 crores in the second. The result was that 1896-97 closed with a deficit of 1.7 crores and 1897-98 with a deficit of 5.36 crores. It will, however, be seen that if these extraordinary charges had not come upon the State, both years would have been years of surpluses, and the surplus for 1897-98 would have been close upon four crores of rupees. In 1898-99, exchange established itself in the neighbourhood of 16*d.*—the average rate realised during the year being 15.98*d.*—and the year closed with a balance of 3.96 crores of rupees, after providing a crore for military operations on the frontier, thus inaugurating the era of substantial surpluses. Now we all know that a rise of 3*d.* in the exchange value of the rupee—from 13*d.* to 16*d.*—means a saving of between four and five crores of rupees to the Government of India on their Home Charges alone, and I think this fact is sufficient by itself to explain the huge surplus of the last four or five years…

If there had been no extra charges for war and famine, the national revenue on the basis of the new rupee would have been found to exceed the requirements of Government by 6¾ crores a year. Allowing for the savings effected in consequence of the absence of a portion of the troops in South Africa and China, as also for the generally reduced level of ordinary expenditure in famine times, and taking note of the fact that the opium revenue has recently turned out somewhat better than was expected and might reasonably be relied on, we still may put down the excess of our present revenue over our present expenditure at about five crores of rupees, which is also the figure of the amount saved by Government on their Home Charges as a consequence of the exchange value of the rupee having risen from 13*d.* to 16*d.* Now, my Lord, I submit with all respect that it is not a justifiable course to maintain taxation at the same high level when the rupee stands at 16*d.* that was thought to be necessary when it stood at 13*d.* During the last sixteen years, whenever deficits occurred, the Finance Member invariably attributed them to the falling rupee and resorted to the expedient of additional taxation, explaining that that was the only way to avoid national bankruptcy. During the first twelve years of this period, from 1885-86—when Sir Auckland Colvin told the Council in his Financial Statement almost in prophetic terms that affairs were 'passing into a new phase', necessitating a reconsideration and revision of the fiscal status established in 1882—down to 1896-97, there was one continued and ceaseless struggle on the part of the Finance Department of the Government of India to maintain at all risks and hazards a 'strong financial position' in the face of a rapidly changing situation, and provide by anticipation against all possible dangers near and remote, fancied and real; and not a year passed—literally speaking—but heralded some change in the financial arrangements of the country. The famine grant was suspended for three successive years, 1886-87 to 1888-89, then reduced for two more, and permanently so in the last year of the period. Twice during these twelve years were the Provincial Contracts subjected to drastic revision (1887-88 and 1892-93), and the total gain secured to the Imperial Treasury on such revision and by a contraction of Provincial resources was full 1.10 crores (64 lakhs in 1887-88 and 46 lakhs in 1892-95)... But the chief financial expedient employed to escape the supposed embarrassment of the time was continuous additions to the taxation of the country. Nine years out of these twelve witnessed the imposition of new taxes. First came the income-tax in 1886, and then followed in rapid succession the salt duty enhancement of 1887-88 (June 1888), the petroleum and patwari-taxes and extension of the income-tax to Burma in 1888-89, customs on imported liquors increased in 1889-90, the excise duty on Indian beer in 1890-91, the import duty on salt-fish in Burma in 1892-93, the re-imposition of the 5 per cent *ad valorem* duties on imports, excluding cotton goods, in 1893-94, and the extension of import duties to cotton goods in 1894-95. In 1896 there were changes in the tariff. The 5 per cent import and excise duties on cotton yarns were abolished and the import duties on cotton goods were reduced from 5 to 3½ per cent—involving a sacrifice of 50 lakhs of rupees as a concession to the clamour of Manchester, but a countervailing excise of 3½ per cent was imposed on cotton goods of all counts manufactured in Indian mills. Lastly came the imposition of countervailing duties on imports of bounty-fed sugar in 1899.

The total additional revenue raised by these measures of taxation during the past sixteen years has been no less than 12.30 crores a year.

But this is not all. The land-tax, too, has come in its own automatic way for large augmentations during the period. Taking the ordinary revenue alone under the head, we find the increase has been Rs. 2.82 crores. One startling fact about these land-revenue collections is that during the six years from 1896-97 to 1901-02 (a period including the two greatest famines of the country) these collections actually averaged £17.43 millions a year as against £16.67 millions, the average for the six preceding years, i.e., from 1890-91 to 1895-96.

Putting these two heads together, the total augmentation of public burden during these years comes to over 15 crores.

Such continuous piling up of tax on tax, and such ceaseless adding to the burdens of a suffering people, is probably without precedent in the annals of finance. In India, it was only during the first few years following the troubles of the mutiny year that large additions were made to the taxation of the country; but the country was then on the flood-tide of a short-lived prosperity, and bore, though not without difficulty or complaint, the added burden. During the past sixteen years the country has passed through a more severe phase of agricultural and industrial depression and yet it has been called upon to accept these fresh burdens—year after year—increasing without interruption, and all this with a view to ensuring and maintaining a 'strong financial position', proof against all assaults.

The broad result of this continued series of taxing measures has been to *fix the taxation of the country at a level far above the actual needs of the situation*. And it is the *fiscal status* so forced up and maintained, and not a normal expansion of revenue, that has enabled the financial administration during all these trying years not only to meet out of current revenue all sorts of charges, ordinary and extraordinary, but to present at the close of the period abounding surpluses which the richest nation in European might well envy.

A taxation so forced as not only to maintain a *budgetary equilibrium* but to yield a well 'large, continuous, progressive surpluses'—even in years of trial and suffering—is, I submit, against all accepted canons of finance. In European countries, extraordinary charges are usually met out of borrowings, the object being to avoid, even in times of pressure, impeding the even, normal development of trade and industry by any sudden or large additions to the weight of public burdens. In India, where the economic side of such questions finds such scant recognition, and the principle of meeting these charges of the year with the resources of the year is carried to a logical extreme, the anxiety of the Financial Administration is not only to make both ends meet in good and bad years alike, but to present large surpluses year after year...

Plea for the Reduction of Taxation

This being my view of the whole question, it was to me, I need hardly say, a matter of the deepest regret that Government had not seen their way, in spite of four continuous years of huge surpluses, to take off a portion at any rate of the heavy burdens which had been imposed upon the country during the last sixteen years. Of course the whole country will feel grateful for the remission of close upon two crores of the arrears of land revenue. The measure is a bold, generous and welcome departure from the usual policy of clinging to the arrears of famine times, till a portion of them has to be abandoned owing to the sheer impossibility of realising them, after they have been allowed to hang over the unfortunate raiyat's head, destroying his peace of mind and taking away from him heart and hope. The special grant of 40 lakhs of rupees to education will also be much appreciated throughout the country. But my quarrel is with the exceedingly cautious manner—a caution, I would venture to say, bordering on needless timidity—in which my Hon'ble friend has framed the Budget proposals for next year. Why should he, with four continuous years of fat surpluses to guide him, and no special cloud threatening his horizon, budget for a surplus of only 1¼ crores, when three times the amount would have been nearer the mark and that, again, as calculated by a reasonably cautious standard? If he had only recognised the ordinary facts of our finance, as disclosed by the surpluses of the last four years, he would have, among other things, been able to take off the additional eight annas of salt duty, raise the taxable minimum of the income-tax to at least Rs.1000 a year, abolish the excise duty on cotton goods, and yet show a substantial surplus for the year. And, my Lord, the reduction of taxation in these three directions is the very least that Government could do for the people after the uncomplaining manner in which they have borne burden after burden during the last sixteen years. The desirability of raising the exemption limit of the income-tax has been frequently admitted on behalf of Government, and, amongst others, by yourself in your Lordship's first Budget Speech. The abolition of the excise on cotton goods is urgently needed not only in the interests of the cotton industry, which is at present in a state of dreadful depression, in large measure due to the currency legislation of Government, but also as an act of the barest justice to the struggling millions of our poor, on whom a portion of the burden eventually falls, who have been hit the hardest during recent years by famine and plague, by agricultural and industrial depression and the currency legislation of the State, and who are now literally gasping for relief. In this connection I would especially invite the attention of Government to a speech delivered at the annual meeting of the Bombay Chamber of Commerce by my friend the Hon'ble Mr. Moses—a by no means unfriendly critic of Government, and one who enjoys their confidence as also that of the public. Mr. Moses in that speech describes with much clearness and force the great injury which the currency legislation of Government has done to our rising cotton industry. That industry, he tells us, has now 'reached the brink of bankruptcy', no less than fourteen mills being about to be liquidated, and some of them, brand new ones, being knocked down to the hammer for a third only of their original cost. Mr. Moses also speaks of the severely adverse manner in which the new currency has affected the economic position of the mass of our countrymen.

Reduction of Salt Duty

As regards the reduction of salt duty, I do not think any words are needed from anyone to establish the unquestioned hardship which the present rate imposes upon the poorest of the poor of our community. Government themselves have repeatedly admitted the hardship; but in these days, when we are all apt to have short memories, I think it will be useful to recall some of the utterances of men responsible for the Government of India in the matter. In 1888, when the duty was enhanced, Sir James Westland, the Finance Member, speaking on behalf of the Government of India, said: 'It is with the greatest reluctance that Government finds itself obliged to have recourse to the salt duty.'

Currency Legislation Necessitates Tax-Reduction

My Lord, the obligation to remit taxation in years of assured surpluses goes, I believe, with the right to demand additional revenues from the people in times of financial embarrassment. A succession of large surpluses is little conducive to economy and is apt to demoralise even the most conscientious Governments by the temptation it offers for indulging in extravagant expenditure. This is true of all countries, but it is specially true of countries like India where public revenues are administered under no sense of responsibility, such as exists in the West, to the governed. A severe economy, a rigorous retrenchment of expenditure in all branches of the Administration, consistently, of course, with the maintenance of a proper standard of efficiency, ought always to be the most leading feature—the true governing principle—

of Indian finance, the object being to keep the level of public taxation as low as possible, so as to leave the springs of national industry free play and room for unhampered movement. Such a course is also imperatively demanded by the currency policy which has been recently adopted by Government. That policy has, no doubt, given the country a stable exchange and brought relief to the Finance Member from his usual anxieties; but when the final adjustment of prices takes place, as is bound sooner or later to happen, it will be found that a crushing burden has been imposed upon the vast majority of tax-payers in the country. It is true that general prices have not been as quick to adjust themselves to the new artificially appreciated rupee, as the rupee itself has been to respond to the restrictions put upon its production. This was, however, to be expected, as the force of tradition in a backward country like India was bound to take time to be overcome. Famine conditions during the last few years also retarded adjustment, but there is no doubt that there would be a general fall of prices sooner or later corresponding to the artificial appreciation of rupee. And when that happens, Government will be taking about 40 per cent more in taxation from producers in this land and paying to its servants a similarly augmented remuneration. This will be a terrible burden for the masses of the country to bear. Already, during the last few years of famine, they have had to suffer most serious losses in converting their stock of silver into rupee when the rupee had grown dearer, but its purchasing power had not correspondingly increased. When the expected adjustment of general prices takes place, one curious result of it will be that the Government will have made a present to moneylenders of about 40 per cent of the loans which these moneylenders have made to agriculturists—a result which surely Government could never have desired. In view of the great injury which the currency policy of Government has thus done, and will do as its results unfold themselves more and more, to the agriculturists and other producers of this country, I submit Government are bound to make to them such slight reparation as is possible by reducing the level of taxation as low as circumstances may permit.

'Deep and Deepening Poverty'

My Lord, in considering the level of taxation in India and the administration of the revenues so raised, it is, I think, necessary to bear in mind two root facts: (1) it is the finance of a country, a considerable part of whose revenues is, by reason of its political and military necessities, spent outside its borders and *ipso facto* brings no commercial equivalent to the country; and (2) that it is the finance of a country which is not only 'poor, very poor', as Lord George Hamilton admits, but the bulk of whose population is daily growing poorer under the play of the economic forces which have been brought into existence by British rule. It is true that the fact of this growing poverty of our people finds no official recognition, and we have even assurances from the highest quarters of their advancing prosperity. With all due deference, however, I venture to submit that we, who live in the midst of the hard actualities of a hard situation, feel that any such comforting views of the condition of the Indian people are without warrant in the facts of the case and we deem it our duty to urge, on behalf of the struggling masses no less than in the interests of good administration, that this fact of a deep and deepening poverty in the country should be frankly recognised, so that the energies of the Government might be directed towards undertaking remedial measures. The Hon'ble Finance Member sees in last year's Customs returns a sign of the advancing prosperity of the people. Now, apart from the fact that it is unsafe to draw conclusions from the returns for any single year, since the imports of particular years often only technically belong to that year, there is, I submit, nothing in the returns of last year to bear out my Hon'ble friend's contention. The bulk of our countrymen, whose economic condition is the point at issue, have nothing to do with the imports of sugar or cotton manufactures, which now are practically only the finer fabrics. The silver imported also could not have concerned them since last year was a famine year, and the poorer classes, instead of buying any silver, parted over large areas with the greater portion of what they possessed. The increase in the imports of petroleum only means the larger replacement of country-oil by petroleum... Petroleum is also in some places now being used for cooking purposes in place of fuel. I do not think, therefore, that the Hon'ble Member is justified in drawing from last year's Customs returns the conclusion which he draws from them. The growth under Land-revenue, Excise and Stamps is sometimes mentioned as indicating increasing prosperity. But the growth of Land-revenue is a forced compulsory growth. It is a one-sided arrangement, and the people have either to pay the increased demand or give up their land and thereby part with the only resource they have. A growth of Excise-revenue, to the extent to which it is secured by increased consumption, only shows that the operations of the Akbari Department, with its tender solicitude for the interest of the legitimate consumer—a person not recognised by the State in India in pre-British times—are leading to increased drunkenness in the land. This, of course, means increased misery and is thus the very reverse of an indication of increasing prosperity. Liquor is not like ordinary articles of consumption, which a man buys more or less as his means are larger or smaller. When a man takes to drink, he will go without food, and will sacrifice wife and children, if necessary, but he will insist on satisfying his craving for the spirituous poison. Similarly, an increase of revenue under Stamps only means an increase in litigation, which undoubtedly shows that the people are quarrelling more, but which is no proof of their growing riches. No, my Lord, the only taxes whose proceeds supply any indication of the material condition of the people are the income-tax and the salt-tax—the former, roughly speaking, for the middle and upper classes and the latter for the masses. Now, the revenue under both these heads has been more or less stationary all these years, and the salt revenue has not even kept pace with the normal growth of the population. They, therefore, lend no support to the contention that the people are advancing in material prosperity...

These and similar facts, taken cumulatively, lead, and lead irresistibly, to the conclusion that the material condition of the mass of the people in India is steadily deteriorating, and I grieve to say that the phenomenon is the saddest in the whole range of the economic history of the world. Here is a peasantry which, taken all in all, is inferior to no other people in industry, frugality and patient suffering. It has enjoyed the blessing of uninterrupted peace for half a century, and at the end of the period the bulk of them are found to be in a worse plight than they have ever been in. I submit, my Lord, that a fact so startling and so painful demands the earnest and immediate attention of Government, and I venture to believe that Government cannot afford to put off facing the situation any longer. An inquiry into the condition of a few typical villages has been suggested, and, if undertaken, will certainly clear many of the prevailing misapprehensions on the subject. It is urged on behalf of Government that no such inquiry is needed, because similar inquiries have been already made in the past. There is no doubt that inquiries of some sort have been made, and the Government have in their possession a large body of valuable information on the subject—information which unfortunately they insist on withholding from the public. Why this should be is difficult to understand, as the field is exclusively economic and Government ought to welcome the co-operation of non-official students of the subject in understanding and interpreting the economic phenomena of the country. I venture to think that if the papers connected with the Cromer [*Major Evelyn Baring (later Lord Cromer), Finance Member, Government of India, 1880–83; he went on to become British Agent and Consul-General in Egypt—Ed.*] inquiry of 1882, the Dufferin [*Marquis of Dufferin and Ava, Governor-General of India, 1884–88—Ed.*] inquiry of 1887-88 and the confidential inquiry undertaken in 1891-92 were published, much valuable assistance would be afforded to the public by Government. The same remark applies to the statistical memorandum and notes on the condition of lower classes in the rural parts furnished to the Famine Commission of 1898 by the Provincial Governments, the official memorandum referred to by your Lordship in the Budget discussion of last year, 'worked out from figures collected for the Famine Commission of 1898', the Appendices to the Report of the Famine Commission of 1901, and the official Memorandum on agricultural indebtedness referred to by the present Lieutenant-Governor of the Punjab in his speech on the Punjab Land Alienation Bill—all of which documents have been kept confidential without any intelligible excuse. I think your Lordship will have done much to bring about a truer appreciation of the economic situation in the country, if you will see your way to publishing these valuable papers and documents, which there is really no reason for withholding from the public…

Necessity of Mass Education

Then the question of mass education must be undertaken in right earnest, and, if it is so undertaken, the present expenditure of Government on public education will require a vast increase. My Lord, it is a melancholy fact that while with us nine children out of every ten are growing up in ignorance and darkness, and four villages out of every five are without a school, our educational expenditure has been almost marking time for many years past; whereas in England, where every child of school-going age must attend a school, the Government expenditure on education has mounted from 4½ millions to 11¼ millions sterling in the course of fifteen years, and Lord Rosebery is not yet satisfied! It may be asked how can the two things that I advocate simultaneously be achieved together, namely, a considerable reduction of taxation and a large increase in the outlay on education and other domestic reforms? My answer is that the only way to attain both objects simultaneously is to reduce the overgrown military expenditure of the country. My Lord, when the strength of the Army was increased in 1885 by 30,000 troops in spite of the protest of the Finance and Law Members of the Government of India, it was pointed out by those two officers that the then existing strength of the Army was really sufficient for all purposes of India—for keeping quiet within the borders and repelling aggression from abroad, and that if the contemplated increase was effected, it would only constitute a temptation to the Indian Government to undertake undesirable schemes of territorial aggrandisement. The Army Commission [*Special Commission appointed by the Government of India with Sir Ashley Eden as President to inquire into the organization and expenditure of the Indian Army—Ed.*] of 1879, after an exhaustive inquiry, had come to the same conclusion, viz., that the then strength of the Army was sufficient not merely for the work of maintaining internal peace but also for repelling foreign aggression, even if Russia acted with Afghanistan as an ally. But the scare of a conflict with Russia was then so great that it carried everything before it, and the proposed additions to the Army were made in India. It may be noted that it was not only in India but in other parts of the British Empire too that large and sudden additions were then made to the existing garrisons, Mr. Gladstone obtaining a large vote of credit for the purpose. But the remarkable circumstance is that, whereas everywhere else the garrisons were reduced to their old proportions as soon as the scare passed away, in India alone the burden came to stay. The result of that was that the prophecy of Sir Auckland Colvin and his colleagues was fulfilled with painful promptitude, and within a year after the increases were made, Upper Burma was invaded, conquered and annexed. Well, my Lord, the contention that the additional troops were not wanted for Indian purposes is again forcibly illustrated by the fact that during the last two years over 20,000 troops are engaged outside India in doing the work of the Imperial Government, and that, though one of these two years saw the severest famine of the last century, the peace of the country has continued absolutely unbroken. I am aware that in one of your first speeches in this Council, Your Excellency was pleased to declare that so long as you were at the helm of affairs in India, no suggestion for a reduction of the strength of the Army would meet with any support at the hands of the Indian Government. Now, even if an opinion, expressed three years ago, be not liable to modification today, what we urge is, I submit, not necessarily a reduction of the strength of the Army located in India, but a reduction of its cost to the Indian people. What strength of the Army should be maintained in India is a question of high Imperial policy in which we are not allowed a voice. But this, I think, we may claim, that if the strength maintained is in excess of India's own requirements, as it is now plainly proved to be, the cost of the excess portion should, as a mere matter of justice, be borne by the Imperial Government. Even on the narrower ground that the Army in India is required for the maintenance of British rule, England, I submit, is as much interested in the maintenance of this rule here as we are, and so it is only fair that a portion of the cost should be borne on the English estimates. If this were done, and if Indians were more widely employed in the public service of the country—more particularly in the special departments—Government will be able to reduce taxation and yet find money for more education, better Provincial finance, active efforts for the industrial development of India after the manner of the Japanese Government, and various other schemes of internal reform. Then will Indian finance be really placed on a truly sound basis, and then will our public revenues be administered as those of a poor country like India should be administered. My Lord, your Lordship spoke the other day in terms of striking eloquence of the need there is of Indians now giving up narrow views or limited ideals and feeling for the Empire with Englishmen that new, composite patriotism which the situation demands. Now that is an aspiration which is dear to the heart of many of us also. But the fusion of interest between the two races will have to be much greater, and the people of India allowed a more definite and a more intelligible place in the Empire, before that aspiration is realised. Let Englishmen exercise a certain amount of imagination and put themselves mentally into our place, and they will be able to better appreciate our feeling in the matter. It has been said that a little kindness goes a long way with the people of India. That, I think, is perfectly true. Who, for instance, ever thought of casting a doubt on the loyalty of the Indian Press in the time of Lord Ripon? There was strong language used then as now in the Press, but it was not in the Indian section of it. What, my Lord, is needed is that we should be enabled to feel that we have a Government national in spirit though foreign in personnel—a Government which subordinates all other considerations to the welfare of the Indian people, which resents the indignities offered to Indians abroad as though they were offered to Englishmen, and which endeavours by all means in its power to further the moral and material interests of the people in India and outside India. The statesman who evokes such a feeling among the Indian people will render a great and glorious service to this country and will secure for himself an abiding place in the hearts of our people. Nay, he will do more—he will serve his own country in a true spirit of Imperialism—not the narrower Imperialism which regards the world as though it was made for one race only and looks upon subject races as if they were intended to be mere footstools of that race—but that nobler Imperialism which would enable all who are included in the Empire to share equally in its blessings and honours. My Lord, I have said all this before your Lordship not merely because you happen to be Viceroy of India at the present moment, but also because everyone feels that your Lordship is destined for even higher honours and for positions of greater responsibility and influence on your return to your native land. And, if this anticipation is realised, your Lordship will be in a position—even more so than today—to influence the character of the Government of this country in the direction we so ardently desire. In this hope I have spoken today, and respectfully trust your Lordship will forgive me if here and there I have spoken with a frankness which may appear to be somewhat unusual, but which, in my humble opinion, is one of the highest forms which true loyalty can take.

3

THE IDEA OF SOCIAL REFORM

While the Indian intelligentsia and the nascent middle class believed in the beneficial effects of British rule on Indian society, they also began to ponder over the conditions which facilitated the takeover of the country by the British East India Company. How did an ancient civilization surrender so abjectly to what was originally just a mercantile firm? How could, as Bipin Chandra Pal so eloquently articulated, three million people be subjugated by three lakh aliens? The practice of caste hierarchy was seen as the major factor which prevented Indians from forging a common bond of nationality. The reformers also addressed the issue of the position of women who had to bear the brunt of evil practices like child marriage and sati. Reform and a radical change in the social vision became an inalienable part of the history of nineteenth-century India. The colonial state too played its part in occasionally siding with the reformer. However, the 'mutiny' of 1857 dealt a blow to such a role as far as the state was concerned. Henceforth, it decided to stay away from any such reform process. The notion of its permanence shaken, the state now started looking for new allies, which it soon found in the conservative section of the Indian population which included native rulers who had helped them in suppressing the revolt of 1857. This aristocracy legitimized traditions and the reformers now had to contest not only large sections of the population who were steeped in prejudices and superstitions, but also segments of the ruling class which fostered adherence to age-old customs. In the latter part of the nineteenth century, at a time when

Indians were organizing themselves politically, the leadership often found itself debating whether they should focus on social reform or on bringing people under one political umbrella. As they realized that one without the other might not have a lasting impact, the question of whether to prioritize social reform over political organization began to agitate their minds.

Till the end of the nineteenth century, the issue of social reform was not very clearly articulated by intellectuals who were more vociferous about increasing political representation. This was primarily because these intellectuals perceived English rule as symbolizing a new agency to help rid Indian society of its moribund and decadent state. The task of demanding political rights was by and large combined with the agenda of social reform with the state seen as the reforming agency. As K.T. Telang says in the significant speech reproduced in this chapter, many leaders like Gokhale symbolized this duality of purpose. However, it was easier to point fingers. For one, there was the matter of the state legislating on social issues, which was always a prickly affair. In some sense, the issue of social reform as it was raised during that early phase of modern Indian history is still very significant as it focused on the role of the state in the affairs of communities.

Moreover, a large section of the intelligentsia had begun taking the view that political agitation and settlement of political questions must take precedence over social and cultural issues. Incidentally, this group also began to argue for change in the modes and goals of political contest in India. The major stream of swadeshi leaders came from this section. On the other hand, for many like G.K. Gokhale and N.G. Chandavarkar and even Telang, social issues were not to be divorced from the political issues of the time. The struggle between the two groups came to such a state that it even split the Indian National Congress. In some sense, the split in the Congress in 1907 into the extremists and moderates, though not directly related to the divide among those who articulated political issues over social ones and those who wanted social reforms to be addressed in tandem with political ones, showed how wide the chasm had become between these two groups.

~

KASHINATH TRIMBAK TELANG

Must Social Reform Precede Political Reform in India?

K.T. Telang (1850–1893) was an advocate and Oriental scholar who vigorously participated in literary, social, municipal and political work, as well as in the affairs of the University of Bombay, of which he was the vice-chancellor from 1892 until his death. He founded the Bombay Presidency Association with Pherozeshah Mehta in 1885. He helped organize the first session of the Indian National Congress. On the issue of social reform he took an interesting 'middle path', or the 'line of least resistance'. The following speech made at the Students' Literary and Scientific Society, Elphinstone College, Bombay, in March 1886, caused a major controversy. In it Telang argued that it was necessary to 'concentrate attention on political reform because political change would be smoother to effect than social'. As he explained, those seeking political changes had allies in the 'citadel of political bureaucracy' while the social roots of Hindu reaction were entrenched. However, within a month he modified his stand saying that he admired those individuals who dared to follow their convictions.

The subject of this address … attracted my attention many months ago when I was writing a letter to my friend Mr. B.M. Malabari in reference to his notes on 'Infant Marriage and Enforced Widowhood'. When I was writing that letter, Sir Auckland Colvin's communication to Mr. Malabari had just been published in the newspapers. And the view had been expressed in it that we ought to turn our attention to social reform, in preference to the endeavours we're making to teach our English rulers what their duties were in the government of the country. In my letter to Mr. Malabari, I ventured briefly but emphatically to express my dissent from this view of Sir A. Colvin.

And first, when we are asked to give precedence to social over political reform, it is necessary to consider whether there is such a sharp line of demarcation between social and political matters as must be drawn in order to give effect to this demand. I confess I think such a line cannot be logically drawn. The division is one which in many respects is one of convenience only. And even those matters which are mainly and to a great extent social have most important political aspects, and vice versa. Take education. It is an agency of vital importance alike for political and social purposes. Or again, take the removal of the prohibition against a voyage to England. The social importance of this is obvious. But the political value of it also is equally manifest, especially now when we have just welcomed the

Indian Delegates back to their own country. Take again the question in reference to which this controversy has been raised. The question of infant marriage is a social one. But the modes suggested for remedying the evil raise great political issues, touching the province of legislation, and the true functions and limits of State activity. Therefore, it is clear that these political and social questions are so intertwined one with the other that a hard and fast line cannot in practice be drawn between them. And consequently, even if the preference suggested could be justified in theory, it would not be feasible to enforce it in practice.

But now, assuming that it is practicable to work on the basis of such a preference being given to social over political reform, let us inquire on what ground of reason such a preference can be laid down. I have endeavoured to follow the whole controversy as it has been going on for some time past. And I have come across only two reasons in favour of the preference thus suggested. First, it is said that slavery at home is incompatible with political liberty. Now, when understood in its true sense, I have no quarrel with this principle. I am prepared to concede, and indeed I hold the doctrine myself very strongly, that the true spirit of political liberty must be only skin-deep, if so much, in the man who can actively maintain or even passively tolerate slavery within his own household. But I apprehend that for the application of this principle, you must have a conscious tyranny on the one side and a slavery that is felt to be slavery on the other. Without this consciousness on both sides, I hold that the principle would be incorrect. Now, how does the matter stand in the case before us? Have we in truth got to deal with a case of conscious tyranny and felt slavery? I say, certainly not. I say that so far as we have tyranny and slavery in the case, we have only a case of the tyranny of the past, the present being bound in slavery to it. It is not, as it is often represented, a case of male tyrants and female slaves to any notable extent. We are all—men and women, widows and widowers, children and adults—slaves, if that is the proper expression, to ancient custom. Remember this further. As regards all those burning questions, which just now trouble us in connection with social reform; as regards enforced widowhood, infant marriage, voyages to England, and so forth, the persons who are supposed to be our slaves are really in many respects our masters. You talk of the duty which lies upon us of breaking the shackles off their feet, but they will have none of this breaking off of the shackles. To a great extent they do not feel the shackles, and they decline to let us break them. They protest against that interference with and desecration of their ancient and venerable traditions, which, from their point of view, is involved in this course of enfranchisement. Therefore I hold, that the phrase 'household slavery', as used in this controversy, is entirely a misnomer. It is these so-called slaves within our households who form our great difficulty. And under these circumstances, I venture to say, that the sort of 'household slavery' that in truth prevails among us, is by no means incompatible with political liberty. The position in fact is this. Here we have what may, for convenience, be treated as two spheres for our reforming activities. There is slavery in the one sphere, and there is slavery in the other, and we are endeavouring to shake off the slavery in the one sphere as well as in the other. I can see no reasonable objection to this course. That course is a perfectly legitimate one, and as Mr. Herbert Spencer has pointed out, it is also shown to be the natural one by scientific observation.

Let us now go on to the next reason alleged in favour of the precedence claimed for social over political reform. It is said that a nation socially low cannot be politically great, that history shows no instance of such a condition. Now if this means that political and social progress go on together, that the spirit of progress working in the political sphere always manifests itself in greater or less vigour in the social sphere, I at once admit it. The passage from Mr. Spencer's essay, which I quoted in my letter to Mr. Malabari, and which merely sums up the result of a full discussion marked by all Mr. Spencer's acumen and comprehensive grasp, shows that very clearly. But this is a very different thing indeed from the proposition involved in the present argument. It is not enough, as thus understood, to justify the preference demanded. For that purpose, it is necessary to prove that in a social condition that is at any given period unsatisfactory, political greatness is unattainable, and political progress not to be achieved. To this proposition, I confess I cannot see that history affords any support. And I hold, indeed, that the lessons to be deduced from history run exactly counter to this. Look at that brilliant episode in the history of India which is connected with the names of Sivaji, and the subsequent Maratha rulers—an episode on which our memories still love to dwell. I have been recently reading several of the Bakhars or chronicles of those times which have been published. And judging from them, I cannot find that the social condition of that period was very much superior to the social condition that is now prevailing. We had then infant marriage and enforced widowhood; we had imperfect female education; we had also the practice of Sati, though that never was a very widespread practice. Confining our attention to the subjects involved in the practical controversy now going on, and to subjects kindred to it, it is plain, I think, that the palm of superiority cannot be awarded to the period covered by the achievements of the great Maratha power. Yet there can be no doubt that politically those achievements were very brilliant, and that they implied great political progress, at least within the limits of their principal home. If we go back to a still earlier period, we have evidence in the writings of that famous Chinese traveller, Hiouen Tsang who came to this country in the seventh century AD, of a prosperous political condition, while the facts of the social condition do not indicate any very great superiority over what prevails now. The caste system was then in force. And we have it expressly and distinctly stated by Hiouen Tsang that in those days widow marriage was not practised. There you have one mark of 'household slavery' certainly, yet the political condition of the provinces in Northern India ruled by Harshavardhana, or of our own part of the country, then governed by the great Pulakesi, was by no means a bad one. But it may be said that our materials for a correct picture of those times are not satisfactory, and that it will not be quite safe to draw such inferences from our imperfect materials. I do not wish to impugn this view. I must admit certainly that the materials are not quite satisfactory. And therefore I will ask you for a little while to join with me in considering the lessons to be derived from the history of a country, whose history we can ascertain from much more satisfactory materials—a history, too, which we are sometimes charged with knowing better than we know the history of our own country. Let us look at the history of the country which we believe, and are happy in believing, to be at the very top of the political ladder today; let us look at the history of England in the seventeenth century AD, the materials for which are easily accessible, and have been digested for us by such classic historians as Hallam, for instance, and Lord Macaulay. The political history of England in the seventeenth century is pretty familiar to us. The beginning of the century synchronises with the close of the reign of Queen Elizabeth, in whose time, after a pretty long period of enjoyment by the Crown of almost uncontrolled power, the rights and privileges of the people had begun to be asserted. I pass over the reign of James I and come to that of Charles I. Here you have the achievements of that brilliant galaxy of political workers, containing Hampden, the Five Members, the great men of the Long Parliament. You have then the battles of the first English Revolution, as it has sometimes been called, winding up with the proceedings of the tribunal over which Bradshaw presided, and the final catastrophe of the execution of King Charles I. A republican might object to the phrase catastrophe, but as there was a destruction of the life of one of God's creatures, it is, I hope, allowable to speak of the event as a catastrophe. Well, we pass on then to the protectorate of Cromwell, a tangible embodiment of the assertion of popular power against the Crown. Then we come after the Restoration to the well known Habeas Corpus Act. And after the short and inglorious reign of James II, we come to the great Revolution of 1688. Then we have the Declaration of Rights and Bill of Rights, till finally we reach the Act of Settlement at the very close of the seventeenth century. It would not be easy, I should say, to find out in history many parallels to the course of political progress indicated by the events I have now alluded to—a course which not merely improved the condition of England at the time, but has been followed up by greater or less progress of a similarly salutary character since, and is being still so followed up in our own day... So much for the political condition. And now let us see what was the social condition of England at the time when her people were achieving these glorious political successes. The materials are collected ready to our hands in an elaborate chapter, the third or fourth, of Lord Macaulay's *History of England*—on the condition of England in 1685. Those who wish to examine the question for themselves must read that chapter in the original. I cannot go now into all the topics there expatiated on. The condition of the working classes, and the agriculturists, the state of the means of communication, the extraordinary extent to which children were overworked for the benefit, in the result, of the adult population, the looseness and obscenity of general conversation, these are all dwelt on in the interesting pages of Macaulay. I will not say more about them. I will only draw attention particularly to two points. The first relates to the state of female education. Macaulay gives us an instance of the miserable state of female education, and merely as an instance of what was only too common at the time, the ignorance of such a person as Queen Mary, the wife of William III—her ignorance of her own vernacular, the classical languages being, of course, out of the question. The ignorance is shown in a sentence endorsed by Queen Mary herself on a copy of a book, a Bible, I think, presented to her. The English is such as a boy in our sixth standard classes could easily improve. I have copied out the words here, and I will read them to you. 'This book,' so runs the endorsement, 'was given the King and I at our crownation.' That is one point. Another, also noted by Macaulay, is that husbands 'of decent station', as Macaulay is careful to note, were not ashamed, in those days, of cruelly beating their wives. Well, as I said before, I need not go into further details. These are enough to demonstrate that at the politically glorious epoch we are now surveying, the social condition of England in regard to the relations of the sexes, was by no means of a highly creditable character. Look again at the England of today. Politically, she continues to be as great, and as prosperous, and as energetic in advancement, as ever. How is she socially? I have noted down here a point or two in regard to this, which is worthy of consideration. But I wish to say a word of warning before I refer to these points themselves. On this as well as on the last point, I refer only to existing social evils. This is necessary for the argument. But I must not be understood as supposing for one instant that these evils afford a satisfactory picture of the social condition of England, taken as a whole, whether in the seventeenth century or at the present day. I have not the privilege of a personal knowledge of the social condition of England even at the present day. But from all I have read and seen here; from all I have heard from those of our friends who have had the inestimable privilege of seeing with their own eyes England and English social life; especially from what I have heard from our distinguished friends who have only just returned; and among them, too, especially my excellent friend Mr. Ramaswami Mudliar of Madras who has publicly spoken on this subject; from all this, I have formed a conclusion, which I have no hesitation in plainly avowing, that in my judgement the social condition of England is, in many important respects, immensely superior to that of any of the section of our Indian community. I hope this open avowal will prevent any misunderstanding of my meaning in what I have said on this subject, and also in what I am going to say. Of the detailed points, then, that I have noted, I pass over one which I had intended to refer to, but which, on second thoughts, I consider to be so liable to misapprehension that it had better be omitted. And I will refer first to the question of women's rights. That was a question on which, as we all know, the late John Stuart Mill felt, thought, and wrote, very strongly. But what has been the result of it? His very eloquent treatise on the subjection of women has not yet had any appreciable result, as regards the practical enforcement of its doctrines, while Mr. Mill himself was, in his lifetime, ridiculed for his out-of-the-way views. Great is truth and it prevails, says the Latin proverb, and our own Sanskrit maxim is to the same effect: Truth alone is victorious, not untruth. But for the present the truth enunciated by Mill is not in the ascendant. Again, it was only the other day, in this very Hall, that we were informed how the relations of the working classes and the aristocratic party in England were constituted, and how the former felt a genuine and fervent sympathy with the wants and wishes of the Indian population, because they felt that in their own country and by their own people, they were treated in much the same way as we are here. Does that indicate a satisfactory social condition? Or again, let me refer to the telegram received only this afternoon, about a grand Socialist meeting of 20,000 people in Hyde Park. One of the Socialist orators there declared that there would be bloodshed, unless social reform—by which I understand him to mean a reform in the relations of the different classes of society—was granted. Can we say that that is altogether as it should be? There is one more point that I would wish to refer to here, especially because it affords an even closer parallel to our condition than those to which I have now alluded. Marriage with a deceased wife's sister is at present prohibited in England. The movement for the removal of this prohibition is not one of yesterday. It is an old one, and has gone on for many years. On the last occasion that it was solemnly discussed, the reform was obstructed, and successfully obstructed, by those who correspond in English society to our priesthood. There you have the case of a social reform which comes as near as possible to the social reforms required among us—reforms, that is to say, of social regulations intertwined closely with religious, or what are regarded as religious ordinances. How, then, does the whole matter stand? In this England of ours, this England, where political reform is advancing by leaps and bounds, where political affairs attract such attention as is shown by the commotion of the General Election just closed—in this England, there are still social evils, huge and serious social evils, awaiting remedy. To them attention is not directed with anything like the force and energy bestowed on political affairs—even until bloodshed is threatened. Where, then, is the lesson of history which we are asked to deduce and act upon? Once more I say that my remarks must not be understood as implying for a moment that I am comparing our social condition with that of England. I am doing nothing of the sort. I am only pointing the lesson taught by the contemporary history of England—that political progress can be achieved, and is being achieved before our eyes, where social evils still remain unremedied, and where they receive but a comparatively small fraction of the attention and reforming energy of the people.

Well, then, having dealt with and shown what I conceive to be the fallacy of the arguments urged in support of the affirmative of the question which forms the subject of this evening's discourse, I will now proceed to state the arguments which appear to me to support the negative answer to that question. And first, it seems to me to be plainly a maxim of prudence and common sense, that reform ought to go, as I may say, along the line of least resistance. Secure first the reforms which you can secure with the least difficulty, and then turn your energies in the direction of those reforms where more difficulty has to be encountered. You will thus obtain all that vigour which the spirit of reform must derive from success, and thus carry out the whole work of progress with greater promptitude than if you go to work the other way. This is the principle we actually act upon within the sphere of political activity itself. How, then, can we be justly twitted for applying the same principle as between the two spheres of political and social activity? Now if this principle is correct, it leads manifestly to the conclusion that more energy ought just now to be devoted to political than to social reform. Remember, I am not asking that our reforming energies should be confined to the political sphere. Far from it. I entirely repudiate that principle. And I don't think you could carry it out if you would. As pointed out in the quotation from Mr. Spencer's essay given in my letter to Mr. Malabari—I must ask to be excused for referring to that letter so frequently—the spirit which impels to political reform must needs burst forth in other directions also, more or less frequently, with greater or less force. I have not the remotest idea of laying an embargo on its outgoings in those directions. But this I do say, that political reform is entitled to a greater share of our energies than social, under the circumstances we have got to deal with. Every one of us cannot devote himself to every one of the numerous reforms which are wanted. Extraordinary natural gifts may enable one person, like, for instance, my friend Mr. Ranade, to devote himself successfully to many modes of activity at one and the same time. But this is not possible to us all. Therefore, in dividing our energies, if we have to divide them, between political and social reform, I hold that the greater portion of our energy legitimately can, and therefore ought to be devoted to the former. And now mark how the result I allege follows from the application of the line-of-least resistance principle. What are the forces opposed to us, if I may use that compendious expression? On the one side, we have a government by a progressive nation, which is the benign mother of free nations—a nation which, by its constituted authorities, has solemnly and repeatedly declared, and in some measure practically shown the sincerity of its declaration, that it is ready to admit us to full political rights, when we show that we deserve them and shall use them well. On the other side, we have an ancient nation, subject to strong prejudices; not in anything like full sympathy with the new conditions now existing in the country; attached, perhaps 'not wisely but too well', to its own religious notions with which the proposed social reforms are closely, intimately, and at numberless points intertwined; loving all its own genuine hoary traditions—and some of its very modern ones also which it supposes to be hoary—yet often failing to understand the true meaning and significance of both classes of traditions. As between these two groups of what I have called, only for convenience of phrase, opposing forces, can there be any reasonable doubt how the line of least resistance runs? If we compare the Government and the Hindu population to two forts facing the army of reform, can there be any doubt that the wisest course for that army is to turn its energies first towards the fort represented by the Government, where we have numerous and powerful friends among the garrison, and which is held against us only in order to test first whether we shall be able to properly use any larger powers that may be conceded to us there? As to the other fort, the case is as far as possible from being one of *veni vidi vici*. The soldiers of the old garrison are not in the least ready to 'give up', and in some respects we have even to forge, and to learn to wield, the weapons by which we have to fight them.

Again, in politics, argument goes a great way; in social reform, it goes for very little, seeing that feeling and tradition are involved in it to a very large extent indeed. In politics, even such a thinker as Sir Fitzjames Stephen is content to resort to reason. He says that if the people of India want free institutions, without wire-pulling from English Radicals, let them by all means have such institutions. Sir Fitzjames Stephen's objection is only to the concession of such institutions, when they are not asked for in India, only to prove a pet theory of English politicians. In presence of such champions of the existing order of things, logic is an instrument of power. But where feeling and tradition are the authorities appealed to, logic is almost impotent. You must then make up your minds—still to use logic, of course, but only as a subordinate agency—and you must rely more on a long, patient, toilsome process of diverting the feelings, or to express it differently, making the soil unfit for the growth of these misplaced sentiments and misunderstood traditions, in the same way as, according to a great scientific teacher, science does not attack the weed of superstition directly, but renders the mental soil unfit for its cultivation. You cannot say, you ought not to say here, 'cut this down, why cumbereth it the ground'. You must improve here, you must infuse new vitality and new vigour into the old growth. In one word, to go back once again to our old political phraseology, we have here got, like Disraeli, to educate our party, which always must be, and in this case must particularly be, a lengthy and laborious operation.

... In political matters we can all unite at once. Hindus, Musulmans, Parsis, the people of Eastern India, Southern India, Western India, Northern India—all can unite, and not only can do so in theory, they have actually done so in fact, as demonstrated at the National Congress held last Christmas. What is the secret of this? The answer is obvious. The evils, or supposed evils, are common; the remedies, not being in any way mixed up with any very powerful traditions, are also the same; and all intelligent Indian opinion is necessarily unanimous. In regard to social matters, the conditions are all altered. The evils, for one thing, are not identical. The surrounding conditions are excessively various. The force of traditions and old memories is not equal all round. And the remedies, therefore, that suggest themselves to different minds are almost of necessity different. It is plain, then, that the advantages to secure which we can all united ought to be tried for first, so that we may obtain the benefit of the fraternal feeling which must be generated by such cooperation. If political reforms is thus secured by the concerted action of all the educated classes in India, that must, and inevitably will, tell favourably on the advancement of social reform. Reading Mr. Cotton's book on *New India* the other day, I came across a passage germane to this topic, which I have copied out here and shall read to you. 'Bereft of political independence,' says he, 'their ideas of collective action cannot have that impress of sound logic and morality which collective action alone can impart to them. A considerable degree of unity in thought and action has lately been established in political matters, and it may be hoped, therefore, that there will shortly be a similar manifestation in regard to moral and social questions.' What Mr. Cotton says here is not only perfectly true, but I venture to think it is somewhat understated. In regard to moral and social questions, in the same way as with regard to political ones, there is a great deal more unity already established than he supposes. The difference there, too—as regards the goal to be reached—is but slight. The real difference is—and that I admit is at present very wide—as to the roads for reaching the goal. Some believe in legislation, some in State aid, and some are inclined to trust to the development from within of the energy of the community. Such and other important differences exist in the modes suggested for effecting reforms. But about the substantive reforms themselves, there is but little—but I don't deny that there is a little—difference of views. But the general unity is not thereby marred. And the want of unity in details here referred to is due to various circumstances like those already indicated, and must gradually cease to exist.

One of our Anglo-Vernacular newspapers recently asked how the progress of political reform was expected to tell on the advance of social reform. I say, we have just indicated one mode in which this operation will take place. In political matters, we are learning—and learning more easily than we should do in any other department of activity—the lesson that we must act in concert, that to this end we must give and take, and sink smaller differences for the one common purpose. This, and lessons like this, when we are thoroughly imbued with them, will form the best possible equipment for the work of social reform that lies before us. We must act together, we must disarm opposition, we must conciliate those opposed to us. Such are the modes of action which we are learning in the course of our political activity. These we shall have to apply in the performance of our duty in the social sphere. Let us remember further that with political independence, to a certain extent, goes a great capacity for social advancement. This is not a mere empty speculation. It is a theory in support of which historical testimony can be adduced. Sir H. Maine has pointed out in regard to the Hindu Law as administered by our Indian courts that it has now assumed a stiffness, rigidity, and inflexibility, which formed no feature of the system before British rule. In the days of the Peshva regime again—a regime which many among us are apt to look upon as very anti-liberal and narrow—there was a liberalising process going on, which, if I may be permitted to use that figure, must make one's mouth water in these days. The story of Parashuram Bhau Patvardhan is a familiar one. That brave soldier–statesman had almost made up his mind to get a favourite daughter, who had become a widow in youth, remarried. He had to abandon that intention, it is true, but still the very fact that such an idea should have entered his mind, and should have been placed by him before those by whom he was surrounded, and that these latter should have deprecated it in the very mild manner that they seem to have done—these are facts worthy of being pondered over. Coupling them with such facts as I see in the Bakhars, regarding the behaviour of the Peshvas with Jivba Dada, the entertainment of Musulmans and Hindus at dinner together on occasion of the marriage of Savai Madhavrao Peshva, the marriage of the Peshva Balaji Bajirao with a daughter of a Desastha family, I confess I am inclined strongly to draw the inference, which I have held for a long time, that if Peshva rule had continued a little longer, several of the social reforms which are now giving us and the British Government so much trouble would have been secured with immensely greater ease.

And now I come to the last of the points I wish to address myself to this evening. I do so the more readily now, because I am afraid I have trespassed already too long on your attention. The remark of Sir A. Colvin which I alluded to at the beginning of this address, assumed that as a matter of fact we were devoting an extravagant proportion of our time and energy to the subject of political reform, and neglecting almost entirely—so it appears to me to have assumed—the subject of social reform. I cannot admit this to be the fact at all. I can well understand, how much an incorrect impression should arise among those whose acquaintance with what is going on in Indian Society is from the outside, and derived from newspapers and other similar sources. In the case of political reform, it is of the very essence of the thing that a great deal should be done through the agency of newspapers. Nobody, I am sure, will suspect me of undervaluing the utility of the press in all works of reform. But I must own that I do not think social questions are much the worse for not being talked about so much through the newspapers as political questions. For see how different the two cases are in regard to this point. In regard to politics, the efforts made so far have, as a general but not by any means as a universal rule, addressed themselves to those who come within the circle of the influence of the press. For one thing, the officers of Government have to be kept informed in regard to what is thought, felt, or desired by the people. One of the best means of effecting this is afforded by newspapers. Again, superior officers of the British Government have often to be informed of the doings of their subordinates, and informed in such a way as to enforce attention. The press is a most potent instrument for use in such cases. But in the case of social evils, the party to be educated is to a great extent beyond the ambit of the newspaper's influence. It does not often get into the way of the newspaper, and, it is too thick-skinned to be touched to the quick on that side. The mode of operation, accordingly, must here be necessarily different, although, of course, even here the newspaper is of use as an indirect means of education by way of 'filtration'; and also as a means of communication with those sections of the old party that come nearest to the new; and further as a means of communication between the various sections or members of the new party itself. However, although reforming activity in the social sphere is thus usually less noisy than in the other sphere, it is not, therefore, any the less real. But before I go into details here, I am free to admit at once that the success we have achieved is excessively slight. But if I admit this, I wish to ask whether anyone is prepared to say that the success we have achieved in the political sphere is so very large after all, even with more favourable conditions? Admitting that we are miles and miles away from the goal in social reform, I hold that we are as yet equally far in political. We have made and are making preparations in both, and in both we have made a similar amount of progress. Let us glance at the facts. Female education is one of our principal items, as it is one of our principal means, of social reform. We have made some progress there. I am myself a great believer in the efficacy of female education, especially in connection with general social reform of all descriptions. And, therefore, I need scarcely say that what we have done is small enough in all conscience. But we have done something. Our Parsi friends, with my venerable friend now in the chair as one of their great leaders, have made progress which puts us to shame. But though we are lagging behind, we too are doing something, as I need scarcely tell the members of the Students' Literary and Scientific Society. The girls at the Society's Schools have been for some time increasing in numbers. And recently we have added an Anglo-Vernacular Department to our schools, which, beginning with twelve girls in the first year, and containing twenty-two in the second, now opens its third year with as many as sixty girls. Again I say this is small enough, as no one can feel more strongly than I do. But it is, I will venture to say, perceptible progress. Then there is also the other great section of the Indian community—the Mahomedan. That section has generally been regarded as averse to improvement—especially of the modern sort. But the important movement started by my excellent friend Mr. Badruddin Tyabji and his colleagues, has by its great success shown that the Mahomedan community, too, is socially moving forward. However, to return to other points connected with the social state of the Hindu community. The question of widow marriage has certainly advanced a great deal beyond the stage at which it was, say twenty years ago. The bonds of caste are getting looser, our friends are going to England with less difficulty, and more frequently, than before. [A Voice: What about infant marriage?] A friend there asks about the position of the infant marriage question. Well, even here we are not so bad as we were within the narrow span even of my own experience. The age of marriage is slowly rising. I admit again it is rising very slowly indeed, and the point it has now reached is low enough. Still there is no retrogression certainly, and there is some progress, however slight. And all these facts being such as I have pointed out, I venture to repeat that we cannot fairly be censured for giving too exclusive attention to political at the expense of social reform.

And now, after all this discussion, I venture to reiterate the opinion which I stated many months ago, that it is not possible to sever political from social reform altogether; that the two must go hand in hand, although the march may not in the case of both be with absolutely equal celerity. I say we must and ought to devote the greater portion of our energy to political reform, but so as still to keep alive a warm sympathy for social reform. To one like myself, who believes to a great extent in the philosophy of Mr. Herbert Spencer, this conclusion is not only a correct one, but almost the only one possible. But even to those who may not accept that philosophy, but who will look beneath the surface of things, to them, too, this conclusion must commend itself. Let us then all devote the bulk of our energies to political reform. Let us keep alive our sympathies with social reform and those who undertake them, and let us all help them to the extent of our powers. At all events, for God's sake, let us not set ourselves in antagonism to social reform. In this way only shall we best discharge the whole of the duty which lies upon us, the duty of reform in social as well as political matters. For I must repeat that in my judgement they are both duties and must both be fairly attended to and discharged according to our circumstances and opportunities.

~

N.G. CHANDAVARKAR

An Address on Social Reform

N.G. Chandavarkar (1855–1923), the foremost intellectual leader of his generation, was the soul of the Prarthana Samaj founded by Ranade and his associates in Bombay in 1867. His discourses at the Prarthana Samaj reveal a fascinating mind. A leading member of the Social Reform Conference, he was at the forefront of advocating social reforms. Chandavarkar delivered a speech at the fourth anniversary meeting of the Madras Hindu Social Reform Association, one of the most active organizations involved in social reform in the country at the end of the nineteenth century, at the Anderson Memorial Hall on Saturday, 28 November 1896, where he discussed the current state of reform as well as the future agenda.

When we say that, though we should not go too far ahead, yet we must go ahead, we are brought to the question, what is going ahead? Are any of the measures of social reform which we advocate so rash and hasty that they propose nothing but a leap in the dark or a sudden revolution in Hindu society? Our critics assume a number of things when they criticise us and base on those assumptions their conclusion that we wish to run headlong into reforms and move too fast. But a careful consideration of the measures of reform we propose ought to satisfy an unbiased mind that our programme is moderation itself.

For instance, in the first item of reform on our list we say that it is our first duty to educate our daughters or other female wards. I do not suppose that there is anyone who will seriously maintain that there is anything radical or revolutionary in this idea about the necessity and importance of female education. But we are told that it is no use talking of that education without or before deciding the kind and character of education that our women must receive. Should they be educated in the vernaculars or in English? Now, I do not care whether you educate your women in the vernaculars or in English, though I consider it absolutely necessary that no one, whether man or woman, should be ignorant of his own vernacular, provided the education they are given is one which fits them to be the guardian angels of their homes—provided, that is, we enable them to be not only good housewives but also good companions of life. There are branches of knowledge which must improve the minds of women as much as they improve the minds of men; but the biographies of great women, whether of India or of foreign countries, the art of domestic economy and housekeeping, ought to form the special features of female education. Let us leave aside the pedantry that makes this question of female education a matter of academic discussion and busies itself, like the schoolmen of old, in idle speculations and subtle disputations. Let us be more practical by insisting upon this, above all, that whatever else may be necessary or not for women, this we deem absolutely necessary that they should know their own vernacular, that they should know all that can be learnt about housekeeping, and sewing and the essential truths and the holier and higher and more ancient traditions of the Hindu religion and society and not merely the corruptions into which the vicissitudes of later ages have cast it. If we can teach them more, so much the better for us. But if we cannot soar higher than that, let us soar so high at least; and see that the work, thus fixed, is done thoroughly. I am entirely with those who hold that such education as we impart to women must not unfit them for the duties and obligations which they have to fulfil as the presiding deities of our homes. There is no fear that our women will neglect those duties because they are educated; they are already good housewives within the circumscribed sphere of knowledge in which society has kept them; but our object is to enlarge that sphere by enabling them to perform those duties more efficiently.

Then, on the question of marriage reform what do we propose and pledge ourselves to? It is undoubtedly our object to get rid of the baneful practice of infant marriages and see that the future progeny is not a progeny born of babies. But since the reform in this direction as in all directions must advance by stages, we propose to refrain from marrying our daughters or other female wards before they are eleven years of age in the case of those with whom marriage before puberty is obligatory and in the case of others before puberty. The eleventh year is fixed provisionally as the limit below which no one should celebrate his daughter's or other female ward's marriage. To some it may seem too low a limit; I myself think it might have safely been put at 12; but whether 11 or 12, it is well to begin at some limit and raise it gradually. Is there anything radical in this? Some perhaps may feel inclined to ask—what is the reform you effect by taking such a low limit? My answer is that by fixing upon a limit and determining not to go below it, you take a step forward at a time when the practice is to marry girls when they are 8 to 10. If our limit is 11 today, we shall be encouraged to raise it to 12 and onwards.

What, again, do we urge in favour of widow remarriage, which is also one of the reforms which we deem essential? We have no quarrel with the sentiment which leads either a woman who having lost her husband or a man who having lost his wife determines to consecrate her or his life to a life of celibacy out of respect for the memory of the dear departed. Such a sentiment has everything in it to evoke our admiration; and among the many virtues which have raised our beloved Sovereign, Queen Empress Victoria, immensely in our estimation and taught us to regard her as a model Queen, is the life of noble widowhood which she has been leading since the death of the Prince Consort. But let us not corrupt such a sentiment by sacrificing at its altar, girls who lose their husbands at tender ages, while we allow even men near their graves to marry. I have heard many an orthodox man and many an orthodox woman deplore this accursed custom of enforced widowhood. The sentiment in favour of it has not indeed taken practical shape to a large extent; but it is steadily though very slowly growing. The object of the reform is only to remove the obstacle enforced by custom, not to compel every widow to marry, but to allow a feeling to grow in society that it is permissive to a widow to marry if she chooses.

And what is our programme about caste? In his address delivered at the anniversary meeting of this Association two years ago, Dr. Bhandarkar said, 'Caste has become so inveterate in Hindu society that the endeavour to do so will only result in the formation of new castes. But the end must steadily be kept in view. We must remember that caste is the greatest monster we have to kill.' There again, recognising the insuperable difficulty, and the necessity of moving gradually by stages, we propose, to begin with, the amalgamation of sub-castes so far as inter-dining is concerned.

One more question remains and that is about the re-admission into caste of what are called England-returned men. There is no special reference to it in the published programme of the objects and measures of the Madras Hindu Social Reform Association and I should have if I consulted my own wishes and inclinations, let that question alone without saying a word about it here for the very good and obvious reason that that question more than any other question of social reform has been solving itself and proving too strong for even caste or other prejudices. Our interests, our aspirations, our hopes of the future are bound up with England and, whether you will or no, to England Hindus have gone and to England Hindus will go. The tide is too strong for even the united forces of caste, superstition and priesthood and it is as idle to think or even dream of checking that tide as it was idle on the part of Mrs. Partington to stop the waters of the Atlantic by means of her broom. In several higher castes that I know of in Western India, many have got quietly back into their caste without any fuss or hubbub. And even those castes which are now losing their heads over the question and making a good deal of fuss over it I feel certain that the force of the times is such that a few years hence their future generations will laugh and wonder at the excitement which their ancestors of the present generation have managed to get up over this question. There are those who maintain that the England-returned men ought not to be taken back into caste without the performance of 'prayaschit', and there are others who hold that England-returned men ought not to be re-admitted into caste at all, because a trip to England necessarily involves a violation of the essential rules of caste on the part of those who undertake it by compelling them to eat forbidden food and get contaminated by contact with the Mlecchas. Now, my answer to those who take the prayaschitta view of this question is this. If prayaschitta is penance for a sin committed, there can be on principle no moral objection to those England-returned men doing that penance, if they sincerely think that they committed a sin in going to England and pledge themselves not to do forbidden things here and act accordingly. But of what use is a prayaschitta if instead of leading to sincere penitence and preventing the commissions, it only becomes a promoter and abetter of sin. I do not think that those of us who are sincerely anxious for the welfare and progress of Hindu society—who think that morality is a greater cementing bond of society than anything else—ought to be parties to a theory which teaches men that they have the license to sin freely, for every time they sin they can do penance and pass for sinless men. And a prayaschitta has already become a license, so to say, for many a sin and many a flagrant departure from the path of virtue. My second objection to prayaschitta in the case of England-returned men is that I do not consider that a trip to England is sinful.

This, indeed, is conceded by many who hold to the prayaschitta theory. They say that prayaschitta is only a formality, and there should be no scruple about it. But no reform ought to be promoted, unless we teach people, both by precept and example that it is a reform which is not only essential but also consistent with the principles of morality. The shastras are invoked in support of the theory that going to England is sinful; but the shastras knew nothing of England when they were written or 'revealed' and all that the shastras say is that it is a sin to cross the sea. But what caste has escaped this sin of crossing the sea in these days without going to England? When our opponents, however, find themselves driven into a corner by this argument, they take shelter behind the plausible contention that a trip to England contaminates those who undertake it by bringing them in contact with Mlecchas and compelling them, through sheer necessity, to partake of forbidden food. But they forget that they play with edged tools when they use this sort of argument. The contamination of contact with Mlecchas and the partaking of forbidden food commenced in the case of many a caste in this very country long before anyone thought of going to England. If men that go to England partake of forbidden food through necessity, what are we to say of those in many castes that partake of it on the sly and for mere pleasure and to gratify their appetite and taste? One would not like to say much on this delicate subject, but the time is coming, and has come for honest men, to speak freely. If the truth were told, we should have to say, in the language used by Queen Sheba: 'The half has not been told.' But it is said that the sin of such men is not detected, whereas the 'sin' of England-returned men is found out. Then are we to understand that while we talk of God and the holy bounds of society, society is to be guided by and its members held together on the degrading, vicious and ungodly principle, so eloquently denounced by the late Cardinal Newman as the worst of moral cancers that must ultimately lead to social decay and ruin, 'that it is not the commission but the detection of sin' that is to be the social standard of sinfulness? Let men beware that they are playing fast and loose with their responsibilities as members of society and unconsciously bringing about its extinction by becoming parties to a doctrine that is so demoralising… It is not England-returned men that are breaking loose the moral bonds of our society; the plague spot is elsewhere and because it requires a microscope to detect its bacilli, let it not be supposed that society is safe. It is the spirit of organised hypocrisy, which sanctions the commission of any sin, provided it is done on the sly, and which the members of every caste tacitly tolerate, that is laying the axe at the root, not only of virtue, but all social union of the true type. It is said that the real difficulty to social reform comes from the stated opposition of our gurus, those who preside over castes as their spiritual and social heads and dictators. However much or little we may differ from the gurus, I do not think we are justified in laying the blame upon them so much or so entirely as many are disposed to do. The institution of gurus is a holy and venerable institution, which, I have no doubt, has done much good in the past, and we should not be blind to the fact that our gurus exercised in the past a vast spiritual and moral influence over the Hindu community, and that enabled that community to keep alive the light of virtue even in the midst of its vicissitudes. I am not one of those who think that an institution which has done so well in the past ought to be lightly dealt with...

Lastly I notice with particular pleasure that both in your programme and in your lectures and in your newspaper, you, the members of the Madras Hindu Social Reform Association, lay stress upon a life of purity. That, indeed, ought to be, as indeed you have made it, the keynote of the social reform movement. All reform must begin with the reform of the individual and the reform of the individual begins when he lives a life of openness and virtue and makes that the basis of all progress, both individual and social. We complain that Hindu orthodoxy has a deep-seated prejudice against social reform; but once convince it that you are men of moral excellence, that you lead and insist upon others leading lives of rectitude, and that all your plans and proposals of reform centre round that as the cardinal principle of your faith, you cannot fail to attract its attention, engage its sympathies and at last secure its support. Men now may make light of and ridicule your attempt to denounce and put down what are called nautch parties; they may laugh at you and take you for visionaries; but be sure enthusiasm in the cause of morality has unrivalled charm and power which does not fail sooner or later to assert itself. Our work of social reform must suffer so long as we do not preach and practise the gospel of godly life; with that life as the animating principle of our movements, we may prove more than a match to all prejudice and opposition. I believe there is a great deal of truth in what my distinguished friend, the Hon'ble Mr. Pherozeshah M. Mehta said at a meeting of the Bombay

Legislative Council, when in reply to a member of that Council who pooh-poohed the ladies and gentlemen in England that have been leading the agitation of purity as mad enthusiasts, he reminded the Council that it is such mad enthusiasts who have, as the pages of English history show, awakened the moral conscience of England and contributed to its progress. The sentiment has taken root in Hindu society that, however good a principle may be, it should not be practiced, if it is opposed to public sentiment; and hence it is whatever a reform is proposed, we are met with the Sanskrit verse, which says—although (a thing) is pure, it should not be done or observed because it is opposed to public sentiment. The sentiment embodied in this verse accounts for all ills and evils; it has proved hostile to all reform and progress ... our lives should be so arranged as to enable us to be living protests against lawless modes of living.

I know that the work before us is gigantic, and our difficulties innumerable. Our hearts faint when we see that there is a Himalaya of prejudice, ignorance, and opposition to be got over before we can hope to win and say our work is, or is about to be, accomplished. But if we have our conditions of difficulty, we are also not without our conditions of hope. We have put our hands to the plough, and it is not for us to look back; and we need not look back and despond, if we only bear in mind that, small as our numbers are, uninfluential, as people say, as we may be, it is not, as Mazzini in his vigorous language points out, the number but the unity of forces that enables a good cause to win and prosper. Nor should we be impatient of results. It is enough for us, it should be enough for us, if we are able to say that we have not remained idle or inactive, but have done something, even if that something be very little, to carry the work of social reform a little further than we found it and helped our successors to carry it further still. We do not wish to make light of the past, nor do we desire to touch ancient institutions in either a spirit of irreverence or thoughtlessness. It is because we think that social growth is continuous, and that not only 'perfect truth' but 'perfect development' is 'beyond the reach of any one generation' that we hold fast to the principle that each generation ought to endeavour to leave society better than it found it by raising its ideals of life and conduct; and if we go on with our work ... we may be able to say that we have not worked in vain.

MAHADEV GOVIND RANADE

Reform or Revivalism?

This is the speech Ranade delivered at the eleventh Social Reform Conference at Amraoti in 1897. Around this time a strong debate raged between reform and revivalism. The reform movement was having a tough time faced with revivalist trends not only in the social reform sector but also in the domain of politics. While defending the initiatives for reform, Ranade's assured voice was trying to locate the whole theme in the larger context of the reform movement in the country.

Such, gentlemen, is the brief record of the principal social events of the year. Many ardent spirits amongst us will no doubt be very much dissatisfied with the poverty of this record. At the same time, we must bear in mind that hundreds and thousands, nay millions of our countrymen will regard this poor record as very revolutionary, and condemn this as one of the unseen causes which has brought about physical and moral catastrophes upon the land by way of punishment for the sins of the reformers. These are two extreme sides of the question, and it is not for me to say to an audience like this on which side the balance of truth may be found. The *Arya Patrika* of the Punjab, which is a recognised organ of the Arya Samaj there, has in its words of advice to the Conference expressed its view that we are radically in the wrong in seeking to reform the usages of our society without a change of religion, and it seriously suggests that we should, in the first instance, become members of their Samaj and this conversion will bring with it all desired reforms. Many enthusiastic friends of the Brahmo Samaj entertain similar views and give us similar advice. All I can say to these welcome advisers is that they do not fully realise the situation and its difficulties. People have changed their religion, and yet retain their social usages unchanged. The Native Christians, for instance, especially the Roman Catholic section among them and many sections of Mahomedans are instances in point. Besides, it has been well observed that even for a change of religion, it is too often necessary that the social surroundings must be liberalised in a way to help people to realise their own responsibilities and to strengthen them in their efforts. Lastly, these well-meaning advisers seem to forget that the work of reform cannot be put off indefinitely till the far more arduous and difficult work of religious conversion is accomplished. It may take centuries before the Arya or

Brahmo Samaj establish their claims for general recognition. In the meanwhile what is to become of the social organisation? Slowly but surely, the progress of liberal ideas must be allowed to work its way in reforming our social customs, and the process cannot be stopped even though we may wish it. In the case of our society especially, the usages which at present prevail amongst us are admittedly not those which obtained in the most glorious periods of our history. On most of the points which are included in our programme, our own record of the past shows that there has been a decided change for the worse, and it is surely within the range of practical possibilities for us to hope that we may work up our way back to a better state of things without stirring up the rancorous hostilities which religious differences have a tendency to create and foster. There is no earthly reason whatsoever why we should not cooperate with these religious organisations, or why they should not rather cooperate with us in this work in which our interests are common, because the majority of our countrymen hold different views about religion from those which commend themselves to these Samajas. I am speaking these words with a full sense of my responsibility, for I am in my humble way a member of one, if not of both the Samajas, and I am a sincere searcher after religious truth in full sympathy with the Arya and Brahmo Samaj movements, and I hope therefore that these advisers of ours will take my reply in the same spirit, and will not misunderstand me. Schismatic methods of propagation cannot be applied with effect to vast communities which are not within their narrow pale.

On the other side, some of our orthodox friends find fault with us, not because of the particular reforms we have in view, but on account of the methods we follow. While the new religious sects condemn us for being too orthodox, the extreme orthodox section denounce us for being too revolutionary in our methods. According to these last, our efforts should be directed to revive, and not to reform. I have many friends in this camp of extreme orthodoxy, and their watchword is that revival, and not reform, should be our motto. They advocate a return to the old ways, and appeal to the old authorities and the old sanction. Here also, as in the instance quoted above, people speak without realising the full significance of their own words. When we are asked to revive our institutions and customs, people seem to be very much at sea as to what it is they seek to revive. What particular period of our history is to be taken as the old? Whether the period of the Vedas, of the Smritis, of the Puranas or of the Mahomedan or modern Hindu times? Our usages have been changed from time to time by a slow process of growth, and in some cases of decay and corruption, and we cannot stop at a particular period without breaking the continuity of the whole. When my revivalist friend presses his argument upon me, he has to seek recourse in some subterfuge which really furnishes no reply to the question—what shall we revive? Shall we revive the old habits of our people when the most sacred of our caste indulged in all the abominations as we now understand them of animal food and drink which exhausted every section of our country's Zoology and Botany? The men and the Gods of those old days ate and drank forbidden things to excess in a way no revivalist will now venture to recommend. Shall we revive the twelve forms of sons, or eight forms of marriage, which included capture, and recognised mixed and illegitimate intercourse? Shall we revive the Niyoga system of procreating sons on our brother's wives when widowed? Shall we revive the old liberties taken by the Rishis and by the wives of the Rishis with the marital tie? Shall we revive the hecatombs of animals sacrificed from year's end to year's end, and in which human beings were not spared as a propitiatory offering? Shall we revive the Shakti worship of the left hand with its indecencies and practical debaucheries? Shall we revive the Sati and infanticide customs, or the flinging of living men into the rivers, or over rocks, or hook swinging, or the crushing beneath Jagannath car? Shall we revive the internecine wars of the Brahmins and Kshatriyas, or the cruel persecution and degradation of the aboriginal population? Shall we revive the custom of many husbands to one wife or of many wives to one husband? Shall we require our Brahmins to cease to be landlords and gentlemen, and turn into beggars and dependants upon the king as in olden times? These instances will suffice to show that the plan of reviving the ancient usages and customs will not work our salvation, and is not practicable. If these usages were good and beneficial, why were they altered by our wise ancestors? If they were bad and injurious, how can any claim be put forward for their restoration after so many ages? Besides, it seems to be forgotten that in a living organism as society is, no revival is possible. The dead and the buried or burnt are dead, buried, and burnt once for all, and the dead past cannot therefore be revived except by a reformation of the old materials into new organised beings. If revival is impossible, reformation is the only alternative open to sensible people, and now it may be asked, what is the principle on which this reformation must be based?

People have very hazy ideas on this subject. It seems to many that it is the outward form which has to be changed, and if this change can be made, they think that all the difficulties in our way will vanish. If we change our outward manners and customs, sit in a particular way or walk in a particular fashion, our work according to them is accomplished. I cannot but think that much of the prejudice against the reformers is due to this misunderstanding. It is not the outward form, but the inward form, the thought and the idea which determines the outward form, that has to be changed if real reformation is desired.

Now what have been the inward forms or ideas which have been hastening our decline during the past three thousand years? These ideas may be briefly set forth as isolation, submission to outward force or power more than to the voice of the inward conscience, perception of fictitious differences between men and men due to heredity and birth, passive acquiescence in evil or wrong doing, and a general indifference to secular well-being, almost bordering upon fatalism. These have been the root ideas of our ancient social system. They have as their natural result led to the existing family arrangements where the woman is entirely subordinated to the man and the lower castes to the higher castes, to the length of depriving men of their natural respect for humanity. All the evils we seek to combat result from the prevalence of these ideas. They are mere corollaries to these axiomatic assumptions. They prevent some of our people from realising what they really are in all conscience, neither better nor worse than their fellows, and that whatever garb men may put on, they are the worse for assuming dignities and powers which do not in fact belong to them. As long as these ideas remain operative on our minds, we may change our outward forms and institutions, and be none the better for the change. These ideas have produced in the long course of ages their results on our character, and we must judge their good or bad quality, as St. Paul says, by the fruits they have borne. Now that these results have been disastrous, nobody disputes or doubts, and the lesson to be drawn for our guidance in the future from this fact is that the current of these ideas must be changed, and in the place of the old worship we paid to them, we must accustom ourselves and others to worship and reverence new ideals. In place of isolation, we must cultivate the spirit of fraternity or elastic expansiveness. At present it is everybody's ambition to pride himself upon being a member of the smallest community that can be conceived, and the smaller the number of those with whom you can dine or marry, or associate, the higher is your perfection and purity, the purest person is he who cooks his own food, and does not allow the shadow of even his nearest friend to fall upon his cooked food. Every caste and every sect has thus a tendency to split itself into smaller castes and smaller sects in practical life. Even in philosophy and religion, it is a received maxim that knowledge is for the few, and that salvation is only possible for the esoteric elect with whom only are the virtues of sanctity and wisdom, and that for the rest of mankind, they must be left to wander in the wilderness, and grovel in superstition, and even vice, with only a colouring of so-called religion to make them respectable. Now all this must be changed. The new mould of thought on this head must be, as stated above, cast on the lines of fraternity, a capacity to expand outwards, and to make more cohesive inwards the bonds of fellowship. Increase the circle of your friends and associates, slowly and cautiously if you will, but the tendency must be towards a general recognition of the essential equality between man and man. It will beget sympathy and power. It will strengthen your own hands, by the sense that you have numbers with you, and not against you, or as you foolishly imagine, below you.

The next idea which lies at the root of our helplessness is the sense that we are always intended to remain children, to be subject to outside control, and never to rise to the dignity of self-control by making our conscience and our reason the supreme, if not the sole, guide to our conduct. All past history has been a terrible witness to the havoc committed by this misconception. We are children, no doubt, but the children of God, and not of man, and the voice of God is the only voice which we are bound to listen. Of course, all of us cannot listen to this voice when we desire it, because from long neglect and dependence upon outside help, we have benumbed this faculty of conscience in us. With too many of us, a thing is true or false, righteous or sinful, simply because somebody in the past has said that it is so. Duties and obligations are duties and obligations, not because we feel them to be so, but because somebody reputed to be wise has laid it down that they are so. In small matters of manners and courtesies, this outside dictation is not without its use. But when we abandon ourselves entirely to this helpless dependence on other wills, it is no wonder that we become helpless as children in all departments of life. Now the new idea which should take up the place of this helplessness and dependence is not the idea of a rebellious overthrow of all authority, but that of freedom responsible to the voice of God in us. Great and wise men in the past, as in the present, have a claim upon our regards, but they must not come between us and our God—the Divine principle enthroned in the heart of every one of us high or low. It is this sense of self-respect, or rather respect for the God in us, which has to be cultivated. It is a very tender plant which takes years and years to make it grow. But there is the capacity and the power, and we owe it as duty to ourselves to undertake the task. Revere all human authority, pay your respects to all prophets and all revelations, but never let this reverence and respect come in the way of the dictates of conscience, the Divine command in us.

Similarly there is no doubt that men differ from men in natural capacities, and aptitudes, and that heredity and birth are factors of considerable importance in our development. But it is at the same time true that they are not the only factors that determine the whole course of our life for good or for evil, under a law of necessity. Heredity and birth explain many things, but this law of Karma does not explain all things! What is worse, it does not explain the mystery that makes man and woman what they really are, the reflection and the image of God. Our passions and our feelings, our pride and our ambition, lend strength to these agencies, and with their help the Law of Karma completes our conquest, and in too many cases enforces our surrender. The new idea that should come in here is that this Law of Karma can be controlled and set back by a properly trained will, when it is made subservient to a higher will than ours. Thus we see in our everyday life, or the Fates are, as our own texts tell us, faint obstacles in the way of our advancement if we devote ourselves to the law of Duty. I admit that this misconception is very hard to remove, perhaps the hardest of the old ideas. But removed it must be, if not in this life or generation, in many lives and generations, if we are ever to rise to our full stature.

The fourth old form or idea to which I will allude here is our acquiescence in wrong or evil-doing as an inevitable condition of human life, about which we need not be very particular. All human life is a vanity and a dream, and we are not much concerned with it. This view of life is in fact atheism in its worst form. No man or woman really ceases to be animal who does not perceive or realise that wrong or evil-doing, impurity and vice, crime and misery, and sin of all kinds, is really our animal existence prolonged. It is the beast in us which blinds us to impurity and vice, and makes them even attractive.

There must be nautches in our temples, say our priests, because even the Gods cannot do without these impure fairies. This is only a typical instance of our acquiescence in impurity. There must be drunkenness in the world, there must be poverty and wretchedness and tyranny, there must be fraud and force, there must be thieves and the law to punish them. No doubt these are facts, and there is no use denying their existence, but in the name of all that is sacred and true, do not acquiesce in them, do not hug these evils to your bosom and cherish them. Their contact is poisonous, not the less deadly because it does not kill, but it corrupts men. A healthy sense of the true dignity of our nature, and of man's high destiny, is the best corrective and antidote to this poison. I think I have said more than enough to suggest to your reflecting minds what it is that we have to reform. All admit that we have been deformed. We have lost our stature, we are bent in a hundred places, our eyes lust after forbidden things, our ears desire to hear scandals about our neighbours, our tongues lust to taste forbidden fruit, our hands itch for another man's property, our bowels are deranged with indigestible food. We cannot walk on our feet, but require stilts or crutches. This is our present social polity, and now we want this deformity to be removed; and the only way to remove it is to place ourselves under the discipline of better ideas and forms such as those I have briefly touched above. Reforms in the matter of infant marriage and enforced widowhood, in the matter of temperance and purity, inter-marriage between castes, the elevation of the low castes, and the re-admission of converts, and the regulation of our endowments and charities, are reforms only so far and no further, as they check the influence of the old ideas, and promote the growth of the new tendencies. The Reformer has to infuse in himself the light and warmth of nature, and he can only do it by purifying and improving himself and his surroundings. He must have his family, village, tribe, and nation recast in other and new moulds, and that is the reason why Social Reform becomes our obligatory duty, and not a mere pastime which might be given up at pleasure. Revival is, as I have said, impossible; as impossible as mass-conversion into other faiths. But even if it were possible, its only use to us would be if the reforms elevated us and our surroundings, if they made us stronger, braver, truer men with all our faculties of endurance and work developed, with all our sympathies fully awakened and refined, and if with our heads and hearts acting in union with a purified and holy will, they made us feel the dignity of our being and the high destiny of our existence, taught us to love all, work with all, and feel for all. This is the Reformer's true work, and this in my opinion is the reason why the Conference meets from year to year, and sounds the harmonies in every ear which can listen to them with advantage.

~

HAR BILAS SARDA

Introducing the Child Marriage Restraint Bill

The condition of women in Indian society had begun to be publicly articulated from the late eighteenth century. One of the most critical issues that a number of reformers addressed was child marriage. The age of marriage of the girl child became the focal point for those who demanded state intervention on this. The colonial state which till 1857 had intervened quite actively in the process of social reform, however, took an increasingly neutral stand and in fact sided with those who argued that the state had no role in the social affairs of the communities. It is against this background that the passing of what is called the Sarda Act in 1929 is historic. Har Bilas Sarda, who had spent his life as a scholar and as an administrator in Ajmer and Agra, introduced the bill in the central legislature and implored the state, which tried to play neutral, to act against child marriage. While introducing the bill in the Imperial Legislative Assembly, he made a strong plea in the form of this speech delivered on 15 September 1927.

... Sir, I rise to move that the Bill to regulate marriages of children amongst the Hindus be taken into consideration.

The primary object of the Bill is to put a stop to child-widowhood. No country in the world, except this unhappy land, presents the sorry spectacle of having in its population child-widows who, according to the customs of the country, cannot remarry. Enforced widowhood is a feature peculiar to Hindu society; and when we consider that some of the victims of this pernicious—I had almost said inhuman—custom were babies eight or ten months old when they were married, Honourable Members will realise how urgent and imperative is the call for legislation in the matter.

The Bill before the House does not attempt to lay down the ages at which boys and girls should marry. For Hindus that was done by their law-giver Manu, who laid down that a girl may marry three years after she attains puberty; and Dhanwantri, the great Hindu authority on the subject, declared that ordinarily girls attained puberty in India at sixteen. The social and domestic environments of the present day have perhaps slightly lowered the age of puberty in India. Yet, according to Manu, who allows marriage three years after puberty, even at the present day the marriageable age of a girl ought not to be below sixteen years.

As it stands, my Bill does not go against the spirit or the letter of any religious behest; for no Sastras, ancient or modern, enjoin that a girl must be married before she attains puberty. And it is an admitted fact that girls do not attain puberty before they are twelve years old. Thus, while it does not come into conflict with any Sastras, the Bill removes what is probably the most oppressive burden under which Hindu womanhood is groaning. The Bill is very modest attempt to recognise that female children even amongst Hindus have certain inalienable rights and that the State with any pretensions to civilisation will deem it its duty to protect them, without heeding the vagaries that masquerade in the guise of social customs.

Sir, a reference to the last Census Report will show how important the matter of the Bill is. That Report says that there were in India in 1921 AD 612 Hindu widows who were babies not even 12 months old; 498 between 1 and 2 years; 1,280 between 2 and 3; 2,863 between 3 and 4; and 6,758 who were between 4 and 5 years of age, making a total of 12,016 widows under 5 years of age. The number of Hindu widows between 5 and 10 years of age was 85,580 and those between 10 and 15, 2,33,533. The total number of widows under 10 was 97,596, and under 15 was 3,31,793. These numbers include Jain and Arya widows, for Jains and Aryas have been separately classed in the Report for political purposes; otherwise they are all Hindus and are governed by the same marriage laws. And if we include Brahmos and Sikhs who are as much Hindus as the so-called Hindus, the total number of Hindu widows under 15 was 3,32,472 in 1921 AD.

The gravity of the question will however be realised when we remember that out of every 1,000 Hindu married women 14 are under 5 years of age, 111 below 10, and 437 under 15 years of age. This means that a little over 11 per cent of the Hindu women are married when they are below 10 years of age, i.e., when they were mere children, and that nearly 44 per cent of them lead married lives when they are less than 15 years of age, i.e., when they are not yet out of their teens and before they have attained true and full puberty and are yet physically quite unfit to bear the strain of maternity.

Sir, the secondary aim of the Bill is to remove the principal impediment to the physical and mental growth of the youth of both sexes and the chief cause of their premature decay and death. The measure, I propose, will help to remove the causes which lead to heavy mortality amongst Hindu married girls. The very high percentage of deaths among them is due to the fact that they are quite immature and are utterly unfit to begin married life when they actually do so. Speaking of the strain imposed on girls by married relations, Dr. Lancaster in his book *Tuberculosis in India*, page 47, says: 'People forget the fearful strain upon the constitution of a delicate girl of fourteen years or less, which results from … the stress of maternity. It is a truism to say that the process connected with reproduction, which, from one point of view, may be regarded as the most important of human functions, should be allowed to take place under the most favourable conditions possible. Surely, it would seem to be of fundamental importance that these processes should be delayed until the body, as a whole, shall have attained its full development and be prepared for this great crisis. For in no other crisis of the life does the ultimate result depend so much upon the physical condition of the body.'

And he pleads: 'Let even so much as two years be conceded, and in place of eighteen years which may be reckoned as the lower limiting age in ordinary cases of marriage in the West, let sixteen years be the age which popular opinion shall regard as the normal one for marriage in this country. The result will be an incalculable gain in the health of the women of India as also in that of the children whom they bear.'

Sir, this is the opinion of an authority on the subject. My Bill falls far short of this aim: it is only a step towards this desideratum.

Leaving this aside—and I confess that I regard this as the most important aspect of the question—I think the Bill deserves the support even of those to whom nothing matters but the political emancipation of the country.

Sir, progress is unity. And if we are to make any advance, and the country is to come into line with, or nearly into line with the progressive countries of the West, or is to become free from their domination, a programme of social reform of a thoroughgoing character, of which the abolition of child marriage will be the principal item, must be taken in hand along with the pursuit of political reform. Much of this social reform is no doubt the domestic or private concern of the people of the country and does not call for legislation. I believe, Sir, that just as the veil, with all that it connotes, has disappeared in the greater part of Turkey and is fast disappearing from the rest of it, so must the *purdah*, the *chauka*, child marriage, enforced widowhood, the ban on inter-dining and inter-marriage, caste in its present rigid and ossified form, and untouchability disappear from India, if we are to be in a position to hold our own in the international conflict of interests, the clash of colour, and the struggle for life that are raging furiously in the world. For, we must remember, that even political emancipation, freedom or Swaraj, by whatever name you call that fact, droppeth not like sweet manna from Heaven. It has to be won. It has to be wrested from unwilling hands; and so long as these evils exist in this country, we will neither have the strength of arm nor the strength of character to win freedom. Once these evils are gone, a spirit will arise in the land which no power on earth will be able to quench; a strength of arm to fight for freedom will be developed, which the might of the mightiest will not be able to resist. I am sure, Sir, that as the day follows the night, so will these evils disappear, and disappear soon. But there are certain matters of a serious nature in which considerations of humanity and the inalienable rights of a human being—and that human being, the innocent and helpless child—call for the immediate intervention of the Legislature. The present Bill, Sir, concerns one of those matters. In order to protect the inalienable rights of the innocent children and to concede to them the right to live their lives, it is necessary that infant marriages and child marriages must come to an end at once and boys and girls grow up unfettered by marital ties and unburdened with family cares, which have not only immensely accelerated the death rate amongst the young married people, especially girls, but have dangerously lowered the vitality of the people, stunted their growth, and barred their way to prosperity and happiness.

Sir, I will say one word more as to the utility of the measure I propose for enactment. The Bill, if passed, will give a real and effective protection to girls, which the Age of Consent Act does not do. That law is a sort of flank attack on the social and physical evil, I might say the crime, of child marriage. The law of the Age of Consent, so far as marital relations are concerned, is a dead letter, and has done little practical good except the slight educative effect which it has had on certain classes of people. The law regarding the Age of Consent has been in existence a pretty long time, yet the last Census Report says: 'There is little evidence in the Census figures to suggest that the practice of infant marriage is dying out.'

How long, Sir, shall we then allow this canker to eat into the vitals of our race? Shall we stand by and see the race sink below the point when regeneration and resuscitation become impossible?

... Sir, Providence, as a just retribution for the woes and sufferings to which our passive acquiescence in the continuance of an evil custom subjects the child widows of this country, has condemned us to centuries of political servitude and national impotence, when in our utter helplessness we have silently to suffer the outrageous insults heaped on our womanhood. Sir, when an insult was offered to the Queen of France, the great Burke in a memorable outburst of impassioned and noble eloquence exclaimed that the age of chivalry had passed, or ten thousand swords would have leapt from their scabbards to avenge that insult.

How fallen are we, and not we alone—pardon my saying so—but also those who having inherited the noble traditions of the English race and being custodians of the honour, the good name and the reputation of this country, allow without a protest the womanhood of India to be so basely traduced and grossly insulted—insulted in a manner which has moved at least one Englishman, a true missionary of Christ, to do public penance in Calcutta for the great crime of a countryman of his.

Sir, if Government have no desire or have not the courage to initiate and carry through legislation prohibiting marriages of girls below twelve years of age, they might very well give at least this private measure their hearty support. But even if the Honourable Home Member is not disposed to do this, as we think the representative of the *Ma Bap* Government, possessing a genuine solicitude for the welfare of the people, ought to do, he will at least take up an attitude of neutrality, release Government members from the mandate handicap and permit them to vote according to their conscience; or, let the fate of the Bill be decided by the vote of the Indian members of this House who are principally affected by it.

I hope Government have noted that all the amendments so far proposed by Honourable Members not only support the Bill, but are directed towards making the provisions of the Bill go much further than I have ventured to do.

... Before I resume my seat, I respectfully and with all the earnestness that I can command, invite the attention of Honourable Members on both sides of the House to the touching appeal of Mahatma Gandhi made at Madras on the 7th September 1927, for the abolition of child-widowhood. He said that there was no warrant for this kind of widowhood in Hinduism; and he exclaimed with intense grief and agony of mental pain, 'I have often said in secret to God; If you want me to live, Oh God, why do you make me a witness to these tragedies?'

4

NATIONALISM ON THE MARCH

At a time when several non-European nations were exhibiting signs of a new assertiveness (Abyssinia had defeated Italy in 1896 while tiny Japan had vanquished powerful Russia in 1905), Indians were witness to a heightened sense of racial arrogance on the part of the British bureaucracy. Lord Lytton's and Lord Curzon's viceroyalties became the byword for such arrogance. In the light of this, Annie Besant, Rajendralal Mitra, Bal Gangadhar Tilak, Bankim Chandra Chatterjee and, above all, Vivekananda took it upon themselves to assert the moral, spiritual and civilizational superiority of India. A new generation of leaders, which included Bipin Chandra Pal, Aurobindo Ghose and Ashwini Kumar Dutt in Bengal, Ajit Singh and Lala Lajpat Rai in Punjab, G. Subramanian Iyer, N.K. Ramaswamy Iyer, C. Vijayaraghavachariar, T. Prakasham and M. Krishan Rao in Madras, worked tirelessly towards generating confidence and creating an upsurge of nationalist feelings among their fellow countrymen.

The era also saw new ways of articulating political desire. The 'moderate' tone of the earlier generation began to be criticized and the new generation began looking for fresh ways and means. Passive resistance, swadeshi, swaraj and national education became buzzwords for this impatient generation. These new ideas in some ways grew out of the work done by the previous generation which had hoped that their ideas would be disseminated and discussed and would raise the consciousness of the common man.

It was in order to strike a blow at the growing political assertiveness primarily in Bengal that the province was partitioned in 1905. A new province was created by amalgamating the eastern part of Bengal with Assam. It was argued that Bengal had become too large and unwieldy for efficient administration. But the real reason behind the move, as revealed by regular official pronouncements since 1903, was to weaken the growing nationalist sentiment in Bengal. The partition, however, provided a fillip to a new breed of nationalists. It gave birth to a new movement, the swadeshi movement, which began officially from 7 August 1905. Boycott of foreign goods and government schools became the prime modes of protest. National schools and swadeshi manufacturing units were opened. On 16 October 1905, when the partition was to come into effect, large numbers of people in Bengal fasted and, at the suggestion of Rabindranath Tagore, tied rakhis on each other's wrist as a mark of solidarity. People took out processions singing patriotic songs written by Tagore and others. The swadeshi movement spread to other parts of the country and provided the first spurt of nationalist activity in Assam, Orissa and Punjab.

The new leaders of the swadeshi movement demanded a more assertive Congress. The early nationalists, however, saw any move challenging the colonial state at this juncture as disastrous not only for the Congress but also for the social reform process that the Congress had initiated. Public agitation was still not part of their political vocabulary. This was not because they belonged to the educated elite or middle classes and thus found such public displays lacking in decorum. It was more due to their perception of the colonial state and their lack of understanding of the political mood of the new generation.

At the annual session in Benares in 1905, the new leaders succeeded in making the Congress adopt swadeshi, boycott of foreign goods and national education as its policies. In 1906, swaraj, in terms of dominion status within the British Empire, was adopted as the goal of the Congress. Now the new leaders, termed 'extremists', wanted to push the moderates out of the Congress. This proved to be disastrous and finally led to the split in the Congress in 1907 during the Surat session. The extremists were ousted from the Congress. The colonial state, taking advantage of the situation, came down heavily on the extremist leaders. Tilak was imprisoned and sent to Mandalay jail in Burma. Moderate leaders, out of tune with reality, began losing popular sympathy.

Parallel to the swadeshi movement and the growth of the new group within the Congress, nationalist politics of the era also witnessed individual acts of terrorism by Khudiram Bose, Aurobindo and Barindra Ghose, Rashbihari Bose, Sachin Sanyal, Ajit Singh, Madanlal Dhingra and Damodar Savarkar, which captured the imagination of the youth in the country. Khudiram Bose and Prafulla Chaki, who hurled a bomb at the magistrate of Muzaffarpur, but unfortunately killed two innocent ladies, became household names when Khudiram was hanged. Rashbihari Bose and Sachin Sanyal hurled a bomb at the viceroy's carriage, hurting Lord Hardinge and others.

Notwithstanding their unalloyed sense of patriotism, the extremists' use of cultural symbols like Shivaji, Ganesh or that of Goddess Kali for organizational or inspirational purposes, along with a lack of concern for the peasantry and absence of any social programme would, in the long run, act as impediments to their ideological development as well as to their organizational growth. But that their actions gave a fresh impetus to the people's demand for freedom cannot be denied.

By the first decade of the new century, another vibrant movement had begun to take shape among the Indians who were travelling or settled abroad. This was the Ghadar movement. Ramnath Puri, G.D. Kumar, Tarak Nath Das and others, with the help of Indians settled in North America, had been, since 1905-06, circulating ideas advocating a free Hindustan. With the arrival of Lala Hardayal in 1911, a movement grew with centres in the west coast of USA. Named after its newspaper, *Ghadar* (Revolution), it became the focus of anti-colonial sentiments among the large Indian population settled in the US and in east Asian countries. The Ghadar revolutionaries wanted to bring revolution in India, and for this they invited Rashbihari Bose to organize and lead the scattered revolutionaries. Bose came to Punjab and, after organizing people, fixed 21 February 1915 as the date for the revolution. It was later changed to 19 February. But the government found out about the plan and suppressed the Ghadar revolutionaries. Forty-five people were hanged while hundreds were imprisoned. The revolutionary vision of the Ghadarites, however, left a permanent imprint on the minds of the people in Punjab and the rest of India.

During the First World War, the Home Rule movement led by Annie Besant and Tilak tried to inspire the scattered nationalist forces into action. Influenced by the Irish movement for home rule, it demanded home rule in India on the ground that Indians were now responsible and capable of managing their affairs on their own. The Home Rule leagues of Tilak (1915) and Besant (1916) enlisted volunteers and published pamphlets in which the demands, the reasons and the modes of the movement were articulated. By 1917, Tilak's leagues in Karnataka, the Central Provinces, Bengal and the United Provinces had 14,000 volunteers while Annie Besant's league, which propagated the Home Rule ideas through two weeklies, *New India* and *Commonweal*, had 7000 volunteers. A number of future leaders of India, including Jawaharlal Nehru and M.A. Jinnah, had their first political lessons as volunteers and supporters of these leagues. The popularity of the movement and the radical tones which it gradually acquired rattled the government. It responded by arresting Besant in early 1917, an act which raised a storm of protest. She was released in September 1917 and, on the request of Tilak, was elected president of the Congress later that year.

Tilak and Besant wanted to revive the Congress by involving it in the Home Rule movement. The movement initiated many from the educated youth in small towns into the political life of the country. Home Rule volunteers came in large numbers to the Lucknow session of the Congress in 1916, where the Congress and Muslim League met. Tilak played a crucial role in cementing the Congress–League pact for electoral representation, popularly known as communal representation. It seemed like a radical solution at that point but eventually proved to be one of the stumbling blocks in the development of the national movement.

~

SWAMI VIVEKANANDA

Assertion of Universality

On 11 September 1893, representatives of all the major religions of the world came together in Chicago for the World's Parliament of Religions, probably the first gathering of its kind in the world. Vivekananda (1863–1902), an unknown swami from Bengal, spoke at this congregation. A speech claiming a universal and eternal character for the world's oldest religion, Hinduism, by a representative of a subject people was an entirely new and exciting idea for those who had gathered there. Since the early nineteenth century, Christian missionaries had relentlessly attacked both Islam and Hinduism, resulting in a double-bind inferiority complex—political subjugation as well as religious insecurities. It was precisely against such attacks on Islam by Christian missionaries that Raja Rammohun Roy had written his masterpiece, Tuhfat-al-muwahiddin, *defending the monotheism of Islam. Vivekananda's speech can be viewed in the context of not only such a complex but also against the backdrop of rising nationalist temper in Asia. These two speeches—Vivekananda delivered the second speech on 27 September 1893 in the final session—give a flavour of the historically significant moment.*

I. Response to Welcome

Sisters and Brothers of America, it fills my heart with joy unspeakable to rise in response to the warm and cordial welcome which you have given us. I thank you in the name of the most ancient order of monks in the world; I thank you in the name of the mother of religions; I thank you in the name of millions and millions of Hindu people of all classes and sects.

My thanks, also, to some of the speakers on this platform who, referring to the delegates from Orient, have told you that these men from far-off nations may well claim the honour of bearing to different lands the idea of toleration. I am proud to belong to a religion which has taught the world both tolerance and universal acceptance. We believe not only in universal toleration, but we accept all religions as true. I am proud to belong to a nation which has sheltered the persecuted and the refugees of all religions and nations of the earth. I am proud to tell you that we have gathered in our bosom the purest remnant of the Israelites, who came to Southern India and took refuge with us in the very year in which their holy temple was shattered to pieces by Roman tyranny. I am proud to belong to the religion which has sheltered and is still fostering the remnant of the grand Zoroastrian nation. I will quote to you, brethren, a few lines from a hymn which I remember to have repeated from my earliest boyhood, which is every day repeated by millions of human beings: 'As the different streams having their sources in different places all mingle their water in the sea, sources in different tendencies, various though they appear, crooked or straight, all lead to Thee.'

The present convention, which is one of the most august assemblies ever held, is in itself a vindication, a declaration to the world of the wonderful doctrine preached in the Gita: 'Whosoever comes to Me, through whatsoever form, I reach him; all men are struggling through paths which in the end lead to Me.' Sectarianism, bigotry, and its horrible descendant, fanaticism, have long possessed this beautiful earth. They have filled the earth with violence, drenched it often and often with human blood, destroyed civilisation and sent whole nations to despair. Had it not been for these horrible demons, human society would be far more advanced than it is now. But their time is come; and I fervently hope that the bell that tolled this morning in honour of this convention may be the death-knell of all fanaticism, of all persecutions with the sword or with the pen, and of all uncharitable feelings between persons wending their way to the same goal.

II. Address at the Final Session

The World's Parliament of Religions has become an accomplished fact, and the merciful Father has helped those who laboured to bring it into existence, and crowned with success their most unselfish labour.

My thanks to those noble souls whose large hearts and love of truth first dreamed this unfearful dream and then realised it. My thanks to the shower of liberal sentiments that has overflowed this platform. My thanks to this enlightened audience for their uniform kindness to me and for their appreciation of every thought that tends to smooth the friction of religions. A few jarring notes were heard from time to time in this harmony. My special thanks to them, for they have, by their striking contrast, made general harmony the sweeter.

Much has been said of the common ground of religious unity. I am not going just now to venture my own theory. But if anyone here hopes that this unity will come by the triumph of any one of the religions and the destruction of others, to him I say, 'Brother, yours is an impossible hope.' Do I wish that the Christian would become Hindu? God forbid. Do I wish that the Hindu or Buddhist would become Christian? God forbid.

The seed is put in the ground, and earth and air and water are placed around it. Does the seed become the earth, or the air, or the water? No. It becomes a plant, it develops after the law of its own growth, assimilates the air, the earth, and the water, converts them into plant substance, and grows into a plant.

Similar is the case with religion. The Christian is not to become a Hindu or a Buddhist, nor a Hindu or a Buddhist to become a Christian. But each must assimilate the spirit of the others and yet preserve his individuality and grow according to his own law of growth.

If the Parliament of Religions has shown anything to the world it is this: It has proved to the world that holiness, purity and charity are not the exclusive possessions of any church in the world, and that every system has produced men and women of the most exalted character. In the face of this evidence, if anybody dreams of the exclusive survival of his own religion and the destruction of the others, I pity him from the bottom of my heart, and point out to him that upon the banner of every religion will soon be written, in spite of resistance: 'Help and not Fight', 'Assimilation and not Destruction', 'Harmony and Peace and not Dissension'.

~

ANANDA MOHAN BOSE

A National Awakening

Born in Mymensingh, now in Bangladesh, Ananda Mohan Bose (1847–1906) was one of the foremost nationalists in Bengal who combined his zeal for the Brahmo Samaj with his brilliance at the Bar. As secretary of the Indian Association, which he founded with Surendranath Banerjea in 1876, Bose convened a 'national conference' in December 1883 in Calcutta to discuss 'the burning questions' of the day. This became a precursor to the formation of the Indian National Congress in 1885. In 1905, the partition of Bengal roused him literally from his deathbed. The memorable speech reproduced here was delivered on 16 October 1905, the day the foundation stone of the Federation Hall at Calcutta was laid, symbolizing the unity of the people. It is probably the last public speech by this brilliant orator.

My beloved friends, Mahomedan and Hindu fellow-citizens of one and indivisible Bengal... I come amongst you as one almost risen from the dead to see this moment of a national upheaval and of national awakening. Drawn from my sick-bed, where I have been secluded from the world by serious illness for nearly a year, allow me to express my grateful thanks to you for the great and the signal privilege you have conferred on me by associating me with yourselves on this great and historic occasion, which will live in the annals of Bengal and mark an epoch in its history. I see around me after a long time the faces of many dear friends and comrades, who have been in the front of the fight, I salute them and I salute you all on this day of solemn recollections and solemn resolves.

It is, indeed, a day of mourning to us when the province has been sundered by official fiat, and the gladsome spirit of union and of community of interest which had been growing stronger day by day, runs the danger of being wrecked and destroyed, and many other evils into which this is not the occasion to enter are likely to follow in its wake. And yet in the dispensation of Providence not unoften out of evil cometh good; and the dark and threatening cloud before us is so fringed with beauteous gold and brightening beams, and so fraught with the prospect of a newer and a stronger national union, that we may look upon it almost as a day of rejoicing. Yes, as our glorious poet has sung in one of his many noble and inspiring utterances, 'Ebar Tor Mora Gange Baan Eseche', the dead, current-less and swampy river has felt the full force and fury of the flood and is swelling in its depths. Have we not all heard the booming of that national call, and its solemn summons to our hearts? Let our souls mount forth in gladness to the throne of the Most High at the sacred fatal hour of the new and united Bengali nation.

... And this Federation Hall, the foundation stone of which is being laid to-day not only on this spot of land, but on our moistened, tearful hearts, is the embodiment and visible symbol of this spirit of union, the memorial to future generations yet unborn, of this unhappy day and of the unhappy policy which has attempted to separate us into two parts.

... I rejoice from my heart that this ceremony is presently to be followed by an inauguration for furthering and consolidating the industrial development of the country, on which depends the material-salvation of millions in this land. And yet the two inaugurations are not separate, but one, and like the sacred Ganges and the holy Jumna they will commingle their waters and unite their waves in one merry march to the azure sea.

... And now, farewell my friends with these, which may, perchance, be the last words which I shall utter to you on the side of eternity. Farewell on this day of fraternal union, when the bond of Rakhi is tied in our arms. Much that comes pouring into my heart must remain unsaid. Ours is not the land of the rising sun, for to Japan, victorious, self-sacrificing and magnanimous, belongs that title: but may I not say that ours is the land where the sun is rising again, where after ages of darkness and gloom, with the help (let me gratefully acknowledge) of England and English culture, the glowing light is bursting once again over the face of the land. Let us all pray that the grace of God may bless our course, direct our steps, and steel our hearts. Let action, and not words, be our motto and inspiring guide. And then shall my dream be realised of a beauteous land, blessed by nature, and filled by men true and manly, and heroic in every good cause—true children of the motherland. Let us see in our heart of hearts the Heavens opening and the angels descending. In ancient books, the gods are described as showering flowers and garlands on the scene of a notable battle. See we not, my friends, those flowers dropped to-day from selfsame hands, welcoming us to the new battle, not of blood, but manly effort and stern resolve in the country's cause?

And Thou, Oh God of this ancient land, the protector and saviour of Aryavrata and the merciful Father of us all, by whatever name we call upon. Thee be with us on this day, and, as a father gathereth his children under his arms, do Thou gather us under Thy protecting and sanctifying care.

~

BAL GANGADHAR TILAK

Tenets of the New Party

Bal Gangadhar Tilak delivered a lecture at a students' meeting held at College Square, Calcutta, on 4 January 1907. Bipin Chandra Pal was in the chair. Tilak spoke about the differences between the two main groups within the Congress—the Extremists and the Moderates—and indicated that these differences were not so much in ideals, as in methods. The new party, started by Lala Lajpat Rai, Tilak and Bipin Chandra Pal—the trio popularly referred to as Lal-Bal-Pal—stressed the need of the fourfold programme, namely, swaraj, swadeshi, boycott and national education. In fact, Tilak's speech hinted at what later came to be regarded as Gandhian ideals and programmes. In this sense, the Indian freedom struggle had a continuously developing programme which each successive generation tried to take forward.

Two new words have recently come into existence with regard to our politics, and they are Moderates and Extremists. These words have a specific relation to time, and they, therefore, will change with time. The Extremists of today will be Moderates tomorrow, just as the Moderates of today were Extremists yesterday. When the National Congress was first started and Mr. Dadabhai's views, which now go for Moderates, were given to the public, he was styled an Extremist, so that you will see that the term extremist is an expression of progress. We are Extremists today and our sons will call themselves Extremists and us Moderates. Every new Party begins as Extremists and ends as Moderates. The sphere of practical politics is not unlimited. We cannot say what will or will not happen 1000 years hence; perhaps during that long period the whole of the white race will be swept away in another glacial period. We must, therefore, study the present and work out a programme to meet the present condition.

It is impossible to go into details within the time at my disposal. One thing is granted, viz. that this Government does not suit us. As has been said by an eminent statesman—the government of one country by another can never be a successful, and therefore, a permanent government. There is no difference of opinion about this fundamental proposition between the Old and New Schools. One fact is that the alien government has ruined the country. In the beginning, all of us were taken by surprise. We were almost dazed. We thought that everything that the rulers did was for our good and that this English Government has descended from the clouds to save us from the invasions of Tamerlane and Chengiz Khan, and, as they say, not only from foreign invasions but from internecine warfare, or the internal or external invasions, as they call it. We felt happy for a time, but it soon came to light that the peace which was established in this country did this, as Mr. Dadabhai has said in one place—that we were prevented from going at each other's throats, so that a foreigner might go at the throats of us all. Pax Britannica has been established in this country in order that a foreign government may exploit the country. That this is the effect of this Pax Britannica is being gradually realised in these days.

It was an unhappy circumstance that it was not realised sooner. We believed in the benevolent intentions of the government, but in politics there is no benevolence. Benevolence is used to sugarcoat the declarations of self-interest, and we were in those days deceived by the apparent benevolent intentions under which rampant self-interest was concealed. That was our state then. But soon a change came over us. English education, growing poverty and better familiarity with our rulers opened our eyes and our leaders, especially the venerable leader who presided over the recent Congress, were the first to tell us that the drain of the country was ruining it, and if the drain was to continue, there was some great disaster awaiting us. So terribly convinced was he of this that he went over from here to England and spent twenty-five years of his life in trying to convince the English people of the injustice that is being done to us. He worked very hard. He had conversations and interviews with Secretaries of State, with Members of Parliament and with what result?

He has come here at the age of eighty-two to tell us that he is bitterly disappointed. Mr. Gokhale, I know, is not disappointed. He is a friend of mine and I believe that this is his honest conviction. Mr. Gokhale is not disappointed but is ready to wait another twenty years till he is disappointed like Mr. Dadabhai.

He is young, younger than myself, and I can very well see that disappointment cannot come in a single interview, from interviews which have lasted only for a year or so. If Dadabhai is disappointed, what reason is there that Gokhale shall not, after twenty years? It is said there is a revival of Liberalism, but how long will it last? Next year, it might be, they are out of power, and are we to wait till there is another revival of Liberalism, and then again if that goes down, and a third revival of Liberalism takes place; and after all, what can a Liberal Government do? I will quote the observation of the father of the Congress, Mr. A.O. Hume. This was made in 1893. Let the Government be Liberal or Conservative, rest sure that they will not yield to you willingly anything. The Liberal Government means that the Government or the members of the Government are imbued with Liberal principles because they want to have the administration of their country conducted on those principles. They are Liberals in England, but I have seen Liberals in England come out to India to get into Conservative ways.

A statesman is bound to look to the present circumstances and see what particular concessions are absolutely necessary, and what is theoretically true or wrong. He has to take into consideration both the sides. There are the interested Anglo-Indians and the Secretary of State is the head of the Anglo-Indian bureaucracy whose mouthpiece he is. Do you mean to say that when the whole bureaucracy, the whole body of Anglo-Indians, is against you, the Secretary of State will set aside the whole bureaucracy and give you rights? Has he the power? If he does, will he not be told to walk away? So then it comes to this, that the whole British electorate must be converted. So you are going to convert all persons who have a right to vote in England, so as to get the majority on your side; and when this is done, and when by that majority the Liberal party is returned to Parliament and bent upon doing good to India and it appoints a Secretary of State as good as Morley, then you hope to get something by the old methods.

The New Party has realised this position. The whole electorate of Great Britain must be converted by lectures. You cannot touch their pocket or interest; and that man must be a fool indeed who would sacrifice his own interest on hearing a philosophical lecture.

The New Party perceives that this is futile. To convert the whole electorate of England to your opinion and then to get indirect pressure upon the Members of Parliament, they in their turn to return a Cabinet favourable to India, and the whole Parliament, the Liberal party and the Cabinet bringing pressure on the bureaucracy to yield—we say this is hopeless. You can now understand the difference between the Old and the New parties. Appeals to the bureaucracy are hopeless. On this point both the New and Old parties are agreed. The Old Party believes in appealing to the British nation and we do not. That being our position, it logically follows we must have some other method. There is another alternative. We are not going to sit down quiet. We shall have some other method by which to achieve what we want. We are not disappointed, we are not pessimists. It is the hope of achieving the goal by our own efforts that has brought into existence this New Party.

There is no empire lost by a free grant of concessions by the rulers to the ruled. History does not record any such event. Empires are lost by luxury, being too much bureaucratic, overconfident, or from other reasons. But an empire has never come to an end by the rulers conceding power to the ruled.

The New Party wishes to put a stop to this. We have come forward with a scheme which if you accept shall better enable you to remedy this state of things than the scheme of the old school. Your industries are ruined utterly, ruined by foreign rule; your wealth is going out of the country and you are reduced to the lowest level which a human being can occupy. In this state of things, is there any other remedy by which you can help yourself? The remedy is not petitioning but boycott. We say, prepare your forces, organise your power, and then go to work so that they cannot refuse you what you demand. A story in Mahabharata tells that Shri Krishna was sent to effect compromise, but the Pandavas and Kauravas were both organising their forces to meet the contingency of failure of a compromise. This is politics.

Are you prepared in this way to fight if your demand is refused? If you are, be sure you will not be refused; but if you are not, nothing can be more certain than that your demand will be refused and perhaps, for ever. We are not armed, and there is no necessity for arms either. We have a stronger weapon, a political weapon, in boycott. We have perceived one fact, that the whole of this administration, which is carried on by a handful of Englishmen, is carried on with our assistance. We are all in subordinate service. The whole Government is carried on with our assistance and they try to keep us in ignorance of our power of cooperation between ourselves by which that which is in our own hands at present can be claimed by us and administered by us. The point is to have the entire control in our hands. I want to have the key of my house, and not merely one stranger turned out of it. Self-government is our goal; we want a control over our administrative machinery. We do not want to become clerks and remain. At present, we are clerks and willing instruments of our own oppression in the hands of an alien Government, and that Government is ruling over us not by its innate strength but by keeping us in ignorance and blindness to the perception of this fact. Professor Seely shares this view. Every Englishman knows that they are a mere handful in this country and it is the business of every one of them to befool you in believing that you are weak and they are strong. This is politics.

We have been deceived by such a policy so long. What the New Party wants you to do is to realise the fact that your future rests entirely in your own hands. If you mean to be free, you can be free, if you do not mean to be free, you will fall and be forever fallen. So many of you need not like arms; but if you have not the power of active resistance, have you not the power of self-denial and self-abstinence in such a way as not to assist this foreign Government to rule over you? This is boycott, and this is what is meant when we say, boycott is a political weapon.

We shall not give them assistance to collect revenue and keep peace. We shall not assist them in fighting beyond the frontiers or outside India with Indian blood and money. We shall not assist them in carrying on the administration of justice. We shall have our own courts, and when time comes we shall not pay taxes. Can you do that by your united efforts? If you can, you are free from tomorrow.

Some gentlemen who spoke this evening referred to half-bread as against the whole bread. I say I want the whole bread and that immediately. But if I cannot get the whole, do not think that I have no patience. I will take the half they give me, and then try for remainder. This is the line of thought and action in which you must train yourself. We have not raised this cry from a mere impulse. It is a reasoned impulse. Try to understand that reason and try to strengthen that impulse by your logical convictions. I do not ask you to blindly follow us. Think over the whole problem for yourselves. If you accept our advice, we feel sure we can achieve our salvation thereby. This is the advice of the New Party. Perhaps we have not obtained a full recognition of our principles. Old prejudices die very hard. Neither of us wanted to wreck the Congress, so we compromised, and were satisfied that our principles were recognised, and only to a certain extent. That does not mean that we have accepted the whole situation. We may have a step in advance next year, so that within a few years our principles will be recognised, and recognised to such an extent that 'the generations who come' after us may consider us as moderates. This is the way in which a nation progresses. This is the way national sentiment progresses, and this is the lesson you have to learn from the struggle now going on. This is a lesson of Progress, a lesson of helping yourself as much as possible, and if you really perceive the force of it, if you are convinced by these arguments, then and then only it is possible for you to effect your salvation from alien rule under which you labour at this moment.

~

LALA LAJPAT RAI

Swadeshi

Popularly known as Punjab Kesari *or the 'lion of the Punjab', Lala Lajpat Rai (1865–1928) led the protests against the Jallianwala Bagh massacre and the non-cooperation movement in Punjab. A fiery orator, a good organizer, and a prolific and versatile writer, Lajpat Rai was one of the three (with B.C. Pal and B.G. Tilak) who headed the 'extremist' faction of the Congress. He died as a result of injuries suffered in a brutal police lathi charge while protesting against the Simon Commission. The speech reproduced here was delivered at the All India Swadeshi Conference in Surat in 1907. Earlier, at the annual session of the Congress at Surat, where the new forces first came into prominence, the leadership under Pherozeshah Mehta tried to prevent the 'extremists' from taking centre stage as this, they argued, would be detrimental to the interests of the Congress and its movement. Lala Lajpat Rai was elected the undisputed leader of the extremists and was put up as the candidate for the post of president of the Congress against the wishes of the leadership. Conscious of the fact that such a course would weaken the movement, Lala Lajpat Rai declined to face the election. He presided over the India Swadeshi Conference, and his speech on the occasion gives a detailed picture of the political scenario of the country.*

Even if I had a hundred lives to sacrifice in the service of my country, they could furnish but poor opportunities of my doing adequate justice to the honour and esteem that I have been shown the last five weeks. They have touched the deepest chords of my heart, and have brightened my vision of the future of my countrymen. The extraordinary outburst of feeling for individuals which has found expression during the last two years throughout the length and breadth of our country, is undoubtedly a striking and new spectacle. It cannot be satisfactorily explained by the public services of these men although some of them have rendered eminent services to the country. It cannot be said of all and least of all, a humble individual like myself.

In my eyes, this outburst of feeling has a deeper reason than the services of individuals. It is one indication of the growing consciousness of the national unity. India was hitherto said to be only a geographical expression. It has now begun to aspire, under the guidance of an All-Wise Providence to a unified political existence, and to a place in the comity of nations. The congeries of nations that are said to inhabit this vast territory have, after a long period of disunion and disorganisation, begun to realise that, after all, they are one people with one common blood running through their veins, with common traditions, common history and a common faith in their future. It is true that communities are divided from communities, sects from sects, and Provinces from Provinces, by differences of religion, language and customs. The wave of Western civilisation, however, with its unifying influence, is levelling down these differences and creating a community of interest and feeling which is the precursor of a new dawn in our life. Some time ago, people began to look back and find that with all their differences, they were, after all, the branches of a common tree, the descendants of the same stock, the inheritors of the same civilisation, with local differences only. Practically they were the speakers of the same language. Even Mahomedans, taken as a whole, could not say that in their traditions, languages and customs, they had nothing in common with the Hindus. This looking backwards made them compare their present position with the position of their people in other parts of the world, and led them to look forward. Thus was awakened the national consciousness which, for want of greater occasions, has begun to exhibit itself in demonstrations and ovations in honour of individuals, who have even by slight sacrifices earned the distinction of being the servants of the country. Interpreting these ovations in this sense, I feel I have every reason to rejoice over them.

I join with you in congratulating myself as being the fortunate recipient of these marks of honour and respect, for which I thank you most sincerely and through you the other classes of my countrymen.

It has, however, been dinned into my ears ever since I reached Lahore and was once more a comparatively free man, that a large number of my countrymen had betrayed me, that my deportation was due principally to Mahomedan machinations, that a number of Hindu gentlemen also had combined, consciously or unconsciously to bring about what they considered to be the ruin of the cause that I had at heart, that a large number of my friends and co-workers deserted me in the hour of my troubles and purchased their safety, either by ignoring me or by disowning me and my principles. I am told that under the circumstances, the political amelioration of the country is a hopeless task, for which I need waste no more of my time and energies. I am further told that in the light of the experience of the last six months, it is futile to base any hope of political salvation upon the union of Hindus and Mahomedans, that such union is impossible, that our people are an inert mass having no life to assert, and too ignorant to understand their rights and that the leading men are mostly corrupt, selfish, ease loving and cowardly, that while talking loudly of political emancipation and liberty, they are wanting in the courage of their convictions, and are not prepared to suffer for the ideas, that the political ideas that obtain in the educated party, and their conception of political right were entirely foreign, borrowed bodily from the West without any reference to their suitability to the genius and traditions of the nation, and that, under the circumstances, the best interests of our people lie in directions other than political, and that we should be contented with the sort of Government we have got, and should studiously avoid doing anything that may be offensive to the authorities.

True to their instincts and traditions, our enemies are trying to bring about schism amongst the patriotic party. Unfortunately, their efforts have already met with success, and a deplorable schism has already taken place which is extremely painful and humiliating to every patriotic Indian. For some time to come the efforts of every true son of India will have to be directed to bring about a reconciliation amongst brothers that have for the present parted. The latest move is to play the Moderates against the Extremists and vice versa. To tell you the truth I do not know whether these words truly represent the principles of the parties that are called after these names. I, for one do not like these names. But if these words are to stick to us, I would beg of my Moderate friends not to play into the hands of the enemies for to do so will be, in the words of the Hon'ble Mr Gokhale, to make confusion worse confounded. It may be that some of the so-called Extremist methods are not to their liking, but for that reason to give them over to the enemy and to force them into the position of perpetual opponents by slighting them or holding them to the persecution of the Government and to the ridicule of the Anglo-Indian will not be wisdom. It would eventually involve us in difficulties and controversies which might exhaust all the time and energy available for national work. To my Extremist friends, I would respectfully appeal not to be impatient of slowness of age and voice of practical experience...

In any case, it is absolutely necessary to observe and maintain discipline in public life. Without it we may be only confounding chaos with progress. I would, therefore, beg of you to do nothing which would hamper the growth of responsible public life in the country. My Moderate and Extremist friends will not, I hope, misunderstand me. I do not say that they have done anything to deserve my remarks. Mine is only a danger signal.

One word more and I have done. The country is now in the grip of a dire famine. The nation that we aspire to serve mostly lives in huts and cottages, and is in great distress. The Government is doing its duty or at any rate professes to do it, in providing relief to the unfortunate victims of famine. Shall we, the blood of their blood, lag behind and do nothing to relieve the distress of the aged and the poor? The highest dictates of patriotism require that our sympathies should go forth to the help of the destitute and the wretched, and that by sharing what has been given to us with our countrymen in distress we should conclusively establish our claims to speak for them and to demand their cooperation with us in the ensuing struggle. Our claims to their regard and love should be based upon substantial services and not merely on lip sympathy expressed in paper resolutions. I, therefore, appeal to any friends and co-workers, to put their shoulders to the wheel, to organise a non-official famine relief campaign in the famine-affected Provinces to collect funds, and to carry sympathy and help to all homes and places in need of the same. The young, the aged and the women, specially called to us for help and it will be a shame if we decline to respond to this call and spend the whole stock of our energies in academic controversies and wordy warfare. I know that work is tremendous, and that the difficulties are still more so. But it affords the most useful and most effective training for disinterested patriotic life. Even partial success in this direction will be a very valuable moral asset, and an object lesson to those who have to continue the work after us.

~

BIPIN CHANDRA PAL

The New Movement

Bipin Chandra Pal (1858–1932) was in a way the voice of the new nationalist mission like Surendranath Banerjea was for the earlier phase. His visit to south India in 1907 and his lectures in Madras fired the imagination of and informed and influenced a large number of educated people in the region and gave the national movement a pan-Indian character. Fresh from the swadeshi agitation in Bengal, Pal introduced the people of south India to the idea of swadeshi and swaraj, the slogans of the movement that began with the partition of Bengal. Part of a series of lectures delivered by him in Madras in 1907, this speech is historic in the way it contextualized the national movement till 1907 and anticipated future political movements led by people like Gandhi.

When, at the close of the last Session of the Indian National Congress in Calcutta (1906), I was asked to come over here (Madras) on a short lecturing tour, and when in response to that kind invitation I agreed to do so, I did not expect the demonstration that I witnessed while progressing along with you in a procession. I refuse to accept it as a procession organised in my honour, and, therefore, I say I was not prepared for the demonstration that I saw. It was not in honour of any particular individual, but of the ideals of *Swadeshi* and *Swaraj* (cries of *Vande Mataram*), to which reference has already been made by my friend in the chair. Nor did I expect such a large gathering as I see before me. I was fortunate enough to address very large audiences in Madras on previous occasions, but this audience I am called upon to face this evening is absolutely out of all proportion to what experience I had even in your enthusiastic city, four to five years ago. This is a proof, Sir, I take it, not merely of the idle curiosity of the people of this great city, (cries of 'certainly not') but I take it—and I am glad of that assurance—that it is a proof at least of the interest that has been awakened among my countrymen here in the New Movement that has already commenced to bring about mighty transformations in the thoughts and ideals of our countrymen all over this great Indian continent. (Hear, hear.)

What is this New Movement? You read in the newspapers the outer manifestations of this movement. You have come to identify this movement with Swadeshi; you have come to identify this movement with something more than Lord Minto's 'honest' Swadeshi; you have come to identify it with Swadeshi that is organically related to boycott; (Hear, hear.) you have come to identify this movement with the new ideal of Swaraj; you have come to identify this movement also, as your chairman told you, with the Partition of Bengal. (Hear, hear.) You see ripples of this movement in the outbreak of lawlessness in the Eastern Provinces; first, in the outbreak of lawlessness by those who are paid by the people of this country (hear, hear and cries of shame) to help in the preservation of law and order. (Cries of shame.) You saw the ripple of this new movement in the kind of lawlessness last year about this time in Barisal. (Cries of shame.) You, I believe, recognised also the outer ripples of this movement in the present outburst of lawlessness in another shape, viz., in the outburst of Mahomedan vandalism in parts of East Bengal. You have come to identify this movement with the incarceration of your young men and old men also, with the arrests of popular leaders (cries of shame) in different parts of Bengal. You have come to identify it with the regulation sticks of the police and the *Vande Mataram* sticks of the people. I know all this; and you also know all these things. But I do not care just now to speak of those outer ripples. They are merely the manifestations of a force that is flowing through the very heart of the nation. They are the outermost fringe, as it were, the outermost course of the mighty currents that have commenced to stir to their very depths the still waters of Indian national life. Some time ago an

English gentleman, a retired Anglo-Indian official, wrote to a friend of mine in Calcutta, wanting to know the inwardness of the New Movement in Bengal. I desire to speak a few words to you this evening on this inwardness of the New Movement.

Partition and the Unity of Bengal

What is this movement due to? What are the forces of its strength and inspiration? What are the forces that lie hidden at the root of this movement? What is it that this movement desires to achieve and how does it propose to achieve that end? Reference, gentlemen, has been made to the Partition of Bengal. Allow me to tell you that the significance of that measure has been considerably exaggerated outside Bengal. It has been, I confess, exaggerated also to some extent even by a section of the Bengali press. The Partition was an evil measure, the Partition was a hateful measure. The Bengalis hated to be divided from their own people, the Eastern Province from the Western Province. We have been living together for how many centuries past nobody knows; we have developed a peculiar culture of our own through a common language and a common literature. Belonging though no doubt to the wide life of Indian Hindus and Indian Moslems, yet Bengal Hinduism has its own peculiarity, as the Moslem ideal and culture of Bengal have also their own peculiarity. Bengal has been for many centuries past a nation speaking one language, belonging to one civilisation, practically trying to develop one culture, and this original unity based upon the unity of language, religion, civilisation and culture, developed and grew—thank God—under the community of civic and political interests. Ever since the establishment of British rule in India, we had been governed practically by one and the same laws, ruled by the same administration; and our political life has, all these years, been controlled by one single policy. Suddenly, however, the Province, united in language, united in past historic associations, united in past historic associations, united in civilisation and culture, united in a common law and administration, this Province was proposed to be cut into two, which gave offence to us. It pained us. We cried, we prayed, we petitioned, we protested, but all to no purpose (cries of shame) and the administrative will—I will not call it administrative necessity because we do not recognise the necessity—had its way. And on the 16th October 1905, two Provinces were made out of the Province of Bengal. The measure was carried out with almost indecent haste, and the reason of the haste was this: Judging from the past experience of Indian political life and agitation, the Government of Lord Curzon evidently believed, that, as long as the measure was not carried out, so long only would this agitation continue. But once it became a 'settled fact', the agitation also would quietly, like all previous agitation, more or less settle down. That was the acute prognosis which the Viceroy made of the situation. For once, superior wisdom was blinded, superior intelligence failed to see through the outer garb and gathering of popular agitation and popular excitement, and the agitation against Partition instead of subsiding, as previous agitations had done, when it was found that they would do no good, continued; it increased, it expanded; it attacked and covered new grounds. It developed new forces and it applied these new forces to the solution of the problem before itself. (Hear, hear.)

The Agitation against Partition

Whence came this new inspiration, this new force? Truth to say, we soon recognised that it is not in the power of the Government, much less is it in the power of an alien Government, to divide a people whom God has united. (Hear, hear, hear.) They might with their pen, dipped in red ink, pass a line on the administrative map of the Province (hear, hear) ... But the stroke of the pen cannot cut the nation into two. The stroke of the pen, though it wounds, wounds in other ways than by cutting things into twos and threes, twenties and thirties. If it were possible for a stroke of the pen to cut up anything, why we have been applying this stroke, my friend in the chair and I, a humble follower of his. (Cheers.) We have been cutting administrations not into two, but into two hundreds almost every day by the stroke of our pens; but the administration remains all the same. We pierce officials by this instrument, but the officials remain all the time hale and hearty. So that when Lord Curzon passed his gubernatorial pen, cut the Province of Bengal in twin, Bengal remained one, and all that this attempt did was to create a deathless determination in the people to continue to be one to the end of their life. (Hear, hear.) So, really, the Partition measure failed, and the failure of it was confirmed by the proceedings of the public meeting that we held in Calcutta on the 7th August 1905. I was addressing an overflow meeting on that memorable evening from the steps of the Calcutta

Town Hall. The audience was as large as this, and when I saw that audience the idea struck me that it would be a very good thing if the Viceroy's astral body could descend from Simla and take its position on the top of the banyan tree that we have near our Town Hall, and if it could see from the top of that tree the crowds that had gathered, and declared their determination to undo the Partition measure. If he could have seen it, he might have known and understood from ocular evidence how Bengal was being partitioned by him. No, gentlemen, the partition has failed. Mr. Morley says it is a 'settled fact'. History declares that it is a settled failure (cheers), and I think settled failure is as good an expression as 'settled fact'. (Hear, hear.) Now, the Partition has failed, and we do not care whether the Partition goes or whether it remains.

The New Movement and Curzon

Why, because in our eagerness to undo this Partition, in the agony of our heart, as our protests, our prayers, our petitions failed to move the obdurate hearts of those who are placed over us to govern us and to rule us, in the agony of despair we looked about and found nothing on which we could lean. All was dark; our faith in all the professions had already commenced to wane long before the Partition measure had been broached. Our faith in the generosity and justice of British policy had commenced to waver before the Partition measure had commenced. Lord Curzon—God bless him (cheers and laughter)—I say it sincerely, God bless him (renewed laughter), because, to my mind, Sir, India has not had a more beneficent Viceroy than Lord Curzon. (Hear, hear.) Lord Ripon was kind. Lord Ripon (cheers) was considerate. Lord Ripon was good. He was tender-hearted. But Lord Ripon's rule was not as beneficent to India as Lord Curzon's has been. Lord Ripon was like a kind mother, and there are circumstances in the life of a child when a kind mother becomes a bad mother, when a kind mother works more mischief than a hating step-mother might have done. Lord Ripon was a kind Viceroy, but Lord Curzon was a beneficent Viceroy. But whether he wished it or not, that is another question. That is not a question that needs trouble you. Let the English people judge it. Let them consider in the light of their own interests the viceroyalty of Lord Curzon. But applying our standard of judgement to that viceroyalty, I do not hesitate to say that it has been one of the most beneficent, if not decidedly the most beneficent, viceroyalties that India ever had. We had been brought up, Sir, for too long a period, upon political lollipops. We had been given for too long a period the beautiful and charming baby-comforter to keep ourselves quiet. Lord Ripon had done it. Others would do it again. But God be thanked, Lord Curzon threw the baby-comforter away, and by throwing it away he made us feel the hunger that is in us, the hunger for *Swaraj* (hear, hear), the hunger for political autonomy, the hunger for occupying our definitely appointed place in the council of nations (hear, hear), the hunger for entering upon our own rights in the universal life of humanity, with a view to deepen, to broaden, to quicken that life by the provisions of our special culture, civilisation and ideals. (Hear, hear.) This is the work that God has done, and chose, in the mysteriousness of His Providence, Lord Curzon as the main instrument for doing this work. Let us thank God for Lord Curzon's viceroyalty, and let us hope and trust that Lord Curzon will live long and enjoy health, and be the Premier of England when India will place before him the ultimatum. (Shouts of *Vande Mataram.*) That will be the fitting end of the drama of which the first act only has been played by that capable Viceroy.

Political Ideal in 1887

Gentlemen, Lord Curzon did this good. He awakened the dormant consciousness of the nation, but he did not create it. The consciousness was there. It lay latent, it flowed as an undercurrent, and recent movements only helped to bring the latent forces in the nation to the surface. What was the preparation for this New Movement? When we call anything new, we do not mean to say that it has no relation to things that can be described as old. New and old are only comparative terms. What was new in 1887 becomes old in 1907. That is all the difference, and you must recognise that difference, when talking and thinking about the New Movement, the New Thought, New Ideal or the New Methods. There is an evolution, there has been an evolution in the history of Indian politics also. I remember the first time that I appeared upon a public platform in your city. It was in 1887, when you had the first Congress here. I miss now some kindly faces whom I first came to know in 1887; and when I appeared for the first time on the platform of the Congress in 1887 in the course of what may be called, so far as Congress platforms are concerned, my maiden speech, I declared that I was a democrat, a democrat of democrats, a radical of radicals; yet I said that neither my democracy nor my radicalism took away in the least measure from my loyalty to the British Government. (Hear, hear.) That was in 1887 and I said it in all sincerity and earnestness. I do not believe that diplomacy is needed or suited to a subject nation. My friend, Mr. A. Choudhury, had declared sometime ago that a subject nation has no politics. By politics I can only mean one thing and that thing is diplomacy. Diplomacy is concealment of ideas and purposes, concealment of sentiments and opinions that is necessary in negotiations between one powerful State and another. It is not necessary between a subject people and its Government, unless that subject people are viciously inclined and desire to bring about a rebellion before the time is ripe for it. In that case, diplomacy may be held good. But, I do not believe, I say, in diplomacy in subject peoples. A subject people must have its politics, but a subject people cannot have any diplomacy. And when I said that my democracy and my radicalism combined together to make me immensely loyal to the British Government, I said what I believed to be true then and I said what numbers of my educated countrymen belonging to that generation absolutely believed to be true. In those days, we had faith in the British nation. We had been brought up with the idea that our salvation and even our political salvation would come from England. We believed in those days that England's mission in India was a conscientiously divine mission. I believe it is a divine mission but I would qualify that old statement by deleting the word conscientiously from it now. But in 1887 we all believed that England was conscientiously and deliberately working for the political emancipation of India. We believed that she would take up by the hand and gradually set us in our own proper place among the nations of the world. We believed that by the gradual expansion of the principles and organisation of Self-Government that had been introduced by Lord Ripon, by the reform and expansion of Legislative Councils, by the introduction of large numbers of people of this country into our public services, by granting us the charter of free citizenship and investing us with the right of organising national militia—we hoped, we believed in 1887, that by these means England would gradually train us to become a free nation and take up our place among the free States of the World; and we believed what Lord Macaulay had said many years ago, that, if such day come when the people of India, trained and educated by England in the arts, sciences, the philosophies and the ideals of the West, would demand the right to government themselves, would desire to have the same free institutions, if such a day came, England would regard it as a most glorious day in her history. For, having found an ancient nation in the very depths of degradation, it took that nation up, gave out to that nation its own wisdom, its own inspiration, its own experience and its own strength, and set that ancient nation once more upon the pedestal of free citizenship. That had been declared by Macaulay and the declaration in one form or other had been repeated by successive British statesmen here in this country and across the seas. We looked up to these declarations. We accepted them as gospel truth and we believed that if really we depended on England for our political emancipation, followed her guidance, accepted her discipline, placed ourselves in her hands for our training, then the day would come when under her guidance, and with her help, we would be able to realise our highest, noblest and deepest political aspirations and be a free nation among the free nations of the world. (Cheers.)

Curzon Destroyed an Illusion

That was the faith that lived in us in the eighties; that was the faith that quickened the activities of the Indian National Congress. That was the faith which governed all our political agitations in the past. I put it to you, have you that faith today? (Cries of no, no.) You need not be afraid of saying that you have no faith. It is clear for the simple reason that Lord Curzon has distinctly stated that there is no ground for entertaining such a faith any more. That declaration, which gave us a greater charter than the Queen's Proclamation itself, is this. (Cheers.) I will just refresh your memory. Speaking on the Budget—it was, I believe, in his lordship's last but one Budget speech—he said that we had misread and misunderstood the Queen's Proclamation. We had been preserving it as our *Magna Carta*. It was a foolish fancy. Sir, the Magna Carta has a peculiar history of its own. The Magna Carta was signed under peculiarly complex circumstances, and in the absence of those circumstances, in the absence of those active political forces that begot the Magna Carta (hear, hear) in the absence of King John, in the absence of Runnymede, in the absence of the armed Barons, in the absence of the pitiable condition of the English King, there could be no Magna Carta. It should be some other Carta, but it would not be Magna Carta. But still, we had looked upon it as our Magna Carta. It was the custom in those days to think of everything

Indian in terms of English life. If there was a great man among us, say Kalidasa, etc., whoever he might be, he must be either a Shakespeare or a Milton or a Byron or a Shelley. If there be a philanthropist, he must be a Howard. He counts for nothing unless he is a Howard. That was the mental attitude of the Indian people then, and, on account of this peculiar mental attitude, we looked about for our political documents and found this precious document in the Queen's Proclamation. We called it the Magna Carta; that is the psychological explanation. Not that our leaders did not know that the forces that created the Magna Carta were not present in India at the time of the Queen's Proclamation. Whatever that might be, we regarded it as our Magna Carta. And we based all our appeals to the Government upon the great Charter; and Lord Curzon thought that it was time to kill this foolish fancy, and from his place in the Viceregal Council, he said that we did not read the Charter, read the Queen's Proclamation as carefully as we should have done. We could repeat it from memory (laughter) with all punctuations from beginning to end. Why, there is nothing in it that we have forgotten, nothing in it that we have omitted. What is the meaning then of this Viceregal declaration that we did not read the Magna Carta, that we did not read the Queen's Proclamation alright? Lord Curzon did not keep us long in suspense, because, in the very next sentence he declared that we did not properly attend to the simple qualifying phrase 'so far as it may be'. We had known of this qualifying phrase, of this conditional clause; but we had interpreted it in our own way; we had thought that this conditional clause had reference to our fitness, to our education, to our character and not to anything else. (Hear, hear.) Lord Curzon said, 'No, it has reference not to your education, fitness or character, but to the permanence of British overlordship in India.' 'So far as it may be' means so far as is consistent with the preservation of the supreme authority of the British in this country. You may be qualified by education and character to manage your own affairs, you may be better qualified than those who are brought out from across the seas to manage or mismanage the British administration; but so long as the administration in India continued to be British, so long the direction of its affairs must necessarily rest with the British. Therefore, you would be given every opportunity of carrying out orders, but not to make one single order. You would be given every opportunity of working the details, but no right to initiate reforms. What Lord Curzon said has been repeated by Lord Minto only two months back in his Budget speech. What does Lord Minto say? He says that 'it is absolutely necessary that whatever reforms are introduced by the Government of India must be initiated by the Government itself; and it would be a mischievous thing for the British Government of India if the idea got abroad that the Government of India had no conviction of their own, that they initiated reforms under pressure of public opinion here or under instructions from the people and the Government in England'.

That is what Lord Minto says, the same thing as Lord Curzon said. It means that the control of affairs, the direction of the administration, the right of initiative shall always be taken by the British people and their representatives here, not by anyone else. It means, Sir, an open declaration by the present Viceroy that they are not amenable and they will never be amenable to Indian opinion in those matters. (Cries of shame.) What right have you to expect the British Government to do anything more than what they are doing? Would you do it, I ask you, if you were in their position? (No, no.) Then, do not cry shame. You regarded them at one time as more than human and little less, if less at all, than gods. It was your folly if the disillusionment has come. Do not in the name of truth and justice think them to be more than human. They are men; they have not come here on an altruistic purpose; they have come here for the expansion of their trade, for the spread of their own empire, for the exploitation of the resources of the country and even the intellect of the land for the improvement of their wealth and intellect. (Cries of shame.) Look facts in the face. Crying shame is a good sentiment, but it is very bad reason.

Minto Morley Process

Now, Sir, Lord Minto has made this distinct declaration, that public opinion in India will not have any influence with the government of this country so far as administration is concerned. For reform must proceed from him. Any other source cannot but be a mischievous thing. Why mischievous, Sir? Why, because, if once you and I get the idea into our head that we can force the hands of the British Government in India, then after that what would you find but the deluge? Then you will clamour for more, more, more, and more, until you have got the whole thing out of their hands. Therefore, Lord Minto warns you. They will do nothing simply because you want them to do it; they will do nothing under pressure of Indian opinion.

And yet we have all these twenty-five years and more been dreaming of this one thing, namely, that, by the application of popular opinion to the problems of administration, by the creation of enlightened public opinion in India and by applying the force of that opinion upon the Government of this country and the British nation at 'home' we would be able to obtain every kind of political reform that we might demand. That has been our belief. That has been the one absolutely settled plan in the programme of the Congress. We have always believed in this, that the Government of India is amenable to Indian public opinion. If it has not been guided by Indian public opinion it has been due to the fact that we have not been able to create a sufficiently strong public opinion. That has been our idea, Sir. But Lord Minto knocks that idea on the head at once and he says, 'No, we shall not budge a fifth, a tenth, a hundredth or a millionth part of an inch. No pressure of Indian public opinion can influence Government.' So, Lord Minto paraphrases Lord Curzon's declaration, and Lord Minto has the support of 'honest John' in this matter; because if Lord Minto's declaration is a paraphrase on the one hand of Lord Curzon's dicta, then, on the other hand, the commentary is John Morley's statement, that 'so far as my imagination reaches, so long the Government in India must be a personal and absolute Government'. An absolute government is that which refuses to be amenable to public opinion; an absolute government is a new euphemism for despotic government: an absolute government is a despotic government. A despotic government is that which is not amenable to public opinion. An absolute government is that which does not agree to be guided and controlled by the opinions, ideals and sentiments of those whom it governs. It is a despotic government. And what Lord Curzon had said some three or four years back, what Mr. John Morley declared last autumn, that is what Lord Minto has represented in other words and in another context in his last Budget speech. And yet this was not what we had been taught and trained to believe of the British Government in India. We had been trained to believe for the last twenty-five years, we have lived upon this one faith, that the British Government in India is a constitutional government. Is it, Sir, a constitutional government?

Constitutional Government

My moderate friends still claim that it is a constitutional Government; they say that the British Government in India is a constitutional

Government. There is some little confusion of thought in regard to this claim. Every government must have a constitution of its own. There can be no government without a constitution, because, if a government had no constitution, there would be no continuity of purpose and policy. If a government had no constitution, there would be nothing to regulate the parts to the parts and the parts to the whole. A government, if it has nothing more, has at least an administrative machinery, and a machinery must have a constitution; though it be a mechanical constitution it must have a constitution of its own. Therefore, every government has a constitution of its own. But every government is not called in political science and in political history a constitutional government. Is it so? The government of the Czar has also a constitution of its own. Even the autocrat of all the Russians is bound by certain laws, certain precedents, certain customs, certain ideas and forms, and, therefore, there is a constitution in Russia. But whoever has called the Government of the Czar a constitutional government? Persia, Sir, had a constitution five years ago. If it had no constitution, government would have been impossible in Persia. But still you say that the people of Persia got a constitution only a few months back! What then do you mean? You mean this: That though they had in Persia a constitution, like all governments, including autocracies, it was only recently that the people of Persia were promised what in political science is called constitutional government.

The word 'constitution' is used in a technical, in a special sense, in political history and political science. What is that sense? It is this: Constitutional government is that which organises the State machinery on the basis of recognised organs through which the opinions of the people may apply themselves on the work of the government. That is what is understood by constitutional government. Constitutional governments are governments that allow, by their very constitution, every right to the people to assert their opinion and ideas effectively upon those who govern. That is constitutional government. And I put it to you, my dear friends, have we any such rights? (Cries of no.) And if we have not these rights, if we have not the organs by and through which the unanimous opinion of the people of India can apply itself to the work of Government of India, how then can we say that the Government of India is a constitutional government? Take Lord Minto's statement. He distinctly declares that nothing will be done by the government under pressure of Indian public opinion. Is that a declaration of the constitutional character of the Government of

India, I ask? (Shame.) My friends, understand before you cry 'shame'. And if the government is not a constitutional government, what becomes of the plea of constitutional agitation?

Constitutional Agitation in India: What it Really Means

The word, in fact, has been used in a very loose way. The words 'constitution' and 'constitutional' have been used in a special sense by our lawyers and politicians. They understand by 'constitution' and 'constitutional' simply that which is regulated by law, that which is within the bounds of law. It does not matter who made the law, or who makes them. 'Constitutional' means legal, lawful and absolutely nothing more in India. Constitutional agitation means an agitation which is consistent with the safety of the agitator. Constitutional agitation thus means an agitation that will not conjure up the dreaded Section 124A of the Indian Penal Code. Constitutional agitation means an agitation within the limits of the Indian Penal Code.

Significance of the New Movement

If that be the meaning of constitutional agitation, the New Movement has not as yet made any declaration against it. We do not as yet proclaim anything which transgresses the existing laws of the Government of India, and we do not, so far as we see now, believe that it will be necessary for us in the near future to transgress those limits. We respect the laws and we shall respect the laws of the present Government as long as those laws respect the primary rights of citizenship. There are certain rights which Governments do not create, but rights which create Governments themselves. Those are not constitutional rights; they are not created rights; they are natural rights; as my friend in the chair suggests, they are primary rights, rights that inherit to every individual human being, rights the charter of which is received from no man but from Him who stands on High, who has endowed every man with his life, with his limbs, who has endowed every man with his human instincts, who has endowed every man with his intellect and every spiritual and ethical endowment. The charter of these primary rights comes not from any crowned head, but it comes from the King of kings, from the throne of God Himself.

And so long as the British Government in India will respect those natural, those primary, those uncreated rights of person and property of individual Indian citizens, so long we shall respect their laws, and our agitation shall be conducted along such lines. In this sense, we may claim to be as constitutional as are those who refuse to accept the constitutional character of our programme and propaganda.

Faith in British People Killed

This word 'constitutional' has been used, I repeat, in Indian politics in a very loose way, to mean not what is meant in political science and political history but simply law-abiding, legal, lawful. Now, Sir, Lord Minto, before him Mr. Morley, before him Lord Curzon, and before Lord Curzon, successive administrators in India had worked together to kill the faith that was in this nation, faith in the British people, faith in the British Government, faith in England's altruistic mission in India. This faith has been killed in the course of the last twenty years, and the New Movement has risen up, for it is a new faith born out of the ashes of the old faith.

In proportion as our faith in the foreign Government has been decaying, in proportion as our dependence on the foreign people and the foreign administration has increased and the realisation of our national destiny has grown weaker and weaker, in that proportion has frustration appeared in Indian politics. On one side there is an overwhelming sense of helplessness. If the Government won't do anything, how are we to achieve our end? If the Government will not listen to our prayers, how can we realise what we want to realise ourselves? It is an attitude of despair on one side. The loss of faith in the foreign nation, in the foreign Government and in the foreign people has grown keen not bitter—I was going to say keen and bitter. And the result is a general sense of despair which leads a lot of people to seek for their own advancement. Since national improvement is impossible why follow the chimera? Go and improve yourself. Make your pile and enter into friendly relations with the Government. The people won't be the better or the worse for your association, year after year, in the participation of this Government. So, why, when all are doomed, should you say, I will not have more than others? I will have 15-9 pies and you keep the three pies in the rupee. That is one attitude that has grown of late in the public life of this country.

New Faith in Our Own People

There is another attitude—that, with the decadence of the faith in the foreign people and in the foreign Government, with the decadence of our faith in the foreign administration which has come to us, we have learnt to look nearer home. Our eyes have been turned away from the Government House, away from the Houses of Parliament, from Simla and Calcutta, and our faces have turned now to the starving, the naked, the patient and long suffering 300 millions of our people, and in it we see a new potency, because we view them now with an eye of love which we never had felt before, and in the teeming, toiling, starving and naked populations of India, we find possibilities, potentialities, germs that have given rise to this New Movement. That is the cornerstone of this Movement, namely, Faith in the People, Faith in the genius of the Nation, Faith in God, who has been guiding the genius of this nation through ages by historic evolution. Faith in the eternal destiny of the Indian People. With the decadence of our faith in the foreign Government and in the foreign nation, has grown up this higher, this dearer, this deeper, this more vital and more divine faith in Indian humanity (cheers). And to understand the New Movement properly, you must look upon it through the prism of this new faith in the Indian people; to understand this New Movement, you must look upon it through the prism of the Indian historic evolution; to understand this New Movement aright, you must look into it through the prism of the highest ideals of your nation, and the highest teachings of your seers and the highest possibilities of your social, economic, industrial and even your political life. It is not an idle dream. This is the message of Indian history, and this is the highest generalisation, I beg to submit, of political science.

Problem of Indian Politics—Seen from a New Angle

After all, what is this Indian problem of politics? Is it a problem of economics? Is it a problem of administration? I refuse to accept it as such. It is not a mere political or an economic problem. What is it then? It is a simple, psychological problem. You do not seem to follow me. How many are the people of this country? Three hundred millions and more. How many are there who govern these people? Less than three lakhs, taking merchants and non-officials together. Now, how can you explain this Government of three hundred millions of people not concentrated upon a tiny bit of space like the great island, which is the home of our rulers, but spread over a continent many times the size of England, the size of Great Britain? You ought to be able to find it for yourself. Now, this problem, this strange problem—the government of three hundred millions and more by aliens of less than three lakhs of persons over a vast continent—can it be anything else than a psychological problem?

England rules India not by force of arms—it would be an impossibility, utter impossibility. The *Times* might show us its sword. The *Pioneer* might remind us of the tiger claws of the Anglo-Saxon, who, I believe, loses his canine character by association with Bengal climate. They might declare that India shall be governed by the sword and by the sword it will have to be kept. British bayonets did not win India. If it was won by the sword, it was the sword of the Indian sepoy that won India for the British nation. And it is not kept by the sword either. How many swords have you got in a district? How many bayonets have you got in your Taluka? Have you one single bayonet in a village or can you keep one military man with a bayonet in every village in India? It is utterly impossible. There is no army in all the world possessed by any power, nay not even by Germany or Russia, who can place one soldier and for his protection another two in every village in India (laughter). The sword never won India.

Conquest of India by the Sword—A Myth

When I hear, Sir, that England won the Empire of India by the sword, when I am threatened with the sword of the *Times*, ah! I am reminded of the story in the Upanishads. In the Taittiriya Upanishad you know the story that though Brahman made the gods conquer their enemies, the gods forgot all about Him. They thought 'it is our glory, it is our conquest'. When the gods were sitting, just as they did in the Delhi Durbar, and Indra was congratulating himself upon the prowess of his thunderbolt by which he had subdued the Asuras, and when Agni was also congratulating himself upon his prowess by which he had conquered and Varuna had been doing the same, there appeared a strange figure near the council of the gods. They looked at it but could not recognise it. Who was that unknown figure? The gods sent Agni, the messenger, 'Go thou and ask who he is.' Agni went and asked. 'Who art thou?' asked this strange figure. Agni said, 'I can burn the earth and the heavens.' That strange figure took up a dry piece of grass and held it before Agni, the god of fire, and said, 'Burn thou this.' Agni applied all his force to burn it and failed. Varuna went. He said, 'I can drown everything.' This strange figure said, 'Drown thou this tiny little reed.' Varuna applied all his force, but the reed could not be drowned. Then Vayu went and said, 'I can blow away everything.' The strange figure said, 'Blow thou this tiny little weed', but he could not do it. They all came back and said, 'We do not know who he is.' Then Indra was asked to go. As soon as he went, this strange figure disappeared. In its place appeared the symbol of Divine Knowledge and it told Indra that this strange person was He by whose power they had conquered the Asuras, but whom they had forgotten. If, Mr. Chairman, the thirty millions of the Indian people could once concentrate, not their strength, but merely their determination, and set that determination up in the neighbourhood of the Delhi Durbar, our rulers would know that the power that won India was not the power of their sword. It was the power of circumstances, it was the power of Divine Will that made the British our rulers for the time being. In this pride, in their ignorance and in their folly they see it not. They are like the scriptural adder that has eyes but seeth not, that has intelligence but the intelligence is not applied to the actualities of the situation about them.

Who Governs India?

Who governs India? Sir, it is we who govern India. (How, how?) Go to any district. How many Englishmen are there in a district? Sometimes two, sometimes three, sometimes four, but never more than half-a-dozen. To whose tune do the Magistrate, the Police Superintendent and the Judge play? The Police Superintendent answers to the tune of the Huzur Sheristadar and the Huzur Sheristadar is your man. It is the Judge who adjudicates. He adjudicates properly more often by the light of the native officials and the native lawyers than by his own imported light. Let me ask, who keeps the peace of the country? It is my Constable, my Chowkidar, my Head Constable and my Sub-Inspector. They are Hindus, Mahomedans or Christians. They are all brown or black, never white. The aliens sit on the top, receive the fattest pay, but we do the most troublesome, the arduous, the most difficult, complex and complicated work. The administrative machinery would come to a standstill, if we drew ourselves away from it (cries of surely). Then, my dear friends, if it is so, what is the secret of this? The secret is hypnotism.

Hypnotic Spell

It is hypnotism. It is *Maya* and *Maya*. And in the recognition of the *Mayic* character of British power in India lies the strength of the New

Movement. What we want is—to prove this *Maya*, to dispel the illusion, to kill and destroy this hypnotism. We have been hypnotised into the belief that, though three hundred millions we may be, yet we are weak. The thing has been dinned into our ears for how many years you all know. For the last fifty years, this thing has been dinned into our ears; for the last one hundred years it has been dinned into our ears that we are weak. They set up one Indian against another, and then they call it their conquest. That is how they write our history.

They are going to celebrate the festival of Plassey, the festival of Clive. But who fought and conquered and who was defeated at the battle of Plassey? Mir Jaffar stood away. The treacherous Mir Jaffar stood away. My Mahomedan friends would take note of it that when the last Mahomedan Nawab was deprived of his Sultanate in Bengal, the only man who fought and was ready to die for him was a Hindu. His Mahomedan general stood aside. Had Mir Jaffar not played the part of a traitor, had Mir Jaffar fought as valiantly and as faithfully as Mohan Lal did, had not Jagat Sett, that treacherous banker, had not another treacherous member of the banking aristocracy, Umichand, had not certain other men, the leaders of the political life of Bengal in those days, conspired in secret against the Nawab, if they had not played themselves into the hands of the tiny little clerk in Fort William, Clive's record of heroism would never have come into existence.

This is how the British Empire in India was established. And this is how India is being administered by them. But we know it not. The Sheristadar knows not his own power, the Inspector knows not the measure of his own power, the Inspector knows not the measure of his own brains, the Deputy Magistrate knows not the important functions that he discharges in the administration of the country. He looks to his pay and looks up to the men who can increase or decrease his pay; he has no time to look into himself, nor about himself, and, therefore, this hypnotism continues. My dear friends, a moment's consideration will show that, if we are weak today this weakness is not real, but illusory.

Cause of Disorganisation in India

If we are disorganised this disorganisation is also caused by this hypnotism. If we are disorganised, we must organise ourselves. We organise when any vital interest is involved in any matter, and for the safety of that interest, organisation is absolutely necessary. But what vital interest have we in this country outside our personal, private family interests? What interest have we in the government of this country? You say, we cannot govern ourselves, because we are divided; you say that we cannot administer our own affairs, because there is caste dividing one group from another; there is religion dividing one community from another; there are the Hindus standing apart from the Mussalmans and the Mussalmans standing apart from the Christians. You say, there are so many religions, so many languages, so many castes and so many differences; how will you organise yourselves? Were there not at one time differences of religion, differences of classes, conflicts of interests, of class against class, in England? Were there not provincial differences and jealousies in Germany before the master-hand of Bismarck, helped by the late Emperor William, welded together these heterogeneous Germans into one great German nation? Common interests, common life, and the same vital community of interests have made other peoples merge their differences in the pursuit of that vital thing.

Have not we lessons in regard to this in our own past? India knows of two instances within the memory of history of nation-building. One was in the Punjab, the recent history of the Sikhs, and the other was in the Deccan, the history of the Mahrattas. And what was peculiar in the Punjab? What was peculiar in Maharashtra? Leave the Punjab alone, because there the problem was sought to be worked out in a very limited field. Take the history of the Mahrattas. Who do you find there? Sivaji combined not only the Hindus but he combined the Hindus and the Mahomedans both. He united the interests of the two great communities in his own ideal of a Maharashtra.

What did Pratapaditya do in Bengal? You talk of disunion between the Hindus and Mahomedans. But at the time of Pratapaditya, the Mahomedan satraps and the princes in Bengal fought side by side with the Hindus against the common foe, the Mogul Emperor, against Man Singh, Akbar's general, when he came to conquer Pratap. There was Isha Khan, one of the great twelve landlords of Bengal, who were really ruling chiefs. He joined Pratap and fought with the Moguls. So, if you can create community of interests, if you can present something that can be regarded by all people as the common ideal, if you can present an ideal that can appeal to every community in India—the development not of their peculiar culture and character, but the fulfilment, according to one's own lines, of the highest aspirations that quicken in them, if you can present such an ideal, then all these differences will disappear.

Our Weakness—A Myth, Not a Reality

We have been told we are disunited and we have believed in it; we have been told that we are weak and we have believed in it; we have been told that we are ignorant and we cannot understand politics, and we have believed in it. And this belief has been the cause of all our weakness, and it is a hypnotic cause. It is induced by *Maya*. And it is upon a recognition of this *Mayic* character of the present sovereignty in India that the New Movement bases itself, and it proclaims, therefore, that the salvation of India must come first and foremost of all through right knowledge. *Maya* can be dispelled by right knowledge whether it be Vedantic or political. It is, therefore, that we proclaim from the house-tops our ideal: it is, therefore, that we make no secret of our propaganda, because the idea that has to be dispelled is this, the sense of helplessness in the people. The thing that has to be fought against is this despair, corroding, killing despair in the nation. What you and I want now, is the message of strength; what you and I want now, is the declaration of some such idea that will quicken our intellect and our emotions as well, and that will take possession of our wills. Such an ideal will lead us to make one united determination to cut asunder this *maya* and make us prepare ourselves for those sacrifices, which this determination will naturally demand in the future. This determination, this sacrifice, this knowledge, this ideal, it is these that would solve the Indian problem. And it is these which I have tried in my lecture on the New Movement to place before you tonight.

Not a Mere Political Movement

But one lecture, though extending over a couple of hours, is not sufficient to explain to you all the aspects, all the principles, much less the great and sublime philosophy that stands behind this New Movement. It is not a merely political movement, though politics has come to receive, perhaps, the largest amount of its attention just now. This movement is not a mere economic movement, though it is applied to the solution of the great problem of Indian poverty. This movement is essentially a spiritual movement. It has its application in social, in economic, in political life of the sublime theosophy of the Vedanta. It means the desire to carry the message of freedom. It is the supreme message of the Vedanta; and we are to carry out that message, to realise that ideal in the social, economic and the political life. What is the message of the Vedanta? The message of the Vedanta is this: that every man has within himself, in his own soul, as the very root and realisation of his own soul, as the very root and realisation of his own being, the spirit of God; and as God is eternally free, self-realised, so is every man eternally free and self-realised. Freedom is man's birth-right. It is inherent in the very making of man. Man is made not out of the image, not in the image, but out of the Substance of the Maker. And as God is eternally free, so are we. Prince or peasant, Brahmin or Pariah, man or woman, Hindu or Mahomedan, Buddhist or Christian, rich or poor, ignorant or learned, we are eternally free.

We realise it not, because we are enveloped in ignorance. We realise it not, because freedom has not organised itself as yet in our social life. We realise it not, because this spirit of freedom has not been able to organise itself as yet in our economic life. We realise it not, because this freedom, this ideal of freedom, has not as yet actualised itself in our political life. It is the freedom of free citizens comprising a Free State. There and there alone can we recognise, can we actualise, can we objectify, can we bring it before ourselves, our own natural freedom. In the citizenship of a Free State we regulate ourselves, we control ourselves, we rule ourselves, we restrain ourselves. And freedom, my dear friends, is not want of restraint but self-restraint; freedom is not want of determination, but self-determination; and it only exists in you as members of a free State, as free citizens of a free State, in the administration of your own affairs, in your submitting yourselves to your own affairs, in your submitting yourselves to the laws that you helped to make and in submitting yourselves to the regulations that you helped to impose upon yourselves and upon the community at large (cheers). That gives the clue to the political life. It is the life of a free citizen in a Free State wherein you realise the freedom of God, which is self-restraint, self-regulation and self-determination for the purpose of self-realisation (cheers). Therefore, I say, this New Movement is not a mere political movement. It is essentially a spiritual movement. They do not understand its meaning; they cannot understand its strength; they have no faith in this Movement, because they do not recognise it as a supremely spiritual movement. And because we recognise it so we believe that the spirit of our race will fulfil and realise itself in and through this Movement and shall realise the divinely appointed destiny of our nation.

Our faith is first in God, faith in the history in and through which God reveals Himself. Our faith is in the history of our own people and in the genius of our own nation. It is the manifestation, within the limits of our national life, of the Spirit of God and God Himself and because we have this faith, we believe in the success of our Movement.

We are disorganised today, but we shall become organised tomorrow. We are weak today, but we can become strong in our own native strength tomorrow. We believe we are incapable of self-sacrifice today, but we shall attain the strength to make the self-sacrifice tomorrow. And by these means, by determination, by self-sacrifice and by combination, we shall be able to realise the end that this New Movement has set up, namely that of Swaraj. (Continued cheers and cries of *Vande Mataram*.)

~

ANNIE BESANT

The Home Rule Resolution

Annie Besant (1847–1933), leader of the theosophist movement who adopted India as her home, led the Home Rule movement which demanded, along the lines of the Irish Home Rule movement, new constitutional arrangements for India. The Home Rule movement mobilized the younger generation in various cities and towns in India. In recognition of her services, the Congress elected her as its president for the 1917 session of the Congress held at Calcutta. She became the first woman president of the Congress and in the speech reproduced here she articulated the mood of the time.

You have just heard the scheme of reforms which has been passed by the All India Congress Committee in conference with the Reform Committee appointed by the All India Muslim League. Those reforms are alluded to in the second clause and you will see that they are meant for a transition period to be passed as soon as possible and to lead up to that change which is to come with the reconstruction of the Empire after the War—that change to Self Government of India on a footing of equality with the Self Governing Dominions. It is to the last clause that I propose to ask your attention. The last clause says that in the reconstruction of the Empire after the War India shall be lifted from the position of Dependency to that of an equal partner in the Empire with the Self Governing Dominions. With regard to that it is said that you ought not to embarrass the British Government by raising such a question as this in the middle of the War. We are only following the example of the Self Governing Dominions. We are only taking the advice of Mr. Bonar Law who advised the Dominions to strike the iron while it was red hot. After the reconstruction of the Empire the iron will be cold and where I ask is the blacksmith who allows the red hot iron to cool down before he strikes it to the shape and form he wants?

We hear at this moment much talk about the five nations who are to form a Federated Empire after the War. Where is India? Oh, She is not one of the five. She is a coloured people and coloured people are to have the right of domination over them by colourless people. Coloured people have only the duty of submission. (Cries of Shame.) But that is not the doctrine that this coloured nation at least is willing to accept. We are not uncivilised natives of South Africa that we should bow our heads beneath the yoke of the five nations. It is not lack of colour that makes clever brains. The Lord Buddha and the Christ were coloured men. All the founders of religion were coloured men. Have the colourless produced a single founder of religion? We will never bow beneath the yoke of the Colonies.

We are told not to spread bitterness against the Colonies. I think the writer of that has begun at the wrong end. Have we excluded the Colonies from India, because they could not talk or write some language of which they knew nothing? Was it this country or was it Australia that passed that Law? Have we said that no North American or Canadian should come to India unless he comes straight from port to port when there is no line of ships that carries straight from one to the other or has Canada made that law against the Indian people? What is this talk of bitterness? Bitterness is caused by the Colonies and not by India. Let this advice be given to the Colonies and not to India. The Indian had no share in the making of that feeling.

Oh we are not fit to govern ourselves and we are divided! Are we? We have shown some power of union during the last few years. Our Congress was split into half nine years ago. But we stand a United Congress today. Hindus and Muslims had a gulf between them not in

Kashmir where a Hindu Prince rules nor in the Deccan where a Muslim Prince is the Sovereign, but only in the British Raj and that gulf has been bridged by Muslims and Hindus themselves and we have linked our hands in love, in trust, in mutual forbearance, in mutual respect and we stand today a united nation that nothing shall hereafter break asunder.

Oh you are not fit for Self Government. You are ignorant. Who has the right to cast that reproach at the masses of our people? It was the late Mr. Gopal Krishna Gokhale who tried to win free and compulsory education cautiously, carefully, step by step for he was not an impatient idealist in the world, however much his heart went with impatient idealism. An Indian tried to educate his brethren but who is it that denied it? It was the Imperial Council with its perpetual majority of officials. Does it then lie in the mouths of Englishmen to reproach us with ignorance when the Government would not educate our people and would not help us to do it?

Then they say: 'You cannot help yourselves'. Did we pass the Arms Act? Did we take away weapons from the hands of our people? Since 1878 there has been no pure blooded Indian whether Hindu or Mussalman who could possess arms without a license to the gaining of which all sorts of difficulties are attached. Is it India's fault that it is undefended? For thirty years the Congress has asked for the repeal of the Arms Act and for permission to volunteer and to open Military Colleges, and those who have treated every demand with contempt say that we are not fit to govern ourselves, because we cannot defend ourselves. It is only Home Rule that will enable us to defend ourselves. Until we have Home Rule we cannot be armed as we should be.

~

MUHAMMAD ALI JINNAH

Protest against Internment

Muhammad Ali Jinnah (1876–1948) was, in the early part of the twentieth century, a staunch nationalist of the liberal fold and a champion of Hindu–Muslim unity. A leading lawyer and a public personality in Bombay, he presided over the meeting convened under the auspices of the Bombay Presidency Association on 30 July 1917. His speech on that occasion, protesting the arrest of Annie Besant, reflected the anger and indignation that had swept across the country in the wake of the internment.

It is said that we are to put out of our thoughts entirely the early grant of Self-Government to India, that we are not going to get anything like the reforms formulated and sanctioned by the Indian National Congress and the All-India Muslim League last December at Lucknow to be given effect to at the close of the War, that we must be content with small minor reforms which the bureaucracy have recommended though we are not yet even accorded the small mercy of knowing what they are, that we are not to raise expectations in the minds of the people which are not going to be fulfilled. We are threatened with Government action if we do not obey these warnings and as an earnest thereof Mrs. Besant and her co-workers are interned—any expression of public opinion recording disapproval of the Government action is not desired. In Bengal and Delhi, public meetings have been stopped already. Now why is India alone of all other parts of the Empire to be marked out for silence—and why should we be at this moment subject to this repressive policy? We are shedding our blood and pouring our money ungrudgingly and unstintingly for the defence of the Empire in this War, the very basis of which is to preserve the liberty and freedom of people of various countries. Is the bureaucracy of India blind? Have they lost their reason to treat loyal India at this juncture in this manner? It is a mistake. It shows an utter want of wisdom and statesmanship. What is His Excellency the Viceroy Lord Chelmsford doing? His silence at this moment is most ominous and worse than the most drastic repressive actions already adopted and enforced by some of the Provincial Governments.

Protest against Internment

We protest against the internments of Mrs. Besant and her co-workers not only on principle, but also because it is an attempt to intern the Home Rule or Self-Government Scheme of Reforms, framed and adopted conjointly by the Indian National Congress and the All-India Muslim League at Lucknow. We declare that we stand by the scheme unswervingly and unflinchingly, and we shall do all that lies in our power for its realisation at the close of the War. We protest against the methods adopted and attempts that are made, to silence the people of India from carrying on their constitutional agitation. We feel that Government are blind to the real public opinion in the country regarding the Reform Scheme passed at Lucknow; and are entirely misled and pursuing a policy which is fraught with most serious consequences. It has already led the people to earnestly consider whether they should not adopt the principle and methods of Passive Resistance.

An Unprecedented and a Most Unfortunate Situation

The present political situation is unprecedented and most unfortunate; it has cast the gravest responsibility upon the leaders, the people and the Government alike, which requires the most careful and immediate attention of us all. Let us not try to muddle through as usual. The times are different and changed. We require at once a clear and definite enunciation of the policy of the Government. We require that the confidence of the people in the Government which has been so severely shaken within the past three months should be restored at once to enable us to win this War, which has been our first and foremost consideration throughout this long and weary struggle which has been going on for nearly three years. The people of India are anxious and are earnestly endeavouring to attain the status of a self-Governing Member of the Empire at an early date; but it is really a folly to think that because of that they are not loyal to the Empire.

In the belief and faith that British statesmanship has not come to the point of utter bankruptcy I appeal to it on behalf of this meeting that they should not lose any time in making a declaration of policy for making India a self-Governing Member of the British Empire at an early date, and order the reversal of the recent repressive policy, in response to the public opinion which is unequivocal and emphatic throughout the country.

5

THE DREAMERS

The political awakening of the nation and the movement for social reforms which addressed superstitions and prejudices also gave shape to the quest for a modern scientific world. A galaxy of scientists—P.C. Ray, J.C. Bose, C.V. Raman, S.N. Bose, Meghnad Saha—emerged in India in the early part of the twentieth century. These scientists lacked basic infrastructure for advanced research but were part of a large socio-political movement that gave them a sense of direction. Overcoming incredible financial and logistical odds, visionaries like Mahendra Lal Sircar set up institutes of scientific research and learning like the Indian Association for the Cultivation of Science in Calcutta which inspired similar institutions in the future. These institutes tried their best to promote a scientific temper among Indians. The Indian Institute of Science, started in 1909 thanks to the pioneering vision of J.N. Tata, became the breeding ground of scientific talent in the country. As vice chancellor of the University of Calcutta, Sir Asutosh Mukherjee brought brilliant Indians, including Sir C.V. Raman, K.S. Krishnan and S.N. Bose, to work in the science department of the university.

While the quest for alleviating poverty and the suffering of the people was the basic social ethos of Indian science from the very beginning, these scientists also dreamt of a modern and developed people free of superstitions, rational in their outlook and capable of working things out through reason rather than blind faith. The institutional structure that Meghnad Saha, S.S. Bhatnagar and others had been envisioning since the 1920s gradually came to be realized in India under the leadership of Jawaharlal Nehru when institutions like the Council of Scientific and Industrial Research, Indian Council of Agricultural Research and National Physical Laboratory came into being after independence.

~

PRAFULLA CHANDRA RAY

Dawn of Science in Modern India

In 1920, Prafulla Chandra Ray (1861–1944) became the first Indian to be elected president of the Indian Science Congress. More than a personal achievement for the great man of science, it was a moment of glory for Indian science which operated under an extremely restrictive colonial environment. As this historic speech—delivered at Nagpur in 1920 as the presidential address of the Indian Science Congress—detailed, Indian scientists had no infrastructural support to speak of and no prospects of growth. The speech articulated the anguish of the suppressed Indian soul. For the first time, the needs of Indian science were voiced from the podium of the Indian Science Congress. A nationalist to the core, P.C. Ray rendered yeomen service to the cause of science in India. To provide infrastructural support for scientific research and training, he started Bengal Chemicals and Pharmaceutical Works, a pioneering venture in indigenous scientific and industrial collaboration, and other factories, all in the face of British obstruction. His The History of Indian Chemistry *provided a foundation and sense of lineage to Indian science and immensely boosted the confidence of scientists in the country vis-à-vis their scientific inheritance.*

With great diffidence I have responded to your call to preside at this conference. It is not, however, my intention today to make a disquisition on any branch of scientific research. I shall content myself with a humble, but by no means a less important, theme.

Our age is pre-eminently an age of science. It has been rightly observed by a great English writer: 'Modern civilisation rests upon Physical Science; take away her gifts to our country, and our position among the leading nations of the world is gone tomorrow; for it is Physical Science only that makes intelligence and moral energy stronger than brute force.' The recent war has amply demonstrated the truth of these observations. While Europe, America and Japan have taken to the field of science with singular vigour and activity, how does the land lie about us in India? The situation fills our mind with sorrow and shame, and you will excuse me if I enter into a short history of the subject.

Dawn of Science in Modern India

Indian culture has been from time immemorial of a peculiar cast and mould. It will not be quite wrong to say that the Hindus are pre-eminently a metaphysical nation. Not that the cultivation of physical science was entirely neglected in India's ancient days, but it proceeded as an adjunct to the study of metaphysics and religion. From the time which marked the decline of Buddhism commenced the dark ages of India, and, for the last 1000 years or more, India has been a *tabula rasa* so far as the cultivation of physical sciences is concerned. In Europe, the lamp of science has been burning dimly from the time of Paracelsus and Basil Valentine and Galileo, Newton and Boyle, but more and more brilliantly in the 18th and 19th centuries. We in the east, on the other hand, have been living all this time in silent and ecstatic meditation. To the Hindu, nursed in the principles of Vedanta, the material world has no real existence: and Sankara, as an exponent of the Vedanta philosophy, is unsparing in his criticism and denunciation of the atomic theory as propounded in the Vaiseshika philosophy, ridiculing the author of the system itself as 'Kanada' or atom-eater. No wonder M. Cousin in his *History of Philosophy* quotes such passages as these: 'Science is superior to practice, and contemplation is superior to Science; prefer contemplation to Science, inaction to action, faith to work, etc.' As M. Senart says—'The Hindu mind is very religious and very speculative; an obstinate guardian of traditions, it is singularly insensible to the joys of action and to the solicitations of material progress.' The attitude of the Indian mind towards the study of the laws of the material world and the incessant activity of the West is aptly summed up in the well-known lines of the poet

> The East bowed low before the blast,
> In patient, deep disdain,
> She let the legions thunder past
> And plunged in thought again

It could not be expected that, with such a bent of mind of the people, there should have been much activity for the cultivation of the physical sciences in this part of the world. Besides, with the decay of the ancient Hindu and Buddhistic culture, an intellectual torpor took possession of the Indian mind and the spirit of enquiry after truth rapidly declined. Authority of the *Shastras* took the place of reason and clouded human intellect. A state of mind was thus fostered which was inimical to the study of Science, which accepts things not on trust, but by verification.

Indian mind lay in this condition till the beginning of the nineteenth century when new conditions of life arose out of the establishment of British rule. This contact with the West brought in new ideas and new modes of thought in Indian life. The introduction of western culture was beset with many difficulties and encountered great resistance at the start.

I shall not enter here into the history of the bitter controversy between the Orientalists and the Anglicists in the days of Macaulay, which ended in the triumph of the latter. The whirligig of time had brought on its own revenge. Rajah Ram Mohan Ray, the maker of modern India and who was the first to resuscitate the Upanishads in Bengal and to translate some of them into English, and who himself was deeply imbued with the Vedanta doctrines, characterised Sanskrit learning as calculated to cause 'a lamentable check to the diffusion of knowledge'. 'Nor will youths be fitted,' cried this great Reformer, 'to be better members of society by the Vedantic doctrines which teach them to believe that all visible things have no real existence, that as father, brother, etc. have no real entity, they consequently deserve no real affection, and therefore the sooner we escape from them and leave the world, the better.' He, therefore, appealed to the then Governor-General of India, Lord Amherst, to discourage 'such imaginary learning, and employ European gentlemen of talent and education to instruct the natives of India in Mathematics, Natural Philosophy, Chemistry, Anatomy, and other useful sciences, which the natives of Europe have carried to a degree of perfection that has raised them above the inhabitants of other parts of the world'. These memorable words were uttered close upon a century ago, but they bear repetition even today.

To the Serampur missionaries, headed by Carey, Marshman and Ward, as also to the founders of the old Hindu School at Calcutta, belongs the credit of being the first to usher in the dawn of intellectual renaissance in Bengal. The earliest systematic attempts to teach the elements of Chemistry were made by John Mack, who was educated at the Edinburgh University and who came out to India in 1821 as professor of the Natural Sciences in the newly founded College at Serampur. Mack used to deliver his lectures to his pupils both in Calcutta and at Serampur. His treatise on Chemistry in Bengali, published in 1834, is perhaps the first rendering of the science in an Indian language. The establishment in 1835 of the Medical College at Calcutta also promoted the study of Chemistry. Among the teachers of this science who have left their mark in our educational history and are remembered even to this day, the name of O'Shaughnessy stands pre-eminent.

O'Shaughnessy was an enthusiast in the teaching of Chemistry. He appeals to the Indian students to take some interest in the pursuit of this science and observes: 'Difficulties will beset his progress, it is true, but to overcome them all, he requires only the qualities which the Indian youth possesses in the most pre-eminent degree. He is quick of perception, patient in reflection, adroit and delicate in experimental manipulation; and, with these endowments, his full success in this study may be most confidently foretold.' How far O'Shaughnessy's words uttered some 80 years ago have come to be true, it is for the scientific public to pronounce an opinion. Two other names also occur to us among the pioneers, namely, Dr. F.N. Macnamara and Kanailal Dey, evidently the first Indian to acquire fame as a pharmacologist and who was elected an honorary member of the Pharmaceutical Society of Great Britain. The appointment of Alexander Pedler in 1874 as professor of Chemistry at the Presidency College, Calcutta, was an eventful one. Pedler's neat manipulation, experimental skill and persuasive lectures contributed not a little to the popularity of the subject, and it was from him that the present speaker, who had the good fortune to sit at his feet for close upon four years, acquired a taste for the cultivation of Chemistry.

A period of 60 years is but a very brief spell in the life history of a nation. This was the preparatory and assimilative stage, at any rate in Bengal, in the cultivation of science. What may be termed the period of reproduction or original contribution began in 1895, for it was in that memorable year that Mr. (now Sir) J.C. Bose read at the meeting of the Asiatic Society of Bengal a paper entitled 'The Polarisation of Electric Waves'. There was activity also in other departments of science. In other provinces too, there has now sprung up a general enthusiasm for the study of science, and instances are not wanting where our countrymen have been able to distinguish themselves in the field. I need not refer to this movement in detail which is within the living memory of all. Suffice it to say that the last quarter of a century has witnessed the dawn of a new spirit in the pursuit of science throughout the country.

Reconstruction and the Need for Research

We stand today at the threshold of a critical period in the history of our country. The war has happily terminated, and we are in the midst of rejoicings over the Peace Celebrations. It has been truly said that the late war called for every ounce of scientific knowledge and effort, that the great nations have been straining their utmost and that the scientific battle has been fought by the laboratory men. Indeed, it was from the nitrogen of the air out of which Germany manufactured synthetic nitric acid and thus defied the world for four years and more in spite of the stringency of the blockade. It is now becoming abundantly clear that the fate of a nation will henceforth depend more upon the achievements of its students of science than upon the skill of its generals or the adroitness of its diplomatists and statesmen. Let me illustrate what I have said by a concrete example. The first thing which America did, when she joined the allies, was to initiate a census of chemists, and in July 1917 a fully detailed description was available of some 15,000 chemists resident in the State, and a research staff consisting of 1,200 technical men with necessary assistants, was enlisted for the research division of the chemical warfare service alone.

Peace hath her victories no less renowned than war. The sudden and unexpected stimulus which chemical research obtained during the war has been the means of calling into existence a trained band of workers especially in the allied countries. In England, for instance, vigorous attempts are now being made to manufacture dyes and fine chemicals backed by heavy subsidies from the state and countervailing duties. It now transpires, however, that Germany, though worsted in the war and her resources enormously crippled, has had her chemical plants practically unimpaired and her army of chemists undiminished in vigour. It is suspected in fact that she is already putting forth mighty efforts to oust her rivals and capture her lost markets. England's preoccupation has also been America's opportunity. During the first three years of the war, secure in her envied neutrality, she reaped a golden harvest by selling raw materials and munitions to the belligerents, and her chemical industries have got such a fillip that in the near future the Indian market bids fair to be flooded with heavy and fine chemicals and dyes manufactured in America...

Emerson says somewhere that a chemist will readily confide his secrets to a carpenter, secrets which he will not impart to a brother chemist for all the world. The accumulated experience of generations of English and French chemists was thus gained by America at almost a bound. Japan has not been slow in stealing a march over us; her volume of exports to India has trebled within the last 2 or 3 years. The question now arises: Where does India stand in this formidable world competition? My answer is, *nowhere.* It is sad to reflect that nothing short of the cataclysm of the late Armageddon could rouse us from our stupor and make us realise that like so many other countries, India must be not only self-contained in the production of her own requirements, but learn to convert vast supplies of raw materials into manufactured products. India has now an enormous amount of leeway to make up. We must now put forth all our energies and make vigorous and sustained efforts so as to be able to stand a fierce world-competition.

Want of General Education—A Bar to Scientific Progress

Unfortunately, educational progress cannot be effected piecemeal and at a moment's notice. It is almost a truism that the nations which have made the greatest advance in science are precisely those which have made ample provisions for the spread of education among the masses. Primary, secondary and higher education—all go together. In fact, America has now authoritatively laid down the dictum that *education is the birthright of every citizen.* Speaking of education in India, Sir Michael Sadler has very aptly observed that you must broaden the base of the pyramid, but not whittle away the apex.

Our people are, however, sunk in abysmal ignorance and their illiteracy is simply colossal—barely 3% of the population are under instruction in all types of educational institutions. Research institutes, such as we have got here at Pusa and elsewhere, are excellent things in their own way. You may wax eloquent over hybridisation and the adoption of improved strain of seeds and the efficacy of fertilisers with their proper percentages of phosphates and nitrogen, and point out that the outturns of the crop may thereby be doubled, but the simple fundamental fact is coolly ignored that you have to deal with a ryot whose excessive subdivision of land and fragmentation of holdings, coupled with his ignorance, conservatism and narrow outlook, renders him incapable of profiting by laboratory experiments. You might as well appeal to deaf ears.

... A widespread diffusion of primary and secondary education among the dumb millions is the only means of making them rely on their own resources. Andrew Carnegie's dictum, 'Educate the people and poverty will take care of itself,' admits of wider application. I should say educate the people and their intelligence and commonsense may be trusted to choose the better path. Without this foundation of primary and secondary education, it is not possible to make any substantial progress in the study of science or its practical application in the field of industry in the country. This is the great handicap imposed on us and it makes itself felt in all directions of life.

It is not the place or the occasion to enter into a detailed criticism of the educational policy of the Government. But I cannot help remarking that the apathy and niggardliness of the Government of India in this respect are lamentable. About the time Sir William Meyer was stating to the Supreme Legislative Council why more funds could not be spared for the extension of education and no schemes of educational progress could be formulated in India, Mr. H. Fisher, President, Board of Education in England, was evolving far-reaching and extensive projects of national education in Great Britain. The British people and the British Government have correctly appreciated the value of the provision of sound education for national efficiency and welfare. In asking for an additional grant of more than £3¾ millions for educational improvement towards the middle of 1917, Mr. Fisher described in the House of Commons in glowing terms what part education had played in giving England a magnificent army to fight for liberty and right. He laid stress upon two things: first, that the Government was earnest in dealing with the problem of education and second, that it was doing it in a systematic and comprehensive manner. Mr. Fisher said—'The mere fact that in the middle of a great war, when the finances of this country are strained to the uttermost, the Chancellor of the Exchequer is willing to fund nearly four millions of additional money for the development of public education is, I think, a sufficient indication that the Government means business. As regards the second point, I can assure the House that all the problems of public education are being considered in relation to one another, and that though in order of time some reforms must necessarily precede others, they are not being dealt with in a fragmentary and opportunist manner.'

In spite of this liberal programme, the cry still in England is that the provision is not adequate. If this be an inadequate provision, indeed, how must the provisions of the Government of India look in this connection compared to the British estimates? I may here observe in passing that the outlay on railways and irrigation is considered as productive, but no outlay is more productive than the outlay on education, which improves and develops the minds of the people. It has well been observed by Mr. Fisher, Minister for Education in England, that 'the capital of a country does not consist in cash or paper, but in the brains and bodies of the people who inhabit it'.

Indianisation of Scientific Departments

I feel it my duty to make a rapid survey of the future of science in India and suggest steps which ought to be taken for the proper culture and development of science in India. By this I mean that educated Indians should take a greater part in original investigations, and steps should be taken for the diffusion of scientific knowledge among the rank and file of the people. The cultivation of science must be entrusted, as is the case everywhere in the civilised world, to the professors in colleges and universities, to the teachers in the secondary schools, and to the officers in the various scientific departments of the state, and there must be a good proportion among the *intelligentsia* in the country to take interest in the pursuits of science and encourage its votaries. The visions of the early educationists, in this respect, have proved quite illusive; the contribution to science by Indians has been extremely meagre. Japan entered the race some 30 years after India, but by what a vast distance she has left us behind! Within the short period of 40 years, she has built up an educational system which is the admiration of the civilised world, while her contributions to Science have been very valuable, and are daily growing in volume and importance.

Let us now see where the fault lies. The scientific services of the Government are posts of great value, prospect, and security; they afford to their holders unique opportunities, rare and valuable materials, for study and investigation.

... Among the occupiers of these posts, there have been many distinguished European savants of great name and fame. I do not for a moment wish to minimise their achievements. The credit of their work, however, belongs to their own native countries, and the results of their experience are enjoyed by their own countrymen. I shall try to make my point a bit clearer. The Indian lives and moves and has his being in the midst of his own people; the European, somehow or other, lives in a world apart, and from his exalted position of aloofness and isolation fails to inspire those who may happen to come into contact with him. Moreover, the European, when he attains the age limit, retires to his own native land, and the accumulated experiences gained at the expense of India are lost to the country for good. In a word, the present system arrests Indian intellectual growth and inflicts a cruel wrong on India.

In Japan, on the other hand, western experts were at first imported for the organisation of the scientific services; but they have gradually been replaced by the Japanese scholars. Japan can thus show an Omori in Seismology, a Kitasato in Bacteriology and a Takamine in Biological Chemistry, not to mention a host of other eminent names.

In India, however, taking, for example, only one instance, the Trigonometrical Survey is entirely reserved for and manned by Royal Engineers with military rank. I do not see why this should be the case. In England, France and Germany, civil graduates with scientific qualifications are being employed in increasing numbers. Even in India, in the early fifties of the last century, we find that Radhanath Sikdar, an alumnus of the old Hindu College, was the right-hand man of Colonel Everest, of the Trigonometrical Survey, from whom the highest peak of the Himalayas has derived its name.

In order to make India self-contained, the Government has proposed to institute a Chemical Service. Probably in the near future, departments of Aerial Navigation, Marine Engineering including Naval Architecture, will have to be organised. The utilisation of Indian brains in these departments should be regarded as pivotal.

Coming now to the second point, viz. the contribution to Science by Indian professors, the result has been disappointing so far as the Government service is concerned. And for this the service system is responsible. Take, for example, the chairs in the Presidency College of Calcutta, probably the premier college in India. The chairs are as well paid as any in the world, and the advantages and facilities afforded to the professors are the best available in India. There is sometimes the honoured tradition of an Eliot or a J.C. Bose or a Pedler connected with some chair. Naturally when a vacancy arises, the aim should be to fill up the posts by able and enthusiastic workers on the subject so as to preserve the tradition and the continuity of the fame attached to such a post. But what happens under the service system? Either a raw untried graduate is brought out from England or it automatically falls to some senior man in the service whose only title to the post is his seniority, which often goes hand-in-hand with senility. In ninety-nine cases out of hundred, the successor so chosen has no single original work to his credit, and may have lost all touch with the progress of his subject. Enormous facilities at his disposal thus remain unused as long as he encumbers that post.

... The selection of men for professorship in our country lies entirely in the hands of a few big officers. In the case of the lower services, it is the Director; in the case of the Imperial Services, it is the India Council. It is a continuation of the old Nawabi system. Generally the Directors, or the officers of the selection bureau, are men who might have achieved some academic distinction at some period of their career (but this is not always necessary), but, having taken to administrative work for long years, are entirely out of touch with the progress in the different branches of knowledge. Such officers are by habit and temperament unfitted to judge the merits of rival candidates, and generally very unfortunate selections are made. The evils of the present method of recruitment to the posts of Professors have been pointed out by the Calcutta University Commission who have suggested organisation of teaching work on a professorial rather than on a service basis.

The authorities in this country are never tired of singing the praise of men trained in the West. In practice, however, even a third class man of London, or a postgraduate of Oxford or Cambridge, is preferred to the best Calcutta graduates...men who have proved their merit by publishing original works in the pages of the journal of learned Societies of the West...

Potentialities of Indigenous Talent

A signal proof of what can be done by Indians, when they are allowed to work under a healthy and free atmosphere, is afforded by the University College of Science, Calcutta. This College grew out of the magnificent and princely gifts of Sir Rashbihari Ghosh and the late Sir T.N. Palit, and was established in 1916; but owing to limitation of funds, the laboratory and the workshop could not be properly organised. In spite of these discouraging conditions, it is the only institution which has shown anything like life and activity as evidenced by the output of original contributions published in the leading scientific journals of England and America. During the academic year 1918-19, there were 17 original contributions from the department of Applied Mathematics, 24 from the Physics department, and 21 from the Chemistry department. Yet this promising institution is treated like a charity boy by the Government and has had only miserable doles ladled out to it.

What little has been done by them only goes to prove their potentiality, their latent capacity for the work to be undertaken in the future. It is, therefore, necessary that steps should be taken to allow Indians to stand on their own legs. The policy which has hitherto been the guiding principle is that everything should be done *for* them and nothing *by* them, and this goes to explain their virtual ostracism from the higher responsible post in the various scientific services. A vast amount of ability and potential energy is thus allowed to run to waste. Japan has all along followed a course which is the very reverse of that adopted here and with what happy results I need not say. A self-contained India, such as the Indian Industrial Commission looks forward to, presupposes that the experts, specialists and workers which the industrial awakening would demand should be created within her own borders.

Pure Science vs. Applied Science

There is at present a popular demand in India for the starting of technological institutes. This is but natural, when we consider the backwardness of our country in point of industrial development and the part played by technological education in the countries of Europe and America. But we must not neglect at the same time the study of Pure Science. We bear in mind that Applied Science cannot stand without Pure Science. As Prof. Huxley says: 'What people call Applied Science is nothing but the application of Science to particular problems.' The advanced nations of Europe have passed through a probationary and evolutionary period of scientific research before they have been able to achieve their industrial supremacy. We are apt to lose sight of the fact that at the bottom of every successful electrical or chemical undertaking lie years of slow, silent and patient research by the devoted students in the laboratory. Almost a century ago, Faraday repeated Oersted's experiment and saw with wonder a magnet going round an electric current. This was the origin of our electric motors, and it would be difficult to calculate how many millions, nay, billions the electric motor has added to the wealth of the world. Wireless telegraphy, which is now an inseparable adjunct of modern life, is not an 'invention' standing alone and conceived apart from all other researches, 'it is a by-product of a consistent and consecutive system of enquiries', to quote Professor Bragg and 'the fruit of many men's work' from Faraday and Maxwell to Hertz and Marconi.

The claims of both Pure and Applied Science are paramount in India as in any other country. I have no intention today to inflict upon you a lengthy dissertation on the comparative merits of Pure and Applied Science. Every country in the world has need of both; no country can do without either. India is just now on the threshold of a political renaissance and no political renaissance is possible without the full development of the intellectual and industrial resources of the country. India, therefore, must not only give her full attention to the cultivation of Pure Science but equally great attention to Applied Science.

Science in Relation to General Progress and Culture

We cannot at the same time afford to disregard the need of a general education and culture or other kinds of social activities. Sir W. Pope has justly observed: 'The entire fabric of any modern state is built up about the manufacturing and agricultural industries of the country. These and the other more obviously intellectual activities of any Western civilisation are as closely interdependent as are the arterial and nervous systems in the animal body; any deficiency or damage occurring in the one systematic component is speedily reflected in a sympathetic deterioration of some seemingly quite disconnected element of the organism. The public neglect of Science in any state is accompanied by poverty of purely intellectual output, by gradual decadence of manufactures, by conservatism of agricultural effort and by the replacement of the statesman by the mere politician.' We find in our own country the consequences of a neglect of these principles. The people are in a state of utter inefficiency and this is nowhere more exemplified than in the shortness of life of an Indian. In India the average expectation of life at birth is about 23 years and in England 46 and in the case of an Indian it is going down from decade to decade.

While the study of Science is essential to our material advancement it has a special need and significance for the culture of Indian youth. A long period of intellectual stagnation, as observed before, had produced in us a habit of dependence on the authority of the *shastras*. Reason was bound to the wheel of faith and all reasoning proceeded on assumption and premises which it was not open to anybody to call in question or criticise. Intellectual progress was handicapped under these conditions and it is no wonder that India cannot point to any notable achievement in this line during the 1,000 years that preceded the advent of British rule. Reason has thus to be set free from the shackles and the function of Science in achieving this end is indisputable. Science takes nothing on trust but applies to them all the methods of investigation and criticism. I look forward to the growth of this scientific spirit in our country to liberalise our intellect. There is no lack of capacity amongst our young men: what are wanted are patience and tenacity of purpose. Science, as Huxley said, requires the virtue of self-surrender. You must patiently observe and interpret the phenomena and events. There is no room for *a priori* reasoning in the realm of Science. The attitude of a scientific mind has been very aptly described by Faraday—'The philosopher,' says he, 'should be a man willing to listen to every suggestion, but determined to judge for himself. He should not be biased by appearances; have no favourite hypotheses; be of no school; and in doctrine have no master. He should not be a respecter of persons but of things. Truth should be his primary object. If to these qualities be added industry, he may indeed hope to walk within the veil of the temple of nature.' It should be the aim of our young men to develop these qualities and nothing is more helpful to their development than the study of Science itself.

Considered from every point of view the progress of scientific knowledge is imperatively necessary to our individual and national growth. For the accomplishment of this object the whole-hearted cooperation of both the Government and the people is indispensable. While the Government must be more liberal in its grants for the cultivation of Science our public-spirited and patriotic countrymen have also a duty to perform. Science owes a great deal to the millionaires of the world. In our country too the examples of Tata, Palit and Ghosh are not wanting. I stand on the platform of a city which is the home of a thriving cotton industry. Here we have merchant princes and successful mill-owners and businessmen. The great philanthropist Andrew Carnegie, himself a self-made man, acted on the motto that 'to die rich is to die disgraced' and gave away more than 100 crores mainly for workingmen's reading rooms and research institutes. I appeal to our wealth and eminence to follow in the footsteps of the great benefactors of men and I am sure that with their help the cause of Science will flourish. The colleges where at present Indian votaries of Science carry on their modest and humble researches have got to be multiplied many times over. More attention should be given in each university now existing in the country to the cultivation of Pure Science particularly Physics and Chemistry, and more colleges and institutes should be established all over the country for the study of Applied Science. It must not be forgotten that the present industrial paralysis of the West offers a golden opportunity to the East to wake up. And if India, by the grace of God, will avail herself of this opportunity to rise equal to the occasion, if her men of Science and industrial pioneers will put their shoulders to the wheel together, if the study of Physics and Chemistry, of Mining and Engineering, of Marine and Aerial Navigation and of the Biological Sciences will succeed in enlisting on their behalf the energy and enthusiasm of thousands of votaries, if the young men of the middle classes will crowd in great numbers the science colleges and the technological institutes more than the law colleges, if the scientific services of the State be thoroughly Indianised, if her rich men will award more scientific scholarships and establish technical schools, India will not take a long time in coming to the forefront of nations and making her political renaissance not a dream but reality.

~

JAGADISH CHANDRA BOSE

The Unity of Life

Jagadish Chandra Bose (1858–1937) was a physicist who pioneered studies in radio and microwave optics. A year after Nikola Tesla made the first public demonstration of radio communication in 1893, Bose conducted experiments in Calcutta to prove that communication signals can be sent without using wires. Though Marconi is generally regarded as the inventor of the wireless, Bose's demonstration of remote wireless signalling is said to have been made before Marconi's. His other stellar contribution to science was in plant physiology where he demonstrated with his crescograph that plants responded to stimuli much like animals do which proved that they had a nervous system and were capable of feeling pain and affection. In the following speech, delivered at the thirteenth session of the Science Congress at Lahore in 1927, Bose explains the process behind his pioneering studies on plant life. It is useful to remember that these studies were conducted in the absence of any technical or research facilities and with no state support to speak of.

In presiding over the Indian Science Congress it is expected that I should give a connected account of my investigations that have been in progress for nearly a third of a century. The results obtained have led to the establishment of the important generalisation of Unity of Life; from this it followed as a corollary, that there must also be an unity of all human efforts and that in the realm of the mind there can be no boundaries and no separations. It is a misreading of the Laws of Nature to regard conflict as the only factor in evolution; far more potent than competition is mutual aid and cooperation in the scheme of life.

Nothing can be more untrue than the ignorant assertion that the world owes its progress of knowledge to any particular race. The whole world is interdependent, and a constant stream of thought has throughout ages enriched the common heritage of mankind. It is the realisation of this mutual dependence that has kept the mighty human fabric bound together and ensured the continuity and permanence of civilisation. Hellenistic Greeks and Eastern Aryans had met here in Taxila to exchange the best each had to offer. After many centuries the East and the West had met once more and it would be the test of the real greatness of the two civilisations that both should be finer and better for the stimulus of contact.

When I commenced my investigations about forty years ago, it was held that by its very peculiar constitution, the Indian mind would always turn away from the study of nature to metaphysical speculations. India was regarded as a land of magic and mysticism where no advance of positive knowledge could be expected. The hypnotic suggestion of inaptitude could only be removed after years of effort, and it is only recently that the generous declaration was made at the Meeting of Intellectual Cooperation, League of Nations 'that India had hitherto been to the West, a land of dreams; they now recognised that these dreams had led to great discoveries. The intellectual cooperation now inaugurated would open out for the world the enormous reserves of thought of Asia, the cradle of civilisation.' It is now my good fortune to see that it is not one but all the provinces of India that are contributing to the advance of different branches of knowledge as is manifest from the activities of the different sections of this Science Congress.

... Previous observers have been misled by the apparent differences between the reactions of animal and plant life. The animal responds to a shock by a twitching movement, while ordinary plants are supposed to be insensitive to a succession of blows. Animals possess sense organs which pick up messages from without, the tremor of excitation being conducted by means of the nervous tissue to the distant motile organ which it causes to move; the plant is supposed not to possess any such conducting tissue. A throbbing organ beats continuously in the animal, for circulation of the nutrient fluid; no similar organ has been suspected in the plant. Two streams of life are thus imagined to flow side by side with little in common between them. This view is wholly incorrect and it is the paralysing influence of wrong speculations that had arrested the advance of knowledge.

In opposition to current views, I was convinced that the mechanism of life of the plant is essentially similar to that of the animal. The demonstration of this would undoubtedly constitute a scientific generalisation of very great importance. For it would then follow that the complex mechanism of the animal machine that has so long baffled us, need not remain inscrutable for all time, since the intricate problems of animal life would naturally find their solution in the study of corresponding problems in the simpler vegetable life. This would mean the possibility of very great advance in the Sciences of General Physiology, of Agriculture, of Medicine and even of Psychology.

The Realm of the Invisible

The real difficulty that thwarts the investigator at every step arises from the fact that the interplay of life action is taking place within the dark profundities of the tree, which our eyes cannot penetrate. In order to reveal the intricate mechanism of its life, it is necessary to gain access to the smallest unit of life, the 'life atom' and record its throbbing pulsation. When microscopic vision fails we have still to explore the realm of the invisible. Until this is done, the intricate problems of life will remain unsolved.

The experimental difficulties have been successfully removed by the invention and construction, in my Institute, of instruments of extreme delicacy and sensitiveness. These new devices by their automatic records, are now revealing the inner mechanism of life, and many regions of inquiry are now opened out which had hitherto been regarded as beyond the scope of experimental exploration. Out of a large number of inventions I will describe a few which render signal service in revealing the hidden activities of life. The *High Magnification Crescograph* instantly records the imperceptible growth, and the variation induced in it under chemical or electrical stimulation. The *Magnetic Crescograph* records movements beyond the highest powers of the microscope, the magnification produced being about 50 million times. Science is measurement and this method of super-magnification has opened out possibilities for great advance in various branches of Science. The *Resonant Recorder* inscribes time as short as a thousandth part of a second, and enables the most accurate determination of the latent or perception period of the plant, and the velocity of transmission of excitation. The *Conductivity Balance* enables the determination of the effect of various drugs in enhancement or depression of the nervous impulse. The *Electric Probe* localises the conducting tissue for the transmission of impulse as also certain pulsating layer of cells in the interior of the tree. The *Electric Phytograph* is the only device for record of the rate of the ascent of sap and the variation induced in it. The *Transpirograph* has enabled determination of the quantity of water transpired by a single stoma of the leaf. The *Optical Sphygmograph* records the pulse-beat of the plant and its modification under various drugs. The *Photosynthetic Recorder* automatically inscribes on a moving drum the rate of carbon-assimilation by plants. It is so extremely sensitive that it detects the formation of carbohydrate as minute as a millionth of a gram. The *Magnetic Radiometer* enables accurate measurement of energy of every ray in the solar spectrum. In conjunction with a special Calorimeter, it has enabled the most accurate determination of the efficiency of the chlorophyll apparatus of green plants in storage of solar energy.

Form and Function

Every organ of a living being is an instrument, subserving a particular function for the advantage of the organism. In Physiology or the study of the phenomena of life, we are primarily concerned with investigations on the function of the organ and not of its form. This will be clearly understood from the comparative study of different types of digestive organs, the primary function of which is to dissolve insoluble organic food by secretion from glands, and the subsequent absorption of the dissolved product. In *Drosera rotundifolia* the leaves are covered with tentacles which discharge a viscid acid secretion. Insects are caught by the secretion and during their struggle the neighbouring tentacles bend over and hold the victims more securely. The insects then become dissolved and digested, the insoluble skeleton being left behind. Nothing could be so strikingly different as this simple type of an open digestive organ from that of the more complex infolded stomach of the animal. Yet functionally one is as much a digestive organ as the other. In the case of Venus Fly-trap or Dionaea, a trap is formed by the two halves of the open leaf, which acts like a gaping mouth closing upon its prey—the captured insect. In the bag-like pitcher of Nepenthe, the digestive organ of the plant approximates more closely to the stomach of an animal.

The plant world affords an unique opportunity for studying the changes by which a simple and primitive organ becomes gradually transformed into one of greater complexity.

The evolutionary process has been active not only in morphological differentiation, that is, in the development of new forms, but also in physiological differentiation, that is, in the development of specialised mechanisms for performance of the various vital functions. There still exists a long-prevalent idea that physiological mechanisms of animals and plants are fundamentally different, because they have been developed along separate lines. The evidence I will adduce will suffice to show that this idea is totally unfounded.

The Sensitiveness of Matter

... How did life make its first appearance on earth? No life, as we understand it now, could have existed when the earth was a mass of molten matter. It has been suggested that the seed of life was imported to this earth by the cosmic dust from other worlds; but this would merely transfer the difficulty backwards. Or perhaps matter itself is sensitive, and has within itself the promise and potency of life, so that at some critical period of the earth's history, the environmental conditions may have favoured the appearance of life in its present form out of non-life.

My investigations have indeed shown that all matter is sensitive, and that they respond to mechanical or electrical stimulation. Over-stimulation was found to cause fatigue from which there was a recovery after a period of rest. Prolonged rest, however, made the substance inert and irresponsive; it had in fact become lazy through lack of stimulation. A strong shock now stirred it up again into readiness for response. Two opposite treatments are thus indicated for fatigue from overwork, and inertness from long passivity! Other experiments showed moreover, that while stimulating drugs cause an enhancement of response, poisons 'kill' it altogether. It would thus appear that sensitiveness is inherent in matter and that there has been a continuous evolution from simple inorganic matter to the highly complex animal life.

Visible Signals of Death

I have succeeded in discovering several exact methods by which the dying organism records its own curve of death. The plant is placed in a thermal bath, the temperature of which is gradually raised. At the definite fatal temperature of 60°C a violent spasm occurs, which corresponds to the death-throe of the animal. An intense electric discharge also takes place at this crisis.

I have recently succeeded in devising a new method, the result of which is somewhat startling. It shows that a plant immersed in a heating bath suddenly loses its buoyancy, and sinks at the fatal temperature.

Automatism

One of the most puzzling phenomena connected with life, is the so-called spontaneous or automatic movements, apparently maintained without any ascertainable cause. Every movement, ordinarily speaking, is due to an antecedent stimulus; but a spontaneously pulsating heart is said to beat of its own accord and therefore regarded as an automatic organ. What is the solution of the mystery of this automatism?

Although such automatic movements are usually associated with animal life, yet similar activities are found in plants like the Telegraph-plant, *Desmodium gyrans*. I have been able to establish the essential similarity between the automatic pulsation of the Telegraph-plant and that of the animal heart, similar effects being induced under variation of temperature, and under different chemical agents, carbonic acid, ether, chloroform and others. Poisonous acids arrest the pulsation of the heart at diastolic expansion; alkaline poison, on the other hand, arrests it at systolic contraction. It is wonderful to discover identical reactions in Desmodium. Poisonous acids arrest the pulsation at diastole, while alkaline poisons produce an arrest at systole. Finally the arrest induced by either of these poisons can be counteracted by the antagonistic action of the other.

These experiments conclusively demonstrate the fundamental identity of the pulsatory mechanism in the animal and in the plant. But the question still remains: what is the cause of these automatic movements?

Wireless Waves on Growth

I investigated the range of perception of the plant in regard to the visible and invisible rays. The plant responds to ultraviolet light with its extremely short wavelength. The effect of light on growth declines towards the yellow and the red. As we proceed further into the infrared region, we come across the vast range of electric radiation the wavelengths of which vary from the shortest wave that I have been able to produce (0.6cm.) to others which may be miles in length. The results of my investigation show that wireless waves produce characteristic variations in growth, depending on the intensity of stimulus. Feeble waves produce an acceleration, while stronger waves produce a retardation of the rate of growth. The perceptive range of the plant is inconceivably greater than ours; it not only perceives, but also responds to the different rays of the vast aetherial spectrum.

It is perhaps as well that our senses are limited in their range. For life would otherwise have been intolerable under the constant irritation of these ceaseless waves of space-signalling to which brick walls are quite transparent. Hermetically sealed metal chambers would then have afforded us the only protection!

The Optical Sphygmograph

Turning next to the plant, any attempt to feel its pulse would, by the very nature of the case, appear to be hopeless. If the plant propelled the sap by periodic pulsation of the active layer, the amount of expansion and contraction of each pulse would be beyond even the highest powers of the microscope to detect. The active cells are, moreover, buried in the interior of the plant; how could the invisible and the hidden be rendered visible?

I nevertheless succeeded in my attempt to record the pulse throb during the passage of the sap-stream as it is pumped up along the stem. The passage of each pulse is attended by an infinitesimal expansion. After the brief passage of the pulse-wave, the stem would revert to its original diameter. In case of identical mechanism in plant and animal, a cardiac stimulant would make the heart-pump of the plant act more energetically, driving the sap faster, causing a greater inflation of the stem. Under depressants the change would be of an opposite character. For recording these infinitesimal dilatations or contractions, it was necessary to construct artificial organs of perception of surpassing delicacy and sensitiveness. The Plant-Feeler or the Optical Sphygmograph, which I have devised, consists of two rods, one of which is fixed and the other movable, the stem of the plant being placed between the two. The movement of the end of the free rod is further magnified by an optical device, the total magnification being about 5 million times. When a dead plant is placed in the apparatus, the indicating line of light remains quiescent, its pulse-beat having been stilled in death. But the imperceptible pulse-beat in the living plant is outwardly manifested by the alternate swings of the beam of light. A depressing agent causes diminished pressure shown by the rush of the light to the left, whereas increased pressure caused by a stimulant produces a rush of light-beam to the right. The waxings and wanings of life are thus for the first time revealed by the moving trail of light.

The Nervous Impulse in Plants

The possession of a nervous system has been denied in the case of plants; my investigations prove, on the other hand, that not only has a nervous system been developed, but that it has attained a high degree of complexity as marked by the reflex arc in which the sensory becomes transformed into a motor impulse. The absence of methods of quantitative measurements has, in the past, led to various unfounded speculations. One of the most grotesque theories recently advanced is that the transmission of excitation in *Mimosa pudica* is due to the excretion of a stimulant by a knife-wound, the stimulant being then carried by the movement of sap caused by the transpiration current. This is a misapplication of the theory of hormone as enunciated by

Starling and Bayliss. There are two different modes of communication between distant organs, by transfer of matter, and by transmission of motion. The first is exemplified by the slow movement of liquids carrying chemical stimulants in solution, such as occurs in the ascent of sap in the plant; the second is the rapid conduction of molecular tremor, from point to point, associated with the propagation of nervous impulse. These two different modes have been aptly likened to communications by post or by telegraph. The difference between the two speeds is so great that it would be an unpardonable mistake to confuse one with the other. The nervous impulse in the plant is sometimes as high as 400 mm per second and is, therefore, several hundred times quicker than the slow rate of ascent of sap. The transpiration current theory presupposes that a wound-stimulus is essential for secretion of a stimulant and that the impulse should always move upwards in the direction of the ascent of sap. I have shown, however, that stimulation can be produced in complete absence of wound and by an electric-shock one-tenth the intensity that evokes human sensation. No demonstration of the totally unfounded character of the transpiration current theory could be more simple and convincing than the observation of the effect of the application of a drop of hydrochloric acid to the tip of the uppermost leaf of Mimosa. The ascent of sap was here impossible; yet an impulse was generated which travelled to a considerable distance downwards, against the direction of the normal ascent of sap. Subsequent chemical examination proved that the stimulant had not been transported, but had remained localized at the point of application.

... From the plant to the animal then, we follow the long stairway of the ascent of life and see the higher and higher expression of that evolutionary process by which life rises above and beyond all the circumstances of the environment and fortifies itself to control them.

~

BIDHAN CHANDRA RAY

The Future of the Medical Profession in India

B.C. Ray (1882–1962) or Bidhan Ray, as he was affectionately referred to, was a leading medical practitioner when he joined the freedom struggle during the non-cooperation movement launched by Gandhi in 1919. One of Gandhi's trusted disciples in Bengal, he became the chief minister of West Bengal after independence. Under his visionary leadership, the state launched a glorious chapter of industrialization, with Durgapur, Kalyani and other industrial clusters and townships coming up. It is not surprising then that people refer to him as the builder of modern Bengal. However, it is as a medical practitioner par excellence that Bidhan Ray is remembered in the world of science and medicine. His profound learning blended with deep empathy for the poor and the underprivileged. In the presidential address of the All India Medical Conference at Lahore in 1929 reproduced below, he calls for integrating the indigenous and ancient systems of medicine in the country with the modern Western system, while criticizing the colonial administration for depriving Indians of a level playing field when it came to medical research and training.

We want to bring together and organise the whole profession, not merely those who profess and practise a particular system of medicine. Our purpose is to secure co-operation amongst all persons whom this Association may consider suitable for membership. Should we restrict the membership to such persons only as follow the Western system of medicine, or open the door to all those who practice, in different parts of the country, any other system with repute and success? If we take medicine merely as a science it may be argued that only those who are trained on scientific methods prevalent in the West should be eligible for the membership. But this, to my mind, is to take a very narrow view of the whole matter. On the other hand, if we define science as a systematised branch of human knowledge, we cannot ignore other systems. I have no doubt whatever that there was a time when the ancient practitioners in medicine—those who elaborated the Ayurvedic system centuries ago—possessed accurate knowledge of the nervous system, of the vascular system, of the changes in pulse in different diseases, and that their knowledge of pathology, such as we understand it today, was of a high order. Speaking in the Imperial Legislative Council in 1916, Sir Pardey Lukis, the then Director-General, said: 'I resent strongly the spirit of trade unionism which leads many modern doctors to stigmatise all Vaids and Hakims as quacks and charlatans. We Allopaths are just emerging from the slough of empiricism. The longer I live in India, the more intimate my connection with Indians, the greater will be my appreciation of the wisdom of the ancients and the more will I understand that the West has still much to learn from the East.'

Other eminent observers also have spoken in a similar strain. Therefore, it is not for us to cut off from the past systems, but it is necessary to resuscitate them, to develop them. If we desire to do so, we cannot ignore them. It is true that the knowledge in those systems has been handed down from generation to generation in the form of sutras, which were committed to memory. The result was that the bulk of information was compressed into a small compass. In the process of transmission the links are gone, the original is mutilated, accretions have gathered and evidence or data on which the conclusions were founded are missing. What we are left with now are dogmatism and perhaps empiricism. On the other hand, if we regard medicine as an art of healing, who is there so bold as to say that this art is the exclusive achievement of one system. Considered thus, the claims of those who practise not the Western but some other system of medicine to be included in the group of medical practitioners become almost irresistible. I would, therefore, desire to see the membership of this Association open to those who honestly believe in their own system of medicine and practice it with real sincerity.

When we organise or attempt to organise any group of people we do so both for the purpose of attacking and defending. Problems connected with the health of the citizens of this country, with the means of preventing diseases and the spread of epidemics, with the method of generating a sanitary consciousness amongst the masses of this country, are items which are to be attacked with determination, courage, resourcefulness, hope and faith. On the other hand, everyone of us realises that we, the medical practitioners in India, are the victims of circumstances and designs which are inimical to the growth of this profession and we have to defend ourselves against them. In the domains of medical education, medical research, medical relief or prevention of diseases, determined and systematic efforts have been made in the past to keep us in a perpetual state of inaction and stagnation. We are told that our education is defective, that we have no original research to our credit, that our ability to provide relief in diseases is of an inferior order, that we cannot administer institutions established for the purpose of affording such relief, that we cannot initiate and successfully carry out schemes for the prevention of diseases. Assuming, for the sake of argument, that this is so, it may pertinently be said, so far as the members who practise the Western system are concerned, that it is clear that the present unsatisfactory condition could grow in it, or the tiller was so careless or ignorant that he did not care, or he did not know how to achieve success in his work. But who are responsible for the training of our youths in medicine?

As far as back as 1912 and 1913, the members of the Indian Medical Service gave evidence before the Public Services Commission that 'the standard of medical education in India is low and that the Indian practitioner is unpractical, that the British schools are far more efficient than Indian colleges', and yet in the year 1913, out of 24 appointments in the Indian Medical Service, 8 Indians got in by competition, and in 1914, out of 35 such posts, 14 were secured by Indians.

We have been blamed because there is no record of research to the credit of the Indian medical practitioners. What is the real root cause? Are Indians incapable of research? Sir J.C. Bose, Sir P.C. Roy, Sir C.V. Raman and Dr Meghnad Saha have won world-wide reputations in research without any guidance or tuition from Westerners. Why cannot the Indian medical practitioners equally succeed? To be successful in medical research it is not only necessary that those who are engaged in it should be provided with laboratories, but hospital facilities should also be secured for them. Till within recent years, all the larger hospitals in this country were manned by members belonging to the Indian Medical Service. All the research appointments were and still are being held by the Service Officers. The process of exclusion has been so carefully, may I say shamelessly, planned and manipulated that even an Indian of established repute has no chance of getting into the group. As regards the management of large hospitals and institutions, the question of the inefficiency of Indians does not arise, because no opportunity is given to Indians to manage any of these hospitals. The indisputable fact remains that in spite of such obstructive methods and in spite of the handicap due to paucity of funds, two large institutions, one in Calcutta and another in Bombay, have been developed and managed entirely under Indian supervision. It is a decisive argument against the charge of inefficiency attributed to Indians. Studied carelessness on the part of the I.M.S. officers in discharging the responsible duties cast upon them, namely, that of developing an Indian Medical Profession, the prearranged method of keeping the Indians out of every opening where they could develop themselves, is responsible for the present state of affairs. Knowledge gives vision to the blind. But perverse attempts have been made to perpetuate the infirmity.

Whatever may have happened in the past, we have now reached a stage when we, as members of the medical profession in India, desire to fulfil our mission, to develop ourselves and to realise the hope with which we adopted the career of a physician. We are prepared to profit by the knowledge of the West, but not under conditions in which it engenders hatred for what is Eastern. I am happy to say our goal is getting clearer, that our vision is getting less obscured, that our self-confidence is being restored and that the whole medical profession in India is being linked together by a common bond of faith and hope.

~

MEGHNAD SAHA

The Present World—One Economic and Cultural Unit

Meghnad Saha (1893–1956), world-renowned astrophysicist, produced what later came to be known as Saha's 'Thermo-Ionisation Equation', or the Saha Equation, which became the foundation for the field of astrophysics. Saha's fundamental contribution to Indian science lies in providing it with an institutional basis. He was at the forefront of organizing scientific societies like the National Academy of Science, the Indian Physical Society and the Indian Institute of Science. He was also associated with setting up the physics department in Allahabad University and the Institute of Nuclear Physics in Calcutta. A visionary in the truest sense of the word, his presidential address at the Indian Science Congress in 1934 is probably the clearest exposition of his vision. While advocating the establishment of an Indian Academy of Science, the speech brought to the fore another of Saha's primary concerns—recurring floods in river embankments. An architect of river planning in India, he made a stellar contribution in the areas of flood control and harnessing river water, framing the original plan for the Damodar Valley Project which became the model for multipurpose river valley projects in India.

The return of the Indian Science Congress to Bombay for the third time after the lapse of eight years bespeaks of the large-hearted liberality for which the citizens of Bombay have been distinguished. On this occasion, specially on behalf of the scientists assembled here, I have to convey to the hosts our heartfelt thanks for the ready response which they made to our call of distress. I have further to remind my colleagues that today at Bombay the Science Congress attains the legal age for majority, when we shall be quite within our rights to claim for the Congress, from the state as well as from the public, those rights and privileges which are enjoyed by similar associations in other countries of the world. But of these demands, I shall speak only during the concluding parts of my address.

At present, the fact is only slowly dawning on the public that the world is fast becoming one great economic unit. A crash in Wall Street leads to a strike in the Bombay Mills, and unemployment in Lancashire leads to fall in the price of jute in Bengal, and ultimately to Hindu-Muslim riots. A prosperous year in India leads to an increased consumption of foreign goods. Overpopulation in Japan and China causes a clash in Manchuria between the two peoples, and is fraught with menace towards Australia and insular India and to world peace. The rulers of countries cannot therefore persist in their Olympian attitude towards other nations—they must become earth-wide in their outlook. But this is prevented by the present faulty system of education which seeks to perpetuate the mediaeval mind, and brings only a small percentage of the population under the humanising influence of Science. The result is disastrous; those who are called upon to guide the nations are mostly men with a rigid outlook, quite unfit to fathom the depths of present-day troubles, or analyse the intricacies of political and economic issues, and unable to hold out any programme of reconstruction. In our country, the result is competitive communalism; among the free nations, a tense atmosphere of competitive nationalism, and between the ruler and subject nations, a spirit of revolt against suffocating imperialism.

But economic and scientific studies show that the world has resources enough for her whole population, and if there be a rational programme of production, and a programme of judicious and equitable distribution, nobody should suffer from hunger, privation, and can even afford to have much better amenities of life. But for this purpose, rivalry amongst nations and communities should give way to cooperative construction and the politician should hand over many of his functions to an international board of trained scientific industrialists, economists, and eugenists who will think in terms of the whole world as a unit, and devise means by which more necessities of life can be got out of the earth; the whole production should be controlled by scientific industrialists, and the distribution should be supervised by the economists. The eugenics should devise means for assigning a fixed quota of population to each geographical unit which it should not be allowed to exceed. It may seem to be a dream, but is perfectly feasible provided the educational programme is thoroughly revised. A new educational scheme should be devised by a World's Congress of foremost thinkers like Bergson, Einstein, Bertrand Russell, Smuts, Spengler, and others, with the special objective of weeding out mediaeval passions from the minds of the coming generation, and for training them to a proper grasp and sufficient appreciation of the beauty and powers of Science. The joy of life for the grown-up men will be provided not in designing means for the plunder or exploitation of our fellow-men in various ways but in administering to their needs, and in free development and display of the finer faculties of the mind.

The Proposals for an Indian Academy of Science

At the present time, the hopes of world peace based on a scientific handling of economic and political problems appear to be, as you are well aware, very distant, for the world forces are moving in such a direction that it is more likely that instead of establishing an era of world peace, and coordinated scientific exploration for the benefit of the whole mankind, the present generation will fulfil Spengler's pessimistic prophecy of the end of a cycle resulting in the crash of modern civilisation. In any case whether we move towards peace or war, it is clear that the prospects of a better future lie entirely with Science. Every country must, for the sake of self-preservation, as well as for the benefit of mankind, husband all its resources scientifically and must foster and stimulate scientific thought. The great industrial ventures, whether private or State, must make increasing use of Science, for otherwise they will not answer the world needs and achieve the desired results.

So in every country, India not excepted, the State must awaken to the need for a proper organisation of her scientific brains.

Confining to our country, it is well-known that a good amount of scientific work, which often led to great industrial enterprises, has been done in the past by the various scientific services. Within the last few years, the Agricultural Research Council has been founded in which a happy departure is noticeable. Unlike the older services, whose organisation probably did not enable them to make use of non-official scientific brain available in the Universities or private institutions, the constitution of the Agricultural Council has been such as to enable it to make full use of all available talent, which is a happy and new departure in the policy of the Government of India.

In this connection, the non-official scientific men have a just cause of grievance against the government. I remember to have read, a few years ago, a short article by our energetic secretary Dr. Agharkar, in the *Modern Review* where he invited attention to the close cooperation existing between workers in the scientific services of the Government, and Professors in Universities in other countries, and complained of its total absence in this country. In other countries, the cooperation is so complete that it is not unusual to find that Universities and Services very often exchange their workers to the mutual advantage of both. I do not see why this cooperation should not be secured in our country as well, and the existing services should not be reorganised on the lines of the Agricultural Research Council.

Need for a River Physics Laboratory

There are many lines in which the Government of India as well as the Provincial Governments can profit immensely if they take the trouble of obtaining proper scientific guidance before launching on large-scale enterprises. As many such cases are not known to you all, I would refer to only one. You are aware that year after year, the Government and other public bodies spend an enormous amount in constructing bridges and water reservoirs, in opening canals, in development schemes, in hydroelectric schemes, and in city drainage schemes which are certainly highly beneficial and undertaken with the best of intentions, but you are certainly also aware that from time to time, very unpleasant facts leak through the columns of the news agency, which show that these schemes are mishandled at some stage or other. Every scientific man knows that before the actual working commences the plans should be scientifically studied in Hydraulic Research Laboratories, with the aid of models and the engineers in charge of constructions should have a clear-cut idea of the work before they are put in charge of it. You may be knowing that in spite of the fact that next to the United States of America, India is the country which has undertaken such works on the most gigantic scale and has spent hundreds of crores of rupees on these works, the Government has not yet thought it fit to establish a single Hydraulic Research or River Physics Laboratory in this country while in other civilised countries no such enterprise is allowed to be undertaken unless the plans are examined in suitable laboratories attached either to the Universities, Technical High Schools, or state departments with the aid of suitable models... I should merely add that I am not against the launching of the schemes, in fact many of them, like the Panjab Canals, have done immense good to the country. But others, like the Orissa and

Midnapur Canals, were constructed on faulty lines, and involved the state in huge financial losses; while other schemes like the laying of railway lines through major parts of Bengal without a proper examination of topography and of the river systems have plunged the country into perpetual outbreaks of malarial epidemics, and led to the sapping of the vitality of the population. I do not hold that either the engineers or the officials are responsible for these failure and disasters. In fact I think that most of them...tried to make the best use of a bad situation. But the fault is due to lack of imagination on the part of those who have taken upon themselves the task of Government and to their failure in devising a proper system of coordinated work in which preliminary scientific study in suitable laboratories should form an essential part of the organisation.

Need for a National Academy of Sciences

It is clear that for these and other reasons which are too numerous to be discussed here, it is necessary that scientific men in India should be better organised, and should try to impress upon the Government, the States, and other public bodies the need for encouragement of scientific research, and for a scientific handling of economic and industrial problems of the country. The best way for them to do so is to organise themselves into a corporate body... Our energetic secretaries have in the pamphlet now in your hands acquainted you with the full history of movement as well as of the various proposals for carrying the idea into action.

... On going through the various proposals, one finds, as is naturally expected, considerable divergence of opinion, regarding the manner and details of organisation and it has appeared to me advisable that it will probably help the general body here to arrive at a practicable course of action, if I were to summarise these views and give my own ideas on them. You are not expected to adhere to my views, but these may be regarded as commentaries on the proposals which the secretaries have brought forward for discussion. These are: 1. whether it is desirable to form an Indian Academy on lines similar to those in Europe or America; 2. if answer to (1) be in the affirmative, whether there should be one Academy for all branches of learning, or there should be separate Academies for Arts and Letters.

I have no reason to doubt that answer to 1 would be in the affirmative. Regarding 2 there are two separate issues involved.

First of all, it is clear that the Academy cannot assume the functions of the sectional societies dealing with different branches of science, consisting of scientists engaged in research in these branches like, the Indian Chemical Society, or the Indian Botanical Society, or the various mathematical societies having an unlimited membership. This is neither necessary, desirable, nor feasible. It is true that many branches of science have not yet organised themselves into societies. It is hoped that they will do so in the near future, and it will be one of the duties of the Academy to help in the organisation of these societies. But as long as they are not in existence, the Indian Academy may continue to take care of these subjects.

The Indian Academy will therefore be a Central Society, on which all branches of science will be represented, or to borrow a simile, it will form like the Royal Society in England, or the Prussian Academy in Germany, the apex of a pyramid of societies devoted to particular subjects. It should have therefore a limited membership. Its membership should be regarded as a mark of distinction and honour and the Academy should be associated with the State in a number of responsible duties involving scientific work.

~

C.V. RAMAN

The Raman Effect

Sir C.V. Raman (1888–1970) was one of the greatest physicists of the twentieth century. After getting his graduate and postgraduate degrees from Presidency College, Madras, he joined the Indian Civil Service as an assistant accountant general in Calcutta. Simultaneously, he started conducting scientific experiments at the Indian Association for the Cultivation of Science. It was here that he came to the notice of Asutosh Mukherjee who brought him over to the physics department of the University of Calcutta. He presided over the Indian Science Congress in 1929 and in the next year received the Nobel Prize for his work on the scattering of light and his discovery of what came to be called the Raman Effect. This speech, the presidential address at the Indian Science Congress in Madras in 1929, was on the Raman Effect.

Your Excellency, Ladies and Gentlemen, it is the privilege of a physicist to concern himself with what may be regarded as the fundamental entities of the material universe we live in. His theories and experiments are directed towards obtaining a clearer understanding of the nature of those entities and of their relationships with each other. His results if expressed in plain language should be intelligible not only to those who profess other branches of Science, but to all who take an interest in the varied phenomena of Nature. The work of the physicist has the closest possible bearing on the interpretation of facts observed in other fields of scientific knowledge. No apology is therefore needed for my decision to devote this address to an exposition of the nature and significance of a new phenomenon recently discovered in my laboratory at Calcutta which has a bearing on the fundamental problems of Physics and Chemistry.

Every one of us is or should be interested in the nature of that phenomenon which we call *light* and which is a species of the genus *radiation*. Light is emitted by matter under suitable conditions of excitation. We heat an atom or excite it by electric discharge. It becomes luminous and gives off radiation. What is radiation? On this point, the physicists of the nineteenth century had come to the very definite conclusion, based on evidence which it seemed impossible could ever be shaken, that light is a kind of wave motion travelling through space, and of the same physical nature as the electromagnetic waves discovered by Hertz and now so familiar to all as the waves of wireless telegraphy and telephony. Remarkably enough, however, the present century has witnessed a re-opening of the question. I will not pause here to trace in detail the history of the development of what is known today as the quantum theory of radiation. It is associated with the names of three great living physicists, namely, Planck, Einstein, and Niels Bohr. It will suffice for my purpose to indicate the very definite and intelligible form it received in Bohr's well-known theory of spectra. According to Bohr, the emission of light from an atom is not a single process but takes place in two distinct stages. The first stage is the energising of the atom, in other words, its passing over from a normal or non-luminous condition into a new state of higher energy content. The second stage is the return of the atom to a condition of lower energy accompanied by the emission of light. Bohr found it necessary, in order to interpret the facts of spectroscopy, to assume that the different states of the atom are sharply differentiated from each other in their energy content. The atom therefore takes up energy or gives up energy as the case may be, in passing from one state to another, in discrete bundles or quanta. Radiation is thus absorbed or emitted by the atom in discrete bundles of energy. It follows naturally that while travelling through space, light also remains as discrete bundles or quanta of radiation. A distinctly unitary character is thus indicated for radiation.

Further powerful support for a corpuscular idea of radiation came to hand a few years ago when Prof. A.H. Compton, now of Chicago University, discovered a remarkable phenomenon which is now known by his name as the Compton Effect, and for which he received the Nobel Prize in Physics a year ago. Briefly, what he found was this: When X-rays fall upon matter and the scattered rays are analysed by an X-ray spectroscope, the lines in the X-ray spectrum are found to be doubled. Prof. Compton gave a very simple and remarkable explanation of this fact. He regarded the incident X-rays as consisting of corpuscles which moved with the velocity of light and on hitting an electron in the scattering material dislodged it and were themselves deviated from their straight path. It is obvious that in such a process the deviated corpuscle would lose part of its energy, this being taken up by the recoiling electron. Prof. Compton's explanation of his effect is supported by the fact that the recoil of the electron is actually observed in experiment. A change in energy of the quantum is equivalent to a change in the frequency of scattered radiation, which therefore appears in the X-ray spectrum as a line in a shifted position. Measurements of the change of wavelength and of the velocity of the recoil-electron appeared strongly to support Prof. Compton's theory, and the latter has therefore gained general acceptance.

We appear thus to have reached the astonishing position that two distinct theories of light both claim our acceptance. In other words, light consists of waves expanding spherically outwards from a luminous atom into ever-increasing volumes of space, and it also consists of a corpuscle shot off in some specific direction from the luminous atom and therefore moving along a straight line to infinity. I have often seen it suggested that there might be no real conflict between these two widely different points of view if we regard the light corpuscle statistically. In other words, if we had a sufficiently large number of atoms giving out corpuscles, the two pictures of radiation may be statistically equivalent. So indeed they would be, if a corpuscle emitted from one atom and a corpuscle emitted from another could be regarded as equivalent. But such a conception would be totally repugnant to wave principles. For, when we consider a luminous gas, the waves emitted by the different atoms in it would not be equivalent unless all the atoms were at the same place and emitting light-waves in identical phase. It is obviously difficult to accept the latter proposition, and in fact we may be fairly certain that it is untrue. The particular suggestion here made for securing a statistical equivalence of the wave and quantum theories of radiation seems therefore untenable. My own feeling is that it is impossible to accept the wave and quantum theories of radiation as simultaneously true if Compton's idea of a localised quantum is a correct and universal description of the process of radiation from atoms. In order to explain the familiar facts of optical interference and diffraction, we are compelled to assume that the light emitted by a luminous atom spreads out spherically with identical velocity and phase in all directions. Theoretically it is possible to analyse a spherical wave into a set of plane-directed waves passing simultaneously through the centre of the sphere in all directions, *provided they are all in identical phases at the centre*. We may, of course, regard a plane wave as equivalent to a directed quantum in the sense of Compton, but as a single atom can only radiate one quantum at a time, it is impossible to explain interference if we assume the emission to consist generally of directed quanta. In Compton's own experiment, we are dealing with the secondary radiation from an atom illuminated by X-rays of wavelength much shorter than the diameter of the atom. This is a very different problem from that of an atom radiating spontaneously in all directions. In a paper appearing in the *Indian Journal of Physics*, I have discussed the case of Compton from what I believe to be rather a novel point of view, and shown that so far from the Compton Effect being opposed to the classical wave principles, the latter actually indicate the existence of such an effect, and quantitatively predict its observed characters. On the view developed in my paper, Compton's experiment is not a disproof of the spreading wave theory. We do not regard the beam of radiation thrown out in a straight line by a light house and travelling for miles without appreciable spreading, as a contradiction of wave principles, but explain it as an effect produced by the lenses and mirrors of the light house. In an analogous way, I utilise the relation between the wavelength of the radiation and the size of the atom to explain Compton's results. The investigation shows that the classical and quantum theories of radiation are indeed statistically equivalent, but this equivalence is secured by the properties of the atom, and not by filling space with localised quanta. I will go so far as to say that in my view, it is entirely futile to regard the light quantum as a particle having any specifiable shape, size or position.

This theoretical paper on the Compton Effect was worked out during a holiday at Waltair in October, 1927. Apart from any little intellectual satisfaction which its writing may have given me, its chief interest is that it prepared the ground for the experimental work of the following months which I shall now mention.

Eight years ago, we commenced at Calcutta a series of experimental studies on the scattering of light in transparent media of all kinds. These studies were largely inspired by a desire to understand and explain fully such natural optical phenomena as the light of the sky, the dark blue colour of the deep sea and the delicate opalescence of ice in glaciers. It soon became evident that the laboratory studies intended in the first place to reproduce these natural phenomena on a small scale would carry us some way towards a solution of such fundamental problems of Physics as the constitution and structure of molecules, their number, arrangement and thermal movements in gaseous, liquid and solid media, and the nature of radiation itself. I will not fatigue you by reciting the numerous experimental and theoretical researches carried out by us on these subjects. Associated with me during these eight years were a great many young physicists from all parts of India who received their research training in my laboratory. Amongst them, I would specially mention the names of Dr. K.R. Ramanathan and of Mr. K.S. Krishnan, both by reason of their conspicuous originality in research and in view of the importance of their personal contributions to the development of the subject now under discussion. To them, and to my numerous other collaborators from Bengal and Madras and Northern India, I owe a debt of gratitude.

At a very early stage in our investigations, we came across a new and entirely unexpected phenomenon. As early as 1923, it was noticed when sunlight filtered through a violet glass passes through certain liquids and solids, e.g., water or ice, the scattered rays emerging from the track of the incident beam through the substance contained certain rays not present in the incident beam. The observations were made with colour filters. A green glass was used which cut off all light if placed between the violet filter and the substance. On transferring the glass to a place between the substance and the observer's eye, the track continued to be visible though feebly. This is a clear proof of a real transformation of light from a violet into a green ray. The most careful chemical purification of the substance failed to eliminate the phenomenon. Subsequent investigations showed the same effect in a considerable number of liquids and solids, and we even attempted a spectroscopic investigation of it.

Though, from time to time, we returned to the study of this new phenomenon and published accounts of it, its real significance as a twin brother to the Compton Effect first became clear to me at the end of 1927 when I was preoccupied with the theory of the subject. I regarded the ejection of the electron in the Compton Effect as essentially a fluctuation of the atom of the same kind as would be induced by heating the atom to a sufficiently high temperature, and the so-called directed quantum of Compton as merely an unsymmetrical emission of radiation from the atom which occurs at the same time as the fluctuation in its electrical state. The conception of fluctuations is a very familiar one in optical and kinetic theory, and in fact all our experimental results in the field of light-scattering had been interpreted with its aid. There was, therefore, every reason to expect that radiations of altered wavelength corresponding to fluctuations in the state of the scattering molecules should be observed also in the case of ordinary light.

The idea was energetically taken up and the experiments showed it to be completely correct. It became clear that we had here a new radiation effect far more general and universal in its character than the Compton Effect, and of which the latter could be regarded as a special case. The ejection of an electron is a very violent type of fluctuation. There are numerous other comparatively mild types of fluctuation possible in the electrical state of atoms and molecules. Such fluctuations correspond to relatively small changes in the energy level of the atomic system in the sense of Bohr. If a change of energy level is produced by the incident radiation and is simultaneous with it, the quantum of radiation emitted under these conditions may be greater or smaller as the case may be than the quantum of incident radiation. We may represent this change as a chemical reversible reaction.

MOLECULE + RADIATION MOLECULE + RADIATION
(normal state) (high frequency) (excited state) (low frequency)

If the reaction proceeds in the direction of the upper arrow, we have a diminution in frequency of the radiation, and if in the direction of the lower arrow, we have an increase of frequency. The relative importance of the two types of reaction would obviously be determined by the law of mass-action, that is to say, upon the populations of the normal and excited states of the molecules present in the irradiated substance. In ordinary cases, the presence of excited states is determined by temperature. Other causes of excitation of molecules if present must also be taken into account.

Since atomic and molecular systems have many possible energy levels as shown by the facts of spectroscopy, we see in the foregoing chemical equation the possibility of observing a great many new lines in the spectrum of the scattered radiation.

The most convenient way of studying the effect is by using the intense monochromatic radiation of the mercury arc and to condense its light into the substance, or better, actually to bring the arc into close proximity with the substance as in the well-known work of R.W. Wood on resonance spectra. The spectrum of the scattered radiation is then readily photographed and shows a multitude of new lines, bands, and in addition continuous radiation. The relation between the frequencies of the incident and scattered radiations will be readily noticed from the equation written above ... The difference between the incident and scattered quanta is equal to the quantum of absorption or emission, or as the case may be, of the molecules. The characteristic frequency of the molecule is, therefore, subtracted from or added to the frequency of the incident radiation to give that of the scattered light.

In one sense, this combination of the incident frequency with the frequency of the molecule is an analogue of the classical phenomena of Tartini's Tones which we are familiar with in acoustical theory, and which are explained in terms of the forced vibrations of a non-harmonic oscillator. This analogy may no doubt be used to find the intensity of the modified radiations approximately, by applying the correspondence principle to a non-harmonic molecular model of suitable type. The difference between this classical analogue and the actually observed optical effect is in the extraordinary disproportion between the intensity of the lines corresponding to the differential and summational tones respectively, which is far greater than in the acoustical analogies.

An extremely interesting and fundamental point regarding the new type of secondary radiation is that, in general, it is strongly polarised. In this respect, the phenomenon is analogous to the experimentally known polarisation of the Compton type of X-ray scattering. We notice, however, that the different lines corresponding to different molecular frequencies are polarised to very different extents. It may be presumed that this is due to the molecular oscillators involved not possessing spherical symmetry. Whether this explanation is sufficient or not remains to be tested by computation and comparison with observation.

We may here pause a little to consider more closely the real significance of our phenomenon. Some, no doubt, will claim to see in it a further confirmation of the quantum theory of radiation. My own view, however, is that there is nothing in the effect that in any way contradicts the wave principles, and that on the other hand the fact that we can cut up or add to the quantum of energy to any arbitrary extent is unfavourable to the idea of a real, corporeal existence for it. We may, of course, get over this difficulty by assuming that the incident quantum in some way disappears on collision with the molecule, and that a new quantum of smaller or larger energy arises from the combination. But the observed fact of the strong polarisation of the lines is unfavourable to the latter idea. As already indicated in the foregoing discussions, the concept of localised quanta is irreconcilable with the phenomena of wave optics, and the necessity for introducing it is even less in the present case than in the Compton type of scattering.

I shall now pass on to consider some applications of the new effect. Its potential value perhaps is greatest in the field of Chemistry. The method of investigation affords us an extraordinarily easy and convenient process of mapping the infrared spectra of chemical compounds. The geometry of the chemical molecule and the forces of chemical affinity determine the frequencies of molecular vibrations. In many cases, they lie in the far infrared, a region of the spectrum which has hitherto been difficultly accessible to observation. The study of light-scattering enables us, as it were, to photograph the whole infrared spectrum with the same facility and ease as the visible and ultraviolet spectra. The determination of the fundamental vibration frequencies of the chemical molecule, their relative importance as gauged by the intensities of the lines, and even more, their peculiar polarisation characters promise to take us deep into the fundamental problems of Chemistry. As an illustration, I will mention a recent paper by Daure in the *Comptes Rendus* of the French Academy. Daure investigated the spectra of the chlorides of carbon, silicon, titanium, arsenic, lead, antimony and bismuth by this method. The investigation revealed hitherto unknown spectra in the far infrared for each of the compounds studied, exhibiting remarkable analogies and differences amongst each other in the position, intensity and polarisation of the lines.

In Organic Chemistry also, the method opens up an illimitable field of research. Numerous lines appear whose positions in many cases are accurately measurable, and are influenced notably by changes in chemical constitution. A very surprising feature is the extreme sharpness of some of the lines. The frequencies of the vibration of the carbon-carbon bond in benzene can be determined, for example, with extraordinary precision unapproachable by other methods. It is precisely this accuracy of measurement and the rich and varied mass of data obtainable that indicate for this method a real future.

The study of the influence of changes of temperature and pressure, and of a change of physical state on the intensity, positions and widths of the spectral lines promises to furnish information of value in the field of Molecular Physics. Already in our earliest observations it was noticed that the spectral lines obtained with ice are sharper and somewhat displaced in position relatively to the broad bands found with liquid water. The sharpness of the lines observed with transparent crystals appears to be a general feature. As an example I may mention the case of selenite in which Mr. Krishnan found that the water of crystallisation also gave well-defined lines instead of the bands observed with water.

Preliminary studies have shown that it is perfectly practicable to photograph the lines in the spectra of vapours. Hence it will be possible in many cases to investigate the changes in molecular spectra in the passage from vapour to liquid as well as those in the passage from liquid to solid. In the change from vapour to liquid, we have a partial destruction of the freedom of rotation of the molecules. Such observations as we have made seem to indicate that exchanges of energy between the incident quantum and the molecule can also occur with respect to the rotational states of the molecule. The optical anisotropy of the molecule appears to be involved in the possibility of such induced molecular rotation. Whether the removal of restriction on rotational freedom when the molecule passes from liquid to vapour results in a fuller development of such rotational spectra remains to be investigated.

At low temperatures, many liquids as is known refuse to crystallise, become highly viscous and ultimately are transformed into glasses. Glycerine is a typical example of such a liquid. Mr. Venkateswaran has observed in it a remarkable development of a continuous spectrum whose intensity falls with rise of temperature or by dilution with water. The precise origin of this phenomenon and the existence of similar effects at low temperatures in the case of other viscous liquids remain to be studied. The problem of the amorphous solid condition is related to this. Already Pringsheim has noted that fused quartz, unlike the crystalline substance, does not show any lines in the scattered spectrum. The explanation of this may be that the lines have become too broad and diffuse to be photographed.

6

TOWARDS FREEDOM

The First World War sowed the seeds for the emergence of a new world order where Great Britain would no longer be the empire 'on which the sun never sets'. Though Britain and the Allied forces emerged victorious, the economic cost of the war was too great and the process of disintegration of the empire, which would reach its apogee almost thirty years later, began now. In India, the national movement for freedom too experienced a paradigm shift. And the man responsible for this was Mohandas Karamchand Gandhi. Gandhi had returned to India in 1915 after spending over two decades in South Africa where he led a heroic struggle on behalf of Indian workers and other oppressed classes against the racial and discriminatory policies of the rulers. It was during this struggle that he first experimented with satyagraha and non-violence as political weapons.

By 1918, Gandhi had established himself as a leader with a unique way of protesting exploitation and injustice. In 1917, the country got its first taste of his style of agitation when he went to Champaran in Bihar to see for himself the plight of the indigo peasants who were being severely exploited. When Gandhi reached Champaran, the district magistrate ordered him to leave the district. He, however, declined to comply with the order, in 'obedience to the highest law of our being', as he said in the courtroom. Not only was the expulsion order withdrawn, Gandhi and his associates were allowed to record the complaints of the peasants, which were then presented to the government. The latter could not ignore the facts and the official committee appointed to look into the peasants' complaint unanimously asked for the abolition of the system whereby the peasants were being forced to grow indigo on part of their land even though its price was falling. This was a new development in the history of the national movement and it made big news all over the country. Gandhi also led the textile workers in Ahmedabad against the mill-owners and organized a satyagraha among the peasants in Kheda against the imposition of land tax. His simple and austere life made the masses identify with him as one of them.

At the same time, the Muslim intelligentsia in the country was agitated at what they saw as a breach of faith on the part of the British. The Ottoman Empire had suffered a major military defeat in the First World War. While the Treaty of Versailles (1919) reduced its territorial extent and diminished its political influence, the Allied forces promised to protect the Ottoman emperor's status as the Caliph. However, under the Treaty of Sevres (1920), a number of territories were carved out of the empire. Mohammad Ali, Shaukat Ali, Abul Kalam Azad and sections of the ulema launched the Khilafat agitation to protest this move. They approached Gandhi, who sympathized with the Khilafat cause, as he believed that the British had violated a promise, and appealed to the Congress to side with the Khilafatists. At this juncture, the government hurriedly passed the Rowlatt Act which provided for incarceration of people even without trial. The act soon became the rallying ground for the non-cooperation movement.

Gandhi suggested the formation of satyagraha sabhas to protest against the draconian law. An all-India hartal was planned for 30 March 1919. The date was later postponed to 6 April. Hartal was observed in Delhi, Orissa, Assam, Madras, Bombay and Bengal. On 13 April, the police opened fire on a peaceful gathering of people at Jallianwala Bagh in Amritsar, killing hundreds of unarmed people. Subsequently, martial law was clamped. The Jallianwala Bagh incident incensed the country. Poet and Nobel laureate Rabindranath Tagore returned his knighthood in protest. The Hunter Commission, set up to inquire into the incident, published a report which Gandhi later termed as 'page after page of whitewash'.

In November 1919, the All India Khilafat Committee met at Allahabad where Gandhi proposed adoption of a non-violent non-cooperation movement. The proposal was accepted and the movement soon engulfed the country. Abul Kalam Azad, Maulana Akram Khan and Muniruzamman Islamabadi made the movement popular in Bengal. Akram Khan's *Mohammadi* propagated the spirit of swadeshi and boycott. Mohammad Ali's *Hamdard* and *Comrade* and Abul Kalam Azad's *Al Hilal* were powerful organs in spreading the message of the movement. In the meantime, Gandhi was trying to bring the Congress round to the idea of non-violent non-cooperation. In September 1920, at a special meeting of the Congress in Calcutta, there was some opposition to the idea. In December 1920, however, the Congress at its annual session at Nagpur unanimously accepted the non-cooperation resolution. The country now plunged into what was its first mass political movement. Khilafat and non-cooperation mingled to produce a powerful mass upheaval. Schools, law courts and foreign cloth were boycotted. People all over the country adopted the charkha and swadeshi cloth. The Congress had already announced in Nagpur that the attainment of swaraj by peaceful and legitimate means was its goal. There was, therefore, a new enthusiasm for an impending freedom, which Gandhi said would come within a year. The peasants joined the movement in Oudh, Bengal, Madras, Bombay, Bihar and Assam. A new leadership, of which a large number came from the rural area, emerged. Tribal movements in Bihar and the Manipur hills were also influenced by the movement and the message of Gandhi. The movement was poised for a new phase when, on 4 February 1922, a group of people in Chauri Chaura, Gorakhpur, provoked by the police, attacked a police station and burnt the policemen alive. Gandhi decided to suspend the movement. He was criticized for the decision by almost all leaders cutting across political affiliations, but he remained unmoved. For him, principles were not to be sacrificed. Non-violence was not to be diluted.

Rise of the Peasantry, the Working Class and the Left

The sudden suspension of the movement created a sense of helplessness. Chittaranjan Das and Motilal Nehru formed the Swaraj Party in a bid to enter the assemblies and wreck them from within. Gandhi's programme had no place for electoral battle. So while the swarajists fought elections and made impressive forays into the legislative assemblies of the Central Provinces, Bengal, and also in the Central Legislative Assembly, Gandhi concentrated on constructive work, which formed part of his social programme. This involved village reconstruction works, upliftment of artisans and propagation of the charkha, and removal of untouchability. For Gandhi, the social and political movements were inseparable. It is here that his ideas of politics and nationalism differed from those for whom nationalism meant just freeing the country from foreign rule.

A large number of people, particularly the youth, inspired by the Russian Revolution, began to gravitate towards Marxism in the 1920s. Kazi Nazrul Islam, the Bengali poet, gave powerful expression to the new vigour that socialist thought had brought into the minds of the nationalists. His *Sarvahara* (*The Proletariat*) and *Bisher Banshi* (*Flute of the Venom*) were proscribed and he was sentenced to jail for a year. M.N. Roy emerged as a prominent leader of the socialist youth. Labour and kisan parties were organized by people like M. Singaravelu, Hemanta Sarkar, Muzaffar Ahmad, S.A. Dange and Shaukat Usmani in Madras (1923), Bengal (1925) and Bombay and in the shape of the Kirti Kisan Party in Punjab. Later on, they were brought under the banner of the Peasants and Workers Party. Workers began to organize themselves into trade unions which articulated issues involving labour at the national level. The formation of the Communist Party of India in 1925 provided the socialist movement a focus and a radical and progressive orientation to the national movement.

Acts of individual heroism, which since the days of Khudiram Bose's martyrdom in 1908, indicated the high watermark of patriotism and selfless sacrifice, still moved the revolutionary terrorists. But now they began to organize themselves along larger social programmes. The new thinking was reflected in the acts of Surya Sen, Bhagat Singh, Jatin Mukherjee, Jadu Gopal Mukherjee, Bhagwati Charan Vohra, Yashpal and Chandrashekhar Azad. Vohra's book *The Philosophy of the Bomb* best expressed this change. This new thinking resulted in the formation of the Hindustan Republican Association in 1924.

Bhagat Singh symbolized this change better than anyone. Born in 1908 and nephew of the famous revolutionary Ajit Singh, he founded the Punjab Naujawan Bharat Sabha in 1926. Bhagat Singh understood the role of the masses in any revolution. He was also one of the first to realize the increasing influence of communalism which he thought was dangerous for society. As early as 1928, he and his friends decided to deny entry into the Naujawan Sabha to anyone who was a member of any religious or communal organization, a decision even the Congress would take as late as 1938. Following his incarceration at the age of twenty-two, he wrote the famous tract entitled 'Why I Am an Atheist', one of the finest written by any political leader.

Surya Sen of Chittagong, popularly known as Masterda, was

another brilliant revolutionary. In 1918, he became the president of the Chittagong branch of the Indian National Congress. He established a number of hardline patriotic organizations, including Jugantar, in various parts of Chittagong. Aware of the limited resources available to freedom fighters, he advocated guerrilla warfare against the colonial government. Of his more daring attempts, mention must be made of the Chittagong Armoury Raid on 18 April 1930. He was arrested in 1933 and hanged on 12 January 1934. An interesting feature of these revolutionary groups was the participation of a large number of women. Pritilata Waddedar, Kalpana Dutt, Shanti Ghose, Suniti Choudhury, Bina Das, Manikuntal Sen and Ashalata Sen would play a very crucial role in the national movement and in organizing the peasant and labour classes.

This period also saw the growth of communal organizations. Some of the greatest leaders of India parted company either with the Congress or the nationalist cause during the 1920s. M.A. Jinnah ironically broke with Gandhi on the question of the latter's integration of the Khilafat demand with the non-cooperation movement, which Jinnah said was a communal step. Despite his impeccable secular credentials, Jinnah would go on to lead the Muslim League in its demand for a separate homeland for Muslims. Lajpat Rai, Veer Savarkar, Asutosh Lahiry and many other patriots began to view the popular phase of the national movement as harmful to the cause of the Hindu community. The post non-cooperation riots at Kohat, North-West Frontier Province (NWFP), at Malabar, and in 1926 in Calcutta added to the heightening communal perceptions. The Ali Brothers, the closest colleagues of Gandhi during the Khilafat days, accused Gandhi of betraying the Muslims. Communal ideas and organizations rapidly proliferated in such an atmosphere. One important reason for this was the success of the national movement in inspiring peasants, labourers and millions of ordinary people cutting across caste and community to join the movement. The entrenched elites, landlords and the upper classes were alarmed by this radical turn in the national movement and the Congress. This also partially explains why most of the communal organizations like the Muslim League and the Hindu Mahasabha were so stridently anti-Congress.

The Civil Disobedience Movement and its Aftermath

It was during this phase of the movement that the British sent the Simon Commission, comprising seven British Members of Parliament, with no Indian representative in it, to study and recommend constitutional reforms for India. In its 1927 session in Madras, the Congress resolved to boycott the commission. The commission was greeted with strikes and hartals everywhere it went, including Lahore where the protestors were led by Lala Lajpat Rai. In a brutal police assault on the protestors, Lala Lajpat Rai was severely injured and succumbed to his injuries. The Congress set up a committee under Motilal Nehru which produced the Nehru Report, proposing a new dominion constitution for India. Jinnah presented some amendments which would have changed the very character of the polity recommended by the report. Subhas Bose and Jawaharlal Nehru too attacked the report for not calling for complete independence.

The Congress met at Lahore in 1929 and proclaimed achievement of complete independence as its official goal, observing 26 January 1930 as independence day. The session also authorized the working committee to launch a programme of civil disobedience. Gandhi was ready for this and he soon sent an ultimatum to the viceroy, writing in detail his programme and asking the government to go ahead if it wanted to prevent him from breaking the salt law. He embarked on the historic Dandi March on 12 March 1930 and reached the coast at Dandi on 6 April where he prepared salt, thereby symbolically breaking the salt law. The act caught the imagination of the whole country. In Bengal, volunteers from the Abhay Ashram in Comilla, East Bengal, went to the coast near Contai, East Midnapur in West Bengal, to break the salt law. C. Rajagopalachari marched from Trichinopoly to Vedaranyam on the Tanjore coast, while on the Malabar coast, K. Kelappan made salt. A new centre of civil disobedience emerged in the NWFP where Khan Abdul Ghaffar Khan and his followers, popularly known as the Khudai Khidmatgars, began non-violent civil disobedience. Large-scale incidents of picketing of liquor shops and those selling foreign cloth, refusal to pay taxes, and giving up of legal practices symbolized the movement. The government decided to take action and arrested Gandhi on 4 May 1930. There were countrywide strikes and demonstrations in protest. The movement was later suspended when the Gandhi–Irwin Pact was signed and Gandhi agreed to participate in the Second Round Table Conference in Britain. Nothing much was achieved at the conference because the authorities were bent on branding the Congress as one of the many voices and openly patronized the princely states, reactionaries, leaders of the oppressed classes and communal leaders against the Congress.

The Government of India Act, 1935 provided for direct elections for the first time. Provincial assemblies were to include more elected Indian representatives, who in turn could lead majorities and form governments. The dilemma of a mass movement entering electoral politics and then accepting office became acute during the 1937 elections which the Congress won in many provinces. In a colonial system, the ultimate source of power remained with the centre and they could manipulate it to counter the anti-colonial forces. After reviewing and debating all aspects, the Congress decided to form ministries in several provinces where they introduced many social and economic reforms. This created apprehensions in some quarters, for example the landlords in the United Provinces. The Muslim League too began to attack the ministries for, what it termed, their atrocities upon Muslims. Though never substantiated, these allegations were used as propaganda to paint the future shape of the society under a Congress-ruled Hindu raj.

The War and the Quit India Movement

The Second World War was declared in Europe on 1 September 1939. The Indian government, in gross disregard of public opinion, declared war on Germany. Indian leaders protested being drawn into the war without being consulted on the issue. However, they refrained from active agitation lest it hamper the war effort against anti-fascist forces. After careful thought, Gandhi launched an individual satyagraha on 17 October 1940 with a carefully chosen band of satyagrahis. Individuals made public speeches against cooperation with the war effort and thereafter courted arrest. In the meantime, Japan joined the war in December 1941 and began threatening the Indian borders. The news of retreating British forces, leaving Indians and others to the mercy of the Japanese, created a sense of anger and helplessness in India. Police atrocities and wartime crises too had made people restive. Gandhi understood this growing unrest and despite strong reservations by a number of leaders, decided to launch a movement. On 8 August 1942 at Bombay he gave the clarion call of 'Do or Die' and 'Quit India'. The authorities arrested Gandhi and other national leaders that same night. From the next day, people across the country came out into the open and one of the most massive anti-colonial agitations began. Government property was damaged, parallel governments were set up in peasant bases in Balia in eastern United

Provinces, Midnapur in Bengal and Satara in Maharashtra. The socialist group within the Congress, including people like Jayaprakash Narayan, Ram Manohar Lohia, Achyut Patwardhan and Aruna Asaf Ali took over the leadership of the movement and made heroic contributions.

After the war ended in 1945, the British realized that they could no longer hold on to India. From then on, things moved at a rapid pace towards independence and transfer of power. Unfortunately, the process was marked by the partition of the country, which resulted in the largest migration of population ever witnessed anywhere in the world and led to some of the worst communal riots in the history of the subcontinent, claiming over a million lives.

~

MOHANDAS KARAMCHAND GANDHI

The Banaras Hindu University Speech

In 1916, Madan Mohan Malaviya invited M.K. Gandhi (1869–1948) to speak on the occasion of the inauguration of the Banaras Hindu University. The viceroy, Lord Hardinge, had come to grace the function as had some of the most eminent political and social leaders of the country and a host of rajas and maharajas. On 4 February 1916, clad in a short, coarse dhoti and Kathiawadi cloak and turban, Gandhi began his speech by apologizing for the delay in reaching the dais because of the security arrangements. This speech heralded Gandhi's arrival on the national scene, and from then on he would largely shape the contours of the freedom movement. Gandhi articulated an outlook to the nation and to its people so different to what had been expressed thus far that the established leaders of the country at that point of time felt uneasy with it, so much so that Annie Besant left the meeting in 'disgust at what he was speaking'. Gandhi's speech was a virtual attack not only on the dress and language of the entire political spectrum but on the whole system of thought that had determined the political voice of the country which, he maintained, had created a gulf between the masses and the leaders.

We have been told during the last two days how necessary it is, if we are to retain our hold upon the simplicity of Indian character, that our hands and feet should move in unison with our hearts. But this is only by way of preface. I wanted to say it is a matter of deep humiliation and shame for us that I am compelled this evening under the shadow of this great college, in this sacred city, to address my countrymen in a language that is foreign to me. I know that if I was appointed an examiner, to examine all those who have been attending during these two days this series of lectures, most of those who might be examined upon these lectures would fail. And why? Because they have not been touched.

I was present at the sessions of the great Congress in the month of December. There was a much vaster audience, and will you believe me when I tell you that the only speeches that touched the huge audience in Bombay were the speeches that were delivered in Hindustani? In Bombay, mind you, not in Benares where everybody speaks Hindi. But between the vernaculars of the Bombay Presidency on the one hand and Hindi on the other, no such great dividing line exists as there does between English and the sister languages of India; and the Congress audience was better able to follow the speakers in Hindi. I am hoping that this University will see to it that the youths who come to it will receive their instruction through the medium of their vernaculars. Our language is the reflection of ourselves, and if you tell me that our languages are too poor to express the best thought, then I say that the sooner we are wiped out of existence the better for us. Is there a man who dreams that English can ever become the national language of India? Why this handicap on the nation? Just consider for one moment what an unequal race our lads have to run with every English lad.

I had the privilege of a close conversation with some Poona professors. They assured me that every Indian youth, because he reached his knowledge through the English language, lost at least six precious years of life. Multiply that by the number of students turned out by our schools and colleges, and find out for yourselves how many thousand years have been lost to the nation. The charge against us is that we have no initiative. How can we have any, if we are to devote the precious years of our life to the mastery of a foreign tongue? We fail in this attempt also. Was it possible for any speaker yesterday and today to impress his audience as was possible for Mr. Higginbotham? It was not the fault of the previous speakers that they could not engage the audience. They had more than substance enough for us in their addresses. But their addresses could not go home to us. I have heard it said that after all it is English-educated India which is leading and which is doing all the things for the nation. It would be monstrous if it were otherwise. The only education we receive is English education. Surely we must show something for it. But suppose that we had been receiving during the past fifty years education through our vernaculars, what should we have today? We should have today a free India, we should have our educated men, not as if they were foreigners in their own land but speaking to the heart of the nation; they would be working amongst the poorest of the poor, and whatever they would have gained during these fifty years would be a heritage for the nation. Today even our wives are not the sharers in our best thought. Look at Professor Bose and Professor Ray and their brilliant researches. Is it not a shame that their researches are not the common property of the masses?

Let us now turn to another subject. The Congress has passed a resolution about self-government, and I have no doubt that the All-India Congress Committee and the Muslim League will do their duty and come forward with some tangible suggestions. But I, for one, must frankly confess that I am not so much interested in what they will be able to produce as I am interested in anything that the student world is going to produce or the masses are going to produce. No paper contribution will ever give us self-government. No amount of speeches will ever make us fit for self-government. It is only our conduct that will fit us for it. And how are we trying to govern ourselves?

I want to think audibly this evening. I do not want to make a speech and if you find me this evening speaking without reserve, pray, consider that you are only sharing the thoughts of a man who allows himself to think audibly, and if you think that I seem to transgress the limits that courtesy imposes upon me, pardon me for the liberty I may be taking. I visited the Vishwanath temple last evening, and as I was walking through those lanes, these were the thoughts that touched me. If a stranger dropped from above on to this great temple, and he had to consider what we as Hindus were, would he not be justified in condemning us? Is not this great temple a reflection of our own character? I speak feelingly, as a Hindu. Is it right that the lanes of our sacred temple should be as dirty as they are? The houses round about are built anyhow. The lanes are tortuous and narrow. If even our temples are not models of roominess and cleanliness, what can our self-government be? Shall our temples be abodes of holiness, cleanliness and peace as soon as the English have retired from India, either of their own pleasure or by compulsion, bag and baggage?

I entirely agree with the President of the Congress that before we think of self-government, we shall have to do the necessary plodding.

~

MOHAMMAD ALI

Justice to Islam and Turkey

Mohammad Ali (1878–1931) came into prominence during the Khilafat agitation in the 1920s which tried to influence the British government to protect the Ottoman Empire which had suffered a major defeat in the First World War. For a brief while in the early 1920s, following Gandhi's integration of the Khilafat demands with the non-cooperation movement, India witnessed a remarkable period of Hindu–Muslim unity. In the following speech delivered at a meeting held at Kingsway Hall, London, on 22 April 1920, one can discern Mohammad Ali's characteristic humour and complete disdain for his position as a colonized subject, as he exposes the duplicity of the Western powers on the issue of Turkey.

The resolution that I have the honour to place before you this evening is: That this meeting urges upon the Government the necessity for taking into serious consideration, in the Turkish settlement, the religious obligations of the Muslims (who in India alone number some 70 million citizens of the British Empire) and the national sentiment of United India.

Before I say anything about the claims that we have come to present, not only to the British and Allied Governments, but to the nations of Europe and America, I should like to make one point clear. And it is this—that we are not Turks. Whether the Turks be good people or bad people, whether they are gentle and humane, as all who have known them say, or murderers of women and children and massacrers, as has been alleged fairly frequently, they are, technically at any rate, the King's enemies. But we are British Indians, fellow-citizens of yours and as good subjects as you are of the King Emperor. When the Turks come they will present a case to the Allies. I hope they will present the case well, and I hope they will succeed in presenting their case. But the case we have got to present is not the case of aliens or enemies, but the case of members of this Empire. I am glad that in the resolution the word 'citizen' is used. To tell you the truth, I have been quite content to call myself a subject. However, I present the case today from the eminence of British citizenship, which I can only feel just a little bit when I am here, and not at all in my own country, where I can be interned or imprisoned without charge or trial, and nobody any the wiser, and where it is rather difficult for me to remember that I am as much a citizen as Mr. Lansbury. For if he is sent to prison, for which I am sure he has qualified himself, the people would soon know the reason why by a few questions asked in the House of Commons—one of our friends here (Colonel Wedgwood) would probably have an all-night sitting—and even if the House of Commons proved as impotent as it sometimes is in these democratic days of Coalitions and Coupons the good people of the Labour Party would see to it that by some sort of action, direct or indirect, I can't tell which, the right of British Citizenship was not denied to Mr. Lansbury.

Now, what is our case? We are told in the 'Times' and other newspapers that the Muslims of India must not dictate the foreign policy of the British Government. Well, ladies and gentlemen, in our wildest dreams it certainly did not occur to us to dictate the foreign policy of the British Government. I wish we could even dictate the internal policy of the Government in connection with India. If this is an Empire (I should like to call it a Commonwealth) in which we are equal partners, as we are very often told we are, and it was certainly demanded of us to be equal partners when sacrifices had got to be made—and at that time we in India neither stinted money nor men—well, then, when the war is over, when the captains and the kings have departed—particularly the kings, for only one or two are now left—when poor, common people, no better than us Indians and people of that sort, very common people, not autocrats and aristocrats, but mere democrats, have assembled to make peace, then I want to know what position I, whose people have given their men and money, have in the making of the peace. If you, ladies and gentlemen, who are of British birth and Christian faith, do not like your policy to be dictated to you by black heathens of the East, then I say we also do not want the foreign policy of our Empire to be dictated to us by a tiny fraction of forty-five millions of people of British birth and Christian faith.

If you desire to have a commonwealth, well and good. If you want the old fashioned Empire, well and good, though not so well and good; but in any case it is not little Englanders who call themselves Imperialists that are going to lay down the policy of the British

Empire. We, who number three hundred and fifteen millions in an Empire of four hundred and fifteen millions, should, I say, have some kind of voice, if not the prepondering voice, in the making of peace, though we had none in the making of a war which, nevertheless, we were called upon to wage.

... When the Queen of England, in the days of my grandfather, took into her hands the reins of office in India, and began to rule over the territories of the East India Company, a trading company which had become a sovereign power entirely against its will, after passing numerous self-denying ordinances...well, when the reins of Government in these territories passed into the hands of the Queen, a proclamation was issued that did her credit and did your people credit...The most important thing that the document contained was that no matter what changes should take place, one thing would remain unchanged—our religious obligations would be respected...

In the House of Commons the hero of Paisley, fresh from his triumph, in the very first debate that he could start on the subject after his election, talked of the connection of the Khilafat and Constantinople as being a fairly modern matter, and maintained that the Sultan as Khalifa has not been there more than four hundred years. Well, that is still 300 years longer than the rule of English kings and queens in India, but I will come to that by and by. Well, Mr. Asquith wanted to 'Vaticanise' the Khalifa. But the Khalifa, as even Mr. Lloyd George could now tell him, was not the Pope, and the moment he would consent to be 'Vaticanised' he would cease to be the Khalifa. He was the Commander of the Faithful, the President of our Theocratic Commonwealth, the Leader of all Muslims in peace and war, though he could neither claim to be infallible like the Pope, nor could he in all circumstances exercise unquestioned authority, for Allah was the only Sovereign, and in case of dispute Muslims were bound to refer back to the Holy Quran and to the Traditions of the Prophet whose successor the Khalifa is.

But whatever he could or could not do, the Khalifa was certainly not a pious old gentleman, whose only function in life was to mumble his prayers and repeat his beads as Mr. Asquith clearly seems to think. If such is the ignorance of Mr. Asquith with regard to such fundamental doctrines of Islam, even after having been enlightened by our Delegation, then is it not a shame and a disgrace to one who has once been, and apparently still dreams of being once more, the Prime Minister of the Imperial Government of Great Britain?

Having claimed to shape the destinies of three or four hundred million Indians, including over 70 million Muslims, if this is the extent of their knowledge, then I say it is a shame and a disgrace. Mr. Asquith said, no doubt humorously that in these days even if a Khalifa goes to war he cannot hope to go to war with limited liabilities. Well, I will say this to him, that even in this twentieth century we are a very backward people in India, and if you will go to war with the Khalifa in order to oust him from the seat of the Khilafat, if you go to war with him in order to dismember his Empire, and if you go to war with him in order to step into the sanctuaries of our faith, because there is oil in Mosul, if you go to war with him because the sanctity of the Holy Land of Islam must be violated by exploiters demanding a mandate in Mesopotamia, no doubt in the Sacred name of Self-Determination spelt with three letters, O-I-L—then even in these days you will have to go to war. I am afraid, with very limited assets indeed.

Therefore, although I do not threaten, although we have not come here to threaten you, it ought to be made clear to you that the situation is now different. Today it is not only the Muslims who feel like this, but the Hindus, and even the Sikhs—after Amritsar. India today is one and united. That is why in our resolution we have asked the Government to show respect not only for Muslim obligations, but also for the national sentiment of United India. How is this sentiment expressing itself? On the 17th October last the Muslims observed the Khilafat Day, a day on which the Muslims suspended business and fasted and prayed, and many Hindus joined them. Now on the 19th March, precisely the day that we were being received in 10, Downing Street by Mr. Lloyd George, from one end of India to another there was a total suspension of business, in which not only Muslims and Hindus and Sikhs, but Parsees and others also participated. In order to realise what this suspension of business means, I will ask you not to think of a railway strike, nor even a general strike in England or in Germany: you have got to think of the total suspension of business throughout the Continent of Europe. Yet, primitive as some of our people are, very impulsive as they seem to be, in spite of this universal demonstration, there was no violence.

... We are being led by a man who believes in Soul-force. If throughout the world today there is anyone who tries to live up to the Sermon on the Mount—that sermon which is often overrated but at the same time always forgotten in the shaping of your foreign policy—if any man tries to live up to that sermon it is Mahatma Gandhi. He is not a Muslim. He is a Hindu of Hindus. Today he is leading the entire continent of India because he has realised that in this matter the Muslims are not carrying on a 'fictitious' and a 'factitious' agitation, and he has carefully ascertained that they cannot possibly 'moderate' the claims that they have put forward without being absolutely false to all the convictions that they have cherished for centuries. Time after time he had pressed us for an irreducible minimum of our claims. He has at last himself drawn up a manifesto, which we have brought with us as the mandate of the Indian Delegation. The claim put forward is a simple claim. It says that it is one of the fundamental doctrines of Islam, absolutely unalterable, that there should always be a Khalifa, and that the Khalifa should have temporal power at all times adequate for the defence of the Faith, and that is the measure of the irreducible minimum of temporal power.

Whatever you like to think about temporal power, I am convinced, and I think I can convince you easily enough, that when you have people like Lord Bryce who want to use the argument of the 'Big Stick', you will be bound to meet the Muslim demand for temporal power for the Khalifa. If, however, there is complete disarmament in Europe, the first person who will desire to bring his arms to the scrap-heap, or to turn them into ploughshares, will be the Muslim Khalifa himself.

The second claim is that the local centre of our Faith, the land known as the Island of Arabia, should be free from non-Islamic control in any shape or form. Arabia to the European geographer is a peninsula bounded only on three sides by water; but to the Islamic religion it has always been an island. You will understand this when I tell you that it is surrounded on one side by the Mediterranean and the Red Sea, on another side by the Indian Ocean, on the third side by the Persian Gulf, and on the fourth by the waters of the Euphrates and the Tigris; and on his deathbed our Prophet gave an injunction, binding on all sections of Muslims, that in that region no kind of non-Muslim control should be allowed.

But even if you disregard our religious requirements, what about your own political principles? We have heard a great deal of the principle of self-determination, and now that we have seen some applications of this principle, we find that it has about as many interpretations as love or religion. There is one interpretation when the principle is applied to Ireland; on this you are all well-informed, and I shall not waste your time. There is another interpretation of self-determination for Montenegro, when it is assured it is not good to be a cock's head when you can be a bull's tail. In spite of Montenegro's desire for independence, she is assured that it is better in her own interest to be part of a larger unit. When we ask that the Arabs should not be forced to get out of the larger unit we are told by Mr. Lloyd George: 'Is the sacred principle of self-determination not to be applied to an Arab simply because he is a Muslim?' But surely the last interpretation of self-determination is the best of all. We never knew that that large mouthful of a word, self-determination, could be spelt with three letters: O-I-L. This is the latest interpretation of self-determination. But whatever Mr. Lloyd George may say, the people of Mesopotamia, as well as those of Syria and Palestine, have clearly determined that they will have no mandates and no protectorates.

... the Muslims cannot permit that their Khalifa is to remain as a hostage. They claim that it is part of their Faith that the Khilafat should exist as an independent sovereignty, and its Empire should not be dismembered any further after the very great spoliation that had already taken place after the Balkan War. After that large spoliation, the Khalifa's Empire has really been reduced to such small proportions that they must insist that in the Holy Lands, even in spite of oil, they would not have a British Protectorate, or French or American mandate.

What do Muslims ask? They say: 'Have an International Commission! Allow the Muslims of India and Hindus to be represented on that Commission, and go into the whole question of massacres before the war, during the war, and now. If the Turks are found guilty they should be punished. But if they are to be punished, equal punishment should be meted out to those who caused the sands of Tripoli to be soaked with Arab blood.' We demand that in the Balkans—the bones of Turks are still bleaching today on Balkan heights—we demand that the people who butchered women and children there in cold blood after unnameable outrages, should be punished. And we Indians have a right to demand that not only should it be the Italians and the Bulgarians and the Greeks, but even the British, the O'Dwyers and the Dyers who have dyed their hands with gore and fired on innocent crowds assembled for lawful purpose on April 13 last year, we demand that they too should be punished.

But if you, Englishmen and women, are not prepared to do justice by your own people, then I say you have no right to talk of doing justice by the Turks, and to deal with this business of massacres.

If you will use force to compel us to submit to a peace that contravenes Islamic religious requirements, and blood is shed for blood, then the guilt of blood will be yours, because you are prepared to use force, but you are not prepared to do justice to the Muslims.

This is what we have come to ask. I tell you this, we have not come to threaten, and we do not threaten you. My friend Mr. Wedgwood, in the House of Commons, said, 'You can get more out of English people by persuasion than by threats,' and I believe him. But he says, 'What can you threaten us with?' Well, that is the worst part of the whole business. There is nothing at all after less than a hundred years of British rule that we can threaten you with. It is true, as Colonel Wedgwood asked, what can we threaten you with? Though the measure of our impotence, in spite of our righteous wrath today, is also the measure of the success of your crushing rule achieved in no more than a century. But having reduced us to this state of impotence, I ask you to consider this. If we want to threaten you, we obviously cannot threaten you with Howitzers and Dreadnoughts and Aeroplanes and Tanks; but we possess a thing that is unconquerable: our determination to die true to our Faith. Money is being poured into the Fund for the Khilafat. But every Muslim who pays is told that this is not money; it is only a draft on the life of every subscriber. We do not threaten to kill you; but we do threaten you with our undying determination to die kings of our consciences and masters of our souls.

~

CHITTARANJAN DAS

The Resolution on Non-cooperation

Deshbandhu Chittaranjan Das (1870–1925) was called to the Bar in 1894 and soon emerged as one of the most successful legal practitioners in Calcutta. He made a name for himself when in 1909 he successfully defended Aurobindo Ghose in the Alipore Bomb Case. An influential leader in Bengal during the non-cooperation movement (1919–22), Das organized a ban on European clothes, leading by personal example. He also set up the Swaraj Party in association with Motilal Nehru. Initially opposed to the idea of non-cooperation, he came to champion it tirelessly. At the annual session of the Congress in Nagpur, December 1920, he moved the historic non-cooperation resolution which marked the beginning of a new phase in the Indian national movement. The speech reproduced below is the concluding part of his celebrated address on the occasion.

Mr. President, Ladies and Gentlemen, I rise to move the Resolution on Non-cooperation. I shall presently read the resolution before you…

Whereas in the opinion of the Congress the existing Government of India has forfeited the confidence of the country; and whereas the people of India are now determined to establish Swaraj; and whereas all methods adopted by people of India prior to the last special session of the Indian National Congress have failed to secure due recognition of their rights and liberties and the redress of their many and grievous wrongs, more specially in reference to the Khilafat and the Punjab; now this Congress, while reaffirming the resolution on the Non-violent Non-cooperation passed at the special session of the Congress at Calcutta, declares that the entire or any part or parts of the scheme of Non-violent Non-cooperation, with renunciation of voluntary association with the present Government at one end and the refusal to pay taxes at the other, should be put in force at a time to be determined by either the Indian National Congress or the All India Congress Committee, and that, in the meanwhile to prepare the country for it, effective steps should continue to be taken in that behalf.

I call upon you, in the name of all that is holy, to carry this Resolution without one single dissentient voice. I want you to declare to the nation to realise their God-given rights. Rights exist, but they have got to be realised. Rights exist because this is the eternal law of life, but still every man and every woman and every nation on earth has got to realise those rights. Realise the fact that we have got those rights, and the moment you realise that, the Bureaucracy or any 'Cracy' in the world cannot stand against you; and I want to tell the Bureaucracy that we have made up our minds to compel it to recognise that which we have got. May God grant us the strength not only to pass this Resolution, but to work upon it and to carry out the great idea of which the Resolution is the expression.

~

MOHANDAS KARAMCHAND GANDHI

Address to Congress Workers, Bardoli

By 1922, the non-cooperation movement had gathered momentum to the extent that the government had become jittery about its inability to control the growing wave of unrest. At this juncture, events took a violent turn in Chauri Chaura, where a police post was attacked by a group of demonstrators, resulting in the death of twenty-two policemen. Shocked into disbelief, Mahatma Gandhi, in a short speech delivered on 10 February 1922 at Bardoli, called for the immediate suspension of the movement. Though the move was criticized by many of Gandhi's close associates who felt that it would undo their achievements and give the government an upper hand, it confirmed Gandhi's assertion that non-violence was an article of faith with him.

I regard those who have assembled here as some of the best workers in the country. In fact I can see the condition of India at the present time truly reflected by this small assembly. What I have heard now confirms me in the belief that most of those who are present here have failed to understand the message of non-violence. This convinces me that the country at large has not at all accepted the teaching of non-violence. I must therefore immediately stop the movement for civil disobedience.

MOHANDAS KARAMCHAND GANDHI

Statement at Trial Court, 1922

After the suspension of the non-cooperation movement, the government came down heavily on political agitators. Gandhi was arrested on 10 March 1922 and tried for inciting disaffection towards the state. During the court proceedings on 18 March, the charges were read out. Before passing his judgment, Justice Robert Broomfield asked Gandhi if he would like to make a statement. The result was one of the most eloquent testimonials to a man's belief and moral courage. So impressive was Gandhi's statement at court that even the judge could not remain unaffected as he pronounced, 'Mr Gandhi you have made my task easy in one way by pleading guilty to the charges. Nevertheless, what remains, namely, the determination of a just sentence, is perhaps as difficult as a judge in this country could have to face … it will be impossible to ignore the fact that you are in a different category from any person I have ever tried or am likely to have to try... I propose in passing sentence to follow the precedent of a case in many respects similar to this case that was decided some twelve years ago, I mean the case against Bal Gangadhar Tilak under the same section. The sentence that was passed upon him as it finally stood was a sentence of simple imprisonment for six years. You will not consider it unreasonable, I think, that you should be classed with Mr. Tilak... And I should like to say in doing so that if the course of events in India should make it possible for the Government to reduce the period and release you, no one will be better pleased than I.'

Before I read this statement I would like to state that I entirely endorse the learned advocate general's remarks in connection with my humble self. I think that he was entirely fair to me in all the statements that he has made, because it is very true and I have no desire whatsoever to conceal from this court the fact that to preach disaffection towards the existing system of Government has become almost a passion with me, and the learned advocate general is also entirely in the right when he says that my preaching of disaffection did not commence with my connection with *Young India* but that it commenced much earlier, and in the statement that I am about to read it will be my painful duty to admit before this court that it commenced much earlier than the period stated by the advocate general. It is the most painful duty with me but I have to discharge that duty knowing the responsibility that rests upon me, and I wish to endorse all the blame that the learned advocate general has thrown on my shoulders in connection with the Bombay, the Madras and the Chauri Chaura occurrences. Thinking over these deeply and sleeping over them night after night, it is impossible to dissociate myself from the diabolical crimes of Chauri Chaura or the mad outrages in Bombay and Madras. He is quite right when he says that, as a man of responsibility, a man having received a fair share of education, having had a fair share of experience of this world, I should know the consequences of every one of my acts. I knew that I was playing with fire. I ran the risk and, if I was set free, I would still do the same. I know that I was feeling it so every day and I have felt it also this morning that I would have failed in my duty if I did not say what I said here just now.

I wanted to avoid violence. I want to avoid violence. Non-violence is the first article of my faith. It is also the last article of my creed. But I had to make my choice. I had either to submit to a system which I considered had done an irreparable harm to my country or incur the risk of the mad fury of my people bursting forth when they understood the truth from my lips. I know that my people have sometimes gone mad; I am deeply sorry for it. I am therefore here to submit not to a light penalty but to the highest penalty. I do not ask for mercy. I do not ask for any extenuating act of clemency. I am here to invite and cheerfully submit to the highest penalty that can be inflicted upon me for what in law is a deliberate crime and what appears to me to be the highest duty of a citizen. The only course open to you, the judge, is as I am just going to say in my statement, either to resign your post or inflict on me the severest penalty if you believe that the system and the law you are assisting to administer are good for the people of this country and that my activity is therefore injurious to the public weal. I do not expect that kind of conversion, but by the time I have finished with my statement you will perhaps have a glimpse of what is raging within my breast to run this maddest risk that a sane man can run.

~

KAZI NAZRUL ISLAM

Deposition of a Political Prisoner

Kazi Nazrul Islam (1899–1976) is known as the rebel poet. His revolutionary poems and essays were regularly proscribed by the British authorities, leading to his arrest on charges of sedition on 23 November 1922. His poem 'Bidrohi' (The Rebel) *was published on 6 January 1922 in* Saptahik Bijli (Weekly Lightning). *In March, Nazrul's first book,* Byathar Daan (Offerings of Pain), *a collection of short stories, was published in Calcutta. On 11 August, a biweekly,* Dhumketu (Comet), *premiered with Nazrul as the editor. On 26 September, Nazrul's poem* 'Anandamoyeer Agamoney' (The Coming of Goddess Durga) *was published in* Dhumketu. *Nazrul was charged with sedition for writing this poem. On 13 October,* Dhumketu *demanded India's complete freedom from the British government. On the same date,* Agni Bina (The Fiery Veena), *a collection of poems, was published in Calcutta and immediately proscribed by the government. On 25 October,* Yuga Bani (The Message of the Age), *a collection of his essays, was published in Calcutta and proscribed by the government. An arrest warrant was issued against Nazrul on charges of sedition on 8 November. He was arrested in Comilla, East Bengal, on 22 November. On 7 January 1923, Nazrul wrote* 'Rajbandir Jabanbandi' (Deposition of a Political Prisoner) *while awaiting trial in Presidency Jail, Calcutta. He delivered the speech in the court of Chief Presidency Magistrate Swinho on 16 January 1923. Nazrul was sentenced to one year of hard labour.* 'Rajbandir Jabanbandi' *was published in the final issue of* Dhumketu *on 27 January. It is an example of Nazrul's superb skill in composing what in today's terms would be considered a 'prose-poem' in which his characteristic holistic interweaving of the poetic, political, spiritual, personal, and universal finds a powerful, uncompromising and eloquent expression.*

The charge against me: I'm a rebel against the Crown. Therefore, I'm now a prisoner, convicted by a royal court. On one side is the Royal Crown, on the other, the flame of the Comet. One is a king, with a scepter in his hand; the other is the Truth, with the scepter of Justice. On the side of the king are state-paid government employees. On my side is the King of all kings, the Judge of all judges, the eternal Truth—the awakened God.

No one has appointed my Judge. In the eye of this Judge Supreme, kings and subjects, rich and poor, happy and sad—all are equal. On His throne are placed side by side the Royal Crown and the beggar's monochord. His law is Justice, Religion. That law is not created by any human conqueror for a particular conquered people. That law is created by the global humanity from its realisation of the Truth. It belongs to the universal Truth. It's the law of the Supreme God. On the side of the king is a molecular piece of the creation; on my side, the primordial, infinite, indivisible Creator.

What is behind the king is insignificant; behind me is Shiva. The goal of the one on the side of the king is selfish, monetary reward; the goal of the one on my side is the Truth, the reward of Bliss.

The message of the king is like bubbles; mine—the boundless ocean. I'm a poet, sent by God to speak the unspoken Truth, to give form to the formless creation. God speaks through the voice of the poet. The message is the revelation of the Truth, the message of God. That message may be judged seditious in a state-court, but in the court of Justice, that message is not against Justice, not against Truth. That message may be punishable in a state-court, but in the light of Religion, at the door of Justice, it is innocent, untainted, untarnished, inextinguishable as the Truth itself.

The Truth reveals itself. No angry look or royal punishment can suppress it. I'm the lyre of that timeless self-revelation—the lyre in which the message of eternal Truth has been resounded. I'm the lyre in the hands of God. A lyre may break, but who can break God? There's Truth, there's God—there's always been and always will be. One who is obstructing the message of Truth today, trying to silence it, he too is but a miniscule, insignificantly powerful, part of God's creation. It is due to God's gesture, God's presence, God's will that he is here today, and may not be here tomorrow. There's no limit to a human being's foolish pride; he wants to imprison, to punish his own creator! But one day, that pride will definitely drown in tears.

Anyway, as I was saying, I'm an instrument for revealing the Truth. Maybe some cruel power may be able to imprison that instrument, may even be able to destroy it; but the One who plays the instrument, in that lyre who plays the message of Shiva, who can imprison Him? I'm mortal! but my God is immortal, I'll die, the king will die—because many rebels like me have died, as have many kings who have brought such charges. But never—for no reason—it's been possible to suppress the Truth, to kill His message. That's how He is revealing Himself today and will do so through eternity. This proscribed message of mine will once again be expressed through other voices. The music of my flute will not die simply because my flute has been confiscated—I can play the music through another flute I can get or create. The music is not in my flute—it's in my heart; and the flute—in my creative skill of constructing it. Therefore, neither the flute nor the music is to be blamed. Rather, I'm the one to be blamed—I, the player of the flute. Likewise, for the message which has flowed out of my voice, I'm not responsible. It's not my fault, nor my lyre's; rather, it's His fault—who, through my voice, plays His lyre. Therefore, it isn't me who is the rebel against the state. The real rebel against the state is that Musician of lyre, God Himself. There's no royal power or a second god who can punish Him. No police force or prison has yet been created who can punish Him. The state-employed translator, in the state-language, has merely translated the language of that message, but not its life-spirit. The translation merely expresses the rebellion against the state, because the purpose of that translation is to please the king. My writing expresses the Truth, Power and life-spirit. My purpose is to worship God; on behalf of the oppressed, distressed global humanity, I'm the shower of Truth, tears of God. I have not rebelled against a mere king, I have rebelled against injustice.

I know and I have seen—I'm not alone standing convicted in this court today. Standing behind me is the beauteous Truth, God Himself. Throughout ages He stands quietly behind His soldiers of Truth turned political prisoners. A state-employed judge cannot be a judge of the Truth. Through farcical trials like this when Jesus was crucified, Gandhi was imprisoned, that day too God quietly stood behind them. The judge could not see Him. Between him and God stood the emperor. In fear of the emperor, his conscience, his two eyes were blinded. Otherwise, he would have trembled in fear and awe in his seat, turn blue, along with his seat of the judge, burn to ashes.

The judge knows that what I've said and written is not unjust in the eyes of God, not a lie in the court of Justice. But he will probably punish me, because he is not on the side of the Truth; he is on the side of the king. He is not on the side of Justice, he is on the side of law. He is not free, he's a servant of the king. Yet, I ask—whose courtroom is it? The king's or of Religion? This judge—is he accountable to the king, or to his conscience, to the Truth, to God? Who rewards this judge? The king or God? Wealth or self-satisfaction?

I hear that my judge is a poet. I'm delighted! A rebel-poet is to be judged by a judge-poet! But the last boat at the day's end is calling this elderly judge; whereas, red-dawn's *naba-shankha* is here to greet my coming. Death is calling him, life is calling me. I can't tell whether our respective setting star and rising star will unite. Nah, I'm talking nonsense again.

Today, India is subjugated. Its people are slaves. This is the absolute truth. In this kingdom, to call a slave a slave, injustice an injustice, is sedition. This cannot be the rule of Justice. This forcible twisting of a truth into a lie, injustice into justice, night into day—can the Truth go on tolerating this? Can such rule last forever? It's been possible this long, maybe because the Truth was oblivious. But today the Truth is awakened—any awakened soul with eyes can see that for sure. Am I a rebel because I voiced the distressed cry of the Truth stricken by this unjust rule? Is it only my own crying? Or, is it the united, loud voice of the entire oppressed Heaven and Earth? I know the cataclysmic roar of my voice is not mine alone—it's the cry of the suffering of the entire world. This cry cannot be silenced simply by intimidating me, even killing me. Suddenly, in someone else's voice, this lost message will be heard thunderously!

Instead of India being subjugated, if England was subjugated by India and if the defenseless, oppressed people of England, like the people of India, would be anxious to liberate their own motherland,

and, if at that time, I was the judge and, like me, this judge, charged with sedition, was to be tried by me, then, what this judge at that time from his defendant's dock would have said, I too am saying the same thing in the same way.

I'm highly self-confident. What I've understood to be unjust, oppression, a lie—I've called it just that—without trying to please anyone or to receive praise or a favour. I have not merely rebelled against the injustices of the king, but my Truth-sword has also attacked and rebelled against the society, race, nation. For this, in and outside my home, I've been subjected to too much ridicule, humiliation, reproach, attacks. But I've not let anything intimidate me into debasing my Truth, my God; out of greed I did not sell off my self-realization; I did not shorten my austerely attained self-satisfaction—because I'm dear to God; a lyre of Truth. I'm a poet, my soul is one with the soul of the truth-seeing saint. I've been born with an unexplainable, boundless sense of fulfilment. This is not my arrogance, but a simple and honest acknowledgment of the truth of self-realisation and self-confidence. I cannot accept a lie out of blind faith, greed, fear of the king or the public. I cannot accept tyranny. Then my God will abandon me. It is because this body-temple of mine is the seat of the awakened God that people worship this temple, show reverence. What will be left of this temple if God abandons it? Who will come seeking in it? That is why in my voice was heard Shiva's trumpet call of cataclysm, in my hand the Comet's fire-flag wavered, behind the flag the temple-God in the guise of Narayan danced the Dance of Destruction.

This Dance of Destruction is a prologue to a new creation. That is why I relentlessly, fearlessly, with my head raised high, held the flag and played His trumpet. I heard the piercing call of the mighty Shiva, I understood the command of his blood-red eyes. I understood instantly that I was a red soldier of the universal cataclysm of protecting the Truth, regaining Justice. He sent me as a precursor to Bengal—the green cremation ground, a land asleep—to blow the trumpet. I'm an insignificant soldier, I have merely obeyed his command with the best of my ability. He knew mine would be the first chest to be hit; I'm therefore honoured to think of myself as the first wounded soldier of this cataclysm. After being released from prison, when I submit myself to His feet with the mark of a wound on my chest and the blood-mark of persecution on my forehead, when I submit myself to His feet, then His compassionate offering of nectar will calm, reliven and inspire me. On that day, once again, I will take my stand under the shadow of His sword. That hope for a crimson dawn, ecstasy, will transform my prison days into a heaven of resounding laughter and songs. I'm a son of the Immortal. Without even my asking for it, God has given me the power to transform the torturous iron rods into precious jewels and gold with the touch of the all-pervasive delight in the heart of the child-eternal. I have no fear, no regrets, because God is with me. My unfinished duty will be completed by someone else. The Truth cannot be suppressed. The comet in my hand will now become a torch of fire in the hands of God to burn the injustices, tyranny. Now the captain of the fiery airplane will be God Shiva himself! Therefore, lo, there's nothing to fear!

My imprisoned mother has called upon her unworthy son, offering him a place in her bosom. I do not know if there's a place for this unfortunate child in the bosom of the subjugated, helpless mother. If there is, then I will thank the judge with tearful eyes. I reassure you—I have no fear, no regrets. I'm a son of the Immortal. I know that the tyrant's tormenting of the Truth comes to an end; in that Truth lies my destiny!

~

MANABENDRA NATH ROY

Leftism in Congress

Manabendra Nath Roy (1887–1954), whose original name was Narendranath Bhattacharya, was a revolutionary, philosopher, political theorist and activist. An exponent of the philosophy of Radical Humanism, he was also an international communist leader and theorist though he denounced communism later. Initially a member of the underground revolutionary movement in Bengal, he escaped and landed in Mexico where he not only converted to Marxism but also founded the Communist Party of Mexico, the first communist party outside Europe. He debated with Lenin (who called him the Oriental Marx) on the relationship that communist movements in colonized countries should have with the nationalist movements in those countries under the leadership of the middle class and bourgeoisie. He had a chequered career after returning to India. A popular speaker and intellectual with an arrogance befitting an original mind, Roy was one of the first to theorize the character of the national movement. However, his originality, dynamism and arrogance often prevented him from having a more broad-based acceptance and he remained at the margins of the national movement. Shifting to an enlightened humanism in the later phase of his life, Roy continued to guide the younger generation of the country through his speeches and writings till he died at Dehradun. The following speech, made at the 'All-India Study Camp of the League of Radical Congressmen' which was convened in Dehradun in June 1940, is a masterpiece where he tries to theorize on the historical location of leftism in India. It shows the originality and brilliance of a genius.

It has been asked why we begin the study of the origin of leftism in 1919. The answer is that, before that time, there did not exist any mass movement. Leftism, as we understand it, can develop only on the basis of a mass movement. Let us start from an elementary point. What is leftism? The term itself is very confusing, and I would suggest its rejection. Nevertheless, it may be useful to know how the term originated. That may enable us to read in it a sensible content. The term originated at the time of the Great French Revolution. When the Estates General first assembled, by accident as it were, the most intransigent revolutionary group occupied seats at the left hand of the Chairman of the Assembly. The people with contrary interests, the upper classes, went farthest away from their opponents, and seated themselves on the right side. Thus originated the terms 'right' and 'left' in politics. The political ideas advocated by the two groups came to be known respectively as 'leftist' and 'rightist'. If the gentleman who presided over the Estates General called those seated at his left hand 'leftists' and those seated at his right hand 'rightists', why should those terms dominate our thoughts even to-day? By an accident the opposing groups might have sat differently, and the meaning of the terms would be reversed. Similarly, mechanical terms were also coined in the history of the Indian nationalist movement… If we identify extremism with leftism then the origin of leftism in the Indian National Congress cannot be traced in 1919. In that sense, Tilak and Aurobindo Ghosh were leftists. But the political ideas of Tilak, for example, were hardly revolutionary. He differed from the older Congress leaders, but the difference was very slight. Ideologically, both were reactionaries. As a matter of fact, in the case of Tilak, the position was very curious. His political ideas might have been slightly more advanced than those of the older Congress leaders. But socially and culturally, men like Gokhale were certainly more advanced than Tilak.

For us, leftism means acceptance of the principles of revolution. A really revolutionary ideology of the nationalist movement was first formulated about 1919-20. Before that time, there was a revolutionary movement, but the conception of the movement was entirely different from ours. However, inside the Congress before 1920, there was no differentiation between revolutionaries and anti-revolutionaries. The extremists wanted a little more than the moderates. Tilak also was prepared to accept even one anna in a rupee, and strive for more. That was not a revolutionary spirit. It was reformism, *par excellence.* That distinction between extremism and moderatism has no place in our discussion. We want to trace the development of a revolutionary ideology in the struggle for national freedom. Therefore, we begin with the year 1919, when the movement became a mass movement.

It has been maintained by one comrade that since Gandhi launched the first mass movement, he is to be appreciated as the originator of leftism in the Congress. That is a wrong point of view. No single individual ever creates a movement. Gandhi did not create the movement of 1920. On the contrary, he himself was the creation of that movement. His merit was that he allowed himself to be so created. We must appreciate that merit on his part. The mass movement was the basis of leftism. But a mass movement does not always necessarily create a revolutionary ideology and revolutionary leaders. On the contrary, it often comes under the domination of reactionary leaders. That was the case with the mass movement of 1920, and Gandhi's subjective role was to degenerate the movement in that way.

... It is very correct to say that, in these days, there can be no absolute standard for leftism. What is leftism today may become rightism tomorrow. A product of a revolution may become an enemy of the revolution. That is usually the case with the products of primitive, immature, elemental forces of revolution. Jesus Christ, the Prophet of Islam, Buddha, were all products of revolutions. But their names in course of time became symbols of counter-revolution.

If there was ever any creator of the struggle for Indian freedom, the credit must go to imperialism. A revolutionary movement primarily is the product of objective conditions. The objective conditions for the growth of a revolutionary movement in India are the products of imperialist exploitation.

Even those who do not regard Gandhi as the creator of the movement hold that he gave expression to the revolutionary urge of the masses, and therefore played a revolutionary role. That also is not a correct view. Facts do not bear out that contention. As a matter of fact, Gandhi did his best to check the movement already in the beginning. He suspended the Satyagraha movement against the Rowlatt Act, immediately upon its being declared, because he had to rush to Ahmadabad to control a strike, which had broken out there as a part of the mass movement which constituted the background of the Satyagraha campaign. He busied himself with the object of controlling the strike at Ahmadabad on the ground that the masses should not be used for political purposes. Judged by the first act, Gandhi can be hardly credited with the role of the leader of a mass movement. He has all along been rather a controller of the mass movement. If he was not there, the movement most probably would have developed more powerfully. As a matter of fact, it did develop in spite of him, notwithstanding all his efforts to check it. Why, then, was he installed in the leadership of the movement? That is a puzzling phenomenon we have to explain. For us, the explanation is this. A movement gets the kind of leadership it deserves.

The mass movement of 1919-20 developed in the background of extreme political backwardness and general ignorance. Gandhi became the leader of the movement, because he was the personification of the ignorance and prejudices of the masses which created the movement. Gandhi occupied the centre of the scene not as a political leader, but as a Mahatma. That fact explains the whole puzzle.

We are back to a question we discussed yesterday, namely the influence of religion on a movement of backward masses. The first expression of the mass movement in India took a religious form. It created a Mahatma. That was the expression of mass awakening. How did that happen? In the absence of the conviction that man can remake the world in which he lives, the belief in some supernatural power is inevitable. With all their dissatisfaction, the masses were not yet conscious of their power. They must rely on a superior power. The Mahatma is the agent of God on earth. Gandhi stabilised his position by exploiting the weakness of the movement. Instead of making the masses conscious of their objectively revolutionary urge, he tried to make them forget it altogether.

Therefore, the question is not whether the movement in 1919-20 was leftist or rightist. It is whether the movement was revolutionary or not. If the question is put in that form, the answer is decidedly in the affirmative. Only then can the historical role of Gandhi be correctly appreciated. As the product of a revolutionary movement, he has a place in history. But it is a different matter to talk about his role. One cannot play a role unconsciously. A role is always performed consciously. Therefore, Gandhi's role in a revolutionary movement was counter-revolutionary from the very beginning.

Again, it will be useful to be accurate about terms. He was not actually counter-revolutionary but anti-revolutionary. Counter-revolution is an active function of social forces. Only a class in power can be counter-revolutionary. The anxiety to prevent a revolutionary outbreak is only anti-revolutionary. Therefore, strictly speaking, Gandhi's role was anti-revolutionary. Gandhism was anti-revolutionary. That was particularly so when a number of Gandhists were in office in seven provinces. Through their instrumentality, Gandhism became a force of counter-revolution.

In so far as he was the product of a revolutionary movement, Gandhi was certainly a factor in that movement. But, as himself, he was not a product of a revolutionary movement, but of feudal-patriarchal reaction. Until 1919, he was purely that. Upon his becoming a factor in the revolutionary movement, the contradiction in him became acute. His being hailed as a Mahatma enabled him to impose his reactionary ideas on an objectively revolutionary movement composed of backward masses. His contribution has indeed been the imposition of an anti-revolutionary, reformist, reactionary ideology on an objectively revolutionary movement.

My difference with Lenin regarding Gandhi and his role was on this point. Lenin thought that, being a creation of a revolutionary movement, Gandhi would be pushed by it to a position where he must play a revolutionary role. Lenin thought so because he was not aware of the solidity of Indian reaction which had been galvanised by imperialism, although, in the beginning, the latter did have disruptive significance. He was also mistaken about the role of the nationalist bourgeoisie. He failed to see that the role of a class may not be the same in different periods of history. Capitalism was once a revolutionary force. But it does not necessarily follow from that the bourgeoisie must always remain a revolutionary factor, even if it wants to establish capitalism. Lenin thought that the leadership of the revolution might well be taken over by the bourgeoisie. He thought that, like in other revolutions, taking place in backward social conditions, a religious man like the Mahatma could be utilised by the bourgeoisie to promote its purposes. I explained to him that in India and other relatively advanced colonial countries, the bourgeoisie could not be a revolutionary force, and therefore the situation was not such as might make a revolutionary weapon out of a religious man. In the Indian situation, the traditions of his own class were bound to assert themselves ultimately, and his actions would be determined by them.

Soon after the appearance of Gandhi, the bourgeoisie did make a feeble attempt to assert its domination over the nationalist movement. That attempt expressed itself through the rise of the Swaraj Party. It should be conceded a place in the process of the development of leftism in the Congress. The founder and leader of the Swaraj Party, C.R. Das, was the first Congress leader to speak of Swaraj for the ninety per cent. He also declared that he did not want to replace the white bureaucracy by a brown bureaucracy, and that Swaraj must be for the masses, and won by the masses. In 1922, those were revolutionary ideas. The Mahatma had stolen the masses. The bourgeoisie wanted to capture them from him. But they failed. Because they could not advocate a revolutionary ideology as against the reactionary ideas represented by the Mahatma which appealed to the prejudices of the ignorant masses.

With the rise of the Swaraj Party, yet another thing happened. That was a very significant incident, although it was largely confined to Bengal. The Swaraj Party established contact between the nationalist revolutionaries of a previous epoch and the mass movement in the postwar years. My appreciation of the old revolutionary movement is already recorded. As far back as in 1921, I expressed the opinion that it was a politically revolutionary movement with a reactionary social outlook. That may help the solution of the problem about the present attitude of the Forward Group in Bengal. Why is the one-time Jugantar Party playing such a dubious role today, confusing issues between right and left, and sabotaging the crystallisation of the left wing in Bengal? I was once connected with that group. From abroad I re-established contact, and I urged them to join the Congress when it was still in a flux. If conscious revolutionaries came in the movement, they might capture its leadership. But they were not very welcome. Gandhi demanded that they must publicly declare that their former activities had been bad and mistaken, and that they were joining the Congress to atone for their past sins. The revolt against Gandhism, raised by C.R. Das, enabled the old revolutionaries to penetrate the Congress. They supported Das. He accepted the programme of transforming the Congress into a political party with a democratic republican programme. All that preceded the Gaya Congress, on which occasion the programme of a National Democratic Revolution was formulated for the first time. A draft of that document had reached C.R. Das before the Gaya Congress.

After Bardoli, Gandhi called the non co-operation movement off. But for the agitation of the pro-changers, the movement would have completely collapsed. The agitation for parliamentary action kept up the political life. From that point of view, the Swaraj Party can be regarded as an expression of the growth of leftism in the Congress. In so far as it expressed the ambition of the bourgeoisie as a class, it was more progressive than the no-changers, representing the feudal-patriarchal ideology of Gandhi. Just as, compared with the older moderates and liberals, the non co-operators of 1920-21 were leftists, so was the Swaraj Party, in so far as it opposed Gandhism, for a time, the left wing of the Congress. But that leftism does not fit into the development of leftism as we conceive it today. The organisation of the Swaraj Party was the first attempt in the direction of converting the Congress into a political party. The attempt failed, because the nationalist bourgeoisie was incapable of leading a revolutionary struggle. It turned out to be an abortion of leftism, just as the Congress Socialist Party and the Forward Bloc were to be abortions of leftism half a generation later. The Swaraj Party was an abortion; the Forward Bloc a posthumous monster.

The purpose of today's discussion is to cure some of our comrades of the feeling of a sham apology for our own existence. They are always on the defensive, as if it is a mistake for us to exist at all. Having committed the mistake, we must justify it somehow. There is a Communist Party, a Congress Socialist party, a Forward Bloc, and now the Forward Group in Bengal. Nobody asks why they exist. Some of our comrades are anxious to measure up to their standards. Yet an investigation into the antecedents and history of those groups shows that they came into existence after we had laid the foundation of leftism, and done considerable spade-work in propaganda and organisation. We exist by our own merit. We are the creation of the movement, just as the Mahatma also was. Our self-confidence must result from that act. We must know something of our own history and origin. This group is not the creation of any individual. It does not require any authority, protection or patronage. It is a creation of the movement. It is the best that the movement in India has produced. It is the positive outcome of the developments during the last twenty years. If there is any future for this country, it belongs to our group. This realisation should be the outcome of our today's discussion.

A number of other questions have been interjected into this discussion. One is about proletarian hegemony. Only about ten years ago, this much talked of but little understood phrase came to be heard in India. Those who talk the most about it may know very little about it. Nevertheless, proletarian hegemony has been actually exercised in Indian politics ever since 1921. And that has been done through the instrumentality of our group. Our group has all along been the organ of proletarian hegemony in Indian politics. We cannot belittle the proletariat. But, it asserts itself on the Indian national life only through our intermediacy. But for us, there is no expression in India of the revolutionary significance of the proletariat. We must be self-critical. We must know our defects and shortcomings in order to remove them. We are not satisfied with whatever we have achieved until now. We want to accomplish much more. But the history of our group since 1921 should make you proud in spite of everything. Every constructive idea introduced in the political life of this country originated with us. Everything sensible that the Congress leaders or the Congress Socialist Party or the so-called Communist Party may do or say today, was initiated by us, at least ten years earlier. But ours is the fate of pioneers. We say a thing when people are not yet capable of understanding it, because they cannot see beyond their nose. The situation develops, and eventually things become so very clear, that others too can also see them at last. They take up the ideas, for which we had been ridiculed and castigated. Plagiarists and vulgarisers are hailed as prophets by the public with a memory even shorter than the proverbial. But recognition or no recognition, that is completely immaterial. We must ourselves know what we are contributing, so that we may not be discouraged when the fate of pioneers weighs heavily on us. That is hegemony. Hegemony is intellectual leadership, leadership without acknowledgement. Hegemony cannot be exercised by shouting from the housetops. It can be exercised only be men who can make the supreme sacrifice. It means that you actually supply the revolutionary inspiration of a movement but do not get the credit for it, though you may get all the blame.

We have been doing that. How could we? Because we have learned our Marxism. Marxist hegemony is already established in the Indian movement. All, including the Gandhists, are under its influence, in some way or other. Therefore, in so far as Marxism is the ideology of the proletariat, proletarian hegemony in the struggle for Indian freedom is already a partially accomplished fact—thanks to our efforts. But in order to exercise hegemony effectively, one must have patience. If you administer a large dose of a strong medicine to a man with a weak heart, he may die instead of being cured. In the given situation, only small doses of revolutionary ideas can be helpfully administered. That is not reformism. To do otherwise would defeat our purpose.

Apart from us, the so-called Communist Party is the only factor of leftism with any significance. All the others are abortions. The C.P. also is a monster. It claims to do what we are actually doing. Only, there is a great difference. They try to do it in a wrong way, and the wrong time—either too early or too late. That is because they cannot think for themselves. In answer to the question, whether we still expect to cure the Communist Party, I should say that as long as a group of people call themselves Communists and profess Marxism, there is some hope. They may not be altogether dishonest, but only mistaken and stubborn. All their mistakes result from the inability to appreciate Marxism. Marxism is the ideology not only of the proletariat. To regard it as the ideology of the proletariat, and nothing more, is wrong. It is a woeful under-estimation of the historical significance of Marxism. We are living in an age in which the guiding principle of all human progress is Marxism. Otherwise, it cannot influence the development of the Indian struggle for freedom, which is not identical with the struggle between labour and capital. Marxism cannot be effectively applied to the Indian situation by those who have narrow, superficial, pedantic, mechanical ideas about it. Intellectual subservience is the misfortune of the so-called Communist Party of India; it is so called, because it is not guided by a correct understanding of Marxism.

At one time, differences arose between ourselves and the so-called C.P. The process of radicalisation was beginning in the Congress. The experience of the movement of 1930-32 was fervent. For many Congressmen the Socialist Party was an expression of that process. Not a few of those responsible for the formation of the C.S.P. are to be found among ourselves. Originally, the tendency represented the reaction to the stupidities of the so-called Communists. It was the tendency towards an organisational crystallisation of all revolutionaries influenced by Marxism. The idea was that the C.P. had gone wrong; a really Communist or Socialist Party must be created anew. But there is more than one way of deviating from Marxism. Together with ourselves, there were others associated with the process of crystallisation of the revolutionary elements inside the Congress. They failed to have a correct understanding about the social character of those elements, and consequently adopted an inappropriate organisational method. They vulgarised Marxism to suit their mistaken course. We had to part company, and keep the flag of leftism flying high.

~

S. SATYAMURTI

Adjournment Motion re the Seizure of Subrahmanya Bharathi's Songs

Celebrated as one of India's greatest poets, Subrahmanya Bharathi's nationalist and political writing routinely invited the wrath of the colonial government. Following the ban imposed by the Government of Burma, the Madras government too imposed a ban on Subrahmanya Bharathi's poems. It asked the police to search and seize the songs from the printer. S. Satyamurti (1887–1943), the radical face of the Congress in Tamil Nadu and one of its most powerful voices, moved an adjournment motion in the legislative council on 8 October 1927 regarding the seizure. After a long procedural wrangling, the motion was debated, put to vote and passed by a majority of 76 to 12. Members cutting across party lines voted in favour of the motion. Introducing the motion, Satyamurti made a blistering attack on the government.

Mr. President, Sir, I beg leave to move that the business of this House do stand adjourned to consider a matter of urgent public importance, namely, the recent action of the City Police in entering upon and searching the premises of the Hindi Prachar Sabha on the High Road, Triplicane, for copies of Bharathi's songs, and seizing nearly two thousand copies of the same.

Sir, in support of this motion, I do not think I need advance elaborate or detailed arguments. For, I know, Sir, I am not exaggerating the feeling of any Member of this House who is a Tamilian, or who knows Tamil, or who is a patriot, or who is not afraid of patriotism, when I say that one wants no arguments to support this vote of censure on the action of the Madras Government in having acquiesced in or directed the City Police to seize what will remain, in spite of the Madras Government's activities, so long as the Tamil language lasts or a single Tamilian exists, as the most priceless and patriotic songs in that great language.

Sir, the late Subrahmanya Bharathi was a man on whose tongue, to use the language of romance for half a minute, the Goddess Saraswathi can honestly be believed to have danced the dance of patriotism. If he had been born in any free country, why in any country of the world except India, that man would have been made the Poet-Laureate of that country, would have been given honours and titles by a Government which knows how to respond to the feelings of the people, and would have lived and died among the most honoured of the nation. But, Sir, being the slave country that we are, he had to live as an exile in Pondicherry, enjoying the hospitality of the French Government, and die a broken wreck, because he found no use for himself under the auspices of this Government. But, Sir, martyrs and patriots before him have gone to the same fate. Subrahmanya Bharathi lived and died a patriot. I want to repeat, Mr. President, that so long as the Tamil language lasts, you may confiscate all the copies which exist—even as our sacred Vedas were handed down from generation to generation, for aeons, without a single piece of writing, by the memory of our ancient Hindu ancestors, even as Macaulay was able to repeat every line of Milton's 'Paradise Lost', I have no doubt, that so long as a single Tamilian lives, these songs will remain the priceless heritage of the Tamil race. I can inform this House, Mr. President, after this ill-advised action of the Government, we are starting a propaganda for getting by heart every song of Subrahmanya Bharathi, and although the Hon'ble Law Member and the Hon'ble Home Member may between them confiscate every printed word of those patriotic songs, human ingenuity has not yet invented any machinery which is able to confiscate thoughts and memories. Thoughts and memories will flourish, and wherever the Hon'ble Law Member or the Home Member goes, they will hear only these songs sung, and they will have to apply cotton wool to their ears if they want to save themselves from being polluted by hearing these brave and patriotic songs.

Sir, the origin of this action is not even complimentary to this Government. This Government is here governing the bulk of the Tamilians in whose language these poems are written. These poems are a quarter of a century old. For nearly twenty-five years, these songs have been sung throughout the province, and I appeal to my Hon'ble friend the Chief Minister, who I know is a very good student of Tamil whether he has not heard and enjoyed these songs, whether he has not heard and felt his pulse beat quicker, and his blood run warmer in his veins, when these magnificent, soul-stirring songs were sung. I am sorry my two other friends who crossed the floor are not here. If they were here, they dare not contradict me when I say that some of the election methods by which they came to this very Council, which gave them the opportunity to cross the floor and become Ministers, were these patriotic songs sung by boys and girls in public meetings. Sir, do you know that in this Tamil country, if you want to get up a magnificent meeting, if you want to sustain the interest of the audience, the most usual method is to get these songs sung? I wish I had voice to sing a few of those songs here, which will melt even the stony hearts of the hon. Law Member and the Home Member. I will read some of them, and even a prosaic reading of these songs will melt the hearts of these people.

Sir, it seems to me that for this Government to obey the dictates of the Burma Government, as if they have no opinion of their own in the matter, is inconsistent with a Government which has any sense of self-respect about it. Sir, the origin of this is the notification published by the Burma Government at Rangoon on 7 August 1928 in the Police Department.

They say: 'In exercise of the powers conferred by section 99-A of the Code of Criminal Procedure, 1898, the Governor in Council hereby declares to be forfeited to His Majesty all copies wherever found of the booklet in Tamil entitled "The National Songs, Parts I and II" composed and published by C. Subrahmanya Bharathi in the Bharathi's Asramam at Triplicane, Madras, on the ground that it contains seditious matter, the publication of which is punishable under section 124-A of the Indian Penal Code as tending to excite disaffection towards the Government established by law in British India.' Sir, section 99-A of the Criminal Procedure Code, which is one of the effects of the recommendations of the Press Act Repeal Committee over which some of our countrymen went enthusiastic, says when a local Government passes the order the Police may seize the same wherever found in British India and any magistrate may authorise any Police officer to enter upon and search for the same in any premises. Now, I want to know from the Hon'ble Law Member or whoever is in charge of this department and is going to reply to me, why this notification was published in the Fort St. George Gazette, dated 11 September 1928. Is there any rule by which notifications of local Governments are automatically republished in the Fort St. George Gazette? I know of no such rule. The only rule or practice I know of is that the resolutions and notifications of the Government of India published in the Gazette of India are republished by Madras Government in the Fort St. George Gazette for the information and guidance of the people of this province. There is no rule which requires, so far as I know, the republication in the Fort St. George Gazette of this order of the Burma Government. I should like to know why the local Government published this order.

The next stage, Sir, comes when the Police applied for a warrant before the Chief Presidency Magistrate to search those premises and to seize those copies. The application was made by Mr. Saptur Hussain, Inspector, Intelligence Department. The application says: 'I beg to submit that under notification, in G.O. Mis.No.739, Public, dated the 7th August 1928 of the local Government, Burma, republished by the local Government of Madras in the Fort St. George Gazette, dated 11th September 1928, the booklet styled "the National Songs", Parts I and II by C. Subrahmanya Bharathi have been forfeited to His Majesty under section 99-A of Criminal Procedure Code. I request this Honourable Court to issue a warrant authorising me to enter upon and search for the same in (1) Hindi Prachar Press, Triplicane, (2) Bharathi Asramam, Talayari Street, (3) O.N. Dandapani and Company, where such booklets are reasonably suspected to be stored.' With regard to this application for warrant, Mr. President, I want to know whether this action was taken by the Commissioner of Police at his own instance and on his own responsibility, or whether the Member of Government in charge of the Police had any knowledge or notice of it. If he had no knowledge or notice of it, I want to know whether it is the policy of the Madras Government that in a first class political matter like this, seizure of proscribed literature under orders of another local Government, the Police are going to be allowed to act on their own responsibility, without so much as 'by your leave' of the Government. Then, Sir, I want to know whether the order was applied for by the Police after taking the permission of Government or at least letting them know that they propose to do it. On that, Sir the Chief Presidency Magistrate passed this order: 'Whereas complaint has been made before me of the possession of undermentioned proscribed booklets and it has been made to appear to me that the production of the copies of the said booklets is essential to the inquiry now being made into the said offence...'

It is not clear, Sir, what the offence referred to is. Whatever it is, the facts are the Police did apply for and the Magistrate issued a warrant, and as many as two thousand copies of this book have been seized and forfeited to His Majesty and kept in the Record office of the Chief Presidency Magistrate.

Apart from the political or literary aspect of this matter, Mr. President, there is the human aspect about it. This man, Subrahmanya Bharathi, as I have said, died a broken man, a poor man, leaving behind him a widow and two daughters whose only means of subsistence is the proceeds of the sales of these books, and some friends have offered themselves to publish these books and to remit the profits out of those sales for the maintenance of this family of this great but poor man. As a consequence, the Bharathi Asramam and the Hindi Prachar Sabha in Triplicane are spending and have spent money on this publication, and after selling these publications they are going to send the profits for the maintenance of the widow and the daughters of this great and patriotic man. Is it consistent with charity or good sense or even ultimately the sense of honour of this Government that they should seek to deprive a widow and two fatherless children of their only means of subsistence in order that they may pursue the Burma Government's vendetta against high and patriotic literature of this kind? Apart from anything else, that must appeal to every Hon'ble Member of this House. Are you going to punish the widow and the daughters of Subrahmanya Bharathi, because he wrote patriotic songs, and punish them in this mean and despicable manner by depriving them of their livelihood? It is contemptible; it is unworthy of any Government which wants to call itself civilised or self-respecting or honourable.

... My Hon'ble friend the Chief Minister, a few months ago, in answer to questions on the floor of this House, said that his Government had no objection to the teaching or singing of Bharathi's songs in Government and aided schools in our Presidency. Look at the action of the Hon'ble Education Minister. He knows Tamil, he knows the songs, and the Council thanks him for his act of patriotism by which he allowed these songs to be sung in the schools provided by the Government. He sits there, he is still the Chief Minister and the most powerful Minister; he makes and unmakes ministers at his will; and yet with all his great powers of formation, destruction and reorganisation, this greater minister is unable to influence his two Colleagues who are now sitting to the right and left of him, the hon. Home Member and the Hon'ble Law Member, who do not say a word to the Chief Minister but listen to the Burma Police directing the Madras Police to seize by warrant and forfeit to His Majesty those very books which the Hon'ble Chief Minister thinks furnish the intellectual pabulum to our young children and on which they could be reared as honourable citizens; but when it comes to the reserved half, it is to be forfeited (laughter). I do not know whether it is a matter for laughter or tears. That is for him to decide. But if I were the hon. Chief Minister, I would rather be a dog and bay at the moon than be such a Minister as to be compelled to look when his own Colleagues snap their fingers at him saying, 'You may sing Bharathi's songs in schools and colleges but we will forfeit them.' I will not say anything more about him; for he is the only good man in the whole piece. Let us go to the villains of the piece, the Hon'ble Home Member and the Hon'ble Law Member, and both of them are Indians. I believe they have not given up their claim to be called Indians. The Hon'ble Law Member was till the other day sitting on this side or that side of the House, and I know he is a very good speaker in Malayalam, one who is listened to with respect. Supposing there are patriotic songs in Malayalam of the nature, I am going to read presently, does he think that he will forfeit those songs because a neighbouring Government called them seditious? And what about the Home Member? He represents Islamic culture there; he is there to protect Islamic interests; he is there, not for any other reason, but to see that the great Islamic culture is preserved intact from the invasion of the secular Government. Is it consistent with Islamic culture which is based on democracy, charity and free thinking, that he should be a party to this deliberate and wicked attempt at poisoning the intellect of the nation at its very fountain source and telling the people, 'You shall not become patriotic, you shall not become proud of your country, you shall not love your country, but you always shout with me that we will be slaves, that Britain shall rule over the waves?' If that is their attitude I can understand their action. If on the other hand these gentlemen claim to be patriots, I put it to my friend the Law Member—he is not a lawyer listening to the arguments of another lawyer on the other side vigorously taking notes and answering argument by counter-argument, that he should keep his heart open, his brains open, if he can, to listen to us and convert himself and have the courage to get up and say, 'Mr. President, I am ashamed of the action of the Madras Government; I shall recall the order.' I do not think he will rise to that occasion, but still I hope he will offer to do so.

Then, Sir, what are these songs? I am not going to dwell on their seditious name, under your ruling. I merely want to tell the House these are songs with the like of which one is familiar in English literature, such as praising the country, praising her natural beauties, praising her great heroes and heroines, praising her great achievements, expressing unmitigated love for the motherland, expressing joy in her present and hope in her future. Are these unworthy of any nation? These have been proscribed. I have got copies here and I can make a present of them to the Hon'ble Home Member or the Law Member, I will make a present of them to the Council Library, and if the Police want them they can go and search there and take them.

... I do not know, Sir, if there is any Tamilian in this House or outside whose heart will not melt at these songs. I ask them to remember this, that these songs are now declared forfeited to His Majesty by the action of a government which are to a certain extent kept in those treasury benches by us; the music of it is so great that even a halting reader of those songs like myself can make an appeal to the members here.

... I have listened to the Hon'ble Law Member shouting here yesterday; he has not even read these songs, but still he has forfeited the book. I can understand if the Government has chosen one of these songs or two and said that those songs should be forfeited. They have not done anything of the kind. These two volumes consist of some of the most moving songs on our religion and letters, apart from pure patriotism.

I shall finish by referring to similar songs in English literature which Englishmen sing in their country, which they sing even in our own country in private dinner parties and other places. They sing of the glories of England—'Britain shall rule the waves, Britons shall never be slaves'—but Indians shall always be slaves. That is the burden of their songs, if they are to be judged by the results of their actions.

... I want to point out three capital differences between the English nationalistic literature and ours. English nationalistic literature boasts of its own strength and speaks of the confusion and destruction of their enemies. 'God save the King, keep him victorious, happy and glorious and confound his enemies.' That is the Englishman's song. The Englishman's psychology is that God has to deal with only two categories, England and her subjects on the one hand her enemies on the other. That is, God must give up all His other work and constantly save England and confound her enemies. Humanity has come under these two categories, England and her subjects on the one hand or England and her enemies on the other. Whereas the message of Subrahmanya Bharathi is the message of all races, of poets, philosophers and seers of all nations. Let India be free and happy and the other nations of the world be free and happy. Is it for preaching this message of peace on earth and goodwill to all men that the Madras Government which does not understand the ABC of patriotism or nationalism has ventured to lay its profane hand on this sacred literature? We are constantly told that we are a nation of many races and creeds. Bharathi was a Brahman by birth, and I appeal to non-Brahmans in the South—several of them were his friends and I do not want to name them—to say whether throughout his literature, there is a single trace of caste or communal bias or superiority or inferiority. He talks only of Indians as a whole, he knows no distinction of class or creed, race or religion. He is the most cosmopolitan that I know of among modern authors. Is it for preaching this harmony among men that his books are sought to be forfeited by this Government? It seems to me that this action of the Government cannot be justified on any basis whatever, either of duty or of reason.

I have only one word, Mr. President. This motion is going to be pressed to a division. This motion, I know, will be passed. But I also know that the present Government, constituted as it is, will not listen to the united voice of this House. But the matter is not going to end here. It is a challenge to the literary genius of the Tamil race; it is a challenge to the self-respect of those whose mother tongue is Tamil. It is a challenge to all those patriotic citizens here and elsewhere who value intellectual freedom and value patriotism. I appeal to them all to see to it that this battle does not end here, but is taken to the hustings, and every elected member who votes against this motion, let him remember that the moment he rises to support the action of the Government, his fate as an elected member is sealed once and for all. I appeal to the Tamil friends on the Treasury benches to see that this order is revoked. I have great pleasure in making this motion.

~

BHAGAT SINGH

Statement before the Lahore High Court Bench

By the late 1920s, Bhagat Singh (1908–1930) had emerged as the undisputed leader of the youth of the country. He led a band of revolutionaries who thought not only of overthrowing British rule but also of the establishment of a socialist, secular and democratic society. Bhagat Singh repeatedly attacked the communalization of politics in the Punjab and in this did not forgive even his own hero Lala Lajpat Rai for turning communal in his later years. His piece entitled 'Why I Am an Atheist' is one of the best documents of rational and progressive thought in the country. In the brilliant statement reproduced here, made in January 1930, Bhagat Singh demolishes the basis of the sessions court judgment, which had sentenced him for hurling bombs in the legislative assembly, and emphasizes the importance of motive. The motive of action, he argued, should be the main consideration while judging the offence of an accused.

We are neither lawyers nor masters of English language, nor holders of degrees. Therefore, please do not expect any oratorial speech from us. We therefore pray that instead of going into the language mistakes of our statement Your Lordships will try to understand the real sense of it.

Leaving other points to our lawyers, I will confine myself to one point only. The point is very important in this case. The point is as to what were our intentions and to what extent we are guilty. This is a very complicated question and no one will be able to express before you that height of mental elevation which inspired us to think and act in a particular manner. We want that this should be kept in mind while assessing our intentions and our offence. According to the famous jurist Solomon, one should not be punished for his criminal offence if his aim is not against law.

We had submitted a written statement in the Sessions Court. That statement explains our aim and, as such, explains our intentions also. But the learned judge dismissed it with one stroke of pen, saying that 'generally the operation of law is not affected by how or why one committed the offence. In this country the aim of the offence is very rarely mentioned in legal commentaries.'

My Lords, our contention is that under the circumstances the learned judge ought to have judged us either by the result of our action or on the basis of the psychological part of our statement. But he did not take any of these factors into consideration.

The point to be considered is that the two bombs we threw in the Assembly did not harm anybody physically or economically. As such the punishment awarded to us is not only very harsh but revengeful also. Moreover, the motive of the offence of an accused cannot be found out without knowing his psychology. And no one can do justice to anybody without taking his motive into consideration. If we ignore the motive, the biggest generals of the world will appear like ordinary murderers; revenue officers will look like thieves and cheats. Even judges will be accused of murder. This way the entire social system and the civilisation will be reduced to murders, thefts and cheating. If we ignore the motive, the government will have no right to expect sacrifice from its people and its officials. Ignore the motive and every religious preacher will be dubbed as a preacher of falsehoods, and every prophet will be charged of misguiding crores of simple and ignorant people.

If we set aside the motive, then Jesus Christ will appear to be a man responsible for creating disturbances, breaking peace and preaching revolt, and will be considered to be a 'dangerous personality' in the language of the law. But we worship him. He commands great respect in our hearts and his image creates vibrations of spiritualism amongst us. Why? Because the inspiration behind his actions was that of a high ideal. The rulers of that age could not recognise that high idealism. They only saw his outward actions. Nineteen centuries have passed since then. Have we not progressed during this period? Shall we repeat that mistake again? If that be so, then we shall have to admit that all the sacrifices of the mankind and all the efforts of the great martyrs were useless and it would appear as if we are still at the same place where we stood twenty centuries back.

From the legal point of view also, the question of motive is of special importance. Take the example of General Dyer. He resorted to firing and killed hundreds of innocent and unarmed people. But the military court did not order him to be shot. It gave him lakhs of rupees as award. Take another example. Shri Kharag Bahadur Singh, a young Gurkha who killed a Marwari in Calcutta. If the motive be set aside, then Kharag Bahadur Singh ought to have been hanged. But he was awarded a mild sentence of a few years only. He was even released much before the expiry of his sentence. Was there any loophole in the law that he escaped capital punishment? Or, was the charge of murder not proved against him? Like us, he also accepted the full responsibility of his action, but he escaped death. He is free today. I ask Your Lordships, why was he not awarded capital punishment? His action was well calculated and well planned. From the motive end, his action was more serious and fatal than ours. He was awarded a mild punishment because his intentions were good. He saved the society from a dirty leach [*sic*] who had sucked the life-blood of so many pretty young girls. Kharag Singh was given a mild punishment just to uphold the formalities of the law.

This principle [*that the law does not take motive into consideration—Ed.*] is quite absurd. This is against the basic principles of the law which declares that 'the law is for man and not man for the law'. As such, why the same norms are not being applied to us also? It is quite clear that while convicting Kharag Singh his motive was kept in mind, otherwise a murderer can never escape the hangman's noose. Are we being deprived of the ordinary advantage of the law because our offence is against the government, or because our action has a political importance?

My Lords, under these circumstances, please permit us to assert that a government which seeks shelter behind such mean methods has no right to exist. If it exists, it is for the time being only, and that too with the blood of thousands of people on its head. If the law does not see the motive, there can be no justice, nor can there be stable peace.

Mixing of arsenic (poison) in the flour will not be considered to be a crime, provided its purpose is to kill rats. But if the purpose is to kill a man, it becomes a crime of murder. Therefore, such laws which do not stand the test of reason and which are against the principles of justice, should be abolished. Because of such unjust laws, many great intellectuals had to adopt the path of revolt.

The facts regarding our case are very simple. We threw two bombs in the Legislative Assembly on April 8, 1929. As a result of the explosion, a few persons received minor scratches. There was pandemonium in the chamber, hundreds of visitors and members of the Assembly ran out. Only my friend B.K. Dutt and myself remained seated in the visitors gallery and offered ourselves for arrest. We were tried for attempt to murder, and convicted for life. As mentioned above, as a result of the bomb explosion, only four or five persons were slightly injured and one bench got damaged. We offered ourselves for arrest without any resistance. The Sessions Judge admitted that we could have very easily escaped, had we had any intention like that. We accepted our offence and gave a statement explaining our position. We are not afraid of punishment. But we do not want that we should be wrongly understood. The judge removed a few paragraphs from our statement. This we consider to be harmful for our real position.

A proper study of the full text of our statement will make it clear that, according to us, our country is passing through a delicate phase. We saw the coming catastrophe and thought it proper to give a timely warning with a loud voice, and we gave the warning in the manner we thought proper. We may be wrong. Our line of thinking and that of the learned judge may be different, but that does not mean that we be deprived of the permission to express our ideas, and wrong things be propagated in our name.

In our statement we explained in detail what we mean by 'Long Live Revolution' and 'Down With Imperialism'. That formed the crux of our ideas. That portion was removed from our statement. Generally a wrong meaning is attributed to the word revolution. That is not our understanding. Bombs and pistols do not make revolution. The sword of revolution is sharpened on the whetting-stone of ideas. This is what we wanted to emphasise. By revolution we mean the end of the miseries of capitalist wars. It was not proper to pronounce judgement without understanding our aims and objects and the process of achieving them. To associate wrong ideas with our names is out and out injustice.

It was very necessary to give the timely warning that the unrest of the people is increasing and that the malady may take a serious turn, if not treated in time and properly. If our warning is not heeded, no human power will be able to stop it. We took this step to give proper direction to the storm. We are serious students of history. We believe that, had the ruling powers acted correctly at the proper time, there would have been no bloody revolutions in France and Russia. Several big powers of the world tried to check the storm of ideas and were sunk in the atmosphere of bloodshed. The ruling people cannot change the flow of the current. We wanted to give the first warning. Had we aimed at killing some important personalities, we would have failed in the attainment of our aim.

My Lords, this was the aim and the spirit behind our action, and the result of the action corroborates our statement. There is one more point which needs elucidation, and that is regarding the strength of the bombs. Had we had no idea of the strength of the bombs, there would have been no question of our throwing them in the presence of our respected national leaders like Pandit Motilal Nehru, Shri Kelkar, Shri Jayaker and Shri Jinnah. How could we have risked the lives of our leaders? After all we are not mad and, had we been so, we would have certainly been sent to the lunatic asylum, instead of being put in jail. We had full knowledge about the strength of the bombs and that is why we acted with so much confidence. It was very easy to have thrown the bombs on the occupied benches, but it was difficult to have thrown them on unoccupied seats. Had we not been of saner mind or had we been mentally unbalanced, the bombs would have fallen on occupied benches and not in empty places. Therefore I would say that we should be rewarded for the courage we showed in carefully selecting the empty places. Under these conditions, My Lords, we think we have not been understood properly. We have not come before you to get our sentences reduced. We have come here to clarify our position. We want that we should not be given any unjust treatment, nor should any unjust opinion be pronounced about us. The question of punishment is of secondary importance before us.

~

JAWAHARLAL NEHRU

'Purna Swaraj', Presidential Address, Lahore Session, 1929

This speech, in which Jawaharlal Nehru (1889–1964) declared Purna Swaraj as the goal of the Congress at its Lahore session held on the banks of the river Ravi in 1929, holds a special significance for the national movement. In many ways it altered the course of the national movement and after this there was no looking back. Demands for abandoning all talk of dominion status had been on the rise and the youth of the country was increasingly veering to the idea that the Congress should declare full independence as its goal. In the 1928 convention in Calcutta, while discussing the report prepared by Motilal Nehru, Subhas Bose and Jawaharlal Nehru had demanded complete independence. As such, when Nehru declared Purna Swaraj as the goal of the Congress in its 1929 session, it had an electrifying effect on the psyche of the people.

Comrades, for four and forty years this National Congress has laboured for the freedom of India. During this period it has somewhat slowly, but surely, awakened national consciousness from its long stupor and built up the national movement. If today we are gathered here at a crisis of our destiny, conscious of our strength as well as of our weakness, and looking with hope and apprehension to the future, it is well that we give first thought to those who have gone before us and who spent out their lives with little hope of reward, so that those that followed them may have the joy of achievement. Many of the giants of old are not with us and we of a later day, standing on an eminence of their creation, may often decry their efforts. That is the way of the world. But none of you can forget them or the great work they have done in laying the foundations of a free India. And none of us can ever forget that glorious band of men and women who have laid down their young lives or spent their bright youth in suffering and torment in utter protest against a foreign domination.

Many of their names even are not known to us. They laboured and suffered in silence without any expectation of public applause, and by their heart's blood they nursed the tender plant of India's freedom. While many of us temporised and compromised, they stood up and proclaimed a people's right to freedom and declared to the world that India, even in her degradation, had the spark of life in her, because she refused to submit to tyranny and serfdom. Brick by brick has our national movement been built up, and often on the prostrate bodies of her martyred sons has India advanced. The giants of old may not be with us, but the courage of old is with us still and India can yet produce martyrs like Jatin Das.

This is the glorious heritage that we have inherited and you wish to put me in charge of it. I know well that I occupy this honoured place by chance more than by your deliberate design. Your design was to choose another—one who towers above all others in this present day world of ours—and there could have been no wiser choice. But fate and he conspired together and thrust me against your will and mine into this terrible seat of responsibility. Should I express my gratitude to you for having placed me in this dilemma? But I am grateful indeed for your confidence in one who strangely lacks it himself.

You will discuss many vital national problems that face us today and your decisions may change the course of Indian history. But you are not the only people that are faced with problems. The whole world today is one vast question mark and every country and every people is in the melting pot. The age of faith, with the comfort and stability it brings, is past, and there is questioning about everything, however permanent or sacred it might have appeared to our forefathers. Everywhere there is doubt and restlessness and the outcome hangs in the balance. We appear to be in a dissolving period of history when the world is in labour and out of her travail will give birth to a new order.

No one can say what the future will bring, but we may assert with some confidence that Asia and even India will play a determining part in future world policy. The brief day of European domination is already approaching its end. Europe has ceased to be the centre of activity and interest. The future lies with America and Asia. Owing to the false and incomplete history many of us have been led to think that Europe has always dominated over the rest of the world, and Asia has always let the legions of the West thunder past and has plunged in thought again. We have forgotten that for millennia the legions of Asia overran Europe and modern Europe itself largely consists of the descendants of these invaders from Asia. We have forgotten that it was India that finally broke the military power of Alexander. Thought has undoubtedly been the glory of Asia and specially of India, but in the field of action the record of Asia has been equally great. But none of us desires that legions of Asia or Europe should overrun the continents again. We have all had enough of them.

India today is part of a world movement. Not only China, Turkey, Persia and Egypt but also Russia and the countries of the West are taking part in this movement, and India cannot isolate herself from it. We have our own problems—difficult and intricate—and we cannot run away from them and take shelter in the wider problems that affect the world. But if we ignore the world, we do so at our peril. Civilisation today, such as it is, is not the creation or monopoly of one people or nation. It is the composite fabric to which all countries have contributed and then have adapted to suit their particular needs. And if India has a message to give to the world as I hope she has, she has also to receive and learn much from the messages of other peoples.

We want to put an end to the exploitation of India's poor and to get the reality of power and not merely the livery of office. Mr Wedgwood Benn has given us a record of the achievements of the past decade. He could have added to it by referring to Martial Law in the Punjab and the Jallianwala Bagh shooting and the repression and exploitation that have gone on continually during this period of 'Dominion Status in Action'. He has given us some insight into what more of Dominion Status may mean for us. It will mean the shadow of authority to a handful of Indians and more repression and exploitation of the masses.

What will this Congress do? The conditions for cooperation remain unfulfilled. Can we cooperate so long as there is no guarantee that real freedom will come to us? Can we cooperate when our comrades lie in prison and repression continues? Can we cooperate until we are assured that real peace is sought after and not merely a tactical advantage over us? Peace cannot come at the point of the bayonet and if we are to continue to be dominated over by an alien people, let us at least be no consenting parties to it.

If the Calcutta resolution holds, we have but one goal today, that of independence. Independence is not a happy word in the world today; for it means exclusiveness and isolation. Civilisation has had enough of narrow nationalism and gropes towards a wider cooperation and inter-dependence. And if we use the word independence, we do so in no sense hostile to the larger ideal. Independence for us means complete freedom from British domination and imperialism. Having attained our freedom I have no doubt that India will welcome all attempts at world cooperation and federation and will even agree to give up part of her own independence to a larger group of which she is an equal member.

British Imperialism

The British Empire today is not such a group and cannot be so long as it dominates over millions of people and holds large areas of the world's surface despite the will of their inhabitants. It cannot be a true Commonwealth so long as imperialism is its basis and the exploitation of other races its chief means of sustenance. The British Empire today is indeed gradually undergoing a process of political dissolution, it is in a state of unstable equilibrium. The Union of S. Africa is not a happy member of the family, nor is the Irish Free State a willing one. Egypt drifts away. India could never be an equal member of the Commonwealth unless imperialism and all it implies is discarded. So long as this is not done, India's position in the Empire must be one of subservience and her exploitation will continue.

There is talk of world peace and pacts have been signed by the nations of the world. But despite pacts armaments grow and beautiful language is the only homage that is paid to the goddess of peace. Peace can only come when the causes of war are removed. So long as there is the domination of one country over another, or the exploitation of one class by another there will always be attempts to subvert the existing order and no stable equilibrium can endure. Out of imperialism and capitalism peace can never come. And it is because the British Empire stands for these and bases itself on the exploitation of the masses that we can find no willing place in it. No gain that may come to us is worth anything unless it helps in removing the grievous burdens on our masses. The weight of a great Empire is heavy to carry and long our people have endured it. Their backs are bent down and their spirit has almost broken. How will they share in the Commonwealth partnership if the burden of exploitation continues? Many of the problems we have to face are the problems of vested interests mostly created or encouraged by the British Government. The interests of the Rulers of Indian States, of British Officials and British Capital and Indian Capital and of the owners of big Zamindaris are ever thrust before us, and they claim our protection. The unhappy millions who really need protection are almost voiceless and have few advocates.

A Test

We have had much controversy about Independence and Dominion Status and we have quarrelled about words. But the real thing is the conquest of power by whatever name it may be called. I do not think that any form of Dominion Status applicable to India will give us real power. A test of this power would be the entire withdrawal of the alien army of occupation and economic control. Let us therefore concentrate on these and the rest will follow easily.

Declaration of Independence

We stand therefore today, for the fullest freedom of India. This Congress has not acknowledged and will not acknowledge the right of the British Parliament to dictate to us in any way. To it we make no appeal, but we do appeal to the Parliament and the conscience of the world, and to them we shall declare, I hope, that India submits no longer to any foreign domination. We are very conscious of our weakness and there is no boasting in us or pride of strength. But let no one, least of all England, mistake or under-rate the meaning or strength of our resolve. Solemnly with full knowledge of consequences, I hope we shall walk on and there will be no turning back. A great nation cannot be thwarted for long when once its mind is clear and resolved. If today we fail and tomorrow brings no success the day after will follow and bring achievements.

The Congress represents no small minority in the country and though many may be too weak to join it or to work for it, they look to it with hope and longing to bring them deliverance. Ever since the Calcutta resolution, the country has waited with anxious expectation for this great day when this Congress meets. None of us can say what and when we can achieve. We cannot command success. But success often comes to those who dare and act; it seldom goes to the timid who are ever afraid of consequence. We play for high stakes; and if we seek to achieve great things it can only be through great dangers. Whether we succeed soon or late, none but ourselves can stop us from high endeavour and from writing a noble page in our country's long and splendid history.

We have conspiracy cases going on in various parts of the country. They are ever with us. But the time has gone for secret conspiracy. We have now an open conspiracy to free this country from foreign rule, and you comrades, and all our countrymen and countrywomen are invited to join it. But the rewards that are in store for you are suffering and prison and it may be death. But you shall also have the satisfaction that you have done your little bit for India, the ancient, but ever young, and have helped a little in the liberation of humanity from its present bondage.

~

MOHANDAS KARAMCHAND GANDHI

On the Eve of the Dandi March

Mahatma Gandhi was master of the symbolic gesture. In 1930, the commonplace salt became the emblem for one of the most historic protests against an imperial power anywhere in the world. He decided to break the salt law by making salt and towards this end embarked upon what is known as the Dandi March. On the eve of the march on 11 March 1930, he spoke to a gathering of almost 10,000 people who attended his prayer meeting. The speech is memorable for its resolute calmness.

In all probability this will be my last speech to you. Even if the Government allows me to march tomorrow morning, this will be my last speech on the sacred banks of the Sabarmati. Possibly these may be the last words of my life here.

I have already told you yesterday what I had to say. Today I shall confine myself to what you should do after my companions and I are arrested. The programme of the march to Jalalpur must be fulfilled as originally settled. The enlistment of the volunteers for this purpose should be confined to Gujarat only. From what I have seen and heard during the last fortnight, I am inclined to believe that the stream of civil resisters will flow unbroken.

But let there be not a semblance of breach of peace even after all of us have been arrested. We have resolved to utilise all our resources in the pursuit of an exclusively non-violent struggle. Let no one commit a wrong in anger. This is my hope and prayer. I wish these words of mine reached every nook and corner of the land. My task shall be done if I perish and so do my comrades. It will then be for the Working Committee of the Congress to show you the way and it will be up to you to follow its lead. So long as I have not reached Jalalpur, let nothing be done in contravention to the authority vested in me by the Congress. But once I am arrested, the whole responsibility shifts to the Congress. No one who believes in non-violence, as a creed, need, therefore, sit still. My compact with the Congress ends as soon as I am arrested. In that case there should be no slackness in the enrolment of volunteers. Wherever possible, civil disobedience of salt laws should be started. These laws can be violated in three ways. It is an offence to manufacture salt wherever there are facilities for doing so. The possession and sale of contraband salt, which includes natural salt or salt earth, is also an offence. The purchasers of such salt will be equally guilty. To carry away the natural salt deposits on the seashore is likewise violation of law. So is the hawking of such salt. In short, you may choose any one or all of these devices to break the salt monopoly.

We are, however, not to be content with this alone. There is no ban by the Congress and wherever the local workers have self-confidence other suitable measures may be adopted. I stress only one condition, namely, let our pledge of truth and non-violence as the only means for the attainment of Swaraj be faithfully kept. For the rest, everyone has a free hand. But, that does not give a license to all and sundry to carry on on their own responsibility. Wherever there are local leaders, their orders should be obeyed by the people. Where there are no leaders and only a handful of men have faith in the programme, they may do what they can, if they have enough self-confidence. They have a right, nay it is their duty, to do so. The history of the world is full of instances of men who rose to leadership, by sheer force of self-confidence, bravery and tenacity. We too, if we sincerely aspire to Swaraj and are impatient to attain it, should have similar self-confidence. Our ranks will swell and our hearts strengthen, as the number of our arrests by the Government increases.

Much can be done in many other ways besides these. The liquor and foreign cloth shops can be picketed. We can refuse to pay taxes if we have the requisite strength. The lawyers can give up practice. The public can boycott the law courts by refraining from litigation. Government servants can resign their posts. In the midst of the despair reigning all round people quake with fear of losing employment. Such men are unfit for Swaraj. But why this despair? The number of Government servants in the country does not exceed a few hundred thousands. What about the rest? Where are they to go? Even free India will not be able to accommodate a greater number of public servants. A Collector then will not need the number of servants he has got today. He will be his own servant. Our starving millions can by no means afford this enormous expenditure. If, therefore, we are sensible enough, let us bid goodbye to Government employment, no matter if it is the post of a judge or a peon. Let all who are cooperating with the Government in one way or another, be it by paying taxes, keeping titles, or sending children to official schools, etc. withdraw their cooperation in all or as many ways as possible. Then there are women who can stand shoulder to shoulder with men in this struggle.

You may take it as my will. It was the message that I desired to impart to you before starting on the march or for the jail. I wish that there should be no suspension or abandonment of the war that commences tomorrow morning or earlier, if I am arrested before that time. I shall eagerly await the news that ten batches are ready as soon as my batch is arrested. I believe there are men in India to complete the work begun by me. I have faith in the righteousness of our cause and the purity of our weapons. And where the means are clean, there God is undoubtedly present with His blessings. And where these three combine, there defeat is an impossibility. A Satyagrahi, whether free or incarcerated, is ever victorious. He is vanquished only when he forsakes truth and non-violence and turns a deaf ear to the inner voice. If, therefore, there is such a thing as defeat for even a Satyagrahi, he alone is the cause of it. God bless you all and keep off all obstacles from the path in the struggle that begins tomorrow.

~

JAWAHARLAL NEHRU

The Karachi Resolution, 1930

In this speech, Jawaharlal Nehru presented the socio-economic vision of India's freedom struggle. A democratic and secular polity and an equitable system were part of the social philosophy of the movement. The Karachi Resolution lay these goals down in writing. In fact, this resolution can also be called the Magna Carta of Fundamental Rights in India.

This Congress is of the opinion that in order to end the exploitation of the masses, political freedom must include real economic freedom of the starving millions. In order therefore, that the masses may appreciate what Swaraj as conceived by the Congress will mean to them, it is desirable to state the position of the Congress in a manner easily understood by them. The Congress therefore declares that any constitution that may be agreed to on its behalf, should include the following items, or should give the ability to the Swaraj Government to provide for them.

1. Fundamental rights of the people such as
   - i. Freedom of association and combination.
   - ii. Freedom of speech and press.
   - iii. Freedom of conscience and the free profession and practice of religion, subject to public order and morality.
   - iv. No disability to attach to any person of religion, caste or creed in regard to public employment, office of power or honour and the exercise of any trade or calling.
   - v. Equal rights and obligations of all citizens. No civic bar on account of sex.
   - vi. Equal rights to all citizens of access to and use of public roads, public wells and all other places of public resort.
   - vii. Right to keep and bear arms in accordance with regulations made in that behalf and such reservations as may be required for public safety.
2. Religious neutrality on part of the state.
3. A living wage for industrial workers, limited hours of labour, healthy conditions of work, protection against the economic consequences of old age, sickness and unemployment.
4. Labour to be freed from serfdom or conditions bordering on serfdom.

5. Protection of women workers, and specially adequate provisions for leave during maternity period.
6. Prohibition against employment of children of school-going age in factories.
7. Right of labour to form unions to protect their interests with suitable machinery for settlement of disputes by arbitration.
8. Substantial reduction of land revenue and rent and in case of uneconomic holdings exemption from rent for such period as may be necessary.
9. Imposition of a progressive income-tax on agricultural income above a fixed income.
10. A graduate inheritance tax.
11. Adult suffrage.
12. Free Primary education.
13. Military expenditure to be reduced by at least one-half of the present scale.
14. Expenditure and salaries in civil departments to be largely reduced. No servant of the state, other than specially employed experts and the like to be paid above a certain fixed figure which should not ordinarily exceed Rs. 500/- per month.
15. Protection of indigenous cloth by exclusion of foreign cloth and foreign yarn from the country.
16. Total prohibition of intoxicating drinks and drugs.
17. No duty on salt.
18. State regulation of the exchange ratio so as to help Indian industries and bring relief to the masses.
19. Control by the state of key industries and mineral resources.
20. Control of usury—direct or indirect.

It will be open to the All India Congress Committee to revise, amend or add to the foregoing so far as such revision, amendment or addition is not inconsistent with the policy and principles thereof.

~

MOHANDAS KARAMCHAND GANDHI

I Give You a Mantra

The Quit India movement of 1942 represented the crowning glory of India's fight for independence. It was the most dramatic of all movements that the

Indian leadership had launched in its struggle against colonial rule. Till 1940, in the midst of the Second World War, the Congress leadership was not inclined to launch any mass movement as they felt that such a move would weaken the government at a time of emergency. However, when Japan entered the war and was, by 1941, knocking at the borders of India, there was a general panic among the people and a sense of demoralization over the way the British Army and bureaucracy had abandoned their posts in South-east Asia, leaving the local population at the mercy of the advancing Japanese Army. Mahatma Gandhi announced the Quit India resolution despite the reservations of the majority of his colleagues. He declared he would prefer anarchy to British apathy. The speech at Gowalia Tank Ground in Bombay on the fateful day shook the foundations of the empire forever. Gandhi began by first congratulating the communist leaders who had opposed the resolution as they thought such a move at this stage would weaken the Allied powers in their war against the fascists. He commended them for their honesty in standing up for a cause.

I congratulate you on the resolution that you have just passed. I also congratulate the three comrades on the courage they have shown in pressing their amendments to a division, even though they knew that there was an overwhelming majority in favour of the resolution, and I congratulate the thirteen friends who voted against the resolution. In doing so, they had nothing to be ashamed of. For the last twenty years we have tried to learn not to lose courage even when we are in a hopeless minority and are laughed at. We have learned to hold on to our beliefs in the confidence that we are in the right. It behoves us to cultivate this courage of conviction, for it ennobles man and raises his moral stature. I was, therefore, glad to see that these friends had imbibed the principle, which I have tried to follow for the last fifty years and more.

... In satyagraha, there is no place for fraud or falsehood, or any kind of untruth. Fraud and untruth today are stalking the world. I cannot be a helpless witness to such a situation. I have travelled all over India as perhaps nobody in the present age has. The voiceless millions of the land saw in me their friend and representative, and I identified myself with them to an extent it was possible for a human being to do. I saw trust in their eyes, which I now want to turn to good account in fighting this Empire upheld on untruth and violence. However gigantic the preparations that the Empire has made, we must get out of its clutches. How can I remain silent at this supreme hour and hide my light under the bushel? Shall I ask the Japanese to tarry a while? If today I sit quiet and inactive, God will take me to task for not using up the treasure He had given me, in the midst of the conflagration that is enveloping the whole world. Had the condition been different, I should have asked you to wait yet a while. But the situation now has become intolerable, and the Congress has no other course left for it.

Nevertheless, the actual struggle does not commence this moment. You have only placed all your powers in my hands. I will now wait upon the Viceroy and plead with him for the acceptance of the Congress demand. That process is likely to take two or three weeks. What would you do in the meanwhile? What is the programme, for the interval, in which all can participate? As you know, the spinning-wheel is the first thing that occurs to me. I made the same answer to the Maulana. He would have none of it, though he understood its import later. The fourteen-fold constructive programme is, of course, there for you to carry out. What more should you do? I will tell you. Everyone of you should, from this moment onwards, consider yourself a free man or woman, and act as if you are free and are no longer under the heel of this imperialism.

It is not a make-believe that I am suggesting to you. It is the very essence of freedom. The bond of the slave is snapped the moment he considers himself to be a free being. He will plainly tell the master: 'I was your bonded slave till this moment, but I am a slave no longer. You may kill me if you like, but if you keep me alive, I wish to tell you that if you release me from the bondage of your own accord, I will ask for nothing more from you. You used to feed and clothe me, though I could have provided food and clothing for myself by my labour. I hitherto depended on you instead of on God, for food and raiment. God has now inspired me with all urge for freedom and I am today a free man and will no longer depend on you.'

You may take it from me that I am not going to strike a bargain with the Viceroy for ministries and the like. I am not going to be satisfied with anything short of complete freedom. Maybe, he will propose the abolition of salt tax, the drink evil, etc. But I will say: 'Nothing less than freedom.'

Here is a mantra, a short one, that I give you. You may imprint it on your hearts and let every breath of yours give expression to it. The mantra is: 'Do or Die.' We shall either free India or die in the attempt; we shall not live to see the perpetuation of our slavery. Every true Congressman or [Congress] woman will join the struggle with an inflexible determination not to remain alive to see the country in bondage and slavery. Let that be your pledge. Keep jails out of your consideration. If the Government keeps me free, I will spare you the trouble of filling the jails. I will not put on the Government the strain of maintaining a large number of prisoners at a time when it is in trouble. Let every man and woman live every moment of his or her life hereafter in the consciousness that he or she eats or lives for achieving freedom and will die, if need be, to attain that goal. Take a pledge with God and your own conscience as witness, that you will no longer rest till freedom is achieved and will be prepared to lay down your lives in the attempt to achieve it. He who loses his life will gain it; he who will seek to save it shall lose it. Freedom is not for the coward or the faint-hearted.

~

SUBHAS CHANDRA BOSE

Message to Gandhi

Along with Jawaharlal Nehru, Subhas Chandra Bose (1897–1945) was one of the prominent young leaders of the Congress in the 1920s and 1930s. He was elected president of the Indian National Congress for two consecutive terms in 1938 and 1939. However, ideological conflicts with Gandhi—Bose advocated violent resistance and was convinced that Mahatma Gandhi's tactics of non-violence would never be enough to secure freedom—forced him to resign. He established a separate political party, the All India Forward Bloc, and continued to call for the full and immediate independence of India. Kept under house arrest by the government, Bose managed to escape and left India in 1941 to organize the Indian National Army (INA) in Japan, planning an attack on India from the Burmese border. Bose's speech reproduced here, broadcast from Azad Hind Radio on 6 July 1944, on the eve of the INA's march on India, not only articulates the trust and camaraderie between Gandhi and Bose who despite their differences had abiding respect for each other, but also demonstrates the high esteem and regard in which Bose held Gandhi.

After the sad demise of Shrimati Kasturba in British custody, it was but natural for your countrymen to be alarmed over the state of your health. For Indians outside India, differences in method are like domestic differences. Ever since you sponsored the Independence

Resolution at the Lahore Congress in December 1929, all members of the Indian National Congress have had one common goal before them. For Indians outside India, you are the creator of the present awakening in our country. The high esteem in which you are held by patriotic Indians outside India, and by foreign friends of India's freedom, was increased a hundred-fold when you bravely sponsored the 'Quit India' Resolution in August 1942 …

It would be a fatal mistake on your part to make a distinction between the British Government and the British people. No doubt there is a small group of idealists in Britain—as in the U.S.A.—who would like to see India free. These idealists, who are treated by their own people as cranks, form a microscopic minority. So far as India is concerned, for all practical purposes, the British Government and the British people mean one and the same thing. Regarding the war aims of the U.S.A., I may say that the ruling clique at Washington is now dreaming of world domination. This ruling clique and its intellectual exponents talk openly of the 'American Century'. In this ruling clique, there are extremists who go so far as to call Britain the 49th State of the U.S.A.

I can assure you, Mahatmaji, that before I finally decided to set out on this hazardous mission, I spent days, weeks and months in carefully considering the pros and cons of the case. After having served my people so long to the best of my ability, I could have no desire to be a traitor, or to give anyone a justification for calling me a traitor. Thanks to the generosity and to the affection of my countrymen, I had obtained the highest honour which it was possible for any public worker in India to achieve. I had also built up a party consisting of staunch and loyal colleagues who had implicit confidence in me. By going abroad on a perilous quest, I was risking not only my life and my whole future career, but what was more, the future of my party. If I had the slightest hope that without action from abroad we could win freedom, I would never have left India during a crisis. If I had any hope that within our lifetime we could get another chance—another golden opportunity—for winning freedom, as during the present war, I doubt if I would have set out for home.

There remains but one question for me to answer with regard to the Axis Powers. Can it be possible that I have been deceived by them? I believe it will be universally admitted that the cleverest and the most cunning politicians are to be found amongst Britishers. One who has worked with and fought British politicians all his life cannot be deceived by any other politician in the world. If British politicians have failed to coax or coerce me, no other politicians can succeed in doing so. And if the British Government, at whose hands I have suffered long imprisonment, persecution and physical assault, has been unable to demoralise me, no other power can hope to do so. I have never done anything which could compromise in the least either the honour or the self-respect or the interest of my country.

There was a time when Japan was an ally of our enemy. I did not come to Japan so long as there was an Anglo-Japanese alliance. I did not come to Japan so long as normal diplomatic relations obtained between the two countries. It was only after Japan took what I considered to be the most momentous step in her history, namely, declaration of war on Britain and America, that I decided to visit Japan of my own free will. Like so many of my countrymen, my sympathies in 1937 and 1938 were with Chunking. You may remember that as President of the Congress I was responsible for sending out medical mission to Chunking in December 1938.

Mahatmaji, you know better than anybody else how deeply suspicious the Indian people are of mere promises. I would be the last man to be influenced by Japan if her declarations of policy had been mere promises.

I should now like to say something about the Provisional Government that we have set up here. The Provisional Government has, as its one objective, the liberation of India from the British yoke, through an armed struggle. Once our enemies are expelled from India, and peace and order is established, the mission of the Provisional Government will be over. The only reward that we desire for our efforts, for our suffering and for our sacrifice is the freedom of our motherland. There are many among us who would like to retire from the political field, once India is free.

Nobody would be more happy than ourselves, if by any chance our countrymen at home should succeed in liberating themselves through their own efforts, or if by any chance the British Government accepts your Quit India Resolution and gives effect to it. We are, however, proceeding on the assumption that neither of the above is possible and that an armed struggle is inevitable. India's last war of independence has begun. Troops of the Azad Hind Fauj are now fighting bravely on the soil of India, and in spite of all difficulty and hardship they are pushing forward slowly but steadily. This armed struggle will go on until the Britisher is thrown out of India and until our Tricolour National Flag proudly floats over the Viceroy's House in New Delhi.

Father of our Nation! In this holy war of India's liberation, we ask for your blessings and good wishes.

~

J.B. KRIPALANI

Partition of the Country

Despite the glorious chapter of the freedom struggle, in the end the country's freedom came at the cost of partition. The communalization of politics that had been visible since the 1920s extracted a severe toll in the days leading up to independence. Communal violence broke out in several parts of the country, particularly the east. Calcutta went up in flames in 1946, followed by some of the most gruesome killings in Noakhali and Bihar. Soon after independence, the theatre of violence shifted to the west as Punjab and Delhi witnessed an orgy of butchery. In the following speech by J.B. Kripalani (1888–1982), president of the Congress during the transfer of power, at the All India Congress Committee on 14 June 1947, one can discern how the joy of impending independence was tempered with a sense of horror at the madness that had overtaken the people.

When I became President of this great organisation, Gandhiji in one of his prayer speeches said that it was not only a crown of thorns that I would have to wear but that I would have to lie on a bed of thorns. I did not realise then that it would be literally so. On the 16th October 1946 my name was announced as the President and on the 17th I had to fly to Noakhali. After that I had to go to Behar and now recently to the Punjab. These visits were a succession of shocks one greater than the other. It is not only that many innocent lives are lost. Much more than the massacre of the innocent, what has affected me profoundly is the fact that our respective religions are being degraded. Both the communities have vied with each other in the worst orgies of violence, so that in the latest communal frenzy more cruel and heartless things have been done than at any previous time. I have seen a well where women with their children, 107 in all, threw themselves to save their honour. In another place, a place of worship, 20 young women were killed by their menfolk for the same reason. I have seen heaps of bones in a house where 307 persons, mainly women and children, were driven, locked up and then burned alive by the invading mob.

These ghastly experiences have no doubt affected my approach to the question. Some members have accused us that we have taken this decision out of fear. I must admit the truth of this charge but not in the sense in which it is made. The fear is not for the lives lost or of the widows' wail or the orphans' cry or of heaping indignities upon each other but that we shall progressively reduce ourselves to a state of cannibalism and worse. In every fresh communal fight the most brutal and degraded acts of the previous fight become the norm. So we keep on degrading each other and all in the name of religion. I am a Hindu and am proud of the fact. But this is because Hinduism for me has stood for toleration, for truth and for non-violence or at any rate for the clean violence of the brave. If it no more stands for these ideals and if in order to defend it people have to indulge in crimes worse than cannibalism then I must hang down my head in shame. And I may tell you that often I have felt and said that in these days one is ashamed to call oneself an Indian.

I have been with Gandhiji for the last 30 years. I joined him in Champaran. I have never swayed in my loyalty to him. It is not a personal but a political loyalty. Even when I differed from him I have considered his political instinct to be more correct than my elaborately reasoned attitudes. Today also I feel that he with his supreme fearlessness is correct and my stand is defective. Why then am I not with him? It is because I feel that he has as yet found no way of tackling the problem on a mass basis. When he taught us non-violent non-cooperation he showed us a definite method which we had at least mechanically followed. Today he himself is groping in the dark. He was in Noakhali. His efforts eased the situation. Now he is in Behar. The situation is again eased. But this does not solve in any way the flare up in the Punjab. He says he is solving the problem of Hindu–Muslim unity for the whole of India in Behar. Maybe. But it is difficult to see how that is being done. There are no definite steps as in non-violent non-cooperation that leads to the desired goal.

And then unfortunately for us today though he can enunciate policies they have in the main to be carried out by others and these others are not converted to his way of thinking.

It is under these painful circumstances that I have supported the division of India. You know I belong by family and birth to the

Pakistan area. My relatives and friends yet live there. When as back as 1906 I began my political career I never thought that I was working for the liberty of any particular portion of India. It was for the whole of India. Every nook and corner, every stream and mountain of the land is sacred for me. It shall so remain even after this artificial partition that separates brother from brother. Already in my opening speech I have said that in India at least one must not think in communal terms but in terms of Indian citizenship and in this respect I commend Mahatmaji's advice given to us yesterday. If there is to be a united India again his policy alone will work.

The fear has been expressed that this decision does not and cannot stop communal rioting. This fear may be well or ill founded. For the time being the prophets of evil seem to be in ascendancy. How are then future riots to be tackled? Will the vicious world revolve, as it has revolved recently on the basis of retaliation? This question I had already answered in my Presidential address at Meerut. I said then that as the Centre had refused to function, the provinces became virtually independent. The Government in Behar should have given a warning to the Government of Bengal that if the Hindus who were living in Bengal were cruelly treated the Behar Government with the best will in the world would not be able to protect lives of the Muslim resident in Behar. This would have meant that the issue had been raised to the international plane where organised government deal with each other. The issue would have been taken out of the hands of the excited mob fury that knows no morality, no law, no restraint. Mob fury is always blind. International violence has at least some system and method about it. I am sure that those who hold the reins of authority after August 16th in India will make it their duty to see that justice is done to the Hindu minorities in Pakistan. If my words could carry weight with the Pakistan section of India I would say: Let the two Constituent Assemblies appoint a Joint Committee to go into the matter of the minority rights. This may insure us against individuals and excited and fanatical mobs from taking the work of vengeance that is outside political moral law in their own hands.

We have passed just now the resolution of the States. In this connection I would suggest one thing. Let the people of all those States who have not yet sent their representatives to the Constituent Assembly do so themselves. Wherever Legislative Assemblies exist let these Assemblies as in British India elect their representatives to the

Constituent Assembly by single transferable vote. Where no such Assemblies exist other devices may be used to elect representatives. Such representatives have a right to sit in our Constituent Assembly which is a sovereign body. In our Fundamental Rights Committee we have postulated one common citizenship of India. Every State citizen is an Indian Citizen and he has a right to be represented in the Indian Constituent Assembly. No Dewan coming from outside the State can limit this right of the citizen. We need the help and advice of the States people in framing a constitution for India. We are no more bound by the document of May 16. In any case today ours is a sovereign assembly. No court of law here in India or outside has any jurisdiction over our Constituent Assembly. Now that it has met and has made its own rules of procedure it cannot even be dissolved except by its own vote. I do not see why the State People's representatives cannot be allowed in our Constituent Assembly.

In conclusion, I would say, let us not rest content with the freedom that we shall be having shortly. Let us bend all our energies to the goal of unification which we have missed in order to achieve our freedom quickly. This can best be done by making India a strong, happy, democratic and socialist state, where all citizens irrespective of religion or caste shall have equal opportunities of development. Such an India can win back the seceding children to its lap. In this task we shall need all the devoted service and sacrifice that we have needed in our fight for freedom. Let us abandon all power politics. Let us not give up the glorious tradition of sacrifice, hardship and voluntary poverty which we built up when we courted jail, lathi, blows and bullets. Let us again absorb ourselves in this new task which is as important as the achievement of freedom, for the freedom we have achieved cannot be completed without the unity of India. Divided India will be a slave India. Let us therefore get out of this second slavery as quickly as we can. Let all the new opportunities we have got to mould our own destiny be henceforward directed to this supreme goal of Indian Unity. In this task may God help us.

7

DEMANDS OF REPRESENTATION

Given India's diversity in terms of geographical spread, religions, languages and castes, a multiplicity of voices demanding to be heard was only to be expected. The nationalist struggle against colonialism and for greater political rights increasingly fostered a feeling among Indians that they belonged to one nation. At the same time, movements for social reform which often went hand in hand with the political struggle, created an awareness of the ills that plagued Indian society and a resolve to address those ills. Paradoxically, these very forces also brought to the fore multiple struggles within society. Increasingly aware of a right to a better life, sections of society started to articulate demands for representation in education, employment and participation in government, administration and other aspects of national life. Many of these groups, which claimed to represent a certain section of society based on caste, professional or religious affiliations, grew within the emerging national movement and went on to constitute the popular base for the movement. Others developed in opposition to the Indian National Congress, drawing sustenance from the direct or indirect help of the colonial administration which had an ulterior motive in encouraging these groups against the national movement.

Caste having been the most visible factor in keeping large sections of the population mired in ignorance and poverty, it is not surprising that the first demands for representation originated from the so-called lower castes which wanted to throw off the yoke of caste oppression. Thanks to the efforts of people like Jyotiba Phule (1827–90), an activist and social reformer from Maharashtra who formed the Satya Shodhak Samaj with the objective of liberating the Shudras and preventing their exploitation by the Brahmins, avenues for education had opened up for the lowest strata of society, which was unthinkable even a generation ago. Interestingly, the Satya Shodhak Samaj merged with the Congress in 1930, thus demonstrating how much the marginal classes had begun to be integrated with the mainstream. A powerful non-Brahmin movement emerged in the south in the early years of the twentieth century. The Brahmins had a stranglehold on higher education and consequently they dominated government service. The first two decades of the twentieth century witnessed a gradual rise in general literacy as well as in English literacy, hitherto the sole preserve of Brahmins, among the non-Brahmin castes. Educated non-Brahmins began to question the inferior position assigned to them. Hailing from landowning and merchant classes, the non-Brahmin leaders in the Madras Presidency aspired to political power and official influence commensurate with their wealth and status in society. This led to the formation of the Justice Party which demanded caste-based reservations in government jobs and government control of temples. The party was actively supported by the colonial state which realized that championing sectional interests was to their advantage. The party came to power in Madras after winning the assembly elections in 1921 and ruled for the next fifteen years. Throughout this era, it opposed the Congress and when one of its prominent leaders, Ramaswamy Naicker, popularly called Periyar, left the Congress on the issue of social reforms to initiate the self-respect movement, his demands on behalf of the movement were accepted by the Justice Party which implemented equal representation for castes based on the caste ratio.

The arrival of Gandhi on the national scene initiated another phase in the struggle of the lower classes for social justice and political empowerment. In the 1920s, Gandhi launched what would be the biggest social movement against the practice of untouchability. He argued against the notion of hierarchy of works that had gradually come to define the varna system, under which some professions became inferior and those who performed these came to be regarded as untouchables. Gandhi wanted to destroy this notion of hierarchy. This period also saw the emergence of B.R. Ambedkar as a leader of what he called the 'depressed classes'. He opposed Gandhi and argued that untouchability was legitimized by the varna system and unless the caste system itself was abolished caste oppression would not go. Gandhi, however, did not agree, because for him the fault did not lie in the institution of caste itself, as it had endured for centuries. What was important was the removal of the cancerous growth in it. Given the fundamental difference of their respective positions, both argued vehemently, but true to the democratic ethos of the national movement, respected each other's opinion and tried to convince each other of the merits of their respective positions. Temple entry movements at Vaikom and Guruvayur in Kerala using satyagraha as the weapon and the countrywide movements for the upliftment of lower-caste people were the direct result of Gandhi's constructive programme. Surprisingly, though Ambedkar hailed from the 'depressed classes', Gandhi was a bigger draw than Ambedkar among these oppressed classes. The colonial administration, however, accepted Ambedkar's claims to represent these classes and invited him to the Second Round Table Conference.

By far the one demand for representation that had the most far-reaching consequence came on the grounds of religion. The Congress annual session of 1916 in Lucknow first accepted the principle of communal representation when it sought to overcome the problem of separate electorates by agreeing to Jinnah's plea to allow weightage of seats in the legislative councils of certain provinces where Muslims were in the minority. The next three decades witnessed increasing communalization of the policy with the atmosphere being further vitiated by the Government of India announcement of the Communal Award in August 1932, granting separate electorates to minority communities, including the 'depressed classes'. With Jinnah's articulation of the two-nation theory at a session of the Muslim League in 1940, the process of the country's bifurcation along religiously defined communal lines was inexorably set in motion.

~

O. TANIKACHALA CHETTIYAR AND OTHERS

Proportion of Non-Brahmins in the Public Services

To begin with, the non-Brahmin members of the Madras Presidency organized themselves in formations which were non-political. Their concerns were restricted to providing facilities to students who came to Madras from different parts of the presidency—which encompassed parts of present-day Kerala, Karnataka, Tamil Nadu, Andhra Pradesh and Orissa—to study. Soon, the educational and welfare activities of the non-Brahmin groups gave way to political mobilization and they began demanding representation in jobs and the legislature, which necessitated the formation of a formal association. Their efforts finally led to the formation of the South Indian Liberal Federation in 1916, popularly known as the Justice Party, with C. Natesa Mudaliar, Dr. T.M. Nair and Sir Pitti Thiayagaraya Chettiyar as its leaders. They began demanding community-wise reservation in government jobs, on the lines of what had transpired in Mysore State in 1916-17. In 1921, O. Tanikachala Chettiyar, a prominent leader of the non-Brahmin groups, introduced a motion in the Madras Legislative Assembly to give preference to non-Brahmins in public appointments. The introduction and the debate that followed provide an interesting glimpse into what constitutes one of the earliest demands for sectoral and caste-based representation.

Mr. President, I beg to move—That this Council recommends to the Government that a standing order be issued to every officer or board or body of officer authorised to make appointments to the public service to give preference to candidates from the non-Brahman communities (including therein Christians, Muhammadans and members of the depressed classes) until a proportion of at least 66 per cent amongst offices carrying a salary of Rs.100 per mensem and upwards and a proportion of 75 per cent amongst offices carrying a salary less than Rs.100 are reached within a period of seven years from the date so long as such candidates possess the minimum qualifications prescribed by the rules relating to opportunities to the public services although such candidates may be less qualified than Brahman candidates.

This resolution provides a remedy for a long-standing, deep-seated and fostering sore from which the non-Brahman communities have been suffering for a long time. It is not invented by me, but, if I may say so, it is a patent of the Mysore Government manufactured under the expert advice of responsible officers of that State constituted into a committee presided over by no less a distinguished civilian than Sir Leslie Miller, who enjoys the confidence of all classes and communities, not merely in British India but also in Mysore. It is a panacea which the Government of Mysore discovered for the many ills which the bulk of its citizens are suffering from. In this Presidency, Sir, the non-Brahmans for decades past have been kept down from rising higher, both in the matter of recruitment to the public services and in the matter of getting promotions, by the Brahman gentlemen who managed to capture the higher appointments in the State leaving the crumbs to their less fortunate brethren. The non-Brahmans kept their feelings pent up and only when the non-Brahman movement was organised that for the first time their grievances and their feelings found expression in newspaper articles and later in interpellations addressed to the Legislative Council. Formerly, they had no means of ventilating their grievances through the public press, for the public press as it existed then was owned by Europeans, e.g. the *Madras Mail* and the *Madras Times*, who did not bother themselves about ventilating the grievances of the non-Brahmans. Nor could the non-Brahmans expect the *Hindu*, owned by a Brahman, to lend its columns for airing their grievances. Their feelings continued to be pent up until, as I said, an organisation of their own could give publicity to those feelings. What has been the result of this agitation in the press and through the Legislative Council? These interpellations and the answers given by government that they could consider these matters sympathetically were received by the Brahman gentlemen who occupy high positions under the Government, like the plague inflicted on the land of the Farrows who would not allow the children of Israel to be freed from their bondage. The more the non-Brahman invoked the aid of the Government the more the hearts of the Brahman superior officers became hardened.

C. Natesa Mudaliyar: I second this resolution. In seconding it I am not doing so with any feeling of apathy or ill will against members of any particular community. For who are they but our own brethren of the soil? But I do so with a sincere desire to safeguard the interests of the suffering millions of the land, who were, who are and who will be a source of strength to the British Government.

Sir, the non-Brahmans assisted the British Government in laying the foundations of the British empire in India. They poured their money into the British treasury in the shape of revenue. They came to the rescue of the British Government whenever they were in trouble. They fight the non-co-operator internally and place their men and money at the disposal of the government when the enemy threatens them from abroad. Sir, it was by a false hypothesis that a good knowledge of English was the standard of efficiency; these valuable and loyal people who held the highest positions of honour and trust under the British Government at its commencement were reduced to the position of mere slaves. They were about to be reduced to be hewers of wood and drawers of water. They suffered at the hands of all the authorities of all the departments—educational, excise, revenue and judicial. They agitated and agitated to liberate themselves. Their cry was a cry in the wilderness. It was a critical period in the history of the real people of this presidency... Fortunately for us, thanks to the efforts of our Grand Old Man, thanks to the patriots that went beyond the seas to fight the cause of the people, and to the sacrifice of one of the greatest sons of India, the most sincere of patriots and bravest of fighters, we got communal representation and we have all communities represented in this very Council. Thanks to the statesmanship of His Excellency the governor we have got the people's minister here. Fortunately for us there was a redeeming clause in the Reforms' Scheme. The franchise was extended. We have got the people's representatives here. If any growth develops rapidly at the expense of the body, emaciating the body, it is a malignant growth and should be operated upon immediately. The council will agree that if one community flourishes at the expense of other communities and leaves the other communities far behind, it retards the growth of the country. Sir, it is the Government that should safeguard the interests of the people of the land, especially the taxpaying majority and see that they are well represented. No representation no taxation.

A.T. Palmer: Mr. President, I have great pleasure in supporting this resolution. I wish I had the ability and the wisdom and the eloquence that the Mover has to give my support to this very laudable resolution which he has brought forward. Sir, in the early part of the 19th century when the English people came to India, it was the non-Brahmans that came near the European and helped them while the Brahmans were suspicious of the intruders. In those days the Brahman thought that it was beneath his dignity to learn the foreign language of English and it was the non-Brahman who gave the British all the help in the administration of the land. As time advanced, the Brahman was able to see that it was no use sticking to his old habits, and readily accepted this new cause and made himself equipped for appointments in Government services and the non-Brahman in his usual want of forethought did not see that he would be handicapped in the race. Eventually, it so happened that the Brahman got over his head and then the struggle for existence for the non-Brahmans became very serious. It is always my plan to explain what I have got to say by an example. It is not for me to criticise the Brahman in his office, but it has always been the peculiar feature of the Brahman to help his own people—we admire the Brahmans for it—with the result that the non-Brahman has been carefully kept away from the government posts in ways which it is difficult even for a very keen officer to understand. The Brahman has the wit to out-wit the European. I remember a certain case where a non-Brahman was aspiring to a Deputy Collector's post. When the opportunity came, the Collector wanted his head clerk to put before him all the men who were eligible for the post. This non-Brahman was anxiously waiting for this opportunity, but he was cleverly set aside with the remark that he could not be spared because he was the only Telugu-knowing man in the office. Now, this clever move took a dozen years for this man to retrieve his chance and it was after 12 years of struggle he got the post of a Deputy Collector. That man is no more, but that is what he told me. Sir, I do not blame the English people for the present state of things. Partly the non-Brahmans are responsible for this, but mostly it is due to other agencies. Now the time has come when the non-Brahman is opening his eyes and is equipping himself for every post in the government and the government should come forward and help the non-Brahman, not because he is a non-Brahman, but because he forms the core of the society, the bulk of the population of this land and as such it is but right that a proportionate representation should be created in all offices. With these few remarks, I beg to support the resolution.

P. Siva Rao: Sir, when the Hon'ble Mr. Knapp held out the olive branch and sued for peace we fully expected that there would be an end of all this unpleasant discussion in this Council. Some of us heartily voted for the amendment in the true belief, that there was some genuine grievance which had to be redressed. We thought that as the principle contained in the Board's Standing Order has been made applicable to all the departments by the amended resolution which has just been carried unanimously, it would satisfy my non-Brahman friends. Now is it the contention of my honourable friend Mr. Tanikachala Chettiyar that the Secretariat is not a department of the Government and why should he put the Secretariat under a special category? While having chosen, and very wisely I may say, not to press that resolution and accepting the amendment, it passes my comprehension why he should have decided to press this resolution.

Now Sir, Mr. Tanikachala Chettiyar has got his party in power. He puts the Brahmans in one category and puts the rest of the world in another and so it is an extremely easy thing for him to pass such a resolution. But I sincerely and solemnly warn him against making the decisions of this Legislative Council the laughing stock of the whole world. Let it not be said, Sir, for a moment that because the non-Brahmans have been returned to power and can pass successfully any measure they like, they are parties to an unwholesome resolution like this. Mr. Tanikachala Chettiyar will do well to remember that it is desirable to have the powers of a giant but it is very undesirable to use them like a giant and I may tell him that if he presses this resolution I would simply characterise it as an abuse of power. I am afraid, Sir, that the proceedings of this Council will go before the eyes of the whole world. The reforms having been started only recently the eyes not only of the British public and the Mother of Parliaments but the eyes of the whole world will be upon us and let us behave with decorum and decency instead of penalising one particular community because they are Brahmans and instead of waking up at one particular moment and saying, 'We have been taking a nap all the time. We want all the departments cleared of all Brahmans.' Instead of saying all that I once more implore Mr. Tanikachala Chettiyar that the interests of his community are quite safe in the resolution the amendment of which we have carried and let him not provoke further antagonism or further unpleasant feeling in this House by pressing this resolution.

Diwan Bahadur L.A. Govindaraghava Ayyar: Mr. President, in opposing this resolution I do not propose to reciprocate the antagonistic spirit which unhappily was apparent in the speech of the honourable mover. I was one of those who were in support of the previous resolution, and if I may say so, I was heartily in support of it because I think it is the duty of every member of this House irrespective of the class, caste or creed to which he may belong to remove all possibilities of any misunderstanding or of irritation that may be legitimately held to exist either in the Government ranks or elsewhere among the classes which go to make the body politic... When we subscribed to the principles underlying the previous resolution to the extent that those principles are capable of application in connexion with the Secretariat Departments, those who were in favour of that resolution had a legitimate right to expect that its principles would be given effect to.

But unfortunately, Sir, this resolution has still been moved and I have only to make two observations in respect of that resolution.

The first is this: The consideration to which the Hon'ble Finance Member has drawn the attention of the House, considerations which are obvious to everybody who without any prepossession of his own is prepared to look at the state of matters to which those considerations are applicable—those considerations make it perfectly clear that if there is a disproportion of non-Brahmans or rather that there is a greater proportion of Brahmans than non-Brahmans in the Secretariat, it is not the intriguing Brahman that is responsible for it, but it is the unfortunately limited field available for selection that is really responsible for it and the remedy for righting this disproportion is not by crying down the Brahman but by coming up to the level of the Brahman.

The second point I wish to lay stress upon, Sir, is this. If we consider that it is legitimate for this House to allow a resolution such as this to be moved notwithstanding the acceptance of the previous resolution, much of the irritation, the heat and the unseemly spirit that is bound to characterise the discussion of questions which bring up communal and racial consideration is bound to appear again and again. And I thought, Sir, that one of the chief reasons why the previous resolution was moved with the approbation of the whole House was that a cool, impartial and composed atmosphere should prevail here, so that we might be able to bring to the consideration of questions that we have to now and then discuss a certain amount of detachment of view, impartiality of judgment, good sense and also good taste. Now, Sir, all that stands a great chance of being jeopardised by honourable members thinking it consistent with their duty to this House and to their electorates that they should, even after the previous resolution has been accepted, be bringing forward resolutions such as this.

C.V. Venkataramana Ayyangar: I have to say just a few words, Sir, and I will begin by saying that my sympathy is entirely with the principle of such resolutions. I thought that the fact that a compromise was supposed to have been arrived at would create a calm atmosphere, and I would have been more glad if all these speeches were made when that proposition was carried instead of a compromise which might reopen this question, I am afraid, once in six months. So far as the principle is concerned, I must once for all say while dissociating myself from all the reasons given by the previous speakers, that I, from some higher point of view want some such remedy as is required by this proposition to be given. My reason is this. Although I think that the Reform Act is unsatisfactory and has not gone so far as it might have, still there is some possibility of our doing some good in this Council. I think so far as we have gone, it is agreed that we are probably doing very good work. But my own view is that but for these communal difficulties, we would have got a more satisfactory Reform Act and probably done much better work in these days. Rightly or wrongly there is a feeling on the part of these non-Brahmans that they have not got the share that they ought to have got. I say rightly or wrongly and it does not matter whether it is due to a little want of desire on their parts. But the fact remains that there is a strong feeling amongst non-Brahmans and all I can say is whether that feeling is justified or not, it is better that they are given an opportunity to see if they can come in more numbers. Therefore I say that whatever possible opportunities can be given to them may be given. Of course, as to the reasons for the difference in percentage, I have got my own views that it was probably because the non-Brahmans preferred and very rightly other than Government service. Many of us know that respectable non-Brahmans although they educate their children up to the B.A. degree or so, don't want them to confine themselves entirely to the precincts of the Government service and therefore they do not care for these appointments. This will be proved if we ascertain the number of applications made for appointments. Of course, our non-Brahman friends have given other excuses that because they knew they won't succeed in getting higher appointments they did not send applications. Now let them enter in the hope that they will get such higher appointments and let us see. From a national point of view I am very strongly in favour of seeing more of our educated Brahmans getting into non-Government services. There was a glamour at one time among Brahmans that the Government service was the summum bonum of existence of every Indian born man whatever the pay might be and whatever the difficulties might be. So far as the material prosperity of these officers is concerned, I know personally of instances where the funerals of Tahsildar and Deputy Collectors had to be paid for by their friends. Now that glamour has extended to other communities also, and if that is so, why should not the non-Brahmans also have the benefit of it? Why not the Brahmans, I say, give them this benefit by not entering into the Government service and take up some public work. My own impression is that it would be better for the nation as well as for the Brahmans themselves if they keep away from the government service and take some sort of trade or industry and move shoulder to shoulder with their non-Brahman friends. There is no doubt that, as matters stand, if statistics are taken, the Brahmans would be nowhere now when compared with the non-Brahmans in industrial pursuits. Therefore in the interest of calm administration of this government, the calm administration of the whole Presidency, and also in the interests of harmonious co-operation in this Council and elsewhere, and both in the interests of political work as well as of the agricultural and industrial advancement also, I suggest that there is no reason why we should not allow our non-Brahman friends to enter into the various departments of government. Of course the Hon'ble Mr. Knapp has very well asked 'how to kick out the people who are already in the service'. That is really a very difficult question. The learned mover Mr. Tanikachalam Chettiyar has suggested one remedy, viz., mutual transfer between the officer in the Secretariat and in the mufassal. Many of them in the mufassal consider that they have got more advantage and better facilities of working there than coming here and being tied down to their desk. But if there is any member of the Provincial service outside who is willing to have an exchange with an officer in the Secretariat, there is no reason why we should not do it. A number of Brahmans and non-Brahmans have come to the Coimbatore district from the Secretariat and they find it more comfortable there and therefore my Brahman friends in the Secretariat will be glad to go outside. There they can have less work, more liberty and probably would get much by way of travelling allowance if today's resolution on that subject is not acted upon. I may also say that we have got efficiency first to maintain and I think there is no way of distinguishing efficiency except by educational qualifications. One thing may be suggested. It would be better to have a statistics showing the number of applications rejected. Possibly there is a good deal of paucity in applications and government could not create applications. I would suggest to government one other way. If they want the best intelligence, they may hold a competitive examination and graduates may be allowed to compete for it and the best men according to their merits may be selected. Probably it may be better to decide purely from the result of the answers than taking into consideration their University or communal qualifications. Anyhow on the assurance given by the Hon'ble Mr. Knapp, I think the resolution need not be pressed.

There is another point also so far as the Hon. Members sitting on the front bench are concerned. I believe all of them have control over the Secretariat departments. Only one of them is a Brahman and two are Europeans who cannot be said to be partial to any community and therefore it can very well be said that whenever vacancies occur in future and when appointments have to be made, the seven gentlemen may be left to see that proper things are done.

... I may say that the appointments hereafter at least may be looked into by the members. The Secretaries will be guided by their notes. The various modifications and qualifications to the existing rules may not after all be satisfactory to my non-Brahman friends and may not be successful for other reasons than communal.

I think, Sir, some such thing could be done, so that these complaints against the various communities might disappear. So that Sir, as I said, although I cannot vote for this resolution as it is worded, I am in full sympathy with the principles underlying the proposition and I will be very glad if some arrangement can be come to and the matter settled.

~

BHIMRAO RAMJI AMBEDKAR

The Depressed Classes

Born into a poor untouchable community, Babasaheb B.R. Ambedkar (1891–1956) spent his life fighting the Hindu caste system and the practice of untouchability. In the 1930s, he emerged as a radical critic of the Congress leadership on the issues of what were officially called the 'depressed classes'. He argued that the Congress did not represent the interests of the depressed classes. Most famously, he refused to accept Mahatma Gandhi's classification of untouchables as 'Harijan'. Though he failed to back his claim of representing the depressed classes through the electoral process, Ambedkar used the opportunities that the colonial state gave him to represent his case against the Congress in many forums, including the Second Round Table Conference held between 12 November 1930 and 19 January 1931. The speech reproduced below was made at the conference where for the first time he robustly articulated that the case of the depressed classes needed to be represented differently and that he was in some sense their representative. A scholar nonpareil and a gifted mind in legal matters, he was the Congress leadership's choice to head the Drafting Committee of the Constitution. As India's first law minister in Nehru's cabinet, it was he who moved the Hindu Code Bill in 1948 which earned him the sobriquet 'modern Manu'. However, he fell out with the Congress and gradually carved out an independent path to mobilize the Dalits and emerge as the undisputed champion of the oppressed classes in India.

Mr. Chairman. My purpose in rising to address this Conference is principally to place before it the point of view of the depressed classes, whom I and my colleague, Rai Bahadur Srinivasan, have the honour to represent, regarding question of constitutional reform. It is a point of view of 43,000,000 people, or one-fifth of the total population of British India. The depressed classes form a group by themselves which is distinct and separate from the Muhammadans, and, although they are included among the Hindus, they in no sense form an integral part of that community. Not only have they a separate existence, but they have also assigned to them a status which is invidiously distinct from the status occupied by any other community in India. There are communities in India which occupy a lower and a subordinate position; but the position assigned to the depressed classes is totally different. It is one which is midway between that of the serf and the slave, and which may, for convenience, be called servile—with this difference, that the serf and the slave were permitted to have physical contact, from which the depressed classes are debarred. What is worse is that this enforced servility and bar to human intercourse, due to their untouchability, involves not merely the possibility of discrimination in public life, but actually works out as a positive denial of all equality of opportunity and the denial of those most elementary of civic rights on which all human existence depends. I am sure that the point of view of such a community, as large as the population of England or of France, and so heavily handicapped in the struggle for existence, cannot but have some bearing on the right sort of solution of the political problem, and I am anxious that this Conference should be placed in possession of that point of view at the very start.

That point of view I will try to put as briefly as I can. It is this: that the bureaucratic form of government in India should be replaced by a government which will be a government of the people, by the people and for the people. This statement of the view of the depressed classes I am sure will be received with some surprise in certain quarters. The tie that bound the depressed classes to the British has been of a unique character. The depressed classes welcomed the British as their deliverers from age-long tyranny and oppression by the orthodox Hindus. They fought their battles against the Hindus, the Mussalmans and the Sikhs, and won for them this great Empire of India. The British, on their side, assumed the role of trustees for the depressed classes. In view of such an intimate relationship between the parties, this change in the attitude of the depressed classes towards British Rule in India is undoubtedly a most momentous phenomenon. But the reasons for this change of attitude are not far to seek. We have not taken this decision simply because we wish to throw in our lot with the majority. Indeed, as you know, there is not much love lost between the majority and the particular minority I represent. Ours is an independent decision. We have judged the existing administration solely in the light of our own circumstances and we have found it wanting in some of the most essential elements of a good government. When we compare our present position with the one which it was our lot to bear in Indian society of the pre-British days, we find that, instead of marching on, we are only marking time. Before the British, we were in the loathsome condition due to our untouchability. Has the British Government done anything to remove it? Before the British, we could not draw water from the village well. Has the British Government secured us the right to the well? Before the British, we could not enter the temple. Can we enter now? Before the British, we were denied entry into the Police Force. Does the British Government admit us in the Force? Before the British, we were not allowed to serve in the Military. Is that career now open to us? To none of these questions can we give an affirmative answer. That the British, who have held so large a sway over us for such a long time, have done some good we cheerfully acknowledge. But there is certainly no fundamental change in our position. Indeed, so far as we are concerned, the British Government has accepted the social arrangements as it found them, and has preserved them faithfully in the manner of the Chinese tailor who, when given an old coat as a pattern, produced with pride an exact replica, rents, patches and all. Our wrongs have remained as open sores and they have not been righted, although 150 years of British rule have rolled away.

We do not accuse the British of indifference or want of sympathy. What we do find is that they are quite incompetent to tackle our problem. If the case was one of indifference only it would have been a matter of small moment, and it would not have made such a profound change in our attitude. But what we have come to realise on a deeper analysis of the situation is that it is not merely a case of indifference, rather it is a case of sheer incompetence to undertake the task. The depressed classes find that the British Government in India suffers from two very serious limitations. There is first of all an internal limitation which arises from the character, motives and interests of those who are in power, which prevents them from appreciating the living forces operating in our society, makes them indifferent and inimical to its aspirations, and apathetic to our education. It is not because they cannot help us in these things but because it is against their character, motives and interests to do so. The second consideration that limits its authority is the mortal fear it has of external resistance. The Government of India does realise the necessity of removing the social evils which are eating into the vitals of Indian society and which have blighted the lives of the downtrodden classes for so many years. The Government of India does realise that the landlords are squeezing the masses dry, and the capitalists are not giving the labourers a living wage and decent conditions of work. Yet it is a most painful thing that it has not dared to touch any of these evils. Why? Is it because it has no legal powers to remove them? No. The reason why it does not intervene is because it is afraid that its intervention to amend the existing code of social and economic life, will give rise to resistance. Of what good is such a government to anybody? Under a government, paralysed between two such limitations, much that goes to make life good must remain held up. We must have a government in which the men in power will give their undivided allegiance to the best interest of the country. We must have a government in which men in power, knowing where obedience will end and resistance will begin, will not be afraid to amend the social and economic code of life which the dictates of justice and expediency so urgently call for. This role the British Government will never be able to play. It is only a government which is of the people, for the people and by the people that will make this possible.

These are some of the questions raised by the depressed classes... This is therefore the inevitable conclusion which the depressed classes have come to: namely, that the bureaucratic Government of India, with the best of motives, will remain powerless to effect any change so far as our particular grievances are concerned. We feel that nobody can remove our grievances as well as we can, and we cannot remove them unless we get political power in our own hands. No share of this political power can evidently come to us so long as the British Government remains as it is. It is only in a Swaraj constitution that we stand any chance of getting the political power into our own hands, without which we cannot bring salvation to our people.

There is one thing, Sir, to which I wish to draw your particular attention. It is this. I have not used the expression Dominion Status in placing before you the point of view of the depressed classes. I have avoided using it, not because I do not understand its implications nor does the omission mean that the depressed classes object to India's attaining Dominion Status. My chief ground for not using it is that it does not convey the full content of what the depressed classes stand for. The depressed classes, while they stand for Dominion Status with safeguards, wish to lay all the emphasis they can on one question and one question alone. And that question is, how will Dominion India function? Where will the centre of political power be? Who will have it? Will the depressed classes be heirs to it? These are the questions that form their chief concern. The depressed classes feel that they will get no shred of the political power unless the political machinery for the new constitution is of a special make. In the construction of that machine certain hard facts of Indian social life must not be lost sight of. It must be recognised that Indian society is a gradation of castes forming an ascending scale of reverence and a descending scale of contempt—a system which gives no scope for the growth of that sentiment of equality and fraternity so essential for a democratic form of government. It must also be recognised that while the intelligentsia is a very necessary and a very important part of Indian society, it is drawn from its upper strata and, although it speaks in the name of the country and leads the political movement, it has not shed the narrow particularism of the class from which it is drawn. In other words what the depressed classes wish to urge is that the political mechanism must take account of and must have a definite relation to the psychology of the society for which it is devised. Otherwise you are likely to produce a constitution which, however symmetrical, will be a truncated one and a total misfit to the society for which it is designed.

There is one point with which I should like to deal before I close this matter. We are often reminded that the problem of the depressed classes is a social problem and that its solution lies elsewhere than in politics. We take strong exception to this view. We hold that the problem of the depressed classes will never be solved unless they get political power in their own hands. If this is true, and I do not think that the contrary can be maintained, then the problem of the depressed classes is I submit eminently a political problem and must be treated as such. We know that political power is passing from the British into the hands of those who wield such tremendous economic, social and religious sway over our existence. We are willing that it may happen, though the idea of Swaraj recalls to the mind of many of us the tyrannies, oppressions and injustices practiced upon us in the past and the fear of their recurrence under Swaraj. We are prepared to take the inevitable risk of the situation in the hope that we shall be installed, in adequate proportion, as the political sovereign of the country along with our fellow countrymen. But we will consent to that on one condition and that is that the settlement of our problem is not left to time. I am afraid the depressed classes have waited too long for time to work its miracle. At every successive step taken by the British Government to widen the scope of representative government, the depressed classes have been systematically left out. No thought has been given to their claim for political power. I protest with all the emphasis I can that we will not stand this any longer. The settlement of our problem must be a part of the general political settlement and must not be left over to the shifting sands of the sympathy and goodwill of the rulers of the future. The reasons why the depressed classes insist upon it are obvious. Every one of us knows that the man in possession is more powerful than the man who is out of possession. Every one of us also knows that those in possession of power seldom abdicate in favour of those who are out of it. We cannot therefore hope for the effectuation of the settlement of our social problem, if we allow power to slip into the hands of those who stand to lose by settlement unless we are to have another revolution to dethrone those whom we to-day help to ascend the throne of power and prestige. We prefer being despised for too anxious apprehensions, than ruined by too confident a security, and I think it would be just and proper for us to insist that the best guarantee for the settlement of our problem is the adjustment of the political machine itself so as to give us a hold on it, and not the will of those who are contriving to be left in unfettered control of that machine.

What adjustments of the political machine the depressed classes want for their safety and protection I will place before the Conference at the proper time. All I will say at the present moment is that, although we want responsible government, we do not want a government that will only mean a change of masters. Let the Legislature be fully and really representative if your Executive is going to be fully responsible.

I am sorry Mr. President I had to speak in such plain words. But I saw no help. The depressed classes have had no friend. The government has all along used them only as an excuse for its continued existence. The Hindus claim them only to deny them or, better still, to appropriate, their rights. The Muhammedans refuse to recognise their separate existence, because they fear that their privileges may be curtailed by the admission of a rival. Depressed by the government, suppressed by the Hindu and disregarded by the Muslim, we are left in a most intolerable position of utter helplessness to which I am sure there is no parallel and to which I was bound to call attention.

Regarding the other question which is set down for discussion I am sorry it was decided to tag it on to a general debate. Its importance deserved a Session for itself. No justice can be done to it in a passing reference. The subject is one in which the depressed classes are deeply concerned and they regard it as a very vital question. As members of a minority, we look to the Central Government to act as a powerful curb on the provincial majority to save the minorities from the misrule of the majority. As an Indian interested in the growth of Indian nationalism, I must make it plain that I am a strong believer in the unitary form of government and the thought of disturbing it I must confess does not please me very much. This unitary government has been the most potent influence in the building up of the Indian nation. That process of unification which has been the result of a unified system of government has not been completed and I should be loathe to withdraw this most powerful stimulus in the formative period and before it has worked out its end. However, the question, in the form in which it is placed, is only an academic question and I shall be prepared to consider a federal form, if it can be shown that in it local autonomy is not inconsistent with central unity.

Sir, all that I, as a representative of the depressed classes, need say on their behalf I have said. May I crave your indulgence to permit me as an Indian to say a word or two generally on the situation which we have to meet. So much has been said regarding its gravity that I shall not venture to add a word more to it, although I am no silent spectator of the movement. What I am anxious about is to feel whether we are proceeding on right lines in evolving our solution.

What that solution should be rests entirely upon the view that British Delegates choose to take. Addressing myself to them I will say, whether you will meet the situation by conciliation or by applying the iron heel must be a matter for your judgment—for the responsibility is entirely yours. To such of you as are partial to the use of force and believe that a regime of *Lettres de cachet* and the *Bastille* will ease the situation let me recall the memorable words of the greatest teacher of political philosophy, Edmund Burke. This is what he said to the British nation when it was faced with the problem of dealing with the American Colonies:

> The use of force alone is but temporary. It may endure for a moment, but it does not remove the necessity of subduing again: a nation is not governed which is perpetually to be conquered. The next objection to force is its uncertainty. Terror is not always the effect of force, and an armament is not a victory. If you do not succeed, you are without resource; for conciliation failing, force remains, but force failing, no further hope of reconciliation is left. Power and Authority are sometimes bought by kindness, but they can never be begged as alms by an impoverished and defeated violence. A further objection to force is that you impair the object by your very endeavours to preserve it. The thing you fought for (to win the loyalty of the people) is not the thing you recover, but depreciated, sunk, wasted and consumed in the contest.

The worth and efficacy of this advice you all know. You did not listen to it and you lost the great continent of America. You followed it to the lasting good of yourself and the rest of the Dominions that are with you. To such of you as are willing to adopt a policy of conciliation I should like to say one thing. There seems to be prevalent an impression that the Delegates are called here to argue for and against a case for Dominion Status and that the grant of Dominion Status will be dependent upon which side is the victor in this battle of wits. With due deference to all who are sharpening their wits, I submit that there can be no greater mistake than to make the formula of logic govern so live an issue. I have no quarrel with logic and logicians. But I warn them against the disaster that is bound to follow, if they are not careful in the selection of the premises they choose to adopt for their deductions. It is all a matter of temper whether you will abide by your logic, or whether you will refute it, as Dr. Johnson did the paradoxes of Berkeley by trampling them under his foot. I am afraid it is not sufficiently realised that in the present temper of the country, no constitution will be workable which is not acceptable to the majority of the people. The time when you were to choose and India was to accept is gone, never to return. Let the consent of the people and not the accident of logic be the touchstone of your new constitution, if you desire that it should be worked.

~

VINAYAK DAMODAR SAVARKAR

Presidential Address, Akhil Bharatiya Hindu Mahasabha, 1937

V.D. Savarkar (1883–1926), or 'Veer' Savarkar, is known for his espousal of a Hindu nationalist political ideology which he termed 'Hindutva'. He appeared on the national scene as a leader in the first decade of the twentieth century, first in India and later in England where he became involved with the revolutionary group India House. His book on the 1857 sepoy rebellion, The Indian War of Independence, *was banned by the British and he was arrested in 1910. After his attempt to escape failed, he was sentenced to fifty years of imprisonment at the Cellular Jail in the Andaman and Nicobar Islands. However, he was released in 1921 after he signed a plea for clemency renouncing all revolutionary activities. He then emerged as a powerful votary of the Hindu cause. As president of the Hindu Mahasabha he advocated the ideal of Hindus as a distinct nation and of India as a Hindu Rashtra as seen from this extract of his presidential speech at the nineteenth session of the Akhil Bharatiya Hindu Mahasabha held at Karnavati, Ahmedabad, in 1937. Interestingly, his claims that Hindus and Muslims constituted two 'antagonistic nations living side by side' and that 'there are two nations in the main: the Hindus and the Moslems, in India' echo M.A. Jinnah's formal articulation of the same notion three years later when he put forward his demand for a separate nation for the Muslims, Pakistan.*

Ladies and Gentlemen, I thank you most cordially for the trust you have placed in me in calling upon me to preside on this 19th Session of the Hindu Mahasabha. I don't take it so much as an honour bestowed upon me by my nation for service rendered in the past as a command to dedicate whatever strength is still left in me to the Sacred Cause of defending Hindudom and Hindustan—our common Motherland and our common Holyland, and pressing on the fight of our National Freedom. So far as the Hindus are concerned there can be no distinction nor conflict in the least between our Communal and National duties, as the best interests of Hindudom are simply identified with best interests of Hindustan as a whole. Hindudom cannot advance or fulfil its life-mission unless and until our Motherland is set free and consolidated into an Indian State in which all our countrymen to whatever religion or sect or race they belong are treated with perfect equality and none allowed to dominate others or is deprived of his just and equal rights of free citizenship as long as everyone discharges the common obligations and duties which one owes to the Indian Nation as a whole. The truer a Hindu is to himself as a Hindu he must inevitably grow a truer National as well. I shall substantiate this point later on as I proceed...

The Definition of the Word 'Hindu'

As the whole superstructure of the mission and the function of the Hindu Mahasabha rests on the correct definition of the word 'Hindu', we must first of all make it clear what 'Hindutva' really means. Once the scope and the meaning of the word is defined and understood, a number of misgivings in our own camp are easily removed, a number of misunderstandings and objections raised against us from the camp of our opponents are met and silenced. Fortunately for us, after a lot of wandering in wilderness, a definition of the word Hindu which is not only historically and logically as sound as is possible in the case of such comprehensive terms, but is also eminently workable is already hit upon when 'Hindutva' was defined as: *Asindhusindhuparyata yasya Bharatbhumika/Pitribhu punyabhuyasachya sa vayee Hinduritismrita.*

Everyone who regards and claims this Bharatbhoomi from the Indus to the Seas as his Fatherland and Holyland is a Hindu. Here I must point out that it is rather loose to say that any person professing any religion of Indian origin is a Hindu. Because that is only one aspect of Hindutva. The second and equally essential constituent of the concept of Hindutva cannot be ignored if we want to save the definition from getting overlapping and unreal. It is not enough that a person should profess any religion of Indian origin, i.e., recognise Hindustan as his punyabhu, his Holyland, but he must also recognise it as his pitribhu too, his Fatherland as well. As this is no place for going into the whole discussion of the pros and cons of the question, all I can do here is to refer to my book, *Hindutva,* in which I have set forth all arguments and expounded the proposition at great length.

I shall content myself at present by stating that Hindudom is bound and marked out as a people and a nation by themselves not by the only tie of a common Holyland in which their religion took birth but by the ties of a common culture, a common language, a common history and essentially of a common fatherland as well. It is these two constituents taken together that constitute our Hindutva and distinguish us from any other people in the world.

... Just as by the first constituent of Hindutva, the possession of a common Holyland—the Indian Mahommedans, Jews, Christians, Parsees, etc. are excluded from claiming themselves as Hindus which in reality also they do not—in spite of their recognising Hindustan as their fatherland, so also on the other hand the second constituent of the definition that of possessing a common fatherland excludes the Japanese, the Chinese and others from the Hindu fold in spite of the fact of their having a Holyland in common with us...

The Hindus are a Nation by Themselves

Some cavil at the position I have taken that the Hindu Mahasabha as I understand its mission, is pre-eminently a national body and challenge me—'How the Hindus who differ so much amongst themselves in every detail of life could at all be called a nation as such?' To them my reply is that no people on the earth are so homogenous as to present perfect uniformity in language, culture, race and religion. A people is marked out a nation by themselves not so much by the absence of any heterogeneous differences amongst themselves as by the fact of their differing from other peoples more markedly than they differ amongst themselves. Even those who deny the fact that the Hindus could be called a nation by themselves, do recognise Great Britain, the United States, Russia, Germany and other peoples as nations. What is the test by which those peoples are called nations by themselves? Take Great Britain as an example. There are at any rate three different languages there; they have fought amongst themselves dreadfully in the past, there are to be found the traces of different seeds and bloods and races. If you say that in spite of it all they are a nation because they possess a common country, a common language, a common culture and common Holyland then the Hindus too possess a common country so well marked out as Hindustan, a common language, the Sanskrit, from which all their current languages are derived or are nourished and which forms even today the common language of their Scriptures and literature and which is held in esteem as the sacred reservoir of ancient scriptures and the tongue of their forefathers. By 'Anuloma' and 'Pratiloma' marriages their seed and blood continued to get comingled even since the days of Manu. Their social festivals and cultural forms are not less common than those we find in England. They possess a common Holyland. The Vedic Rishis are their common pride, their Grammarians Panini and Patanjali, their poets Bhavabhooti and Kalidas, their heroes Shri Ram and Shri Krishna, Shivaji and Pratap, Guru Govind and Banda are a source of common inspiration. Their Prophets Buddha and Mahaveer, Kanad and Shankar, are held in common esteem. Like their ancient and sacred language—the Sanskrit—their scripts also are fashioned on the same basis and the Nagari script has been the common vehicle of their sacred writings since centuries in the past. Their ancient and modern history is common. They have friends and enemies in common. They have faced common dangers and won victories in common. One in national glory and one in national disasters, one in national despairs and one in national hope and Hindus are welded together during aeons of a common life and a common habitat. Above all the Hindus are bound together by the dearest, most sacred and most enduring bonds of a common Fatherland and a common Holyland, and these two being identified with one and the same country our Bharatbhoomi, our India, the National Oneness and homogeneity of the Hindus have been doubly sure. If the United States with the warring crowds of Negroes, Germans and Anglo-Saxons, with a common past not exceeding four or five centuries put together can be called a nation—then the Hindus must be entitled to be recognised as a nation par excellence. *Verily the Hindus as a people differ most markedly from any other people in the world than they differ amongst themselves.* All whatsoever of a common country, race, religion, and language that go to entitle a people to form a nation, entitle the Hindus with greater emphasis to that claim. And whatever differences divide the Hindus amongst themselves are rapidly disappearing owing to their awakening of the national consciousness and the Sanghatan and the social reform movements of today.

Therefore the Hindu Mahasabha that has, as formulated in its current constitution, set before itself the task of the maintenance, protection and promotion of the Hindu race, culture and civilisation for the advancement and glory of 'Hindu Rashtra' is pre-eminently a national body representing the Hindu Nation as a whole.

Is this Mission of the Mahasabha Narrow, Anti-Indian and Parochial?

Some of our well meaning but unthinking section of Indian patriots who look down upon the Mahasabha as a communal, narrow and anti-Indian body only because it represents Hindudom and tries to protect its just rights, forget the fact that communal and parochial are only relative terms and do not by themselves imply a condemnation or curse. Are not they themselves who swear by the name of Indian Nationalism in season and out of season liable to the same charge of parochialness? If the Mahasabha represents the Hindu nation only, they claim to represent the Indian nation alone. But is not the concept of an Indian Nation itself a parochial conception in relation to Human State? In fact the Earth is our motherland and Humanity our Nation. Nay, the Vedantist goes further and claims this Universe for his country and all manifestation from the stars to the stone his own self. *Amcha swadesh. Bhuvantrayamadhye wasa*, says Tukaram! Why then take the Himalayas to cut us off from the rest of mankind, deem ourselves as separate Nation as Indians and fight with every other country and the English in particular who after all are our brothers-in-Humanity! Why not sacrifice Indian interests to those of the British Empire which is a larger political synthesis? The fact is that all Patriotism is more or less parochial and communal and is responsible for dreadful wars throughout human history. Thus the Indian Patriots who instead of starting and joining some movement of a universal state, stop short of it, join an Indian Movement and yet continue to mock at the Hindu Sanghatan as narrow and communal and parochial succeed only in mocking at themselves.

But if it is said justification of Indian Patriotism that the people who populate India are more akin to each other bound by ties of a common ancestry, language, culture, history, etc., than they are to any other people outside India and therefore we Indians feel it our first duty to protect our Nation from political domination and aggression of other non-Indian nations then, the same reason could be adduced to justify the Hindu Sanghatan Movement as well....

The Hindu Mahasabha Is Perfectly National in Its Outlook

For what does the Hindu Mahasabha aim at? As the national representative body of Hindudom it aims at the all-round regeneration of the Hindu people. But the absolute political independence of Hindustan is a sine qua non for that all-round regeneration of Hindudom. The fortunes of the Hindus are more inextricably and more closely bound up with India than that of any other non-Hindu sections of our countrymen. After all the Hindus are the bedrock on which an Indian independent state could be built.

Whatever may happen some centuries hence, the solid fact of today cannot be ignored that religion wields mighty influence on the minds of men in Hindustan and in the case of Mohammedans especially their religious zeal, more often than not, borders on fanaticism! Their love towards India as their motherland is but a handmaid to their love for their Holyland outside India. Their faces are ever turned towards Mecca and Madina. But to the Hindus Hindustan being their Fatherland as well as their Holyland, the love they bear to Hindustan is undivided and absolute. They not only form the overwhelming majority of Indian population but have on the whole been the trusted champions of Her cause. A Mohammedan is often found to cherish an extra-territorial allegiance, is moved more by events in Palestine than what concerns India as a Nation, worries himself more about the well-being of the Arabs than the well-being of his Hindu neighbours and countrymen in India. Thousands of Mohammedans could be found conspiring with the Turkish Khilaphatists and Afghans with an object to bring about a foreign invasion of India if but a Mohammedan rule could thus be established in this land. But to a Hindu, India is all in all of his National being. That is the reason why the Hindus predominate in the struggle that is going on for the overthrow of the political domination of England over this country. It is the Hindus who went to the gallows, faced transportation to the Andamans by hundreds and got imprisoned by thousands in the fight for the liberation of Hindustan. Even the Indian National Congress owes its inception to Hindu brain, its growth to Hindu sacrifice, its present position to Hindu labours in the main. *A Hindu Patriot worth the name cannot but be an Indian patriot as well.* In this sense the consolidation and the independence of Hindu Nation is but another name for the independence of the Indian Nation as a whole. For, the Hindu Sanghatanists know full well that no regeneration of Hindudom could be brought about and no honour and equal place could be secured for the Hindu Nation amongst the Nations of the world unless swarajya and swatantrya are won for Hindustan, their Fatherland and Holyland.

But What Does This Independence of India—This Swarajya or Swatantrya—Mean?

In common parlance swarajya is understood as the political Freedom of our country, of our land, the independence of the geographical unit called India. But the time has come when these expressions must be fully analysed and understood. A country or a geographical unit does not in itself constitute a nation. Our country is endeared to us because it has been the abode of our race, our people, our dearest and nearest relations and as such is only metaphorically referred to, to express our national being. The independence of India means, therefore, the independence of our people, our race, our nation. Therefore, Indian swarajya or Indian swatantrya mean, as far as the Hindu Nation is concerned, the political independence of the Hindus, the freedom which would enable them to grow to their full height.

... India is dear to us because it has been and is the home of our Hindu Race, the land which has been the cradle of our prophets and heroes and gods and godmen. Otherwise land for land there may be many a country as rich in gold and silver on the face of the earth. River for river, the Mississippi is nearly as good as the Ganges and its waters are not altogether bitter. The stones and trees and greens in Hindustan are just as good or bad stones and trees and greens of the respective species elsewhere. Hindustan is a Fatherland and Holyland to us not because it is a land entirely unlike any other land in the world but because it is associated with our History, has been the home of our forefathers, wherein our mothers gave us the first suckle at their breast and our father cradled us on their knees from generation to generation.

... The real meaning of swarajya then, is not merely the geographical independence of the bit of earth called India. To the Hindus independence of Hindustan can only be worth having if that ensures their Hindutva—their religious, racial and cultural identity. We are not out to fight and die for a 'swarajya' which could only be had at the cost of our 'swatva' our Hindutva itself!...

The Anti-national Designs of the Mohammedans

Fortunately for the Hindus, Mr. Jinnah and the Moslem Leaguers have deliberately disclosed their real intentions this year at the Lucknow session of the Moslem League more authoritatively, more frankly and even more blatantly than they used to do before. I thank them for it. An open enemy is safer than a suspicious friend in dealing with him. Their resolutions at Lucknow are in fact no news to us. But up to this time the onus of proving the existence of the Moslem anti-national attitude and their Pan-Islamic ambitions more or less lay on the Hindus. But now we need do no more than point out to the authoritative speeches and resolutions of the League delivered and passed at that Lucknow Session to explain the anti-Hindu, anti-Indian and extra-territorial designs of the Moslems. They want the unalloyed Urdu to be raised to the position of the national tongue of the Indian state, although it is not spoken as a mother tongue by more than a couple of crores of Moslems themselves and is not understood by some twenty crores of people in India, Moslems included; in spite of the fact that it can claim no more literary merit than Hindi which is the mother tongue of some seven crores of people and is easily understood by some ten crores more! While the Arabian language itself, on which Urdu is fed is deemed outlandish by Kemal and the Turks in the land of the Khaliphas itself, the Moslems expect some twenty-five crores of Hindus to learn it and to adopt it as their national tongue! As to the national script, the Moslems insist on adopting the Urdu script and would have nothing to do, at any rate so far as they are concerned, with the Nagari! Why? Kemal may have discarded the Arabian script itself as unsuited to the present-day needs, the Nagari may be more scientific, more amenable to printing, more easy to learn, may already be current amongst or known to twenty crores of people in Hindustan, yet the Urdu script must be the state script and Urdu the state language for the only merit that attaches to them of being recognised by the Mohammedans as their cultural asset and therefore, to make room for it, the cultures of the Hindus and other non-Moslem sections in Hindustan must go to dogs! The Moslems will not tolerate the 'Vande Mataram' song. The poor unity-hankers amongst the Hindus hastened to cut it short. But the Moslem would not tolerate even the piece of it cut to order. Drop the whole song and you will find that the Moslems would demand that the very words 'Vande Mataram' are a standing insult to them! Get a new song composed even by an over-generous Ravindra, Moslems would have nothing to do with it because Ravindra being a Hindu could not but commit the heinous offence of using some Sanskrit words as 'Jati' instead of 'Kaum', 'Bharat' or 'Hindustan' instead of 'Pakistan'! They cannot be satisfied unless a national song is composed by an Iqbal or Jinnah himself in unalloyed Urdu, hailing Hindustan as a Pakistan—the land dedicated to Moslem domination!

When will our unity-hankers understand that the real question at the root of this Moslem displeasure is not a word here or a song there! We would have sacrificed a dozen songs or a hundred words of our own free will if thereby we could really contribute to the unity and solidarity of Hindustan. But we know the question is not so simple as that. It is the strife of different cultures and races and nations and these trifles are but the passing and outward symptoms of this malady deep seated in the Moslem mind. They want to brand the forehead of Hindudom and other non-Moslem sections in Hindustan with the stamp of self-humiliation and Moslem domination and we Hindus are not going to tolerate it any longer not only in the interests of Hindudom alone but even in the interests of Indian nation as well.

But if we do not tolerate this the Hon. Mr. Fuzlul Huq told there and then at Lucknow what would happen to us! From the high altitude of a Prime Minister's gaddi he promised to 'satana' the Hindus in Bengal (*main Hinduoko sataunga*) if other Hindus proved recalcitrant elsewhere to the orders of the Moslem League. Now the gaddi of the Prime Minister of Bengal was the outcome of the reforms which were wrested out from the English hands by the martyrdom and sacrifice of the Hindu Patriots in Bengal. *The Moslems there as everywhere did not claim a special representation or weightage in those sufferings and sacrifices.* But as soon as the reforms came, who could occupy and deserve the gaddi of a Prime Minister but the Hon. Mr. Fuzlul Huq! And now he threatens the very Hindus in Bengal who struggled most and suffered most, to whose sufferings alone Mr. Huq owes his gaddi that he will 'satana' (*sataunga*) them, in all shades of the meaning of that word from teasing to oppressing! I should like to assure the Honourable Mr. Fazlul Huq that the Bengal Hindus are a hard nut to crack. They have at times forced some of the prancing Proconsuls of even the powerful British Empire like Lord Curzon to climb down! But if he ever does persecute our Bengal Hindus then let him not forget that we Hindus also can in Maharashtra and elsewhere deal out to his comrades the same treatment, measure for measure, full to the brim and well shaken!

I need not refer to the attitude of the Moslems as regards the Communal Award and the Federation in which case also they want to humiliate the Hindus and Shylock-like insist on having their pound of flesh! I don't want to tire you out with a plethora of figures which you all know by heart. It is only enough to remind you of the audacious proposal openly debated in the League regarding the

Moslem demands to cut up the body politic of our Motherland right in two parts—the Mohammedan India and the Hindu India—aiming to form a separate Moslem country—Pakistan—comprising of the provinces of Kashmir, Punjab, Peshawar and Sind!

Hands off, sir, hands off! If you aim thus to reduce the Hindus to the position of helots in their own land, you should do well to remember that a succession of Aurangzebs when they wielded an Imperial power here had failed to perform that feat and in their attempt to carry out that design only succeeded in digging their own graves! Surely, Jinnahs and Huqs cannot accomplish what Aurangzebs failed to achieve!

Two Antagonistic Nations Living in India Side by Side

As it is, there are two antagonistic nations living side by side in India. Several infantile politicians commit the serious mistake in supposing that India is already welded into a harmonious nation, or that it could be welded thus for the mere wish to do so. These our well-meaning but unthinking friends take their dreams for realities. That is why they are impatient of communal tangles and attribute them to communal organisations. But the solid fact is that the so-called communal questions are but a legacy handed down to us by centuries of a cultural, religious and national antagonism between the Hindus and the Moslems. When time is ripe you can solve them; but you cannot suppress them by merely refusing recognition of them. It is safer to diagnose and treat deep-seated disease than to ignore it. Let us bravely face unpleasant facts as they are. India cannot be assumed today to be a unitarian and homogenous nation, but on the contrary there are two nations in the main: the Hindus and the Moslems, in India. And as it has happened in many a country under similar situation in the world the utmost that we can do under the circumstances is to form the Indian State in which none is allowed any special weightage or representation and none is paid an extra-price to buy his loyalty to the State. Mercenaries are paid and bought off, not sons of the Motherland to fight in her defence. The Hindus as a nation are willing to discharge their duty to a common Indian State on equal footing. But if our Moslem countrymen thrust on a communal strife on the Hindus and cherish anti-Indian and extra-territorial designs of establishing a Mohammedan Rule or supremacy in India then let the Hindus look to themselves and stand on their own legs and fight single-handed as best as they can for the liberation of India from any non-Hindu yoke, be it English or Moslem or otherwise.

Vote Only for Those Who Pledge to Defend Hindutva and are Tried Sanghatanists

With this end in view I exhort you all to assert yourselves as Hindus! Down with the apologetic attitude that makes some of us feel shy to proclaim themselves as Hindus, as if it was something unnational, something like a disgrace to be born of the line of Shri Ram and Shri Krishna—Shivaji and Pratap and Govind Singh! We Hindus must have a country of our own in the Solar System and must continue to flourish there as Hindus—descendants of a mighty people… The Mohammedans only vote for those who openly and boldly pledge to guard and aggressively secure rights for the Mohammedan people. But we Hindus commit the suicidal blunder of voting for those who openly declare that they are neither Hindus nor Mohammedans and yet are never tired of recognising Mohammedan organisations and dealing with them and of adjusting compromises in the name of the Hindus, ever against Hindu interests and to unbearable humiliation of the Hindus. You must henceforth vote for those who are not ashamed themselves of being Hindus, openly stand for the Hindus and pledge themselves not to keep burning incense, always at the cost of the Hindus before the fetish of a dishonourable unity-cult… let no Hindu vote for a man who is not a Sanghatanist and you will find then that your own ministries will be championing the just cause of our Hindu Nation as boldly as the Mohammedan ministries are doing theirs. This alone will save not only the Hindu Nation of ours but even the Indian State to come. For truly Hindus are and cannot but be the mainstay of our Indian State! We shall ever guarantee protection to the religion, culture and language of the minorities for themselves, but we shall no longer tolerate any aggression on their part on the equal liberty of the Hindus to guard their religion, culture and language as well. If the non-Hindu minorities are to be protected then surely the Hindu majority also must be protected against any aggressive minority in India!

MUHAMMAD ALI JINNAH

Presidential Address, All India Muslim League, Lahore Session, March 1940

On 23 March 1940, Muhammad Ali Jinnah, the president of the All India Muslim League, declared that the 'the Hindu–Muslim problem' was not an inter-communal problem but an international one as Muslims in India constituted a separate nation. The official demand of the Muslim League henceforth would be the creation of a separate state of Pakistan in the areas where Muslims were in a majority. Though many intellectuals, including poet Allama Iqbal, had broached such an idea, it was Jinnah's invocation of the same at Lahore which can be described as the official declaration of the two-nation theory whereby Hindus and Muslims were seen as belonging to two different religio-cultural entities and were therefore required to have two independent and separate nations. The Lahore Resolution, as it was referred to thereafter, heralded the foundation of Pakistan.

Ladies and Gentleman, we are meeting today in our session after fifteen months. The last session of the All-India Muslim League took place at Patna in December 1938. Since then many developments have taken place. I shall first shortly tell you what the All-India Muslim League had to face after the Patna session of 1938. You remember that one of the tasks which was imposed on us and which is far from completed yet, was to organise Muslim Leagues all over India. We have made enormous progress during the last fifteen months in this direction. I am glad to inform you that we have established Provincial Leagues in every province. The next point is that in every by-election to the Legislative Assemblies we had to fight with powerful opponents. I congratulate the Musalmans for having shown enormous grit and spirit throughout our trials. There was not a single by-election in which our opponents won against Muslim League candidates. In the last election to the U.P. Council, that is the Upper Chamber, the Muslim League's success was cent per cent. I do not want to weary you with details of what we have been able to do in the way of forging in the direction of organising the Muslim Leagues. But I may tell you that it is going up by leaps and bounds.

Next, you may remember that we appointed a committee of ladies at the Patna session. It is of very great importance to us, because I believe that it is absolutely essential for us to give every opportunity to our women to participate in our struggle of life and work. Women can do a great deal within their homes even under purdah. We appointed this committee with a view to enable them to participate in the work of the League. The objects of this central committee were: (1) to organise provincial and district Muslim Leagues; (2) to enlist a larger number of women to the membership of the Muslim League; (3) to carry on an intensive propaganda amongst Muslim women throughout India in order to create in them a sense of greater political consciousness...; (4) to advise and guide them in all such matters as mainly rest on them for the uplift of Muslim society. This central committee, I am glad to say, started its work seriously and earnestly. It has done a great deal of useful work. I have no doubt that when we come to deal with their report of work done we shall really feel grateful to them for all the service that they have rendered to the Muslim League.

We had many difficulties to face from January 1939 right up to the declaration of war. We had to face the Vidya Mandir in Nagpur. We had to face the Wardha Scheme all over India. We had to face ill-treatment and oppression to Muslims in the Congress-governed provinces. We had to face the treatment meted out to Muslims in some of the Indian States such as Jaipur and Bhavnagar. We had to face a vital issue that arose in that small state of Rajkot. Rajkot was the acid test made by the Congress which would have affected one-third of India. Thus the Muslim League had all along to face various issues from January 1939 up to the time of the declaration of war. Before the war was declared the greatest danger to the Muslims of India was the possible inauguration of the federal scheme in the Central Government. We know what machinations were going on. But the Muslim League was stoutly resisting them in every direction. We felt that we could never accept the dangerous scheme of the Central Federal Government embodied in the Government of India Act, 1935. I am sure that we have made no small contribution towards persuading the British Government to abandon the scheme of Central Federal Government. In creating that mind in the British Government the Muslim League, I have no doubt, played no small part. They are also very conservative, and although they are very clever, they are slow in understanding. After the war was declared, the Viceroy naturally wanted help from the Muslim League. It was only then that he realised that the Muslim League was a power. For it will be remembered that up to the time of the declaration of war, the

Viceroy never thought of me but of Gandhi and Gandhi alone. I have been the leader of an important Party in the Legislature for a considerable time, larger than the one I have the honour to lead at present, the Muslim League Party in the Central Legislature. Yet the Viceroy never thought of me before. Therefore, when I got this invitation from the Viceroy along with Mr. Gandhi, I wondered within myself why I was so suddenly promoted and then I concluded that the answer was the 'All-India Muslim League' whose President I happen to be. I believe that was the worst shock that the Congress High Command received, because it challenged their sole authority to speak on behalf of India. And it is quite clear from the attitude of Mr. Gandhi and the High Command that they have not yet recovered from that shock. My point is that I want you to realise the value, the importance, the significance of organising yourselves. I will not say anything more on the subject.

But a great deal yet remains to be done. I am sure from what I can see and hear that Muslim India is now conscious, is now awake and the Muslim League has by now grown into such a strong institution that it cannot be destroyed by anybody whoever he may happen to be. Men may come and men may go, but the league will live for ever.

Now, coming to the period after the declaration of war, our position was that we were between the devil and the deep sea. But I do not think that the devil or the deep sea is going to get away with it. Anyhow our position is this. We stand unequivocally for the freedom of India. But it must be freedom for all India and not freedom of one section or, worse still, of the Congress caucus and slavery of Musalmans and other minorities.

Situated in India as we are, we naturally have our past experiences and particularly by experience of the past 2½ years of provincial constitution in the Congress-governed provinces we have learnt many lessons. We are now, therefore, very apprehensive and can trust nobody. I think it is a wise rule for everyone not to trust anybody too much. Sometimes we are led to trust people but when we find in actual experience that our trust has been betrayed, surely that ought to be sufficient lesson for any man not to continue his trust in those who have betrayed him. Ladies and gentlemen, we never thought that the Congress High Command would have acted in the manner in which they actually did in the Congress-governed provinces. I never dreamt that they would ever come down so low as that. I never could believe that there would be a gentlemen's agreement between the Congress and the Britishers to such an extent that although we cried hoarse, week in and out, the Governors were supine and the Governor-General was helpless. We reminded them of their special responsibilities to us and to other minorities and the solemn pledges they had given to us. But all that had become a dead letter. Fortunately, Providence came to our help and that gentlemen's agreement was broken to pieces and the Congress, thanks Heaven, went out of office. I think they are regretting their resignations very much. The bluff was called off. So far so good. I, therefore, appeal to you, in all seriousness that I can command, to organise yourselves in such a way that you may depend upon none except your own inherent strength. That is your only safeguard and the best safeguard. Depend upon yourselves. That does not mean that we should have ill-will or malice towards others. In order to safeguard your rights and interests you must create that in yourself that you may be able to defend yourselves. That is all that I want to urge.

Now, what is our position with regard to the future constitution? It is that, as soon as circumstances permit or immediately after the war at the latest, the whole problem of India's future constitution must be examined *de novo* and the Act of 1935 must go once for all. We do not believe in asking the British Government to make declarations. These declarations are really of no use. You cannot possibly succeed in getting the British Government out of this land by asking them to make declarations. However, the Congress asked the Viceroy to make a declaration. The Viceroy said, 'I have made the declaration.' The Congress said, 'No, no; we want another kind of declaration. You must declare and at once that India is free and independent with the right to frame its own constitution by a Constituent Assembly to be elected on the basis of adult franchise or as low a franchise as possible. This assembly will of course satisfy the minorities' legitimate interests.' Mr. Gandhi says that if the minorities are not satisfied then he is willing that some tribunal of the highest character and most impartial should decide the dispute. Now, apart from the impracticable character of this proposal and quite apart from the fact that it is historically and constitutionally absurd to ask the ruling power to abdicate in favour of a Constituent Assembly—apart from all that, suppose we do not agree as to the franchise according to which the Central Assembly is to be elected, or suppose we, the solid body of Muslim representatives, do not agree with the non-Muslim majority in the Constituent

Assembly, what will happen? It is said that we have no right to disagree with regard to anything that this Assembly may do in framing a national constitution of this huge subcontinent except those matters which may be germane to the safeguards for the minorities. So we are given the privilege to disagree only with regard to what may be called strictly safeguards of the rights and interests of minorities. We are also given the privilege to send our own representatives by separate electorates. Now, this proposal is based on the assumption that as soon as this contribution comes into operation the British hand will disappear. Otherwise there will be no meaning in it. Of course, Mr. Gandhi says that the constitution will decide whether the British will disappear and, if so, to what extent. In other words, his proposal comes to this: First give me the declaration that we are a free and independent nation, then I will decide what I should give you back! Does Mr. Gandhi really want the complete independence of India when he talks like this? But whether the British disappear or not, it follows that extensive powers must be transferred to the people. In the event of there being a disagreement between the majority of the Constituent Assembly and the Musalmans, in the first instance, who will appoint the tribunal? And suppose an agreed tribunal is possible and the award is made and the decision given, who will, may I know, be there to see that this award is implemented or carried out in accordance with the terms of that award? And who will see that it is honoured in practice, because, we are told, the British will have parted with their power mainly or completely? Then what will be the sanction behind the award which will enforce it? We come back to the same answer: the Hindu majority would do it—and will it be with the help of the British bayonet or Mr. Gandhi's 'ahimsa'? Can we trust them any more? Besides, ladies and gentlemen, can you imagine that a question of this character, of social contract upon which the future constitution of India would be based affecting 90 millions of Musalmans, can be decided by means of a judicial tribunal? Still that is the proposal of the Congress.

Before I deal with what Mr. Gandhi said a few days ago I shall deal with the pronouncements of some of the other Congress leaders—each one speaking with a different voice. Mr. Rajagopalachari, the ex-Prime Minister of Madras, says that the only panacea for Hindu-Muslim unity is the joint electorates. This is his prescription as one of the great doctors of the Congress organisation! (Laughter.) Babu Rajendra Prasad on the other hand only a few days ago said, 'Oh, what more do the Musalmans want?' I will read to you his words. He says, referring to the minority question: 'If Britain would concede our right of self-determination surely all these differences would disappear.' How will our differences disappear? He does not explain or enlighten us about it.

But so long as Britain remained and held power, the differences would continue to exist. The Congress has made it clear that the future constitution will be framed not by the Congress alone but by the representatives of all political parties and religious groups. The Congress has gone further and declared that the minorities can have their representatives elected for this purpose by separate electorates though the Congress regards separate electorates as an evil. It will be representative of all the peoples of this country, irrespective of their religious and political affiliations, who will be deciding the future constitution of India and not this or that party. What better guarantee can the minorities have? So, according to Babu Rajendra Prasad, the moment we enter the Assembly we shall shed all our political affiliations, and religions and everything else. This is what Babu Rajendra Prasad said as late as 18th March 1940. And this is now what Mr. Gandhi said on the 20th of March 1940. He says: 'To me Hindus, Muslims, Parsis, Harijans, are all alike, I cannot be frivolous'—but I think he is frivolous—'I cannot be frivolous while I talk of Qaid-I-Azam Jinnah. He is my brother.'

The only difference is this, that brother Gandhi has three votes and I have only one vote! (Laughter.)

'I would be happy indeed if he could keep me in his pocket.' I do not know really what to say to this latest offer of his.

'There was a time when I could say that there was no Muslim whose confidence I did not enjoy. It is my misfortune that it is not so today.'

Why has he lost the confidence of the Muslims today? May I ask, ladies and gentlemen?

'I do not read all that appears in the Urdu press, but perhaps I get a lot of abuse there. I am not sorry for it. I still believe that without Hindu-Muslim settlement there can be no Swaraj.'

Mr. Gandhi has been saying this now for the last 20 years.

'You will perhaps ask in that case why do I talk of a fight? I do so because it is to be a fight for a Constituent Assembly.'

He is fighting the British. But may I point out to Mr. Gandhi and the Congress that you are fighting for a Constituent Assembly which, the Muslims say, we cannot accept, which, the Muslims say, means three to one, about which the Musalmans say that they will never be able, in that way, by the counting of heads, to come to any agreement which will be a real agreement from the hearts, which will enable us to work as friends and, therefore, this idea of a Constituent Assembly is objectionable, apart from other objections. But he is fighting for the Constituent Assembly, not fighting the Musalmans at all.

He says, 'I do so because it is to be a fight for a Constituent Assembly. If Muslims who come to the Constituent Assembly'—mark the words—'who come to the Constituent Assembly through Muslim votes'—he is first forcing us to come to that Assembly—and then says, 'declare that there is nothing common between Hindus and Muslims then alone I would give up all hope, but even then I would agree with them because they read the Koran and I have also studied something of that holy Book.' (Laughter.)

So he wants the Constituent Assembly for the purpose of ascertaining the views of the Musalmans and if they do not agree then he will give up all hope, but even then he will agree with us! (Laughter.) Well, I ask you, ladies and gentlemen, is this the way to show any real, genuine desire, if there existed any, to come to a settlement with the Musalmans? (Voices of no, no.) Why does not Mr. Gandhi agree, and I have suggested to him more than once and I repeat it again from this platform, why does not Mr. Gandhi honestly now acknowledge that the Congress is a Hindu Congress, that he does not represent anybody except the solid body of Hindu people? Why should not Mr. Gandhi be proud to say, 'I am a Hindu, Congress has solid Hindu backing.' I am not ashamed of saying that I am a Musalman. (Hear, hear and applause.) I am right and I hope and believe even a blind man must have been convinced by now that the Muslim League has solid backing of the Musalmans of India. (Hear, hear.) Why then all this camouflage? Why all these machinations? Why all these methods to coerce the British to overthrow the Musalmans? Why this declaration of non-co-operation? Why this threat of civil disobedience? And why fight for a Constituent Assembly for the sake of ascertaining whether the Musalmans agree or they do not agree? (Hear, hear.) Why not come as a Hindu leader proudly representing your people and let me meet you proudly representing the Musalmans? (Hear, hear and applause.) This is all that I have to say so far as the Congress is concerned.

So far as the British Government is concerned, our negotiations are not concluded yet, as you know. We had asked for assurances on several points, at any rate we have made some advance with regard to one point and that is this. You remember our demand was that the entire problem of the future constitution of India should be examined *de novo*, apart from the Government of India Act of 1935. To that the Viceroy's reply, with the authority of His Majesty's Government, was—I had better quote that—I will not put it in my own words. This is the reply that was sent to us on 23rd December: 'My answer to your first question is that the declaration I made with the approval of His Majesty's Government on October the 13th last does not exclude'—mark the words 'does not exclude'—'examination of any part either of the Act of 1935 or of the policy and plans on which it is based.' (Hear, hear.)

As regards other matters, we are still negotiating and the most important points are: (1) that no declaration should be made by His Majesty's Government with regard to the future constitution of India without our approval and consent (hear, hear and applause) and that no settlement of any question should be made with any party behind our back (hear, hear) unless our approval and consent is given to it. Well, ladies and gentlemen, whether the British Government in their wisdom agree to give us that assurance or not, I trust that they will still see that it is a fair and just demand when we say that we cannot leave the future fate and the destiny of 90 millions of people in the hands of any other judge. We and we alone wish to be the final arbiter. Surely that is a just demand. We do not want that the British Government should thrust upon the Musalmans a constitution which they do not approve of and to which they do not agree. Therefore the British Government will be well advised to give that assurance and give the Musalmans complete peace and confidence in this matter and win their friendship. But whether they do that or not, after all, as I told you before, we must depend on our own inherent strength and I make it plain from this platform, that if any declaration is made, if any interim settlement is made without our approval and without our consent, the Musalmans of India will resist. (Hear, hear and applause.) And no mistake should be made on that score.

Then the next point was with regard to Palestine. We are told that 'endeavours, earnest endeavours, are being made to meet the reasonable national demands of the Arabs'. Well, we cannot be satisfied by earnest endeavours, sincere endeavours, best endeavours (laughter). We want that the British Government should in fact and actually meet the demands of the Arabs in Palestine. (Hear, hear.)

Then the next point was with regard to the sending of the troops of outside [*sic*]. Here there is some misunderstanding. But anyhow we have made our position clear that we never intended, and, in fact, language does not justify it, if there is any misapprehension, or apprehension, that the Indian troops should not be used to the fullest in the defence of our own country. What we wanted the British Government to give us assurance of was that Indian troops should not be sent against any Muslim country or any Muslim Power. (Hear, hear.) Let us hope that we may yet be able to get the British Government to clarify the position further.

This, then, is the position with regard to the British Government. The last meeting of the Working Committee had asked the Viceroy to reconsider his letter of the 23rd of December having regard to what has been explained to him in pursuance of the resolution of the Working Committee dated the 3rd of February and we are informed that the matter is receiving his careful consideration.

Ladies and gentlemen, that is where we stand after the war and up to the 3rd of February.

As far as our internal position is concerned, we have also been examining it and, you know, there are several schemes which have been sent by various well-informed constitutionalists and others who take interest in the problem of India's future constitution, and we have also appointed a sub-committee to examine the details of the schemes that have come in so far. But one thing is quite clear. It has always been taken for granted mistakenly that the Musalmans are a minority and of course we have got used to it for such a long time that these settled notions sometimes are very difficult to remove. The Musalmans are not a minority. The Musalmans are a nation by any definition. The British and particularly the Congress proceed on the basis, 'Well, you are a minority after all, what do you want?' 'What else do the minorities want?' Just as Babu Rajendra Prasad said. But surely the Musalmans are not a minority. We find that even according to the British map of India, we occupy large parts of this country, where the Musalmans are in a majority—such as Bengal, Punjab, N.W.F.P., Sind and Baluchistan.

Now the question is, what is the best solution of this problem between the Hindus and the Musalmans? We have been considering, and as I have already said, a committee has been appointed to consider the various proposals. But whatever the final scheme of constitution, I will present to you my views and I will just read to you in confirmation of what I am going to put before you, a letter from Lala Lajpat Rai to Mr. C.R. Das. It was written, I believe, about 14 to 15 years ago and that letter has been produced in a book by one Indra Prakash recently published and that is how this letter has come to light. This is what Lala Lajpat Rai, a very astute politician and a staunch Hindu Mahasabhite said. But before I read this letter it is plain that you cannot get away from being a Hindu if you are Hindu! (Laughter.) The word 'nationalist' has now become the play of conjurers in politics. This is what he says:

> There is one point more which has been troubling me very much of late and one which I want you to think carefully and that is the question of Hindu-Mohammedan unity. I have devoted most of my time during the last six months to the study of Muslim history and Muslim law and I am inclined to think it is neither *possible* nor *practicable*. Assuming and admitting the sincerity of Mohammedan leaders in the non-co-operation movement, I think their religion provides an effective bar to anything of the kind.
>
> You remember the conversation I reported to you in Calcutta which I had with Hakim Ajmal Khan and Dr. Kitchlu. There is no finer Mohammedan in Hindustan than Hakim Ajmal Khan, but can any Muslim leader override the Koran? I can only hope that my reading of the Islamic law is incorrect.

I think his reading is quite correct. (Laughter.)

> 'And nothing would relieve me more than to be convinced that it is so. But if it is right then it comes to this that although we can unite against British we cannot do so to rule Hindustan on British lines. We cannot do so to rule Hindustan on *democratic lines*.'

Ladies and gentlemen, when Lala Lajpat Rai said that we cannot rule this country on democratic lines it was all right but when I had the temerity to speak the same truth about 18 months ago there was a shower of attacks and criticism. But Lala Lajpat Rai said 15 years ago that we cannot do so, viz., to rule Hindustan on democratic lines. What is the remedy? The remedy according to Congress is to keep us in the minority and under the majority rule. Lala Lajpat Rai proceeds further:

> What is then the remedy? I am not afraid of the seven crores of Musalmans. But I think the seven crores in Hindustan plus the

> armed hosts of Afghanistan, Central Asia, Arabia, Mesopotamia and Turkey, will be irresistible. (Laughter.)
>
> I do honestly and sincerely believe in the necessity or desirability of Hindu-Muslim unity. I am also fully prepared to trust the Muslim leaders. But what about the injunctions of the Koran and Hadis? The leaders cannot override them. Are we then doomed? I hope your learned mind and wise head will find some way out of this difficulty.

Now, ladies and gentlemen, that is merely a letter written by one great Hindu leader to another great Hindu leader fifteen years ago. Now, I should like to put before you my views on the subject as it strikes me taking everything into consideration at the present moment. The British Government and Parliament, and more so the British nation, have been for many decades past brought up and nurtured with settled notions about India's future, based on developments in their own country which has built up the British constitution, functioning now through the Houses of Parliament and the system of cabinet. Their concept of party government functioning on political planes has become the ideal with them as the best form of government for every country, and the one-sided and powerful propaganda, which naturally appeals to the British, has led them into a serious blunder, in producing the constitution envisaged in the Government of India Act of 1935. We find that the most leading statesmen of Great Britain, saturated with these notions, have in their pronouncements seriously asserted and expressed a hope that the passage of time will harmonise the inconsistent elements in India.

A leading journal like the *London Times* commenting on the Government of India Act of 1935, wrote, 'Undoubtedly the differences between the Hindus and Muslims are not of religion in the strict sense of the word but also of law and culture, that they may be said, indeed, to represent two entirely distinct and separate civilisations. However, in the course of time, the superstition will die out and India will be moulded into a single nation.' So, according to the *London Times*, the only difficulties are superstitions. These fundamental and deep-rooted differences, spiritual, economic, social and political, have been euphemised as mere 'superstitions'. But surely it is a flagrant disregard of the past history of the subcontinent of India as well as the fundamental Islamic conception of society vis-à-vis that of Hinduism to characterise them as mere 'superstitions'. Notwithstanding a thousand years of close contact, nationalities, which are as divergent today as ever, cannot at any time be expected to transform themselves into one nation merely by means of subjecting them to a democratic constitution and holding them forcibly together by unnatural and artificial methods of British Parliamentary Statute. What the unitary government of India for 150 years had failed to achieve cannot be realised by the imposition of a central federal government. It is inconceivable that the fiat or the writ of a government so constituted can ever command a willing and loyal obedience throughout the subcontinent by various nationalities except by means of armed force behind it.

The problem in India is not of an inter-communal character but manifestly of an international one, and it must be treated as such. So long as this basic and fundamental truth is not realised, any constitution that may be built will result in disaster and will prove destructive and harmful not only to the Musalmans but to the British and Hindus also. If the British Government are really in earnest and sincere to secure peace and happiness of the people of this subcontinent, the only course open to us all is to allow the major nations separate homelands by dividing India into 'autonomous national states'. There is no reason why these states should be antagonistic to each other. On the other hand, the rivalry and the natural desire and efforts on the part of one to dominate the social order and establish political supremacy over the other in the government of the country will disappear. It will lead more towards natural goodwill by international pacts between them, and they can live in complete harmony with their neighbours. This will lead further to a friendly settlement all the more easily with regard to minorities by reciprocal arrangements and adjustments between Muslim India and Hindu India, which will far more adequately and effectively safeguard the rights and interests of Muslims and various other minorities.

It is extremely difficult to appreciate why our Hindu friends fail to understand the real nature of Islam and Hinduism. They are not religions in the strict sense of the word, but are, in fact, different and distinct social orders, and it is a dream that the Hindus and Muslims can ever evolve a common nationality, and this misconception of one Indian nation has gone far beyond the limits and is the cause of most of your troubles and will lead to destruction if we fail to revise our notions in time. The Hindus and Muslims belong to two different religious philosophies, social customs, literatures. They neither intermarry nor interdine together and, indeed, they belong to two different civilisations which are based mainly on conflicting ideas and conceptions. Their aspects on life and of life are different. It is quite clear that Hindus and Musalmans derive their inspiration from different sources of history. They have different epics, different heroes, and different episodes. Very often the hero of one is a foe of the other and, likewise, their victories and defeats overlap. To yoke together two such nations under a single state, one as a numerical minority and the other as a majority, must lead to growing discontent and final destruction of any fabric that may be so built up for the government of such a state.

History has presented to us many examples, such as the Union of Great Britain and Ireland, Czechoslovakia and Poland. History has also shown to us many geographical tracts, much smaller than the subcontinent of India, which otherwise might have been called one country, but which have been divided into as many states as there are nations inhabiting them. Balkan Peninsula comprises as many as 7 or 8 sovereign states. Likewise, the Portuguese and the Spanish stand divided in the Iberian Peninsula. Whereas under the plea of unity of India and one nation, which does not exist, it is sought to pursue here the line of one central government when we know that the history of the last 1200 years has failed to achieve unity and has witnessed, during the ages, India always divided into Hindu India and Muslim India. The present artificial unity of India dates back only to the British conquest and is maintained by the British bayonet, but termination of the British regime, which is implicit in the recent declaration of His Majesty's Government, will be the herald of the entire break-up with worse disaster than has ever taken place during the last one thousand years under Muslims. Surely that is not the legacy which Britain would bequeath to India after 150 years of her rule, nor would Hindu and Muslim India risk such a sure catastrophe.

Muslim India cannot accept any constitution which must necessarily result in a Hindu majority government. Hindus and Muslims brought together under a democratic system forced upon the minorities can only mean Hindu raj. Democracy of the kind with which the Congress High Command is enamoured would mean the complete destruction of what is most precious in Islam. We have had ample experience of the working of the provincial constitutions during the last two and a half years and any repetition of such a government must lead to civil war and raising of private armies as recommended by Mr. Gandhi to Hindus of Sukkur when he said that they must defend themselves violently or non-violently, blow for blow, and if they could not, they must emigrate.

Musalmans are not a minority as it is commonly known and understood. One has only got to look round. Even today, according to the British map of India, 4 out of 11 provinces, where the Muslims dominate more or less, are functioning notwithstanding the decision of the Hindu Congress High Command to non-co-operate and prepare for civil disobedience. Musalmans are a nation according to any definition of a nation, and they must have their homelands, their territory and their state. We wish to live in peace and harmony with our neighbours as a free and independent people. We wish our people to develop to the fullest our spiritual, cultural, economic, social and political life in a way that we think best and in consonance with our own ideal and according to the genius of our people. Honesty demands and the vital interest of millions of our people impose a sacred duty upon us to find an honourable and peaceful solution which would be just and fair to all. But at the same time we cannot be moved or diverted from our purpose and objective by threats or intimidation. We must be prepared to face all difficulties and consequences, make all the sacrifices that may be required of us to achieve the goal we have set in front of us.

Ladies and gentlemen, that is the task before us. I fear I have gone beyond my time limit. There are many things that I should like to tell you, but I have already published a little pamphlet containing most of the things that I have been saying and I think you can easily get that publication both in English and in Urdu from the League office. It might give you a clearer idea of our aims. It contains very important resolutions of the Muslim League and various other statements. Anyhow, I have placed before you the task that lies ahead of us. Do you realise how big and stupendous it is? Do you realise that you cannot get freedom of independence by mere arguments? I should appeal to the intelligentsia. The intelligentsia in all countries in the world have been the pioneers of any movements for freedom. What does the Muslim intelligentsia propose to do? I may tell you that unless you get this into your blood, unless you are prepared to take off your coats and are willing to sacrifice all that you can and work selflessly, earnestly and sincerely for your people, you will never realise your aim. Friends, I therefore want you to make up your mind definitely and then think of devices and organise your people, strengthen your organisation and consolidate the Musalmans all over India. I think that the masses are wide-awake. They only want your guidance and your lead. Come forward as servants of Islam, organise the people economically, socially, educationally and politically and I am sure that you will be a power that will be accepted by everybody. (Cheers.)

8

THE BIRTH OF A NATION

The Second World War came to an end in 1945 with the dropping of the atom bomb on Hiroshima and Nagasaki. Elections for the Central Legislative Assembly were announced and as a precursor to that, Congress leaders were released from jail. In the meantime, the Indian National Army (INA)—formed in 1940 by Mohan Singh and others of the British Indian Army who were taken as prisoners of war by the Japanese—had captured popular imagination. After he left the country in a dazzling display of courage and enterprise, Subhas Bose took the lead in organizing the army afresh. Announcing the formation of the Provisional Azad Hind Government, Bose declared a war against the British Indian Army and the INA marched towards India. Facing all sorts of discrimination at the hands of the Japanese Army, the soldiers braved the difficult terrain and reached the border in Kohima. But soon the Japanese reversal began and the hopes of the INA to hoist the Indian flag atop the Red Fort were shattered. The soldiers of the INA were taken prisoners by the British who decided to try them for treason. The trials began in November 1945 in the Red Fort. The entire country burst into angry protests against the trials and the sentencing of these heroes of Indian independence.

It was amidst this nationalist wave that elections to provincial and central legislatures took place. Though the right to vote was limited to a small section of the population, the elections were seen as a test of the ideological penetration of the nationalist forces and their opponents. While the Congress candidates were victorious in overwhelmingly large numbers, the Muslim League, which had fared dismally in a similar exercise in 1937, won all the Muslim seats. This vindicated its claim that it alone represented the Muslims of the subcontinent.

Communal Riots, Independence and Partition

The mutiny by the Naval Ratings at Bombay and Karachi made the signs of disaffection within the army apparent. Demoralization of the bureaucracy was also evident. It was clear that Britain could not hold on to India any longer. The Muslim League, actively patronized by the bureaucracy, was opposed to any move by the British to leave India without first granting Pakistan. A Cabinet Mission arrived in 1946 to recommend future arrangements. The Mission rejected Pakistan as a viable alternative but its recommendation to group provinces on the basis of religious majority was taken by the League as an endorsement of its demand for Pakistan. Congress leaders like Jawaharlal Nehru firmly rejected the Mission's recommendations regarding the mandatory character of the grouping system. To force its demand for Pakistan, the League now rejected the Cabinet Mission recommendations, after initially accepting them, and declared a phase of 'direct action' on 16 August 1946. With no anti-colonial programme or pretensions, 'direct action' could be targeted only against the Congress and against those who opposed Pakistan. The result was a communal carnage in Calcutta in which more than 5000 people were killed. Noakhali, which had been a major outpost of the peasant movement since the non-cooperation–Khilafat days, erupted in an anti-Hindu frenzy. The ideology of communalism by now held complete sway. To avenge the Noakhali killings, village after village in Bihar was burned down and Muslims killed in thousands with such savagery that Nehru reacted by saying that he would bomb the area if the riots did not stop.

These riots convinced a wide cross-section of the population and political leaders that partition was inevitable. The leaders realized that any further opposition to partition would only lead to more Noakhalis and Bihars. Thus partition was seen as a panacea to the problem of communalism.

On 15 August 1947, India became free, marking a triumphant culmination of years of struggle against the British Empire. At the stroke of midnight on 14 August 1947, Nehru addressed the Constituent Assembly, memorably invoking India's 'tryst with destiny'.

As Sarojini Naidu pointed out in her speech, it was an epic struggle of millions of anonymous heroes. It was one of the longest anti-colonial battles, the likes of which had not been seen anywhere else in the world. Those who participated in the battle consistently invoked the ideas of democracy, liberty and equality that came from British philosophers and political leaders themselves. They fought for institutions—modern, secular and democratic—so that the discrimination by the colonialist as well as by the Indian could be addressed at a higher level. They gave the nationalist movement a strong democratic and secular ethos which is primarily why India could retain a democratic and secular fabric after independence while many other countries which became independent around that time gave in to tyranny and dictatorship.

Some parts of India, for example Goa, continued to remain under colonial rule. The Portuguese authorities ruthlessly suppressed the internal struggle for independence to which the Indian government provided moral and material support. The issue was even internationalized with the Portuguese dictator Salazar making it a point to get the support of US President John Kennedy. The Indian government refused to blink in the international battle of nerves and in 1961 initiated military action to free Goa, Daman and Diu. Thus, the last vestige of colonial presence was removed.

~

JAWAHARLAL NEHRU

Tryst with Destiny

In 1929, Jawaharlal Nehru's momentous address on the banks of the river Ravi, in which he declared Purna Swaraj as the goal of the Congress, changed the course of the nation's history. It was Nehru again who in the midnight hour of 14 August 1947 announced the dawn of India's freedom to the world. An epoch-making speech depicting the human quest for freedom, this address represents not only the feelings and emotions of Nehru but also the spirit of a people whose non-violent struggle for freedom was unparalleled in the annals of freedom movements anywhere in the world.

Long years ago we made a tryst with destiny, and now the time comes when we shall redeem our pledge, not wholly or in full measure, but very substantially. At the stroke of the midnight hour, when the world sleeps, India will awake to life and freedom. A moment comes, which comes but rarely in history, when we step out from the old to the new, when an age ends, and when the soul of a nation, long suppressed, finds utterance. It is fitting that at this solemn moment we take the pledge of dedication to the service of India and her people and to the still larger cause of humanity.

At the dawn of history India started on her unending quest, and trackless centuries are filled with her striving and the grandeur of her success and her failures. Through good and ill fortune alike she has never lost sight of that quest or forgotten the ideals which gave her strength. We end today a period of ill fortune and India discovers herself again. The achievement we celebrate today is but a step, an opening of opportunity, to the greater triumphs and achievements that await us. Are we brave enough and wise enough to grasp this opportunity and accept the challenge of the future?

Freedom and power bring responsibility. The responsibility rests upon this Assembly, a sovereign body representing the sovereign people of India. Before the birth of freedom we have endured all the pains of labour and our hearts are heavy with the memory of this sorrow. Some of those pains continue even now. Nevertheless, the past is over and it is the future that beckons to us now.

That future is not one of ease or resting but of incessant striving so that we might fulfil the pledges we have so often taken and the one we shall take today. The service of India means the service of the millions who suffer. It means the ending of poverty and ignorance and disease and inequality of opportunity. The ambition of the greatest man of our generation has been to wipe every tear from every eye. That may be beyond us, but as long as there are tears and suffering, so long our work will not be over.

And so we have to labour and to work, and work hard to give reality to our dreams. Those dreams are for India, but they are also for the world, for all the nations and peoples are too closely knit together today for any one of them to imagine that it can live apart. Peace has been said to be indivisible; so is freedom, so is prosperity now, and so also is disaster in this One World that can no longer be split into isolated fragments.

To the people of India, whose representatives we are, we make an appeal to join us with faith and confidence in this great adventure. This is no time for petty and destructive criticism, no time for ill-will or blaming others. We have to build the noble mansion of free India where all her children may dwell.

I beg to move Sir, that it be resolved that:

(1) After the last stroke of midnight, all members of the Constituent Assembly present on this occasion do take the following pledge: 'At this solemn moment when the people of India, through suffering and sacrifice, have secured freedom, I,..., a member of the Constituent Assembly of India, do dedicate myself in all humility to the service of India and her people to the end that this ancient land attain her rightful place in the world and make her full and willing contribution to the promotion of world peace and the welfare of mankind';

(2) 'Members who are not present on this occasion do take the pledge (with such verbal changes as the President may prescribe) at the time they next attend a session of the Assembly.'

SAROJINI NAIDU

The Battle for Freedom Is Over

Known as the Nightingale of India, Sarojini Naidu (1879–1949) was a poet and a freedom fighter. She played a pivotal role in bringing women to the forefront of the freedom movement. She was the first Indian woman to become the president of the Indian National Congress and the first woman governor of a state in independent India. In this speech, broadcast from the Delhi station of All India Radio on the afternoon of 15 August 1947, she captured the cosmopolitan and universal nature of the Indian national movement and the idea of universal freedom that the movement enshrined as its core philosophy.

Oh, world of free nations, on this day of our freedom, we greet you. Oh, world of nations not yet free, on the day of our freedom we pray for your freedom in the future.

Ours has been an epic struggle, covering many years and costing many lives. It has been a struggle, a dramatic struggle. It has been a struggle of heroes chiefly anonymous in their millions. It has been a struggle of women transformed into strength and power like the Kali, the goddess of strength they worship. It has been a struggle of youth suddenly transfigured into power itself, sacrifice and ideals. It has been a struggle of young men and old men, of rich and poor, the literate, the illiterate, the stricken, the outcast, the leper and the saint. It has been the only revolution in the whole history of the world that has been without bloodshed; and for this we thank one man, one tiny person, who on this day that he has brought to us, is somewhere remote in a little far-off corner of India, wiping the tears of those who feel themselves exiled from our midst. Mahatma Gandhi, our prophet of non-violence, our general of victory, he taught us a new way of deliverance from evil. He had no device of his banner excepting non-violence. He had no weapons for his legions excepting self-sacrifice and suffering. We marched to the tune of faith and hope and charity that forgives all sins of trespassers that ruined our country through the ages. We have to thank him, our leader, whose life is immutable, immortal, in the love of his countrymen, whose days are imperishable, who has created a new civilisation for the world to be based in the years to come, of his gospel of love, truth and non-violence.

But we wish to offer today our thanks to the men and women of all races who have striven for India's freedom, the scholars of Europe who restored to us our pride and ancient culture, to the antiquarian and the archaeologist who has discovered for us our own ruined cities, to the missionaries of all countries who chose the life of poverty in far-off villages and served the poor and the needy and the desolate. To all we owe thanks.

Today I remember those abroad who were the pioneers of our dream of freedom, men who are exiles if they are alive, forgotten if they are dead, who never sought nor received recognition or reward, only privation, persecution and death. But all these today are immortal in our minds. We thank the Englishmen who were our friends, though many Englishmen were our enemies, not personal enemies but the victims themselves of a system of iniquitous imperialism. But those Englishmen who served us, became part of our Indian history, part of our struggle for India's independence. And it seems somehow poetical, it seems somehow romantic, it seems somehow logical that the great grandson of Queen Victoria, Louis Mountbatten, should have, by grace and generosity, dissolved the empire that Disraeli built for her. All of them we thank.

The battle of freedom is over. The struggle for peace begins. And my country, my India, that has never excluded friend or foe from her hospitality, my India that has taken knowledge from all over the world, that has offered knowledge and wisdom to the world, once more will she stand in the forefront of the world civilisation, once more will she bring the message of peace, once more will she carry her lamp into the darkness of strife and struggle and hatred; and the nations of the world who are free, nations of the world who are not free, we pledge you our comradeship, our fellowship, our understanding, our love. Let us move together towards the great world fellowship of which we dream. Let us work together for the peace that will never be ended. Let us work for justice, for equity, for human rights but no privileges, for human duties but no prerogatives, let us be citizens of a great free world of which our ancestors dreamed and for which we have striven. Men and women together, men and women of a common humanity, let no religion, no community, no text, no tongues divide us, for ours is a common destiny. Ours is a common purpose. Ours is a common wish and ambition to rebuild this broken world into the image of our heart's desire. And which country but India can take the lead in restoring the world to its pristine glory. We, who have been the dreamers of dreams, the seers of visions, the creators of wisdom, the followers of renunciation, we, who have given the heroes of the independence struggle, for India, we have rung through the whole gamut of the world's adventures, of the world's emotions. We are the wise. We are reborn today of the crucible of your sufferings.

Nations of the world, I greet you in the name of India, my mother, my mother whose home has a roof of snow, whose walls are of living seas, whose doors are always open to you. Do you seek peace or wisdom, do you seek love and understanding, come to us. Come to us in faith, come to us in hope, come to us believing that all gifts are ours to give. Today, in the name of India, I give for the whole world the freedom of this India that had never died in the past that shall be indestructible in the future and shall lead the world to ultimate peace.

~

J.B. KRIPALANI

The End of Centuries-old Slavery

In this address broadcast from the Delhi station of All India Radio at 2 p.m. on 15 August 1947, J.B. Kripalani, the Congress president, spoke about the end of slavery. If Jawaharlal Nehru's speech was poetic, Kripalani's was an expression of the pent-up passion of millions who felt the burden of repression suddenly lifted and who wanted to cry out 'Ah Freedom!'

The long-awaited day of India's freedom is come. Here centuries-old slavery has ended. The people's representatives are at last in the seats of the mighty. Those who were reviled and despised have come into their own. For this day our patriots through the last several decades worked and suffered. Many of them who fought for this day are not in our midst to rejoice with us. They suffered so that others may enjoy. They died so that others may live in peace, freedom and honour. To the memory of all those known and unknown patriots we pay our humble tribute of love and honour.

We are thankful that our leader in this righteous fight, the Father of our Nation, Mahatma Gandhi, under whose saintly guidance we have lived to see this day, is yet in our midst. To him as a free people we pay our homage. He has written a new chapter in the history of the world, for he has led this nation to achieve by truth and non-violence what always was achieved through war and violence, through bloody revolution and its trail of misery and war. May he live long in our midst to guide us in the constructive tasks that lie ahead of us.

His and his nation's dream has not been completely fulfilled as often happens in human affairs; our achievement has fallen short of our goal. We wanted a free and united India. What we have got is a free India, divided and distracted. The result is that many of our countrymen whose hearts are lacerated at the division of the motherland are in mourning today. Our joy cannot therefore, be as complete as it would have been had India on this historic day remained one and undivided. Maybe our suffering and sacrifice were not great enough for the double task of unity and freedom.

However, we may not forget that the unity we had under the British rule was a unity in slavery. It was an artificial unity imposed from above by our masters who held both Hindus and Muslims in their iron grip. What we need is a free, spontaneous and organic unity—unity not only of political institutions and laws imposed upon us by the foreigner but the unity of hearts of common purpose, common effort and a common goal. This can only be achieved by our own efforts and such efforts can fructify only when communities that have been kept apart by the foreigner are free to think and act independently.

Let us, therefore, not rest content with the liberty we have achieved today. Let us henceforward bend all our energies to the unification of this land of ours. In this task we shall need all the undivided effort and devotion that we brought to the cause of freedom. Let us abandon all thoughts of ease, comfort and self and resume the path of sacrifice and suffering that has brought us where we are. This unity that we so ardently derive can only be achieved if we, who are privileged to be the citizens of the Indian Union, cease to think in communal terms. Let no citizen of the Indian Union think of himself as a Hindu, Muslim, Sikh, Christian or Parsi but as an Indian—Indian first and Indian last. Let him also not think in terms of retaliation and reprisal. The two major communities have tried this long enough and today there is murder, loot and arson in many parts of India. We are as far from unity today as ever before. Let us, therefore, after this bitter experience, change the methods that we have employed so far. Maybe, as in the case of our liberty, so in the case of our unity, the salvation lies, even as Mahatma Gandhi has indicated, through non-violence and truth.

Above all let us try to make the Indian Union great and prosperous. If we in our portion of India are able to evolve a new order of society based on democracy and social justice, where all power and profit belong to where they should—to the workers in the field and factory—we would provide the great inducement to our seceding countrymen to rejoin us and work with us. This is also the way to preserve our newfound liberty.

~

MAULANA ABUL KALAM AZAD

To the Muslims in Delhi

In the aftermath of partition, Delhi was a smouldering cauldron. The influx of refugees from Pakistan had aggravated a situation already tense with reports of riots and large-scale killings of Hindus in Pakistan. Hindu communal elements roamed the streets of the capital, rioting and urging the extermination of Muslims who had stayed back. A large number of Muslims, particularly the poorer sections of the population, had been moved to special refugee camps and there loomed the very real danger of a backlash originating from these camps. Homeless and afraid, having lost their political and national identity, these

Muslims needed reassuring. In such a situation, Maulana Abul Kalam Azad (1888–1958), who had right through the freedom struggle espoused the cause of Hindu–Muslim unity, so much so that the Muslim League called him 'the Showboy of the Congress', took it upon himself to reason with members of his community and urge restraint. In an evocative speech, delivered on 23 October 1947, he not only castigated the politics of communalization, but also assured the Muslims of their place in free India. At the same time, he lambasted them for contemplating leaving the land of their forefathers and chasing after the false chimera of Pakistan.

My brethren! You know what has brought me here today. This congregation at Shahjehan's historic mosque is not an unfamiliar sight for me. Here, I have addressed you on several previous occasions. Since then we have seen many ups and downs. At that time, instead of weariness, your faces reflected serenity, and your hearts, instead of misgivings, exuded confidence. The uneasiness on your faces and the desolation in your hearts that I see today, reminds me of the events of the past few years.

Do you remember? I hailed you, you cut off my tongue; I picked my pen, you severed my hand; I wanted to move forward, you broke off my legs; I tried to turn over, and you injured my back. When the bitter political games of the last seven years were at their peak, I tried to wake you up at every danger signal. You not only ignored my call but revived all the past traditions of neglect and denial. As a result the same perils surround you today, whose onset had previously diverted you from the righteous path.

Today, mine is no more than an inert existence or a forlorn cry; I am an orphan in my own motherland. This does not mean that I feel trapped in the original choice that I had made for myself, nor do I feel that there is no room left for my aashiana. What it means is that my cloak is weary of your impudent grabbing hands. My sensitivities are injured, my heart is heavy. Think for one moment. What course did you adopt? Where have you reached, and where do you stand now? Haven't your senses become torpid? Aren't you living in a constant state of fear? This fear is your own creation, a fruit of your own deeds.

It was not long ago when I warned you that the two-nation theory was death-knell to a meaningful, dignified life; forsake it. I told you that the pillars upon which you were leaning would inevitably crumble. To all this you turned a deaf ear. You did not realise that fleet-footed time would not change its course to suit your convenience.

Time sped along. And now you have discovered that the so-called anchors of your faith have set you adrift, to be kicked around by fate. Their understanding of the word fate does not correspond with the lexicon of your belief. For them, fate is another name for lack of courage.

The chessboard of British gamesmanship has been upturned. Those pawns called 'leaders' which you had carved and installed, have disappeared overnight. You believed that the chessboard had been spread forever and forever, and the worship of those pawns was the summum bonum of your existence. I do not want to lacerate your wounds, or aggravate your agony. However, if you look into the past you will find that through hindsight you can unravel several mysteries.

There was a time, when exhorting the need for achieving India's Independence, I had called out to you. No nation, however depraved, can stop the inevitable turn of events. A revolutionary political change has been inscribed in India's book of destiny. The twentieth century maelstrom of freedom is about to break India's chains of slavery. If you falter and fall behind the march of the times, if you remain inert and lethargic, the future historian will record that your flock, a cluster of seven crores, adopted an attitude towards freedom, which was characteristic of a community heading towards extinction. Today, the Indian flag has been hoisted in all its majestic splendour. This is the very same flag which evoked sneers and contemptuous laughter from the rulers of the time.

It is true that time did not accede to your wishes; instead, it bowed in deference to a nation's birthright. This turn of events has struck fear in your heart. Perhaps, you believe that something good has been taken away from you, and has been substituted with something evil. Yes, you are restless; because you had not prepared yourselves for the good, and believed that the evil was, in fact, manna from heaven. I refer to your years of slavery under a foreign rule, under which you were treated as play puppets. There was a time when our nation had plunged herself in pitched battle to overthrow the foreign rule; and, today, the outcome of that struggle is causing you consternation. How should I berate you for your unbecoming haste? Hardly have we completed our journey that you are showing signs of going astray.

My brothers! I have always attempted to keep politics apart from personalities, thus avoiding those thorny valleys. That is why some of my messages are often couched in allusions. But what I have to say today needs to be direct and to the point. The partition of India was a fundamental mistake. The manner in which religious differences were incited inevitably led to the devastation that we have seen with our own eyes. Unfortunately, we are still seeing it at some places.

There is no use recounting the events of the past seven years, nor will it serve any good. Yet, it must be stated that the debacle of Indian Muslims is the result of the colossal blunders committed by the Muslim League's misguided leadership. These consequences, however, were no surprise to me; I had anticipated them from the very start.

Now that Indian politics has taken a new direction, there is no place in it for the Muslim League. Now the question is whether or not we are capable of any constructive thinking. For this, I have invited the Muslim leaders of India to Delhi, during the second week of November.

The gloom cast upon your lives is momentary; I assure you we can be beaten by none save our own selves! I have always said, and I repeat it again today; eschew your indecisiveness, your mistrust, and stop your misdeeds. This unique triple-edged weapon is more lethal than the two-edged iron sword which inflicts fatal wounds, which I have heard of!

Just think about this life of escapism that you have opted for, in the sacred name of Hejrat. Get into the habit of exercising your own brains, and strengthening your own hearts. If you do so, only then will you realise how immature your decisions were.

Where are you going and why? Raise your eyes. The minarets of Jama Masjid want to ask you a question. Where have you lost the glorious pages from your chronicles? Was it only yesterday that on the banks of the Jamuna, your caravans performed wuzu? Today, you are afraid of living here! Remember, Delhi has been nurtured with your blood. Brothers! Create a basic change in yourselves. Today, your fear is as misplaced as your jubilation was yesterday.

The words coward and frenzy cannot be spoken in the same breath as the word Muslim. A true Muslim can be swayed neither by avarice nor apprehension. Don't get scared because a few faces have disappeared. The only reason they had herded you in a single fold was to facilitate their own flight. Today, if they have jerked their hand free from yours, what does it matter? Make sure that they have not run away with your hearts. If your hearts are still in the right place; make them the abode of God. Some thirteen hundred years ago, through an Arab ummi, God proclaimed, 'Those who place their faith in God and are firm in their belief, no fear for them nor any sorrow.' Winds blow in and blow out; tempests may gather but all this is short-lived. The period of trial is about to end. Change yourselves as if you had never been in such an abject condition.

I am not used to altercation. Faced with your general indifference, however, I will repeat that the third force has departed, and along with it, its trappings of vanity. Whatever had to happen has happened. Politics has broken out of its old mould and a new cast is being prepared. If your hearts have still not changed and your minds still have reservations, it is a different matter. But, if you want a change, then take your cue from history and cast yourself in the new mould. Having completed a revolutionary phase, there still remain a few blank pages in the history of India. You can make yourselves worthy of filling those pages, provided you are willing.

Brothers! Keep up with the changes. Don't say, 'We are not ready for the change.' Get ready. Stars may have plummeted down but the sun is still shining. Borrow a few of its rays and sprinkle them in the dark caverns of your lives.

I do not ask you to seek certificates from the new echelons of power. I do not want you to lead a life of sycophancy as you did during the foreign rule. I want to remind you that these bright etchings which you see all around you are relics of the Qafilas of your forefathers. Do not forget them. Do not forsake them. Live like their worthy inheritors, and, rest assured, that if you do not wish to flee from this scene, nobody can make you flee. Come, today let us pledge that this country is ours, we belong to it and any fundamental decision about its destiny will remain incomplete without our consent.

Today, you fear the earth's tremors; once you were virtually the earthquake itself. Today, you fear the darkness; once your existence was the epicentre of radiance. Clouds have poured dirty waters and you have hitched up your trousers. Those were none but your forefather who not only plunged headlong into the seas, but trampled the mountains, laughed at the bolts of lightning, turned away the tornados, challenged the tempests and made them alter their course. It is a sure sign of a dying faith that those who had once grabbed the collars of emperors, are, today, clutching at their own throats. They have become oblivious of the existence of God as if they had never believed in Him.

Brothers! I do not have a new prescription for you. I have the same old prescription that was revealed to the greatest benefactor of mankind, the prescription of the Holy Quran: 'Do not fear and do not grieve. If you possess true faith, you will gain the upper hand.'

The congregation is now at an end. What I had to say, I have said, briefly. Let me say once again, keep a grip on your senses. Learn to create your own surroundings, your own world. This is not a commodity that I can buy for you from the market-place. This can be bought only from the market-place of the heart, provided you can pay for it with the currency of good deeds. May God's grace be on you.

~

B.T. RANADIVE

Opening Report on the Draft Political Thesis

On 29 February 1948, the Communist Party of India (CPI), in the course of its second congress in Calcutta, adopted an extraordinary strategic and tactical position vis-à-vis the independence of the country. As declared by its general secretary, B.T. Ranadive (1904–90), the line which marked a break with the past had been arrived at after looking at the international situation. The political slogan that the CPI adopted was 'Azadi jhuthi hai'*—the freedom is false. The resolution, an extract from which is reproduced here, labelled the government of Jawaharlal Nehru as a lackey of imperialist forces and insisted that the slogan of building a self-reliant economy under a sovereign national state as dreamt by the leadership was a hoax.*

... We characterise here the National Government as the Government of national surrender, of collaborators, a Government of national compromise. Thus in place of our former wrong characterisation about the Government as one of an advance with whom we should have a joint front, we have now the characterisation that it is a Government of national surrender and collaboration; the conclusion that follows, therefore, is that it is the basic policy of the working class and its Party to oppose this Government, and this is what we have sharply underlined.

People ask what happens to the Government? Does a time come when somebody else may be prepared to take power and turn this Government out? Yes. That is what we visualise.

We have given the slogan of a People's Democratic Front based on the alliance of the working class, peasantry and the oppressed middle class and the intelligentsia. We visualise that as the Front grows we can marshal all people around the slogan of the democratic revolution, disillusion them about the present Government and develop sufficient strength to demand: A People's Democratic State. If we do not visualise the prospect of coming into sharp opposition to this Government, then all that we say about unmasking the compromising policy of this Government has no meaning. In fact, the central question is the question of power and we are answering that question by demanding a People's Democratic State.

Many have said that this Government is a Kerensky Government. But, at the same time, one should not forget the other significant fact that in our country we have not yet a strong Bolshevik Party like that of Russia. We say yes, it is a Government of compromise, it is a Government of national surrender, it is a Government of collaborators. But, at the same time, we must keep in mind that it is a Government manned by those who still have the loyalty and admiration of a good section of the people. To be a Marxist and forget this fact will land us in very serious difficulties. We must consistently and continuously unmask before the masses the compromising, collaborating face of this Government. Our first job today is to run an unceasing campaign and win the majority of the masses over to our side. It is this alone that will enable us to achieve our objective of replacing the present collaborationist Government by a Government representing the workers, peasants and other sections of the petty bourgeoisie.

Therefore, our immediate task is to win the majority of the working class, the peasantry, the toiling masses, to mobilise the people through partial struggles. How quickly we are able to develop these struggles, how quickly we are able to develop the consciousness of the working class, how quickly the independent strength of the Communist Party is developed—on these main factors depend the future of our country. Mobilise the people through the partial struggles, through the political struggles, into a common stream and give it a common consciousness, a clear understanding that the essential changes, the abolition of landlordism, the nationalisation of industries, in a word, the programme of the democratic revolution cannot be achieved without a Government based on the working class, peasantry and middle classes.

How is the slogan of Democratic Front fundamentally different from our old slogan of Congress–League–Communist unity? The old slogan was a slogan based on the oppositional role of the Congress leadership and the national bourgeoisie. We then said: Here is a national movement; strengthen it and fight for it. We tried to make the Congress the basis of the anti-imperialist front. Later on, when we said Congress–League-Communist joint front, it was our idea of the maximum unity and mobilisation of the people for the purpose of the common fight against imperialism. Today, because the bourgeois leadership is no longer oppositional, because the bourgeois leadership is collaborationist, the main brunt of the fight falls on the Party of the working class. Our responsibility has tremendously increased. The national bourgeoisie is playing a disruptive role. We have to achieve the maximum unity of the people, fighting the bourgeois policy of compromise. Our task, therefore, is one of fighting its policy, of defeating its policy. Here, therefore, is the basic shift in which the main unity of the people must be based on the working class and its Party and the mass organisations behind the Communist Party.

In fact, our whole outlook towards reforms must be really Communist. We have always considered reforms as by-products of revolutionary struggles. We will take them. Every quarter of a loaf of bread that we win must become a weapon in the fight for the whole bread. In working-class struggles, in agrarian struggles, because we failed to understand the depth of the movement, we began to apply the old criteria whenever small concessions were won and boost them up as something big that had been achieved. But, in fact, those concessions were won out of the fear of the masses developed by the bourgeoisie. We have tended to welcome minor reforms as major victories and thus slow down the tempo of agrarian revolution. We have to understand the tempo of the present struggle. The programme is there; the urgent question is: what is the relation between the programme and the immediate movement? Till now we were only propagandists. We are now in a new period in which, in fighting for the immediate realisation of this programme of democratic revolution, we consolidate and strengthen the Democratic Front.

~

LAKSHMI N. MENON

Republic Day Broadcast to the People of Goa

By 1960, Goa remained the only part of Indian territory under foreign control. The Government of India under the leadership of Jawaharlal Nehru mobilized international support and internal consensus to free Goa of Portuguese control. Nehru was scathing in his attack on international powers, including the US, whose support had legitimized the Portuguese occupation of Goa. Goa was finally liberated in 1961 following a military operation. Lakshmi Menon, the deputy minister for foreign affairs in the central government, addressed the people of Goa in the course of the Republic Day broadcast by All India Radio in 1962.

Today we are celebrating perhaps the first Republic Day of India; for without Goa the freedom of India was incomplete, not to say inadequate. For four hundred and fifty years Portugal and France held on to certain regions of India and the efforts of the Republic of India to get these territories back succeeded with France but failed with Portugal. Negotiations failed; for fourteen years the people of Goa and the other territories were subjected to hardships of various kinds and they were denied the advantages of freedom and comradeship with the rest of the mother country. Then the people of Dadra and Nagar Haveli liberated themselves and declared their wish to be merged with India, which has taken place to the joy and satisfaction of all of us. Today, the rest of the Portuguese territories, Daman, Diu and Goa, have also joined their motherland and hence this is a happy occasion, a day of rejoicing, a day also to take our pledge for the future.

The first fine rapture of freedom will subside, and in its place we have to develop a faith in our common destiny, a dedication to work hard for the realisation and fulfilment of that common destiny. Many of us, by long familiarity have accepted inequalities, the contrast of opulence and poverty, as the necessary evils of human society. Yet we see in the West as well as in many so-called backward social systems, a method of producing wealth and a juster method of distribution by which dirt, poverty and disease are gradually eliminated. Countries which have been under colonial administration and denied the opportunity to work in freedom are characterised by an unhealthy dependence on external sources for their needs and an indifference to utilise their internal resources for their own development. The great strides taken by India during the period of her freedom show how by cooperative human effort we can achieve things undreamt of and bring happiness to ourselves and others in need.

All of us are proud of our great heritage of tolerance and social traditions which have enabled us not only to resist the impact of other cultures but also to hang on to prejudices and values which are perhaps out of place in a progressive society. India is a secular state in which the followers of all faiths are given equal status and recognition and equal freedom to preach and practice the respective faiths. The State does not give any subvention to any particular faith or encourage any denomination. The strength of the religion is the faith of the believer, and full freedom is given to the followers of the different faiths to carry on their work without let or hindrance, and indeed without any financial assistance from the administration.

The fact that many religions have flourished in the country where the minarets, spires and gopurams mingle in harmony and where the muezzin's call is accompanied by temple and church bells is a symbol of our tolerance. This spirit of tolerance should be seen in our daily life and activities, in our dealings with others, in the understanding of our problems and our effort to realise the common destiny of our people. May we, the people of India, realise the great responsibility which has come to us and join hands to pursue the tasks which lie ahead of us. Today, on the auspicious occasion of our First United Republic Day, let us take one pledge—not to stop working till we have made our green and pleasant country the land of dreams for our children. Jai Hind.

9

THE ASSASSINATION OF MAHATMA GANDHI

Mahatma Gandhi was assassinated on 30 January 1948 by Nathuram Godse. Contemporary accounts, the testimony of Nathuram's brother Gopal Godse, and circumstantial evidence pieced together by the Justice Jivan Lal Kapoor Commission, appointed in 1965 by the central government to ascertain the facts of conspiracy behind the murder, found that the assassination was the result of an all-round campaign of hate against Gandhi organized by Hindu communalists.

The assassination shocked not only the country but the entire world. Given the stature of Gandhi, his contribution to India's freedom struggle, the extraordinary work he had undertaken over the previous year in reining the communal madness that had overtaken the nation, and his presence in the public consciousness, this was understandable. Popular reaction to the killing ranged from outrage and indignation to a surprising advocacy of the need to act responsibly and adhere to the teachings of the departed leader. As Swami Ranganathananda of the Ramakrishna Mission aptly put it, 'Even those who were critical and doubtful about some of his recent policies have become, after the tragedy, deeply affected by the personality of Gandhiji and the strength it has been to the national cause. The entire nation is thus with Gandhiji today in a much more real sense...'

The response of the Congress leadership, many of whom had been colleagues of Gandhi through the years of the freedom struggle, brings out the significance of his presence amidst them. While the

Congress leaders displayed the composure they had shown during the course of the largest mass movement in modern history, one can feel in their reactions a deep sense of loss and an attempt to come to terms with the magnitude of the tragedy. Though a sense of helplessness is palpable in their responses, leaders like Sardar Patel and Nehru also articulated the responsibilities that Gandhi's demise left on their shoulders. Patel, for example, reminded people of their responsibilities, coaxing them not to 'lose heart'.

Expressing the collective sense of loss was Jawaharlal Nehru's broadcast. 'The light has gone out of our lives,' said Nehru. He found 'darkness everywhere'—a sentiment echoed by the country. Nehru was verbalizing not only a personal loss but that of an entire civilization. One sympathizes with him and the leadership when he says, '…we will not run to him for advice and seek solace from him'. Nehru, who more than anyone else was aware of world history, was also expressing the loss of Gandhi in the context of the world: 'For that light represented something more than the immediate present; it represented the living, the eternal truths, reminding us of the right path, drawing us from error, taking this ancient country to freedom.'

S.A. Dange's response located the assassination in the context of Gandhi's political beliefs. A critic of Gandhi and the way he conducted the freedom movement, the communist leader gave a different perspective to the killing. According to him, Gandhi was murdered neither for his philosophy nor because he was a saint. He was killed because he wanted to politically intervene in the struggle for freedom in a way inimical to the thinking of certain people and their political ideology.

~

VALLABHBHAI PATEL

Do Not Lose Heart

Sardar Vallabhbhai Patel (1875–1950) had been Mahatma Gandhi's right-hand man since the days of the Bardoli satyagraha of 1928. He was for all practical purposes the man who shaped the organization of the Congress since the 1920s. As India's first home minister, his was a trial by fire in the aftermath of partition. The violence that marked the country's independence and partition culminated in the assassination of Gandhi. As home minister,

Patel was criticized for the breach of security and inefficiency was insinuated. These events must have taken a heavy toll. But true to his sense of duty and his reputation as 'the iron man of India', in his address to the nation on the evening of 30 January 1948, he strove to inspire confidence and composure in the people. While remorse at the tragedy is very discernible, the speech also informs the people of the country of what happened and what their responsibilities were at this hour of trial.

My heart is full of grief and sorrow! I do not know what to say to you. What happened today is a matter of grief and shame.

I went to see Mahatmaji today at four o'clock in the afternoon and was with him for an hour. At five, he took out his watch and told me that it was time for his prayers; and, as he walked towards the prayer-ground, I left Birla House for my place. As soon as I arrived at my house, I was given the ghastly news.

On going back to Birla House immediately, I saw him after the tragedy. His face had the same calm and serene expression. Kindness and forgiveness were writ large on his face.

Of late, Gandhiji was dissatisfied with the state of affairs in the country. The fast which he undertook recently was an outcome of it. How good would it have been if he had laid down his life during that fast! But he had work to do and he survived it. A bomb was thrown on him by a misguided youth the other day, and he escaped that also but today his life could not be spared for us.

The occasion today is for grief and not anger. Anger is sure to make us forget the great teachings which Gandhiji preached all his life. We did not take his advice during his life and let it not be said that we did not follow him even after his death. That will be a great blot on our name.

Whatever we may feel, we must not forget that now is the test for us. We must stand firmly and solidly without any division in our ranks. The burden which of late India has been called upon to bear is a tremendous one. It would have broken our backs if we had not the support of that great man. That support has now gone. But Gandhiji will still be with us always because his teachings and noble ideals will always be before us. Tomorrow at 4 p.m. his body will turn into ashes but his soul will be with us for all times to come because it is eternal.

What could not be achieved during his lifetime may be fulfilled now! This ghastly tragedy may startle the conscience of the young men of India and make them alive to their duty. Do not lose heart. Stand together and complete the work started by Mahatma Gandhi.

~

JAWAHARLAL NEHRU

The Light Has Gone Out

Gandhi and Nehru were two completely contrasting personalities who differed on a number of issues like modernity, civilization, socialism and capitalism, the role of the machine in a modern state. Yet, they understood each other and respected each other's judgements. There was no denying the strong bond between the two. Gandhi had for all practical purposes anointed Nehru his successor to lead the country through its birth as an independent nation. Nehru's sense of grief and helplessness come across clearly in the poignant speech broadcast on All India Radio on the evening of 30 January 1948. It gives a glimpse into the intimate relationship that existed between two individuals who more than anyone else shaped the modern Indian nation.

Friends and Comrades, the light has gone out of our lives and there is darkness everywhere. I do not know what to tell you and how to say it. Our beloved leader, Bapu as we called him, the Father of the Nation, is no more. Perhaps I am wrong to say that. Nevertheless, we will not see him again as we have seen him for these many years. We will not run to him for advice and seek solace from him, and that is a terrible blow, not to me only but to millions and millions in this country. And it is a little difficult to soften the blow by any other advice that I or anyone else can give you.

The light has gone out, I said, and yet I was wrong. For the light that shone in this country was no ordinary light. The light that has illumined this country for these many many years will illumine this country for many more years, and a thousand years later, that light will still be seen in this country and the world will see it and it will give solace to innumerable hearts. For that light represented something more than the immediate present; it represented the living, the eternal truths, reminding us of the right path, drawing us from error, taking this ancient country to freedom.

All this has happened when there was so much more for him to do. We could never think that he was unnecessary or that he had done his task. But now, particularly, when we are faced with so many difficulties, his not being with us is a blow most terrible to bear.

A madman has put an end to his life, for I can only call him mad who did it and yet there has been enough of poison spread in this country during the past years and months, and this poison has had an effect on people's minds. We must face this poison, we must root out this poison, and we must face all the perils that encompass us, and face them not madly or badly, but rather in the way that our beloved teacher taught us to face them.

The first thing to remember now is that none of us dare misbehave because he is angry. We have to behave like strong and determined people, determined to face all the perils that surround us, determined to carry out the mandate that our great teacher and our great leader has given us, remembering always that if, as I believe, his spirit looks upon us and sees us, nothing would displease his soul so much as to see that we have indulged in any small behaviour or any violence.

So we must not do that. But that does not mean that we should be weak, but rather that we should, in strength and in unity, face all the troubles that are in front of us. We must hold together, and all our petty troubles and difficulties and conflicts must be ended in the face of this great disaster. A great disaster is a symbol to us to remember all the big things of life and forget the small things of which we have thought too much. In his death he has reminded us of the big things of life, the living truth, and if we remember that, then it will be well with India...

It was proposed by some friends that Mahatmaji's body should be embalmed for a few days to enable millions of people to pay their last homage to him. But it was his wish, repeatedly expressed, that no such thing should happen, that this should not be done, that he was entirely opposed to any embalming of his body, and so we decided that we must follow his wishes in this matter, however much others might have wished otherwise.

And so the cremation will take place on Saturday in Delhi city by the side of the Jumna river. On Saturday forenoon, about 11.30, the pier will be taken out at Birla House and it will follow a prescribed route and go to the Jumna river. The cremation will take place there at about 4 p.m. The place and route will be announced by radio and the Press.

People in Delhi who wish to pay their last homage should gather along this route. I will not advise too many of them to come to Birla House, but rather to gather on both sides of this long route from Birla House to the Jumna river. And I trust that they will remain there in silence without any demonstrations. That is the best way and the most fitting way to pay homage to this great soul. Also, Saturday should be a day of fasting and prayer for all of us.

Those who live elsewhere, out of Delhi and in other parts of India, will no doubt also take such part as they can in this last homage. For them also, let this be a day of fasting and prayer. And at the appointed time for cremation, that is 4 p.m. on Saturday afternoon, people should go to the river or to the sea and offer prayers there. And while we pray, the greatest prayer that we can offer is to take a pledge to dedicate ourselves to the truth, and to the cause for which this great countryman of ours lived and for which he has died. That is the best prayer that we can offer him and his memory. That is the best prayer that we can offer to India and ourselves. Jai Hind.

~

SRIPAD AMRIT DANGE

Mahatma Gandhi's Death

S.A. Dange was one of the founders of the communist movement in India. A brilliant student, Dange left his studies quite early to participate in the national movement. He went on to become the undisputed leader of the Bombay textile labourers, and as secretary of the Girni Kamgar Union organized the historic strike against mill owners in 1928. In February 1948, when the formal proposal for a condolence motion on the assassination of Mahatma Gandhi was moved in the Bombay Legislative Assembly, Dange spoke with a passion and directness that symbolized his political style and character. He not only attacked the assassins but also directed his anger at the political ideology behind the killing. Even at this stage, when most mourners only eulogized the departed, Dange did not give up his original critical position on Gandhi's politics, criticizing him for siding with capitalists and for failing to lead a social revolution. This is what makes his obituary different from other run-of-the-mill condolence speeches.

Sir, I join in the deep sorrow and condolence that the Honourable Premier has expressed in moving the Resolution which is now before us. The condolence that this House expresses is not a formal matter, because this House, according to its own claims and according to the constitution under which it functions, is supposed to speak for the people. The condolence of a democratic body cannot be a formal affair, just recounting the good deeds and the philosophies of the man who died—in this case the 'Founder of the Indian nation', like Mahatma Gandhi. While one may analyse his life, and take lessons from his philosophy, it is our responsibility today to give to the public, who have sent us to this House, a clear-cut directive as to what is their duty in the face of the dastardly murder that took place of one of the greatest men in the world. Mahatma Gandhi was murdered and people go on arguing about his philosophy. But he was not murdered for his philosophy; he was not murdered because he was a Saint; he was not murdered because of his experiments with diet; he was not murdered because he was a journalist; nor was he murdered because he wrote beautiful Gujarati. No, he was not murdered because he was a saint; saints are not murdered. He was murdered because he intervened in the political affairs of this country in his own way and his intervention in the political conditions of this country on the crucial point of Hindu-Muslim Unity was not liked by communal reactionaries. He was guilty of this one single sin and for that particular sin he was murdered—not because he preached peace, love and brotherhood in the abstract. He preached love between the landlords and the tenants and many landlords and their sympathisers who are in the Government or outside it took action against the tenants because they too wanted peace, love and brotherhood among the *Kisans* on the basis of abolishing landlordism. Fire and sword were used against these *Kisans*, but the infuriated *Kisans* did not threaten to murder Mahatma Gandhi in their holy anger. No, no peasant ever thought of killing the Mahatma on the ground that the Governments which were established with his blessings denied to the peasant even the ordinary democratic rights. No Warli peasant, no worker, no communist murdered him. It is the reaction of the princes, landlords and Capitalists which organised itself, conspired and murdered him! In one of the speeches made here today, I was surprised to hear the plea for forgiveness even in this case. I do not stand for forgiveness in this respect and, therefore, while joining wholeheartedly in the tributes paid to the Mahatma's great services, I do not join in the call for forgiveness. Uproot the policy, the conspirators and their supporters, who committed this foul murder. That should have been the ringing call at the end of the resolution which is placed before us today. However, I am not adding any amendments to the resolution.

Sir, according to me, we are not here today to write the Mahatma's biography. History has yet to evaluate his contribution to the struggle for national freedom and world freedom. However, one cannot deny he was as much the product of his times as other great men. The great movements that he launched were the products of the world crisis and not the products of merely his will, genius or love. The 1920 movement, the 1930 movement, the 1940 movement and the 1942 movement—all were born out of the world crisis in which society of exploiters was collapsing. Mahatma Gandhi had the genius to seize the opportunity and impress the crisis in his own way.

In 1948 after the division of India, he told us that if the people based their activities on the Hindu-Muslim hatred and involved two great communities in a war—if that be their guiding principle—then the people of both the states would surely come to ruin. His advice was not heeded. The leadership of the Governments had failed to solve a single problem of people's needs and to organise democracy against the exploiters for a real peaceful life; ... To drown this, the reactionaries let loose communal strife...when they found that Mahatma Gandhi was trying to establish Hindu-Muslim unity... To avoid a civil war, they conspired and murdered him. The Premier spoke of personal security, and people taking the law in their own hands. The reactionaries had so manned the whole bureaucratic structure the Government could not offer personal security even to the greatest Indian. What kind of personal security is there in this country? What kind of law and order have we in this country? The person of Mahatma Gandhi could not be protected by Governments which were conducted by his own disciples. If the House will permit me—I do not think it is within our rights today—I would move a Resolution impeaching the Government who failed to protect the life of Mahatma Gandhi. All these months, these Governments had time to suppress only the legitimate struggles of workers, peasants and students for simple democratic rights but they did nothing to prevent the spread of the virulent poison that was being injected in the life of society by the R.S.S. leadership. What kind of law and order does exist in this country? While workers are shot down for conducting peaceful strikes, an organisation of two million men, an organisation based purely on the doctrine of reactionary force was allowed to carry on its activities uninterrupted! In these circumstances, it is no wonder that people should try to take possession of law and order because they know that the law and order which exists is for the exploiters and against the exploited. So the lesson that we ought to learn from this great tragedy—it is a cruel lesson—is that there is a huge conspiracy in this country to involve the two States in a war, to establish a Fascist military dictatorship in this country and drown the peoples' struggles for decent life and living. That is the essence of this conspiracy and its first victim was Mahatma Gandhi, because he stood against such a Hindu-Muslim war. For our future guidance, we must note the warning that Mahatma Gandhi gave as his last act, namely, that there should be complete Hindu-Muslim unity in this country and no war between the two States. All through his life he preached non-violence, although his so-called non-violent struggles against the British rule always led to violent risings. He himself admitted it but he said that he was not responsible for it. And finally he added that he preferred holy violence for the defence of the people to non-violent retreat in cowardice. Therefore rely on the people to do that. The people have expressed their anger on the action of the murderer and on the murderous organisation and their supporters. That anger should be controlled and well directed and not condemned, because it is the people alone who can defend their democracy,... When even the papers containing the evidence against the murderer have disappeared from the strongly guarded police bags, can we rely upon the State? No; we cannot. Therefore, we must rely on the people. Yes, it is the people's tribunal which should judge the murderer, it is the people's tribunal which will judge those princes, landlords and capitalists who defended the murderous organisation and financed it. It is the people's tribunal which will judge the actions of those who occupy the high seats of Government and who, by their statements, gave a certificate of patriotism to this reactionary movement aimed at the people. With that lesson, Sir, I would again say that the death of Mahatma Gandhi is a great loss to the country and to the people, but it is not a loss because, as some say, the experiment of non-violence would be ended. No. While the leonine violence is being conducted on the side of the very Governments which sing his praises, the experiment of non-violence, that is real peaceful society, will be conducted on the side of the people alone and certainly real peace, love and brotherhood will prevail only when the working class and peasantry are in charge of the State and when a socialist democracy is organised in this country. It is this lesson that we have to draw. We must beware of the enemies of the toiling people and we should not prevent the people from properly expressing their holy anger and hatred against their enemies, the exploiters.

~

SWAMI RANGANATHANANDA

The Legacy of Mahatma Gandhi

Born as Shankaran Kutty, Swami Ranganathananda (1908–2005) joined the Ramakrishna Mission in 1926 and rose to become one of the most powerful exponents of the message of not only the Mission but also of Indian society and its values. He served the Mission in Rangoon and Karachi. As president of the Ramakrishna Math, he was a brilliant and influential advocate of Indian philosophical and religious ideas for over fifty years. Swami Ranganathananda lived the last days of his life in the headquarters of the Ramakrishna Mission at Belur, West Bengal. In this speech delivered at the premises of the Ramakrishna Math and Mission in Karachi on 15 February 1948, Ranganathananda places Gandhi in the long civilizational history of the world and tries to analyse the reasons behind the universal condemnation of the assassination.

It is, indeed, a happy occasion for us all this evening to gather here in this Math premises in order to remember the greatness of Mahatma Gandhi and to pay our respectful homage to him. It is now sixteen days since he passed away; these have been days of national and international mourning. Never before in history has the death of an individual evoked human sorrow on so vast a scale. From the response that Gandhiji's passing away has evoked from millions and millions of people in India and abroad, we can have an idea of the great thirst in the hearts of men and women today for the universal and abiding spiritual and moral values which the great martyr strove so successfully to express in his fully lived life of 79 years. This form of universal appreciation of the nobility of Mahatma Gandhi's life and character strengthens us in our faith that the heart of man is sound and that it can stand up against the creeping cynicism of the age, and greet, in hopeful joy, greatness which is fundamental and benevolence which is universal.

The nation has mourned and, while mourning, has also done a

certain amount of heart-searching. The truly great benefit the world as much by their death as by their life. The death of Gandhiji has produced a wave of revulsion against the communal poison which was creeping relentlessly into the Indian body-politic and has roused the nation—now divided into India and Pakistan—to a sense of its duty and responsibility. There is urgent need for re-thinking on the part of our people and for assessing the nature and scope of the great legacy bequeathed to us by our departed leader.

There is no denying the fact that the manner and circumstances of Gandhiji's death make of it an unparalleled tragedy. Even natural death in his case would have been a national calamity. The extraordinary measure of tragedy in this case proceeds from the anomaly and unnaturalness of that death—the death, at the hands of an assassin, of one who was an embodiment of gentleness and love and who had no enemies. In all such cases, the assassin strives to play the part of the hero; but in this case, the entire episode, beginning with the arrival of the gentle and harmless Gandhiji, unprotected, at the prayer ground, and moving to its climax in the stepping forward of the assassin and his firing, at point blank range while feigning to bow down in salute, reveals it as the meanest and most cowardly among the assassinations of world history. Leaders, well protected by the military and the police, and shielded by every conceivable precautionary measure, have yet been assassinated in various parts of the world by reckless individuals. Any person, however protected he may be, can be assaulted, insulted, or killed by another who is so determined. There is, therefore, nothing very extraordinary or special about the circumstance of one Godse assassinating a person like Mahatma Gandhi, who was, though fearless, childlike and approachable by all.

But there is one important feature of this tragedy which gives us cause for hope; this relates to the public reaction to the tragedy. I would like to lay particular emphasis on this point which, I fear, has been somewhat overlooked in the general sorrow of the hour. The universal condemnation of the assassination, and the expression of spontaneous loyalty by millions and millions of people in this country and abroad to the person of the great leader, and their resolve to follow his lead, constitute an invaluable legacy of hope and cheer left to humanity by Gandhiji, through his fruitful life crowned by an equally fruitful death. The steadying influence of that final service of his is already becoming visible on the tortured mind and face of our nation.

The world honoured, respected, and loved Gandhiji in his lifetime; it honours, respects and loves him today, after his death, a thousand times more. This is a rare phenomenon in history; in fact, we have hardly a parallel instance. Those who spoke in terms of national guilt may have had in mind the crucifixion of Jesus. In the case of Jesus, apart from his eleven disciples, almost all of whom denied their master at the moment of crisis, and a handful of devotees who clung fast to him throughout, all else around him considered him a weak undesirable person and an impostor, deserving of that sad end; there were only a handful of people to mourn his death, but that too privately. But that has not detracted from the greatness of Jesus or the truth of his message, or from the fruitfulness, to be realised later, of that supreme tragedy at Calvary. But in the case of Gandhiji, barring the members of a small unworthy gang who seem to have planned the nefarious act before, and appreciated it after, the entire world of mankind, both inside India and outside, mourns his loss as a personal bereavement and as a human calamity. Not only that; the Indian nation gave a royal send-off to the mortal remains of the great 'Father of the Nation'.

The New Testament gospels depict the moving scenes of the Christ tragedy in the last chapters. The tragedy begins with the arrest of Jesus by the Roman soldiers with the help of one of his own disciples, Judas, and then moves onward with deepening intensity. Jesus is insulted, slapped, made to carry his own cross, and crowned with a crown of thorns. The drama becomes pathetic when his own disciples, out of selfish fear, deny and forsake him at the moment of crisis; gloom and despair descend on the handful of the faithful when the tragedy reaches its climax at Calvary. It will be fruitful to compare this with the present tragedy; here we find everything reversed from the beginning to the end. And after the tragedy, the affirmations of loyalty have become tumultuous; and gloom and despair have descended, not on the multitudes of the faithful whose only share is sorrow at the bereavement, but on the foolish few who constitute the misguided group of murderers. Even those who were critical and doubtful about some of his recent policies have become, after the tragedy, deeply affected by the personality of Gandhiji and the strength it has been to the national cause. The entire nation is thus with Gandhiji today in a much more real sense than what we can say regarding any other political leader in the world, past or present.

Among contemporary leaders of people, Gandhiji stands alone in his eminence and uniqueness. His is the staggering example of a leader who practiced what he professed and gave out to the people only what he had tested in his own life, whether it be in the fields of politics or economics, religion or personal morality.

... He passionately worked to increase the moral stature of the Indian people and to better their material conditions; he struggled with a singular passion to wipe away the stain of long standing social injustice on the body-politic, to give cheer to the oppressed, and redeem the lowly and the lost; he endeavoured to impart to the nation the inspiration of a religion of divine love and human service; he successfully worked our programmes intended to instil courage and dignity in the two neglected sections of Indian society, namely, women and the masses; he readily responded to individual appeals for help, advice, and guidance in the fields of life, ranging from personal and spiritual problems, to dietetics and health, care of the infant and the village cattle, down to the problems of the profitable utilisation of human refuse and dead cattle.

In the context of [India's] political struggles and social aspirations, Gandhiji stands as a symbol, as an archetypal man. To every one of our problems in these fields, we have seen him responding with a readiness, as if he and the national environment were fused into one. This type of identification with the achievements and sufferings of a struggling nation of 400 million people is what makes him a leader of a unique type, a true representative of the ideals and aspirations of the people, whom he leads, without being led by their passing whims and moods, as is the case with most leaders of the world—a unique leader of struggling people.

... Gandhiji is the example of a leader who is not guided by the passing moods and passions of the populace, but who turns and guides these in the direction of the vision of human excellence he has experienced for himself. His stress on truth and non-violence is the only beacon light in a world enveloped in the darkness of selfishness and exploitation, hatred and violence. He alone could look calmly and compassionately into the blood-shot eyes of contemporary man. Modern world conditions engendered by science and technology call for the transformation of energies of hatred and violence, competition and strife, into the moral forces of cooperation and service, love and peace. The moral education of modern man, in step with his intellectual attainments and technical achievements, is the most urgent task facing humanity today. In India itself, as also in Pakistan, the urgent task is the stilling of communal passions and the channelling of their energies into the moral fields of collective human welfare. The stress on love and service may sound unrealistic in the present national context of suspicion and hatred in the wake of political partition. But in human relations, hatred and destruction can never be a long-term measure. After short spells, it has to be transformed into, and yield place to, love and construction.

By holding high this banner of love and service through thick and thin in the midst of his socio-political programmes and activities, and the banner of truth and non-violence in his personal life, Gandhiji has left an imperishable legacy which, as years pass, humanity in India and elsewhere will recognise as the only values capable of expressing the dignity and worth of man, as the only hope of civilisation and progress, and as the only guarantee of the march of man everywhere to all-round growth and fulfilment.

10

THE CONSTITUTION: EMBODIMENT OF THE NATIONAL SPIRIT

In the history of India's struggle for independence, 15 August 1947 was not an end in itself. With independence, leaders now had to find ways to resolve the many social and economic problems that had merely been debated during the freedom struggle. The idea of the early nationalists that India was a *nation in the making* still held true. The violence in the wake of the partition had demonstrated that the foundations of the Indian nation were not very strong. The nationalist fervour that had forced the British to quit now had to be harnessed to address the issues of poverty, illiteracy and development, commensurate with the development of a democratic and secular polity. These were the considerations that went into the making of the Indian constitution, echoing the spirit of the freedom movement.

Independence had come after a long and arduous struggle. It was quite natural for the aspirations which guided the vision of this struggle to be reflected in the constitution written for the governance of the people. Embedded in India's struggle for independence was a constitutional struggle. Beginning with intellectuals like Surendranath Banerjea and Dadabhai Naoroji, who first articulated the need for greater representation, to Mahatma Gandhi, who advocated the idea of complete severance of colonial ties, nationalists of different hues had put up a legal and constitutional fight of a high intellectual order. Their meditations on swaraj and swadeshi, on what a sovereign state would imply, their critique of the economic order of the colonial state, and their pronouncements on the existing social and economic order and the one envisaged in a free nation shaped the framing of the Indian constitution. It is to the credit of these visionaries that what had taken centuries to evolve in many democratic Western countries, was achieved in a matter of less than a century in India.

The words which appear in the preamble to the constitution—sovereign, democratic, republic—are significant as they not only capture the collective spirit of the times but also a collective resolve. Sovereignty generally indicates the supreme legal and political authority that a state has over its subjects inside its own territory and in some cases even in a foreign territory. It gives a state a distinctive identity in the international system. Sovereignty is quite often treated as a matter of academic discourse or that of legal status. In the case of India, too, imperialist historians, the colonial establishment and some radical quarters in India have tried to argue that the change in sovereignty involved only a transfer of power. A careful study of the struggle for independence, however, demonstrates that there is a more substantial story behind the word 'sovereign' than a mere textbook analysis can ever convey. It shows that juxtaposing the word 'sovereign' with 'democratic' and 'republic' in the preamble was not a mere coincidence but indicative of a deep and symbiotic relationship between them which reflects the will of the people.

Two simultaneous processes made the collective resolve possible. First, there were efforts to constitute 'the people' living in the geographical and colonized territory of India into a nation and second, make them aware of the grounds on which they would demand self-rule for this nation. There was definitely a consciousness of a geographical and cultural terrain called India and a medium through which people had entered into dialogue with each other for centuries. But the idea of being part of an identity called 'nation' and contesting a colonial power was entirely new. This identity needed to be nurtured.

Racial and cultural markers had earlier been used to provide the justification for such a unity. The revolt of 1857 had united a section of the people on religious and racial grounds. These people even wanted to restore the old order. But a large number of people remained untouched and saw British rule as modernizing and enlightened. For decades after the revolt, there continued to be segments of the population who saw British rule with its modern education, communication and rule of law as providing opportunities to emerge from centuries-old servitude. There were also efforts to show racial similarities between Europeans and Aryans who, it was argued, constituted a vast segment of the Indian population. Thus, the use of racial and religious symbols as justification for self-rule was fraught with problems and could never take root.

A very conscious intelligentsia and a political leadership emerged in the nineteenth century to propagate and disseminate these ideals and demands. They poured all their creative energies into uniting Indians as a people, urging them to break the shackles of caste, antiquated traditions and inhuman customs, and strive for a common progressive bond against the colonial power. Only such a progressive unity, they argued, could make the demand for self-rule meaningful and morally and politically justifiable.

The economic critique of the colonial state also intensified the craving for self-rule. That colonial rule, notwithstanding its claims of benevolence, was making Indians poorer by exploiting their economy was brought to the fore by people like Naoroji, G.K. Gokhale, M.G. Ranade and R.C. Dutt. Freedom from economic exploitation and freedom to steer an independent developmental path became a significant component of the people's demand for independence. Now self-rule was demanded for the well-being of the Indian people. There was an increasing congruence in people's well-being and aspirations and the demand for self-rule. The economic critique and its resonance with the people's understanding was so strong that even after years of powerful intellectual and political attacks, it has held firm as the most powerful basis of Indian nationalism.

Those who laid the foundations of this economic nationalism in the late nineteenth and early decades of the twentieth centuries were, however, not demanding complete freedom in the sense of sovereignty for India. They demanded that the British act according to their self-professed sense of justice and law in developing and modernizing India. They demonstrated that the British claims of development were not true and that British rule was actually impoverishing Indians.

Even people like Bal Gangadhar Tilak, Bipin Chandra Pal or Aurobindo Ghose—who were opposed to the early nationalists—did not call for what can be understood as complete freedom. They only came up with a demand for 'swaraj' in 1906 when Dadabhai Naoroji chaired the Calcutta session of the Indian National Congress. Their demand for swaraj envisaged a constitutional arrangement with more powers of representation to Indians. What they highlighted, however, was an increasing loss of faith in the British system of justice. This was significant as only this could have produced sufficient disillusionment among the masses with regard to their belief in British benevolence.

The idea of 'self-rule' (in the sense of sovereignty) was not espoused by the political leadership till the 1920s. This, however, did not mean that they desired colonial rule. They were putting forth the most radical demand of their generation and preparing the grounds for subsequent generations to demand this freedom. The act of demanding total freedom required a people to believe that they could sever relations with their colonial masters and yet survive as a state, as a rule-bound society and a society which could develop, modernize and prosper. This is the confidence that Gandhi instilled in the people when he arrived on the scene in the 1920s. His declaration that he would win swaraj in one year made people realize their own sense of commitment to the idea of freedom. The Gandhian movement prepared a generation of leaders which shaped the idea of 'self-rule' in close ties with the people. In 1928, when the Motilal Nehru Committee, appointed by the All India Congress Committee to draft a constitution, demanded dominion status like that of other British colonies, Australia and Canada, the new leadership which had emerged and captured the imagination of the masses opposed the recommendations and demanded that the Congress put forward the demand for Purna Swaraj.

What was different about the demands for freedom being made in the 1930s was not only that these were demands for nothing less than total freedom but also that these demands were being articulated by the masses. The nationalist awakening witnessed among the intellectual elite in the latter half of the nineteenth century, which had for long remained confined to the Western-educated youth, had spread to the common man. Gandhi had brought the masses to the centre stage, thus providing a popular basis to the demand for sovereignty. This popular involvement also signified the importance of democracy. Sovereignty implied the ability to take decisions for ourselves, and it was only natural that this ability be extended to deciding on the form of government. Given our diversity, democracy was the only way, even though there were some who feared that democracy could mean majority rule. Only in a democratic system of government would people have a sovereign say in the affairs of running the nation. The Constituent Assembly being a representative body with members belonging to different communities and regions of India as also members representing different political persuasions, it is not surprising that the constitution enshrined protective measures for religious and ethnic minorities and women. Through this Constituent Assembly it could be said that the people gave themselves a constitution which made them sovereign. In this way, the constitution truly imbibed one of the ideals of the French Revolution—that of popular sovereignty, advocated by people like Rousseau, which despite its shortcomings had stirred the imagination of so many people over the last century.

Even those who criticized the social and political vision of the freedom struggle approved of the constitution, agreeing that the spirit with which it had been conceived was the surest way to safeguard democracy in a country plagued by poverty and illiteracy. It is a tribute to the vision of its framers that Indian democracy and society still stands tall despite many weaknesses in its body politic, while countries which became independent long after India have either turned towards dictatorship or have disintegrated into chaos.

The composition of the Constituent Assembly, which was responsible for drafting the constitution, was based on the proposal of the Cabinet Mission which had advocated that the recently elected members of the provincial assemblies elect the members of the Constituent Assembly. The people who finally made it to the Constituent Assembly were the most popular leaders of the era. All the presidents of political parties were there as well as those who represented sectional interests, including the president of the Indian Landholders Association, Maharaja Kameshwar Singh of Darbhanga. There were eight chief ministers of provinces including T. Prakasham (Madras), B.G. Kher (CP), Harekrishna Mehtab (Orissa) and Gopinath Bordoloi (Assam). There were members of the Governor General's executive council, speakers of provincial assemblies, and many other prominent public personalities. The chief women representatives were Hansa Mehta, Ammu Swaminathan, Malati Choudhury, Sucheta Kripalani, Purnima Banerjee, Rajkumari Amrit Kaur and Sarojini Naidu. It was, however, the leaders of the national movement, Jawaharlal Nehru, Vallabhbhai Patel, Rajendra Prasad, Govind Ballabh Pant, Maulana Abul Kalam Azad and others, who played an important role in formulating the frame of reference for the constitution and giving it its final shape.

The most striking feature of the Constituent Assembly was the catholicity that was displayed by the Congress as an organization which, in the larger spirit of the national movement, tried to bring representatives of all sections of the population to the Assembly so that their voices could be heard. The Congress saw to it that capable public men were invited to join and contribute to the making of the constitution. Thus it was that they could enlist the services of the great administrator N. Gopalaswamy Ayyangar, the scholar–philosopher Sarvepalli Radhakrishnan, the great legal personality Alladi Krishnaswamy Iyer, the erudite scholar and legal mind Hirday Nath Kunzru, and one of the greatest teachers that Calcutta University has produced, Professor Harindra Kumar Mookherjee who also headed the minority committee. It is this inclusive nature that made the party and its leadership appoint one of its bitterest critics, Dr B.R. Ambedkar, as chairman of the Drafting Committee in August 1947.

On 20 November 1946, H.V.R. Iengar, secretary of the Constituent Assembly, sent the invitation of the viceroy to 296 members to attend the first meeting of the Assembly on 9 December 1946. At this meeting, the Congress president, J.B. Kripalani, requested Dr Sachidananda Sinha, the grand old man of the Imperial Legislative Council (1910–20), to take the chair as temporary chairman of the Assembly. Dr Sinha had not only been in the Imperial Legislative Council but had also been deputy president of the Imperial Legislative Assembly in 1921. The inaugural speech of Dr Sinha added to the grandeur of the occasion when he quoted the poet Iqbal's famous couplet, '*Yunan-o-Misr-o-Roma sab mit gaye jahan se, baki magar hai ab tak naam-o-nishan hamara/Kuch baat hai ki hasti mit'ti nahi hamari, sadiyon se hai dushman daur-e-zaman hamara*' (Greece, Egypt, Rome have all disappeared from the face of the earth; but the name and fame of India, our country, has survived the ravages of time and cataclysm of ages. Surely there is an eternal element in us which has frustrated all attempts to obliterate us).

The issues before the members of the Assembly were many and contentious. The question of the princely states, whom the Cabinet Mission Plan had given ninety-three seats in the Assembly and therefore a dominant voice, had to be resolved. In light of the fact that the Objectives Resolution envisaged setting up a republic, these monarchies, numbering more than 500, presented a real problem. Another issue pertained to the members of the Muslim League who had decided not to join the Assembly. This had to be viewed against the backdrop of the charged communal atmosphere which was gradually dividing areas in Bengal and Punjab into communal war zones. Issues pertaining to caste and language needed to be addressed as well.

The Assembly appointed several committees like the Advisory Committee on Fundamental Rights and Minorities, the Union Power Committee, the Union and Provincial Constitutions Committee, and a Finance Committee. One of the most important committees was the Advisory Committee on Fundamental Rights and Minorities which met for the first time under the chairmanship of Vallabhbhai Patel. In this meeting it appointed five subcommittees on Fundamental Rights, North East Frontier Areas and Assam, North West Frontier Tribal Area, Excluded and Partially Excluded Areas, and Minorities.

These committees submitted their respective reports between April and August 1947. With the inputs from these committees and the notes prepared by various members, the Constitutional Advisor, B.N. Rau, presented a draft with 240 clauses and 13 schedules by October 1947. The draft contained the generally agreed broad outline and the foundation on which the Assembly as well as the Drafting Committee worked to give final shape to the constitution. The Assembly appointed the Drafting Committee on 29 August 1947. The Drafting Committee was 'to scrutinize the draft of the text of the constitution prepared by the constitutional advisor giving effect to the decision taken already in the Assembly and including all matters which are ancillary thereto or which have to be provided in such a constitution, and to submit to the Assembly for consideration the text of the draft constitution as received by the committee'.

From 27 October 1947, the Drafting Committee sat regularly for forty-two days and finally submitted the draft constitution to the president of the Assembly on 21 February 1948. This draft included 315 articles and 8 schedules. The clause-by-clause consideration began on 15 November 1948 and concluded on 17 October 1949. The crucial issue of language was discussed at the end in November 1949 and it turned out to be a passionate, acrimonious and partisan debate. With the language issue settled, the constitution was finally adopted on 26 November and with the election of the president of the Constituent Assembly as the President of the country on 26 January 1950, India came into being as a republic.

VALLABHBHAI PATEL

Speech at the First Meeting of the Advisory Committee on Fundamental Rights

Vallabhbhai Patel was in many ways responsible for giving the nascent nation the confidence of meeting the challenges that lay ahead. A man of few words and deep understanding, he was the architect of the chapter on fundamental rights in the Indian constitution. As chairman of the Advisory Committee on Fundamental Rights and Minorities and through its subcommittees he ensured that minorities were assured all possible rights and that the division of the country over the demand made by a religious minority did not cloud the judgement of the constitution makers. Patel's speech at the first meeting of the Advisory Committee on 27 February 1947, where he speaks of the Indian resolve to have a place for minorities in the new republic, therefore, has a special place in the history of India.

Gentlemen, I thank you most sincerely for the honour—the great honour—that you have conferred upon me by reposing your confidence in electing me as chairman of a committee which is composed of various interests. This committee forms one of the most vital parts of the Constituent Assembly and one of the most difficult tasks that has to be done by us is the work of this committee. Often you must have heard in various debates in British parliament that have been held on this question recently and before when it has been claimed on behalf of the British Government that they have a special responsibility—a special obligation—for the protection of the interests of the minorities. They claim to have more special interest than we have. It is for us to prove that it is a bogus claim, a false claim and that nobody can be more interested than us in India in the protection of our minorities. Our mission is to satisfy every one of them and we hope we shall be able to satisfy every interest and safeguard the interest of all the minorities to their satisfaction. Let us hope that our deliberations will be so conducted that we can disillusion those who are looking with a critical eye from outside that we know how to conduct our business and we know how to rule better than those who claim that they can rule others. At least let us prove we have no ambition to rule others. In this committee, therefore, we begin our work today with a determination and a desire to come to decisions not by majority but by uniformity. Let us sink all our differences and look to one and one interest only, which is the interest of all of us—the interest of India as a whole.

~

JAWAHARLAL NEHRU

The Objectives Resolution

Before the Constituent Assembly could begin its work to frame a constitution for free India it was but appropriate that the leaders of the national movement present before the members of the Assembly, and through them the people, a statement of the principles, objectives and vision of an independent India that they envisioned through a document like the constitution. The Objectives Resolution moved by Jawaharlal Nehru is a watershed event in the history of India. It was presented on 13 December 1946 and was followed by debates on the legality, procedures and other substantive matters contained in the constitution.

I beg to move:

(1) This Constituent Assembly declares its firm and solemn resolve to proclaim India as an Independent Sovereign Republic and to draw up for her future governance a Constitution;
(2) WHEREIN the territories that now comprise British India, the territories that now form the Indian States, and such other parts of India as are outside British India and the States as well as such other territories as are willing to be constituted into the Independent Sovereign India, shall be a Union of them all; and
(3) WHEREIN the said territories, whether with their present boundaries or with such others as may be determined by the Constituent Assembly and thereafter according to the Law of the Constitution, shall possess and retain the status of autonomous Units, together with residuary powers, and exercise all powers and functions of government and administration, save and except such powers and functions as are vested in or assigned to the Union, or as are inherent or implied in the Union or resulting therefrom; and
(4) WHEREIN all power and authority of the Sovereign Independent India, its constituent parts and organs of government, are derived from the people; and

(5) WHEREIN shall be guaranteed and secured to all the people of India justice, social, economic and political; equality of status, of opportunity, and before the law; freedom of thought, expression, belief, faith, worship, vocation, association and action, subject to law and public morality; and
(6) WHEREIN adequate safeguards shall be provided for minorities, backward and tribal areas, and depressed and other backward classes; and
(7) WHEREBY shall be maintained the integrity of the territory of the Republic and its sovereign rights on land, sea, and air according to Justice and the law of civilised nations, and
(8) this ancient land attains its rightful and honoured place in the world and make its full and willing contribution to the promotion of world peace and the welfare of mankind.

Sir, this is the fifth day of this first session of the Constituent Assembly. Thus far we have laboured on certain provisional and procedural matters which are essential. We have a clear field to work upon; we have to prepare the ground and we have been doing that these few days. We have still much to do. We have to pass our Rules of Procedure and to appoint Committees and the like, before we can proceed to the real step, to the real work of this Constituent Assembly, that is, the high adventure of giving shape, in the printed and written word, to a Nation's dream and aspiration. But even now, at this stage, it is surely desirable that we should give some indication to ourselves, to those who look to this Assembly, to those millions in this country who are looking up to us and to the world at large, as to what we may do, what we seek to achieve, whither we are going. It is with this purpose that I have placed this Resolution before this House. It is a Resolution and yet, it is something much more than a resolution. It is a Declaration. It is a firm resolve. It is a pledge and an undertaking and it is for all of us I hope a dedication. And I wish this House, if I may say so respectfully, should consider this Resolution not in a spirit of narrow legal wording, but rather to look at the spirit behind that Resolution. Words are magic things often enough, but even the magic of words sometimes cannot convey the magic of the human spirit and of a Nation's passion. And so, I cannot say that this Resolution at all conveys the passion that lies in the hearts and the minds of the Indian people today. It seeks very feebly to tell the world of what we have thought or dreamt of so long, and what we now hope to achieve in the near future. It is in that spirit that I venture to place this Resolution before the House and it is in that spirit that I trust the House will receive it and ultimately pass it. And may I, Sir, also, with all respect, suggest to you and to the House that when the time comes for the passing of this Resolution let it be not done in the formal way by the raising of hands, but much more solemnly, by all of us standing up and thus taking this pledge anew.

The House knows that there are many absentees here and many members who have a right to come here, have not come. We regret that fact because we should have liked to associate with ourselves as many people, as many representatives from the different parts of India and different groups as possible. We have undertaken a tremendous task and we seek the cooperation of all people in that task; because the future of India that we have envisaged is not confined to any group or section or province or other, but it comprises all the four hundred million people of India, and it is with deep regret that we find some benches empty and some colleagues, who might have been here, absent. I do feel, I do hope that they will come and that this House, in its future stages, will have the benefit of the cooperation of all. Meanwhile, there is a duty cast upon us and that is to bear the absentees in mind, to remember always that we are here not to function for one party or one group, but always to think of India as a whole and always to think of the welfare of the four hundred millions that comprise India. We are all now, in our respective spheres, partymen, belonging to this or that group and presumably we shall continue to act in our respective parties. Nevertheless, the time comes when we have to rise above party and think of the Nation, think sometimes of even the world at large of which our Nation is a great part. And when I think of the work of this Constituent Assembly, it seems to me, the time has come when we should, so far as we are capable of it, rise above our ordinary selves and party disputes and think of the great problem before us in the widest and most tolerant and most effective manner so that, whatever we may produce, should be worthy of India as a whole and should be such that the world should recognise that we have functioned, as we should have functioned, in this high adventure.

There is another person who is absent here and who must be in the minds of many of us today—the great leader of our people, the father of our Nation (applause)—who has been the architect of this Assembly and all that has gone before it and possibly of much that will follow. He is not here because, in pursuit of his ideals, he is ceaselessly working in a far corner of India. But I have no doubt that his spirit hovers over this place and blesses our undertaking.

As I stand here, Sir, I feel the weight of all manner of things crowding around me. We are at the end of an era and possibly very soon we shall embark upon a new age; and my mind goes back to the great past of India to the 5000 years of India's history, from the very dawn of that history which might be considered almost the dawn of human history, till today. All that past crowds around me and exhilarates me and, at the same time, somewhat oppresses me. Am I worthy of that past? When I think also of the future, the greater future I hope, standing on this sword's edge of the present between this mighty past and the mightier future, I tremble a little and feel overwhelmed by this mighty task. We have come here at a strange moment in India's history. I do not know but I do feel that there is some magic in this moment of transition from the old to the new, something of that magic which one sees when the night turns into day and even though the day may be a cloudy one, it is day after all, for when the clouds move away we can see the sun later on. Because of all this I find a little difficulty in addressing this House and putting all my ideas before it and I feel also that in this long succession of thousands of years, I see the mighty figures that have come and gone and I see also the long succession of our comrades who have laboured for the freedom of India. And now we stand on the verge of this passing age, trying, labouring, to usher in the new. I am sure the House will feel the solemnity of this moment and will endeavour to treat this Resolution which it is my proud privilege to place before it in that solemn manner. I believe there are a large number of amendments coming before the House. I have not seen most of them. It is open to the House, to any member of this House, to move any amendment and it is for the House to accept it or reject it, but I would, with all respect, suggest that this is not the moment for us to be technical and legal about small matters when we have big things to face, big things to say and big things to do, and therefore I would hope that the House would consider this Resolution in this big manner and not lose itself in wordy quarrels and squabbles.

I think also of the various Constituent Assemblies that have gone before and of what took place at the making of the great American nation when the fathers of that nation met and fashioned out a constitution which has stood the test of so many years, more than a century and a half, and of the great nation which has resulted, which has been built up on the basis of that constitution. My mind goes back to that mighty revolution which took place also over 150 years ago and to that Constituent Assembly that met in that gracious and lovely city of Paris which has fought so many battles for freedom, to the difficulties that that Constituent Assembly had and to how the King and other authorities came in its way, and still it continued. The House will remember that when these difficulties came and even the room for a meeting was denied to the then Constituent Assembly, they betook themselves to an open tennis court and met there and took the oath, which is called the Oath of the Tennis Court, that they continued meeting in spite of Kings, in spite of the others, and did not disperse till they had finished the task they had undertaken. Well, I trust that it is in that solemn spirit that we too are meeting here and that we, too, whether we meet in this chamber or other Chambers, or in the fields or in the market-place, will go on meeting and continue our work till we have finished it.

Then my mind goes back to a more recent revolution which gave rise to a new type of State, the revolution that took place in Russia and out of which has arisen the Union of the Soviet Socialist Republics, another mighty country which is playing a tremendous part in the world, not only a mighty country but for us in India, a neighbouring country.

So our mind goes back to these great examples and we seek to learn from their success and to avoid their failures. Perhaps we may not be able to avoid failures because some measure of failure is inherent in human effort. Nevertheless, we shall advance, I am certain in spite of obstructions and difficulties, and achieve and realise the dream that we have dreamt so long. In this Resolution which the House knows has been drafted with exceeding care, we have tried to avoid saying too much or too little. It is difficult to frame a resolution of this kind. If you say too little, it becomes just a pious resolution and nothing more. If you say too much, it encroaches on the functions of those who are going to draw up a constitution, that is, on the functions of this House. This Resolution is not a part of the constitution we are going to draw up and it must not be looked at as such. This House has perfect freedom to draw up that constitution and when others come into this House, they will have perfect freedom too to fashion that constitution. This Resolution therefore steers between these two extremes and lays down only certain fundamentals which I do believe no group or party and hardly any individual in India can dispute. We say that it is our firm and solemn resolve to have an independent sovereign republic. India is bound to be sovereign, it is bound to be independent and it is bound to be a republic. I will not go into the arguments about monarchy and the rest, but obviously we cannot produce monarchy in India out of nothing. It is not there. If it is to be an independent and sovereign State, we are not going to have an external monarchy and we cannot have a research for some local monarchies. It must inevitably be a republic. Now, some friends have raised the question: 'Why have you not put in the word "democratic" here.' Well, I told them that it is conceivable, of course, that a republic may not be democratic but the whole of our past is witness to this fact that we stand for democratic institutions. Obviously we are aiming at democracy and nothing less than a democracy. What form of democracy, what shape it might take is another matter. The democracies of the present day, many of them in Europe and elsewhere, have played a great part in the world's progress. Yet it may be doubtful if those democracies may not have to change their shape somewhat before long if they have to remain completely democratic. We are not going just to copy, I hope, a certain democratic procedure or an institution of a so-called democratic country. We may improve upon it. In any event whatever system of government we may establish here must fit in with the temper of our people and be acceptable to them. We stand for democracy, it will be for this House to determine what shape to give to that democracy, the fullest democracy, I hope. The House will notice that in this Resolution, although we have not used the word 'democratic' because we thought it is obvious that the word 'republic' contains that word and we did not want to use unnecessary words and redundant words, but we have done something much more than using the word. We have given the content of democracy in this Resolution and not only the content of democracy but the content, if I may say so, of economic democracy in this Resolution. Others might take objection to this Resolution on the ground that we have not said that it should be a Socialist State. Well, I stand for Socialism and, I hope, India will stand for Socialism and that India will go towards the constitution of a Socialist State and I do believe that the whole world will have to go that way. What form of Socialism again is another matter for your consideration. But the main thing is that in such a Resolution, if, in accordance with my own desire, I had put in, that we want a Socialist State, we would have put in something which may be agreeable to many and may not be agreeable to some and we wanted this Resolution not to be controversial in regard to such matters. Therefore we have laid down, not theoretical words and formulae, but rather the content of the thing we desire. This is important and I take it there can be no dispute about it. Some people have pointed out to me that our mentioning a republic may somewhat displease the Rulers of Indian States. It is possible that this may displease them. But I want to make it clear personally and the House knows that I do not believe in the monarchical system anywhere, and that in the world today monarchy is a fast disappearing institution. Nevertheless it is not a question of my personal belief in this matter. Our view in regard to these Indian States has been, for many years, first of all that the people of those States must share completely in the freedom to come. It is quite inconceivable to me that there should be different standards and degrees of freedom as between the people in the States and people outside the States. In what manner the States will be parts of that Union, that is a matter for this House to consider with the representatives of the States. And I hope in all matters relating to the States, this House will deal with the real representatives of the States. We are perfectly willing, I take it, to deal in such matters as appertain to them, with the Rulers or their representatives also, but finally when we make a constitution for India, it must be through the representatives of the people of the States as with the rest of India who are present here...

Well, Sir, we are going to make a constitution for India and it is obvious that what we are going to do in India, is going to have a powerful effect on the rest of the world, not only because a new free independent nation comes out into the arena of the world, but because of the very fact that India is such a country that by virtue, not only of her large size and population, but of her enormous resources and her ability to exploit those resources, she can immediately play an important and a vital part in world affairs. Even today, on the verge of freedom as we are today, India has begun to play an important part in world affairs. Therefore, it is right that the framers of our constitution should always bear this larger international aspect in mind.

We approach the world in a friendly way. We want to make friends with all countries. We want to make friends in spite of the long history of conflict in the past, with England also. The House knows that recently I paid a visit to England. I was reluctant to go for reasons which the House knows well. But I went because of a personal request from the Prime Minister of Great Britain. I went and I met with courtesy everywhere. And yet at this psychological moment in India's history when we wanted, when we hungered for messages of cheer, friendship and cooperation from all over the world and more especially from England, because of the past contact and conflict between us, unfortunately, I came back without any message of cheer, but with a large measure of disappointment. I hope that the new difficulties that have arisen, as everyone knows, because of the recent statements made by the British Cabinet and by others in authority there, will not come in our way and that we shall yet succeed in going ahead with the cooperation of all of us here and those who have not come. It has been a blow to me, and it has hurt me that just at the moment when we are going to stride ahead, obstructions were placed in our way, new limitations were mentioned which had not been mentioned previously and new methods of procedure were suggested. I do not wish to challenge the bona fides of any person, but I wish to say that whatever the legal aspect of the thing might be, there are moments when law is a very feeble reed to rely upon, when we have to deal with a nation which is full of the passion for freedom. Most of us here during the past many years, for a generation or more have often taken part in the struggle for India's freedom. We have gone through the valley of the shadow. We are used to it and if necessity arises we shall go through it again. (Hear, hear.) Nevertheless, through all this long period we have thought of the time when we shall have an opportunity not merely to struggle, not merely to destroy, but to construct and create. And now when it appeared that the time was coming for constructive effort in a free India to which we looked forward with joy, fresh difficulties are placed in our way at such a moment. It shows that, whatever force might be behind all this, people who are able and clever and very intelligent, somehow lack the imaginative daring which should accompany great offices. For, if you have to deal with any people, you have to understand them imaginatively; you should understand them emotionally; and of course, you have also to understand them intellectually. One of the unfortunate legacies of the past has been that there has been no imagination in the understanding of the Indian problem. People have often indulged in, or have presumed to give us advice, not realising that India, as she is constituted today, wants no one's advice and no one's imposition upon her. The only way to influence India is through friendship and cooperation and goodwill. Any attempt at imposition, the slightest trace of patronage, is resented and will be resented. (Applause.) We have tried, I think honestly, in the last few months in spite of the difficulties that have faced us, to create an atmosphere of cooperation. We shall continue that endeavour. But I do very much fear that that atmosphere will be impaired if there is not sufficient and adequate response from others. Nevertheless, because we are bent on great tasks, I hope and trust that we shall continue that endeavour and I do hope that if we continue we shall succeed. Where we have to deal with our own countrymen, we must continue that endeavour even though in our opinion some countrymen of ours take a wrong path. For, after all, we have to work together in this country and we have inevitably to cooperate, if not today, tomorrow or the day after. Therefore, we have to avoid in the present anything which might create a new difficulty in the creation of that future which we are working for. Therefore, so far as our own countrymen are concerned, we must try our utmost to gain their cooperation in the largest measure. But, cooperation cannot mean the giving up of the fundamental ideals on which we have stood and on which we should stand. It is not cooperation to surrender everything that has given meaning to our lives. Apart from that, as I said, we seek the cooperation of England even at this stage which is full of suspicion of each other. We feel that if that cooperation is denied, that will be injurious to India certainly to some extent, probably more so to England, and to some extent to the world at large. We have just come out of the World War and people talk vaguely and rather wildly of new wars to come. At such a moment this New India is taking birth—renascent, vital, fearless. Perhaps it is a suitable moment for this new birth to take place out of this turmoil in the world. But we have to be clear at this moment, we, who have this heavy task of constitution building. We have to think of this tremendous prospect of the present and the greater prospect of the future and not get lost in seeking small gains for this group or that. In this Constituent Assembly we are functioning on a world stage and the eyes of the world are upon us and the eyes of our entire past are upon us. Our past is witness to what we are doing here and though the future is still unborn, the future too somehow looks at us, I think, and so, I would beg of this House to consider this Resolution in this mighty prospect of our past, of the turmoil of the present and of the great and unborn future that is going to take place soon. Sir, I beg to move.

~

J.J.M. NICHOLS ROY

On the Objectives Resolution

At the time of independence, J.J.M. Nichols Roy (1884–1959) along with Gopinath Bordoloi personified the political and other aspirations of the north-eastern part of India. An extremely dynamic leader, he was also the most vocal representative of the hill people from Assam and the tribal areas. Speaking on the Objectives Resolution on 18 December 1946, Nichols Roy articulated how India should be viewed and the way the representatives should go about drafting the constitution. The speech also spells out certain reservations that many people had on issues of minority rights.

Mr. President Sir, thank you for giving me this opportunity to speak on this Resolution. I stand here to support the Resolution moved by Pandit Nehru, with all the force that I can command. This Resolution contains all the principles that need to be enunciated in such a kind of Resolution to be placed before this House. First of all, it has stated the objective that we all in India have in our minds, that is, to proclaim at a certain date the independence of India. Here we have only resolved that we shall proclaim the independence of India and we have that firm resolve in our mind to get the independence of India. That is the desire of everyone in India. I cannot imagine that there will be anybody in India from one end of India to the other end, who will be against that kind of objective. Then it proclaims also that the kind of Constitution that we shall make will be a republican form of Government,—a democratic form of Government, a Government by the people and for the people. That is surely the desire of all the people of India. It is true that there are some monarchies in India but we envisage the time when all these monarchies will become at least wholly constitutional monarchies like the Monarchy of England, and we believe that even the people of all the States envisage that in their own States, there will be a democratic form of Government. Therefore there can be no objection at all to these declarations that we have in this Resolution. Then it speaks of the territories which will be included in the Union of India and it is comprehensive enough. Then in the third para it speaks of autonomous units—that those autonomous units which are now autonomous according to present boundaries or with such other boundaries as they may have afterwards—these units or territories will remain autonomous units together with residuary powers and will exercise all powers and functions of government and administration, save and except such powers which are assigned to the Central Government. This is our desire, this is the desire of all the people of this country. It is the object before us that each Province will be autonomous. In this connection, Sir, I want to say that it is very unfortunate that the idea of Sections was introduced in the Cabinet Mission Declaration and that in a Section according to the latest interpretation given by His Majesty's Government a certain Province will be outvoted by the majority of members of another Province. I speak especially in connection with Section 1C which relates to Assam: Assam is a non-Muslim Province. There are 7 non-Muslims who are representatives of Assam in this Constituent Assembly and 3 are Muslims. I am sorry that my Muslim friends are not present here, in this Assembly. I wish they were here. In Bengal, Sir, there are 27 non-Muslims and 33 Muslims. If we are brought into a Section, there will be 36 Muslims and 34 non-Muslims and if the voting in that Section will be by a majority vote, a simple majority vote as interpreted by His Majesty's Government, it will mean that our Constitution, our Assam Constitution, will be framed by the majority of the people of Bengal, that is the Muslim League. We cannot conceive of anything that is so unjust as this, Sir (Cheers). It is a matter which should be considered by all the members of this Constituent Assembly.

... The principle of driving by force a non-Muslim Province to come under a Muslim Province is absolutely wrong. Mr. Jinnah has forced His Majesty's Government to commit this great injustice to our Province, and we feel, Sir, that we shall have the sympathy and support of this august body, that our Province may not be driven to that pitiable condition. I want Mr. Jinnah and the League Members to be here and I want them to come here to take part in the framing of the constitution of India. I will expect him and all the others to be just. I do not want anything else except that they will act like gentlemen and be just. It is unjust, everybody knows, that we should be forced into such a position in which we are now placed by the recent interpretation of His Majesty's Government. We are an autonomous Province and a non-Muslim Province... Now, Sir, it may be said that this will at once bring a conflict between the British Government and this Constituent Assembly. This need not be... I believe that we can adopt a friendly attitude. We shall say to the British Government: 'We thank you for the good effort you made to bring a compromise between the Hindus and the Muslims. You have given to us good advice and made good recommendations. You have acted as makers of peace. We shall, as far as practicable, implement your recommendations, but we shall, like responsible persons, be free to deviate from them whenever we find it is impracticable and unjust to carry out literally to the letter any of your recommendations. We shall frame a constitution which will do justice to all minorities and which shall not overlook any community. If the members of the Muslim League will cooperate, we shall heartily welcome them. After we have finished framing the constitution, the whole of India will get the opportunity to see what kind of constitution this Constituent Assembly has framed; we request you, British gentlemen, not to make speeches in Parliament which will suggest revolutionary activities in India. Kindly cooperate with us quietly until we finish our work, and then judge our work. Then only the British Government will have the opportunity to see what kind of a constitution this Assembly has framed. Then, and not till then, can they say that this Constituent Assembly has been just or unjust to a certain community or to the Muslims. We do expect that the Muslim community will come here and cooperate in framing the Constitution of India. There is no one who wishes their attendance here more than I do. I have some very good friends among the members of the Muslim League and I would like to see them come here and cooperate with this Assembly.

... Now, to turn to paragraph 5. In this paragraph we have provisions regarding justice and freedom, social justice, justice in the economic and political field, ensured to all. Political justice, no doubt, will mean that every community will get representation in the legislatures as well as in the administration of the country. Therefore, there need be no fear in the mind of any community that this Constituent Assembly will not look after their interests.

Then there is mention here of the freedom of thought, expression, belief, faith and worship. There was a propaganda made in this country by some parties that when there will be self-government in India, some religious faiths will not be allowed to propagate their faith. This is really false propaganda. This Resolution has declared that this will not be the case. There will be provision in the constitution of India for the freedom of all religious faiths and for the propagation of those faiths according to their own desire. I am particularly glad that this para speaks of association and action, subject to law and public morality. Public morality needs to be protected by government and righteousness needs to be exalted. 'Righteousness exalteth a nation, but sin is a reproach to any people.'

I would like to speak on other points of this Resolution but I don't think I need dwell on them at all. There are difficulties and hindrances before us. India is not an exception to difficulties of this nature; such difficulties confronted Canada, Australia and even the United States when they were engaged in the work of framing their constitutions, and some parts of those countries did not come into the constitution at the beginning, although they came in afterwards. That very same thing may be repeated here in India. We shall have to go on framing the constitution and then when that is placed before the world and before this country, it will then and then only be the proper time for the people of England or the British Government to say that it is not a constitution according to their Declaration. Before that happens, they should not try to prejudge what this Constituent Assembly will do and thus cause obstruction to its work.

I want to speak on only one more point, which has impressed me from the speech of Viscount Simon in the House of Lords. Viscount Simon has said that this Constituent Assembly if it carries on the work of framing a constitution for India will 'threaten' India 'with a Hindu Raj'. I was very much surprised when I saw these words in a newspaper this morning. When I was in Western countries, in England and also America, I was impressed by the fact that some people in those countries had an idea that a Hindu is a man who is steeped in his caste system and who worships a cow. If this is the idea which Viscount Simon has when he refers to a Hindu Raj i.e., that the people of India will be forced to perpetuate the caste system and to worship a cow, then he is entirely wrong. If the people who are assembled here—whether they be Hindus, Muslims, or Christians, or whatever other religion they may profess—if they frame a constitution which will be a democratic constitution, which will do justice to everybody, why should that constitution be called a Hindu Raj? And if by 'Hindu' is meant people who live in India, surely we should have a constitution for the people of India. That is exactly what we want: we want a constitution to be made by the people of India, but if some people in India do not want to come into the constitution just now, they will come afterwards and I envisage a time when they will all enter into this constitution and make India one country—one united country—with a democratic form of government. I have faith that all these hindrances will be removed by prayer to God. Let us follow the example of Mahatma Gandhiji—our Bapuji and pray to God. Let us pray to God that all these hindrances may be removed from our way and that we may be able to carry on the work of framing a constitution which will be a blessing to our whole country.

~

JAWAHARLAL NEHRU

Objectives of the Constitution

After a prolonged and often heated debate on the Objectives Resolution during which questions were raised even on the authority of the Constituent Assembly to give itself the right to prepare the constitution, the Objectives Resolution was put to vote on 22 January 1947. Jawaharlal Nehru spoke on the occasion, authoritatively addressing the doubts about the authority of the Constituent Assembly. At the same time, in this speech one can see Nehru laying down the foundation of India's foreign policy, one of friendship towards all nations, including Britain, irrespective of camps and blocs into which nations were aligning themselves.

Mr. President, it was my proud privilege, Sir, six weeks ago, to move this Resolution before this Hon'ble House. I felt the weight and solemnity of that occasion. It was not a mere form of words that I placed before the House, carefully chosen as those words were. But those words and the Resolution represented something far more; they represented the depth of our being; they represented the agony and hopes of the nation coming at last to fruition. As I stood here on that occasion I felt the past crowding round me, and I felt also the future taking shape. We stood on the razor's edge of the present, and as I was speaking, I was addressing not only this Hon'ble House, but the millions of India, who were vastly interested in our work. And because I felt that we were coming to the end of an age, I had a sense of our forbears watching this undertaking of ours and possibly blessing it, if we moved aright, and the future, of which we became trustees became almost a living thing, taking shape and moving before our eyes. It was a great responsibility to be trustees of the future, and it was some responsibility also to be inheritors of the great past of ours. And between that great past and the great future which we envisage, we stood on the edge of the present and the weight of that occasion, I have no doubt, impressed itself upon this Hon'ble House.

So, I placed this Resolution before the House, and I had hoped that it could be passed in a day or two and we could start our other work immediately. But after a long debate this House decided to postpone further consideration of this Resolution. May I confess that I was a little disappointed because I was impatient that we should go forward? I felt that we were not true to the pledges that we had taken by lingering on the road. It was a bad beginning that we should postpone even such an important Resolution about objectives. Would that imply that our future work would go along slowly and be postponed from time to time? Nevertheless, I have no doubt that the decision this House took in its wisdom in postponing this Resolution, was a right decision, because we have always balanced two factors, one, the urgent necessity in reaching our goal, and the other, that we should reach it in proper time and with as great a unanimity as possible. It was right, therefore, if I may say with all respect, that this House decided to adjourn consideration of this Motion and thus not only demonstrated before the world our earnest desire to have all those people here who have not so far come in here, but also to assure the country and everyone else, how anxious we were to have the cooperation of all. Since then six weeks have passed, and during these weeks there has been plenty of opportunity for those who wanted to come, to come. Unfortunately, they have not yet decided to come and they still hover in this state of indecision. I regret that, and all I can say is this, that we shall welcome them at any future time when they may wish to come. But it should be made clear without any possibility of misunderstanding that no work will be held up in future, whether anyone comes or not. (Cheers.) There has been waiting enough. Not only waiting six weeks, but many in this country have waited for years and years, and the country has waited for some generations now. How long are we to wait? And if we, some of us, who are more prosperous can afford to wait, what about the waiting of the hungry and the starving? This Resolution will not feed the hungry or the starving, but it brings a promise of many things—it brings the promise of freedom, it brings the promise of food and opportunity for all. Therefore, the sooner we set about it the better. So we waited for six weeks, and during these six weeks the country thought about it, pondered over it, and other countries also, and other people who are interested have thought about it. Now we have come back here to take up the further consideration of this Resolution. We have had a long debate and we stand on the verge of passing it. I am grateful to Dr. Jayakar and

Mr. Sahaya for having withdrawn their amendments. Dr. Jayakar's purpose was served by the postponing of this Resolution, and it appears now that there is no one in this House who does not accept fully this Resolution as it is. It may be, some would like it to be slightly differently worded or the emphasis placed more on this part or on that part. But taking it as a whole, it is a resolution which has already received the full assent of this House, and there is little doubt that it has received the full assent of the country. (Cheers.)

There have been some criticisms of it, notably, from some of the Princes. Their first criticism has been that such a Resolution should not be passed in the absence of the representatives of the States. In part I agree with that criticism, that is to say, I should have liked all the States being properly represented here, the whole of India—every part of India being properly represented here—when we pass this Resolution. But if they are not here it is not our fault. It is largely the fault of the Scheme under which we are functioning, and we have this choice before us. Are we to postpone our functioning because some people cannot be here? That would be a dreadful thing if we stopped not only this Resolution, but possibly so much else, because representatives of the States are not here. So far as we are concerned, they can come in at the earliest possible moment, we will welcome them if they send proper representatives of the States. So far as we are concerned, even during the last six weeks or a month, we have made some effort to get into touch with the Committee representing the States Rulers to find a way for their proper representation here. It is not our fault that there has been any delay. We are anxious to get everyone in, whether it is the representatives of the Muslim League or the States or anyone else. We shall continue to persevere in this endeavour so that this House maybe as fully representative of the country as it is possible to be. So, we cannot postpone this Resolution or anything else because some people are not here.

Another point has been raised: the idea of the sovereignty of the people, which is enshrined in this Resolution, does not commend itself to certain rulers of Indian States. That is a surprising objection and, if I may say so, if that objection is raised in all seriousness by anybody, be he a Ruler or a Minister, it is enough to condemn the Indian States system of every Ruler or Minister that exists in India. It is a scandalous thing for any man to say, however highly placed he may be, that he is here by special divine dispensation to rule over human beings today. That is a thing which is an intolerable presumption on any man's part, and it is a thing which this House will never allow and will repudiate if it is put before it. We have heard a lot about this Divine Right of Kings, we had read a lot about it in past histories and we had thought that we had heard the last of it and that it had been put an end to and buried deep down into the earth long ages ago. If any individual in India or elsewhere raises it today, he would be doing so without any relation to the present in India. So, I would suggest to such persons in all seriousness that, if they want to be respected or considered with any measure of friendliness, no such idea should be even hinted at, much less said. On this there is going to be no compromise. (Hear, hear.)

But, as I made plain on the previous occasion when I spoke, this Resolution makes it clear that we are not interfering in the internal affairs of the States. I even said that we are not interfering with the system of monarchy in the States, if the people of the States so want it. I gave the example of the Irish Republic in the British Commonwealth and it is conceivable to me that within the Indian Republic, there might be monarchies if the people so desire. That is entirely for them to determine. This Resolution and, presumably, the Constitution that we make, will not interfere with that matter. Inevitably it will be necessary to bring about uniformity in the freedom of the various parts of India, because it is inconceivable to me that certain parts of India should have democratic freedom and certain others should be denied it. That cannot be. That will give rise to trouble, just as in the wide world today there is trouble because some countries are free and some are not. Much more trouble will there be if there is freedom in parts of India and lack of freedom in other parts of India.

But we are not laying down in this Resolution any strict system in regard to the governance of the Indian States. All that we say is this that they, or such of them, as are big enough to form unions or group themselves into small unions, will be autonomous units with a very large measure of freedom to do as they choose, subject no doubt to certain central functions in which they will cooperate with the Centre, in which they will be represented in the Centre and in which the Centre will have control. So that, in a sense, this Resolution does not interfere with the inner working of those Units. They will be autonomous and, as I have said, if those Units choose to have some kind of constitutional monarchy at their head, they would be welcome to do so. For my part, I am for a Republic in India as anywhere else.

But whatever my views may be on that subject, it is not my desire to impose my will on others; whatever the views of this House may be on this subject, I imagine that it is not the desire of this House to impose its will in these matters.

So, the objection of the Ruler of an Indian State to this Resolution becomes an objection, in theory, to the theoretical implications and the practical implications of the doctrine of sovereignty of the people. To nothing else does any one object. That is an objection which cannot stand for an instant. We claim in this Resolution to frame a constitution for a Sovereign, Independent, Indian Republic—necessarily Republic. What else can we have in India? Whatever the States may have or may not have, it is impossible and inconceivable and undesirable to think in any other terms but in terms of the Republic in India.

Now, what relation will that Republic bear to the other countries of the world, to England and to the British Commonwealth and the rest? For a long time past we have taken a pledge on Independence Day that India must sever her connection with Great Britain, because that connection had become an emblem of British domination. At no time have we thought in terms of isolating ourselves in this part of the world from other countries or of being hostile to countries which have dominated over us. On the eve of this great occasion, when we stand on the threshold of freedom, we do not wish to carry a trail of hostility with us against any other country. We want to be friendly to all. We want to be friendly with the British people and the British Commonwealth of Nations.

But what I would like this House to consider is this: When these words and these labels are fast changing their meaning and in the world today there is no isolation, you cannot live apart from the others. You must cooperate or you must fight. There is no middle way. We wish for peace. We do not want to fight any nation if we can help it. The only possible real objective that we, in common with other nations, can have is the objective of cooperating in building up some kind of world structure, call it 'One World', call it what you like. The beginnings of this world structure have been laid down in the United Nations Organisation. It is feeble yet; it has many defects; nevertheless, it is the beginning of the world structure. And India has pledged herself to cooperate in that work.

Now, if we think of that structure and our cooperation with other countries in achieving it, where does the question come of our being tied up with this group of Nations or that group? Indeed, the more groups and blocks are formed, the weaker will that great structure become.

Therefore, in order to strengthen that big structure, it is desirable for all countries not to insist, not to lay stress on separate groups and separate blocks. I know that there are such separate groups and blocks today and because they exist today, there is hostility between them, and there is even talk of war among them. I do not know what the future will bring to us, whether peace or war. We stand on the edge of a precipice and there are various forces which pull us on one side in favour of cooperation and peace, and on the other, push us towards the precipice of war and disintegration. I am not prophet enough to know what will happen, but I do know that those who desire peace must deprecate separate blocks which necessarily become hostile to other blocks. Therefore India, in so far as it has a foreign policy, has declared that it wants to remain independent and free of all these blocks and that it wants to cooperate on equal terms with all countries. It is a difficult position because, when people are full of fear of each other, any person who tries to be neutral is suspected of sympathy with the other party. We can see that in India and we can see that in the wider sphere of world politics. Recently an American statesman criticised India in words which show how lacking in knowledge and understanding even the statesmen of America are. Because we follow our own policy, this group of nations thinks that we are siding with the other and that group of nations thinks that we are siding with this. That is bound to happen. If we seek to be a free, independent, democratic republic it is not to dissociate ourselves from other countries, but rather as a free nation to cooperate in the fullest measure with other countries for peace and freedom, to cooperate with Britain, with the British Commonwealth of Nations, with the United States of America, with the Soviet Union, and with all other countries, big and small. But real cooperation would only come between us and these other nations when we know that we are free to cooperate and are not imposed upon and forced to cooperate. So long as there is the slightest trace of compulsion, there can be no cooperation.

Therefore, I commend this Resolution to the House and I commend this Resolution, if I may say so, not only to this House but to the world at large so that it can be perfectly clear that it is a gesture of friendship to all, and, that behind it there lies no hostility. We have suffered enough in the past. We have struggled sufficiently, we may have to struggle again, but under the leadership of a very great personality we ought always to think in terms of friendship and goodwill towards others, even those who opposed us. How far we have succeeded, we do not know, because we are weak human beings. Nevertheless, the impress of that message has found a place in the hearts of millions of people of this country, and even when we err and go astray, we cannot forget it. Some of us may be little men, some may be big, but whether we are small men or big, for the moment we represent a great cause and therefore something of the shadow of greatness falls upon us. Today in this Assembly we represent a mighty cause and this Resolution that I have placed before you gives some semblance of that cause. We shall pass this Resolution, and I hope that this Resolution will lead us to a constitution on the lines suggested by this Resolution. I trust that the constitution itself will lead us to the real freedom that we have clamoured for and that real freedom in turn will bring food to our starving peoples, clothing for them, housing for them and all manner of opportunities of progress, that it will lead also to the freedom of the other countries of Asia, because in a sense, however unworthy we have become—let us recognise it—as leaders of the freedom movement of Asia, in whatever we do, we should think of ourselves in these larger terms. When some petty matter divides us and we have difficulties and conflicts amongst ourselves over these small matters, let us remember not only this Resolution, but this great responsibility that we shoulder, the responsibility of the freedom of 400 million people of India, the responsibility of the leadership of a large part of Asia, the responsibility of being some land of guide to vast numbers of people all over the world. It is a tremendous responsibility. If we remember it, perhaps we may not bicker so much over this seat or that post, over some small gain for this group or that. The one thing that should be obvious to all of us is this that there is no group in India, no party, no religious community, which can prosper if India does not prosper. If India goes down, we go down, all of us, whether we have a few seats more or less, whether we get a slight advantage or we do not. But if it is well with India, if India lives as a vital free country, then it is well with all of us to whatever community or religion we might belong.

We shall frame the constitution, and I hope it will be a good constitution, but does anyone in this House imagine that, when a free India emerges, it will be bound down by anything that even this House might lay down for it? A free India will see the bursting forth of the energy of a mighty nation. What it will do and what it will not,

I do not know, but I do know that it will not consent to be bound down by anything. Some people imagine that what we do now may not be touched for 10 years or 20 years, if we do not do it today, we will not be able to do it later. That seems to me a complete misapprehension. I am not placing before the House what I want done and what I do not want done, but I should like the House to consider that we are on the eve of revolutionary changes, revolutionary in every sense of the word, because when the spirit of a nation breaks its bonds, it functions in peculiar ways and it should function in strange ways. It may be that the constitution this House may frame may not satisfy that free India. This House cannot bind down the next generation, or the people who will duly succeed us in this task. Therefore, let us not trouble ourselves too much about the petty details of what we do; those details will not survive for long if they are achieved in conflict. What we achieve in unanimity, what we achieve by cooperation is likely to survive. What we gain here and there by conflict and by overbearing manners and by threats will not survive long. It will only leave a trail of bad blood. And so now I commend this Resolution to the House and may I read the last para of this Resolution? But one word more, Sir, before I read it. India is a great country, great in her resources, great in her manpower, great in her potential, in every way. I have little doubt that a Free India on every plane will play a big part on the world stage, even on the narrowest plane of material power, and I should like India to play that great part in that plane. Nevertheless today there is a conflict in the world between forces in different planes. We hear a lot about the atom bomb and the various kinds of energy that it represents and in essence today there is a conflict in the world between two things, that atom bomb and what it represents and the spirit of humanity. I hope that while India will no doubt play a great part in all the material spheres, she will always lay stress on that spirit of humanity, and I have no doubt in my mind that ultimately in this conflict that is confronting the world, the human spirit will prevail over the atom bomb. May this Resolution bear fruit and may the time come when in the words of this Resolution, this ancient land attains its rightful and honoured place in the world and makes its full and willing contribution to the promotion of world peace and the welfare of mankind.

~

SARVEPALLI RADHAKRISHNAN

The Flag of Dharma

On 22 July 1947, Jawaharlal Nehru moved the motion to adopt the national flag with the words '...the National Flag of India shall be horizontal tricolour of deep saffron (Kesari), white and dark green in equal proportion. In the centre of the white band, there shall be a Wheel in navy blue to represent the Charkha. The design of the Wheel shall be that of the Wheel (Chakra) which appears at the abacus of the Sarnath Lion Capital of Asoka. The diameter of the Wheel shall approximate to the width of the white band. The ratio of the width to the length of the Flag shall ordinarily be 2:3.' Speaking on the motion, the second president of the Indian republic, Sarvepalli Radhakrishnan (1888–1975), put the flag in the context not only of the national movement but also placed it in the ambit of the civilizational ethos of the country. India's foremost philosopher and exponent of its rich philosophical heritage, professor of Calcutta University and Oxford University and vice chancellor of Banaras Hindu University, Dr S. Radhakrishnan headed the First Education Commission of independent India in 1948. Known for his moving and extremely erudite speeches all over the world, in this speech he presents the essence of India through its flag.

... The Flag links up the past and the present. It is the legacy bequeathed to us by the architects of our liberty. Those who fought under this Flag are mainly responsible for the arrival of this great day of Independence for India. Pandit Jawaharlal has pointed out to you that it is not a day of joy unmixed with sorrow. The Congress fought for unity and liberty. The unity has been compromised; liberty too, I feel, has been compromised, unless we are able to face the tasks which now confront us with courage, strength and vision. What is essential today is to equip ourselves with new strength and with new character if these difficulties are to be overcome and if the country is to achieve the great ideal of unity and liberty which it fought for. Times are hard. Everywhere we are consumed by phantasies. Our minds are haunted by myths. The world is full of misunderstandings, suspicions and distrusts. In these difficult days it depends on us under what banner we fight. Here we are putting in the very centre the white, the white of the Sun's rays. The white means the path of light. There is darkness even at noon as some people have urged, but it is necessary for us to dissipate these clouds of darkness and control our conduct—by the ideal light, the light of truth, of transparent simplicity which is illustrated by the colour of white.

We cannot attain purity, we cannot gain our goal of truth, unless we walk in the path of virtue. The Asoka wheel represents to us the wheel of the Law, the wheel of Dharma. Truth can be gained only by the pursuit of the path of Dharma, by the practice of virtue. Truth, Satya, Dharma, Virtue, these ought to be the controlling principles of all those who work under this Flag. It also tells us that the Dharma is something which is perpetually moving. If this country has suffered in the recent past, it is due to our resistance to change. There are ever so many challenges hurled at us and if we have not got the courage and the strength to move along with the times, we will be left behind. There are ever so many institutions which are worked into our social fabric like caste and untouchability. Unless these things are scrapped we cannot say that we either seek truth or practise virtue. This wheel which is a rotating thing, which is a perpetually revolving thing, indicates to us that there is death in stagnation. There is life in movement. Our Dharma is Sanatana, eternal, not in the sense that it is a fixed deposit but in the sense that it is perpetually changing. Its uninterrupted continuity is its Sanatana character. So even with regard to our social conditions it is essential for us to move forward.

The red, the orange, the Bhagwa colour represents the spirit of renunciation. It is said: *Sarve tyage rajadharmesu drsta*. All forms of renunciation are to be embodied in Raja Dharma. Philosophers must be Kings. Our leaders must be disinterested. They must be dedicated spirits. They must be people who are imbued with the spirit of renunciation which that saffron colour has transmitted to us from the beginning of our history. That stands for the fact that the world belongs not to the wealthy, not to the prosperous but to the meek and the humble, the dedicated and the detached.

That spirit of detachment that spirit of renunciation is represented by the orange or the saffron colour and Mahatma Gandhi has embodied it for us in his life and the Congress has worked under his guidance and with his message. If we are not imbued with that spirit of renunciation in these difficult days, we will again go under.

The green is our relation to the soil, our relation to the plant life here on which all other life depends. We must build our Paradise here on this green earth. If we are to succeed in this enterprise, we must be guided by truth (white), practise virtue (wheel), adopt the method of self-control and renunciation (saffron). This Flag tells us, 'Be ever alert, be ever on the move, go forward, work for a free, flexible compassionate, decent, democratic society in which Christians, Sikhs, Moslems, Hindus, Buddhists will all find a safe shelter.'

VALLABHBHAI PATEL

Cultural and Educational Rights

On 1 May 1947, Sardar Vallabhbhai Patel, who headed the panel on minorities, moved clause 18 which is the heart and soul of minority rights and which went a long way not only in assuring the minorities that the newly independent state was going to be truly democratic but that it would also embody a truly republican spirit. The speech was brief but one can imagine the magisterial figure of Vallabhbhai Patel presenting this to be approved by the members of the Constituent Assembly at a time when the country was going through the worst kind of communal carnage. This short speech symbolizes the true character of the leadership at the time, undaunted by transient failures and looking beyond the immediate present to a glorious future.

I move clause 18 now.

(1) Minorities in every Unit shall be protected in respect of their languages, script and culture, and no laws or regulations may be enacted that may operate oppressively or prejudicially in this respect.
(2) No minority whether based on religion, community or language shall be discriminated against in regard to the admission into State educational institutions, nor shall any religious instruction be compulsorily imposed on them.
(3) (a) All minorities whether based on religion, community or language shall be free in any Unit to establish and administer educational institutions of their choice.
(b) The State shall not, while providing State aid to schools, discriminate against schools under the management of minorities whether based on religion, community or language.

I move this clause for the acceptance of the House.

~

N. GOPALASWAMY AYYANGAR

The Official Language

The issue of official language was probably the most volatile of all issues addressed by the framers of the constitution. Recognizing the potential for controversy over the issue, the discussion pertaining to it was taken up only towards the end. The debate was acrimonious and generated a lot of heat with allegations and counter-allegations. Realizing that a balanced outcome was impossible in the charged atmosphere, it was decided that neither a committee of the Constituent Assembly nor the Congress Party would move a resolution on the matter. Rather, K.M. Munshi, Gopalaswamy Ayyangar and B.R. Ambedkar were asked to move the motion privately. N. Gopalaswamy Ayyangar was one of the ablest administrators the country had at the time of independence. An asset to the Constituent Assembly, he along with K.M. Munshi provided the foundation of the text of the constitution which the constitutional adviser B.N. Rau and his secretariat finally prepared. On 12 September 1949, Gopalaswamy Ayyangar adroitly presented the motion on the official language to the Assembly.

... Then Sir we had to consider the other aspect of this problem. We had to consider, for instance, the question of the numerals about which I shall have to say something more detailed in the few remarks that I shall permit myself. Then we shall have to consider the question of the language of the states and we took a decision that, as far as possible, a language spoken in the state should be recognised as the language used for official purposes in that state and that for the interstate communications and for communications between the state and the centre the English language should continue to be used, provided that where between two states there was an agreement that inter-communication should be in the Hindi language, that should be permitted.

... Then we have to recognise one broad fact, viz., that while we could recognise 'Hindi' as the language for the official purposes of the Union, we must also admit that that language is not today sufficiently developed. It requires a lot of enrichment in several directions, it requires modernisation, it requires to be imbued with the capacity to absorb ideas, not merely ideas but styles and expressions and forms of speech from other languages. So we have put into this draft an article which makes it the duty of the State to promote the development of Hindi so that it may achieve all these enrichments and will in due course be sufficiently developed for replacing adequately the English language which we certainly contemplate should fade out of our officially recognised proceedings and activities in due course of time. Those, generally speaking, are the basis of this particular draft which I have moved.

Now, in considering this draft, I wish to place before the House one or two facts. The first that I wish to place before the House is that this draft is the result of a great deal of thought, a great deal of discussion. It is also...a compromise between opinions which were not easily reconcilable and therefore when you look at this draft, you have to take it not as a thing which is proposed by an individual member like me or by three members if I include my two colleagues whose names are set down here. It is not to be looked upon as something which we have put forth. It is the result of a compromise...great sacrifices of opinion, of very greatly cherished views and interests, for the purpose of achieving this draft in a form that will be acceptable to the full House.

Now I wish to draw the attention of the House to one or two of the basic principles underlying this draft. Our basic policy, according to the framers of this draft, should be that the common language of India for Union purposes should be the Hindi language and the script should be the Devanagari script. It is also a part of this basic policy that the numerals to be used for all official Union purposes should be what have been described to be the All-India forms of Indian numerals. The authors of this draft contemplate that these three items should be essential parts of the basic policy in this respect for practically all time. I wish to emphasise that fact because I know there is a school of opinion in this House that so far as the international forms of Indian numerals are concerned they should be placed in this scheme on the same footing as the English language. Those of us who are responsible for this draft, do not subscribe to this proposition. We consider that to the same extent the Hindi language and the Devanagari script for letters in that language should form a permanent feature of the common language of this country, to the same extent should the international forms of Indian numerals be part of this basic policy. That is at the root of this draft.

It is true that in order to effect a compromise with those who hold a different view we made one or two concessions in this behalf which we thought would persuade the others to fall in line with us. One concession was that though the international forms of Indian numerals would be a permanent feature, the President, even during the first fifteen years during which the English language will continue to be used practically for all purposes, during that period he may direct that the Devanagari numerals also should in addition to the international forms of Indian numerals be used for one or more official purpose of the Union.

... Now, I do not think it will be necessary for me to recommend the claims of the international forms of Indian numerals to this House. They must have read a great deal about it already, and I am sure those who will follow me here will have a lot more to say about it and so I do not go into the history of this question. I will only mention one or two facts. These forms of numerals originated in our country, and therefore, we should be proud to continue the almost universal use of these numerals which is now made in this country as a part of the future language set-up in this country. (Hear, hear). Secondly, the whole world, perhaps with one or two exceptions, has adopted these numerals. It is but right that we should keep in step with the whole world, or it should be really the other way, the whole world is already ready to keep in step with us who really gave these numerals to the world. And shall we throw away this proud position in the world with all the attendant advantages that it brings to us? Shall we do so, in order to take to something which is not universally used even in this country and which it is impossible for the world at large to use in the future? Those facts I should like to place particularly before this House before they reach a conclusion on this matter.

Now, Sir, with regard to this particular point, a number of alternatives have been proposed, but I would refer only to the latest...and that is the proposal which says it will place the international forms of Indian numerals practically on the same footing as the English language in the scheme of things. That means that for the first fifteen years, the international forms of Indian numerals will continue to be used and after that period Parliament might be left to decide for what purposes the international form or the Devanagari form should be used, or both should be used. It looks a very attractive proposition. But at the back of it is this feeling that you visualise the prospect of displacing that international form of Indian numerals altogether in this country. To those of us who are responsible for the draft, that is not a prospect which we can contemplate with anything like equanimity in the largest interests of the country and the world. And therefore it is because of the wrong approach to the whole problem that I am constrained to say that it is not possible for those who hold our particular view to consider this alternative.

Now, Sir, a few words as regards the provision we have made in Chapter III, that is, the language of the courts. We consider it very fundamental that English shall continue to be used in the Supreme Court and the High Courts until Parliament, after full consideration, after Hindi has developed to such an extent that it can be a suitable vehicle for law-making and law-interpretation, comes to the conclusion that it can replace the English language. My own feeling is that English will last in the form of Bills and laws and interpretations of such laws, much longer than fifteen years. That is my own expectation. Now, it is important that we should realise why this Chapter has been put in. Law-making and law-interpretation require an amount of precision; they require a number of expressions and words which have acquired a certain definite meaning: and until we reach that stage in regard to the Hindi language—and I do not think at present the Hindi language is anywhere near it, ignorant as I am of Hindi myself (hear, hear)—I have seen a good deal of the Hindi translations of what happens in this House and I am constrained to say that even the little Hindi I know does not enable me to make out anything from that kind of translation. Perhaps people more versed in Hindi may be able to understand it; perhaps I do understand it sometimes, because of the large number of Sanskrit words that are used in these translations. But that is not Hindi, in the sense that you could use it for court or legislative purposes.

I can tell you a story within my own experience. Ten years ago, I was making a constitution for the State of Jammu and Kashmir. The language of the Legislature had to be described in a section, and those who were drafting it, those officers had simply copied out the language in the Government of India Act, that is to say, English should be the language but if any member was unacquainted with it or was not sufficiently acquainted with the English language he might be allowed to speak in any language with which he was familiar. Well, it so happened that the late Sir Tej Bahadur Sapru happened to be in Srinagar when I was considering this draft, and I thought that I might take advantage of his presence there for advice and sent this draft to him. The only portion to which he objected initially was this section about the language of the Legislature. He said: 'What, in an Indian State where Urdu is the language of the courts and schools, and so on, could you really put in the English language as the language of your

Legislature?' I had a long discussion with him; I told him: '...I am willing to agree that the language of the Legislature should be Urdu to the extent that those people who are not acquainted with English should be permitted to speak in Urdu. But you are a great lawyer and supposing tomorrow I want you to appear before either the High Court here or the Privy Council and argue and interpret a section of the constitution, if it is framed in Urdu would you feel happy?' He appreciated my point. I told him as a compromise: 'I will put in Urdu as the language of the Legislature for debates with a proviso that the authoritative texts of Bills and Acts shall be in the English language.' He instantly agreed to my suggestion and thought that this was the most sensible solution of the problem that confronted us both.

I am mentioning that to you because at the present moment in India we have a similar problem. Our courts are accustomed to English; they have been accustomed to interpret in English. It is not always possible for us to find the proper equivalent to an English word in the Hindi language and then proceed to interpret it with all the precedents and rulings which refer only to the English words and not the Hindi words. That is why we felt it absolutely necessary—almost fundamental—to this constitution if it is to work that this Chapter should go into it.

Sir, I do not wish to go into other matters, because I am afraid I have already exceeded the time you have fixed for me. I would only appeal to the House that we must look at this problem from a purely objective standpoint of practicability. We have to adapt the instrument which would serve us best for what we propose to do in the future and I for one agree with you, Sir, that it will be a most unhappy thing, a most disappointing illustration of our inability to reach an agreed conclusion on so vital a matter if on this point we have to divide the House. I am sure that good sense will prevail.

~

SYAMA PRASAD MOOKERJEE

On the National Language

Syama Prasad Mookerjee (1901–53), son of the legendary vice chancellor of the University of Calcutta, Sir Asutosh Mukherjee, emerged as a major political voice in Bengal in the 1940s. He joined the Fazlul Haq ministry in

Bengal in 1941 but resigned in 1942. A vocal spokesperson for Hindus, he joined the Hindu Mahasabha in 1939 and became its president in 1944. Under his presidentship, the Mahasabha projected a very aggressive Hindu communal position at a time when the Muslim communal demand for Pakistan was reaching a crescendo. Notwithstanding his being a vociferous critic of the secular politics of the Congress, he was one of the most respected political leaders of the country and was therefore invited to not only join the Constituent Assembly but also the interim central cabinet. A scholar of the Bengali language, Syama Prasad was part of the committee which tried to shape a resolution on language. In 1951, he founded the Bharatiya Jana Sangh, the precursor to the Bharatiya Janata Party.

... Why do we accept Hindi? Not that it is necessarily the best of Indian languages. It is for the main reason that that is the one language which is understood by the largest single majority in this country today. If 14 crores of people out of 32 today understand a particular language, and it is also capable of progressive development, we say, let us accept that language for the purposes of the whole of India, but do it in such a way that in the interim period it may not result in the deterioration of our official conduct of business or administration and at no time retard true advancement of India and her other great languages. We accept that proposition, and the scheme which Mr. Gopalaswami Ayyangar has placed before you includes certain principles which we consider, taken as a whole, meet this viewpoint and will be not in the interests of the people coming from the south of India, but in the interests of the people of India as a whole. (Hear, hear.)

You have got some time, fifteen years, within which English will have to be replaced. How is it to be replaced? It will have to be replaced progressively. We will have to decide realistically whether for certain special purposes English should still be continued to be used in India. As some of my friends have already stated we might have rid India of British rule—we had reasons for doing so—but that is no reason why you should get rid of the English language. We know fully well the good and the evil that English education has done to us. But let us judge the future use of English dispassionately and from the point of view of our country's needs. After all, it is on account of that language that we have been able to achieve many things; apart from the role that English has played in unifying India politically, and thus in our attaining political freedom, it opened to us the civilisation of large parts of the world. It opened to us knowledge, specially in the realm of science and technology which it would have been difficult to achieve otherwise. Today we are proud of what our scientists and our technical experts have done.

I say, Sir, we would be suffering from a sense of inferiority complex if we examine the role that the English language should play in this country from any narrow standpoint. There is no question of the English language being used today for political purposes or for dominating any system of national education. It will be for us, the representatives of the people of free India, to decide as to how progressively we will use Hindi and other Indian languages, how progressively we will get rid of the English language; if we feel that for all time to come for certain purposes, we will allow English language to be used or taught we need not be ashamed of ourselves. There are certain matters which we have the courage to speak out, not in individual or sectional interest but where we feel that such a step is to be taken in the interests of the country as a whole. Sir, with regard to regional languages, I am now happy that the amendment proposes to include in the body of the Constitution itself a list of the principal regional languages of India. I hope we will include Sanskrit also. I shall speak here with frankness. Why is it that many people belonging to non-Hindi speaking provinces have become a bit nervous about Hindi? If the protagonists of Hindi will pardon me for saying so, had they not been perhaps so aggressive in their demands and enforcement of Hindi, they would have got whatever they wanted, perhaps more than what they expected, by spontaneous and willing cooperation of the entire population of India. But, unfortunately, a fear has been expressed, and in some areas that fear has been translated into action, where people speaking other languages, not inferior to Hindi by any means, have not been allowed the same facilities which even the much-detested foreign regime did not dare to deprive them of.

I would beg of those who represent the Hindi-speaking provinces in this Constituent Assembly to remember that while we accept Hindi, they in their turn, take upon themselves a tremendous responsibility. I was glad to find that some weeks ago at a meeting of the Hindi Sahitya Sammelan, a resolution was passed that in these Hindi-speaking provinces, there will be compulsory arrangements for the study of one or more of the other Indian languages. (An honourable member: A pious resolution.) Let that not remain a pious resolution. It will depend upon leaders like Pandit Govind Ballabh Pant, Babu Purushottam Das Tandon, Babu Shri Krishna Sinha, and Pandit Ravi

Shankar Shukla to see to it that within the next few months, arrangements are made, if necessary by statute, for the due recognition in their areas of other important regional languages, specially if there are people speaking those languages residing in those areas. I shall watch with interest and see how these facilities are given and the resolution unanimously passed under the leadership of Babu Purushottam Das Tandon is carried into effect in provinces like Bihar and the UP.

... Lastly, I shall say a few words about the numerals. Much has been made about the numerals. We are having a minor war on numerals. But, this suggestion which has been made is not in the parochial interest of the people who come from South India. That is a point which must be understood by every section of this House. The continuance, until otherwise decided, of the international numerals, which really have come back to the land of their birth in a somewhat modified form, is vitally necessary in our own interests, at least for many years to come. Later on, if, on the recommendation of the Commission, the President feels that a change is to be made, that change may be made. You have got your statistics; you have got your scientific work to be done. You have your commercial undertakings, banks, accounts, audit. You have so many other things in respect of which the use of international numerals is necessary.

... It pains to find that in some areas, acceptance of international numerals may become a first class political issue. It depends on the leaders of those provinces to take courage in both hands, get up here and say that they have accepted this compromise for the good of India and that they are going to stand together. If the leaders say so, I have not the slightest doubt that the people also will accept it. We have not banned the circulation of Hindi or Devanagari numerals in any province where the State legislature so decides or even for all-India purposes. All that we have recommended is the acceptance of a formula which we feel will be fair and just to all. I hope that before the debate concludes it will be possible for the representatives of the different view-points to meet together and come forward before the House with the declaration that the proposition of Mr. N. Gopalaswami Ayyangar is going to be unanimously accepted.

JAIPAL SINGH

In Defence of the Adivasi Language

What is not being said on the issue of the language of the tribal population of India even after sixty years of independence was articulated by a brilliant thinker among the tribals of India. Jaipal Singh, a Munda by birth, had the privilege of receiving the best possible education which included an Oxford degree. He had foresight and could think on behalf of the tribal people in a more universalistic manner than any latter-day champion of tribals could. He had championed the cause of the tribal since the days of the statutory commission in 1928, where he presented the case of the tribals of central India in what is possibly the best articulation of their demand for the states of Jharkhand and Chhattisgarh. The founder leader of the Jharkhand Party which spearheaded the movement for a separate Jharkhand state in the 1940s and 1950s, Jaipal Singh and his cause were defeated by the overwhelming odds against the tribal people. This was despite the presence of Jawaharlal Nehru, the foremost champion of tribal welfare, at the helm of affairs. In this speech on the issue of language, Jaipal Singh demonstrates his power of reasoning, which was sharp, precise and confident. The issue is still unresolved and in the politics of language, where numbers matter, the tribal people and their languages are the prime victims.

Mr. President, Sir, I feel that I would not be discharging my duty properly if I did not plead with the House that in Schedule VIIA some of the Adivasi languages that are spoken, not by a few, but, literally, by millions, should also be included. My amendment No. 272 says: That in amendment No. 65 of Fourth List, in the proposed new Schedule VIIA, the following new items be added:

14. Mundari
15. Gondi
16. Oraon.

Sir, if you look at the list of Scheduled Tribes in the last census, you will find there enumerated 176 of them. Of course there are not 176 languages. There may be dialects, in patois form, and the same language may be a shade different in different areas. You might ask me why I have singled out only three out of 176. Sir, I do not wish that the Schedule should be overburdened with numerous languages and that is why I have selected only three important ones. To deal first with the Mundari language, the first in my amendment, I may say that I have not mentioned Santhali because Mundari is the generic term given to the family of languages sometimes called Austric and at other times called Mon-Khmer. I find that in the last census, forty lakhs of people have been recorded as speaking the Mundari language. In the list of the Schedule as it is I find that there are included in it languages spoken by fewer people than the Mundaris. Similarly my reason for including Oraon is that the Oraons are not a small group in our country. There are as many as eleven lakhs of Oraons. Of course, this language finds a place in the Schedule under the language called Kanarese. So, actually, if Kanarese were to embrace Oraon, and if my friend Mr. Boniface Lakra who speaks that language is satisfied that it does I would withdraw item 16 Oraon.

I have asked also that Gondi should be one of the languages as it is spoken by 32 lakhs of people. My main reason to asking the House to accept these three languages is that I feel that by accepting them we will be encouraging the cause of unearthing ancient history.

The House, somehow or other, finds itself divided into two groups—the Hindi purists and others who are generous enough to accept that it should be left to time to evolve a language. Let me confess that I am prepared to accept whatever the House decides. But I do feel very strongly opposed to the puritanical fanaticism that has gripped many people. What is a language? A language is that which is spoken. I think we are taking a retrograde step in trying to think that we can enrich the language that is spoken today by Sanskritising it one hundred per cent for sentimental reasons. I am a great admirer of Sanskrit. I do speak Hindi as it is spoken in my province of Bihar, but that is not the Hindi which my friends want me to accept here. Let Hindi be the language as it is spoken everywhere. Let it enrich itself by taking words from other languages. Let us not think that, if other words are brought into Hindi or Hindustani, we shall be impoverishing it. A language grows and is enriched because it has the courage to borrow words from other languages. I do not mind whether you call it Hindustani or Hindi. Whatever you decide I will readily learn. The Adivasis will learn it. They are bilingual or trilingual. In West Bengal, the Santhals speak Bengali as well as their mother-tongue. Wherever you go you find that the Adivasi has accepted the language of the area in addition to his mother-tongue.

There is not a single Member here from Bihar who has had to learn an Adivasi language. Does my friend Pandit Ravi Shankar Shukla tell me that although there are 32 lakhs of Gonds in the

Central Provinces he has tried to learn the Gondi language? Has any Bihari tried to learn Santhali though the Adivasis are asked to learn the other languages? It is a matter of pride with us that we can talk in other languages also.

I think there should be some reciprocity. There should be some spirit of accommodation, and the provinces that speak Hindi should make it a point to learn another language. That is the spirit that should be shown by us. We should not move in a groove and say that the rest of the country must learn our language because we ourselves shall not learn anything else.

Sir, as I said, we have yet to unearth the hoary antiquity of India. We know very little of ancient India and there is only one way of learning about ancient India and that is by learning the languages that existed in this country before the Indo-Aryan hordes came into this country. Then alone shall we know what India in ancient days was like. I know my friend, Mr. Munshi, has the idea that every time I use the word 'Adivasis' I think in terms of Adivasi republics. He thinks perhaps that by this amendment I am trying to create three linguistic republics. Sir that is not the case. Take Santhali. If my amendment is accepted, it is going to affect West Bengal, Assam, certainly Bihar and Orissa. Take the case of Gondi. Gondi exists mainly in the CP but it stretches to Hyderabad a little bit to Madras and a little bit to Bombay also. Not one of these is an isolated area. They spread over distant provinces. All that I want is that these languages should be encouraged and developed so that they themselves can become enriched and by their enrichment they enrich the Rashtrabhasha of the country. I do not want that linguistic imperialism should get the better of us. Wherever I have been, it has been a pleasure to learn the language of the place I have had to live in.

So far as the script is concerned, I have very strong views and for practical reasons. I feel that we are making a wrong choice in accepting Devanagari. I belong to that school of thought which has been led for the last thirty years by Dr. Suniti Kumar Chatterjee who has advocated international phonetics for all the Indian languages. By international phonetics, I can pronounce Tamil as a Tamilian speaks it. I can speak Kanarese as a Kanarese speaks it. Without knowing a language, I can read and pronounce it as a person whose language it is pronounces it, but I know that the House is not in a mood to accept it. So long as my friends suffer from a complex, the fear complex, I am afraid it is useless to appeal to them to have a script that is practical not only for the purpose of teaching others or teaching oneself.

There is the commercial aspect of it also. It is a well-known fact that the Devanagari script has given headache to all the producers of printing machinery. In the time you can print something like fifteen thousand copies or twenty thousand copies in English, you cannot print even one-tenth of this number in Devanagari. Now, that is the commercial and practical aspect of it. I am not being sentimental. I think the country would have been wise to have done nothing which would retard its progress. By accepting Devanagari, we are impeding ourselves; we shall not be able to move fast enough, until such time as my friends can produce machinery that will move as fast as the international alphabet or something which is only slightly less speedy.

Sir, there is not very much more that I want to say. All that I plead, is that the languages of the most ancient peoples of this country should find a place of honour in the Schedule. I need not say more. I want to assure the Members on both sides that I do not wish to be drawn into this quarrel about language and script. Whatever the House accepts, I and my people will readily accept, and it is in that spirit that I ask the House also to show a spirit of accommodation in accepting my amendment.

~

V.I. MUNISWAMY PILLAY

The New Constitution

Speaking on 17 November 1949, Muniswamy Pillay, representative from Madras, echoed the spirit of freedom that the representatives of the depressed classes felt at the time when the new constitution was being finalized in the realization that free India was ushering in a new era of democracy.

Mr. President, Sir, I stand before this august Assembly to support the Motion moved by my honourable friend, Dr. Ambedkar. Sir, I will be failing in my duty if I do not refer to the magnanimous way in which you have conducted the proceedings of this august Assembly in preparing the Constitution of this great land of ours. Sir, as one of the signatories of the epoch-making Poona Pact, you will be happy today that we have opened a new chapter in the history of India by giving equal opportunities to all classes and sections of the people who inhabit India. Sir, Mahatma Gandhi laid the seed for the amelioration of the condition of the Depressed Classes and that took shape in a formidable way and today we find ourselves in the company of men who have thought it necessary to afford facilities for the common man in our great country.

Sir, I proceed now to appreciate the great services that have been rendered by the Drafting Committee whose services are so valuable to us; they have not spared days and nights in coming to decisions on important articles. I must say a word of praise to the calibre and capacity of the Chairman of the Drafting Committee Dr. B.R. Ambedkar. (Loud cheers.) Coming as I do from a community that has produced Dr. Ambedkar, I feel proud that his capacity has now been recognised, not only by the Harijans but by all communities that inhabit India. The Scheduled Castes have produced a great Nandanar, a great devotee, a Tirupazanalwar, a great Vaishnavite saint, and above all a Tiruvalluvar, the great philosopher whose name and fame is not only known throughout the length and breadth of India but of the whole world.

To that galaxy of great men of Harijans now we have to add Dr. Ambedkar who as a man has been able to show to the world that the Scheduled Castes are no less important but they can rise to heights and give to the world their great services. I know, Sir, that he has served the community of the Harijans and also of India by his great service and sacrifice in preparing a Constitution which will be the order of the day from the 26th of January 1950 and I also feel, Sir, of the Chief Draftsman and of the staff that have worked in preparing the Constitution cannot be belittled; they equally receive our praise.

Now coming to the Constitution itself, Sir, I feel proud that our countrymen have thought it necessary that the Fundamental Rights should give no discrimination to any man who is considered to be lower in the rank and file of the nation. Articles 15 and 16 go to give no discrimination; at the same time they give equal opportunities of employment. I specially welcome these provisions.

The great thing that this Constitution brings to notice, not only to this country but to the whole world is the abolition of untouchability. The fair name of India was a slur and a blot by having untouchability. Great avatars and great saints tried their level best to abolish untouchability but it is given to this august Assembly and the new Constitution to say in loud terms that no more untouchability shall stay in our country.

Again, Article 29 gives power to the would-be Government throwing open all Hindu religious institutions to all classes and sections of Hindus. At one time dogs and swine might enter the sacred precincts of temples but the shadow of an untouchable was considered a great abomination. I feel proud, Sir, that by this article that slur has been removed away. Due to this discrimination...my people have been converted to various faiths and thereby our population has dwindled as also their merit, but today I am proud that under Article 29 not only all Hindu religious institutions have been thrown open to all classes and sections of Hindus but all educational institutions maintained by the State or are receiving aid from Government will be thrown open to all the sections of the people.

Another thing, Sir, is that Mahatma Gandhi has told in unequivocal terms that prohibition must be the order of the day. We declare that if he were to be a dictator for even one day he would have proclaimed prohibition for the whole of India. Article 47 rightly puts in the Constitution that there shall be prohibition through the length and breadth of India. Article 46 gives the Scheduled Castes and Scheduled Tribes a very important place and I welcome that. Another Article, 48, deals with the preservation of milch cow and prohibition of cow slaughter. As a Hindu I feel that the great value of a cow is felt in India and it is a religious sentiment that the cow must be preserved and I feel happy that an article has been brought in this Constitution. Under Article 343 we have been able to agree for a common official language for the whole of India. Fifteen years has been set as the target period by which India must get into the common language, but coming as I do from a non-Hindi area, my community especially have not the occasion or the opportunity to train themselves in the language of Hindi. Whatever it may be, the future Government that will come to stay will think over this matter and see that, if a great section of the non-Hindi area or population have not developed to that state to take up Hindi, they will see that some more time is given.

Coming to Article 74 which allows the choice of ministers, I am one of those, Sir, who believe in the political rights of a community. During the past years when the Act of 1935 was in force there was a convention that the unrepresented communities must be given a choice to be ministers but that has been taken away from here but I am sure the people who will be in charge in future will see that the unrepresented communities in the ministries are given a chance so that the backwardness of such communities may be removed and they may keep an equal status with others. Coming to Article 81 I find that in the composition of the Peoples Assembly no reservation has been given. When I questioned this matter in this august Assembly, the Chairman of the Drafting Committee told us that the Minorities Advisory Committee have not made any special recommendation as to this matter, but I am sure the President who will be responsible for getting the composition of the provisional Parliament will find ways and means later whereby a certain reservation may be got for these people.

Sir, I am proud that the Drafting Committee has understood the views of the members of the Scheduled Castes and others and have brought in articles 320 and 335 which deal with the representation of Scheduled Castes in the services. I feel it is very important that a community that was at the outskirts of the society for centuries must be given a place and I think these articles go a long way to protect the interests of the Scheduled Castes in the matter of representation in the services.

Another important factor in the Draft Constitution is the giving of adult franchise in India. This will open the door to all the adults in this country, especially to the Scheduled Castes, who form one-sixth of the population of India, to equal opportunity to send proper representatives to the various assemblies. My only fear is, whether these people who have not yet been duly educated will be able to exercise their vote intelligently and send proper representatives. But, I am sure that with the help and assistance of the various communities in India, they will be able to send their proper representatives in the various assemblies.

Sir, in the matter of reservation of seats for the Scheduled Castes in the provincial assemblies, it was necessary to put a time limit of ten years... It is due...to the generosity of Sardar Patel who so ably conducted the meetings of the Minorities Advisory Committee that we have agreed to a time limit of ten years and also to the appointment of a Special Officer to see to the needs of the Harijan community and the Scheduled Tribes. If in that period we have developed properly, we will not hesitate to remove the time limit; but if it is found that these people have not risen up to the level of the other communities, it is my humble belief that the future parliamentarians and the Government will see that the time limit is extended.

Sir, another important thing is that a definition has been given of Scheduled Castes and Scheduled Tribes. Before the Provincial

Parliament comes into effect, it is said that the President by a declaration will say which are the communities that come under the category of Scheduled Castes and Scheduled Tribes. It has come to my knowledge and of other members of my community that some people have been playing to eliminate some of the communities that really come under the category of Scheduled Castes. I think, Sir, proper care will be taken to see that no community that comes under the category of Scheduled Castes is eliminated.

The great thing in this Constitution that is before the House is that the word 'minorities' has been removed. I know, as a matter of fact, it is not the desire of myself or of my community to be ever called a minority or Scheduled Caste; we want to merge with the thirty crores of people in this country. But, as Mahatma Gandhi rightly said, it is the change of heart that is required. If the caste Hindus and those people who predominate in this country only show that change of heart, it will be time, Sir, that we ourselves merge into the great community of Indians and I do not want to perpetuate this seclusion for ever.

In conclusion, I may, on behalf of the members of the Harijans that are present in this House and of Harijans outside ... assure you and the august Assembly and the Government ... and the future Government of India that the Harijans to the last man will uphold the Constitution that has been passed by the Constituent Assembly and work it to the very letter and spirit.

BHIMRAO RAMJI AMBEDKAR

On the Draft Constitution

As chairman of the Drafting Committee, B.R. Ambedkar had to perform a Herculean task in coordinating the recommendations and decisions of various committees and compiling them as constitutional provisions and then getting them amended and approved by the Constituent Assembly. On 4 November 1948, he introduced the draft constitution and moved it for consideration of the Constituent Assembly. In the course of his speech on the occasion, he responded to some basic criticisms of the draft constitution.

... It is said that there is nothing new in the Draft Constitution, that about half of it has been copied from the Government of India Act of 1935 and that the rest of it has been borrowed from the Constitutions of other countries. Very little of it can claim originality.

One likes to ask whether there can be anything new in a Constitution framed at this hour in the history of the world. More than hundred years have rolled over when the first written Constitution was drafted. It has been followed by many countries reducing their Constitutions to writing. What the scope of a Constitution should be has long been settled. Similarly what are the fundamentals of a Constitution are recognized all over the world. Given these facts, all Constitutions in their main provisions must look similar. The only new things, if there can be any, in a Constitution framed so late in the day are the variations made to remove the faults and to accommodate it to the needs of the country. The charge of producing a blind copy of the Constitutions of other countries is based, I am sure, on an inadequate study of the Constitution. I have shown what is new in the Draft Constitution and I am sure that those who have studied other Constitutions and who are prepared to consider the matter dispassionately will agree that the Drafting Committee in performing its duty has not been guilty of such blind and slavish imitation as it is represented to be.

As to the accusation that the Draft Constitution has produced a good part of the provisions of the Government of India Act, 1935, I make no apologies. There is nothing to be ashamed of in borrowing. It involves no plagiarism. Nobody holds any patent rights in the fundamental ideas of a Constitution. What I am sorry about is that the provisions taken from the Government of India Act, 1935, relate mostly to the details of administration. I agree that administrative details should have no place in the Constitution. I wish very much that the Drafting Committee could see its way to avoid their inclusion in the Constitution. But this is to be said on the necessity which justifies their inclusion. Grote, the historian of Greece, has said that: 'The diffusion of constitutional morality, not merely among the majority of any community but throughout the whole, is the indispensable condition of a government at once free and peaceable; since even any powerful and obstinate minority may render the working of a free institution impracticable, without being strong enough to conquer ascendancy for themselves.'

By constitutional morality Grote meant 'a paramount reverence for the forms of the Constitution, enforcing obedience to authority acting under and within these forms yet combined with the habit of open speech, of action subject only to definite legal control, and unrestrained censure of those very authorities as to all their public acts combined too with a perfect confidence in the bosom of every citizen amidst the bitterness of party contest that the forms of the Constitution will not be less sacred in the eyes of his opponents than in his own'. (Hear, hear.)

While everybody recognises the necessity of the diffusion of constitutional morality for the peaceful working of a democratic Constitution, there are two things interconnected with it which are not, unfortunately, generally recognised. One is that the form of administration has a close connection with the form of the Constitution. The form of the administration must be appropriate to and in the same sense as the form of the Constitution. The other is that it is perfectly possible to pervert the Constitution, without changing its form by merely changing the form of the administration and to make it inconsistent and opposed to the spirit of the Constitution. It follows that it is only where people are saturated with constitutional morality such as the one described by Grote the historian that one can take the risk of omitting from the Constitution details of administration and leaving it for the Legislature to prescribe them. The question is, can we presume such a diffusion of constitutional morality? Constitutional morality is not a natural sentiment. It has to be cultivated. We must realise that our people have yet to learn it. Democracy in India is only a top-dressing on an Indian soil, which is essentially undemocratic. In these circumstances it is wiser not to trust the Legislature to prescribe forms of administration. This is the justification for incorporating them in the Constitution.

Another criticism against the Draft Constitution is that no part of it represents the ancient polity of India. It is said that the new Constitution should have been drafted on the ancient Hindu model of a State and that instead of incorporating Western theories the new Constitution should have been raised and built upon village Panchayats and district Panchayats. There are others who have taken a more extreme view. They do not want any Central or Provincial Governments. They just want India to contain so many village Governments. The love of the intellectual Indians for the village community is of course infinite if not pathetic (laughter). It is largely due to the fulsome praise bestowed upon it by Metcalfe who described them as little republics having nearly everything that they want within themselves, and almost independent of any foreign relations. The existence of these village communities each one forming a separate little State in itself has according to Metcalfe contributed more than any other cause to the preservation of the people of India, through all the revolutions and changes which they have suffered, and is in a high degree conducive to their happiness and to the enjoyment of a great portion of the freedom and independence. No doubt the village communities have lasted where nothing else lasts. But those who take pride in the village communities do not care to consider what little part they have played in the affairs and the destiny of the country; and why? Their part in the destiny of the country has been well described by Metcalfe himself who says: 'Dynasty after dynasty tumbles down. Revolution succeeds to revolution. Hindoo, Pathan, Mogul, Maharatha, Sikh, English are all masters in turn but the village communities remain the same. In times of trouble they arm and fortify themselves. A hostile army passes through the country. The village communities collect their little cattle within their walls, and let the enemy pass unprovoked.'

Such is the part the village communities have played in the history of their country. Knowing this, what pride can one feel in them? That they have survived through all vicissitudes may be a fact. But mere survival has no value. The question is on what plane they have survived. Surely on a low, on a selfish level. I hold that these village republics have been the ruination of India. I am therefore surprised that those who condemn Provincialism and communalism should come forward as champions of the village. What is the village but a sink of localism, a den of ignorance, narrow-mindedness and communalism? I am glad that the Draft Constitution has discarded the village and adopted the individual as its unit.

The Draft Constitution is also criticised because of the safeguards it provides for minorities. In this, the Drafting Committee has no responsibility. It follows the decisions of the Constituent Assembly. Speaking for myself, I have no doubt that the Constituent Assembly has done wisely in providing such safeguards for minorities as it has done. In this country both the minorities and the majorities have followed a wrong path. It is wrong for the majority to deny the existence of minorities. It is equally wrong for the minorities to perpetuate themselves. A solution must be found which will serve a double purpose. It must recognise the existence of the minorities to start with. It must also be such that it will enable majorities and minorities to merge someday into one. The solution proposed by the

Constituent Assembly is to be welcomed because it is a solution which serves this twofold purpose. To diehards who have developed a kind of fanaticism against minority protection I would like to say two things. One is that minorities are an explosive force which, if it erupts, can blow up the whole fabric of the State. The history of Europe bears ample and appalling testimony to this fact. The other is that the minorities in India have agreed to place their existence in the hands of the majority. In the history of negotiations for preventing the partition of Ireland, Redmond said to Carson, 'Ask for any safeguard you like for the Protestant minority but let us have a United Ireland.' Carson's reply was: 'Damn your safeguards, we don't want to be ruled by you.' No minority in India has taken this stand. They have loyally accepted the rule of the majority which is basically a communal majority and not a political majority. It is for the majority to realise its duty not to discriminate against minorities. Whether the minorities will continue or will vanish must depend upon this habit of the majority. The moment the majority loses the habit of discriminating against the minority, the minorities can have no ground to exist. They will vanish.

The most criticised part of the Draft Constitution is that which relates to fundamental rights. It is said that Article 13 which defines fundamental rights is riddled with so many exceptions that the exceptions have eaten up the rights altogether. It is condemned as a kind of deception. In the opinion of the critics fundamental rights are not fundamental rights unless they are also absolute rights. The critics rely on the Constitution of the United States and to the Bill of Rights embodied in the first ten Amendments to that Constitution in support of their contention. It is said that the fundamental rights in the American Bill of Rights are real because they are not subjected to limitations or exceptions.

I am sorry to say that the whole of the criticism about fundamental rights is based upon a misconception. In the first place, the criticism in so far as it seeks to distinguish fundamental rights from non-fundamental rights is not sound. It is incorrect to say that fundamental rights are absolute while non-fundamental rights are not absolute. The real distinction between the two is that non-fundamental rights are created by agreement between parties while fundamental rights are the gift of the law. Because fundamental rights are the gift of the State it does not follow that the State cannot qualify them.

In the second place, it is wrong to say that fundamental rights in

America are absolute. The difference between the position under the American Constitution and the Draft Constitution is one of form and not of substance. That the fundamental rights in America are not absolute rights is beyond dispute. In support of every exception to the fundamental rights set out in the Draft Constitution one can refer to at least one judgment of the United States Supreme Court. It would be sufficient to quote one such judgment of the Supreme Court in justification of the limitation on the right of free speech contained in Article 13 of the Draft Constitution. In *Gitlow Vs. New York* in which the issue was the constitutionality of a New York 'criminal anarchy' law which purported to punish utterances calculated to bring about violent change, the Supreme Court said: 'It is a fundamental principle, long established, that the freedom of speech and of the press, which is secured by the Constitution, does not confer an absolute right to speak or publish, without responsibility, whatever one may choose, or an unrestricted and unbridled license that gives immunity for every possible use of language and prevents the punishment of those who abuse this freedom.'

It is therefore wrong to say that the fundamental rights in America are absolute, while those in the Draft Constitution are not. It is argued that if any fundamental rights require qualification, it is for the Constitution itself to qualify them as is done in the Constitution of the United States and where it does not do so it should be left to be determined by the judiciary upon a consideration of all the relevant considerations. All this, I am sorry to say, is a complete misrepresentation if not a misunderstanding of the American Constitution. The American Constitution does nothing of the kind. Except in one matter, namely, the right of assembly, the American Constitution does not itself impose any limitations upon the fundamental rights guaranteed to the American citizens. Nor is it correct to say that the American Constitution leaves it to the judiciary to impose limitations on fundamental rights. The right to impose limitations belongs to the Congress. The real position is different from what is assumed by the critics. In America, the fundamental rights as enacted by the Constitution were no doubt absolute. Congress, however, soon found that it was absolutely essential to qualify these fundamental rights by limitations. When the question arose as to the constitutionality of these limitations before the Supreme Court, it was contended that the Constitution gave no power to the United States Congress to impose such limitation, the Supreme Court invented the doctrine of police power and refuted the advocates of absolute fundamental rights by the argument that every state has inherent in it police power which is not required to be conferred on it expressly by the Constitution. To use the language of the Supreme Court in the case I have already referred to, it said: 'That a State in exercise of its police power may punish those who abuse this freedom by utterances inimical to the public welfare, tending to corrupt public morals, incite to crime or disturb the public peace, is not open to question...'

What the Draft Constitution has done is that instead of formulating fundamental rights in absolute terms and depending upon our Supreme Court to come to the rescue of Parliament by inventing the doctrine of police power, it permits the State directly to impose limitations upon the fundamental rights. There is really no difference in the result. What one does directly the other does indirectly. In both cases, the fundamental rights are not absolute.

In the Draft Constitution the fundamental rights are followed by what are called 'Directive Principles'. It is a novel feature in a constitution framed for Parliamentary Democracy. The only other constitution framed for Parliamentary Democracy which embodies such principles is that of the Irish Free State. These Directive Principles have also come up for criticism. It is said that they are only pious declarations. They have no binding force. This criticism is of course superfluous. The constitution itself says so in so many words.

If it is said that the Directive Principles have no legal force behind them, I am prepared to admit it. But I am not prepared to admit that they have no sort of binding force at all. Nor am I prepared to concede that they are useless because they have no binding force in law.

The Directive Principles are like the Instruments of Instructions which were issued to the Governor-General and to the Governors of the Colonies and to those of India by the British Government under the 1935 Act. Under the Draft Constitution it is proposed to issue such instruments to the President and to the Governors. The texts of these Instruments of Instructions will be found in Schedule IV of the Constitution. What are called Directive Principles is merely another name for Instruments of Instructions. The only difference is that they are instructions to the Legislature and the Executive. Such a thing is to my mind to be welcomed. Wherever there is a grant of power in general terms for peace, order and good government, it is necessary that it should be accompanied by instructions regulating its exercise.

The inclusion of such instructions in a Constitution such as is proposed in the Draft becomes justifiable for another reason. The Draft Constitution as framed only provides a machinery for the government of the country. It is not a contrivance to install any particular party in power as has been done in some countries. Who should be in power is left to be determined by the people, as it must be, if the system is to satisfy the tests of democracy. But whoever captures power will not be free to do what he likes with it. In the exercise of it, he will have to respect these Instruments of Instructions which are called Directive Principles. He cannot ignore them. He may not have to answer for their breach in a Court of Law. But he will certainly have to answer for them before the electorate at election time. What great value these Directive Principles possess will be realised better when the forces of right contrive to capture power.

That it has no binding force is no argument against their inclusion in the Constitution. There may be a difference of opinion as to the exact place they should be given in the Constitution. I agree that it is somewhat odd that provisions which do not carry positive obligations should be placed in the midst of provisions which do carry positive obligations. In my judgment their proper place is in Schedules IIIA and IV which contain Instruments of Instructions to the President and the Governors. For, as I have said, they are really Instruments of Instructions to the Executive and the Legislatures as to how they should exercise their powers. But that is only a matter of arrangement.

Some critics have said that the Centre is too strong. Others have said that it must be made stronger. The Draft Constitution has struck a balance. However much you may deny powers to the Centre, it is difficult to prevent the Centre from becoming strong. Conditions in the modern world are such that centralisation of powers is inevitable. One has only to consider the growth of the Federal Government in the USA which, notwithstanding the very limited powers given to it by the Constitution, has outgrown its former self and has overshadowed and eclipsed the State Governments. This is due to modern conditions. The same conditions are sure to operate on the Government of India and nothing that one can do will help to prevent it from being strong. On the other hand, we must resist the tendency to make it stronger. It cannot chew more than it can digest. Its strength must be commensurate with its weight. It would be a folly to make it so strong that it may fall by its own weight.

The Draft Constitution is criticised for having one sort of

constitutional relations between the Centre and the Provinces and another sort of constitutional relations between the Centre and the Indian States. The Indian States are not bound to accept the whole list of subjects included in the Union List but only those which come under Defence, Foreign Affairs and Communications. They are not bound to accept subjects included in the Concurrent List. They are not bound to accept the State List contained in the Draft Constitution. They are free to create their own Constituent Assemblies and to frame their own constitutions. All this, of course, is very unfortunate and, I submit, quite indefensible. This disparity may even prove dangerous to the efficiency of the State. So long as the disparity exists, the Centre's authority over all-India matters may lose its efficacy. For, power is no power if it cannot be exercised in all cases and in all places. In a situation such as may be created by war, such limitations on the exercise of vital powers in some areas may bring the whole life of the State in complete jeopardy. What is worse is that the Indian States under the Draft Constitution are permitted to maintain their own armies. I regard this as a most retrograde and harmful provision which may lead to the break-up of the unity of India and the overthrow of the Central Government. The Drafting Committee, if I am not misrepresenting its mind, was not at all happy over this matter. They wished very much that there was uniformity between the Provinces and the Indian States in their constitutional relationship with the Centre. Unfortunately, they could do nothing to improve matters. They were bound by the decisions of the Constituent Assembly, and the Constituent Assembly in its turn was bound by the agreement arrived at between the two negotiating committees.

But we may take courage from what happened in Germany. The German Empire as founded by Bismarck in 1870 was a composite State, consisting of 25 units. Of these 25 units, 22 were monarchical States and 3 were republican city-States. This distinction, as we all know, disappeared in the course of time and Germany became one land with one people living under one Constitution. The process of the amalgamation of the Indian States is going to be much quicker than it has been in Germany. On 15 August 1947 we had 600 Indian States in existence. Today by the integration of the Indian States with Indian Provinces or merger among themselves or by the Centre having taken the Centrally Administered Areas there have remained some 20–30 States as viable States. This is a very rapid process and progress. I appeal to those States that remain to fall in line with the Indian

Provinces and to become full units of the Indian Union on the same terms as the Indian Provinces. They will thereby give the Indian Union the strength it needs. They will save themselves the bother of starting their own Constituent Assemblies and drafting their own separate constitution and they will lose nothing that is of value to them. I feel hopeful that my appeal will not go in vain and that before the Constitution is passed, we will be able to wipe off the differences between the Provinces and the Indian States.

Some critics have taken objection to the description of India in Article 1 of the Draft Constitution as a Union of States. It is said that the correct phraseology should be a Federation of States. It is true that South Africa which is a unitary State is described as a Union. But Canada which is a Federation is also called a Union. Thus the description of India as a Union, though its constitution is Federal, does no violence to usage. But what is important is that the use of the word Union is deliberate. I do not know why the word 'Union' was used in the Canadian Constitution. But I can tell you why the Drafting Committee has used it. The Drafting Committee wanted to make it clear that though India was to be a federation, the federation was not the result of an agreement by the States to join in a federation and that the federation not being the result of an agreement no State has the right to secede from it. The federation is a Union because it is indestructible. Though the country and the people may be divided into different States for convenience of administration the country is one integral whole, its people a single people living under a single *imperium* derived from a single source. The Americans had to wage a civil war to establish that the States have no right of secession and that their federation was indestructible. The Drafting Committee thought that it was better to make it clear at the outset rather than to leave it to speculation or to dispute.

The provisions relating to amendment of the constitution have come in for a virulent attack at the hands of the critics of the Draft Constitution. It is said that the provisions contained in the Draft make amendment difficult. It is proposed that the constitution should be amendable by a simple majority at least for some years. The argument is subtle and ingenious. It is said that this Constituent Assembly is not elected on adult suffrage while the future Parliament will be elected on adult suffrage and yet the former has been given the right to pass the Constitution by a simple majority while the latter has been denied the same right. It is paraded as one of the absurdities of the Draft Constitution. I must repudiate the charge because it is without foundation. To know how simple are the provisions of the Draft Constitution in respect of amending the Constitution one has only to study the provisions for amendment contained in the American and Australian constitutions. Compared to them those contained in the Draft Constitution will be found to be the simplest. The Draft Constitution has eliminated the elaborate and difficult procedures such as a decision by a convention or referendum. The powers of amendment are left with the Legislature, Central and Provincial. It is only for amendments of specific matters—and they are only few—that the ratification of the State legislatures is required. All other Articles of the Constitution are left to be amended by Parliament. The only limitation is that it shall be done by a majority of not less than two-thirds of the members of each House present and voting and a majority of the total membership of each House. It is difficult to conceive a simpler method of amending the Constitution.

What is said to be the absurdity of the amending provisions is founded upon a misconception of the position of the Constituent Assembly and of the future Parliament elected under the constitution. The Constituent Assembly in making a constitution has no partisan motive. Beyond securing a good and workable constitution it has no axe to grind. In considering the Articles of the Constitution it has no eye on getting through a particular measure. The future Parliament if it met as a Constituent Assembly, its members will be acting as partisans seeking to carry amendments to the Constitution to facilitate the passing of party measures which they have failed to get through Parliament by reason of some Article of the constitution which has acted as an obstacle in their way. Parliament will have an axe to grind while the Constituent Assembly has none. That is the difference between the Constituent Assembly and the future Parliament. That explains why the Constituent Assembly though elected on limited franchise can be trusted to pass the constitution by simple majority and why the Parliament though elected on adult suffrage cannot be trusted with the same power to amend it.

I believe I have dealt with all the adverse criticisms that have been levelled against the Draft Constitution as settled by the Drafting Committee. I don't think that I have left out any important comment or criticism that has been made during the last eight months during which the constitution has been before the public. It is for the Constituent Assembly to decide whether they will accept the constitution as settled by the Drafting Committee or whether they shall alter it before passing it.

But this I would like to say. The constitution has been discussed in some of the Provincial Assemblies of India. It was discussed in Bombay, CP, West Bengal, Bihar, Madras and East Punjab. It is true that in some Provincial Assemblies serious objections were taken to the financial provisions of the constitution and in Madras to Article 226. But excepting this, in no Provincial Assembly was any serious objection taken to the Articles of the Constitution. No constitution is perfect and the Drafting Committee itself is suggesting certain amendments to improve the Draft Constitution. But the debates in the Provincial Assemblies give me courage to say that the constitution as settled by the Drafting Committee is good enough to make a start with. I feel that it is workable, it is flexible and it is strong enough to hold the country together both in peace time and in war time. Indeed, if I may say so, if things go wrong under the new Constitution, the reason will not be that we had a bad Constitution. What we will have to say is that Man was vile.

~

RAJENDRA PRASAD

Let Posterity Judge

On 26 November 1949, the president of the Constituent Assembly, Dr Rajendra Prasad (1884–1963), made a brilliant speech not just outlining some of the features of the constitution, but also congratulating all the members for completing a work of such magnitude with a sense of cooperation and courtesy. Dr Rajendra Prasad put the whole work in a perspective which Jawaharlal Nehru desired when he moved the Objectives Resolution. This speech is in essence a summary of the process by which the constitution was framed and of the various provisions which were discussed, debated and adopted by the framers.

Before I formally put the motion which was moved by Dr. Ambedkar, I desire to say a few words.

I desire to congratulate the Assembly on accomplishing a task of such tremendous magnitude. It is not my purpose to appraise the value of the work that the Assembly has done or the merits or demerits of the Constitution which it has framed. I am content to leave that to others and to posterity. I shall attempt only to point out some of its salient features and the method which we have pursued in framing the Constitution.

Before I do that, I would like to mention some facts which will show the tremendousness of the task which we undertook some three years ago. If you consider the population with which the Assembly has had to deal, you will find that it is more than the population of the whole of Europe minus Russia, being 319 millions as against 317 millions. The countries of Europe have never been able to join together or coalesce even in a Confederacy, much less under one unitary government. Here, in spite of the size of the population and the country, we have succeeded in framing a Constitution which covers the whole of it. Apart from the size, there were other difficulties which were inherent in the problem itself. We have got many communities living in this country. We have got many languages prevalent in different parts of it. We have got other kinds of differences dividing the people in the different parts from one another. We had to make provision not only for areas which are advanced educationally and economically; we had also to make provision for backward people like the Tribes and for backward areas like the Tribal areas. The communal problem had been one of the knottiest problems which the country has had before it for a pretty long time. The Second Round Table Conference which was attended by Mahatma Gandhi failed because the communal problem could not be solved. The subsequent history of the country is too recent to require narration here; but we know this that as a result, the country has had to be divided and we have lost two big portions in the north-east and north-west.

Another problem of great magnitude was the problem of the Indian States. When the British came to India, they did not conquer the country as a whole or at one stroke. They got bits of it from time to time. The bits which came into their direct possession and control came to be known as British India; but a considerable portion remained under the rule and control of the Indian Princes. The British thought at the time that it was not necessary or profitable for them to take direct control of those territories, and they allowed the old Rulers to continue subject to their suzerainty. But they entered into various kinds of treaties and engagements with them. We had something near six hundred States covering more than one-third of the territory of India and one-fourth of the population of the country. They varied in size from small tiny principalities to big States like Mysore, Hyderabad, Kashmir, etc. When the British decided to leave this country, they transferred power to us; but at the same time, they also declared that all the treaties and engagements they had with the Princes had lapsed. The Paramountcy which they had so long exercised and by which they could keep the Princes in order also lapsed. The Indian Government was then faced with the problem of tackling these States which had different traditions of rule, some of them having some form of popular representation in Assemblies and some having no semblance of anything like that, and governing completely autocratically.

As a result of the declaration that the treaties with the Princes and Paramountcy had lapsed, it became open to any Prince or any combination of Princes to assume independence and even to enter into negotiations with any foreign power and thus become islands of independent territory within the country. There were undoubtedly geographical and other compulsions which made it physically impossible for most of them to go against the Govt. of India but constitutionally it had become possible. The Constituent Assembly therefore had at the very beginning of its labours, to enter into negotiations with them to bring their representatives into the Assembly so that a constitution might be framed in consultation with them. The first efforts were successful and some of them did join this Assembly at an early stage but others hesitated. It is not necessary to pry into the secrets of what was happening in those days behind the scenes. It will be sufficient to state that by August 1947 when the Indian Independence Act came into force, almost all of them with two notable exceptions, Kashmir in the north and Hyderabad in the South, had acceded to India. Kashmir soon after followed the example of others and acceded. There were standstill agreements with all of them including Hyderabad which continued the status quo. As time passed, it became apparent that it was not possible at any rate for the smaller States to maintain their separate independent existence and then a process of integration with India started. In course of time not only have all the smaller States coalesced and become integrated with some province or other of India but some of the larger ones also have joined. Many of the States have formed Unions of their own and such Unions have become part of the Indian Union. It must be said to the credit of the

Princes and the people of the States no less than to the credit of the States Ministry under the wise and far-sighted guidance of Sardar Vallabhbhai Patel that by the time we have been able to pass this constitution, the States are now more or less in the same position as the provinces and it has become possible to describe all of them including the Indian States and the provinces as States in the constitution. The announcement which has been made just now by Sardar Vallabhbhai Patel makes the position very clear, and now there is no difference between the States, as understood before, and the provinces in the New Constitution.

It has undoubtedly taken us three years to complete this work, but when we consider the work that has been accomplished and the number of days that we have spent in framing this Constitution, the details of which were given by the Honourable Dr. B.R. Ambedkar yesterday, we have no reason to be sorry for the time spent.

It has enabled the apparently intractable problem of the States and the communal problem to be solved. What had proved insoluble at the Round Table Conference and had resulted in the division of the country has been solved with the consent of all parties concerned, and again under the wise guidance of the Honourable Sardar Vallabhbhai Patel.

At first we were able to get rid of separate electorates which had poisoned our political life for so many years, but reservation of seats for the communities which enjoyed separate electorates before had to be conceded, although on the basis of their population and not as had been done in the Act of 1919 and the Act of 1935 of giving additional representation on account of the so-called historical and other superiority claimed by some of the communities. It has become possible only because the Constitution was not passed earlier that even reservation of seats has been given up by the communities concerned and so our Constitution does not provide for reservation of seats on communal basis, but for reservation only in favour of two classes of people in our population, namely, the depressed classes who are Hindus and the tribal people, on account of their backwardness in education and in other respects. I therefore see no reason to be apologetic about the delay.

The cost too which the Assembly has had to incur during its three years' existence is not too high when you take into consideration the factors going to constitute it. I understand that the expenses up to the 22nd of November come to Rs 63,96,729. The method which the

Constituent Assembly adopted in connection with the Constitution was first to lay down its 'terms of reference' as it were in the form of an Objectives Resolution which was moved by Pandit Jawaharlal Nehru in an inspiring speech and which constitutes now the Preamble to our Constitution. It then proceeded to appoint a number of committees to deal with different aspects of the constitutional problem. Dr. Ambedkar mentioned the names of these committees. Several of these had as their Chairman either Pandit Jawaharlal Nehru or Sardar Patel to whom thus goes the credit for the fundamentals of our Constitution. I have only to add that they all worked in a business-like manner and produced reports which were considered by the Assembly and their recommendations were adopted as the basis on which the draft of the Constitution had to be prepared. This was done by Mr. B.N. Rau, who brought to bear on his task a detailed knowledge of Constitutions of other countries and an extensive knowledge of the conditions of this country as well as his own administrative experience. The Assembly then appointed the Drafting Committee which worked on the original draft prepared by Mr. B.N. Rau and produced the Draft Constitution which was considered by the Assembly at great length at the second reading stage. As Dr. Ambedkar pointed out, there were not less than 7,635 amendments of which 2,473 amendments were moved. I am mentioning this only to show that it was not only the Members of the Drafting Committee who were giving their close attention to the constitution, but other Members were vigilant and scrutinising the Draft in all its details. No wonder, that we had to consider not only each article in the Draft, but practically every sentence and sometimes, every word in every article. It may interest honourable members to know that the public were taking great interest in its proceedings and I have discovered that no less than 53,000 visitors were admitted to the Visitors Gallery during the period when the constitution has been under consideration. In the result, the Draft Constitution has increased in size, and by the time it has been passed, it has come to have 395 articles and 8 schedules, instead of the 243 articles and 13 schedules of the original Draft of Mr. B.N. Rau. I do not attach much importance to the complaint which is sometimes made that it has become too bulky. If the provisions have been well thought out, the bulk need not disturb the equanimity of our mind.

We have now to consider the salient features of the constitution. The first question which arises and which has been mooted is as to the category to which this constitution belongs. Personally, I do not attach any importance to the label which may be attached to it—whether you call it Federal Constitution or Unitary Constitution or by any other name. It makes no difference so long as the constitution serves our purpose. We are not bound to have a constitution which completely and fully falls in line with known categories of constitutions in the world. We have to take certain facts of history in our own country and the Constitution has not to an inconsiderable extent been influenced by such realities as facts of history.

You are all aware that until the Round Table Conference of 1930, India was completely a Unitary Government, and the provinces derived whatever power they possessed from the Government of India. It was there for the first time that the question of Federation in a practical form arose which would include not only the provinces but also the many States that were in existence. The Constitution of 1935 provided for a Federation in which both the provinces of India and the States were asked to join. But the federal part of it could not be brought into operation, because terms on which the Princes could agree to join it could not be settled in spite of prolonged negotiation. And, when the war broke out, that part of the Constitution had practically to be abrogated.

In the present Constitution it has been possible not only to bring in practically all the States which fell within our geographical limits, but to integrate the largest majority of them in India, and the Constitution as it stands practically makes no difference so far as the administration and the distribution of powers among the various organs of the State are concerned between what were the provinces and what were Indian States before. They are all now more or less on the same footing and, as time passes, whatever little distinction still exists is bound to disappear. Therefore, so far as labelling is concerned, we need not be troubled by it.

Well, the first and the most obvious fact which will attract any observer is that we are going to have a Republic. India knew republics in the past olden days, but that was 2,000 years ago or more and those republics were small republics. We never had anything like the Republic which we are going to have now, although there were empires in those days as well as during the Mughal period which covered very large parts of the country. The President of the Republic will be an elected President. We never have had an elected Head of the State which covered such a large area of India. And it is for the first time that it becomes open to the humblest and the lowliest citizens of the country to deserve and become the President or the Head of this big State which counts among the biggest States of the world today. This is not a small matter. But because we have an elected President, some of the problems which are of a very difficult nature have arisen. We have provided for the election of the President. We have provided for an elected legislature which is going to have supreme authority. In America, the legislature and the President are both elected and both have more or less equal powers—each in its or his own sphere, the President in the executive sphere and the legislature in the legislative sphere.

We considered whether we should adopt the American model or the British model where we have a hereditary king who is the fountain of all honour and power, but who does not actually enjoy any power. All the power rests in the legislature to which the Ministers are responsible. We have had to reconcile the position of an elected President with an elected legislature and, in doing so, we have adopted more or less the position of the British Monarch for the President. This may or may not be satisfactory. Some people think too much power has been given to the President; others think that the President, being an elected President, should have even more powers than are given to him.

If you look at it from the point of view of the electorate which elects the Parliament and which elects the President, you will find that practically the entire adult population of the country joins in electing this Parliament and it is not only the Members of the Parliament of India but also the Members of the Legislative Assemblies of the States who join in electing the President. It thus comes about that, while the Parliament and Legislative Assemblies are elected by the adult population of the country as a whole, the President is elected by representatives who represent the entire population twice over, once as representatives of the States and again as their representatives in the Central Parliament of the country. But although the President is elected by the same electorate as the Central and State Legislatures, it is as well that his position is that of a Constitutional President.

Then we come to the Ministers. They are of course responsible to the legislature and tender advice to the President who is bound to act according to that advice. Although there are no specific provisions, so far as I know, in the Constitution itself making it binding on the President to accept the advice of his Ministers, it is hoped that the convention under which in England the King acts always on the advice of his Ministers will be established in this country also and, the President, not so much on account of the written word in the Constitution, but as the result of this very healthy convention, will become a Constitutional President in all matters.

The Central Legislature consists of two Houses known as the House of People and the Council of States which both together constitute the Parliament of India. In the provinces, or States as they are now called, we shall have a Legislative Assembly in all of them except those which are mentioned in Parts C and D of Schedule I, but every one of them will not have a Second Chamber. Some of the provinces, whose representatives felt that a Second Chamber is required for them, have been provided with a Second Chamber. But there is a provision in the Constitution that if a province does not want such a Second Chamber to continue or if a province which has not got one wants to establish one, the wish has to be expressed through the legislature by a majority of two-thirds of the Members voting and by a majority of the total number of Members in the Legislative Assembly. So, even while providing some of the States with Second Chambers, we have provided also for their easy removal or for their easy establishment by making this kind of amendment of the constitution not a Constitutional Amendment, but a matter of ordinary parliamentary legislation.

We have provided for adult suffrage by which the legislative assemblies in the provinces and the House of the People in the Centre will be elected. It is a very big step that we have taken. It is big not only because our present electorate is a very much smaller electorate and based very largely on property qualification, but it is also big because it involves tremendous numbers. Our population now is something like 320 millions if not more and we have found from experience gained during the enrolment of voters that has been going on in the provinces that 50 per cent roughly represent the adult population. And on that basis we shall have not less than 160 million voters on our rolls. The work of organising election by such vast numbers is of tremendous magnitude and there is no other country where election on such a large scale has ever yet been held.

I will just mention to you some facts in this connection. The legislative assemblies in the provinces, it is roughly calculated, will have more than 3,800 members who will have to be elected in as many constituencies or perhaps a few less. Then there will be something like 500 members for the House of the People and about 220 Members for the Council of States. We shall thus have to provide for the election of more than 4,500 members and the country will have to be divided into something like 4,000 constituencies or so. I was the other day, as a matter of amusement, calculating what our electoral roll will look like. If you print 40 names on a page of foolscap size, we shall require something like 20 lakhs of sheets of foolscap size to print all the names of the voters, and if you combine the whole thing in one volume, the thickness of the volume will be something like 200 yards. That alone gives us some idea of the vastness of the task and the work involved in finalising the rolls, delimiting constituencies, fixing polling stations and making other arrangements which will have to be done between now and the winter of 1950-51 when it is hoped the elections may be held.

Some people have doubted the wisdom of adult franchise. Personally, although I look upon it as an experiment the result of which no one will be able to forecast today, I am not dismayed by it. I am a man of the village and although I have had to live in cities for a pretty long time, on account of my work, my roots are still there. I, therefore, know the village people who will constitute the bulk of this vast electorate. In my opinion, our people possess intelligence and commonsense. They also have a culture which the sophisticated people of today may not appreciate, but which is solid. They are not literate and do not possess the mechanical skill of reading and writing. But, I have no doubt in my mind that they are able to take measure of their own interest and also of the interests of the country at large if things are explained to them. In fact, in some respects, I consider them to be even more intelligent than many a worker in a factory, who loses his individuality and becomes more or less a part of the machine which he has to work. I have, therefore, no doubt in my mind that if things are explained to them, they will not only be able to pick up the technique of election, but will be able to cast their votes in an intelligent manner and I have, therefore, no misgivings about the future, on their account. I cannot say the same thing about the other people who may try to influence them by slogans and by placing before them beautiful pictures of impracticable programmes. Nevertheless, I think their sturdy commonsense will enable them to see things in the right perspective. We can, therefore, reasonably hope that we shall have legislatures composed of members who shall have their feet on the ground and who will take a realistic view of things.

Although provision has been made for a Second Chamber in the Parliament and for Second Chambers in some of the States, it is the popular House which is supreme. In all financial and money matters, the supremacy of the popular House is laid down in so many words. But even in regard to other matters where the Upper Chamber may be said to have equal powers for initiating and passing laws, the supremacy of the popular House is assured. So far as Parliament is concerned, if a difference arises between the two Chambers, a joint session may be held; but the Constitution provides that the number of Members of the Council of States shall not be more than 50 per cent of the Members of the House of the People. Therefore, even in the case of a joint session, the supremacy of the House of the People is maintained, unless the majority in that very House is a small one which will be just a case in which its supremacy should not prevail. In the case of provincial legislatures, the decision of the Lower House prevails if it is taken a second time. The Upper Chamber therefore can only delay the passage of Bills for a time, but cannot prevent it. The President or the Governor, as the case may be, will have to give his assent to any legislation, but that will be only on the advice of his Ministry which is responsible ultimately to the popular House. Thus, it is the will of the people as expressed by their representatives in the popular Chamber that will finally determine all matters. The Second Chamber and the President or the Governor can only direct reconsideration and can only cause some delay; but if the popular Chamber is determined, it will have its way under the Constitution. The Government therefore of the country as a whole, both in the Centre and in the provinces, will rest on the will of the people which will be expressed from day to day through their representatives in the legislatures and, occasionally directly by them at the time of the general elections.

We have provided in the Constitution for a judiciary which will be independent. It is difficult to suggest anything more to make the Supreme Court and the High Courts independent of the influence of the executive. There is an attempt made in the Constitution to make even the lower judiciary independent of any outside or extraneous influence. One of our articles makes it easy for the State Governments to introduce separation of executive from Judicial functions and placing the magistracy which deals with criminal cases on similar footing as Civil Courts. I can only express the hope that this long overdue reform will soon be introduced in the States.

Our Constitution has devised certain independent agencies to deal with particular matters. Thus, it has provided for Public Service Commission both for the Union and for the States and placed such Commission on an independent footing so that they may discharge their duties without being influenced by the executive. One of the things against which we have to guard is that there should be no room as far as it is humanly possible for jobbery, nepotism and favouritism. I think the provisions which we have introduced into our Constitution will be very helpful in this direction. Another independent authority is the Comptroller and Auditor-General who will watch our finances and see to it that no part of the revenues of India or of any of the States is used for purposes and on items without due authority and whose duty it will be otherwise to keep our accounts in order. When we consider that our Governments will have to deal with hundreds of crores, it becomes clear how important and vital this Department will be. We have provided another important authority, i.e., the Election Commissioner whose function it will be to conduct and supervise the elections to the legislatures and to take all other necessary action in connection with them. One of the dangers which we have to face arises out of any corruption which parties, candidates or the Government in power may practise. We have had no experience of democratic elections for a long time except during the last few years and now that we have got real power, the danger of corruption is not only imaginary. It is therefore as well that our Constitution guards against this danger and makes provision for an honest and straightforward election by the voters. In the case of the legislature, the High Courts, the Public Services Commission, the Comptroller and Auditor-General and the Election Commissioner, the Staff which will assist them in their work has also been placed under their control and in most of these cases their appointment, promotion and discipline vest in the particular institution to which they belong thus giving additional safeguards about their independence.

The Constitution has given in two Schedules, namely Schedules V and VI, special provisions for administration and control of Scheduled Areas and Scheduled Tribes. In the case of the Tribes and Tribal Areas in States other than Assam, the Tribes will be able to influence the administration through the Tribes Advisory Council. In the case of the Tribes and Tribal Areas in Assam, they are given larger powers through their District Councils and Autonomous Regional Councils. There is further provision for a Minister in the State

Ministries to be in charge of the welfare of the Tribes and the Scheduled Castes and a Commission will also report about the way in which the areas are administered. It was necessary to make this provision on account of the backwardness of the Tribes which require protection and also because of their own way of solving their own problems and carrying on their Tribal life. These provisions have given them considerable satisfaction as the provision for the welfare and protection of the Scheduled Castes has given satisfaction to them.

The Constitution has gone into great details regarding the distribution of power and functions between the Union and the States in all aspects of their administrative and other activities. It has been said by some that the powers given to the Centre are too many and too extensive and the States have been deprived of power which should really belong to them in their own fields. I do not wish to pass any judgment on this criticism and can only say that we cannot be too cautious about our future, particularly when we remember the history of this country extending over many centuries. But such powers as have been given to the Centre to act within the sphere of the States relate only to emergencies, whether political or financial and economic, and I do not anticipate that there will be any tendency on the part of the Centre to grab more power than is necessary for good administration of the country as a whole. In any case the Central Legislature consists of representatives from the States and unless they are convinced of their overriding necessity, they are not likely to consent to the use of any such powers by the Central executive as against the States whose people they represent. I do not attach much importance to the complaint that residuary powers have been vested in the Union. Powers have been very meticulously and elaborately defined and demarcated in the three lists of Schedule Seven, and the residue whatever it may be, is not likely to cover any large field, and, therefore, the vesting of such residuary powers does not mean any very serious derogation in fact from the power which ought to belong to the States.

One of the problems which the Constituent Assembly took considerable time in solving relates to the language for official purposes of the country. There is a natural desire that we should have our own language, and in spite of difficulties on account of the multiplicity of languages prevalent in the country, we have been able to adopt Hindi which is the language that is understood by the largest number of people in the country as our official language. I look upon this as a decision of very great importance when we consider that in a small country like Switzerland they have no less than three official languages and in South Africa two official languages. It shows a spirit of accommodation and a determination to organise the country as one nation that those whose language is not Hindi have voluntarily accepted it as the official language. (Cheers.) There is no question of imposition now. English during the period of British rule, Persian during the period of the Muslim Empire were Court and official languages. Although people have studied them and have acquired proficiency in them, nobody can claim that they were voluntarily adopted by the people of the country at large. Now for the first time in our history we have accepted one language which will be the language to be used all over the country for all official purposes, and let me hope that it will develop into a national language in which all will feel equal pride while each area will be not only free, but also encouraged to develop its own peculiar language in which its culture and its traditions are enshrined. The use of English during the period of transition was considered inevitable for practical reasons and no one need be despondent over this decision, which has been dictated purely by practical considerations. It is the duty of the country as a whole now and especially of those whose language is Hindi to so shape and develop it as to make it the language in which the composite culture of India can find its expression adequately and nobly.

Another important feature of our Constitution is that it enables amendments to be made without much difficulty. Even the constitutional amendments are not as difficult as in the case of some other countries, but many of the provisions in the Constitution are capable of being amended by the Parliament by ordinary acts and do not require the procedure laid down for constitutional amendments to be followed. There was a provision at one time which proposed that amendments should be made easy for the first five years after the Constitution comes into force, but such a provision has become unnecessary on account of the numerous exceptions which have been made in the Constitution itself for amendments without the procedure laid down for constitutional amendments. On the whole, therefore, we have been able to draft a Constitution which I trust will serve the country well.

There is a special provision in our Directive Principles to which I attach great importance. We have not provided for the good of our people only but have laid down in our Directive Principles that our State shall endeavour to promote material peace and security, maintain just and honourable relations between nations, foster respect for international law and treaty obligations and encourage settlement of international disputes by arbitration. In a world torn with conflicts, in a world which even after the devastation of two world wars is still depending on armaments to establish peace and goodwill, we are destined to play a great part, if we prove true to the teachings of the Father of the Nation and give effect to this Directive Principle in our Constitution. Would to God that he would give us the wisdom and the strength to pursue this path in spite of the difficulties which beset us and the atmosphere which may well choke us. Let us have faith in ourselves and in the teachings of the Master whose portrait hangs over my head and we shall fulfil the hopes and prove true to the best interests of not only our country but of the world at large.

I do not propose to deal with the criticism which relate mostly to the articles in the part dealing with Fundamental Rights by which absolute rights are curtailed and the articles dealing with Emergency Powers. Other members have dealt with these objections at great length. All that I need state at this stage is that the present conditions of the country and tendencies which are apparent have necessitated these provisions which are also based on the experience of other countries which have had to enforce them through judicial decisions, even when they were not provided for in the Constitution.

There are only two regrets which I must share with the honourable members. I would have liked to have some qualifications laid down for members of the legislatures. It is anomalous that we should insist upon high qualifications for those who administer or help in administering the law but none for those who made it except that they are elected. A law giver requires intellectual equipment but even more than that capacity to take a balanced view of things to act independently and above all to be true to those fundamental things of life—in one word—to have character. (Hear, hear.) It is not possible to devise any yardstick for measuring the moral qualities of a man and so long as that is not possible, our Constitution will remain defective. The other regret is that we have not been able to draw up our first Constitution of a free Bharat in an Indian language. The difficulties in both cases were practical and proved insurmountable. But that does not make the regret any the less poignant.

We have prepared a democratic Constitution. But successful

working of democratic institutions requires in those who have to work them willingness to respect the viewpoints of others, capacity for compromise and accommodation. Many things which cannot be written in a Constitution are done by conventions. Let me hope that we shall show those capacities and develop those conventions. The way in which we have been able to draw this Constitution without taking recourse to voting and to divisions in lobbies strengthens that hope.

Whatever the Constitution may or may not provide, the welfare of the country will depend upon the way in which the country is administered. That will depend upon the men who administer it. It is a trite saying that a country can have only the Government it deserves. Our Constitution has provisions in it which appear to some to be objectionable from one point or another. We must admit that the defects are inherent in the situation in the country and the people at large. If the people who are elected are capable and men of character and integrity, they would be able to make the best even of a defective Constitution. If they are lacking in these, the Constitution cannot help the country. After all, a Constitution like a machine is a lifeless thing. It acquires life because of the men who control it and operate it, and India needs today nothing more than a set of honest men who will have the interest of the country before them. There is a fissiparous tendency arising out of various elements in our life. We have communal differences, caste differences, language differences, provincial differences and so forth. It requires men of strong character, men of vision, men who will not sacrifice the interests of the country at large for the sake of smaller groups and areas and who will rise over the prejudices which are born of these differences. We can only hope that the country will throw up such men in abundance. I can say this from the experience of the struggle that we have had during the period of the freedom movement that new occasions throw up new men; not once but almost on every occasion when all leading men in the Congress were clapped [*sic*] into prison suddenly without having the time to leave instructions to others and even to make plans for carrying on their campaigns, people arose from amongst the masses who were able to continue and conduct the campaigns with intelligence, with initiative, with capacity for organisation which nobody suspected they possessed. I have no doubt that when the country needs men of character, they will be coming up and the masses will throw them up. Let not those who have served in the past therefore rest on their oars, saying that they have done their part and now has come the time for them to enjoy the fruits of their labours. No such time comes to anyone who is really earnest about his work. In India today I feel that the work that confronts us is even more difficult than the work which we had when we were engaged in the struggle. We did not have then any conflicting claims to reconcile, no loaves and fishes to distribute, no powers to share. We have all these now, and the temptations are really great. Would to God that we shall have the wisdom and the strength to rise above them, and to serve the country which we have succeeded in liberating.

Mahatma Gandhi laid stress on the purity of the methods which had to be pursued for attaining our ends. Let us not forget that this teaching has eternal value and was not intended only for the period of stress and struggle but has as much authority and value today as it ever had before. We have a tendency to blame others for everything that goes wrong and not to introspect and try to see if we have any share in it or not. It is very much easier to scan one's own actions and motives if one is inclined to do so than to appraise correctly the actions and motives of others. I shall only hope that all those whose good fortune it may be to work this Constitution in future will remember that it was a unique victory which we achieved by the unique method taught to us by the Father of the Nation, and it is up to us to preserve and protect the independence that we have won and to make it really bear fruit for the man in the street. Let us launch on this new enterprise of running our Independent Republic with confidence, with truth and non-violence and above all with heart within and God over head. Before I close, I must express my thanks to all the members of this august Assembly from whom I have received not only courtesy but, if I may say so, also their respect and affection. Sitting in the Chair and watching the proceedings from day to day I have realised as nobody else could have, with what zeal and devotion the members of the Drafting Committee and especially its Chairman, Dr. Ambedkar in spite of his indifferent health, have worked. (Cheers.) We could never make a decision which was or could be ever so right as when we put him on the Drafting Committee and made him its Chairman. He has not only justified his selection but has added lustre to the work which he has done. In this connection, it would be invidious to make any distinction as among the other members of the Committee. I know they have all worked with the same zeal and devotion as its Chairman, and they deserve the thanks of the country.

I must convey, if you will permit me, my own thanks as well as the thanks of the house to our Constitutional Adviser, Shri B.N. Rau, who worked honorarily all the time that he was here, assisting the Assembly not only with his knowledge and erudition but also enabled the other members to perform their duties with thoroughness and intelligence by supplying them with the material on which they could work. In this he was assisted by his band of research workers and other members of the staff who worked with zeal and devotion. Tribute has been paid justly to Shri S.N. Mukerjee who has proved of such invaluable help to the Drafting Committee.

Coming to the staff of the Secretariat of the Constituent Assembly I must first mention and thank the Secretary, Mr. H.V.R. Iengar, who organised the Secretariat as an efficient working body. Although latterly when the work began to proceed with more or less clockwork regularity, it was possible for us to relieve him of part of his duties to take up other work, but he has never lost touch with our Secretariat or with the work of the Constituent Assembly.

The members of the staff have worked with efficiency and with devotion under our Deputy Secretary Shri Jugal Kishore Khanna. It is not always possible to see their work which is done removed from the gaze of the members of this Assembly but I am sure the tribute which member after member has paid to their efficiency and devotion to work is thoroughly deserved. Our reporters have done their work in a way which will give credit to them and which has helped in the preservation of a record of the proceedings of the Assembly which have been long and taxing. I must mention the translators as also the Translation Committee under the Chairmanship of Honourable Shri G.S. Gupta who have had a hard job in finding Hindi equivalents for English terms used in the Constitution. They are just now engaged in helping a Committee of Linguistic Experts in evolving a vocabulary which will be acceptable to all other languages as equivalents to English words used in the Constitution and in law. The Watch and Ward offices, and the Police and last though not least the Marshall have all performed their duties to our satisfaction. (Cheers.) I should not forget the peons and even the humbler people. They have all done their best. It is necessary for me to say all this because with the completion of the work of Constitution-framing most of them who have been working on a temporary basis, will be out of employment unless they could be absorbed in other Departments and Ministries. I do hope that it will be possible to absorb them (hear, hear) as they have considerable experience and are willing and efficient set of workers. All deserve my thanks as I have received courtesy, cooperation and loyal service from all.

It now remains to put the motion which was moved by Dr. Ambedkar, to the vote of the House.

11

THE SPIRIT OF FREEDOM: QUEST FOR A JUST AND MORAL SOCIETY

A study of India's march to nationhood reveals a pattern unique in modern history. Whereas 'nation' and 'nationalism' in many parts of the world have come about by advocating exclusivity and the creation of barriers among populations, in the Indian context nation-making was a refreshingly liberating experience. It enlarged not only the frontiers of the political landscape but also the possibilities of human freedom. Many people miss this very basic reading of the history of the subcontinent. Terms like 'Muslim nationalism' that M.A. Jinnah tried to popularize (and many Western as well as Indian authors use for the sake of theoretical convenience, superimposing it on the more appropriate Muslim communalism in the Indian context) and the idea of what is referred to as Hindu nationalism as well as later developments like Sikh communalism (also referred to as Sikh nationalism to give it legitimacy—both political and intellectual) were antagonistic to the spirit of Indian nationalism as they restricted the boundaries of the possibilities inherent in the appeal of what was called Indian nationalism. Yet, very rarely did the national movement try to block the ideological or practical expression of such divergent mobilization of aspirations, believing that a true nation ought to provide space for a large number of liberating experiences and opportunities. The modern Indian renaissance in terms of literature, music, arts and social reform has been coterminous with these movements along with the overarching movement for freedom from colonialism. Very rarely has the creative expression of human freedom come from the philosophical bases of Hindu nationalism or Muslim nationalism while the more inclusive national movement fostered within it a large number of movements for freedom from myriad bondages like a patriarchal society, caste, class and feudal set-up.

The essence of the history of the idea of India has been a republican quest for equality in all spheres of life. This went beyond even the French idea which quite often degenerated into Gallic chauvinism. Equality has been an intellectual as well as political idea enveloping in it ethical and social movements. It is this idea of equality that made people demand justice and try and unsettle institutions which impeded human self-realization, set up new codes of public and private morality and moral order, and finally critique all bounded notions of human survival. Caste, for example, has been one such institution which was considered abominable by people from Rammohun Roy and Jyotiba Phule to Mahatma Gandhi who saw in its hierarchical nature the denial of not only human self-respect but also a denial of basic survival needs. Thus, at the first opportunity during the framing of the constitution, R.R. Diwakar, who had been closely involved in the movement for political freedom, demanded legislation to eliminate caste from official records. Likewise, political stalwarts wasted little time after independence in passing an act providing for the abolition of the practice of untouchability, a long-cherished dream of many who had fought for the nation's freedom.

In 1947, India emerged out of almost two hundred years of colonial experience. A major political drive at the onset of freedom was the one against the feudal structure which was primarily characterized by native rulers, zamindars and Indian princes who had been the bulwark of colonialism, its foremost apologists. Since the beginning of the struggle for freedom, the leadership which guided the struggle came primarily from the modern, quite often English-educated intellectual and not the native rulers and traditional leaders. The national leaders wanted to do away with feudal structures, and towards that end demanded an amalgamation of the native states into the democratic order that was to be born. While Nehru echoed the overall sentiments of the people in this respect, it was Sardar Patel who gave effect to those sentiments through his arduous efforts in dismantling these structures. The voice of a legislator from Bihar, Tajamul Hosain, in the Constituent Assembly in 1947-48 gives one a sense of the popular anger against the feudal set-up.

A democratic society, modern and enlightened, not only demanded the abolition of caste and feudal structures but also a new legal framework of rules and norms that fostered equality. Of primary importance was ushering in a world of equality for women, on whom the weight of tradition and religiously sanctioned laws was the heaviest. The need for a common Hindu code had been felt since the 1940s, and in 1941 the Hindu Law Committee had been appointed under B.N. Rau. The committee's report was overwhelmingly in favour of modernizing the legal structure and codifying Hindu laws so that a common Hindu code could be promulgated. In the vitiated atmosphere of the 1940s, this was seen as too radical a project and the communal and conservative elements which held sway opposed all initiatives in this regard. With independence, one thought that Nehru and a leadership with a new zeal would see it through. The new law minister, B.R. Ambedkar, who was seen as the new Manu, moved the motion in 1948 to get the Hindu Code Bill passed. The bill came up against massive opposition which more or less killed it. Eventually, a truncated version of the bill, broken up into four separate bills, was passed in 1955-56. However, the failure cost the republic badly as the idea of a common civil code (for all communities) got drowned in the whole episode and remained a dream for progressives.

Despite such hiccups, the spirit of freedom and a vision for a just and equal society pulsated through the Indian political panorama. The leadership which framed the contours of the nation never lost sight of the common man. From the time of Dadabhai Naoroji, debates on poverty and development, the suffering of the poor and the establishment's responsibility towards alleviating this remained the centrepiece of India's political and intellectual life. Whether it was acquiring tribal land for development projects or the treatment of Dalits and tribal people or even the issue of capital punishment, a deep sense of empathy for the lowest common denominator guided those who represented the Indian people. The Indian Parliament, being the largest public space for such representatives, has often reverberated with the speeches of those who never allowed the establishment to forget the poor, the underprivileged and the marginalized. These speeches articulate the Indian quest for freedom, for a just and humane society and an equal and moral site of humanity.

N.G. CHANDAVARKAR

The Children of Light

On 30 December 1905 at Benares, N.G. Chandavarkar addressed the Indian National Social Reform Conference which M.G. Ranade and Chandavarkar had founded as a forum for those who were trying to bring reforms in Indian society. The extraordinary address tried to structure a moral universe in a purely non-religious and rhetorical way, drawing examples from the Upanishadic thought of the progression from darkness to light.

The ancient world, said Mr. John Morley in his lecture on Machiavelli, delivered in the Sheldonian Theatre on the 2nd of June 1897, thought that Man existed for the State, whereas we, in modern times, think that the State exists for Man. Aristotle, he continued, could not conceive of a good life apart from the State; for, according to the ancient Greeks, outside it a man's moral obligations disappeared. The relation of man to humanity at large, to the universe of which humanity is but a part, was not an integral factor of the common morality of the ancient world, though Socrates made an approach towards universal morality. The same opinion is shared by other thinkers of our times. For instance, Mr. Bernard Bosanquet, in his 'Civilisation of Christendom and Other Studies', remarks that the conception of a universal humanity...is absolutely modern and is the outcome of the conviction that 'a single principle or will lies at the root of nature and is also embodied in the minds and actions of men' forming 'the inspiring conviction of every progressive society, as of all science and practical energy'.

These remarks are suggestive of the question, all important to us who are gathered here to think on and promote the cause of social reform—the question whether the ancient Hindus fall within the description of Mr. John Morley and Mr. Bernard Bosanquet. I am not the man to go into hysterics over our ancient civilisation and paint it in colours of exaggeration because it suits our pride at the present moment; but, viewing it in a spirit of calmness and making due allowance for its defects, it appears to me that the Rishis of old, who laid down our laws and conceived the ideas, out of which Hindu society emerged, started with the conception of a universal morality and the birthright of humanity as the deep-down basis of life. What is familiar to us in these days as the 'Eternal Verities' or, as the

'Everlasting yea' and the 'Everlasting Nay', in the expressive language of Carlyle, had found its eloquent exponents in the Rishis, who never tired of their faith in the principle of unity underlying the mind and actions of men as well as the mind and actions of nature. They gave it the name of Sanatana Dharma or the Shaswata Dharma, i.e., the religion of the eternal verities unconditional and applicable to all human beings of whatever caste, class, or creed, embodying the laws of the universal mind, and the principle of universal morality, as distinguished from the Varnashrama Dharma or the laws applicable to particular castes or conditions of life. For instance, in the Apaddharma Parva of the Shanti Parva of the Mahabharata, Truth is represented as the Sanatana Dharma or the Religion of the Eternal Verities and Truth is described as comprehending the virtues of *Samata* (equity or justice), *Dama* (self-control), *Amatsaryam* (freedom from jealousy), *Kshama* (mercy), *Hri* (self-respect), *Titiksha* (patience), *Anusuyata* (freedom from fault-finding), *Tyaga* (liberality), *Dhyana* (meditation), *Aryatva* (magnanimity), *Dhriti* (resolution), *Daya* (sympathy) and *Ahinsa* (humanity). And in the Bhagavat Gita, God after saying that he has established the Dharmas of the four castes, according to qualities and actions—not, mind you, according to birth—declares that He is the Creator and Founder of the Shaswata Dharma, i.e., the religion of the Eternal Verities or Universal Morality. This conception of the fundamental unity and universal morality is acknowledged by Emerson as finding 'its highest expression' in our Vedas, the Bhagavat Gita, and the Vishnu Puran, which, he observes, 'rise to pure and sublime strains in celebrating it'. But it is not the purely religious books alone that dwelt upon it, even the legislator took notice of it, as may be judged from the immortal stanza of Yajnyavalkya on universal morality.

Starting with this idea of the fundamental unity and universal morality, the Rishis conceived of man, as a spiritual being, standing for the spiritual interests of the world. Get into the heart of the best of their description of man in relation to the universe surrounding him, pore over their subtlest analysis of his actions and emotions and you find that man, the individual, stood to them not as 'a mere fraction of society' or what the ancient Greeks and Romans, according to Mr. John Morley, regarded 'as a mere cog or pinion on the vast machine of the State' but as an 'epitome' of the Society and of the State as well. Hence our ancient law books begin not with the duties of the king and subjects or the rules of the complicated machinery of

Judicature, State or Society, but the first place is given to the development of the individual and family life. The deep significance of that is, as I conceive it, that to the ancient Rishis, the true social bond was the moral ideal; spiritual evolution was the end of Society and State, and progress which consisted in fulfilment of the moral ideal, was to be attained through Man, the individual and the Family as the unit of Society and the State.

Hence the perfection of the individual was the first problem to which the Rishis applied themselves. They seemed to say: 'Get hold of your individual first, develop him and your ideal of State and Society will be realised.' They laid down rules for his education when young, his daily life in adult and old age. These rules may indeed seem to us in several particulars, minute and tedious and here and there crude. But we must not judge of a people's civilisation by the details of the rules and laws prescribed for a particular period of their growth. The cardinal fact is to find the central idea underlying them, and the ideal by which those rules were evolved. The rules were merely applications to the details of life as it existed at that time: they were mere forms and machinery. But they recognised that the forms and machinery are transient, the central idea of them as the root of the civilisation stood for permanence. It was on that account that they laid down the rule that custom was above the Shastras. But whether over custom or the Shastras, one law was intended to stand supreme—the law of the Sanatana Dharma or the Shaswata Dharma: the law of Universal Morality or Eternal Verities embodied in the single word Truth—Truth standing for Justice, Love and Mercy. What was the central idea round which the machinery of Society was made to move by the Rishis of old? In the mass of the detailed performance of duties, prescribed for the individual one idea stands out most prominently, viz., that he was to pray, to yearn, and to seek for 'light'. The Gayatri, which the individual was to utter with unerring regularity morning and evening, is no more and no less than the cry of the human soul for Light. It is an appeal to God that His Light may be shed on the mind of the individual to illuminate it. It is a national prayer, because it is the form enjoined on each individual; and we are taught there to pray, not for bread, because 'man was not born for bread alone' but for 'Heaven's Light, our Guide'—it teaches us 'to bask in the great morning which rises forever out of the eastern seas and be ourselves children of Light'. It is not the Gayatri or Sandhya alone which points to the ideal yearning. The Upanishads too emphasise it, for there again we are taught to pray every day of our lives for light, the light of truth. '*Asatomam Sadyamaya, Tamsomam Jotirgamaya*' i.e., 'Lead me from Untruth to Truth: from Darkness to Light'. Such was yearning for light that, according to the Gita, men learned in Brahma are said to find salvation when they depart in 'fire, light, day time, the bright fortnight and the six months of the northern solstice'. When God reveals Himself to Arjuna, it is the refulgence of Light that Arjuna saw. And, realising the value of the symbol as the best argument, the Rishis sought to enforce this ideal yearning of Light by means of ceremonies. The ceremony by means of which the boy, when he is eight years of age, is invested with sacred thread and initiated into the responsibilities of serious life is performed before Fire, the emblem of Light, to teach the boy that his principal duty is to be a child of Light. The marriage ceremony, too, is performed in the same presence; ... the man and woman, wedded as husband and wife, are enjoined to preserve the sacred fire in whose presence the material bond was tied, and to worship it. Family life was thus conceived and represented as the centre of the social system; the home was made a shrine or a sanctuary, not a mere lodging house but 'a haven of rest and strength' where God dwelt because Light shone.

This was the central idea and ideal of ancient Hindu life—the pivot round which society was enjoined to move. 'We were children of Light.' And what did this national yearning for Light, prescribed in the best of our prayers, solemnised in symbolic worship and idealised in spirit of grace and grandeur by the sweetest of our prophets and poets, mean? For what did it stand? It stood as a lesson to us—a lesson to sink into our hearts and animate our lives—that we should always move with the times by means of the light of knowledge acquired, experiences gained, and events revealed; that we should ever move forwards, instead of standing still. It stood for the light of the seer, the insight of the sage and the foresight of the statesman. Are we children of Light now? Institution and customs, good enough perhaps for the times for which they were devised, intended to meet the wants, the necessities and surrounding circumstances of particular age, as suited to the environment, according to the Light that then shone on the minds of our ancestors, have exalted themselves at the sacrifice of their end; and the central ideal of the people, the yearning for light which discovers a new age, new necessities, new aspirations, has been obscured by the ideal of blind usage and customs, with the result that we have become seekers after the very darkness which we are taught by the Rishis to avoid. Life has become monotonous and the sacredness of personality—that which contributes to the growth and greatness of people—has gone out, making us, as Mr. John Morley would say, mere cogs or pinions on the vast machine of society. The Rishis said, 'Seek Light' and the Hindu went to foreign lands, founded colonies and spread abroad his religion, and returned with his love for his country made all the stronger for the excursion. We all know what becomes of the man who always stays at home and never gets out. Browning in two of his poems 'Parting in the Morning' and 'Meeting at Night' illustrates the common-place truth that that man is happy who leaves his house in the morning, spends his day abroad and returns home at night, rejoins his family and then his home becomes all the sweeter and brighter for the day's outing. These two little gems of a poetic piece are intended by the poet to convey the truth that the two supreme necessities of human existence, whether individual or national, are going out and coming in, going abroad and returning to one's own country. One learns one's country better, loves it more by looking about and travelling abroad.

But we have put a ban on foreign travel—and this is how we yearn for Light. The Rishis said husband and wife are one and are to seek Light—the light of Truth, Justice and Mercy—together. They enjoined upon them both together the worship of Grihyagni or the Domestic Light, because by means of it they sought to impress upon them the lesson that both together should be seekers of the Divine Light of intelligence, i.e., Truth. ... they laid down the law that a man shall marry again on the death of his first wife, because he cannot seek Light without the cooperation of a wife. But they hedged that around with the restriction that no man shall marry a second time who has a son by his first wife. But now who thinks of the Grihyagni or the yearning for Light? That is gone; and an old dotard with one foot in the grave, who has sons, is not ashamed but thinks he is only carrying out the injunctions of the Rishis when he marries a babe of a girl and society encourages him in the name of the Sanatana Dharma. Woman to yearn with the husband for Light must have intelligence cultivated—but she is steeped in darkness and has taken her revenge upon us, and we have become the children of superstition. And yet we talk of this as our Sanatana Dharma! What would the Rishis have thought of this! Where is their religion of the Eternal Verities, the Universal Religion, the Religion of Humanity on which, Mr. John Morley points out, all conception of modern progress is based, constituting 'the only safe foundation of modern polities', while we will not raise even a finger to help the fallen but will uphold the tyranny of caste, and the ignorance or seclusion or miseries of womanhood. The Rishis of old said, 'This poisonous tree, the World, has produced two species of sweet fruits, Love and Poetry.' And they made Ahimsam (Humanity) the first leading principle of the Sanatana Dharma. But we use that sacred word, are proud of our Sanatana Dharma, while we go on perpetuating castes in minute sub-divisions and think nothing of and do nothing for those whom custom has treated as the lower classes. Our love is for ourselves and our castes and the neighbour is nothing to us. And yet we stand up for the Sanatana Dharma.

If we are to fit ourselves as a people for the work of the world in the modern times, we must rise to a juster and nobler conception of that which, according to Mr. John Morley, forms the moving spring of modern civilisation. And such a conception ought not to be difficult for us to attain, because, after all is said against our ancient civilisation, it forms its central ideal. To a people for whom their Rishis have laid down the prayer for Light, as the very essence of their daily lives, when truly lived, who in the spirit of that Light conceived the idea of universal morality and humanity which is the foundation of modern progress, it ought not to be a great effort if only the educated among them will go back to this national yearning for Light and use the sacred words Sanatana Dharma not lightly but in the spirit of seriousness and will not confound it with the narrow morality of castes. But we shall never get to a just conception and proper realisation of that inspiring ideal of our ancients so long as we fail to perceive what the Rishis perceived that the home and family life are the real units of Society and State. Truly has it been said by one of the greatest sages: 'Domestic events immediately concern us; public events may or may not; that which is done and cared for at home—not what is carried on or left undone in the State-house—must be the history of times and the spirit of the age to us.'

And this is what the ancient Rishis realised. Hence in their utterances we see the grand strokes of Light typified as the emblem of Truth and Holiness. To those who cry down and oppose the Social Conference as the enemy of Hindu ideals and of the Sanatana Dharma, here is the answer. We appeal to the tenets of the Dharma as the very key-note of the mission of social reform. Times change but eternity remains—the times are a mere masquerade of the 'eternities'. We do not seek anything new—we desire to cast into the mould of the new times the very oldest of thoughts which has been bequeathed to us as a precious legacy of the Rishis in the form of the Sanatana Dharma. What is the very first virtue prescribed by that Dharma? Ahimsa or Humanity. Samata, Equity or Justice. And we ask is it consistent with Ahimsa or Humanity to neglect the fallen, to treat any man, however low his birth, as beyond care and kindness, and doom child widows to lifelong misery?

And I am not afraid to ask this question when we are met in this holy city of Benares, sacred to Hinduism—a city the very look of which 'breathes grandeur upon the very humblest face of human life'. We are met on the bank of the holy Ganges, the source of which the Rishis of old, indulging in one of the brightest of their divine illuminations, drew from 'a skily fount' ...

And I am glad to say the question is not asked in vain. Day by day the stream of Social Reform, drawing its source like the Ganges from the skily fount of Light which we are taught by the Sanatana Dharma to worship and cherish is slowly but surely flowing onwards, to make the people part of the living ocean of the life of the present age. I speak in no spirit of boast when I say that the year just ending has written its word of encouragement and hopefulness on the page of our history. Of some of the years preceding I spoke in my inaugural addresses as years of Social Conferences, provincial, district or communal. But the year 1905 has a brighter record on its credit. While Social Conferences in several provinces have not been wanting, it has been a year of ladies' gatherings and widow marriages. The experiment made in Bombay in the December of 1904, by holding a gathering of ladies, presided over by that model of a Hindu woman, Mrs. Ramabai Ranade, and similar gatherings in several places have followed during the year. The good example has caught and our womankind are to the fore slowly but surely. And the holding of a ladies' gathering here in connection with our Social Conference, under the presidency of the Rani of Partapgarh, is more eloquent of the growing spirit of our cause than any words of mine. As to widow marriages, I have not the exact figures before me just at this moment, but I am, I think, under the mark when I say that there have been during the year no less than 30 widow marriages throughout British India—a great advance upon any of the preceding years. And I repeat what I have said in every inaugural address of mine on the platform of the Social Conference—the right of the Hindus to be in the vanguard of progressive peoples will be judged according as they plead for the widow and the so-called lower classes of society. The question about these classes is a very serious one. But even there the movement is not without its effects of awakening. My friend, Mr. Shinde, missionary of the Prarthana Samaj of Bombay, has been making a tour in the country to find out what is being done for the elevation of those whom we treat as the outcastes of society, and he has published in the papers an interesting account of what he has seen. The signs are so far hopeful.

In the name of the Sanatana Dharma then, the Religion of Universal Morality and Humanity, in the name of the ideal of old, which enjoins us to be 'Children of Light,' I call upon you to go back to the heart of your religion and by means of the ancient light to learn to speak the language of today, to make use of Light to fulfil the obligation imposed on us by the requirements of modern times. The Sanatana Dharma does not mean rites and ceremonies which come and go but equity and right which stand for ever. We see degeneracy everywhere because we do not produce great minds, and it is a universal law of nature, attested by history that 'great minds are not produced in a country where the test of a great mind is agreeing in the opinions of the small minds'. Let us rise to a sense of man-worthiness which can only come of woman-worthiness. The one need of the age is men with convictions, not men with mere opinions who will ring changes on such sacred words as the Sanatana Dharma without the will and the daring to practise it. There is enough of talk but the great thing is action conceived in the spirit of sobriety, self-restraint and self-respect. 'Nothing is impossible to the lover.' Not by hatred of others, not by jealousy of others, not by petty controversies and party conflicts is regeneration possible to any people. Sir Francis Younghusband said the other day in his speech at one of the English Universities that we of this dear land of ours are fitted to be the spiritual leaders of the world. In every sense—in more senses than perhaps he meant, that is true—the people who see Visions will never perish. But we must see Visions as the old Rishis—in a spirit of calmness, of truth, love and resolution, and the Vision must be the ideal of the man who thinks his mission is to uplift the fallen, and relieve the miseries and inequalities of life.

The idea that no man is bound to act up to what he thinks right, what he is convinced is right, but that he must submit to customs, however bad, because society is bound by them, is, I say, un-Hindu because it is in our own Hindu sacred book—the Bhagavat Gita—written, that 'children only and not the learned speak of the speculative and the practical faculties as two. They are but one, for both obtain the self-same end and the place which is gained by the followers of the one is gained by the followers of the other. That man seeth who seeth that the speculative and the practical doctrines are one. These are your ideals, 'children of light' that you were, sanctify yourselves as a people consecrated to the cause of the Social Conference because it draws its inspiration from the genuine Sanatana Dharma of the Rishis and is broad-based upon the great truth, illustrated by the rise and fall of nations, and emphasised by Mr. John Morley in his lecture on Machiavelli that whether it is a Society or State, that which will not cooperate with 'the Universal Mind' and move on the lines of humanity and love, truth and justice, equity and right, self-control..., is doomed to starve, to decay and perish as a dead carcass.

~

MOHANDAS KARAMCHAND GANDHI

Swaraj

Mahatma Gandhi's ideas of swaraj have been widely discussed. While many talk about it as a return to the pristine days of pre-industrial civilization, some link it to an individualistic quest for a simple life. Intellectually, many have tried to attack the attempt to create a modern society by contrasting it with Gandhi's idea of a non-modern society based on handicrafts, gram panchayats and simple living. It needs to be remembered that in leading one of the largest mass movements in human history, and that too through non-violent means, he was articulating ideas in a general manner. The Gandhian programme of swaraj had a radical agenda of social transformation notwithstanding contemporary criticism against it. This can be seen in the address to the open session of the Congress in Karachi in 1930. It was at this session that Jawaharlal Nehru moved what has come to be known as the Karachi Resolution which talked about fundamental rights, land reforms and many other progressive ideas. Knowing that the resolution might face opposition, Gandhi, displaying his trademark acumen, spoke before Nehru so that he could indicate his support for the resolution well before it was moved. Gandhi was in many ways the architect of modern India and its political and social sensibilities, and this speech is testimony to his vision.

But by passing this resolution we make it clear to the world and to our own people what we propose to do as soon as we come into power. Let Government also take note of it. Let those who may have to deal with us at the Round Table Conference also take note of the fact that the Viceroy, under Swaraj, should not get more than Rs. 500 per month. The position has been made as clear as possible, in order that we may not be accused of having sprung sudden surprises on those who have to deal with us. They are also meant to forewarn all concerned. Let them prepare themselves for the coming legislation by modelling their lives in the light of the coming changes.

I shall take a few instances. Clause IV of the fundamental rights protects the culture, language and scripts of the minority. Now though I am sure that Islamic and Aryan cultures are not mutually exclusive and fundamentally different, I must recognise that Musalmans look upon Islamic culture as distinctive from Aryan. Let us therefore cultivate tolerance. Let us try to learn the Urdu language and Urdu script and understand the Musalmans' insistence on it.

Then there is abolition of all disabilities attaching to women, in regard to public employment, office of power or honour etc. The moment this is done, many of the disabilities to which the women are subjected will cease. So far as the Congress is concerned, we have admitted no such disability. We have had Dr. Besant and Shrimati Sarojini Devi as our Presidents and in the future free state it will be open to us to have women presidents.

Religious neutrality is another important provision. Swaraj will favour Hinduism no more than Islam, nor Islam more than Hinduism. But in order that we may have a state based on religious neutrality, let us from now adopt the principle in our daily affairs. Let not a Hindu merchant hesitate to have deserving Muslims as his employees, and let every Congressman make religious neutrality his creed in every walk of life.

Item number five deserves the immediate attention of all mill and factory owners who should anticipate human legislation foreshadowed in the clause.

The last item relates to the control of usury. Islam strictly prohibits the charging of interest but there is no reason why usury should not be regarded as criminal by a Hindu. The Pathans have forgotten the Islamic injunction, have followed our bad example and are known to charge from 200 to 300 per cent interest. I wish I could persuade Khan Abdul Ghaffar Khan to go to our parts to wean his co-religionists from usury. Let also our bankers and moneylenders make drastic reductions in their rates of interest, lest drastic legislation should find them unprepared. The farmers are being crushed to extinction. So let the moneylenders adopt 8 per cent as the maximum rate to afford the same relief.

Let the Zamindars and the Maharajas be assured that the Congress does not seek to destroy them, but is determined to destroy all wrong and injustice. Let them make an earnest endeavour to understand the grievances of their tenants and introduce adequate measures of relief before legislation overtakes them. It is open to them to join the Congress as Raja Saheb of Kalakankar and Chowdhary Raghuvir Narayan Sinha have done.

Let it be understood that this resolution by no means has any finality. It is open to the AICC to revise, amend or add to the twenty points and so let no one oppose the resolution for mere difference on matters of details. Those, however, who are opposed to the policy and principle must reject it, but they must bear in mind that the poor man's Swaraj is soon coming and let them not be found unprepared when it actually comes.

~

M. SINGARAVELU

Fearlessly Expose the Sham of Casteism and Oppression

An advocate and a pioneer of the communist movement in the country, M. Singaravelu (1860–1946) was also a fervent atheist. This presidential address, delivered at the Atheists Conference held at Madras on 31 December 1933, reveals a passionate and logical mind at work. It not only gives a brilliant exposition of the origin of the word 'God' and the history behind theism but also invokes the need to cultivate a rational outlook while providing an idea of the political and social situation in which the conference was held.

Dear Comrades, I think this conference is the first of its kind in the whole of India. One can boldly assert that this conference will bring good to the country and people. Unfortunately some people out of ignorance ridicule this conference. As usual theists indulge in slander. The bureaucrats try to indulge in repression under some pretext or other. This is not new. In the past many progressive movements had been persecuted and ridiculed.

Not content with ridiculing the progressive movement this mad and ignorant world had always tried to stop the spread of scientific knowledge. Ingersol, the famous atheist of America, was not taken note of during his lifetime. He was even ridiculed. But now his birth anniversary is being celebrated in America. Bradlaugh, the British atheist, was put behind bars during his lifetime. Now what happens in Britain? Commemoration meetings in honour of Bradlaugh are now being held in Britain. I am sure in due course still bigger conferences of this kind would be held in this country. It is quite likely that people may forget the name of the atheists but their ideas will remain forever in the minds of the people.

Atheism is one of the ancient doctrines. This doctrine originated and developed side by side with theism. When the concept of god was ushered in along with it and by its side came the doctrine of 'no-god'. Till the time man acquired his faculty to speak, man was not aware of any god. Some of the primitive tribesmen have confessed their ignorance about god. These people can aptly be called Primitive Atheists.

In this connection it is really interesting to note the history of religion. Every religion had proclaimed that people belonging to the other religion were atheists. A non-Hindu is an atheist to a Hindu. To a Muslim any non-Muslim is an atheist. Likewise many more people were termed as atheists. Hence I would like to say I am really proud to be an atheist, as an atheist is not only non-religious but also does not accept the belief in God.

Nasthigam (Atheism) is derived from the Sanskrit root 'naasti', which means no or non-existent. But this has come to denote a person who does not believe in god. We shall see how far this idea can hold water. Among Hindus, Vaishnavites do not believe in Siva and vice-versa. To us it is not a question of disbelieving Siva or Vishnu but both! No wonder bigotry and fanaticism of all kinds are against atheism.

God is an ancient word. It is not a matter nor does it denote any matter. Nobody has seen, touched, tasted or sensed god. But at the same time he is said to have appeared in the form of deer, ox etc. Even a child in these days does not believe these stories. But the fear and respect the word 'god' commands is beyond anybody's comprehension. Millions of people almost daily utter the word. Wars have been waged in the name of this word. People have been harassed and hunted down in the name of this word. The tragedy is in spite of such an impact nobody has seen nor known what god is like. It is something like a blind man trying to locate a black cat in a dark room! No wonder the theists named him 'marai porul' (Hidden). Out of sheer convention and upbringing people believe in the belief of the existence of god. This belief is called Theism. To contend that there is no basis for such a belief is Atheism.

Origin of Belief

Millions of years ago, man had no faculty to speak. Hence the word god would not and could not have been in use at that time. It is claimed by the scientists that nearly 100 millions of years ago, life first came into existence in this world and during those periods millions of lives came into existence and perished too. During those days, the word god could not have been in existence. In the course of evolution, man climbed down from tree and gradually developed human form and physique. After some thousands of years, he began to speak and only after reaching a stage of perfection of expression of his ideas, the word 'god' was uttered. Mr. Frazer, the famous anthropologist, explains in detail this aspect of human development. It goes without saying that the word god came into vogue only after the human race came into existence and only after a stage of perfection of his features. The primitive man referred to abracadabra etc. as gods. They meant five-eyed man, eleven-headed person etc. After a lapse of millions of years, even today that word god is respected and revered. Such is the miracle of this word.

Why and How This Miracle?

Surrounded by wild beasts, the primitive man was afraid of them just as they were afraid of him. Rain, storm, cyclone, thunder, lightning etc. caused him fear. This fear was communicated to his fellow-men by signs. Fear of the natural phenomena against which he was helpless forged into an idea. These forces should be more powerful than him, he concluded. Thus originated the primitive concept of god and the word. When human society advanced, his power for expression developed and in course of time many means of exchanging his ideas by words he developed. This became a fertile soil to attribute thousand and odd words to the idea of god. Like a parrot, man has been repeating this word for centuries.

As the word was his own creation, he began to build houses (temples) for his god. Just as he respects his superiors and elders, he began to respect his god. What all he indulged in such as music, dance, rituals, feasts, etc. were also offered to his god. Thus god slowly developed and advanced as man advanced.

Some shrewd men of those days found an easy way to live and this paved the way for replacing the word with an idol. To make man live perpetually in fear of god, these men did everything possible and thus priesthood came into existence. These priests lived and thrived on the fear and ignorance of men. Thus around the single fiction of the word god the whole edifice of religious and philosophical system of rituals and prayers was built.

What is the earthly benefit of this word? Since time immemorial, wars have been waged in the name of god. Has any one of the so-called vices such as greed, avarice to others' property and land etc. been reduced all these years? Do not thieves, rapists and murderers also pray to god?

Human Sufferings

Who is responsible for epidemics, war, fire, floods and other calamities? Are devils responsible for such calamities? If so who created devils? Tiger attacks and eats cow. Who created cow and also tiger? Snake eats frogs. Who created frogs and also snakes? If human sufferings are caused by devils, why did god create devils? Worse still god is called the merciful and the benevolent. Can theists answer any one of the above questions? No, they cannot.

Is it not an irony that in the name of the most merciful, the most bloody wars have been waged? That thousands of Jains have been burnt alive, that temples have been razed to the ground and crusades fought for centuries? The only benefit is that pundits and purohits lead a happy life in the name of god.

These pundits pose a question, rather a threat. They claim that once the fear of god is removed from the minds of men, it would lead to increase in vices and other anti-social activities. Men will be devoid, they assert, of beauty, goodness, hope, love, morals and ethics. How far is it correct?

Take for example the inmates of a jail. Are they atheists or theists? Were not social crimes prevalent in those good old days? Were not the guilty and culprits ruthlessly punished? Does not the capitalist of today deceive the worker and defraud him of his lawful wages? And who are the capitalists? Are they not theists? Does not the trader adulterate and deceive the consumer? And who is a trader? Is he an atheist or theist? And who loots the major portion of the temple festivities? The same capitalists, traders and business people spend lakhs of money on god and temples. The exploited money, the money that is accumulated by cheating and deceiving the worker and ordinary people, is spent lavishly on the temples.

Now let us go to the root of this problem. What are the causes that lead to social crimes and other so-called vices? The social conditions and social consciousness are the key points. If the present social conditions change, they will bring about a change in the social consciousness of the people. And mind you, this alone will put an end to the so-called sins and vices. The vices and sins have nothing to do with god.

The theists again argue: Fear of hell or heaven is necessary for man, failing which he will not give alms to the poor. Our answer to this question is this: Charity is an insult to human dignity. Further, it demoralises both the giver and the taker of alms.

Now what is this alms giving about? Is it out of poverty a man begs? If so what is poverty due to? Is it not because of the inequality that a man is poor and he begs? What is inequality due to? The capitalist steals from the worker the wages due to him and thus becomes wealthy. And out of the stolen wages a negligible portion is given away as alms! This is nothing but downright deceit.

Thirdly: The theists claim that god is associated with beauty, values, ethics and morals and if once god is rejected the whole edifice of human values will fall down. Our objection is: Beauty, value, etc. differ from people to people. A she-scorpion looks beautiful to a he-scorpion but to us it is incarnation of ugliness. What is beauty to one does not appear so to another. Hence beauty or ugliness depends on individual tastes. The creation of god looks beautiful to one, but it is not so to another.

Darwin has, in detail, explained another aspect of this question. Birds, insects and animals which do not know the name of god, enjoy beauty and nature. Hence appreciating and enjoying beauty has nothing to do with god. To cite an example, a hunter is elated when he finds new means and methods of tracing an animal. A poet is thrilled if he finds a new expression to express his imagination. Thus pleasure is made by men and for men.

The theists claim that if a man is to be gifted with love, compassion, kindness, generosity etc. it needs belief in the existence of god. But we see even animals manifest these qualities even though they have no consciousness of god, let alone getting his blessings.

In the course of history, many beliefs have become obsolete and I am sure even this belief, viz. theism, will also become obsolete in due course. You know that Brahmins of today do not perform their daily rites. Temple-going crowds are becoming thin and thin. Dean Inge has recently expressed with regret that atheism is slowly gaining ground in the Christian World.

Quite recently there was a cyclone havoc in Tamil Nadu. Instead of praying people began to think of finding out ways and means of providing relief to the grief-stricken people.

The first and dangerous effect of theism is that it saps the initiative of man. Ignorance takes deeper roots in him. People are prevented from acquiring scientific knowledge. Theism is not only a negative evil; it is positively harmful to the people. The atheist challenged the theist to point out at least one single good effect of theism that benefited mankind. This challenge has never been accepted till this day. 'The blood of the martyrs is the seed of the church,' goes the saying. 'Whatever may be the future of god, we can never forget and forgive his past.'

Mr. Bradlaugh in his book *Humanity's Gain from Unbelief* has well explained this point.

1. While all religions were in favour of slavery, atheism alone stood against it and saved the people.
2. Atheism fought against all kinds of superstitions and saved humanity from disease and other natural calamities.
3. Fortune-telling, prophecy and other blind superstitious beliefs have been reduced, thanks to atheism.
4. Torturing people in the name of driving out evil spirits, has been now stopped.
5. The arrogance of kings and tyrants has been claimed because of atheism.
6. The axiom of 'Question-not' has been challenged by atheism and this paved the way for the growth and development of ideas of Freedom and Equality.

To crown it all, it is only atheism that instils confidence in man. It is only atheism that proclaims that social and economic inequalities are only manmade. Hence it goads man to seek out ways of removing the obstacles in the way of progress. It is only atheism that proclaims to man: 'Man! Be a man! You alone can convert this earth into a paradise!'

Mr. Laplace, a French Astronomer, had discovered the Nebular Hypotheses. When Napoleon the Great questioned the scientist as to why he had not referred to god, the scientist boldly replied that god was superfluous and hence he had been left out.

Matter consists of millions of atoms and these atoms in the course of development combined and gradually the earth evolved. At a particular stage of development, vegetation came about and this paved the way for evolution of plants and animals. After some thousands of years man evolved from Ape. He climbed down from the tree, began to stand erect and walk. He settled on land and developed his tongue. Out of necessity he made tools and implements. He improved the tools and began a well-settled life in villages first and then in towns. He codified laws, made moral and ethical codes. In all these processes, man developed out of his own attempts and work. At a particular stage of development, when he was not in a position to understand the forces of nature, he feared and the concept of god was ushered in. Thus man invented god and the same man now disowns him, on the solid achievements of science. It is upon this impregnable rock that the atheist builds his edifice.

In the last three centuries, science has made a tremendous headway. When theists said that god created the universe, the Nebular theory scientifically rejected it. The other claim of theists that god created the world has been refuted by geologists. When they argued that god created life, Darwin has punctured this theory. After facing defeat after defeat they have changed fronts. Now they claim that Matter is different from life. Even this has been refuted by science. Science has proved that Life is not a separate matter but it is a combination of several atoms and at a particular stage of development life evolves. It has also been proved that life is the quality of matter. Thus theism has been hunted from pillar to post. Now they have opened a new front viz. consciousness. This is also a figment of imagination. After all what is consciousness? It is only the sum total of movements of the sense organs. The behaviour scientists say 'If you express your ideas through words it is speech. But if you think aloud it is consciousness.'

Thus science is expanding its horizons and theism is now put on docks. It has to lose its ground as the development of science has vindicated the correctness of atheism.

Comrades, crucial battles are ahead of us. So we cannot rest on our oars now. Though it is put on defence, theism has not been completely routed. Power, money, propaganda, etc. still side with theism. Further, the majority of people, out of ignorance, still remain in the camp of theism and we have to reclaim them. The rulers are interested in keeping them within the camp of theism. No wonder religion and theism always go together. Theism with the help of power and money may again and again attempt to bar the growth and development of human initiative. The concrete example is the development of Hitlerism and Fascism. Religious beliefs and other age-old obscurantist ideas are thrust down the throat of people. This is a dangerous trend.

Take again some of the views expressed by Gandhiji. He is openly advocating theism. Further he is trying to make some readjustment in caste system, at best to reform it. In our view these are against the principles of atheism.

The so-called removal of untouchability is a mere device to strengthen religious beliefs among the people. The untouchables numbering about 6 crores are economically poor and downtrodden. What they need is not god or religion. They need a square meal a day and an opportunity to earn a decent livelihood.

There is another danger ahead. The Hindu Mahasabha, the Sanatanists, Muslim communalist etc. are still striving hard to capture the legislative assembly so that Theism can be enthroned again. These are the worst reactionaries in the unfortunate land. Beware comrades, not to lose this opportunity for contesting and capturing every seat in every village and panchayat, in every taluk and district boards.

Fearlessly expose the sham of casteism and oppression. Dethrone ignorance and theism. Please enthrone in its place Atheism and Socialism.

~

RABINDRANATH TAGORE

Crisis in Civilisation

The Renaissance man of modern India, Rabindranath Tagore (1861–1941) strove all his life for a civilizational synthesis of the East and the West. Through his Visva-Bharati University at Santiniketan, he made a conscious effort towards dialogue and harmony between civilizations. He spoke and wrote extensively on the scourge of aggressive nationalism which he held squarely responsible for the conflicts that afflicted the world. On his birthday on 8 May 1941, Tagore made his customary address at Visva-Bharati. In what was to be his last speech before his death later that year, Tagore expressed his hope for humanity despite the uncertainties at home and abroad. This classic speech articulates his quest for a just and moral world order.

Today, I complete eighty years of my life. As I look back on the vast stretch of years that lie behind me and see in clear perspective the history of my early development, I am struck by the change that has taken place both in my own attitude and in the psychology of my countrymen—a change that carries within it a cause of profound tragedy.

Our direct contact with the larger world of men was linked up with the contemporary history of the English people whom we came to know in those earlier days. It was mainly through their mighty literature that we formed our ideas with regard to these newcomers to our Indian shores. In those days the type of learning that was served out to us was neither plentiful nor diverse, nor was the spirit of scientific enquiry very much in evidence. Thus their scope being strictly limited, the educated of those days had recourse to English language and literature. Their days and nights were eloquent with the stately declamations of Burke, with Macaulay's long-rolling sentences, discussions centred upon Shakespeare's drama and Byron's poetry and above all upon the large-hearted liberalism of the nineteenth-century English politics.

At the time though tentative attempts were being made to gain our national independence, at heart we had not lost faith in the generosity of the English race. This belief was so firmly rooted in the sentiments of our leaders as to lead them to hope that the victor would of his own grace pave the path of freedom for the vanquished. This belief was based upon the fact that England at the time provided a shelter to all those who had to flee from persecution in their own country. Political martyrs who had suffered for the honour of their people were accorded unreserved welcome at the hands of the English. I was impressed by this evidence of liberal humanity in the character of the English and thus I was led to set them on the pedestal of my highest respect. This generosity in their national character had not yet been vitiated by Imperialist pride. About this time, as a boy in

England, I had the opportunity of listening to the speeches of John Bright, both in and outside Parliament. The large-hearted, radical liberalism of those speeches, overflowing all narrow national bounds, had made so deep an impression on my mind that something of it lingers even today, even in these days of graceless disillusionment.

Certainly that spirit of abject dependence upon the charity of our rulers was no matter for pride. What was remarkable, however, was the wholehearted way in which we gave our recognition to human greatness even when it revealed itself in the foreigner. The best and noblest gifts of humanity cannot be the monopoly of a particular race or country; its scope may not be limited nor may it be regarded as the miser's hoard buried underground. That is why English literature which nourished our minds in the past does even now convey its deep resonance to the recesses of our heart.

It is difficult to find a suitable Bengali equivalent for the English word 'civilisation'. That phase of civilisation with which we were familiar in this country has been called by Manu 'Sadachar' (lit. proper conduct), that is, the conduct prescribed by the tradition of the race. Narrow in themselves these time-honoured social conventions originated and held good in a circumscribed geographical area, in that strip of land, Brahmavarta by name, bound on either side by the rivers Saraswati and Drisadvati. That is how a pharisaic formalism gradually got the upper hand of free thought and the ideal of 'proper conduct' which Manu found established in Brahmavarta steadily degenerated into socialised tyranny.

During my boyhood days the attitude of the cultured and educated section of Bengal, nurtured on English learning, was charged with a feeling of revolt against these rigid regulations of society. A perusal of what Rajnarain Bose has written describing the ways of the educated gentry of those days will amply bear out what I have said just now. In place of these set codes of conduct we accepted the ideal of 'civilisation' as represented by the English term.

In our own family this change of spirit was welcomed for the sake of its sheer rational and moral force and its influence was felt in every sphere of our life. Born in that atmosphere, which was moreover coloured by our intuitive bias for literature, I naturally set the English on the throne of my heart. Thus passed the first chapters of my life. Then came the parting of ways accompanied with a painful feeling of disillusion when I began increasingly to discover how easily those who accepted the highest truths of civilisation disowned them with impunity whenever questions of national self-interest were involved.

There came a time when perforce I had to snatch myself away from the mere appreciation of literature. As I emerged into the stark light of bare facts, the sight of the dire poverty of the Indian masses rent my heart. Rudely shaken out of my dreams, I began to realise that perhaps in no other modern state was there such hopeless dearth of the most elementary needs of existence. And yet it was this country whose resources had fed for so long the wealth and magnificence of the British people. While I was lost in the contemplation of the great world of civilisation, I could never have remotely imagined that the glaring example of it stares me in the face in the utter and contemptuous indifference of a so-called civilised race to the well-being of crores of Indian people.

That mastery over the machine, by which the British have consolidated their sovereignty over their vast Empire, has been kept a sealed book, to which due access has been denied to this helpless country. And all the time before our very eyes Japan has been transforming herself into a mighty and prosperous nation. I have seen with my own eyes the admirable use to which Japan has put in her own country the fruits of this progress. I have also been privileged to witness, while in Moscow, the unsparing energy with which Russia has tried to fight disease and illiteracy, and has succeeded in steadily liquidating ignorance and poverty, wiping off the humiliation from the face of a vast continent. Her civilisation is free from all invidious distinction between one class and another, between one sect and another. The rapid and astounding progress achieved by her made me happy and jealous at the same time. One aspect of the Soviet administration which particularly pleased me was that it provided no scope for unseemly conflict of religious difference nor set one community against another by unbalanced distribution of political favours. That I consider a truly civilised administration which impartially serves the common interests of the people.

While other imperialist powers sacrifice the welfare of the subject races to their own national greed, in the USSR I found a genuine attempt being made to harmonise the interests of the various nationalities that are scattered over its vast area. I saw peoples and tribes, who, only the other day, were nomadic savages being encouraged and indeed trained, to avail themselves freely of the benefits of civilisation. Enormous sums are being spent on their education to expedite the process. When I see elsewhere some two hundred nationalities—which only a few years ago were at vastly different stages of development—marching ahead in peaceful progress and amity, and when I look about my own country and see a very highly evolved and intellectual people drifting into the disorder of barbarism, I cannot help contrasting the two systems of governments, one based on cooperation, the other on exploitation, which have made such contrary conditions possible.

I have also seen Iran, newly awakened to a sense of national self-sufficiency, attempting to fulfil her own destiny freed from the deadly grinding stones of two European powers. During my recent visit to that country I discovered to my delight that Zoroastrians who once suffered from the fanatical hatred of the major community and whose rights had been curtailed by the ruling power were now free from this age-long repression, and that civilised life had established itself in the happy land. It is significant that Iran's good fortune dates from the day when she finally disentangled herself from the meshes of European diplomacy. With all my heart I wish Iran well.

Turning to the neighbouring kingdom of Afghanistan I find that though there is much room for improvement in the field of education and social development, yet she is fortunate in that she can look forward to unending progress; for none of the European powers, boastful of their civilisation, has yet succeeded in overwhelming and crushing her possibilities.

Thus while these other countries were marching ahead, India, smothered under the dead weight of British administration, lay static in her utter helplessness. Another great and ancient civilisation for whose recent tragic history the British cannot disclaim responsibility is China. To serve their own national profit the British first doped her people with opium and then appropriated a portion of her territory. As the world was about to forget the memory of this outrage, we were painfully surprised by another event. While Japan was quietly devouring North China, her act of wanton aggression was ignored as a minor incident by the veterans of British diplomacy. We have also witnessed from this distance how actively the British statesmen acquiesced in the destruction of the Spanish Republic.

On the other hand, we also noted with admiration how a band of valiant Englishmen laid down their lives for Spain. Even though the English had not aroused themselves sufficiently to their sense of responsibility towards China in the Far East, in their own immediate neighbourhood they did not hesitate to sacrifice themselves to the cause of freedom. Such acts of heroism reminded me over again of the true English spirit to which in those early days I had given my full faith, and made me wonder how imperialist greed could bring about so ugly a transformation in the character of so great a race.

Such is the tragic tale of the gradual loss of my faith in the claims of the European nations to civilisation. In India the misfortune of being governed by a foreign race is daily brought home to us not only in the callous neglect of such minimum necessities of life as adequate provision for food, clothing, educational and medical facilities for the people, but in an even unhappier form in the way the people have been divided among themselves. The pity of it is that the blame is laid at the door of our own society. So frightful a culmination of the history of our people would never have been possible, but for the encouragement it has received from secret influences emanating from high places.

One cannot believe that Indians are in any way inferior to the Japanese in intellectual capacity. The most effective difference between these two eastern peoples is that whereas India lies at the mercy of the British, Japan has been spared the shadow of alien domination. We know what we have been deprived of. That which was truly best in their own civilisations, the upholding of the dignity of human relationship, has no place in the British administration of this country. If in its place they have established, with baton in hand, a reign of 'law and order', in other words a policeman's rule, such mockery of civilisation can claim no respect from us. It is the mission of civilisation to bring unity among people and establish peace and harmony. But in unfortunate India the social fabric is being rent into shreds by unseemly outbursts of hooliganism daily growing in intensity, right under the very aegis of 'law and order'. In India, so long as no personal injury is inflicted upon any member of the ruling race, this barbarism seems to be assured of perpetuity, making us ashamed to live under such an administration.

And yet my good fortune has often brought me into close contact with really large-hearted Englishmen. Without the slightest hesitation I may say that the nobility of their character was without parallel—in no country or community have I come across such greatness of soul. Such examples would not allow me wholly to lose faith in the race which produced them. I had the rare blessing of having Andrews—a real Englishman, a real Christian and a true man—for a very close friend. Today in the perspective of death his unselfish and courageous magnanimity shines all the brighter. The whole of India remains indebted to him for innumerable acts of love and devotion. But personally speaking, I am especially beholden to him because he helped me to retain in my old age that feeling of respect for the English race with which in the past I was inspired by their literature and which I was about to lose completely. I count such Englishmen as Andrews not only as my personal and intimate friends but as friends of the whole human race. To have known them has been to me a treasured privilege. It is my belief that such Englishmen will save British honour from shipwreck. At any rate if I had not known them, my despair at the prospect of Western civilisation would be unrelieved.

In the meanwhile the demon of barbarity has given up all pretence and has emerged with unconcealed fangs, ready to tear up humanity in an orgy of devastation. From one end of the world to the other the poisonous fumes of hatred darken the atmosphere. The spirit of violence which perhaps lay dormant in the psychology of the West has at last roused itself and desecrates the spirit of Man.

The wheels of the Fate will some day compel the English to give up their Indian empire. But what kind of India will they leave behind, what stark misery? When the stream of their centuries' administration runs dry at last, what a waste of mud and filth they will leave behind them! I had at one time believed that the springs of civilisation would issue out of the heart of Europe. But today when I am about to quit the world that faith has gone bankrupt altogether.

As I look around I see the crumbling ruins of a proud civilisation strewn like a vast heap of futility. And yet I shall not commit the grievous sin of losing faith in Man. I would rather look forward to the opening of a new chapter in his history after the cataclysm is over and the atmosphere rendered clean with the spirit of service and sacrifice. Perhaps that dawn will come from this horizon, from the East where the sun rises. A day will come when unvanquished Man will retrace his path of conquest, despite all barriers, to win back his lost human heritage.

Today we witness the perils which attend on the insolence of might; one day shall be borne out the full truth of what the sages have proclaimed: 'By unrighteousness man prospers, gains what appears desirable, conquers enemies, but perishes at the root.'

~

MOHANDAS KARAMCHAND GANDHI

The Last Fast

Of all Gandhian methods of protest and mass mobilization, the fast continues to be the most significant in democratic India. It has become a powerful device in the hands of agitators demanding rights and dues. To Mahatma Gandhi, a fast was as much a way of self-purification as it was a potent weapon in his struggle against colonial rule and other forms of injustice. In a couple of instances, his fasts looked like attempts at coercing the authority to release him from jail or accept his demands. For this reason, his fasts were quite often cited as a denial of his own non-violent methods. However, on more than one occasion he clarified that through fasts he was only purifying himself and that all his demands were raised only after he had carefully gone through them and thus fasting only gave him the strength to bring his demands to the forefront. In the communally charged atmosphere of Delhi in 1948, Gandhi undertook what was to be his last fast. He embarked on it as a protest against the communal violence witnessed in Delhi and against the Indian government's decision to stop the payment of Rs 55 crore to Pakistan as per the post-partition settlement of accounts between the two nations. He began his fast on 12 January and it had the desired effect both in government circles, with the Government of India reconsidering its decision on the payment to Pakistan, and among the general public as seen in the restoration of peace. But it also hardened the attitude of Hindu communal elements who viewed this as another in a series of acts appeasing Muslims and Pakistan. Within twelve days of the day he called off his fast (18 January), Gandhi was assassinated by a Hindu fanatic. This speech is the closest anyone has come to evolving a philosophy of a fast.

One fasts for health's sake under laws governing health, fasts as a penance for a wrong done and felt as such. In these fasts, the fasting one need not believe in Ahimsa. There is, however, a fast which a votary of non-violence sometimes feels impelled to undertake by way of protest against some wrong done by society, and this he does when as a votary of Ahimsa he has no other remedy left. Such an occasion has come my way.

When on September 9th, I returned to Delhi from Calcutta, it was to proceed to the West Punjab. But that was not to be. Gay Delhi looked a city of the dead. As I alighted from the train I observed gloom on every face I saw. Even the Sardar, whom humour and the joy that humour gives never desert, was no exception this time. The cause of it I did not know. He was on the platform to receive me. He lost no time in giving me the sad news of the disturbances that had taken place in the Metropolis of the Union. At once I saw that I had to be in Delhi and 'do or die'. There is an apparent calm brought about by prompt military and police action. But there is storm within the breast. It may burst forth any day. This I count as no fulfilment of the vow to 'do' which alone can keep me from death, the incomparable friend. I yearn for heart friendship between the Hindus, the Sikhs and the Muslims. It subsisted between them the other day. Today it is non-existent. It is a state that no Indian patriot worthy of the name can contemplate with equanimity. Though the Voice within has been beckoning for a long time, I have been shutting my ears to it, lest it may be the voice of Satan, otherwise called my weakness. I never like to feel resourceless, a Satyagrahi never should. Fasting is his last resort in the place of the sword—his or other's. I have no answer to return to the Muslim friends who see me from day to day as to what they should do. My impotence has been gnawing at me of late. It will go immediately the fast is undertaken. I have been brooding over it for the last three days. The final conclusion has flashed upon me and it makes me happy. No man, if he is pure has anything more precious to give than his life. I hope and pray that I have that purity in me to justify the step.

Worthy of Blessing

I ask you all to bless the effort and to pray for me and with me. The fast begins from the first meal tomorrow. The period is indefinite and I may drink water with or without salts and sour limes. It will end when and if I am satisfied that there is a reunion of hearts of all the communities brought about without any outside pressure, but from an awakened sense of duty. The reward will be the regaining of India's dwindling prestige and her fast fading sovereignty over the heart of Asia and through the world. I flatter myself with the belief that the loss of her soul by India will mean loss of the hope of the aching, storm-tossed and hungry world. Let no friend, or foe if there be one, be angry with me. There are friends who do not believe in the method of the fast for the reclamation of the human mind. They will bear with me and extend to me the same liberty of action that they claim for themselves. With God as my supreme and sole counsellor, I felt that I must take the decision without any other adviser. If I made a mistake and discover it, I shall have no hesitation in proclaiming it from the housetop and retracing my faulty step. If there is clear indication, as I claim there is, of the Inner Voice, it will not be gainsaid. I plead for all absence of argument and inevitable endorsement of the step. If the whole of India responds or at least Delhi does, the fast might be soon ended.

But whether it ends soon or late or never, let there be no softness in dealing with what may be termed as a crisis. Critics have regarded some of my previous fasts as coercive and held that on merits the verdict would have gone against my stand but for the pressure exercised by the fasts. What value can an adverse verdict have when the purpose is demonstrably sound? A pure fast, like duty, is its own reward. I do not embark upon it for the sake of the result it may bring. I do so because I must. Hence, I urge everybody dispassionately to examine the purpose and let me die, if I must, in peace which I hope is ensured. Death for me would be a glorious deliverance rather than that I should be a helpless witness of the destruction of India, Hinduism, Sikhism and Islam. That destruction is certain if Pakistan ensures no equality of status and security of life and property for all professing the various faiths of the world, and if India copies her. Only then Islam dies in the two Indias, not in the world. But Hinduism and Sikhism have no world outside India. Those who differ from me will be honoured by me for their resistance however implacable. Let my fast quicken conscience, not deaden it. Just contemplate the rot that has set in in beloved India and you will rejoice to think that there is a humble son of hers who is strong enough and possibly pure enough to take the happy step. If he is neither, he is a burden on earth. The sooner he disappears and clears the Indian atmosphere of the burden the better for him and all concerned.

I would beg of all friends not to rush to Birla House nor try to dissuade me or be anxious for me. I am in God's hands. Rather, they should turn the searchlights inwards, for this is essentially a testing time for all of us. Those who remain at their post of duty and perform it diligently and well, now more so than hitherto, will help me and the cause in every way. The fast is a process of self-purification.

~

JAIPAL SINGH

Damodar Valley Corporation and Tribal Displacement

One of the most accomplished men to ever enter the Indian Parliament, Jaipal Singh had an acute understanding of the way tribals were being made to pay for developmental activities after independence. The speech reproduced below was delivered during the debate on the Damodar Valley Corporation Bill brought before the Constituent Assembly (Legislative) on 14 February 1948 by the minister for mines N.V. Gadgil. As a member from the area which was going to be submerged, Singh had first-hand knowledge of the issues that the government was overlooking. His speech was a thorough yet witty criticism of the government. He pointed out the problems of displacement inherent in development, emphasizing the need to rehabilitate people thus displaced. Years later, in the 1980s, the issue came to the forefront in the struggle of the people against the construction of many projects such as Tehri, Silent Valley and the Narmada Valley.

... I congratulate my friend, Mr. Gadgil, for presenting this Bill. It augurs well for the Nehru Government that the first adventure in planning should affect the Adivasi tracts. It has taken Congressmen nearly 65 years to do for the Adivasis something concrete, something big and something bold is being done; it is going to be model for future river projects throughout India.

... There is one thing on which I feel I must again make my emphasis and it is in regard to the promise which the Honourable Minister made for displaced persons and their resettlement. When he first begged leave to introduce this Bill, he promised the displaced people heaven. He said that he would give them houses better than they ever had and that every consideration would be paid to make their suffering as little as possible in the interim period. I would like to suggest to my Honourable friend the Minister that he might experiment with this promised heaven of his in a temporary way. For example, the villages will have to be evacuated. Obviously people must live somewhere. If this is an adventure in planning, surely we shall have some time to think, some time to experiment with our ideas on these displaced people. I know the area very well. I come from the area myself and let me tell the House quite clearly that this Bill provided Free India an opportunity. This project is the first one of its kind to enable Free India to put right a damage on Adivasis that has been there for the last 6000 years. Most of the villages will be Santhal villages but, though they are not entirely populated by Santhals, banias and other undesirable elements have got in and they have been for years and years a serious menace to the moral and material welfare of the people. Now banias also will evacuate, I ask my Honourable friend, the Minister, is he going to reinstate the banias in the villages again, just because they are also evacuees from these villages or is he going to take a bold step and see that this disease, this terrible virus that has crept into the simple body politic of these villages is completely uprooted and put at the bottom of the project? What is he going to do? Is he going to experiment? I am not trying to be inhuman: all that I am trying to say is this. Let us be realistic in our endeavour. It is no good saying that we are going to give them better houses. What is really important is, are you going to give them their self-respect? Are you going to give them a *modus vivendi* whereby they will be able to contribute as men of honour, compatriots having a place of honour in the national life of India? This is the issue. I am not looking at it merely from a material point of view. We are not going to make my fellow Santhals happier simply by making them live in palaces. We do not want your palaces. We want to live for things whereby we can be compatriots in the common endeavour. I am thinking more of the spiritual aspect of the problem of rehabilitation, and this is not a matter with which we can play light-heartedly. We shall have to have the help of experts, of social workers, say from the Tata Social Institute at Bombay, or we may have to take the help of anthropologists, so that it will not be merely a matter of lay experiment. When I talk of displaced persons, I am not merely thinking of the 300 and odd villages that will be displaced. I think we have to go temporarily a little backward. We have to think of the roughly 5 lakhs of Santhals who have been crimped from that particular area and who, because of economic circumstances, have been forced to make their habitat in the tea gardens of Assam. I think most of us are old enough to realise what Mahatma Gandhi tried to do in the tea gardens of Assam. I think most of us still remember that noble march of his, which he endeavoured to make with these same Santhals, so that they might be repatriated back to their homes. I suggest while we are thinking of the displaced villagers and the inhabitants of those 300 and odd villages, we might as well bear in mind that perhaps we would be reintegrating the Santhals by making an endeavour, as far as is possible, to get back the persons, the families, which have had to desert those villages in order to find a living elsewhere, because this particular area is no longer going to be a desert. It is no longer going to be subject to the ravages of a terrible and obstreperous river. This project is going to make this river walk and not run: that is the whole idea of it. We are going to harness the waters, which means that we shall have the water under control.

That brings me, as I said, to one rather particular aspect that is bound to be lost by people who are not Adivasis. When we think of submerging a village we think merely of the submersion of the lands and the houses. But we forget that there are things that an Adivasi values very much. For example, they have their *Sarnas*, the sal or other groves where most of the worship is done by them. They think very highly of their burial places called *Sasana*. In fact though he is now there, the march of his race, his ancestors from one part of the country to another part of the country is known by the menhirs, slabs of stones that they leave behind them. All these will have to be submerged. I want to ask my friend, the Minister, has he any idea of the spiritual rehabilitation of the men I have spoken of? Of course, we cannot reproduce the graves but we are going to destroy their worshipping places. In the scheme of resettlement that we have, have you any plan in detail that these people are going to have their worshipping places again? Or, is it merely that we are going to give them big cement houses and say that they are better off than in their kutcha ones? That is the spiritual aspect that should not be forgotten.

Similarly, there is the question of akharas. Every Santhal village has a plot, an arena, in the heart of it for their dancing. Dance is rhythm of the life of Santhals. Most of you may be inclined to laugh at the aboriginal dances...

But believe me there is much that the rest of India has to learn from Adivasis in regard to the rhythm of life. It was Tagore who chose a typical Santhal area to interpret to the world the rhythm of Indian life such as is found in all its nakedness at Bolpur and the other villages surrounding it. I would ask my Honourable friend the Minister not to forget that aspect of it either.

I would like to say something in regard to what my Honourable friend Pandit Hirday Nath Kunzru said. He seems to be under the impression that there will be such a surplus of energy that some machinery would have to be improvised which would compel and increase the consumption of electrical energy. So far as I have been able to understand the situation we shall not have a surplus of energy. The scheme is such that it is in the heart of the industrial country. It is not very far removed from the big industrial areas. It is surely intended that the energy, as much of it as we can produce, will be utilised by all the industrial concerns as well as by the population. So far as I can see there will not be much surplus energy. In any case the whole purpose of the project will be defeated if there is not full use made of the energy. It is surely hoped that new industries will be attracted by the project. So I think on that account the fears expressed by my friend Pandit Hirday Nath Kunzru are unfounded. His reference to coal which was also supported by Professor Shah to my mind is equally ungrounded. Admittedly we have not as much coal as we would like to have. The Mahindra Committee Report shows that if we were to exploit our coal deposits a little more scientifically we can still carry on for about a century but this project will mean that coal that is now being used for industry will be available for other purposes. In other words the consumption will not be as much as had been in the past because coal, it is hoped, will be replaced by the electrical energy which should be available in abundance and at a much cheaper rate.

In the speeches that I have heard T.V.A. [*Tennessee Valley Authority—Ed.*] has been mentioned a good deal. I have been at pains to try to understand the underlying principles behind the T.V.A. and I find that there is much we have to learn from the T.V.A. But all the while we must remember that we have in the last resort to deal with human beings. The T.V.A. had to deal with America. The Damodar Valley Project has to deal with Indians and that is exactly where the differences come in. I know my friend Mr. Gadgil has taken the very best advice possible. After all what more can any Government do than to get Mr. Voorduin and Mr. Savage who are experts and who have had long experience of Tennessee Valley Authority that is in the technical aspect of it and the construction of the dam itself. I do not think there can be much doubt that the very best has been done to ensure the finest expert knowledge and that knowledge is being utilised for this and other projects. I understand that Mr. Savage has made a survey of the Hirakud Project also. But when it comes to dealing with human being his project has to deal with Indians and I think that is where the difference comes in. A suspicion has been thrown that unless the personnel were very carefully selected they would abuse their power; it has also been hinted that there might be friction between the two provincial governments and various other local authorities that are situated in the area of operation and so forth.

My own attitude to this is: Certainly have the very best men possible running this Authority, I am one of the co-signatories to the minute of dissent in which my friend Mr. Naziruddin Ahmad and I have made it quite clear that we would like the Authority to be unhampered, unfettered and unmanacled by interference from a bureaucracy about 700 miles away. We do want the thing to work smoothly and the whole essence of democracy is that we do not lose faith in our fellow human beings. We say let the good in man outweigh the evil in him. When we come to discuss the clauses my friend Mr. Naziruddin Ahmad and I will have our own arguments to place before the Assembly but for the time being Sir I notice it is nearly time to adjourn and if I may just say so I think we must trust this Authority. Of course the very best men must be appointed and they must not be political appointments. There is no doubt whatever that the biggest project, the first colossal project that Free India is going to undertake must be run on such lines that it will be a complete success so that all other projects, be it Hirakud, Bhakra, Tungabhadra and what not, will look to this as a model and guide.

~

R.R. DIWAKAR

Caste Should Go

In the course of the Constituent Assembly debates, R.R. Diwakar, a prominent Congress leader from Karnataka, moved a resolution for the abolition of caste from government records. His speech on 17 February 1948, from which an extract is reproduced below, reflects the mood of the freedom fighter who had a cosmopolitan humanism as his guiding spirit and who believed that the liquidation of any exploitative system began with a simple first step.

My Resolution is very modest and it really wants to undo what has been done. In the first place, it says 'that the Government shall not recognise any caste, sub-caste, sect or religion' so far as the State and the State services are concerned. This is the first part. Now, here, certain vested interests have been created by conventions or by rules or by deliberate administrative action, and it is natural for those people to think that this is possibly an attack against such vested interests. I positively deny any such charge simply because, if at all there are any educationally backward or economically backward sections in the body polity, it is the duty of every Government, much more so of a National Government, still more so of a democratic National Government, to see that all backward peoples, whether they are backward in the economic field, in the social field or in the educational or cultural field, are supported and given special facilities for culture, for education and for the improvement of their economical condition. I shall fully support anyone who would suggest any method of improving the condition of the backward people in this country. There is no question about it. Therefore, I say that this first part which says that there should be no recognition of any caste, sect or religion in the matter of the State and the State services is a very desirable and necessary one, and I fully believe that any kind of privilege or right bestowed on any person or any group on account of his or its caste is really not so much a healthy and good encouragement, but I say positively that it is a part of the vicious circle which is created by caste consciousness and caste patriotism. It is only perpetuating that consciousness, it brings in evils which it really wants to negate or destroy. Therefore, that is not the proper remedy for really removing that kind of backwardness which is the cause for asking for certain special privileges or rights. I would therefore suggest that while trying to remove the causes of this kind of consciousness, let us try by all means possible to see that everyone in our nation, be he of any caste, be he of any creed, or be he of any religion, is really brought up to a certain common level of education, of economic condition and of culture.

~

RENUKA RAY

Rescue and Rehabilitation of Women

Post-partition riots clouded the joy of independence. Noakhali in Bengal passed into folklore for the savagery witnessed there and for being regarded as Mahatma Gandhi's finest hour. One component of the riots was the large-scale kidnappings of Hindu women by Muslim men and their forced marriages thereafter, which added to the already tense communal atmosphere. Sucheta Kripalani launched a campaign in Gandhi's presence in Noakhali to rescue these women. Once the riots spread to the western front, the need to protect women from the horrors being inflicted on them and to rescue and rehabilitate such womenfolk was increasingly felt. Renuka Ray, a legislator from Bengal, raised the issue in the Constituent Assembly on 12 March 1948.

Mr. Speaker I shall speak specifically on the problem of rescue and restoration of women on which I have tabled a cut motion.

No one in this House or in the world outside will dispute the fact that the worst horror that has come as an outcome of the communal frenzy and bestiality in this country is the treatment that has been meted out to women. This dreadful aspect of it which first arose in Noakhali, has since spread far and wide and has assumed a magnitude and a proportion that is unparalleled in human history. Sir, the rescue and the restoration to the social fold of women who have been the victims of this outrage is the most difficult and yet the most essential part of rehabilitation work. The little experience that I have had in the rescue of such women makes it impossible for me to discount or minimise in any manner the very great difficulty of this type of work. I hope that the Honourable Prime Minister...will realise that any suggestions that I have to offer are not in the nature of destructive criticism.

Apart from the question of rescue itself, on which I will say a few words later, the mental rehabilitation, the restoration of such women who have been the victims of outrage, is a problem which requires very intricate and delicate handling. I will not have the time to go into any great detail or any descriptive analysis, nor do I think it is necessary. I should like to confine my remarks as far as possible to some concrete suggestions.

In the first place, I feel strongly that women who have been so grievously hurt and wounded should be kept apart from other refugees until such time as they are in a position to take up the threads of normal life. They should be kept under the individual care and supervision of women who are skilled and competent to help them and nurse them back to take up their positions in the social fold. Even if the families of such women are anxious to take them back, I think it is undesirable that they should go back until such time as they are mentally as well as physically restored. There is a great likelihood of their being crippled and maimed for life unless some action is taken to see that they are not required to readjust themselves to ordinary life until they have had time to get back to normalcy. I think some competent authority such as the women's section of the Relief and

Rehabilitation Ministry with the help of women's organisations should be in charge of this work and it is they who should decide when such women are fit to return to their homes. A much more important matter is the question of unmarried girls in regard to the return of these girls to those who claim to be their relatives. Unless they are their own parents, I think the authenticity as well as the desirability of such relatives should be gone into before they are handed over; unless this is done there is the likelihood and danger of further exploitation of these girls. If there is any dispute over this there should be some such machinery as a Court of Wards which should be set up to decide the matter. I do think that the Government or the Ministry of Relief and Rehabilitation should immediately empower itself legally in both these types of cases so as to be in a position and have the right to decide what is best for the women concerned.

I will now turn to the question of rehabilitation. The last speaker has made a very eloquent speech on this subject and I only want to point out some specific points with regard to the rehabilitation of women. I do not think that the establishment of homes where some little occupation is given which has not been properly planned is enough. In this country there is a very great dearth of women who come forward to be trained in the different fields of nation building services that are so necessary for the development of the nation. This great tragedy has left thousands and thousands of women homeless and alone. Why should we not utilise even their circumstances to whatever extent possible to our advantage. The opportunity should be taken to train these women to become useful and purposeful citizens. Tinkering with the problem by doing a little here and there will not be sufficient. What is required is a properly planned scheme of vocational training on a long-term basis. The women can be trained in a variety of occupations according to their aptitude and inclination—such as nurses, teachers, social workers, training them in useful occupations such as running laundry services, co-operative restaurants, community kitchens and various other things. I would request, in fact I would earnestly appeal to the Rehabilitation Minister to take up this question immediately. It is quite unnecessary to draw up a scheme with large overhead expenses which may mean delay. Simple schemes which can be implemented immediately should be taken up. But I think a good deal of time has already been wasted, and I hope that there will be no more delay!

I will now turn to another aspect and that is the question of rescue. I think that this House is aware of the fact that there is an apparent reluctance on the part of a certain number of women to return to their homes. There are two main causes for this. One is (and I have seen cases like this myself) where women act as hostages for the protection and the safe conduct of their families. Until and unless these families are returned from the danger zone these women would rather sacrifice themselves than jeopardise the future of their dear and near ones. The second point is that a great deal of propaganda has been done in regard to the bigotry and prejudices of Hindu society. If these women come to know that the compelling force of circumstances has broken down these prejudices to a large extent, and if they also know whether they have homes to come back to or not, the Government of India with the help of the women's organisations of this country are willing to take up the responsibility and see to it that they are not victimised, they would come back. I think that every avenue should be explored to see that this news reaches them through the Indian newspapers which have circulation in Pakistan, or through transit camps or High Commissioner's offices. Systematic propaganda to make the truth of the matter known should be taken up immediately.

Sir, there is one other point which I would like to make if you would give me the time and that is that the customs barriers that have been imposed since March have raised a new problem. We have heard from reliable witnesses about women being searched across the border in Eastern Pakistan and of the outrages that have been committed on them… I do think that the Government should approach the Pakistan authorities and both Governments should appoint women investigators or women police to search women on both sides. It is true that the Government of India can only show its own good faith, its own effectiveness and can only request and not compel Pakistan. But I think that if we on our side show that we are sincere and earnest about this problem then whatever is or is not done on the other side this itself will be the most compelling force on our side. This is the way that Mahatma Gandhi wanted us to act. We cannot pay him tribute only by changing the name of towns, townships and roads, nor by engraving his name or picture on stamps. If we wish to honour and pay tribute to him, which we failed to do during the last many months, let us put our minds to this problem, about which he was so deeply agitated. Let us each and every one of us help the Government of India to see to it that women are not victimised further. We can show our own good faith, as I said, and I am sure that in the end this will have its effect on the other side. Neither retaliation nor lukewarm behaviour, because of lack of response on the other side, will achieve what we desire.

~

TAJAMUL HOSAIN

Nizamat Should Go

Tajamul Hosain, a legislator from Bihar, reflected the radical mood of the country against all hierarchical forms of exploitation, particularly now that the biggest of them all, colonialism, was gone. In this passionate speech, delivered in the Constituent Assembly on 15 March 1948, he argued for the immediate liquidation of the nizamat from Hyderabad state as it depicted a feudal order whose days were over.

Sir, history tells us that there was a time when everything existed for the ruler. The people existed for the ruler, whose word was law. Louis XIV of France is reported to have said, 'Letat, c'est moi' (I am the State). But now the times have considerably changed and they have changed for the better. Now the rulers do not count; it is the people who count and everything now exists for the people and tiny rulers are simply the servants of the people. Sir, most of the States were at one time merely the provinces of the Central Government. I do not think that there was any State in India which was independent with external sovereignty. And all these States which were really provinces of the centre had as their rulers people called Subahdars who are now called Governors. The difference between the Governors of those days and the Governors of present day is only this that in those days the period of office was not fixed; he might be Governor for life or in perpetuity or from generation to generation. But now the term of office of the Governor is fixed. When the British came out to this country and became its rulers they thought they would not be able to remain in India long if they had direct contact with the people. They did not want to have any connection with the people, and they devised two methods for this. They created two institutions; those who were Subahdars of provinces were recognised as perpetual rulers of the province which was called a principality; and the petty holders of land scattered everywhere were called Zamindars or jagirdars or talukdars. The princely order, whether they had or did not have internal powers, were the real backbone of British rule, and they did everything to support the British people in ruling this country. And in recognition of their services titles were showered upon them, like Maharaja and Knighthood, and so on. But the British did not realise that the world's greatest man in modern times would be born in this country and open the eyes of the people who would see that they were slaves, who by his non-violent methods would succeed in turning them out of this country. Alas, he is no longer with us though he is with us in spirit. But the point is that the British had to go. As soon as they went away we had the rule of the people here. The first thing we did was to abolish this feudal system and the intermediaries known as Zamindars. And in every province there is an attempt—which I hope will succeed in the end—to abolish these intermediaries. But then I am unable to understand the anomalous position that is being created. In the centre there will be a republic—I presume and hope it will be socialist republic. In the province there will be the rule of the people but in some part of India the old feudal system will continue as before. Our Government say there is some difficulty about it; we cannot get rid of these people because when the British were going away they told these so-called Princes, 'We are going away after creating two Dominions; it is for you to accede to either of them or to become independent. Paramountcy has lapsed.' But are we going to act up to the wishes of these people who have gone from here? Were they not our enemies throughout? Did they not try to throttle us in every way when we tried to achieve our freedom? I will advise my Government to abolish this princely order forthwith as the Zamindaris are being abolished. There should be no princely order anywhere and every State without exception should go. There should be our Governors; they were Governors in perpetuity and now they should be our Governors for a fixed period say, five or six years, and nothing beyond that. Why should the Princes be given any compensation? I am not in favour of giving anything to them. They have extracted enough money in cash and kind from the poor people of the land: they hoarded enormous amounts of cash and jewellery and they are far more wealthy than anyone of us. Let them go away unsung and unhonoured. But there is one class of people on whose behalf I will appeal to the Prime Minister, and these are the rulers and Zamindars who were the first people to fight against the British in 1857. Some died on the battlefield while others were hanged or shot dead, their properties and estates were confiscated. With regard to such people I want to know what the policy of Government is, whether they are going to be compensated or not. I submit, Sir, that these are the only people entitled to compensation and compensation must be given to them.

There is one aspect of the matter which I want to mention before I deal with Hyderabad. Supposing there is a war and some foreign power invades India, do you think for a moment that these so-called ruling Princes will side with us? Are they not sorry now that the British have left and some of them have to merge with other States or provinces? If left as they are—as feudal lords—they will become fifth columnists and attack us when we are attacked by a foreign power. Therefore I submit that the princely order must be abolished forthwith.

Now I will deal with Hyderabad. In 1713 the ancestor of the present Nizam of Hyderabad—Asaf Jah—was appointed Subahdar by the then Central Government. In 1800 there was a treaty of alliance between the East India and the then Nizam in which the latter has been described as Subahdar…

… the Nizam never exercised external powers, and a State which does not exercise external powers cannot be described as an independent sovereign State. No doubt the British created the Nizam perpetual ruler of that principality but the Nizam always remained a subordinate vassal of the British Empire. He received titles and honours like Farzand and Arjumand of Britannia and so on, and also 'His Exalted Highness' etc. But it was only twelve years ago in 1936 that the present Nizam agreed to accede to the Federation of India. Does that not show that he has always been a subject and a vassal of the Central Government? Sir, the British have always claimed to be the successors of the Moghul Empire and no doubt we are the successors of the British Government; and so the Nizam is nothing better than a Subahdar. He was Subahdar during the East India Company and during the British rule he was Subahdar. Now that the real ruler in the shape of the people has come in, he says, 'No I will not accept you.' I am afraid he is making a fool of us and we are showing weakness. Our Government is showing weakness. I cannot understand the idea of appointing an Agent General. Does the Honourable Prime Minister think that by sending him the State will accede to the Indian Dominion? Do you think the Nizam will ever come down? I say that negotiations are a waste of time, money and energy. The Honourable

Prime Minister the other day in answer to a supplementary question of mine said that he wanted to know the wishes of the people of Hyderabad as to whether they will accede or not. But I will ask the Prime Minister how he is going to ascertain the wishes of the people as long as the people are under him. Unless you take possession of the State you cannot get the people over to you.

I would advise the Honourable Prime Minister that the first thing he should do is to stop negotiations; secondly recall the Agent General; and thirdly march an army there at once. I am sure that within a couple of days you will capture the whole of Hyderabad. It is not Kashmir and nobody can come to the help of Hyderabad.

My time is up although I would like to say more. I however believe that there should be no princely order. It does not matter whether Kashmir goes over to Pakistan or not but in the Dominion we must have one Government throughout.

~

BHIMRAO RAMJI AMBEDKAR

The Hindu Code Bill

As minister of law in the first cabinet of independent India, Dr B.R. Ambedkar was given the task of codifying Hindu laws so that one could move towards a uniform civil code. Jawaharlal Nehru, who believed that Hindu society needed to change its laws in keeping with modern times, was keen that this bill be piloted through by a progressive law minister like Ambedkar. For Ambedkar, the Hindu Code Bill was the first step towards a radical change in the Hindu social order. He finally introduced the resolution to refer the bill to a select committee on 9 April 1948. The committee included three women members, namely, Durgabai Deshmukh, Renuka Ray and Ammu Swaminathan. The bill continued to be debated till 1951 when it was finally dropped in the face of stiff opposition.

Sir, this Bill, the aim of which is to codify the rules of Hindu Law which are scattered in innumerable decisions of the High Courts and of the Privy Council, which form a bewildering motley to the common man and give rise to constant litigation, seeks to codify the law relating to seven different matters. Firstly, it seeks to codify the law relating to the rights of property of a deceased Hindu who has died intestate without making a will, both female and male. Secondly, it prescribes a somewhat altered form of the order of succession among the different heirs to the property of a deceased dying intestate. The next topic it deals with is the law of maintenance, marriage, divorce, adoption, minority and guardianship. The House will see what is the ambit and the periphery of this Bill. To begin with the question of inheritance, under this head the Bill enacts a new principle, at least for certain parts of British India. As many members who are lawyers in the House will know, so far as inheritance is concerned, the Hindus are governed by two different systems of law. One system is known as Mitakshara and the other is known as Dayabhag. The two systems have a fundamental difference. According to Mitakshara, the property of a Hindu is not his individual property. It is property which belongs to what is called a coparcenary, which consists of father, son, grandson and great grandson. All these people have a birthright in that property and the property on the death of any one member of this coparcenary passes by what is called survivorship to the members who remain behind, and does not pass to the heirs of the deceased. The Hindu Code contained in this Bill adopts the Dayabhag rule, under which the property is held by the heir as his personal property with an absolute right to dispose it of either by gift or by will or any other manner that he chooses.

That is one fundamental change which this Bill seeks to make. In other words, it universalises the law of inheritance by extending the Dayabhag rule to the territory in which the rule of the Mitakshara now operates.

Coming to the question of the order of succession among the heirs, there is also fundamental difference of a general character between the rule of the Mitakshara and the rule of the Dayabhag. Under the Mitakshara rule the agnates of a deceased are preferred to his cognates; under the Dayabhag rule the basis of heir-ship is blood relationship to the deceased and not the relationship based on cognates or agnatic relationship. That is one change that the Bill makes; in other words, here also it adopts the rule of the Dayabhag in preference to the rule of the Mitakshara.

In addition to this general change in the order of succession to a deceased Hindu, the Bill also seeks to make four changes. One change is that the widow, the daughter, the widow of a pre-deceased son, all are given the same rank as the son in the matter of inheritance. In addition to that, the daughter also is given a share in her father's property; her share is prescribed as half of that of the son. Here again, I should like to point out that the only new change which this Bill seeks to make, so far as the female heirs are concerned, is confined to the daughter; the other female heirs have already been recognised by the Hindu Women's Right to Property Act of 1937. Therefore, so far as that part of the Bill is concerned, there is really no change in the Bill at all; the Bill merely carries the provisions contained in the Act to which I have made reference.

The second change which the Bill makes so far as the female heirs are concerned is that the number of female heirs recognised now is much larger than under either the Mitakshara or the Dayabhag.

The third change made by the Bill is this that under the old law, whether the Mitakshara or the Dayabhag, a discrimination was made among female heirs, as to whether a particular female was rich or poor in circumstances at the death of the testator, whether she was married or unmarried, or whether she was with issue or without issue. All these considerations which led to discrimination in the female heirs are now abolished by this Bill. A woman who has a right to inherit gets it by reason of the fact that she is declared to be an heir irrespective of any other considerations.

The last change that is made relates to the rule of inheritance in the Dayabhag. Under the Dayabhag the father succeeds before in preference to the mother; under the present Bill the position is altered so that the mother comes before the father.

So much for the order of succession of heirs to a deceased male Hindu. I now come to the provisions in the Bill which relate to intestate succession to females. As Members of the House who are familiar with Hindu Law will know, under the existing law the property held by a Hindu female falls into two categories; one is called her stridhan, and the other is called 'woman's property'. Taking first the question of stridhan, under the existing law, stridhan falls into several categories; it is not one single category, and the order of succession to the stridhan of a female under the existing law varies according to the category of the stridhan; one category of stridhan has a different law of succession than another category and these rules are alike both as to Mitakshara as they are to the Dayabhag. So far as stridhan is concerned the present Bill makes two changes. The one change it makes is that it consolidates the different categories of stridhan into one single category of property and lays down a uniform rule of succession; there is no variety of heirs to the stridhan in accordance with the different categories of the stridhan—all stridhan is one and there is one rule of succession.

The second change which the Bill seeks to make with regard to the heirs is that the son also is now given a right to inherit the stridhan and he is given half the share which the daughter takes. Members will realise that in formulating this Bill and making changes in rules of succession, it is provided that while the daughter is getting half the share in the father's property, the son is also getting half the share in the mother's property so that in a certain sense the Bill seeks to maintain an equality of position between the son and the daughter.

Coming to the question of the 'woman's estate', as members of the House will know under the Hindu Law where a woman inherits property she gets only what is called a 'life estate'. She can enjoy the income of the property, but she cannot deal with the corpus of the property except for legal necessity; the property must pass after the death of the woman to the reversioners of her husband. The Bill, here again, introduces two changes. It converts this limited estate into an absolute estate just as the male when he inherits gets an absolute estate in the property that he inherits, and secondly, it abolishes the right of the reversioners to claim the property after the widow.

An important provision which is ancillary to the rights of women to inherit property contained in this Bill is the provision which relates to dowry. All members of the House know what a scandalous affair this dowry is; how, for instance girls who bring enormous lot of property from their parents either by way of dowry or stridhan or gift are treated, nonetheless, with utter contempt, tyranny and oppression. The Bill provides in my judgment one of the most salutary provisions, namely, that this property which is given as dowry to a girl on the occasion of her marriage shall be treated as a trust property, the use of which will inure to the woman and she is entitled to claim that property when she comes to the age of 18, so that neither her husband nor the relations of her husband will have any interest in that property; nor will they have any opportunity to waste that property and make her helpless for the rest of her life.

... There is another part of the Bill which is important and it relates to the rights of a wife to claim separate maintenance when she lives separate from her husband. Generally, under the provisions of the Hindu Law, a wife is not entitled to claim maintenance from her husband if she does not live with him in his house. The Bill, however, recognises that there are undoubtedly circumstances where if the wife has lived away from the husband, it must be for causes beyond her control and it would be wrong not to recognise the causes and not to give her separate maintenance. Consequently the Bill provides that a wife shall be entitled to claim separate maintenance from her husband if he is (1) suffering from a loathsome disease, (2) if he keeps a concubine, (3) if he is guilty of cruelty, (4) if he has abandoned her for two years, (5) if he has converted to another religion and (6) any other cause justifying her living separately.

The next topic to which I wish to make a reference concerns the question of marriage. The Code recognises two forms of marriages. One is called 'sacramental' marriage and the other is called 'civil' marriage. As members will know, this is a departure from the existing law. The existing Hindu law recognises only what is called 'sacramental' marriage, but it does not recognise what we call a 'civil' marriage. When one considers the conditions for a valid sacramental marriage and a valid registered marriage, under the Code there is really very little difference between the two. There are five conditions for a sacramental marriage. Firstly, the bridegroom must be 18 years old, and the bride must be 14 years old. Secondly, neither party must have a spouse living at the time of marriage. Thirdly, parties must not be within prohibited degree of relationship. Fourthly, parties must not be *sapindas* of each other. Fifthly, neither must be an idiot or a lunatic. Except for the fact that similarity of sapindaship is not a bar to a registered marriage, so far as other conditions are concerned, there is no difference between the sacramental marriage and the civil marriage. The only other difference is that the registered marriage must be registered in accordance with the provisions in the Bill while a sacramental marriage may be registered if parties desire to do so. Comparing the rules of marriage contained in the Bill and the existing law, it may be noticed that there are three differences which the Bill makes. One is this, that while the existing law requires identity of caste and sub-caste for a valid sacramental marriage, the Bill dispenses with this condition. Marriage under the Bill will be valid irrespective of the caste or sub-caste of the parties entering into the marriage.

The second provision in this Bill is that identity of gotrapravara is not a bar to a marriage while it is under the existing law. The third distinctive feature is this, that under the old law, polygamy was permissible. Under the new law it is monogamy which is prescribed. The sacramental marriage was a marriage which was indissoluble. There could be no divorce. The present Bill makes a new departure by introducing into the law provisions for the dissolution of marriage. Any party which marries under the new Code has three remedies to get out of the contract of marriage. One is to have the marriage declared null and void; secondly, to have the marriage declared invalid; and thirdly, to have it dissolved. Now, the grounds for invalidation of marriage are two: One, if one party to the marriage had a spouse living at the time of marriage, then such a marriage will be null and void. Secondly, if the relationship of the parties fell within what is called the ambit of prohibited degrees, the marriage could be declared null and void. The grounds for invalidation of the marriage are four. First, impotency. Second, parties being sapinda. Third, parties being either idiotic or lunatic. Fourth, guardian's consent obtained by force or fraud. In order not to keep the sword of dissolution hanging on the head, the Bill, in my judgment very wisely, has provided a limit to an action for invalidation. It provides that a suit for the invalidation of marriage must be filed within three years from the date of the marriage; otherwise the suit will be barred and the marriage will continue as though there was no ground for invalidity. The Bill also provides that even though the marriage may be invalidated and may be declared invalid by a Court of Law, the invalidation of marriage will not affect the legitimacy of the children born and they would continue to be legitimate just the same.

Then coming to the question of divorce, there are seven grounds on which divorce could be obtained: (1) desertion, (2) conversion to another religion, (3) keeping a concubine or becoming a concubine, (4) incurably unsound mind, (5) virulent and incurable form of leprosy, (6) venereal diseases in communicable form, and (7) cruelty.

Coming to the question of adoption, there again, most of the rules embodied in the Bill are in no way different from the rules obtaining under the present law. There are two new provisions in this part dealing with adoption. Firstly, under the Code it will be necessary for the husband if he wants to make an adoption to obtain the consent of his wife and if there are more than one, at least the consent of one of them. Secondly, it also lays down that if the widow wants to adopt, she can only adopt if there are positive instructions left by the husband authorising her to adopt and in order to prevent litigation as to whether the husband has, as a matter of fact, left instructions to his wife, the Code provides that the evidence of such instructions shall be either by registered deed or by a provision in the will. No oral evidence would be admissible, so that chances of litigation are considerably mitigated. The Code also provides that the adoption may also be evidenced by registration. One of the most fruitful sources of litigation in this country is the question of adoption. All sorts of oral evidence is manufactured, concocted; witnesses are suborned; widows are fooled; they one day declare that they have made one adoption and subsequently they make an avowal that they have not adopted and in order that all this litigation may be put a stop to the Code makes a salutary provision that there may be registration of adoption by a Hindu.

Then there is the question of minority and guardianship, the last subject which the Bill seeks to codify. There is nothing new in this part of the Code and, therefore, I do not propose to say anything so far as that part in the Bill is concerned.

As members will realise, the points which arise out of this Bill for consideration and which are new are these: First, the abolition of birthright and to take property by survivorship. The second point that arises for consideration is the giving of half-share to the daughter. Thirdly, the conversion of the women's limited estate into an absolute estate. Fourthly, the abolition of caste in the matter of marriage and adoption. Fifthly, the principle of monogamy and sixthly the principle of divorce. I have sought to enumerate these points separately and categorically because I felt that in view of the limited time we have at our disposal, it would be of help to the Members of this House if I could point out what are the points of debate on which attention may be concentrated. These departures which are made in this Bill undoubtedly require justification, but I think it would be a waste of time if I at this stage undertook any defence of the departures enacted by this Bill. I propose to hear Honourable Members as to what they have to say on the points which I have enumerated, and if I find that it is necessary for me to enter upon a justification, I propose to do so in the course of my reply. Sir, I move.

~

HANSA MEHTA

Suggestions for the Hindu Code Bill

A prominent Congress leader, Gandhian and educationist, Hansa Mehta was president of the All India Women's Conference in 1945. In the debate on the Hindu Code Bill in the Constituent Assembly, she represented the voice of the progressive woman who supported the bill and yet had certain reservations about it not addressing many issues which she articulated in the speech.

Sir, I congratulate the Honourable Minister for bringing this Bill even at this late hour of the Session. I also congratulate, or rather I express my sense of gratitude to Sir B.N. Ban and his colleagues for the great labour they have bestowed on the Report on which these recommendations are based. This Bill to codify the Hindu Law is a revolutionary Bill and though we are not quite satisfied with it, it will be a great landmark in the social history of the Hindus. But since this Bill was drafted many things have happened and one of the biggest things that has happened is the achievement of our political freedom. Our new Constitution is in the making, we have already agreed upon the fundamental principles on which this new Constitution is to be drafted. The new State is going to be a democratic State and democracy is based on the equality of individuals. It is from this point of view that we have now to approach the problems of inheritance and marriage etc. that are before us. The Select Committee will therefore have to see that the new Bill is drafted on these principles.

It is true that the Code has abolished the sex discrimination with regard to inheritance. A woman is recognised as an heir and she is also entitled to enjoy her property in her full rights; that is, the Code has abolished the limited estate of the woman. Even then we feel that it does not go far enough. A daughter who is recognised an heir inherits the property, but she inherits half the share of the son. This violates the principle of equality on which we have again and again said that our new Constitution is going to be based—a Constitution which aims to secure for the people of this country justice, social, political and economic. We therefore feel that the daughter should get an equal share in the property of her father with the son, and the son also should get an equal share in the property of his mother with the daughter. It is also argued that a daughter gets her share from her father as well as from her husband, while the man does not get anything from his wife. We have already proposed, that is the Women's Organisations have said that the husband can also inherit the property of his wife in the same way that the wife inherits the property of her husband. In the Indian Succession Act the provision for the inheritance of husband is already there and I think we shall do well to copy that provision.

People have argued, and the Honourable friend who spoke before me has said that if a daughter is given her share, especially in a landed property, there will be fragmentation of land. But why is this argument trotted out in the case of a daughter's inheritance? The same thing applies if a man has more than one son; if he has, say, four or five sons the land has to be fragmented; why is the argument not trotted out then, and only trotted out when the question of daughters inheriting the property comes up? The better thing would be that there should be law against fragmentation and the property should be sold if it goes below the prescribed limit. Or there is another alternative and that is collectivisation of the land.

Then with regard to the question of marriage, I am gratified, and the women of India will be very happy to know, that the principle of monogamy is recognised, and if the Code comes into being then the principle of monogamy will be established. Sir, we have felt that all civilised nations, all civilised communities have adopted the principle of monogamy. Disrespect for women and all the atrocities that we hear of perpetrated on women are I think due to the fact that this principle of polygamy exists. If we had monogamy I do not think that women would have been abducted, married off or other things would have happened to them. This is a very wholesome principle and I hope the House will accept it.

But with regard to some of the conditions of marriage there are one or two points that I would like to suggest. With regard to the marriage of the sapindas and the definition of sapinda, that requires a little revision; we are not quite satisfied with the definition that is given in the Code. Then again, we would like the age of marriage also to be a condition of a valid marriage. We have got the Sarda Act but that is not satisfactory; that has not satisfied the people because it has not been able to prevent child marriages; it is not effective. For that reason we would like the law to be more drastic. If we want sixteen to be the age of marriage, then it is very necessary that it should be included as one of the conditions of valid marriage and I would like the Select Committee to make that change.

Then with regard to divorce, even that, from the point of view of some, does not go far enough. There is, however, one thing that I would like to bring to the notice of the members of the Select Committee and that is the time given for desertion. If a man or a woman deserts his or her spouse, it has been provided, he or she can divorce her or him after five years. Five years is the period given in the Code. Even in 'Narad Smriti' it is given that a childless woman should wait for three years. After three years she can marry again. So why not also bring that particular provision here, that if a woman is childless, she need not wait till five years, but can divorce her husband after three years? If a woman has got children, then five years would be the right period, but for a childless woman three years would be a reasonable period.

With regard to guardianship, here also the Code has not made any changes in the present law. Father is the natural guardian of the children. The mother does not come in. We would like the mother also to be a co-guardian of the children with the father.

With regard to adoption, I think the whole chapter should be scrapped. We are a secular State. We want to be a secular State. Adoption in Hindu law is for religious purposes. Why should a secular State have anything to do with a religious custom? What we are concerned with is whether adoption which is for religious purposes should be recognised by the State for purposes of inheritance. We say that it should not. If a child is adopted—whether it is a boy or a girl—we would like a daughter also to be adopted—if a child is adopted not for religious purpose, but for real purpose, i.e. that the parents want a child, then that child should have the same rights as the natural child. But if there is adoption for religious purposes, only then I think that adoption should not be recognised for purposes of inheritance.

These are some of the important points that I would like the Select Committee to consider. Speeches have been made—at least my Honourable friend Dr. Pattabhi has made a very long speech—praising all sorts of things about our past traditions. We have looked too much to the past. We must now look to the future. It is for the future generation that we are making this law. It is not for us, but for the future generation that is coming after us that this law will be applied. We have to look to the future conditions. After all, it is the conditions that determine the law. The law reflects the society. The law reflects the conditions in which the people live. We have to see that the future generation is not fettered by our own prejudices with regard to marriage or divorce or with regard to any other ideas that we may have today. I hope the Select Committee will consider that and produce a Bill which will be a great boon to the future Hindu society.

JAIPAL SINGH

On the Report of the Commissioner for Scheduled Castes and Scheduled Tribes

The constitution of India enjoined the Government of India to appoint a commissioner for Scheduled Castes and Scheduled Tribes who had to report to Parliament. It was conceived as one of the most powerful instruments by means of which Indian democracy, through its watchdog the Parliament, would keep an eye on the promise of development and prosperity made by the nation to its most underprivileged people. The first report of the commissioner was presented to the Lok Sabha in December 1952 and was followed by animated discussions. While certain members like Shrimati Khongmen, who talked about the state of women and people in the Khasi Hills, were very optimistic about the report and its possible implementation, others like Jaipal Singh were cynical and minced no words in criticizing the government's half-hearted measures with regard to the deprived classes, cogently pointing out that while the constitution provided for many safeguards for the deprived people, there was little scope in it for direct action. He also made an earnest plea for rising above party politics when dealing with the upliftment of these people. And in his mention of the land acquisition for the Chittaranjan Loco Works, one sees how issues of displacement and rehabilitation have been constantly voiced in the Indian public space since 1948.

I regret I find it very difficult indeed to feel enthused over this report. Apart from thanking the Government for setting apart a meagre day, one day only, to discuss this report, I have nothing more to say by way of congratulating the Government. The introductory speech of the venerable Minister is proof in itself of the lack of seriousness of the gravity of this problem. There are empty Treasury Benches. Is that how the Treasury Benches receive this very, very important subject? I know there will be the reported materials that they will read and perhaps in their own time try to digest. But surely, those of us who are inarticulate most of the time in this House deserve a little more consideration from the Treasury Benches than we are getting... The Treasury Benches must have en masse to listen to the difficult voice of the Scheduled Castes, the Scheduled Tribes, the backward classes and others who might be interested in the problem of the depressed section of our community.

I know it for a fact that there is no greater friend in this country today of the minorities and the group we are discussing today are a minority, but a very important minority—some have been neglected for a century, others have been neglected always, for thousands of years. There is one person about whom I would like to say a few words. I am not at all concerned with what the Special Officer has written. But there is one propaganda officer, a natural one, who has been saying things from his heart, whenever he has had opportunities of visiting the tribal areas, who deserves the thanks not of mine only, but of the many tribal millions and the depressed classes, and that is Jawaharlal Nehru. He is the only one who, as far as I can see it, in an India that is infested with obscurantists, is the champion, of the minorities.

Having said that I do not want to throw any more bouquets, because I would like to get down to realism, get down to brass tacks and try to give my own suggestions. I know it has become the habit in this country for speakers to screen themselves behind big names. Mahatma Gandhi's name has been mentioned, Dr Ambedkar's name has been mentioned, and the names of many others have been mentioned. Even the name of the Indian National Congress has been dragged into picture. I can think of no poorer way of presenting one's case than to shield behind big names. I am not here to defend my party or to abuse the other parties. All that I request of this House and the country is to look at this problem above party politics, because if it is going to be treated as a matter of party politics—what the Congress men have done or not done—then...we shall be lost completely. For that very reason I urge my friends, whether they are with me politically or against me, to accept whatever I say in that particular light, in the light of this tremendous problem being kept above party politics. And it is because of that I have to criticise the various Governments of the States about whatever, in my opinion, they have failed to achieve... Unfortunately, it is because everything is handled from the political angle that we have failed in this... We have failed to achieve what we might have achieved even in these couple of years.

I know there will be speakers after me, particularly people wearing white caps, who will eulogise everything that has been done by their fellow white capwallas. Let us go to Bihar and see the areas where Adivasis suffer and also glory. What is happening in Bihar? I have only just mentioned that people screen themselves behind big names. The name of Adimjati Seva Mandal has been mentioned in this connection. There are annual conferences held in Rashtrapati

Bhavan. Why? Are these people prepared to tell me here that the Mandal has any confidence in any of the places where it has been constituted? How is it that in South Bihar, in Jharkhand, despite my Honourable Friend, Mr Jawaharlal Nehru—whom we worship, because he is the only hope of this country—despite his visit to that area the Congress faced a holocaust...?

... I do not want our reverend Leader to be exploited by unscrupulous people. I am advisedly using these rather strong words. I do not mean to abuse anybody. But what I want to say is this. There are people who call themselves social workers. They are not social workers. There are some people who call themselves social workers and are exploiting the fair name of the Indian National Congress and Government funds; and they are not doing the tremendous, noble party any good. I want my friends on the other side to realise and to appreciate the fact. We do not mind who does good—whether it is Western missionaries, Ramakrishna Mission, Indian National Congress, anybody. We will welcome everyone who will come to help us to grow bigger and better and become prosperous. How is it, can my friends on the other side tell us why is it that non-aboriginals in the Naga Hills are suspect? It is all very well for my friends to say that during the British regime non-aboriginals were not allowed to go to the Naga Hills. Would Dr. Katju have visited the Naga Hills those days? If he had done so, perhaps he would have come back minus his head. I am not in any way supporting this isolationism of the British. But there were certain definite reasons. My friend, Dr. Katju, suggested that more people should go and mix there. God help if that is going to happen! If you are going to bring more baniyas and money-lenders, Heaven help the Adivasis in those jungles! What we want are genuine workers. I agree with him. We do not want that lovely speeches should be made and nothing more happen. We want something definite and concrete...

The whole question is this. I think the Ministry of Home Affairs in this particular regard have completely forgotten what their duty is as enjoined by the constitution. They have completely forgotten it. I am not interested in how many Commissioners and Special Officers are appointed and how many reports are written. What I am interested in is how 'my people'—I do not mean only the tribal people; I mean all the backward people—how they are being enabled to coming up to the general level. A report is not going to make them just come up. In fact the report is ignominiously lacking in any information. The

Special Officer himself admits that nobody thinks anything of him. Even with the Prime Minister's letter people do not take notice of him. What do you expect? As Thakkar Bapa himself once wrote to me—I have read this letter in this House before and I dare not read it again—'After all he is a Government servant, and he has his limitations.'

Let us forget the Special Officer. Whatever has happened or not happened is not his fault. But I do accuse the Ministry of Home Affairs for lacking in an integrated policy. They have no policy at all. It is now two years. What has happened? Precious time is being lost. And according to the Constitution, we are supposed to be making up the leeway in ten years. Nothing will happen, may I say, because everywhere constitutionally your safeguards may be there, but there is lacking the sanction for direct intervention. What is actually the fact is that the centre is imbecile, is unable to tell the other people what they should do.

It has happened only yesterday. What did my friend the Deputy Minister of Irrigation and Power say? Here the Prime Minister and Planning Minister and everybody has assured us on the floor of this House and told us that the Adivasis evacuated from the places submerged by water as a result of the multipurpose river valley projects would get land for land, house for house. Now we are told, like a bolt from the blue: no. I can repeat the words. But they are so fresh. It happened only yesterday, and I do not think the House would like to be burdened with a repetition of that. A complete change. What is happening? We hear of a wonderful thing, the Hirakud Dam. Yes, the Hirakud Dam is an excellent thing. But is that all? Is a fine piece of engineering all that my honourable friends on the other side want to enthuse over, and make me completely forget what is going to happen to my people? Should not these people who are transplanted be rehabilitated elsewhere or enabled to live with any self-respect? Is an engineering feat the only thing we should brag about in this country?

What happened at the time of land acquisition for the Chittaranjan Loco Works? The Santhals there were given cash. Within about three weeks they were landless labourers.

Yesterday a question was asked about the Maithon project. I would urge upon my friends, it may be that they are not quite near the spot where all the tragedies happen. They do not quite appreciate the tragedy that is brought about. Do we want to increase the army of landless workers in this country? If we do not, then the Government should adopt a firm policy that no one should be made to evacuate village—Santhal or no Santhal—unless he is given land for land, house for house and more if possible.

I know the difficulties of the Government. Miracles obviously cannot be worked overnight. I do appreciate the fact that any big change that has to come, whether it is for the Harijans or any other backward group, must come from within. I have to stress the fact that I do not want any non-official agency to work this. In the name of patriotism, people go about the country and abuse the trust the various political parties and Government have put in them. I have seen it before my eyes. I do not want to mention names. But it is a fact. The House must accept it when I say that we have to screen these non-official agencies carefully. It is not that only Congress men are patriots, that only non-official agencies that are sponsored by the Congress must qualify for ameliorative measures. It should not be like that. It should be above party politics.

All that I would urge on my friends opposite is this. Mr. Jawaharlal Nehru, a couple of years back, when a representation had been made by the father of this House, Mr. B. Das, after his tour of Assam wrote back saying that for some time he had been thinking of having a Ministry of Social Services. Perhaps my Honourable Friend would like me to remind him of it, in case he thinks I am just pulling something out of my hat. It is not that. This is what he said: 'Long time ago I was of opinion that we should have a Minister of Social Service. But there is no point in having a minister unless there is something to be done.'

Well, quite frankly, I do not understand what the latter part means. But the first part says that for a long time my leader there, our leader, the Leader of this House has been thinking of establishing a Ministry of Social Services. But then he finds himself confronted with the terrible problem of the question of finance.

~

N.C. CHATTERJEE

The Special Marriage Bill

The Special Marriage Bill evoked strong responses after it was introduced in Parliament in 1954. The Bill envisaged making marriage a civil contract rather than a religious one and provided grounds and avenues for dissolution (divorce) of marriages registered under this Act. This was in keeping with their opposition to the Hindu Code Bill of 1948 (of which the Special Marriage Bill was a component) on the grounds that a state which calls itself secular should not interfere with community and customary laws. It was passed by the Rajya Sabha but conservative communal elements in the Lok Sabha left no stone unturned to delay the bill. The Lok Sabha spent a record twelve hours over the motion for the consideration of the bill. N.C. Chatterjee, renowned lawyer and spokesperson for the Hindu Mahasabha, voiced his strident opposition to the bill. Notwithstanding stiff opposition, the Bill was passed.

The honourable Law Minister, my friend Shri Biswas, in his very elaborate opening speech has tried to emphasise the aspect that it is a permissive Bill, it is not a compulsory measure, it is a non-communal and non-sectarian measure, it is meant to be all-pervasive and that, therefore, it is not a measure which ought to provoke very much comment. I am afraid, it is not quite correct and I shall endeavour to point to my honourable friends in this House that, although it is prima facie permissive, it has got certain features which will lead to very serious effects on sacramental marriages, specially the Hindu marriages.

There is a clause which is rather extraordinary, and is of a revolutionary character. This is a clause which was not in the original Special Marriage Act as it was passed in 1872. You know, as my friend the honourable Law Minister has pointed out, this Bill was passed at the instance of Shri Keshab Chandra Sen and Brahmo leaders who wanted a particular kind of civil marriage not restricted by the injunctions of Hindu laws, because they wanted to marry outside the caste, in the same gotra and so on. These were not permissible at that stage and therefore they wanted such a Bill. But, these restrictions are now gone. Two legislations have come into being in 1941 and 1949 and a good deal of the *raison d'être* of that old Act has now gone. First of all, under the Hindu Law as it now stands there is no restriction with regard to caste or sub-caste, or gotra or pravara. Anyone can marry outside the caste and that marriage will be perfectly valid. The law has been put beyond any doubt. I am reading to you from the latest edition of *Principles of Hindu Law* by Mr. D.F. Mulla—the latest edition has been edited by a great judge and great jurist, Mr. Justice Mukerjea. He has pointed out that in two respects the law is now perfectly clear. First of all he has pointed out: 'It is now provided by the Hindu Marriage Disabilities Removal Act, 1946, that notwithstanding any text rule or interpretation of the Hindu Law or any custom or usage, a marriage between Hindus, which is otherwise valid, shall not be invalid by reason only of the fact that the parties thereto belong to the same gotra or pravara.'

This, Sir, is one important change which was effected. The second important change which has been effected is this, that by the Act of 1949 restrictions with regard to inter-caste marriages have gone.

... I maintain and I ask all my honourable friends to consider seriously this aspect of the problem. Is it right that Upper House should take charge of this Bill in the initial stage? Which is the proper forum for the consideration of such an important and controversial measure which will affect the lives of millions of people, the welfare of individuals, the welfare of society at large and the welfare of the entire nation? I am very happy to find that some honourable Members on the opposite benches also feel like that and first speaker who followed the honourable Law Minister, Shri C.C. Shah said: 'If I may respectfully say so, Sir, I regret that this Bill which is so important and which is so controversial, should have been introduced and discussed first in the Council of States and then brought to this House. And I am also urging that the convention should be immediately introduced that all important and controversial measures like this should first be introduced in this House before they are taken by the other House.'

It is not a question of prestige, it is not a question of dignity; but, it is a question of principle, the essential question of this bi-cameral parliamentary system. We have been elected by adult suffrage. We reflect the popular will and in respect of any measure like this, which will have tremendous consequences on the whole national set-up, it is important and vital that the popular House democratically elected should have the first say in the matter. Shri C.C. Shah has also rightly pointed that it will save a lot of time and it will also save a good deal of complication. Sir, you know that certain amendments have been made by the Upper House which have made the Bill more controversial and the honourable Prime Minister who addressed this House on the last day of the last session, also said that this Bill as it has emerged from the Council of States requires amendment. I am reading, Sir, the exact language of Pandit Nehru: 'I think that as the Bill has emerged from the Council of States it would be desirable to make some alterations and amendments.'

He did not specify what amendments and what alterations should be made, but I have no doubt that the honourable Prime Minister was thinking of a very revolutionary clause which has been inserted by the Upper House, namely, the clause regarding divorce by consent. Divorce by consent is repugnant to the basic principles of Hindu marriage, repugnant to the entire system on which Hindu family life rests. This is unknown in English Law. As a matter of fact, if you go to any Divorce Court in England, you will find that the first issue that is adjudicated upon by the divorce judge will be: has there been any consent between the parties to get divorce? It may not be raised at any pleading, but in the English courts, French courts and also in most of the Continental Courts, the first thing that requires adjudication is: is there consent between the parties to get the divorce? Is it a matter of friendly compact between the husband and wife so that the holy union should be disrupted? As you know—you are a distinguished lawyer yourself—in the English courts there is a Proctor attached to every divorce judge and that Proctor makes an independent enquiry, because on the face of things there may be a good case, and good lawyers may be engaged, whole thing goes on for days, elaborate evidence is taken and then the judge makes his finding, but it may be that there were some facts which were not placed before the court deliberately although eminent lawyers might have appeared. Therefore, in the western countries where you have provision for divorce, they take this important precaution: let there be no divorce by consent, by arrangement or by contract.

I am honestly of the opinion that it will lead to companionate marriages, it will lead to convenient marriages, it will lead to some kind of *muta* marriages, maybe for seven days or ten days...

I know that some people, who think they are progressive, are in favour of divorce by consent. I maintain I am also progressive and that is why I accepted a seat on the Untouchability Bill Committee. I honestly feel as the President of the biggest organisation in India of Hindus that, if Hinduism has to live untouchability must die and that is why I joined the Committee. That is the cardinal principle of the organisation to which I belong and of which I am the temporary head. What I am pointing out is that you must know and realise the basic principles of Hindu marriage.

[Shri S.S. More (Sholapur): May I make a submission that this Bill does not refer to Hindu marriages?]

It does refer and I am sorry that Mr. More has not read the Bill. If Mr. More had taken the trouble of reading the Bill, he would have realised that one of the most important clauses is this, namely, that under this Bill, after it is enacted, Mr. More, who married Mrs. More years ago, can go with her to the Marriage Registrar and have their marriage registered under this law, and then he will cease to be governed by the Hindu law of succession and will be governed by the Indian Succession Act. Not only that. Under this Bill, there is provision for retrospective application of the law of divorce to sacramental marriages which took place twenty or thirty years back. I am opposed to that on principle. I am saying that you have no right to tamper with sacramental marriage. A man marries a woman under the Hindu law and a Muslim gentleman marries a Muslim lady under the Muhammadan Law, knowing perfectly well the obligations of the respective laws. When a Hindu marries a Hindu woman under the Hindu Law he knows that there is an indissoluble union, there can be no divorce and it must be a permanent partnership, eternal fellowship for self-fulfilment and for the development of society—*dharma, artha, kama, moksha*. It is incapable of termination by bilateral arrangement or contract. The man and the woman accept their union with the full knowledge of their obligations—and they live together. As a matter of fact, there may be children who are born to them. Suppose a man was married thirty years ago and has sons about 25 or 20 years of age...

Look at the absurdity of the thing. Immediately that marriage is registered, that man is governed by the Succession Act. Not only that. His son, who is 25 years old and who may have married under the Hindu law or the Hindu sacramental system and who may have children, will cease to be governed by the Hindu law; he will be governed by the Indian Succession Act.

I am pointing out that this retrospective application of the provisions of the Bill to sacramental marriages is not proper and is not desirable and it is destructive of the basic principles of the Hindu ideals of marriage. You should not, therefore, tamper with sacramental marriages. The Doctor behind me is saying 'Nobody is forcing you.' He does not know our society, he does not know our country and he does not know at least the women of India.

According to this Bill, in India if a man gets the signature of his wife to an application for registration, he can file it and get the marriage registered, and immediately—the next day or the day after—he can go to the court and apply for divorce on certain grounds specified, maybe cruelty, maybe adultery or any one of the grounds prescribed for the purpose. You know our country, you know how helpless the people are and you also know the standard of literacy in the country. I think Acharya Kripalani was quite right when he said that it will be the easiest thing for the husband to get the consent of the wife. Is it desirable, having regard to the state of society—they are not economically competent; they are not hundred per cent literate as in other countries—that you should allow the husband to get the consent or signature of his wife, and next day get it registered and then apply the Indian Succession Act? Not only that. The man can go and have a divorce in the court. I beg of this House to consider whether it would be desirable to have sacramental marriages interfered with, the Hindu marriages tampered with by the provisions of this Bill.

... For effecting this remarkable change or a revolutionary change like this, the House should have got the mandate of the nation. It was not there in the Hindu Code Bill; it was not in Sir B.N. Rau Committee's report... Did you ever consult the nation? Did you ever consult the electorate? Did you ever ask for the mandate of the country? You want divorce by consent. The honourable Law Minister himself has pointed out—I think he is right there, although we differ on many points—that something like this law was existent only in Soviet Russia. Outside the communist countries, not in the United States of America, not in Australia, not in Canada, there is this kind of law. I am quoting Soviet civil law, a portion of which was read out by the Law Minister: 'Either spouse had complete freedom to discontinue without stating the reasons thereof.'

Therefore, you can say 'I do not like any longer my wife.' Finished. The divorce was recorded by the registry office not only upon a declaration by both the spouses but also upon a unilateral declaration by spouse of his or her desire to discontinue conjugal life. You send a postcard to the Registration Officer: 'I do not like any longer my wife.'

... The Soviet civil law said that not only upon a declaration by both the spouses but also by the unilateral declaration by the spouse, conjugal life could be discontinued. Therefore, it would be quite all right if we have unilateral declaration. One may like it, and say it is very desirable. I say it is very undesirable: it is destructive of the basic principles of Hindu concept of marriage. So many empires have crashed into ruin; so many dynasties have sprung and have gone into oblivion; so many civilisations have ceased to function at all, but Hindu civilisation and Hindu society still live. Why? Not because of anything else but because of certain vital principles to which it clings and one of the principles was this: the purity of domestic life, and the high standard of chastity of women which it enforced. That purity and chastity have been the great principles which are vital and which have preserved Hindu society and Hindu civilisation. Will you in any way destroy that? Will anyone want to affect that organism and that great principle? ... In Soviet Russia itself they have changed the law, and they are trying to tighten it up. The same thing is happening even in countries like England and America. They know that family life is going to pieces and they are trying to make divorce stricter. I am only saying this: Men and women have married under the Hindu Law, or under Muslim Law or under personal laws and they have entered into sacramental marriages accepting the full liabilities and the full obligations of such sacramental marriages. What business have you to interfere with or to tamper with such marriages? Why do you give loophole in these cases and say that even then, the divorce clauses will be applicable on registration? Then, what is the *raison d'être*? What is the object of having a Hindu marriage taken to a divorce court? I cannot understand. You have already a Bill dealing with all Hindu marriages with the possibility of divorce of such Hindu marriages. Make it an all-pervasive Bill applicable to all citizens, if you have the courage to say that by having one marriage law in secular India, you are trying to implement the basic or directive policies of the Constitution-makers. I can understand that. But you are not doing it. You are having a Hindu Marriage and Divorce Bill. The Select Committee is going on. When you are having provision for Hindu marriage and divorces of such Hindu marriages, why do you allow, by a side-wind, this kind of attack and this kind of dissolution of Hindu marriage? It is not logical. With great respect, I would say that it is not right.

~

N. RACHIAH

The Untouchability (Offences) Bill

The campaign against untouchability by Mahatma Gandhi in the 1920s and 1930s was one of the most revolutionary of its kind launched by any leader in modern history. He traversed the country, visiting thousands of villages, arguing, debating and trying to convince the upper castes, those who practised untouchability, that it was an immoral practice. It was not only a blot on human existence but also on Hinduism. For Gandhi, the political question and the social question were never separate and he made the removal of untouchability the major plank of his political campaign. The constitution makers, when they passed the right to equality as a fundamental right, were in fact echoing the sentiment of the national movement that equality was the sine qua non of modern India. However, old, established practices die hard and as such it was felt imperative to introduce legislation to make untouchability a legal offence. It was a radical piece of legislation and N. Rachiah, who rose to become one of the foremost leaders from Karnataka, spoke in Parliament about the philosophy behind the Untouchability (Offences) Bill on 27 August 1954.

I wholeheartedly welcome this piece of legislation and this is the first time in the Parliament that a social legislation of this type is going to be placed on the statute book of our country. While welcoming this Bill, I must be very grateful to Gandhiji who sacrificed his life for the emancipation of particularly the Harijans or the Scheduled Castes of India. As Mr. Somana said, we are more than one-fifth of the population in this country, and yet it is so unfortunate and so sorrowful to see that for thousands of years these human beings were degraded to the lowest strata of society where even animals have got a better place than these human beings.

Our constitution, the sacred document of our democracy, assures equal opportunities, justice and liberty to all its citizens and articles 15 17, 25, 29, 38 and 46 aim at securing equal justice, social, economic and political. Can we say that in this country there is any social justice? I can tolerate any inequality but not social inequality, because social equality is the basis or foundation for the rapid progress of any country or any individual. The cancer of untouchability, which has been banned by article 17 of the constitution, has devoured millions or crores of our people, who have given their lives without seeing what life is.

Crores of our people have been subjected to this type of tuberculosis. As we all know, the disease tuberculosis eats away the body. So this tuberculosis of untouchability will eat away the country if allowed any longer. Now, we talk of oneness, we talk of democracy. We see that Government have not provided large sums of money in the Five Year Plan and in the next Five Year Plan for the emancipation of these people. Gandhiji, who sacrificed his life for the cause of the Scheduled Castes, said in the year 1933 when the resolution was passed in Bombay with regard to temple entry: 'It was the last September that leading Hindus claiming to represent the whole of Hindu India met together and unanimously passed a resolution condemning untouchability and pledging themselves to abolish it by law if possible even during the existing regime, and failing that, when India had a parliament of her own.'

This is a great day that this parliament, which is the true representative of more than 36 crores of the people of India, is going to pass this Bill and I am sure that this is a landmark in the Indian society which seeks to consolidate and unify the Indian society and also gives salvation to more than 80 million people in the country. In this connection, I am reminded of the struggle that was going on between patricians and plebeians in the Roman society. Till that struggle ended, the Romans could not build a Roman empire; India cannot be great till caste Hindus and Harijans end their struggle. The patricians could be compared to the caste Hindus here and we the Harijans, have been like the plebeians in the Hindu society. Our leaders talk of oneness, but where is it? Even in the hostels, schools and colleges, this is not to be found, and communal divisions are there. Cannot the Government abolish the communal institutions, mutts, etc., in the interest of democracy and in the name of a Welfare-State? I am sure democracy cannot survive in India if those institutions are allowed to go on in this way.

We, the Harijans, are in favour of a peaceful, constitutional, rapid revolution, both social and economic. The social revolution cannot be achieved without the economic revolution, and the economic revolution cannot be achieved without the social revolution; both are closely knit together, and I do know that they are inseparable. Many Members say that the economic revolution must be given first priority, but Government do not grant lands to Harijans. If the Government do recognise the acute problems of Harijans let them at least give them land—at least the remaining land now available and which has been lying there for the last thousands of years. There has been no dearth of land lying waste in the country. At least now, can the Government make a central legislation that all the remaining Government wasteland, whether forest or non-forest areas, that could be cultivated, be given to the Harijans? They are reluctant. I cannot but agree with what Shri Shrikant, Scheduled Caste Commissioner, has said, namely, the emancipation of Harijans can be achieved only if there is honest effort on the part of the people and Government. Not only that. I do not think that a Harijan can now get even a *chaprasi's* post, ordinarily. What is the meaning of reservation of certain posts in services, if the Central Government order or a State Government order is not given effect to? In Mysore, the Central Government's order was received regarding reservation of posts in services for Harijans. But there is no Harijan representative in the Public Service Commission there, though the Harijans were more than one-sixth of the population in Mysore. The Public Service Commission there is composed of caste Hindus. They (the Government of Mysore) delayed the implementation of the order for two years within which period they appointed all caste Hindus in vacant places where the Harijans should have been appointed. According to the order, the Harijans were to be given 22 per cent of the posts. So, for another 20 years, Harijans are not going to get any job, because they have already overrecruited the non-Harijans in filling the posts. The same thing is going on elsewhere. If this is the position, we do not want this concession. We do not want any of these concessions whatsoever, if this is the position. Still, if they are interested in democracy, if they are interested in the Welfare State, let them do it properly. We want the proper thing to be done. Gandhiji said that the practice of untouchability was repugnant to the reason, love and the spirit of mercy. He said once, 'If I were to be re-born, I want to be re-born as an untouchable, to share all their sorrows and pleasure—and also the impediments to which they are subject to.' Is it not a great statement, Sir?

Mr. Shrikant, the Commissioner for Scheduled Castes and Scheduled Tribes, has said as follows in his report: 'The progress made in this direction at the moment is still very slow, though I realise that complete eradication of this evil will take a little time on account of the deep-rooted prejudice—deeper than the ones against the Negroes in America of old—customs and habits prevailing in the Country.' He concludes with what an American wrote: 'The whole commerce between slave and master is a perpetual exercise of the most boisterous passions, the most unremitting despotism on one part and degrading submissions on the other.'

... ours is a degrading submission which we do not tolerate... I must be very grateful to Mr. Shrikant who has been very bold and sympathetic and who is really the disciple of Gandhiji. He has made out his report very clearly in the interests of the emancipation of these backward classes, particularly the Harijans... If they [*the government—Ed.*] are really honest in their opinion, let them appoint a commission or a board or a committee to investigate the working of the schemes for Harijan welfare i.e., Scheduled Castes and Scheduled Tribes. They do not want to do so. They want to wait till the Backward Classes Commission's report is submitted. Why should it be so? ...

With regard to the temples, I should like to mention this: wherever the Ministers go to the temple or such other places, why should they not have a programme for taking Harijans also along with them? I am sure, however, that this cancer, this demon of untouchability is going to be rooted out of the country. I am sure of this because all the Harijans are awakened today. But still, the Government and the people as a whole—whether caste Hindus, or non-Hindus—should cooperate together: particularly the legislators and the leaders.

~

JAWAHARLAL NEHRU

A Socialistic Pattern of Society

Speaking at the sixtieth annual session of the Indian National Congress in Avadi, Tamil Nadu, on 21 January 1955, Jawaharlal Nehru as the Congress president moved the motion regarding a socialistic pattern of society. Like millions of his contemporaries, Nehru had been influenced by socialism and socialist thought. But his was not a doctrinaire socialism and he rebuked those who held a bookish notion of it. In this resolution, he articulated his credo and the way he envisioned the development of the country.

Yesterday I had the honour to present a resolution before you, which you passed. In it we stated that we wanted it to be clearly understood that we aim at a socialistic pattern of society. In the present resolution which deals with the economic policy, we have to give effect to that decision of yours, because ultimately it is the economic policy which is going to reshape that picture of India which you call the 'socialistic pattern'. This resolution is therefore of the highest importance.

This resolution contains a brief reference to the objective to be achieved. First of all, after expressing appreciation of what has been done, the resolution says that the time has now come for substantially increasing production, for raising the standards of living and for having progressively fuller employment so as to achieve full employment within a period of ten years. The first thing to note about this resolution is that it does not merely repeat what we have said before. It points out that the time has come for us to advance on the economic and social plane. In a sense we have been doing it, but we have not been doing it adequately. The time has come to put an end to unemployment in ten years. By ten years we mean two Five-Year Plan periods. I wish you to appreciate that we try not to word our resolution in what might be called bombastic language. We are an old and mature organisation with a great deal of experience. It is not desirable, therefore, that we should use words which are vague or bombastic. On the whole we understate what we propose to do. If we really give effect to this resolution it means bringing about revolution in this country, an economic revolution bigger than any that has taken place in our times. Take the simple fact of putting an end to unemployment within ten years. Just try to think what it means in this country with its population growing year by year. It is a terrific job, the like of which has not been done in these circumstances in any other country.

Yesterday, we had the President of Yugoslavia here. It was a great privilege to have had amidst us such a great revolutionary, soldier of freedom and builder. Whatever Yugoslavia's troubles, unemployment has never been one of them. In fact, they are short of human beings to do their work. For us to compare ourselves with Yugoslavia in the matter of unemployment will not therefore lead us anywhere. Take the Soviet Union—a great big country, four or five times the size of India, with a population which is only about one-third of India's. The problem is different for them—a vast area with a small population. Our problem is different—a big country, heavily populated, and underdeveloped. Similarly, we cannot compare our problems with those of America, England and Western Europe where they have had two hundred years of industrial growth. These comparisons may sometimes be helpful but they mislead. We have to understand our problem as it is in India, no doubt learning from what has been done in America, England, Yugoslavia, Russia or China, but at the same time bearing in mind that the conditions in India are special and particular. Further, we have also to understand that our background is in many ways peculiar, particularly the Gandhian background.

We talk about planning. As you all know, planning is essential, and without it there would be anarchy in our economic development. About five years ago, planning was not acceptable to many people in high places but today it has come to be recognised as essential even by the man in the street. Our First Five-Year Plan is now about three years old, and we are now thinking about our Second Five-Year Plan. A phrase in this resolution says that the Second Five-Year Plan must keep the national aims of a Welfare State and a socialistic economy before it. These can only be achieved by a considerable increase in national income, and our economic policy must, therefore, aim at plenty and equitable distribution. The Second Five-Year Plan must keep these objectives in view and should be based on the physical needs of the people. These are really the important and governing words of the resolution and ought to be the controlling factors in drawing up the Second Five-Year Plan. Before going on to other aspects of the question may I say that a Welfare State and a socialistic pattern of economy are not synonymous expressions? It is true that a socialistic economy must provide for a Welfare State but it does not necessarily follow that a Welfare State must also be based on a socialistic pattern of society. Therefore the two, although they overlap, are yet somewhat different, and we say that we want both. We cannot have a Welfare State in India with all the socialism or even communism in the world unless our national income goes up greatly. Socialism or communism might help you to divide your existing wealth, if you like, but in India, there is no existing wealth for you to divide; there is only poverty to divide. It is not a question of distributing the wealth of the few rich men here and there. That is not going to make any difference in our national income. We might adopt that course for the psychological good that might come out of it. But from the practical point of view, there is not much to divide in India because we are a poor country. We must produce wealth, and then divide it equitably. How can we have a Welfare State without wealth? Wealth need not mean gold and silver but wealth in goods and services. Our economic policy must therefore aim at plenty. Until very recently economic policies have often been based on scarcity. But the economics of scarcity has no meaning in the world of today.

Now I come to this governing clause which I just referred to with regard to the Second Five-Year Plan, namely, that the Second Five-Year Plan should be based on the physical needs of the people. You will remember that yesterday the President also emphasised the necessity for basing planning on the people's physical needs. Our First

Five-Year Plan was based on the data and the material we had at our disposal as well as on things that were actually being done at the time. Take these big river valley schemes. All these things were being done at the time and we had no choice but to continue them. We had to accept what had been done. Of course, we added one or two new schemes and rearranged the priorities. That is to say, our Plan was largely based on the finances available and consisted in taking up those schemes which were most useful. But it was limited planning, not planning in the real sense of the word. The conception of planning today is not to think of the money we have and then to divide it up in the various schemes but to measure the physical needs, that is to say, how much of food the people want, how much of clothes they want, how much of housing they want, how much of education they want, how much of health services they want, how much of work and employment they want, and so on. We calculate all these and then decide what everyone in India should have of these things. Once we do that, we can set about increasing production and fulfilling these needs. It is not a simple matter because in calculating the needs of the people, we have to calculate on the basis not only of an increasing population but of increasing needs. I shall give you an instance. Let us take sugar. Our people now consume much more sugar than they used to, with the result that our calculations about sugar production went wrong.

Now, why do they eat more sugar? Evidently because they are better off. If a man fetching a hundred rupees finds his income increased to a hundred and fifty, he will eat more sugar, buy more cloth, and so on. Therefore, in making calculations, we have to keep in mind that the extra money that goes into circulation because of the higher salaries and wages, affects consumption. So we find out what in five years' time will be the needs of our people, including even items needed by our Defence Services. Then we decide how to produce those things in India. In order to meet a particular variety of needs we have now to put up a factory which will produce the goods that we need five years hence. Thus, planning is a much more complicated process than merely drawing up some schemes and fixing a system of priorities.

Behind all this is another factor—finance. Finance is important but not so important as people think. What is really important is drawing up the physical needs of the people and then working to produce things which will fulfil such needs. If you are producing wealth, it does not matter very much if you have some deficit financing because you are actually putting money back through goods and services. Therefore it does not matter how you manipulate your currency so long as your production is also keeping pace with it. Of course there is the fear of inflation. We must avoid it. But there is no such fear at present in India. On the other hand, there is deflation. Nevertheless, we have to guard against inflation. We have to produce the equivalent of the money pumped in. Sometimes there is a gap between investment and production, when inflation sets in. For example, let us say we put in a hundred crores of rupees in a river valley scheme which takes seven or eight years to build. During the years it is being built we get nothing out of it but expenditure. This can be balanced in cottage industries, in which the gap in time is not large. The additional money that you have put in is not locked up for long. Therefore in planning we have to balance heavy industry, light industry, village industry and cottage industry. We want heavy industry because without it we can never really be an independent country. Light industry too has become essential for us. So has cottage industry. I am putting forward this argument not from the Gandhian ideal, but because it is essential in order to balance heavy industry and to prevent the big gap between the pumping in of money and production.

But production is not all. A man works and produces something because he expects others to consume what he produces. If there is no consumption, he stops production. Therefore whether it is a factory or a cottage unit, consumption of what is produced should be taken care of. Mass production inevitably involves mass consumption, which in turn involves many other factors, chiefly the purchasing power of the consumer. Therefore planning must take note of the need to provide more purchasing power by way of wages, salaries and so on. Enough money should be thrown in to provide this purchasing power and to complete the circle of production and consumption. You will then produce more and consume more, and as a result your standard of living will go up.

I have ventured to take up your time in order to give you some idea of the approach that is intended in this resolution when we say that the Second Five-Year Plan should be based on the physical needs of the people. I hope it has helped you to understand the way we are thinking. I myself do not see any other way of rapid progress. The financial approach to planning is not rapid enough. I should like you to explain this to people when you go home to your respective towns and districts. We are responsible for giving effect to this resolution. We have to fulfil our promise.

~

PRITHVIRAJ KAPOOR

Capital Punishment Should Go

Theatre and cinema artiste Prithviraj Kapoor (1906–72) was a nominated member of the Rajya Sabha. On 25 April 1958, he moved the motion for abolishing capital punishment. What comes through in this speech most eloquently is the respect he had for the members of Parliament, something that is completely missing now. His vision of the political leadership of his age is an eye-opener for the present generation. The leadership seemed worthy of such admiration. To top it, Kapoor brought a motion which was progressive in its content and some of the best minds worked on the debate that followed the introduction of the motion.

Sir, while moving this Resolution, I do not presume to know more than other people know, the wiser people, the elder people, the experienced people, people who have dealt with the life of the nation for such a long time. I do not presume that I know better in this matter; nor do I presume that their attention is not drawn towards this subject, a very great subject, a very important subject; nor do I presume that it is not there in the hearts of the people to do away with this stigma from the face of humanity; nor do I presume that statesmen and elders and the wiser people, people who are leading the nation today, do not realise the importance of this fact that this is something which should be done away with and if our nation, our country, takes the first step, so much the better—first in the sense that there are countries, there have been countries who have abolished capital punishment and then recalled that Act, gone back on that step on some grounds, on some fears. I know that. We all know about their fears, but the fears of one man may not be the fears of others, the circumstances of one man may not be the circumstances of another man, the circumstances of one country may not be the circumstances of another country, the ambitions, hopes and dreams of one country may not be the hopes, ambitions and dreams or ideals of another country. Ours is absolutely a different case and hence it is that most humbly I am moving this Resolution in that humble spirit that we have turned a page, not only a page, but a very big chapter in the life of our nation. After centuries—I will not be wrong at any rate if I say that—in the history of our country perhaps this is the first time that we are leading a life in which all that has to be said and all that has to be done is to be done by the people, by the chosen of the people, the chosen leaders of the people. Hence whenever we take any step or we want to take any step, the past should not frighten us nor the history or the acts or the deeds or opinions of other countries and what has happened in other countries should frighten us or deter us in any way from taking any bold step. From taking a step in the right direction when we feel that we are right, when once we are convinced that we are right, nothing should hinder us, nothing should stop us from taking that step.

We have to take a bold step and decide once and for all now that we shall not have this form of punishment. 'Thou shalt not kill' was said long long ago. Nobody has bothered about it but it is open to us to say now that we shall not kill but that we shall change the hearts, the term given to us in English by the Father of the Nation, 'change of heart'. Why cannot we do that in our own country and then perhaps the world will take the cue therefrom and follow it tomorrow? I know that there are so many countries which are not doing it but we shall not have to follow other countries. Our circumstances are different, our background is different, our culture is different, our traditions are different and our people are different. Therefore, our approach should be based on our circumstances, on our background, on our traditions and on our dharma, way of life. A great philosopher, sitting right in front of me, said once that dharma is one which brings people together. This will be the greatest of dharma, to do away with capital punishment, to do away with that which does away with life and thus give people a chance to become better, to become improved, giving a chance to people to live in amity, brotherhood, love and affection.

So, Sir, when I move this Resolution, I move it with the humblest of spirit, with the humblest of motives, without this presumption that other people do not know about it, without the presumption that other people do not want to do it. No, Sir, I believe our fare goes by lots and this has fallen to the lot of an artiste who can perhaps give the viewpoint of an artiste on this subject.

PANDURANG VAMAN KANE

Time Has Not Come

Dr P.V. Kane (1880–1972) was a great Sanskrit scholar whose knowledge of Indian tradition and philosophy was unsurpassed. He translated and edited the four-volume History of Indian Dharmashastras. *He was nominated to the Rajya Sabha in 1953 and again in 1958. However, after being appointed national professor of Indology (on a salary) he resigned from the Rajya Sabha in 1959. In this speech, he defends the death penalty, upholding the state's prerogative on it, and provides a counterpoint to the motion moved by Prithviraj Kapoor.*

… Do you want to punish or not? That is the point. If you want to punish, then it must be of a severe kind; otherwise what is the use of punishing? If you take a thief and a murderer and place them on the same level, then what is the difference? It is better to be a murderer than to be a thief because in that case he can escape. Of course, one set of people will never accept these arguments while another set of people will accept them. I can tell you that from the days of Mahabharata this point has been argued. In the Mahabharata a very good case has been made out. When a man commits a murder, and he is sentenced to death by the king, his wife and children suffer and they perish. So in order to avenge one murder, you kill many people. That is the plea made before the king. Then the king replies, 'You are wrong. My position as a king calls upon me to maintain the wife and the children who have lost their breadwinner. So, about their breadwinner there is no difficulty. I shall do it.' But I want that such people should not go unpunished and I want that this should be a deterrent punishment. If these people know that they may commit dacoity with murder, take the money, pass it on to their wives and children and they themselves may go to jail for nine years, that is bad for you. You and I sitting here in this well-sheltered House will say nothing. People outside will be afraid. They will say what are those Parliamentarians doing? There, outside, even if you are suspected to be telling the police that illicit liquor is being made, you are stabbed. What protection is there for the ordinary man? The protection is that the man who stabs should be sent to the gallows, that he will get no benefit out of the murder of this man. That is the reason why this punishment is there. I do not justify it. When all of us become sadhus, men given to non-violence, then, no punishment will be required. But as the world goes at present, this punishment must be there. The fear must be there that by committing the murder and taking away the money you will not be there to enjoy it. You must remember that you are dealing with the common man. The law is made for the generality of men. There may be exceptions.

And then there is that other fear, which some lady member, I suppose, stressed, that the innocent may be sent to the gallows. I may tell you frankly that during about 45 years of my life at the Bombay High Court appellate side, there was only one case in which the wrong men were found to be guilty of murder. And their innocence came out later on. But they were not sent to the gallows. The judges were careful and the evidence was circumstantial and it appeared to them to be rather cooked up. Therefore, they gave this punishment, transportation for life. After five years it transpired in another case that some other persons were the guilty men. You will find that there is no reviewing in such cases. When the matter came up I was among the pleaders there. The High Court was asked by the Government as to what they thought of the new evidence and the old evidence and what recommendation they would make. And the judges recommended that their former decision appeared to be wrong and the new decision was that the new fellows were the persons who were guilty. They said that those other men should be at once released and compensation paid to them.

Then there are other remedies. Do not think that it ends with the judges. The Governor has got the right of reprieve. The President, under the constitution, can actually condone or pass a lesser sentence. My point is that there are so many safeguards provided that it will not be in one case out of thousand cases brought before the court that a wrong man will be sent to the gallows by the judicial process... Why don't you apply your non-violence? Let somebody who believes in non-violence say, 'You kill me first. Don't shoot them down.' Has any one man done like that? Very rarely. All profess non-violence. I do not find ten people or twenty people saying 'Unless you kill us first, nothing can be done, you can go and burn the buses' and so forth. This is all tall talk. I do not believe in this talk. Unless I find twenty men going when there is a riot and saying, 'First kill us, then only you can go', it cannot be accepted. Nothing has been done like that. Perhaps there may be one case; it may be an exception. My point is that people will have to live without the dread of goondas, and goondas are the people who should know that they will not be there to enjoy the fruit and they will be sent to the gallows. Therefore, this sentence has four characteristics; most of them have four characteristics. It is retributive, maybe 'eye for an eye'. The society requires that those who are guilty should be punished. In what way is for the judges, it was for the king in those days and now it is for the President, to decide. Then, there is the compensatory character also. Suppose a man beats me. I can file a suit for the physical trouble caused and also he may be prosecuted. So, it has, as I said, a compensatory character. Another thing is, suppose I am beaten by somebody and that man is allowed to go on paying Rs. 25. My mind feels I have suffered so much, but he pays Rs. 25 and goes scot-free. Then I also wish that there should be a retributive punishment. You may not express it. But every man feels that if he is wronged by another, that man must come to grief in some other way. That is another character. There is the fourth character, namely, preventive. Every king, ancient king, made a proclamation, 'Whoever does this will be punished by the king, in the same manner.' So, that has got some preventive or some terrorising—if I may use a strong word—character about it. My point is that the facts have not proved sufficiently that we should jump at once. At present there are so many safeguards and therefore, in my opinion, nothing need be done.

~

RAM MANOHAR LOHIA

Daily Earnings of an Indian

One of the most famous speeches ever delivered in Parliament was Dr Ram Manohar Lohia's speech on 6 September 1963 in Hindi. The debate on the distribution of national income, during the course of which the speech was delivered, came to be known as the 'three annas versus fifteen annas' debate. Dr Lohia's fierce argumentative skill, his enviable command over data and facts, and his fervour to improve the lot of the common man all came to the fore. His disclosures startled the nation and put the ruling party, the Congress, to shame as he quoted government figures to show how wrong and misleading the claims of the government were. Dr Lohia disputed the government's assertion that the average daily income of an Indian was fifteen annas (one rupee equalled sixteen annas in those days) and proved through facts and figures that it was just three-and-a-half annas or four annas.

The conclusion drawn from the discussion held so far is, I believe, that the daily earnings of twenty-seven crore Indians are three annas according to me, the honourable prime minister thinks it is fifteen annas, whereas the planning minister says it is seven-and-a-half annas. Now it is between the honourable prime minister and the planning minister to decide who is right.

My argument is not that the daily earnings of the common man, particularly of twenty-seven crore Indians, is three annas or three-and-a-half annas or two-and-a-half annas. But the point is that the government has turned a blind eye to the poverty in the country and unless there is a will to eradicate poverty a tangible formula cannot be worked out. I have to say one thing about the figures that have been placed here by the planning minister. They were meant for the taxation enquiry committee. The finance ministry desired to know the income and expenditure of people so that a substantial amount could be recovered by imposing higher taxes. Therefore, the figures of this committee were even otherwise doubtful because they were meant for a different purpose.

They wanted to substantiate that Indians spend more, therefore, higher taxes should be imposed. This is quite clear. It is there in the report which is published by the national survey. The taxation enquiry committee has recommended it so that the finance ministry could carry on its job effectively...

Secondly, instead of taking prices prevalent in 1948-49 as base, generally current prices are taken into account. I fail to understand who these statisticians are who furnish these figures. When fifty lakh people died in the Bengal famine, they proved that only five lakhs had died. Therefore, the ministers should remain cautious and give them some guidelines. I would not take their figures as it is but I shall use my own sense of judgement as far as possible. According to the figures of the planning minister, rural expenditure comes to about Rs. 8700 crores whereas income from agriculture which includes income from livestock also comes to about Rs. 6600 crores. This is clear from the figures placed before us by the planning minister. I should have kept the income from livestock and agriculture separate but even without doing so there is a variation of Rs. 2000 crores. In a way the variation is of about Rs. 3000 to 3500 crores if we take the two heads separately. The government may say that there is variation between the income and expenditure because donations, charity and debts are also included in the expenditure. In this connection, I would like to say that one cannot be under debt forever. Debts can be for a limited period for two, four, five or ten years. After all, the figure of income and expenditure should be the same. There may be a slight variation between the two.

A major mistake that is committed in the figures of consumer index is that the price difference is added. For example, the data pertaining to fuel and electricity which have been published so far relate to the thirteenth series but the planning minister has referred to the seventeenth series. We cannot verify it. On the basis of the data of the thirteenth series, I would like to tell that expenditure on fuel and electricity by the lowest income group has been computed as twenty paise and other expenditure as ninety-one paise whereas other expenditure is rupee one and two paise. For sugar, cash expenditure is fifteen paise whereas other expenditure is nineteen paise. In this way, the total expenditure is inflated but if it is inflated from Rs. 6600 crores to Rs. 8700 crores, it will not be proper.

I would tell you another way of calculation. In 1960-61 the daily earnings of thirty-two crore agricultural labourers was forty-five paise and in 1961-62 the daily earnings of thirty-five crore agricultural labourers came down to forty-three paise. Now how I calculated this is a long story. I would like to make it clear that the official figures are the basis of my calculation. Ordinarily, it is believed that ten per cent of the upper strata swallow fifty per cent of their earning. As a result thereof, actual daily earning of agricultural labourers in 1960-61 was twenty-five paise and in 1961-62 it was twenty-three paise. This is evident from the official figures. Suppose we add the income from livestock even then the earnings will not be more than twenty-seven paise i.e. four-and-a-half annas. But we should not add this income because the people about whom we are discussing cannot afford to keep the cattle to augment their income. Therefore, the official figures prove that over twenty-seven crore people in this country survive on four annas a day. This is based on figures of national income published by the government.

In this connection, I would like to share a piece of information which I have collected. I cannot say whether it is correct or incorrect.

Anyway, I would like to submit that the government has fudged the national income by twenty per cent from the very beginning. One reason might be that they wanted to show that India is rich. Second can be that they wanted to facilitate taxation and everyone knows that the figures are fudged.

Now I would like to submit one thing more and that is about per capita income in poor states. The figures that the planning minister had placed were based on the second census of the country. Uttar Pradesh, Bihar, Rajasthan, Madhya Pradesh, Orissa and Andhra Pradesh are the six poorest states. Their total rural population is twenty crores, though in fact it is twenty-three crores. I know about Uttar Pradesh. The government has published those figures. At one time, the per capita income in rural areas was Rs. 182. We can go by the same argument that the top ten per cent swallow fifty per cent of the income or I can adopt another method, which I generally use, viz., that the top twenty per cent consume sixty per cent of the income whereas remaining eighty per cent of the populace is left with forty per cent. I have got these figures from the official sources. It is another thing that these figures are official whereas my calculation is personal. I would like to advise the government not to take the figures provided by experts as such, there should be some guidelines otherwise consequences can be bad. The per capita income of Uttar Pradesh would come down to Rs. 101 from Rs. 182 if we do not count the top ten per cent who swallow fifty per cent of the income. Similarly, it would be reduced to ninety-one rupees if we include those twenty per cent who swallow sixty per cent of the income. This means that the daily earnings per head remain under four annas. It is evident from the figures provided by the government itself that twenty-seven crore people in this country survive on a daily earning of less than four annas. Then there is another figure of Rs. 193 per head. If it may be a little more, even then it would be about four annas or three-and-a-half annas or three-and-a-quarter annas. There will not be much difference. This is about Uttar Pradesh…which is so poor. The plight of the people of Orissa, Madhya Pradesh, Bihar and Rajasthan is also the same. Crores of people, say twenty crore rural people—out of which leave apart two at the rate of ten per cent or four crores at the rate of twenty per cent—or eighteen crore or sixteen crore people are surviving on a daily earning of four annas or three-and-a-half annas according to official figures.

… The honourable prime minister had stated on 22 August 1960 that national income had increased by forty-two per cent and per capita income by twenty per cent. However, he was surprised to find as to where that increase evaporated. In a way the government had already accepted that it was not aware as to where that increase had gone. Thereafter, a committee on the distribution of national income was constituted. Now my question, where has that committee disappeared? I will go into the details of this matter a little later but before that I would like to draw your attention to another point. In India, thirty-four per cent of the families own less than one acre of land and fourteen per cent of the land is owned by only one per cent of families. From this figure certain dangerous result can be observed. Previously I had submitted that twenty-seven crores of Indians earn only three annas for their livelihood. Now I submit that ten to fifteen crores of our people subsist on only two annas. I have received several letters condemning me for my statement about our people earning only three annas for their living. If these figures are analysed differently we will find that there are about seven crore agricultural labour in our country. We can deduct half or one crore out of this because they may be slightly better off.

As regards the small farmers...at least fourteen to fifteen crore own less than two-and-a-half acres of land. The number of artisans is about two to three crore. Then in urban areas also the plight of twenty to twenty-five per cent people is pitiable who find it difficult to make both ends meet.

In fact they live in such horrible conditions that it is surprising as to how they are surviving. They live on pavements, *jhuggi-jhonpri* clusters, and somehow manage to survive by picking grains from garbage dumps. As regards those who have migrated from rural areas and have some means of income, they try to spend minimum on themselves as they have to support their families living in the rural areas. Then there are adivasis, widows and I may be allowed to say so, the carefree monks. The total number of all these categories of people is twenty-seven to thirty crore.

Apart from referring to the aforementioned figures, I would like to present a first-hand account of the situation which the honourable prime minister, the honourable minister of planning and the government should keep in view. In Benares, I have seen cows eating corpses. In Orissa, where little fish is available in the rivers, I have seen hundreds of people spreading their fishing nets to catch fish. At Salem in Tamil Nadu, I have seen lakhs of artisans earning only ten, twelve or fourteen annas per day. If calculations are made about the average income of these people, the average is bound to work out to less than three annas per day. Similarly, if we look into the income of the other weaker sections, we will find that they also earn the same amount per day...

These are government figures. The statisticians also compete with each other in presenting a brighter picture. One such organisation is based in Delhi and is called the National Council of Economic Research. It has given the names of twenty-nine districts where the per capita income is less than one hundred rupees. I am mentioning here the names of some of these districts—in Darbhanga, in Saran and Chapra it is ninety-six rupees; in Deoria it is ninety-eight; in Tehri Garhwal it is eighty-four. If the method of calculation which I had previously submitted is applied here, that is, to deduct fifty per cent income for the ten per cent upper strata and sixty per cent of the amount for next twenty per cent people, the daily income of the remaining lower sections in these districts comes to less than three annas. I have referred to only four districts. There are forty similar districts where the income is Rs. 110, Rs. 120 and Rs. 125...

If we refer to the thirteenth series it will become evident as to how our living standard is going down. In 1952 the per capita expenditure of thirty per cent of the population was ten rupees and twenty-five paise and in 1957-58 it was reduced to ten rupees and fourteen paise. The figures which I have quoted are government figures. The honourable prime minister should go through the publication of his own government in order to know about the declining standards of living. Similarly, the expenditure of thirty per cent families was reduced from fifteen rupees and seventy paise to fourteen rupees and fifty paise. The expenditure of only two per cent families has increased from forty-five rupees to forty-eight rupees. This is how the standard of living of the people is constantly declining.

Previously per capita income used to increase by seven rupees per year. This holds good no longer. It now increases by two naya paise every year and if this is the pace of our progress, we shall be vulnerable to outside threat. In this connection I would particularly like to refer to China and Ghana and not the USSR and USA. In Ghana, the per capita income is increasing by thirty to forty rupees and in China it is increasing by fifty rupees to sixty rupees. Why have we not been able to make similar progress? Because the pattern of consumption underwent change and modernisation but without corresponding modernisation in our production process; we started aping the Western countries in our consumption patterns but it did not reflect in our production system. The standard of living of our leaders, businessmen and bureaucrats went up day by day so that they came at par with their counterparts in Europe and USA but the standard of living of the common man remained where it was.

Two or three lakh persons grow rich every year. It is the only effect of the five year plans and a major portion of the increased national income is siphoned off for that purpose. In my opinion there are fifty lakh rich people at the moment and three lakh people are becoming rich every year. During the last twelve to fifteen years three lakh people have been becoming rich. The British government functioned with the support of three lakh people and the present government is run by fifty lakh people.

If we examine the figures of the income of the people and the income tax which they are paying, we will find that 9,52,000 persons are paying taxes and they are paying Rs. 200 crores as income tax having an income of Rs. 120 crore. But it is common knowledge that their actual income is double of this amount of Rs. 120 crore. Moreover a very huge expenditure is being incurred on the facilities being provided to ministers, etc. In this way the total expenditure comes to about Rs. 250 crore. This amount is taken away by only one per cent of the population as is evident from government statistics. The figures which I have collected from my own sources are, however, even more.

I think that we can easily save Rs. 100 to Rs. 120 crore according to one method and Rs. 150 to Rs. 200 crore according to the other by rationalising the expenditure. The government can function more effectively, the income tax burden can be reduced and there can be better development of agriculture and industries. But only the person whose heart bleeds for the common man can do it.

This government has turned into a government of directionless experts and whatever recommendations the experts make, the government blindly follows them. The ministers have little knowledge about agriculture, industries, national income, etc. The honourable ministers should apply their own mind instead of blindly following the recommendations of the experts. They should think over the recommendations and then give directions because the statisticians and the economists are like poisonous snakes who dance to the tune of the snake charmers. But if you are incapable of playing the flute the results are bound to be disastrous.

I would like to claim that if the distribution of national income is rationalised, it can be increased by twenty rupees every year and this can be done by any ordinary individual but only when everyone gets a share in the increase in the national income.

~

INDIRA GANDHI

To Martin Luther King

Martin Luther King (1929–68) is the most famous leader of the American civil rights movement. In 1964, he became the youngest man to be awarded the Nobel Peace Prize (for his work as a peacemaker, promoting non-violence and equal treatment for different races). Having closely studied Mahatma Gandhi's method of non-violent satyagraha, King applied its principles in his struggle against the oppression of coloured people in America. In this sense, he was a pioneer in trying and working out the efficacy of a non-violent mass movement in different societal and political conditions. He was assassinated on 4 April 1968. On 24 January 1969, the Indian government posthumously conferred the Jawaharlal Nehru Award for International Understanding on Martin Luther King, which was accepted by his widow Coretta Scott King. Speaking on the occasion, the Indian prime minister, Indira Gandhi (1917–84), remarked on the similarities of the lives and struggles of Mahatma Gandhi and Martin Luther King.

This is a poignant moment for all of us. We remember vividly your last visit to our country. We had hoped that on this occasion, Dr. King and you would be standing side by side on this platform. That was not to be. He is not with us but we feel his spirit. We admired Dr. King. We felt his loss as our own. The tragedy rekindled memories of the great martyrs of all time who gave their lives so that men might live and grow. We thought of the great men in your own country who fell to the assassin's bullet and of Mahatma Gandhi's martyrdom here in this city, this very month, twenty-one years ago. Such events remain as wounds in the human consciousness, reminding us of battles yet to be fought and tasks still to be accomplished. We should not mourn for men of high ideals. Rather we should rejoice that we had the privilege of having had them with us, to inspire us by their radiant personalities. So today we are gathered not to offer you grief, but to salute a man who achieved so much in so short a time. It is befitting, Madam, that you whom he called the 'courage by my side', you who gave him strength and encouragement in his historic mission, should be with us to receive this award.

You and your husband both had foreseen that death might come to him violently. It was perhaps inherent in the situation. Dr. King chose death for the theme of a sermon, remarking that he would like to be remembered as a drum major for justice, for peace and for righteousness. When you were once asked what you would do if your husband were assassinated, you were courage personified, replying that you might weep but the work would go on. Your face of sorrow, so beautiful in its dignity coupled with infinite compassion, will forever be engraved in our hearts.

Mahatma Gandhi also had foreseen his end and had prepared himself for it. Just as training for violence included learning to kill, the training for non-violence, he said, included learning how to die. The true badge of the satyagrahi is to be unafraid.

As if he too had envisaged the martyrdoms of Mahatma Gandhi and Martin Luther King, Rabindranath Tagore once sang:

> In anger we slew him,
> With love let us embrace him now,
> For in death he lives again amongst us,
> The mighty conqueror of death.

This award, Madam, is the highest tribute our nation can bestow on work for understanding and brotherhood among men. It is named after a man who himself was a peace-maker and who all his life laboured passionately for freedom, justice and peace in India and throughout the world. Dr. Martin Luther King's struggle was for these same values. He paid for his ideals with his blood, forging a new bond among the brave and the conscientious of all races and all nations.

Dr. King's dream embraced the poor and the oppressed of all lands. His work ennobled us. He spoke of the right of man to survive and recognised three threats to the survival of man—racial injustice, poverty and war. He realised that even under the lamp of affluence which was held aloft by science, lay the shadow of poverty, compelling two-thirds of the peoples of the world to exist in hunger and want. He proclaimed that mankind could be saved from war only if we cared enough for peace to sacrifice for it.

Dr. Martin Luther King drew his inspiration from Christ, and his method of action from Mahatma Gandhi. Only through truth can untruth be vanquished. Only through love can hatred be quenched. This is the path of the Buddha and of Christ, and in our own times, that of Mahatma Gandhi and of Martin Luther King.

They believed in the equality of all men. No more false doctrine has been spread than that of the superiority of one race over another. It is ironical that there should still be people in this world who judge men not by their moral worth and intellectual merit but by the pigment of their skin or other physical characteristics, some governments still rest on the theory of racist superiority—such as the governments of South Africa and the lawless regime in Rhodesia. Unregenerate groups in other countries consider one colour superior to another. Our own battle is not yet over. Caste and other prejudices still survive, but most of us are ashamed of them and recognise them as evils to be combated. We are trying hard to eradicate them.

While there is bondage anywhere, we ourselves cannot be fully free. While there is oppression anywhere, we ourselves cannot soar high. Martin Luther King was convinced that one day the misguided people who believed in racial superiority would realise the error of their ways. His dream was that white and black, brown and yellow would live and grow together as flowers in a garden with their faces turned towards the sun. As you yourself said, 'All of us who believe in what Martin Luther King stood for, must see to it that his spirit never dies.' That spirit can never die. There may be setbacks in our fight for the equality of all men. There may be moments of gloom. But victory must and will be ours. Let us not rest until the equality of all races and religions becomes a living fact. That is the most effective and lasting tribute that we can pay to Dr. King.

~

JAYAPRAKASH NARAYAN

Revolution on the Agenda

In post-independence India, if anyone can be said to have truly experimented with Mahatma Gandhi's method of mobilization for social and political purposes, it was Jayaprakash Narayan and Vinoba Bhave. Both directed their efforts at changing society by mobilizing people for mass action. In the 1950s, Vinoba Bhave organized the Bhoodan movement in the course of which he travelled the length and breadth of the country asking those with big landholdings to gift land to him which he then redistributed to the landless poor. Jayaprakash Narayan was closely involved with this. He also played a major rôle in the peace process in Nagaland in 1965 by actively participating in the peace mission with the chief minister, B.P. Chaliha. In 1974 he organized the surrender of the dreaded dacoits of Chambal.

In 1969, even as the country celebrated the birth centenary of Mahatma Gandhi, there were efforts to denigrate Gandhi and mar the celebrations.

Gujarat witnessed severe communal violence which, as was later revealed, had been carefully planned and orchestrated. Addressing the National Conference of Voluntary Agencies in New Delhi in 1969, Jayaprakash, while talking about the social agenda, fell back on his mentor, Mahatma Gandhi, providing a fresh perspective on the revolutionary aspects of Gandhi's social work which he mentions are as relevant in the modern age.

Nowadays in India there is a conscious effort to denigrate Gandhiji and his ideas. There is an organised effort to say 'what is all this talk of satyagraha, what is Gandhiji's contribution in bringing freedom to India, how is he responsible for that', etc. As one who had participated in the struggle, I make bold to say that if Gandhiji had not created a mass awakening and sustained it over a period of twenty-seven years, I don't think it would have been possible to raise the Azad Hind Fauj under the leadership of Netaji. Today, we hear that in Ludhiana or somewhere a statue of Gandhiji was blackened. After all, Gandhi was murdered in this capital of India.

Gandhiji was asked: 'You do this constructive social work. You take up a programme and make a countrywide propaganda and campaign for the purpose of converting the people to your scheme. If some people refuse to be converted what will you do? Will you go on trying to convert everyone till doomsday?' Gandhiji said: 'Certainly not.' He explained: 'If I am convinced that I have done enough and there are still some people who refuse to be persuaded then I will use my unfailing weapon of non-violent non-cooperation. This Brahmastra is to be used as a part of the strategy of a vast movement of change and reconstruction.' Therefore, I say that we should give some thought to this—how all of us can join hands together in fashioning one simple programme like the salt satyagraha?

There is one simple programme of mass action which we can place before the people from today and then go on covering and persuading the people to launch a mass movement of change in a non-violent way. A non-violent revolution, unlike a violent revolution, cannot take place just in ten days... A non-violent movement develops step by step and it, therefore, takes time.

I think it was given to Vinobaji's genius to find out that the constructive organisations in the field were losing the spirit and losing their perspective and were slowly getting tied to the chariot wheels of this big juggernaut, the State of India, because one has to go for this subsidy or that grant in aid. In that case, we will end up by merely becoming good people who perform some kind of service without being able to change the society. I do not think that any political party can do it by winning elections alone. Vinobaji, instead, laid emphasis on constructive work organisations already in the field set up by Gandhiji. He also launched a programme of Bhoodan to which people responded. In a country like India, redistribution of land is absolutely essential as a measure of social and economic justice. The problem of fragmentation is not difficult to solve. It could be solved by consolidation of holdings. It could be solved by cooperative agriculture. When you have a society in which there is scarcity of land and many people, with 85 or 90 per cent of the people living in the villages and depending on agriculture; if you have a situation where a few people own hundreds of thousands of acres and the rest, millions of them, are landless, then truly it is an explosive situation. You have an unjust situation. Many people laughed at Bhoodan and said it was a failure. I do not think you are aware of the programme in all its aspects. You may not have taken the trouble to find out the facts about Bhoodan. It has been a failure in the sense that it has failed to solve the problem of landlessness. But let me tell you frankly that the problem of landlessness is insoluble in India. Nobody can solve it because our population is too vast. Therefore, along with Khadi and village industries, there should be a widespread network of small rural industries. But to the extent to which land redistribution has been effected in India, many times more acreage of land has been redistributed by Bhoodan than by legislation.

Jawaharlal Nehru always laid emphasis on questions of land reform, redistribution of land and security for tenant. These three things always figured in his letter to chief ministers and also in his speeches. In spite of that, in my state [Bihar], even though the ceiling law was passed, not one acre of land was redistributed…, whereas we have been able to distribute 365,000 acres of land which are fit for cultivation. We have rejected as unfit for cultivation about sixteen lakhs of acres in Bihar. In UP not more than 10,000 to 12,000 acres of land have been redistributed through legislation, but 310,000 acres through Bhoodan. Recently I went to Bombay. This is a Ryotwari area and I wanted to know the position. The revenue department wrote to me a letter saying that as a result of the Ceiling Act they were expected to get surplus land totalling 129,000 acres. But in Maharashtra we have redistributed 106,000 acres of land. This is the social and economic change brought about by Bhoodan…

Now we have launched Gramdan. We should look upon it as a voluntary organisation, and Gandhiji was an incarnation of voluntarism. But this is where he wanted his voluntarism to begin. You see now the French revolutionaries are talking of decentralisation. But when a Gandhian talks of decentralisation, immediately our learned people in Delhi University, in the Planning Commission and in the Government of India turn round and say, 'In this age of technology, Mr. Jayaprakash Narayan, do you think that decentralisation is possible?' France is one of the two most technologically developed countries of western Europe, next only to West Germany. Yet the French are talking about decentralisation. If the dimensions of our social, economic and political institutions are beyond human scope, then man is going to be crushed under the juggernaut organisation, under over-mechanisation. The students in western Europe are revolting against exactly this very corruption of civilisation in which the autonomy of the individual is being completely suppressed. Gandhiji has said that man is the supreme consideration for him. He wanted the highest possible material and physical development of the individual being. He begins from there. If you do not believe in the machine, if we don't believe in organisation, but if we believe in man and in the dignity of man, then let us take a second look at understanding man better. In this Centenary Year, we have to snatch the initiative from the hands of politicians, from the parliament and the legislatures and give it back to the people. This is our job.

~

INDIRA GANDHI

For a Just and Moral International Order

In a landmark speech at the first United Nations Conference on Human Environment in Stockholm, 1972, Indira Gandhi set the terms of reference for the global struggle in the field of environmental concerns. While rich nations had been targetting the poor countries on the subject of pollution, Indira Gandhi put the discourse on a more fundamental level. She forcefully argued that any discussion on a global environmental policy could not take place without reference to the aspects of equity and justice.

It is indeed an honour to address this Conference—in itself a fresh expression of the spirit which created the United Nations—concern for the present and future welfare of humanity. It does not aim merely at securing limited agreements but at establishing peace and harmony in life—among all races and with nature. This gathering represents man's earnest endeavour to understand his own condition and to prolong his tenancy of this planet. A vast amount of detailed preparatory work has gone into the convening of this Conference guided by the dynamic personality of Mr. Maurice Strong, Secretary-General of the Conference. I have had the good fortune of growing up with a sense of kinship with nature in all its manifestations. Birds, plants, stones were companions and, sleeping under the star-strewn sky, I became familiar with the names and movements of the constellations. But my deep interest in this our 'only earth' was not for itself but as a fit home for man.

One cannot be truly human and civilised unless one looks upon not only all fellow men but all creation with the eyes of a friend. Throughout India, edicts carved on rocks and iron pillars are reminders that twenty-two centuries ago Emperor Ashoka defined a king's duty as not merely to protect citizens and punish wrongdoers but also to preserve animal life and forest trees. Ashoka was the first and perhaps the only monarch until very recently to forbid the killing of a large number of species of animals for sport or food, foreshadowing some of the concern of this Conference. He went further, regretting the carnage of his military conquests and enjoining upon his successors to 'find their only pleasure in the peace that comes through righteousness'.

Along with the rest of mankind, we in India—in spite of Ashoka—have been guilty of wanton disregard for the sources of our sustenance. We share your concern at the rapid deterioration of flora and fauna. Some of our own wild life has been wiped out, miles of forests with beautiful old trees, mute witnesses of history, have been destroyed. Even though our industrial development is in its infancy, and at its most difficult stage, we are taking various steps to deal with incipient environmental imbalances. More so because of our concern for the human being—a species which is also imperilled. In poverty he is threatened by malnutrition and disease, in weakness by war, in richness by the pollution brought about by his own prosperity.

It is sad that in country after country, progress should become synonymous with an assault on nature. We who are a part of nature and dependent on her for every need, speak constantly about 'exploiting' nature. When the highest mountain in the world was climbed in 1953, Jawaharlal Nehru objected to the phrase 'conquest of Everest' which he thought was arrogant. Is it surprising that this lack of consideration and the constant need to prove one's superiority should be projected onto our treatment of our fellow men? I remember Edward Thompson, a British writer and a good friend of India, once telling Mr. Gandhi that wild life was fast disappearing. Remarked the Mahatma: 'It is decreasing in the jungles but it is increasing in the towns!'

We are gathered here under the aegis of the United Nations. We are supposed to belong to the same family sharing common traits and impelled by the same basic desires, yet we inhabit a divided world.

How can it be otherwise? There is still no recognition of the equality of man or respect for him as an individual. In matters of colour and race, religion and custom, society is governed by prejudice. Tensions arise because of man's aggressiveness and notions of superiority. The power of the big stick prevails and it is used not in favour of fair play or beauty, but to chase imaginary windmills—to assume the right to interfere in the affairs of others, and to arrogate authority for action which would not normally be allowed. Many of the advanced countries of today have reached their present affluence by their domination over other races and countries, the exploitation of their own masses and their own natural resources. They got a head start through sheer ruthlessness, undisturbed by feelings of compassion or by abstract theories of freedom, equality or justice. The stirrings of demands for the political rights of citizens, and the economic rights of the toiler came after considerable advance had been made. The riches and the labour of the colonised countries played no small part in the industrialisation and prosperity of the West. Now, as we struggle to create a better life for our people, it is in vastly different circumstances, for obviously in today's eagle-eyed watchfulness, we cannot indulge in such practices even for a worthwhile purpose. We are bound by our own ideals. We owe allegiance to the principles of the rights of workers and the norms enshrined in the charters of international organisations. Above all, we are answerable to the millions of politically awakened citizens in our countries. All these make progress costlier and more complicated.

On the one hand the rich look askance at our continuing poverty. On the other they warn us against their own methods. We do not wish to impoverish the environment any further and yet we cannot for a moment forget the grim poverty of a large number of people. Are not poverty and need the greatest polluters? For instance, unless we are in a position to provide employment and purchasing power for the daily necessities of the tribal people and those who live in or around our jungles, we cannot prevent them from combing the forest for food and livelihood, from poaching and from despoiling the vegetation. When they themselves feel deprived, how can we urge the preservation of animals? How can we speak to those who live in villages and in slums about keeping the oceans, the rivers and the air clean when their own lives are contaminated at the source? The environment cannot be improved in conditions of poverty. Nor can poverty be eradicated without the use of science and technology.

Must there be conflict between technology and a truly better world or between enlightenment of the spirit and a higher standard of living? Foreigners sometimes ask what to us seems a very strange question, whether progress in India would not mean a diminishing of her spirituality or her values. Is spiritual quality so superficial as to be dependent upon the lack of material comfort? As a country we are not more or less spiritual than any other but traditionally our people have respected the spirit of detachment and renunciation. Historically, our great spiritual discoveries were made during periods of comparative affluence. The doctrines of detachment from possessions were developed not as rationalisation of deprivation but to prevent comfort and ease from dulling the senses. Spirituality means the enrichment of the spirit, the strengthening of one's inner resources and the stretching of one's range of experience. It is the ability to be still in the midst of activity and vibrantly alive in moments of calm; to separate the essence from circumstances; to accept joy and sorrow with the same equanimity. Perception and compassion are the marks of true spirituality.

I am reminded of an incident in one of our tribal areas. The vociferous demand of elder tribal chiefs that their customs should be left undisturbed found support from noted anthropologists. In its anxiety that the majority should not submerge the many ethnical, racial and cultural groups in our country, the Government of India largely accepted this advice. I was amongst those who entirely approved. However, a visit to a remote part of our north-east frontier brought me in touch with a different point of view—the protest by the younger elements that while the rest of India was on the way to modernisation they were being preserved as museum pieces. Could we not say the same to the affluent nations?

For the last quarter of a century, we have been engaged in an enterprise unparalleled in human history—the provision of basic needs to one-sixth of mankind within the span of one or two generations. When we launched on that effort our early planners had more than the usual gaps to fill. There were not enough data and no helpful books. No guidance could be sought from the experience of other countries whose conditions—political, economic, social and technological—were altogether different. Planning, in the sense we were innovating, had never been used in the context of a mixed economy. But we could not wait. The need to improve the conditions of our people was pressing. Planning and action, improvement of data leading to better planning and better action, all this was a continuous and overlapping process. Our industrialisation tended to follow the paths which the more advanced countries had traversed earlier. With the advance of the sixties and particularly during the last five years, we have encountered a bewildering collection of problems, some due to our shortcomings but many inherent in the process and in existing attitudes. The feeling is growing that we should reorder our priorities and move away from the single-dimensional model which has viewed growth from certain limited angles, which seems to have given a higher place to things rather than to persons and which has increased our wants rather than our enjoyment. We should have a more comprehensive approach to life, centred on man not as a statistic but an individual with many sides to his personality. The solution of these problems cannot be isolated phenomena of marginal importance but must be an integral part of the unfolding of the very process of development.

The extreme forms in which questions of population or environmental pollution are posed, obscure the total view of political, economic and social situations. The Government of India is one of the few which has an officially sponsored programme of family planning and this is making some progress. We believe that planned families will make for a healthier and more conscious population. But we know also that no programme of population control can be effective without education and without a visible rise in the standard of living. Our own programmes have succeeded in the urban or semi-urban areas. To the very poor, every child is an earner and a helper. We are experimenting with new approaches and the family planning programme is being combined with those of maternity and child welfare, nutrition and development in general.

It is an over-simplification to blame all the world's problems on increasing population. Countries with but a small fraction of the world population consume the bulk of the world's production of minerals, fossil fuels and so on. Thus we see that when it comes to the depletion of natural resources and environmental pollution, the increase of one inhabitant in an affluent country, at his level of living, is equivalent to an increase of many Asians, Africans or Latin Americans at their current material levels of living.

The inherent conflict is not between conservation and development, but between environment and the reckless exploitation of man and earth in the name of efficiency. Historians tell us that the modern age began with the will to freedom of the individual. And the individual came to believe that he had rights with no corresponding obligations. The man who got ahead was the one who commanded admiration. No questions were asked as to the methods employed or the price which others had had to pay. The industrial civilisation has promoted the concept of the efficient man, he whose entire energies are concentrated on producing more in a given unit of time and from a given unit of manpower. Groups or individuals who are less competitive and, according to this test, less efficient are regarded as lesser breeds—for example the older civilisations, the black and brown peoples, women and certain professions. Obsolescence is built into production, and efficiency is based on the creation of goods which are not really needed and which cannot be disposed of, when discarded. What price such efficiency now, and is not reckless a more appropriate term for such behaviour?

All the 'isms' of the modern age—even those which in theory disown the private profit principle—assume that man's cardinal interest is acquisition. The profit motive, individual or collective, seems to overshadow all else. This overriding concern with self today is the basic cause of the ecological crisis.

Pollution is not a technical problem. The fault lies not in science and technology as such but in the sense of values of the contemporary world which ignores the rights of others and is oblivious of the longer perspective.

There are grave misgivings that the discussion on ecology may be designed to distract attention from the problems of war and poverty. We have to prove to the deprived majority of the world that ecology and conservation will not work against their interest but will bring an improvement in their lives. To withhold technology from them would deprive them of vast resources of energy and knowledge. This is no longer feasible nor will it be acceptable.

The environmental problems of developing countries are not the side-effects of excessive industrialisation but reflect the inadequacy of development. The rich countries may look upon development as the cause of environmental destruction, but to us it is one of the primary means of improving the environment for living, or providing food, water, sanitation and shelter; of making the deserts green and the mountains habitable. The research and perseverance of dedicated people have given us an insight which is likely to play an important part in the shaping of our future plans. We see that however much man hankers after material goods, they can never give him full satisfaction. Thus the higher standard of living must be achieved without alienating people from their heritage and without despoiling nature of its beauty, freshness and purity so essential to our lives.

The most urgent and basic question is that of peace. Nothing is so pointless as modern warfare. Nothing destroys so instantly, so completely as the diabolic weapons which not only kill but maim and deform the living and the yet to be born; which poison the land, leaving long trails of ugliness, barrenness and hopeless desolation. What ecological project can survive a war? The Prime Minister of Sweden, Mr. Olof Palme, has already drawn the attention of the Conference to this in powerful words.

It is clear that the environmental crisis which is confronting the world will profoundly alter the future destiny of our planet. No one among us, whatever our status, strength or circumstance, can remain unaffected. The process of change challenges present international policies. Will the growing awareness of 'one earth' and 'one environment' guide us to the concept of 'one humanity'? Will there be more equitable sharing of environment costs and greater international interest in the accelerated progress of the less developed world? Or will it remain confined to a narrow concern, based on exclusive self-sufficiency?

The first essays in narrowing economic and technological disparities have not succeeded because the policies of aid were made to subserve the equations of power. We hope that the renewed emphasis on self-reliance, brought about by the change in the climate for aid, will also promote a search for new criteria of human satisfaction. In the meantime, the ecological crisis should not add to the burdens of the weaker nations by introducing new considerations in the political and trade policies of rich nations. It would be ironic if the fight against pollution were to be converted into another business, out of which a few companies, corporations, or nations would make profits at the cost of the many. Here is a branch of experimentation and discovery in which scientists of all nations should take interest. They should ensure that their findings are available to all nations, unrestricted by patents. I am glad that the Conference has given thought on this aspect of the problem.

Life is one and the world is one, and all these questions are interlinked. The population explosion, poverty, ignorance and disease, the pollution of our surroundings, the stockpiling of nuclear weapons and biological and chemical agents of destruction are all parts of a vicious circle. Each is important and urgent but dealing with them one by one would be wasted effort.

It serves little purpose to dwell on the past or to apportion blame, for none of us is blameless. If some are able to dominate others, this is at least partially due to the weakness, the lack of unity and the temptation of gaining some advantage on the part of those who submit. If the prosperous have been exploiting the needy, can we honestly claim that in our own societies, people do not take advantage of the weaker sections? We must re-evaluate the fundamentals on which our respective civic societies are based and the ideals by which they are sustained. If there is to be change of heart, a change of direction and methods of functioning, it is not an organisation or a country—no matter how well intentioned—which can achieve it. While each country must deal with that aspect of the problem which is most relevant to it, it is obvious that all countries must unite in an overall endeavour. There is no alternative to a cooperative approach on a global scale to the entire spectrum of our problems.

I have referred to some problems which seem to me to be the underlying causes of the present crisis in our civilisation. This is not in the expectation that this Conference can achieve miracles or solve all the world's difficulties, but in the hope that the opinions of each nation will be kept in focus, these problems will be viewed in perspective and each project devised as part of the whole.

On a previous occasion I had spoken of the unfinished revolution in our countries. I am now convinced that this can be taken to its culmination when it is accompanied by a revolution in social thinking. In 1968 at the 14th General Conference of UNESCO the Indian delegation, along with others, proposed a new and major programme entitled 'a design for living'. This is essential to grasp the full implications of technical advances and its impact on different sections and groups. We do not want to put the clock back or resign ourselves to a simplistic natural state. We want new directions in the wiser use of the knowledge and tools with which science has equipped us.

And this cannot be just one upsurge but a continuous search into cause and effect and an unending effort to match technology with higher levels of thinking. We must concern ourselves not only with the kind of world we want but also with what kind of man should inhabit it. Surely we do not desire a society divided into those who condition and those who are conditioned. We want thinking people, capable of spontaneous self-directed activity, people who are interested and interesting, and who are imbued with compassion and concern for others.

It will not be easy for large societies to change their style of living. They cannot be coerced to do so, nor can governmental action suffice. People can be motivated and urged to participate in better alternatives.

It has been my experience that people who are at cross-purposes with nature are cynical about mankind and ill-at-ease with themselves. Modern man must re-establish an unbroken link with nature and with life. He must again learn to invoke the energy of growing things and to recognise, as did the ancients in India centuries ago, that one can take from the earth and the atmosphere only so much as one puts back into them. In their hymn to Earth, the sages of the Atharva Veda chanted, and I quote: 'What of thee I dig out, let that quickly grow over, Let me not hit thy vitals, or thy heart.'

So can man himself be vital and of good heart and conscious of his responsibility.

~

BABA AMTE

My Colleagues in Conscience

One of India's most revered social and moral leaders, Murlidas Devidas Amte, or Baba Amte as he is popularly known, is a part of the great march that began with people like Rammohun Roy, M.G. Ranade, Jyotiba Phule, Rabindranath Tagore, Mahatma Gandhi and thousands of others who have given India its political, intellectual and social ethos. India's democracy, its republican status, its constitution and elections are results of this march. However, the struggle for moral freedom goes on and in this Baba Amte remains true to the traditions that Gandhi invoked, of renunciation while engaging with life. Baba Amte has devoted his life to the care and rehabilitation of leprosy patients at his community development project at Anandwan, near Nagpur. He also launched the 'Bharat Jodo' (Unite India) movement for the purpose of establishing peace and raising environmental consciousness, travelling from one end of the country to the other. In 1990, Baba Amte left Anandwan to live along the Narmada river and fight for the rehabilitation of tribals affected by the construction of large dams on the river. Since then he has been an integral part of the Narmada Bachao Andolan which has been fighting the establishment and the advocates of development through the moral force of the people. Baba Amte received the Ramon Magsaysay Award for Public Service in 1985. In this, his written speech delivered by his son Dr Vikas Amte in Manila, Philippines, on 31 August 1992, Baba Amte comes across like a sentinel, reminding us of our commitment to build a nobler, more humane and just society.

I want to fly like a Madia tribesman's arrow, quivering with sun-intoxicated raptures, to thank you for the honour of conferring on me this highest Asian award for public service. But as I am tied to my torture-stake of pain, I am deputising my son, Dr. Vikas Amte, to receive it on my behalf and on behalf of my big family at Anandwan: all those afflicted with leprosy, the lame and the blind, the deaf and the mute, the orphans and the homeless.

It is a privilege to accept this prestigious award presented in the name of Ramon Magsaysay, an outstanding leader, yet a man of the people who believed firmly in dignity, liberty and supreme sovereignty. Motivated by this mighty belief he could ensure a government that listened to the voices of the people. (Government should always be skilful in binding up the gaping wounds and drying its people's tears.) Magsaysay had this lofty ideal in his heart—an ideal which he proclaimed and practised in his lifetime.

I am really distressed by my disability; it is better to be healthy than to be famous. But God has given me supreme power to smile through the tears. Confidence and courage are my strongest and sharpest weapons.

Public service is not merely something that occupies the hours you are doing it, but invades all your life and experience and affects them in one way or the other. In public service people test you before they entrust themselves to you.

I never have wanted to commit the sin of turning a deaf ear to the plaintive cries of thousands of leprosy patients; of people who are physically handicapped; of people who though present in the world are absent—the deaf, the mute; of youths united only in the fraternity of frustration; of people whose intestines are gnawed by hunger, whose minds are darkened by ignorance and hatred, whose eyes open into perpetual night; of tribesmen who have remained unprotesting for an agonisingly long time. People who remain silent for a long time become a silenced minority; that is detrimental to any democracy.

I sought fellowship with the primitive Madia tribes of central India. My love for these people cleansed my polluted heart, sanctified my ambitions, sweetened my relationships, glorified my undertakings and transformed the valley of shadows in my life into the bursting dawn of eternal day. Those walking in the twilight of life, those seeking honestly the last harvest of their lives, those desiring and striving with shaky confidence to add new life to their years, those leading life in stark loneliness—I wanted to be their companion on their long, lonely voyages.

I wanted to be a contemporary of those 'Lords of Conspicuous Scars'—Christ, Damien, Gandhi. I saw the imprint of those nails with which Christ was crucified on the palms of Damien and on the breast of Gandhiji. Every time I stand in the company of a leprosy patient I see the imprint of Christ's kiss on his forehead.

'I have infirm wings, a heart—weary and insolent, a restless will, a broken backbone but I am still not weary of long voyages and uncertain things.' Thus like Macintyre, I will attempt to shape a community united in a shared vision of the good for man.

All service to be truly effective and of permanent value must be wrought in love. Your work is your life made visible. In public service you have to bait death in pursuit of your aims. You cannot afford to indulge in desires and pleasures. War kneads the earth with blood. In public service the distressed world begs your attention and you have to drench it with love and compassion. Goodwill and dedication alone do not suffice. Public service challenges us to discover and accept new values, new attitudes and most important, new commitments.

The award will lead me to deeper commitments.

12

ECONOMY AND DEVELOPMENT

The paradigm of development that India adopted after independence was based on the consensus arrived at over the previous hundred years of struggle. There were no disagreements on certain basic objectives—eradication of poverty, industrialization along modern lines and developing the capabilities of the country and its people to the fullest. The development model also had social and economic equity as its inalienable goals. The intelligentsia had from the beginning shown that the policies of the colonial state had been depriving the country of its potential for growth and development. They argued that these policies had to change to enable India to become an industrialized, modern and self-reliant country. Almost all major segments of the Indian leadership, including the capitalist class which organized itself in contradistinction to the sections which had vested interests in the colonial system and policies, felt that no development was possible without developing the agrarian sector which held the key to the life of the economy and that of the largest section of the Indian population.

From the beginning there was a consensus that in any development project the Indian state had to be the lead actor. This was primarily because only the state had the capacity to mobilize resources on the scale required for development projects of such magnitude. Secondly, it was also thought that the Indian state, organized along democratic lines, would ensure that the fruits of development were distributed equitably so that a foundation for a just society could be laid. The state's role was envisaged in relation to external forces also where it was thought that the Indian state would act as a buffer against any unequal distribution of economic and political power in the world that could threaten the Indian economy. In the Constituent Assembly, several leaders had pointed out that links with the global economy had to be sustained with care and prudence. So, unlike the present perception of the Indian leadership of the era, it was not ostrich-like in its responses to the world economy. The policy makers were aware that India had missed the first Industrial Revolution and that it had to catch up fast in order to deal with the comity of nations on equal terms. They realized that relationships between nations are most often defined by their respective economic strengths. It was not an easy task given that in the 1950s countries were getting increasingly divided into camps. India wanted to retain its independence and self-respect and at the same time required aid to develop itself industrially. These considerations were reflected in the Industrial Policy Resolution of 1956 which laid down that heavy industries were to be the springboard of India's industrial growth.

By the 1960s, there were strong critics of the developmental process. Though there were no major criticisms of the planned process itself, some of the tendencies that were developing in the economy came in for a lot of flak. In the name of state control, rapidly increasing bureaucratization of the production and distribution processes and mechanisms was leading to mismanagement and inefficient handling of resources. Though it was recognized that there was a need to review the developments in the economy, the Chinese attack in 1962, the war with Pakistan in 1965 and the subsequent droughts of 1965-66 followed by the adverse international situation arising out of the American war in Vietnam and the war in the Middle East in 1967 did not allow the leadership the time and space to try out a new approach.

Apart from the economy, there were threats to India's independent foreign policy too as India had to face the wrath of the United States which declined food relief. All of these exacerbated the crisis and in 1967, the government devalued the currency in an attempt to address the emergency. This was vehemently attacked by various sections in the country who saw it as capitulation to the US and to institutions like the World Bank and the International Monetary Fund (IMF). The resolution of the leadership amidst such an overwhelming crisis was twofold. While it decided to make the country self-sufficient in food production by sponsoring the Green Revolution, it also enlarged the state's role by placing many private large-scale businesses like mining and banking under government control. Thus, by 1970, the country was poised for a new kind of economic mechanism.

The late 1960s saw the Congress hegemony in many provinces of the country beginning to come apart. Keen to arrest this decline and establish herself as the undisputed leader, Indira Gandhi ushered in the next decade with radical economic programmes like nationalization of banks and the abolition of privy purses. At the same time, a number of regulatory devices like the Monopolies and Restrictive Trade Practices Act (MRTP) and Foreign Exchange Regulation Act (FERA) were enforced to give the state greater control over the processes of production. Though these acts were ostensibly meant to prevent concentration of economic power in the hands of a few and ensure more equitable distribution of wealth and income, they led to unparalleled corruption in bureaucratic and government circles in what was generally regarded as the zenith of the 'licence-permit-quota raj'. By the mid-1970s, growth had stagnated at 3.5 per cent per annum or what was derisively known as the 'Hindu rate of growth'. The 1980s saw the first efforts at liberalizing trade policies, encouraging the telecom and information technology sectors and reducing the sway of the bureaucracy and the government on the economy. The political instability towards the end of the decade resulted in a grave economic crisis which saw India's foreign exchange reserves falling to alarmingly low levels and necessitating the mortgaging of gold reserves to finance foreign currency requirements. The crisis led to a paradigm shift in the government's economic policies. The process of liberalizing the economy which had tentatively begun in the early 1980s climaxed with the budget of 1992-93. The prime minister, P.V. Narasimha Rao, brought in Manmohan Singh, an economist turned policy maker, as his finance minister to initiate and implement policies to open up the trade and industrial regime and liberalize financial institutions so that the creativity and entrepreneurship of Indians would not become a casualty at the altar of official and bureaucratic controls. The opening up of the economy to market forces and the dismantling of regulatory mechanisms have resulted in a phenomenal change in the economic and social landscape of the country. With annual growth rates reaching an all-time high of 8 per cent, India is now being looked at as a potential economic superpower. At the same time, there has been a concomitant decline in public services and an increasing disparity in the distribution of wealth with a substantial proportion of the population unable to receive the benefits of the new initiatives. In the new millennium, the Indian economy presents a strange paradox whereby glitzy shopping malls and booming consumerism exist side by side with stagnation in agriculture and instances of farmers' suicides.

~

G. SUBRAMANIAN IYER

Industrialization of the Country

Born in Tiruvadi, Tanjore district, G. Subramanian Iyer began his career as a teacher at Pachayappa's High School in Madras and later became the headmaster of the Anglo Vernacular School, Triplicane. With Veeraghavachariar and a few others he started The Hindu *as a weekly. A respected national leader at the beginning of the twentieth century, Iyer enthusiastically championed the cause of industrialization. He was one of the first to voice the demand for the country's industrial development as part of the nationalist demand for swadeshi. This constituted the foundation of the swadeshi model of development on which the vision of India's future industrialization was based. The following speech, made at the seventeenth session of the Indian National Congress held at Calcutta in 1901, provides a strong and clear-cut enunciation of this nationalist's vision.*

Mr President, Ladies and Gentlemen, in the resolution I have the honour to move is embodied our conviction as well as the conviction of all that have studied the economic condition of the country, namely, that the time has come for serious attention being given by the State to the inauguration of a policy by which the latent resources of the country may be developed for the benefit of the people and the exploitation of these resources by foreign capitalist may be arrested so that the constant drain of the wealth of the country to foreign countries may not continue to deepen the impoverishment of the people. In this matter as in many other matters, Government and the people hold entirely different opinions. In our opinion the material regeneration of the country cannot be effected until the people themselves are able to develop and utilize their resources for their own good, sell the produce of their industries in their own market, meet their wants with articles of their own manufactures, keep out foreign capital and foreign enterprise, in fact, maintain their industrial independence like other great countries of the world. On the other hand, it seems to be the opinion of Government that no such elaborate process is required, but that the gates have only to be thrown wide open for the advent of foreign capital in order that the hidden wealth of India may be brought out to make the Indian people happy and contented. It is in this view that Lord Curzon, in his last Budget speech, made the memorable statement that in order to increase the non-agricultural sources of income he welcomed the investment of foreign capital in India. In his Lordship's opinion the investment of foreign capital in the construction of Railways, Canals, Factories, Workshops, Mills, Coal-mines, Metalliferous-mines, cultivation of Tea, Sugar and Indigo, is the path to the salvation of India. While making the statement, His Excellency made no reference whatever to the part which the people of India should be called upon to fulfil in the protection of their own interests and the conservation of their own wealth. Is India to be always in the position of labourers working for daily wages under foreign employers or are her people to be made sooner or later fit to take their own independent share as employers of labour and as labourers themselves in the expansion of industries and in their own ultimate material regeneration? It is apparent that the latter event is not in the contemplation of our rulers. They seem to think that, while foreign capitalists sweep away the wealth of the country, the Indian people would have enough in the petty daily wages they may receive from their alien employers. It need not be said that we entirely disapprove of a policy so disastrous to our future. I am not aware of any instance of a country, either in modern or in ancient times, where a number of foreign capitalists with all the political and social advantages of their being of the ruling race, have helped in bringing about the industrial prosperity of the people ruled. Other countries do borrow foreign money for the development of their resources, but the borrowed money is invested by the countries themselves using indigenous agency, talent and labour, whereas in India the foreign capitalist brings his capital with himself, invests it as he likes and carries away the profits of his investment. In other countries the need to borrow foreign capital and to employ foreign agency is looked upon as a temporary evil and everything possible is done to replace foreign by indigenous capital and talent and to dispense with foreign aid in the development of the country's resources. In India far from this increasing foreign exploitation being looked upon as a temporary evil and from a time in the early future being looked forward to when the Indian people will effect their own industrial regeneration, the State is satisfied that the present anomalous condition of subjection to foreign capitalists is the only possible and beneficial order of things in the commercial career of India.

I am not in the least disposed to advocate the exclusion of the investment of foreign capital, but while no obstruction is placed against its investment we press Government for such measures being adopted as will enable the people themselves by their knowledge and training to take their own part by the side of their English competitors in industrial expansion of the country. The great object of increasing the non-agricultural wealth of the country cannot be attained by inviting foreign capitalists to work our mines, to cultivate our fields, utilise our raw materials and supply the daily wants of our people by their own articles at the cost of indigenous industries. Such a policy, far from producing this desirable result, only goes to make our people more and more helpless and confirms their state of dependence on foreign aid. Lord Curzon may be pleased to call those that differ from him in this matter as talkers of platitudes; still, at the risk of being included in this category, I do not hesitate to say that it is only in this way, that is, by educating and training our own people so as to enable them to take into their own hands the manufacture of our raw materials that non-agricultural wealth can be created. For over fifty years, specially since the opening of the Suez Canal, has foreign capital been freely flowing into India and at this moment millions of British money is invested here giving employment to about two millions of Indian labourers. Yet there is absolutely no evidence to show that non-agricultural wealth has thereby increased and that relief has been afforded to the overflowing population of agriculturists.

India has no alternative in the solution of the problem of its industrial future but to adopt the same methods and follow the same policy as other countries under similar circumstances have done. There is no country in the world whose modern history furnishes such valuable and extremely interesting object-lessons to India as Japan, which within the last thirty years has revolutionised her industrial condition with an aptitude, courage and foresight as marvellous as have characterised her political revolution. Before the Restoration of 1868, Japan was industrially in the same mediaeval and backward state as India is at the present moment, but along with the political revolution was inaugurated an era of industrial revolution also which upset her old indigenous system of industries. Japan's emergence from her isolation and her contact with the progressive nations of Europe were accompanied by radical changes in the habits and tastes of the people and the new craze for novelties and for European articles was such that the old class of producers were unable to supply the new demand. An industrial crisis was brought about; the nation which from time immemorial was self-contained and self-dependent in regard to her industrial requirement, began, of a sudden, to import all things from other countries, from the costly implements of modern warfare and expensive machinery down to trifling food-stuffs and toilet articles. Either the political and social conditions had to be made to adjust themselves to the old industrial system or the industrial system to adjust itself to the new political and social conditions. Naturally the latter was decided upon and the Japanese statesmen made up their minds that no obstacles, however great, should be allowed to hinder the nation's victorious march on the path of progress. The measures that were adopted in view of this end are of the greatest interest to leaders of Indian economic thought. One of the earliest of these measures was to educate the people, grown-up, as well as young men, high officials as well as others. Officials were sent to European countries for the purpose of observing and examining their industries and political institutions with a view to transplanting to the Japan soil whatever promised to bear good fruit. A great many students also were sent abroad to study the different branches of modern science. In Japan itself educational institutions were established by the State, and the Government established various factories without scruples as to financing and managing them, with a view to the manufacture of costly articles required for its own use. Meanwhile, the young men trained in foreign countries were available to cooperate with the capitalists, merchants and patriots of their country in pushing forward the industrial upheaval of the nation. Japan has now passed the stage of doubt and trial and she now entertains the ambition of rivalling England, Germany and America as a manufacturing country. Her natural resources are unlimited, and she has inestimable advantage of a patriotic Government and patriotic people who know the wants of the country and pursue the means of supplying them with forethought, patience and undaunted determination. In one respect she feels that she has not sufficiently advanced and that is the training of men to lead industrial movements along different lines as their pioneers, and to inspire capitalists and merchants with confidence and courage.

In the opinion of a former Prime Minister of Japan, the number of such men is yet sadly small as compared with the demand... Some time ago Japan used to employ a large number of foreign professors in her educational institutions, but their number has of late considerably diminished. But still their number is large. According to the *Japan Times*, a journal published in English at Tokyo, there were in the year 1899 altogether 52 foreign professors, of whom 16 were Germans, 12 were English, 6 were Americans, 6 French, 3 Koreans, 2 Russians, 2 Italians, 2 Chinese, 1 Belgian, 1 Spaniard, and 1 Swede. 'It is satisfactory to notice,' writes this paper, 'that strenuous efforts are being made by the Department of Education to afford means to the University Professors to keep up with the progress of Science in the West by personal visits of more or less extended period, to the leading seats of learning there, as well as to provide supplies of Professors by sending young graduates to complete their studies abroad.' The number of students ordered to go abroad for these purposes during the year under consideration was 58, the great majority of whom proceeded to Germany, while those that returned from abroad after finishing their studies there numbered fifteen. The total number of the professors and graduates studying abroad at the expense of the Government and for the purposes mentioned above was 100 at the end of March 1900, showing an increase of 92 over the number for the corresponding period of the preceding year.

Thus the recent history of Japan and of other countries in Asia as well as in Europe points to the important fact that the prosperity of every progressive country depends to a great extent upon the development of its resources by the application of high scientific process of manufacture. Much as His Excellency Lord Curzon ridiculed our effort to rouse Government to an adequate sense of the paramount importance of this fact, still statesmen of the foremost rank in other countries, in England, in Germany, in France, in Canada, and, not the last among these, the late remarkable ruler of Afghanistan, have laid the utmost stress on a departure in this direction in their respective educational systems. It may be there are other means which Lord Curzon has in his mind of redeeming India from her present industrial degradation, yet if the wisdom of contemporary statesmen burdened with the most awful imperial responsibilities is a guide to us, the most effective means of maintaining material progress and prosperity is certainly to so educate the mind and talent of the people as would enable them not only to meet their own wants with their own resources, but also to compete successfully with other countries in the markets of the world. I do not know what is Lord Curzon's faith in this matter, but I do not share in the belief that in the direction he points out, lies the solution to the problem of Indian poverty. And I do not hesitate to say that in wasting almost a crore of rupees on his favourite project of a museum of antiquities in Calcutta, he is not doing what is best calculated to enhance the material happiness of the people. At all events, in this period of fierce international competition for the wealth of the world, the greatest anxiety of thoughtful men is not to erect monumental buildings, but to advance industrial and scientific education, side by side with general education of the most liberal kind.

India has had the benefit of foreign capital invested in Indian industries and we have had 25,700 miles of Railways built; yet where is the promised millennium? It seems to be as far off as ever. Only the Indian people are becoming more and more helpless and the process of industrial extinction is becoming more and more complete. In the eyes of eminent men the only salvation of India consists in replacing, as far as may be, foreign enterprise by native effort. In remarkable accord with Mr. Dadabhai Naoroji's opinion, such a conservative politician as Sir M. Bhaonagiri said in the House of Commons last year, that 'the great cause which leads to the impoverishment of the resources of India and exposes her population to the ravages of scarcity and famine was the drain of the wealth of India by the enormous volume of the foreign manufactured articles imported into India every year'. To stop this ceaseless and enormous drain of wealth, which amounts to no less than 40 millions a year, by stemming the tide of foreign importation and by substituting in the place of foreign articles those manufactured in the country with Indian capital, Indian knowledge, and Indian agency, is not a problem to be solved by the establishment of a dozen small schools at a cost of a few thousand rupees, where a few Indian artisans may receive training. It is not the hand of the artisan that has to be trained so much as the mind of the higher class of young men who will pioneer the way to the industrial upheaval of India. For almost every article of daily use the Indian people now depend upon foreign manufacturers. Not only are cotton fabrics imported, but among other manufactured goods imported from abroad are : (1) Apparel, including boots and shoes, (2) Building materials, (3) Cabinet ware and furniture, (4) Candles, (5) Clocks and watches, (6) Earthenware and porcelain, (7) Glass and glassware, (8) Leather and leather goods, (9) Matches, (10) Paints and colours,

(11) Paper and paste-board, (12) Soap, (13) Stationery, (14) Toys, (15) Umbrellas, (16) Ironware. Now there is not a single article in this list which cannot be manufactured in India and of which the raw materials are not to be found in abundance in this country. Instead of these raw materials being manufactured here and the manufactured articles being sold in the markets of our country at comparatively cheap prices, they are exported to foreign countries where they are converted into finished articles to be imported back to this country and sold here for enormous profits. In fact, India supplies raw materials to other countries and is content to receive from them finished articles of use. It is this anomalous state of India's foreign trade that is proving so disastrous to her economic condition. The Indian people not only lose the wages and profits that can be obtained from the manufacture of raw materials, but have also to pay for the profits of the foreign capitalists and merchants, for the freight, insurance fees and so forth. To remove this anomaly and to place India's trade on a natural basis, the basis, namely, that the large and unlimited market supply by her teeming population should be mainly reserved for the products of her indigenous industries and that what may remain as surplus should be exported to foreign countries in exchange for what cannot be produced or manufactured here, to do this is the only means of averting the disaster that threatens to work India's complete economic ruin in the near future.

The real problem, then, is how the present industrial condition of India can be adjusted as that of Japan was adjusted to her new political conditions, which have dragged this country from her old isolated, self-contained state into the vortex of the fierce commercial competition marking the interrelation of the great community of nations. India cannot possibly remain idle or move backward in the face of modern conditions. She must either gird up her loins and march forward or get annihilated. Nor can India put up with the destiny which foreign nations hold out to her, as the Right Honourable Jesse Callings only the other day held out to her, that she should supply labour while British capitalists appropriate the profits of Indian industries. The ancient and civilised people of India cannot submit to such a condition of virtual slavery. If the British rulers of India are really interested in our future well-being and if the nation is not to be reduced to a state of slavery, they must adopt the policy which Japan has adopted with such striking results. The Indian people must be trained so as to enable them to organise and manage their own industries and stem to some extent the ceaseless inflow of foreign commodities. Prompt steps should be taken to provide sufficient facilities for such training, selected young men and even professors of colleges being sent at the expense of Government to foreign countries such as Germany and Japan to be trained there, so that on their return they might be able to apply their training and knowledge to our industrial development. It cannot be said in the face of instances such as Dr. J.C. Bose, Mr. Paranjpe, Dr. Roy, Professor Gajjar, and a number of other names, that Indians have no aptitude for the highest scientific training or for the prosecution of original researches. On the other hand, there is plenty of evidence to show that a strong inclination in favour of scientific and specialised studies is growing in the minds of the educated classes and no more striking illustration of this inclination can be given than the memorable enterprise of Mr. J.N. Tata and the legacies and endowments of rich men here and there in favour of industrial institutions. Only it is a lamentable fact that the Government of India should be so lukewarm in stimulating these tendencies. If only Lord Curzon wished it, he could have already made Mr. Tata's Research Institute an accomplished fact. And in the failure of the attempt made by some of our English well-wishers, scientists of the highest reputation, to get a Laboratory established in Calcutta for making scientific researches, we behold another of this sad prejudice of Government against scientific and practical education.

We know that at present the Government of India has this subject of technical education under consideration. But unfortunately it is not the large question of bringing out a general industrial upheaval of the country but only the narrower and less important one of reviving Indigenous Manual industries of the country that is under consideration. Why this should be so I cannot understand. On the other hand an entirely different view is held in other countries, as I have already said. The Royal Commissioners on Technical Education in England have recorded their opinion that 'the success which has attended the foundation of extensive manufacturing establishments, engineering shops, and other works on the Continent, could not have been achieved to its full extent in the face of many retarding influences, had it not been for the system of high technical institution in these Schools, for the facilities for carrying on original scientific investigation, and the general appreciation of the value of that instruction and of original research, which is felt in these countries'. And yet Lord Curzon ridicules this method recommended with such warmth and talks of 'a baton of institutes and a cluster of Polytechnics' as scarcely capable of producing a 'ripple in the great ocean of social and industrial forces'. We suppose that importation of foreign capital, in His Lordship's opinion, is a more efficacious remedy.

I am not by any means disposed to underrate the importance of technical education in its middle and elementary branches. By all means let Government do what it can in this direction, and the country will duly appreciate the benevolence of Government's policy. But what the country most needs in its present impoverished condition is not the creation of a class of trained labourers to serve under alien employers or a few nice articles of luxury which will be used by the small and limited class of princes and noblemen in this country. It is the articles of daily consumption by the great mass of the people that we should be able to produce; and our other natural springs of wealth should be exploited by us and for our benefit and not by the people of other countries. This should be the first stage in our country's career, while at the same time it is Government's duty to direct a general survey to be taken of the hundreds of old indigenous industries which still linger and decay in obscure corners of the country. It would be a great pity indeed if these small village industries which afford occupation to hundreds of thousands of people were allowed to die. What the condition of these industries is, what can be done to improve their methods, what new appliances may be introduced, how better markets can be opened to them—these and other kindred matters will form legitimate subjects of enquiry. It will be a very interesting enquiry to consider whether the principle of cooperation, the principle of the old guilds and leagues of the West cannot be adopted. It cannot be denied that these obscure industries deserve every encouragement that Government can give them. Still in the great problem before us the training of the mind and not that of the hand or the eye is the foremost factor.

Over and above the inferior industries carried on by artisans and mechanics, there are industries which consist in the manufacture of vegetable products into articles of utility and which cannot be undertaken by the people themselves without large capital or specially trained knowledge. These industries are now gradually being seized by the foreign capitalists thereby closing future outlets for indigenous enterprise. Recently in Southern India a syndicate has been formed to manufacture fibre from the aloe plant. This plant is found in great abundance over large areas in that part of the country, and I dare say the profits of this industry will go to swell the outflow of India's wealth. Similar industries are possible everywhere in India, and who knows they will not soon be brought within the sweep of Anglo-Indian enterprise, of which the latest outcome is the 'India Development Company' presided over by a retired Lieutenant-Governor and other high officials, who, having accumulated capital from the salaries received at our cost, bring their savings back for further accumulations.

There is no lack of comparatively small and simple industries which, before they are taken up by others, should be undertaken by our own countrymen. I need not say that I refer to industries like weaving, metal works and so forth, or to cultivation on scientific principles, of trees, plants, flowers, fruits, cattle farming, etc., which in other countries afford a paying occupation to large number of people. What can be done in order to give facilities to indigenous effort in the direction of developing these simple but paying means of livelihood by Government and the people themselves, might be profitably included in the industrial survey that we ask Government to undertake. I further venture to say that our countrymen themselves, such as are assembled at this Congress, have a duty to perform in this important matter. The great complaint is that there is no capital in this country. Though this is certainly true to a great extent, still there is some capital which would be organised and made available, but lies scattered in extremely small sums and is often wasted on useless luxuries and imaginary wants. Thus we can start Banks, industrial as well as agricultural, and Insurance Societies, and adopt other means which will induce thrift and providence and create a general spirit of saving and industry amongst our people. Societies must be started to diffuse knowledge and to watch the interests and the condition of our producers, leaflets and pamphlets should be issued...in order that a general taste for industries and other practical pursuits of life might be created. I have referred to the new inclination that is coming over our people in favour of practical education and independent pursuits of life. If the Congress will bear with me for a few minutes I shall mention the following instances which I have recently noted.

The Maharajah of Baroda is maintaining a large number of students in foreign countries. The Government of Travancore has lately announced the foundation of two scholarships for the same purpose. Mr. J.N. Tata, the enlightened and patriotic millionaire of Bombay whose name is fast becoming a household word throughout India, has for some time past done the same thing. Through the exertion of the late Mr. Ranade, the request of the late Sir Munguldai Nathubai for educational charity was made available for scholarships of this kind. H.H. The Nizam has already sent some students for liberal education in England and there is every reason to hope that that enlightened ruler would be pleased to depute some students for practical industrial training also. The Maharajah of Mymensing has shown enlightened and practical sympathy with this plan. He had sent to Italy for practical training in architecture a student named Rohini Kanto Nag who, however, on return after the completion of his study died... Another student, by name Sasi Kumar Hesh, was also sent to Italy by this patriotic Prince, and he has returned a master of the arts of painting and has already won fame in European countries. It is stated that the Maharajah intends sending two more youths to Europe for the same purpose. An association has recently been founded in Bombay with the object of promoting industrial education in India, and in its latest report we read the following significant passage. 'To refute an objection which a few people had raised sometime ago, that no youths would, on account of religious and other difficulties, be forthcoming, it may be stated that 57 students have of their own accord applied for our help and that 8 of them are graduates of Indian Universities in arts or sciences, that 5 are L.M.E.'s of the Bombay Technical Institute, that 24 are practical Engineers, and that the remaining 20 are undergraduates, applications from students who have studied up to the Matriculation Examination are numerous and have not here been taken into account. Besides, during the course of the three years past, about 2 dozen qualified students have gone to foreign countries for learning industries, either on their own account or supplemented by help from others.'

It is no use of saying that these students studying industries in foreign countries will find no suitable employment on their return. In the first place, the fact that so much is being done by private efforts is a sufficient refutation. If there is any sufficient reason for the belief that such will be the result, all the spontaneous effort that I have referred to will not be made. In the second place, some of the students who have thus returned have found profitable and honourable employment. I have already mentioned the name of Mr. Hesh who is doing very well as a painter. Mr. Godbole, who was trained in pottery and chocolate manufacture in Belgium, has started a chocolate factory in Baroda. An enterprising Parsee gentleman, Mr. Talati, who was with great difficulty trained in England, is now running a thriving leather factory in Bombay, which the Railway Companies and Lord Northcote and Lord Curzon have thought worthy of their patronage. Mr. Wagle will soon establish a glass factory in Bombay. I recently read in a Bengali Newspaper of a Bengali mining expert, Babu Sarat Chunder Rudra, who travelled all over the world, and visited the mines of distant Korea. His services have been utilised by a European Mining Company in Bengal. Mr. H.P. Chatterjee of Umballa, who studied the art of pencil making in Japan, has, on his return, issued a prospectus inviting shares for the modest capital of Rs 6,000 to establish a pencil factory. There must be other instances of which I am not aware. These instances unmistakably go to prove the new tendency of the national mind against the old beaten track of official and professional service in favour of independent industrial pursuits.

Now, I should bring these rather lengthy observations to a close. I shall briefly summarise as follows the chief points to which I desire to draw public attention through this Congress.

(1) The first and most important step that should be taken under any intelligent system of technical education is to provide facilities either by institutions established in this country like Tata's Institute or by endowing foreign scholarships for our own people to become the pioneers and captains of our industries.

(2) Indian students should be trained in industrial schools as managers and foremen etc., of local industries. There is no reason why Indians, if they cannot supply the capital and organising talent should not be employed in the higher and more responsible offices in established industrial and commercial firms, in the Kolar Gold Mines and in the coal mines in other parts of India. There are absolutely no openings for native technical skill and is it not a pity that no effort is made by those in power to arrange matters so that the people may derive some permanent benefit from the enterprises carried on in their midst? The Native State of Mysore has made a small beginning in this direction. It has established in connection with its gold industry a meteorological laboratory. It has also established an Institute which might be easily converted, it is said, into a first-class technical school of a special character. In the long run Indians trained in such an Institute will take the place of European engineers and materially reduce the cost of industry. It is further suggested that in the celebrated Cauveri Falls Electric Power Transmission Scheme, it is possible to establish a school of mines and mineralogy which, by arrangement with the managers of the Kolar mines, could be made an

institution equal to any in the world for the opportunities it could offer for both theoretical and practical training in all that belongs to mines and minerals. There is no reason why a similar attempt should not be made to utilise for this purpose the facilities afforded by other mining establishments in different parts of the country.

(3) There are other industries in connection with which schools should be established for the training of Indian students. Recently the intelligent and enterprising community of weavers in Madura, reflecting on the decay of their industry brought on by French and German competition prayed to Government for the establishment of a (i) Textile School, (ii) a Technical Dye-house for natural colours, (iii) an alizarine factory for preparing alizarine from madder roots, (iv) a gilt thread making factory, and woollen clothes from hand-loom driven by electric power.

(4) A survey of the indigenous industries of the country by means of a mixed commission of officials and non-officials, which would travel from place to place and make a personal investigation of local industries. This is not a new idea but it has been pressed on to the Government for years by the Congress. I may add that on a recent occasion our good friend Lord Reay made the same suggestion. Most of these industries possess great merit as works of art and of utility and so long as the industrial system of India remained a system of domestic or family occupation, they thrived well. But in these days their conditions have changed, they have lost their old market, the labourers themselves have degenerated, and public state has altered. It is believed that most of these industries can be greatly improved and introduced into distant markets by a system of pecuniary help to the artisans and by giving them the help of improved appliances. An investigation such as I propose can include these matters with benefit within the scope of the labour of the commission.

Gentlemen, such are the proposals this Congress makes to Government for the industrial regeneration of India. We maintain that the non-agricultural wealth such as His Excellency Lord Curzon depends upon for the relief of the agricultural classes is not to be created by the importation of foreign capital. In our opinion the only secret of India's industrial salvation is that which other countries, more especially Japan, have discovered and employed with marvellous success. Why our own Government should be blind to this great fact and should assume an attitude of scepticism, it is difficult to understand. Issues of the gravest character are involved in this problem. And the disposition to put off the solution rather than tackle the problem with energy and promptitude cannot but be regarded as a most lamentable fact. Whether this attitude is in any way connected with a regard for the vested interests of the governing country, interests which are in a sense incompatible with India's industrial progress, I cannot say, I only hope that in this question Indian interests alone will receive consideration. According to the repeated declarations and assurances of our Government, made in the most solemn manner possible, the interests of India take precedence over the interests of the ruling country when there is a conflict between both, and we are confident that the sense of justice and fair play will prevail over the selfishness of vested sectional interests, in the solution of this problem, most vitally affecting the future, under the guidance of British rule.

~

PURUSOTTAMDAS THAKURDAS

Presidential Address, FICCI, 1928

The Federation of the Indian Chamber of Commerce and Industries (FICCI) was set up in 1927 by leading Indian entrepreneurs to voice the concerns and demands of the Indian business and industrial class. From the outset, the clash between British interests and those of the Indian business groups began to emerge through the speeches and debates of FICCI. Very soon, FICCI became the voice of the Indian capitalist class and began to take a strong and independent position on economic matters. One of the strongest notes of dissent that FICCI articulated in its annual demands through its presidential speeches pertained to the matter of free trade. Indian entrepreneurs were of the opinion that free trade should be a matter of mutual interest and benefit between Indian business houses and those in the ruling country. However, foreign mercantile groups and agencies, in league with the colonial administration, put hurdles in the way of local industry and trade, preventing it from prospering, and used the free trade argument to suit their own business and economic interests. At its second annual meeting in 1928 in Calcutta, Purusottamdas Thakurdas, a powerful and articulate spokesperson for Indian businessmen, in his presidential address clearly enunciated the position of the Indian capitalist class vis-à-vis the colonial attitude towards it. He also articulated why it was not desirable to separate business and economic interests from political ones.

Indian trade and industry have a long and ancient history. Their importance was recognised and the mercantile community was an integral part of Indian polity from the earliest time. Since the advent of British Rule, however, foreign trade has tended...to engage a larger measure of official interest, than indigenous commerce and industry. Indian thinkers for over a generation have felt that the fiscal and economic policies of the Government require to be adapted to the economic needs and conditions of the country and the germ of the present movement is to be found in their writings and speeches. The most prominent names in this school of thinkers, which I recall with gratitude, are Dadabhai Naoroji, Romesh Chunder Dutt and Ranade; two of these were the originators of the Swadeshi movement, which for many years remained in a latent state until it gained strength on the Partition of Bengal in 1905. Indian commerce and industry then became conscious of its distinctive rights and responsibilities. First, an Indian industrial exhibition, and then an industrial conference became associated with the Indian National Congress movement. One often hears it said that economics should be entirely dissociated from politics. This is impossible, even if it be admitted for the sake of argument that it is desirable. Every year sees the power of organised industry exercised more strongly on Governments, either in the form of social legislation, trade control, or tariffs to protect listing and encourage nascent industries. We can no more separate our politics from our economics than make the sun and moon stand still. On the contrary, we ardently desire to see the two more closely associated, and the power of Government steadily directed, raising the economic standard of our people and so build up a more prosperous and happier India. The Indian Merchants' Chamber of Bombay had its origin in the political and economic renaissance to which I have referred. Other chambers followed and in 1915 the idea of a commercial congress for all India took birth; the first Congress was held that year under the Presidentship of Sir Fazulbhoy Currimbhoy. The fifth and last Industrial Congress was held last year at Madras under the Presidentship of Sir Ibrahim Rahimtoola. Hereafter it is expected that the Annual Meeting of the Federation will obviate the necessity of having a commercial congress, except under special circumstances.

This brief review of the history of this movement is necessary to understand that Indian commerce and industry are intimately associated with and are indeed an integral part of the national movement growing with its growth and strengthening with its strength. Much misunderstanding is due to this important fact not being sufficiently recognised. The ideal of the national movement in the political sphere, namely to make the Indian nation united, prosperous and progressive is also the ideal of Indian commerce and industry in the economic sphere. Many of our European friends and even some Indians do not realise that deprived of its inspiration in Indian nationalism, Indian commerce and industry might be reduced to mere exploitation. The attitude of the Indian commercial world to Government and British commercial interests can be rightly appreciated only if this great fact is understood. Indian commerce and industry cannot make terms with the one or the other at the expense of national interest. At the same time peace and order, security of person and property, are in India, as elsewhere, the first requirements of commercial and industrial well-being; and Government may count upon the support of Indian commerce to every well-considered measure having for its object the promotion of these prime interests. If on some occasions Indian commercial representatives have found themselves unable to accord their support to Government measures, it is because they were not convinced that the security aimed at could not be assured by the use of the existing powers of Government. They also felt that excessive powers in the hands of an executive not responsible to or removable by the legislature are apt to be used in ways which would lead to serious and widespread discontent in the country, which is not a condition favourable to economic progress. Indian merchants and businessmen are in close contact with the masses, and are the first to feel the effect of any serious discontent in the country. They are, therefore, in the best position to appreciate the probable effect of any legislative action and if they find it necessary to oppose a measure specially designed to ensure public safety it should be presumed to be dictated by motives not only of self-interest, but also of the public welfare. Mutual confidence and more frequent consultations between Indian commercial bodies and Government will lessen the opportunities of difference, and ensure for Government measures the support not only of those directly interested in commerce and industry, but also of the large body of the public.

As for British commercial interests, once they realise that Indian commerce is a phase of Indian nationalism, they will cease to misunderstand its attitude on some important questions which affect them. For my own part, I look forward to the time when the distinction between Indian and British in the commerce and industry of the country will disappear, and both British and Indian industrialists and businessmen will work harmoniously together in promoting the economic well-being of the country. Such cooperation even now is not rare, and it is bound to grow as Englishmen in India understand that Indian leaders have no predatory intentions, and that in a self-governing India, British interests will be as secure as at the present day. They should recognise, however, that Indians have the same right to a predominant share in the commerce and industry of their country, as other nationals have in their countries, and should not misinterpret their attempts to obtain it as an attack upon British interests in India. One sometimes hears of claims to a stake in the country computed in terms of amounts of British capital invested. I cannot help thinking that arguments against our national aspirations based on such claims are derogatory to the high plane on which the relations between Britain and India should always rest. Otherwise, it is not difficult to argue on the other side that, even in terms of money, Britain has recovered from this country much more than the amount of British capital invested in India, and that after all the stake of the Indian Merchants in India is very considerably larger, in fact many thousand times larger. But the relation between the two countries must be decided by higher considerations and on broader grounds than those of rupees, annas and pies. This Federation recognises that the prosperity of the commercial and industrial classes is, and can only be, founded on the prosperity of the masses in India, namely, the agricultural classes. We are, therefore, keenly alive to, and grateful to Your Excellency for your personal interest in the well-being of India's agriculture. Lord Mayo established the Department of Agriculture with the help and advice of A.O. Hume, the founder of the Indian National Congress, some sixty years ago. Several Viceroys after him, especially Lord Curzon, interested themselves in the improvement of agriculture and the condition of the agriculturists. The Linlithgow Commission's opinion on the present condition of the industry, however, is that these efforts have not appreciably improved the lot of the cultivator, or of the state of the industry. The central recommendation of the Commission is to institute a Board of Research. Research has been of great utility in helping agriculture in advanced countries, but the capacity to utilise the results of research presupposes a wide diffusion of, at least, elementary education, and the financial resources to invest capital in the necessary fertilisers, machinery, etc. The former does not as yet exist in this country. The establishment of a nationwide system of elementary education on a free and compulsory basis is, therefore, a most urgent condition of agricultural, as of all industrial development. I may add that more substantial results are to be expected in this, as in other directions, by utilising the immemorial tradition of Indian experience, than by discarding it as useless, and establishing in the country a system entirely foreign to its genius and habits. Regarding the financial resources of the agriculturists, the credit of the bulk of them is still so low that at least in one important Presidency the Central Co-operative Bank finds it difficult, in spite of having resources at its command, to assist more than about 18 per cent of the agriculturist borrowers in typical cotton areas. The rest have to borrow from the local sowcar and the much-abused moneylender at rates of interest varying from 10 to 50 per cent per annum.

There is one point which has perhaps been overlooked by the Agricultural Commission—or which was possibly beyond its scope—namely, the price which Indian raw material secures in the markets of the world. There are many directions in which Indian interests can be better safeguarded and Indian raw materials be given fairer valuation in these markets than at present. As Your Excellency knows, the Agricultural Department of the United States of America by passing the Cotton Standards Act in 1923 compelled the whole world to trade in American cotton on no other standards except those prepared by that Department for American cotton. The Act imposes heavy penalties (up to six months' imprisonment) on any American citizen buying, selling, either quoting, or receiving quotations based on any standards other than those of the United States of America. The cotton trade of the whole world has more or less been compelled to fall in a line with this. The latest information from America is that American shippers have been successful in securing the establishment at Bremen, Havre, Rotterdam, Ghent and Brussels of super appeal Boards or communities by which all disputes regarding the quality, etc., of American cotton will be decided. On these Committees the American shippers are represented equally with European buyers of American cotton, no unwarranted running down of the raw material of America is thus risked, and this somewhat exceptional measure has been successful only because the cotton trade of America has behind it the wholehearted support of the Government of the United States of America who are actuated by the ideals of increasing the reputation and good name of American cotton and securing a fair price to its growers. I do not pretend that Indian raw material is, in every respect, exported in the most perfect condition, but it cannot be claimed, either, that American cotton is marketed in such a satisfactory state as to be incapable of improvement. At the moment, the Indian shipper has no voice in the cotton exchanges; or for that matter in any exchanges, where Indian raw materials are traded in, in any part of the world. I may say that even in India the Central Government has not yet been able to devise uniform standards for trading in the same variety of cotton all over the country.

Regarding the export of jute which is the monopoly of India, and a necessity of the world, the commercial Sale Rooms of London where the jute business is transacted, if they keep any nationals from their precincts, they keep out Indians. There are other Sale Rooms in London which definitely refuse to take Indians as their members. I mention this in order that Your Excellency may realise, in correct perspective, the feelings with which Indians who see those conditions in foreign countries return here owing to such handicaps. I am sure that if the Government of India took some interest in removing these handicaps on Indians, they would not have to work long in securing this redress. I need hardly add that such a step, when achieved, will materially assist the Indian grower in several directions. It would help against an unwarranted lowering of the value and reputation of Indian raw materials in world markets, and would further facilitate the marketing of Indian produce abroad.

~

NALINI RANJAN SARKAR

Indian Economy

Nalini Ranjan Sarkar (1882–1954) rose from humble beginnings (he had to leave school due to financial constraints) to become one of the country's leading thinkers on finance and industry. He joined the non-cooperation movement and between 1937 and 1939 was a member of the Bengal cabinet under Fazlul Huq. He was also a member of the viceroy's executive committee. Possessing a good understanding of the insurance sector, Sarkar entered the Hindustan Cooperative Insurance Society in 1911 and went on to become first its general manager and ultimately its president, a position he held till his death. He was also president of the Bengal National Chamber of Commerce and Industry, member of various economic and business committees, and a delegate to the Indo-Japanese Trade Conference in 1923. Sarkar had a deep understanding of education and its relation to society. As vice-president of the National Council of Education, Bengal, a fellow of the Calcutta University Senate in 1934, a member of the Court of the University of Dacca in 1940-41, pro-chancellor of Delhi University during 1941-42, and president of the Presidency College Governing Body in 1942, he made a significant contribution to the cause of education in the country. It was the committee headed by Sarkar in 1946 which recommended setting up the IITs on the lines of the Massachusetts Institute of Technology, a futuristic idea which envisioned a clear break from the British educational and technological system. Sarkar was also one of the three experts who constituted the Expert Committee on Finance in the Constituent Assembly. A close confidant of Gandhi, Sarkar had a very clear position on the political role of Indian capitalists. His presidential address at FICCI in 1934, after the civil disobedience movement was suspended, is significant because he was speaking at a time when almost all national leaders were either in jail or in hiding following Linlithgow's imposition of martial law-like conditions. Sarkar not only spoke on the ongoing debate about trade and currency but also clearly enunciated the need for planning and a vision thereof. This speech is one of the most comprehensive expositions on the economic situation of the country, effortlessly weaving in the importance of infrastructure to economic development and the ideal relationship between the political and the business classes.

Although foreign trade generally receives greater attention in economic discussions, it is necessary to realise that, as far as India is concerned, her internal trade, like that of America, is of much greater value and importance.

At the outset, I must say that the Government has paid very inadequate attention to the development of internal trade. The fact that they are vitally interested in India's foreign obligations has induced them to pay almost exclusive attention to foreign trade to the neglect of the problem of the expansion of internal trade. This was perhaps also due to the fact that the British business community have much larger interests in the foreign trade than in the internal trade of the country...It should be fully realised that our internal trade, important as it is even today in volume and value relatively to our external trade, must still be very much more developed. For, Indian industries must grow at a fairly rapid pace and their success would depend largely upon exploiting the internal market to the fullest extent, in other words, upon the development of facility for the movement of goods from one part of the country to another. In our country, happily enough, nature seems to have provided some excellent opportunities for the exchange of commodities between one part of the country and another—that is, for natural division of labour. Jute, cotton, oil-seeds, wheat, tea, are all grown in fairly well-defined separate regions, and any facilities given for the mutual exchange of these commodities are bound to increase the internal trade of the country. Similarly, the major industries of India like cotton, cement, iron and steel, etc. are located in accordance with the natural advantages possessed by a certain area, and the encouragement given to a wider distribution of their products in India would ultimately increase the volume of internal trade.

What is necessary, therefore, is to plan out the development of internal trade. Its present volume requires careful calculation, and having ascertained this, the scope of its further development should be investigated.

Having decided to expand internal trade, our next attempt should be the removal of the existing obstacles like high freight rates, differential excise duties, etc. and the establishment of conditions conducive to its steady development.

While it is obvious that we should seriously address ourselves to the task of creating conditions for the steady and unhampered development of the internal trade of the country, it is well to remember that we might, at the same time, develop and expand our foreign trade, particularly our exports, in view of the fact that we have heavy annual external obligations to meet. An expanding export surplus is consequently a necessity for India not only to meet our immediate requirements of foreign goods, but also for the purpose of steadily diminishing the volume of our foreign obligations. The growth of our foreign trade during the present century is certainly encouraging but the shrinkage in India's percentage share of world's trade in recent years, which can hardly be explained by the present depression, is a disquieting feature of her foreign trade demanding organised efforts for its redress and improvement. By far the preponderating proportion—not less than two-thirds of our export trade—consist of raw materials and 'food, drink and tobacco'. It reveals India's predominantly agricultural economy, indicating how any serious diminution in the volume of her exports would react disastrously upon the mass of India's agricultural population.

Another unwelcome feature of India's foreign trade is the

preponderating importance of a few countries. England, Germany, France, America and Japan between them account for more than half the total value of India's foreign trade. The danger of thus putting too many eggs into a few baskets should be obvious.

The problems of our foreign trade thus pertain to both the maintenance and expansion of our markets abroad and it requires closer study and the continuous attention of the government. The volume, the direction, the competition encountered, and the facilities needed—all require careful watching. At the present moment, the functions of the Government of India in this respect cease with the collection and publication of foreign trade figures. There is no organisation whose duty it is to watch the tendencies revealed by these figures and take necessary steps in the national interest. The present Department of Commercial Intelligence is ill-equipped for that purpose, and without any further delay, machinery should be set up conforming to a real Board of Trade. Until such an institution is set up, the planned development of our foreign trade would be almost impossible. This is all the more important in these times when the fiscal and commercial policies of foreign countries are undergoing rapid changes with their inevitable reactions upon our own foreign trade. During the last few years, the development of foreign trade by trade agreements between countries has become a widely accepted method. Nearly every European country of any importance has entered into one or more of these agreements with their customers. The main features of such agreements have been the most-favoured nation treatment, export, and import quotas or exchange clearing arrangements. They have not only led to the lowering and simplification of tariff barriers between the countries entering into such trade understandings, but also tended to increase the volume of trade between them, by facilitating the exchange of goods mutually advantageous to them. An approximate approach to such methods was made in the series of agreements entered into at Ottawa between the various parts of the Empire. While the method is unexceptionable, it must be said that, as far India is concerned, the actual agreements were hastily concluded with insufficient knowledge and preparation by persons whose greatest handicap was a basic misconception of India's foreign trade position. This has been proved by subsequent events. The Ottawa Agreements were only the starting point for the United Kingdom and other parts of the Empire to enter into a network of economic understandings with non-Empire countries. England took the lead and concluded a series of carefully planned agreements with a large number of other countries such as Argentina, Germany, Norway and Sweden, while a similar agreement was entered into by Canada with France. So far as India is concerned, the possibilities of evolving such agreements have so far been practically neglected, and this bears an eloquent testimony to the absence of any real trade policy on the part of our Government. The recent Indo-Japanese Agreement makes a departure in this respect but even this Agreement was not, as I have already pointed out, the outcome of a predetermined plan calculated to expand the foreign trade of India. The Bombay–Lancashire Pact is worse than futile, judged by the criterion of trade expansion.

The most important part of a trade plan for India would, in the present circumstances, consist in the negotiation of commercial agreements with her foreign customers on a strictly scientific basis, securing real advantage to the interests of this country. A complete survey of possibilities of such agreements concluded at Ottawa may, in the light of experience, require fundamental alteration in order to serve Indian interests better. The possibility of the greater expansion of India's trade outside the Empire than within it should be kept in view, and mere political affiliations should not be allowed to stand in the way of its realisation.

In view of the increasing complexities of foreign trade and the keener competition experienced by our products abroad, the watchful assistance of Trade Delegation is essential. Without further delay, Trade Commissioners should be appointed in the Far East, the Middle East, East Africa and America. A definite policy should be laid down for developing a really efficient Consular Service, manned by well-trained and experienced people.

One discouraging feature of India's foreign trade is the small share of Indians in it. Apart from ignorance of foreign conditions and traditional economic conservatism, the absence of an Indian exchange bank is the most serious handicap. There is no dearth of exchange banks in India, but they are all foreign institutions and the Indian merchants cannot hope to, and do not, get the same facilities the British, American or a Japanese gets from the Bank of his own nationality. Japan realised very early that an exchange bank of her own was necessary for developing her foreign trade and for increasing the share of her own nationals in it. She started an exchange bank fully backed by her Government. I am convinced that, on identical grounds, an Indian exchange bank should be established with adequate assistance from the Government.

Transport

In a large country like India, internal transport is of much greater importance than in a small country. The transport problems of a country of long distances consist mainly in the carriage of goods and passengers quickly, and cheaply, consistent with efficiency. The system and methods of transport now serving India should be tested by this standard, and it would be generally found that they would not come out of the test quite well.

In the machinery, policy and organisation of India's transport there are glaring inconsistencies and anomalies. Nowhere does one find a unity of purpose, a coordination of services or desire to obtain the maximum benefit out of whatever natural facilities the country may provide. Railways compete with railways, and railways combine to compete with waterways. Waterways compete with railways, and coastal sea transport agencies try to take trade away from railways. An unholy war is further waged between railways and road motors. While this struggle is in full swing the country looks on unconcerned and the government is slow in moving. Every day of inactivity adds to the confusion and renders the establishment of a coordinated internal transport system more and more difficult.

A survey of the transport map of India, today, betrays a lamentable lack of policy, and impresses the urgency of a coordinated development of all the various transport systems with a view to avoid waste and ensure efficiency. For this purpose, a Central Ministry of Communications should be considered, and every Province should have a Department of Transport working under the general guidance of the central authority.

Currency and Exchange

By far the most important feature of economic planning is the planning in monetary matters. In the absence of planned money, prices of commodities will be subjected to fitful influences, trade and industry could not have the assurance of adequate finance at reasonable rates, and confusion would prevail in the capital, gilt-edge and exchange markets. The well-being and prosperity of all the sections of the community are profoundly affected by the way in which the currency authority controls the standard supplies or withdraws currency and otherwise undertakes varied operations which affect the value of money and prices of goods. The currency mechanism can either do great good or great harm according as it functions in a wholesome fashion. The good it can do embraces the entire country and no section of the population remains unaffected if harm accrues. It is for this reason that the utmost emphasis should be laid on a correct and scientific plan for money.

In the evolution of a proper currency standard our authorities should revise their ideas as regards the proportion of gold in our external reserve. Conservative in every other respect, and fighting shy of experiments in every other sphere, the Finance Member has, however, professed ultra-modern ideas in regard to gold. Gold is a fetish to him. It is sterling that is the be all and end all. He visualises a day when countries which have been grabbing all the gold that they could lay their hands on would be sorry that they did so. In this view, George Schuster has no use for even the policy of Great Britain. While England has been rapidly strengthening her gold reserve in the period following the abandonment of gold standard, the Indian Government has allowed gold to flow out of the country, without any attempt on their part to secure a portion for the strengthening of their currency reserve. From the published figures in the Bank of England returns and from the reported accumulations of gold in the Exchange Equalisations Fund, it may be said that Britain has gained an additional $150 millions of gold within two and a half years. India, on the other hand, has exported gold to the amount of Rs. 175 crores. Our currency reserve has not gained one ounce of gold during all this period. We are asked to feel very pleased with ourselves as sincere philanthropists who have helped international finance by exporting gold without let or hindrance. If it is certain that the important countries of the world would go back to gold standard as soon as conditions permit; and if, therefore, it is essential that India too should re-establish gold standard, the present attitude of the Government in regard to gold exports must be considered extremely detrimental from the point of view of planned money. There must be definite plans for the acquisition of gold on account of the currency reserve for such amounts as would ensure the smooth function of gold standard in a country which has two kinds of notes in circulation, namely, paper notes and silver notes; and which has an annual recurring liability of about $30 million by way of overseas commitments.

In this, as in other matters, the currency policy of India has been fashioned at the dictation of White Hall and in the interests of the

City of London. It is negligence of the Indian interests and the policy of drift which have most adversely affected the economic life of India; what is worse, it has seriously jeopardised the prospects of satisfactory reform in the future. The conflict between the currency system of India and the larger economic interest of the country has become more and more pronounced. Considerations connected with our foreign obligations have exerted undue influence over the outlook of the government and they have failed to realise that the best guarantee for a proper discharge of such obligations can be provided by stimulation of our export trade and expansion of our favourable balance to both of which the high ratio has proved a serious impediment.

From a survey of the history of the past, it is obvious that we have had no plan or definite aim in currency and monetary affairs. Those who have been shaping the currency and exchange policy have been content to live for the day. They have evinced no desire to place it on a suitable and permanent basis; yet, of all issues affecting economic destiny of a country, nothing requires more urgently and more imperatively to be placed on a definite and permanent basis than currency and monetary policy.

Although the canons of a sound currency system are universal in their character and are fairly well-known, the principles which in the circumstances prevailing in India, should be regarded as most important to the policy best suited to this country, need to be fully emphasised. We should aim, in the first place, at a comparative stability of internal price level. As I have already stated less attention has been paid to this most important consideration, and, not infrequently, it has been absolutely ignored in the anxiety of the Government to maintain a stable exchange value. A fair measure of elasticity should be one of the essential characteristics of our future exchange and currency policy. Special attention will have to be paid to the fact that seasonal variations in economic conditions are very marked in India. Lastly, in its management, interference from abroad and international influences should be eliminated as completely as possible.

Further, we should aim at a coordination of the currency and credit policies of the government which are now conspicuous for their complete divorce from each other, not infrequently reacting most disastrously on the internal price level. The establishment of the Reserve Bank is expected to solve the problem to some extent, but with very little effective control of the Reserve Bank over exchange its complete control over the current policy will be doubtful. Besides, the influence of the Treasury Bills policy of the Government over the volume of money in circulation cannot be ignored. Money is at present pumped out and pumped into the market at the discretion of the Government, often with scant regard to the effect of such actions on price level. The plan for our future currency and exchange policy of the country will have to provide for safeguards against such unsettlement of the market.

So far as the wider questions of banking development and the credit policy are concerned, the Reserve Bank, even if it had been an ideal institution, could do little in the matter of acting as the monetary authority, without there being a network of banks in the country. The number of cities having a banking office is too small as compared with the total number of cities in the country. A considerable number of towns, not to speak of villages, have no modern banking institution and it is necessary to establish a large number of commercial banks spread throughout the country. As I have already stated, banking development of the country, meagre as it is, has been entirely lopsided. Industry and agriculture have been sadly neglected. The need is at present keenly felt for developing a more diversified system of banking by the establishment of banks of all kinds, for financing agriculture, industry (both for long-term requirements, as well as for short period), and trade (both internal and foreign). To bring all these banks within the orbit of the effective influence of the Reserve Bank, it will be necessary to establish discount houses and licensed warehouses. The absence of a bill habit has resulted in the popularity of the system of cash credits which is at present a weak link in the banking system of the country. The problems of loan officers in Bengal and Nidhis in Madras and the problem of indigenous bankers remain also to be solved. Reform of these agencies must be made essential feature of planned money.

Finance

The logic of circumstances demands that the new sources of revenue should be tapped, the need for which is also evident from a review of the position of the Provincial Governments. Land revenue, their principal source, is extremely inelastic and has shown considerable resistance to any substantial increase; the receipts from excises also have not in all the provinces yielded the desired result, leaving stamps as the only important dependable item. But as in the case of income-tax, dependence on a single source for a considerable portion of the revenue receipts is extremely precarious, and suggests the necessity for making the tax system more broad-based.

At the same time, we have to take into consideration the limited taxable capacity of the people. The people of India are admittedly very poor as compared with those of other countries, and the proportion of the total tax revenue to the total national income cannot naturally be as high as in other more fortunately placed countries; which leads to the conclusion that not much can be raised by imposing new taxes or increasing the present rates of taxes. We cannot ignore, on the other hand, that if the present practice of expending larger sums on the primary services of the Government to the exclusion of the more important developmental works is abandoned or even modified, and if, in future, increasing sums are allotted for the latter, the consequent improvement in the economic condition of the people will enable them to bear the burden of increased taxation to a greater extent than is possible at the present moment.

The minimum total amount of additional revenue to be placed at the disposal of the Provincial Governments for making a fair beginning in regard to the nation-building services has been estimated by Sir Walter Layton in his Financial Report appended to the Report of the Simon Commission at between Rs. 40–50 crores. It is extremely problematic whether it is feasible to raise this amount of additional tax revenue, while it is equally doubtful whether the money thus raised will be available for being spent for the secondary services of the Government in India, in view of probable shrinkage in Customs Revenue—a loss which will also have to be made up from the new levies.

These facts inevitably lead to the conclusion that to enable the Provincial Governments to adopt beneficial measures, it will be necessary not merely to tap new sources of revenue but also to exercise strict control over items of expenditure, particularly those relating to the maintenance of internal and external security in order to leave a larger margin for productive purposes. It is, however, well to recognise that this economy in expenditure will not dispense with the necessity for additional taxation.

As regards the new sources of taxation which can be tapped, careful enquiries will have to be made into the equity, incidence and the probable yield from taxation of agricultural income, the institution of a tobacco monopoly (and, for that matter national monopolies in regard to other commodities of similar nature), excise duties on certain specific commodities, stamp duties on railway receipts, etc. I do not propose to deal with these specific suggestions here, but I would suggest that possibilities of raising additional tax revenue from these and other sources should be carefully investigated. Simultaneously, steps should also be taken to increase the productive power of the existing sources of revenue by varying the rates. Besides, attempts should be made for making Post and Telegraphs Department a revenue-earning department instead of being a burden on the general revenue as is now the case. This principle has been widely accepted in countries like Switzerland and Canada. But while State revenue is to be the objective, full and sympathetic investigation should be made of the taxable capacity of the people before any scheme of indirect taxation is undertaken through the regulation of postal and telegraph rates. The existing financial position of the department as is now administered by the Government of India is extremely unsatisfactory. Year after year it is being run with deficits and for the last few years it has been almost a fashion to make of the general depression a scapegoat and put the whole blame on it. The crying necessity is, however, greater economies in administration, for which there is a vast scope.

The question of India's debt burdens will also have to be tackled in a scientific manner. The influence which our external debts and Home charges have on our Balance of Accounts with foreign countries can hardly be exaggerated. In spite of the fact that we have ordinarily had a large visible balance of trade, our huge foreign obligations have not infrequently caused serious anxiety to the Government in meeting the annual charges.

To my mind the best method of meeting these obligations is to create a separate Fund, into which should be annually allocated sums determined in accordance with certain fixed principles; these annual allocations should be utilised not merely for paying interest charges but also for redeeming portions of the original debts, in such a way as to wipe off the entire amount of our external debts at an early date. A similar provision made for our internal debts would facilitate conversion of loans bearing higher interest charges into those bearing lower rates, thereby relieving the burden on the general revenues.

As regards future borrowings, I would suggest that a Central Loan Council or a Council of National Debt be set up to accord sanction to the floatation of all loans and also to coordinate central and provincial borrowings. For the purpose of raising loans abroad, India must shake off her exclusive dependence on the London market and should tap other markets as well.

Allied with the question of our external debts is that of the Home charges which are a source of immense concern to the country. The reduction in these charges, which mainly consist of pensions and allowances to the past and present government officials recruited from England, has become imperative; and while the stopping of further recruitments in England altogether will in course of a number of years result in the ultimate extinction of these charges, the question of regulating their payment by paying an annuity for a fixed number of years to the British government in return for their undertaking the entire liability on this account should be carefully considered.

In view of the fact that the provinces are to secure greater autonomy with greater responsibilities for their own development and advance, the question of an equitable allocation of the resources is of primary importance. While the question has been discussed by a number of Government Committees and Commissions and settled to be only unsettled again and again, the solution still remains remote. The fundamental defect of the system, which has persisted since the Meston Award, is the allotment of comparatively inelastic sources of revenue to the provinces. Land settlement of land tenure does not prevail; excise is one in which diminishing returns have set in with the growth of an enlightened public opinion. Irrigation and forests are likewise mostly unproductive, mainly due to the fact that Governmental expenditure in these directions is quite meagre. It is, therefore, necessary to make a satisfactory re-allotment of sources of revenue with full consideration of the needs and potential of respective provinces before the Federal constitution is actually inaugurated and fresh burdens and responsibilities devolve upon the provinces. Financial justice to the federal units will constitute in itself not only a source of strength to themselves but also a reserve of potential support to the Federation.

That the administrative machinery in India is exceptionally top-heavy is an admitted fact. A poor country like India can ill afford the luxury of such expensive administration, which has always hampered the prosecution of schemes for national development. Reductions in government expenditures are also urgently required for releasing adequate funds to help in the launching of a constructive economic plan for India. I would suggest in this connection the establishment of a Commission on the lines of the American Efficiency and Economy Commission to thoroughly examine the whole question of government expenditures and suggest necessary economies consistent with efficiency. I am firmly convinced that government expenditures can be considerably curtailed without in the least impairing the efficiency of administration.

Machinery for Planning

The work which faces us requires a regulating or planning body in possession of all relevant and accurate statistical materials for a correct assessment of economic and social happenings.

The central idea is to set up a Supreme Economic Council or a National Planning Commission which will in no sense supersede either the executive or legislative limit of the government. From the working of the Tariff Board, a fruitful scheme for such a Council or Commission could be drawn. It should be composed of a permanent personnel of experts with the right to co-opt from time to time members having expert and specialised knowledge of particular problems when the Council will have to deal with such matters. Such a procedure will ensure the availability of specialised knowledge for special problems while guarding against a too circumscribed outlook or unwieldiness on the part of the Council itself. In the task of planning each particular industry, manufacturing, agricultural or extractive, must be dealt with as a whole, and the several units in any one industry must organise themselves for cooperative work. The next step would be establishment of organisations for the whole of Industry, Agriculture, Retail Trade, Foreign Trade, Banking etc., which should be able not only to represent as organised functional bodies their respective cases to the Council but also to carry out such schemes of work as may be entrusted to them. Where such embracing organisations for the whole or any particular economic aspect of life or for the separate units in any one industry do not exist, the setting up of such associations should be actively encouraged.

In respect of the provinces, too, we should have similar Economic Councils, although, in so far as the services of experts will be needed to elucidate particular problems, it will be open to them to draw on the experiences of the Central Council in addition to their right to co-opt members with specialised knowledge of mainly provincial matters.

An important function which the provincial councils will subserve is the compilation of all relevant data in regard to the various aspects of the economic life of the respective provinces. Towards this end, voluntary cooperation of universities and colleges on the one hand and of Chambers of Commerce on the other, would be found extremely valuable.

While facts and figures bearing on the situation in each province will be gathered, sifted, analysed and compiled by the provincial bodies, the Central Council will have to coordinate the results of the provincial investigations and, what is more important, to take all those measures for the expansion and enlargement of the economic statistics of the country, so as to bring them into line with the statistics maintained by progressive countries like America. The Economic Intelligence Bureau will have to be organised on a thorough and efficient basis. It would be necessary, in this connection, to ascertain how far the existing machinery of the Department of Commercial Intelligence and Statistics admits of expansion and strengthening, so as to make the kind of Economic Intelligence Bureau which it will be the prime purpose of the Central Council to provide itself with. I should again like to impress upon you a point which I have already stressed, viz., that the basic necessity of our plan is for developmental purposes. And India should be developed mainly in the interest of Indians. It is therefore incumbent that in any machinery we may set up for the formulation and execution of the plan, we should constantly bear this fact in mind.

Urgency of Action

In examining such vast problems within the limited time at my disposal, I have necessarily had to content myself with a reference to some of the principal subjects only, omitting reference to a lot of other connected subjects. An economic plan itself is only part of national planning, and the latter comprises the coordination and harmonisation of a number of other human activities which go to make up the physical, mental, moral and material well-being of the people of the country.

The great need of the moment is not only a policy of action to deal with a pressing situation, but also the provision of a new conception of social and economic organisations which will facilitate the evolution towards a healthy and stable economic system. Such a system need not involve a radical reconstruction of the economic structure. Nor need it eliminate from business the motive of personal reward. Once we have laid the foundations of a plan for economic betterment of the country as a whole, there will still be a large field of useful work for even the most hardened individualist. But unless something is done quickly, I feel, there is a limit to the sufferings that will be borne by even a traditionally patient people; and when their balance of mind has been upset by continued privations and their judgment warped by severe economic adversity, they may develop into the most fertile soil in which the violent and ruthless could sow the seeds of revolution.

Political Outlook

I have confined myself so far to the consideration of economic problems with which as businessmen we are so intimately concerned. The political situation also affects us no less vitally. Frequently, we have experienced how political conditions have thwarted activities to a greater extent than we imagine. I need not therefore apologise to you for making certain observations on the political situation.

The country had been following a certain political programme in accordance with a policy that was laid down by the most dominant political organisation of the people. The whole nation for a time supported it and the commercial community, even while it could not as a body actively participate in it, genuinely sympathised with it and helped it in various ways. It did not bring us that measure of success that was universally hoped for. The very nature of the programme is such that there are serious practical limitations to its continuance for any length of time. An extreme programme of non-violent direct action imposes severe sufferings upon and demands great sacrifices from its adherents. The stringent measures adopted by the government have also seriously affected the chances of its continuance as a mass movement. In an atmosphere of intense inter-communal clash and sectional differences, the continuance of such direct action of this kind may easily become a dangerous method. To continue to use such a weapon and at the same time prevent its inevitable reactions require a degree of national unity and discipline that is not found in India today. Civil resistance as understood and practised in India, by itself, need not necessarily be a dangerous method. But among its advocates is a group of people who view it merely as a preliminary to further extreme action for the promotion of aims and ideals about which there is not the least unanimity. In short, their ideas appear to favour a social and economic revolution, if necessary. When we examine Civil Disobedience as a method, we should not be too greatly influenced by the aims of its saintly originator, but we must also ponder deeply over what are likely to be the results, if its control and direction passed into the hands of those whose purity of motives and selfless devotion we may admire, but whose reckless disregard of consequences cannot be defended. And who can say it will not happen? As businessmen we cannot risk the creation of an atmosphere of national confusion and disintegration. It is not that Indian businessmen are afraid of financial loss. If they could be sure of achieving the aim, they would never recoil at sacrifices. But if they feel these sacrifices will not bear fruits, they cannot in fairness to themselves support that policy. This is the simple and understandable position of Indian businessmen.

At the same time we are quite aware that the government by their lack of vision and sympathy and the adoption of harsh and indefensible methods may be adding fuel to the fire of national resentment, which might at any time blaze forth again into the terrible conflagration of revolution. We are powerless to prevent it. The responsibility for it, if such a position occurs, must rest entirely with the government. We have warned against it; but warnings go unheeded, for what does government care for the opinion of the people of this country?

Now the old programme is, for all practical purposes, suspended, and no new programme has been adopted in its place. But as far as it can be seen the feeling is widespread, not merely among the commercial community but even among erstwhile active adherents of the policy and the country in general, that a definite change in the political programme, and the political methods and tactics is necessary. It is a feeling that is fully shared by businessmen all over India and I fully trust it will be given due consideration when the time for decision arrives.

Government's Attitude

Apart from the transformation in popular feelings and ideas, there have also occurred perceptible changes in the situation of the government. After the success which they feel they have achieved in checking the nationalist movement, they are naturally feeling more confident of their own powers and less inclined to respect the country's wishes. The Assembly and Councils everywhere have ceased to function as guardians of national rights or champions of national interests. The government has been able to persuade them to pass the most reactionary measures with indecent haste and surprising ease. The most unwarrantable interference with individual freedom has been openly exercised. Above all, ruthlessly oppressive measures have been incorporated into the framework of the administration. While a cloak of justification for them, however thin, might have been provided by the conditions that existed some time ago, their indefinite continuance and the continual addition to their number are not warranted by the present circumstances. But the government are arming themselves and strengthening their defences, lest under the petty concession that they contemplate in the White Paper, real power and effective control should slip out of their hands. Under the next regime it may be difficult for the government to force the legislatures to accept such measures; but under extensive and undefined powers that will certainly be vested in the Governors and the Governor-General, all attempts at their repeal can be effectively thwarted.

Paradoxical as it may appear, simultaneously with the strengthening of the bureaucratic buttresses, the Imperial Government are also considering the extension of some political concessions. The wearisome delay which marks the progress of their proposals through the interminable stages of Conferences and Committees, before they are finally placed before the Parliament signifies the seriousness with which the whole question is viewed by Britain. India's own opinion of the constitutional proposals embodied in the White Paper and the subsequent discussions in London, which constitute Britain's prescription for the solution of the Indo-British problem, has been given frank expression. Even the moderate-minded representatives that gave evidence before the Joint Parliamentary Committee did not consider them as acceptable. 'India desires,' they say, 'to shake hands with Great Britain in token of friendship based on a recognition of equality. A proposal that she should be handcuffed before she is allowed to shake hands, lest she be tempted to strike, is hardly the most expedient method of beginning a new era of cordiality and mutual understanding.' The spirit that runs through them is one of open mistrust and the proposals themselves are grossly inadequate judged even by the declaration of policy made by the Prime Minister at the end of the First Round Table Conference. They are characterised by a carefully concealed unwillingness to part with real power. Wherever there has been any concession of power it has been effectively nullified by artfully contrived checks and balances. The Governor-General's extraordinary powers and 'special responsibilities' will overshadow whatever powers may be delegated to the Ministers. The Defence Budget will be determined by the Governor-General and the Commander-in-Chief. In matters of currency, credit and exchange the previous sanction of the Governor-General will be necessary for any substantial change in the present order of things. That the Governor-General should have a special Financial Adviser (a function which in all countries is fulfilled by the Finance Minister) is an unmistakable indication that the Finance Minister is not expected to share his confidence. The constitution and powers of the new Reserve Bank have been so devised that real Indian interests will still find it difficult to gain influence. The proposal for a Statutory Railway Board is another measure that has been devised to diminish the powers of the legislature and segregate the transport organisation from popular control. The provisions relating to commercial discrimination have been so framed that, in the form which they finally assume, they may prove a powerful impediment to India's economic progress and freedom, and the strongest guarantee of the economic control of India by foreign capital. Under the plea of preventing commercial discrimination Britain is really attempting to force India to confer upon the British businessman every right, every privilege that an Indian businessman can ever enjoy. Even the idea of so-called reciprocity is receding to the background, and nobody in India can enjoy greater rights than a British businessman. This is a position which may lead to a future economic conflict many times more severe than the present political struggle.

If the situation does not improve and if the present struggle is continued, India will remain a source of increasing weakness and troubles to Great Britain. While her apparent control and the outward forms of political domination may continue, her real influence over India's life, ideas and outlook is fast dwindling. The antipathy she has aroused cannot be eradicated by 'strong measures', political palliatives or half-hearted concessions. While these facts suffice to show that under the new constitution the position will remain substantially unchanged, Britain's attitude towards India has not undergone any basic alteration. There is not even an indication as to when the tutelage will end. The position is both unsatisfactory and uncertain.

But the government seem to be changing their tactics. New methods are under their contemplation. The devices they will adopt under the new regime to retain control of the country will differ widely from the old weapons. For this reason, again, the country also would require to change its methods and instruments.

But it would be difficult to prescribe them just now before knowing the exact position and attitude of the British Government; and neither is it possible immediately to define our attitude towards them under the next regime, and even if it were possible, at the present stage, it would be eminently inadvisable. There is time yet to do that. We do not yet know in what shape the Bill will finally emerge and, therefore, it strikes me that it would not be wise to enter into speculation about our future action.

There is a section of people who seem anxious to express their willingness to work the new constitution for what it will be worth. They do not even know the ingredients of the medicine manufactured and patented in England, but they are eager to prescribe it for India. In my judgment such an attitude is not warranted by the present state of things. There is nothing to justify or support the assumption that our readiness to make an unequivocal declaration of cooperation will induce the British people to make any change in their policy or concede greater powers to us. You will pardon my inability to understand those whose zeal for cooperation under all or any circumstances still remains unabated.

Duty of the Commercial Community

I do not think the time has yet arrived for the commercial community to make any immediate decision on the question of Council entry. Our readiness to go to the Councils cannot be of any avail unless the country also decides upon such a policy. Representatives of the commercial community may go to the Councils to oppose unacceptable measures and help the initiation of beneficent ones; but unless the nation also decides to enter them the few representatives of Indian commerce can expect to do neither successfully. Some of them are in the Councils today. Are they able to prevent the enactment of any unjustifiable measures, even in the economic sphere? Are they able to influence legislation for the benefit of our economic progress? The Councils can be of some advantage to us only if they consist of the real representatives of the people on whom our representatives can rely and with whom they can work in cooperation. Until, therefore, the country decides to enter the Councils, it will be premature to make any decision ourselves in this matter. What we really ought to do is to express our views frankly so that they may exercise due influence upon the leaders when they assemble to make the final decision and, having done so, to await the decision before adopting any definite policy ourselves.

As I have already stated, the general feeling is growing that a review of our political situation and resources and a reconsideration of our political methods and tactics are necessary. The great lesson brought home to us by the events of the past few years, as I read them, is that too great a sanctity should not be attached to one particular method. Political tactics often necessitate the adoption of several weapons at the same time. The value of a method is sometimes so exaggerated, and invested with almost divine sanctity that not infrequently there is the danger of our losing sight of the goal. There may grow up an impatience of any other methods suggested for the attainment of the same goal. A tenacious loyalty to a given method is often a political asset of great value; but when you mistake it for an unalterable political principle, it may become a terrible handicap to political progress.

The soundness of a given political method should be tested not merely by its theoretical excellence, but also by its adaptability to the conditions actually prevailing and which are necessary for the achievement of success. It might be eminently desirable to have an army composed of men, every one of whom is six feet high, but by prescribing this condition as an indispensable for entry into the army you will hardly gather more than a few hundred men.

Support for Council Entry

We have in the past employed certain political methods. We should not be afraid to admit that they have not brought us the success we had hoped for. Ordinary prudence demands a change. There is nothing derogatory to a change in political methods. Considerations of false political prestige should not deter us from grasping the realities of the situation which call for a change, so long as our goal remains unchanged and our ideals unaltered. A river in its course to the sea encounters many an obstacle. If it encounters a hill in the course of its progress, it circumvents it and continues its course to the sea. So should it be with our politics.

Within the bounds of the principles of morality and the tenets of the philosophy of our life, we should have no hesitation in adopting any method that is likely to further our ends and strengthen our cause. I do not believe that we should not approach an evil thing even to mend it, not even to end it. If the leaders think that the Councils can give us strength to achieve our goal they must capture them and work them. If they believe the Councils are impediments in the path of our political progress, they must capture them and break them. In any circumstance we must prevent others from using them to pass bad laws and utilise the support of these black-legs as justification for their black laws. As instruments of self-government these Councils may not excite our enthusiasm; but when they are filled with unworthy men, they have been freely utilised as weapons against national economic interests and political aspirations. There are men in the present Assembly and Councils, who, merely to win the applause of the Treasury Bench and gain the favour of the Government, have deprived great national institutions, political and commercial. There are yet others who could not have retained their seats except by fanning the same hateful flame. The opinions and actions of these men are being paraded before the world as those of the country. Should this at least not be prevented from happening again?

The Indian commercial community has always helped the political organisations in all legitimate endeavours to attain Swaraj, and will, I am sure, continue to do so. But the national leaders should take into consideration all our circumstances and limitations so that our humble cooperation and services may also be useful for the advancement of the country's cause. Our future political methods should be such that every man who loves his country will have an opportunity to make some contribution, however small, towards its advancement. We the commercial community desire to march with our countrymen. Do not exclude us by taking a route we cannot follow or prescribing methods we cannot use.

Conclusion

Gentlemen, I have now about done, but before I resume my seat I must extend to you my sincere thanks for the honour you conferred on me by electing me your President for the year. It is an honour which I highly covet, it is a privilege to have served you and this is the happiest moment of my life. There are few more honourable positions to which an Indian may aspire than the presidentship of this important body representing the vast interests of Indian trade, commerce and industry. I would ask you to pardon the length of my speech but I thought it necessary to bring to your attention these matters which are so greatly exercising our minds today, and also what urgently calls to be done to improve the country's economic condition. I hope, therefore, that the proceedings which follow will be really constructive and helpful. It is hardly necessary for me to urge upon you, that a tremendous responsibility rests on the Indian commercial community; for, on them devolves to a larger extent than any other section of the people, the duty of sailing the economic vessel past the shoals and quick sands that threaten a safe anchorage.

~

SUBHAS CHANDRA BOSE

National Planning

As president of the Indian National Congress in 1938, Subhas Chandra Bose constituted the Planning Committee under the chairmanship of Jawaharlal Nehru. This speech delivered at the inauguration of the All-India National Planning Committee at Bombay, on 17 December 1938, spells out the vision Bose had for the Indian economy.

During the last few weeks I have noticed an apprehension in certain quarters as to the possible effects of our efforts at industrial planning on the movement that has been going on since 1921 for the production of *khadi* and the promotion of cottage industries under the auspices of the All-India Spinners Association and the All-India Village Industries Association respectively. It may be remembered that at Delhi I made it perfectly clear that there was no inherent conflict between cottage industries and large-scale industries. As a matter of fact, I divided industries into three classes: cottage, medium-scale and large-scale industries, and I pleaded for a plan which would lay down the scope of each of these classes. Not only that. In the National Planning Committee we have reserved a seat for a representative of the All-India Village Industries Association and a similar seat could also be arranged for the All-India Spinners Association. It would be doing us a grave injustice if it be urged or even apprehended that the promoters of the

National Planning Committee want to sabotage the movement for the revival of cottage industries.

Everybody knows or should know that even in the most industrially advanced countries in Europe and Asia e.g., Germany and Japan, there are plenty of cottage industries which are in a flourishing condition. Why then should we have any apprehension with regard to our own country?

I may now add a few remarks on the relation between cottage industries and large-scale industries. Among large-scale industries, mother industries are the most important because they aim at producing the means of production. They put into the hands of artisans necessary appliances and tools for facilitating quicker and cheaper production. For example, if in the city of Banaras we could supply electrically-driven looms along with electrical power at the rate of half-anna per unit, it would be possible for the artisans working in their own homes to turn out *sarees* and embroidered cloth of different varieties at about five or six times the present rate of production, and it would enable them to compete successfully with foreign imported goods of this description. With a good marketing organisation and an organisation for the supply of raw materials, these artisans can be rescued from the depths of poverty and misery to which they have fallen.

This is not the only instance which I can give. If the power industry and the machinery manufacturing industries are controlled by the State for the welfare of the nation, a large number of light industries like the manufacture of bicycles, fountain pens and toys can be started in this country by men of the artisan class working with the family as a unit. This is exactly what has been done in Japan: success depends entirely upon the fact that power and machinery are extremely cheap and the Japanese Government have set up boards for the supply of raw materials and for proper marketing. I believe that this is the only way by means of which the handloom industry and the silk industry of our country can be revived.

The National Planning Committee will have to tackle specific problems. It will have first to direct its attention to the mother industries i.e. those industries which make the other industries run successfully—such as the power industry, industries for the production of metals, heavy chemicals, machinery and tools, and communication industries like railway, telegraph, telephone, and radio.

Our country is backward in respect of power supply compared

with industrially advanced countries. In the matter of electrical power particularly, India's backwardness can be gauged from the fact that while we have at present only seven units per head, a backward country like Mexico has ninety-six units per head and Japan about five hundred units per head. In developing electrical power, the Government has squandered money: take the instance of the Mandi hydro-electric scheme on which the Government have spent ten times as much as other countries have done on similar efforts.

How I wish an enquiry could be made into the manufacture of machinery and machine tools with a view to keeping up supplies in the event of interruption of communications with foreign countries owing to war or any other causes. The other key industries into which an enquiry should be started are the fuel, metal production and heavy chemical industries. In this respect the resources of the country have not been properly investigated. Whatever little industries there is, is being controlled by foreigners, with the result that there is a lot of wastage. This is particularly true of the fuel industry.

The last key industry is the transport and communications industry which includes railways, steamships, electrical communications, radio, etc. At present the railways are controlled by the Railway Board which is entirely under European management, and only a small fraction of the requirements of railways is manufactured in the country. As regards steam navigation, excepting coastal traffic, the entire communication is in the hands of non-Indians owing to unfair privileges enjoyed by them. Electrical goods are entirely supplied by foreign countries. As regards radio, I would like to suggest the setting up of a special sub-committee to investigate its possibilities.

Lastly, we will have to consider the most important problem of finding the necessary capital and credit for our plan of industrialisation. Unless this problem is solved, all our plans will remain mere paper schemes and we shall not make any headway in industrial progress.

~

PRASANTA CHANDRA MAHALANOBIS

Studies Related to Planning for National Development

P.C. Mahalanobis (1893–1972) was a reputed scientist and statistician, best known for the Mahalanobis Distance, a statistical measure, and for his pioneering contribution to large-scale sample surveys. He was the founder of the Indian Statistical Institute which was responsible for the operational research related to the planning for the Second Five Year Plan (1956–61) which envisaged the rapid industrialization of India. The following speech was delivered at the Indian Statistical Institute, Calcutta, on 3 November 1954 in the presence of Jawaharlal Nehru who had come to inaugurate the discipline of studies relating to planning for national development. The speech details the scientific model—the Mahalanobis Model—adopted for the Second Five Year Plan and the vision behind it.

Different models of economic growth are being constructed and studied on the basis of different sets of relations (sometimes expressed in a mathematical form) between relevant varieties. The object of making different models is to explore a wide range of possibilities which would give some guidance in the choice of the basic approaches. A brief explanation is given in this note of one type of approach. It is convenient to use numerical examples to explain the general procedure. But the figures given here are used purely for purposes of illustration and no special significance should be attached to them. In fact, the aim of the group studies relating to planning is to make realistic estimates of these figures.

We assume that the net output of the economy is 100 of which 94 is consumer goods and services and 6 is capital goods. We desire to increase the share of capital goods to an average of 10 per cent. This would have to be done gradually. In the beginning, we may have to import much capital goods from abroad. But it would be clearly more economical to manufacture capital goods within the country. (For example, we are at present importing machinery from abroad to build factories for the production of steel. It is obviously desirable to construct a sufficiently large workshop to build factories for steel production.) This means developing the capital goods industries, that is, increasing the production of investment in capital goods enterprises as much as possible. At present only a small portion, possibly less than 10 per cent, of all investments goes to capital goods industries. From preliminary studies it seems that this proportion would have to be increased to, say, 30 per cent to double the national income in 20 years. From the long-range viewpoint, it would do still better to push up the share of heavy industries to 40 or over 50 per cent but this may be too difficult to accomplish and too great a sacrifice of the present for the benefit of the future. We may, therefore, adopt 30 per cent as the share of capital goods industries for purposes of illustration—this means an allocation of 3 per cent of net national income or about Rs. 300 crores for investment in capital goods industries every year.

Having allocated 30 per cent of the investment to capital goods industries, we may proceed to give, say, 20 per cent to investments in large factories to manufacture consumer goods, 25 per cent to agriculture and small industries, and 25 per cent to services. On the basis of an initial investment rate of Rs. 600 crores per year allocated in the way mentioned above it is possible to study the changes in the national economy in 10 years. We shall assume that the ratio of new income generated to capital investment is one-fourth in the case of large-scale enterprises to produce both capital and consumer goods, half in the case of agriculture and small industries, and one in planned services. We also assume for purposes of illustration that the average amount of investment required per engaged person is Rs. 10,000 for capital goods industries, Rs. 7,500 for consumer goods factories, and Rs. 1,000 for agriculture, small industries and services. On certain plausible assumptions (and using a particular form of a model of economic growth) it seems that at the end of 5 years the rate of investment would increase to about Rs. 860 crores per year; national income would increase by 17 per cent, and new jobs created every year would be as large as nearly 48 lakhs. The rate of development would, however, become more rapid as time progresses.

At the end of 10 years, the rate of investment would rise to over Rs. 1,200 crores, national income would increase by 42 per cent, and employment by nearly 70 lakhs of jobs. (In fact, such an increase of employment may not be even necessary in which case the investment in small industries may be fixed at a lower level.)

In addition to the planned or directed investments (through, for example, the existing control over capital issues) it is assumed that there would be an unplanned sector; and also that it is possible to work out the relation and interaction between the planned and the unplanned sectors. On the basis of such interaction it would be possible to make a rough estimate of the total increase in national income and the portion available for consumption.

At this stage it is necessary to consider the distribution of the increase in income among the population. In principle, the distribution of income can be controlled to some extent through taxation and other financial measures. It is, therefore, possible, in principle, to lay down certain targets in the distribution of income. (This in fact is one of the important responsibilities of Planning Authorities.)

Once the desired distribution of income is settled, it would be possible to consider the change in the demand of consumer goods and services. Purchasing power would increase with rising income; and the demand for goods and services would increase in a definite way depending on the nature of the commodities or services. Intensive studies have been started on the basis of the data collected by the National Sample Survey to find out how the consumption of particular commodities or services actually changes with increasing levels of per capita expenditure. For example, it seems that if the income increases by 30 per cent, the consumption of salt may increase by only 8 per cent, of cereals by 12 per cent and of cotton textiles by 25 per cent. (These are illustrative figures and should not be taken as actual estimates.)

The above change in consumption with increasing income refers, of course, to different households or individuals at the same point of time. It is not unreasonable to assume that, as a first approximation, a similar change would take place when the income of the same households or individual increases over time. On this assumption and with any given (desired) distribution of income it is possible, in principle, to make a rough estimate of the total increases in demand of different consumer goods and services. This gives a basis to settle the supply of goods required to meet the increased demand. But it is not necessary to accept the figures exactly as estimated. It is possible, within certain limits, to make suitable adjustments from social or administrative considerations. For example, the supply of certain luxury items may be deliberately kept low or the supply of certain items like, say, education or health services may be increased. (Such adjustments would be naturally the responsibility of the Planning Authorities.) After such adjustments, the requirements of consumer goods would become available.

At the same time it would be necessary to decide the requirements of capital goods which would naturally depend on the programme of investment. Consideration would be also given to imports and exports. It may be decided, for example, to meet certain portions of the requirements (of both capital and consumer goods) through imports. It would be necessary at the same time to settle what additional quantities of which commodities would have to be produced and exported to meet the cost of imports. In this way the final planned bill of goods (to meet estimated requirements of consumption, investment, and export) which would have to be produced in the country, would become known.

Next comes the crucial step of examining whether the required additional bill of goods and services can be in fact produced and supplied with the help of the investments of different types for which allocation had been actually made. It would be necessary at this stage to consider the detailed breakdowns of production of commodities and the supply of services. The economic and technological relations between investment, income, and employment in different industries would have to be used at this stage for which intensive studies would be indispensable. (Work on a small scale has been already started.) If the desired requirements of goods and services can be supplied through appropriate investments in different industries within the limits of the allocated resources, then a solution would have been reached. It would be then possible to proceed with the detailed planning within the broad frame of the solution adopted by the Planning Authorities.

Further problems would arise as the programme of investment and production becomes more and more concrete. One industry would sell its products to various other industries. Also it would get its needs from other industries. For example, to produce one additional million ton of steel it is necessary to produce (or import) two additional million tons of coal, two additional million tons of iron ore, and additional quantities of many other materials such as manganese ore, dolomite, magnesite, fluxes, refractories, etc. Moreover, fixed and working capital requirements of one industry would be supplied by many other industries, and its own product would be used as fixed and working capital in other industries. Thus the whole industrial structure is closely interlocked, and in order to conceive of a change in the level of production of one commodity it is necessary to give consideration to the change in output of many other industries. When an approximate allocation of investments is ready, the anticipated consumer expenditure is known, and the requirements of final flows of consumer goods have been settled, it would be necessary to work out the total output of the different industries (inclusive of all intermediate products and consistent with the bill of final goods). This can be done with the help of inter-industry relations (sometimes called input-output tables). Work is already in progress in 12 sectors (that is, a 12 x 12 table); and arrangements are being made to prepare a 90 x 90 table. Later on, it is proposed to consider the interrelation and two-way distribution of fixed and working capital.

In the present approach the essential aim is to adopt a pattern of investments which by developing the capital goods industries would make available a larger and larger supply of capital goods produced within the country and thus make it possible to increase progressively the rate of investment and hence the rate of economic development in the desired way. A larger rate of investments would mean an increase in employment and in salary and wage payments leading to an increase in purchasing power which in its turn would create a larger demand for goods and services. One aim of planning must be to meet the increase in demand by a commensurate increase in the production of the required goods and in the supply of the required services. If this is feasible, a possible solution at the technological level would be available (which may or may not be acceptable depending on other considerations). If the expected requirements cannot be met by the anticipated production, then changes would have to be made in the investment plan until this condition is broadly satisfied. The acceptable solution must also satisfy, as far as possible, the condition of attaining full employment in, say, 10 years. If there is more than one solution satisfying the two basic conditions mentioned above, it would be possible to introduce supplementary conditions relating to the increase of income or the distribution of income.

One condition in the aggregate is, of course, that the total production of consumer goods should equal the total personal income after tax deductions together with current payments by public administration other than transfers and factor incomes. It is desirable that this balance should be maintained year by year, and not merely reached at the end of the plan period. It would be difficult to attain this balance during periods of large-scale capital construction because the new capital stock realised is not consumable. Gaps between demand and supply would no doubt sometimes emerge and short-range correctives (in the way of price controls, rationing, etc.) may be necessary from time to time.

It is necessary but not sufficient to work out a plan, in physical terms; the financial counterpart must also be worked out. The most important question here is to find financial means to increase investment from, say, 5 or 6 to 10 per cent of national income. It is possible to use the investment plan itself to help in this matter. For example, new investments can be made entirely or mostly in the public sector so that 'profits' or the surplus can be utilised for further investments. (Ploughing back of profits in existing private enterprises can be permitted to the desired extent to enable production being increased at marginal outlay.) Excise duties can be levied at the point of production in large-scale industries in the private sector and the proceeds used for national development. Further expansion of large-scale manufacture of such consumer goods as can be produced through handicrafts or small industries can be discouraged or prohibited for some time which would make available more resources for capital goods industries and other sectors. Factory production of consumer goods may, however, be arranged, preferably in the public sector, in the case of essential commodities, or goods for export, or finally, 'luxury' goods on which it is possible to earn very high profit.

The model described here, however, definitely contemplates a large increase in small industries to supply as much as possible the increasing demand in the short run. After full employment has been attained, and the capital goods industries have been developed fairly well, it would be possible and desirable to increase the rate of industrialisation by drawing away labour from agriculture and small industries. At this stage there would be no danger of creating unemployment through the expansion of large-scale factory industries.

It would be probably desirable to give immediate attention to increase production to full capacity in both large and small industries, and also to increase productivity by all other means such as working 2 or 3 shifts, because all this can be done with a very small outlay of capacity and also because this would create a good deal of employment. The question of surplus production would emerge which may require government purchases on a large scale to build up inventories which would be used to meet the increase in demand later on. Government trading may be of help in this connexion and may also be useful in earning profits to be utilised for economic development. Suitable excise duties at the point of production and planned profits at the stage of distribution can serve the dual purpose of securing resources for investment and of promoting an egalitarian level of living by imposing higher differential duties or profits on luxury goods.

In dealing with the programme of industrial production one most important question would be an adequate supply of trained personnel at all levels. This may indeed prove to be a serious bottleneck. Attention would, therefore, have to be given to estimate the requirements of trained personnel and to make necessary provision to give training to the required number in each field. Input-output tables in respect of manpower would be of help in this connexion. Studies are also being started in this field. In addition, suitable provision will have to be made to ensure an adequate supply of services personnel including health, education, research, etc.

~

JAWAHARLAL NEHRU

The Second Five Year Plan

Economic planning in India is carried out through five-year plans, developed, executed and monitored by the Planning Commission. In the history of India's five-year plans, the Second Five Year Plan is crucial because it laid down industrialization as the basis for the all-round economic growth of the country. The plan focused on industry, particularly heavy industries. Nehru (in association with P.C. Mahalanobis) was personally responsible for drafting the plan and hence his speech initiating the debate on the plan in the Lok Sabha on 23 May 1956 is one of the most important speeches in the economic history of the nation.

We are engaged in the shaping of the future of India. Surely, there could be few subjects more exciting than this. It is, therefore, with a sense of the burden of history upon me and upon this House, that I face this problem. It is also with a great sense of humility, because, however great and however competent we may consider ourselves, we are small in relation to this mighty theme of building up our country and taking its millions of people forward during the next five years.

These five years are only some kind of a period that we fix for our convenience, because there are no isolated periods in the march of a nation. It is a continuous march. We must really think in terms of even longer periods and in terms of several Five-Year Plans. This is the second. Nobody thinks that at the end of the Second Plan we shall have been at the end of our journey. There is no journey's end when a nation is marching. Leaving out the ultimate ends, even such a goal as we envisage, the objective of a socialist pattern of society, is not going to be achieved at the end of the First Five-Year Plan or the Second. It may require three or four Five-Year Plan periods before we can say with some confidence that we have very largely achieved it. Therefore, we must keep this larger perspective in view. In planning, especially, we are apt to forget the larger perspective and lose ourselves in some particular aspect which is of importance and yet which may very well come in the way of the larger perspective. For example, take the question of regional development. We are all agreed that there should be a uniform development all over India. We are all agreed that disparities, not only as between individuals in regard to income, but as between the various areas in India, should be removed, that there should be equality of growth and opportunity all over India. But, if we start applying that principle regardless of the other objectives and perspectives, we may spoil the whole Plan. We may not have very much to give to any region. Therefore, in looking at the Five-Year Plan, we have to think really of several Five-Year Plans. That is why it is becoming more and more important that we should, in addition to the period we are dealing with, have a longer perspective in view.

The Second Five-Year Plan necessarily deals with what might be called material objectives. They are very important because it is on the basis of certain material achievements that we can build other achievements. The Plan deals to some extent, no doubt, with culture and like matters. Nevertheless, it confines itself chiefly to material advance. That does not mean that we in this House attach no importance to other aspects of human life. Indeed, all the material advance that we may achieve may, perhaps, be worth nothing at all and may avail us little, if we forget the moral, spiritual and other aspects of human life.

We stand in the middle of the twentieth century, and this period has seen far-reaching changes all over the world. There have been wars and revolutions. The tempo of change is very great. Any plan that we make, like this Five-Year Plan, is subject to the great political, economic and technological changes that we are witnessing.

All of us have some kind of ideology, some kind of philosophy of life. We may not be philosophers, but without some kind of philosophical or ideological approach, we would have no yardstick to measure things by. And yet, our ideologies and philosophies of life somehow do not fit in with this middle of the twentieth century. This may be due to the fact that though facts change and circumstances become different, we still hold on to old lines of thinking. The human mind is singularly conservative, and it does not change easily. We hold on, if I may venture to say so, to some out-of-date philosophical or ideological approaches. Take the question of war. Many people say that because of various developments in the world, war has become, or ought to become, out of the question. War was useful—whether good or bad—if it helped you to realise your objective. When it does not do that, when in fact it does the reverse, then no person should indulge in war.

I should like to extend that parallel a little further. If a war, atomic or other, is now something that can only be considered excessively foolish, cold war becomes more and more absurd. Cold war exists; it goes on, but really, analysed in the circumstances of today, it has little meaning.

Likewise, certain other approaches—some economic approaches, which may have a great deal of truth—just do not fit in with the present circumstances. The major fact of today is the stupendous growth of technology, the tremendous growth of the productive apparatus of society, the tremendous power that human beings possess and are likely to possess in the form of atomic energy. These things are not quantitative changes, but qualitative changes in society.

Of course, in India we have not been very powerfully affected by the technological process. We have read about it, but we have no real sensation of it. In planning, however, we have to think in technological terms, because it is this growth of science and technology that has enabled man to produce wealth on a scale nobody could even dream of earlier. It is technology which has made other countries wealthy and prosperous, and it is only through the growth of technology that we shall become a wealthy and prosperous nation.

If you looked at the picture of India—and that would apply to many other countries under colonial rule—ten years ago or twelve years ago, you would find a static, even a stagnant society. Either we remained where we were or we even went backwards. I shall mention a few figures. Take, for instance, the post-war period. In 1948-49, the national income was Rs. 8,650 crores, and the per capita income Rs. 246.9. In the next year, the national income was Rs. 8,820 crores, and the per capita income Rs. 248.6. In 1950, just before the First Five-Year Plan, the national income was Rs. 8,850 crores, and per capita income Rs. 246—that is, it had slightly come down even from 248. You see the national income remaining more or less the same, or very slightly creeping up, and the per capita income remaining the same or going down. Meanwhile, of course, the population has kept growing.

This was the state of affairs for several decades before the First Five-Year Plan began functioning. At the end of the First Five-Year Plan, we have a national income of Rs. 10,800 crores—nothing very remarkable, but nevertheless significant. The per capita income has gone up from Rs. 246 to Rs. 281 at the end of the First Five-Year Plan period.

As I said, there have been far greater increases in other countries where the pace of development has been greater. Nevertheless, the First Five-Year Plan made a significant change in the nature of our static and stagnant economy. It broke that barrier of poverty which is the curse of a poor country and out of which it can hardly grow, because poverty breeds poverty. I do not say that the First Five-Year Plan has broken down the entire barrier, but it has made the first effective breach in that barrier in regard to national income and in regard to per capita income. Now, in the Second Plan, we have to make a bigger breach.

In many countries, it so happens, the old rule prevails: unto those that have, more shall be given, and from those that have not, even what they have might be taken away. So the poor countries remain poor and the rich countries become richer and richer, with more surplus, more investment, more production. So it goes on. The rate of progress in some countries, from reports that we see, is 5 per cent per annum, 6 per cent or even 10 per cent or 11 per cent.

We have aimed at 5 per cent in this Plan, and 5 per cent is going to be a hard job. We shall have to work very hard, because we have started at such a low level, with such low surpluses. India is almost at the lowest rung of the income ladder. Even China, I believe, is a little higher. So was Russia at the time of the Revolution.

The First Five-Year Plan has, as I said, made a significant breach in this barrier which prevents a poor country from going ahead. How does the Planning Commission think of the future? Naturally, it is an estimate; nevertheless, it is not purely guesswork; it is based on such thinking and statistics as we possess. I have just told you that at the end of the First Five-Year Plan period, the national income is Rs. 10,800 crores. At the end of the Second Plan period, we expect it to reach Rs. 13,480 crores and the per capita income to go up from Rs. 281 to Rs. 331. For the Third Plan period, we envisage the national income going up to Rs. 17,260 crores and the per capita income to Rs. 396. For the Fourth Plan—that will take us to 1971—the national income is expected to go up to Rs. 21,680 crores and per capita income to Rs. 546. This is some kind of a rough estimate of what we think the progress of India might be in the next twenty-year period.

This depends on many factors that are uncertain. The whole idea of the Planning Commission may be upset to our advantage by new developments in science and technology. The Planning Commission cannot tell us what scientific and technological developments will come about. Therefore, we may go ahead faster. On the other hand, if by some misfortune we cannot work as hard as we hope the country will, we may not achieve our target.

We have often repeated that this Plan is a flexible Plan. What does that mean? It does not mean that it is a vague Plan for us to change and throw about, or for us to say, 'If we cannot achieve this, we shall fix a lower target or extend the period by another year or two.' It does not mean that. Naturally, if by *force majeur* it becomes absolutely impossible for us to do anything, we cannot help it. But by flexible I do not mean that these targets are loose targets. We want to achieve them; we are going to try to achieve them.

I may tell the House that even after the preparation of this report there has been a change. While considering it, just previous to its printing, the National Development Council refused to accept one of the main targets that we had laid down, something of vast importance to us, the target for production of food grains. The National Development Council thought the target was too low. It directed that it must be raised, not raised by a little. The figure that is given in the book, I believe, is 15 per cent additional food production in the next five years. The National Development Council felt that this was totally inadequate and said we must try to achieve 40 per cent or at least 35 to 40 per cent. It is a very great jump from 15 to 40 per cent. Were we just engaging in wishful thinking? No, I think it is possible to achieve nearly 40 pet cent increase.

So the House will see that even as the report is prepared, and even as we here in Parliament are considering it, our minds go further. It is in that sense that the Plan is flexible. We shall consider the targets every year, and vary them, if we think it necessary.

We are now going to have annual plans. Every year a report of the Annual Plan will be placed here which will give a more precise indication of the targets for that year. I hope to place a report of the Annual Plan of the first year of the Second Five-Year Plan before this House during the next session.

~

JAWAHARLAL NEHRU

Temples of the New Age

Dedicating the Bhakra Nangal Dam to the nation, Jawaharlal Nehru called it and others like it the 'temples of Modern India', monuments to a nationalistic vision of modernization and growth. After independence, India went on to build more than 3000 dams which it believed would improve quality of life by providing drinking water to many, while supporting economic growth by diverting water for power and irrigation to fields. And indeed, India's irrigation systems have enabled the country to be self-sufficient in food production since 1974. For the idealistic generation of leaders immediately after independence, involved in the task of building a nation, projects like Bhakra Nangal, Damodar Valley and Hirakud were part of a sacred vision. This is a translation of the speech Nehru made in Hindi while inaugurating the Nangal Canal on 8 July 1954.

I have occasion frequently these days to participate in functions marking the inauguration of some new work or completion of some other. Today, you and I and all these persons have gathered here on one such occasion. I want to know from you what you think and feel in your minds and hearts on this occasion, because in my heart and mind there is a strange exhilaration and excitement, and many kinds of pictures come before me. Many dreams we have dreamt are today drawing near and being materialised. For the materialisation of these dreams, we may praise one another, and those who have done good work should be praised. But how many can be praised when the list runs to thousands, nay, lakhs?

Let us give praise where it is due. The work which we see today, and in the inauguration of which we are participating, is much bigger than our individual selves. It is a tremendous thing. I have told you that I, and undoubtedly many of you, have frequent occasion to participate in various functions. A foundation stone is laid somewhere; a building, a hospital, a school or a university is opened elsewhere. Big factories are going up. Such activity is taking place all over the country because Mother India is producing various kinds of things. Among them, Bhakra-Nangal has a special place—Bhakra-Nangal where a small village stood, but which today is a name singing in every corner of India and in some parts of the world too; because this is a great work, the mark of a great enterprise.

About fifty years ago, an Englishman came here and for the first time had the idea that something could be done at this place, but the idea did not materialise. The matter was raised many times. Some rough plans were made but they were not pursued. Then India became free. In the process, the Punjab suffered a great shock and a grievous wound. But despite the shock and the wound, freedom brought a new strength, a new enthusiasm. And so with the wound, the worries and calamities, came this new enthusiasm and new strength to take up this big work. And we took it up. I have come here frequently. Many of you also must have come and seen this slowly changing picture and felt something stirring deep within you. What a stupendous, magnificent work—a work which only that nation can take up which has faith and boldness! This is a work which does not belong only to the Punjab, or PEPSU or the neighbouring States, but to the whole of India.

India has undertaken other big works which are not much smaller than this. Damodar Valley, Hirakud and the big projects of the South are going on apace. Plans are being made every day because we are anxious to build a new India as speedily as possible, to lead it forward, to make it strong and to remove the poverty of its people. We are doing all this, and Bhakra-Nangal in many respects will be one of the greatest of these works, because a very big step in this direction is being taken here today after years of endeavour. Every work we complete in India gives fresh strength to the nation to undertake new tasks. Bhakra-Nangal is a landmark not merely because the water will flow here and irrigate large portions of the Punjab, PEPSU, Rajasthan and fertilise the deserts of Rajasthan, or because enough electric power will be generated here to run thousands of factories and cottage industries which will provide work for the people and relieve unemployment. It is a landmark because it has become the symbol of a nation's will to march forward with strength, determination and courage. That is why, seeing this work, my courage and strength have increased, because nothing is more encouraging than to capture our dreams and give them real shape.

Just before coming to Nangal, I was in Bhakra where the dam is being built. I stood on the banks of the Sutlej and saw the mountains to the right and left. Far away, at various spots, people were working. Since it was a holiday, there was not much work going on, for all the people had come here. Still there were a few persons working. From a distance they looked very small against the mighty-looking mountain through which a tunnel was being bored. The thought came to me that it was these very men who had striven against the mountains and brought them under control.

What is now complete is only half the work. We may celebrate its completion but we must remember that the most difficult part still remains to be done—the construction of the dam about which you have heard so much. Our engineers tell us that probably nowhere else in the world is there a dam as high as this. The work bristles with difficulties and complications. As I walked round the site I thought that these days the biggest temple and mosque and gurdwara is the place where man works for the good of mankind. Which place can be greater than this, this Bhakra-Nangal, where thousands and lakhs of men have worked, have shed their blood and sweat and laid down their lives as well? Where can be a greater and holier place than this, which we can regard as higher?

Then again it struck me that Bhakra-Nangal was like a big university where we can work and while working learn, so that we may do bigger things. The nation is marching forward and every day the pace becomes faster. As we learn the work and gain experience, we advance with greater speed. Bhakra-Nangal is not a work of this moment only, because the work which we are doing at present is not only for our own times but for coming generations and future times.

Another thought came to my mind when I saw the Sutlej. Where has it come from? What course has it traversed to reach here? Do you know where the Sutlej springs from? It rises near Mount Kailash in the vicinity of Mansarovar. The Indus rises nearby. The Brahmaputra also flows from that place in a different direction, reaching India and Pakistan after traversing thousands of miles. Other rivers rise from places nearby and flow from Tibet towards China. So the Sutlej traverses hundreds of miles through the Himalayas to reach here and we have tried to control her in a friendly way. You have seen the two big diversion channels. At present the whole river has been channelled through one canal. After the rains we will divert the river completely in the two channels so that the dam might be built there.

I look far, not only towards Bhakra-Nangal, but towards this our country, India, whose children we are. Where is she going? Where have we to lead her, which way have we to walk and what mighty tasks have we to undertake? Some of these will be completed in our lifetime. Others will be taken up and completed by those who come after us. The work of a nation or a country is never completed. It goes on and no one can arrest its progress—the progress of a living nation.

We have to press forward. The question is which way we have to take, how we should proceed, what principles, what objectives we have to keep before us. All these big questions crop up. This is not an occasion to tell you about them but we have to remember them always and not forget them. When we undertake a big work we have to do so with a large heart and a large mind. Small minds or small-minded nations cannot undertake big works. When we see big works our stature grows with them, and our minds open out a little.

~

HOMI JEHANGIR BHABHA

Development of Atomic Energy in India

A nuclear physicist who played a major role in developing India's atomic energy programme, H.J. Bhabha (1909–66) is considered the father of India's nuclear weapons programme. He was instrumental in setting up the Tata Institute of Fundamental Research while at the same time guiding India into the atomic age, albeit for peaceful purposes. Towards this end he established the Atomic Energy Commission in 1948. The construction of India's first atomic power plant began at Tarapur, Maharashtra, in 1963. The process reached its climax on 18 May 1974 when India became the sixth country to join the nuclear club, following the explosion of a nuclear device at Pokaran. On 3 August 1964, Bhabha delivered a talk over the radio in which he discussed the strides the country had made in atomic energy since 1954 when the Department of Atomic Energy was created by the Government of India.

The decision of the Government of India to develop atomic energy in India in an important way may be said to have been taken when the Department of Atomic Energy was created on August 3, 1954. Some limited steps had already been taken before that date. An Atomic Energy Commission, which acted essentially as an advisory body to the Department of Scientific Research and later the Ministry of Natural Resources and Scientific Research, was established in 1948. It had virtually to start from scratch as it did not have the benefit of a nucleus of scientists who had participated in the development of atomic energy during the war years, as did several advanced countries.

Fortunately, the Commission could draw upon the help of the Tata Institute of Fundamental Research which was founded in 1945 as a joint endeavour on the part of the Sir Dorab Tata Trust and the then Government of Bombay. The Government of India had already joined the enterprise; and the Institute, which is today the National Centre of the Government of India for Advanced Study and for Fundamental Research in Nuclear Science and Mathematics, owes its great development to the support it has received from the Government of India.

One of the first activities undertaken by this Institute for the Atomic Energy Commission was the setting up of a small electronics group which has developed today into the Electronics Division of the Atomic Energy Establishment at Trombay, the largest research and development group in electronics in the country, with over 170 scientists and engineers and a total staff of about 760. It is of interest to recall that the control system of Apsara, India's first reactor, was built in a wartime hutment on the site where the Institute stands today. If the Trombay Establishment has been able to develop so rapidly, it is largely due to the assisted takeoff which was provided by the Institute, which can rightly be called the cradle of India's atomic energy programme. The Tata Institute of Fundamental Research is today the largest of India's national laboratories with the sole exception of the Atomic Energy Establishment at Trombay, and is a centre of world renown in its specialised fields of physics and mathematics.

The decision to set up the Atomic Energy Establishment at Trombay was taken by the Atomic Energy Commission in January 1954. The Trombay Establishment is today by far the largest scientific and technical research institution in the country, with a staff of some 1,550 scientists and engineers, and a total staff of nearly 7,000. Indeed, this centre has a larger scientific and technical staff than the entire Council of Scientific and Industrial Research or the Defence Organisation of the Government of India.

The policy has been followed from the very beginning to develop all the technology of atomic energy at Trombay without reliance on foreign assistance. The decision to build our first reactor was taken by the Commission in March 1955, and the reactor became critical for the first time on August 4, 1956. Although the fuel elements for it, which contain enriched uranium, were supplied by the United Kingdom Atomic Energy Authority, the reactor itself was designed and built entirely by Indian scientists and engineers. It is interesting to note that at that time, except for the United Kingdom, France, Sweden and Norway, most other European countries still had no reactors of their own, but were in the course of purchasing them from the United States. Apsara was the first reactor in Asia outside the USSR, and helped to push forward India's atomic programme in an important way.

The next reactor, the Canada-India Reactor, was built with Canadian assistance. It is a powerful 40 MW research reactor adapted for engineering experiments, and also one of the largest isotope producers in the world. While the reactor itself was supplied by Canada and its erection was Canadian responsibility, most of the erection was in fact done by Indian personnel. The largest number of Canadian staff at any time did not exceed 30, while the total number of engineers and skilled artisans employed was about 1,200. The first charge of the reactor was supplied half from Canada and half from India. To do this a uranium metal plant was designed and built by Indian engineers at Trombay which produced its first ingot of uranium metal in January 1959. A fuel element fabrication plant was also set up by Indian scientists and engineers and the first prototype fuel element for the Canada-India Reactor was ready in June 1959. Indian fuel elements have been very satisfactory from the very beginning. The performance of the fuel elements fabricated at Trombay has been as good as those of any corresponding fuel elements. When one recalls that the production of fuel elements is considered to be one of the most difficult and critical jobs in this field, the achievement of Indian metallurgists and engineers is something to be proud of. It has placed India among about half-a-dozen countries in the world which make their own fuel elements today.

The next step was to build a plant for treating used fuel elements and extracting from them the very valuable fissile material, plutonium. It is this material which will form the bridge to the use of thorium for the generation of electricity from atomic energy. The construction of a plutonium plant was completed early this year, and it is now undergoing trial runs with active fuel. A plutonium plant is one of the most sophisticated types of chemical plants and has several special features. First of all the plant treats highly radioactive material, the activity of which may run into hundreds of thousands curies, i.e. an activity equivalent to that of several hundred thousand grammes of radium. Consequently all its operations have to be done by remote control from behind 4 to 6 feet thick walls of concrete.

At the last stage, when plutonium has been separated in a pure form another danger has to be guarded against. Plutonium being a fissile material, a chain reaction starts spontaneously if more than a certain critical amount of it accumulates in any one place, and this may result in an explosive liberation of radiation and fission products. The plant has therefore to be so designed that such an accidental criticality is virtually impossible. The design and construction of this plant by Indian scientists and engineers is a considerable achievement. There are only four other countries with operating plutonium plants—France, the UK, the USA, the USSR; Norway also has a small pilot plant.

India has long been known to have the largest deposits of thorium in the world in the monazite sands of Kerala, but the efforts of the Atomic Minerals Division have led to the discovery of even larger deposits of monazite on the borders of Bengal and Bihar. It has also led to the discovery of substantial deposits of uranium in Bihar. One of these deposits is being developed industrially, and a uranium mine is being opened in this area. A uranium mill to produce uranium-concentrates from this ore by treating a thousand tonnes of ore per day is also being set up near the mine at Jaduguda in Bihar. This mill again has been designed by Indian scientists and engineers, and is being erected by them. Further prospecting work during the last three years has quadrupled our established reserves of uranium, which are now sufficient to support a nuclear power capacity of over 9 million KW of electricity, which is much more than envisaged even at the end of the Fifth Five-Year Plan. The rate of discovery leads one to expect that much more uranium will be discovered and India can, therefore, say now with confidence that her uranium position is comfortable.

The Planning Commission included a nuclear power station of 300,000 KW in the Third Five-Year Plan (1961–1965) at an estimated cost of Rs. 510 million. This station will be located at Tarapur. But such is the progress of technology in this field that the station will now have a capacity of 380,000 KW, and will cost only Rs. 485 million. Since then a decision has been taken to set up the second nuclear power station near Rana Pratap Sagar in Rajasthan with a capacity of 200 MW in one reactor. While the first station is of the boiling water type, and uses enriched uranium as fuel and light water as moderator—a type which has been very successfully developed in the United States—the second station, of a type developed in Canada, will use natural uranium as fuel, which can be produced in the country, and will be moderated by heavy water.

Recently the Planning Commission has also a proposal of the

Atomic Energy Commission to set up the station in Rajasthan and to construct a similar station of 400 MW in Madras. Tarapur is expected to be ready by the end of 1968, and the other two stations during the Fourth Five-Year Plan period; so that by the end of the Fourth Plan, India will be generating nearly 1.2 million KW of electricity from atomic energy. It is now agreed that electricity from these stations will be slightly cheaper than electricity from thermal stations in these areas, where coal would have to be brought by rail over long distances. It will also be cheaper than electricity which might be obtained in these areas by long distance transmission from large stations located at the pit-head.

The installation of an additional 1.8 million kilowatts of nuclear power in the Fifth Five-Year Plan is now under consideration. Even the acceptance of this proposal will give India 3 million kilowatts of power generated by atomic energy by the end of the Fifth Plan. This will still be only a small fraction of the country's total power generation at the time. However, power is the basic necessity of industrialisation and the needs of power are expected to rise to such an extent within the next couple of decades that we shall have to depend increasingly on atomic energy. There is little doubt that before the end of the century, atomic energy will be producing a substantial part of the power in India, and thereafter practically all the additions to our power generation will come from it at that time.

Atomic energy has its uses also in agriculture, biology, industry and medicine. Isotopes and radioactive substances can be used for improving the strains of crops, for studying the best application of fertiliser, for pest control, for the preservation of food, for the refined control of processes in industry, and lastly for diagnosis and therapy in medicine. The Atomic Energy Establishment has developed and already made most of the electronic instrumentation required for these uses and is in a position to produce it for the country as a whole. Radioisotopes are already being produced in quantity, not only for all the needs of the country but also for export to other countries, and indeed some are being sold, for example, to Ceylon, France, Pakistan, South Korea, Thailand and the International Atomic Energy Agency.

The period of ten years which has just elapsed may be considered to be the period of adolescence of atomic energy work in India. The country's atomic energy programme can now be said to have reached maturity and India can look forward to the period ahead as a developed and mature atomic power, but one whose efforts are solely directed towards using atomic energy for peaceful purposes. Atomic energy has come to be accepted today as a growing part of a growing industry. But when the decision was taken to go in for it in an important way ten years ago, atomic energy for the generation of electricity had not been proved even in the industrially advanced countries. At that time it needed great vision, imagination and courage to embark on such a programme and to give it the necessary financial support. It is appropriate to remember that if India today is one of the half-a-dozen most advanced countries in atomic energy it is thanks to the farsighted vision of the country's late Prime Minister, Jawaharlal Nehru.

~

INDIRA GANDHI

Nationalization of Private Commercial Banks

At its Avadi session in 1954, the Indian National Congress adopted the establishment of a socialistic pattern of society as its objective. Towards that end a number of steps were initiated which gave the state a bigger role to play in the economy. One of the most far-reaching of such steps was the nationalization of private commercial banks. In 1956, S. Gurupadswamy, an ardent socialist, put forward a resolution in Parliament for nationalizing banks. In 1963, K. Brahmananda Reddy again moved the same resolution which was fervently supported by the Communist Party and particularly by Bhupesh Gupta. By 1966, the political situation had changed with Indira Gandhi taking over as prime minister, with the backing of a group of strong regional satraps, popularly known as the Syndicate which comprised leaders like K. Kamaraj, Atulya Ghosh and S. Nijalingappa, who thought that a callow and inexperienced leader could be easily managed. Indira Gandhi began to assert her independence soon enough and the Congress suffered a historic split in 1969. She now began to look for support among the younger elements in the Congress and among leftist leaders. Advised by a group of brilliant young intellectuals, which included people like G. Parthasarathy, P.N. Haksar and D.P. Dhar, she began to take steps which the radical section within the Congress was articulating. The nationalization of banks was as much a means to keep the leftists happy as an instrument to bolster her image of being pro-people. It also gave her a handle to acquire the wherewithal to finance social goals in the future. On 21 July 1969, two days after Indira Gandhi promulgated the ordinance nationalizing fourteen commercial banks, she announced her decision in the Lok Sabha.

Mr. Deputy Speaker Sir, an Ordinance was promulgated the day before yesterday nationalising fourteen of the major commercial banks incorporated in India. With your permission I should like to share with the House the considerations which weighed with Government in taking this momentous decision and the spirit in which they propose to implement it.

Nearly fifteen years ago Parliament approved that we should set before ourselves the goal of a socialist pattern of society. Since then Government have taken several measures towards the achievement of this goal. Public ownership and the control of commanding heights of national economy and of its strategic sectors are essential and important aspects of the new social order which we are trying to build in the country. We regard this as particularly necessary in a poor country which seeks to achieve speedy economic progress consistent with social justice in a democratic political system one which is free from the domination of a few and in which opportunities are open to all.

Financial institutions are among the most important levers that any society has at its command for the achievement of its social and economic objectives. It is in recognition of this fact that we nationalised life insurance business and the then Imperial Bank of India over a decade ago. Since then we have also set up in the public sector other institutions for the provision of medium or long-term finance to industry and agriculture. The nationalisation of major banks is a significant step in this process of public control over the principal institutions for the mobilisation of people's savings and canalising them towards productive purposes.

After the serious difficulties which we have had to encounter in recent years our economy is once again poised for fresh growth and development. There has been a notable breakthrough on the agricultural front, technologically and otherwise. The increase in our exports has been impressive. There has been substantial progress in power supply and the development of transport as also the availability of trained manpower. Our industrial base has been strengthened and diversified. It is in this context that we launched the Fourth Plan earlier this year with confidence and determination.

The question which has been engaging our attention for some time is how best to impart an element of dynamism and new vigour into the process of our development so that the targets of the Fourth Plan in the public and private sectors cannot only be fulfilled but if possible exceeded. Our major concern has been to accelerate the tempo of investment and production so as to improve living standards and increase employment opportunities consistent with our determination to achieve self-reliance. It is necessary to mobilise the savings of the people to the largest possible extent and to utilise them for productive purposes in accordance with our plans and priorities. Government believes that public ownership of the major banks for which there has been widespread public support will help in the most effective mobilisation and deployment of national resources so that our objectives can be realised with a greater degree of assurance.

The ordinance promulgated by government provides for the nationalisation of all scheduled banks incorporated in India which have minimum deposits of not less than Rs. 50 crores at the end of June last. The fourteen banks in this category together with the State Bank of India and its subsidiaries which already operate under public ownership account for more than 85 per cent of bank deposits in this country. The House will appreciate that in view of the very nature of the measure and also to forestall any possibility of manipulations which may not be in the public interest it was essential to make a swift and sudden move which could only be achieved through an ordinance. The fact that speculation about government's intentions had assumed an acute phase in the last few days rendered it all the more necessary to act without any further loss of time and in anticipation of the approval of Parliament which will be sought through a Bill which government proposes to bring during the current session.

So far as foreign banks are concerned they provide by and large business of a specialised nature such as facilitating foreign trade and tourism. The operation of banks of one country in another subject to the laws of the land is mainly for such purposes and is part of an international facility. Our Indian banks also maintain their branches in many countries. It has been government's general policy to confine the opening of new branches of foreign banks to major port towns where their specialised services are needed. Having regard to all these factors, government has decided to exclude branches of foreign banks incorporated outside India from the purview of the Ordinance.

As I stated the other day this is not the beginning of a new era of nationalisation. Whatever the pattern of the economy, it is widely recognised that the operations of the banking system should be informed by a larger social purpose and should be subject to close public regulation. Government has come to the conclusion that the desired regulation and rate of progress consistent with the urgency of our problem could be secured only through nationalisation.

I should like to reiterate my assurance that even after nationalisation the legitimate credit needs of private industry and trade big or small will be met. Indeed it shall be our endeavour to ensure that the needs of productive sectors of the economy and in particular those of farmers, small-scale industrialists and self-employed professional groups are met in an increasing measure. It will be one of the positive objectives of nationalised banks to actively foster the growth of new and progressive entrepreneurs and to create fresh opportunities for hitherto neglected and backward areas in different parts of the country. The banks will now be better placed to serve the farmer and to promote agricultural production and rural development generally. Public ownership will also help to curb the use of bank credit for speculative and other unproductive purpose. By severing the link between the major banks and the bigger industrial groups which have so far controlled them government believes that the step they have taken will also bring about the right atmosphere for the development of adequate professional managements in the banking field. Government attaches the utmost importance to modern managerial techniques and practices.

~

MANMOHAN SINGH

General Budget Speech, 1992-93

Delivered on 29 February 1992 at 1720 hours Indian time, the 1992-93 budget speech—whose concluding part is reproduced here—marked the most radical break from the economic policies the country had pursued since independence. It altered the course of India's economic and social structure. Though the country had been liberalizing its economy since the 1980s and Rajiv Gandhi's tenure as prime minister saw important changes in the attitude of the government and the administration towards economic issues, it was the Narasimha Rao government with Manmohan Singh as finance minister which gave India a complete economic overhaul, integrating the economy with the emerging world order and changing the way India's economy and economic institutions would look in times to come.

... Our nation will remain eternally grateful to Jawaharlal Nehru for his vision and insistence that the social and economic transformation of India had to take place in the framework of an open society, committed to parliamentary democracy and the rule of law. India's development is of tremendous significance for the future of the developing world. To realise our development potential, we have to unshackle the human spirit of creativity, idealism, adventure and enterprise that our people possess in abundant measure. We have to harness all our latent resources for a second industrial revolution and a second agriculture revolution. Our economy, polity and society have to be extraordinarily resilient and alert if we are to take full advantage of the opportunities and to minimise the risks associated with the increasing globalisation of economic processes. We have to accept the need for restructuring and reform if we are to avoid an increasing marginalisation of India in the evolving world economy. The economic policy changes brought about by our Government under the inspiring leadership of Prime Minister Narasimha Rao in the last eight months are inspired by this vision. Our party is an inheritor of great traditions of national service. True to this heritage, we commit ourselves to providing a firm and purposeful sense of direction to the reform process so that this ancient land of India regains its glory and rightful place in the comity of nations. This budget represents a contribution to the successful implementation of this great national enterprise, of building an India free of war, want and exploitation, an India worthy of the dreams of the founding fathers of our republic. We shall pay any price, bear any burden, make any sacrifice to realise those dreams. India is on the move again. We shall make the future happen.

Sir, I have come to the end of my labour. Tonight, I feel like going to the theatre. Let the assassins be informed, I am prepared to meet their onslaught. As a poet says, '*Sarfaroshi ki tamanna ab hamare dil me hai, dekhna hai zor kitna bazu e katil me hai.*' Sir, I commend the budget to this August House.

~

NANI PALKHIVALA

On the General Budget of 1992-93

Nani Palkhivala (1920–2002) was an eminent jurist and economist. Apart from being a leading interpreter of constitutional law in the country and an ardent defender of the civil liberties guaranteed by the constitution, he was also an expert on economic matters, particularly the budget. His annual lectures explaining the intricacies of the budget were attended by industrialists, lawyers, economists and the common man, and made him a household name with the country's middle and upper classes. This particular address was made in Bombay.

This year's budget is not a budget for the greedy, paid for by the needy. The budget provisions properly so called (as distinct from the proposed amendments to the direct tax laws) are well-conceived, and deserve the support of the well-informed irrespective of party affiliations.

Liberalization is the key to the budget. It is a watershed budget which marks the beginning of a new chapter in India's economic history. It was our ideological socialism which had been responsible for India remaining the twentieth poorest nation on earth. Our gross domestic product is smaller than that of Greater Los Angeles (population 14 million). This year's historic budget for the first time reflects the consciousness of our government that fast economic growth would be impossible with outdated socialism.

Dr Manmohan Singh has rightly emphasized that unless certain values are adhered to by the nation, it cannot come out of the recession. The Finance Minister has no Midas touch; he has no snake oil which can be used as having a magical healing power in matters economic.

The proposed integration of India into the global economy has not come a day too soon. The emerging world economy has erased national boundaries. Capital and companies no longer stop at the border. If India is to grow and prosper, it has no alternative but to be integrated into the world economy.

Reduction of taxes is one of the avowed aims of the budget. In a global economy, cutting taxes has become a matter of national interest: high tax countries inevitably lose out. The days when the government could adopt any tax policy, as if the nation existed within a vacuum, are over.

If India is to have a stable and healthy balance of payments, it can only be through increased exports. Even Holland, one of the tiny countries of the world with a population of 15 million, has six times the exports of India!

The least justified criticism of the budget is that it has been framed under the dictates of the World Bank and the International Monetary Fund. The censure is levelled by those whose critical perception does not exceed forty watts. They should credit India with enough intelligence to make the right decision for itself after forty years of mistaken policy. Some of the ablest men in the two international institutions are Indians: to say that the Indian Government cannot think for itself is gratuitous self-condemnation.

In any event we must judge the policy underlying the budget on its merits, and it is wholly irrelevant to be concerned about who suggested the path of wisdom. One of the great failings of democracy is the mistaken belief that it is the duty of the Opposition to oppose.

Secondly, the fear has been expressed in some quarters that India will be swamped by multinationals. The truth is that India runs no risk whatever of being dominated by foreign corporations. We must get rid of the illusion that we are still fighting the East India Company.

Thirdly, the view has been expressed that the budget has not done enough to check inflation or to counter recession. To control inflation is possible, but to eliminate it is beyond hope at this juncture. The last time we had 'negative inflation' (to use bad English) was when Mr Morarji Desai was the Prime Minister (1977–79). The spirit of the nation—the spirit of national dedication and confidence which then emerged after the tyranny of the Emergency—had as much to do with the fall in prices as any budget.

Inflation is a worldwide phenomenon. A dollar today is worth only 13 cents in 1945 money; a pound is worth six pence. Even the Deutschemark is only one-third of its value in 1948 when it replaced the worthless Reichsmark.

Again, the world economy is going through a period of recession. The current economic depression in the United States is billed as 'the mother of all recessions'—the longest since 1945. General Motors, the giant among corporations, incurred a loss of $4.5 billion in 1991—unparalleled in the Company's 84-year history. The critics claim that in Britain the recession is deeper than in any other country. About 20,000 companies went into liquidation in 1991, which works out to one in every 50 British companies.

There are several points on which the budget deserves to be commended.

(1) It is the first budget which aims at breaking the shackles of the bureaucratic command system.
(2) It reflects consciousness of the risk to the nation of an unbridled increase in the total liabilities of the government. We are stealing from the future. No less than Rs. 32,000 crore will be spent next

year merely on servicing the loans. That would constitute almost one-fourth—23 per cent to be precise—of the total governmental expenditure: more than what will be spent on Plan or Defence.

(3) It has restored the balance of payments to a less critical level than before. We have a reserve of $4.4 billion. The risk of defaulting or having to ask for rescheduling of debts no longer looms over the horizon.

(4) Partial convertibility of the rupee is a sensible step. That this step is in the national interest is proved by the example of Pakistan.

(5) The confidence of foreign investors has been restored. The scramble by non-resident Indians to withdraw their deposits from banks has ceased.

(6) The abolition of the office of the Controller of Capital Issues is an essential step in the process of liberalization.

(7) The decision to abolish deduction of tax from interest on term deposits with banks is in the public interest. When Bonn introduced ten per cent withholding tax from interest on bank deposits, there was a flight of capital. Deposits worth DM 100 million vanished from West German banks and re-appeared next door in tiny Luxembourg. The law was promptly scrapped.

(8) Permitting the import of gold is a prudent decision.

(9) The reduction of the statutory liquidity ratio from 38.5 per cent to 30 per cent would release larger bank funds for loans to business and reduce the heavy bank interest rate by one percentage point.

(10) The lowering of the vertiginous customs tariffs to a less unreasonable level is welcome. It is the inevitable step which has to be taken if India is to be integrated into the global economy.

(11) The lowering of the maximum marginal rate of income-tax on individuals would, in the long run, have no detrimental effect on government revenues, because it would result in better compliance. Professor Lawrence Lindsey of the Harvard University has given cogent evidence to prove that income-tax revenues are most buoyant when the maximum rate is 40 per cent. This phenomenon, called 'the Lindsey effect', has been accepted in the United States where the maximum rate is 33 per cent and in Britain where it is 40 per cent. The reduction of the maximum marginal rate on non-corporate assesses to 44.8 per cent (including surcharge) will bring India closer to the fast developing countries which have slashed their rates.

~

SOMNATH CHATTERJEE

Surrendering Self-reliance

In this speech delivered on 4 March 1992, on the President's address to the joint session of Parliament, Somnath Chatterjee, the leader of the Communist Party of India (Marxist), spoke aggressively and passionately about the anti-people character of the 1992-93 general budget. This is an important speech because the line of argument adopted in it has since then provided the outline for the discourse by those who oppose economic reforms and globalization on the grounds that in an attempt to integrate the Indian economy with the emerging world order we are sacrificing national interests at the behest of international organizations like the World Bank (WB) and the International Monetary Fund (IMF).

... Sir, the contents of the President's Address prove that we were fully justified in boycotting the Joint Session of Parliament because we did not wish to participate in the ritualisation of a very solemn occasion which has the sanctity of Constitution behind it.

If one goes through the Address, one hears the voice, not of the President of a vibrant and progressive India, but the voice of a President of a country which has lost its self-reliance and self-dignity. That is why the President of this country was made to indulge in banal platitudes and sterile homilies without any indication of any independent and pro-people thinking or of any basic policy formulation in the whole Address.

Sir, I am very sorry to say that the Address is the product of a Government which is in bondage, a Government which is on leash led by the nose by the combine of Bush, Camdessus and Preston who have become the arbiters of our nation. That is why we find that the Address does not enthuse the nation but condemns the people, compromises their dignity and ridicules their commitment to self-reliance. This Narasimha Rao Government, now headed by a sober-gentleman-turned-arrogant within a sphere of a few months, will go down in history as the one which has mortgaged our country to the imperialist financial marauders for some tainted lucre. Our economic sovereignty and national prestige have become negotiable and we are projected to the whole world as cringing supplicants to those agencies whose imperialist and capitalist design so far as the Third World countries are concerned is very well known. They are more anxious to maintain their hegemony than to come to the real rescue of the developing and the Third World countries. That is why very serious problems faced by the ordinary people, common people of the country, not the highest income brackets of this country, like the steep and unabated price rise of essential commodities, have received a tongue-in-cheek reference of about six lines in an Address covering 19 pages while 16 lines have been devoted for the fulsome praise of Bush and Company's so-called humanitarian philanthropic and democratic pretensions.

... the current year's Budget has put the final nail in the coffin of the principle of self-reliance and mixed-economy which was the dream of Pandit Jawaharlal Nehru and which was adopted, by and large, as our national policy. But Pandit Jawaharlal Nehru has become an inconvenient name to the Congress party. And Nehruvian economic policy is being projected as dirty words. ... And the Nehruvian economic policy is being projected as an anti-growth concept. We do not any longer hear that the public sectors occupy the commanding heights of our economy... Those who still believe in the same, in the primacy of the public sector, are being dubbed as anti-nationals. Now to the Congress Party and to the Congress Government, market economy of the US variety has become the mantra and Pandit Jawaharlal Nehru has been given an indecent burial. Our objection to the Centre's economic policies so far has been against the tardy implantation of the principles of self-reliance.

Our objection so far has been against the weakening of the public sector and the Congress Government's continuous pampering to a handful of monopolists and speculators in the country and perpetuating the miseries of the common people. But what has happened now? This Government has not only reversed the policy without any mandate from the people, without there being even a mention in the election manifesto, without having a majority support from the people of this country but they have also changed the path of our economic growth or direction and they have adopted brazen facedly the capitalist path of market economy which will only multiply the miseries and sufferings of the common people. And it has already resulted in surrendering to the stranglehold of monopolists, foreign agencies and even compromising our ability to decide our own future.

Today, the Prime Minister's intervention was very significant. Why I say this is because he has become arrogant, he has become insensitive. He is very happy. He said that the people outside were very, very happy with his Budget and with his economic policy.

According to the Prime Minister, people are praising this Budget sky high. But who are these people? It is *Washington Post*, a newspaper of the American imperialists, NRIs, FICCI, ASSOCHAM and the like. Dr. Manmohan Singh is being projected as having saved this country. But has the Budget been welcomed by the common people, by the toiling masses? No. They—the common people—considered the Finance Minister and the Prime Minister of our country as the messiahs of our financial doom and of economic perfidy… We want to make it very clear that we can never be and we shall not be a party to this process of dismantling and defilement. We shall protest both here and outside… We shall protest both inside and outside this House, on the streets, in the factories, in the fields and in every nook and corner of the country. We are giving this advance warning to them.

They are very happy also that some sarkari economists and some sarkari journalists are made to sing paeans of praise of the Budget. These people always do. They always praise the Government Budget, whichever is the Government and whichever is the Budget. They praised Rajiv Gandhi's Budget and now they are criticising Rajiv Gandhi's Budget and applauding Narasimha Rao's Budget. But nobody is able to deny the effect of the IMF and the World Bank conditionalities on the preparation of their Budget. And very significantly this Government deliberately kept suppressed from the people and this Parliament those documents which ultimately they were forced to disclose by pressure of public opinion and opinion in the House. It had disclosed a very sorry and serious state of affairs.

I would request my honourable friends from the treasury benches not to make it a partisan issue and to please go through the documents very carefully for the sake of their Government only, if this temporary majority they wish to perpetuate. You may now ignore and you may play with the future of this country. That is why, in one of my earlier interventions, I had requested my very good friends from the treasury benches to please go through them. Please do not mortgage your conscience. This is not a matter of whip. When so many people are raising this question, please try to go through those documents and find out what commitments this Government has already made.

… We charge that this Government has compromised our economic sovereignty and this Budget is the faithful implementation of the fiats of the IMF and the World Bank. I am not today dealing with the Budget in detail. That will be dealt with when we come to the Budget discussions.

... In 1991-92 the total debt servicing was estimated to be Rs. 11,936 crores of which the share of commercial borrowings was Rs. 4,158 crores. It was 35 per cent of the total debt servicing which means a debt trap. These are not my figures. Who is responsible for this and how are you trying to solve this? The only way they have chosen is to go on bended knees to the IMF and to the World Bank.

We had even opposed the '1981 approach' to the World Bank, when the present Rashtrapatiji was the Finance Minister. He had gone to the IMF to take loan. I would like to know as to what agreement was entered into then. Would you please disclose the 1981 agreement with the IMF and the World Bank? We would like to know as to what were the conditionalities there. What has forced you to completely surrender your rights and completely bind your hands and feet, so far as our economic policies are concerned?

So far as the borrowings from the commercial banks are concerned, the solution was not to go to the IMF, but to restrict non-essential imports and to increase the exports. But, that was not the policy that was adopted.

What is the direction of the present plan? The present Deputy Chairman circulated some documents containing the outline of the plan. It was said that the success of the plan depends on and it can only succeed if there is an increase in the export to the extent of 13.6 per cent every year. It is impossible to reach that. They are no longer making that forecast. Then, the Planning Commission itself says that the planning process will come to a halt. Who is responsible for this and what are the ways out? Is it only to go to the IMF and the World Bank? Is there no other way in this country? Is it for this that this country has been fighting, dismantling everything? What was the role of the public sector when this country became independent and after that? Who came to the core sector?

Not a single monopolist came to the core sector in this country. In the steel sector, in the oil sector, who were the people, who were the industrialists-friends of yours who made investments? It was the public sector which came there and Jawaharlal Nehru realised that the public sector was the only panacea, the only way out. On the basis of his experience, he presented the Industrial Policy in the House in 1956, which the Congress Party adopted. But, that Congress, of course, is dead and gone.

... The public sector undertakings like ONGC, Indian Oil Corporation, Steel Authority of India, etc. have helped this country to grow. With nascent democracy which was to develop under the trauma of partition and huge mass transfer of people from one place to another, the public sector has taken the role and now it is being ridiculed. Who is responsible for the mismanagement of the public sector? Today you are selling the shares of the public sector undertakings, of profitable concerns, to whom? To the multinationals and to the monopolists.

... What is the provision made and what is the indication given in the President's Address as to how the price rise will be dealt with? Just a casual reference was made to that. Their manifesto—I hope they have not torn out page 25, because 25 is rather unfortunate for them—says at page 25, that Congress is determined to roll back the prices to levels obtaining in July 1990 in case of diesel, kerosene, salt, edible oils, etc. Either that has been torn away or you have put ink on this. Page 26 is also the back of 25. Tearing of that page will help them. It is said, 'The Congress will create 10 million new jobs per year and 100 million jobs by the end of the century.'

... The annual rate of inflation has been 13.5 per cent for wholesale price index—the highest in the decade as the seasonal downturn in prices proved to be rather modest. Between April and December, the major portion of which this Government has functioned with the blessings of IMF, the rate of increase in prices stood at 13.7 per cent compared to 9.3 per cent. Even Mr. Chandra Shekhar performed better than you. An analysis of the trends in a month-wise rise in prices for 1991 shows inflation at 16.3 per cent which was the highest in September as compared to 12.2 per cent in June. The rate of rise in prices for primary articles during the calendar year on a point to point basis has been estimated at 18.9 per cent.

... Neither the Budget nor the President's Address makes any provision as to how to contain the price rise, far less to bring it down...

Another very serious situation which the country is facing, specially the common people is the problem of unemployment. Sir, in 1951, number of persons who were unemployed were 3.29 lakhs. The wonderful Congress contribution to this country at the end of 1989 was 3.27 crores. This figure refers to the registered unemployed people.

... In March 1991, with the help of the Congress, the Chandra

Shekhar Government's performance resulted in having 34,890,000 as registered educated unemployed persons. And what was the average number of vacancies notified during that period? It was 38,000. For one year, the figure comes to 33.48 lakhs against unemployed persons in the exchanges and only a maximum of 4.56 lakhs could be employed. What will happen to these unemployed people? What is the source of livelihood for these people? Where will they go? Can the agricultural sector or the industrial sector bear any further employment? From where will they earn their livelihood? Please tell us. I would like to know about it. And now, over and above, what is happening? We are told of employees being redundant. Four lakhs of Railway employees are going to lose their jobs. Government offices are being closed and you are encouraging Exit Policy. You have not adopted a policy for reviving a single sick industry. The new modern hi-tech industries will provide very little employment to the ordinary people because they are highly mechanised and automatic machines are used, so far as we know. Then, where will these people go for jobs? What are you doing to help them to earn their livelihood through small-scale industries? What entrepreneurial assistance are you giving them? Sir, over two lakhs of sick companies are in private sector about which they are so enamoured. Why so many private sector industries are closed or sick?

What are you going to do to help these people and now, you are getting rid of employees of the public sector. You are sending the units to the BIFR for closure and winding up. But what will happen to the employees? What is the hoax about the National Renewal Fund? It is said that it will be for retraining and redeployment. With all sincerity and seriousness, I am asking as to where will you redeploy them. What alternative training will you give them? How many people will you train with the amount in your Renewal Fund? For heaven's sake, please tell us about this. What is the fate of those people who are unemployed who are not criminals or anti-social elements? They want to live a decent life with an ordinary amount and not crores of rupees. They want to look after their families and lead a decent life. Where will they get deployed? Please tell us so that we can inform them not to worry and that this benign Government will give them jobs.

Sir, the Exit Policy has been thrust upon this country by the IMF. If you go through the history of Latin American countries which had gone to the IMF and the World Bank, you will find that exactly similar and identical words were used. We hear the very same words 'macro-economic policy', 'structural adjustments' and so on. This is the jargon that Dr. Manmohan Singh is using now and we have heard every word before. Brazil, Peru and many other countries had to swallow these words. Have you become completely blind and insensitive just for some foreign exchange? Have you given up your right to think and to decide for yourself? What will happen now? Even the Rashtrapatiji is being made to utter words, if I may say so, which are against the interests of the common people of this country. He says that there should not be any strike and there should not be any industrial action. People may lose their jobs and die of starvation. But they should not protest. Is this country a country of slaves or sheep or goats? That they silently starve and die and shall not protest against all this? This country will never accept an attempt by the Government to prohibit industrial action. It is not a charity from the Government. It has been earned by the working class through their struggle over a long period of time and they will never give up their right of industrial action to fight for their own rights.

Today we find that there is a very grave economic situation. Is it reflected in the President's Address? What is the policy statement that has been made in the Address as to how to solve this grave economic situation? Nobody is denying it. Even the Government is saying that there is a grave economic situation. But where is the reflection of that in the President's Address? Earlier, we were at least told that the Address was prepared in a great hurry and they could not even think about it properly. But now, they had seven months of informed assistance from IMF also to prepare the President's Address. But this is the position. This Address is nothing but a parchment in which every thing that this country needs has been consciously omitted to be mentioned. Without meaning any disrespect to Rashtrapatiji, personally, I may say that it has become a useless document and it should be thrown into the wastepaper basket.

There has to be an alternate approach. We have suggested it many times. But who is listening? This Government is under the bondage of the IMF and the World Bank. Were they listening? We have circulated an alternate proposal. They did not even have the courtesy to come and discuss with us or even to call us and discuss this alternate approach.

Now, what about land reform? Have you ever thought of bringing about land reforms in this country? We have suggested that without land reforms and without wider dispersal of ownership in industrial capital, without the use of a technology which is both modern and labour-intensive, a technology which will use labour and not replace it, we can never improve our economy. When we bring about this type of reforms, then and then alone, we can increase the purchasing power of the common people and then and then alone agricultural and industrial growth can follow on the basis of expansion of domestic market and not otherwise. But that is never an area to which they pay any attention.

Instead, we find that in the economic sector, this Government has launched an outright attack, a comprehensive attack on the public sector. Even the Parliament has not been taken into confidence when they took the decision with regard to 49 per cent disinvestment in the public sector. And this is one of the most dangerous policies. Then they have adopted the Exit Policy. With a sleight of hand, they dismantled the provisions of FERA and MRTP in the inter-session period and the FERA has become a useless document. Now they are supposedly thinking on the Dunkel proposals, which will bring ruin to the agriculturists of this country and drug industry in the country. But this Government is thinking on those lines. Today we find it in the newspaper. It has been discussed in the other House also. The Minister has said that there are some positive features in the Dunkel proposal so far as the agriculture sector is concerned. But, Shri Chidambaram has said that without discussing the matter in Parliament, the Government will not take any decision. But, Sir, we are hearing not a word about any action taken against any of these big industrial houses. Rs. 50,000 crores of black money are circulating in this country. Is this not a pressure on our economy? Is there any step taken to unearth this black money? On the other hand, we know what this Government has done.

The top ten industrial houses in this country have taken loans up to 31st March, 1991 from the following financial institutions:

IDBI Rs. 1486 crores
IFCI Rs. 553 crores
ICICI Rs. 626 crores

The total comes to Rs. 2666 crores which is outstanding from these ten business or industrial houses to these important Governmental agencies. When the small-scale sector or the medium-scale sector go to these banks for the purpose of loans and advances, no money is made available for them. They are working overtime for the purpose of giving loans to these big industrial houses which have been allowed to remain unrealised for years and years.

Even the interest is not paid. What is the credibility of this Government or of this Party which has ruined this country by their misrule of over forty years?

What is the performance of the present Government—Shri Narasimha Rao's Government? Overnight, they have taken a somersault. Nobody is saying anything these days about Shri Rajiv Gandhi.

The overall rate of growth is minus 2.3 per cent. The GDP growth instead of 8 per cent is 2.5 per cent. The overall rate of growth was minus 8 per cent from April to October. Food grains output has dropped by 1.5 per cent during this Government's regime. Agricultural production is stagnant. Population is increasing but agricultural production is not increasing. The Balance of Payments position was a little difficult. I do not know whether they would have agreed to give us the copy of the World Bank Report but we have somehow managed to get a copy of the Report. There, you will find that the only reason for going to the World Bank was to get some foreign exchange for imports. Then, why this performance of our economy? Why industrial production is going down? Why agricultural production is going down? Why GDP is going down? What have you done for the last seven or eight months? This is the performance of this Government? We are told today by the Prime Minister that they have nothing to say... Now, the Prime Minister is only reading FICCI's circulars, not even the ordinary papers of this country. He has lost touch with the common people of this country. That is my fear. That is our misfortune. Probably, our Prime Minister is not allowed to think of his own until IMF and World Bank permits him to think.

~

AMARTYA SEN

Development as Freedom

Nobel laureate Amartya Sen has been one of the leading economists in the modern world. With his keen eye on the economic development in India and China, and the philosophy of distribution behind the political set-up, he has argued that development in fact satisfies the most enduring human need, that of freedom. On 31 July 2003, Sen addressed a seminar organized by FICCI in New Delhi on 'Development as Freedom: An Indian Perspective'. Sen's speech covers a range of theoretical issues and conveys the essence of development.

... Given the globally undivided nature of the basic approach, there can be, in a foundational sense, no specifically 'Indian perspective' of 'development as freedom'. The Indian perspective has to be—and that is clearly the intention of the organizers of the seminar—only one part of a larger global perspective. The approach I have tried to pursue involves a universalism, which finds expression in different ways... including the diagnosis of a set of common concerns and basic aspirations that we share across the world, despite the diversity of their manifestations in different countries, cultures and societies. For example, the food we like to eat, the clothes we want to wear, the entertainment we seek, the uses we make of our liberties vary greatly between one society and another, and yet the general freedom of being well-fed, well-clothed, well-entertained and well-emancipated is, I have argued, a shared objective. This point is important to me in my attempt to resist the separatism generated by political nationalism and also the growing influence of cultural sectarianism. Our robust uniqueness can, I would argue, go hand in hand with our shared commonality, without any conflict whatsoever.

Along with the happiness in receiving attention, I am also, as I mentioned earlier, somewhat embarrassed since the basic approach presented...is not really new. Indeed, very far from it. In one form or another, they have figured in the thoughts of people across the world over thousands of years. They were prominent, for example, in the deliberations of Gautama Buddha—arguably the greatest Indian of all times—when, twenty-five hundred years ago, he left his princely home in search of wisdom. Gautama was deeply bothered by the unfreedoms of ill health, disability, mortality and ignorance, which he saw around him in the foothills of the Himalayas, but which he knew existed all around the world. The questions that moved him—and sent him in search of enlightenment—throw significant light on a great many subjects, including the need to overcome unfreedoms that motivate the pedestrian approach of 'development as freedom'. Even though Buddha himself went on, as we all know, into rather abstruse issues involving the nature of life and the transcendental predicament of living beings, nevertheless the nature of Buddha's motivating questions remains profoundly relevant for practical public policy as well. In the transcendental context it may appear trivial that some of the earliest interregional meetings to settle differences of views were arranged by Buddhist intellectuals (respectively in Rajagriha in the sixth century BCE, in Vaisali in the fifth century BCE, in Pataliputra in the third century BCE, and in Kashmir in the second century AD), and that every early attempt at printing—in China, Korea and Japan—was undertaken by Buddhist technologists (the first printed book in the world was a Sanskrit Buddhist text, *Van Vajrachedikaprajnaparamita*, translated into Chinese in early fifth century and printed in 868 AD). But these were major steps in the development of a deliberative and communicative tradition in the world and in enhancing the reach of public reasoning, a proper history of which is yet to be written.

Similar connections can be identified in the immensely diverse writings of such thoroughly disparate thinkers as Kautilya, Ashoka, Shudraka or Akbar, in our country, or of Aristotle, Adam Smith, Condorcet, Mary Wollstonecraft, Karl Marx or John Stuart Mill, in the West (to name just a few writers). Valuing substantive freedoms is not at all novel, nor is the search for the ways and means of advancing these freedoms, through public deliberation and social organization. Many of these earlier authors paid specific attention to the inequality of the adversities we face, related to class, gender, race, location, community, and other stratifications that divide us. The need to address these structured inequalities is a critically important part of development as freedom.

Freedoms as Ends

Development as Freedom proceeds from the basic recognition that freedom is both (1) the primary objective, and (2) the principal means of development. The former is a normative claim and includes the understanding that the assessment of development must not be divorced from the lives that people can lead and the real freedoms that they can enjoy. Development can scarcely be seen merely in terms of enhancement of inanimate objects of convenience, such as a rise in the GNP (or in personal incomes), or industrialization, or technological advance, or social reforms. These are, of course, valuable and often crucially important influences on our lives, but they are not valuable in themselves: their importance depends on what they do to the freedoms of the people involved.

Even in terms of being at liberty to live reasonably long lives (free of escapable ailments and other causes of premature mortality), it is remarkable that the extent of deprivation for particular groups in very rich countries can be comparable to that in the so-called 'third world'. ...In the United States, African Americans (that is, American blacks) as a group have no higher—indeed have a lower—chance of reaching an advanced age than do people born in the immensely poorer economies of China, or Jamaica,...or for that matter, substantial parts of India. The freedom from premature mortality is, of course, helped by a larger income (that is not in dispute), but it also depends on many other features of social organization, including public health care and medical security, the nature of schooling and education, the extent of social cohesion, and so on. It is critically important, therefore, to take an adequately broad view of development.

Interdependence of Freedoms

The starting point of our analysis is the nature of our ends; the capacious freedoms that we have reason to seek. However, we cannot stop there. Freedom of one kind tends, by and large, to help the advancement of freedoms of other kinds, so that each type of freedom, while an end in itself, is also a means to other freedoms. These connections require empirical investigation and scrutiny...

Freedoms can be of many different kinds... I (have) tried to make the task more manageable by classifying diverse freedoms into five different categories, namely: economic empowerment, political freedoms, social opportunities, protective security and transparency guarantees. There is nothing particularly sacrosanct about this classification, but it does cover the ground, and since the programme of this seminar includes, I am happy to see, discussion of each of these aspects of overall freedom, and I am greatly looking forward to the results of those deliberations.

In the rest of this talk, I want to comment on the interrelations between these distinct kinds of freedoms—how they can assist as well as complement each other. I start specifically with one particular issue that has figured prominently in Indian debates as well as international discussions in recent years. Doubts about the merits of Indian democracy—and about democracy in general—have been aired with much frequency recently. These doubts can be, I believe, well addressed in the perspective of development as freedom.

Democracy and the Ends and Means of Development

The first point to note in assessing Indian democracy is that democracy cannot be evaluated in primarily instrumental terms. Political freedom and civil rights have importance of their own. Their value to the society does not have to be indirectly established in terms of their contribution to economic growth or other such economic or social achievements. Politically unfree citizens are deficient in freedom even if they happen to enjoy a very high level of income.

The second point goes beyond this purely valuational issue. Despite the commonly made generalization that democracy tends to slow down economic growth, extensive cross-country comparisons—by Robert Barro, Adam Przeworski and others—have not provided any empirical support for this often-repeated belief. More specifically, when comparative statements are made that try to show the failure of Indian democracy, it is typically assumed that had India not been a democracy, it would have had experiences rather similar to South Korea, Singapore, or China, rather than other non-democratic countries such as North Korea, Afghanistan, or Sudan. In fact, the proximate comparison of India with a not-always democratic country must be with Pakistan, and somehow that does not tend to be the focus of the rosy portrayals of the non-democratic alternative that India is supposed to have missed.

There is, however, a deeper issue of methodology here. The policies and circumstances that have led to the economic success of Asian economies to the east of India—whether South Korea or Singapore or China—are by now reasonably well understood. A sequence of empirical studies have identified a general list of 'helpful policies', with much internal diversity, which includes the role of economic competition, use of international markets, a high level of literacy and school education, successful land reforms, easier availability of credit (including micro-credit), good public health care, and appropriate incentives for investment, exporting and industrialization. There is absolutely nothing to indicate that any of these policies is inconsistent with greater democracy and actually have to be sustained by the elements of authoritarianism that happened to be present in South Korea or Singapore or China. The basic point is that economic growth is helped by the friendliness of the economic climate, rather than by the fierceness of the political regime. If India has failed to do enough to create such a favourable climate and to learn from the positive experiences of China or South Korea, the blame can hardly be put on the shoulders of political freedoms of citizens. Indeed, more engaging public discussion on what needs to be done can help to change India's deficiencies. This calls for more democracy—not less.

Further, it is not sufficient to look only at the growth of GNP or other such indicators of overall economic expansion. In assessing democracy and political freedoms, we have to see their impact on the lives and capabilities of the citizens. For this it is particularly important to examine the connection between political and civil rights, on the one hand, and the prevention of major disasters (such as famines), on the other. The availability and use of political and civil rights give people the opportunity to draw attention forcefully to general dangers and vulnerabilities, and to demand appropriate remedial action.

Governmental response to acute sufferings of people often depends on the political pressure that is put on it, and this is where the exercise of political rights (such as voting, criticizing, protesting) can make a real difference. The role of democracy in preventing famines has received attention precisely in this context, including the fact that India has not had a real famine since independence (despite continued endemic under-nourishment and often precarious food situation), whereas China had the largest famine in recorded history during 1958-61, when the ill-calculated public policies that led to the disaster were continued by the government without any substantial emendation for three years, while nearly 30 million people died. The association of famines with authoritarianism can be seen also in the experiences of Cambodia in the 1970s, Ethiopia and Sudan in the 1980s, North Korea in the 1990s—and indeed even today.

At a less extreme level, the recent experiences of the so-called 'Asian economic crisis' during 1997-99, which affected many of the economies of East and South-east Asia, bring out, among other things, the penalty of undemocratic governance. Once the financial crisis led to a general economic recession, the protective power of democracy—not unlike that which prevents famines in democratic countries—was badly missed in these countries. The suddenly dispossessed in many of these countries did not have the voice and the hearing that a democratic system would have given them. Not surprisingly, democracy has become a major issue in many countries in East and South-east Asia today.

India and China

Democracy gives an opportunity to the opposition to press for policy change even when the problem is chronic and endemic rather than acute and disastrous (as in a famine). So the limited reach of Indian social policies on education, basic nutrition, health care, land reform and gender equity reflects the weakness of democratic practice in India. It is, in fact, as much a failure of the opposition parties as of the governments in office in India's post-independent history, since the opposition need not have allowed those in power to get away with gross neglect.

Comparison of the experiences of China and India bring out some interesting lessons, which can take us well beyond the frequently repeated simple generalizations. The comparative perspectives in life expectancy, which is quite central to the approach of development as freedom, can throw interesting light on a complex reality that requires a more discriminating analysis. In the middle of the twentieth century, post-revolution China and newly independent India had about the same life expectancy at birth, around 45 years or so. The Chinese leaders were immediately more successful in rapidly expanding health care and life expectancy than their Indian counterparts were, and in these fields (leaving out the temporary interruptions in famines), China clearly got more from the egalitarian commitment of its authoritarian leadership than India did from its democratic system. When the economic reforms were introduced in China in 1979, China had a lead of 14 years or more over India, with the Chinese life expectancy at 68 years while India's was less than 54 years.

The speed and composition of Chinese economic growth were, however, in many ways in great need of improvement in the pre-reform period. Radical economic reforms, which were introduced in 1979, ushered in a period of extraordinary growth in China over the last two decades. We run, however, into an odd conundrum as far as life expectancy is concerned. China's life expectancy, which is now just about 70 years, compares with India's figure of 63 years or more, and the life-expectancy gap in favour of China, which was 14 years before the Chinese reforms, has been halved to almost 7 years now.

How is this possible given what we know about the dreadful state of health care in India? I might perhaps mention here that in the latest round of investigative research done by the Pratichi Trust, which I was privileged to set up in 1999 (with the help of my Nobel money), the terrible state of public health care in India is even more obvious to me than it was earlier. Not only do two-thirds or more of the surveyed population get no assistance at all from the public health services, a high proportion has ended up going to private service providers who are not only not qualified in any system of medicine, but are nothing but quacks. The proportions going to quacks in the sample population in the two districts studied are, respectively, 29 per cent in Birbhum in West Bengal, and as much as 69 per cent in Dumka in Jharkhand.

We all know about the terrible state of health care in India. But that exactly is its saving grace. Indeed, the continuing improvement—slow as it is—comes just from that fact and public pressure that this eventually generates (I hope our Pratichi Trust report on health will generate some response—as our report in the form of a critique of the delivery of primary education in West Bengal, to some extent, already has). This is precisely why freedom of information is so critically important. Secrecy is not good for health care (as was rather dramatically confirmed recently with the spread of the SARS epidemic which had been kept under a lid in Southern China for five months), and China's stagnation in health care has something to do with that. It also has something to do with the fact that since the economic reforms, Chinese health care system has abandoned its earlier commitment to social insurance for all, in favour of privatized insurances which people have to buy (unless they are lucky enough to have employers who buy it for them).

Aside from the importance of public scrutiny of social services such as health delivery, the opportunities of democracy include the possibility of debating changes in general economic policy. The abandonment of the general entitlement to health care in China, which was carried out very smoothly through compliant politics, would have almost certainly received far greater resistance in more plural political systems. China's spectacular achievement in health entitlement and egalitarian distribution in the pre-reform period may have been largely the result of visionary political commitment, but the preservation of those gains and their further expansion would certainly have been helped by wider political engagement and more democratic participation.

Indeed, if we look at Kerala, which has had a long history of egalitarian politics not altogether dissimilar to the kind that China had in its early period, but also has the benefit of democracy and oppositional politics, we find a life expectancy of about 74 years, which is significantly ahead of China's 70 years. The contrast is even sharper if we look at specific points of vulnerability, such as infant mortality rate, in which Kerala's figure now is less than half of China's.

While India has much to learn from China's past experience in rapidly expanding health care and basic education, which led to speedy expansion of life expectancy in the pre-reform period, and also from its post-reform experience in pursuing intelligent and undogmatic economic policies that make excellent use of global economic opportunities (in both these China has been a world leader), there is little that India need learn from China on the alleged virtues of authoritarian politics.

Freedoms, Rights and Public Discussion

It can, in fact, be argued that India can get much more from its own democratic system. If freedoms are important, then their implications in terms of people's rights—and the duties of others to help in safeguarding and advancing those rights—must call for probing public discussion. Democracy is not merely a system of elections, but also one of public reasoning, which can play a robustly constructive role in bringing about changes in policies and priorities to advance substantive freedoms.

Let me illustrate the point with some examples. One of the major failures of the Indian economy is that despite the elimination of famines and despite the presence of exceptionally large stocks of food grains, there remains a massive level of endemic hunger across the country. For example, judged in terms of weight for age, whereas 20 to 40 per cent of sub-Saharan African children are undernourished, that proportion is 40 to 60 per cent in India. A gigantic sum of public money is spent in the field of food in India, but much of that expenditure goes to keep the producers' price high, and to meet the cost of carrying large stocks from one year to the next. It is, of course, possible to make good use of a sensible proportion of those stocks to reduce undernourishment, particularly of the children. Indeed, it is possible to consider even very ambitious schemes of food guarantee for the undernourished in India through appropriate variations in public policy. But more modestly, much can be achieved even by such humble programmes as the serving of mid-day meals to all Indian school children—an arrangement that is already in operation in parts of the country. This would generate, simultaneously, a great many benefits: enhance nutrition, increase school attendance, raise the proportion of girls who go to school, help to break down caste barriers through communal eating, and reduce the common syndrome of attention deficit that standardly affects a considerable portion of the poorer school children who come to the school underfed.

The policy reform that is needed is largely a matter of clarity of economic and social thinking, and here public reasoning can certainly help. The Supreme Court has already identified the entitlement to a cooked mid-day meal as a right of Indian school children, but that right has been very partially implemented across the country. To proceed further, it is extremely important to generate political pressure about remedying the deprived state of Indian children. Public concerns can be made more effective through greater use of the opportunities that democracy offers, including quality newspapers and other media, which we are very fortunate to have.

Similar issues of public reasoning arise in a number of other problem areas, including the neglect of school education in general (despite the achievements of specialized technical and higher education in India), the poor state of basic health care (despite the quality of expensive private medicine), the deep insecurities suffered by vulnerable minorities (despite the secular form of the Indian polity), continued neglect of the interests and freedoms of women (despite the prominent role of many women leaders in politics and the professions), and so on. Political freedoms and transparency guarantee (particularly in the form of freedom of information) are direct requirements of democracy, but they in turn can be immensely powerful in expanding economic empowerment, social opportunities and protective security. There is nothing as contrary as grumbling about the limitations of Indian democracy without trying to do what we can to extend its reach. Since I do know that many of the participants in this seminar have made great contributions to expanding the scope and effectiveness of democracy, I am sure we will have the opportunity of benefiting enormously from the fruits of their experience.

The point is sometimes made that democracy cannot help those who do not form a majority. This thesis, based on a mechanical identification of democracy with just majority rule, is not only a mischaracterization, it also profoundly underestimates the role of public reasoning in politicizing social failures. Democracy is more than majority rule, and goes also beyond legal guarantees of minority rights (though making these guarantees effective can indeed be extremely important, as we know from recent events). Democracy must, in addition, include the availability and use of the opportunity of open public reasoning based on public knowledge which helps us to understand and value the freedoms of all members of the society without exception.

In illustrating the reach of public reasoning, I might consider one of the well recognized successes of the democratic system, namely the absence of famines in democratic countries. In fact, the proportion of famine victims in the total population is always comparatively small—very rarely more than 10 per cent. If elections are hard to win after a famine, and if criticisms from newspapers and the other media, and from the opposition parties, are difficult to brush off, the effectiveness of this mechanism lies in the ability of public discussion to make the predicament of famine victims generally understood by the population at large. Indeed, even the knowledge of a relatively small number of starvation deaths, as in say Kalahandi, can immediately generate massive public concern. It is the reach of public reasoning on which the effectiveness of democracy depends, and it is for us to make the reach as wide and extensive as possible.

I will end there, except for recounting a small event. Some years ago, I was talking with and trying to entertain a young child by telling her about Alice in the Wonderland. I thought she would be amused by Alice's question: 'What is the use of a book without pictures or conversations?' The child was indeed amused and readily agreed with Alice, but went on to retaliate by asking me whether my own books had pictures and conversations. I told her that, alas, my books did not really have anything that she would accept as a proper picture (I expected her to be sceptical of the picturesque quality of my statistical charts), but I added that my last book did begin with a conversation—indeed one that occurred thousands of years ago.

The child was quite impressed, but so—on reflection—was I. Why does it make sense...to pay attention to what we tell each other, and in this case, to listen to what Maitreyee told her husband, more than two and a half thousand years ago (with which my book began)? Maitreyee was, as it happens, talking about the unimportance of wealth in comparison with longevity. The answer to the puzzling question must be that talking to each other—arguing, debating and when necessary hollering—is the way we express our priorities, and then go on to examine and re-examine them, which give effectiveness to the results of our deliberations. All this is crucial for private comprehension, but particularly for public reasoning, involving unobstructed information, open scrutiny and political confrontation. It is also, for much the same reason, pivotal for the dynamism of the approach of development as freedom.

13

THE CHINESE AGGRESSION

The Chinese Army launched a major offensive against India in 1962. Commencing in September and ending with a unilateral ceasefire announced by China on 21 November, the war left in its wake a shattered army, a humiliated leadership and a bewildered nation plagued by self-doubt and unsure of its security.

With the conclusion of the Chinese Revolution in 1949, China had emerged as the second biggest communist country in the world with the erstwhile nationalist forces of Chiang Kai-shek confined to the island of Formosa (Taiwan). This coincided with the heightening of the Cold War during which the United States and the Western Bloc positioned themselves against the communist powers led by the Union of Soviet Socialist Republics. The People's Republic of China was considered a satellite of the Soviet Union and was not given a seat in the Security Council of the United Nations while even tiny Formosa had one. The United States did not recognize the claims of the People's Republic of China.

It was India and particularly Jawaharlal Nehru who advocated granting China its rightful place in the comity of nations. India fought for China's inclusion in the United Nations. At international forums, Nehru kept harping on China being independent of the Soviet Union and that Chinese communism was not, as Cold War theoreticians proclaimed, merely another chapter in the onward march of communism that had to be contained. The 1950s marked the high point of Indo-Chinese relationship, with its attendant slogan of

'Hindi–Chini bhai bhai'. However, dark clouds were just round the corner.

The Chinese aggression had its roots in China's efforts at consolidation, both internal and external. And in both these arenas, India, notwithstanding the friendly relations between the leadership of the two countries, became a roadblock. In consolidating its territorial boundaries just after the revolution, communist China looked towards Tibet, a region of great strategic importance which it considered under its sovereign control and which it had tried to capture many times in the past. Tibet had declared its independence in 1913 and at a conference in Simla in 1914, Tibetan, Indian and Chinese authorities had met to discuss the Tibetan demand for de facto sovereignty. China had refused to accede to the demand. The conference had decided to divide Tibet into inner and outer Tibet with the latter agreeing to acknowledge Chinese suzerainty if its autonomy was accepted. However, China did not sign the treaty. There was also an agreement between Indian and Tibetan representatives, with Sir Henry McMahon fixing the boundaries between Tibet and India. China was not a party to the meeting. It never accepted the McMahon Line and it disputed three Indian positions: in the eastern sector, called the North Eastern Frontier Area (NEFA), it claimed about 20,000 square km of Indian territory; a large chunk in the middle Himalayan sector; and in the western sector about 30,000 square km of high plateau known as the Aksai Chin in Ladakh district of Jammu and Kashmir bordering Tibet and the Xinjiang province of China. Not only that, China began to push its claims by defeating the Tibetan army at Chambdo in 1950 and forcing Lhasa to recognize Chinese sovereignty in 1951. The Chinese were in control of the area by 1952.

With these changes and the territorial boundaries now coming under close scrutiny, Indian and Chinese representatives met at Beijing in 1953-54. At the conclusion of a series of meetings, the Chinese premier Zhou Enlai and Indian Prime Minister Jawaharlal Nehru in their joint communiqué in June 1954 recognized the five principles of coexistence (Panchsheel or Pancha sila) as the foundation for future relations. These principles were: 1) mutual respect for each other's territorial integrity and sovereignty; 2) mutual non-aggression; 3) mutual non-interference in each other's internal matters; 4) equality and mutual benefit; and 5) peaceful coexistence. Later on, in the Bandung conference of Asian and African nations, this was popularized and Panchsheel became widely recognized and adopted as principles of international and interstate relations. In fact, at the conclusion of the 1954 meetings, China seemed to be in agreement with India and did not raise any objections to the Indian position which it questioned later on.

However, soon after this, reports started coming in that the Chinese were developing infrastructure in the Aksai Chin area. They planned a road from China to Tibet and from there via the Karakoram Range to Sinkiang and Mongolia and back to China. Aksai Chin was an obstruction on this road and soon China published maps showing the area as part of Chinese territory. It also asserted that it had never accepted the McMahon Line. A couple of meetings between Zhou Enlai and Nehru failed to resolve the issue. To further complicate the dynamics of the situation, the Dalai Lama, the temporal and spiritual leader of the Tibetan people, crossed over to India in March 1959 with 20,000 of his followers. The Indian government provided him with appropriate hospitality. This humiliated the Chinese leadership which attacked Nehru as a tool of the US-led anti-communist and particularly anti-Chinese bloc trying to sabotage their position in Tibet with the backing of the CIA.

Another bone of contention between India and China was their relative importance in world affairs. By 1956, India had emerged as the leader of the Third World, particularly after the Suez crisis which pitted Egypt against Israel, the United Kingdom and France. Nehru played a crucial moderating role during the crisis and prevented it from taking on an anti-West tone. In fact, he found an ally in the US which exerted pressure on the UK, France and Israel to withdraw. China desperately wanted to take on the leadership of the Third World and give it an anti-American slant. The Chinese attack on India was thus not just an effort to humiliate India but to finish off Nehru's leadership in the Third World. And it succeeded. After 1962, India retreated from making its claim to the leadership of the Third World.

By August 1959, incursions of the Chinese Army into Indian territory became frequent. In September 1962, a battalion of 600 Chinese soldiers crossed the Thagla Ridge at Leh. On 20 October 1962, the Chinese Army launched a full-scale offensive at the Chip Chap Valley in Ladakh which almost wiped out two Indian regiments positioned there. In the north-eastern sector also, Chinese forces made rapid inroads into Indian territory and by 18 November they had reached Tezpur, a major frontier town in Assam. Indian soldiers fought bravely but were no match for the well-prepared, strategically located and well-equipped Chinese Army.

The Chinese attack created a national crisis. The Communist Party of India with its sympathies for the communist movement across the world found itself at the receiving end of intense persecution. There were widespread attacks on members of the party and a large number of communists were arrested throughout the country under the Defence of India Rules. Nehru and his policy on China had been the object of criticism in India right through the 1950s, particularly from the Socialist Party with their anti-China stance and the right-wing Jana Sangh and Swatantra parties. On 21 August 1959, for example, a young Jana Sangh leader, Atal Bihari Vajpayee, had moved a resolution in the Lok Sabha to refer the Tibetan issue to the United Nations. J.B. Kripalani's critique of Nehru's Tibet policy was one of the most trenchant criticisms of Nehru's foreign policy with regard to China which became a handle to attack the entire gamut of government policies including the sympathies for the left and the championing of the Non-aligned Movement. In the aftermath of the Chinese invasion, there was naturally a massive nationalist upsurge which right-wing and communal parties exploited to discredit the communists whose loyalty to India was put under the scanner. Nehru too was savagely criticized for the military disaster.

It was, however, a victory of the spirit of the Indian freedom movement and her nascent democracy that India weathered the crisis notwithstanding the defeat at Chinese hands. The presence of Nehru and the indomitable sprit of communist leaders like Bhupesh Gupta, H.N. Mukherjee and A.K. Gopalan in and outside Parliament prevented the Indian state from becoming tyrannical as had happened with many other countries at the time. The tradition of democracy had been nurtured well enough for India to retain its democratic functioning and institutions even after such a national disaster. In the various debates that originated on the crisis, one discerns how leaders acted as sentinels of freedom and democracy.

~

JAWAHARLAL NEHRU

Massive Aggression on Our Frontiers

This was a speech Nehru would never have dreamt of making—asking the country to defend itself against external aggression. Though an ambassador of peace, Nehru nevertheless was a statesman and his address to the nation on

All India Radio, 22 October 1962, shows the hallmark of a statesman leading a country from the front. While it is essentially an attempt to rouse the nation in the face of a national emergency, there is also a tacit admittance of the fact that India might have been too trusting of a neighbour she should have been wary of given the latter's posturing in the years immediately preceding the aggression.

Comrades, Friends and Fellow countrymen, I am speaking to you on the radio after a long interval. I feel that I must speak to you about the grave situation which has arisen on our frontiers because of continuing and unabashed aggression by the Chinese forces. A situation has arisen which calls upon all of us to meet it effectively.

We are men and women of peace in this country, conditioned to the ways of peace. We are unused to the necessities of war. Because of this, we endeavoured to follow a policy of peace even when aggression took place on our territory in Ladakh five years ago. We explored avenues for an honourable settlement by peaceful methods. That was our policy all over the world, and we tried to apply it even in our own country. We know the horrors of war in this age today and we have done our utmost to prevent war from engulfing the world.

But all our efforts have been in vain in so far as our own frontier is concerned, where a powerful and unscrupulous opponent not caring for peace or peaceful methods, has continuously threatened us and even carried the threats into action. The time has therefore come for us to realise fully this menace which threatens the freedom of our people and the independence of our country. I say so even though I realise that no power can ultimately imperil the freedom which we have won at so much sacrifice and cost to our people after long ages of foreign domination. But to conserve that freedom and integrity of our territory we must gird up our loins and face this greatest menace which has come to us since we became independent. I have no doubt in my mind that we shall succeed. Everything else is secondary to the freedom of our people and of our Motherland. If necessary, everything else has to be sacrificed in this great crisis.

I do not propose to give you the long history of continuous aggression by the Chinese during the last five years and how they have tried to justify it by speeches, arguments and the repeated assertion of untruths and a campaign of calumny and vituperation against our country. Perhaps there are not many instances in history where one country that is India has gone out of her way to be friendly and cooperative with the Chinese Government and people and to plead their cause in the councils of the world and then for the Chinese Government to return evil for good and even go to the extent of committing aggression and invade our sacred land. No self-respecting country and certainly not India with her love of freedom can submit to this, whatever the consequences may be.

There have been five years of continuous aggression on the Ladakh frontier. Our frontier in NEFA remained largely free from this aggression. Just when we were discussing ways and means of reducing tension and there was even some chance of the representatives of the two countries meeting to consider this matter a new and fresh aggression took place on the NEFA border. This began on the 8th of September last. This was a curious way of lessening tension. It is typical of the way the Chinese Government have treated us.

Our border with China in the NEFA region is well known and well established from ages past. It is sometimes called the McMahon Line. This line which separated India from Tibet was the line of the high ridges which divided the watersheds. This has been acknowledged as the border by history, tradition and treaties long before it was called the McMahon Line. The Chinese have in many ways acknowledged it as the border, even though they have called the McMahon Line illegal. The Chinese laid claim in their maps to a large part of NEFA which has been under our administration for a long time... Even the maps which the Chinese produced were acknowledged by them repeatedly to be old and out-of-date maps which had little relevance today.

Yet on this peaceful border where no trouble or fighting had occurred for a long time the Chinese committed aggression and that in very large numbers and after vast preparations for a major attack.

I am grieved at the setbacks to our troops that have occurred on this frontier and the reverse that we have had. They were overwhelmed by vast numbers and by big artillery, mountain guns and heavy mortars... There may be some more reverses in that area. But one thing is certain that the final result of this conflict will be in our favour. It cannot be otherwise when a nation like India fights for her freedom and the integrity of the country.

We have to meet a powerful and unscrupulous opponent. We have therefore to build up our strength and power to face this situation adequately and with confidence. The conflict may continue for long. We must prepare ourselves for it mentally and otherwise. We must have faith in ourselves and I am certain that the faith and our preparations will triumph. No other result is conceivable. Let there be this faith and fixed determination to free our country from the aggressor.

We must steel our wills and direct the nation's energy and resources to this one end. We must change our procedures from slow moving methods of peacetime to those that produce results quickly. We must build up our military strength by all means at our disposal.

But military strength is not by itself enough. It has to be supported fully by the industry of the nation and by increase in our production in every way. I would appeal to all our workers not to indulge in strikes or in any other act which comes in the way of increasing production. That production has to be not only in the factory but in the field. No anti-national or anti-social activities can be tolerated when the nation is in peril.

We shall have to carry a heavy burden whatever our vocations may be. The price of freedom will have to be paid in full measure and no price is too great for the freedom of our people and of our Motherland.

I earnestly trust and I believe that all parties and groups in the country will unite in this great enterprise and put aside their controversies and arguments which have no place today and present a solid united front against all those who seek to endanger our freedom and integrity.

The burden on us is going to be great. We must add greatly to our savings by the purchase of bonds to help to finance production and meet the increasing cost of national defence. We must prevent any rise in prices and we must realise that those who seek to profit at a time of national difficulty are anti-national and injure the nation.

We are in the middle of our Third Five Year Plan. There can be no question of our giving up this Plan or reducing any important element of it. We may adapt it to the new requirements here and there. But essentially the major projects of the Plan must be pursued and implemented because it is in that way that we shall strengthen our country not only in the present crisis but in the years to come.

There are many other things which our people can do and I hope to indicate some of them at a later stage. But the principal thing is to devote ourselves to the task of forging the national will to freedom and to work hard to that end. There is no time-limit to this. We shall carry on the struggle as long as we do not win because we cannot submit to the aggression or to the domination of others.

We must avoid any panic because that is bad at any time and there is no reason for it. We have behind us the strength of a united nation. Let us rejoice because of this and apply it to the major task of today which is preserving our complete freedom and integrity and the removal of all those who commit aggression on India's sacred territory. Let us face this crisis not light-heartedly but with seriousness and with a stout heart and with firm faith in the rightness of our struggle and confidence in its outcome. Do not believe in rumours. Do not listen to those who have faint hearts. This is a time of trial and testing for all of us and we have to steel ourselves to the task. Perhaps we were growing too soft and taking things for granted. But freedom can never be taken for granted. It requires always awareness, strength and austerity.

I invite all of you, to whatever religion or party or group you may belong, to be comrades in this great struggle that has been forced upon us. I have full faith in our people and in our cause and in the future of our country. Perhaps that future requires some such testing and stiffening for us.

We have followed a policy of non-alignment and sought friendship of all nations. I believe in that policy fully and we shall continue to follow it. We are not going to give up our basic principles because of the present difficulty. Even this difficulty will be more effectively met by our continuing that policy.

I wish you well and whatever may befall us in the future, I want you to hold your heads high and have faith and full confidence in the great future that we envisage for our country. Jai Hind.

~

HARI VISHNU KAMATH

The 1962 War: A Critical Evaluation

H.V. Kamath, an ardent supporter of Subhas Chandra Bose, had been a vocal leader in Parliament since 1948. Critical of the communists, Kamath was an articulate and often vociferous critic of Nehru's policies too. His speeches, particularly on civil liberty and other domestic issues, were of a very high quality. In a speech delivered in the Lok Sabha on 9 November 1962, during the discussion on the resolution regarding the proclamation of emergency on account of the Chinese aggression, he launched a fierce attack on international communism and criticized Nehru and his supporters, asking them to show some fight and lead from the front. The concluding part of the speech is reproduced here.

... The Himalayas are not today a physical barrier; they are not a physical mountain. They are an ideological frontier between democracy and communism. The eternal snow-capped sentinel of our sages, of our munis, of our poet Rabindranath Tagore '*Ambar chumbit bhal Himachal.*' That Himalaya is now the dividing line between democracy and communism. And this communist conspiracy, the international communist conspiracy, must be scotched on the heights, not at the foot-hills of the Himalayas.

The heart of the nation is sound. The heart of the Indian nation and the Indian people is sound. They are only asking for a strong, determined, courageous and dedicated leadership. When Gandhiji was with us, when Netaji was with us, and when Nehruji was marching shoulder to shoulder with those two great leaders, did not the nation respond? What was the secret of that? It was leadership, and again, leadership. And if that leadership is forthcoming in abundant measure, I have no doubt in my mind the people will respond and give all that they have, even their lives. Leadership must rise to the occasion, and give that kind of leadership to this country. I hope that the Prime Minister who has done so much in the past for the country, worked and fought for the country in the company of Mahatmaji and Netaji, now after having streamlined his Cabinet, after having reshuffled his Cabinet to some extent—he may do a little more—should rise to the occasion and give such leadership to the Indian people, the men and women and children of this country, of this vast land. If that is done, then, as was said by one of the Sikh gurus in a different context, '*Sava Lakh Se Ek Ladau*' our forty crores of Indians will be more than a match for the seventy crores of Chinese in their country, and we will drive them back. There is no doubt about that. I am sure about that. If that is forthcoming, under God with hope and faith, the nation will march undaunted, and avenge our reverses, avenge those defeats of the past, the shame and humiliation of the past few weeks, and will go on marching not merely to victory in war but to a victorious peace, and that I am sure will come within the lifetime of this very Parliament. I am sure of that, and we shall all acclaim the victorious peace. Jai Hind!

~

J.B. KRIPALANI

Motion Regarding the White Paper on Indo-Chinese Relations

J.B. Kripalani was one of the staunchest critics of Jawaharlal Nehru's policy on China and the lack of preparedness on the part of the country in the face of external aggression. His sharp and sarcastic tone and his language were more than a match for Nehru's eloquence. However, in spite of the bitter criticism, his words never crossed the boundaries of decency and parliamentary decorum. This speech, delivered while moving the motion on 12 September 1959 in the Lok Sabha, was by far the most significant one attacking Nehru for all the sins of omission and commission on the China question. It did not merely demonize Nehru on the issue, like many other political parties and personalities did during the aggression as well as in later years; it laid down his understanding of the nature of the Chinese revolution, the 'totalitarian regime' in power there, and its possible impact on its neighbours which India had chosen to overlook at its own peril. It also criticized the Indian government's response to China's takeover of Tibet, suggesting the 'morally right' course India should have adopted vis-à-vis the Chinese occupation of Tibet.

It is a very serious matter we are discussing here today. You will not, therefore, mind if I make constant reference to my notes. I have been speaking upon this topic inside and outside the House since 1950. In connection with Tibet, in 1950, I said: 'Our Government's attitude is understandable on the assumption that Tibet is a far-off country, and none of our business. But supposing what has happened in Tibet happens to Nepal, supposing the Chinese liberation forces come to Nepal, then, I am sure we will fight, whether we are ready or not.'

Again, in 1954, after signing of the Indo-Chinese agreement, I said that the destruction of a buffer state was an unfriendly act, and was dangerous for the security and safety of India. Many nations have gone to war on that issue. I am not saying this to remind the House that I said so. We have more serious business than that. Why did I say all these things? It was because I had taken note of the serious nature of the revolution that had taken place in China. Our Prime Minister while speaking in the Rajya Sabha said that 'the revolution was a major factor in history, and any appraisal of the situation neglecting the fact of the revolution would be utterly wrong; and many of the troubles in the international world were due to the fact that a deliberate attempt was made not to recognise the major events in human history'.

I entirely agree with the Prime Minister. I may submit that if some countries in the West have failed to recognise the significance of the Chinese Revolution, I am afraid we have done no better. This Revolution, by whatever name we may call it, has established in China a totalitarian government. Such a regime can only be a military regime. It is based upon power and force. Its appeal is to authority and not to reason. It does not believe in cooperation but strict obedience and regimentation. All education is turned into propaganda. Truth is subject to party loyalty. Such a regime is fanatical. It pays no regard to the purity of means. It is controlled either by a dictator or by a self-perpetuating junta of politicians. Whatever such a regime may do at home may not be the concern of neighbouring countries. But it is a concern of every peaceful neighbour to see what its international policy is.

The foreign policy of a totalitarian government cannot but be expansionist. It is natural. Power, if not increased, will fade away. Therefore, if we are really to take note of the tremendous revolution that has taken place in China, we must not forget its aggressive nature.

History has also proved that whatever effect a revolution may have in internal politics, it does not change the foreign policy of a nation. The French Revolution did not change the foreign policy of France initiated by Louis XIV. The Fascist revolution in Italy and Germany did not change the foreign policy of these countries. Bolshevik Russia follows the foreign policy of Peter the Great and the Czars of nibbling at its neighbours. We see today China is following the expansionist policy of its predecessor imperial regimes. There is nothing to wonder at that.

I submit that if some Western nations have overemphasised the totalitarian and militarist and expansionist character of the Chinese Revolution, we in India have minimised it. May I submit that if there is a choice in international affairs, it is better to overemphasise danger than to underemphasise it? If we do the latter, we shall be caught unaware and unprepared and our people will also be caught so.

So, we had the taste of this new totalitarian regime in China. Immediately after the Communists had established their rule on the mainland the old Imperial policy was followed in Tibet, a helpless and a disarmed country. While the former imperial regimes in China were content and were satisfied with the exercise of suzerainty, the new regime wanted complete control of Tibet. They would have nothing less than that.

Again, we had other indications about the character of this regime. In October 1949, in reply to a telegram of congratulations from the Indian Communist Party on the success of the communists in China, Mr. Mao Tse-tung sent the following telegram: 'I firmly believe that relying on the brave Communist Party of India and the unity of all patriots, India will not certainly remain long under the yoke of imperialism and its collaborators. Like China, India will one day merge in the socialist democratic family.'

It is family indeed, for there is one and the same family for communists all over the world, wherever they may be born. Further, in Chinese eyes, and unfortunately in the communists' eyes here, we were not free even in 1949, and our Government was a collaborator. Our Government was collaborating with Western imperialists. I suppose in the eyes of China and in the eyes of some of our own countrymen, we do not seem to have achieved our freedom yet; liberation is yet to come, and, therefore, we see the march of Chinese armies on our borders; and they are liberation forces. The idea that we were stooges of Western imperialism was again made clear to us when instinctively, our Prime Minister protested against Chinese excursion in Tibet. He said, 'It was not quite clear from whom the Chinese were liberating Tibet.' History has given the answer. Every fanatical creed, whether it be religious or political, undertakes to make people free from themselves, and make them happy against their will. We are familiar with it. This apart, we got a prompt answer to our protest; we were told that we had made our protest because we were stooges of Western imperial powers. In fact, the language was more vulgar. This vulgarity has continued all through the years. Our Prime Minister has politely called it the language of the cold war. Instead of resenting these insults, we merely submitted to them and recognised Chinese sovereignty over Tibet. This proved to the Chinese that we would submit to their bullying tactics. I am afraid we have been doing so throughout these years.

Some people have asked: What could India have done? Could it have gone to war on the issue of Tibet? It need not have. But while recognising the de facto sovereignty of China on the mainland, India should have refused to recognise Chinese rule in Tibet. It would have put us morally in the right. We do not recognise the right of France over Algeria. Are we, therefore, at war with that country? Do we not have diplomatic and friendly relations with it? By submitting to the rape of Tibet, I am very sorry to say, the Prime Minister has repudiated what he has often said, that wherever there is injustice and tyranny, India shall not remain neutral; it will always stand for justice and fair play. It is but fair that I remind him of these words.

I want the House and the country to know and to mark that China in her internal and international advance is even more quick and thorough than Russia. Russia began its expansion only when its revolution was 23 years old, and even then when Europe was in the throes of the world war. China began its campaign as soon as its power was established on the mainland. I want the House to mark that difference between the two regimes.

I have talked of the totalitarian and military character of the new Chinese regime. This fact comes out more clearly more recently. In a statement of the Chinese Ambassador made to our Foreign Secretary as late as May this year, he says: 'China will not be so foolish as to antagonise the United States in the East and again to antagonise India in the West.'

This, Sir, reminds me of Hitler's theory of war on one front. But strangely enough, the Chinese have chosen not the eastern, but the western front … which they have done in spite of the fact that in the east, the territory that they want to liberate is undoubtedly Chinese territory and the people are also Chinese people and not foreign people. Of course, they tried the eastern front a couple of years back when they attacked the off-shore islands under the sway of Chiang Kai-shek. It should not have been difficult for the Chinese to take possession of these islands. They were not useful to the United States or to Chiang Kai-shek. But the USA resisted the attack on these islands which were not of much use to it. The late Mr. Dulles made it plain that communists will move out of the mainland only at the expense of a third world war. For this, China with her population of 600 million was not prepared. They were not prepared for a war. Therefore, what remained for Communist China was an incursion in the west, on the Indian frontier. They think they are avoiding a second front as Hitler did. But who knows one day they may have no choice but to fight on both the fronts?

In 1954, we entered into a treaty with the Chinese Government. I am sorry to say that by that treaty, we recognised not only the suzerainty, but also the sovereignty, of China over Tibet. If we did that, it was very necessary to try and settle the borders with China. All along, we had common borders with Tibet. Now, these were turned into common borders with China. We are told that there was some talk of borders at the time the treaty was signed, but nothing was decided. Later too, there was some talk about that in 1956 when the two Prime Ministers met here, but there was nothing in writing. We knew, or ought to have known, that between China and Burma, there are border disputes and they have not yet been decided, and the Chinese Government has not been able to carry out its own promises. This, I quote from the Prime Minister. In international dealings, treaties or other documents, it is dangerous to leave matters at the level of talk without any signed documents. It is best to have everything in writing. Even when there is a talk, the notes of the talk must be accepted by both parties and signed. This seems not to have been done, in spite of the fact that semantic difficulties were felt by both the parties, as we are told by the Prime Minister. Our Prime Minister is too shrewd a politician not to know that in international intercourse, words have today ceased to have ordinary dictionary meaning. Therefore, it was the more necessary that everything should be in black and white. Even then, there are apprehensions of misinterpretation, but the field of misunderstanding is narrowed down. At least, the neutrals can see what is right and what is wrong in a document.

Some members in the Rajya Sabha said that the Chinese had become wild with us after the grant of asylum to the Dalai Lama and the Tibetan refugees. The Prime Minister seemed to endorse this view. It may be that their wrath has increased after these events. But in this, too, the Chinese are different from the Russians: the Chinese are more unreasonable. The Hungarian refugees sought asylum in many European countries, but Russia has not on that account indulged in border aggression against those countries. However, the Chinese aggression began earlier. According to Dr. Kunzru, aggression began in 1952. In 1954 we had Panchsheel—the five principles of peaceful co-existence. I need not discuss here these principles except to say that all these principles are based upon the maintenance of the status quo, however cruel and iniquitous it may be.

The principles were enunciated in order to put a seal of approval on the sovereignty of China over Tibet. Therefore, on one occasion, I was constrained to say in this House that the Panchsheel was born in sin. In spite of the agreement and the Panchsheel, aggression on our borders began three months after the signing of the treaty, as pointed out in the White Paper. It has since been going on and it has been increasing. It would appear as if the Chinese were waiting simply for the signing of the treaty which recognised their sovereignty in Tibet. Every time they have indulged in the aggression, they have blamed us and drawn our attention to the Panchsheel. I am reminded of a Hindi proverb which I need not quote here. It has something to do with the Kotwal and the danda.

Our territories have been occupied, our people have been kidnapped, our guards have been fired at, taxes have been collected, roads have been built leading towards India; check and observation posts established along our borders and even, as the report says, trenches have been dug in many places along the frontier. In Ladakh a regular motor road has been built and it is said that an aerodrome has been established in our territory.

Sir, much as I dislike Chinese aggression on our borders, I am much more concerned with what our Government has done or proposes to do about it. After all, the Chinese, as I have said, are working in consonance with the genius of their regime and in pursuance of their international goal. But, whatever aggressions have been there so far I regret to say that the country has been kept in ignorance of this aggression for a long period, even though many notes, through the years, have passed between the two countries. The Parliament elicited this through questions in this and the other House. No information was even given voluntarily. Even then, it has been meagre, and, often, the acts of aggression have been minimised—may I say almost excused. Sometimes, it would appear there has been special pleading for the Chinese.

Recently, Sir, when there was a question about the road built by China in Ladakh, the House was told, if I remember aright and speaking subject to correction, that it was not a regular road but stones were kept to mark the passage. But, now, we know it is a motor road. No mention was made of the aerodrome built in our territory. We were told that the territory was mountainous—where nothing could grow, not even a blade of grass—and no people lived there.

There are places in Rajasthan today where all these conditions exist. May I know what the Government would do if some of those parts are invaded by Pakistan? Sir, then, another question arises. If these places are so uninhabitable for man and vegetable, then, why do the Chinese want to occupy them? It is a strange thing that they should earn the ill-will of India and occupy portions of territory that are of no use to them. Our people have a shrewd suspicion and it is this that these uninhabitable places are occupied to serve as springboards for future action. A springboard has not to be green or populated. Our people are not thinking in terms of a few miles of barren rock. They are thinking in terms of the honour of the country which has some meaning for them. Apart from that, they are thinking of something more and it is this that they are thinking about the safety and the freedom of their country in the near future. Here then lies the trouble which people with their horse-sense are able to sense.

... While there are acts of aggression on our territory, while violent and angry notes are sent to us, on our side we are satisfying ourselves merely with sending back polite notes or protests. Also, all the time, what is more painful, our people are being encouraged to keep on repeating the mantram, 'Chini Hindi Bhai Bhai'. This, I am sure, makes our people, if not our leaders, look ridiculous before the world. Such conduct lowers our dignity of which we are reminded so often by our Prime Minister.

Sir, I also do not understand this over-politeness of ours. After all, in ordinary conversation, we regulate the pitch of our voice according to the hearing capacity of the listener. If he is hard of hearing, we raise our voice; if a man does not understand polite language, we may not abuse him, but we must speak in plain and unvarnished language. Nobody would be more polite and courteous than Gandhiji. But many times, he had to use hard and harsh words against British Imperialism. On one occasion, I remember he wrote an article in *Young India* with the caption 'Shaking the Mane of the British Lion'. It formed part of the prosecution which he had to face and for it he was awarded six months' imprisonment. (Some Hon. Members: Six years.) Six years. Sir, we cannot be more polite than the Father of the Nation when dealing with aggression. It is natural for us to be anxious to avoid a major complication which may precipitate a war. A war between the two countries is bound to develop into a global war whether one likes it or not. But we cannot avoid war through appeasement. Appeasement is always at the expense of one's honour. It has also never saved peace. It did not save peace in Europe in 1939.

I would like to know what the Government proposes to do under the present circumstances. I have read the Prime Minister's speech in the Rajya Sabha several times. I am afraid, I find no indication of this in the Prime Minister's speech. Is there any idea to throw back the Chinese out of the territories they have occupied? As their aggression is described by our communist friends as merely 'border incidents', so will our action in turning them back be a 'border incident'. When we have cleared our borders of aggression, we can, then, think in terms of negotiations, but always on the basis of McMahon line. The maintenance of the status quo can only be when aggression has been stopped and the territories occupied by the Chinese re-occupied by our people. Our Prime Minister has as a last resort proposed arbitration. It is not usual to submit the cases of national territories to arbitration. National territory belongs to the people of the country. (Hear, hear.) It cannot be the subject of arbitration. Apart from this, who can arbitrate in this case? What country except Russia will be acceptable to China? All other countries, whether they are capitalist or socialist, in the world are capitalist and as such imperialist! Even communist Yugoslavia, if it is not capitalist, is a stooge of capitalists and the imperialists, though it may call itself communist or Marxist. However, all this can come after our territory has been cleared of aggression.

During the course of his speech in the Rajya Sabha, our Prime Minister has, in answer to Dr. Kunzru, said that there could be no change in our foreign policy and that it stands as firm as a rock though today even the Himalayas are shaking. I am afraid that, when the Prime Minister says this, he is thinking merely in terms of the basic principles of our policy. What are these principles? India stands for peace. India stands for disarmament. India stands for non-alignment with the power blocs. That is not all. There is a furthersome thing. India also stands for international justice and fair play. The Prime Minister himself has often said that in the case of injustice and tyranny, India will not remain neutral. I am afraid we have not acted upon this principle in the case of Tibet.

In this House talking about our foreign policy two years back, I have said that it is a mistake to suppose the foreign policy of a country consists merely in enunciating abstract and basic principles. It must also think in terms of appropriate strategy and tactics, through which these principles are to be given effect to. We have failed to embody our principles into appropriate strategy and tactics for effective action. It may be that in evolving these, we may have to modify our principles to some extent. There will always be a gulf between principles and practice, between the ideal and the actual. That cannot be avoided in this defective world. I submit for the consideration of the Prime Minister that we have failed in our foreign policy at the level of strategy and tactics. Herein some modification is surely necessary if we are to be effective.

Sir, in conclusion, I would beg of the Government to be firm.

Their vacillation and the Prime Minister's varying statements confuse the public minds. A confused people cannot be ready for an emergency. Even in his Press interview yesterday, the Prime Minister talked of restraint. Restraint without action is meaningless. I can quite understand that there should be restraint in giving expression to the feelings when our people go and demonstrate against an Embassy. That is not desirable and I am one with the Prime Minister when he condemns these things. But how are the feelings of the people to get expression unless there is action behind what they want to be done? Talking of this restraint is just like talking of restraining a horse and tightening when the damn horse does not exist. I can assure the Prime Minister, if he needs any assurance that the country will be behind him to a man—and even to a woman—if he takes effective action against foreign aggression.

~

BHUPESH GUPTA

Communist Support to the War Effort

In the wake of the Chinese aggression, communists in India came under attack from right-wing communalists, nationalists of every hue, and even government agencies. Their patriotism was questioned and many were hauled up and imprisoned on the suspicion of sympathizing with the Chinese. The irresponsible behaviour of its cadres in some places worsened what was to begin with a difficult situation. In this speech, regarded by some as one of the most powerful in the history of Indian parliamentary democracy, made in the Rajya Sabha on 8 November 1962, Bhupesh Gupta not only defended the communists, strongly asserting their patriotic credentials, but also stood up for Jawaharlal Nehru on his handling of the crisis. The speech played a significant role in blunting the attacks on Nehru across the political spectrum.

May I at the outset pay the respectful homage of our Group in this House to the men and officers of our Armed Forces who have made the supreme sacrifice in defending our frontiers and the honour and integrity of our country? The story of their bravery and sacrifice is yet to be fully told, but we cannot but record our deep appreciation of the manner in which they have held aloft the banner of our Motherland. Fighting against overwhelming manpower and firepower, our jawans and their officers have displayed their flaming patriotism and their irrepressible courage. In their martyrdom once again it has been demonstrated that the honour and integrity of our country are not going to be bartered away or surrendered. Permit me also on this occasion to send our deep sympathies and condolences to the bereaved families of our martyrs on the frontiers. We also fervently wish that those men and officers who have been injured will soon recover.

The unity and resolve of the entire nation to face the Chinese aggression is perhaps the greatest tribute to the heroism and sacrifice of India's sons in soldiers' uniforms. The nation's abundant best wishes go to these men and officers who are fighting so valiantly to defend our country and to regain the territories that have been lost as a result of the recent Chinese aggression.

Sir, the nation is now in the midst of a grave situation face to face with the challenge to its territorial integrity and its honour. This has forced upon us the state of emergency and compelled us to direct our energies to the maximum possible extent so that India's honour and integrity are upheld at all costs. It is a tragedy that the Indian Republic and its Government which have been pursuing a policy of peace and tirelessly working for friendship among nations for the promotion of peaceful co-existence should have today been subjected to this open aggression.

The Chinese aggression has rightly roused the indignation of the entire Indian people. The manifold barriers of party, region and other affiliations which divide our people have as far as this issue is concerned simply disappeared. The nation has risen as one man to meet the challenge. We fully share the just patriotic indignation of our people. It would be the greatest folly on anyone's part to imagine that a great nation like India can be intimidated, humbled and humiliated. India has not fought for long years and won her national independence to see it trampled underfoot on her frontiers. We have not become a free nation to have our freedom thus attacked and menaced. Hence along with the entire nation our Party joins hands with all patriotic people and stands behind the Prime Minister's appeal for national unity in defence of the country.

The national defence is the supreme task of the hour. It is a sacred task which calls for sacrifice, unity and dedication. So long as China maintains its present posture and refuses to see the way of reason, so long as she persists in the aggression and occupies India's territory, all-out efforts for the defence of the Motherland naturally remain the crucial and central task. Defence efforts mean the efforts not only on the frontiers but also in the rear. Everything must be done to improve the fighting capacity of our Armed Forces. The needs of equipment and other needs must receive the topmost priority. Let it not be said that when they were fighting on the mountains with so much courage and spilling their warm blood, we who live in the rear did not rise equal to the occasion. We are sure, now that the Prime Minister himself is in charge of national defence, every step will be taken to improve the position of our men and officers on the frontiers and meet all their needs. At this testing moment, the Prime Minister, if I may say so, symbolises the will and resolve of the entire nation.

... May I now say a word or two about the totally wrong, unobjective and hence untruthful evaluation of Prime Minister Nehru by the Chinese authorities. We are shocked that the Chinese radio and press are calling Prime Minister Nehru an agent of US imperialism, expansionist, tool of US imperialism, etc. Since when has he become a US agent? Since when has he become an expansionist? When the Panchsheel was signed in 1954, and the Bandung Conference took place in 1955, the Chinese had exactly the opposite things to say in praise of Prime Minister Nehru. At that time they were of course telling the truth. What has happened since then? In the years that have followed the signing of the Panchsheel, and the Bandung Conference, Prime Minister Nehru has played an even greater part in upholding the cause of world peace, in supporting the liberation struggles against imperialism. His voice has been heard in championing such causes not only on the floor of this Parliament but also from the forum of the United Nations Organisation. Indeed, under his able leadership, as a champion of peace and non-alignment, our country has played such a remarkable, constructive part for safeguarding world peace and against colonialism. Did he not stand up against aggression in Egypt? Did he not acclaim the Cuban struggle, recognise the Algerian freedom movement? Did he not extend full-throated support to the Congolese people and the people of Angola? Did he not liberate Goa defying the anger of imperialist quarters and Portuguese imperialism? Is he not even today supporting the cause of the People's Republic of China in the United Nations while some others are opposing it? Is he not maintaining good and friendly relations with the Soviet Union and other socialist countries as well as with the non-aligned newly liberated nations? Why then is he so maligned and attacked? We totally repudiate this politically wrong and otherwise harmful propaganda by China. This does not certainly help to improve the situation. Today the newly liberated non-aligned nations are a big progressive force in the world. They are playing a great historic role, and how can you explain that role if you leave out India? In the forefront of the camp of peace-loving and non-aligned nations playing a constructive role for the sake of peace and freedom, India occupies clearly the first place and we are proud of it. And is this position of India imaginable today without the role and leadership of Prime Minister Nehru?

May I mention that the progressive people the world over do not share the view of the Chinese in regard to Prime Minister Nehru? On the contrary, they acknowledge with profound respect and gratitude the constructive part Prime Minister Nehru has been playing in the international arena today. The sooner the Chinese side returns to truth and objectivity in regard to the assessment of Prime Minister Nehru and his Government, the better for them and for all those who are interested in strengthening the camp of peace and freedom. Normal relations with India can never be restored on the basis of this totally wrong assessment.

Our Party has pledged itself to participate fully in all activities for promotion of national unity, defence and strengthening of the morale of the people. In many States our comrades are already taking their posts and sharing the responsibilities in this hour of difficulty. It is a question of principle for us as citizens of India, as sons and daughters of our Motherland. Whatever may be the provocation from any quarter, we propose unflinchingly to play our part along with the rest of our people in fulfilling the assignments the Prime Minister's call embodies. We only hope that while taking practical steps or making arrangements, the Prime Minister's call for unity will be borne in mind. Unity cannot be built on the basis of pettiness, prejudices or by trying to take narrow sectarian political advantage out of the situation.

Let the fundamental greatness of the nation be displayed in its unity, in its resolve, in its patriotism, in its readiness to make sacrifices and in its dedication to the service of our country and its honour. We are convinced that our cause which is just and honourable will triumph and India shall emerge out of this grim test with flying colours. Let us then rally to this call of the nation, pledge ourselves altogether and all in unity. Once again on behalf of my Party, we extend our full support to the Prime Minister and to the Government in the tasks that lie ahead.

But before I sit down may I make a complaint with deep sorrow and agony? I wish I did not have to refer to it. You have read in today's newspapers that a number of Communists have been arrested in different parts of the country. It pains us that the Government should have taken this action against our comrades when we are mobilising our Party in response to the Prime Minister's call for national unity and for national defence and for the defence of our Motherland. I fervently hope that the Prime Minister, the Home Minister, for whom I have great regard naturally, and the leaders of the State Governments will realise that all this is absolutely needless and unwarranted and a waste of energy on their part. I hope they would find their way to releasing the comrades who have been arrested. The line of our Party has been clearly set forth by the recent resolution of our Party's National Council and we, as a disciplined Party, every member of the Party, are in dead earnest in implementing this line in all seriousness and with all sincerity. I once again appeal to the Government of India and to the State Governments not to take recourse to such needless actions against the members of our Party.

Finally, Mr. Chairman, I reiterate the pledge of our support in this hour, of crisis in every way, in this hour of peril or threat to our security and independence. No matter what the Government does, no matter how many Communists are put in prison, the Communists, every one of them, the leaders and the rank and file, shall take their place and posts alongside our compatriots in the defence of our Motherland and for the protection of the honour and integrity of our country. I support the Resolution.

P.N. SAPRU

Defence of India Bill, 1962

The year 1962 was an important milestone in Indian democracy. The Chinese attack, barely fifteen years after independence, was a matter of grave concern as it was quite possible that a nascent democracy would fail in the face of its first major crisis. There was a danger that taking advantage of the emergency, either the military would take over or a strong dictator would emerge or some foreign power would start dictating terms in the name of saving India from further attacks. The aggression could have given rise to a totalitarian regime, forever impairing individual freedom. However, when national emergency was proclaimed in 1962, there were vigilant members present who saw to it that it did not curb individual freedom more than what was necessitated by the situation. P.N. Sapru, a sharp legal mind and a prominent jurist, was one such ever-watchful presence in Parliament. While speaking on the debate on the Defence of India Bill, 1962, on 7 December 1962, he talked of something extremely significant—judicial review.

As to the emergency there can be no doubt, and I am not going to argue that there is emergency. No person howsoever much he might value personal freedom—and I confess that I value it very very much—can deny that there is a great emergency facing the nation. Therefore, one cannot object to the scheme of this Bill. I, therefore, support the Bill. I have, however, to make a few observations regarding one or two points.

The first question of importance is that of the reviewing authority. The reviewing authority in cases of detention should be a judicial authority. It should be a judicial officer. It should be a High Court judge or a retired High Court judge or a judicial officer within the meaning of Article 236 of the Constitution. It is a well-known principle embedded in our jurisprudence that the prosecutor must not be the judge. The judge here will have to decide whether there are any grounds for suspicion. He will not have to pass a verdict on the guilt or otherwise of the person concerned. He will have to apply his mind to the question whether there are any grounds for suspicion. For that task a person who is judicially trained is better qualified than a person who has had experience in administrative life... I would not like the Chief Secretary to sit in judgement over the orders of the District Magistrate. I would not like Members of the Board of Revenue to sit in judgement over an order passed by District Magistrates... Justice must not only be done but must seem to be done. We must remember that it is a democracy which is fighting a totalitarian State. It is not a totalitarian State which is fighting another totalitarian State. We must not, in fighting a totalitarian State, ourselves become a totalitarian State. That is my point number one.

The second point to which I would like to draw your attention is that of the constitution of Special Tribunals. Here I must say that the Home Minister has shown a commendable spirit of liberalism. He has accepted some of the suggestions which were made by us at the Informal Committee meeting which we had with him. But I would by way of answer to Mr. Santhanam say that the right of special appeal which you cannot deny under the Constitution to the accused would become farcical if the evidence is not recorded. Most of the cases triable under this Act are cases which would be covered by existing provisions and I therefore welcome the liberalisation of the clause in question. I would further point out that so far as the right of appeal is concerned, there is another remedy open to the applicant, which has not been emphasised here. That remedy is an application for a writ of prohibition or *certiorari* under Article 226 of the Constitution. The Tribunal will also be subject to the superintendence of the High Court under Article 227 of the Constitution. Now, I know that the powers of the High Court exercised under Article 226 are of a limited character. But even so, they are of a revisory [*sic*] character and in a proper case it can interfere even where there is no evidence to support a conviction. It can interfere where there is an error apparent on the face of the record. Therefore there is a remedy which is available to an accused person.

Writ of *habeas corpus* is also possible. That right may have been taken away so far as the Criminal Procedure Code is concerned but that right has not been taken away so far as the Constitution is concerned. And it cannot be taken away so far as the Constitution is concerned.

So far as the right of special appeal is concerned, there is no such thing as a right. Article 226 gives discretion to the Supreme Court to do justice in all manner of cases, and in the exercise of that power, it entertains appeals and there is therefore no question, as far as I know, of any deposit such as is required in ordinary appeals in the Supreme Court. Therefore, in a fit case it will be open to the Supreme Court to grant special leave of appeal to a person convicted by these Tribunals. Therefore, there are some judicial safeguards of a healthy character in this Bill.

There is one further observation which I may make with your leave. I am not opposed to your taking action against individual Communists or individual Fascists or other individuals who are hampering the war effort. But I would not like this House or this Parliament becoming an anti-Communist body. We are not professionally anti-Communist. We must remember that the leader of the largest Communist Party in Europe, Mr. Togliatti, accused China of being unreasonable the other day at the International Congress of Communists in Italy. There are elements in the Communist world which have deplored the activities of China, and it is not desirable for us to irritate or annoy those elements.

Finally, I would like to say that while victory must be ours, we cannot rule out the path of negotiation. We have to think in terms of negotiation from strength and I am therefore happy that President Nasser who has—I repeat—been a good friend of this country is sending his special representative to the Colombo Conference. I hope that the Colombo Conference will be able to evolve a formula which China may not disregard. The difficulty with China is that, outlawed by the comity of nations, she acts and feels like an outlaw. It is a vicious circle which we have to break and we have got to combine strength with reasonableness, we have to combine the capacity for firm negotiations with the capacity for adjustment and elasticity. I am not indulging in language of undue moderation when I say all this. I would like our war effort to be strong and effective. But I do not believe in brave words unless they are backed up by military strength of a character which can overawe the Chinese people. We are grateful to the United States and the United Kingdom for coming to our help. But I may just remind some Members that British papers like *The Guardian* or *The New Statesman* or *The Tribune* have been suggesting to this country in their own inimitable way that we should not rule out negotiations on certain terms. Well, that is what I would say by way of answer to Mr. Santhanam.

Then, Sir, there is one suggestion which has been made by Mr. Santhanam, which I whole-heartedly endorse and that is that the Home Minister should present annual report to us on the working of this measure which is undoubtedly of a very drastic character. We know that he is a man of great humanity, and we can be certain that the powers with which the executive has been vested by the unanimous vote of this House will be used in a moderate manner in a manner befitting a great Government.

14

STATE OF THE NATION—I

The diversity of India presents its own problems. The administrative unity that the British had brought about was in some sense an imposed one. Under British administration, homogeneous linguistic and cultural zones were either scattered across different political and administrative units or were clubbed together arbitrarily. Thus, Madras and Bombay presidencies had in them different linguistic, cultural or even geographical units which began to be articulated with the rise of political consciousness. Quite often they reflected an insider–outsider dichotomy. For example, the demands of colonial administration necessitated the presence of Bengali babus in Assam or Tamil clerks in the Andhra region. With increasing awareness of one's identity and affiliation, the idea of a linguistic, cultural and administrative congruence began to take shape, preparing the ground for anti-Bengali or anti-Tamil consciousness in these regions.

On the eve of India's independence, the political leadership was faced with not only the problem of communal violence but also a fragmented political entity. One of the major problems that vexed the leadership in those trying times was the issue of the princely states. There had been over 500 native states under British paramountcy. Their sizes ranged from that of a village to a whole state like Jammu and Kashmir. Many of these princely states were loath to give up the privileges they had hitherto enjoyed and merge with India. The government under the new home minister, Sardar Patel, began to amalgamate these states with the Indian union through different policy instruments. States like Hyderabad required military action given the communal and blackmailing tactics used by the Nizam and his ministers and this added another prickly dimension to the issue. Jammu and Kashmir was another problematic state which wanted to retain its independent status. Pakistan's interest and involvement in the state queered the pitch further. Soon after independence, intruders backed by the Pakistani Army entered the state, pillaging and burning villages, looting and raping. When the intruders had almost reached the vicinity of Srinagar, Maharaja Hari Singh, who had till then toyed with the idea of staying out of both India and Pakistan, requested military assistance from the Government of India. The maharaja signed the Instrument of Accession with India, which was accepted by the then Governor-General. The Government of India took the case of Pakistani aggression in its territory (Kashmir was now part of India) to the United Nations. This was just the beginning of the sordid saga that has played out in Kashmir ever since. Over the years, India and Pakistan have fought four battles over Kashmir and the issue remains as contentious as ever.

Another controversial issue that came to the fore after independence was the demand for reorganization of provinces on a linguistic basis. P. Sundarayya, the fiery communist leader from Andhra, raised this issue in the first session of the Rajya Sabha in 1952. Coming so soon after the partition of the country, the national leadership was against taking any steps that could be construed as divisive and these sentiments were echoed by none other than Prime Minister Nehru himself. However, popular aspirations as expressed by P. Sundarayya, C.G.K. Reddy and others forced the Government of India to constitute, in December 1953, the State Reorganization Committee (SRC) under the chairmanship of Fazl Ali. The committee, which submitted its report in 1955, recommended the linguistic division of the states of Hyderabad, Bombay and CP–Berar. With regard to Bombay, the committee recommended a bilingual state which included Saurashtra (part of CP–Berar) but excluded Vidarbha and Belgaum–Karwar. The recommendations of the report sparked off unprecedented opposition. Huge rallies took place to oppose its recommendations. Barely a month after the tabling of its report, the SRC came up with a new proposal which envisaged three states—a city–state of Bombay, Maharashtra (which included Vidarbha and whose centre was to be Nagpur) and Gujarat (which would include Saurashtra). The city–state of Bombay would be administered independently. This proposal sparked off a greater opposition, with the demand for Bombay to remain a part of Maharashtra gaining ground and leading to widespread violence. The issue was finally settled with the formation of the new state of Gujarat with Bombay becoming the capital of Maharashtra.

The issue of linguistic reorganization of states continued to simmer for over a decade and in 1965-66 the demand for a Punjabi suba began to boil over, leading to the new states of Punjab and Haryana being carved out of the erstwhile state of Punjab. By the time some more new states were inaugurated in 1972 in the north-east of the country, politically, the Indian union looked very different from what it had been in 1947.

Meanwhile, the issue of official language exploded with a fresh round of violence. By 1959, the statutory ten years after the promulgation of the constitution by which time there was to be a switchover to Hindi as the official language was drawing closer. Hindi enthusiasts in the government as well as outside began to get restive as were those who were opposed to Hindi as the compulsory official language. The issue rapidly snowballed into an anti-Hindi agitation in the southern part of India, taking a violent turn in Tamil Nadu. The issue was eventually settled with the announcement that Hindi would not immediately replace English and as Nehru had advised and agreed on, the three-language formula would guide the state's language policy wherein English would continue as the link language. However, the controversy changed the political landscape of the country. It helped the Dravida Munnettra Kazhagam (DMK) to finally oust the Congress from power in Tamil Nadu, forever redefining the politics of many parts of south India. Hindi enthusiasts in northern India also became politically active through this plank.

The war with Pakistan in 1965, followed by famine and drought and resultant food scarcity in the mid-1960s, exerted considerable strain not only on the economy but also on the polity. The overwhelming presence of the Congress began to fragment for the first time since independence. The year 1967 was a sort of watershed. A number of states—Rajasthan, Punjab, Uttar Pradesh, Bihar and West Bengal—saw the formation of non-Congress ministries. In a fragile political situation, the role of the centre and its representative, the governor, became crucial. The office of governor was increasingly seen to have become a political pawn in the hands of the centre which used it to further its own interests. The late 1960s also witnessed ideological battles turning violent in the form of the Naxalites who claimed to follow in the footsteps of the leader of the Chinese revolution, Mao Tse-tung, and tried to usher in an armed peasants' revolution from their base in Naxalbari in northern Bengal. The movement, which unleashed a series of violent episodes, was brutally crushed by the West Bengal government under Siddhartha Shankar Ray.

~

VALLABHBHAI PATEL

The Mantle Will Now Fall on Young Shoulders

Speaking at a public meeting in Jaipur on 17 December 1947, Sardar Patel outlined his policy of uniting all the native states under one administrative and political formation. Looking back, the task may look simple but in 1947 it was extremely difficult with the native states enjoying British patronage and possessing huge resources. The sheer number of such states, more than 500, added another dimension. This speech ties Patel's ideal of a modern India with his work of uniting these entities.

There are about 500 small Indian Princely States—more than the total number of independent States in the world. The former alien rulers of India preserved them like pickles, but now Paramountcy has gone, foreign rule has gone and India has become free. But we have not yet breathed the real air of freedom. So many people do not know that we have got Swaraj, though they know that foreign rule is gone. People do not yet have any taste of it. They do not know whether we have gained anything from it. We must make them realise the difference between foreign rule and Swaraj.

It is true we have not yet had time. During the short time that has elapsed, we have had, due to our misfortune, communal troubles. The poison of hatred generated by the League gripped us. We accepted even partition of India in the hope that it would restore peaceful conditions. That was not to be. If we had not been hit by this cataclysm, we would have been much better off. Fortunately Jaipur has escaped and I congratulate its people and government on it. The model which you have placed before the world is one which your people can be proud of, but what about the future? We will not stand still, we have to march forward. I am confident that it will not be necessary for me or you to ask for responsible government from the Jaipur Maharaja. Whatever you want you are sure to get. The Maharaja of Jaipur and his advisers have worked together with us in unifying India. I know they are with us and have shared with us in the achievement of freedom.

In every State people demand responsible government. The Rulers are aware of this and know that they have to march with the times. At the same time we should be clear about our own duty. It is our right to take over government from them, but if we cannot improve upon it and provide better administration, what is the advantage?

The Congress has not demanded power for the sake of power but for the sake of service. If you have narrow ideas like Sikhistan, Jatistan and Rajasthan, I should like to say that the world today is different. We cannot think of any such narrow ideology. Government must be that of the people—rich, poor, Hindu, Muslim, Parsee and Christian.

We have to conduct governmental affairs in a manner that each one feels it is his own government. Times are such that government is of those who exert and not of those who sit idle. You should be certain how and for what purpose you use power. We have to utilise power for the welfare of the downtrodden.

I find in the State there are the Praja Mandal and Congress, Hindu Sabha, R.S.S., Rajput Sabha, Jat Sabha and so on. This will not do. You have yet to get together and work together.

You have expressed the hope that Hyderabad shall also join the Indian Union within one year. I have no doubt that it will. It will realise that its interests demand it. The people demand self-government in Hyderabad. They have a right to do so. How can Hyderabad remain isolated? It will come of its own accord.

Muslims demand parity when Hindus are 85 per cent and Muslims 15 per cent. Responsible men should not talk like this. Some say they have connections with Pakistan. If that is so, they will have to bear the consequences.

Kashmir is a different problem. The Pakistan Government is saying that the tribesmen have become infuriated and are attacking, looting, etc. But everyone knows it is not the work merely of raiders. There can be no doubt that there are some regular troops armed with automatic weapons. It is our duty to stand by Kashmir and we will discharge that duty. India will not desert Kashmir even if the struggle goes on for ten years. But ultimately it will be for the people of

Kashmir to decide their own fate, and this can be possible only when the last raider has left the State. There is, therefore, no cause for worry, but the people of Jaipur can assist the Government of India by spreading the message that there should be no trouble elsewhere.

I have received complaints against the Rashtriya Swayamsevak Sangh. If so many complaints are received, the Sangh should realise that there must be something wrong. I appreciate the enthusiasm of young men, but that should be diverted into constructive channels.

There is a great deal to be done to make India militarily strong. Very substantial industrial effort must back the army. All that cannot be achieved by the lathis of the Sangh which are being used for breaking the heads of a handful of Muslims. There is no point in your hoping to get Pakistan back into the Indian Union. It will come of its own accord and we should, therefore, let the Pakistanis remain as they are. I am certain that whether they grow strong or weak, ultimately it would be better for us to get them back when they themselves feel like doing so.

A strong army requires strong support in the matter of supply and food. The people have, therefore, to husband their resources and for that purpose they must forget their quarrels.

We old men have completed our mission. India has secured her freedom. The mantle will now fall on young shoulders and they should be ready to undertake it. They cannot do this if they waste their efforts over trifles. If they follow the path, which the Sangh has been following, they would be doing a disservice to the country.

Everyone realises that in order to subsist as a great nation India must produce more, but instead of that, agitators are compelling workers to strike, the latest instance being in Calcutta where the popular government wants special powers but obstruction is placed in its way. Firing had to be resorted to, but the reply is a threat of a general strike to compel the withdrawal of the Bill.

There is no question now of foreigners being given special powers. It is a representative government which can be changed if people want it to be changed. Let those who feel that urge to advise a general strike ponder over the reception which was accorded to our leader, Pandit Nehru, when he went to Calcutta. He was greeted by a million people.

It is only agitators who clamour for strikes. India is not going to benefit by these tactics. We cannot afford to waste a single hour. It is essential for our existence that we should produce. If we still do not realise this, we are doomed.

Land has been concentrated in the hands of a minority of people in States like Jaipur. I appeal to landholders not to live on the earnings of those who shed their sweat and blood to make the soil productive. It does not behove Rajputs whose duty it is to protect others to live at the expense of others. Let them make sacrifices so that others may live.

It was by disunity that India lost its freedom. Hundreds of years ago, despite the feats of valour and heroism performed by men and women in Rajputana, India became a slave to foreigners. The people should not repeat those mistakes now.

In the address, I have also been asked to say something about Junagadh, but there is hardly anything to be said. The people of Junagadh will deal with the problem. The problem of the States now consists of Hyderabad and Kashmir. I have every hope Hyderabad will do the right thing before the year is out. In this world the popular will can be ignored only at one's peril.

When such a big power as the British had to quit India under the pressure of popular opinion, how can the Nizam hope to do otherwise? However, the new government which has just assumed office should be given a chance. Some people fear that in the interim period Hyderabad will be prepared for a struggle. Even if that is true, it is foolish to imagine that we would sit idle while these preparations are being made.

I appeal to you to follow implicitly the constructive programme laid down by Mahatma Gandhi.

~

N. GOPALASWAMY AYYANGAR

Situation in Kashmir

N. Gopalaswamy Ayyangar was one of India's foremost constitutional experts and participated in the making of the constitution. He had also been the prime minister of Kashmir. Through this speech made on 15 January 1948, the issue of Pakistan's aggression on Kashmir was first brought to the notice of the United Nations.

The situation in the Jammu and Kashmir State is grave today. It is growing graver every day, thanks to the difficult nature of the country where the sanguinary fight is in progress and to the wintry weather conditions. Even so, the situation need be no matter of concern to us, if we proceed to handle it in an exclusively military way and to deal with the invaders and raiders in the way they deserve to be dealt with and in the manner in which under other circumstances we would not have hesitated to deal with them. Such handling, in the present case, might, however, involve risks of an armed conflict with our neighbour, and, with due regard to the principles we have subscribed to as a member of the United Nations, we would like to exhaust every possible resource for avoiding war, particularly war with people of a neighbouring state with whom centuries of common living, culture and tradition incline us, in spite of ephemeral recent happenings, to continue and develop the ties that bind us together. We have come, therefore, to invoke your assistance in persuading the Pakistan Government, where we so far have failed, and in thus helping to save the lives and honour of thousands in the Jammu and Kashmir State. Freed from the scourge of invasion, and with normal life restored, this land of beauty and its hard-working and self-awakened people will thus be enabled to carve out for themselves, by a free choice of their own, the economic and political destiny that awaits them.

We have referred to the Security Council a simple and straightforward issue. There is at this very moment a small war going on in Kashmir. Every day that passes brings in its wake added sorrow and suffering to the people of Kashmir. Furthermore, every day that the war is prolonged the danger of the extension of the area of conflict grows. Who can derive satisfaction from such a state of affairs? Is it not really a matter of extreme urgency that the raiders be withdrawn and fighting should cease? Is not the withdrawal of these raiders and the averting of a threatened breach of the peace the sole issue demanding priority and urgent consideration? Are we making any unreasonable demands when we ask our neighbouring state of Pakistan to discharge its neighbourly duties? We only desire to see peace restored in Kashmir and to ensure that the people of Kashmir are left free to decide in an orderly and peaceful manner the future of their state. We have no further interest, and we have agreed that a plebiscite in Kashmir might take place under international auspices after peace and order have been established. Everything that we have done has been in discharge of our legal, constitutional, and moral responsibilities and obligations.

~

SHEIKH ABDULLAH

The Real Issue

Sheikh Abdullah (1905–82) is one of the most important political figures in the modern history of Jammu and Kashmir. He founded the Muslim Conference in 1931 (the name was changed to National Conference in 1938) and launched an agitation against the rule of Maharaja Hari Singh. He urged self-rule for Kashmir. The inspiration for the struggle came from the Indian national movement. Indian leaders, particularly Jawaharlal Nehru and Mahatma Gandhi, sympathized with his movement. After Pakistan's infiltration in Jammu and Kashmir in 1947 and the signing of the Instrument of Accession, Sheikh Abdullah took a very strong position. In this speech at the United Nations on 5 February 1948, where he spoke immediately after the Pakistani spokesperson Zafrullah Khan had delivered his speech, Sheikh Abdullah eloquently articulated a clear vision of the struggle of the Kashmiri people, exposing Pakistani duplicity in the matter, and clearly laying down his position on the presence of the Indian Army in the troubled state.

There are many troubles in Kashmir. I have listened patiently to the debate in the Security Council, but I feel that I am rather confused. After all, what is the point in dispute? The point in dispute is not that the sovereignty of the Prince is in question, as the representative of Pakistan stated yesterday. After all, I have suffered the punishment of being sentenced to nine years' imprisonment for saying what the representative of Pakistan said with regard to the Treaty of Kashmir of 1846. I am glad that he said it in the Security Council, where he is immune from any punishment. Therefore, I am not disputing that point, and that is not the subject of the dispute before the Security Council.

The subject of the dispute before the Security Council is not the maladministration of the Princely State of Kashmir. In order to set right that maladministration, I think I have suffered the most and today when, for the first time, I heard the representative of Pakistan supporting my case, it gave me great pleasure.

After all, what is the dispute between India and Pakistan? From what I have learned from the complaint brought before the Security Council by my own delegation, the dispute revolves around the fact that Kashmir acceded legally and constitutionally to the Dominion of India. There was some trouble about the democratisation of the Kashmir administration within the state, and the tribesmen from across the border have poured into my country. They have been helped and are being helped by the Pakistan Government with the result that there is the possibility of a greater conflagration between India and Pakistan. India sought the help of the Security Council so that Pakistan might be requested to desist from helping the tribesmen, and to desist from supporting the inside revolt, should I say, the lawful authority.

Pakistan's Denial

I should have understood the position of the representative of Pakistan if he had come boldly before the Security Council and maintained: 'Yes, we do support the tribesmen; we do support the rebels inside the state because we feel that Kashmir belongs to Pakistan and not to India, and because we feel that the accession of Kashmir to India was fraudulent.' Then we might have discussed the validity of the accession of the state of Kashmir to India. But that was not the position taken by the representative of Pakistan. He completely denied that any support was being given by the Government of Pakistan to either the tribesmen or those who are in revolt within the state against the constituted authority.

How am I to convince the Security Council that the denial is absolutely untrue? I am sitting before the Security Council at a distance of thousands of miles from my country. I have fought many battles, along with my own men, on the borders of Jammu and Kashmir. I have seen with my own eyes the support given by the Pakistan Government, not only in supplying bases, but in providing arms, ammunition, direction and control of the tribesmen; and I have even seen the Pakistan Army forces from across the border.

The denial has come so flatly that it becomes very difficult for me to disprove it here before the Security Council, unless the Security Council accedes to our request to send a Commission to the spot and to first find out whether the allegations brought before the Security Council with regard to the aid given by the Government of Pakistan are correct or incorrect. If they are incorrect, the case fails; if they are correct, then the Security Council should take the necessary steps to advise the Government of Pakistan to desist from such support.

I was explaining how the dispute arose—how Pakistan wanted to force this position of slavery upon us. Pakistan had no interest in our liberation or else it would not have opposed our freedom movement.

Pakistan would have supported us when thousands of my countrymen were behind bars and hundreds were shot to death. The Pakistani leaders and Pakistani papers were heaping abuse upon the people of Kashmir who were suffering these tortures. Then suddenly, Pakistan comes before the bar of the world as the champion of the liberty of the people of Jammu and Kashmir. The world may believe this, but it is very difficult for me to believe.

When we refused the coercive tactics of Pakistan, it started full-fledged aggression and encouraged the tribesmen in this activity. It is absolutely impossible for the tribesmen to enter our territory without encouragement from Pakistan, because it is necessary for them to pass through Pakistan territory to reach Jammu and Kashmir. Hundreds of trucks, thousands of gallons of petrol, thousands of rifles, ammunition, and all forms of help that all army requires, were given to them. We know this. After all, we belong to that country. What Pakistan could not achieve by the use of the economic blockade it wanted to achieve by full-fledged aggression.

I had thought all along that the world had got rid of Hitler and Goebbels, but from what has happened and what is happening in my poor country I am convinced they have only transmigrated their souls into Pakistan.

We are being attacked daily. Thousands of armed men come across the Pakistan border and raze each and every village of our country to the ground. That is what is actually happening. We see it daily with our own eyes, and yet we are being told that Pakistan has nothing to do with this—that it is not at all interested.

What do we request? We request nothing more than that the Security Council send some members to this area to see for themselves what is happening there. If Pakistan comes forward and says: 'We question the legality of the accession,' I am prepared to discuss whether or not the accession of Jammu and Kashmir to India was legal. However, now they say: 'We want a plebiscite; we want to obtain the free and unfettered opinion of the people of Kashmir. There should be no pressure exerted on the people and they should make the free choice as to the state to which they wish to accede.'

Aid from India

We realised that Pakistan would not allow us any time, that we had either to suffer the fate of our kith and kin of Muzaffarabad,

Baramulla, and see the same happen to Srinagar and other towns and villages, or to seek help from some outside authority.

Under these circumstances, both the Maharajah and the people of Kashmir requested the Government of India to accept our accession. The Government of India could easily have accepted the accession and could have said: 'All right, we accept your accession and we shall render this help.' There was no necessity for the Prime Minister of India to add the proviso, when accepting the accession, that 'India does not want to take advantage of the difficult situation in Kashmir. We will accept this accession because without Kashmir's acceding to the Indian Dominion we are not in a position to render any military help. But once the country is free from the raiders, marauders and looters, this accession will be subject to ratification by the people.' That was the offer made by the Prime Minister of India.

That was the same offer which was made by the people of Kashmir to the Government of Pakistan, but it was refused because at that time Pakistan felt that it could, within a week, conquer the entire Jammu and Kashmir State and then place the fait accompli before the world, just as it happened some time ago in Europe. The same tactics were used.

But, having failed in those tactics, Pakistan now comes before the bar of the world, pleading: 'We want nothing; we only want our people to be given a free hand in deciding their own fate. And in deciding their own fate, they must have a plebiscite.' There is no dispute as to that. After all, this very offer was made by the Prime Minister of India and by the people of Kashmir.

They then continue and say: 'No, a plebiscite cannot be fair and impartial unless and until there is a neutral administration in the State of Jammu and Kashmir.' I have failed to understand the terminology 'neutral administration'. After all, what does 'neutral administration' mean?

The Neutrality Myth

The representative of Pakistan has stated that Sheikh Abdullah, because he is a friend of Jawaharlal Nehru, because he has had sympathy for the Indian National Congress, because he has declared his point of view in favour of accession to India, and because he is head of the emergency administration, cannot remain impartial. Therefore, Sheikh Abdullah must depart.

Let us suppose that Sheikh Abdullah goes. Who is to replace Sheikh Abdullah? It will be someone from amongst the four million people of the Jammu and Kashmir state. But can we find anyone among these four million people whom we can call impartial? After all, we are not logs of wood; we are not dolls. We must have an opinion one way or the other. The people of Kashmir are either in favour of Pakistan or in favour of India.

Therefore, Pakistan's position comes down to this: that the four million people of that State should have no hand in running the administration of their own country. Someone else must come in for that purpose. Is that fair? Is that just? Do the members of the Security Council wish to oust the people of Kashmir from running their own administration and their own country?

Then, for argument's sake, let us assume that the four million people of Jammu and Kashmir State agree to have nothing to do with the administration of their country; someone else must be brought into the country for this purpose. From where do the members of the Security Council propose that such a neutral individual may be secured? From India? No. From Pakistan? No. From anywhere in the world? No. Frankly speaking, even if the Security Council were to request Almighty God to administer the state during this interim period, I do not feel that He could act impartially. After all, one must have sympathy either for this side or that side.

If elections were to be held in the United Kingdom sometime with the Labour Government in power, would anyone say to Mr. Attlee: 'The elections are now going on. Because you happen to belong to the Labour Party, your sympathies will be in favour of the Labour vote. Therefore, you had better clear out. We must have a neutral man as Prime Minister until our elections are finished.'

However, we have been told that Sheikh Abdullah must walk out because he has declared his point of view in favour of India. Therefore, he cannot be impartial. We must have some impartial man; we must have some neutral man.

As I have submitted to the members of the Security Council, Sheikh Abdullah happens to be there because the people wish it. As long as the people wish it, I shall be there. There is no power on earth which can displace me from the position which I have there. As long as the people are behind me, I will remain there. Once the people cease to have any faith in me, I cannot hold that position.

Impartial Vote

We have declared, once and for all, that there shall be freedom of voting, and for that purpose we have said: 'Let anyone come in; we have no objection. Let the Commission of the Security Council on India come into our state and advise us how we should take a vote, how we should organise it, and how it can be completely impartial. We have no objection.' My Government is ready to satisfy, to the last comma, the impartiality of the vote.

But to have an impartial vote is one thing; to have a say in the administration of the state is a different thing entirely. After all, with what are we concerned? We are concerned only with the fact that no influence shall be exercised over the voters, one way or the other. The people shall be free to vote according to their own interests. We are ready to accept that.

Backdoor Tactics

It is then said: 'You cannot have freedom of voting as long as the Indian army remains in the Jammu and Kashmir State.' It is probably very difficult for me to draw a full picture of what is going on in that country. There is absolute chaos in certain parts of the country, fighting is going on and thousands of tribesmen are there, ready to take advantage of any weakness on the part of the State of Jammu and Kashmir.

Once we ask the Indian army, which is the only protective force in Kashmir against these marauders, to clear out we leave the country open to chaos. After all, one who has suffered for the last seventeen years, in attempting to secure the freedom and liberation of his own country, would not like an outside army to come in and to remain in the country.

However, what is the present situation? If I ask the Indian army to clear out, how am I going to protect the people from looting, arson, murder, and abduction, with which they have been faced all these long months? What is the alternative? The Prime Minister of India long ago declared that the Government of India had no intention of keeping its army permanently stationed in Kashmir. He stated: 'We are there only as long as the country is in turmoil. Once law and order is established, once the marauders and the tribesmen leave the country, we will withdraw our army.' That pledge is already there.

There need be no fear, since the Indian army is there, that they will interfere in the exercise of a free vote. After all, a Commission of the Security Council will be there in order to watch. It will be stationed at certain strategic points, so that in the event of danger from any border, the army will be there to protect that border. The army is there to curb disorders anywhere in the State; that is all. The army will not be in each and every village in order to watch each and every vote.

It is then said: 'Can we not have a joint control? Can we not have the armies of Pakistan and India inside the state in order to control the situation?' This is an unusual idea. What Pakistan could not achieve through ordinary means, Pakistan wishes to achieve by entering through the back door, so that it may have her armies inside the state and then start the fight. That is not possible.

After all, we have been discussing the situation in Kashmir. I should say that we have been playing the drama of *Hamlet* without the Prince of Denmark. The people of Kashmir are vitally interested in this question. Four million people in Kashmir are keenly interested in this entire issue. I have sympathies with the peoples of Poonch and Mirpur.

The representatives of Pakistan will probably concede that I have suffered greatly for the people of Poonch as well as for the people of Mirpur. There is no difference on this issue of internal democratisation of the administration between me, my party and the people of Poonch. We are one; we want our own liberty; we want our own freedom; we do not want autocratic rule. We desire that the 4,000,000 people in Jammu and Kashmir, Hindus, Sikhs and Muslims, shall have the right to change their destiny, to control their country, and to administer it as best they can. On that point there is absolutely no difference. However, it is not a question of internal liberation. The Security Council should not confuse the issue. The question is not that we want internal freedom; the question is not how the Maharajah got his state, or whether or not he is sovereign. These points are not before the Security Council.

According to my understanding there are two points at issue: first, how to secure this neutral, impartial administration; second, whether or not the Indian army shall remain.

It is not at all disputed that we must have a plebiscite and that the accession must be ratified by the people of Kashmir, freely and without any pressure on this or that side. That much is conceded;

there is no dispute about that. The dispute arises when it is suggested that, in order to have the free vote, the administration must be changed. To that suggestion we say, 'NO'.

United People

I do not know what course future events will take. However, I may assure the Security Council that, if I am asked to conduct the administration of this state, it will be my duty to make the administration absolutely impartial. It will be my duty to request my brothers, who are in a different camp at this time, to come to lend me support. After all, they are my own kith and kin. We have suffered together; we have no quarrel with them. I shall tell them: 'Come on; it is my country; it is your country. I have been asked to administer the state. Are you prepared to lend me support?' It is for me to make the administration successful; it is for me to make the administration impartial. It is not for Pakistan to say: 'No, we must have an impartial administration.' I refuse to accept Pakistan as a party in the affairs of the Jammu and Kashmir State; I refuse this point-blank. Pakistan has no right to say that we must do this and we must do that. We have seen enough of Pakistan. The people of Kashmir have seen enough. Muzaffarabad and Baramulla and hundreds of villages in Jammu and Kashmir depict the story of Pakistan to the people of Jammu and Kashmir. We want to have no more of this.

The only issue before the Security Council is that Pakistan must observe its international obligations and must not support any outside raiders. Pakistan should not encourage inside revolt. Pakistan has denied that it has. In order to verify the statements made by the representatives of India and Pakistan, the Security Council must send a commission to the spot to see whether the complaint brought before the Security Council is valid or invalid. If the Security Council finds that the complaint brought before it by India is valid, Pakistan should be asked to desist, or India should be permitted to use its means to carry out the decision of the Security Council.

~

VALLABHBHAI PATEL

Defence of India Rules, 1950

Vallabhbhai Patel had the unenviable task of being home minister in the chaotic period immediately following independence. The introduction of the Defence of India Rules in Parliament provides a classic example of the difficulties the leadership experienced in introducing such measures as they themselves had been victims of such regulations in the past under the British. The government was faced with a piquant situation where the vast corpus of fundamental rights granted by the constitution came into conflict with the necessity of taking preventive measures to tackle the communal problem, the issue of communist uprisings in Telangana and other parts of the country and various other threats to internal security. The introduction of the Defence of India Rules, 1950, which empowered the government to make preventive arrests, evoked criticism as many people felt it violated the spirit of fundamental rights given in the constitution. Patel's response on 2 August 1950 was terse as always though not lacking in passion and logic.

We have not been detained for weeks, but years without cause. We did not know for what we were being detained. Several times we were not allowed to know whether our relatives were living or not. We were not allowed to know what was happening outside. The facilities that have been given to these people in jail, many people would prefer them to the liberty outside. Those people who have made sacrifices for civil liberty are not less able to appreciate what civil liberty is. But, my friend does not know or does not appreciate that the very liberty for which we have fought and which we hold dear is at stake.

See what is happening all round India! See where the world is today! Debating in a House like this where there is complete protection, you think that it is so all round. You talk of civil liberty. My friends, I would like any of you to go to Old Delhi where meetings are held every day and where speeches are made that were never made before in the whole history of India. The vulgar speeches they make, the vituperative language that they use and the violence that they preach, you should go and hear!

There are two challenges that we have to meet. There is a challenge from a class of people who delight in, and who believe it their duty to widen the gulf between community and community, to create hatred between community and community. There is another class of people who want to disrupt the society and the democratic institutions with violence, without any scruples. We are going to meet both the challenges with all our resources.

My friend referred to the case of Mr. Bhopatkar. I know Mr. Bhopatkar is a revered leader. I have worked with him as a comrade. But, the Hindu Mahasabha to a certain extent is an organisation which has a complex... You must remember that when the Father of the Nation was murdered, it was by a group of people who belonged to that organisation. I am ready to prove to anybody that there was a group of people there who were determined to take his life. They were not satisfied even after taking his life. He tells me that the Magistrate did not know who was the Minister to be murdered. He wants to know it. Well, I shall meet his challenge. The Minister meant was the Prime Minister of India.

What do you get by knowing that? And the information was given by an associate of Mr. Bhopatkar. You wish everything to be divulged! Is it in the public interest? Can the police take risks? When Mahatma Gandhi was murdered, the Ministry was being attacked for not protecting his life. I was not spared. When we take precautions, you say civil liberty is at stake. Where are we to go?

We do not arrest people in order to stifle opposition. I challenge anybody to show an instance in which a single individual has been arrested during our regime for stifling opposition. On the contrary, I have told the communists often, and so has our revered leader the Prime Minister, that the communists are free to contest the polls if they adopt the method of non-violence. If they do not, if they persist in their methods, they must take their chance; I cannot help it.

What we have done up to now is that we have given a freedom which was never enjoyed by the country before. Read the newspapers...which continuously incite violence. What is the meaning of your reading a sentence from a judgment of the Chief Justice where he says that there should be no objection to criticism of or disaffection against government? See the volume of preaching of disaffection against the government: such as was never heard of before us! Our own colleagues preach disaffection. We do not mind it. Many people do it. Everywhere you find it.

He says that this Act gives greater powers and it is more severe. Has he balanced the thing? In this Act we have given power for the scrutiny of cases...by a judicial officer of the rank of a High Court Judge, whose decision is mandatory and we are bound to accept it. It was not so in the past. What is it that you want? I know the defects of this Act. We know the circumstances in which we were forced to bring in this Act. But, the defects are on both sides.

I am going to bring in, I promise, a well-considered measure either in the next session or at least in the Budget session, because I think that the aim of this government must be clear, the objective of this government must be understood properly, not only in this House, but outside also, in the country as a whole, that no amount of propaganda however violent will deter this government from maintaining law and order in this country. In the whole of South East Asia, this is the only stable country where democracy can function. We are still proud of the performance that we have put in in the short period of our office. We may have failed; a beginner may make mistakes. But, will you not appreciate and encourage our governments, our units who are functioning in very difficult circumstances?

Take a province like Bombay, the centre of communist activity since its birth, the place of revolutionaries who claim that there should be a Hindu communal government in this country, perhaps not only a Hindu, but a sectional Brahminical government of this country. If that is the aim and object of a set of people, then I tell you that we are performing the elementary functions of a civilised government in detaining these people. We are not keeping them a day longer than is necessary. We do not take delight in it. But we are prepared to take up any challenge from any quarter.

~

SYAMA PRASAD MOOKERJEE

On Jammu and Kashmir

Syama Prasad Mookerjee was one of those who stridently criticized what he called the Nehru administration's favouritism to India's Muslims. The Bharatiya Jana Sangh, which he founded, called for a uniform civil code for both Hindus and Muslims and an end to the special status of Jammu and Kashmir. The Praja Parishad, a Hindu communal outfit in Jammu, was also demanding the state's integration with India and was opposed to the National Conference's idea of autonomy. This statement delivered by Mookerjee on 17 February 1953 in the Lok Sabha is the clearest exposition of the official position of the Bharatiya Jana Sangh and its offshoot the Bharatiya Janata Party on the Kashmir issue. Mookerjee visited Kashmir in 1953 and went on a hunger strike to protest the law prohibiting Indian citizens from settling in the state and the need to carry ID cards. He was arrested in Kashmir on 11 May. Although the ID card rule was revoked owing to his efforts, he died in jail under mysterious circumstances on 23 May.

... With regard to the position in Jammu and Kashmir...which has been engaging the attention of the public and of the Government for the last so many weeks.

I know we have been maligned; we have been attacked and abused, and all sorts of motives have been hurled at us. Motives have been hurled at the Praja Parishad. I would beg of the House, and I would beg specially of the Prime Minister...I would beg of everyone to examine the issues dispassionately. Let us not hurl abuses at each other...

I know the Prime Minister levels the charge of communalism on all of us. Whenever he cannot meet an argument that is the answer that he has to give... I am getting sick of this charge which is unfounded. If we want to consider whether communalism exists in the country or whether it is openly advocated as a plank by any political organisation, let us fix a date for a debate and let us discuss the matter. Let Government bring forward its charges. Let us have a chance of replying. We do not want communalism in this country. We do not want that on the basis of religion or on the basis of caste one section of Indians should go on hating other sections. We want to see developed a society where people of diverse religions will be able to live as common citizens and enjoy common rights. If there is a feeling that something is being done opposite to this policy—which we say not—instead of talking in an abstract way, let us meet...let us all against whom such charges are levelled sit together and discuss. We are not enemies of this country... Therefore, if Government comes forward with such a charge-sheet it is only fair and just that it must be a real charge-sheet and we must be able to understand each other's point of view...

What is this Jammu and Kashmir agitation for? A few months ago I went to Jammu. In fact I spoke here just the day before I left for Jammu. I do not know much of that State, certainly not even perhaps one hundredth of what the Prime Minister does. But yet I came into contact with people during my short stay there, and I saw those people and the working of the minds of those people whom the Prime Minister and Sheikh Abdullah would not touch. There may be men whose minds may be working in one direction. There may be persons who may think in a particular way, different from what I do. But certainly there cannot be anybody hundred per cent bad or hundred per cent good. Their approach has to be examined; their fears and doubts have to be examined and dispelled.

The Dogras against whom this fight is going on are not a race of cowards. They are a community that has given the finest martial strength of India. They fought for the liberty of their country; they shed their blood for the good of this country. They are being shot down and their women are being molested and sent to jail, and the whole state is now in the midst of a terrible repression which was not witnessed perhaps even in the worst days of the British regime.

... Their fears have to be examined. It is not communal at all. If you want to give it a communal colouring, someone may come and say 'the majority are Muslims and only Hindus are being attacked'. Somebody may say 'this is a communal attack against Hindus'. But it is an attack by the State for certain reasons, good or bad.

What are the things they want? They want that the question of accession should be finalised. I know there are constitutional difficulties. But this is a matter which has to be settled, after understanding what their fears and doubts are. It is no use either Sheikh Abdullah or Shri Jawaharlal Nehru saying 'we are satisfied that everything is all right'. They have to be satisfied. And if you can satisfy them with regard to this question, then one big hurdle goes.

I have suggested various methods. I will not go into details at the moment. But I have suggested to the Prime Minister a number of possible alternatives through which the question can be decided. There is the question of finality of accession.

... There is the question of applicability of the Constitution of India. Now, let us see how this question arises. Sheikh Abdullah says that the Jammu and Kashmir Assembly enjoys a limited sovereignty. I can understand one sovereign Parliament in India, and that is the Parliament here. There cannot be two sovereign Parliaments in this country. But he is under the impression that according to the terms of the Constitution that we have approved he has got certain limited powers. I do not want to go into technicalities. Jammu and Kashmir is a part of the Indian Union, and that State has to be governed according to some Constitution. The suggestion is: accept the Indian Constitution. This is a Constitution framed by a Constituent Assembly which was dominated by Shri Jawaharlal Nehru himself. This is a

Constitution which is based on secular considerations. It is not a Constitution dictated by any communal motives. If it is good enough for four crores of Muslims in India why can it not be good for the people of Jammu and Kashmir?

But there again there is a compromise suggested, namely, let those provisions of the Constitution which relate to fundamental matters be implemented. Some of them were declared here on the floor of the House in July. They have not been implemented till now. It is said that they have not been implemented because the movement has started! A more frivolous and fantastic reply could not have been given. The agreement was reached in July, and till November nothing was done. And in November, only a part application of that agreement was sought to be made. And it is suggested that because the movement started the agreement could not be implemented. They are not ready with the implementation yet. It is only today that the announcement has been made that a Committee has been set up for clarifying certain issues. The Prime Minister knows this better than anybody. Certain issues have to be clarified. There are a number of matters, fundamental rights, Supreme Court, President's powers, financial integration, abolition of customs duty. I have added conduct of election under one authority for the whole of this country.

If in respect of these matters Sheikh Abdullah and his party say 'we will not accept one hundred per cent of your constitution', well, let us know which portion they desire...but as friends, consider and agree that for special reasons certain exemptions should be made.

For instance lands. If you want to have a special law for Jammu and Kashmir, that for acquisition of land no compensation should be paid, and if it has succeeded in the State, provide for it. We will not question it. But finalise matters with regard to civil rights, financial integration, abolition of customs duties. It is a disgrace that we should have today in India customs duties for one part. The answer given is that they will lose one crore of rupees... Well, that one crore we will have to provide for. All parties in this House will support the Finance Minister if he says that for the purposes of full integration of that State to India we will have to make a separate grant of that sum to Jammu and Kashmir. You can forgo fifty crores of rupees for enforcing prohibition. You must do something for unifying the economic life of our country of which Jammu and Kashmir is a part. Do you suggest that we will continue this customs duty, which is operating so harshly against the people of the State themselves?

These are matters which have got to be finalised. On the question of the flag let me say it is not a question of mere sentiment. The Prime Minister said the other day: oh, these people who are agitating about this want their Bhagwa flag to be raised over the Red Fort if the occasion arises. He mistakes the issue. It is not a question of the Bhagwa flag. The Congress accepted its flag with some alterations. It is the National flag of India now. Supposing some party, when they come into power, decide to change the design or the colour of the flag. That is not a crime. We have not said that the Bhagwa flag should be flown where the RSS rule; the Communist Party will have the red flag where they rule or the Socialist Party will have their red flag where they rule or the Congress will have their own flag flying where they govern. Nobody has suggested that. Let there be one flag for the whole country. The Prime Minister has assured me and he has publicly stated that the Indian flag is supreme flag and the other flag is subordinate to it. Very well. Let us accept it. Through that way I see the path of compromise. Let the Indian flag fly over Jammu and Kashmir State every day like other States. That point can be settled—the State flag may be used on special occasions.

Then there is the question of going into their grievances. A Commission has been appointed. What Commission? The Commission consists of 4 persons. The Chief Justice is one of them—I need not say anything now about him—he is the Chief Justice of the State... One is the Revenue Commissioner, the second is the Accountant General and the third is the Conservator of Forests. These are the three officers of the State who have been put into that Commission of Enquiry. Is it suggested that a Commission consisting of three officers of that State will sit and go into very vital matters which challenge the soundness of the position of that State? Is this ever done when any controversy arises? Why not have an impartial Commission consisting of the Chief Justice and two judges of High Court in India and why not widen the terms of reference and say that whatever grievances there are, that Commission will go into—any economic matter or a social matter or an educational matter, whatever that may be? ... Now, I ask the House which are the matters which savour of communalism. You start referring to their past history, their father's history, grandfather's history. Why drag the poor Maharaja? He was loyal to the country, what offence did this Maharaja commit? He accepted accession. He handed over power to the Government of India. He handed over power to Sheikh Abdullah. Sheikh Abdullah's ascendancy on the political throne there was possible through the legal decision of the Maharaja himself. So, why drag him? Now he has gone. He is finished. Now you say that the agitation is going on for vested interests. What vested interests? Will the people of Jammu, if they succeed in the agitation, take charge of the entire State? They have made it clear that they have no political ambition as such. How can they possibly give help to vested interests in such a manner that that will disturb the stability of the State, the unity of the State? I entirely agree with the Prime Minister that the unity of the State of Jammu and Kashmir must be preserved at any cost. In fact we must recover one-third of the territory of the State which we lost, if we have a sense of national prestige. It is a matter of disgrace that one-third territory of ours is now in the hands of the enemy.

I am not suggesting that you break the State of Jammu and Kashmir into bricks. The suggestion which I once made as a compromise formula to Sheikh Saheb was that if the whole State cannot accept India's Constitution immediately, it may do so in parts. That was a second alternative, but even then Kashmir would remain within India. Let us declare that Jammu will remain as one State. Let us declare that the provincial boundaries also will not be disturbed. Already the province of Jammu is now being divided on communal grounds. Of course the reply is that the intention is not communal but the decision may be communal. You are creating Hindu zones and Muslim zones within the province. Keep the province of Jammu intact, keep Ladakh intact, even if you want to have the scheme of provincial autonomy provided for them. These are matters of negotiations. They can be settled without breaking heads or without creating any controversy.

So far as the origin of the movement is concerned, you can rightly say, as the Prime Minister has told me a number of times 'do you expect that I shall tolerate this sort of disobedience, deliberate disobedience of law? This deliberate disobedience is a challenge to authority.' I agree that on normal occasions, this should not be the procedure. We expect that in a democratic Constitution such as ours, we should be able to proceed in a manner that we get redress of our grievances through constitutional means. Undoubtedly, that should be our aim and I hope that that will be the ultimate result of our joint endeavours. Supposing a situation arises where through the adamant attitude taken up by the Government, because of the majority at its command, they refuse to do anything for the people who are opposing their policy and you goad them to a certain course of action of your own, what happens then? It is your own inability to cope with the situation that may exasperate people. Is it not a fact that the Praja Parishad sent representations during the last two years to the President, to the Prime Minister, to Sheikh Saheb? They begged for an interview from the Prime Minister who refused to grant an interview only about a year ago. They could not get an interview from the President... Sheikh Abdullah was not prepared to move. You have removed social untouchability under your Constitution but you are creating political untouchability because you cannot see eye to eye with certain people whose politics you do not approve. Do you believe you will be able to run this Government in this way? I say this without any fear of contradiction that this movement would never have been started if only there was a chance of representing their view to the people in authority... Now, practically the movement has been forced upon them. Before the movement started, when I came back from Jammu, I saw Pandit Nehru, I saw Sheikh Abdullah. Believe me. I went out of my way and pleaded for a change of attitude. I was extremely anxious that in view of the possible repercussions and the war that was impending with Pakistan and also the experiment which Sheikh Abdullah has made, I was anxious—even today I am anxious—that we should forget the past and proceed in a statesmanlike way and settle all our differences. I have not concealed my admiration over the manner in which Sheikh Abdullah has conducted himself whatever might be said against his policy. I told him personally and I said it in public that here was a man who was making an experiment which our national leaders failed to make and which resulted in the vivisection of the country. I appealed to him, 'For heaven's sake, go to Jammu and make the people feel that they are not outsiders and you are the real leader for the Hindus and Muslims.' I saw the danger signal in Jammu... I regret to say that both Sheikh Abdullah and Pandit Nehru have been unable to cope with the situation and to go near the minds of the people of Jammu.

... It may be that the Maharaja, a Dogra, was at the head of the Government which was not liked by the majority of Muslims but when the table was turned, it was essential that these Dogras should not be singled out as a community which had been guilty of bad conduct or bad motives. There was a ruthless attack on the Maharaja personally. It was unnecessary because he had gone out of the picture. The Dogras have been branded as a community which had gone and dominated over the Kashmir Valley. Psychologically, you could not bring the people nearer you. That is why I appeal to you to go near them even at this stage. You talk to them, send for their representatives, understand their viewpoints and thus create a situation which will make it possible for all of us to stand united.

Now, what is the remedy? I come to my last, the last point which I would like to place before the House. What is the remedy? Is repression a remedy? The Prime Minister said yesterday in the Council of States that he had a list of 100 persons, policemen, etc., who had been attacked, buildings which have been mobbed and other kinds of outrage which have been committed. Pamphlets have been circulated to us. I have got about 8 or 10 of them with me but there is the other side of the picture also. I have got here reports of the repression which have been carried on. If I read them I know you will stand aghast. I have not the proof to show that whatever said is true or not, just as I have not the means to say whatever has been circulated by the Abdullah Government is true or not. I wanted to send a small delegation of responsible people including three legislators. Such is the state of Jammu and Kashmir within the Indian Union: permits were refused. Certain political parties are allowed to go; certain political parties are not allowed to go. I had declared that they would not interfere; only they will go, see and come back. Even that was not allowed. They say, they are out for violence…

You talk of Gandhism, Gandhian style and the healing touch… If I come forward and say, let us have an honourable settlement and bring this to an end, what right has any democratic leader to say, we will not touch you, we will not talk to you, you are guilty of communalism? Has any Muslim been killed? Has any section of Muslims been attacked in the province of Jammu where the Muslims form a majority? What is it that you have decided now? The National Militia consisting of Sheikh Abdullah's party men, mostly Muslims, are to be let loose on these people in these villages. You say they are communalists. You are fanning the fire of communalism and you do not know where it will lead to. I do not want this to continue. Let us put an end to it. How to put an end to it? What is the suggestion that I make publicly to the Prime Minister? Let us not judge who was right and who was wrong. Let us take them at their word and hear their demand and their needs. Release them and send for them. Do not make any commitment now. Send for them. Let us understand the difficulties, constitutional and political. Tell them, here we are to give an assurance with regard to the future status. Their grievances will be enquired into by an impartial Commission. Let us make an attempt. We talk of Gandhism. We hold a school here and make it an international show as to what Gandhism has been and how India is being ruled. Is this the type of Gandhism that you refuse to talk to some people because they are your political opponents, because their past is bad? Who is there to probe into the past of every one of us? You judge the present difficult political situation according to the present requirements. What did the British Government do? Did not the British Government carry on repression? Did they not then say that they will not touch the Naked Fakir? Did not the gentleman who is the present Prime Minister of England say, no compromise with the Naked Fakir and did not that Naked Fakir bring freedom to this country? How do you say that you will not talk to your opponents because of their past? What did Sheikh Abdullah do? Did not the Maharaja and he fight with each other? Did not the Maharaja shake hands with him and did he not himself in his own writing make Sheikh Abdullah the Chief person in the State of Jammu and Kashmir? Are we to carry in our breasts past stories, past history, and thereby aggravate a situation which will destroy not only certain sections but the entire peace and prosperity of this country? Take us as friends. If we are wrong, correct us. We are not sitting here with any outsiders. This Table does not divide us. This Table is your Table. It does not divide the minds of men. Why should we go on quarrelling in this way? Trust us. Sit down with us. If anybody has committed any wrong, tell them that in the national interests this should not be done. Give them a chance. Let us see whether we can proceed in that manner or not. You will not be able to destroy the Dogras. I have seen some of them, fine elements. It brought tears to my eyes. I saw some men, the women; great people, patriotic people, fearless people. They have not been violent up till now. I advised them that if any movement, if any protest is to be carried on, it must be on the basis of non-violence. Because, you cannot fight the organised violence of the State and you will lose the sympathy and cooperation of the people. It is a question of civil right. It is a question of their life and death, of their very existence. Believe them. I have seen Prem Nath Dogra, whom I respect with all my heart… He is a loyal citizen, a quiet sufferer. He is a leader who does not lose his head. Do you know how many years ago his pension was stopped? I myself did not know. When I met him a few months ago in Jullundur, he was talking about his private affairs. He said, 'Doctorsab, I am a poor man.' I said, 'Why, you are a Government pensioner?' He said, 'Sheikh Abdullah Saheb has deprived me of that long ago.' I asked, 'You never protested?' He said, 'Why should I?' Democracy is functioning in this way. The pension given by the Jammu and Kashmir Government has been withdrawn because his politics was not liked. He has started the movement today. But, when was the pension withdrawn?

There are people belonging to Jammu, refugees, who have their money in the Jammu and Kashmir Bank. Does the Finance Minister know that they are not allowed to draw their money because they cannot produce their documents? They went to the High Court of Jammu and Kashmir and the High Court gave an order that the money should be paid. An Ordinance had been passed prohibiting the Bank from paying this money. These are the grievances which have to be looked into. What about the Dharmartha Trust which Raja Gulab Singh and his successors created? It may be for the preservation of Hindu temples. Is that a crime? Preservation of Hindu temples in India can be done by means of Trust. That money is not allowed to be paid. Why is it not done? These are matters which have to be gone into. Each may be a small matter or a big matter. It is the cumulative effect of these as also the persistent refusal of the authorities to sit down and talk to the representatives of the people that have brought about this situation.

Even now, my appeal to the Prime Minister is this. Let us forget the past. Let him take up the matter. He can rise equal to the occasion. He can deliver the goods with Sheikh Abdullah. I do not say for a moment that you should minimise the stature of Sheikh Abdullah. I do not wish for a moment that you should humiliate the Government because then whom do I humiliate? Our own Government elected by the people of the country. It is not a question of mutual humiliation or gaining one point here or losing another point there. It is the question of the settlement of an issue which is of national importance and which may create serious problems and destroy the peace and happiness of large parts of India and I appeal to the Prime Minister to move before it is too late. We have been charged and branded as encouraging the movement. I repudiated it earlier on the floor of the House and repudiate it now. It is not our movement. The movement is theirs, spontaneous; not a Praja Parishad movement; the movement has spread and various classes of people have come into it. We have sympathised with it. We have supported it. We have extended our blessings to it. We have done that because it is not a struggle of Jammu, it is a struggle of the people of India.

... If somebody has gone wrong let us sit down even at this stage. That was Gandhism. He did not decry his opponents. He sent for everyone who differed from him even to the utmost extent, sat with them, talked with them, and tried to capture their hearts. I have not the least doubt in my mind that if that attempt is made by Shri Nehru and Sheikh Abdullah, if these people are sent for and we say to them: 'We are your friends. Let us sit down and discuss the matter, and not raise any other issue and your legitimate grievances will be looked into,' the matter will be settled in ten minutes' time. It is that magnanimity, that generosity and statesmanship to which I ask the Prime Minister to rise at this critical juncture.

... Let us try to find out some formula whereby the Jammu question can be settled. Whatever may be said against us, whatever motives may be ascribed to us, I can give this assurance to the Prime Minister that in case an emergency arises in this country...on behalf of the party that I represent, including the much-maligned groups, I offer our unconditional allegiance and support to the Government. If such a condition arises, it will be the duty of everyone to stand by the Government so that the interests of the country may be kept supreme. The maintenance of peaceful atmosphere in the country is imperative. I hope, Sir, by means of mutual discussion and understanding we will be able to make the interest of the people of Jammu and Kashmir safe. Let us consider the case on its merits dispassionately and reach a solution which will be to the lasting benefit of the State as also of the entire country.

~

JAWAHARLAL NEHRU

Resolution on Linguistic Provinces

On 7 July 1952, the Lok Sabha debated the resolution on linguistic states. It was an intense debate with tempers running high over the issue of reorganizing the states on linguistic lines. To many, including Nehru, any talk of partitioning states brought memories of the partition of 1947. Intervening in the debate, Nehru attacked the communist members, who had argued 'theoretically' about a linguistic basis of nationalities which, the communists said, made India the home of several nationalities. He also criticized others whose arguments were based on other practical considerations. During the intervention, he also mentioned that he preferred people taking a party line rather than the emotionally charged lines premised on primordial loyalty to language. Though his response came towards the conclusion of the debate, it is significant as it shows a statesmanlike understanding of an emotive issue.

... I shall refer to some points that have been mentioned and some ideas which I have on the subject. Right from the beginning it was said—I think it was Dr. Lankasundaram who said it—that we should keep away from passion and prejudice. I entirely agree with him. Dr. Mookerjee said that this is not a matter which might be considered a party matter. I also entirely agree with him. And yet, may I say that perhaps it would have been better if it was a party matter. I shall explain myself. Not that I want things to become party matters, but a party matter is something that cuts across provincial feelings. It may be good, or it may be bad. But anyhow it is not on a provincial basis that a party would consider it. Well, this particular question is in the nature of things a provincial question. Therefore, where division comes or where friction comes as between representatives of one province and another—which I think is worse than party divisions—perhaps it would have been better if it was a party matter, if it is considered on the basis of some principle, if you like. There are different ways of looking at it, but not on the basis of provincial differences, or thinking.

Now, an honourable Member—one of the noted poets we have in this House—referred to the policy, the old British policy of divide and rule. He seemed to conclude, to hint that in this matter of linguistic provinces, the policy of the present Government is a continuation of this divide and rule policy. Now I must confess that I have failed to understand that. It may be a flight of poetic fancy, perhaps. Whatever one's view on this question may be, how it is a policy of divide and rule I do not understand.

Now repeated references have been made to the Congress policy for a large number of years and one honourable Member said that some time or other in the past I used to go about shouting from the house-tops or street corners about linguistic provinces. I am not aware of having done so at all. In fact, I have never been very anxious about linguistic provinces. I might say—and this is entirely, if I may say so, a confidential aside to the House—I have had peculiar views about our provinces and coming as I do from the biggest of India's provinces, I think that provinces should be very small in this country, but not provinces as we have them today with all the paraphernalia of a Governor, a High Court and this and that. But my voice has been a lonely voice, even when the Constituent Assembly was considering it. We were so used to existing conditions that we followed more or less what we have been used to.

Now talking about the Congress, everybody knows that thirty years ago or thereabouts, the Congress stood for linguistic provinces. Then skipping over the period, in 1945-46 (seven years ago) the Congress in its election manifesto said: 'It (the Congress) has also stood for the freedom of each group and territorial area within the nation to develop its own life and Culture within the larger framework and it is stated that for this purpose such territorial areas or provinces should be constituted, as far as possible, on a linguistic and cultural basis.'

That was seven years ago. The latest position is as embodied in the election manifesto of the last General Elections drawn up at Bangalore. May I read that out?

> The demand for a redistribution of provinces on a linguistic basis has been persistently made in the South and West of India. The Congress expressed itself in favour of linguistic provinces many years ago. A decision on this question ultimately depends upon the wishes of the people concerned. While linguistic reasons have undoubtedly cultural and other importance, there are other factors also, such as, economic, administrative and financial, which have to be taken into consideration. Where such a demand represents the agreed views of the people concerned, the necessary steps prescribed by the Constitution, including the appointment of a Boundary Commission, should be taken.

That more or less represents the policy and the position of Government in this matter.

Now, in regard to the Andhra Province, for instance, honourable Members have said: go and take a vote or plebiscite; 95 or 97 per cent, would vote for it. I entirely agree. But that does not get over my difficulties. I am all in favour of the Andhra Province. But what will happen if you take the votes of the Andhras and the Tamilians and others in regard to the issue and conflict like Madras city? Then you will not get 90 per cent, this way or that. It is quite clear that if you take the vote of the Andhras on the Andhra Province on principle they will vote for it en bloc. And rightly so, if I may say so: just as if you take the votes of large numbers of our friends on the Karnataka question they will vote for the Karnataka Province. I have no doubt about that. Or Maharashtrians. If they did not do so, or if they were not expected to do so, the question does not arise for our discussion. So we proceed on the basis of the assumption that considerable numbers of people in certain areas desire a province—more or less a linguistic province you may call it, although it is too limited a phrase—but they want a province where more or less their language prevails.

But the other question is where two such areas overlap, where they come into some friction with each other, how is one to decide about that overlapping and that friction?

... Therefore, the policy that Government stated previously, a year ago and more, was this that where a demand is made which is by general consent—of course, it was taken for granted that the people of that area as a whole more or less wanted it, but the consent meant of those who were concerned in regard to those overlapping and border areas—if that is obtained, then one can go ahead.

... Speaking for myself, I have been overburdened by the thought that in these critical days or years we must give topmost priority to developing a sense of unity in India and that anything that might come in the way of that unity might perhaps be delayed a little, till we have laid that strong foundation. Because of that I have, frankly—and I should be quite frank with this House—not taken any aggressive or positive step for my own part in regard to the formation of these linguistic provinces. Although I agreed with the demand in many cases I left it at that, and if there is general consent well and good, we will do it and I am prepared to do it... towards the end of 1949 we had practically come to the conclusion to have an Andhra Province, because most matters had been settled by compulsion by us... I think a Committee was formed and the Local Government had practically settled matters, when suddenly we found that two or three important matters, very vital matters, were not settled. Were we to give some kind of a decision to compel acceptance of that? This was just on the eve of the New Constitution of the Republic. The question was whether in this New Constitution we should not include Andhra as a separate Province. We as a Government were perfectly prepared to do it. But we could not do it when at the last moment conflicts arose: so that for the last two and a half years or more we were on verge of doing this, but something happened outside our own competence that delayed matters. I have no doubt at all in my mind, taking an individual case like the Andhra Province, that there is a great deal of justification for it. It is bound to come, and I have no doubt that the Andhras want it. And in the final analysis that is the final justification for it.

But when we get into difficulties about the City of Madras or Rayalaseema—I am not putting this just trying to create difficulties, I hope the question of Rayalaseema would by mutual consent be settled—whatever it is, when you get into these difficulties what is the Government to do, except that it can follow two courses. One is to allow a better atmosphere and to try to encourage a settlement by consent. The other is to come down with a heavy hand and overrule this party or that and give its own consent. The second can be done. Governments do it. But in a matter of this kind honourable Members will no doubt realise that strong feelings are roused, and if we make a new province by some kind of coercive method and leave a trace of intense bitterness behind between those two provinces which used to be one and were divided up later, it would not be good for either to start with that trail of inheritance of ill-will and bitterness against your neighbours just at the time when you are starting from scratch, when you have to settle down and build yourself anew. Therefore it is infinitely better, even though it takes a little more time, to do it with the goodwill and consent of your neighbours and others.

That was our general approach, and I submit that is the right approach because it will ultimately save you more time this way than to try to do something apparently quickly but in effect by a method which may entangle you into long arguments for years. After all, even the simplest of partitions brings problems and all kinds of difficulties, administrative, financial, this, that and the other. The Burma partition was very different, of course. Nevertheless, it was a complete partition with our goodwill. There was no conflict in it; still it took ten years, I think, to work itself out gradually, while it has not quite worked out yet in some ways. And those other partitions, the unfortunate ones, which happened in this country undoubtedly made many of us and many in the country become rather hesitant about changing the map of India too much. It is not in that way, of course, and I am not comparing it with that. But it does rather upset things. Of course, where it is necessary, let us change it. I am perfectly agreeable that it is necessary in some cases. But, the resolution that has been put forward, as it is worded, seems to me, not only completely unacceptable, but, if I may add, completely objectionable. It is all very well for our friends from Andhra or Maharashtra or Kerala or Karnataka, to put forward a definite proposal which could be considered and then accepted or not. But, a general proposition saying 'let us take the map of India, and on the basis of language, let us reshape and cut it up anew', is one which, I submit, no reasonable person can support. Because, it means your cutting up everything that you have got, upsetting everything that you have got, and just at the moment when you are more or less settling down in some way or other, unsettling everything. It will be dangerous at any time. More so, at a time when the world hangs on the verge of a crisis—one does not know what tomorrow or the day after might bring—for us to unsettle and uproot the whole of India for a theoretical approach or a linguistic division seems to me an extraordinarily unwise thing.

Then, again, in this matter, we have got a magnificent inheritance of India. We want, of course, to better that inheritance, to further it, to advance it. In doing so, if we think too much parochially or provincially, which is sometimes justified—I do not say that one should not think of his parish or his province; one should. If one applies that parochial way of looking at the whole of India, it is a dangerous thing. This resolution is for transferring the parochial or provincial outlook to the whole of India, and upsetting everything.

My honourable friend Dr. Syama Prasad Mookerjee spoke eloquently about West Bengal. I have no doubt that every Member in this House realises the tremendous burden that West Bengal has had to shoulder and face. I have no doubt at all that of all the States in India, West Bengal has had to shoulder more burdens than any other as a result of the partition and the rest of it, and other matters connected with that. I am sorry that he rather strayed away into other matters in regard to East Bengal; those are other questions. He advanced an argument that because of the heavy population of West Bengal, some adjoining areas may be added on to it. Now, I am not giving an opinion. Logically or theoretically speaking, that seems to be a valid argument. But, you cannot always be logical in these matters. I am quite sure that Members from Bihar did not wholly approve of what Dr. Mookerjee might have said, regardless of party or anything else. I am not going into whether they are right or he is right.

Let us take another thing. Dr. Mookerjee talked about certain districts, etc. Two or three months ago, I was in the Darjeeling area of North Bengal and there was a deputation from the Gurkha league demanding a Gurkha or Nepali province in North Bengal. Now, I am quite sure Dr. Mookerjee does not approve of that. It means taking away something even from this restricted Bengal. I might inform the House of my own reaction to that. But, instead of using my own words, I shall read out an answer that Sardar Patel gave in this House, with which I entirely agree. When this question of Gurkha province or Uttarkhand came up, his answer was: 'The Government of India consider this move of Uttarkhand in North Bengal as unreal, misconceived and harmful to national interests. The Government of India are determined not to give any quarter to any agitation for the formation of any such province and will not allow the solidarity of the country to be disturbed by such mischievous moves.'

In this matter, Dr. Mookerjee and I are in complete hundred per cent agreement. My point is this. If Dr. Mookerjee starts the question of re-distribution round about Bengal, all these questions arise, not only in the west, but in the north too. Everything comes up in the boiling cauldron of distribution all over India and one does not know what will emerge out of it ultimately.

It is all very well to say, as some honourable Members have said, as Dr. Mookerjee has said, as Dr. Khare has said, 'Decide this question this way or that way; do not leave it undecided.' Well, I confess I do not understand that. I can understand even a specific matter being decided. But, a general question of re-distribution in India being decided this way or that, I do not understand. In fact, such things, normally, are not decided this way or that way. You may lay down some general principles if you like. But, principles come into clash. There is the principle of linguistic provinces. There is the principle of economic self-sufficiency or whatever it is. There are financial considerations; this, that and the other; there are so many considerations. You have to balance all these things and then come to a particular decision in a particular place. No single general principle will apply. Normally speaking, you take what you have got. You have got the present structure of India, geographically. In fact, in the last three, four or five years, it has changed very greatly. First of all by the partition which took away a part of India and secondly by the merger of a large number of the old Indian States, the picture has changed greatly. But, nevertheless, roughly speaking, the old provinces of India remain more or less the same. That does not mean that they should not change. Certainly, they may change. You start with the basis that you do not upset it. You take one particular demand, and if it is reasonable, you consider it and give effect to it, if you like. But, to say that you should give effect to the principle all over India, there is no particular meaning.

In great countries like India, like China, there is always this great difficulty about provincialism. They are huge countries and inevitably, different parts of the country differ from other parts, sometimes in language, sometimes in ways of living and so many other things. In China they have some great advantages over us. They have, at any rate, one written language for the whole of China although the spoken language differs. Both these great countries have had to contend against provincialism. I do not know enough about the past or the recent history of China as to how they have dealt with this question for me to go into details about it. But, generally speaking, they have tried to get over it by getting rid of the provinces themselves. I believe they have divided China into a number of what they call Zones, five or six or seven or eight, whatever, the number may be. Apart from two or three autonomous areas, which are Mongolia and Tibet, the rest are Zones, which, presumably, cut across the old provincial boundaries. I cannot judge about China; I merely mention this because the problem is, in regard to size and provinces, much the same here. Maybe, it is more difficult here or more different here. But, our thinking too much in terms of anything that leads to an intensification of provincial feelings will, undoubtedly, weaken the conception of India as a whole. That is one aspect of it.

Another aspect, which is equally important, is that we have certain very important languages in India. A language by itself may be good or bad; but round that language clusters ways of living, sometimes ways of thought and all kinds of ways have grown round it and it is but right that that particular aspect of cultural manifestation should have an opportunity for full growth.

So far as language is concerned, I think that we should encourage almost every hill dialect in India. I am not in favour of suppressing these languages, and certainly the major languages must go ahead. So, in order to encourage the growth of the people, the best way is through the language they speak, and every State should do that; if it is multilingual, it should do it in the different languages. Why the political boundary should necessarily be a linguistic one, I do not see.

If there are within the same boundary different languages, they can have pride of place and be given full opportunity. But I think that although the linguistic demand is mentioned so often, it is not really the question of language that counts in this. Here and there it comes, but behind that there is something which is a little more difficult to deal with. It is a feeling of not having a square deal, if I may say so. That feeling comes in; otherwise, probably the language issue would not arise—a feeling that if they were separate and managed their own affairs, well, they will see to it that they get the square deal. If the feeling is there—and it is there—I cannot say whether there is much justification or not...

That is bad for us. That we should still function in this narrow provincial way of showing favour to one group and distinguishing the other group from it—that certainly is a bad thing, which means that we are still limited in our outlook, and however big our talk may be, we do not really think or function in a national way. We have to admit that. Having admitted it, we have to try to get over it. If we get over it, we should not do something which encourages that rather limited outlook. So you come up against two things. One is that we should not encourage that limited outlook; secondly, we must encourage the growth of the people in every way through their own language—cultural and other growth. You can balance these things. As a matter of fact, roughly speaking, in parts of the south of India, certain parts of the south of India—there is more or less a linguistic division in India; it may overlap here and there, but it is there—in the south you have two great States, Bombay and Madras which are multilingual. I should have thought that to live in a multilingual State gave greater opportunities of growth and for developing the wider outlook than to live in this, if I may say so, as somebody said, big leviathan of a State like Uttar Pradesh. Then you will find...in history and elsewhere, that countries, small States are forced to think in large terms. The people living in small States are forced to think in large terms. They are forced to learn languages of other States. Because people live in huge States and countries, they become so content with the vast area that they do not think of the other areas or other people. They become self-complacent and all that. It is not a good thing, this business of size by itself. It never connoted either intelligence or anything else. I do not know why people are intent on greatness in size, geographically or otherwise. This idea of size, if I may say so, comes from olden days and is connected with land; a man owning more and more land, therefore, getting more and more income; therefore, if he is a king, more and more people calling him Your Majesty or whatever it is. The size does not mean growth in any sense, but still we seem to think so—I am quite sure, for my part I am perfectly agreeable for Uttar Pradesh to be made into four provinces if you like; have three, four or as many as you like, but I doubt very much if many of my colleagues of Uttar Pradesh will relish that idea and they probably would like another chunk from another province.

... Some honourable Members referred to Hyderabad and the desirability or necessity for it to be cut up. May I say that I think it would be undesirable and unfortunate and injurious for Hyderabad to be disintegrated. Some honourable Members may not agree with me. That is a different matter. I am not challenging their bona fides in this matter, and I am not speaking about ever and ever. I am speaking of the present and the near future, and I think any attempt at splitting up Hyderabad would upset the whole structure of south India.

I am expressing my opinion. It would upset the whole structure of south India. For years you go about trying gradually to settle down. Here you have got a certain administrative and other continuity. As a matter of fact, we should have thought in terms of these provinces or States purely as administrative units, and nothing more. Whatever is convenient we have. In regard to other matters we do not think in terms of the provinces necessarily.

... The position, therefore, of Government in this matter is this: that we feel, that we realise that there is a strong demand by large numbers of people for certain linguistic provinces in India to be constituted. More or less this is so in south India—in other parts also as Dr. Mookerjee has pointed out. Almost every province has some petty demand, but those are not important.

Now in regard to these demands in south India which are old demands, which have great justification behind them, we are perfectly prepared to go ahead. We are not going to take up the question of India and shape it on a linguistic basis, but we are prepared to take up any particular matter, to consider it and I would repeat what we have said before; in regard to them nobody expects agreement by everybody, 100 per cent agreement, but in regard to the major matters which are at the present moment dividing the States concerned, on that there should be a fair measure of agreement. If that is so, if I may give an example with regard to the Andhra claim, I believe it was Dr. Lankasundaram who said that no Andhra will ever give up his claim to the city of Madras...

I am sure many Members from the Tamil areas would equally vehemently assert something to the contrary. But there it is. Let them come together and come to some kind of settlement. So far as I am concerned, or so far as we are concerned as a Government, I do not suggest that we should remain passive in this matter. I am prepared to do all I can to help in that settlement, I am certainly prepared to bring them together, but I just cannot see how I can go with a flaming sword to the Tamils or the Andhras and say, 'You must submit to the other's demand.' That I find very difficult to do. If I do that, even so the result will not be good, because you leave this trail of bitter memories behind; then maybe they will have a feeling of recovering the lost territory later on from another province. But the difficulty is this. We talk about Vishala Andhra, the Maha Gujarat or the Samyukth Maharashtra. If we see a map, we find that they all overlap.

If you look at the maps of Maha Gujarat, Vishala Andhra or the Samyukth Maharashtra, you find that they overlap and come into conflict with each other. So long as you are discussing the theory of it, many people from the Maha Gujarat will vote for the Vishala Andhra and so on. But as soon as they see the maps, they will come, after the poet said, to brass tacks—it is not very poetical, if I may say so. As soon as they come to brass tacks, then you find conflicts arising all over.

And we may be told, and ancient history may be invoked to say that 'in the year 1000 AD or something like that, Maha Gujarat spread right up to there,' or 'Look at history, at the time of the Rashtrakutas, the Maharashtra empire was up to here or there.' It was there; very interesting history no doubt, to say that the Andhra empire at the time of Ashoka or later had spread up to… We get back to these ancient historical memories, and try to claim that territory. Those ancient empires in their day were rather warring empires or imperial entities conquering other places. If the Andhras think of the ancient Andhra empire, and if the Maharashtrians think of the old Maharashtra and so on …

… This talk of linguistic provinces and historical parallels of where they were, leads quite inevitably to thinking that way and of spreading out in a sense, not a dominating one, but still of being in a more important position vis-à-vis the neighbour. Obviously you cannot possibly produce all those things. You cannot divide and give the same territory to two provinces, because they overlap. So there are all these difficulties.

Why have an agitation to convince me? I am convinced. If you are an Andhra go and talk to the Tamils or others who are concerned, and I will join the talks too if necessary, not that I want to keep out of it. It is no good trying to convince me because I am convinced about the same. I am not convinced about the same, as I said, if somebody talks to me about Uttarkhand, I am very much opposed to it; if somebody else talks of a Sikh province, I say 'Nothing doing.' I am not going to play about with my potters there. That is a different matter. But in regard to these major claims like Andhra or Karnataka or Kerala or Maharashtra...

West Bengal and other places are not questions of new provinces. They are merely questions of frontier rectification, if you like to put it that way. I have no objection to that. I do not myself see why conditions should arise between the State of Bihar and the State of Bengal such that people should feel unhappy in crossing over from this side or that, either refugees or others. I think it is all one country.

I do not think that there is universal agreement in that matter. However we shall consider that separately, but again that has to be considered, in a spirit of goodwill, because the odd thing is that the more the one side agitates about it, the more the other side gets rigid...

... But it must be realised that this kind of one-side agitation really comes in the way of the solution of these problems because the people of the other provinces get excited the other way.

... If the States concerned agree to the plebiscite, let us have it, but imposing a plebiscite where it may be a decision, let us say, by 45 to 55 or something like that, would not help, bitterness will remain and you cannot dispose of all these things normally by plebiscite.

... Prof. Saha referred to the case of the Soviet Union. Well I do not think it applies here. That is helpful, no doubt, but not very much so. First of all, the Soviet Union emerged as it is today after years of fire and civil war and slaughter. All kinds of things happened there. There was invasion from outside and what not. Out of that it is in a sense easier to build up. Secondly, India is much more, if I may say so, of a unity than the Soviet Union. The Soviet Union is no longer an Empire as a whole, but it is a collection of a number of totally different countries, Russia plus other countries and Siberia. They have formed a political unit and are happy about it. That is very good. So they proceeded on a different basis, on the basis, in theory of independent republics federating together. Now, India is completely different from that position. You cannot have that here, on the basis of independent republics federating together. We are a much more unified country. The question would arise if you took Russia, that is, not the Soviet Union, but Russia which is more of a unified country, and compare that to India. That will be a better comparison than taking large tracts of Asia which belong to the Soviet Union, which have been added to it and which follow a common policy etc. Even so, as a matter of fact probably the theory there is somewhat different from the practice—I mean the theory of secession. I think it is perfectly clear that no part of it can secede at all and as it happens, there has been a progressive decentralisation there. In spite of the theory of secession, the process of centralisation has gone pretty far.

~

O.V. ALAGESAN

On Linguistic States

On the resolution regarding linguistic states moved in the Lok Sabha in 1952, the issue of Andhra as a new state was the centre of debate. O.V. Alagesan, the legislator from Chingleput (Madras Province) which was proposed to be part of the new Andhra state, mounted a strong criticism of the whole idea of language being the criterion of new state formation, pointing out the ridiculous lengths to which the criterion could be applied to satisfy partisan interests. The speech was made on 12 July 1952.

The debate has gone on for more than six hours and at long last I am glad that one representing the Tamil area has been called to speak. It looked as if there are no representatives in this House from the Tamil area, more so from Madras. There was much bandying of words about the city of Madras. Several honourable Members spoke about the position that it should take under the future redistribution scheme. I was wondering what happened to representatives from the city of Madras in this House. There are several of them. The south of Madras is very ably represented by my honourable friend Mr. T.T. Krishnamachari, who fortunately or unfortunately has got into the Treasury Benches and therefore his mouth is shut. But, that does not mean that nobody in this House knows his opinion about the city of Madras. Again, three-eighths of the city of Madras is represented equally ably by my honourable friends Mr. Natesan and Shrimati Chandrasekhar. I hope they will be given an opportunity to speak their minds. They will be really voicing the opinion of the people of Madras in this matter, where they want to remain, and where they want to be tagged on. Up till now, the debate has assumed a tilted and unreal aspect, because the real representatives of the city of Madras in this House have not been called upon to give their opinion in this matter.

I shall first deal with the immediate background of this resolution and then take up some of the controversial points that have been raised by my friends from Andhra area. If I have counted rightly, so far five of them, including you, Sir, have, spoken, and several from the Kerala area, and several others from the Karnataka area have also spoken. This demand for linguistic provinces is more emotional in content than either political or economic. People are deeply stirred over this question, and very much agitated and in the Andhra area people are going on fast. I do not know whether to call it satyagraha or otherwise and they demand linguistic province. It is a sort of glorification of the past. When the achievements of the people become memories of the past, it is language that holds up the mirror to those achievements and reminds them of those. When everything else decays and dies, language alone lives. It is because of this that language evokes the deepest emotions in the human heart. Take the Maharashtrian, for instance. He dreams of the valiant days of Shivaji and longs to relive them.

… He contemplates the great saint of Maharashtra and his sacred abhangs, and feels very much elevated. So also Andhra friends dream of the empire of the pre-Christian era, which has nothing in common with the Telugu except the name, Andhra.

… The Tamil poets…have sung how Tamilian kings conquered North Indian chieftains and planted their flag on the Himalayas. They have very discreetly omitted all mention of the defeats that they suffered at the hands of others. The honourable Finance Minister, the clever man that he is, quoted a simple Kural from the book of Tiruvalluvar, ending his reply to the general discussion on the Budget and the whole of Tamil Nadu was aglow with pride that, here is a Finance Minister, who is himself a Maharashtrian, but has chosen to quote Kural. Even if he had set apart about ten crores to the Tamil area, he would not have evoked such a response, because the people would have still said, here is a Finance Minister who could have given much more, but he has given only this much.

That is the magic that language exercises over the mind of men. If the people and their representatives are agitated over it, I can perfectly understand that.

Just as my honourable friend Mr. Nijalingappa said a few minutes ago, our friends opposite have not been slow to seize this question of high emotional value and they have come out as the champions of linguistic provinces. They are the foremost in demanding redistribution on linguistic basis. That is perfectly understandable. It would be very interesting to know from them how many languages and dialects they have recognised for the purpose of linguistic redistribution. There are certain languages in this country which do not have any script. Yet, my honourable friends opposite would give him the luxury of a separate State, because they would recognise even dialects. We should improve them; we should develop them; that is what they would say. There is another language called Tulu, which is spoken in a portion of South Kanara. Half of that district will go to Tulu and half to Konkani. If my friends opposite have their way, they will have the entire country cut up into all sort of little linguistic bits so that there may not be the requisite amount of unity and solidarity in the country. They would ask us to follow blazing example of the Fatherland and ask us to develop every little dialect because it serves their purpose eminently well. We now carry on our public affairs through the medium of language and that too a foreign language. Though the language is one we could voice different opinions. Yesterday, we saw how the honourable Home Minister had his opinion changed and introduced a major change in the Bill in deference to the wishes of the Opposition.

When our friends opposite have it all their own way, they would not have any diversity of opinion. They will enforce total conformity and uniformity. Having ensured that, they would allow any amount of diversity in language. What if there are 100 languages? They will all sing the same chorus; they will sing the greatness of the State symbolised in its Head. So, it suits them very well to bring up this question at this moment and try to weaken this country. It will be very profitable to enquire how our friends who believe in ultra centralism seemingly adopt a course which decentralises power in the hands of the various linguistic units. Therein lies the secret of their strategy. They adopt methods which are diametrically opposite to the ends that they desire.

I shall pass on to the various controversial points that have been raised by my honourable friends coming from the Andhra area. First of all, it was said that the people's wishes should be consulted. We have no objection to that. Only I say that the people's wishes have already been consulted. They have given their opinion and verdict in the last election. I shall prove it. There is a very eminent Andhra leader. The House heard the story from the Prime Minister how the Andhras were within an inch of having their province and they let it slip through their fingers. It was one man who said that he will not accept Andhra province without the city of Madras, and so it had to be given up. And that gentleman had the wisdom to seek election from one of the city constituencies to demonstrate the accuracy of the opinion he was voicing. Then the people gave their verdict and said: 'You have to lose the deposit: you have no hold on the place.'

... That is why they gave their vote against him, because they knew that the vote would be misappropriated for the purpose of claiming the city of Madras for the Andhra province and so they anticipated this and asked him to go. Of course, I recognise that my Andhra friends are highly emotional. The Tamilians do not clamour as much for their own province. But why? It is not because we do not want the province. It is because we have a greater sense of realism. Even if the Andhra State is separated, the remainder will still be a composite State. There will be the Malayalees in it, there will be the Canarese in it. We are not going to ask them to go away. So, we have developed that sense of practical values and we are carrying on. That is why you do not find here any clamour for a separate Tamil province, but that does not mean that we do not want one.

I shall give you a simple example how this question not being solved comes in the way at all times. Recently, just a little time ago, the Postal Department proposed to issue certain new stamps with the ensigns of various poets of the country on them. I found Meera and Tagore and Tulsidas—perhaps he is the only poet in Hindi—and some others. I asked the Deputy Minister of Communications why he had omitted the famous Tamil poet Subrahmanya Bharathi. His reply was: 'We considered this question. We wanted to have Bharathi, but then, we could not think of a Telugu poet so that both can be issued at the same time. And so Bharathi had to be left out.' That is the wonderful understanding that even our Ministers and the central Government have of this issue. Hence, we will be happier if this issue is solved at an early date...

~

JAWAHARLAL NEHRU

The Naga Issue

The British brought the tribal areas in the north-east under political control and declared these 'excluded areas' and 'backward tracts'. They adopted a policy of non-interference in local tribal affairs. One of the most critical challenges the Indian state faced after independence pertained to these areas. The Naga National Council led by Angami Zapu Phizo declared independence for the Naga people on 14 August 1947, a day before India's independence. The Indian constitution provided for the inclusion of such areas inhabited by the Nagas as part of the territory of the Indian Union. Phizo was arrested in 1948 for his anti-India activities but was released soon after. Over the next few years, he consolidated his position and influence and declared that in a referendum he had conducted, 99 per cent had voted in favour of independence. Despite repeated peace offers by the Government of India, the movement for a separate Naga state continued unabated. When Phizo once again declared Nagaland's independence on 22 March 1956, the Indian Army was inducted to crush the insurgency. Nehru's stand as represented in his speech in Parliament on 1 August 1960 is the idealized stand of the Indian state for every conflict—that Indian democracy will solve all problems through dialogue and not through violence.

Mr. Speaker sir, I have on many previous occasions referred in this House to the problem of the Nagas. As Honourable Members are aware, we have always regarded the territory inhabited by the Nagas, as by other tribal people all over India, as part of independent India as defined in our constitution. We looked upon all these tribal people as citizens of independent India having all the privileges and obligations of such citizenship.

... Our policy has always been to give the fullest autonomy and opportunity of self-development to the Naga people, without interfering in any way in their internal affairs or way of life.

Unfortunately the process of devolution of local autonomy could not be implemented in full because troubles arose in the area as a result of the hostile activities of a section of the Nagas. The ostensible object of this hostile section was to carve out an independent Naga territory entirely separate from India. This was a demand which no government in India could ever agree to. These hostile elements among the Naga people thereafter took to violent methods, and we had to take steps to meet these illegal activities. The hostile Nagas indulged in arson, loot and extortion of money from their own fellow Nagas. They also committed a number of gruesome murders. It became our duty to give protection to the large number of other Naga residents of these areas and to meet the menace of this continued violence. The help of our Army and the Assam Rifles was taken in this conflict and various steps were taken to give the necessary protection and to maintain law and order. This conflict inevitably caused much suffering to the people of those areas, most of whom were anxious to live a peaceful life and carry on their avocations. The story of the last five and six years has been a sad and depressing one. Gradually, there was an improvement in the situation and over large areas in the Naga districts peaceful conditions were established. One bright feature was the extension of our development work and the establishment of school, hospitals and communications. But in spite of this considerable improvement, a hard core of the hostile elements continued their violent activities even though they were driven back into the remoter parts of these hills.

... I take this opportunity to express our satisfaction at the agreement reached with the Naga leaders. We have regarded the Nagas as full Indian citizens. I have said to the Naga people several times in the past that there could be no question of independence for the Nagas. India achieved her independence thirteen years ago and the Nagas are as independent as other Indian citizens. We have not the slightest desire to interfere with the tribal customs and usage of the Nagas or in their distinctive way of life. The Nagas have been anxious to have a separate state within the Indian union. The agreement now reached with them should enable them to find the fullest opportunity of self-expression and we sincerely hope that the new arrangement will result in the rapid restoration of normal conditions in the area. I must, however, make it clear that no government can permit hostile activities on its soil, and while we are ready to give our fullest support to those who will cooperate in giving effect to the agreement just reached we shall continue to deal firmly with the hostile elements. This is an unpleasant but unnecessary task and I trust that the Naga leaders will cooperate fully in putting an end to the disloyal activities of a minority of their people.

~

C.N. ANNADURAI

Dravida Nadu

C.N. Annadurai (1909–69), popularly known as Anna, was the first non-Congress chief minister of Tamil Nadu after independence. In 1949, he founded the Dravida Munnettra Kazhagam (DMK) and in the wake of the anti-Hindi agitation became its most sober and articulate face in Parliament. He became a member of the Rajya Sabha in 1962 and carried his campaign against Hindi to Parliament, viewing it as an Aryan cultural invasion. In April 1962, on the motion to thank the President on his address to Parliament, Anna presented a scathing indictment of the Government of India. For the first time, the demand for a separate and independent 'Dravida Nadu' comprising the four southern states was seriously raised in Parliament. However, the Chinese attack and the change in the tone of the central government, coupled with the victory of the DMK in Tamil Nadu, gradually brought such demands to a halt. Soon, Anna became the chief minister of Tamil Nadu and with him began the complete domination of the political space in the state by the Dravida parties.

I claim Sir, to come from a country, a part in India now, but which I think is of a different stock, not necessarily antagonistic. I belong to the Dravidian stock. I am proud to call myself a Dravidian. That does not mean that I am against a Bengali or a Maharashtrian or a Gujarati. As Robert Burns has stated, 'A man is a man for all that.' I say that I belong to the Dravidian stock and that is only because I consider that the Dravidians have got something concrete, something distinct, something different to offer to the nation at large. Therefore it is that we want self-determination.

After coming here I must say that many times I have found great kindness in the Honourable Members. I did not expect so much kindness when I came here. I find that this kindness even makes me forget the animosities that had been created by certain Hindi-speaking people. I would very much like to be one with you. I would very much like to be with you as one nation. But a wish is one thing and facts are another. We want one world, one government. But we forget national frontiers. The other day I found the Honourable Member Mr Dayabhai Patel speak and when he spoke about Gujarat, there was such fire in his words and about such an industrially advanced state. Take my state of Madras. It is backward taking into consideration everything. You have here four steel plants. We have been crying hoarse for a decade and more for a steel plant, but what have they given us? They gave the portfolio to a new Minister, not the steel industry to us. Perhaps, if the Honourable Subramaniam had not come here he might have been pressing for the steel industry from there. Is it diplomacy or prudence or political expediency? I don't know which—but you have brought him here and you are going to ask him to reply to the demand of the south. That is what the British were doing—divide and rule, barter and get money, marshal out figures and demolish arguments.

The fact that we want separation is not to be misconstrued as being antagonistic. Of course, I can understand the feelings that would very naturally arise in the minds of people in the northern area, whenever they think of partition. I know the terrible consequences of partition and I am deeply sympathetic towards them. But our separation is entirely different from the partition which has brought about Pakistan. I would even say that if sympathetic treatment is afforded, there need be no heat generated. There would not be any dire consequences. Fortunately, the south itself is a sort of a geographical unit. We call it the Deccan plateau or the peninsula. There will not be a large number of people migrating from this place to that. There will not be any refugee problem. I would ask you to very calmly bestow deep and sympathetic thought on the problem.

The language and other details will be worked out by a Constituent Assembly. The position today is, whatever may be your reading of the situation, for whatever we do not get in the south, the masses are ready to lay the entire blame on the Indian Government. There will be very natural reasons for not opening certain industries there, but the moment we are denied a steel plant, the moment we are denied new railway lines, the moment we are denied an oil refinery, the man in the street in the south gets up and says, 'This is the way of Delhi. This is the way of northern imperialism and unless you come out of that imperialism you are not going to make your country safe, sound, plentiful and progressive.' When I talk about separation, I represent the resurgent view of the south and as the illustrious person, Mira

Behn, stated some time ago, the natural unity that we found when we were opposing the British is not to be construed as a permanent affair. The principle of separation or, to put it more explicitly, the principle of self-determination, has been accepted by leaders of international repute and more than that, by the Prime Minister of this subcontinent of ours. During the days of the Pakistan controversy, Pandit Jawaharlal Nehru, speaking, if I remember correctly, on the Kapurthala grounds, stated categorically that they, the Congress, as an organisation, would try to keep every unit within the Indian Union; but if any Indian unit decided to secede, the Congress would give its consent. Thus, the Congress has recognised the principle of self-determination. I make this bold appeal to that liberal thought, to that democratic spirit. Despite the fact that he has become the Prime Minister, I think part of the old fire is still burning in his heart. Why don't you give self-determination to peninsular India? After that, India will not be impoverished. I would say that that decision would pave the way for raising the stature of India. I am inviting those people who want to keep India one and indivisible to make it a comity of nations instead of it being a medley of disgruntled units here and there.

~

JAYAPRAKASH NARAYAN

The Nagaland Peace Mission

In May 1964, the Government of India constituted a peace mission consisting of Jayaprakash Narayan, B.P. Chaliha, then chief minister of Assam, and Michael Scott, an English pastor sympathetic to the Nagas, which worked out a ceasefire agreement between the Government of India and the Naga underground rebels. The agreement was a prelude to political negotiations to peacefully resolve the conflict. Jayaprakash Narayan presented the peace mission's agenda before the Tatar Hoho (the parliament of the Naga Federal Government) on 24 February 1965. This frank and honest speech made by him on the occasion demonstrates the Gandhian strategy to resolve conflict by means of dialogue which Jayaprakash Narayan tried to adopt in his peace mission.

India is a family made up of equal nations, a multinational state. The Naga people are unquestionably a multinational. The United Kingdom itself is one, containing English, Scottish, Welsh and Irish nations. There are also multiracial and multi-religious states. Different nations may, and do, share a common citizenship and membership of one state.

After the creation of the state of Nagaland it is possible for the Naga people to govern themselves. They are free within the present framework of the Union–state relation to govern their state. No one rules Assam but Assamese; no one rules Bengal but the Bengalis; no one rules Madras but the Madrasis. Each state in USA is an autonomous unit. The range of powers vested in the state may be great or small, but the nature of power and control is a matter of negotiation between the state and the Government of India. The situation is therefore entirely different from that which prevailed under the British rule.

There is no doubt that your struggle is not a mere law and order question. But I have tried to show that the Naga freedom movement may take on a different character if it is placed in the context of a union consisting of self-governing states represented in the Union Parliament. We have suggested these recommendations as we are aware of the nature of the Union of India. If it had been otherwise we would never have made such suggestions. What kind of relation we want may be negotiated; it is entirely open, and an agreement is also possible. Participation has many possible meanings. It is possible for Nagaland to participate in the Indian Union as an equal, free and self-governing partner. Even today as the constitutional position exists the laws of the Government of India cannot be applied to Nagaland unless the assembly of Naga people first approve them.

If the Nagaland Federal Government feels it should have nothing to do with this constitution, it may by all means throw it away. But a new constitution has to be drawn up.

I must admit that I had little idea of the seriousness of the situation here before my association with this work. So little news appeared in the press. But in the last two months its seriousness has been brought home to me in all its depth, danger and frightfulness. By the grace of God wisdom has dawned on both parties. We have got now some kind of peace. The people of Nagaland now breathe more freely; people in India too feel relieved. The scanty news of firings, ambushes, sabotage had filled them with anxiety; but there is now relief and thankfulness.

Rise of Extremists

But we have not yet overcome the danger. This session of the Tatar Hoho has to consider how to meet the threat looming large on the horizon. This is not only a threat to Nagaland; it is also a threat to India. If the present negotiations break down its immediate result in India will be disastrous. In every country there are extremists as well as liberals, reasonable people as well as fanatics; there are those who appeal to humanity and those who appeal to violence. If the talk fails, the hands of the extremists who have been demanding the deportations of Michael Scott and the arrest of Jayaprakash Narayan will be strengthened. In such an event, the real India—the voice of reason and humanity—will be the first casualty. There are some people who are engaged in sabre-rattling. If the peace mission fails this will provide an opportunity to those who wish to fish in troubled waters. This would be a disaster for our country, the land of Mahatma Gandhi. Failure of the peace talks would be our spiritual defeat. It involves the loss both of men and materials, but this is insignificant in comparison to the spiritual loss. The peace mission is therefore determined not to give up hope but will continue its efforts to preserve peace and make it permanent. We have all staked our lives to achieve our propose.

For we realise that India's involvement in a violent struggle in Nagaland would not only harm people in India but would also besmear India's image internationally.

Failure of Peace Efforts

For the people of Nagaland failure of the peace efforts would mean terrible suffering. I need not elaborate. You know too well how the people in this unfortunate land have suffered in the past. I wish to say one thing more: We regard the Naga freedom fighters as Naga patriots, not as outlaws. They are not breaking laws; they are fighting for freedom. We have the greatest respect, affection and regard for them, and we are here as their friends.

... The mission has staked its life on this peace work. We shall not rest... We had requested an extension of six months at the peace talks at Khensa. All we were able to get was one month and nine days. We shall plead again for a long extension. These matters cannot be settled with the threat of firing hanging over our heads; there must be peace in our hearts for this work...

As for the question of the extension of the powers of the armed forces for another year, this was a routine matter. It is no new step. The security forces are here to aid the civil power; they have no power themselves. We in the peace mission would like to see the security forces of India withdrawn tomorrow. We made an attempt earlier to get them withdrawn from all internal security duties, but we did not succeed. This single fact, of their presence here, makes the Naga people feel they are not free. They feel the security forces are a visible expression of their lack of freedom.

~

KAPUR SINGH

Punjabi Suba

Kapur Singh (1909–86) was selected for the Indian Civil Service and served in various administrative posts. He joined active politics in 1962 and was elected to the Lok Sabha and later to the Punjab Legislative Assembly in 1969. He was the moving spirit behind the Anandpur Sahib Resolution adopted by the Shiromani Akali Dal in 1973, which enunciated the modern Sikh communal political formula and policy. Kapur Singh was also a prolific writer and his Parasarprasna *ranks as a classic on Sikh philosophy. The speech reproduced here, delivered on 6 September 1966 in the Lok Sabha, shows his grasp of politics as well as the biting directness with which he criticized the Punjab Reorganisation Bill of 1966 dividing the state into two, Punjab and Haryana, on the basis of language, which he said slighted 'Sikh aspirations'.*

Madam Chairman, I have gone through this draft bill most carefully and I have heard the honourable home minister with the most diligence and respect which his speeches and utterances always deserve.

… as it is I have no option but to oppose this bill. Like the curates' egg though it might be edible…but it is devoid of nutritional qualities and since its putrefaction is far gone, it is really unfit for human consumption.

I am convinced that it is deleterious for the Sikhs however strong their stomachs might be supposed to be, as Mr. Tyagi hinted. I oppose this bill on behalf of my constituents and I reject it on behalf of my parent party, Shiromani Akali Dal. I do so for three reasons, firstly, it is conceived in sin; secondly, it has been delivered by an incompetent and untrained midwife and thirdly, it is opposed to the best interests of the nation as it will almost certainly lead to a weakening of national integration and loss of faith in the integrity of those who exercise political power in the country.

It is not an illicit child but it is conceived in sin. It may have the vigour of the hybrid offspring but unfortunately it is an offspring of a miscegenous union, and therefore, I oppose it. I say, it is conceived in sin, because it constitutes the latest act of betrayal of solemn promises—series of solemn promises—given to the Sikh people by the accredited leaders of the majority community, by the revered leaders of the Congress national movement, and by the unchallenged spokesmen of the ruling party.

It will do this House good, it will do the public a lot of good, it will do the people of India a lot of good, and it will do the international community a world of good, to listen to a brief narration of this story of betrayal of a people...

Here is the brief story of a callous betrayal of such a people—the Sikhs of India—by those whose flesh and bones the Sikhs are and whose ancestors—common ancestors of the betrayed and betrayers both—had upheld the highest and the noblest notions and standards of Ethical conduct in respect of the subject of keeping faith with fellow men and redeeming promises solemnly made.

I quote from Mahabharata Adi Parvam, sub chapter 74 and verse 25: 'He who has one thing in mind but represents another thing to others, what sin he is not capable of committing? For, he is a thief and a robber of his own self.'

I ask the honourable members to take their minds back to the year 1929, when the All India National Congress met, at the banks of the river Airavati of our ancestors, fixed complete independence as its political goal. On that bitterly cold night of destiny, I was present as one of the student volunteers in the service of the Nation. On the previous day, the Sikhs had taken out a procession with veteran Baba Kharak Singh leading it on elephant back....

It was on this occasion that Mahatma Gandhi, Motilal Nehru and Pandit Jawaharlal Nehru went to meet Baba Kharak Singh, at his place on Chauburji Road, and gave the Sikhs a solemn assurance that after India achieves political freedom, no Constitution shall be framed by the majority community unless it is freely acceptable to the Sikhs. This promise was then reduced into a formal policy resolution of the All India Congress Committee.

Afterwards, this policy resolution was repeatedly reiterated, officially and semi-officially, throughout the period up to August 1947, and it was not officially repudiated till 1950 when the present Constitution was framed. The trusting Sikhs, who in their daily prayer extol keeping faith as the noblest human virtues, placing complete reliance in this solemn undertaking given to them by the majority community, resisted and refused all offers and proposals made to them by the British and the other people... This is the first link of the history which I am going to narrate here so as to provide background to the conclusion as to why the bill should be rejected. The second link is that in the year 1932, at the time of the Second Round Table Conference, the British Government, through Sardar Bahadur Shivdev Singh, then a member of the Indian Secretary of States Council, made an informal proposal to the Sikhs that if they dissociate finally with the Congress movement, they would be given a decisive political weightage in the Punjab, such as would lead to their emerging as a third independent element in India after the British transfer to the inhabitants of this subcontinent.

The much maligned, the naïve Master Tara Singh, to my personal knowledge, promptly rejected this tempting offer. I was then a student at the University of Cambridge and was closely associated with these developments.

In April 1947, Mr. Jinnah, in consultation with certain powerful leaders of the British Cabinet in London offered to the Sikhs, first through Master Tara Singh and then through the Maharaja of Patiala a sovereign Sikh state, comprising areas lying to the west of Panipat and east of the left bank of the river Ravi, on the understanding that this state then confederates with Pakistan on very advantageous terms to the Sikhs. Master Tara Singh summarily rejected this attractive offer and Maharaja of Patiala declined to accept it in consultation with Sardar Patel and Jawaharlal Nehru.

... On the 9th December 1946, when the first meeting of the Constituent Assembly was held under the chairmanship of Babu Rajendra Prasad, Pandit Jawaharlal Nehru moved the first and the fundamental resolution in which it was said: 'Adequate safeguards would be provided for minorities... It was a declaration, a pledge and an undertaking before the world, a contract with millions of Indians and, therefore, in the nature of an oath which we must keep.'

What happens in case of political perjury is not a point which I propose to discuss today, for, when neither the feelings of shame, the reproaches of conscience, nor the dread of punishment is there, the sufferers can only pray to God, which the Sikhs are doing today. But since it is the prerequisites of power to invent its own past, I am putting the record straight for the public opinion and the posterity by recapitulating this sorry tale of betrayal of Sikhs, a trusting people.

... In the month of May 1947, precisely on the 17th May, Lord Mountbatten, Pandit Jawaharlal Nehru, Nawab Liaqat Ali Khan and Sardar Baldev Singh, flew to London on the invitation of the British Cabinet, in search of a final solution of the Indian communal problem. When the Congress and the Muslim League failed to strike any mutual understanding and Pandit Jawaharlal Nehru decided to return to India, the British Cabinet leaders conveyed to Sardar Baldev Singh that if he stayed behind, arrangements might be made so as to 'enable the Sikhs to have political feet of their own on which they may walk into the current of world history'.

Sardar Baldev Singh promptly divulged the content of the offer to Pandit Jawaharlal Nehru and in compliance with the latter's wishes, declined to stay back and flew back to India after giving the following brief message to the press: 'The Sikhs have no demands to make on the British except the demand that they should quit India. Whatever political rights and aspirations the Sikhs have, they shall have them satisfied through the goodwill of the Congress and the majority community.'

... In the month of July 1947, the Hindu and Sikh members of the Punjab Legislative Assembly met at Delhi to pass a unanimous resolution favouring partition of the country, in which resolution occur the following words: 'In the divided Indian Punjab, special constitutional measures are imperative to meet just aspirations and rights of the Sikhs.'

It is these very Hindus of Punjab, who, with the ready aid of the Government of India leaders, even when their understanding was not qualified to keep pace with the wishes of their heart, adopted every conceivable posture and shrank from no stratagem to keep Sikhs permanently under the political heel, first by refusing to form a Punjabi speaking state in which the Sikhs might acquire political effectiveness and second, by falsely declaring that Punjabi was not their mother tongue.

The bill before the house is a calculatedly forged link in the chain, the sordid story of which I have just now narrated. When in 1950, the present Constitution Act of India was enacted, the accredited representatives of the Sikhs—the Shiromani Akali Dal—declared vehemently and unambiguously in the Constituent Assembly that 'the Sikhs do not accept this Constitution Act: the Sikhs reject this Constitution Act'. Our spokesmen declined to append their signatures to the Constitution Act as a token of this clear and irrevocable rejection.

I will, for want of time, skip over the story of the Sikhs' sufferings during the last 18 years in an independent India under the political control of political and anglicised Hindus, and will merely refer to the reply which Pandit Jawaharlal Nehru gave to Master Tara Singh in 1954, when the latter reminded him of the solemn undertaking previously given to the Sikhs on behalf of the majority community. Pandit Jawaharlal Nehru replied, 'The circumstances have now changed.' If there is one thing that the Sikhs know too well, it is that now the circumstances have changed.

Let us now briefly examine the immediate ancestry of the present bill. It was on 21st March 1966 that the Minister of Home Affairs set up a Commission presided over by a Supreme Court Judge, requiring the Commission, firstly, to examine existing boundaries of Hindi and Punjabi regions of Punjab to set up Punjab and Haryana states; secondly, applying linguistic principles as they have resulted in the 1961 census figures; and thirdly, to determine boundaries that do not involve breaking up of tehsils. All these three guidelines given to the Commission by the Government of India are, when they are properly examined by people who understand the realities of politics, heavily loaded against the Punjab state, and have the effect of reducing Sikhs to even more political ineffectiveness than at present. Nor has the Shah Commission failed to take full advantage of the instruments of discrimination thus placed in their hands by the Government of India. They have, firstly, arbitrarily truncated and reduced, as much as they could, the existing Punjabi region, and secondly, applied all principles of demarcation with a left-handed justice—made use of a principle where it could harm the Punjab and not used it where it could harm the resultant territorial interest of Haryana or Himachal Pradesh. For instance, Dalhousie has been taken out of Punjab and given to Himachal because it is hilly, while Morni which is of a higher altitude than Dalhousie has been taken away to be bestowed on Haryana, because its residents are Hindus, which is the same thing as saying that they are Hindi-speaking.

Thus, this story goes on and every conceivable stratagem has been adopted, through truncating its areas, through divesting it of its utility undertakings in public sector, and through neutralising its limbs of governmental apparatus and by robbing it of its capital city, and by forging the so-called common links to reduce the Punjab state into a glorified Zila Parishad, and to achieve these sordid and unedifying objectives, the judiciary has been made use of.

Madam Chairman, permit me to say that if there is one political crime greater than any other, the ruling party has committed during the post-independence era, it is frequent employment of judiciary for quasi-political purposes, and the result is that the Working Committee of the Shiromani Akali Dal has passed a resolution on the 20th July 1966 which reads: 'After having carefully viewed the findings, the reports and judgments of judicial and quasi-judicial Tribunals and Forums...comes to the conclusion, that the entire judicial machinery and the judicial process of the independent India, under influences of a certain section of political Hindus, is prejudiced and has been perverted against the Sikh people in India in relation to their just and legal rights.'

... A modern state...has four estates: the Parliament, the executive, the judiciary and the press. The concrete realities of these four alone can furnish an acid test as to whether the Sikh problem in India is a real problem or not. To the executive and the judiciary, reference has already been made by me. I now propose to make a reference to Parliament, this august House, which is deserving of our highest respect, and its dignity is the dignity of the people of India and hence inviolable. Nevertheless, the Sikhs are aware that, under the existing constitutional arrangements, they cannot send more than a couple of their own representatives to the Parliament and even they may not always be heard freely. How many times has it happened in this House, in the recent past, that particular members of the minority communities have been made aware, in no uncertain manner, that they must not—must never—say this thing or that, or else a hearing might be denied them...

And, lastly the press. We have a free press here and a lively and impartial press on the whole. But, what is it like when it comes to dealing with Sikhs, that is, politically vocal Sikhs or questions largely concerning the Sikhs? In the days of his clash with Beaverbrook, Baldwin said of the press: 'Power without responsibility, the privileges of harlots throughout the ages.'

And, I say no more. I have said enough to explain the background of the Resolution No. 2 of the Working Committee of the Shiromani Akali Dal passed on the 20th July 1966 wherein occur the following passages in relation to the scope of this bill:

Sikhs resolve and proclaim, their determination to resist, through all legitimate means, all such attempts to devalue and liquidate the Sikh people in a free India, and consequently demand that the following steps should be taken forthwith by the rulers of India to assure and enable the Sikhs to live as respectable and equal citizens of the Union of India, namely, first, the Sikh areas deliberately and intentionally cut off and not included in the new Punjab to be set up, namely, the areas of Gurdaspur District including Dalhousie, Ambala District including Chandigarh, Pinjore, Kalka and Ambala Saddar, the entire Una Tehsil of Hoshiarpur District, the areas of Nalagarh, called Desh, the Tehsil of Sirsa, the sub-Tehsils of Tohana and Guhla and Rattia block, District Hissar, Shahbad block of District Karnal and the contiguous portions of the Ganga Nagar District of Rajasthan must now be immediately included in the new proposed Punjab so as to bring all contiguous Sikh areas into an administrative unit, to be Sikh Homeland, within the Union of India.

Second, such a new Punjab should be granted an autonomous constitutional status on the analogy of the status of Jammu and Kashmir as was envisaged in the Constitution Act of India in the year 1950.

I am coming to a close. Madam, on behalf of the Sikh people represented by the Shiromani Akali Dal, I reject the entire schemata of this bill, and oppose it. I call upon the Government to take necessary legislative measures to solve the problem of the Punjab in the light of the resolution of the Shiromani Akali Dal, just referred to.

~

NATH PAI

Governors of States

Nath Pai was a leader of the Socialist Party, a powerful orator whose speeches were marked by a keen sense of factual details, and the most prominent non-communist voice which criticized the government in the Lok Sabha. In the 1960s, his speeches, along with those of Ram Manohar Lohia, gave the socialists a lead in the country's parliamentary politics. Their speeches also inspired the youth and students. When, after the 1967 elections, for the first time a range of non-Congress parties and formations began to wrest initiatives in the states, the post of the governor became important. There were widespread allegations of the governor's post being misused or abused by the party at the centre, the Congress, to install its own party in power in the states or dislodge ministries of other parties. It was in such a situation that Nath Pai's motion in the Lok Sabha on 15 November 1967 presented one of the sharpest critiques of the government in the history of Parliament till that time.

... The Constitution says that the Governor of a State shall be appointed by the President by warrant under his hand and seal. Why was this provision made? It was in order to avoid a clash between an elected Governor and the elected representatives of a State. What do we find in practice the Congress doing? The sanctity of the office of the Governor is totally ignored... The then Prime Minister in his remarks in the Constituent Assembly had said, 'I regard it as a vital link.' This is what Pandit Jawaharlal Nehru said. There was somebody who said: 'Today, we have him as the Prime Minister. He perhaps has no axe to grind. But we may get a Prime Minister who may have an axe to grind. What shall we do then?'

This is Mr. Viswanath Das speaking in the Constituent Assembly. I think such a state of affairs has already come to pass. Here, we find that the office which was created to maintain the unity of the country—Pandit Nehru said, 'I want this as a check against separatist tendency'—has been converted into the office of a patronage to be distributed by the Union Government to discredited, defeated and discarded politicians from the ruling party. We have to look at the galaxy of the men who came to be the Governors of the States in free India after 1947. What happens? A man runs for an election and seeks the mandate, in his little constituency, and 100,000 Indians do not think him worthy of their confidence to represent them in the Assembly and they reject him. But what is not good enough for 100,000 Indians is quite good for the whole State to put him as the Governor there. The man who cannot enjoy the confidence of his constituency is to be imposed on the whole State of as big an area of 50 million Indians. Here is a direct mockery of the very spirit of the Constitution. It was in this sense that I tried to move a censure motion against Mr. Chavan.

May I draw your attention to Article 355 of the Constitution which says that it shall be the duty of the Government of India to ensure that the Government of every State is carried on in accordance with the spirit of Constitution? Every opportunity was taken by this Government to bring the Constitution into contempt. The appointment of the Governors of States is one such thing. The latest example is provided by the appointment by the Government of India of the Governor of Bihar.

... We are told that there was a healthy convention evolved by the late Prime Minister, Pandit Jawaharlal Nehru, i.e., he normally consulted the Chief Ministers about the appointment of Governors in their respective States. The truth was that even for Pandit Jawaharlal Nehru, these provincial satraps of the Congress Party were too strong *dadas*; he could not disregard them; he sounded them but normally he appointed Governors whom they wanted. Now with the change of Government what is happening? Mr. Chavan, very subtle in the use of words, told us that there is consultation; and 'consultation is consultation' he quipped in Parliament. When we asked whether it was approval, he stopped there and took shelter behind his famous thing, the smile.

... The Governor pledges to protect and preserve the Constitution of India and to devote himself to the service and well-being of the people of State. Nowhere does he take the oath that 'I will serve the party at the Centre'; that is not the oath of office; the oath of office is that 'I will serve the Constitution', the oath is not to serve the Congress, but the oath is to serve the people of India or the people of the State.

I now come to one sinister thing that is happening, this new fashion in India—this new danger to our democracy—defections. I have no kind of illusion in my mind and I have spoken publicly about it, and I had made a sporting offer to the Prime Minister when the defection became clear in Rajasthan... I said it should be possible to identify these ten gentlemen, let us identify them, take the initiative in a resolution for expelling them from the Assembly and hounding them out from public life. The Congress would not accept it because it was inconvenient for them.

But then, when the defections occur the other way round, suddenly we hear Mr. Chavan and the Prime Minister talking about the necessity of evolving a code of conduct, that defections are dangerous...

My party was a victim, I know it, so I have the guts to say it and to condemn it also. It gains all the force because I know there have been defections from my party too.

We take the powers about the summoning or dissolving the Government. The whole frame of the Constitution of India is the supremacy of the will of the people; that the will of the people will triumph in this country and that the will of the people shall not be defeated by the executive; that the executive shall be answerable and responsible to and removable by the legislature which represents the will of the people. We are now seeing that in West Bengal, the Governor thinks that the ruling United Front has lost its majority. And what does he do? He therefore thinks that he is justified in ordering the Chief Minister to call a meeting. Here, I must make a distinction. In the first, the essence of democracy lies in the fact that the Chief Minister, claiming popular support, should never hesitate to call the Assembly. It is not the part of the functions of a Governor to order a Chief Minister to summon the Assembly.

Before I conclude I want to make this plea once again to my friend, Shri Chavan, and also the Prime Minister, now that she has been good enough to come and listen to this important debate. I have my political differences. I never hide them. Those with whom I have, they are there. Whether anybody meets me at my residence or in the Parliament or in public, they are there. I do not have two standards as some are in the habit of having. Having said that, let me try once again to emphasise what is at stake. What is at stake is the very fabric of the Constitution of India. It is a very delicate thing that we have inherited. Let us not be guided by the temporary gains which our respective parties may make. If the price is weakening the strong fabric of the Constitution, if the price is to be paid in breaking the main concept of democracy, no party gain should persuade us to follow that dangerous path. I hope Shri Chavan will try to see what is at stake. Allow the Governments to prevail till the people there through the Assembly pass their verdict—be it the Government of Haryana, the Government of Punjab or the Government of Kashmir.

I would have liked to say something about what is happening in Kashmir. I see double standards of the Government functioning. What happens there is totally different. Nobody can interfere because the Government happens to be of a party which is the same as at the Centre. Therefore, danger to the security of the country, to the law and order and Constitution in Kashmir cannot be made by the Governor any matter for reference to the President of India.

I, therefore, submit, let not different standards prevail—one in Rajasthan, one in Bengal, one in Kashmir, one in Maharashtra and one in Bihar. Standards to be applied will have to be uniform because in the uniformity of standards we give new strength to the Constitution. I am not concerned about the fate of Shri Mahamaya Prasad or Shri Ajoy Mukherjee. I am concerned with the continuance of democratic values and the Constitution. These are our greatest heritages. Let not anybody light-heartedly tamper with these two heritages.

~

KANU SANYAL

Declaration of the Formation of CPI(M-L)

The radical communists who were critical of the policies of both the communist parties—the Communist Party of India and Communist Party of India (Marxist)—began to organize themselves in the late 1960s and came to be known as 'Naxalites'. The term comes from Naxalbari, a small village in northern West Bengal, where a radical section of the CPI(M) led by Charu Mazumdar and Kanu Sanyal spearheaded a militant peasant uprising in 1967. They tried to develop a 'revolutionary opposition' in order to establish 'revolutionary rule' in India. In 1967, the 'Naxalites' organized the All India Coordination Committee of Communist Revolutionaries (AICCCR), and broke away from the CPI(M). Uprisings were organized in several parts of the country. In 1969, the AICCCR gave birth to the Communist Party of India (Marxist-Leninist). On 1 May 1969, Kanu Sanyal declared the formation of the third communist party in a meeting at Shaheed Minar in Calcutta.

Comrades and friends! I feel ashamed and embarrassed at the high regard that is shown to me. I am an ordinary cadre, a servant of the people, and my abilities are very limited.

The reason why Naxalbari stirred the whole of India and the whole world is that it was a correct application of Mao Tse-tung's thought in the concrete conditions of India. It was our respected leader Comrade Charu Mazumdar who pointed out the path along which Naxalbari developed; that is, it was under his leadership that the correct application of Mao Tse-tung's thought in the concrete conditions of our country was carried out for the first time and provided the basis on which the heroic peasants of Naxalbari rose in armed revolt against imperialism, feudalism, comprador capital and the old and new revisionists. This is how they advanced along the path blazed by the Chinese revolution and lighted the torch of Indian revolution, and thus proved in the concrete conditions of India that it is not men like Indira Gandhi, Morarji, Dange, Namboodiripad and Jyoti, but the people of India who are the really decisive force of history, it is the people who are the real heroes. So when people applaud me, I cannot but remember the faces of Comrades Tribeni Kanu, Sobhan Ali, Appalaswamy Naidu, Rengim and Babulal Biswakarmakar, and realise how small I am compared to them!...

... In the revolutionary situation which prevails in India today, class struggle has intensified to such a degree that the revisionists are finding it impossible to retain their deceptive mask, and yet, retain it they must. The revisionists and neo-revisionists, in their eagerness to serve their masters well have landed themselves in a fix, and do not know how to get out of it!...

Truly, the reactionaries the world over have grown so weak that they have to change their policy every other day. No matter how hard they try to deceive the people, they are very soon compelled by the prevailing revolutionary situation to attack the people, and with this, it becomes impossible for them to keep up their pretence any longer.

The great Communist Party of China has declared that by the year 2001, that is, only 31 years from now, the people of the whole world will be liberated from all kinds of exploitation of man by man and will celebrate the worldwide victory of Marxism, Leninism, Mao Tse-tung's thought. This is no mere declaration, it is a historic directive. Through this the great Communist Party of China points out to the communists of the whole world how excellent the world situation is for making revolution, and, at the same time, directs all of them to march forward boldly. Also, the historic responsibility of carrying forward the Indian revolution has fallen on our shoulders.

Internationally and nationally, the reactionaries have grown so weak that they crumble wherever we hit them. In appearance they are strong but in reality, they are only giants made of clay, they are truly paper tigers. They themselves have no reliance on their own strength; rather, it is we, who, unable to get rid of our old ideas, try to paint them in awe-inspiring colour and imagine them to be quite powerful. It can be quite confidently said that once we dare boldly to build up peasants' armed struggle in the rural areas with the poor peasants as the leader, such struggle is certain to develop more and more. In this new era, the characteristic feature of a semi-colonial and semi-feudal country like India is that the peasants' armed struggle is the only main form of struggle which can rouse and unite all the revolutionary masses, and quicken the process of India's liberation.

The reason why such struggles have not yet become widespread in all parts of the country is not that the reactionaries are very strong or that the revisionists still have considerable potential for deceiving the people; the reason is, we have been rather late in understanding what particular task has to be emphasised at a given moment, and old conservative ways of thinking are obstructing us at every step and preventing us from marching forward resolutely.

It is perfectly true that we cannot correctly lead a revolution forward unless there is a revolutionary party. Our great teacher Chairman Mao Tse-tung has taught us that there must be a revolutionary party, because the world is full of enemies who exploit and oppress the people. The people want to overthrow their exploitation and oppression. So, Chairman Mao teaches us that in the era of capitalism and imperialism there must be a revolutionary party like the Communist Party, and without such a party it is impossible for the people to overthrow the exploitation and oppression of their enemies.

He further teaches us that such a party must be able to apply Marxism-Leninism. Mao Tse-tung's thought in the given condition of the country will be able to develop itself by using the method of criticism and self-criticism to correct its mistakes, and be intimately linked with the masses. Only such a Communist Party can lead the people for overthrowing the exploiting classes and their running dogs.

In India there never has been such a party. The agents of imperialism, feudalism and comprador capital have hitherto prevented the Communist Party from adopting a correct line. The Indian people have repeatedly risen up in revolt and the Indian peasants have repeatedly carried on valiant armed struggles against imperialism and feudalism. But all this heroism and sacrifice ended in failure, not because imperialism and its running dog, the Congress government, could suppress the people with bullets and lathis; the reason for this failure lies in the fact that the old and new revisionist leading clique in the communist movement stabbed the people's movements in the back. From the very beginning, these revisionists, acting as faithful lackeys of imperialism, feudalism and comprador capital, compounded revisionism with native Gandhism and consistently and cynically betrayed the country and the Indian people in their frantic effort to keep the mass struggles securely confined within the limits of parliamentary democracy. This is why the cause for which the heroic workers of the Punnapra-Vayalar struggle of 1946-47 shed their blood has remained unfulfilled to this day; this is how the heroic struggle of Telangana peasants (1946-51) was smothered by these renegades. Whenever the party ranks revolted against these treacherous actions this revisionist leading clique repeatedly managed to fool the ranks by substituting a 'new' individual from among their own clique for the discredited one and then frantically resumed once more, through this 'new' leadership, their old game of imprisoning the mass struggles within the musty dungeon of electioneering and parliamentary democracy. But how can a few flies ever shut out the blazing brightness of the sun? Similarly, it is not possible for a few traitorous renegades to stop the working of the inexorable laws of history. And so, we find that all the trickery and opposition of this traitorous leading clique of the communist movement could not prevent the victorious onward march of Chairman Mao Tse-tung's thought in India. Thus, the conditions for the emergence of a genuine communist party in India were created.

Of course, it has not been easy, nor smooth. When, in 1965, our respected leader, Comrade Charu Mazumdar rebelled against the neo-revisionist leading clique of Sundarayya, Ranadive, Namboodiripad, Promode, Jyoti and company and called upon the revolutionaries in the CPM to build peasants' armed struggle, he was subjected to the vilest slanders. People like Promode Babu, Harekrishna Babu raved that he was a mad man, a man who was mentally sick, and in open statements termed him a police agent and created a fascist atmosphere inside the party with a view to preventing comrades from knowing what Comrade Charu Mazumdar had written and from meeting Charu-da. But what has been the result? Were these lackeys of reaction able to smother the revolutionary clarion call of Marxism, Leninism, Mao Tse-tung's thought? No, they couldn't; on the contrary, the call given out by Comrade Charu Mazumdar created a stir throughout India. The analysis made by Comrade Charu Mazumdar inspired us, the revolutionaries of Darjeeling district. When we went among the peasant masses in the Terai region with a view to applying through concrete practice the great teaching of Chairman Mao: 'Learn warfare through warfare,' we saw how eagerly the peasant masses accepted our views and how an idea was transformed into a material force—and thus was created Naxalbari—the Chingkang Mountain of India! Having failed in their attempt to prevent the revolutionary application of Marxism-Leninism and seeing that the parliamentary path, which they had been so frantically peddling, was going completely bankrupt, the traitorous revisionist clique adopted the method of the notorious Congress reactionaries and madly tried to drown the Naxalbari struggle in blood. Cloaked as communists, this traitorous bunch of revisionists shot down ten peasant women. (*Altogether eighteen peasants—men, women and children—were killed and hundreds were arrested, tortured and persecuted by the UF government in 1967—Ed.*) In their mad attempt to smother the ringing call of Mao Tse-tung's thought, they even drowned the thirteen-year-old son of a peasant in a well by tying a rope round his neck. But they failed all the same. Inspired by the success of the correct application of Mao Tse-tung's thought in India, the communist revolutionaries all over the country, led by our respected leader Comrade Charu Mazumdar, formed the All India Co-ordination Committee of Communist Revolutionaries (AICCCR) and, thus, laid the basis for building a genuine communist party in India. It is under the leadership of the Co-ordination Committee that peasants' armed struggle has been organised in Srikakulam in Andhra, Lakhimpur Kheri in Uttar Pradesh, Mushahari in Bihar, Koraput in Orissa, that the communist revolutionaries of Assam, Maharashtra, Rajasthan, Madhya Pradesh, Mysore, Kerala, Punjab, Haryana, Tamil Nadu and Kashmir have rallied under the banner of revolution and boldly established throughout India the path of seizing power through armed struggle as opposed to the rotten and stinking parliamentary path peddled by the revisionists, and were able to present before the international communist movement the decision that in the post-Second World War period boycott of parliamentary elections has become a matter of strategy.

The task before the AICCCR was to lay the basis for building a genuine communist party. That task has been successfully completed.

With great pride and boundless joy I wish to announce today at this meeting that we have formed a genuine communist party—the Communist Party of India (Marxist-Leninist). Our party was formed on the memorable day of the international communist movement—the 100th birthday of the great Lenin. When our party was born, the historic Ninth National Congress of the great Communist Party of China was in session under the personal guidance of Chairman Mao Tse-tung. I feel proud that the task of making this historic announcement has been given to me. I firmly believe that the great Indian people will warmly welcome this event, will realise the formation of this party as a historic step forward for the Indian revolution and will come forward to raise the struggle to a higher stage under the leadership of the party. On the other hand, I am also convinced that the announcement of the formation of the party will strike terrible fear in the hearts of all the enemies of the people—open or disguised.

The revolutionary situation in our country is very mature and the people are in a revolutionary mood, and lastly, our people have boundless loyalty to the great leader Chairman Mao and the great Communist Party of China. Taking advantage of all these factors, various trends of petty bourgeois revolutionism have appeared as represented by individuals and groups. Whatever they may do or not, one thing is clear: by refusing to recognise the authority of the revolutionary party they are flouting the chief condition for making revolution. Thus they are, willingly or unwillingly, creating obstacles in the way of carrying forward the revolutionary struggle. This is a counter-revolutionary trend within the revolutionary movement. We must struggle against this trend and rally all genuine revolutionaries under the banner of our party.

Comrades and friends! A high tide of revolution is sweeping through the whole world. The Vietnam people's armed struggle is achieving one victory after another. The people of the whole world are realising through bitter sacrifice and bloodshed the great truth of Chairman Mao's words: 'Political power grows out of the barrel of a gun.' The raging flames of people's armed struggles are sweeping through the colonial, semi-colonial and semi-feudal countries of Asia, Africa and Latin America. The struggles of workers, students and youth are surging forward in the capitalist countries of Europe and North America. In the USA itself, the struggles of students and workers are on the upswing. In the Soviet Union, a revolutionary party has been formed and Soviet workers and people are rising up in struggle against the Soviet social-imperialist clique. Students and youth are already rising up in revolt against the revisionist capitalist rule in Czechoslovakia, Hungary, Yugoslavia and Poland. Chairman Mao Tse-tung, the greatest Marxist-Leninist of the present era and the great teacher and leader, is at the helm of the world revolution which is being led by the great Communist Party of China. A heavy responsibility rests on us. The whole world is looking towards India with great expectation. We can achieve success only if we resolutely march forward ready to make every sacrifice in order to serve the people. The Chairman has said: 'Bitter sacrifice strengthens bold resolve, which dares to make sun and moon shine in the new sky.' We will certainly be able to make a new sun and a new moon shine in the sky of our great motherland—India. It is certain that our great people of India, led by the newly-formed communist party, will march forward in unison with the people of all other countries and build a free, happy and prosperous India free from exploitation of man by man. The Chairman has said that he who defies death and remains undaunted in face of a thousand difficulties can make an emperor dismount. I am firmly convinced that we shall be able to achieve success.

The all-conquering thought of Mao Tse-tung has already struck firm roots into the soil of India, people's revolutionary struggles are bursting forth everywhere—from Kashmir in the north to Kumarika (*Cape Comorin—Ed.*) in the south, and from Assam in the east to Maharashtra in the west—and the sparks of Naxalbari are spreading far and wide. In such a situation we may justifiably hope that our cherished revolutionary dream will come true—the dream that India, our great motherland, will liberate herself by sending all the reactionaries to their graves. Shouldn't the revolutionaries dream? Yes, they must not lose sight of our achievements, must see the bright future… This is what is meant by dreaming revolutionary dreams. It is not enough for us to have such dreams ourselves, we must encourage the people also to dream of a bright future. How was it possible for our heroic comrades like Tribeni Kanu, Sobhan Ali, Babulal Biswakarmakar, Barka Majhi, Naidu and Rengim to raise the banner of revolution higher still by shedding their own blood and to sacrifice their lives displaying total unconcern for their own selves? This was possible only because they had dreams—revolutionary dreams, dreams of liberating India and the people from exploitation and oppression.

I have spoken at length and there may well be some errors in what I have said. This is possible and natural because I have not yet been able to assimilate well the thought of Mao Tse-tung. I am sure you will help me rectify my mistakes by making criticism of my errors.

Inquilab Zindabad! Long live India's People's Democratic Revolution! Long live the Communist Party of India (Marxist-Leninist)! Long live the great Communist Party of China! Long live Chairman Mao—the great leader of the world's people!

INDIRA GANDHI

Inauguration of New States

In the early 1970s, a large number of territories in the north-eastern part of the country got their statehood, resulting in the emergence of a new picture of the Indian Union. The first in the series was Meghalaya. While taking part in the inaugural ceremony of the new state of Meghalaya, on 2 April 1970, Prime Minister Indira Gandhi placed the new state in the context of Indian polity and society, reiterating that in this 'new constitutional experiment' the need was to take everyone along.

It is a day of rejoicing, and yet, from today begins your high responsibilities and burdens, to carry on the administration of this area, to take all your people forward towards the even development of this region. This is a new constitutional experiment and we sincerely desire its success. Whatever help we can give will be forthcoming for the defence, security and well-being of the people inhabiting this beautiful and strategic part of our country. No one of us can escape the compulsions of geography. Hence, it is essential for the Government and the people of Assam, and the Government and the people of Meghalaya to work in close cooperation and collaboration. Any barrier or feeling of distance between the hills and plains impedes the progress of both, for each is dependent on the other. Together, we can all galvanise our resources, unearth our rich minerals and give to the people of Meghalaya a better deal in life.

We are proud of our multiracial, multilingual variety. Our Constitution safeguards the religious and linguistic freedom of all our people. It is our endeavour to see that opportunities for growth and development reach every part of our land and every section of our people. The people of every region should be enabled to grow in freedom and in the hope of a life that is worth living. But the quality of a nation is judged not by the number of its people, nor by the extent of its area, but by the loftiness of its ideals, the excellence of its policies and the endeavour made to achieve its objectives.

15

EDUCATION

India is one of the few Third World countries which has developed a large network of educational institutions, and which possesses an intellectually and politically vibrant academia. This is despite the resourcefulness and pull of the developed world which is often detrimental to the cause of Third World institutions and their educational autonomy. One needs only to look at African and Latin American institutions to realize the fortitude our educational system has displayed.

What accounts for not only the survival but also the growth of educational institutions in India? While one may thank the British colonial authorities for laying the foundations of an enduring system of education, a close reading of history will reveal that the inherent strengths of our educational institutions are the result of the untiring efforts of the Indian intelligentsia and leadership. Almost all national leaders of repute were agitators for the cause of education. M.G. Ranade, G.K. Gokhale, Pherozeshah Mehta, Surendranath Banerjea and Lala Lajpat Rai spent their life fighting for the expansion of educational facilities and for the independence and autonomy of educational institutions. They agitated against colonial apathy to education and ceaselessly demanded investment in the area while taking steps on their own to establish institutions of learning to enable their countrymen to take part in the administration of their own country.

It is often argued that the nationalist intelligentsia emphasized university education at the cost of primary education. The argument has been iterated and forwarded as the reason for the neglect and poor funding of primary education by the state. The truth is that the nationalist intelligentsia clamoured for increase in the overall education budget and more so in the primary segment of education. In fact, it was Gokhale who moved the motion for free primary schooling way back in 1910. If anything, the colonial state was against spending in the higher education segment as well. In fact all other countries in the British Empire suffered from a lack of higher education and did not have capable people to man responsible positions when they became free. India was unique in the sense that on the eve of independence it had a bank of capable and educated manpower though small in number. This was not so much due to British munificence as it was because of the relentless struggle by the intelligentsia. The British projected the intelligentsia's fight for educational institutions and higher budgetary spending on education, particularly higher education, as a sign of its eagerness to safeguard its own interests. The administration repeatedly tried to play primary education against higher education in this context despite demonstrations by the Indian leadership that there was no rupture between the two and that higher education was as much a necessity, as the products of higher educational institutions would in the ultimate analysis train those who would man primary and secondary schools.

It is interesting that after the Gandhian phase of the national movement, university education suffered some neglect as the need to move away from colonial education was increasingly realized. Many people started national colleges. Mahatma Gandhi himself experimented with the development of an indigenous curriculum. These national colleges, however, did not survive as alternative educational institutions and within a couple of decades joined the existing educational pattern. At the same time, the national movement saw a large number of public men opting out of forums and discussing regulating university and other educational institutions. By the 1920s, a powerful critique of colonial education began to develop, thanks to the writings of people like Rabindranath Tagore and Gandhi. Also, the freedom movement drew people out to the fields and to jails, not to university syndicates and senates. One hardly hears Sardar Patel, Jawaharlal Nehru or Subhas Bose fighting it out in a senate meeting, unlike their earlier generation of Gokhale, Mehta or Badruddin Tyabji who actually participated in such meetings. Thus the governing bodies of premier universities filled up with brokers, property dealers and caste and community leaders with short-sighted parochial interests. Universities became institutions without any universal vision. Nehru, for example, notwithstanding his tremendous zest for science, was not seen as eager to supervise an institutional redesigning. By the 1970s and 1980s, it was apparent that the Indian university system had become a means for providing jobs to those affiliated with local political parties and a site for implementing all sorts of ideas of social justice that the ruling parties at the provincial and national levels thought would pay electoral dividends. Prominent universities like Nagpur, Bombay, Madras, Calcutta, Patna, Kerala, Allahabad, Visva-Bharati, Punjab, Osmania and Mysore which once attracted talent and scholarship from all across the country were reduced to local employment bureaus with caste and community, religion and language defining the criterion for employment right from the vice chancellor to a peon.

This is in sad contrast to the way leaders involved themselves in the affairs of education prior to and immediately after independence. In independent India, it was largely the communists who demonstrated a passion for developing universities and determining their character. Some of the most brilliant interventions on higher education in the country have come from communist leaders. S.A. Dange's intervention in the debate on Poona University is one of the best expositions on the university system. The tradition was carried forward by Bhupesh Gupta. Speaking in the course of the debate on the Jawaharlal Nehru University Bill in the mid-1960s, Gupta expressed the need to create, as Dange had said in 1947, a university of the people.

The developments in education post-independence, as reflected in the speeches here, are more about the nature of the institutions. What, for example, would be the place of the university in the educational system and what kind of education should be imparted? These were contentious issues and the speeches here reflect these concerns.

~

SYED AHMAD KHAN

Foundation of the Mohammedan Anglo-Oriental College

The Mohammedan Anglo-Oriental College, Aligarh, was established by Sir Syed Ahmad Khan in 1877. Sir Syed envisioned the college not merely as an institution to impart education but also as a means of modernizing the

Muslims and taking them forward to an enlightened intellectual and social plane. Like Raja Rammohun Roy's efforts to reform the Hindus half a century earlier, Sir Syed tried to initiate an overall reform process among the Muslims. Ever since the revolt of 1857, Muslims had felt alienated vis-à-vis the British rulers who viewed them with suspicion. Sir Syed realized that if the Muslims were to make any progress in national life, it had to come in cooperation with the British, and the only way to bring that about was by educating them and providing them with a common meeting ground with the British. The Mohammedan Anglo-Oriental College, later Aligarh Muslim University, played a stellar role in realizing his dream. This speech was delivered at the Aligarh Institute Hall on 8 January 1877, on the occasion of the public dinner in honour of the foundation of the Mohammedan Anglo-Oriental College.

The enthusiasm with which you have drunk my health fills me with feelings of a mixed nature. I feel obliged to you for the great honour you have done me; I feel sincerely happy that the events of today have passed off well, but along with these feelings there is a consciousness that I am neither worthy of the honour you have done me, nor that the success which the Mohammedan Anglo-Oriental College has hitherto secured, is due to my exertions to the extent you imagine. But, gentlemen, there is one thing which I admit sincerely, and without any hesitation, and that is that the College of which the founding-stone has been laid today, has been for many years the main object of my life. Ever since I first began to think of social questions in British India, it struck me with peculiar force that there was a want of genuine sympathy and community of feeling between the two races whom Providence has placed in such close relation in this country. I often asked myself how it was that a century of English rule had not brought the natives of this country closer to those in whose hands Providence had placed the guidance of public affairs. For a whole century and more, you gentlemen have lived in the country in which we have lived; you have breathed the same air, you have drunk the same water, you have lived upon the same crops as have given nourishment to millions of your Indian fellow subjects. Yet the absence of social intercourse, which is implied by the word friendship, between the English and the natives of this country, has been most deplorable. And whenever I have considered the causes to which this unsatisfactory state of things is due, I have invariably come to the conclusion that the absence of community of feeling between the two races was due to the absence of the community of ideas and the community of interests. And, gentlemen, I felt equally certain that so long as this state of the things continued, the Mussalmans of India could make no progress under English rule. It then appeared to me that nothing could remove these obstacles to progress but education. And education, in its fullest sense, has been the object in furthering which I have spent the most earnest moment of my life, and employed the best energies that lay within my humble power. Yes, the college is an outcome to a certain extent of my humble efforts, but there are other hands, whose existence has not only been most valuable but absolutely essential to the success of the undertaking. And I feel sure that the honour of the success is due to them, rather than to me. But gentlemen, the personal honour which you have done me tonight assures me of a great fact, and fills me with feelings of a much higher nature than mere personal gratitude. I am assured that you, who upon this occasion represent the British rule, have sympathies with our labours. And to me this assurance is very valuable, and a source of great happiness. At my time of life, it is a great comfort to me to feel that the undertaking which has been for many years, and is now, the sole object of my life, has roused on one hand the energies of my own countrymen, and on the other, it has won the sympathy of our British fellow-subjects, and the support of our rulers; so that when the few years I may still be spared are over, and when I shall be no longer amongst you, the college will still prosper and succeed in educating my countrymen to have the same affection for their country, the same feelings of loyalty for British rule, the same appreciation of its blessings, the same sincerity of friendship with our British fellow-subjects as have been the ruling feelings of my life. Gentlemen, I thank you again for the honour you have done me, and sincerely reciprocate the good wishes you have so kindly expressed this evening.

~

PHEROZESHAH MERWANJI MEHTA

Speech at the Seventh Annual Meeting of the Bombay Graduates' Association

The British government constantly complained about not having enough revenue to spend on education in the provinces. Pherozeshah Mehta was a sharp critic of such a position. His radical tongue lashed out at the officials in the precincts of the Legislative Council, both provincial and central. In this speech delivered at the Seventh Annual General Meeting of the Bombay Graduates' Association, held in the hall of the Framji Cowasji Institute at Dhobi Talao, Bombay, on 4 April 1893, Pherozeshah Mehta was in his element, full of sarcasm and wit as he launched a scathing attack on British policy with regard to education. A stronger indictment of government policy is hard to come by.

Gentlemen, this is the fifth time that you have done me the honour of electing me your President; and it was represented to me that the most appropriate method of thanking you for so signal a mark of your confidence would be to give one of my performances as the recognised ventriloquist of this city, created by special appointment under what might be almost considered a Government Resolution, if not under the written signature, at least under the declaration of the versatile and accomplished Chief Secretary to the Government. I confess, gentlemen, I received the proposal at first with hesitation and doubt. But my fears mostly vanished when I recollected that a similar performance given by me at Poona at the last Provincial Conference was fortunate enough to earn the generous and grateful appreciation of one who is himself no mean performer in this line, as this very hall as well as those of Elphinstone College and various other institutions can bear eloquent testimony; for a good many of you present here can, I believe, recall the delight and admiration with which we have heard Mr. Lee-Warner discourse on a variety of topics in this very hall and elsewhere. On one point, however, on which I might have felt discouraged, I think I can rely on your support with confidence. This entertainment is given gratis; and presiding at the prize-distribution at St. Peter's School, Mr. Lee-Warner is reported to have said that people do not value that which they get for nothing. For example, he pointed out that you are apt to value the education you receive in proportion to the amount of fees you are made to pay for it. Now, gentlemen, I venture to dissent from this proposition. I think we can make bold to assure Mr. Lee-Warner that the people of this country will not, for example, value the services of Anglo-Indian officers any the less, if they will accept the depreciated rupee in payment of their salaries instead of vigorously agitating for some measure to make up for the loss, no doubt with the view of preventing us from valuing their services. On the contrary, they may be sure that the country would think of them all the more highly, if, with a deficit of a crore that has ended, and a budget deficit of a crore and a half for the next year, and with a still gloomier outlook in the future, they would not lend themselves to the powerful agitation that has been organised to attack the Indian Exchequer in their interests. For as H.E. the Governor told us the other day, in earnest and impressive terms, when warning us not to ask for a higher expenditure on education, it is these Government officers who are better aware than any of us 'of the needs of the poorest classes of the many millions of this Presidency, that *they* know better than we do how many hundreds of villages there are which need improved sanitary surroundings, mainly in the shape of better water, and which may be induced to undertake these improvements with the aid of a little Government assistance, that *they* know better than we do of the many square miles of jungly tracts, the inhabitants of which are in sore need of better roads to get their produce to market, that they know better than we do of the hundreds of thousands of poor people who are in dire need of medical assistance, but whom such assistance may by degrees be brought with the addition of Government contributions.' I think, gentlemen, our honoured friend Mr. Dadabhai Naoroji will feel extremely gratified to find that H.E. the Governor and the officers at least of this Presidency have been at length converted to his views of the poverty of the country, and of the inadequacy of its revenue to meet the most urgent and elementary wants of the people, unless he chooses to be sarcastic and say, as he did in the Currency debate in Parliament, that 'India is rich or poor, prosperous or otherwise, just as it suits an argument'. However that may be, I feel sure, gentlemen, that whatever the intrinsic worth of this entertainment laid before you, you will think none the worse of it for getting it free of cost.

I should like, first of all, gentlemen, to impress upon you the great utility and necessity of such an organisation as this Graduates' Association. It has now been in existence for seven years, and its regular reports show that it has been steadily doing good and useful work. If all our graduates rallied round its standard, it seems to me that its usefulness could be immeasurably extended. Educational problems are increasing in number and complexity, and it is of the highest importance that we should recognise it as our duty to organise ourselves and watch the development of the educational policy of Government, and to lend all such help as our knowledge and experience may enable us to render, in the proper solution of educational questions. The past year, gentlemen, has had its full quota of questions of great interest, affecting the educational progress of this

Presidency. Among them all, there is none of more surpassing importance than that of the attempted withdrawal of Government from the direct control and management of institutions for higher education. In presiding at the Poona Provincial Conference last year, I ventured to urge that it was high time that public opinion should express itself, in no uncertain voice, with regard to the grave perils that threatened our educational interests. This warning, gentlemen, has been severely criticised and resented as altogether unfounded and unwarranted. I have been told by some of the publicists of this city that they have searched in a variety of quarters for these grave perils and not a shade or shadow of them could they discover anywhere. I have been told that the expenditure on education has been larger this year than any previous year. I have been told that no educational earthquake has brought Elphinstone College or any other educational building to the ground, and that no educational whirlwind has laid the University Tower low. Now, gentlemen, I am ready to confess that none of these catastrophes has overtaken us. And still, gentlemen, if you search for a thing in every possible quarter except where it is, it is no wonder that you cannot discover it. The grave perils of which I spoke at the Conference were not a sudden discovery of mine. I had spoken of them in Lord Reay's time and in his Lordship's presence, when at the celebration of the new Elphinstone College buildings I ventured to say that 'the cause of education, of literary education as it is called, but which I prefer to call by its old-fashioned name of liberal education, may just now be compared to a tempest-tossed bark in mid ocean'. So grave had the perils become that, speaking from the fullness of close and intimate personal knowledge of the policy and tendencies of Government, of which he was himself a distinguished member, Sir Raymond West deemed it his imperative duty not to leave these shores without publicly raising his voice, in the hall of the University itself, against the dangers that threatened the cause of higher education. That danger, gentlemen, lies in the persistent attempts that have been made for the last seven or eight years to enforce the policy of the withdrawal of Government from the direct provision, control and management of higher education. It is difficult, gentlemen, to imagine a policy more mischievous and disastrous in its effects on the welfare and progress of the country. I know, gentlemen, that in the first place, it is sought to be justified by the recommendations of Lord Ripon's Education Commission. Now I think, gentlemen, it is time to expose the utter disingenuousness of this appeal to authority which is so constantly made. In dealing with the subject of the withdrawal of the State from the direct provision and management of education, especially of higher education, the Commission at the very outset had to acknowledge that 'perhaps none of the many subjects we have discussed is encompassed with greater difficulty or has elicited more various shades of opinion, alike among the witnesses we have examined and within the Commission itself, than this'. On one point, it was able to record an unanimous opinion that withdrawal of direct departmental agency should not take place in favour of missionary bodies, and that departmental institutions of the higher order should not be transferred to missionary management. With regard to all the rest, the Commission was brought to any recommendations at all with the greatest difficulty. In fact, careful perusal of the Report shows that what little unanimity is recorded in it is more of words than conviction. In dealing with the course of discussion on this subject in para 534, the Report says that 'it seems desirable to describe the course of our deliberations upon this subject with greater fullness than we have deemed necessary in other portions of the Report. Our main difficulty was as to the initial recommendation from which all others would naturally follow. It was proposed to find such a starting point in the motion: "That, under adequate guarantees for the permanence and efficiency of the substituted institutions, the gradual closing of Government institutions, especially those of the higher order or their transfer to native management under the general control of, and aided by the State, should be regarded as not only an important stimulus to private effort, and consequently to any sound grant-in-aid system, but as urgently needed in view of the social and political education of the people." This motion was negatived by a large majority. A motion substantially the same, but adding that such withdrawal was desirable "as conducive to the advancement of the social, moral, and political education of the people", shared the same fate.' In summing up the general conclusion arrived at, the Report proceeds to state that 'our discussions brought out clearly the fact that while anxious to encourage *any natural transfer of institutions*, we are not prepared as a body to adopt any form of expression that may be construed into a demand for the immediate or general withdrawal of the State from the provision of the means of high education. We are convinced that, while the transfer of management under the conditions stated is eminently desirable, it is only by slow and cautious steps that it can ever be really attained. The Department should cordially welcome every effort of the kind, and should accept it, if it can be accepted without real loss to the community; but while encouraging all such offers, its attitude should be, not that of withdrawing from a charge found to be burdensome, and of transferring the burden to other shoulders, but of conferring a boon to those worthy of confidence, and of inviting voluntary associations to cooperate with the Government in the work and responsibilities of national education. We have certainly no desire to recommend any measures that will have the effect of checking the spread and continuous improvement of higher education.' Now, Gentlemen, while the Commission thus carefully guarded its recommendations, they are now mostly forgotten in the attempt to carry out a policy of precipitate withdrawal. The attempted transfers, instead of being natural and unforced and spontaneous, have more the character of Tudor 'benevolences', and, in one case, it was tried to be enforced at the point of heavy penalty which has been actually carried into execution. Instead of being by slow and cautious steps, they are tried to be rushed through without any reasonable guarantees of efficiency. Instead of being a boon and a favour, the attitude of Government is openly that of withdrawing from a charge found to be burdensome and of transferring the burden to other shoulders. And lastly, the recommendations of the Commission are made use of for the very result that it deprecated, *viz*., of checking the spread and continuous improvement of higher education. In the second place, it is attempted to delude us by patriotic reference to the great benefits to be derived from the bringing out and encouraging of private effort and enterprise; and we are even told that it would be a means of advancing our political education. 'This history of education in Bombay since 1885,' writes Mr. Lee-Warner, 'will hereafter be mainly known by systematic efforts made to encourage private enterprise and to give education a practical turn. Variety and freedom have been generally introduced. Self-help had been evoked by the transfer of the management of schools to local bodies, and the Department has learned to look upon itself as responsible rather for the direction and encouragement of educational activity than as a State Department for giving education and managing schools.' Mr. Lee-Warner must pardon us if we look with suspicion on language so strange in the mouth of an Anglo-Indian bureaucrat. Last year Mr. Lee-Warner solemnly protested that he did not know what was meant by a bureaucrat. As he does not seem to be satisfied with the brief answer which I attempted to give him at the time, I will, with your permission, gentlemen, endeavour to describe that eminent personage at somewhat greater length. Among the many delightful and inimitable delineations of typical character immortalised by Dickens, many of you, perhaps, remember the faithful portraiture of Sir Joseph Bowley, the Poor Man's Friend and Father. You remember, gentleman, how Sir Joseph discoursed on their respective duties: 'Your only business, my good fellow, is with me. You need not trouble yourself to think about anything. I will think for you; I know what is good for you; I am your perpetual Parent. Such is the dispensation of an all-wise Providence. What man can do, I do. I do my duty as the Poor Man's Friend and Father; and I endeavour to educate his mind, by inculcating on all occasions the one great lesson which that class requires. That is, entire Dependence on myself. They have no business whatever with themselves.' Now, gentlemen, can there be an apter description of the Anglo-Indian bureaucrat after his own heart than as the exact counterpart of Sir Joseph Bowley in relation to the poor Indian—the poor Indian's Friend and Father? When, therefore, this superior person, who has always bitterly resented any introduction of private enterprise and local self-government, and who is not even yet reconciled to what he still devoutly believes to be the imbecile vagaries of Lord Ripon, talks glibly of bringing out and encouraging self-help and private enterprise only in the sphere of higher education, surely we are warranted in receiving such strange and unfamiliar utterances with some degree of caution and suspicion. And in sooth, gentlemen, the meaning of it all is that higher education is supposed to be advancing at too rapid a pace, and the numbers of men it turns out, clamouring for Government employ, are regarded as what is termed a distinct political danger. In his Convocation address this year at the Allahabad University, in many respects singularly thoughtful and instructive, Sir Charles Crosthwaite frankly gives voice to this view. After stating that 'by one party the Universities and Colleges have been accused of flooding the country with half-educated young men who will look nowhere but to the service of Government for employment, whose knowledge is superficial, whose conceit is boundless, who are fluent and turgid in language, but who have no accurate conception of the meaning of the words they use or the phrases they repeat,' Sir Charles goes on to say, 'there is no doubt that in the cases of some of the older Universities, the number of men who have taken degrees is in excess of the demand for men of their stamp. In this country there is a distinct danger in creating a class of needy scholars who are in excess of and above the only employment open to them. There are two ways in which it can be met with by those who have the control of education. One is by making college education more expensive and self-supporting and restricting it to those whose parents can afford to pay for it, and to boys of exceptional merit who can win scholarships and contribute to the cost of their schooling.' Sir Charles Crosthwaite has here laid down the esoteric doctrine of those who justify the withdrawal of Government from directly helping higher education, on the diplomatic grounds of evoking self-help and private enterprise, and of developing, as Mr. Lee-Warner puts it, 'variety of freedom'. I do not, as indeed I cannot within the scope of this address, propose to attempt to expose the main fallacy which underlies the conception of higher education as being only in the interests and for the advancement of the comparatively few individuals who receive it, and not as being one of the most important and indispensable factors in the general progress and welfare of the people at large. It would require more time than is at my command on this occasion, to point out that those who consider the downward filtration theory as untenable and exploded, have never been able to understand it, and realise the extremely slow and indirect manner in which social modification works itself out. I will content myself with giving only one illustration of the narrow conception of the benefits of higher education being confined only to its immediate recipients. In the admirable address from which I have already quoted, Sir Charles Crosthwaite bore ungrudging testimony to its beneficial influence on the administration of the country. 'On one point,' he says, 'I can speak with experience. I had many years' practice in Indian administration, and I am able to bear testimony to the fact that the efficiency of the administration and its purity, especially in the matter of dispensing justice, had made very great progress, of education, and especially of the higher education of which a knowledge of English and English literature had formed the chief part.' The excellent work of our Subordinate Judicial service, manned by judges who are the products of our higher education, is admitted on all hands. But is it not apparent that, in turning out such men, higher education had done the most signal services to the masses of the people by securing to them a pure, and intelligent, and comparatively cheap administration of justice, than which nothing is more essential to their well-being, prosperity, and contentment. We can easily multiply these instances. In turning out medical graduates, for example, have not our Universities and Colleges not only benefited the recipients of their various culture, but conferred the most invaluable boon on the people at large by helping to bring into existence dispensaries and hospitals with their cheap assistant surgeons, and carrying medical relief to their very doors? It is because of this wide-reaching beneficial action of higher education that it has now come more and more to be recognised in most European countries that it is the State that must assume direct charge of it. I think this Association can do no more useful service than in organising the most strenuous opposition to the retrograde policy which Anglo-Indian interest and alarm is trying to palm off under the false enticements of an appeal to our patriotic feelings for self-help and self-government. This is the grave peril of which I spoke at the Poona Provincial Conference as threatening our most vital educational interests, and this is the grave peril against which I trust you will wage unceasing war, despite hollow arguments and sarcastic sneers. On one thing, however, gentlemen, you have some reason to congratulate yourselves. The attempts to carry out this policy have hitherto not been very successful. In his account of Lord Reay's Administration, Sir William Hunter ruefully confesses that though 'an attempt was made to transfer the Government High Schools to local authorities, it proved immediately successful only with the Ahmednugger High School'. The attempt to economise, as it was said, the educational resources of the Presidency, by practically abolishing the Poona Deccan College of unrivalled historical interest, and indissolubly connected with the name of its founder, Mountstuart Elphinstone, was also frustrated through the force of public opinion, in giving expression to which this Association did good service by its vigorous remonstrance. Unfortunately, gentlemen, the baffled foe has in his rage and disappointment sought to console himself in his retreat by wreaking vengeance in another quarter. If the anxiety to stimulate private enterprise and self-help were not simply another name for confiscating the funds devoted to higher education, if the devotion to the policy laid down by the Education Commission was not something like the devotion of Mr. Pecksniff to the virtues of Faith and Charity, then no institution, as you are aware, had a right to more fostering and tender treatment than the Poona Fergusson College. It was formed and conducted by a band of young men of culture and education, who unhesitatingly sacrificed their own interests and prospects to the cause of education. It was assisted by a grant, long before the proposal to amalgamate it with Deccan College was conceived. But when that proposal fell through, the prestige of Government required some sacrifice to appease its ruffled dignity, and orders were at once issued to stop the grant to the College. There is absolutely no justification, gentlemen, for what might be fairly called almost a breach of faith. I am aware, gentlemen, that the resources of official ingenuity are not easily exhausted, but when it is urged that two full Colleges are too many for a small place like Poona, surely those who urge this argument cannot be ignorant of the patent fact that the area which these Colleges serve is not confined to the city of Poona only, but extends over the whole of the Deccan, the incontrovertible proof of which lies in the full attendance on the rolls of the two Colleges, Fergusson College numbering about 300 students, and Deccan about 250. The action of Government in the matter can be easily defended on the principles consistently avowed by Mr. Maclean, whom I have always admired for his unflinching logic, if not for his farsightedness. To him every Indian College is a nursery for hatching broods of vipers; the less, therefore, the better. But it is entirely indefensible on the part of those who always protest their innocence of any idea to starve higher education. Frustrated in the attempt to cut adrift the higher schools of the Presidency, and to abolish Deccan College, the advocates of the new policy of withdrawal have not been incapable of much mischief. They have triumphantly served the University with notice after notice, by which the paltry contribution of Rs. 15,000 has been successively reduced to Rs. 10,000 and then to Rs. 5,000. Various are the reasons given for striking this blow at the very fountain-head of all higher education. The University must be made self-supporting. Primary education would go to the dogs but for the Rs. 10,000. The Empire would be insolvent if Rs. 10,000 were not speedily called in. It is difficult, gentlemen, to speak with patience of this miserable maltreatment of the University or to characterise it in the terms it deserves. For years the University has been unable to move in the direction of urgent reform for want of funds, and yet when it is most in need of them this decree for retrenchment is fulminated. Let us respectfully beseech the Chancellor of the University to make an earnest appeal to the Governor, who, trained in the manly and healthy discipline of public life in England, cannot but know when to yield, as he surely knows when to hold his own, and entreat him not to allow his administration to be permanently marred by a blot, which, tiny as it is, may never be effaced. Then, gentlemen, in two other directions also, the new doctrine has come in the way of a full advance. Gujarat and Sind by this time ought to have had two better equipped Colleges than they have. Great credit is due to the local promoters of the two existing Colleges in these provinces; but in congratulating these public-spirited men, we are apt to forget that each of these provinces, especially Sind, were entitled to be provided by the State with a model College. But, gentlemen, where the new doctrine has done most mischief is in stopping the further development and improvement of existing institutions. In a written Minute which Sir R. West sent to the Education Commission, he pointed out how much remained to be done before the existing High Schools and Colleges could be called model institutions. He showed how insufficiently equipped they were in many essential respects. But all hope of their reform and improvement seems to be now gone for ever; for the cry is that other demands are more urgent. I have already had occasion to partly refer, gentlemen, to the impressive utterances of the Chancellor at our last University Convocation. On that occasion he further said, 'I am but too aware, from the reception that has been given to my public utterances on educational questions elsewhere, that these remarks of mine are likely to be construed as indicating the intention on the part of Government to shirk what are regarded as its own duties by laying them on institutions or private individuals.' And his Lordship added: 'But if those who criticise what I have said, and may criticise what I say now, were as well aware as I am of the needs of the poorest classes of the many millions of this Presidency; if they knew, as well I do', the various things I have quoted above, 'then,' his Excellency went on to say, 'they would appreciate the feelings which actuated me to express a preference for the expenditure of a larger portion of Government funds on the undoubted poor than has hitherto been allotted to them.' When, gentlemen, I first heard these words delivered in his Excellency's quiet but impressive way, I confess that for a moment I felt that I and others who think with me ought to be ashamed of ourselves for our hasty short-sightedness. But it was only for a moment, for a change soon came over the spirit of my dream, and it seemed to me that the picture which his Excellency had drawn in so touching a fashion, took a remarkable resemblance to that of the amiable and well-meaning father of a somewhat numerous family, addicted unfortunately to slipping off a little too often...to the house over the way, who, when the mother appealed to him to do something for the education of the grown-up boys, begged of her with tears in his eyes to consider if her request was not unreasonable, when there was not even enough food and clothes for the younger children. The poor woman could not gainsay the fact, with the hungry eyes staring before her; but she could not help bitterly reflecting that the children could have food and clothes, and education to boot, if the kindly father could be induced to be good enough to spend a little less on drink and cards. Similarly, gentlemen, when we are reminded of the crying wants of the poor masses for sanitation and pure water and medical relief and primary education, might we not respectfully venture to submit that there would be funds, and to spare, for all these things, and higher education too, if the enormous and growing resources of the country were not ruthlessly squandered on a variety of whims and luxuries, on costly residences and sumptuous furniture, on summer trips to the hills, on little holiday excursions to the frontiers, but above and beyond all, on the lavish and insatiable humours of an irresponsible military policy, enforced by the very men whose view and opinions of its necessity cannot but accommodate themselves to their own interests and ambitions. Gentlemen, this plea of robbing Peter to pay Paul is one that will not bear close examination. We do not ask that primary education should be starved, or that technical education should be stunted. On the contrary, we assert that it is incumbent upon the State to provide the necessary funds for them from the proper sources; what we protest against is, that it should be attempted to provide those funds by curtailing others urgently required for the maintenance and advancement of higher education. Never was a plea more unstatesmanlike and hollow than that which tried to justify the confiscation of the University grant by pleading that it was to be carried to the account of primary education. Something of this aspect of the question must have forced itself on the minds of our rulers, for they have recently surprised us beyond all belief by turning a most remarkable somersault in regard to it. Hitherto we were ruefully told that it was all because of the dearth of funds that in this country so small a percentage of the revenue was applied to educational objects. When, therefore, gentlemen, we woke one morning, not very long ago, and read a report in the daily papers of the speech made by his Excellency the governor at the opening of the Madressa-I-Anjuman-I-Islam, I will not attempt to guess what your state of mind might be; but for myself, I rubbed my eyes harder than ever Aladdin did when he woke up in the enchanted palace. You know, gentlemen, that in the highest flight of his ambition for the

Educational Department, Sir Alexander Grant never soared beyond a dream of 2 per cent. But it seems we have all been under an entire delusion. His Excellency states frankly how he came to make the discovery. 'I was led some months ago,' he says in his speech, 'into a consideration of this subject by a statement that Bombay spent less on education in proportion to its revenue than most civilised countries. If that was in any way true, I felt we were bound to make an extraordinary exertion to find the wherewithal to increase our educational expenditure.' His Excellency has now discovered that the expenditure on education in this Presidency in proportion to its gross revenues has increased from 4 per cent in 1882-83 to nothing less than 6 per cent in 1891-92, while the boasted European countries, whom we have been perpetually dragging into the comparison, have been spending—United Kingdom, 5 per cent; France, 2; Prussia, 3; Belgium, 2; Italy, 2; Holland, 5; and Sweden and Norway, 3 per cent. This is sufficient in itself to cover with confusion all the people like us who have been talking blatant nonsense all these years about the niggardliness of our Government, and its failure to do its duty with regard to education. And the Accountant-General has further confounded us by solemnly publishing an imposing array of figures. It is a venturesome task to go at a department so fearfully and wonderfully constructed as that of the Accountant-General, and which can pour columns and columns of figures without pause or mercy. But Mr. Cox will pardon me if I say that he has let the cat out of the bag. Not that it could not have been seen till he opened the bag, which was really too transparently thin. I suppose nobody knows better than Mr. Cox that, when you institute a comparison between ratios of expenditure in different countries, the least you can do is to take in each case the same factors for the ratio. Otherwise there is no comparison at all. Now, gentlemen, the wonderful figure of 6 per cent alleged to be spent by this Government is arrived at by taking the ratio between the expenditure on education and a *portion only* of revenues of the Presidency, while the 2, 3 and 5 per cent of the European countries is calculated on the ratio between their respective expenditure on education and their whole and entire revenue. Of course, one is at perfect liberty to say that the Bombay Government spends 6 per cent of the funds allotted to it out of its revenues for local expenditure; but then you cannot compare that percentage with a percentage in other countries calculated on an entirely different basis, and then crow over that false superiority. I think his Excellency the Governor will not, on consideration, thank his advisers and informants, whoever they may be, for leading him into such a quandary. Whatever other excuses Government may plausibly put forward, the fact is undeniable that the percentage spent on education in the different provinces of India compares most lamentably with the percentage spent in civilised countries. That percentage is just about 1.5 per cent, whatever figures you take, the total net revenues of the Presidency according to the last Administration Report of 1891-92 being Rs. 13 crores and 30 lakhs and the total State expenditure on education being Rs. 19,65,632 (Administration Report 1892-93, and D.P.L.'s Report 1891-92). It is absurd to compare this percentage with that in the different countries and states of Europe and America. In the United Kingdom, the parliamentary grants-in-aid of primary education alone amounted in 1892 to £6,262,350, which, on the Imperial revenue for that year of 91 millions, gives a percentage of over 6.5 per cent, for simply primary education. This is without taking into account the magnificent endowments for secondary and collegiate education which exist in the United Kingdom, in its great public schools, its wealthy universities, and in the colleges attached to them, nearly twenty-three in Oxford and nineteen in Cambridge. His Excellency himself admits that the expenditure on primary education alone is in France 2 per cent; in Prussia, 3; in Belgium 2; Italy, 2; Holland, 5; and Sweden and Norway, 3; while taking 9 lakhs as the expenditure on primary education in Presidency, as his lordship himself puts it, we have, on our net revenue of 13 crores and 30 lakhs, the magnificent percentage of 0.7. But the state expenditure in France, Prussia, and other European countries is not confined to primary education only. They spend large sums in maintaining a magnificent series of institutions for secondary and collegiate education, with which our high schools and colleges can bear no comparison whatever. In the French budget for 1892, 122,110,425 francs was set down for primary education, and 16,888,504 for secondary, which, on the ordinary revenue for that year, gives a percentage of 4.7. In Sweden and Norway the percentage is over 5 and 7 per cent respectively. In the different states of Germany, the percentage ranges from 5 to 9 per cent. In Belgium and Denmark it is over 5 per cent. In Italy it is about 2.5 per cent, but there is besides, large annual revenue vested in its universities. But the most instructive instance is that of despotic, autocratic, semi-barbarous Russia, which spends on public instruction nearly 2.5 per cent of her revenues. However, gentlemen, though the grand discovery made by the Accountant-General and the other informers and advisers of his Excellency proves to be only a mare's nest, there is one comfort to be derived from the discussion which it has raised; there is one ray of light piercing through the surrounding gloom. You remember, gentlemen, Lord Harris's words I quoted above. 'If it was in any way true,' he told us, 'that Bombay spent less on education in proportion to its revenue than most civilised countries, I felt we were bound to make an extraordinary exertion to find the wherewithal to increase our educational expenditure.' Gentlemen, now that I think we have shown that it is a fact that Bombay does spend less, and grievously less, on education than other civilised countries, let us appeal to Lord Harris to redeem his promise to make an extraordinary effort to bring up the percentage to a figure, not larger than that for which Sir Alexander Grant sighed more than twenty-five years ago, pointing out that 'if 2 per cent per annum on the presidential revenues were allowed to Bombay, the whole aspect of the Department and the Universities might, in my opinion, be speedily changed for the better'. I am afraid, Gentlemen, I have detained you too long with my ventriloquism. But one word more and I have done. Our departing Commander-in-Chief told us the other day that while it was right and proper that India should be governed with wisdom and justice, the maintenance of the empire must, in the last resort, depend not on the loyalty of the people but upon the power and strength of the army to repel foreign invasion. It is perfectly true that loyalty, perhaps like all other virtues, is founded on self-interest. But it is no less true that if that self-interest is allowed to be enlightened and developed, as nothing can enlighten and develop it as a wise system of education in the centre of righteous policy, then that self-interest, as in the case of the other virtues, grows out of and beyond itself, and becomes transformed into a sentiment of earnest, devoted, and enlightened loyalty, which, in the hour of danger, will not wait to calculate the chances, but throw its lot with, and stand by, the object of its loyalty, not as a matter of interest, but as a matter of affection and duty. In India, gentlemen, the soldier is abroad, and must be; but the humble schoolmaster is no less indispensable; he alone can add stability and permanence to the work of the soldier.

~

GOPAL KRISHNA GOKHALE

Free and Compulsory Primary Education

The colonial administration consistently attacked the Indian leadership's demand for higher education, berating the nationalist intelligentsia for its obsession with higher education, while trying to position itself as the champion of primary education. Its policy of advocating primary education as against higher education created an antagonistic relation between the two. Indian leaders argued that they were demanding all-round educational development of the people and that the 'primary education versus higher education debate' was pointless. One led to the other and one without the other was impossible. They demonstrated time and again that the British authorities were the ones who were not interested in the development of primary education. The following speech by G.K. Gokhale shows the nationalist leadership's overarching concern for the development of education in India. He moved this resolution at the Imperial Legislative Council on 18 March 1910, seeking provisions for free and compulsory primary education.

I beg to place the following Resolution before the Council for its consideration:

That this Council recommends that a beginning should be made in the direction of making elementary education free and compulsory throughout the country, and that a mixed Commission of officials and non-officials be appointed at an early date to frame definite proposals.

My Lord, I trust Council will note carefully what is exactly that this resolution proposes. The resolution does not ask that elementary education should be made compulsory at once throughout India. It does not even ask that it should be made free at once throughout the country, though this was the course which the Government of India themselves were decidedly inclined to adopt three years ago. All that the resolution does is to recommend that a beginning should now be made in the direction of making elementary education free and compulsory and that a Commission should be appointed to consider the question and frame definite proposals. In other words, I propose the State should now accept in this country the same responsibility in regard to mass education that the Governments of most civilised countries are already discharging, and that a well-considered scheme should be drawn up and adhered to till it is carried out.

My Lord, a French writer has just described the nineteenth century as pre-eminently the century of the child. The question of the education of the child occupied the attention of statesmen during that century as much as any other important question, and there is no doubt that the enormous expansion of popular education that has taken place during the period in the Western world ranks in importance with its three other great achievements, viz., the application of science to industrial processes, the employment of steam and electricity to annihilate distance, and the rise of democracies. My Lord, three movements have combined to give to mass education the place which it occupies at present among the duties of a State—the humanitarian movement which reformed prisons and liberated the slave, the democratic movement which admitted large masses of men to a participation in Government, and the industrial movement which brought home to nations the recognition that the general spread of education in a country even when it did not proceed beyond the elementary stage, meant the increased efficiency of the worker.

My Lord, the time is long past when anybody could seriously contend that the bulk of human beings were made for physical labour only and that even the faint glimmer of rudimentary knowledge was not for them. On the contrary, it is at present universally recognised that a certain minimum of general instruction is an obligation which society owes to all its future members, and in nearly the whole civilised world every State is trying to meet this obligation only in one way, namely, by making elementary education compulsory and free. And thus it is, that led by the German States, country after country in Europe and America and Japan in the East have adopted this system of free and compulsory education; and we find today all the countries in Europe, excepting Russia and Turkey, and the United States of America and Canada and Australia and Japan and several even of the smaller Republics in South America—all having this system in operation. And even within the borders of India itself it is gratifying to note that the enlightened and far-seeing rulers of Baroda, after an experiment of 15 years carried out in one of the talukas of the State, namely, the Amreli Taluka, has since last year extended this system to the whole of his State.

My Lord, one word more and I have done. I will frankly confess that I have not introduced this resolution in the Council today in the hope that it will be adopted by the Council. Constituted as this body is, we all recognise that unless a resolution finds favour in the eyes of the Government, there is no chance of its being carried, and I recognise further that it is not reasonable to expect Government to accept this resolution without further consideration. Even if they are inclined to take a favourable view of my proposals, they are proposals which will naturally have to be referred to the Secretary of State before any decisive step is taken. I have not therefore the least expectation that this resolution will be adopted by the Council. But though the Government may not be able to accept the resolution, they certainly can undertake to examine the whole question at an early date in a sympathetic spirit. If this is done, I shall be satisfied. In any case the Government, I trust, will not do two things. I trust they will not make a definite pronouncement against the principle of free and compulsory education today and I also trust that the resolution which I have moved will not be brushed aside on the plea that the condition of the finances does not admit of the proposals being maintained. My Lord, there is much truth in the homely adage that where there is a will there is a way. I think that this question of compulsory and free primary education is now in this country the question of questions. The well-being of millions upon millions of children who are waiting to be brought under the humanising influence of education depends upon it. The increased efficiency of the individual, the higher general level of intelligence, the stiffening of the moral backbone of large sections of the community, none of these things can come without such education. In fact, the whole of our future as a nation is inextricably bound up with it. My Lord, however this resolution may be disposed of here today I feel that in this matter we are bound to win. The practice of the whole civilised world, the sympathies of the British democracy and our own natural and legitimate aspirations of which your Lordship has more than once admitted the reasonableness, all these are united in its favour. This resolution will come up again and again before this Council till it is carried to a successful issue. My Lord I earnestly hope that the Government will read aright the needs of the situation and not fail to move with the times in this matter. To my mind the call of duty to them is clear, and it is also the call of statesmanship—that statesmanship which pursues unhasting but unresting, the highest interests of the people committed to its care.

RABINDRANATH TAGORE

The Education Mission of Visva-Bharati

One of the most original thinkers on education, Rabindranath Tagore's contribution to every aspect of the life of the nation has been so great that it is not easy to do justice to it in a short profile. He wanted to root Indian education to its ancient richness without losing sight of the benefits that opening up to the West could provide. He believed that education did not mean merely collecting and transmitting information but that it had a higher purpose: opening the mind's eye to the world which surrounds us. The relationship between nature, man and his education was an integrated one, and for this education had to be closely tied to the environment. Unlike many others who spoke and debated on the subject of education, Tagore was not merely content with words. He had the vision and the courage to give practical shape to what he believed in, leading him to set up the Visva-Bharati University, a revolutionary attempt at overhauling the system of education. This lecture, broadcast by Radio New York on 10 November 1930, brilliantly summarizes his educational philosophy.

I have been asked to speak this evening to my invisible audience about the educational mission to which I have devoted my life and I am thankful for this opportunity.

I am an artist and not a man of science, and therefore my institution necessarily has assumed the aspect of a work of art and not that of a pedagogical laboratory. And this is the reason why I find it difficult to give you a distinct idea of my work which is continually growing for the last thirty years. With it my own mind has grown, and my own ideal of education found freedom to reach its fullness through a vital process so elusive that the picture of its unity cannot be analysed.

Children's minds are sensitive to the influences of the great world to which they have been born. This delicate receptivity of their passive mind helps them, without their feeling any strain, to master language, that most complex instrument of expression full of ideas that are indefinable and symbols that deal with abstractions. Through their natural gift of guessing, children learn the meaning of the words which we cannot explain.

But it is just at this critical period that the child's life is brought into the education factory, lifeless, colourless, dissociated from the context of the universe, with bare white walls staring like eyeballs of the dead. The children have to sit inert whilst lessons are pelted at them like hailstones on flowers.

I believe that children should be surrounded with the things of nature that have their own educational value. Their minds should be allowed to stumble on and be surprised at everything that happens before them in the life of today. The new tomorrow will stimulate their attention with new facts of life.

The minds of the adults are crowded; the stream of lessons perpetually flowing from the heart of nature does not fully touch them; they choose those that are useful, rejecting the rest as inadmissible. The children have no such distractions. With them every new fact comes to a mind that is always open, with an abundant hospitality. And through this exuberant, indiscriminate acceptance they learn innumerable facts within a short time, amazing compared to our own slowness. These are the most important lessons of life that are thus learnt in the first few years of our career.

Because, when I was young I underwent the mechanical pressure of a teaching process, one of man's most cruel, and most wasteful mistakes, I felt it my duty to found a school where the children might be free in spite of the school.

At the age of twelve I was first coerced into learning English. Most of you in this country are blissfully unconscious of the mercilessness of your own language. You will admit, however, that neither its spelling, nor its syntax, is perfectly rational. The penalty for this I had to pay, without having done anything to deserve it, with the exception of being born ignorant.

When in the evening my English teacher used to come I was dragged to my daily doom at a most unsympathetic desk and an unprepossessing textbook containing lessons that are followed by rows of separated syllables with accent-marks like soldiers' bayonets.

As for that teacher, I can never forgive him. He was so inordinately conscientious! He insisted on coming every single evening, there never seemed to be either illness or death in his family. He was so preposterously punctual too. I remember how the fascination for the frightful attracted me every evening to the terrace facing the road; and just at the right moment, his fateful umbrella—for bad weather never prevented him from coming—would appear at the bend of our lane.

Remembering the experience of my young days, of the schoolmasters and the classrooms, also knowing something of the natural school which nature herself supplies to all her creatures, I established my institution in a beautiful spot, far away from the town, where the children had the greatest freedom possible under the shade of ancient trees and the field around open to the verge of horizon.

From the beginning I tried to create an atmosphere which I considered to be more important than the class teaching. The atmosphere of nature's own beauty was there waiting for us from a time immemorial with her varied gifts of colours and dance, flowers and fruits, with the joy of her mornings and the peace of her starry nights. I wrote songs to suit the different seasons, to celebrate the coming of spring and the resonant season of the rains following the pitiless months of summer. When nature herself sends her message we ought to acknowledge its compelling invitation. While the kiss of rain thrills the heart of the surrounding trees if we pay all our dutiful attention to mathematics we are ostracised by the spirit of universe. Our holidays are unexpected like nature's own. Clouds gather above the rows of the palm trees without any previous notice; we gladly submit to its sudden suggestion and run wildly away from our Sanskrit grammar. To alienate our sympathy from the world of birds and trees is a barbarity which is not allowed in my institution.

I invited renowned artists from the city to live at the school, leaving them free to produce their own work which the boys and girls watch if they feel inclined. It is the same with my own work. I compose my songs and poems, the teachers sit round me and listen. The children are naturally attracted and they peep in and gather, even if they do not fully understand, something fresh from the heart of the composer.

From the commencement of our work we have encouraged our children to be of service to our neighbours from which has grown up a village reconstruction work in our neighbourhood unique in the whole of India. Round our educational work the villages have grouped themselves in which the sympathy for nature and service for man have become one. In such extension of sympathy and service our mind realises its true freedom.

Along with this has grown an aspiration for even a higher freedom, a freedom from all racial and national prejudice. Children's sympathy is often deliberately made narrow and distorted, making them incapable of understanding alien peoples with different languages and cultures. This causes us, when our growing souls demand it, to grope after each other in ignorance, to suffer from the blindness of this age. The worst fetters come when children lose their freedom of heart in love.

We are building up our institution upon the ideal of the spiritual unity of all races. I hope it is going to be a great meeting place for individuals from all countries who believe in the divine humanity, and who wish to make atonement for the cruel disloyalty displayed against her by men. Such idealists I have frequently met in my travels in the West, often unknown persons, of no special reputation, who suffer and struggle for a cause generally ignored by the clever and the powerful. These individuals, I am sure, will alter the outlook for the future. By them will be ushered a new sunrise of truth and love, like that great personality, who had only a small number of disciples from among the insignificant, and who at the end of his career presented a pitiful picture of utter failure. He was reviled by those in power, unknown by the larger world, and suffered an inglorious death, and yet through the symbol of this utmost failure he conquers and lives for ever.

For some time past, education has lacked idealism in its mere exercise of an intellect which has no depth of sentiment. The one desire produced in the heart of the students has been an ambition to win success in the world, not to reach some inner standard of perfection, not to obtain self-emancipation.

Let me confess this fact, that I have my faith in higher ideals. At the same time, I have a great feeling of delicacy in giving utterance of them, because of certain modern obstacles. We have now-a-days to be merely commonplace. We have to wait on the reports in the newspapers, representative of the whole machinery which has been growing up all over the world for the making of life superficial. It is difficult to fight through such obstructions and to come to the centre of humanity.

However I have this one satisfaction that I am at least able to put before you the mission to which these last years of my life have been devoted. As a servant of the great cause I must be frank and strong in urging upon you this mission. I represent in my institution an ideal of brotherhood where men of different countries and different languages can come together. I believe in the spiritual unity of man, and therefore I ask you to accept this task from me. Unless you come and say, 'We also recognise this ideal', I shall know that this mission has failed. Do not merely discuss me as a guest, but as one who has come to ask your love, your sympathy and your faith in the following of a great cause.

There is no meaning in such words as spiritualising the machine, we can spiritualise our own being which makes use of the machine, just as there is nothing good or bad in our bodily organs, but the moral qualities are in our mind. When the temptation is small our moral nature easily overcomes it, but when the bribe that is offered to our soul is too big we do not even realise that its dignity is offended. Today the profit that the machine brings to our door is too big and we do not hesitate to scramble for it even at the cost of our humanity. The shrinking of the man in us is concealed by the augmentation of things outside and we lack the time to grieve over the loss. We can only hope that science herself will help us to bring back sanity to the human world by lessening the opportunity to gamble with our fortune. The means of production constructed by science in her attempts to gain access into nature's storehouse are tremendously complex which only proves her own immaturity just as simplicity is wanting in the movements of a swimmer who is inexpert. It is this cumbersome complexity in the machinery which makes it not only unavailable to the majority of mankind but also compels us to centralise it in monster factories, uprooting the workers' life from its natural soil and creating unhappiness. I do not see any other way to extricate us from these tangled evils except to wait for science to simplify our means of production and thus lessen the enormity of individual greed.

I believe that the social unrest prevalent today all over the world is owing to the anarchy of spirit in the modern civilisation.

What is called progress is the progress in the mechanical contrivances; it is in fact an indefinite extension of our physical limbs and organs which, owing to the enormous material advantage that it brings to us, has tempted the modern man away from his inner realm of spiritual values. The attainment of perfection in human relationship through the help of religion, and cultivation of our social qualities occupied the most important place in our civilisation up till now. But today our homes have dissolved into hotels, community life is stifled in the dense and dusty atmosphere of the office, men and women are afraid of life, people clamour for their rights and forget their obligations, and they value comfort more than happiness and the spirit of display more than that of beauty.

Great civilisations in the East as well as in the West have flourished in the past because they produced food for the spirit of man for all time; they tried to build their life upon the faith in ideals, the faith which is creative. These great civilisations were at last run to death by men of the type of our precocious schoolboys of modern times, smart and superficially critical, worshippers of self, shrewd bargainers in the market of profit and power, efficient in their handling of the ephemeral, who presume to buy human souls with their money and throw them into their dustbins when they have been sucked dry, and who, eventually, driven by suicidal forces of passion, set their neighbours' houses on fire and are themselves enveloped by the flame.

It is some great ideal which creates great societies of men, it is some blind passion which breaks them to pieces. They thrive so long as they produce food for life; they perish when they burn up life in insatiate self-gratification. We have been taught by our sages that it is truth and not things which saves man from annihilation.

The reward of truth is peace, the reward of truth is happiness. The people suffer from the upsetting of equilibrium when power is there and no inner truth to which it is related, like a motor car in motion whose driver is absent.

~

MOHANDAS KARAMCHAND GANDHI

The Wardha Scheme

Mahatma Gandhi's ideas on education, particularly in the Indian context, were entirely different from those of his contemporaries. He looked upon the English education system in India as a soulless attempt at imitation. His ideas were different from those of people like Tagore or other thinkers on education in the emphasis he placed on vocational development which he thought would make a person mentally independent. He made his own children undergo education along these lines and tried to popularize this kind of education in his ashram. Gandhi's inaugural address at the Wardha Conference on 22 October 1937, an extract from which is reproduced below, is probably the most important document of his thoughts on education. The conference was attended by renowned educationists and ministers like Zakir Husain, Vinoba Bhave and P. Subbarayan, among others. The Congress, which formed ministries in as many as seven provinces in 1937, tried to implement the recommendations originating from this conference which came to be known as the Wardha Scheme. The Muslim League used this to attack the Congress on the grounds that it was pushing Gandhi's Hindu ideas. Notwithstanding such criticism, the conference at Wardha proved to be a revolutionary step as far as thinking on education in the country was concerned.

The ideas that I wish to place before you today are new in their method of presentation at least to me, although my experience behind those ideas is very old. The proposition that I wish to put forward refers to both the primary and college education. I have included secondary in primary education, because the primary education so called is available to a very small fraction of the people in our villages, many of which I have seen during my peregrinations since 1925. And I have seen, perhaps, more than anybody else, the conditions of the Indian villages. I gained good experience of the rural life of South Africa as well. I know fully well the type of education that is given in Indian villages. And now that I have settled down in Segaon I can study the whole problem of national education from closer quarters. I am convinced that if we wish to ameliorate the rural conditions, we must combine secondary with primary education. The educational scheme that we desire to place before the country must be primarily for the villages. I have no experience of college education, though I have come in contact with hundreds of college boys, have had heart to heart chats and correspondence with them, know their needs, failings and diseases they suffered from. But we must restrict ourselves to a consideration of the primary education. For, the moment the primary question is solved, the secondary one of college education will be solved easily.

I am convinced that the present system of primary education is not only wasteful, but is positively harmful. Most of the boys are lost to their parents and to the occupation they are born. They pick up evil habits, affect the urban ways, get a smattering of something which may be anything but education. What then should be the form of primary education? I think the remedy lies in educating them by means of vocational or manual training. I have some training. I have some experience of it myself, having trained my sons and other children on the Tolstoy Farm in South Africa through some manual training, that is, carpentry or shoe making which I learned from Kallenbach, who had his training in a Trappist monastery. My sons and all children, I am confident, have lost nothing, though I could not give them an education that either satisfied me or them, as the time at my disposal was limited and my preoccupations were numerous.

But the scheme that I wish to place before you today is not the teaching of some handicrafts side by side with liberal education. I want that the whole education should be imparted through some handicraft and industry. It might be objected that in the middle ages only handicrafts were taught to the students; but the occupational training, then, was far from serving an educational purpose. The crafts were taught only for the sake of the crafts, without any attempt to develop the intellect as well...and were lost to the countryside. As a result, it is now impossible to find an efficient carpenter or smith in an average village. The handicraft is nearly lost and the spinning wheel is being neglected...

The remedy lies in imparting the whole art and science of a craft through practical training... Teaching of takli spinning, for instance, presupposes the imparting of knowledge of the various varieties of cotton, different soils in different provinces of India, history of the ruin of handicraft, its political reasons, which will include the history of British rule in India, knowledge of arithmetic and so on. I am trying the same experiment on my grandson, who scarcely feels that he is being taught, for he all the while plays, laughs and sings. I am especially mentioning the takli and emphasising its utility, because I have realised its power and its romance; also because the handicraft of making cloth is the only one which can be taught throughout the country and because the takli is very cheap. If you have any other suitable handicraft to suggest, please do so without any hesitation, so that we might consider it as well...

I have placed the scheme before the ministries; it is for them to accept it or reject it. But my advice is that the primary education should centre round the takli. During the first year everything should be taught through takli; in the second year, other processes can be taught side by side. It will also be possible to earn quite enough through takli because there will be sufficient demand for the cloth produced by the children. Even the parents of the children will be sufficient to consume the products of their children. I have contemplated a seven years' course which so far as takli is concerned would culminate in practical knowledge of weaving, including dyeing, designing, etc.

I am very keen on funding the expenses of a teacher through the product of the manual work of his pupils, because I am convinced that there is no other way to carry education to crores of our children. We cannot wait until we have the necessary revenue and until the viceroy reduces the military expenditure. You should bear in mind that this primary education would include the elementary principles of sanitation, hygiene, nutrition, of doing their own work, helping parents at home, etc. The present generation of boys knows no cleanliness, no self-help, and are physically weak. I would, therefore, give compulsory physical training through the musical drill.

I have been accused of being opposed to literary training. Far from it, I simply want to show the way in which it should be given. The self-supporting aspect has also been attacked. It is said, whereas we should be expending millions on the primary education, we are going to exploit the children. It is also feared that there would be enormous waste. This fear is also falsified by experience. As for exploiting or burdening the children, I would ask whether it was burdening the child to save him from a disaster? Takli is a good enough toy to play with. It is no less a toy because it is a productive one. Even today children help their parents to a certain extent. The Segaon children know the details of agriculture better than I, for having worked with their parents on the fields. Whilst the child will be encouraged to spin and help his parents with agricultural jobs, he will also be made to feel that he does not belong only to his parents but also to the village and to the country, and that he must make some return to them. That is the only way. I would tell the ministers that they make the children helpless by doling out education to them. They would make them self-confident and brave by their paying for their own education by their own labour. The system is to be common to all Hindus, Muslims, Parsis and Christians. Why do I not lay any religious instructions, people ask. Because I am teaching them practical religion, the religion of self-help.

The state is bound to find employment if needed, for all the pupils thus trained. As for teachers, Professor K.T. Shah has suggested conscription. He has demonstrated its value by citing Italy and other lands.

If Mussolini could impress the youth of Italy for the service of his country, why should not we? Was it fair to label as slavery the compulsory enlistment of service of our youth for a year or longer before they began their career? The youths had contributed a lot to the success of the movement for freedom during the past seventeen years, and I would call upon them to give freely a year of their lives to the service of the motherland. Legislation, if it was necessary in this respect, would not be compulsion, as it could not be passed without the consent of the majority of our representatives.

College education was largely an urban proposition. I would not say that it was an unmitigated failure, as primary education was, but the results were fairly disappointing. Why should anyone of the graduates have to be unemployed?

... We have communal quarrels—not that they are peculiar to us. England had also its War of the Roses, and today British Imperialism is the enemy of the world. If we want to eliminate the communal strife, we must start on the education I have now adumbrated. That plan springs out of non-violence... We have to make our boys true representatives of our culture and our civilisation, of the true genius of our nation. We cannot do so otherwise than by giving them a course of self-supporting primary education.

~

SRIPAD AMRIT DANGE

On the Poona University Bill

Since the 1920s, there had been a demand for a university separate from Bombay University which would encourage Marathi language and culture. It was proposed to set up Poona University for this purpose. When the bill to establish the university was taken up by the premier of Bombay, B.G. Kher, on 31 October 1947, S.A. Dange used the opportunity to present a fine critique of the education system and the whole structure of colonial education.

Sir, I will try to be as brief as possible in my remarks, and I shall limit myself to stating my views on the scheme as presented by the honourable Prime Minister, and, in considering the subject, try to follow strictly his own scheme.

I completely agree with him that university education is the crown of education, though sometimes the crown does not bring much of an income to the wearer thereof. On the contrary, it might perhaps bring him unemployment. Nevertheless, university education is the crown of education. University education is the apex of education, and the primary or basic, the base. Secondary education is more or less interwoven between primary and university education.

The Government in defining its relation to education has a definite viewpoint and that viewpoint is that basic education henceforth shall take note of the dignity of labour, shall be allied with the processes of labour and shall not neglect them. So, when a child gets basic education and goes to higher education, it will not be handicapped by the difficulty inherent in mere arts education. A child with basic education gets a technical bias; the child will have a bias towards handicraft. That is all to the good, though one may have differences as to what should be the type of labour used in basic education. The idea of imparting basic education to children is correct. Then we go to the primary education. There also the viewpoint of the Government is good. The Primary Education Bill, which we passed the other day, in its preamble stated that the guiding motive of primary education, that is education given to a child from the age of six years to the age of ten or so, shall be universal, free and compulsory. The proposal to give basic and primary education to every child, that will grow into a citizen of the country, irrespective of considerations of caste, creed, colour, wealth etc., is very welcome. This approach of the Government to the problem of primary education is, as I said the other day, fundamentally democratic.

Now, coming to the crown of education, university education, let us see whether it fits in with the scheme of the basic and primary stages of education. Sir, when we look into the whole thing, we find that the claim made by the honourable Prime Minister that the University Bill is fundamentally new, that it is a departure from the old Act, is partly true and partly untrue, because the crown does not fit in with the basic and primary stages. I do not say that it is the fault either of the honourable Prime Minister or of the Government. I must say that the Prime Minister has not fostered those conceptions. In his general remarks he said that the Bill is intended to turn out a new type of citizen; that the Bill is meant for the people as a whole. But, I say that the scheme does not fit in with that ideal, for the simple reason that our society today has not got the necessary resources to make secondary and university education fit in with the fundamental conception which underlies primary education which is to be made universal, free and compulsory. Under the present-day conditions university education is such that it is not, and cannot be made, universal, free and compulsory. Thus the very foundation of democratic application is missing in the University Bill, for the simple reason that it cannot be made universal, free and compulsory. That is why it is a crown which does not fit in over the structure of basic and primary education. It is neither universal nor free. It is a crown which is conferred upon a restricted and selected few.

What is the principle of that selection? What is the principle by which this crown is handed over to certain people only and is not available to others? The basic and primary education is available to every child born, irrespective of race, caste, wealth, or anything. It is universal, free and compulsory, but the crown is not so. Everyone is not going to get it. Some people are selected for it. It is going to be conferred upon those select few. What is the process by which some people get the crown and the others do not get this logical and continuous development of their primary education? That depends upon the capacity to pay for it. After the primary education, only if the parents have got the capacity to pay for the child's secondary and university education, can the child have an opportunity for university education irrespective of its ability to get the crown, the university degree—this is the fundamental concept which we ought to grasp in the present-day university education. It is not the fault of the honourable Prime Minister. Nor is it the fault of the Government. The limited national resources which we have got in our hands are such that we cannot apply the principle of the basic and primary education to the university education and make it as wide and fundamentally democratic as we have done in the primary field. Therefore, this is the handicap from which the honourable Prime Minister and all of us suffer.

[Mr. B.G. KHER: On a point of information, Sir, is the honourable member in favour of making university education compulsory?]

Yes, I am, if you make the parents capable of maintaining the children up to the university. The parents must have the power to maintain the child till he gets complete university education. They should be able to pay for his textbooks and fees in the absence of the income which the child after the age of 15 or 16 fetches for the parents. That is why I was referring to the national wealth and resources. If the parents can do without the income which the child may fetch, and can pay the child's fees and hostel charges in the university, then alone will they send the child up to the crown. Who does not want his child to become a graduate, engineer or a technician? Why should only some people get the crown? Why should others not get the crown? It does not depend upon the voluntary will of the parent. Everyone cannot get the crown because of the compulsion in the payment of fees.

The limitation of finance compels the Government to limit the universality and the freeness of education to the primary. We will come to such a stage in our society when university education will not be limited to the class which can pay for it, but will be universal, free and compulsory. We shall work for a society, the whole of which will be a working intelligentsia, and in which there will be no differentiation between manual labour and intellectual labour. We are going to have such a society, and if today in this Bill we cannot do that, it is because we have not got the requisite productive capacity. As society advances, we shall have that capacity. This is exactly the point we are going to reach where the full products of social labour will be available to every man. To that stage we have not come in any country. University education is not universal, free and compulsory as yet even in the Soviet Union. But there they have made the preconditions ready for it. There the intelligentsia rise from the ranks of the working class, and does not belong to the exploiting classes which have been completely abolished. Still, even in that country this university education has not become universal, free and compulsory, because the productive sources of the State have not come to that level where the abundance of wealth is of such type that it can have universal, free and compulsory university education. The manufacturing and turning out of intelligentsia is the function of the university. If society has to be run, an intelligentsia has to be prepared to run the state machinery, whether in the interest of this class or that. The University Bill seeks to train an intelligentsia to run the machinery of capitalism. That is why I say that this Bill is not fundamentally democratic and fully popular, and does not fulfil the final ambitions of society which we have in view. It does not satisfy all the fine aims and ideals that a social man should have, namely, to destroy the differentiation between class and class and between intellectual labour and manual labour.

I was saying that this Bill is limited in scope and cannot carry forward all our people beyond the basic and primary stage. Society as a whole is still handicapped for want of advancement. True, it is not the fault of this Government; it is a historical fault. But I am pointing it out, because I do not want any single citizen of this province to go away with the idea that we have got a measure which finally sums up all our ambitions. Let us, therefore, look at it from a limited point of view. When we come to that view, we come to the fact that the function of the university here is limited to the turning out of the intelligentsia, which has to run the machinery of the State, and increase the productive capacity of our society but on a capitalist–landlord basis. That is why in this Bill a departure is made. The Hon.

Prime Minister himself distinguished this Bill from all previous Bills. He made certain references. They were to the education that we used to get under the British. Everyone knows what education was under the British. I fully agree with him in most of the criticisms which he made. But the question is whether he is making a departure from the previous practice while making criticisms of that practice. I would say he is partly making a departure from the past and partly sticking to the past. Therefore, while trying to lift us out of the past, he has carried over some of the defects of the past. Take, for example, the question of English language as medium. The Bombay University is the emblem of English education. By accident, it turned out Ranade, Bhandarkar and others. The honourable Prime Minister gave us the names of the first four graduates who became great: Ranade, Bhandarkar, Modak and Wagle. They became great not because the Bombay University conferred degree on them. In fact they denied everything the Bombay University stood for. They became great by negating everything that the university stood for. Take for example Rajawade. Every student of Marathi knows him. Similarly, the Deccan Education Society has produced great men. These people became great because they negated the very principles of the institution which brought them forth. Is this Bill going to continue that? Are we going to produce through the Maharashtra University great men who would be great only by denying the very tradition of this university education, just as Ranade and others became great by denying their university education?...

The Hon. Premier was describing the greatness of some of the Oxford and Cambridge professors. Unfortunately, I have not got much respect for the professors of Oxford and Cambridge. If we are going to imitate Oxford and Cambridge, we shall be turning out Churchills to conquer other peoples' lands and not people like Mahatma Gandhi or Pandit Jawaharlal Nehru. Oxford or Cambridge is a house of snobs. And even today they treat our students who go there with snobbery. One of the best surgeons in the K.E.M. Hospital wanted to get the F.R.C.S. degree...and he went to Edinburgh. One of the questions that was put to him in the oral test was what he thought about Pakistan and Hindustan and whether the Indians could manage their own affairs without the British. The doctor, like any other self-respecting Indian, replied that it was none of their business to put him such a question in a medical examination. The doctor, of course, failed in the oral test but he passed in surgery. Another experienced doctor, who had gone to England with the help of a scholarship of the Government or the college, was for six months given the ordinary work of a novice and asked to stand by at the operation table, because the surgeons there thought that this doctor, though he had practised for several years, was unfit even to stand by them at the operation table because he was taught in an Indian college. That man surrendered his scholarship, and was booking his passage to India when I met him.

We, therefore, Sir, need not imitate the foreigners. Our professors are of a higher calibre than those of Oxford and Cambridge, and the professors turned out according to the scheme of education that we have now in view may be even better than the Laskis and others whom our Premier mentioned. If we take the calibre of an average American student and that of our student, our university student will be found to be more serious and more political than an average American student. That is my experience. I, however, do not want to go further in the matter, because, if I do so, it will be rather hard on the honourable Premier, and the people will lose whatever little respect they have got for Oxford and Cambridge.

... Lastly, Sir, the new State that we are having is not a Hindu–Muslim State, and, therefore, the new education, as defined in clause 6 as being non-religious and secular, is a welcome feature of the Bill. However, whatever further mechanism that should be provided in the Bill to ensure against communalism in education should be thought about by the Select Committee along with clause 6. It should be seen that the content of education is not allowed to go on wrong lines, and a safety mechanism should be introduced by the Select Committee. Otherwise, you will only mean to demarcate from the past but will not lay down any programme for the future. Then the medium of Marathi also should be laid down. The question of financing of education should not be subject to the whims of private financiers whose wealth should be made subject to popular need and will. The control should be more democratised than it is today.

~

MEGHNAD SAHA

Reforms in Higher Education

Meghnad Saha, one of India's pioneering scientists who led the growth of applied physics in the country, was also closely involved in a number of public causes. As a member of the Lok Sabha, he played an important role in furthering science and education. He was the first to talk about the setting up of a University Grants Commission. He moved two cut motions on 13 June 1952 in the course of the debate on the demand for grants for the Union education ministry. In support of his cut motions, he highlighted the paramount need for reform in the sphere of higher education, emphasizing more budgetary allocation for education.

I am to tell the House that the University Commission was appointed by the Government of India in 1948, to survey the position of higher education in this country. It was presided over by no less a personage than Dr. Sarvepalli Radhakrishnan, who is one of the most eminent educationists of our country, a philosopher of international importance and now Vice-President of the Republic. There are many useful recommendations which the University Commission has made. One would have thought that a set of resolutions coming from such a highly placed body would receive the serious attention of the Government of India. But I regret to see that all these three years, action has not been taken on any one of them. I cannot give in detail all the recommendations, but I shall just invite the attention of the House to only a few. These are:

Firstly, University education should be on the Concurrent List. Under the present circumstances, University education is a State subject. The Commission found that this has led to a deterioration of University education standards and to many other unpleasant things;

Secondly, that the President of the Republic should be the Visitor of all the Universities of India;

Thirdly, it should be the concern of the Central Government to provide ample finance for the development of Universities; and

Fourthly, the money so provided should be spent through an autonomous University Grants Commission, which should be properly constituted.

The University Commission visited almost all the Universities and higher educational institutions in India. They collected evidence from all kinds of people, from the heads of States, Education

Ministers, distinguished educationists, men and women interested in public life and all of them said that it was rather bad when the Constitution was framed, to have made education a State subject. I shall just read an extract from their report: 'Nearly all our witnesses have expressed their opinion as to the proper category for University education, as to whether it should be Central, Concurrent or Provincial. A minority, but a minority including very important witnesses thought that it should be wholly Central; a very large majority of University spokesmen and public men and women thought that it should be Concurrent. Practically the only witnesses who thought that it should be Provincial were representatives of only one or two State Governments. The consensus of opinion was that it should be a Concurrent subject.'

I find that the Planning Commission has also stated that it should be a Concurrent subject. Why should it be a Concurrent subject? The University provides us with the best brains of the country. We found that almost in all the Provinces the Universities are pulling in different directions; there is no unity of purpose. We found that sometimes they are following policies which are highly provincial and detrimental to the cause of unity. We found that many of the Universities were being made tools of State politics. We were convinced that education should be free from all taints of Provincialism, that our Universities should train a number of high class workers, brain workers, in the interests of the country as a whole. Therefore, it was thought that it should be a Central subject, and if not wholly a Central subject, at least a Concurrent subject.

Then we found that Universities were grossly underfinanced for the tasks they are attempting. We want to undertake reconstruction of the country on a vast scale. We require very good workers, we require good lawyers, good doctors, good engineers, technical men, scientific men of all types who can undertake the vast work of reconstruction. If you read the Russian Five Year Plan, you will find that a very good part of the Plan is devoted to the question of training of personnel. Why? Because without good personnel, without properly trained engineers, technicians, and scientists, you cannot reconstruct this country. All your thoughts of reconstruction in this country without highly trained personnel would be idle daydreams. We found that for this purpose, the Universities were grossly underfinanced, and the State Governments had absolutely no money with which they could come to the help of the Universities; we saw no possibility that the

Provinces could provide the whole of the necessary expenditure. The Commission, therefore, came to a sort of compromise that as far as education up to B.A. or B.Sc. stage was concerned, it should be wholly a State subject, as far as postgraduate studies were concerned, that is, M.A., M.Sc. and research work and higher professional education, like medical, engineering, and technical, the expenditure should be shared half and half between the State Governments and the Centre. We wanted to ensure that the States should not wash off their hands entirely from the responsibility of higher education. They should give as much money as they can afford. At the same time, the Centre also should be interested in the work.

I might perhaps say in this connection that the grants of most of the Universities have remained what they were before the Second World War, while the price of a rupee has gone down to one-fourth of its pre-war value. This is a very sad state of affairs. You find that most of the teachers are underpaid, and our laboratories are without equipment, standard of education is very unsatisfactory and there is a state of despondency everywhere in University quarters. You find in several Universities—my own old University of Allahabad for example—there is an Enquiry Committee because overenthusiastic University authorities have overspent their budget. Actually, there people were actuated with the highest of motives. They wanted to provide education for the growing needs of the country and it was a mockery of fate that they should be punished for their enthusiasm.

~

M.C. CHAGLA

Structure of Education

M.C. Chagla (1900–1981) was a renowned jurist and diplomat who served as the chief justice of Bombay High Court from 1948 to 1958. He was also the Indian ambassador to the USA from 1958 to 1961 and Indian high commissioner to the UK from April 1962 to September 1963. Between 1963 and 1966, he served as union education minister. This was a period when the education system in India had started showing signs of strain. Chagla was enthusiastic about cleaning it up and doing something new. The significance of the following speech, delivered in the Lok Sabha on 26 March 1965, lies in the fact that it suggests that the government was seriously thinking of amending the constitution to make education a part of the concurrent list. On 12 March 1965, Dr L.M. Singhvi had moved a resolution in the Lok Sabha which said: 'This House is of the opinion that the pattern and structure of education should be purposefully recast and reorganized with a view to promoting greater educational uniformity and the cause of national integration.' M.C. Chagla's intervention came in response to this resolution.

May I compliment my hon. friend, Dr. Singhvi, for whom I have very great regard, on moving this Resolution? I appreciate the spirit underlying it, the object he has of improving the whole structure of education. But may I appeal to him not to press this Resolution, because we are trying to do exactly what he wants by appointing the Education Commission which will go into the whole spectrum of education, primary, secondary, higher, technical and so on. It will deal with all the points he has raised in his Resolution.

Two of my hon. friends have talked about primary education. I agree that the situation is far from satisfactory. But look at what has happened since independence? Fifty million boys are there in primary schools today. It is what I call an expansion explosion. We have not sufficient teachers, trained teachers, we have not sufficient schools, we have not sufficient textbooks. The children want to come and are clamouring for education. Therefore, I have been emphasising that while we cannot prevent expansion, we must also pay some attention to quality.

May I point out two things? We are trying to make primary education production oriented. I agree with what my hon. friend over there said that students should have the opportunity of self-expression. The student should do something creative and not grind his nose at the desk and merely read textbooks and pass examinations. Also we are doing our best with regard to textbooks. We have set up a committee here. We are writing textbooks on a national basis. We are going to send them to every state so that they can be translated into different national languages.

I do not know whether my colleague was good enough to note down all points Dr. Singhvi made. I cannot deal with all the points he has made in this short time. I will try to reply to as many as I can.

I agree with him that education is of basic importance. I think there is nothing in India today which is of greater importance than education. It is investment in human beings. Unless we can raise the educational standards of our people, we can never go far as a nation.

Therefore, I entirely agree with him that education too should be given priority. Unfortunately, whenever there is an economy drive, education becomes the first casualty.

That is how it is because we cannot show results. They say: 'We cannot produce steel, we cannot produce fertilisers, we cannot put up irrigation dams. What is the value of education?' But we are creating human beings, and no nation can progress without creating the right type of human beings.

... As regards the teachers' profession, I entirely agree with what he says. I have said so often on the floor of the House, I have said it at public meetings, and I go on repeating that I think that our teachers are very poorly paid. But look at what we have done. We have offered 50 per cent for increase in the emoluments of teachers, if the state government can spare the other 50 per cent.

Therefore, I do feel that the system of matching grants has not succeeded, and we are trying to evolve a better system for the fourth plan.

I entirely agree that our education cannot improve unless we raise the standard of our teachers. We are doing everything possible to raise the status of our teachers. We give them national awards. Teachers are selected for these awards. We have a national foundation to relieve the distress of the teachers. As I have said, we are giving every incentive to the states to raise the dignity and status of the teachers. Still they are very poorly paid.

I wish I were both Education Minister and Finance Minister, and then I could write cheques for education, but I am not. Therefore, for everything I want for education, I have to beg, to go down on my knees before the Finance Minister and say, 'Please give me some money for education,' because I think this is the greatest national activity that we can have.

Then my hon. friend wants that a high-power commission should be appointed. This has already been done. He says that the recommendations of the Mudaliar commission have not been implemented. I cannot implement the recommendations of the Mudaliar commission when by March next year I hope to have the report of this educational commission, and I give an assurance to this House that this commission's report will not be pigeonholed. Once we have taken a decision, we will implement whatever the commission recommends.

I agree with the suggestion of Dr. Singhvi that there should be an all-India pattern of secondary education. At various conferences of Education Ministers, we have laid down the pattern—so many years of schooling, three years' degree course, etc. Most of the states are conforming to it, and today we are giving the greatest importance to secondary education.

... Secondary education is a state subject. A suggestion has been made by the teachers that I should set up a Secondary Education Grants Commission like the University Grants Commission. We consulted the law ministry, and they said it was not constitutional. So unless we make secondary education either a Union subject or a concurrent subject, this cannot be done.

But I must admit, as I have said before, that although there is no concurrence in law, to a large extent there is a concurrence in substance, because all the Education Ministers agreed at the last Education Ministers' conference that in all matters affecting quality in secondary education, the schemes should be Centrally sponsored or Central schemes, and that the states would abide by the directions given by the Centre. Therefore, we are having a crash programme with regard to teaching of science and teacher training. These are two very important subjects so far as secondary education is concerned. Unless we attach the greatest importance to science our country will not progress. We are very backward in science. We have a special commission consisting of Russians and Americans financed by UNESCO. It has gone around and given a report on how to improve science education in secondary schools and we have started implementing it. Dr. Singhvi says that education must be in the concurrent list. I am trying to get at least higher education in the concurrent list. That is in Sapru committee's report. So far only one state, Punjab, had agreed to it. My friend who is an eminent lawyer knows that constitution cannot be amended unless a majority of states ratify this particular amendment. So that even if I get the whole House to agree, I think very likely I would, that higher education at least should be in the concurrent list, it is no good till I get a majority of the states to agree to it. With regard to the Indian Education Service, a Resolution had been moved this afternoon in the Rajya Sabha and we will set up the Indian Education Service almost immediately. I am very happy that at least in that respect all the states have agreed that we should have an all-India Educational Service. That will be a great integrating factor. The constitutional requirement is that it has to be carried by a two-third majority in the Rajya Sabha.

A Resolution had been moved and I hope the vote will be taken on Monday. Another suggestion of Dr. Singhvi is: what about the president being vested with visitorial powers for all the universities? The universities are autonomous. The university acts are passed by state legislatures. We have had model universities bill committee and they have made certain suggestions about the appointment of Vice Chancellors. I have forwarded this report to the various states but again, I cannot compel the states to accept this.

... The other suggestion is the establishment of national colleges to serve as the peak of excellence for other institutions. I agree that our colleges are in a bad way. 85 per cent of our students are in colleges. There are some very good colleges but the majority of them are bad colleges. We have now decided to concentrate on improving the standard of colleges. I agree with my honourable friend that we should take up one or two colleges and make them models.

Since you have already indicated, I must conclude my remark as quickly as possible. Shri S.N. Das has moved an amendment. It conforms to the reference we have made to the commissions. Our education system should be according to our national pattern. My friend Mr. Mahida supported the Resolution and had spoken about primary education and moral education and it was said that convocations should be made simpler. The other day, I delivered a convocation address at Wardha at the rural institute. We had an entirely Indian ceremony but again this must be left to the universities as they are autonomous.

... In all these things, what we have to remember is that the numbers are astronomical: 50 million students in primary school, about 10 million in secondary schools and a million and a quarter in colleges and universities. In any scheme which we device, we are faced with these enormous numbers. I agree that the students should have training, as my hon. friend Shri Chakravarty suggests, but it is a question not only of resources but of teachers and the equipments.

I would not take any more time of the house. I again thank Dr. Singhvi for having moved the Resolution. The debate has been interesting. I would appeal to him not to press this to a division. I can assure him that all these points will be taken into consideration by the commission. I shall forward copies of the proceedings of this House on this Resolution to the commission.

~

BHUPESH GUPTA

On the Jawaharlal Nehru University Bill

The Jawaharlal Nehru University (JNU) was the idea of M.C. Chagla during his tenure as education minister. He wanted to set up a university of international standards which would deal with cutting-edge areas of science and technology including agricultural technology. After he placed the bill introducing the idea and initial concept of the university in the Rajya Sabha on 1 September 1965, Bhupesh Gupta spoke on the motion. He thought that the idea as articulated by the education minister was good but 'pedestrian'. He wanted the new university to be different from traditional universities granting degrees annually. When JNU finally came into existence, it reflected more of Bhupesh Gupta's vision than that of M.C. Chagla.

Mr. Chairman, Sir, we have heard some speeches, especially from the Congress benches. I do not think it is necessary to talk about this university in order to settle the name of a personality in history. We are told that the name of Pandit Jawaharlal Nehru would be immortalised by this particular university as though that is how we are now going to immortalise him; otherwise, according to them—it seems to me he would not be immortal. I think this is an entirely wrong approach. It is understandable if honourable members take the opportunity of expressing certain good and noble sentiments for their leader and for, undoubtedly, a very great man. But we are here discussing the specific proposal for a university, and let us not try to waste much time on the name itself, although points were made about him, or the biographical sketch of Pandit Jawaharlal Nehru was drawn. What we should do here is to look at the problem and examine the question that is before us on merits. We are having another university in Delhi as indeed we should have got one much earlier. Delhi's requirements of higher education are not squarely met and Delhi certainly deserves to be given a university by the Central Government and arrangements for providing higher education by the Central Government should have been made. That was not done. Naturally, people have suffered and our education has suffered here. Mr. Chairman, therefore I am happy that Delhi will perhaps have a larger scope for higher education in humanities, in science and in technology. But it is a pedestrian way in which the Bill has been conceived of by our esteemed friend, Mr. Chagla. One should have thought that when you are giving this name to this university and are being guided by certain sentiments which would be cherished, undoubtedly, honestly you would have also introduced some new ground in the matter of approach. But what we have is just a common-place legislation which more or less repeats the picture of the universities that we have in our country. There is nothing particularly new in it, nothing particularly exciting in it, nothing particularly hopeful in it. That is what I wish to say.

The very first thing that comes to my mind in this connection is: for whom we are arranging this education. Yes, technological education, scientific education and other educational facilities should be extended. We agree, but preference should be given, especially when income disparities continue in the country in a very serious manner, when we find that the young boys and girls coming from the poorer classes do not have the opportunity or wherewithal to enter the portals of our university, naturally the question arises whether this university is going to be open for them, those who do not have enough money or whose families do not have enough money or whether it is going to be just another one which will be accessible only to the sons and daughters of the rich. This question is very important and has to be answered and settled from the standpoint of those who need the care of the country most. Still, we talk about the Oxford University and so on. I do not know how long it will take—perhaps another five centuries we will require at this rate—in order to forget the Oxford and Cambridge Universities.

Mr. Chairman, let us not go into all these things. These are very pedantic, high-sounding and perhaps very, very attractive to those people who have, in the corner of their hearts, still a lingering admiration for everything that is Anglo-Saxon. I am not one of those people. Certainly, there are a lot of things to be got from every country and England is not excluded from them. But why cannot the problems of our universities be considered from the standpoint of the requirements of our country in the light of the experience about education in the contemporary world? And I think the contemporary world points to one thing and it is this that the type of educational system that we have in Oxford and Cambridge in modern times, with very high-flown expenses and with a different set-up of values and functions of our people or any people for that matter, does not meet the requirements of the situation. That is what I wish to say. Therefore, let us not go into it. Here, Mr. Chagla should consider for whom the university is intended. Why should we like more money to be given to this without any assurance given by the Government that this university will particularly cater to the needs of the poorer classes and poorer people?

Mr. Chairman, let us not have Cambridges and Oxfords and Princetons and Harvards here; let us create universities and colleges that our people need, that our development needs, for the remaking of our material and cultural being. That is what I say and therefore the first thing is to ensure that the sons of the working people, the worker, the peasants and the middle classes do have the doors of the universities thrown wide open to them. That is the first thing and for that you have to provide not only money but also a different outlook. Money must come; we must have subsidised education; it must be highly subsidised because the investment that you will be making in imparting higher scientific and technical education to the poorer sections of the community will have been repaid in course of time in creative and even constructive labour which would go to the benefit of the entire society. That is how I view this matter. But Mr. Chairman, if the cost of education becomes expensive—from Rs. 125 to Rs. 200—I should like to know how many even of the great officers of the Government would be in a position to send their sons to these universities. That is what I would like to know. We know of those days when the tuition fee in the colleges was Rs. 10. Now, to go to the college, one requires to spend Rs. 30. That is the position. Then, we pay the tuition fees and spend on books and other things. Therefore, if Mr. Chagla feels and honourable members who expressed good sentiments about Pandit Jawaharlal Nehru feel that he had some socialist ideas and a socialist way of looking at things, let the emphasis be shifted from the upper classes to the classes that are economically at bottom layers of the society. This is the first suggestion.

Secondly, the university should be run on a broad basis. I would not like the bureaucratic set-up to come in. The autonomy should be completely guaranteed. I think we can give autonomy in a larger measure to a university of this kind. Since Jawaharlal Nehru's name is associated with it I feel there should be a faculty which educates the students in the sprit of world power. Now, we have got all faculties... We want, therefore, in a university of this kind a special faculty to be created that would impart learning and education in the spirit of the worldwide struggle for peace because nothing today is so novel and great as that one which teaches our younger generation...the struggle that humanity is waging for peace. Therefore, this thing should be there. Let there be a new faculty. Show some originality... There are new faculties to be created. That is a matter for the Select Committee to consider. Maybe it is not possible to include everything in a Bill. But an indication should be there. That is what I say.

Then, Mr. Chairman, I should also like this university to educate students in various matters connected with development of democratic institutions and democracy in the country. This should be a special subject. It should be there in other universities also. Sir, many names are taken here. We find special faculties in a given situation are brought into existence in order to educate the people in special branches of learning so that students may become useful, enlightened citizens when they are educated in world affairs and the affairs of the State. Therefore, I say such suggestions should also be considered.

Some honourable members talked about student indiscipline. Sir, we are elder people. Therefore, we can talk about student indiscipline. But, Mr. Chairman, let us look at the ruling class and at the elders in a particular State from which Pt. Jawaharlal Nehru came. I see the greatest indiscipline going on among those teaching about discipline to the students. Take the example of UP. What is happening there? Among the leaders, as you know, they talk glibly about student indiscipline. Sir, by and large, I do maintain that our student community are a fine lot, a very disciplined body. We know the student communities in other countries also and we should have no hesitation in extending to the student community as a whole our best feelings and deep appreciation of the manner in which they conduct themselves. There will be some bad people. And where there are not bad people, I should like to know. If you take percentages, you will find a much higher percentage of bad people in the Treasury Benches than in any college or university in the country. Therefore, let us not talk about this business. Sir, students should have ideals before them. I should like this university to have a clear faculty, I maintain, for the studies of scientific socialism. And why should it not be there? Everybody talks about socialism. Mr. S.K. Patil talks about socialism. Mr. G.D. Birla talks about socialism. Mr. J.R.D. Tata talks about socialism. Mr. Haridas Mundhra talks of socialism when he gives money to a particular election fund. Everybody these days talks of socialism. But one does not know what it is....So, there should be a faculty for the study of scientific socialism.

... I know, in the postgraduate courses Marxism is taught but the books are always from the United States of America which display no knowledge of Marxism at all. Therefore, Mr. Chairman, I should like a faculty to be created to impart proper education of this kind.

As far as other things are concerned, I do not wish to say anything because we will have another chance I believe when the thing comes back from the Select Committee. But I think the poor should be kept in view. Noble ideas should be kept in mind. And certainly when Parliament has declared for the establishment of, what they call, a socialist State, socialism should be studied as a special subject, as it prevails in this country, in this particular university.

~

R.K. NARAYAN

Burden on Childhood

All of us are witness to the sight of little children trudging out of their homes, bleary-eyed, at an ungodly hour of the morning, bent over with a sack full of books on their backs. On 27 April 1989, author R.K. Narayan (1906–2001), who was a nominated member of the Rajya Sabha, spoke on the burden of modern-day education on children and its role in robbing them of the joys of childhood. This short speech brings out the joylessness and ineffectiveness of the modern system of education and urges Parliament to take practical steps to mitigate children's suffering and restore them their childhood.

Madam Chairman, I am taking this honourable House to another world. In the stress and concerns of adult world, the problems or rather the plight of children are unnoticed. I am not referring to any particular class but to the childhood itself. The hardships start right at home when straight from the bed the child is pulled out and got ready for the school even before his faculties are awake. He or she is groomed and stuffed into a uniform and packed off with a loaded bag on her back. School bag has become an inevitable burden for the child. I am now pleading for abolition of the school bag by an ordinance, if necessary. I have investigated and found that an average child carries strapped to his back like a pack mule not less than 6-8 kg of books, notebooks and other paraphernalia of modern education in addition to lunch box and water bottle. More children on account of this daily burden develop a stoop and hang their arms forward like a chimpanzee while walking and I know some cases of serious spinal injuries in the children too. Asked why not leave some books behind at home, the child replies it is her teacher's order that all books and notes must be brought every day to the class. For what reason God alone knows. If there is a lapse the child invites punishment which takes the form of being rapped on the knuckles with a wooden scale, a refinement from our own days when we received cane cuts on our palm only. The child is in such terror of the teacher whether you call her sister, mother superior or just madam that she is prepared to carry out any command issued by her who has no imagination, sympathy or whatever.

The dress regulation particularly in convent schools is another senseless formality. Tie, laced shoes and socks, irrespective of the climate is compulsory. Polishing a shoe and lacing it becomes a major task for the child first in the day. When the tie has become an anachronism even in the adult world, it is absurd to enforce it on children. After the school hours, the child returns home only to find her mother or her tutor waiting to pounce upon her, to snatch her bag and compel her to go through special coaching and home work. For the child, the day has ended with no time for play or dream. It is a cruel harsh life imposed on her and I present her case before this House and the hon. members to think over and devise a remedy by changing the whole educational system and outlook so that childhood has a chance to bloom rather than wilt in the dreadful process of learning. Other areas where the child needs protection is their involvement in adult activities such as protest marches, parades, lining up on roadsides and waiting for VIPs. Children are made to stand in the hot sun for hours without anyone noticing how they suffer from fatigue, hunger and thirst. Children must be protected and cherished which would seem especially relevant in the Year of Nehru Centenary. Now how it is to be done, it is up to the members and administrators to consider but perhaps not by appointing a commission of inquiry but in some other practical and peaceful manner.

16

LABOUR

The labour movement in India was greatly influenced by similar movements in Britain and by the rise of communism in Europe. However, due to the peculiar conditions which prevailed in India—the colonial situation and the anti-colonial national movement—very soon it acquired an additional dimension. In the initial stages, the labour movement flowered as part of the national movement and the first president of the All-India Trade Union Congress (AITUC) was Lala Lajpat Rai. From its beginning in the 1880s, when people like Sasipada Banerjee in Bengal and later N.M. Joshi in Maharashtra began to organize labour, through the rise of militant unions in 1928-29 in Bombay, to the post-independence period which witnessed powerful unions exerting considerable influence on economic decision making, the Indian labour movement has been led by a galaxy of charismatic leaders which has included S.A. Dange, B.T. Ranadive, S.M. Banerjee, Jyoti Basu, V.V. Giri, George Fernandes, A.K. Ray, Indrajit Gupta and Gurudas Dasgupta, among others. Interestingly, unlike other developed and developing countries, the labour movement in India, due to its links with the national movement prior to independence, was not perceived as antithetical to the political leadership after independence and hence did not have to suffer the state repression that such movements had to in other countries. For over forty years till the late 1980s, trade unions were a very vociferous and dominant presence in the economy. In the 1980s, labour leaders like Datta Samant wielded considerable clout in the Bombay–Pune industrial belt. Since then, however, the state, under pressure from changing global economic patterns, began to see the trade union movement as an impediment to growth. In the meantime, the nature of the labour movement too had altered. In the rapidly changing political and economic situation where organized labour is being fast replaced by the unorganized segment, a new vision for the labour movement, incorporating the peasantry, temporary and migrant labourers and workers from special economic zones, is yet to find a clear political articulation. No political party or labour organization has come out clearly with an understanding of the new industrial world and the role of labour in it.

~

JOSEPH BAPTISTA

Address at the First All-India Trade Union Congress

The All-India Trade Union Congress (AITUC) opened its first session at the Empire Theatre, Bombay, on Sunday, 31 October 1920. The theatre, as was reported later, 'was crowded to the utmost capacity by delegates and visitors'. The delegates came from different parts of the country and represented practically all branches of labour in India. Among those present, besides the president and the chairman of the reception committee, were Annie Besant, M.A. Jinnah and Motilal Nehru. The proceedings commenced with the singing of labour songs after which Joseph Baptista (1864–1930), or Kaka Baptista as he was called, one of the founders of the AITUC and mayor of Bombay in 1925-26, made a speech welcoming the delegates to the session.

Brothers and Sisters, Delegates, the high honour of welcoming you to the First All-India Trade Union Congress devolves upon me and I welcome you with feelings of much pleasure and pride. I can assure you that the originators of the idea of this congress, Mr. Chaman Lall and Mr. Pawar, and their collaborators have all been working with edifying energy and enthusiasm. Nevertheless, I anticipate that some of you will be subjected to discomfort and inconvenience. I must, therefore, request you to forgive our faults and overlook our shortcomings, and I am confident you will respond with customary oriental indulgence.

Sowing the Seed

The agenda of business is not formidable, but the chief business of this congress will be to sow the seed, which like the proverbial mustard will germinate and grow into the mighty tree of the Federation of Labour in India, which we all desire. To nurse and water the seedling and sapling will be a labour of love for the Knights of Labour in India but their reward will be sweet. The supreme need of the moment is really for some light from the east to illumine the darkness of the west; for the humanising spiritualism of the east to chasten the brutalising materialism of the west. I believe we can achieve this object by the power and principles of organised labour in India. Among labourers, I include the hewer of wood and drawer of water and the tiller in the fields. These too ought to be the chief objects of solicitude for the state. This has never been denied in theory by any government, ancient or modern, but it has never been enforced in practice by the governing classes.

The Via Dolorosa for the labourer has been slavery, serfdom, or indentures or statutes of labour, combination laws and similar beds of roses. The emancipation of labour from this oppressive system is not yet fully attained as our own people are experiencing in some parts of the world Christian governments. But even where there are no indenture conditions or combination laws, labour is dominated by capital. Capitalists have ceased to buy slaves, but they still buy labour, and pay for it according to the eternal and infernal law of demand and supply. This idea of buying is the root of the evil. Till it is eradicated and supplanted by the higher idea of partnership the well-being of the workers will never be secured. They are partners and co-workers and not buyers and sellers of labour. They are all engaged in promoting the well-being of the society. Capital does not buy or employ labour. Society is the ideal we must strive to achieve... Without the political power of the purse and the lawmaker we cannot go far, but we can go a good way towards the goal by the power of union, strikes and boycotts.

~

LALA LAJPAT RAI

Presidential Address, AITUC, 1920

Lala Lajpat Rai was elected the first president of the All-India Trade Union Congress in 1920. The labour leader B.P. Wadia proposed the election of Lala Lajpat Rai to the presidential chair. The father of labour unionism in western India, N.M. Joshi, seconded the resolution and said that Lala Lajpat Rai was the fittest man to be president and would be able to 'lay the solid foundation of this and allied movements'. Mr Miller of the North Western Railways and Diwan Chaman Lal further supported the resolution. Chaman Lal commented that 'the Lala had been asked to preside over the first session...not simply because he was an eminent leader of public opinion...or because he had the high distinction of being an ex-president of the Indian National Congress, but principally because he was the heart and soul of the cause of the working classes of this country'. A workmen's delegate further supported the resolution, and the whole assembly stood and cheered. Joseph Baptista then garlanded Lala Lajpat Rai amid renewed cheering. This is an extract from the presidential speech delivered by Lala Lajpat Rai on the occasion.

Mr. Baptista, Ladies and Gentlemen, permit me to thank you from the bottom of my heart for the honour you have done me by asking me to preside over the first session of the All-India Trade Union Congress.

It is a unique occasion, the first of its kind even in the history of this ancient country of ours. In her long history extending over thousands of years, India has surely seen many a great gathering in which parts of this vast subcontinent and all classes of its population were represented, gatherings at which were discussed and settled important and nice questions of religion, philosophy, grammar, law and politics, gatherings in which foreign scholars and foreign ambassadors and foreign diplomats took part. But history records no instance of an assemblage that was convened solely to consider the interests and welfare of workers not of this city or that, not of this province or that, but of Bharatvarsha as a whole.

Even under British rule we have had all-India gatherings of various kinds, political, religious, social, literary, scientific, etc., etc., but never an all-India meeting of the workers of the country or one where people assembled to consider the interests and the present and future welfare of the workers as such. This by itself should show, if there was nothing else to remind us of the fact, that the India of today is very different from the India of ancient and medieval times, nay even from the India of yesterday. We are living in an age quite different from anything that the world has seen or known before. That being so, the problems that face and the questions that confront us are from the very nature of things of a different kind from those that confronted our immediate and remote ancestors. This fact, whether we like it or not, has to be recognised.

National Isolation Impossible

Then there is another fact also which receives scant attention from those who profess to guide the destinies of this great nation, namely that we are living in times in which no nation can live an isolated life of its own. Whatever happens in the world outside of our shores affects us in our daily life very closely and intimately. It makes our food dearer, our clothing more costly, our possession more or less valuable and similarly affects other relations of life very deeply. In the same way whatever happens in our country affects the outside world also equally deeply and intimately. This is not limited to any single sphere of life but is virtually true of almost all spheres, but particularly so of the political and economic. So whether we like it or not, we are a part and parcel of the modern world.

This modern world is characteristically a world of machinery, of steam, gas and electricity. This is a world of mass production, of organised capital, organised industry and organised labour. Organised mass production involves the organisation of capital and the organisation of labour on a scale never heard of before. So far, organised capital had its way. It has ruled the world for the last 150 years, and the world today is groaning under its burden. It has destroyed many an old civilisation, enslaved religion, chained science and placed in bondage all the forces of nature and human intellect. Humanity is its bond slave.

Old China with its four to five hundred millions of industrious, hard-working and art-loving people, with its ancient culture, science and art, has been broken on the wheel and thrown to the wolves. India with its hoary civilisation, its mighty spiritualism, its great philosophy and its beautiful art, with a family consisting a one-fifth of the whole human race, has also been bled white by the forces of organised capital and is today lying prostrate at its feet. Militarism and imperialism are the twin children of capitalism; they are one in three and three in one. Their shadow, their fruit and their bark, all are poisonous. It is only lately that an antidote has been discovered and that antidote is organised labour.

India's Economic Bondage

We in India have been rather slow to find and apply this antidote. The reasons are obvious. We are politically impotent and economically helpless. Our political impotence has made us a nation of pariahs in relation to the rest of the world. Our masters used us to conquer and police the world for their benefit and glorification. They also used us to develop their colonies, cultivate their fields, operate their mines, man their industries, and increase their wealth. By way of adding insult to injury they maligned our religion, caricatured and painted us so black as to be considered unfit for being accepted as equals or even as men by the so-called civilised races of the world.

In the eyes of the latter, we are a nation of coolies, inferior in everything that distinguishes a mere animal from man. This was a trick by which organised British capital managed to create a prejudice against us in the minds of the white workers of Europe, America and Africa. It was necessary for their purpose. Any bond of brotherhood or of mutual interest between the workers of Europe and America, on the one hand and those of Asia on the other would have destroyed the spell by the force of which they exploited and sweated both. To the workers of Manchester was always presented the bugbear of the cheap labour of India. We in India were kept in fear of the competition of Manchester.

The war however has broken the spell. The workers of Europe and America have now discovered that the cause of the workers is one and the same all the world over, and that there can be no salvation for them unless and until the workers of Asia were organised, and internationally affiliate labour in Europe threatens to turn the tables against their masters, the employers, and they recognise that the success of their movement demands a close association of European workers with the workers of Asia.

So long as there is cheap labour in China and India, and so long as India is helpless to keep out foreign capital and to prevent the latter using Indian and Chinese labour to the detriment of the European workers, the cause of the European proletariat is neither safe nor secure. The movement we are inaugurating today is thus of more than national importance. It is a matter of international significance.

The workers of India are joining hands and brains not only to solidify the interest of Indian labour, but also to forge a link in the chain of international brotherhood. The future is on the laps of god and prophecy is unsafe but it may be safely predicted that the success of the movement to which we are giving birth today may eventually turn out to be an event of world importance.

Not at the Expense of Labour

If the development of the Indian industries requires the organisation of Indian capital, it still more requires the organisation of Indian labour. Labour and capital must meet on equal ground and join hands to develop Indian industries. As at present neither the government nor the capitalist is disposed to treat the worker fairly and equally. The former sacrifices him at the altar of princely salaries to a higher rank of the European...and also for the exigencies of militarism. The capitalist wants to sweat him for his hundred or two hundred per cent profit. Surely, that is not the way to develop Indian industries if it is to be done at the expense of labour alone.

I maintain, therefore, that it has become absolutely necessary for Indian labour to organise itself on national lines in order to be able to negotiate with their employers on equal terms and with due regard to national interests. I refuse to admit that the interests of Indian industries must in every case override the human needs of workers.

In all discussion about the demands and rights of labour in India labour is still treated as a commodity to be sold and purchased in open market. In every discussion it is the interests of industry that are held supreme. The question asked is: 'Will the industry bear it?' The proper question in my judgment should be: 'How can the industry be made to bear it consistently with the minimum human requirements of the worker and his family, on the standard of a moderately comfortable healthy life for him and his children, a provision for the education of the latter and for the rainy day?'

If however Indian capital wants to ignore the needs of labour and can think only of its huge profits, it should expect no response from labour and no sympathy from the general public. If labour must remain half-starved, ill-clothed, badly housed, and destitute of education, it can possibly have no interest in the development of Indian industries, and appeals in the name of patriotism must fail.

On these grounds and several others it is desirable that Indian labour should lose no time to organise itself on a national scale. Capital is organised on a worldwide basis; it is backed up by a financial and political strength beyond conception; its weapons are less perishable than those employed by labour; it presents dangers which apply universally. In order to meet these dangers Indian labour will have to join hands with labour outside India also, but its first duty is to organise itself at home.

The most important business then before this congress is to bring into existence a central organisation which would protect the interests of labour all over India. The organisation cannot be perfected without bringing all the unions in India into its orbit of influence. But a beginning can certainly be made with as many organisations as are willing to join hands at once. Those who are pioneers must exercise patience, tolerate criticism and show readiness to subordinate individual opinions and predilections to the interests of the general body of workers in such a way as to convince those that are hesitating and faltering of their sincerity and earnestness.

It is easy to criticise, it is sometimes convenient to stay out till the pioneers have cleared the field and borne the brunt of opposition.... But it is neither manly nor patriotic to do so. Anyway, the pioneers must proceed in a spirit of brotherhood working in the interests of all, and always willing to share the gains with all.

PARVATHI KRISHNAN

Industrial Disputes (Amendment and Miscellaneous Provisions) Bill, 1956

Parvathi Krishnan, daughter of a legendary Congress leader of Madras Dr P. Subbarayan and wife of communist leader N. Krishnan, was a very popular and articulate member of Parliament. On 9 August 1956, Parvathi spoke in the Rajya Sabha, linking the industrial dispute resolution mechanism to the newly evolved Second Five Year Plan and the idea of a socialist pattern of society. The speech gives the reader a glimpse of the goal the leaders of the era envisaged when they spoke of a 'progressive socialistic pattern of society'.

Mr. Deputy Chairman, Sir, as I see it and as a few speakers have also mentioned, we have to view this Bill in the background of its being within the framework of the Second Five Year Plan. All the time there has been reference to the fact that for the successful implementation of the Plan this, that and the other has to be done, and so forth. Sir, what do we mean by the Second Five Year Plan? I mean, what does it express by itself, as it has been put before the people of this country? The Second Five Year Plan is supposed to aim towards more rapid industrialisation, increased production and the economic and social progress of free India. If these are the aims of the Second Five Year Plan, if these aims and objects are to be achieved, then indeed it is really very important that industrial relations should be given very serious consideration. Because, Sir, in a period of industrial advance, in a period of building up a nation's economy, certainly, industrial relations will play a very, very important role.

Therefore, Sir, one would have expected from this Bill a basis for improvement in relations between employers and employees, and I must say that it is a sad disappointment that great limitations are being placed by this Bill rather than the path being opened up for an improvement in such relations. Certainly, there are advantages. One cannot offhand or outright say that this Bill is an employers' Bill or a workers' Bill or a Government Bill—whatever it is. As I see it, there are certain advantages and one has to welcome those advantages. For instance, the extending of the definition of 'workman'; it does not go far enough, but something is there. Secondly, the provision that notice of change in Standing Orders will have to be given to workmen. The principle of voluntary arbitration being accepted, the principle that the worker should also have the right to move the certifying officer for a change in Standing Orders, the abolition of the Appellate Tribunal and a very hesitant and a very timid step towards speeding up the working of the dispute machinery—these are all very welcome aspects of the Bill. But, at the same time, Sir, I would like to draw the attention of the House to the fact that serious drawbacks continue to exist, and certain very essential safeguards for the workers have been removed. I will come to the removal of these safeguards later.

The fundamental basis for industrial peace I would like to point out is the acceptance and the active implementation of the principle of collective bargaining and agreements. So long as that principle is not guaranteed by the provision of a bill like this, no attempt, no good feeling either on the part of the Government or the so-called 'enlightened' employer, or on the part of the working class is going to help. In my opinion, Sir, any Government or any party that claims to strive for a socialist society must recognise that if workers are to play their part in building a new society they must be given the necessary prerequisites as every other section of society.

However, in the light of the socialist pattern of society, within which setting the Second Five Year Plan has been framed, suitable alterations in labour policy require to be made. A socialist society is built up not solely on monetary incentives, but on ideas of service to society and the willingness on the part of the latter to recognise such service. The creation of industrial democracy, therefore, is a prerequisite to the establishment of a socialist society.

Are we going forward, in however hesitant a manner, towards creating the prerequisites for the creation of an industrial democracy? It is by this yardstick that I would request all Members of the House to measure this Bill, including the honourable Deputy Minister himself. Because I notice how carefully, while waxing eloquent about the Second Five Year Plan, while waxing eloquent over how the workers will have to be 'responsible', must not be 'undisciplined' and how the employers also will be 'brought to book', waxing eloquent on all these subjects, he remained singularly and significantly silent on the question of industrial democracy. It is an easily forgotten matter and I would like to draw the attention of all Members of the House to that very central point which is very, very important if the Second Five Year Plan is to have any meaning whatsoever to the people of our country.

Now, Sir, industrial democracy can only grow if there is a strong trade union movement, speaking from the angle of the working class. In our country today, this is not the case. We do not have a strong organised trade union movement; a vast majority of the workers in our country continues to be unorganised. If the trade union movement is to grow, is to become a strong force and play its full and essential role in society; if indeed industrial democracy is to grow and the future of industrial democracy is to be assured; if that is to happen, Sir, we come back to the basic principle of collective bargaining and we come back to the necessity for the guarantees of that principle being put into practice.

Sir, I would like to point out that collective bargaining is very closely linked with the principle of recognition of the trade union. What exactly is the role of the trade union? As I see it, on the one hand it is the task of the trade union to safeguard the interests of the employees and to uphold them and also to fight and strive for further safeguards for better and better conditions for the workers. On the other hand—and this is where the dual role of the trade union comes in—it is also incumbent on the trade unions to make their workers conscious of their duty towards society, of fulfilling their obligations towards the task of building the nation, towards the task of contributing to the economic and industrial progress of the country and of the people. Since the passing of the Industrial Disputes Act in 1947 what has really happened in the absence of the principle of recognition of trade unions being implemented? What has happened is that the workers are being asked to become lawyers; they are being asked to become litigation-minded; they are being asked to school themselves into the role of public prosecutors and assistant public prosecutors and so on. Or on the other hand you will find that many outsiders who come into the trade union are not brought in because of their qualifications as a result of serving the people or serving the working class or doing any work with regard to social welfare, but because of their legal qualifications. The ability to argue this or that point, the interpretation of what is dependent and what is independent and so on—becomes the necessary qualification for a trade union leader. He may or may not be qualified to serve the interests of the working class and to help in the building up of an organised trade union movement which will play its part in society and which will play its part in helping to better industrial relation. This is what has happened.

The workers have become litigation-minded. Why is it so? Because when trade unions, even with a membership of the vast majority of workers, go forward to meet management, go forward to place their demands in order to discuss them with the management, the management does not want to meet them. Obviously, it is very easy to understand why. Here Sir, I am talking particularly of the bigger employers including the Government. And, as a result, one has to go to the Government which sometimes may be wise, sometimes may be otherwise, and the Government may or may not refer the dispute to a tribunal. And months and years go by while all the ramifications and somersaults and the legal implications are gone into and meanwhile the trade union goes its own way, the management goes its own way and here we sit in Parliament and pass legislation that is supposed to further help matters.

Now, Sir, I come to the most controversial clause, and that is the amendment to section 33. It is indeed amazing that this amendment should be brought in when we are on the threshold of the Second Five

Year Plan. That is the protection, Sir, that the worker has had against any unfair action. It has always been open to the employers to take action against the workers, with permission from the court even when a dispute was before a tribunal. Now, Sir, we are told that there is the new class of protected workmen and that after all in the building of a socialist pattern of society—emphasis on pattern, socialist pattern of society—it is necessary to see that other interests are also protected, etc. etc. And then we are told of the indiscipline of workers, indiscipline of so and so, indiscipline all round, and that the employers, after all the poor, suffering, starving employers, will have to be safeguarded so that they can also put in their bit in building the new India, and that section 33 was really preventing the employers from pulling their complete weight in the First Five Year Plan, 'let us guarantee them at least now so that they will do their best to cooperate'. This seems to be the strange logic. Then it is said, 'the Standing Orders are there, and only within the Standing Orders action can be taken against workers, and after that approval has got to be got from the Court; therefore why worry?' Firstly, one must remember that the Standing Orders apply to those factories, those establishments which employ a hundred or more workers, and in our country there are certainly a large number of workers that belong to establishments that have smaller number—for instance, the small workshops, match factories, etc. where there are much less than a hundred workers. How the Standing Orders will help them I do not understand.

Secondly, Sir, we are told, that the employers must have some safeguard. It seems to me, Sir, that the Government, wedded to the principle of compensation, imagining that the rest is all going against the employer, feel 'why not give the employer something'. As far as section 33 is concerned most blatantly in the Statement of Objects and Reasons, it is said that 'Employers have complained that they are prevented from taking action even in obvious cases of misconduct and indiscipline unconnected with the dispute till long after the offence has been committed'. Well, Sir, if this is the only argument that can be brought forward, all I can say is that workers are also complaining that they are unable to take action against 'undisciplined' employers who may be taking advantage of a dispute being there before the tribunal. (Laughter.) Sir, I hear laughter. That, of course, comes from certain sections. I can, of course, guess the sections from where it comes.

I am glad it is evident to others, but I was not sure. Apparently, all I was saying so far seems to have rung a bell in certain quarters. To take away the protection that is being given to the workman by section 33, all these arguments are used, and it is amazing what acrobatics the defenders of this amendment have to go through. If you say that this right is being taken away without laying the rest of the cards on the table—that is, victimisation of active trade unionists being made possible—then you are told, 'Oh, but it was only a notional right that the worker had, because after all the employers used to sack the people and, then go to the court, and then the case went on. Now we are speeding up legislation. Therefore, it won't be so bad', etc. etc. When you point out, Sir, that there are positive cases, where trade union workers, where among the more conscious sections, the working class have been protected by section 33, you are told that there are cases of indiscipline also. 'There are those guilty of theft, guilty of rudeness to employers'; you say that they are responsible trade union workers but the employers say that they are undisciplined. Well, Sir, in such cases in industrial establishments action can be taken under the Criminal Procedure Code, and there are other laws. Why section 33 has to be done away with in order to enable the employer to take action against antisocial elements I fail to understand.

Then, Sir, there is another thing about the matters unconnected with the dispute before the tribunal. Now this is a very dangerous thing, because maybe the dispute is about bonus, maybe the dispute is about wages, maybe the matter unconnected happens to be rationalisation, or maybe the matter unconnected happens to be retrenchment of a large number of workers. In a country that is full of the interpretation of law, there is always the danger of further and further interpretation. Therefore, it is very necessary to give a categorical protection to the workmen against any vindictive action on the part of the employers, and on the part of the management. This is why, Sir, we oppose this amendment of section 33 and demand that the protection that the workmen had till now should continue. The workman also should know that there is the possibility for him to stand up for his rights, when the occasion demands it. These are the main points that I would like to bring to the notice of this honourable House.

Then, Sir, there is one more point, and that is with regard to clause 31. Clause 31 on page 21 reads as follows: 'If, immediately before the commencement of this Act, there is in force in any State any provincial Act or State Act relating to the settlement or adjudication of disputes, the operation of such an Act in that State in relation to matters covered by that Act shall not be affected by the Industrial Disputes Act, 1947 as amended by this Act.'

Now, Sir, this is a very blanket clause and it is fraught with danger. Perhaps Sir, one of the Acts it refers to may be the Bombay Industrial Relations Act, and that is sacrosanct and will not be touched by the Government. So, if they want to mention a particular Act, let it be mentioned specifically. If you have a clause of this type, there are other States which are affected. I am told, Sir, that in UP for instance, the working journalists have been told that the Working Journalists Act that has been passed by Parliament cannot come into operation there and there are various Acts already existing in that State which are quoted in order to deny to the working journalists the rights that have been conferred on them. Therefore, Sir, I have got great apprehensions about this particular clause, and I would suggest to the honourable Minister that if he has any particular legislation in mind, let that legislation be mentioned specifically, and the matter can be considered by the House. But this overall and blanket sort of exemption that is given is certainly one that cannot be accepted without being looked into very carefully.

Finally, Sir, I would just like to deal with this phrase 'enlightened employer'... It is so difficult, Sir, in our country to find an 'enlightened' employer. Certainly, there are the smaller employers, those who are struggling against the stream of big monopolistic business that is trying to squeeze them out of existence. There are, no doubt, some smaller employers with whom the trade unions are on the best of terms and who, certainly, listen to the voice of the workers and who, with their limited financial resources, Sir, try to give a more sympathetic hearing to the workers. They also attempt to give better condition wherever possible. Now, Sir, my question is: Who is this 'enlightened' employer? In Valparai, in the Annamalais where there are a large number of tea estates, who are responsible for flouting every single bit of legislation, for flouting any conciliation or agreement that is signed, for flouting any award that is given by any tribunal? There is one particular estate, the Sholayar Estate, and I am sure everyone is aware as to who is this 'enlightened' employer who is the owner of that estate. That estate belongs to the big Birla group of estates. That is the example of an 'enlightened' employer. The owner of that estate fiddles with his registers of those workers who have been there as permanent employees for a number of years under the management, from whom this estate was bought over; and he converts them into temporary employees so that he can save something in the matter of maternity benefit, in the matter of casual leave and in the matter of all those amenities which are guaranteed by law to the working class of his country. These are the 'enlightened' employers, on behalf of whom we have last heard from one spokesman. With all the sentiments that are being expressed with regard to the Second Five Year Plan and with all the sentiments that are being expressed time and again as to the welfare of the toiling sections in this country, we have had the statements made here about the non-existent enlightened employers. I could understand if the spokesmen of smaller employers were here who would demand and receive the cooperation of the working class and of the toiling sections in order to make their industry or their concern stable. I could understand that, Sir. But it really leaves a very bad taste in the mouth—to use that hackneyed phrase—when some of our friends talk about the enlightened employer who will have to pass the burden of the expenses of his industry on to the consumer, because after all he must have that extra money to pay for his palatial house, that extra money to pay for his new Cadillac and that extra money to pay for the air-conditioning plant in his house. When we talk of better industrial relations, certainly, this is not the enlightened employer to whom we refer. But this is the enlightened employer who has been responsible for the deaths of workers in the mines of Parasia and in the mines of Amlabad, and who is not prepared to take those safety precautions that are enjoined upon him by the law of the land. He is simply there to have his huge profits. It is not only the consumer who has to pay, but it is also the worker who pays with his sweated labour and with his life. Therefore, Sir, it is not a question whether this is a Bill for the enlightened employers, whether this is a Bill for the small employers. But this is a Bill, Sir, which does not fulfil the principles of industrial democracy, does not fulfil those principles which are necessarily to be accepted and implemented, if the people of this country and if the working class and all other sections of the masses are to pull their weight unitedly and with all their support and all their enthusiasm for taking the country forward in the coming few years.

~

SRIPAD AMRIT DANGE

Second Pay Commission, 1957

A prominent labour leader, particularly of workers in Bombay whom he organized in the 1920s, S.A. Dange was a powerful speaker whose erudition and first-hand knowledge of the conditions of workers in India made him one of the finest communist leaders of the country. Since the 1930s there had been demands to raise the wages of workers in keeping with the increase in production as well prices of commodities. In 1950, Sucheta Kripalani, Satya Priya Bannerjee and others raised the issue of appointing a pay commission to look into the matters of wages, productivity and price indices comprehensively and periodically to ensure that workers derived some benefits from the growth of the economy. The Second Pay Commission set up in August 1957 was the first such commission in independent India (the First Pay Commission had been set up in May 1946 and had submitted its report a year later). This speech in the Lok Sabha on 19 July 1957 on the Second Pay Commission is worth reading for its attempt to link industrial production to the living standard of the wage-earning class.

Sir, the subject that is before us is quite serious, not because threats of strikes are held or counter-threats of suppressing them are given; because, threats on either side, either of carrying out strikes or suppressing strikes, do not lead us anywhere. After all, there are two parties to the whole question; one is the working class which makes the demand, and the other is the employing class—either the State or the private sector.

... It is already admitted that production is increasing; nobody denies it. It is admitted we are working hard; nobody denies that. The question is, where should the increased production go. It is admitted that part of it must go into greater investments. We do not deny that. But it is also admitted in the Plan that the disparities in income should be reduced as the Plan proceeds and production grows. This is exactly the demand for the Pay Commission. The disparities in income, even in the context of growing production still remain. They should go.

Now, what is socialism if it is not raising real wages? I am not talking of money wages, nor would you permit me to go into discussions of how wages are reflected in prices. But let me submit that it is a wrong theory in economics to say that higher wages always lead to higher prices. This theory has been blown up even in capitalist economies, let alone socialist economies. Wages are the central point around which prices revolve. But prices are not in every section made by wages. Otherwise you would not have such a category as is called monopoly wages. Monopoly wages run away from the wage structure and have nothing to do with wage structure. It is a well-known phenomenon in economics throughout the world that, for example, the prices of manufactured goods and prices of raw materials fluctuate differently and the prices of manufactured goods are controlled by manufacturers irrespective of the wage claims. This is already admitted. Therefore, I would not go into economic theory here, because it is a wrong theory to tell the working class or the community that price, at all times, in all its quantum, is always governed by the quantum of wages. The quantum of wages has nothing to do with the quantum of prices, because prices are a market phenomenon while wages are a production phenomenon. Therefore, I should not go into it, and our Prime Minister would not like to be bothered with the theory of it. But I certainly would like to contradict, if he permits, the statement that wages have nothing to do with the socialist pattern. What we are saying in the resolution is simply this that socialist pattern should not mean falling living standards at least. If you cannot satisfy the demands for some time and if you say do not ask for a higher and rising standard until I complete a certain stage of production that is a reasonable demand. I can understand it. But you should at least guarantee to me a standard which is not a falling standard of living.

But here what are we getting? Prices are rising up while wages are pegged, salaries are pegged. Therefore, what is happening is that real wages are falling. Where annual bonus is obtainable in factories, there alone we are able to get a certain level of real wages in proportion to certain level of productivity. But with regard to government servants there is no question of a link up of process and dearness allowance. Therefore, our submission is that even in a socialist pattern the question of wages is the most important because in a socialist pattern wages is the form of income and is in fact the only income. I would therefore say that if you accept socialist pattern please remember that falling standards at least have to be stopped.

If prices are pegged, I can understand. Stop prices from rising. But with every taxation measure or even without taxation, prices are jumping up. What is the poor man to do? He is pegged up at Rs. 30 plus dearness allowance with a rising scale up to Rs. 35 after ten years. In this country let us do away with the medieval pay structure of thirty or sometimes even twenty-five rupees at the lowest rung and higher pay scales of three or five thousand rupees with allowances and so on and so forth. Should there not be a Pay Commission to judge not only the salaries of government servants but including the whole administrative structure, instead of simply having good words about voluntary cuts? If ten per cent is cut from two thousand rupees it comes to Rs. 200 no doubt. But ten per cent cut from thirty rupees would be a bad blow for the man who is getting a low wage. Therefore voluntary cut is no good. If people were to propose a rationalisation of the whole cost structure including even the MPs then for persons getting above a thousand rupees there should be cut of thirty or forty per cent, those getting between five hundred and thousand rupees should get something less and those who are getting below five hundred should have no cut but they should get a rise. If such a system of arriving at wages is come to, then our Finance Minister will surely find that the saving is enough to meet at least a part of the rise that is claimed by the government servants in the lower categories.

Therefore, the first point is let us not discuss abstract economics. But abstract economics is affecting real life. There I deny the theory that wages in every place determine the quantum of prices and therefore a rise in wages will always lead to a rise in prices. Even in the history of countries with capitalist economies we have found that a very big rise in wages has led actually to a fall in prices many a time. This is recorded in economic literature, and our Finance Minister certainly knows about it. There is no such theory which is valid in capitalist economy and certainly not in socialist economy.

With regard to the question of politics being involved in this, I can say on behalf of my party that we do not approach this question from the point of view of politics at all. Because our main question is would you hold the price line for us? If you give me thirty rupees and rice is selling at two rupees, please hold it at two rupees. But you cannot hold, you have admitted your inability to hold. You cannot hold the profit line.

There was a progressive manufacturer who proposed in another conference that prices be frozen, wages be frozen and dividends be frozen. Only after dividends he added the words at current level. The banks are paying dividends at the rate of 30 per cent. Plantations are paying dividends at the rate of 40 per cent or 50 per cent. And he wants freezing of dividends at the current level, prices to be frozen at the current level and wages also to be frozen at the current level—very impartial community thinking. This is an impartial thinking which leads to an impartial starvation of the fixed wage earner. Surely this is not the way of thinking. I am not referring to any Minister having said that. I am speaking about some manufacturer who made a plea like that.

... Our only request is, please look at the human side of the whole thing. You are thinking of building up a plant; production is going to be planned. I say there is the human side also along with that. There are engines of iron and steel, you must have them; but there is also the human side in the scheme. That means he must get rice, house, clothing etc. You only want to determine the standards of coal for the engine. In that case the engine may probably start running; it cannot run continuously if my human engine fails. I only request that human values be imported into the whole consideration and politics be set aside. The human value should be translated very simply in terms of a Pay Commission. I do not think that everything should be admitted. But enquire with a precondition that the climate of higher production does require, the climate of higher prices does require higher wages. That should be the precondition of understanding of the work of the Commission.

The relief should not be merely in some small field say education. But supposing 10,000 employees have not got children to be educated, what is the use of that benefit? His rice will cost as much as before; in fact more. The educational concession is not going to give him any relief in the rice, wheat or house. Therefore the proposal to give only small benefits is not correct. It may give you satisfaction that in any case we have carried our point and we have not given Pay Commission. Call it a Pay Committee call it an Ad hoc Committee, call it a non-Ad hoc Committee, call it an unorthodox committee—I am not worried with the name provided it functions openly, enquires correctly and judges properly.

But I would say some interim relief would be necessary. Or give some rice, wheat, cloth at exact price which neutralise the rise in cost of living to a large extent. Do not give me money. I do not mind that. Of course that would be reverting back to the medieval system of wages. But, if today under present condition it is necessary, let us do it. In the war days when dearness allowance could not be given in money, it was given in terms of rice, wheat or cloth. Please give like that. But neutralise the rising cost of living and make them live a little better. At least stop the standard of living from falling. We are not even asking for any rise in standard of living immediately; at least stop the fall in standards. If that is not done, then what can I say. I am not here to give threats or anything of that sort. We have not got the power to give threats because it is the trade unions that have to decide and certainly, the trade unions want to decide in a way that compromise and settlement is arrived at. I can assure on behalf of our party that we want settlement, we want understanding, we want the Plan to go ahead but we won't do it on the basis of starving the government employees, whether high or low, whether drawing Rs. 1,000 or drawing Rs. 20.

When production is increasing it is my right that a part of it must come to me in the form of a higher wage, a higher real wage. Therefore the demand for wages is not against the rising needs of productivity, it is not against the economy. Now they are talking about inflation. We cannot go into the whole theory now. In fact, I should have proposed that some of the Ministers who are interested in it and the Opposition Members should once for all thrash it—this whole question as to what is inflation, what is wages, what determines prices etc. Let us sit down and arrive at a concrete understanding on this question.

Then there is the habit of suggesting that higher wages will lead to higher prices and there will be inflation and then again you will lose wages. Somebody says, No. Let us have some understanding, therefore, if possible by a joint discussion on this question also. I would suggest a committee to determine this question so far as this House is concerned to guide us properly on questions of economy. Because economy is not such a small thing like the days of old when you can take a packet of wheat to the neighbour chamar and buy a pair of shoes and walk away. It is not merely village economy. International standards and international prices and production and many other things now enter into the economy. Therefore, economy has become a complicated thing. Therefore, let us not be taken in by slogans. I am sure if the Finance Minister wants he can find the money without inflation. The only trouble is whether he wants it or not. If he wants it he can find the money. He can, I am sure, find that without even having a threat of inflation. It is not that always inflation leads to higher prices. I think he knows it because if he can hold the price line whatever the amount of inflation, the price will not rise and the cost of living will come down. Therefore, it is not an automatic relation that increase in money quantum necessarily leads to inflationary rise in prices...

17

STATE OF THE NATION—II

With the onset of the 1970s, a deep contest over the way Indians perceived themselves vis-à-vis their fellow countrymen began to colour the boundaries of politics, culture and sensibilities. Within the framework of a broad agreement over the secular, socialistic arrangement and a democratic polity, there were discordant voices. In marked contrast to the vision of the earliest nationalists, who argued for India as one nation and Indians as one people, a different conception of nation-making emerged in the 1970s which argued that language or religion or other such parochial loyalties should form the basis for nation formation. Pakistan was held up as an example by those who either supported or opposed such claims. Political formations articulating such ideas, which had remained dormant for close to two decades, began to surface by the mid-1960s once the euphoria of a newly independent nation had worn off. Large-scale communal riots, the result of the ideas spread by such political formations, erupted. As the birth centenary of Mahatma Gandhi approached, the country witnessed intense communal propaganda and ironically, Gujarat, his birthplace, was a site for the expression of such politics of hatred. It was a humiliating sight that one of Gandhi's greatest disciples, Khan Abdul Ghaffar Khan, who had come to India from across the border as a special guest for the centenary celebrations, had to witness such a calamitous situation. He had to remind Indians of Gandhi's principles and urge the people to put some of them into practice.

The violence and gradual decline in the moral order had its

implications on the polity in the 1970s. Radical steps like bank nationalization, abolition of privy purses and other pro-poor rhetoric created a mood of euphoria in the first couple of years of the decade. This, coupled with the heady feeling of victory over Pakistan in the 1971 war which resulted in the creation of Bangladesh, rallied the entire nation behind the leadership of Indira Gandhi. However, the euphoria began to wane soon enough with mounting unemployment, rising prices and increasing corruption of an insensitive bureaucracy. The quality of leadership, particularly within the Congress, too began to decline. Initially, these had a greater impact on the states than at the centre. Bombay witnessed the first spark of urban agitation against the state of affairs with urban middle-class women coming out to protest against the rise in prices. Gujarat was next on the list. Here it was students who began an agitation against the reservation policies of the government which soon evolved into the Nav Nirman movement targetting corruption of the political leadership. The Nav Nirman movement spread to Bihar where students came out in huge numbers under the leadership of Jayaprakash Narayan. Jayaprakash called for a 'sampoorna kranti' (total revolution), urging the police and army not to obey any order they deemed unconstitutional and immoral, leading to the imposition of Emergency on 26 June 1975.

Seen as progressive and charismatic not long ago, Indira Gandhi suddenly became the major target of the middle-class youth, the intelligentsia and the literati. The Nav Nirman movement which began by articulating specific student grievances grew into a strong anti-establishment movement whose initial anti-corruption social and economic vision became increasingly clouded by a virulent anti-Congress and anti-Indira Gandhi rage. In a society where politics is an essential part of life, Indira Gandhi began to symbolize the root of the decline of the moral world of Indian politics. This image was bolstered by an extremely personalized campaign sponsored by communal forces like the Rashtriya Swayamsevak Sangh (RSS). The viciousness of the campaign was one of the reasons cited by Indira Gandhi for imposing the Emergency.

The Emergency remains an interesting question about the limits to which a democracy can allow mass movements against itself. It needs to be remembered that the movement against the Emergency was dictated by organizations like the RSS which were not democratic in their set-up. At the same time, Jayaprakash Narayan's idea of a party-less democracy failed to lead to a stronger parliamentary system.

After the Emergency, India was a different nation. The history of independent India can be neatly divided into two parts, pre- and post-Emergency. The nation would never be the same again. The greatest negative consequence of the Emergency was the cavalier way institutions were treated. Higher educational institutions, institutions of parliamentary democracy, the judicial system and administration were all affected. This would prove disastrous for the nation's efforts at becoming a progressive society through an institutional setting rather than through political intervention from outside. Communal organizations also had a vested interest in the collapse of institutions of higher learning, universities and advanced study centres. By the 1990s, the country could hardly boast of any institution of excellence, an absence which would be deeply felt during one of the most violent eras of the Indian state.

Another equally disturbing fallout of the Emergency, one that would have violent repercussions during the next two decades, was that the communal forces which Indira Gandhi said she was quelling through the Emergency in fact got legitimized by virtue of having been part of the anti-Emergency movement. They could now project the Emergency as a major event and their role in opposing it akin to participating in the national movement for freedom in which their role was rather insignificant. Communal demands of every shade, which contested the broadly agreed ideas of the freedom movement (that of a secular democratic polity with justice and equality being the primary goals), began to be aggressively articulated. And these communal forums, while standing in opposition to each other, strengthened and legitimized each other.

The Akali Dal, which had earlier led the Punjabi Suba movement, was now heard talking about discrimination against the Sikhs. Muslim communal groups began talking abut Muslim votes, reservations, special status and such like. To cap them all were the Hindu communal arguments on Article 370 for Jammu and Kashmir, appeasement of Muslims and a uniform civil code. The ideological drive was soon to be matched by political mobilization which not only upped the rhetoric but also organized the polity along parochial lines which would take Indian society to the brink.

The Sikh communal rhetoric began to take shape in the form of a demand for a separate homeland called Khalistan. By the 1980s, the militant form of the demand transcended the liberal demands for autonomy or special provisions for Sikhs. The demand for a Sikh state also meant creation of a Sikh identity separate from Hindu Punjabis, and spiralling communal violence began to drive a wedge between Hindus and Sikhs. By 1984, Punjab seemed to be slipping out of control of Indian hands. Backed by support from Pakistan, which was still smarting from the loss of Bangladesh, and Western powers, not to speak of non-resident Sikhs, the Khalistan movement changed the politics and nature of violence.

It was around this time that the first signs of Hindu communal mobilization started to show. The RSS spearheaded a movement to popularize its leaders like K.B. Hedgewar and others. It found a handy tool to spread its ideology in the movement to liberate the Ram temple in Ayodhya which, it claimed, Mughal emperor Babar had razed to build the Babri Masjid. The Ram Janmabhoomi movement of the Hindu right-wing forces, the RSS and its political outfit the Bharatiya Janata Party (BJP), gave Indian politics another language and direction. So strong was the communal polarization that for the first time in the history of independent India, a non-Congress government, led by the BJP, came to power at the centre in 1998.

The 1990s also saw a major change in the economic model of the country. The post-1992 reform era is characterized by a drive to change the economy on the one hand and communal polarization on the other, while a third front emerged articulating the slogan of social justice which tried to polarize society on caste lines.

The effect of all such trends was the emergence of an India completely unrecognizable, seen in the light of the 1940s and 1950s. The innocent ideological striving for nation, society and moral order no longer influenced politics, society and institutions. Violence, based on caste and religion, was the new driving force of society. In 1984, the state stood as a mute spectator for a couple of days while hundreds of Sikhs were killed. Violating the age-old Indian tradition of mutual respect for places of worship, the Babri Masjid was destroyed by a mob of Hindu fanatics, and in Gujarat the state actively encouraged a pogrom against Muslims.

In an atmosphere of increasing intolerance, there are voices of sanity and reason which have kept the ideal of a nation and its secular ethos intact. In the new millennium, these progressive sections, including the common man struggling to make a living, are engaged in a veritable fight for the soul of India. The nation gave ample proof of this as a strong public opinion prevented even the BJP from following a strident communal agenda while in power. The party was voted out in the general elections of 2004 which saw the Congress return to centre stage albeit with its clout considerably reduced. In Sonia Gandhi, the Congress had found a new leader with a pan-Indian appeal which was considerably enhanced with her refusal to accept the post of the prime minister.

~

KHAN ABDUL GHAFFAR KHAN

I Have Come to Serve You

After the orgy of violence witnessed during the partition, India remained free of communal tensions for the next two decades. The presence of leaders of the stature of Jawaharlal Nehru was undoubtedly responsible for this. Despite contentious issues like language and the demands for linguistic reorganization of states, and barring the odd conflagration in the south with regard to Hindi, controversies were largely sorted out amicably without resorting to violence. Things began to change from the mid-1960s. A number of factors—wars, food crisis, political instability—had resulted in a restive society that was straining at the leash. Communal clashes began recurring with alarming frequency, and in 1969, the riots in Gujarat took a vicious turn with indications that they were engineered to coincide with the birth centenary of Mahatma Gandhi. Khan Abdul Ghaffar Khan (1890–1988) or Badshah Khan—also known as the Frontier Gandhi for his non-violent leadership of the tribes in the North West Frontier Province—Gandhi's only living political companion of the independence movement, was the guest of honour during the centenary celebrations. Addressing a gathering at the Ramlila Ground, Delhi, on 2 October 1969, he admonished the people for indulging in violence. He said he had come to India to remind Indians of the teachings of Gandhi.

The purpose of my coming to this country is mainly to emphasise to you Indians that you have departed from the path shown by your leader, Mahatma Gandhi. I have not come to take anything. I have not come to become your leader or your father. I have come to serve you and nobody can deter me from doing this. If you do not accept my services the loss will be yours. I want to offer my services to establish unity, love and affection among the people of various communities.

The only purpose of my coming here was to protest against violence, mutual distrust and hatred. The love and affection of Indian people and the remembrance of Gandhiji have attracted me to come here. Strange stories are circulating in India and Pakistan about the purpose of my visit. I have come to serve you. I have not come to take money from you. I have not even come to ask help for Pakhtoonistan. The type of Pakhtoonistan we wanted we are about to achieve.

Many people suggested to me that I should not go to India and lodge my protest against violence. But I thought if I protest here how will it help India and Pakistan. On the other hand if I go there and protest how it would help the two countries. I came to the conclusion that I should go to India and if I have to protest at all I should protest there. If I go to India I will be able to have consultations with the people of India. I have decided to undertake a three-day fast to atone for the general atmosphere of hatred and violence in India and the abandonment by the people of this country of the path shown by Gandhiji.

~

JAYAPRAKASH NARAYAN

Time for Struggle, Not for Studies

Jayaprakash Narayan was one of the prominent leaders of the freedom movement during the 1930s and 1940s. After returning from the United States, where he had gone in 1922 for higher studies, he joined the Indian National Congress on the invitation of Jawaharlal Nehru. While in jail in 1932 for his involvement in the civil disobedience movement, he met leaders like Acharya Narendra Dev, Achyut Patwardhan and Ram Manohar Lohia. After his release, he floated the Congress Socialist Party (CSP), a left-wing group within the Congress, in 1934, with Narendra Dev as its president. During the Quit India movement of 1942, Jayaprakash, along with Lohia and Aruna Asaf Ali, took charge of the agitation in the absence of senior Congress leaders who had been arrested. After independence, he led the CSP out of the Congress to form the Socialist Party, which later became the Praja Socialist Party and emerged as the leading opposition party to the government headed by Nehru. In 1954, however, Jayaprakash dedicated himself to Vinoba Bhave's Sarvodaya movement and its Bhoodan campaign. In 1957, he formally broke from the Praja Socialist Party and began what he called lokniti, *as opposed to* rajniti. *In the early 1970s, he was instrumental in getting the dreaded dacoits of the Chambal terrain to surrender and return to normal life. Together with V.M. Tarkunde, he founded the Citizen for Democracy in 1974 and the People's Union for Civil Liberties in 1976 to uphold and defend civil liberties.*

The atmosphere of unemployment, rising prices and increasing corruption which resulted in large-scale unease with the system in the early 1970s saw him return to active politics, leading the students' movement which began in Gujarat as the Nav Nirman movement and soon moved to Bihar where it became an anti-Congress and anti-establishment movement of mass proportion. Jayaprakash Narayan demanded the resignation of, initially, the Bihar chief minister, Abdul Ghafoor, and later, when the movement was joined by other political leaders and parties, of Indira Gandhi after she was found guilty of violating electoral laws by the Allahabad High Court. He advocated a programme of social transformation which he called 'sampoorna kranti' *or total revolution. It was in response to the spread of this movement that Indira Gandhi imposed Emergency in June 1975. Jayaprakash Narayan was put in jail and later released when his health deteriorated. In 1977, when the Emergency was revoked, the Janata Party which he helped form won the election and came to power with Morarji Desai as the prime minister. In the speech reproduced here, delivered on 29 June1974, he called upon the students of Bihar to rise against corrupt political institutions and asked for a closure of colleges and universities for a year during which he wanted the students to devote their time to rebuilding the nation.*

In the programme I announced on June 5 after consulting students leaders and other friends, I said that colleges and universities should remain closed for one year. But the government seems to be itching for a confrontation with the students. There has been an official announcement that colleges and universities will reopen on the 15th of July…

This struggle is not for any petty or small aim. It is a revolutionary movement. To the students of Bihar goes the credit of having initiated and led this movement. It is now becoming a people's struggle, and at many places has already become a people's movement.

In the past students agitated for their own demands concerned with studies or examinations. Sometimes they even agitated for wrong objectives, while the mass of students supported such agitations for the sake of student unity. This time a conference of students leaders was called in which students of 135 colleges were invited to send their representatives; 250 representatives from 65 colleges attended. They adopted an eleven point charter of demands, which included some that were not related to issues concerning students alone.

Take the question of corruption; it has crossed all bounds. Of course, corruption existed even earlier. But as you all know, if something crossed a particular limit there is qualitative change. There has been such a qualitative change in the matter of corruption. If it is not checked, the whole country will be drowned in the bog of corruption.

All of you know about conditions in Bihar. The state has earned the notoriety of being the most corrupt in the country, and it is correct. Corruption is rampant. But where are the roots of corruption? If those who are in power and authority become corrupt, then no section of society remains unaffected.

In an undeveloped country the state has the dominating place in society. It is not so in developed countries. The newspapers are not filled with ministers' speeches. If a minister or even a prime minister goes somewhere, it is not treated as a world-shaking event. There the government is not run merely with the help of the police, with guns and bayonets, with politics dominating everything, as is the case here. It is natural that the people should consider political change to be important. The students also thought so.

There are indications that if this movement becomes countrywide, it will be the most important event in our history since the country attained independence. Our dream, the dream of those who fought for the country's freedom, will also be realised.

There are some students and parents, some teachers and vice-chancellors, who do not understand this. They do not understand the significance of the movement. They still think that degrees and examinations are important. But such things are wholly insignificant in the context of a revolutionary movement...

To think along old stereotyped lines, to remain confined in mental grooves in a revolutionary situation like the present is to behave like the proverbial ostrich. Remaining blind to what is going on all around you, and thinking only of personal gains would be wholly wrong and incorrect... Would it not be better if the education ministers and the educationalists take the opportunity of utilising this one year to plan a new system of education for Bihar?

The new system should be such as enables boys and girls to stand on their own feet, to become independent, to be able to face the problems of life. Why are they so anxious to carry on this old and thoroughly useless system of education? They should make the best use of this opportunity to change the set-up. If the colleges and universities are opened now, the same old routine will continue.

When we left our colleges during Gandhi's non-cooperation movement, did we not learn anything? I was a student of Patna College when Gandhi gave a call to students to leave their studies. Our examinations were only twenty days away. We were good students, some of us were gold-medallists. Our parents also hoped that we should continue our studies and have good careers. But we thought that any delay on our part would amount to a betrayal of the country. So, hundreds of us left to join the national movement.

It was during that period that we really learnt to live. We had an opportunity to breathe in a golden age of our history. What we learnt during those months was more than I could have learnt after ten years in college. I imbibed then the spirit of independence so that I have never looked again to the institutions of slavery. It was the same spirit that took me to America where I worked for one year to earn money to pay for my studies. The work was in itself a great education.

Now we have a similar situation. The students won't lose anything in one year. Education has been confined to classrooms, lectures and books. It has no relation to life, and so is completely useless. I urge all those who wish to open colleges and universities to consider if it is proper to continue to ruin the students' lives. What the students get in the name of education equips them for nothing but salaries and white collar jobs…

So many of your comrades are in jail. It is now for you to fill the jails. So many of you should come forward to go to jails that even a score of new camp jails should prove inadequate.

Come out of your narrow physical and mental confinement. Brick and stone walls have confined even the minds. Outside them are the people suffering from hunger, from scarcity and high prices. I am afraid that if the rains do not come in time, there will be famine, and Bihar will be ruined. The pre-monsoon crop of maize is already more than half destroyed. I do not know what will happen. Are you not going to be affected by it? Are you not concerned with it? Corruption, soaring prices and unemployment, are they not already corroding your lives? Are they not already creating nightmarish conditions in your lives?

So, I ask you, I appeal to you, give away one year of your life. Sacrifice it to the cause of a peaceful total revolution. Then see what happens, what fruits it brings.

~

N.G. GORAY

Opposing the Emergency

In the Rajya Sabha, the motion for approval of the proclamation of Emergency was brought by K. Brahmananda Reddy. Bhupesh Gupta, Professor V.P. Dutt and V.B. Raju spoke for the motion and then N.G. Goray, the veteran socialist leader, spoke in opposition to the motion on 22 July 1975.

Sir, let me begin my speech by making a candid admission that our perception of the situation and your perception of the situation differ in a fundamental manner. There is a wide gap between the two perceptions. It seems that all of you on that side have come to the conclusion that the best and the safest place for people like me is in jail. And we have come to the conclusion that an egalitarian democracy is impossible in India unless you are removed from power. This is the contradiction which we should not try to hide, because if you hide this, it will be difficult to understand the developments that have taken place during the last three or four years.

Sir, without meaning any disrespect to the speakers who have spoken from that side, I would like to single out three speeches. One, that of Shri Brahmananda Reddy, who initiated the debate, then that of Shri Raju who was frank enough to tell us that there is no question of going back to where we were so far as democratic rights were concerned and the last, but not the least, that of my friend, Professor Dutt, who told us that what is necessary is to speak honestly and I am assuring him that I shall try to be honest. I shall try to present to you my point of view as frankly and as honestly as possible.

Sir, I begin with the speech of Shri Brahmananda Reddy. He presented to us a long charge sheet in which the accused No. 1 was, of course, Shri Jayaprakash Narayan. I would like to ask him if he would allow me to publish a white paper as they have published, detailing all the shootings and all the butchery that they have indulged in during the last 25 years, or, is it going to be only a one-sided affair and I have to listen time and again on the radio, on the TV, in the press that we are the people who have stood in the way of progress, who have stood in the way of democracy, who have stood in the way of social reform. I would like to ask him whether such a liberty of the press, liberty of expression is available?

Just now, Sir, I pointed out to the Chairman that only what the

Minister has spoken will be published and that what we have said here will not be published. The Chief Censor has given guidelines to the press that only the names of those who participate will be mentioned, not the contents. Is this the ideal democracy? Is this the tryst with destiny about which Jawaharlal Nehru had spoken? Therefore, Sir, let us be very frank and let us admit that what has happened today is considered by some of you as the dawn of a new era while we on our side consider that it is the beginning of a long night of authoritarian rule, of suppression of liberty and, maybe, even of disintegration of this country. I do not know…

Now coming to the various charges that have been levelled against this movement as such, let us try to understand what the charges are. Charge No. 1 is that those who have been duly elected are being deprived of their right to continue in the Legislatures for the full term of five years. I would like to ask you: Who has given you the right to prolong this tenure? You say under the Constitution you have the right. Just now you have heard that the Kerala Legislature is being extended by six months. What was the mandate? The mandate of the people was only for five years. Now under the Constitution you are going to extend it for six months. Under the Constitution, if you like it, you can cut it short. What is your authority? No authority at all! It is as if under the Constitution you have a right to subvert the Constitution and if we say that the people have lost faith in you and therefore you should resign, then you say, 'What atrocity are these people committing! How can they ask us to vacate the seats?' But you can ask them to continue in the seats for one year more, two years more or three years more as it suits you. There is no bar on you. You do not want to go to the people. Sir, this particular instance is being flung into our face again and again even by so eminent a person as Prof. Dutt, and I would ask him: Why is it that elections are not held in Kerala? Is the Kerala population in revolt? What is happening in Kerala? Because you know that this emergency is not accepted by the people of Kerala and it will be very difficult for Achutha Menon and his group to come back to power, you give them six months more.

Now the charge is about violence. I would like to ask you: How many people your police and your border police have killed by shooting innocent people? Jayaprakash had asked for a judicial inquiry which was never granted. I have been to the places in Bihar where young students who had committed no offence at all were shot at sight simply because they were on the road when they should not have been on the road. Have you got any remedy against it? Will you please publish your records and say how many times, after independence, police opened fire and how many people were killed? Without any fear of contradiction I will tell you that the British never shot at people like this.

I am not saying that they were angels. But how many times you fired without the least provocation? Will you give account of that? Is it not true that in West Bengal—if there is anything wrong that I am stating, I would say the representatives from West Bengal should stand up and contradict me—the finest flower of youth has been liquidated under the pretext that they belong to the Naxalites…

I would like to ask this from our Professor from Jadavpur University. Simply because you did not want them, the finest flower, the first-class students who always topped in the examinations, they were shot. I say this is nothing short of genocide.

Therefore, when you practice this violence, when the police shoot like that, has not a man like Jayaprakash every reason to appeal to the police to consult their conscience, not to shoot whenever the orders are given, because they are shooting their own brothers and sisters? Don't forget what happened in My-Lai in Vietnam. There also the American soldiers were carrying out orders, but American society is a comparatively free society; the press brought out everything and those who indulged in these atrocities were punished. Nearer home, what did the Pakistani Army do in Bangladesh? Were not terms and conditions laid down by Mujib that all those people would be tried for genocide? Were not the Army people carrying out the orders of the superiors? They were. They were not acting on their own. Therefore, if a man like Jayaprakash says that whenever an order is given to you to shoot, don't shoot; you try to understand whom you are shooting, try to understand who those people are; don't shoot on innocent people, what is wrong? And the question that has been asked again and again—and I was sorry to hear it from Dutt; he was again and again repeating it—was: What have you to say when Jayaprakash appealed to the Army?

… Simply because Jayaprakash said something to the Army, to the people, to the students, you hold the entire country to ransom! Why do you prevent me from speaking? Why do you prevent the press from publishing whatever we say? The press is duty bound to publish what you say, but they will not publish all that we say…

What is a responsible press? I am coming to that point. I say the

Indian press has played a very prominent part in our national struggle and after Independence also. I remember I was in the other House. The Chinese aggression at Ladakh was first reported by our press and there is a record of Jawaharlalji saying that he did not want this news to leak to the people because he wanted friendship between China and India to continue. Who were the people who told us of the Chinese aggression? It was the press. Who told us about the arms supply that was resumed by America to Pakistan? It was the press. At that time, Sardar Swaran Singhji was the Defence Minister. He did not know and then he made enquiries and he came to know that what was reported in the press was true. Why are you afraid of that press? I would like to ask my friends like Dr. Dutt, are you going to make democracy a woman in purdah that nobody should look at her, nobody should touch her and nobody should speak to her? Is that democracy? Many of you must have read that the Japanese Prime Minister was knocked down while he was going to a meeting and presented with a dagger and a request that he should kill himself. That was an attack from the rightists. They did not like his signing the non-proliferation treaty. Did the Japanese Parliament declare emergency because the Prime Minister was attacked? There is a photograph; he is lying on the ground and the attacker is with a dagger.

Just imagine what happens in England. Dr. Dutt had asked can you imagine Wilson leading a morcha against the Parliament? Certainly not. But can you imagine Heath shooting down the coalminers when they declared a national strike? He will not do it and, therefore, Wilson also does not do it. Both sides must play the game. When you cannot answer the people, all the answer that you have is to put them in jail, throw them in jail and put them behind the bars. Is this the answer? And even what we speak here, I know, will not be allowed to go out. When we come to attend Parliament session, you arrest us. Sir, I am reminded of an incident when I attended the British Parliament in a delegation. I was taken aback. Sir, it was a Conservative Government and one member from the Labour Party got up and said: 'A man who was avoiding arrest, came to me in the morning because he belonged to my constituency and he was arrested at my doorsteps. Why did you arrest him when he was approaching his MP?' And, Sir, to my surprise, the Conservative Minister for Home got up and said: 'I apologise for what has been done and I assure you that this thing will not happen again.' Sir, yesterday, I pointed out to you, the President calls us here for attending the Parliament and as soon as we come here, we are arrested. You ask us to go to a meeting and when we go to the meeting, we are arrested. My friend Madhu Dandavate was arrested; Mr. Advani was arrested, Mr. Mishra was arrested. Why? Because they were attending a meeting which you yourself had called. What is this? Is this democracy? I wanted Mr. Dutt and others to raise their powerful voice and say that while we would like to have emergency, we would not have this sort of emergency which is running amuck. If you say that Jayaprakashji's forces were running amuck, are you as counter measure running amuck yourself? So, Sir, my plea is that it is really an action and reaction. You are angry with us; we are angry with you. This will not save democracy. This will not take our country anywhere except towards chaos...

Mr. Dutt yesterday talking about the RSS said that it is a Brahmin-dominated organisation. Who are these people on the front benches? Mr. Umashankar Dikshit, I suppose, is the greatest Sudra. Then, this gentleman, Mr. Kamlapati Tripathi, is the most secular of secular people. Mr. Dutt, if you are engaged in a really serious discussion I will tell you that in this unfortunate land everything has been decided by twenty per cent people. It is they who fight and it is they who rule. It is they who build and it is they who destroy. It is they who legislate and it is they who dispense justice. This is what has happened for centuries.

... Therefore, do not say that this is what you are doing for the downtrodden. You are doing that for yourself, including this twenty-point programme. If you are really serious, then it is not by eliminating us who have been all the while for the implementation of this, but it is by eliminating many on your side that you can fulfil this programme. I ask you a straight question: Are you ready for such a showdown with your own people? I am not blaming anybody, but it is these people who have stopped all these programmes from being implemented. Now, they say there is no land for distribution. It is because they have distributed land to a grandchild which is yet to be born. This is what is happening. I have not said a word against Indira Gandhi. Since I came here or even outside I did not say anything against Indira Gandhi because it is not personal. You say that she is being attacked. Naturally it is because she is the Prime Minister. If she is not the Prime Minister, nobody will mention her. Therefore, when she is the Prime Minister of the country and she is leading the party that is ruling this country for the last so many years, naturally the attack will be on her. Naturally they attacked Mr. Wilson because he was trying to take his country to the European Common Market. He had to go and plead with his people and he conducted a referendum. He never said: You people are opposing me. I will put you in jail. This is not the way of democracy. Democracy ought to be a sturdier plant which can stand all the blows and all the winds, however harsh they may be. Therefore, before I conclude I would say about this twenty-point programme, why does not the Prime Minister propose that this is the programme? Let all the parties come together and discuss it. Maybe we shall have to add two more or subtract two and make it a shorter programme. It does not matter. In fact, as I have said, have five or six main items. Hammer them out and complete them and then move to the next item. Why not ask Jayaprakash Narayan, why not ask all those people whom you have incarcerated? Bring them round the table. Say, this is the programme and anybody who goes against it you will set him aside. Do not put him in jail, but set him aside. Do not suppose that all the bridges need to be blown up. Do not think that you will be able to manage India with only Shrimati Indira Gandhi and your party behind her; it is too vast a country, with so many people, so many shades of opinion, so many religions.

Sir, I know that the contradictions are glaring. I know that we have differed. Still there is no other way for us. If you think that the only way is to shut the mouths of all the Opposition, then I tell you, you are not only harming the Opposition, you are not only harming democracy, you are harming yourself. And with this appeal I conclude.

~

UMA SHANKAR JOSHI

In Opposition to the Emergency

Uma Shankar Joshi (1911–88) is one of the most respected names in Indian literature. He received the Jnanpith Award in 1967 and Sahitya Akademi Award in 1973. He was the vice chancellor of Gujarat University between 1966 and 1972 and later became the chancellor of Visva-Bharati University, Santiniketan. Joshi was a nominated member of the Rajya Sabha during the Emergency and spoke strongly against the way democracy was being throttled, castigating particularly those who live a public life but never take a stand.

Mr. Deputy Chairman, Sir, this is the most agonising moment in five years of my association with this august House. I came here as a poet and a Vice-Chancellor with what fond hopes and dreams. I thought it was possible for India—an ancient people, though a new nation—to achieve socialistic aims through democracy. One thought that India was cut out for this role, that it would achieve social justice through peaceful means. However, yesterday our Home Minister came forward with a plea in favour of emergency, giving up all hopes for democracy in this great land.

He was pleased to lay the blame at the doors of opposition parties and certain happenings in our country. I belong to no party and I would take this opportunity to refer to one detail, about Gujarat. He was not holding this charge when the Nav Nirman movement started in Gujarat. I would like to point out to him that in the beginning it was the Congress Party people themselves who saw the rebirth of Mahatma Gandhi in the Nav Nirman youth. The Communist Party also, as far as I remember, was with the Nav Nirman youth. It was a different story after the ouster of the Ministry. Why did this happen? My plea is for a little self-searching rather than laying the whole blame at the door of the opposition. I have been crying hoarse that the ruling party like the muskdeer runs in vain all around for the opposition, for it is within its own self. The learned friends from the ruling party, the younger people, say that the emergency should have been clamped down on the country two years before or so. It would have been good if something had been done to implement the economic programme two years—I would say many more years—before. But that was not done and a political style developed which only hankered after having a huge majority, unmindful of heterogeneous elements which were counterproductive and which would not allow forward-looking policies of the party to be implemented.

Sir, I do not want to enter into further details. But even if what the Home Minister said was right regarding opposition parties, does it behove of him to suggest that 'If they, the opposition parties, are running democracy in our country, why should not we ourselves deal a death blow to it?' That would be a tragic hour in the life of our country. George Bernard Shaw said that the English people did everything on principle. If they beheaded a king, they beheaded him on principle. Our learned Home Minister says that everything is within the framework of the Constitution. So today, he will be able, with the majority that his party commands, to stifle the Constitution constitutionally. What does it lead to?

A clamp down of pre-censorship has never happened in India, not even under a foreign regime. We are afraid of truth. Where does this fear emanate from, fear which has engulfed the length and breadth of this vast land? Wherefrom has emanated this dark cynical shadow of fear—I mean, terror—which shows its ugly face all around? How many walls have been created after the 26th of June? You want to see that the country is not disintegrated. By switching off all information, rumours run amuck and truth is stifled. This is the fear of truth in a country which has a reputation of being a seeker after truth. This has damaged the image of India all over the world more than anything else.

I should like to press this point and to convey this through this august House to the Prime Minister that when Nehru and Shastri were our Prime Ministers, India, though a developing country trying to pull herself out, almost by the boot-strap, from poverty, was a respected country. It held its head high. Nehru, before laying down his pen, before writing 'Tamam Shud' to his book *Glimpses of World History* quoted from Tagore—where the mind is devoid of fear, where the head is held high, into that heaven of freedom let my country awake.

As Nehru himself said, he was more in tune with Tagore than Gandhiji. So long as he was on the world stage, even though his colleagues, as some people observed, were just Tito, Nasser and Sukarno, he himself always stood taller by a head. He represented a country which held its head high. What will happen to our Prime Minister when she goes abroad? She thinks very much of foreigners' opinions and rightly so, but the image has been damaged.

... If some leaders were found hatching a conspiracy, they should have been brought before a court of law. He may be J.P. He may be Mr. Morarji Desai. He may be Mr. Atal Behari Vajpayee, whoever he may be... But why penalise the people, who the ruling party thinks are, by and large, with them?

I appeal to the Members of the ruling party because now there is only one party. Already there are signs of their heading towards one-party rule, towards the destruction of the federal structure, replacing it by the unitary structure. Already there are signs that the Gujarat and the Tamil Nadu Governments may find themselves in trouble sooner rather than later.

Not being a politician I do not want to enter into a discussion with the Home Minister, but how many Governments have been toppled by the ruling party? How many people have migrated from the opposition parties even here in this House to the ruling party? We are Nominated Members. Independent Members not belonging to any party. The ruling party on that side sucks from this side and whatever is left of the opposition is perhaps the best of them. So put them behind the jail. Have a one-party rule.

... Younger men and women talk lightly of the freedom of the press. People like me who have fought as a young college student have other views in the matter. There are elderly people here. I find the Home Minister himself and white-bearded, very revered writer of Punjabi, Shri Gurmukh Singh Musafir and others are here. What have you been doing all these years? What have you done for Indian democracy? We are here today at a very crucial hour. Have you gone to the Prime Minister and said that you will be blown but you hold these ideas. Is the Prime Minister on talking terms with thinking people in this country?

... Sir, before I conclude I would like to say one word...though words have lost their significance. I am a votary of words. I cannot live without the word. I am a poet. I am an artist first and last. By chance I happen to be here. But what can word do to-day? We have been brought to such a catastrophe. All around there is an unthinking conformism...which does injustice to their own selves and ultimately, to the Prime Minister and more important, to the country.

My appeal to the ruling party in particular and through them to the leader is: Do not be in hurry to ring down the curtain on the First Republic.

INDIRA GANDHI

In Defence of Democracy

Jagjivan Ram, the minister for agriculture and irrigation, moved a resolution for approval of the Emergency at 12.50 hours on 21 July 1975. After a heated debate for two days, the resolution was put to vote at 11.50 hours on 23 July and passed with 336 members of the Lok Sabha supporting it while 59 were against it. Prime Minister Indira Gandhi's defence of the proclamation was a spirited one. She spoke about the fascism of communal forces that had compelled her to declare a state of Emergency. She analysed and portrayed the

RSS and Jana Sangh as communal and fascist organizations and asked why no other party was taking a grim view of the communal passion and hatred unleashed by these organizations. Significantly enough, she attacked the opposition for their supposed championing of democracy.

... Yesterday a charge was made that the Government action was aimed at right reactionaries...this is not my word by the way, it is their word—but against the leftists. It was instructive for me to note during the speech, which I heard very carefully, never once was any of the communal parties criticised.

Some people have been arrested. The largest number are not political, they are people who normally indulge in violence or criminal acts, people who are known as antisocial elements. But next to them the largest number amongst the political people, although some of the groups say they are not political, are the communal parties or groups wedded to terror and murder.

It was said that Government has launched an onslaught on workers. Perhaps the honourable member has not noticed that workers from all over have welcomed our move and have given us full support. The programme that we have announced helps workers to achieve a larger share of real power, and that is why the labour organizations have overwhelmingly welcomed this economic programme and offered their full cooperation: industrial relations have improved almost beyond our imagination in a short while.

It seems to me that the honourable member was speaking not to this House but his own cadres outside. As Shri Deshmukh has said, there is confusion in their ranks because of the nature of the groups and people outside the country who are supporting us and the others which are supporting the opposition front. Some friends are preaching radicalism and socialism to us. I have never claimed to be doctrinaire socialist. I have my own version of socialism and my own vision of what Indian society should be like, and I have been working and going ahead towards that vision and in that direction steadfastly. It is a slow movement, but I believe that it is a surer way of moving ahead. And this is why, although the people may sometimes be angry with us and may sometimes want to reject us as the House will notice, in all times of crisis, all sections of the people have stood solidly behind us.

... The next speaker seemed to be apologising all the time, trying to explain away history and historical facts. He said that the sword of the RSS was a wooden one. Quite frankly I don't see the point of it; either you have a sword or you do not have it; but why a toy sword? What games are they going to play with it? Much as I deplore the type of training that is given to young people in their *shakhas*, much as I condemn the violence which they preach, their real weapon has been something else. It has been the whispering campaign.

Yesterday another member of the opposition said he would like to know what is fascism. I have spoken about this on earlier occasions. Fascism does not merely mean repression; it does not merely mean that the police use excessive force, or that people are imprisoned; it is falsehood, over and above everything, it is the propagation of big lies. It is this whispering campaign; it is the finding of scapegoat to sacrifice and divert the people's attention so that you can go ahead. And this has been the major weapon of the Jan Sangh and the RSS. It was interesting to notice that although sometimes the two organisations want to be regarded as separate, in yesterday's speech, the names of the two parties were used as if they were interchangeable.

What has been appearing in their newspapers? If any party had a feeling for democracy, and for the truth, they could have dissociated themselves from the lies. What falsehood have they left out and not propagated? What insinuation have they not made? Not merely since the Emergency has been declared, but consistently for four whole years day in and day out.

Even today there is a massive whispering campaign: somebody is supposed to be under house arrest, somebody is supposed to be on fast, somebody is supposed to have died, something is supposed to have happened. This is their way of following democracy and this is their vision of truth. Well, if this is so, I must emphatically say that this is not our way. We do not believe in untruth, in falsehood, and we do not believe in that type of democracy.

I am not in habit of quoting, either outside or in the House. But today I should like to do so because I find that some honourable members often deny the truth of what has been said by their side. In a book called *Our Nationhood Defined*—first published in 1939, and later reprinted—with regard to Hitler's Germany, Golwalker wrote: 'The national pride of the Germans is the talk of the whole world. The Germans drove out of their country the Jews only in order to maintain their racial and cultural purity. Germany has also shown that it is very difficult for fundamentally different races to live together. This is a lesson which India could learn and profit by.'

With reference to the Muslims who remained in India after partition, this has been said, and I quote: 'It would be suicidal to delude ourselves into believing that they have turned patriots overnight after the creation of Pakistan. On the contrary, the Muslim menace has increased hundred-fold by the creation of Pakistan which has become a springboard for all their future aggressive designs on our country.'

Much was made of the words in our report—and it was maintained that the RSS was not involved 'as such'. I do not know what the words 'as such' mean. I am not a legal luminary. I am glad I am not. But I quote this from the Ahmedabad Enquiry Committee Report: 'This evidence shows that organised attacks were made on Muslim properties and lorries being used to carry rioters and weapons, the crowd being led and directed by a worker of Jan Sangh.'

This was in September 1969.

In December 1971 there were riots in Tellicherry. What does the Report say? 'I have no doubt the RSS had taken an active part in rousing up the anti-Muslim feeling among the Hindus of Tellicherry.' What do RSS say about Christians? 'So far as the Christians are concerned, to a superficial observer they appear not only quite harmless... They are not only irreligious but anti-national.'

It is quite a long statement, I am not reading it, but this statement reveals their attitude. On Gandhiji's leadership, in a book called *Bunch of Thoughts*, page 153: 'This leadership came as a bitter climax of the despicable tribe of so many of our ancestors who during the past 1200 years sold their national honour and freedom to foreigners and joined hands with the inveterate enemies of our country and religion in cutting the throats of their kith and kin to gratify their personal egoism, selfishness and rivalry.'

On women—this is not by any person, it is in their newspaper, the *Organiser*—'Also it is becoming clear that female franchise in this country is an unnecessary duplication of effort.' On democracy—this was in a speech in October 1965: 'The democracy we speak of is a borrowed hotchpotch...the name does not strike responsive chord in the common man.'

Of course you all know what Sardar Patel wrote in his letter of September 11, 1948: 'Organising the Hindus and helping them is one thing but going for revenge for its suffering on innocent and helpless men, women and children is quite another. Apart from this, is their (RSS) opposition to Congress; that too of such virulence, disregarding all considerations of personality, decency, decorum, created a kind of unrest among people. All their speeches were full of communal poison. It was not necessary to spread poison in order to enthuse Hindus and organise for their protection. As a final result of that poison, the country had to suffer the sacrifice of the invaluable life of Gandhiji. Even an iota of sympathy...no more remained for RSS.'

I spoke just now about fascism. Apart from this whispering campaign of spreading falsehood and finding scapegoats, its main feature is the total advocacy of violence, training youth in ways of violence and terror. We know which groups are wedded to violence today, and they are all with the Morcha. The Congress is the only party which has a consistently unsullied record of opposition to fascism since before independence, and this continues.

Some snide remarks were made about our saying that we had acted according to the constitution and it was suggested or hinted that Hitler also had done the same thing. Of course there is no similarity. If you like you can read the history books of that period. I do not have to read them because I was there and witnessed a great deal of what was happening in Germany at that time.

I should like to know from the honourable members of the opposition whether he can name any one head of state who would have tolerated so much for so long. Which country in the world do you think would have tolerated the campaigns of falsehood, calumny, and violence? And now they talk of democracy. Who is lecturing to us on democracy?

I am going to quote some more. In the *Indian Express* of 8 May 1967, Shri Jayaprakash Narayan was quoted as saying that he was toying with the idea of military dictatorship in India and suggesting that 'in the political instability created as a result of the General Elections in 1967, the nation should summon the services of the army to fill the vacuum and set right the instability'. At that time the honourable member opposite, Shri Gopalan, is quoted as having said, '... warned that Shri Jayaprakash Narayan's remarks amounted to patronising flattery of the armed forces and utter contempt of the people and their democratic and patriotic aspirations.'

Another great leader and sympathiser of the Morcha made the following speech: 'We are now entering a revolutionary situation. For some time, extra-constitutional forces will take over... I would prefer temporarily a patriotic army rule which takes a pragmatic economic line, gives the people a good life, stops population growth.'

This was the version of democracy that was being preached (it is here in black and white) by the leaders of the Morcha. Today they are lecturing us on what democracy should be! One could speak on this subject for hours.

Many points were made in the speeches yesterday. After the judgement of the Allahabad High Court, it was not I who suggested that we should go out on the streets. That call came from the so-called Morcha that the issue should be decided on the streets. It had openly been stated that the movement in Bihar was unconstitutional—not by me but by the person who was at the head of the movement. He said that it may be unconstitutional but that does not necessarily mean that it was undemocratic. I can say that our actions are not against anybody—neither against a person nor against a party. Whatever we are doing is pro-something; it is pro-India, it is pro-Indian people, it is pro the direction and the future of India.

As was said yesterday, the very summoning of Parliament is proof that democracy is functioning in India. The large number of opposition members present is evidence that not every one of them is in detention or behind bars. This action is totally within our constitutional framework. It was undertaken not to destroy the constitution but to preserve the constitution, to preserve and safeguard our democracy.

Our constitution makers had foreseen that a situation might be created, not only external aggression but internal disturbances, when the fabric of national life might be threatened. That is why they provided an entire part entitled 'Emergency Provisions'. Democracy has not been endangered by what Government has done, but democracy was being weakened, was being endangered and would have been destroyed had the opposition front been allowed to launch the direct action and its plan of sabotage under RSS guidance and to go ahead with its campaign to create dissatisfaction in the army, the police and amongst our industrial workers. So, each one of us has to search our hearts and ask ourselves solemnly who was for the destruction of democracy as it has evolved in this country. Whenever this discussion has come up, we have always said that there are faults in the system, let us talk about them, let us see how they can be removed. No system is perfect and each country, as it goes ahead, may find new situations and must find ways in which to deal with them.

The House is aware of the violent agitation in Gujarat. Some honourable members have spoken about it. But I do not remember whether any member drew attention to the manner in which resignations were demanded and obtained. What type of intimidation was resorted to? A mother or father was told 'to sign a resignation letter or we shall kidnap your child'. Is that democracy? When a senior member of the Congress was lying in hospital with heart attack, some students went in there, beat him up and wanted to throw him out of the window. Was that democracy? Was that normal life? Did it show respect for democracy and the constitution?

After the dissolution of the Gujarat Assembly, it was proclaimed openly in public meetings that Parliamentary institutions were unsuitable to India. The electoral system provided in the constitution was under constant attack. Who was responsible for this? Who withstood this challenge and fought to uphold the sanctity of the constitution and of Parliament? The so-called leaders of this disruptive agitation had no qualms at all about handing over the management of their campaign to the RSS in spite of the known record of the RSS in national life, in fermenting communal riots and communal hatred. Was the call for a gherao of Parliament during its Winter Session and appeal to the cause of total revolution an exercise in democratic politics?

It was obvious that certain political elements who do not have anything in common had chosen to come together for the sole purpose of paralyzing and removing a duly elected Government. Groups and parties, whose ideologies were poles apart, joined together. Established democratic norms and political practices were done away with.

It is time now to think seriously about basic matters, about democracy and the functioning of democratic institutions. Political liberty and political rights can exist only so long as political order remains. A state of anarchy can lead only to the quick erosion of every freedom and political right of the individual. There is no doubt about the need for a regulated expression of public discontent against the policies of even an elected Government. We have always accepted that: we have never tried to stop criticism. If we have lost any election, we have never said that the election was rigged or that somebody had done wrong. Now if the opposition wins an election, they say it is free and fair but if they lose it, then they talk of some secret ink, which has mysteriously helped the other person to win. Or some other flights of fancy are indulged in.

However, when protest and resistance is conceived to destroy the very fabric of society and undo the stability of the political system, such action becomes a disguise for action to destroy democracy. Every right that the State concedes to the individual imposes an obligation on him. Similarly, groups and organised associations who enjoy political freedom in a democracy must respect the limits within which those rights have to be exercised. Such are the norms of any functioning democracy anywhere in the world. The makers of almost every constitution have made provisions to deal with elements who try to undo the democratic process through methods and liberties made available to them by the democratic process itself. In no modern democracy can the question of economic betterment and social justice be separated from the proper functioning of democracy.

Democracy implies the existence of representative institutions, the expression of the will of the people as to who their representatives would be and the participation of the people in national tasks. It also implies that once representatives are chosen and Government comes into being with the approval of the majority, it functions freely to bring about the social and economic change that it promised to the people.

When we had a majority, but had a small percentage of votes, we were taunted about it in the House. Now when in Gujarat we have got 41 per cent of the votes and the entire Morcha together—I do not know how many parties there were, I think five parties, together—got 34 per cent then the question of percentage is conveniently ignored.

Here in India, democracy is evolving in a set of unique circumstances. Millions of extremely poor people are hankering for a better life, for greater equality of opportunity, for social justice and they are electing Governments and participating in the process of Government in order to realise these aspirations. Therefore, it is a question of striking a balance, a balance between the political rights of the individual and the social and economic rights of the collective mass of people. Any narrow definition of democracy which tries to ignore these realities can only mean the growth of political ideas which are anti-democratic. The challenges to Indian democracy must be seen in the light of the general problems that this particular system of Government faces in the world and the very unique problems that it faces within India. The essence of the democratic system is the continuous participation of people in political, social and economic processes. The existence of representative Governments and institutions would facilitate such participation and this has been our endeavour. It is true that it has not always worked. The Panchayat system came about in order to give people at a particular level a chance of participation. It sometimes went into wrong hands. That does not mean that the institution is wrong. It does mean that we have to correct its functioning, remove its faults and weaknesses and make whatever changes are necessary.

By the same definition, it is incumbent on a democratic regime to remove all obstacles and impediments to such participation for social, political and economic progress. The great national task we face makes it necessary for us to evolve a political system, in which the right balance is struck, in which the essence of freedom is maintained, while conditions are created for a higher level of social discipline and economic progress.

As I said earlier, the people's response to the Emergency has been wholesome. Why is this so? Because the people genuinely believe that the opposition front was holding the country to ransom and was weakening us at a time of delicate alterations in international power relations and structures. The opposition, used to hearing its own voice and that of a few newspapers, imagined it to be the voice of the people and now it is sadly disillusioned.

But a few determined and unreconciled elements are still at large and are at work. They are announcing plans of sabotage of essential service and strategic installations. Desperadoes belonging to criminal organisations like the Anand Marg are still busy with their plots to murder and kill people. And a few newspapers outside the country, either out of mistaken analysis or by deliberate design, are building this up as a resistance movement. So vigilance cannot be relaxed at the moment.

The question is asked: where do we go from here and when do we return to normalcy? I dealt with this question the other day. First we have to decide what is normalcy. People are free to move about on the roads. Does this mean that some people should decide that although the rule of the road is to drive on the left, they are free to drive on the right side? Is that the meaning of freedom of the road? What kind of chaos would be created if some people did so? Unfortunately, this has happened a couple of times, resulting in tragic accidents.

There has been greater freedom of speech in India than anywhere else in the world. Most countries which are today lecturing us on democracy, what kind of regimes are they supporting morally and materially? Would you like to look at their list?

The Emergency is very young. What was happening in the four

years before that? This is what I am asking. And even today, all those people who are talking the loudest about democracy, what democracy have they had in their regime? Earlier did they lay claim to democracy at any time?

Today's situation is an exceptional one. But so far as you are concerned, there has been no change because you have been calling me dictator all these four years. So what is the change? I was a dictator before and I am a dictator now!

... I should only like to say that anybody who wants to read the newspapers of that period can know about the murders and the insecurity in Bengal when the Marxist Government was there. That is all that I want to say. The Marxist Party's adherence to democracy is very new. So, perhaps, they are more vocal in its support.

The political ill-health which prevailed before the Emergency is certainly not normalcy in any language or in any part of the world. There can be no return to the days of total licence and political permissiveness. Democracy demands self-restraint of all. It is the responsibility of the Government to allow the opposition to function, to allow freedom of speech and freedom of association. But it is equally the responsibility of the opposition not to take advantage of them to destroy democracy or to 'paralyse the Government'. The words 'paralyse the Government' are not mine. I am using them in quotes; they were used by them in public meetings here in Delhi and elsewhere.

There has to be greater self-restraint. When individuals or groups do not learn to cultivate self-restraint, the constitution has to tell them where they have to stop.

The people at large have come to associate Emergency with the beginning of a new era in national life. We should demonstrate during this period how to bring about an atmosphere of self-discipline, an atmosphere when each group tries not to get what it can for itself, but to join together in a common endeavour. We have to convert this painful necessity into a new opportunity for forward movement and towards the realisation of our programmes.

Some honourable members said yesterday that there is not much new in the programmes that were announced. What is new is that there is an atmosphere today when it is easier to implement what we want to do. The workers have assured us and it is our duty to protect them and see that because of their assurance, they do not suffer any hardship. Similarly, all sections of the people should combine in this endeavour.

We have announced some programmes. But very much more has to be done to change life in our cities, in our villages, in our desert areas and in our hilly areas. I would respectfully and humbly request the opposition to try and help in this positive effort. Many of them who have criticised the Emergency, have welcomed the economic programmes. Therefore, at least in this area, let us come up with new suggestions pointing out what we have left out and what can be done. If they come up with new suggestions, let us try to see whether we can convert this 'painful necessity', as I said, into an opportunity to work together and to take this country forward. Thank you.

~

G.G. SWELL

Communal Violence in Gujarat

The 1980s was a crucial decade for India. While the country took the first hesitant steps in opening its economy to the world outside, important changes were taking place in the industrial and other sectors within the country. However, the one defining characteristic of the decade was the rise of communalism and widespread communal violence. The decade ended with the opening of the lock on the disputed site of the Ram temple at Ayodhya, thus igniting the Ram Janmabhoomi–Babri Masjid controversy which would claim many lives in the decade that followed. Gujarat, Uttar Pradesh, Delhi, Bihar and many other states became communal flashpoints, severely testing the secular fabric of the nation. In 1986, during the Gujarat riots, Madhu Dandavate moved a resolution on 21 July 1986 in the Lok Sabha against the communal violence in various parts of the country. Veteran parliamentarian G.G. Swell's impassioned response to the resolution reiterated the dangers of the communal frenzy enveloping the country, memorably pointing out how the real danger to India's freedom and prosperity lay within the country and not in the machinations of foreign powers inimical to its interests.

... In this country we have inherited the legacy of Mahatma Gandhi. He gave his life; he died in order to bring conscience to us, to the different communities in this country after the madness of a partition, and to emphasise that the continuity, the salvation of this country lay in different communities living in peace, in coexistence and in cooperation with one another.

... India has a lot of things to say about herself in the comity of nations. It is the one country in the whole of Asia, excepting Japan, that has maintained, nurtured and has grown in democracy; it is the one country among half a dozen or a dozen of the countries in the world where real democracy has prevailed. If you look at it more objectively, the vastness, the size and the diversity, the in-built contradictions that India has in terms of historical legacies, in terms of differences in religion, in terms of differences in languages, in terms of economic disparities... And yet we have survived ever since Independence, and grown from strength to strength in democracy. We have a lot to say, a lot to be proud about... We have been able to do this because in spite of the differences and lot of conflicts which are inherent anywhere in the world, we have been able to hold together. The different communities in this country, the Hindus, the Muslims, the Christians and the Sikhs have understood this, that in living together, in functioning together there lies the salvation not only of this country, but the salvation, the upliftment of each individual of this country. It is this bond that has held us together. And if there is anything that is going to destroy this country, it will not be external aggression—we have had external aggressions in the past and each time there has been external aggression the country has stood up united as a man; it will not be the machinations of the big powers and the countries inimical to this country, it will not be the international manipulations for geo-strategic advantages, it will be the conflicts within the country and if we allow those conflicts, if we are not able to control and contain those conflicts, they will grow into a monster, and cut up and destroy this country. We have to understand this.

I am very happy that Mr. Dandavate by bringing this subject before the House has served that purpose. I would like to congratulate him for bringing this spirit of objectivity, for having been constructive in his suggestions. There is hardly anywhere where I can differ with him, when he speaks of the freedom of the different religions to practise their religion. There is freedom given to everyone, and of course we have to draw a line. While every religion has the right to practise, has the right to express itself, collectively indoors and outdoors, has a right to take out processions, it should be seen that it does not have a right to flout and to wound the sentiments of the other religions. This is where we should find a way how this thing should be done.

~

P.V. NARASIMHA RAO

Countering Communal Forces

Of all the disputes which have rent asunder Indian society in the recent past, resulting in the loss of thousands of lives, the one pertaining to the Ram Janmabhoomi–Babri Masjid is probably the most important. In 1989, the Congress government under Rajiv Gandhi, in a misguided effort to pander to the Hindu vote-bank, unlocked the gates of the temple and opened it to worshippers despite the fact that it had been disputed property for close to forty years. Hindu right-wing and communal elements like the Vishwa Hindu Parishad and Bajrang Dal, aided and abetted by their parliamentary face, the BJP, exploited the issue for electoral gains, generating a wave of hysteria and hatred all over the country which culminated in the destruction of the Babri Masjid on 6 December 1992. As prime minister at the time, P.V. Narasimha Rao (1921–2004) copped a major share of the blame for his failure to ensure the safety of the disputed structure. While he maintained, as is clear from the speech reproduced here, that he had to believe the assurances given by the chief minister of the state to the Supreme Court and those of the leaders of the BJP on the floor of Parliament, his critics held him squarely responsible for failing to take adequate measures to prevent the demolition. Despite being a scholar of repute and a political leader of standing—who will be remembered as the architect of a new India for initiating the country's economic liberalization, inaugurating a new education policy, and articulating a new foreign policy initiative—in the final analysis his legacy will be forever marred by the incidents of 6 December 1992 and the riots that followed.

I am speaking to you this evening under the grave threat that has been posed to the institutions, principles and ideals on which the constitutional structure of our republic has been built. During the struggle for freedom under the leadership of Mahatma Gandhi, we had promised to ourselves an India free of exploitation, hunger and pestilence recognising the right of every citizen to the fruits of democracy and also his right to practise and preach his own religion without any interference. This resolve was enshrined in our Constitution and the founding fathers of our country sanctified this in the written Constitution of India.

In a country of the size and diversity like ours, it is only the concern and care for the sensibilities of each other which can ensure a smooth functioning of the institutions that we have created. This is the only way to maintain peace and harmony amongst the people of

India. Whatever may be our differences on political, social and economic issues, they have to be acted upon keeping this wider concept in view. The delicate fabric of our nation woven around democracy and secularism is the only anchor-sheet for our country's existence.

The country has witnessed in the last few years an attempt by certain political parties who have in their pursuit of power not been able to exercise restraint and keep their actions within the limitations of propriety, law and the demands of national integration. They have used the differences revolving around the Ram Janma Bhoomi-Babri Masjid dispute to excite base communal passions and utilise the same for political purposes. We have pleaded with them, we have made our efforts to bring different people together in an effort to resolve this matter amicably through peaceful negotiations. We have gone to the fullest extent to create an atmosphere in the country which would be conducive to this effort. We have posed to all parties to the dispute, ways and means to get a judicial determination to this vexed problem. I see no other way in a democratic polity to determine matters on which strong views are held on all sides.

I have personally done whatever I could to help reach a negotiated settlement or a judicial determination to this issue. While all democratic and secular forces have helped in this effort, I am sad to state that the BJP-VHP combine has not only failed to respond to my efforts but as a matter of fact have gone about deliberately to not only thwart my efforts but also to mislead the nation about my intention. What has happened today in Ayodhya where the Babri Masjid structure has been demolished, is a matter of great shame and concern for all Indians. Each and everyone of us want and I have stated so repeatedly that we want to see a temple of Lord Rama being built at Ayodhya. As a matter of fact, people of all faiths in India were even prepared to actively help in this. The BJP-VHP combine have, however, continued to pursue a different line because they felt that this is the only route to carry them to the seats of power. This is a betrayal of the nation and a confrontation with all that is sacred to all Indians as the legacy which we have all inherited and is a part of our national ethos. A great affront has been caused to this. As the first servant of the people of India it is not only my duty but also my mandate to ensure that all such communal forces who are out to confront the nation itself, must be met resolutely. We will go to any extent to preserve and protect secularism and the democratic credentials of our nation. In this onerous task I seek the support and blessings of all the citizens of this country. I would like to say very clearly that we shall no longer suffer the Machiavellian tactics of the communal forces in this country.

I appeal to all those misguided people who have assembled at Ayodhya, on the inspiration of persons who do not have the well-being of the nation at heart, to disperse peacefully and let the law of the land have full sway there. It is to achieve this that my Government has dismissed the Government of UP headed by Shri Kalyan Singh which has totally failed in its primary duty, to which they pledged themselves time and again, to protect the structure. I would like to sound a note of warning to everyone who may try to help such elements who have put the peace and tranquillity of the nation in jeopardy that we shall not spare any action against them in the interest of the nation. I appeal to all of you to maintain calm, peace and harmony at this grave moment of crisis. We have faced many such situations in the past and have overcome them. We shall do this again with firm determination and conviction in the rightness of our path.

~

SONIA GANDHI

Follow My Own Inner Voice

Rajiv Gandhi, prime minister of India from 1984 to 1989, was assassinated in 1991. After his death, his widow Sonia Gandhi kept herself out of government and refrained from taking up any major political assignments. By 1995-96, in the light of the party's electoral slide all over the country and requests from party members and workers, she agreed to enter the political fray. She was elected leader of the Congress and gradually set about revamping the party, bringing it back to power in 2004 against all expectations. However, way back in 1996, senior Congress leaders, keen to wrest the leadership, had argued that Sonia Gandhi was a foreigner and could not be projected as the prime minister of India. This was taken up in a big way by the BJP which saw in this an issue to further polarize the people on communal lines. When the Congress was poised to form a government in coalition with leftist partners in 2004, her name figured prominently as a candidate for prime minister. BJP leaders went overboard in attacking her credentials and threatened to launch a nationwide agitation. In a political masterstroke, she declined to become the prime minister and recommended the name of Dr Manmohan Singh. Her renunciation not only turned the tables on the BJP's virulent attack, shocking them into silence, but also raised her esteem with the public. Sonia Gandhi's address to the Congress Parliamentary Party meeting on 18 May 2004, where she announced her decision not to accept the prime minister's post, is historic in the sense that it probably was the first instance of a politician in India declining public office.

Friends, throughout these past six years that I have been in politics, one thing has been clear to me. And that is, as I have often stated, that the post of prime minister is not my aim. I was always certain that if ever I found myself in the position that I am in today, I would follow my own inner voice. Today, that voice tells me I must humbly decline this post.

You have unanimously elected me your leader, in doing so, you have reposed your faith in me. It is this faith that has placed me under tremendous pressure to reconsider my decision. Yet, I must abide by the principles which have guided me all along.

Power in itself has never attracted me, nor has position been my goal. My aim has always been to defend the secular foundation of our nation and the poor of our country—the creed sacred to Indiraji and Rajivji. We have moved forward a significant step towards this goal. We have waged a successful battle. But we have not won the war. That is a long and arduous struggle, and I will continue it with full determination.

But I appeal to you to understand the force of my conviction. I request you to accept my decision and to recognise that I will not reverse it. Our foremost responsibility at this critical time is to provide India with a secular government that is strong and stable.

Friends, you have given me your generous support; you have struggled against all odds with me. As one of you and as president of the Congress party, I pledge myself to work with you and for the country. My resolve will in fact be all the more firm, to fight for our principles, for our vision, and for our ideals.

18

INDIA AND THE WORLD

As the crown of the British imperial structure, India was central to the international system Britain had built over a couple of centuries. India's relations with the outside world were entirely designed to supplement the imperial policies of the British Empire. It was as citizens of the empire that early Indian intellectuals were able to conceptualize the weaknesses and strengths of the Indian connections to the empire and become aware of the plight of Africans and Asians in other parts of the empire as well as in other imperial systems. The critique of the imperial foreign policy emanating from India voiced this understanding. The birth of an independent foreign policy is located in this intellectual milieu. The earliest criticism of imperial foreign policy came in the shape of an attack on the military policies of the British Indian government. It was argued, and quite convincingly, that military expeditions of the British Indian armies, which were financed out of Indian resources, were primarily meant to advance British imperial interests.

As the freedom movement gathered momentum and became organized under the aegis of the Indian National Congress, Indian leaders began to take up the cause of Indian indentured labourers in far-off colonies and express their opposition to the exploitation of other people on the grounds of colour and race. By the 1940s, India had emerged at the forefront in the struggle against colonialism. India's independence itself acted as a catalyst in defeating colonial forces in other parts of the developing world, particularly in Africa. In

1946, India became the first country to raise the question of racial discrimination in South Africa. At the same time, Indian leaders were enthusiastic votaries of parliamentary democracy and despite the fact that they were fighting for freedom from Britain, they supported the British war effort during the Second World War only because it was a question of the survival of democracy in the face of fascism.

Therefore, when India emerged on the world stage as an independent nation, it already had the foundations of its foreign policy chalked out. In the course of the freedom struggle, the leaders had developed a consensus on the basic principles which would guide India's relationship with the world: friendship with all countries, resolving conflicts by peaceful means, the sovereign equality of all states, and equity in the conduct of international relations. The decision to remain part of the Commonwealth despite having suffered at the hands of British colonialism, the position India took on the Korean imbroglio in the early 1950s, and Jawaharlal Nehru's leadership during the Suez crisis in 1956 were the result of these principles. The idea of non-alignment with any power bloc and pursuing an independent foreign policy was also based on the experiences India had gleaned during the freedom struggle.

However, India's independence coincided with the onset of the Cold War which saw the world being divided into two powerful and estranged camps. India's resolve to not align with these blocs and its efforts to carve out an independent way, which would try to bring the warring blocs closer to each other in the quest for world peace, entailed strengthening multilateral world institutions like the United Nations. From the beginning, India took an active part in founding, maintaining and engaging with similar institutions. It took the lead in efforts to organize Asian and African nations to address issues of development. India had already taken steps towards this end with the Asian Relations Conference which it had organized in March 1947.

India has played a crucial role in the debate and discussion on nuclear non-proliferation and disarmament. The ideas of peace and non-violence that constituted the core of the anti-colonial struggle came to define India's quest for a peaceful international order. However, in spite of championing the cause of disarmament, there was a practical side to the issue which the leadership realized very early: the desire for peace could not come at the cost of national security. Modern science and technology were the sine qua non not only for development but also to create a strong state capable of defending itself. Thus, even while the Indian state rooted for a nuclear weapon-free world, it did not close itself to developments in the field of nuclear energy. In 1974, India tested its first nuclear device and in 1998 it declared itself a nuclear state. All the while, India had to fight the double standards of Western powers which, in the name of non-proliferation, refused to allow developing countries to perform even basic scientific experiments in nuclear or allied fields while piling their own backyards with nuclear weapons. On many occasions, it was the Indian voice which openly fought Western hypocrisy on the nuclear issue in international forums. At the same time, India continued advocating total global disarmament and made constant efforts to gather willing parties towards the quest as the initiative taken by Rajiv Gandhi in 1988 shows.

The last decade of the twentieth century witnessed the dissolution of the Soviet Union and widespread change in Eastern Europe, with the fall of the Berlin Wall symbolizing the collapse of the Iron Curtain which separated the two worlds. It was in such a situation that rapid economic changes swept over India. One of the architects of India's new economic outlook, P.V. Narasimha Rao, was also a perceptive thinker on external affairs who gave India's foreign policy a new orientation in the world that had dawned after the Cold War. In its understanding of the changing world order and the new basis of international relations, Narasimha Rao's speech at the French Institute of International Relations, Paris, on 29 September 1992, is probably as significant as Nehru's speech in September 1946 in the interim government which laid down the basis of India's foreign policy.

JAWAHARLAL NEHRU

India's Foreign Policy

There is an underlying assumption in today's intellectual world that India's foreign policy was single-handedly designed and crafted by Jawaharlal Nehru. The truth is that the progress of the national movement saw the evolution of a vision of the world and India's place in it which was best articulated by Nehru. The idea of non-alignment, the desire and campaign for peace, the disavowal of the use of force in another country's internal matters and a very powerful anti-colonial thrust were all views voiced by Indian intellectuals and leaders since the late nineteenth century. In fact, people like Surendranath Banerjea protested against British Indian soldiers being sent to Afghanistan; D.E. Wacha consistently criticized the British government for using India's resources for British imperial designs. Similarly, in the 1920s and 1930s, the Indian leadership and a large cross-section of intellectuals took a stand against the rise of fascism in Europe. Thus, there was already a strong convergence of ideas regarding India's position in the world from which its foreign policy would spring. Thus, when Nehru spoke on 7 September 1946, six days after the interim government was formed, he was broadcasting the message of the Indian nation and heralding its arrival on the international scene. Nehru's speech is characterized by its lucid language and style and the forceful way in which he outlined the significant features of the foreign policy of independent India.

Friends and comrades, Jai Hind. Six days ago my colleagues and I sat on the chairs of high office in the Government of India. A new Government came into being in this ancient land, the Interim or Provisional Government we called it, the stepping stone to the full independence of India. Many thousands of messages of greetings and good wishes came to us from all parts of the world and from every nook and corner of India…

The Interim National Government is part of a larger scheme which includes the Constituent Assembly which will meet soon to give shape to the Constitution of free and independent India. It is because of this expectation of an early realisation of full independence that we have entered this Government and we propose to function so as to progressively achieve that independence in action both in our domestic affairs and our foreign relations. We shall take full part in international conferences as a free nation with our own policy and not merely as a satellite of another nation. We hope to develop close and direct contacts with other nations and to cooperate with them in the furtherance of world peace and freedom.

We propose, as far as possible, to keep away from the power politics of groups, aligned against one another, which have led in the past to world wars and which may again lead to disasters on an even vaster scale. We believe that peace and freedom are indivisible and the denial of freedom anywhere must endanger freedom elsewhere and lead to conflict and war. We are particularly interested in the emancipation of colonial and dependent countries and peoples, and in the recognition in theory and practice of equal opportunities for all races. We repudiate utterly the Nazi doctrine of racialism, wheresoever and in whatever form it may be practised. We seek no dominion over others and we claim no privileged position over other peoples. But we do claim equal and honourable treatment for our people wherever they may go, and we cannot accept any discrimination against them.

The world, in spite of its rivalries and hatreds and inner conflicts, moves inevitably towards closer cooperation and the building up of a world commonwealth. It is for this One World that free India will work, a world in which there is the free cooperation of free peoples, and no class or group exploits another.

In spite of our past history of conflict, we hope that an independent India will have friendly and cooperative relations with England and the countries of the British Commonwealth. But it is well to remember what is happening in one part of the Commonwealth today. In South Africa racialism is the state doctrine and our people are putting up a heroic struggle against the tyranny of a racial minority. If this racial doctrine is going to be tolerated it must inevitably lead to vast conflicts and world disaster.

We send our greetings to the people of the United States of America to whom destiny has given a major role in international affairs. We trust that this tremendous responsibility will be utilised for the furtherance of peace and human freedom everywhere.

To that other great nation of the modern world, the Soviet Union, which also carries a vast responsibility for shaping world events, we send our greetings. They are our neighbours in Asia and inevitably we shall have to undertake many common tasks and have much to do with each other.

We are of Asia and the peoples of Asia are nearer and closer to us than others. India is so situated that she is the pivot of Western, Southern and South-East Asia. In the past her culture flowed to all these countries and they came to her in many ways. Those contacts are being renewed and the future is bound to see a closer union between India and South-East Asia on the one side, and Afghanistan, Iran, and the Arab world on the other. To the furtherance of that close association of free countries we must devote ourselves. India has followed with anxious interest the struggle of the Indonesians for freedom and to them we send our good wishes.

China, that mighty country with a mighty past, our neighbour, has been our friend through the ages and that friendship will endure and grow. We earnestly hope that her present troubles will end soon and a united and democratic China will emerge, playing a great part in the furtherance of world peace and progress.

... India is on the move and the old order passes. Too long have we been passive spectators of events, the playthings of others. The initiative comes to our people now and we shall make the history of our choice. There is no question of who wins and who loses, for we have to go forward and together as comrades and either all of us win or we all go down together. But there is going to be no failure. We go forward to success and to freedom and well-being of the hundreds of millions of India. Let us all join in this mighty task and make India, the pride of our heart, great among nations, foremost in the arts of peace and progress. The door is open and destiny beckons to all.

~

JAWAHARLAL NEHRU

Membership of the Commonwealth

The Indian constitution provided for a republican form of government. However, Britain and many other Commonwealth countries desired that India remain with the Commonwealth for historical reasons, if not for anything else. But how could India, which fought the British Empire for its freedom, be a member of an organization which was a symbol of colonial power and which had the British monarch as its functional head? Facing strong resentment from different quarters, Nehru and his colleagues decided that India would continue to be a part of the Commonwealth of Nations under titular headship of the British monarch. Coming so soon after a long struggle for independence, the decision surprised many but is illustrative of Nehru's thinking on international affairs. In his broadcast to the nation on 10 May 1949, soon after he attended a meeting of the heads of Commonwealth countries in London, Nehru presented a defence of his stand, reiterating that India did not believe in living with wounded memories of the past and would rather like to make its presence felt in the world with no enmity towards any nation and be part of the struggle for justice. With India becoming a republic, its joining the Commonwealth ultimately changed the character of the organization, with the British monarch becoming a voluntarily accepted ceremonial head of a group of free and independent countries.

I have naturally looked to the interests of India, for that is my first duty. I have always conceived that duty in terms of the larger good of the world. That is the lesson that our Master taught us and he told us also to pursue the ways of peace and of friendship with others, always maintaining the freedom and dignity of India. The world is full of strife today and disaster looms on the horizon. In men's hearts there is hatred and fear and suspicion which cloud their vision. Every step, therefore, which leads to a lessening of this tension in the world, should be a welcome step. I think it is a good augury for the future that the old conflict between India and England should be resolved in this friendly way which is honourable to both countries. There are too many disruptive forces in the world for us to throw our weight in favour of further disruption and any opportunity that offers itself to heal old wounds and to further the cause of cooperation should be welcomed.

I know that much is being done in parts of the Commonwealth which is exceedingly distasteful to us and against which we have struggled in the past. That is a matter to be dealt with by us as a sovereign nation. Let us not mix things up which should be kept separate.

It has been India's privilege in the past to be a meeting place for many cultures. It may be her privilege in the present and the future to be a bridge to join warring factions and to help in maintaining that most urgent thing of today and the future—the peace of the world. It is in the belief that India could more effectively pursue this policy of encouraging peace and freedom and of lessening the bitter hatreds and tensions in the world that I willingly agreed to the London agreement. I associated myself with the decisions taken in London at the Prime Ministers' meeting in the full belief that they were the right decisions for our country and for the world. I trust that the Indian people will also view them in that light and accept them in a manner worthy of the stature and culture of India and with full faith in our future. Let us not waste our energy at this critical moment in the world's history over empty debates, but rather let us concentrate on the urgent tasks of today, so that India may be great and strong and in a position to play a beneficent part in Asia and the world.

~

JAWAHARLAL NEHRU

Asia Finds Herself Again

The Indian freedom struggle inspired many other colonized countries to fight for their independence. The leaders of the Indian National Congress had immense prestige among the struggling masses and their leadership in many countries in Asia and Africa. India's independence, therefore, had a tremendously powerful impact on other movements for freedom in Asia and Africa. In 1947, the people of Indonesia, China, Malaysia, Burma, Ceylon, Indo-China, Iraq, Syria, and many others were fighting against colonial rule. A newly independent India brought the leaders of the Asian countries together at the first Asian Relations Conference in New Delhi in March 1947 to further direct the freedom movements in their respective countries and project an organized front. It was also thought of as a platform for a larger interrelated movement for the freedom and well-being of the Asian people who had suffered colonial rule for centuries. In his inaugural address on 23 March 1947, Nehru expressed solidarity with the Asian people, particularly in their fight against colonial exploitation, and laid down his vision for Asia in the emerging world order.

Friends and fellow Asians, what has brought you, the men and women of Asia, here? Why have you come from various countries of this mother continent of ours and gathered together in this ancient city of Delhi? Some of us, greatly daring, sent you invitations for this Conference and you gave a warm welcome to that invitation. And yet it was not merely the call from us, but some deeper urge that brought you here.

We stand at the end of an era and on the threshold of a new period of history. Standing on this watershed which divides two epochs of human history and endeavour, we can look back on our long past and look forward to the future that is taking shape before our eyes. Asia, after a long period of quiescence, has suddenly become important again in world affairs. If we view the millennia of history, this continent of Asia, with which Egypt has been so intimately connected in cultural fellowship, has played a mighty role in the evolution of humanity. It was here that civilisation began and man started on his unending adventure of life. Here the mind of man searched unceasingly for truth and the spirit of man shone out like a beacon which lighted up the whole world.

This dynamic Asia from which great streams of culture flowed in all directions gradually became static and unchanging. Other peoples and other continents came to the fore and with their new dynamism spread out and took possession of great parts of the world. This mighty continent became just a field for the rival imperialisms of Europe, and Europe became the centre of history and progress in human affairs.

A change is coming over the scene now and Asia is again finding herself. We live in an age of tremendous transition and already the next stage takes shape when Asia assumes her rightful place with the other continents.

It is at this great moment that we meet here and it is the pride and privilege of the people of India to welcome their fellow Asians from other countries, to confer with them about the present and the future, and lay the foundation of our mutual progress, well-being and friendship.

The idea of having an Asian Conference is not new and many have thought of it. It is indeed surprising that it should not have been held many years earlier; yet perhaps the time was not ripe for it and any attempt to do so would have been superficial and not in tune with world events. It so happened that we in India convened this Conference, but the idea of such a conference arose simultaneously in many minds and in many countries of Asia. There was a widespread urge and an awareness that the time had come for us, peoples of Asia, to meet together, to hold together and to advance together. It was not only a vague desire, but the compulsion of events that forced all of us to think along these lines. Because of this, the invitation we in India sent out brought an answering echo and a magnificent response from every country of Asia.

We welcome you, delegates and representatives from China, that great country to which Asia owes so much and from which so much is expected; from Egypt and the Arab countries of Western Asia, inheritors of a proud culture which spread far and wide and influenced India greatly; from Iran whose contacts with India go back to the dawn of history; from Indonesia and Indo-China whose history is intertwined with India's culture, and where recently the battle of freedom has continued, a reminder to us that freedom must be won and cannot come as a gift; from Turkey that has been rejuvenated by the genius of a great leader; from Korea and Mongolia, Siam, Malaya and the Philippines; from the Soviet Republics of Asia which have advanced so rapidly in our generation and which have so many lessons to teach us; and from our neighbours Afghanistan, Tibet, Nepal, Bhutan, Burma and Ceylon to whom we look especially for cooperation and close and friendly intercourse. Asia is very well represented at this Conference, and if one or two countries have been unable to send representatives, this was due to no lack of desire on their part, but because circumstances beyond our control came in the way. We also welcome observers from Australia and New Zealand, because we have many problems in common, especially in the Pacific and in the south-east region of Asia, and we have to cooperate together to find solutions.

As we meet here today, the long past of Asia rises up before us, the troubles of recent years fade away, and a thousand memories revive. But I shall not speak to you of these past ages with their glories and triumphs and failures, nor of more recent times which have oppressed us so much and which still pursue us in some measure. During the past two hundred years we have seen the growth of Western imperialisms and of the reduction of large parts of Asia to colonial or semi-colonial status. Much has happened during these years, but perhaps one of the notable consequences of the European domination of Asia has been the isolation of the countries of Asia from one another. India always had contacts and intercourse with her neighbour countries in the north-west, the north-east, the east and the south-east. With the coming of British rule in India these contacts were broken off and India was almost completely isolated from the rest of Asia. The old land routes almost ceased to function and our chief window to the outer world looked out on the sea route which led to England. A similar process affected other countries of Asia also. Their economy was bound up with some European imperialism or other; even culturally they looked towards Europe and not to their own friends and neighbours from whom they had derived so much in the past.

Today this isolation is breaking down because of many reasons, political and other. The old imperialisms are fading away. The land routes have revived and air travel suddenly brings us very near to one another. This Conference itself is significant as an expression of that deeper urge of the mind and spirit of Asia which has persisted in spite of the isolationism which grew up during the years of European domination. As that domination goes, the walls that surrounded us fall down and we look at one another again and meet as old friends long parted.

In this Conference and in this work there are no leaders and no followers. All countries of Asia have to meet together on an equal basis in a common task and endeavour. It is fitting that India should play her part in this new phase of Asian development. Apart from the fact that India herself is emerging into freedom and independence, she is the natural centre and focal point of the many forces at work in Asia. Geography is a compelling factor, and geographically she is so situated as to be the meeting point of Western and Northern and Eastern and South-East Asia. Because of this, the history of India is a long history of her relations with the other countries of Asia. Streams of culture have come to India from the West and the East and been absorbed in India, producing the rich and variegated culture which is India today. At the same time, streams of culture have flowed from India to distant parts of Asia. If you should know India you have to go to Afghanistan and Western Asia, to Central Asia, to China and Japan and to the countries of South-East Asia. There you will find magnificent evidence of the vitality of India's culture which spread out and influenced vast numbers of people.

There came the great, cultural stream from Iran to India in remote antiquity. And then began that constant intercourse between India and the Far East, notably China. In later years South-East Asia witnessed an amazing efflorescence of Indian art and culture. The mighty stream which started from Arabia and developed as a mixed Iran-Arabic culture poured into India. All these came to us and influenced us, and yet so great was the powerful impress of India's own mind and culture that it could accept them without being itself swept away or overwhelmed. Nevertheless, we all changed in the process and in India today all of us are mixed products of these various influences. An Indian, wherever he may go in Asia, feels a sense of kinship with the land he visits and the people he meets.

I do not wish to speak to you of the past, but rather of the present. We meet here not to discuss our past history and contacts, but to forge links for the future. And may I say here that this Conference, and the idea underlying it, is in no way aggressive or against any other continent or country? Ever since news of this Conference went abroad some people in Europe and America have viewed it with doubt imagining that this was some kind of a Pan-Asian movement directed against Europe or America. We have no designs against anybody; ours is the great design of promoting peace and progress all over the world. For too long have we of Asia been petitioners in Western courts and chancelleries. That story must now belong to the past. We propose to stand on our own legs and to cooperate with all others who are prepared to cooperate with us. We do not intend to be the playthings of others.

In this crisis in world history Asia will necessarily play a vital role. The countries of Asia can no longer be used as pawns by others; they are bound to have their own policies in world affairs. Europe and America have contributed very greatly to human progress and for that we must yield them praise and honour, and learn from them the many lessons they have to teach. But the West has also driven us into wars and conflicts without number, and even now, the day after a terrible war, there is talk of further wars in the atomic age that is upon us. In this atomic age Asia will have to function effectively in the maintenance of peace. Indeed, there can be no peace unless Asia plays her part. There is today conflict in many countries, and all of us in Asia are full of our own troubles. Nevertheless, the whole spirit and outlook of Asia are peaceful, and the emergence of Asia in world affairs will be a powerful influence for world peace.

Peace can only come when nations are free and also when human beings everywhere have freedom and security and opportunity. Peace and freedom, therefore, have to be considered both in their political and economic aspects. The countries of Asia, we must remember, are very backward and the standards of life are appallingly low. These economic problems demand urgent solution or else crisis and disaster may overwhelm us. We have, therefore, to think in terms of the common man and fashion our political, social and economic structure so that the burdens that have crushed him may be removed, and he may have full opportunity for growth.

We have arrived at a stage in human affairs when the ideal of One World and some kind of a World Federation seem to be essential, though there are many dangers and obstacles in the way. We should work for that ideal and not for any grouping which comes in the way of this larger world group. We, therefore, support the United Nations structure which is painfully emerging from its infancy. But in order to have One World, we must also, in Asia, think of the countries of Asia cooperating together for that larger ideal.

This Conference, in a small measure, represents this bringing together of the countries of Asia. Whatever it may achieve, the mere fact of its taking place is itself of historic significance. Indeed, this occasion is unique in history, for never before has such a gathering met together at any place. So even in meeting we have achieved much and I have no doubt that out of this meeting greater things will come. When the history of our present times is written, this event may well stand out as a landmark which divides the past of Asia from the future. And because we are participating in this making of history, something of the greatness of historic events comes to us all.

This Conference will split up into committees and groups to discuss various problems which are of common concern to all of us. We shall not discuss the internal politics of any country, because that is rather beyond the scope of our present meeting. Naturally we are interested in these internal politics, because they act and react on each other, but we may not discuss them at this stage, for if we do so, we may lose ourselves in interminable arguments and complications. We may fail to achieve the purpose for which we have met. I hope that out of this Conference some permanent Asian Institute for the study of common problems and to bring about closer relations will emerge; also perhaps a School of Asian Studies. Further, we might be able to organise an interchange of visits and exchanges of students and professors so that we might get to know one another better. There is much more we can do, but I shall not venture to enumerate all these subjects for it is for you to discuss them and arrive at some decisions.

We seek no narrow nationalism. Nationalism has a place in each country and should be fostered, but it must not be allowed to become aggressive and come in the way of international development. Asia stretches her hand out in friendship to Europe and America as well as to our suffering brethren in Africa. We of Asia have a special responsibility to the people of Africa. We must help them to their rightful place in the human family. The freedom that we envisage is not to be confined to this nation or that or to a particular people, but must spread out over the whole human race. Universal human freedom also cannot be based on the supremacy of any particular class. It must be the freedom of the common man everywhere and full opportunity for him to develop.

We think today of the great architects of Asian freedom—Sun Yat Sen, Zaghlul Pasha, the Ataturk Kemal Pasha and others, whose labours have borne fruit. We think also of that great figure whose labours and whose inspiration have brought India to the threshold of her independence—Mahatma Gandhi. We miss him at this Conference and I yet hope that he may visit us before our labours end. He is engrossed in the service of the common man in India, and even this Conference could not drag him away from it.

All over Asia we are passing through trials and tribulations. In India also you will see conflict and trouble. Let us not be disheartened by this; this is inevitable in an age of mighty transition. There are powerful creative impulses and a new vitality in all the peoples of Asia. The masses are awake and they demand their heritage. Strong winds are blowing all over Asia. Let us not be afraid of them, but rather welcome them; for, only with their help can we build the new Asia of our dreams. Let us have faith in these great new forces and the dream which is taking shape. Let us, above all, have faith in the human spirit which Asia has symbolized for those long ages past.

~

CHAKRAVARTHY RAJAGOPALACHARI

On the Korean Situation

Born in Thorapalli village of Salem district, Tamil Nadu, on 10 December 1878, C. Rajagopalachari (1878–1972), known to the people of India as Rajaji or CR, was quite often referred to by Mahatma Gandhi as 'the keeper of my conscience'. He in a sense became the symbol of the Gandhi-led movement which incorporated social reform, constructive work and the fight for national freedom. No wonder he was known as the Gandhi of south India. As the first chief minister of Madras after the 1935 Act, he was instrumental in introducing many far-reaching measures and laying the foundation of a modern welfare government. After independence, he became the first Indian Governor-General of India. An intellectual stalwart, he possessed a clear and logical mind, uncompromising uprightness and an unparalleled command over English, Tamil, Sanskrit and many more languages. In the speech reproduced here, Rajaji's maiden speech in Parliament in 1950, he launched a spirited defence of India's foreign policy in the light of Jawaharlal Nehru committing India to the Korean imbroglio without taking Parliament into confidence.

In this country of ours we sit quite a long time in Parliament, and we seem to love it, and yet sometimes it happens that very urgent matters calling for immediate action come up for decision just when the House is not sitting. It is for this reason we chose a leader who can be trusted to act in accordance with our wishes and with our general policies on such occasions. I have no doubt the House will approve of my statement if I say that our Prime Minister is a little more democratic than he need be sometimes. On this particular occasion he had to act at once, and I think he acted as he did because he knew that he could get the approval of the House and because also there is a provision in the Constitution that if the House would not give that approval it would be at liberty to alter the policy and at the same time to change its Prime Minister also. I do not, therefore, think that any great point arises out of the fact that when he had to meet the demands of the situation, when the Korea aggression took place, he had not the time to consult the House. He has immediately taken steps to call the House to a special session in order that he may be sure of his ground. I do not think, therefore, that there is any great point in this objection that was repeated by more than one including, I think, even the Deputy-Speaker of the House. I think it was not very important for one of the Deputy-Speaker's position to raise—I would not have minded if other speakers who have fundamental objections to the policy had made it. If one who has no objection to the policy raises it, it looks somewhat odd and might even confuse the issue. I do not think that the people of this country who are still new to democracy should be led to believe that in matters of such urgent importance in foreign matters, unless the whole Parliament is asked to come and decide, the Prime Minister is not entitled to act. I think, as in England, our people should be educated to the fact that very often we entrust the whole matter to the leader in whom we have confidence.

Then, the issue has been somewhat clouded by the form which amendments have taken. I see in the revised list of amendments as it stands, amendments 1, 2 and 3 are really opposition and not amendments. It is convenient perhaps that you may dispose of them in the form of amendments. I just wish to explain that in substance, amendments 1, 2 and 3 are really opposite to what the motion comes to and that therefore these amendments should be rejected totally in case the House approves of the policy which the government has pursued. Regarding the other amendments, No. 4 and amendment No. 5 really are of no great importance by way of debate. Amendment No. 4 wants that we should make an appeal to all people to support the policy which the Prime Minister has pursued. Amendment No. 5 wants to reinforce the army in India, which might be brought up on a suitable occasion in quite a different way; but it is not now very relevant. The last amendment is really a true amendment. It suggests that a token army should be sent to oppose the aggression in Korea in pursuance of the policy that we have adopted.

The first thing to be settled is, what is our attitude in regard to United Nations? I make bold to say, though I am new to this Parliament, that the whole House would approve of the position taken in this regard, namely, that India stands for the conservation and strengthening of the machinery of the United Nations. It definitely stands for the conservation of that organisation and for the strengthening of that organisation. If this is settled, then, the issue before us gets clarified. If we merely discuss it on the basis of Asiatic progress or Asiatic nationality or the unity of some parts of Asia and so on, we get somewhat confused over the issue. The present question is, are we to support and strengthen the United Nations, or do we stand for a policy of overlooking this point whenever any particular issue arises. I have no doubt in my mind as to what we should do. There is no hope for any nation in Asia unless we strengthen the forces that stand for peace and order in this world. If we encourage anything that disturbs the peace of world, there is no hope for any nation in Asia as there is no hope for any nation in other parts of the world. So far as we are concerned, progress either of democracy or progress in the nature of prosperity for any nation in Asia depends entirely on peace being maintained in the world. That is why whenever any issue comes up, the Prime Minister, naturally, sees along with that the linked issue of maintenance of peace in the world... In Asia, just now, looked at from the point of view of human affairs, the peace of the world is linked with every issue that comes up for decision before the citizens of Asia to whatever nation they may belong. If any people believe that introducing a certain economic order or new Government to take charge of affairs by force, which may lead to its conflagration throughout the world, would help, I must say emphatically that they are foolish and that they are taking a suicidal line of action.

Now, therefore, the issue is clear before us. Let us by all means sympathise with the aspirations of Korea. Let us by all means sympathise with those who stand for the unification of the nations of Asia and against any artificial barriers being raised dividing them, for the sake of peace between other nations of the world. The 38th Parallel is one such thing. The 38th Parallel was simply an artificial arrangement by which the armies of the USSR on the one hand and the armies of America on the other were asked to stop at a particular geometrical point or rather a straight line in order that there may be no further confusion in the affairs of the world. But, that has divided Korea as a matter of fact, just now, into two administrations. The issue now is whether an aggressive expedition in order to remove this barrier will produce world conflagration or not and if it is likely to produce a world conflagration, what is India's attitude in that respect. This is the approach which I should like the House to make so that it may judge the policy which the government has followed. If India stands for statesmanly action in the United Nations Security Council, and for the conservation and strengthening of the authority of the United Nations, without unduly attempting to strangle the individual sovereignty of the nations that compose the United Nations, then, we can see the logic behind the Prime Minister's policy and the action taken by him after the announcement made by him as to policy.

If we examine the criticisms—the House was very critical as Mr. Shiva Rao pointed out—whatever might be the impression of a casual visitor, the fact remains that the House is going to give overwhelming support and approval to the policy that has been pursued by the government, which has been announced by the Prime Minister and followed by action on his part. But, there has been some criticism. We should not object to criticism. Nobody is going to be misled by criticism. I do not think the nations of the world are so stupid as to get away with the impression that because several speeches are made here, the confidence which the country is reposing in the Prime Minister has become a matter of doubt. The nations of the world are alive and vigilant and they are not going to commit any such mistake. Let us not be too nervous about expression of opinion. Let us be frank and understand one another. We have not much opposition in our House. Let us not try to discourage criticism.

What is this criticism? This criticism takes one or other of three lines as far as I can see. One is that the Government of India should have kept rigorously aloof. The word 'neutrality' has been used in a somewhat loose style. There is no war for us to decide whether we should be neutral or not. The only question is what should be our attitude in regard to this matter. Some have said that the Government of India should have kept entirely and rigorously aloof. The other line which some members have taken is that the Prime Minister should have done a little less than what he did or he should have done something else. The third line of criticism is that he should have gone much farther than what he has done just now. Let us examine these three positions.

The first position that the Government of India should have kept entirely aloof, I think, is an impossible position. It is impossible even if it were consistent with our national dignity and national interest. How can we ignore the position that somehow we have reached in the world? Can India say, we have no opinion in this matter? That is the simple question. To keep aloof would mean that India is of the opinion that she cannot say anything on this subject. Surely, this is impossible. Neither in my personal capacity, nor as representative of my country, do I wish that we should be arrogant or proud or be conceited. Our power is very little; but our importance is not as little as our power. There is a great difference between the power that we now possess and the importance which without our seeking has been thrust upon India. We could not possibly remain silent in this connection. Keeping aloof is an impossibility.

Then, could we have done anything else than what the Prime Minister has done? If we did anything else than what he has done, it would mean practically encouragement of the very aggression which he seeks to resist and check, very rightly. If India seeks to resist and check violent aggression anywhere, in order that we people in Asia may have a chance of progress in all directions, the Prime Minister of India could not possibly have done less than what he has done; nor could he have kept aloof as I have already said. I imagine that by analysing the history of Korea and by attributing motives, conjecturally and otherwise to the various nations of the world, and by letting ourselves morbidly to fear every powerful nation in the world, we would be acting contrary to what Gandhiji told us to do. He said, 'Shed your fears. Why are you afraid? Strength is not the only means to power. Spiritual strength is as good as physical strength. Do not, therefore, be afraid of anybody.' If you follow that advice, I do not think that either Prof. K.T. Shah or any other member would express such dreadful fear of America, rightly or wrongly, on all occasions. Of course, America is very strong and very powerful too; but why should we be afraid of her? This suspicion, in my humble opinion, is somewhat morbid and we should shed this suspicion.

What is the real issue? Do we or do we not want to check violent aggression in any part of the world in the present state of things? I do not talk total pacifist logic. Let no one make that mistake. But violent jingo logic is as labyrinthine as pacifist logic, and the contrary is also true. I am not talking to you of mere pacifist logic. But in the present state of the world, can we allow violent aggression? On the one side America is interested in her own interests for peace; and on the other the USSR is interested in her own interests for peace. Now, when these two powers are so near to a seat of disturbance, can India possibly look calmly and disinterestedly on a match being thrown near a powder magazine of this kind? I want you to allow me to put a hypothetical case before the House. I am confident that if America had not taken this step of rushing her forces into Korea, and if this violent aggression of North Korea had been permitted to strangle and capture the whole of Korea, every member of this House would have risen in protest and said that at that time America failed in her duty. Everyone of us would have shouted: 'She was so near in Japan. She had all her forces there, and yet she kept looking on. Is this the way a Member of the United Nations should behave on a critical occasion like this?' Everyone would have severely, and I say rightly criticised the American Government for not having done its duty by the United Nations at that juncture. Now, if we follow up this picture, we can settle the present question of right and wrong easily, if we would have blamed a certain nation for not doing a particular thing, can we blame them for doing the thing? I submit that it is wrong to blame them and that is why the Prime Minister of India had no doubt in his mind what to do. Aggression has to be checked, he said, and we offer our moral support to that checking. We are a member of the United Nations and we support the resolutions of the Security Council. India fully supports the policy of checking aggression.

As to what a particular nation should do in order to contribute to the checking of aggression, it is a matter depending on so many things, to be taken together. Its capacity, geographical propinquity and several other matters have to be taken into account in order to decide what particular assistance should be given in order to check aggression. If we are therefore clear in our minds that we ought to check aggression wherever it takes place and whenever it takes place in a dangerous area—apart from any question of pacifism—where there is likely to be a start for world conflagration when such aggression takes place, our first duty irrespective of the merits of the issue is to stop that aggression and to nip violence in the bud, so to say. If we do that there is hope for peace, and it is on that basis that the Prime Minister, on behalf of India, gave full support to the resolutions of the Security Council in regard to this matter. It does not matter how the 38th Parallel came to exist. It does not matter how America came to be independent. It does not matter how Bulgaria came to be independent. If a nation is there, or a government is there and armed aggression is going to disturb its existence, then those who are interested in the peace of the world should prevent this beginning of the conflagration in that area.

Now, if that is settled, then the question that arises is, could we do more? Is the criticism that the Prime Minister should have done more than he did, right criticism? If we think it out, the House will see that if anything more were done by India, instead of checking aggression it might lead to the very conflagration which we wish to prevent. If country after country rushed to Korea with its armies, what can follow, except world conflagration? That was the great problem which our Prime Minister had to face. He had to see where the line should be drawn. He had to see how far we could go and where further progress would have been dangerous. Now here it is that statesmanship comes to play. In attempting to check aggression we should not do anything to accelerate that very conflagration which we fear might be produced and for which we wish to check that aggression. People say that I always try to explain things by means of analogies. Let me indulge in an instance here. Suppose there is a patient who requires a warm fire, or who requires a meal to be cooked by a fire. Can we light that fire if there is a powder magazine nearby? It is true that we should uphold Korea. It is true that we should check aggression, but we should not do it in a manner which would lead to a world conflagration. It is a simple issue. It is difficult to solve, but simple in enunciation. The Prime Minister had no doubt in his mind that we ought not to indulge in any armed movements in the Pacific or in the Indian Ocean or send armies out in ships or make, so to say, any gesture which might be quite enough to light a conflagration in the whole world. That is my answer to the amendment, that the action already taken to implement the policy of the government is not enough, and that government should send a token army. It may be that some time or other we may have to do a thing like that. That is the meaning of the Prime Minister's policy of independence in foreign affairs. What the Prime Minister has been repeatedly urging is not that we are bound to pacifism, or that we are bound to neutrality, as it is called. What he has been urging is that India should not previously commit itself to be an ally of any bloc whose decision it is bound to contribute to in implementation. What he has been saying is that we should keep ourselves independent in our foreign policy and we should decide from time to time as occasions arise as to what he should do in any matter.

There has been criticism that the action taken is likely to lead to a breach of the neutrality we were pledged to. Assuming various things that do not exist, criticisms are offered. But what has India stood for? It has stood for its own independence and for freedom from bloc-alliances. Now that has not been broken in any manner by the Prime Minister's action or the announcement of the government. In fact he has gone almost to the dangerous limit, so to say, of being misunderstood, in order to maintain that independence, by refusing to send any regiment to Korea. It is very easy for people to misunderstand his attitude and imagine that India does not stand for checking aggression and that she is silently, secretly sympathising with the aggressors. He has preferred to risk being misunderstood in that manner, because any other step would have been encouragement to world conflagration, to a world war.

It is true that there are some people—Dr. Syama Prasad gave expression to something of that kind—who think that peace can be preserved only by force being met by stronger force, that if there is aggression it must be met by stronger force and that is the only way and all other talk is moonshine. If this logic were carried to its end it will certainly lead to a world war sooner than later. It is true, as we all know, that generally force can be met only by force. But it is not so in the present case. Why did we build the United Nations Organisation and why do we wish to conserve it? Because we feel that aggression can be checked by the strength of the opinion of the world expressed in such an organisation and that open discussion and postponement of aggressive activities finally lead to checking aggression. That is the principle on which the United Nations Organisation has been formed.

There are some people who think that unless we have a complete World Federation all talk of regulating the force of nations in the UNO is moonshine. Academically it may be a correct position that unless we have a world government and a world army and we are able to oppose that army against every rebel nation, we cannot succeed cent per cent. While that is academically right, we do hope in this world that without strangling individual nationality we can build up slowly, steadily and surely a world organisation to prevent world wars. It has become a passion with the Prime Minister and that is why he as well as the country which he represents, our motherland have risen in the opinion of the world at the present juncture. The steadiness with which he has pursued that aim has raised him and India in the eyes of the world more than we realise ordinarily. It is acknowledged that we are in no way a military power but yet our importance has risen, because of the courage with which we pursue this policy.

Everyone in the world wants peace but they do not know how to get it and maintain it. But India seems to be on the right track and that is why this phenomenal popularity of our Prime Minister throughout the world. We must strengthen his arms. We must give more grease to his elbow, as it is said. We must enable him to help the world to maintain peace.

If we understand these difficulties and those views which I have attempted to explain, the very imperfections that have been pointed out in the policy and the action taken by our Prime Minister will be seen to be their best features. The seeming imperfections, inconsistency and halting character of the action that is now the subject of our debate are its very virtues and its essential virtues. We have to balance what is necessary to check aggression and also avoid and discourage a world conflagration. It is a delicate balancing and that is the virtue of the attitude that the Government of India has taken.

The Prime Minister has taken what action he thought proper and has been almost ploughing a lone furrow. His courage I might say is great in this matter and should be appreciated. He has been ploughing this lone furrow boldly and without any doubt in his own mind and we should appreciate it. That is why he has gone much more into the hearts of the peoples of the world than he might himself have expected at the outset, considering the position which India occupies at the present day. That is why also the same people who criticise him and who are somewhat annoyed by his lukewarmness so far as partisanship is concerned, appreciate his action and welcome it. As a matter of fact they hope that he will, in spite of their own annoyance, carry on in this manner and bring about the confirmation of peace in the world. At any rate, I make bold to say that on account of South Korea there will be no world war. What has been done so far and what has not been done so far taken together make it quite clear to my mind that there will be no world war now. On this very important thing we may rest assured and if any merchant is hoarding his stock to sell them at a higher price, I warn him that he will lose and will make no profit. Prices will begin to go down everywhere hereafter and will not go up.

The line which our Prime Minister has been pursuing has for the moment failed. But there is nothing to be ashamed of; there is nothing to feel discouraged on account of the fact that it has failed.

Things appear to fail but they come out all right later on. It will grow because it has found root in the hearts of people. Only we have to wait for a time and you will see that his peace programme will be taken up.

There are two issues before the United Nations which cannot be ignored. The checking of aggression we support. Let us not be discouraged by the first phase of the fight. Aggression will be checked and Russia knows it very well. That is why I take it that she has come back to take her seat in the Security Council. The other issue is, what then? That is the main and great issue which bas been troubling the mind of our Prime Minister. He is continually asking the question 'Aggression has to be checked. I am for that. But what then?' Are you going to garrison Korea for all time and keep off the enemy at the point of the bayonet? No, it is impossible. Therefore something should be done in order to relieve the tension. What can be done? The things to do and he has suggested them are, get Russia and the real China into the Security Council and let us discuss it together and find a solution for Korea. Without finding a solution for Korea, simply depending on the 38th Parallel, which is merely an astronomer's straight line, as a sacrosanct frontier, is of no use. Independently of checking aggression, let us get all the nations together around a common table and decide. That is why we want China to be recognised. Whether the new China is to be recognised or not, the new China is a fact and sooner or later the United Nations have to recognise not only China but every properly established government in the world. Otherwise there is no strengthening of the United Nations and gradually the United Nations Organisation will deteriorate into a bloc combining to work out their own programme rather than the programme of the world. That is why our Prime Minister is so eager that all opponents should be brought together. Even in this House do we keep out people who may advocate even the most extreme opposition to the government? They are allowed to find a place here and the Speaker rightly gives them far more time than to the supporters of the government. And that is what should be done in the United Nations. Let us burn the gun powder at a common discussion table. The gun powder will exhaust itself at the table, because ultimately gun powder is the anger of mind and that anger, if given an outlet at the table, will finish itself. Even in this very House does not an honourable member after he has lashed out, come outside with a blossoming smile? When the talk is over we are all friends. It is the same principle. Human nature is one in all such matters and I am certain that if the policy of India is accepted by the United Nations, it is bound to be, in course of time, the beginning of peace. We shall then be able to solve the problems of Asia. Otherwise there is confusion, confusion between the forces of nationalism and the forces of Communism and of anti-Communism. All these are mixed up. One does not know what is going on in any particular place. Are they opposing Communism or the foreigner? Are they supporting nationalism? All the confusions will be cleared if people would gather together and discuss the matter. I wish to apologise for any irrelevance and I hope in a maiden speech it will be tolerated.

~

V.K. KRISHNA MENON

India and the United Nations Agenda

V.K. Krishna Menon (1896–1974) gave voice to the anger that the Third World felt about Western hegemony in the international scenario. His was the voice that expressed the fearless confidence of the colonized in their fight against colonialism and racialism. After his studies at Presidency College, Madras, he came into contact with Annie Besant and then left for England in 1925 where he was involved with and became the secretary of the Commonwealth of India League (later, the India League). In 1935, he met Jawaharlal Nehru when the latter came to England and both became friends for life. Krishna Menon was India's high commissioner to the United Kingdom from 1947 to 1952. Between 1953 and 1963, he was the chairman of India's delegation to the United Nations. In between, he became India's defence minister but had to resign in 1962 after India's debacle during the Chinese attack. This speech, his first at the United Nations General Assembly, delivered on 28 September 1953, is a succinct and masterful statement of India's position in the world order and the possible agenda that the United Nations should adopt vis-à-vis equality among nations, the fight against racism and colonialism, and solving the world's problems through peaceful means and not through external aggression as was happening in Korea at that time.

… I should now like to address myself to some of the current problems on the agenda. The first problem relates to the representation of China in the United Nations Assembly. This question will no doubt come up when the report of the Credentials Committee is presented, at which time we shall challenge the report. For four years the legitimate Government of China, the government that has control of the country, the government to which the people owe allegiance and whose authority alone is able to fulfil its obligations, has applied for admission to the United Nations and requested that its delegation be received. The Assembly has not accepted the credentials of the representatives of this government. We regret that this question was again the subject of controversy at the beginning of this session of the General Assembly. In our humble view it is unfortunate that the Soviet Union and the United States fought the issue at large. It should properly be debated at the time of the submission of the credentials report. I submit, with all the deference one can have towards the Chair, that we are doubtful concerning not only the wisdom but also the propriety of raising the question at the early stage, because that is anticipating the finding of the Credentials Committee. We are unable to accept the view, subject to the Chair's ruling, that the matter has been disposed of by the resolution submitted by the United States and adopted by the Assembly that may relate to the problem of the recognition of China or to anything of that kind...

Therefore, I wish to restate our attitude, which is the same as it was last year. The Government of China, which has applied for representation in the United Nations for the past four years, which is the only government that can carry out the obligations in respect of the Charter, and which is the only government entitled to be here, ought to be here. When I was dealing with questions concerning Asia, I should have stated that denying this representation to the proper Chinese government really means disenfranchising 500 million people.

I wish to state, as regards the representatives of the authorities of Formosa who take the place of the Chinese government here, that we have no quarrel with them as persons and that we make no derogatory references of any kind to the personalities concerned. Here we are dealing with a political issue. We have due regard for those who occupy those seats. But at the same time it is our duty to point out that the present situation renders the representation of nearly a third of the Asian continent to this Assembly null and void.

... The next item on the agenda to which we should like to address ourselves is the problem of race conflict. The item which is termed 'race conflict' is, I think, a bit of a euphemism; it is really race domination. This question has been before us for six successive sessions, that is, in the form of the 'Treatment of people of Indian origin in the Union of South Africa', or, more recently, the question of apartheid itself. For six sessions, one or the other of these problems has been before us. The General Assembly has passed five resolutions in regard to the matter. It offered the Government of the Union of South Africa four alternatives, and on three occasions it condemned the Group Areas Act and asked the South African government not to put it into operation. The South African government has turned a deaf ear to all this, except to the extent of intervening in the debate in the attempt to show that these are matters of domestic jurisdiction. This again is another of those expressions of the doctrine of legitimism: if people do not protest, then they are not dissatisfied enough; if they protest, then they are rebels; in either case, the people are wrong.

The next item to which we should like to address ourselves in this general debate is the colonial issue. It is not our intention to allude particularly to the problems of Morocco or Tunis or South West Africa. However, I think it is necessary to say that, in the case of the first two, which are partly under the administration of the French Republic, it is not merely a problem of colonial rule. To our mind and in our approach, it is a problem of the violation of international treaties. It is disregard of the Charter and of treaty obligations and the intervention against and violation of the sovereignty of a territory. Morocco and Tunis are territories that are externally sovereign because the regime of the French government is regulated by treaty obligations. By violation of the treaties, therefore, the authorities responsible have put themselves in a position where they are subject to challenge, not only—as colonial rulers—on the general problem of colonial rule, but also with regard to the sanctity of treaties and the sovereignty of territories which they have violated. We shall deal with this matter in due course when it comes before the Committee.

... Since the time of the war, in the Asian continent some 600 million people have ceased to be members of dependent States. One is happy to say that today, in the whole Asian continent, there are only 14 million people who are under colonial rule. Most of them are under the aegis of the United Kingdom and the rest are under France. But there are only 14 million people who are what might be called subject peoples. It should be possible to bring this subjection to an end. These subject peoples occupy only a very small area of Asia. On the continent of Africa, the problem is rather different. We have a situation where the United Kingdom, which has a home territory of somewhere about 94,000 square miles—less than 100,000 square miles—has an empire in Africa of somewhere about 2,250,000 square miles; whereas France, which has a home territory of less than 250,000 square miles, holds sway over nearly 4,500,000 square miles; 6,750,000 square miles are colonial areas, and, if you include the Trust Territories, it amounts to 8,750,000 square miles. Out of a total population of 191 million people, 139 million people are either subject to colonial rule or are in Trust Territories. Therefore, the vast continent of Africa, which is 130 or 150 times the size of the United Kingdom, is still in part the latter's private domain, the rest being shared by France, Portugal and Spain. Not only was the whole continent retained for the purpose of exploitation, but certain sections of humanity are kept out of it by various devices, indeed even on the basis of apartheid. Therefore, in viewing colonialism, it is not sufficient for us to determine whether the people are worse or better off, or whether the metropolitan countries can find a certain number of convenient local allies to be against their own people. It is time that the sovereign countries, in the context of the provisions of the Charter, faced this colonial issue—which involves discrimination as to race and creed and militates against the self-determination of peoples and national independence—not in the way of entertaining complaints or of merely meeting agitation, but as part of the more constructive endeavours to liberate the entire world by the conscious attempts of humanity, and particularly by the metropolitan countries.

With the best of intentions and feeling—and I feel I can do so—I particularly say to the United Kingdom, which has before it the experience which has often been stated in the words, she has lost an empire to win a commonwealth, she has lost domination to win a fraternity, should not the notable example of Libya and West Africa be extended so that the United Kingdom should no longer have colonial countries any more than it should have slaves at home?

That brings me to the last item on which I want to speak, and that is Korea. The question of Korea has cast its shadow not only over this Assembly but over the entire world. It is a very distressing and dark shadow, the spectre of a country drenched in blood where millions of people on one side and the other have died, where millions of children have been orphaned and where reconstruction, even if it begins today, will take many years before it can make of Korea a homeland in which all its people can live. In addition to this, Korea stands today as the symbol of something which will test our wisdom, our humanity and our political sense. Solutions in Korea represent one of the ways of resolving world tensions. Together with Germany, people look to Korea and what happens there as an indication of what is likely to happen in the rest of the world. The shadow of Korea is drawn long over the face of this Assembly and indeed over the world. It is a story of tragedy, not only of the Korean people but of the peoples in China, the United States, the United Kingdom, France and everywhere else where troops have gone and engaged in war for purposes which their sides believed to be right. It is our business to see that our efforts of the last three years, which have made very slow progress, now become embodied in the terms of a truce.

The position of India in this matter is very well known. Speaking from this rostrum only a few weeks ago [430th meeting] I made it entirely clear that anything that we say in this matter or indeed on any other is not intended to add to the heat of the debate. We think that in the progress that we have made in Korea and in the winning of an armistice, we have reached one milestone. But still, what happens in Korea today is only part of the implementation of the Armistice Agreement, namely, the handing over of the prisoners in pursuance of the Armistice Agreement. When that is over, or simultaneously with it, there comes the other problem of peace. At this present moment I satisfy myself with saying that it would be wrong, in our humble opinion, to approach this problem of peace with the same mentality and in the same atmosphere as prevailed at Panmunjom. There an armistice was negotiated by two sets of warring peoples. The war has stopped now, and it is the common desire of either side to establish peace, and we must therefore approach the problem of peace in an atmosphere of conference.

If I may say so without it being regarded as inappropriate, and I hope the Assembly will bear with me, I think it is appropriate for us to mention that gallant band of men who are today performing the act of repatriation in Korea. I refer to the Indian army. The Indian army is charged with the onerous duty of dealing with the problems of law and order, objective problems, but with very little material power. Our men and our officers have covered themselves with the kind of glory that is not usual in war. For the first time a peace army, on foreign territory, without arms, has been called upon to deal with turbulence and, according to all our information, has done so gallantly and well. I hope this situation continues. They have performed their duty in such a way as to create a feeling of pride not only in our nationals but in this organisation itself. They are part of an international machinery—and I hope it is appropriate for me to refer to this, because one thing that comes out of what has been happening with regard to repatriation is that, given the will, and if we are able to throw away the accepted and conventional views of approach, we can sometimes achieve results. Therefore, an unarmed army is today dealing with a situation in a way which is not only glorious from their point of view, but full of lessons for others who have to resolve political problems.

~

V.K. KRISHNA MENON

On Kashmir

V.K. Krishna Menon has the distinction of delivering the longest speech in the history of the United Nations—an eight-hour-long marathon spread over three successive meetings of the United Nations Security Council on 23 and 24 January 1957. Coming soon after the statement of Feroz Khan Noon, the foreign minister of Pakistan, made in the Security Council on 16 January, in which he had argued that the Kashmir issue was about dispute over territory and not about external aggression, Krishna Menon not only held forth on the history and the context of the Kashmir issue but also lashed out at the brazenly partisan behaviour of British and Australian representatives at the UN. Rarely has such a combination of understanding of international law, mastery over facts and analytical vigour, laced with biting sarcasm been displayed in any debate at a forum like the UN. This is an extract from that masterly speech.

... We felt, as indeed my predecessor in this chair [*Gopalaswamy Ayyangar—Ed.*] pointed out to the Council at that time, that there is no dispute about territory. If it were a dispute about territory, I say with great respect that the Security Council would be incompetent to deal with it because that would be either a political or a juridical question, and under Chapter VI or Chapter VII of the Charter the Security Council would only deal with questions of international peace and security. So we brought here a situation and not a dispute.

But that is not the most important part. We went on to say: 'The

Government of India request the Security Council to call upon Pakistan to put an end immediately to the giving of such assistance,'—immediately, on 1 January 1948, and today we are nine years away from it—'which is an act of aggression against India.'

I shall quote these words more than once before I have concluded, in order to discharge my responsibility as the representative of my government: '…which is an act of aggression against India'. That is the crux of this question. What we are considering here is not merely various resolutions or the method by which a problem may be resolved otherwise. What is before us, and I shall point out later, is this question of aggression, because the whole United Nations is founded upon the basic principles of international law and behaviour. That is based upon equity, and he who asks for equity must come with clean hands. After all, there are difficulties sometimes. Therefore, our starting point is that we came here in order to file a complaint, to ask for redress on a charge of aggression. If Pakistan does not mention this starting point, then we have to point out why we were so concerned about it.

Even today we have frontier raids one way or another. But why did we then ask the Security Council to deal with this matter? If Pakistan does not do so, that is to say, halt the aggression, the Government of India may be compelled in self-defence—and I interpolate that self-defence is not only a right of the Member States of the United Nations but, I submit it is an obligation that Member States have under the Charter because they have an obligation to maintain the sovereignties of their own countries—the Government of India may be compelled in self-defence to enter Pakistan territory, which we did not do, in order to take military action against the invaders. The matter is, therefore, one of extreme urgency and calls for immediate action by the Security Council for avoiding a breach of international peace.

As the delineation of this picture becomes more complete it will be clear that the efforts of India and of the Security Council and the approaches made to Pakistan by mediators and so on have at earlier stages been primarily addressed to the halting of hostilities.

Therefore, our country was faced with the position that part of its territory was invaded, and that invasion had to be resisted; it had to be pushed back. The normal practice of war would have been to defend by attacking the invader. But this was in 1947, and it was a fact, which remains true to us at any rate today, that these were the same people who were part of our country but ten years ago. What is more, between January 1947, when we came here, and October, when these things started, our two countries had only just passed through the holocaust of fratricide, that is, of Indian people killing Pakistanis, and Pakistanis killing Indians. We had witnessed an orgy of violence, and it was the desire of our government that nothing should be done to re-kindle these embers which were still burning at that time.

That was the original position, and I shall keep coming back to it. We are here on a complaint of aggression. That aggression has not been resolved, it has not been got rid of. So long as there are forces of other countries in a place where they have no right to be, irrespective of our rights, I think the Security Council is called upon under the provisions of the Charter to act accordingly.

In this context, so many trees have grown, and a very considerable amount of undergrowth, that it is impossible to see the wood properly, and it will be my attempt to present it as best we can. We shall try to assist the Security Council to see this picture as it was. As I said, five years ago we debated this, and in five years—even apart from the nine years—a great many things happen. It is part of the inevitable practice of nations that the changes in conditions that time brings about and which may go to the root of a question have also to be taken into account.

From there, with great respect to my colleague, the Foreign Minister of Pakistan, I shall follow his example of looking at this problem from the time of the partition of India.

... The Security Council, therefore, adopted its resolution of 20 January and, having done so went on to inquire about various things. Meanwhile the Security Council changed the title to the 'India-Pakistan Question'. We stated at that time that we had no objection to the use of any words which might be desired, but we maintained that the Kashmir question was the subject of the complaint.

... On 21 April 1948, the Council adopted another resolution (S/726). That resolution was a modification, and it gave new instructions to the Commission providing for the withdrawal of the troops and the holding of a plebiscite, and the membership of the Commission was increased to five. On 5 May of that year, the Government of India formally informed the Security Council of its rejection of certain parts of this resolution, and that correspondence is contained in document S/734/Corr.I. India, however, expressed its willingness to confer with the Commission. The letter stated: 'The Government of India have given the most careful consideration to the resolution of the Security Council concerning their complaint against Pakistan over the dispute between the two countries regarding the State of Jammu and Kashmir. The Government of India regret that it is not possible for them to implement those parts of the resolution against which their objections were clearly stated by their delegation, objections which, after consultation with the delegation, the Government of India fully endorse. If the Council should still decide to send out the Commission referred to in the preamble of the resolution, the Government of India would be glad to confer with it.' (S/1100, annex 3.) That letter was signed by Mr. Nehru, the Prime Minister and Minister for External Affairs of India.

... Irrespective of the fact that we did not agree to the expansion of the terms of reference, the Government of India felt that it would be inhospitable and discourteous to the United Nations not to see the members of the Commission. There are cynics who say that that was where our troubles began, but it would be wrong to take that view, because if nations, out of risks and fears in this direction, would not enter into negotiations, then they would not be able to assist in the implementation of the functions of the Charter. But, and I say this in all sincerity, that carries with it the fact that one should not penalise those who necessarily do not stick to the letter of their communication, that is to say, they do not confine themselves to that, but are prepared to go a little further in exploration. Therefore, while we rejected this resolution and refused to accept it, we agreed to receive the Commission.

At that time, Mr. Gopalaswamy Ayyangar, who was the Minister in the Indian Cabinet responsible for these affairs, spoke before the Security Council and he registered objections. I will not read the whole of his speech which was very long, but it is apparent from the preliminary discussion in January 1948 that it all turns upon what we agreed to... Mr. Gopalaswamy Ayyangar said: 'I would now proceed to review briefly some of the detailed provisions of the draft resolution presently under consideration. By way of anticipating a possible claim from the other side, I desire to say a few words on the question of accession...whether the State of Jammu and Kashmir is to accede to India or Pakistan. The contention has been advanced'—and this is our position—'that the accession is for a temporary period'—to do that it will be necessary to repeal an Act of Parliament—'and a limited purpose, and when that period elapses and that purpose has been served, it ceases to be operative.'

That was the contention. Mr. Gopalaswamy Ayyangar went on to say: 'We, on our side, repudiate this claim.' This is as early as 1948, so it is not an afterthought. The accession which took place on 26 October 1947 was both legal and lawful. It has been followed up by India in the discharge of all the obligations that her acceptance of the accession has imposed upon her. She has saved the Jammu and Kashmir State from disintegration. She is now resisting those who are attacking the integrity even today. She is protecting the State's large population from the unfriendly attention of raiders from outside. 'The accession therefore subsists today and will subsist even after the fighting ceases and peace and order have been restored.' That has been the basis of our position from 1948 onwards, it has never moved. Mr. Gopalaswamy Ayyangar went on to say: 'Until then, Pakistan has no constitutional position in Jammu and Kashmir.'

He went on to make a statement which is very important from our point of view: 'After the fighting ceases, the whole of the State will have to come under one Government. By the whole of the State, I include also the area which is now under the control of the rebels and raiders. When the whole of the State thus comes under one administration—and that, the administration of the State of Jammu and Kashmir—India's garrisons will need to be planted at her outer frontiers on the west of the Jammu and Kashmir State. This planting is necessary for enabling India to discharge her obligations for the defence of the State which she has taken over under the Instrument of Accession.'

This is an undertaking which is not only sanctified by our Constitution. It is enjoined by an Act of Parliament of the United Kingdom, which is the basis of our Constitution. These obligations that we are carrying out were also agreed to by the Security Council. The Security Council at no time challenged either the sovereignty of Jammu and Kashmir or the validity of the accession, and that is the only thing that stays. Therefore, wherever the resolution of 21 April 1948 goes into the question of treating the two countries as though they were two parties to a complaint, we have resisted that position and we have not subscribed to that part.

If it were necessary, I would go into the details of the 21 April resolution, but I do not think it is necessary because we are now covered by the resolution that followed. The Commission was appointed by the 21 April resolution. We did not accept that resolution, but what did Pakistan do? Pakistan protested against the resolution without accepting it. It, however, chose Argentina as a member of the Commission on the same day. We objected to certain parts of it, but we agreed to receive the Commission. Pakistan protested and said they would not accept the resolution.

... It was the presence of these troops—which had been denied all along, but was admitted by the Foreign Minister of Pakistan when the Commission arrived in Karachi—that created a new state of affairs. At a later stage, the Pakistan Government gave the reasons for this invasion. The report continues: 'Sir Mohammed Zafrullah Khan stated that three main reasons had motivated the entry of Pakistan troops into Kashmir: protection of the territory of Pakistan from possible aggression by Indian forces; prevention of a fait accompli in Kashmir by the Government of India, and prevention of the influx of refugees into Pakistan.'

... I submit that none of these reasons have anything to do with the people of Kashmir. We have heard a great deal about their future and their destiny, but if the protection of the territory of Pakistan from Indian forces does not sound like a preventive war I do not know what it is—that is the situation where a Member State gets the right to go into a neighbouring territory for fear that it might be attacked from that State. So protection of its territory, the first reason, is not a reason that is sanctioned by the principles of the Charter.

... With regard to the prevention of a fait accompli in Kashmir by the Government of India, so far as the legal position is concerned, whether the Pakistan Government accepted it or not, it had been put before the Security Council; and if the view was that a fait accompli must not be brought about, then the Pakistan Government intended, in spite of the resolution of the Security Council, to decide this by force of arms, that is to say, to use its troops in order to prevent a fait accompli.

... The third reason was to prevent the influx of refugees into Pakistan, and I would say that of all the reasons given this is the one that least holds water. After the partition there were seven or eight million people leaving in each direction. Refugees came from Pakistan into India and from India into Pakistan—one of those horrid scenes in our common history which I hope we shall be able to forget someday. But the idea of troops moving in to prevent the influx of refugees into Pakistan is difficult to understand. The only refugees who went into Pakistan presumably were those who preferred Pakistan as a home. Are we to understand that the Pakistan Government was going to prevent these refugees by the use of an army?

... So there are three reasons given, none of which in my submission have any substance.

... The Foreign Minister made some arithmetical calculations: India told us that India had 80,000 troops in this area and, what is more, that that constituted one-twelfth of the population. I think that if we applied these mathematics in one place it might be useful to apply them in some other place. There are today forty-five battalions in those outposts around 'Azad' Kashmir, and there are only half a million people there. Therefore the Security Council can work out the mathematics on that. I am not referring to other areas at the moment; I am referring to that half million people in what is called the 'Azad' area, where there were, at the time when the Commission was investigating, thirty-two battalions, which have now become forty-five battalions. Therefore, if we face the question of having troops, that is the position.

... On this matter, I also wish to submit that Kashmir is the northern extremity of India. The Indian Army is deployed in the various sectors of the country, and this is one area where it has to function, not only for the protection of Kashmir and all that is involved therein, but because it is the place where it normally would be located.

... If we are to take this into account, then, as I shall point out later, we shall have to take into account the divisions of the Pakistan Army that are located about five, ten and twenty miles from our border. That is, if it is right to have the Pakistan Army in Abbottabad or in Murree or in any of these areas, then it is necessary for the Indian Army to be held somewhere. Therefore, the idea that this is an occupation, which is what has been represented to the Security Council, is a total misnomer.

... Then we come to Part III of the resolution of 13 August 1948, which is the crucial part. Part M states, and I would request you, Mr. President, to give your very careful attention to this: 'The Government of India and the Government of Pakistan reaffirm their wish that the future status of the State of Jammu and Kashmir shall be determined in accordance with the will of the people and to that end, upon acceptance of the truce agreement both governments agree to enter into consultations with the Commission to determine fair and equitable conditions whereby such free expression will be assured.'

... The commitment about a plebiscite is usually spoken of as though it were the law...but what does it amount to? It amounts to an expression of a wish on the part of the two governments. The expression of a wish is far less than what may be called an international obligation. However, I do not wish to argue that point. But take the other one, that it should be carried out upon the acceptance of the truce agreement. There has been no truce agreement signed, because Pakistan armies have not vacated and, what is more, there are continued violations.

... As I shall point out later, there are large numbers of changed conditions under which it is no longer possible to consider the matter in these terms. So any suggestion that the Government of India—and this is the burden of the apprehension about us, and there is no further charge—has a commitment that it is not honouring, I deny totally. So far as we are concerned, the commitment is for the acceptance of a truce agreement. It is not to take a plebiscite but to enter into consultations. That is a very different thing from doing something. First of all, there is no truce agreement. Therefore, if number two does not happen, number three is out of court. Number one, the cease-fire, we have performed. Number two is the truce agreement. I have given the reasons why the truce agreement is not being carried out. Therefore, number three means that it is only when number two has been accomplished that number three comes into the picture at all. The character of number three is not just a matter of taking a plebiscite, but that the government enters into consultations. This means that the two parties shall enter into consultations in the same way, shall we say, as was arranged in connexion with elections in Indo-China. That is all there is to it. Those consultations have taken place, even without a truce agreement, and nothing has come of them.

... From what we have heard in the Security Council, from all the discussions, the debates, the writings and everything else that goes on in Pakistan and which have been communicated in the views expressed by the foreign Press, there is some idea that over and above the Security Council decisions there is a basis for the affiliation of Kashmir to Pakistan, that there is some natural affinity.

... What are these considerations? We accept some of these considerations, but we argue that they are either equally or more applicable to us. For the moment, I am putting to one side whatever title we may have derived. I am talking of the extra-legal considerations and the extra-security considerations.

... The first of these is geographical contiguity, which is commonly accepted by all of us. The answer to that is that Kashmir has a frontier with Pakistan on the west and slightly to the north-west. It has a frontier with India and communications with India. It has a frontier with Russia in Sinkiang and China and Tibet. Therefore, Kashmir has a large number of frontiers.

... Geographical contiguity is very often governed to a considerable extent by the historical past, and Kashmir's economic relations and commercial relations have been very much more with India than with Pakistan. This did not arise in the old days, because it was one country. Therefore, if it is a question of a common frontier and of contiguity, it is not as though the accession of Kashmir to India is the accession of some far-off island which is separated from the rest of our territory. To put it at its worst, contiguity is a common factor.

... The other matter is one on which my government will not in any circumstances alter its position. We refuse to recognise what is called the 'two-nation theory'. India is a secular State, where any person, Hindu, Muslim, Christian, Buddhist, or whatever he is, is an equal son or daughter of India, with rights of citizenship guaranteed by our Constitution. India claims Islam as one of the Indian religions, just as it does Christianity or any other.

Therefore, we refuse to accept the thesis that because the population of a particular area is of one religion, some political issue is involved. We are not a theocracy; we are a modern, secular State governed on democratic principles, where the right of citizenship is based on residence, upon domicile, and upon loyalty to the Constitution. Therefore, we totally disregard this argument with regard to Muslim majorities and Hindu minorities, and everything else.

... Some of you may say that that is a very nice view, but it is not how the world is run. Then how do we look at it? Pakistan has a population—I am subject to correction—of between 70 and 80 million, because I believe that their census, like ours, was taken in 1951, and our populations increase by 1.6 per cent a year. Roughly speaking, Pakistan has a population of somewhere about 75 million; but the proximity of Kashmir is to West Pakistan (Pakistan is in two parts and is separated by the Indian mainland extending for about 1,000 miles). Therefore, the proximity of Kashmir, ethnically and otherwise, is to West Pakistan, and I have no accurate figures of the Muslim population of West Pakistan. However, at the very outside, it cannot be more than about 30 million, and there are nearly 50 million Muslims in India. If our government were to accept the view that because people are Muslims, they should belong to another State, I ask the Security Council, in all conscience, to consider what would happen to the considerable Muslim minorities in my country. They are distributed over the whole of our land. In some places they are sparse minorities, in some places they almost form the majority in the area. Are we to say that they are second-class citizens? We refuse to accept that position in India.

... We have almost as many Muslims in India—and I qualify the word 'almost'—as in the whole of Pakistan. We do not regard it as either a foreign culture or a foreign religion. What is more, whether it be in Pakistan or in India, whether they be Hindus, Muslims, Christians, or whatever they are, their ancestries are pretty much the same. One religion does not mean one race, nor does it mean that there is a separation between two religious groups.

... We have this considerable Muslim population inside India, but it is not regarded as a minority. There is no question of the Muslims having any special sheltered treatment; they would not have it. They are equal citizens in our country, taking their place in our government, in our public services, in our industry, in our agriculture, and in everything else, just like everybody else. The secular State is one of those ideas and one of those possessions which we regard with great jealousy, because in this world the rivalry of religion and the amount of violence that has been carried out in the name of religious loyalty has been to an extent that should shame humanity at any time. Therefore, we are not prepared at any time to accept any view, whatever resolutions anybody may pass, that there is any justice or anything that a modern community can entertain in this idea of what was spoken of in the address of the Foreign Minister of Pakistan, who attributed it to Lord Mountbatten, about what is called communal representation or communal affinity, or something of that kind.

... The whole connexion of Kashmir is, as I said a while ago, with the mainland. Its capital was founded in the third century BC. I am not an antiquarian, I have not studied it, but the history of Kashmir is a continuous one. It has been ruled by Hindu kings, by Muslim kings, by Sikh kings, by Afghans, and by all kinds of people, but it has always been part of the mainland of India.

... Therefore, those are extra-constitutional, extra-legal, extra-United Nations considerations, by which I mean they are considerations which are outside the principles of the Charter, on the one hand, and which do not come into any of the resolutions or any of the decisions which we have made. However, it was necessary for me to put them forward because it was on them that the other argument was based: that the accession was wrong, that we got it by force or by fraud.

... I should like to restate that there was no question of this Kashmir question being on the agenda of the Commonwealth conference of Prime Ministers. The Government of India has objected and will continue to object to the discussion of this problem in any international forum other than the Security Council, which is seized of it. There has been participation by the United Kingdom, the United States, Pakistan, France, Iraq, the Philippines and various other countries in attempts to raise this matter, in however superficial a way, in other forums, and we have on each occasion protested to each government and said that it was the wrong action to take. We continue to do so, irrespective of the responses they make.

... It would be very wrong for me simply to say that there was no Prime Ministers' meeting dealing with this, or that no formal objection was made. There were conversations in 1951—I believe it was the second conference after India decided to become a republic. There were talks with Mr. Menzies, the Prime Minister of Australia. I believe that there were talks before with Mr. Mackenzie King. There were always talks on large numbers of subjects; some of them had nothing to do with this matter at all. There was also an occasion when Mr. Menzies and Mr. Attlee sat together with Prime Minister of India, for a private conversation, and Mr. Liaquat Ali Khan, the Prime Minister of Pakistan, was also present.

... In view of the delicate nature of Commonwealth relations and the bringing in of the names of these Prime Ministers, and for various other reasons, which will become more apparent when I read this resolution—and if I can claim the attention of the representative of the United Kingdom—I should like to read this note recorded at that time by the Prime Minister of India: 'This evening I attempted an informal conference about the Kashmir question. This was originally fixed to be held at 10 Downing Street, but, owing to Mr. Menzies' illness, it was decided to hold it in Mr. Menzies room at the Savoy. We met at 8.30 p.m. The Prime Ministers of the United Kingdom, Canada, Australia, New Zealand, Ceylon and Pakistan were present. We discussed the matter for about an hour.'

I might recall here that the reason for having this informal meeting was that we had refused to have the matter discussed formally in the Prime Ministers' conference.

Mr. Menzies and Mr. Attlee made some preliminary remarks about the extreme desirability of the Kashmir issue being settled, more especially because of the world situation. They referred to a plebiscite having been agreed to and only the conditions relating thereto being subject to dispute. Mr. Menzies expressed his opinion that probably a limited plebiscite would be more desirable. He added that, as there were legitimate apprehensions in the mind of India in regard to the security of the State, it should be easily possible for a brigade or so of Commonwealth troops to be placed there for security reasons till the plebiscite ended. Australia would be glad to provide such troops as it was thought it would be a service rendered to the cause of world peace. Some reference was also made to the heavy expenditure on the defence of India and Pakistan.

Then my Prime Minister gave his reply: 'Mr. Attlee then turned to me. I said I was at least equally desirous of a settlement of the Kashmir question. This was to the advantage of both India and Pakistan, and we had made many attempts but this far without success. They show obviously that it was not quite so simple as it appeared on the surface, or otherwise it would have been settled long ago. No doubt it will be settled sooner or later. I gave a very brief account of some of the difficulties and points that had arisen, and added that two aspects were prominently before me. One was that no steps should be taken which might lead to an upsetting of the somewhat unstable equilibrium that had been gradually established between India and Pakistan during these past few years. There was a grave danger that if a wrong step was taken it would rouse passions all over India and Pakistan and raise new issues of vital importance. That would be a tragedy.

'The second point was that I could not deal with any proposal without reference to my colleagues in Delhi and Kashmir. So far as the Government of India was concerned, we had gone there on the invitation of not only the legally constituted government but also the largest popular party. Our responsibility was confined to defence, foreign affairs and communications. For the rest, the State government was responsible, and we could not interfere with its discretion though we could advise them. It was neither possible nor advisable for us to come to a decision without the concurrence of the State government.'

This was in the early stages of our accession. The relations had not yet been built up.

'Then the Prime Minister of Pakistan said that the state government was just made up of puppets appointed by me, and I could remove them or change them at any time. I took exception to this and told them something about the background of Kashmir and the National Conference and Sheikh Abdullah.

'I had given a very brief resume of the events at Kashmir in the last few years, finishing up with Dixon and the proposals. I pointed out that Dixon had concluded that an overall plebiscite was not feasible and had therefore explored the possibility of a partial plebiscite. To the general principle of this I had agreed, subject of course, to the other matters connected with it being considered and decided upon. I made it clear that there was no point in discussing these matters until the principle was accepted by Pakistan.'

Because at that time, in the discussions with Mr. Menzies, this agreement was to be given by Pakistan and not by us. Because we had agreed, subject to details, to the principle that Sir Owen Dixon had put forward.

'Mr. Liaquat Ali Khan indignantly repudiated this. The Prime Minister of Pakistan thereupon said there was no question of an overall plebiscite not being feasible. There might be some difficulties, but obviously, it could be done. I agreed that it could be done, though it might take time. The question of feasibility did not refer to the practical difficulty of having an electoral roll, but according to Dixon, to various other factors.'—which are set out in the Dixon report and some of which are referred to briefly in these conversations—'Mr. Menzies stated that he had not been able to understand why the Government of the States'—this is important because it comes from Mr. Menzies—'should be pushed aside or suspended because of the plebiscite'—and here I would point out that that was exactly what Pakistan was pressing for—'it could very well continue, although matters connected with the plebiscite might be handed over to the Plebiscite Administrator. Attlee agreed with this.'

Now the Government of India, I would recall, has raised no objection in this connexion—provided other conditions are satisfied... The conversations among the Prime Ministers then touched on the ethnic and linguistic divisions of the State. I quote from the conversations:

'I told them, also, that there was a basic difference between our approach and Pakistan's to the two-nation theory, and the insistence on religious difference coming into politics. While we had reluctantly accepted certain facts, we never accepted Pakistan's theory, and we were not prepared to apply it to Kashmir in any event.'—And here the reference is to the theory of a Muslim State and a Hindu State—'That would be bad for Kashmir, but would be worse still for India and for Pakistan. It would go counter to the principles that governed us and might produce upheavals both in India and in Pakistan. We had only recently witnessed an upheaval of this kind in Bengal, which had with difficulty between controlled by the Agreement between the two Prime Ministers.

'Mr. Attlee pointed out rather warmly that past history did not quite fit in with what I had said. The division of India had largely been based on a religious basis. He did not like this religious basis at all, and he had tried to avoid it, but facts were too strong. Further, he said that ethnic and linguistic divisions were equally dangerous, and we in India were having to face this difficulty in various parts of the country. I said that we were not enamoured of ethnic and linguistic divisions, but, in the circumstances, we certainly thought that any religious approach to a political problem was dangerous and explosive. We had never accepted that principle, and we did not propose to do so in the future. Right from the beginning of the Kashmir trouble, we had laid stress on this fact and had informed the United Nations Commission repeatedly that this appeal to religion must be avoided. In spite of this, the Pakistan Press was full of religious appeals and calls for "Jehad"—that is, holy war.

'If this kind of thing was going to take place before and during the plebiscite period, then there would be no plebiscite, but civil upheaval, not only in Kashmir but all over India and Pakistan. Mr. Menzies then said that he quite agreed that religion should be kept out of the picture, and he had been much disturbed when he saw the Pakistan Press in Karachi'—and this is Mr. Menzies speaking, not the Government of India—'which was writing most irresponsibly on this subject…

'The Prime Minister of Ceylon was silent throughout. Mr. Attlee then referred to river water in connexion with Kashmir and mentioned the international committee set up by Canada and the United States. I mentioned that Mr. Saint-Laurent had drawn our attention to this last year, and I had stated subsequently that I would be perfectly agreeable to having subsequent consideration of the water problem as between India and Pakistan.'

The delegation of Pakistan had not raised this objection during this series of meetings of the Security Council but, had it done so, we should have had the answers... I continue to quote from the conversation of the Prime Ministers:

'The Prime Minister of Pakistan at one stage referred to ethnic divisions of Kashmir and said that, if necessary, a plebiscite could be held separately in these areas. At no time, however, did he accept the idea of partial plebiscite. He insisted on an overall plebiscite for the State, though this might be taken separately in different areas—presumablv to allow these areas to decide for themselves.

'As Mr. Menzies was not feeling too well and had a temperature, the conversations ended rather suddenly at about 10 p.m. Mr. Menzies concluded by saying that we might perhaps think over the various suggestions made in the course of the conversations. These were, according to him, that, firstly, the State Government should not be touched.'—now, this is Mr. Menzies' opinion—'and should continue except in regard to functions relating to the plebiscite; secondly, the Commonwealth might provide a security force, and, thirdly, the plebiscite might be held in different areas. In the course of the conversations, no reference was made either by Mr. Liaquat Ali Khan or by me to the proposal about a Commonwealth force being sent. There was no mention of these talks being resumed.'

... I am sorry to have had to read out this long document. However, we have other matters to consider in relation to the countries involved—particularly in relation to Australia, which though separated from India by miles of sea, is a very close neighbour of ours, in fact, we hope, as time goes on, to establish even closer relations with Australia than we now have. That is why I have read out this document.

... Reference has been made to Sheikh Abdullah. I have already read from his statement to the Constituent Assembly to show what his political position is. Sheikh Abdullah was placed under detention by the Government of Kashmir. There is a detention law in Kashmir, just as there is a detention law in India. This is a piece of legislation which, in spite of our desires to maintain an abstract liberty, we found to be necessary in view of subversive movements in the country. Today, under this law, there are forty-nine people under detention in the whole of Kashmir, a good many of them for acts which have nothing to do with political crimes.

... What is the procedure under this law? First of all, their offences must be stated in the 'detenus'. A man cannot just be detained, he must he told why. They have access to a tribunal of high level, to judicial persons who have to investigate the cases. Objection might be taken to this legislation, and there are some people in India who seriously object to it. The cases are examined by the judicial tribunal, which can order the release of a 'detenu', and the government cannot refuse that release. The 'detenus' are not brought to public trial because there are reasons which may affect relations between states, not only with the state of Pakistan, but with other states. You have already heard, when I read from a document this morning, that my colleague from the United Kingdom quite rightly felt very concerned. I was more concerned, but I did not get any remedy for my concern, though he did for his. That is how the world is, Mr. President. If some of these men were brought to trial, the government could not withhold any evidence under our system, whoever that evidence might affect. It would create an enormous number of difficulties, but I do not want to ask the council to go into all the details. I simply wish to say that, even taking the quantum of it, there are forty-nine persons under detention, some for short period, some for longer.

... It is quite true that the former Prime Minister of Kashmir is under detention, but may I say, without any offence whatever, that the present Prime Minister of Pakistan was arrested in 1948. It is one of those things that happen in times of social changes. My Prime Minister was under detention for a long time, and he has said that he learned a great deal during that period. The present Prime Minister of Pakistan was a prisoner of the former Pakistan government, but I must say that he has not retaliated in the same way.

With regard to Sheikh Abdullah, in a document which I am now going to put in, there are at least five or six extracts from testimonials to Sheikh Abdullah given in previous times by Pakistan publicists and ministers, and there is no name that was too bad for Abdullah at that time. The question is, at which time did he turn quisling.

The letter of the former Prime Minister, Sheikh Abdullah, has been put in as a document by Mr. Khan Noon, and I am sure that he will agree with me that the only way to understand correspondence is to put in both the letter and the reply. Therefore, I have assisted him by providing technical assistance in putting in the reply of Mr. Sadiq, the President of the Kashmir Constituent Assembly. The letter of Sheikh Abdullah, which was put in as a criticism of the government and against accession and so on, was sent to the President of the Constituent Assembly in order to make certain protests. The

President of the Constituent Assembly was elected. He sent a reply; so if the Security Council looks into one letter it must look into the other. Therefore, in the annexes to my statement (S/PV.762/Add.1, annex VII) we have put the two together.

I have a great many more notes here about which I wished to talk, but I think you have heard me long enough. I shall only deal with the essential point that remains. I have no time to contradict every paragraph that appears in the statement of the Foreign Minister of Pakistan. There is, however, a misquotation from a commission document which gives a totally erroneous impression of its meanings. I think that in saying that I am being moderate enough.

The present series of meetings are being held because of the letter dated 2 January 1957 from the Minister for Foreign Affairs of Pakistan to the President of the Security Council. In presenting his case, the Foreign Minister of Pakistan has done two things. First, he delivered what amounts to threats. He indicated that trouble would brew. We have had an opportunity of comparing some of these statements with the statement made in 1947. They have, shall I say, a very close family resemblance, especially if you read them parallel to the other statements I read out a while ago, that is to say, if this was a beginning, then this would not end with the Security Council; Pakistan would propose to do something itself, and so on.

... Then Mr. Khan Noon said: 'Here I would like to say that it is sometimes argued by India that everything is peaceful'—we have only said it is peaceful now on the Indian administered side; on the contrary, we have said it is not on the other side—'so why bother about Kashmir? But I warn you,'—he warns the Security Council—'that is a calm before the storm ... We have just seen a telegram which states that on 11 January, our Minister for Information, Mr. Amir Azam Khan, made statement in Karachi that the Indians have massed their troops on our border. The excuse that Mr. Nehru gives is that he fears an attack from Pakistan, whereas we have not sent one solider to our border. The fact that he is afraid of a war breaking out because of the Kashmir problem should assure the Security Council and the world that it is peaceful on the surface, but if the Security Council closes the door on a peaceful settlement we cannot say what will happen. If the Indian troops are there because India fears war between India and Pakistan, that should be a sufficient answer to those people who say that "all is quiet in the Kingdom of Kashmir"'—it is not a kingdom any more—'and India and Pakistan and the Security Council need not take any action'.

... Therefore, my government, in full faith, believing in the allegiance of the Security Council to the principles of the Charter, believing in its rights in law, in morality and in ethics, and what is more, knowing what are the interests of the people of India and Pakistan, knowing the consequences of unsettlement, remembering the grim tragedy of 1947, knowing the passions that are aroused when there is a quarrel between neighbours, asks you to be careful. We ask for your prudence, we ask for your sound judgement in not jumping into a situation without taking all these facts into consideration.

... The Government of India here is not in the dock. We came here as complainants. A distinguished colleague of ours appears to have mentioned this today; why should we be so much on the defence? If it sounds to people that we are on the defence, it may be because we indulged in some understatements both in the past and in the present. We are here not in order to ask for condemnation of anybody, but we are here in order to state what are our rights under the Charter. Have we the right for the security of our territory? Have we the right to be free from threat? Have we the right to feel assured that the machinery of the Security Council and its resolutions are not going to be used as a smoke-screen for the preparation of aggression against us? Have we the right so far as the Council is concerned—and I say that it cannot impose it—to live side by side with our neighbour, free from the threats of a holy war? Have we the right to enable our people, the great majority of whom are below subsistence levels, to devote their energies, their attention, our resources, our friendships, for their economical and political development?

... These are the questions that face us. And while I have no desire to conclude in this way, I cannot but help referring—and I would have done this if it had come from any other representative of the Government of Pakistan except our old friend Mr. Khan Noon—to what he told this council when he said that between the friendship of the India and Pakistan people stands Mr. Nehru. I ask the Council to consider that statement, coming from a leading Indian personality only ten years ago, who is a family friend of most of what may be called the ruling families, if you like, the persons in government positions in India, who knows our intentions and who represented the Government of India as a whole in many circumstances, and telling our people that between the two of us lies the personality of our Prime Minister.

... If that is not incitement to revolt against the government, I ask what is? It is the only part of that statement that has caused our delegation intense pain. That comes on top of the kind of thing that is written in Pakistan.

... What I have here is from *Dawn*. I am ashamed to read it, but it is my duty to do so. *Dawn* is a paper founded by the founder of Pakistan. It is still regarded as a kind of most important organ, I believe. It says: 'The Security Council will have barely ten days to decide upon some concrete, tangible, unequivocal and compelling step whereby the rapacious brigand of Asia, that hypocrite masquerading as an apostle of peace with his hand red with the blood of Kashmiris as well as Bharati Muslims, that double-facing, double-talking and double-dealing Brahmin Janus who shamelessly woos both Moscow and Washington in order to have the best of both the worlds—can be prevented from accomplishing his designs. Will the United Nations this time act, or will it again temporise and shirk its responsibility?'

This is about the Prime Minister of India...It goes on to say: 'Let us hope for the best, but be also prepared for the worst. The one thing certain is that Bharat shall not be allowed to grab Kashmir finally.'—So there is no question of the plebiscite deciding—'If the United Nations fails, and those with whom we have thrown in our lot prove faithless'—those are the six military allies—'let the world take note that the prospect of a peaceful settlement will vanish forever. The inevitable alternative need not be spelled out—but come it will.'

... I do not say it is a statement of the Pakistan Government. But considering that while the Security Council is sitting here, demonstrations against our missions are taking place in Pakistan territory, and what is more, that those demonstrations are addressed and spoken to in cordial terms by the Prime Minister of Pakistan, I hope the Security Council will pardon me if I make references to this. Even where there are hostilities, even when there are greatly strained relations, there are proprieties to be observed. We have also a very sentimental population, not different from theirs. We have a larger country; we have pockets of Muslims all over. I come from a part of India where a considerable Muslim population forms a pocket. We do not want the conditions to be created where they will be the victims of fanaticism and of passion.

... The Security Council regards this as a dispute. It is not a dispute for territory. There is only one problem before you—whether you will face it or not, and if you do not face it, I say with great respect it is a matter between yourselves and the instructed judgement of your governments—and that problem is the problem of aggression.

My government, when once that is resolved and when all these elements of aggression are withdrawn, will not be wanting, in its allegiance to the Charter, in finding an arrangement by adjustment with our neighbours which will be of our common good. Any other procedures you may adopt will not only put off that day, but will aggravate the relations which we are trying very hard to make otherwise. It will also prove to those vast millions of the Indian people—and irrespective of all circumstances, they have many friends in this world, in all continents—to the masses of them, that the politics of power alignments, religious fanaticisms, personal antagonisms, take precedence over the fundamental principle of the Charter.

... The Charter enjoins upon you, Mr. President, and your colleagues, an action consistent with the crime of invasion.

~

HOMI JEHANGIR BHABHA

Presidential Address, First International Conference on the Peaceful Uses of Atomic Energy

The United Nations General Assembly convened the First International Conference on the Peaceful Uses of Atomic Energy (the Geneva Conference) between 8 and 20 August 1955. One of the largest gatherings of scientists and engineers, the conference saw thousands of scientific papers being presented in an effort to convince the world that there were several non-war or peaceful uses to which nuclear power could be put. The conference helped bring the nuclear issue out of the veil of secrecy and suspicion under which it had been kept, and paved the way for the setting up of the International Atomic Energy Agency. Homi Bhabha, an eminent nuclear physicist who had embarked on a nuclear programme in India with the establishment of the Atomic Research Centre at Bombay, was the president of the conference. His presentation and interventions on the history of energy and in locating the nuclear issue in the course of human history was most encouraging for the atomic scientists.

The purpose of this Conference is to discuss the peaceful uses of atomic energy, and to exchange scientific and technical knowledge connected with it. The importance of this exchange of knowledge can hardly be overestimated. Knowledge is perhaps the most important possession of Man. It is the accumulated knowledge of centuries which differentiates modern Man from his ancestor in the dawn of civilisation. It is this knowledge, and not any notable change in his physical or mental equipment, which has enabled him to build the civilisation of today. One can hardly foresee the far-reaching developments to which this Conference may lead.

In a broad view of human history it is possible to discern three great epochs. The first is marked by the emergence of the early civilisations in the valleys of the Euphrates, the Indus, and the Nile, the second by the industrial revolution, leading to the civilisation in which we live, and the third by the discovery of atomic energy and the dawn of the atomic age, which we are just entering. Each epoch marks a change in the energy pattern of society.

In a practical sense, energy is the great prime mover, which makes possible the multitude of actions on which our daily life depends. Indeed, it makes possible life itself...

The total consumption of energy in the world has gone up in a staggering manner. It is convenient in dealing with such enormous amounts of energy to use an appropriately large unit, denoted by a Q which is equal to a million-million-million British thermal units of energy, corresponding to the combustion of some thirty-three thousand million tons of coal.

The total economically recoverable world reserves of coal, oil, gas and oil shale are equivalent in energy value to under 100Q. Some have put the figure under 40Q. It is probable that, at the rate at which the world consumption of energy is increasing, these reserves will be exhausted in under a century.

Let us pause to see what this means. The bulk of our coal, the bituminous coal, comes from the Carboniferous Age, some 250 million years ago. We are exhausting these reserves, which have been built-up by nature over long periods of time, in a few centuries, in a flash of geological time...

Of the total world consumption of energy, amounting to 1Q per decade in 1950, 37 per cent was in the United States. If the entire population of the world were to consume energy per capita at the same rate as in the United States, the total consumption of energy in the world would be over 5.5Q per decade instead of the present 1Q. Coupled with a doubling of the world's population within the next hundred years, which is the least that we can expect, this would exhaust the known reserves of fossil fuels in under a century.

In this simple arithmetic no allowance has been made for the fact that the standard of living of the industrially advanced countries is rising and, we hope, will continue to rise.

This conclusion is of great significance. It shows that our presently known reserves of coal and oil are insufficient to enable the underdeveloped countries of the world, which contain a major part of its population, to attain and maintain for long a standard of living equal to that of the industrially most advanced countries. It shows the absolute necessity of finding some new source of energy, if the light of our civilisation is not to be extinguished, because we have burnt out our fuel reserves.

It is in this context that we turn to atomic energy for a solution. The Conference will discuss the known reserves of uranium and thorium in individual countries and in the world as a whole. It has been estimated that the total recoverable world reserves of uranium and thorium contain an amount of energy of the order of 1700Q. If this is really so, then atomic energy could, first, provide the energy necessary to enable the underdeveloped countries to reach the standard of living of the industrialised countries, and secondly, enable the entire world to maintain a constantly rising standard of living for very many decades, and possibly for several centuries. For the full industrialisation of the underdeveloped areas, for the continuation of our civilisation and its further development, atomic energy is not merely an aid; it is an absolute necessity. The acquisition by man of the knowledge of how to release and use atomic energy must be recognised as the third great epoch in human history.

There is no longer any question that atomic energy can be used for power-generation…There is little doubt that many atomic power stations will be established in different parts of the world during the next ten years. The extent to which atomic energy contributes in future to the total energy production will depend on the capital and running costs involved, and will vary from country to country. Generally, the basic ideas of atomic energy are simple but its technology is sophisticated and difficult…

It is well known that, unlike coal furnaces which may differ in detail but are basically all of the same design, atomic furnaces can be of at least half dozen basically different patterns, which differ in the physical and chemical state of the fuel, the moderator used, if any, and the method employed for extracting heat. Perhaps some of the greatest interest will attach to the series of technical sessions which are to be devoted to reactor technology. These sessions will throw important light on the merits and disadvantages of the different types of reactors...

The immense concentration of atomic energy has made possible other developments whose immediate results have been less happy, and which have placed a pall of fear over the peoples of the world. I refer, of course, to the development of, atomic and hydrogen bombs. The powerful and technically advanced nations have suffered most from this fear. Atomic weapons lie outside the scope of this Conference, but we cannot entirely separate the applications of peace from the applications of war. The rise of an atomic power industry in many parts of the world, the development of which is necessitated by the growing demands for power, will put into the hands of many nations quantities of fissile material, from which the making of atomic bombs will be but a relatively easy step. A widespread atomic power industry in the world will necessitate an international society in which the major States have agreed to maintain peace...

One has every reason to hope that the intelligence of man will overcome his fear and his weaknesses. The areas of social organisation and orderly peaceful existence have on the average increased continuously with the advance of technology. At no previous period in history have such large and closely integrated States existed. It is, therefore, not surprising that in the atomic age major wars should ultimately become impossible, and that the area of peaceful existence should eventually cover the entire globe...

The historical period we are just entering in which atomic energy released by the fission process will supply some of the power requirements of the world may well be regarded one day as the primitive period of the atomic age. It is well known that atomic energy can be obtained by a fusion process as in the H-bomb, and there is no basic scientific knowledge in our possession today to show that it is impossible for us to obtain this energy from the fusion process in a controlled manner. The technical problems are formidable, but one should remember that it is not yet fifteen years since atomic energy was released in an atomic pile for the first time by Fermi. I venture to predict that a method will be found for liberating fusion energy in a controlled manner within the next two decades. When that happens, the energy problems of the world will truly have been solved forever for the fuel will be as plentiful as the heavy hydrogen in the oceans.

~

V.K. KRISHNA MENON

On South Africa

Towards the end of the nineteenth century, South Africa had a large number of Indians working in the plantations or as labourers in farmlands. The white population, the British as well as the Boers, the descendants of the Dutch settlers, in league with the government adopted a series of oppressive measures towards these Indians including a number of restrictive laws. These discriminatory laws led to Mahatma Gandhi's satyagraha in the first decade of the twentieth century. The 1940s witnessed a spate of new unjust laws which the Indian leadership took upon itself to criticize. In 1943, Natal passed the Pegging Act, restricting the right of Asians to acquire land. Then, in 1946, the Union Government passed the Asiatic Land Tenure and Indian Representation Act to segregate Indians in trade and residence. The Indian community launched a passive resistance campaign on 13 June 1946. India complained to the United Nations in 1946 on racial discrimination against Indians in South Africa. On 7 July 1946, the Government of India prohibited all trade with South Africa. At that time, South Africa accounted for 5.5 per cent of India's exports and about 1.5 per cent of India's imports. Emboldened by the tacit support it received from major European powers, the government in South Africa enacted a series of racist and repressive measures in the 1950s to consolidate white supremacy. The African National Congress and the South African Indian Congress launched a 'Joint Campaign of Defiance against Unjust Laws', demanding the abrogation of a number of obnoxious laws. Over 8000 people of all racial origins were imprisoned in this multiracial non-violent campaign in 1952-53. India and twelve other Asian–Arab states proposed a discussion in the United Nations General Assembly on the 'Question of Race Conflict Resulting from the Policies of Apartheid of the Government of the Union of South Africa'. During the discussion in November 1956, Krishna Menon, with his detailed knowledge of affairs in South Africa and his close relationship with many of the leaders, repeatedly argued that South Africa belonged to all its people, and not to its white minority alone, and paid tribute to all those struggling against apartheid under great difficulties. His speech made a case for democracy and freedom and put forward, in clear terms, India's opposition to the policy of apartheid practised by South Africa.

… I should like to express my regret that our colleagues of the Union of South Africa are not present with us today. Their absence is regrettable from many points of view. There has never been an occasion in this Assembly when anyone has expressed any adverse view in regard to the Union's right to express its opinion, totally unacceptable as that opinion is, I dare say, to every member state in this Assembly. That provides all the more reason why we should regret the absence of the Union's representative.

... We are not trying to create a voting record. But I hope that at the end of this debate, especially in view of the attitude taken by those on whom this policy makes an adverse impact—and it would be only human nature to react to it with more hostility than we have—I hope that this resolution will have passed by a larger vote, and with no votes against it, even if one or two delegations, for whatever reasons, should desire to abstain. I mention this because it is a matter on which the Assembly has very strong feelings, feelings which are not divided by the boundaries of continent or race or political opinion or by the unfortunate dividing line of blocs.

When our colleagues of the Union do not participate in spite of the attitude we take, their action is not directed against those who submit this item, it is not directed against what may or may not be the decision of the Assembly, but it is against the repeatedly recorded decision of the Assembly over a period of years. It is a question—and my colleague from Ireland will understand this reference—of everybody being out of step except my Johnny.

... I would like now to go back a little into the past. Somewhere in the second half of the nineteenth century, the British Colonial Secretary, in order to assist the economic development of South Africa, persuaded the British Indian Government of that day to send numbers of people to work on the sugar plantations in Africa. From that time onwards there has been a racial problem in South Africa. Perhaps there was even one before that, but the newer view is that the Bantu tribes came after the Dutch. But I am not going into the history of this. There are two views about it.

There was a racial problem and no one was aware of it more than General Smuts. But in spite of that and after the League of Nations had been founded, at which he made similar statements, and it died, and the problems of racial discrimination had come to the forefront under the benighted rule of Adolf Hitler, General Smuts, speaking in San Francisco, in words which should be inscribed in letters of gold, states: 'The new Charter should not be a mere legalistic document for the prevention of war. I would suggest that the Charter should contain at its very outset and in its preamble, a declaration of human rights and of the common faith which has sustained the Allied peoples in their bitter and prolonged struggle for the vindication of those rights and that faith.' Part of the vindication was the persecution of the Semitic peoples in Germany by Hitler and also the rape of countries like Czechoslovakia, mainly on a racial basis.

Field Marshal Smuts went on to say: 'In the deepest sense it has been a war of religion perhaps more so than any other war of history. We have fought for justice and decency and for the fundamental freedoms and rights of man, which are basic to all human advancement and progress and peace. Let us in this new Charter of humanity, give expression to this faith in us, and thus proclaim to the world and to posterity, that this was not a mere brute struggle of force between the nations but that for us, behind the mortal struggle, was the moral struggle, was the vision of the ideal, the faith in justice and the resolve to vindicate the fundamental rights of man, and on that basis to found a better, freer world for the future. Never have all peace-loving peoples been so deeply moved. This is what our men and women feel'—meaning the men and women of the Union of South Africa—'they are fighting for on the war fronts, and have been labouring and slaving for on the home fronts in these long years of steadfast endurance. Let us put it into the Charter of the United Nations as our confession of faith and our testimony to the future. Our warfare has been for the eternal values which sustain the spirit of man in its upward struggle toward the light. Let us affirm this faith of ours, not only as our high cause and guiding spirit in this war but also as our objective for the future. The peace we are striving for, and are taking such pains to safeguard, is a peace of justice and honour and fair-dealing as between man and man, as between nation and nation. No other peace would be worth the sacrifices we have made and are prepared to make again and the heavy responsibilities we are prepared to take under this Charter.'

It is hardly necessary to say that this was not a sermon for one day of the week. This was a statement made in the formulation of the Charter. But if that stood alone it would not be adequate. At another part of the session at San Francisco, Field Marshal Smuts said: 'Looking farther afield for precautions and remedies against war beyond the war machine itself, the Charter envisages also a social and economic organisation of the peoples, intended to raise the levels and standards of life and work for all, and, by thus removing social unrest and injustice, to strike at the very roots of war.'

What other thing can raise greater social injustice and unrest than the doctrine of apartheid where the vast majority of people who live in their own countries are foreigners and strangers, outcasts, and where, what is more, any action which they take by not moving out of the house is crime under the law of the country?

Field Marshal Smuts states: 'Great as our achievement is, I feel that more is needed than a mere machine of peace. Unless the spirit to operate it is there, the best plan or machine may fail... And in our faith in the future we expect that those who come after us and who will have to carry our Charter in the generation to come, will also show no less goodwill and good faith in their part of the great task of peace.'

So what we are doing here now has the authority of one of the greatest statesmen not only of South Africa, but of the world, who lived in the context of these racial troubles. I am not for a moment saying that racial laws were not passed in his time. But here is a full statement of the case in which at San Francisco we were enjoined to carry out these principles into the open and to pass them on to posterity.

Since then what has happened? ... I want to preface my observations by saying that my country would be the last to question the right of South Africa to pass whatever laws it wants in its own territory. That Government has a sovereign right to do so. But we as adherents of the Charter also have equal rights to point out if those laws are violation of the Charter...

During this period, nine measures have been under consideration of the South African Government, and some of them have been passed. I must say at this point that it is not sufficient to look merely at the titles of the laws in South Africa. Some of these titles might be misleading.

First, there is the elimination of non-whites from 'open' universities and the establishment of university colleges for non-whites: If you look at the law you think it would be a good thing to establish university colleges for non-whites. But the essential part of it is that they cannot go into the colleges which they were in. This is in the one field of education, in the liberal arts, where people are discriminated against on the very grounds which are contrary to the studies of the humanities.

... Another law is the 'abolition of African representation in Parliament and the Cape Provincial Council'. It is not merely an objectionable law but a violation of undertakings given by the South

African Government from time to time. Another law under consideration is: 'The strengthening of the powers of the Minister of Labour, so that he can apply job reservations unhindered by court decision.' I am sure that the trade union movement of the world will take note of this... The question is not whether there is a man who is an electrician or an engineer, but: what is the colour of his skin or the colour of the skin of his parents?

Fifth, there is: 'The establishment of a Bantu Investment Corporation'—another misleading title—'the capital for which will come from African savings and state contributions.' The effect of this is that Bantu development must come only from that place. Again, this is putting apartheid into the whole business of economic development.

Then there is: 'The transfer of Coloured special schools from the Union Department of Education to the Department of Coloured Affairs.' That also looks very good. It looks as though the so-called Coloured people are going to a big show and look after their own affairs. What happens is this: the state as a whole and its resources no longer become responsible, but the Coloured people are shunted off into an ante-room and become a kind of poor relation.

Then there is: 'The extension of the concept of Bantustan to the towns.' That is the real building of ghettos, territorial segregation. Bantustan, I suppose, means the territory of the Bantus, borrowed from Indian analogies.

Next is: 'Amendment of the Group Areas Act to overcome difficulties with local authorities in the establishment of townships for race groups.' The Group Areas Act is an old friend of ours. It was first introduced to remove the Indians from various parts of South Africa. The groups who are discriminated against were to be denoted by the executive. That is, the executive says, 'You are a group that is objected to, you must go from where you are.' Then they are moved bag and baggage from the place. We have been asking them in this Assembly time after time to withdraw the Group Areas Act... What has happened is, instead of withdrawing the Group Areas Act, which has been the demand of all concerned, they amended the Act so as to overcome the difficulties of the local authorities in establishing townships. It means that the power was given to them for forcible eviction and pushing them out from their original homes to the wilderness.

The last of these is: 'The abolition of Native Advisory Boards when African representation in Parliament is abolished.' That is to say, any function that African peoples could have in regard to administration of Advisory Boards is a concomitant of the abolition of their representation in Parliament.

Legislation in regard to three or four of these has been completed, and the rest is in progress. Despite these new measures, it must be remembered that not only has there been no progress in this matter, but also there has been considerable regress and a total disregard of the resolutions.

... These are the reasons why we bring this matter here year after year. It is not because this is a hardy annual. The draft resolution before us ... does not express the very legitimate indignation of large numbers of people. It does not express words of condemnation. It speaks more in sorrow than in anger. The reason why the draft resolution before us is drafted in this way is in order that the lowest common denominator of adverse opinion may make some impact, if not on the Government of South Africa immediately, on those large numbers of people who, as in Hitler's Germany, are against racial discrimination as such, a thing that cannot be worked...

I hope that the restraint, the moderation, that is shown in these matters will not be regarded by those who do not agree with it as timidity. Our country does not believe that hard words find solutions, but there should be no doubt in the mind of anyone that this disease is fast spreading...

My delegation wishes to make it perfectly clear that we could not solve this problem merely by setting up committees from outside, writing reports going into the anthropology or the physics or the chemistry of this business. We would be the last people to promote or encourage any move which recreates further hostilities. Our attitude is one of appeal to South Africa to join in this general attempt to remove these evils.

Secondly, we do not want it in any way to be understood by anyone that these racial evils are a blot on South Africa and South Africa alone. We have plenty of them in our own country. There are not many countries in the world where discrimination of one kind or another does not take place. But there is not a country in the world which defends discrimination. We all try to get away from the evil. We would not stand up on a platform and proclaim that discrimination is a virtue. We know it is with us, we fight against it, we organise our public opinion against it, we even fight our own countrymen, our political colleagues. But here not only are we told that this has arisen in the context of history, and what are we to do about it. That is not what we are told. We are told that there is apartheid, that there must be apartheid; and not only that there must be apartheid in Africa, but that it must be everywhere else...

I did not want to introduce emotionalism into this matter. I did not want to refer to the enormous amount of hardship it has cost in the uprooting of peoples and families who have been in places for generations and yet being turned out into the jungles and prevented from having the opportunity of earning their livelihood, being separated from employers, who are humane people, who do not subscribe to this but who must obey the law, where bitterness is creeping in. All of those processes which make a society unstable are being promoted by legislation.

A distinguished South African judge once said: 'There are so many laws that have been made in South Africa that if an African gets out of his house, he can commit a crime.' Because if you do something or look at somebody, or tilt your hat in the wrong way, or forget your passbook, or whatever it is, they are statutory crimes. We have moved from the time when the poll tax was the only inhibition in order to obtain control over the African peoples or populations of that character.

We appeal to the Assembly to give full support to the draft resolution, and once again we would like to say to South Africans who are here by proxy that in spite of all that has happened, we fervently hope that whatever procedures they adopt, whether it be formal or informal, whether it be through those who are not so committed as we are, whether it be by any action they take themselves, whether it be by negotiations with their sister states in the African continent, whether it be by some convention to which they could agree, they would make a breach, create some disengagement of this problem, so that it will prevent its spreading into the rest of the continent and will avoid the horrors of racial conflict.

In that connexion, I am instructed by my Government to draw the attention of all of us to the fact that one of the evil by-products of this may be the division among the non-white peoples themselves. An old English official once spoke of 'a subject peoples speaking two languages, one for itself and one for the ruler'. Similarly, it is possible—it has happened in the questions in which we are more intimately related—that attempts will be made to create divisions among the people on whom apartheid makes its impact. There are always those who are prepared to buy a junior partnership in imperialism.

So far as the Indian populations on the African continent are concerned, it is the deliberate policy of my Government to point out to them that nationalism is territorial. An Indian in Africa is an African-Indian or an Indian-African, the same way as the Dutch is an African. It is only on this basis that we can proceed...

~

M.C. CHAGLA

India and West Asia

India was caught in a peculiar bind with regard to its foreign policy in the late 1960s. It had taken a strong stand against Israel and its claims in West Asia particularly in view of its recent occupation of Gaza. This was also the high tide of the American involvement in Vietnam and US President Johnson was bent on blackmailing India into supporting the United States. India's refusal meant delay in the committed food aid to India at a time when the country had undergone two successive droughts, and famine conditions prevailed in most parts of the country. Right-wing opinion at home as well as American lobbyists and Western powers were trying their best to bulldoze India's new prime minister, Indira Gandhi, to change the course of India's foreign policy. In fact, the country's definite shift towards Soviet Russia and West Asian countries can be seen against this background. It was under such circumstances that M.C. Chagla became the foreign minister. Chagla's speech in the United Nations General Assembly on 21 June 1967 clarified India's stand on the issue gently, yet firmly.

Even in this gloomy hour it should perhaps hearten us that the international community has so spontaneously, and with such a measure of unanimity, agreed that the United Nations is the proper forum for arriving at decisions which ensure that the principle gets established that in the second half of the twentieth century, aggressors are not permitted to retain the reward of their aggression, however successful on the field of battle they might be. It would be an understatement to say that peace in West Asia is in peril. Barely a week ago, a short but savage war in that area was brought to a halt, by continuous and persistent efforts of the Security Council, and unless the world community can arrange—and arrange firmly and speedily—a durable and just peace, it is not inconceivable that a world conflagration may follow. We, therefore, hope that the return of peace to the area will be such as to guarantee that there shall be no recurrence of war again; that the human problems created by this war, further compounding the tragedy which already existed in the area as a result of the happenings in 1948 and 1956, will be redressed with the help of all men of goodwill, all over the world, and through the instrumentality of the United Nations. Conditioned by the teachings of Mahatma Gandhi during our struggle for independence, and conditioned earlier, through the centuries, by the tradition of the deep and abiding philosophy of humanism, centuries that produced Buddha and Ashoka, our land has been a crucible for integrating people of different faiths and diverse ethnic origins. For centuries, people have lived in India who practised all the major religions of the world: Buddhism, Hinduism, Islam, Christianity, Judaism, Zoroastrianism. To us, therefore, the philosophy of tolerance, peace and coexistence, is natural and the ideas of violence and war repugnant. Settlement of international disputes through peaceful means, respect for territorial integrity and sovereignty of States, the right of all nations to live in freedom and enjoy fruits of freedom, are all cherished articles of faith with us. Where peace is threatened, or aggression committed, we find it impossible to remain silent and passive. We have, therefore, voiced our sincere and wholehearted sympathy for and solidarity with the Arab peoples in their hours of trial and tribulation.

~

BRAJESH MISHRA

Statement on Pokaran, 1974

India tested its first nuclear device in 1974 at Pokaran, shocking the international community which was caught entirely unawares. The whole Western world as well as a large number of other countries became hostile to India's show of strength through this demonstration, more so because India had steadfastly refused to sign the Nuclear Non-Proliferation Treaty. India was strongly criticized at all international forums including the United Nations. In this speech made on 9 July 1974, Brajesh Mishra, Indian envoy to the United Nations at the time, clarified India's stand on the nuclear issue, insisting that India's nuclear programme was meant for peaceful and scientific uses. In a twist of fate, nearly twenty-five years later, as National Security Adviser and principal secretary to Prime Minister A.B. Vajpayee, Brajesh Mishra was at the helm of affairs when India conducted her second nuclear explosion in 1998.

... Our reasons for not adhering to the NPT are fundamental reasons. They go to the very philosophy of international relations which we have tried to follow since we became independent; and one of the basic points of this philosophy is equality in international life. We have considered and we continue to consider that the NPT is not an equal legal instrument. It is a discriminatory instrument; and I must categorically state here that we will not become a party to that instrument us long as the discriminatory character of that instrument remains as it is today. When the Review Conference takes place—but naturally we have no right to propagate this view, since we are not a party to that Treaty—perhaps it will take a look at this character of the NPT and try to change it so as to make it acceptable universally.

The second point—and I must thank the Minister for taking note of the assurances given by the Government of India in regard to its peaceful intentions—which is perhaps forgotten sometimes is that these assurances, although they were reiterated after the explosion on 18 May, had been given for the last twenty years. I can go back to 1954 or I can go back to even earlier years and quote from the statements of my Government on this question. Now these are solemn statements, solemn declarations which have not been violated so far, and they must be treated as solemn declarations.

After all, even if we were to join the NPT there is a clause for withdrawal. In this sense is the Treaty more solemn than the declarations which we have made? This is a point which I believe should be taken note of and should be welcomed as far as the Government of India is concerned; that it continues to abide by solemn declarations which are not new but have been given over the years, and which have been reiterated very recently, and which I reiterate on behalf of my Government here today. We intend to use nuclear energy solely for peaceful purposes.

There was also a reference—and this has also been made from time to time not only here but also in other fora—that nuclear explosions for peaceful purposes are something which is not immediately of benefit to the international community, and that in any case the

NPT provides for giving the benefit of this technology to non-nuclear-weapon States parties to the NPT. Well, since we are not a party to the NPT we do consider that it is our right to develop this technology for peaceful purposes.

Moreover, it will not be contended by any side that a technology which is limited or which is being developed by five nuclear States alone—if all of them are developing it I do not know—should be the end of the story and that it is not possible that another State with some knowledge, with some experience will be able to contribute towards the development of this technology and thus give the benefit to the international community as a whole, as the nuclear States parties to the NPT have undertaken to do. Again, we feel that there should be no discrimination in this regard. If we are able to contribute, we should be allowed to contribute keeping in mind the very solemn declaration that we have made in regard to peaceful uses of this technology.

~

INDIRA GANDHI

Support to the Palestinian Cause

Indira Gandhi was one of the strongest champions of the Palestinian cause and she held Yasser Arafat, chairman of the Palestine Liberation Organisation, in high esteem. India was one of the first countries to accord recognition to the cause of a free Palestinian state. Yasser Arafat came to India to express his gratitude for the solidarity that India had shown. This speech, delivered at a dinner hosted in honour of Yasser Arafat in New Delhi in 1982, provides a glimpse of the admiration that Indira Gandhi had for the leader of the Palestinian struggle. It also demonstrates how Indira Gandhi was trying to steer the Non-Aligned Movement towards economic issues.

You are the symbol of a people afire with the spirit of freedom. We welcome you as a gallant fighter for a just cause. Your vision, courage and determination have galvanised the Palestinian movement. Your leadership has given it dynamism and strength. We are glad you were able to come once again in our midst.

... Over decades, the people of India have consistently supported the Palestinian people in their struggle to regain their land. As long ago as 1920, before many around this table were born, Mahatma Gandhi spoke up for the people of Palestine. Jawaharlal Nehru wrote about the Palestinian cause and the Indian National Congress repeatedly affirmed its solidarity with the aspirations of the Palestinians. In 1936, the Congress Party observed a 'Palestine Day'. Support to Palestine was a plank of our foreign policy. In the United Nations, newly independent India opposed the partition of Palestine.

Since then, much to our satisfaction, your struggle has gathered considerable international support. Two years ago, it was our privilege to accord full diplomatic recognition to the PLO. But the Palestinian lands are still occupied and your people remain uprooted from their homes and are subjected to many kinds of deprivation.

The denial of rights to any people is an affront to the rights of all others. The plight of your people constitutes a challenge to human dignity. That is why India and the entire Non-Aligned Movement have supported your fight. The Non-Aligned Bureau, which met in Kuwait recently, has rightly decided to redouble its endeavours in the United Nations to find a solution.

We express our strong opposition to the organised repression of the Palestinian inhabitants of the West Bank through large-scale attacks on the civilian population, through the dismissal of popularly elected mayors, and by the economic exploitation of the region. How can there be peace at the expense of the inalienable rights of the Palestinian people?

Iran and Iraq are amongst the foremost supporters of the Palestinian cause. Their continuing conflict is a cause for anxiety to us both. It is bringing destruction and hardship to the people of the two countries and deep anguish to their common friends. At this time, the Palestinian people need complete solidarity among their supporters and well wishers... This war and the unresolved crisis in West Asia, as well as political developments in other parts of the Asian continent, are being used as convenient excuses for the induction of armaments on a large scale, and the increase of foreign pressures into this entire region. Such actions are not conducive to security. On the contrary, by encouraging suspicion and confrontations, they add to insecurity.

Peace is the world's greatest need, without which the developing countries cannot hope to end poverty, nor can the affluent countries maintain their levels of welfare. We encourage any move which lowers tensions. In the gathering gloom, there is some glimmer of light. Leaders of the big powers are suggesting limiting the expansion of armaments. We can only hope that these small beginnings will lead step by step towards meaningful disarmament. This is in line with our own desire and the spirit of non-alignment. India believes in bringing people together and in blunting hostility where it exists. We have tried to strengthen goodwill and friendship with all our immediate neighbours as also with countries in other regions and continents irrespective of their political affiliations.

We have been urging the non-aligned countries to put greater emphasis on economic cooperation. There is concern at the widening chasm between the developed and developing countries, but we can and must do more to establish closer economic relations among the developing countries themselves. The pooling and sharing of our resources and skills will be mutually and collectively beneficial. Cooperation between the developing countries will be mutually and collectively beneficial. Cooperation between the developing countries will help to bring about better cooperation between the developing and the developed. Excellency, we know of your personal interest in these matters. I can assure you that India will continue to do all in its capacity to serve the common good of the developing countries.

Your visit is a major event in the growth of Indo-Palestinian and Indo-Arab friendship which we value and want to nurture, and which we are determined to expand.

~

RAJIV GANDHI

On Disarmament

India has been a strong advocate of general and total disarmament. Towards this end, it has taken several initiatives within the United Nations and outside. In the 1980s, India was part of the Six-Nation Five-Continent Peace Initiative which sought to highlight international concern about the unprecedented nuclear arms race. Rajiv Gandhi (1944–1991), prime minister of India from 1984 to 1989, attended a conference of the Peace Initiative in Stockholm, Sweden, in 1988. In this speech, delivered on 21 January, he calls for a complete elimination of nuclear weapons.

We have come together in the New Year, a year which begins with a breath of hope for the survival of life upon our planet. We are gathered in a city known for its love of peace and harmony. In this bracing winter afternoon, Stockholm seems suffused with the freshness of a new stirring in the air. We thank Prime Minister Carlsson and the friendly people of Sweden for giving us an opportunity in this beautiful city to reflect upon the distance we have covered and the horizons that lie ahead. As Dag Hammarskjold said, 'Only he who keeps his eye fixed on the horizon will find his right road.'

When Olof Palme, Indira Gandhi and our distinguished colleagues in the Six-Nation Five-Continent Peace Initiative issued their first Appeal in May 1984, the dialogue between the nuclear powers had collapsed into accusations of ill-faith and mutual recrimination. When we met in New Delhi three years ago, the dialogue had just resumed. At Ixtapa, there was a glimmer of hope. Now, we have a treaty on the complete elimination of a category of nuclear missiles.

Something of the credit for this must go to the good sense of ordinary people, whose hopes and aspirations we have sought to articulate. Millions across the globe, including those in the nuclear weapon States and the military alliances, have instinctively perceived the incompatibility between nuclear confrontation and lasting of peace. The Six-Nation Five-Continent Peace Initiative has given voice to their perceptions.

We sincerely congratulate General Secretary Gorbachev and President Reagan on their vision and on the sensitivity they have shown to the need to dismantle and destroy nuclear weapon systems. The INF Treaty is a historic beginning, historic, certainly, but, equally certainly, just a beginning. There can be no relapsing into the comfortable complacency of coexisting with the instruments of our own destruction.

What has been achieved will prove a pyretic victory unless it leads irreversibly and without interruption to the complete elimination of nuclear weapons. The process may involve the phased reduction of levels of nuclear weaponry. But the goal must remain the dismantling of all nuclear arsenals, as the precursor to general and complete disarmament.

Warheads have been uncoupled from missiles in one class of nuclear weapons. This is not enough. Warheads must be eliminated. Equally, the pursuit of peace must be uncoupled from strategies of nuclear deterrence, and such strategies must be universally repudiated. The militarization of international relations must end. The international order must be based on peaceful coexistence. We have to have a world free of nuclear weapons. Indeed, eventually, we have to have a world free of all weapons.

It is disturbing that, in certain quarters, there is a strident assertion that disarmament is not only utopian but dangerous. We must change the thinking of establishments reared in the theology of nuclear deterrence. They argue that nuclear weapons keep the peace. This is false. If nuclear weapons exist, they will one day be used, as they were in Hiroshima and Nagasaki, as all weapons have been throughout history. And, on the last day, it will make little difference whether their use was by design or by accident. The nuclear debris will bury all hopes of reprieve. There will be no going back, no survival, none to tell the tale. There will be no lessons to be drawn for the future—for there will be no future.

Therefore, even as we congratulate the United States and the Soviet Union, we seek assurance that the treaty they have signed in Washington constitutes the commencement of a time-bound process of nuclear disarmament. What has been covered so far is just a tiny fraction of the awesome armouries of global annihilation—97 per cent remains. Only the United States and the Soviet Union have initiated this small step.

This small step must lead to many more. The other three nuclear weapon powers must be inducted into the process. The process of global nuclear disarmament must be reinforced by those countries which are able to cross the threshold of not doing so. There must be no assistance, surreptitious or overt, to those trying to acquire nuclear weapons.

There must be no adding of new dimensions to nuclear weaponry. The chimera of an impenetrable shield in space must be abandoned. There is no 'ultimate defence' that can be devised by technology. The search for technological answers thwarts the real search for durable peace. There is no technological solution to the problems of war and peace. It is in the human mind that the defences for peace are built. Human destiny cannot be mortgaged to a machine.

All quantitative improvements in nuclear weapons must be foregone so that reductions in stockpiles are not offset by weapons of greater destructive power, more accurate and even more swift. Hence, the ineluctable need for an immediate moratorium on all nuclear tests, to set the stage for a Comprehensive Test Ban Treaty.

Another great danger arises from new weapons systems and subtle refinements in sophisticated armaments. We should cry halt to this arms race in emerging technologies. The race is on in conventional and nuclear weapons. It is also insidiously penetrating totally new areas. We should identify these technological developments, debar their military applications, and prevent the emergence of new ways of dealing death.

What we need to end is the option of unleashing global devastation or holding the survival of humanity to ransom. We must protect humanity as much from the known dangers of extinction as from those that are still unknown.

There must also be radical reductions in conventional armaments. The process of conventional disarmament should begin where the bulk of such arms is concentrated and extends to other regions of the world. The ultimate objective should be general and complete disarmament.

What we seek is not a marginal adjustment in the machinery of nuclear confrontation, nor a partial or temporary scaling down of the arms race. What we seek is an effective structure of international security, a structure that discards obsolete mindsets, dangerous delusions, and destructive strategic doctrines. Distant though the prospect of a nuclear-free world might seem, it is a prospect. We must start giving thought now to the international order we would like to see prevail in a world which is rid of nuclear weapons. We have to revert to first principles of non-violence and tolerance, of compassion and understanding—of one world for one humanity. Coercion must give way to reason. Spheres of influence and special privileges must yield to a true democracy of nations. The cornering of resources for weaponry must be transmuted into the sharing of resources for global development. The pursuit of dominance must be replaced by coexistence and cooperation.

~

P.V. NARASIMHA RAO

Challenge and Opportunity in the Post-Cold War Era: An Indian Perspective on the Emerging Structure of Interstate Relations

The international scenario changed in the 1990s with the collapse of the Soviet Union and the emergence of the USA as the sole superpower. Given that right through the Cold War era India had been a staunch ally of the Soviet Union, the new state of affairs had important ramifications for the country. With India also embarking on a regime of economic liberalization around this time, the country found itself at economic and political crossroads where it was imperative to understand the international situation and its position in the new political dispensation. The depth of Prime Minister Narasimha Rao's political acumen was thankfully available to India at the time and he brought his wealth of experience in national and international affairs to project India's vision in the new world order. This speech, delivered at the French Institute of International Relations, Paris, on 29 September 1992, reveals his astute understanding of the dynamics of world affairs.

Certainly, India owes some of the inspiration for its own struggle for independence to the ideas of Liberty, Equality and Fraternity bequeathed to us by the French Revolution. In France, we see mirrored our own dedication to democracy, a zealous attachment to independence and a cultural sensitivity that transcends ethnic, national and religious confines.

... During the past few years, the processes of history have suddenly accelerated, transforming the international landscape beyond recognition. What is especially remarkable is, first, the global scope of the change and second, the pace of the change.

Another notable feature of the change is that several contradictory trends are in simultaneous motion. On the one hand there are integrative trends fired by developments in technology and the emergence of a global marketplace. On the other hand, there are disintegrative forces at work, fracturing national entities along ethnic, religious and even tribal lines. There is a welcome surge of democracy and concern for human rights all over the globe. At the same time, the pervasive lack of development and growing poverty in many parts of the world are already creating conditions for the return of totalitarianism. And while the end of the Cold War has erased East-West confrontation, the North-South gulf threatens to make the world a grotesque and extremely ugly place to live in, if living is at all conceivable.

What should be the main features of the new structure of interstate relations? Here, by interstate, I mean total and multilateral. Quite clearly, it must be a structure capable of dealing with challenges that are global in scope. These include issues which affect the interests of the vast majority of countries such as environmental degradation, weapons of mass destruction, cross-border terrorism, drug-trafficking etc., to name a few. There are also other issues which may be specific in location, but nevertheless have a global impact. Thus, the famine and civil war in Somalia, even if it is in a distant part of the world, impinges upon the consciousness of people all over the world.

Secondly, not only must our structure be geared to global challenges, it must also be capable of responding promptly and effectively to the rapidity of change. Problems must be contained before they degenerate into chaos. Crises must be arrested and reversed before they turn into tragedy.

Does our national experience provide us with any pointers in this regard? I think our experience as democracies certainly does. Democracy is effective precisely because it offers a mechanism through which a national consensus can be evolved behind preferred policies. Democracy allows for orderly change. These same principles must now be extended to interstate relations mutatis mutandis. International cooperation to deal with global challenges will be effective only if it is backed by international consensus. Such a consensus can only be evolved through a truly democratic and multilateral process, with the participation of equal and sovereign States.

As a democracy, India has welcomed that popular upsurge that swept across the globe, bringing freedom and opportunity to peoples of countries long suppressed by unrepresentative governments. Here, it would be wrong to assume that this resurgence of democracy in several parts of the world is a permanent and irreversible condition. There is nothing automatic about democracy. It is a political form which has evolved over many centuries. There is a certain temper, a certain way of thinking which lies behind the institution of democracy. Democracy needs to be nurtured. It is not a ready-made garment that fits everyone. It needs to be consciously evolved and practised.

Similar considerations are relevant in devising an appropriate development strategy. The experience of many countries indicates that a market-oriented economy is best suited to bring about an efficient allocation of resources, and consequently more rapid economic development. We ourselves have therefore given a strong market orientation to our economic policy, reducing the degree of government control over productive activity, and providing an environment which encourages the spirit of enterprise in our people. However, the role of the state in economic life will continue to be crucial. There is no mechanistic equation between a free market and economic development, just as free market is not necessarily equal to democracy. This is particularly true in developing countries, where neither the affluence of the few, nor their philanthropy, can be assumed to go down to the base of the pyramid. Large numbers of our populations are outside the operation of market forces and state intervention is necessary if we are to alleviate poverty and distress for these sections of society and to raise their living standards, at least in the foreseeable future. Besides, in developing countries the state often has to play an active role to create the conditions in which markets can work, for example, by providing the necessary infrastructure and often even institutional support not to speak of conditions of law and order, conditions of equal opportunity, conditions of fairness in society as a whole. These are the things which need to be ensured even for a free market economy to function in a state.

If this is the case, then the international structure we seek must be very different from the direction in which we are presently headed. Firstly, we must recognise our responsibility for supporting and nurturing democracy everywhere. The fragile institutions of democracy in the developing world as well as in countries which have just emerged from the collapse of the socialist system are threatened most by economic deprivation and lack of development. All these countries are reorienting their economic policies to utilise the many advantages of market orientation. But we must not assume that this reorientation alone will solve all problems, independent of the international environment. We must also not assume that this reorientation is going to be automatic or easy or it can be possible within a short time. It will take its time, it will take its effort, it will have ups and downs and it will pass through many, many bumps before it really arrives. Such economic reorientation takes time to have its full effect and in this process all these economies can be greatly helped by appropriate international support. They need a greater injection of financial resources to support their reform efforts. They also need assured access to markets in industrialised countries. Their opening up to the world will be most effective only if the world also opens up to them. All this calls for renewed commitment to multilateral international cooperation. Unless this is done we run the risk of discrediting economic reform and also democracy in many countries. I am sure you are aware of the trends that threaten to develop in some of these countries where they find that the advent of democracy, the advent of liberalisation, the advent of opening up has not given results in the short run and people are getting restive. So, some result which gives them hope that there is a possibility of much more coming is necessary. I am not recommending anything to anyone. I am only trying to analyse the way the minds are working in these countries because we have all these inputs coming in from these countries. If such scepticism really takes hold, namely that nothing is going to happen, the road to totalitarianism will not be very distant. This is the danger which I would like to point out because the fragility of democracy itself is a hurdle. If there had been democracy in these countries for the last two hundred or three hundred years they would take all the ups and downs in their stride. But today when there is a sudden change in the system and the change has not been properly assimilated, properly internalised, what is needed is the result in the short run, howsoever slight, howsoever symbolic, howsoever halting, but if it is not there and they are worse off than what they were three or four years ago then there will be the danger of a backlash.

Building an international environment supportive of democracy and helping countries overcome problems of economic transition must, therefore, be the aim of the international community. So, it is a great responsibility, the responsibility for the whole world. For the system of democracy to take root in the whole world, this is the real measure of the responsibility that is implied in this. In the final analysis, democracy within nations can only be sustained if there is democracy among nations. If certain countries with relatively greater political, military and economic power seek to exploit the current fluid situation to perpetuate their dominant status, then others will feel obliged to resist at some point through whatever means are available. Totalitarianism finds its best argument in national insecurity and perception of threat.

~

ATAL BIHARI VAJPAYEE

The Nuclear Tests at Pokaran

India conducted its second nuclear test in May 1998. The test was seen as a declaration of the country's intention to stand up to strong Western pressure and exercise its nuclear option for national security purposes. Prime Minister Atal Bihari Vajpayee, who had long been a votary of India going nuclear, made a powerful statement in Parliament on 27 May 1998.

Sir, I rise to inform the House of momentous developments that have taken place while we were in recess. On 11 May, India successfully carried out three underground nuclear tests. Two more underground tests on 13 May completed the planned series of tests. I would like this House to join me in paying fulsome tribute to our scientists, engineers and defence personnel whose singular achievements have given us a renewed sense of national pride and self-confidence. Sir, in addition to the statement I make, I have also taken the opportunity to submit to the House a paper entitled 'Evolution of India's Nuclear Policy'.

In 1947, when India emerged as a free country to take its rightful place in the comity of nations, the nuclear age had already dawned. Our leaders then took the crucial decision to opt for self-reliance, and freedom of thought and action. We rejected the Cold War paradigm and chose the more difficult path of non-alignment. Our leaders also realised that a nuclear-weapon-free world would enhance not only India's security but also the security of all nations. That is why disarmament was and continues to be a major plank in our foreign policy.

During the 50s, India took the lead in calling for an end to all nuclear weapon testing. Addressing the Lok Sabha on 2 April 1954, Pt. Jawaharlal Nehru, to whose memory we pay homage today, stated 'nuclear, chemical and biological energy and power should not be used to forge weapons of mass destruction'. He called for negotiations for prohibition and elimination of nuclear weapons and in the interim, a standstill agreement to halt nuclear testing. This call was not heeded.

In 1965, along with a small group of non-aligned countries, India put forward the idea of an international non-proliferation agreement under which the nuclear weapon states would agree to give up their arsenals provided other countries refrained from developing or acquiring such weapons. This balance of rights and obligations was not accepted. In the 60s our security concerns deepened. The country sought security guarantees but the countries we turned to were unable to extend to us the expected assurances. As a result, we made it clear that we would not be able to sign the NPT.

The Lok Sabha debated the issue on 5 April 1968. Prime Minister late Smt. Indira Gandhi assured the House that 'we shall be guided entirely by our self-enlightenment and the considerations of national security'. This was a turning point and this House strengthened the decision of the then Government by reflecting a national consensus.

Our decision not to sign the NPT was in keeping with our basic objectives. In 1974, we demonstrated our nuclear capability. Successive Governments thereafter have taken all necessary steps in keeping with that resolve and national will, to safeguard India's nuclear option. This was the primary reason behind the 1996 decision for not signing the CTBT, a decision that also enjoyed consensus of this House.

The decades of the 80s and 90s had meanwhile witnessed the gradual deterioration of our security environment as a result of nuclear and missile proliferation. In our neighbourhood, nuclear weapons had increased and more sophisticated delivery systems inducted. In addition, India has also been the victim of externally aided and abetted terrorism, militancy and clandestine war.

At a global level, we see no evidence on the part of the nuclear weapon states to take decisive and irreversible steps in moving towards a nuclear-weapon-free world. Instead, we have seen that the NPT has been extended indefinitely and unconditionally, perpetuating the existence of nuclear weapons in the hands of the five countries.

Under such circumstances, the Government was faced with a difficult decision. The touchstone that has guided us in making the correct choice clear was national security. These tests are a continuation of the policies set into motion that put this country on the path of self-reliance and independence of thought and action.

India is now a nuclear weapon state. This is a reality that cannot be denied. It is not a conferment that we seek; nor is it a status for others to grant. It is an endowment to the nation by our scientists and engineers. It is India's due, the right of one-sixth of humankind. Our strengthened capability adds to our sense of responsibility. We do not intend to use these weapons for aggression or for mounting threats against any country; these are weapons of self-defence, to ensure that India is not subjected to nuclear threats or coercion. We do not intend to engage in an arms race.

We had taken a number of initiatives in the past. We regret that these proposals did not receive a positive response from other nuclear weapon states. In fact, had their response been positive, we need not have gone in for our current testing programme. We have been and will continue to be in the forefront of the calls for opening negotiations for a Nuclear Weapons Convention, so that this challenge can be dealt with in the same manner that we have dealt with the scourge of two other weapons of mass destruction—through the Biological Weapons Convention and the Chemical Weapons Convention.

Traditionally, India has been an outward-looking country. Our strong commitment to multilateralism is reflected in our active participation in organisations like the United Nations. This engagement will continue. The policies of economic liberalisation introduced in recent years have increased our regional and global linkages and my Government intends to deepen and strengthen these ties.

Our nuclear policy has been marked by restraint and openness. We have not violated any international agreements either in 1974 or now, in 1998. The restraint exercised for 24 years, after having demonstrated our capability in 1974, is in itself a unique example. Restraint, however, has to arise from strength. It cannot be based upon indecision or doubt. The series of tests recently undertaken by India have led to the removal of doubts. The action involved was balanced in that it was the minimum necessary to maintain what is an irreducible component of our national security calculus.

Subsequently, Government has already announced that India will now observe a voluntary moratorium and refrain from conducting underground nuclear test explosions. We have also indicated willingness to move towards a de-jure formalisation of this declaration.

The House is no doubt aware of the different reactions that have emanated from the people of India and from different parts of the world. The overwhelming support of our citizens is our source of strength. It tells us not only that this decision was right but also that our country wants a focussed leadership, which attends to their security needs. This, I pledge to do as a sacred duty. We have also been greatly heartened by the outpouring of support from Indians abroad. They have, with one voice, spoken in favour of our action. To the people of India, and to Indians abroad, I convey my profound gratitude. We look to the people of India and Indians abroad for support in the difficult period ahead.

In this, the fiftieth year of our independence, we stand at a defining moment in our history. The rationale for the Government's decision is based on the same policy tenets that have guided us for five decades. These policies have been sustained successfully because of an underlying national consensus. It is vital to maintain the consensus as we approach the next millennium. In my statement today and in the paper placed before the House, I have elaborated on the rationale behind the Government's decision and outlined our approach for the future. The present decision and future actions will continue to reflect a commitment to sensibilities and obligations of an ancient civilisation, a sense of responsibility and restraint, but a restraint born of the assurance of action, not of doubts or apprehension. Avoiding triumphalism, let us work together towards our shared objective in ensuring that as we move towards a new millennium, India will take its rightful place in the international community.

SELECT BIBLIOGRAPHY

Paucity of space prevents me from providing a detailed bibliography. I have also not listed works in Hindi, Bengali, Marathi and other languages which I consulted and which helped me to understand the currents and cross-currents of Indian history.

A. PRIMARY SOURCES

Institutional Documents and Papers

All India Congress Committee Papers, Nehru Memorial Museum and Library, New Delhi

Constituent Assembly (Legislative) Debates, 1947–49, Nehru Memorial Museum and Library, New Delhi

Constituent Assembly Debates, Vol. I-X, JNU Library, New Delhi

Indian Annual Register, Calcutta, 1919–47, edited by H.N. Mitra and N.N. Mitra, Nehru Memorial Museum and Library, New Delhi

Lok Sabha Debates, 1950–2005, Nehru Memorial Museum and Library, New Delhi

Official Proceedings of the Rajya Sabha, 1950–2005, Nehru Memorial Museum and Library, New Delhi

Pamphlets of the Communist Movement of India (1930–2000), P.C. Joshi Archives on Contemporary History, Jawaharlal Nehru University, New Delhi

Papers of the Communist Party of India, 1925–2000, P.C. Joshi Archives on Contemporary History, Jawaharlal Nehru University, New Delhi

Tracts on the Akali Movement (1920–47), Bhai Veer Singh Sahitya Sadan, New Delhi

Tracts on the Panjabi Suba Movement (1950–67), Bhai Veer Singh Sahitya Sadan, New Delhi

Private Papers

A.P. Patro (1875–1946)

Asutosh Lahiry (1892–1975)

B.N. Rau (1887–1953)
C.R. Reddy (1880–1951)
G.N. Bordoloi (1891–1979)
K.V. Rangaswamy (1880–1960)
M.C. Rajah (1883–1943)
N.G. Ranga (1900–1995)
O.P. Ramaswamy Reddiar (1895–1970)
Sibnath Banerjee (1897–1982)

Printed Government/Institutional Documents

Collected Works of Mahatma Gandhi, Volumes 1–90, Navajivan Publishing House, Ahmedabad, and Publications Division, Government of India, New Delhi

Occasional Speeches and Writings of S. Radhakrishnan, May 1962–May 1964, Publications Division, Government of India, New Delhi, 1965

P.V. Narasimha Rao, Selected Speeches 1992–93, Publications Division, Government of India, New Delhi

Sardar Patel's Correspondence 1945–50, 10 volumes, Navajivan Publishing House, Ahmedabad, 1971–73

Satyam Eva Jayate, A Collection of Articles Contributed to *Swarajya* and Other Journals from 1956 to 1961, Bharatan Publishers, Madras, 1961

Selected Speeches and Writings of Indira Gandhi, 1972–77, Publications Division, Government of India, New Delhi, 1985

Selected Works of Jawaharlal Nehru, Second Series, 16 Vol's, Jawaharlal Nehru Memorial Fund, New Delhi

Speeches of C. Rajagopalachari (1947-48), Publications Division, Government of India, New Delhi

Speeches of Har Bilas Sarda, Arya Yantralaya, Ajmer, 1935

Speeches of Jawaharlal Nehru, 1946–64, Publications Division, Government of India, New Delhi, 1949–68

Speeches of Maulana Azad, Publications Division, Government of India, New Delhi, 1956

Speeches of Rajendra Prasad, Publications Division, Government of India, New Delhi

Speeches of Rajiv Gandhi, Publications Division, Government of India, New Delhi

The Years of Endeavour, August 1969–August 1972: Speeches of Indira Gandhi, Publications Division, Government of India, New Delhi

B. SECONDARY SOURCES

Ahmad, Jamil-ud-Din, *M.A. Jinnah: Speeches and Writings*, Volume I, Lahore: Ashraf, 1960

Austin, Granvile, *The Indian Constitution: Cornerstone of a Nation*, London: Oxford University Press, 1966

Banerjea, Surendranath, *Speeches and Writings, Selected by Himself*, Madras: G.A. Natesan, 1924

———, *A Nation in Making: Being the Reminiscences of Fifty Years of Public Life*, 1925, Reprint, Calcutta: Oxford University Press, 1963

Banerjee, Sumanta, *In the Wake of Naxalbari: A History of the Naxalite Movement in India*, Calcutta: Subarnarekha, 1980

Bardhan, Pranab, *The Political Economy of Development in India*, New Delhi: Oxford University Press, 1984

Basu, Aparna, *The Growth of Education and Political Development 1989-1920*, New Delhi: Oxford University Press, 1974

Batabyal, Rakesh, *Communalism in Bengal: From Famine to Noakhali, 1943-47*, New Delhi, London and New York: Sage Publications, 2005

Best, Geoffrey, *The Permanent Revolution: The French Revolution and its Legacy, 1789–1989*, London: Fontana, 1989

Bhagwati, Jagdish N., and Padma Desai, *India: Planning for Industrialisation—Industrialisation and Trade Policies Since 1961*, London: Oxford University Press, 1970

Bhalla, G.S., *Indian Agriculture Since Independence*, New Delhi: National Book Trust, 2007

Bhambri, C.P., *Bureaucracy and Politics in India*, New Delhi: Vikas Publishing House, 1971

———, *The Indian State: Fifty Years*, New Delhi: Shipra, 1997

Bhattacharya, Ajit, *Jayaprakash Narayan: A Political Biography*, New Delhi: Vikas Publishing House, 1975

Birla, G.D., *In the Shadow of the Mahatma: A Personal Memoir*, Bombay: Vakils, Feffer, and Simons, 1968

Bondurant, Joan V., *Conquest of Violence: The Gandhian Philosophy of Conflict*, Princeton: Princeton University Press, 1958

Brahmananda, P.R., and V.R. Panchmukhi, *The Development Process of the Indian Economy*, Bombay: Himalaya Publishing House, 1987

Buch, M.A., *Rise and Growth of Militant Nationalism in India*, Baroda: Good Companions, 1940

Chagla, M.C., *Roses in December: An Autobiography*, Bombay: Bharatiya Vidya Bhawan, 1973

Chakravarty, Suhas, *V.K. Krishna Menon and the India League, 1925–47*, 2 volumes, New Delhi: Har Anand, 1997

Chakravarty, Sukhamoy, *Development Planning: The Indian Experience*, New Delhi: Oxford University Press, 1987

Chand, Tara, *History of the Freedom Movement in India*, Vol. 1, New Delhi: Publications Division, Government of India, 1961

Chandavarkar, N.G., *Speeches and Writings*, Bombay: Manoranjak Grantha Prakashan Mandali, 1911

Chandra, Bipan, *The Rise and Growth of Economic Nationalism in India*, New Delhi: People's Publishing House, 1966, reprint, 1984

———, *Nationalism and Colonialism in Modern India*, New Delhi: Orient Longman, 1979, reprint, 1987

———, *The Indian Left: A Critical Appraisal*, New Delhi: Vikas Publishing House, 1983

———, *India's Struggle for Independence*, New Delhi: Viking, 1989

———, *Essays on Contemporary India*, New Delhi: Har Anand, 1999

———, et al., *India after Independence, 1947–2000*, New Delhi: Penguin, 2000

Chatterjee, Basudeb, *Trade, Tariffs and Empire: Lancashire and British Policy in India*, New Delhi: Oxford University Press, 1992

Chatterjee, Partha, *Nationalist Thought and the Colonial World: A Derivative Discourse?*, London: Zed Books, 1986
Chatterji, Bhola, *Conflict in JP's Politics*, New Delhi: Ankur Publishing House, 1984
Chattopadhyay, Kamaladevi, *Inner Recesses Outer Spaces: Memoirs*, New Delhi: Navrang, 1986
Chaube, Shivanikinkar, *Constituent Assembly of India: Springboard of Revolution*, New Delhi: Manohar, 2000
Collet, Sophia Dobson, *Life and Letters of Rammohan Roy*, third edition, edited by D.K. Biswas and P.C. Ganguly, Calcutta: Sadharan Brahmo Samaj, 1913
Dadabhai Naoroji, *Poverty and Un-British Rule in India*, First published 1901, Reprint, New Delhi: Bharatiya Kala Prakashan, 2006
Dandavate, Madhu, *As the Mind Unfolds: Issues and Personalities*, New Delhi: Shipra Publishers, 1983
Das Gupta, Jyotindra, *Language Conflict and National Development: Group Politics and National Language Policy in India*, Berkeley: University of California Press, 1970
Dastur, J. Aloo, and Usha Mehta, *Congress Rule in Bombay, 1952 to 1956*, Bombay: Popular Book Depot, 1958
Datt, Subimal, *With Nehru in the Foreign Office*, Calcutta: Minerva Associates, 1977
Desai, A.R., *Agrarian Struggles in India after Independence*, New Delhi: Oxford University Press, 1986
———, *Social Background of Indian Nationalism*, Bombay: Popular Prakashan, 1948, fifth paperback edition, 1976
Deshpande, G.P, *Writings of Jyotiba Phule*, New Delhi: Left Word, 2000
Deshmukh, C.D., *The Course of My Life*, New Delhi: Orient Longman, 1974
Dutt, R.C., *The Economic History of India in the Victorian Age*, 1904, Reprint, New Delhi: Publications Division, Government of India, 1960
———, *The Economic History of India Under Early British Rule*, 1904, Reprint, New Delhi: Publications Division, Government of India, 1960
Dutt, V.P., *India's Foreign Policy*, New Delhi: Vikas Publishing House, 1984
Fox, Richard, *Gandhian Utopia: Experiments with Culture*, Boston: Beacon Press, 1986
Frankel, Francine R., *India's Political Economy, 1947–1977: The Gradual Revolution*, Princeton: Princeton University Press, 1978
Gandhi, M.K., *An Autobiography or The Story of My Experiments with Truth*, Ahmedabad: Navajivan Publishing House, 1946
Gandhi, Rajmohan, *The Rajaji Story 1937–72*, Bombay: Bharatiya Vidya Bhawan, 1984
Ganguli, B.N., *Indian Economic Thought: Nineteenth Century Perspectives*, New Delhi: Tata McGraw-Hill, 1977
Gellner, Ernest, *Nations and Nationalism*, New York: Cornell University Press, 1983
Ghatate, N.M. (editor), *Four Decades in Parliament: Atal Bihari Vajpayee*, New Delhi: Shipra Publications, 1996
Gokhale, Gopal Krishna, *Speeches of Gopal Krishna Gokhale*, Madras: G.A Natesan, 1920

Golwalkar, M.S., *We or our Nationhood Defined*, Nagpur: Bharat Prakashan, 1947
Gopal, S., *British Policy in India, 1858-1905*, Cambridge: Cambridge University Press, 1965
———, *Jawaharlal Nehru: A Biography*, vols. 1–3, New Delhi: Oxford University Press, 1979, 1984
———, *Sarvepalli Radhakrishnan: A Biography*, New Delhi: Oxford University Press, 1986
Gopalan, A.K., *In the Cause of People: Reminiscences*, New Delhi: Orient Longman, 1973
Goyal, D.R., *Rashtriya Swayamsevak Sangh*, New Delhi: Radha Krishna Prakashan, 1979
Greenfield, Liah, *Nationalism: Five Roads to Modernity*, Cambridge: Harvard University Press, 1992
Guha, Ranajit, *Subaltern Studies, I–IV*, New Delhi: Oxford University Press, 1982–86
Gupta, Sisir K., *Kashmir: A Study in India–Pakistan Relations*, Bombay: Asia Publishing House, 1967
Gwyer, Maurice, and A. Appadorai, *Speeches and Documents on the Indian Constitution 1921–47*, London: Oxford University Press, 1957
Habib, Irfan, *Essays in Indian History: Towards a Marxist Perspective*, New Delhi: Tulika, 1995
———, *Indian Economy, 1858–1914*, New Delhi: Tulika, 2005
Hardt, Michael, and Antonio Negri, *Empire*, Cambridge: Harvard University Press, 2000
Harrison, Selig S., *India: The Most Dangerous Decades*, Princeton: Princeton University Press, 1960
Heimsath, Charles H., *Indian Nationalism and Hindu Social Reform*, Princeton: Princeton University Press, 1964
Hobsbawm, Eric, *Nations and Nationalism since 1789: Program, Myth, Reality*, Cambridge: Cambridge University Press, 1990
Hutchins, Francis, *Spontaneous Revolution: The Quit India Movement*, New Delhi: Manohar Books, 1971
Iqbal, Afzal (compiler and editor), *Select Writings and Speeches of Maulana Mohamed Ali*, Lahore: Shaikh Muhammad Ashraf, 1944
Jagirdar, P.G., *Studies in the Social Thought of M.G. Ranade*, Bombay: Asia Publishing House, 1967
Joshi, G.V., *Writings and Speeches*, Poona: Aryabhushan Press, 1912
Joshi, Vijay, and I.M.D. Little, *India: The Macroeconomics and Political Economy 1964-1991*, Washington: World Bank, 1994
Karunakaran, K.P., *India in World Affairs, February 1950 to December 1953: A Review of India's Foreign Relations*, London: Oxford University Press, 1958
——— (editor), *Outside the Contest: A Study of Nonalignment and the Foreign Policies of Some Nonaligned Countries*, New Delhi: People's Publishing House, 1963
Karve, D.G., and D.V. Ambekar (editors), *Speeches and Writings of Gopal Krishna Gokhale*, 3 volumes, Bombay: Asia Publishing House, 1962–67
Kohli, Atul, *The State and Poverty in India: The Politics of Reform*, Cambridge: Cambridge University Press, 1987

Kothari, Rajni, *Politics in India*, New Delhi: Orient Longman, 1982
Kripalani, J.B., *Gandhi: His 'Life and Thought'*, New Delhi: Publications Division, Government of India, 1975
———, *My Times: An Autobiography*, New Delhi: Rupa and Co., 2004
Lahiry, Ashutosh, *Gandhi in Indian Politics: A Critical Review*, Calcutta: Firma KLM, 1976
Landes, David, *The Wealth and Poverty of Nations: Why Some Are So Rich and Others So Poor*, London: Abacus, 1998
Limaye, Madhu, *Politics after Freedom*, New Delhi: Atma Ram Publishing House, 1982
Madhok, Balraj, *Portrait of a Martyr: A Biography of Dr Shyama Prasad Mookerji*, New Delhi: Rupa and Co., 2001
Madison, Angus, *The World Economy: A Millennial Perspective*, Paris: OECD, 2001
Mahajan, Sucheta, *Independence and Partition: The Erosion of Colonial Power in India*, New Delhi and New York: Sage Publications, 1999
Majumdar, Bimanbehari, *History of Indian Social and Political Ideas: From Rammohun to Dayanand*, Calcutta: Bookland Private Limited, 1967
Malhotra, Inder, *Indira Gandhi*, New Delhi: National Book Trust, 2006
Masani, R.P., *Dadabhai Naoroji: The Grand Old Man of India*, London: George Allen and Unwin, 1939
McCully, Bruce T., *English Education and the Origins of Indian Nationalism*, New York: Columbia University Press, 1940
Mehrotra, S.R., *The Emergence of the Indian National Congress*, Delhi: 1971, reprint: Rupa and Co., 2004
Mehta, Pherozeshah M., *Speeches and Writings*, edited by C.V. Chintamani, Allahabad: Indian Press, 1905
Menon, V.P., *The Transfer of Power in India*, Princeton: Princeton University Press, 1957
Menon, Visalakshi, *From Movement to Government, UP, 1937-39*, Delhi, London, New York: Sage Publications, 2002
———, *Gender and Nationalism*, New Delhi: Har Anand, 2004
Mody, Homi, *Sir Pherozeshah Mehta: A Political Biography*, Bombay: Asia Publishing House, 1963
Mohammad, Shan (editor), *Writings and Speeches of Sir Syed Ahmad Khan*, Bombay: Nachiketa Publications Limited, 1972
Mukherjee, Aditya, *Imperialism, Nationalism and the Making of the Indian Capitalist Class, 1920-1947*, New Delhi: Sage Publications, 2002
Mukherjee, Haridas, and Uma Mukherjee, *India's Fight for Freedom or the Swadeshi Movement, 1905-1906*, Calcutta: Firma KLM, 1958
Mukherjee, Mridula, *Colonializing Agriculture: The Myth of Punjab Exceptionalism*, New Delhi: Sage Publications, 2005
———, *Peasants in India's Non-violent Revolution: Practice and Theory*, New Delhi: Sage Publications, 2004
Nag, Kalidas, and Debjyoti Burman, *The English Works of Raja Rammohun Roy*, Calcutta: Sadharan Brahmo Samaj, 1945
Nairn, Tom, *The Break-up of Britain: Crisis and Neo-Nationalism*, London: Verso, 1977

Namboodiripad, E.M.S., *Economics and Politics of India's Socialistic Pattern*, New Delhi: People's Publishing House, 1966

Nanda, B.R., *Gokhale, The Indian Moderates and the British Raj*, New Delhi/London: Oxford University Press, 1977

———, *Mahatma Gandhi: A Biography*, New Delhi: Oxford University Press, 1981

———, *Gokhale, Gandhi and Nehru*, New Delhi: Oxford University Press, 2004

Narain, Iqbal, *State Politics in India*, Meerut: Meenakshi Publishers, 1967

Natarajan, S., *A Century of Social Reform in India*, Bombay: Asia Publishing House, 1959

Nayar, Baldev Raj, *Minority Politics in Punjab*, Princeton: Princeton University Press, 1966

North, Douglas C., and Robert Paul Thomas, *The Rise of the Western World: A New Economic History*, New York: Cambridge University Press, 1973

Omvedt, Gail, *Cultural Revolt in a Colonial Society: The Non Brahmin Movement in Western India, 1873–1930*, Bombay: Scientific Socialistic Education Trust, 1976

Overstreet G.D., and M. Windmiller, *Communism in India*, Bombay: Perennial Press, Bombay, 1960

Palme Dutt, R., *India Today*, Bombay: People's Publishing House, 1949

Pradhan, G.P., and A.K. Bhagwat, *Lokmanya Tilak: A Biography*, Bombay: Jaico, 1959

Prasad, Bimla, *The Origins of Indian Foreign Policy: The Indian National Congress and World Affairs, 1885-1947*, Calcutta: Bookland Private Limited, 1960

Raghuvanshi, V.P.S., *Indian Society in the Eighteenth Century*, New Delhi: Associated Publishing House, 1969

Rai, Lajpat, *Writings and Speeches*, edited by V.C. Joshi, 2 volumes, Jallandhar: University Publishers, 1966

Rajamohan, C., *Crossing the Rubicon: The Shaping of India's New Foreign Policy*, New Delhi: Viking, 2003

Rajendra Prasad, *India Divided*, Bombay: Hind Kitab Limited, 1947

———, *Mahatma Gandhi and Bihar: Some Reminiscences*, Bombay: Hind Kitab, 1949

Ranade, M.G., *Essays on Indian Economics*, Bombay: Thaker and Company, 1898

———, *The Miscellaneous Writings*, edited by Ramabai Ranade, New Delhi: Sahitya Akademi, 1992, first published in Bombay, 1915

Ray, Renuka, *My Reminiscences: Social Development During the Gandhian Era and After*, Calcutta: Stree, 2005

Reddy, E.S., and A.K. Damodaran, *Decolonisation, Peace and the United Nations: Krishna Menon Speeches at the United Nations*, New Delhi: Sanchar Publishing House, 1997

Saraswati, Dayanand, *Satyartha Prakash*, English translation by Durga Prasad, New Delhi: Jan Gyan Prakashan, 1972

Savarkar, V.D., *Hindu Rashtra Darshan: A Collection of the Presidential Speeches*, Bombay: Veer Savarkar Prakashan, 1949

———, *My Transportation for Life*, translated by V.N. Naik, Bombay: Veer Savarkar Prakashan, first edition 1949, reprint, 1984

Sen, Amartya, *Poverty and Famines in South Asia*, New Delhi: Oxford University Press, 1981

Sen, Ashok, *Ishwarchandra Vidyasagar and His Elusive Milestones*, Calcutta: Papyrus, 1977

Sen, Mohit, *A Traveller and the Road*, New Delhi: Rupa and Co., 2003

Sen, Sunanda, *Colonies and the Empire, India 1890–1914*, Calcutta: Orient Longman, 1992

Setalvad, Chimanlal H., *Recollections and Reflections: An Autobiography*, Bombay: Padma Publications, 1946

Singh, Amrik, *Fifty Years of Higher Education in India: The Role of the University Grants Commission*, New Delhi: Sage Publications, 2003

Singh, K.S., *Birsa Munda and His Movement 1874–1901: A Study of a Millenarian Movement in Chotanagpur*, Calcutta: Oxford University Press, 1984

Singh, Randhir, *Marxism and Indian Politics*, New Delhi: Ajanta Prakashan, 1990

Singh, Sita Ram, *Nationalism and Social Reform in India*, New Delhi: Ranjit Printers, 1968

Singh, V.B. (editor), *Economic History of India 1857–1956*, Bombay: Asia Publishing House, 1965

Sitaramayya, B. Pattabhi, *The History of the Indian National Congress (1885-1935)*, Madras, 1935, Bombay: Padma Publications, 1946

Spear, Percival, *Oxford History of India*, New Delhi: Oxford University Press, 1974

Subramanian Iyer, G., *Some Economic Aspects of British Rule in India*, Madras, 1903

Sugar, P.F., and I.J. Lederer (editors), *Nationalism in Eastern Europe*, Seattle: University of Washington Press, 1969

Sundarayya, P., *Telangana People's Struggle and its Lessons*, Calcutta: A Communist Party of India (Marxist) Publication, 1972

Tahmankar, D.V., *Lokamanya Tilak: Father of Indian Unrest and Maker of Modern India*, London: John Murray, 1956

Talukdar, Mohammad H.R., *Memoirs of Huseyn Shaheed Suhrawardy: With a Brief Account of His Life and Work*, Bangladesh: University Press, 1987

Telang, K.T., *Select Writings and Speeches*, Volumes 1-2, Bombay: Samyukta Gauda Saraswat Brahmana, 1916

Tendulkar, D.G., *Mahatma: Life of Mohandas Karamchand Gandhi*, 8 volumes, New Delhi: Publications Division, Government of India, 1951–69

Tilly, Charles (editor), *The Formation of National States in Western Europe*, Princeton: Princeton University Press, 1975

Tripathi, Amales, *The Extremist Challenge: India Between 1890 and 1910*, Bombay: Orient Longman, 1967

Vanaik, Achin, *The Painful Transition: Bourgeois Democracy in India*, London: Verso, 1990

Vira, Dharma, *Reminiscences*, New Delhi: Vikas Publishing House, 1990

Wedderburn, William, *Allan Octavian Hume*, London: T. Fisher Unwin, 1913

Wolpert, Stanley, *Jinnah of Pakistan*, New York: Oxford University Press, 1984

Zaidi A.M., and S.G. Zaidi, *The Encyclopaedia of the Indian National Congress, Volume Eleven: 1936–1938*, New Delhi: Indian Institute of Applied Political Research, 1975

Newspapers and Magazines

Amrita Bazar Patrika, Calcutta
Ananda Bazar Patrika, Calcutta
Asian Survey, 1961–2000
Desh, Calcutta
Dharmayug, Bombay
Dinman, Bombay
Economic Weekly (Later, *The Economic and Political Weekly*), Bombay
Janata, New Delhi
Journal of Economic Perspectives, PA, USA
Mainstream, New Delhi
Modern Review, Calcutta
Newsweek, New York
Saptahik Hindustan, New Delhi
Social Scientist, New Delhi
Swatantra, Bombay
The Hindustan Standard, Calcutta
The Statesman, Calcutta, Delhi
The Times of India, Bombay
Times, New York
World Politics, New Delhi

SOURCES AND COPYRIGHT ACKNOWLEDGEMENTS

The editor and the publisher would like to thank the following for permission to reproduce copyright material:

The Rajya Sabha Secretariat, Parliament of India, for speeches reproduced from the Rajya Sabha Debates dated 25 April 1958, 1962 (Vol. XLI), 1 September 1965, 22 July 1975, 27 April 1989

The Indian Council for Cultural Relations, New Delhi

Bharatiya Vidya Bhavan, Bombay

Dr Deepak J. Tilak, Kesari-Mahratta Trust, Pune

Sajed Kamal

Indian Science Congress Association, Calcutta

Jawaharlal Nehru Memorial Fund, New Delhi, for the speeches of Jawaharlal Nehru, Indira Gandhi, Rajiv Gandhi and Sonia Gandhi

The Secretary, Tamil Nadu Legislative Assembly

The Lok Sabha Secretariat, Parliament of India; a special thanks to Raghav Das

The United Nations Information Centre, New Delhi

The Navajivan Trust, Ahmedabad

1. CONCEIVING A NATION

Surendranath Banerjea, 'Rammohun Roy: The Father of Modern India', *The Father of Modern India*, commemorative volume of the Rammohun Roy Centenary Celebrations, 1933, edited by Satis Chandra Chakravarty, Calcutta, 1935, pp. 193–99

Syed Ahmad Khan, 'Hindu and Mussalman', *Writings and Speeches of Sir Syed Ahmed Khan*, Edited by Shan Mohammad, Nachiketa Publications, Bombay, 1972, pp. 159-60

Surendranath Banerjea, 'Indian Unity', *Speeches and Writings of Honourable Surendranath Banerjea, Selected by Himself*, G.A. Natesan and Company, Madras, 1924, pp. 211–31

Mahadev Govind Ranade, 'The Evolution of a New India', R.K. Prabhu (compiled), *An Anthology of Modern Indian Eloquence*, Bharatiya Vidya Bhavan, Bombay, 1960, pp. 19–28

Bal Gangadhar Tilak, 'Empires: Old and New', *Samagra Tilak*, Vol. 7, Kesari Prakashan, Poona, 1975, pp. 546-47

2. CRITIQUE OF COLONIALISM

Dadabhai Naoroji, 'Maiden Speech in the House of Commons', *Speeches and Writings of Dadabhai Naoroji*, Second Edition, G.A. Natesan & Co., Madras, 1917, pp. 121–23

Dadabhai Naoroji, 'Poverty of India', *Speeches and Writings of Dadabhai Naoroji*, Second Edition, G.A. Natesan & Co., Madras, 1917, pp. 20–64

Romesh Chandra Dutt, 'The Economic Condition of India', *Open Letters to Lord Curzon and Speeches and Papers by R.C. Dutt*, Gian Publishing House, Delhi, pp. 69–88

Dinshaw Eduljee Wacha, 'Congress Resolution on Military Expenditure', *The Encyclopaedia of the Indian National Congress*, Vol. II: 1891-1895, Edited by A. Moin Zaidi and Shaheda Zaidi, Indian Institute of Applied Political Research, New Delhi, 1977, pp. 148–158

Pherozeshah M. Mehta, 'The Budget Speech, 1895-96', *Speeches and Writings of Honourable Sir Pherozeshah Mehta*, C.Y. Chintamani (ed.), with an introduction by Dinshaw Eduljee Wacha, The Indian Press, Allahabad, 1905, pp. 443–59

Pherozeshah M. Mehta, 'The Ilbert Bill Controversy', *Speeches and Writings of Honourable Sir Pherozeshah Mehta*, C.Y. Chintamani (ed.), with an introduction by Dinshaw Eduljee Wacha, The Indian Press, Allahabad, 1905, pp. 158–69

Surendranath Banerjea, 'The Vernacular Press Act', *Speeches and Writings of Honourable Surendranath Banerjea, Selected by Himself*, G.A. Natesan & Co, Madras, 1924, pp. 232–55

Badruddin Tyabji, 'Presidential Address, 1887', *The Indian Nation Builders, Part II*, Ganesh and Co., Madras, 1918, pp. 137–49

Gopal Krishna Gokhale, 'Excessive Surpluses "A Double Wrong": The First Budget Speech in the Imperial Legislative Council', D.G. Karve (ed.), *Speeches and Writings of Gopal Krishna Gokhale,* Asia Publishing House, Bombay, 1962, pp. 1–21

3. THE IDEA OF SOCIAL REFORM

K.T. Telang, 'Must Social Reform Precede Political Reform in India?' K.T. Telang, *Selected Writings and Speeches*, printed and published by K.R. Mitra at Manoranjan Press, Girgaum, Bombay, 1916, pp. 269–299

N.G. Chandavarkar, 'An Address on Social Reform', *Speeches and Writings of Sir N.G. Chandavarkar*, Manoranjak Grantha Prakashan Mandali, Girgaon, Bombay, 1911, pp. 47–77

Mahadev Govind Ranade, 'Reform or Revivalism?', *Miscellaneous Writings of the Late Hon'ble M.G. Ranade*, Edited by Ramabai Ranade with an introduction by D.E. Wacha, Sahitya Akademy, 1992, pp. 188–197

Har Bilas Sarda, 'Introducing the Child Marriage Restraint Bill', *Speeches and Writings of Har Bilas Sarda*, printed and published by Chand Mal Chandak, Manager, at Arya Yantralaya, Ajmer, 1935, pp. 33-44

4. NATIONALISM ON THE MARCH

Swami Vivekananda, 'Assertion of Universality', http://www.ramakrishna.org/chcgfull.htm

Ananda Mohan Bose, 'A National Awakening', *The Indian Nation Builders, Part I,* (Sixth Edition) Ganesh & Co., Madras, 1918, pp. 42–52

Bal Gangadhar Tilak, 'Tenets of the New Party', *Samagra Tilak,* Vol. 7, Kesari Prakashan, Poona, 1975, pp. 553–61

Lala Lajpat Rai, 'Swadeshi', *The Indian Nation Builders, Part I,* Ganesh & Co., Madras, 1918, pp. 336–45

Bipin Chandra Pal, 'The New Movement, Bipin Chandra Pal, *Swadesh and Swaraj,* Yuga Prakasha, Calcutta, 1953, pp. 117–48

Annie Besant, 'The Home Rule Resolution', *Speeches and Writings of Annie Besant* (Third Edition), G.A. Natesan & Co., Madras, 1921, pp. 245–48

Muhammad Ali Jinnah, 'Protest against Internment', Moin Zaidi, *Evolution of Muslim Political Thought in India,* Vol. 2, Published under the auspices of Indian Institute of Applied Political Research by Michiko and Panjathan, New Delhi, 1975, pp. 670–72

5. THE DREAMERS

P.C. Ray, *Dawn of Science in Modern India,* N.N. Mitra (ed.), *The Indian Annual Register,* Calcutta, 1920

Jagadish Chandra Bose, 'The Unity of Life', *Everyman's Science,* Vol. XXXIX, No. 4, October-November, 2003, Indian Science Congress Association, Calcutta, pp. 206–24

Bidhan Chandra Ray, 'The Future of the Medical Profession in India', *Towards Development, Bidhan Chandra Ray Memorial Volume,* Bidhan Chandra Ray Memorial Committee, West Bengal Legislative Assembly Secretariat, Calcutta

Meghnad Saha, The Present World—One Economic and Cultural Unit', N.N. Mitra (ed.), The Indian Annual Register, *Calcutta 1934,* pp. 493-94

C.V. Raman, 'The Raman Effect', *Everyman's Science,* Vol. XXXIX, No. 6, February-March, 2004, Indian Science Congress Association, Calcutta, pp. 350–57, http://sciencecongress.org/ html/pdf/

6. TOWARDS FREEDOM

Mohandas Karamchand Gandhi, 'The Banaras Hindu University Speech', *The Collected Works of Mahatma Gandhi,* D.G. Tendulkar, *Mahatma: Life of M.K. Gandhi,* Vol. 1, Publications Division, 1960, New Delhi, pp. 179–84

Mohammad Ali, 'Justice to Islam and Turkey', *Select Writings and Speeches of Maulana Mohammad Ali,* compiled and edited by Afzal Iqbal, Published by Shaikh Muhammad Ashraf, Lahore, 1944, pp. 183–93

Chittaranjan Das, 'The Resolution on Non-cooperation', *Deshbandhu Chitta Ranjan: Brief Survey of Life and Work*, Published by Rajen Sen, Calcutta, 1926, pp. 116–23

Mohandas Karamchand Gandhi, 'Address to Congress Workers, Bardoli', *Collected Works of Mahatma Gandhi*, Vol. XXII, Publications Division, Government of India, New Delhi, p. 377

Mohandas Karamchand Gandhi, 'Statement at Trial Court, 1922', *Collected Works of Mahatma Gandhi*, Vol. XXIII, Publications Division, Government of India, New Delhi, 1966, pp. 114-15

Kazi Nazrul Islam, 'Deposition of a Political Prisoner', Sajed Kamal, *Kazi Nazrul Islam: Selected Works*, Dhaka: Nazrul Institute, 1999, pp. 211–19

M.N. Roy, 'Leftism in Congress', *Origin of Radicalism in the Congress*, Renaissance Publications Pvt. Ltd, Calcutta, 1942, pp. 1–14

S. Satyamurti, 'Adjournment Motion re the Seizure of Subrahmanya Bharathi's Songs', P. Ramamurty (ed.), *Mr. President Sir, Parliamentary Speeches of Satyamurti*, Book Venture, Madras, 1988, pp. 24–38

Bhagat Singh, 'Statement before the Lahore High Court Bench', *Selected Writings of Shaheed Bhagat Singh*, edited with introduction by Shiv Verma, National Book Centre, New Delhi, pp. 92–96

Jawaharlal Nehru, '"Purna Swaraj", Presidential Address, Lahore Session, 1929', Jagat S. Bright, *Most Important Speeches of Jawaharlal Nehru*, published by Narain Das Kumar, Indian Printing Works, Lahore, 1945, pp. 125–41

Mohandas Karamchand Gandhi, 'On the Eve of the Dandi March', *The Collected Works of Mahatma Gandhi*, Vol. XLIII, Publications Division, Government of India, New Delhi, pp. 46–48

Jawaharlal Nehru, 'Karachi Resolution, 1930', Moin Zaidi, *The Encyclopaedia of the Indian National Congress*, Vol. X, pp. 111-12

Mohandas Karamchand Gandhi, 'I Give You a Mantra', *The Collected Works of Mahatma Gandhi*, Vol. LXXVI, Publications Division, Government of India, New Delhi, pp. 384–86

Subhas Chandra Bose, 'Message to Gandhi', S.A. Iyer, *Selected Speeches of S.C. Bose with a Biographical Introduction*, Publications Division, Government of India, 1962 (reprinted 1983), pp. 233–36

J.B. Kripalani, 'Partition of the Country', N.N. Mitra (ed.), *The Indian Annual Register*, Calcutta, 1947, pp. 124–26

7. DEMANDS OF REPRESENTATION

O. Tanikachala Chettiyar and Others, 'Proportion of Non-Brahmins in the Public Services', Madras Legislative Assembly Debates, 5 August 1921, Vol. 2, pp. 424–46

Bhimrao Ramji Ambedkar, 'The Depressed Classes', Official Report of the Second Round Table Conference, 1932, pp. 131–37; See also, Babasaheb Ambedkar, *Writings and Speeches*, Vol. 2, compiled and edited by Vasant Moon, Government of Maharashtra, Bombay, 1982, pp. 503–09

V.D. Savarkar, 'Presidential Address, Akhil Bharatiya Hindu Mahasabha, 1937', V.D. Savarkar, *Hindu Rashtra Darshan*, Veer Savarkar Prakashan, Bombay, 1984

Muhammad Ali Jinnah, 'Presidential Address at the All India Muslim League, Lahore Session, March 1940' Jamil-ud-din Ahmad (ed.), *Speeches and Writings of Mr. M.A Jinnah*, Published by Shaikh Muhammad Ashraf, Lahore, 1960, pp. 143–63

8. THE BIRTH OF A NATION

Jawaharlal Nehru, 'Tryst with Destiny', Constituent Assembly Debates, Vol. V, No.1, Publications Division, Government of India, New Delhi, pp. 3–5

Sarojini Naidu, 'The Battle for Freedom Is Over', R.K. Prabhu (compiled), *An Anthology of Modern Indian Eloquence*, Bharatiya Vidya Bhavan, Bombay, 1960, pp.142–44

J.B. Kripalani, 'The End of Centuries-old Slavery', R.K. Prabhu (compiled), *An Anthology of Modern Indian Eloquence*, Bharatiya Vidya Bhavan, Bombay, 1960, pp. 205–07

Maulana Abul Kalam Azad, 'To the Muslims in Delhi', Syeda Saydain Hameed (ed.), *India's Maulana*, Abul Kalam Azad Centenary Volume II, *Selected Speeches and Writings*, Indian Council for Cultural Relations, Delhi, 1990, pp. 170–73

B.T. Ranadive, 'Opening Report on the Draft Political Thesis', Party Pamphlet, CPI 1948, People's Publishing House, Bombay, P.C. Joshi Archives on Contemporary History

Lakshmi N. Menon, 'Republic Day Broadcast to the People of Goa', AIR Miscellany, 1962, Director General, All India Radio, New Delhi, 1964, pp. 96-97

9. THE ASSASSINATION OF MAHATMA GANDHI

Vallabhbhai Patel, 'Do Not Lose Heart', *In Tune with Millions*, edited by G.M. Nandurkar, coordinating editor, Manibehan Vallabhbhai Patel, Sardar Vallabhbhai Patel Smarak Bhawan, Ahmedabad, 1975-76, Volume I, pp. 217-18

Jawaharlal Nehru, 'The Light Has Gone Out', *Jawaharlal Nehru Speeches, 1946-49*, Publications Division, Government of India, New Delhi, 1949, pp. 42–44

S.A. Dange, 'Mahatma Gandhi's Death', Bombay Legislative Assembly Proceedings, Bombay, 16 February 1948, pp. 10–12

Swami Ranganathananda, 'The Legacy of Mahatma Gandhi', Swami Ranganathananda, *Eternal Values for a Changing Society*, Vol. IV, Bharatiya Vidya Bhavan, Bombay, 1987, pp. 276–82

10. THE CONSTITUTION: EMBODIMENT OF THE NATIONAL SPIRIT

Vallabhbhai Patel, 'Speech at the First Meeting of the Advisory Committee on Fundamental Rights', B. Shiva Rao (ed.), *The Framing of India's Constitution*, Vol. I, IIPA, Delhi, 1966, pp. 66–67

Jawaharlal Nehru, 'The Objectives Resolution', Constituent Assembly Debates, Manager Publications, Government of India, New Delhi, 1947, Vol. 1, No. 5, pp. 55–62

J.J.M. Nichols Roy, 'On the Objectives Resolution', Constituent Assembly Debates, Manager Publications, Government of India, New Delhi, 1947, Vol. 1, No. 8, 109–13 cc

Jawaharlal Nehru, 'The Objectives of the Constitution', Constituent Assembly Debates, Vol. I, Manager Publications, Government of India, New Delhi, 318–23 cc

Sarvepalli Radhakrishnan, 'The Flag of Dharma', Constituent Assembly Debates, Vol. I, Manager Publications, Government of India, New Delhi, 318–23 cc

Vallabhbhai Patel, 'Cultural and Educational Rights', Constituent Assembly Debates, Vol. III, No. 4, Manager Publications, Government of India, New Delhi, 497 cc

N. Gopalaswamy Ayyangar, 'The Official Language', B.N. Rau, *Framing of India's Constitution: Selected Documents*, Vol. IV, IIPA, New Delhi, 1968, pp. 623–28

Syama Prasad Mookerjee, 'On the National Language', Constituent Assembly Debates, Vol. IX, No. 33, Manager Publications, Government of India, New Delhi, 1389–93 cc

Jaipal Singh, 'In Defence of the Adivasi Language', Constituent Assembly Debates, Vol. IX, No 34, Manager Publications, Government of India, New Delhi, 1439–1441 cc

V.I. Muniswamy Pillai, 'The New Constitution', Constituent Assembly Debates, Manager Publications, Government of India, New Delhi, Vol. XI, No.4, 608–10 cc

Bhimrao Ramji Ambedkar, 'On the Draft Constitution', Constituent Assembly Debates, Vol. VII, Manager Publications, Government of India, New Delhi, 31–44 cc

Rajendra Prasad, 'Let Posterity Judge', Constituent Assembly Debates, Vol. IX, 984–95 cc

11. THE SPIRIT OF FREEDOM: QUEST FOR A JUST AND MORAL SOCIETY

N.G. Chandavarkar, 'The Children of Light', *Speeches and Writings of Sir N.G. Chandavarkar*, Manoranjak Grantha Prakashan Mandali, Girgaon, Bombay, 1911, pp. 133–43

M. Singaravelu, 'Fearlessly Expose the Sham of Casteism and Oppression', C.S. Subramaniam and K. Murugesan, *Singaravelu: The First Communist in South India*, People's Book House, Bombay, 1975, pp. 213–20

Rabindranath Tagore, 'Crisis in Civilisation', Sisir K. Das, (ed.), *The English Writings of Rabindranath Tagore*, Volume Three, A Miscellany, Sahitya Akademy, New Delhi, 2002, pp. 722–26

Mahatma Gandhi, 'The Last Fast', *Harijan*, 18 January 1948, p. 523

Jaipal Singh, 'Damodar Valley Corporation and Tribal Displacement', Lok Sabha Debates, 2 February 1948, Vol. 1, No. 3, 1948, 736–50 cc

R.R. Diwakar, 'Caste Should Go', Resolution Regarding Abolition of Entries of Castes and Religion from Government Registers, Forms and Records, Constituent Assembly of India (Legislative), 17 February 1948, 836–40 cc

Renuka Ray, 'Rescue and Rehabilitation of Women', Constituent Assembly Debates (Legislative), 12 March 1948, Manager Publications, Government of India, New Delhi, 2009–11 cc

Tajamul Hosain, 'Nizamat Should Go', Constituent Assembly of India (Legislative), 15 March 1948, Manager Publications, Government of India, New Delhi, 2166–68 cc

Bhimrao Ramji Ambedkar, 'The Hindu Code Bill', Constituent Assembly of India (Legislative), 9 April 1948, 3628–33 cc

Hansa Mehta, 'Suggestions for the Hindu Code Bill', Constituent Assembly of India (Legislative), 9 April 1948, 3642–44 cc

Jaipal Singh, 'On the Report of the Commissioner for Scheduled Castes and Scheduled Tribes', Lok Sabha Debates, 13 December 1952, 2278–84 cc

N.C. Chatterjee, 'The Special Marriage Bill', Lok Sabha Debates, 1 September 1954, 745–59 cc

N. Rachiah, 'The Untouchability (Offences) Bill', Lok Sabha Debates, Vol. VI, 27 August 1954, 459–65 cc

Jawaharlal Nehru, 'A Socialistic Pattern of Society', Address at the 60th Session of the Indian National Congress at Avadi, 22 January 1955, *Jawaharlal Nehru's Speeches 1953-1957*, Publications Division, Government of India, New Delhi, pp. 15–20

Prithviraj Kapoor, 'Capital Punishment Should Go', Resolution Regarding Abolition of Capital Punishment, 25 April 1958, Rajya Sabha Debates, Vol. XXI, No. 4, Rajya Sabha Secretariat, New Delhi, 431–41 cc

P.V. Kane, 'Time Has Not Come', Resolution Regarding Abolition of Capital Punishment, 25 April 1958, Rajya Sabha Debates, Vol. XXI, No. 4, Rajya Sabha Secretariat, New Delhi, 502–09 cc

Ram Manohar Lohia, 'Daily Earnings of an Indian', Lok Sabha Debates, 6 September 1963, Vol. XX, pp. 4875–88

Indira Gandhi, 'To Martin Luther King', *The Years of Challenge: Selected Speeches of Indira Gandhi, 1966-1969*, Publications Division, 1973, pp. 312-13

Jayaprakash Narayan, 'Revolution on the Agenda', Ramjee Singh and Uttam Kumar Sinha (eds), *JP: 100 Years, Text and Context*, Commonwealth Publishers, New Delhi, 2004, pp. 261–69

Indira Gandhi, 'For a Just and Moral International Order', *Years of Endeavour: Selected Speeches of Indira Gandhi, Aug. 1969-Aug. 1972*, Publications Division, Government of India, New Delhi, 1977, pp. 447–53

Baba Amte, *My Colleagues in Conscience*, http://baba.niya.org/index.php?page=magsaysay_award

12. ECONOMY AND DEVELOPMENT

G. Subramanian Iyer, 'Industrialization of the Country', *The Encyclopaedia of the Indian National Congress*, Vol. 2, Edited by A. Moin Zaidi and Shaheda Zaidi, Institute of Applied Political Research, Delhi, 1977, pp. 92–107

Purusottamdas Thakurdas, 'Presidential Address, FICCI', *Speeches of Sir Purusottamdas Thakurdas, President, Federation of Indian Chambers of Commerce and Industry,* FICCI, 1928, pp. 1–7

Nalini Ranjan Sarkar, 'Indian Economy', N.N. Mitra (ed.), *Indian Annual Register*, 1934, pp. 441–52

Subhas Chandra Bose, 'National Planning', S.A. Iyer, *Selected Speeches of S.C. Bose with a Biographical Introduction*, Publications Division, Government of India, 1962 (reprinted 1983), pp. 96–99

P.C. Mahalanobis, 'Studies Related to Planning for National Development', *Papers on Planning*, edited by P.K. Bose and M. Mukherjee, Statistical Publications Society, Calcutta, 1985, pp. 6–12

Jawaharlal Nehru, 'The Second Five Year Plan', *Jawaharlal Nehru Speeches 1953-1957*, Publications Division, Government of India, 1970 (1958), pp. 90–105

Jawaharlal Nehru, 'Temples of the New Age', *Jawaharlal Nehru Speeches 1953-1957*, Publications Division, Government of India, pp. 1–4

Homi Jehangir Bhabha, 'Development of Atomic Energy', All India Radio, 3 August 1964, see *India and Foreign Review*, 15 October 1964, pp. 8–10 as cited by J.P. Jain, *Nuclear India*, Vol. II, Radiant Publishers, New Delhi, 1974, pp. 145–50

Indira Gandhi, 'Nationalization of Private Commercial Banks', Lok Sabha Debates, 21 July 1969, Vol. 30, 1969, pp. 275–280

Manmohan Singh, 'General Budget Speech, 1992-93', Lok Sabha Debates, 29 February 1992, cc. 10–58

Nani Palkhivala, 'On the General Budget of 1992-93', *We the Nation: The Lost Decades*, Strand Bookshop, Bombay, 1984, p. 169

Somnath Chatterjee, 'Surrendering Self-reliance', Lok Sabha Debates, 4 March 1992

Amartya Sen, 'Development as Freedom', FICCI, 31 July 2003

13. THE CHINESE AGGRESSION

Jawaharlal Nehru, 'Massive Aggression on Our Frontiers', All India Radio, 22 October 1962, *Jawaharlal Nehru's Speeches, September 1957-April 1963*, Vol. IV, Publications Division, New Delhi, 1964, pp. 226–230

Hari Vishnu Kamath, 'The 1962 War: A Critical Evaluation', Resolution Regarding Proclamation of Emergency and Aggression by China, 9 November 1962, 398-99 cc

J.B. Kripalani, 'Motion Regarding the White Paper on Indo-Chinese Relations', Lok Sabha Debates, 12 September 1959, 8005–20 cc

Bhupesh Gupta, 'Communist Support to the War Effort', Rajya Sabha Debates, 8 November 1962, Vol. XLI, No. 1, Rajya Sabha Secretariat, New Delhi, 1962, 214–26 cc

P.N. Sapru, 'Defence of India Bill, 1962', Rajya Sabha Debates, Vol. XLI, No. 22, Rajya Sabha Secretariat, New Delhi, 1962, 3330–33 cc

14. STATE OF THE NATION—I

Vallabhbhai Patel, 'The Mantle Will Now Fall on Young Shoulders', *For a United India: Speeches of Sardar Patel 1947-1950*, Publications Division, Government of India, New Delhi, 1967

N. Gopalaswamy Ayyangar, 'Situation in Kashmir', Security Council Official Record as cited in S.L. Poplai (ed.), *Select Documents on Asian Affairs: India, 1947-1950*, Oxford University Press, Bombay, 1959, pp. 10–30

Sheikh Abdullah, 'The Real Issue', Security Council Official Records, Third Year, Nos 16–35, pp. 18–21, cited S.L. Poplai (ed.), *Select Documents on Asian Affairs: India, 1947-1950*, Oxford University Press, Bombay, 1959, pp. 417–25

Vallabhbhai Patel, 'Defence of India Rules, 1950', Motion on Address by the President, Lok Sabha Debates, 2 August 1950, 115–119 cc

Syama Prasad Mookerjee, 'On Jammu and Kashmir', Lok Sabha Debates, 315–34 cc

Jawaharlal Nehru, 'Resolution on Linguistic Provinces', Lok Sabha Debates, 7 July 1952, 3346–61 cc

O.V. Alagesan, 'On Linguistic States', Lok Sabha Debates, 12 July 1952, 3724–29 cc

Jawaharlal Nehru, 'The Naga Issue', Girja Kumar and V.K. Arora, *Documents on Indian Affairs*, Asia Publishing House, New Delhi, 1961, pp. 94–99

C.N. Annadurai, 'Dravida Nadu', S. Ramachandran (ed.), *Anna Speaks at the Rajya Sabha 1962-1966*, Orient Longman, Bombay, 1975, pp. 3–12

Jayaprakash Narayan, 'The Nagaland Peace Mission', Brahmananda (ed.), *Nation Building in India*, Nachiketa Prakashan, Varanasi, pp. 329–42

Kapur Singh, 'Punjabi Suba', Lok Sabha Debates, 6 September 1966, 9490–98 cc

Nath Pai, 'Governors of States', Motion regarding Governors of States, Lok Sabha Debates, 15 November 1967, 796–811 cc

Kanu Sanyal, 'Declaration of the Formation of CPI(M-L)', *Liberation* (Party Organ of the CPML), Vol. II, No.7, 1969, pp. 110–22

Indira Gandhi, 'Inauguration of New States', *The Years of Endeavour: Selected Speeches of Indira Gandhi, August 1969–August 1972*, Publications Division, Government of India, New Delhi, pp. 192–95

15. EDUCATION

Syed Ahmad Khan, 'Foundation of the Mohammedan Anglo-Oriental College', *Writings and Speeches of Sir Syed Ahmed Khan*, Edited by Shan Mohammad, Nachiketa Publications, Bombay, 1972, pp. 128-29

Pherozeshah Mehta, 'Speech at the Seventh Annual Meeting of the Bombay Graduates' Association', C.Y. Chintamani (ed.), *Speeches and Writings of Sir Pherozeshah Mehta*, The Indian Press, Allahabad, 1905, pp. 43–55

Gopal Krishna Gokhale, 'Free and Compulsory Primary Education', *Speeches of G.K. Gokhale*, Third Edition, G.A. Natesan and Co., Madras, 1920, pp. 590-91, 604-05

Rabindranath Tagore, 'The Education Mission of Visva-Bharati', *The English Writings of Rabindranath Tagore*, Volume Three, Sahitya Akademy, 2002, pp. 626–630

Mohandas Karamchand Gandhi, 'The Wardha Scheme', D.G. Tendulkar, *Mahatma: Life of M.K. Gandhi*, Vol. 4, Publications Division, 1960, New Delhi, pp. 190–92

S.A. Dange, 'On the Poona University Bill', Bombay Legislative Assembly Debates, 31 October 1947, 1669–85 cc

Meghnad Saha, 'Reforms in Higher Education', Lok Sabha Debates, 13 June 1952, Part II of First Session, Vols 1–4, 1723–30 cc

M.C. Chagla, 'Structure of Education', Lok Sabha Debates, Vol. XL, 6308–14 cc

Bhupesh Gupta, 'On the Jawaharlal Nehru University Bill', Rajya Sabha Debates, 1 September 1965, 2300–05 cc

R.K. Narayan, 'Burden on Childhood', Rajya Sabha, Special Mentions, 27 April 1989, Vol. CL, number 4, 183–85 cc

16. LABOUR

Joseph Baptista, 'Address at the First All-India Trade Union Congress', *Labour Movement in India 1918-1920*, ICHR, pp. 315–18

Lala Lajpat Rai, 'Presidential Address, AITUC, 1920', *Labour Movement in India 1918-1920*, ICHR, pp. 320–24

Parvathi Krishnan, 'Industrial Disputes (Amendment and Miscellaneous Provisions) Bill, 1956', Rajya Sabha Debates, cc. 944–60

S.A. Dange, 'Second Pay Commission, 1957', Lok Sabha Debates, 19 July 1957, cc. 4384–92

17. STATE OF THE NATION—II

Khan Abdul Ghaffar Khan, 'I Have Come to Serve You', *Badshah Khan: India Pakistan Relations*, S.S. Publishers, New Delhi, p. 91

Jayaprakash Narayan, 'Time for Struggle, Not for Studies', Satish Kumar (ed.), *Essential JP*, pp. 107–10

N.G. Goray, 'Opposing the Emergency', Rajya Sabha Debates, Official Report, 22 July 1975, Vol. XCIII, No. 2, 33–43 cc

Uma Shankar Joshi, 'In Opposition to the Emergency', Rajya Sabha Debates, Official Report, 22 July 1975, Vol. XCIII, No.1, 66–70 cc

Indira Gandhi, 'In Defence of Democracy', Lok Sabha Debates, 22 July 1975, 44–59 cc

G.G. Swell, 'Communal Violence in Gujarat', Discussion Regarding Communal Situation in Various Parts of the Country, Lok Sabha Debates, 21 July 1986, 361–67 cc

P.V. Narasimha Rao, 'Countering Communal Forces', *P.V. Narashimha Rao: Selected Speeches*, Publications Division, Government of India, pp. 63–65

Sonia Gandhi, 'Follow My Own Inner Voice', aicc.org.in/renunciation-details.php?id=1

18. INDIA AND THE WORLD

Jawaharlal Nehru, 'India's Foreign Policy', A. Appadorai (ed.), *Select Documents on India's Foreign Policy and Relations, 1947-1972*, Vol. I, Oxford University Press, New Delhi, pp. 3–5

Jawaharlal Nehru, 'Membership of the Commonwealth', *Jawaharlal Nehru Speeches 1946-1949*, Publications Division, New Delhi, pp. 269–72

Jawaharlal Nehru, 'Asia Finds Herself Again', *Jawaharlal Nehru Speeches 1946-1949*, Publications Division, New Delhi, pp. 297–304

Chakravarthy Rajagopalachari, 'On the Korean Situation', Lok Sabha Debates 1950, Vol. V, Part II, 344–56 cc

V.K. Krishna Menon, 'India and the United Nations Agenda', E.S. Reddy and A.K. Damodaran, *Decolonisation, Peace and the United Nations: Krishna Menon Speeches at the United Nations*, Sanchar Publishing House, New Delhi, 1997

V.K. Krishna Menon, 'On Kashmir', E.S. Reddy and A.K. Damodaran, *Decolonisation, Peace and the United Nations: Krishna Menon Speeches at the United Nations*, Sanchar Publishing House, New Delhi, 1997

Homi Jehangir Bhabha, 'Presidential Address, First International Conference on the Peaceful Uses of Atomic Energy', *Proceedings of the First International Conference on the Peaceful Uses of Atomic Energy, Geneva*, United Nations Publications, New York, 1956, Vol. 16, as cited by J.P. Jain, *Nuclear India*, Vol. II, Radiant Publishers, pp. 31–35

V.K. Krishna Menon, 'On South Africa', E.S. Reddy and A.K. Damodaran, *Decolonisation, Peace and the United Nations: Krishna Menon Speeches at the United Nations*, Sanchar Publishing House, New Delhi, 1997

M.C. Chagla, 'India and West Asia', A. Appadorai (ed.), *Select Documents on India's Foreign Policy and Relations, 1947-1972*, Vol. II, Oxford University Press, New Delhi, pp. 360–68

Brajesh Mishra, 'Statement on Pokaran, 1974', cited in J.P. Jain, *Nuclear India*, Volume II, Radiant Publishers, New Delhi

Indira Gandhi, 'Support to the Palestinian Cause', *Selected Speeches and Writings of Indira Gandhi*, NMML, New Delhi, 1986, pp. 359-60

Rajiv Gandhi, '*On Disarmament*', http://Indianembassy.org/policy/disarmament/disarm14.htm

P.V. Narasimha Rao, 'Challenge and Opportunity in the Post-Cold War Era: An Indian Perspective on the Emerging Structure of Interstate Relation', *P.V. Narasimha Rao: Selected Speeches*, Vol. II, Publications Division, Government of India, New Delhi, 1994, pp. 392–400

Atal Bihari Vajpayee, 'The Nuclear Tests at Pokaran' www.indianembassy.org/news/mayjune1598

INDEX